Pro Football Prospectus 2008

THE ESSENTIAL GUIDE TO THE 2008 PRO FOOTBALL SEASON

AARON SCHATZ

WITH BEN ALAMAR, BILL BARNWELL, WILL CARROLL,

DOUG FARRAR, STUART FRASER, BRIAN FREMEAU, RUSSELL LEVINE,

KEVIN LYNCH, NED MACEY, SEAN MCCORMICK, BILL MOORE,

ROB PITZER, BEN RILEY, MICHAEL DAVID SMITH, MIKE TANIER,

VINCE VERHEL, AND RYAN WILSON

A PLUME BOOK

PLUME
Published by Penguin Group
Penguin Group (USA) Inc., 375 Hudson Street, New York, New York 10014, U.S.A.
Penguin Group (Canada), 90 Eglinton Avenue East, Suite 700, Toronto, Ontario, Canada M4P 2Y3
(a division of Pearson Penguin Canada Inc.)
Penguin Books Ltd., 80 Strand, London WC2R 0RL, England
Penguin Ireland, 25 St. Stephen's Green, Dublin 2, Ireland (a division of Penguin Books Ltd.)
Penguin Group (Australia), 250 Camberwell Road, Camberwell, Victoria 3124, Australia
(a division of Pearson Australia Group Pty. Ltd.)
Penguin Books India Pvt. Ltd., 11 Community Centre, Panchsheel Park, New Delhi – 110 017, India
Penguin Group (NZ), 67 Apollo Drive, Mairangi Bay, Auckland 1311, New Zealand
(a division of Pearson New Zealand Ltd.)
Penguin Books (South Africa) (Pty.) Ltd., 24 Sturdee Avenue, Rosebank, Johannesburg 2196, South Africa

Penguin Books Ltd., Registered Offices:
80 Strand, London WC2R 0RL, England

First published by Plume, a member of Penguin Group (USA) Inc.

First Printing (2008 edition), July 2008
1 3 5 7 9 10 8 6 4 2

 REGISTERED TRADEMARK—MARCA REGISTRADA

ISBN 978-0-452-28973-4

Printed in the United States of America
Set in Utopia
Design by Jane Raese

Contents

Introduction

Aaron Schatz

Thank you for purchasing the 2008 edition of *Pro Football Prospectus*. If this is your first time picking up our book, allow me to tell you a story.

Once upon a time, there was a guy near Boston who really enjoyed both baseball and football. He really enjoyed advanced statistical analysis in baseball, reading everything from Bill James and every edition of Baseball Prospectus, and he wondered why nobody was doing something similar with the NFL. He started playing around with some goofy little formulas, and his friends thought they were interesting, so one of them designed a Web site to share them with the world. And thus, five years ago this August, Football Outsiders was born.

The basic idea was simple. I was tired of listening to conventional wisdom that didn't make any sense, like the idea that running Eddie George into the line over and over for two yards was supposed to somehow "establish the run" and lead to wins. After breaking down the play-by-play and looking at what was really leading to wins and losses, I discovered that football statistics are heavily dependent on context. It remains a core tenet of a lot of the work we do at Football Outsiders. If you want to see which teams are good and which are bad, which strategies work and which do not, you first need to filter out that context.

Down and distance, field position, the current score, time left on the clock, the quality of the opponent—all of these elements influence the objective of the play and/or its outcome. Yet, conventional statistics will add together all yardage gained by a specific team or player without considering the impact of that particular yardage on wins and losses.

A close football game can turn on a single bounce of the ball. In a season of only 16 games, those effects can have a huge impact on a team's win-loss record, thus obscuring the team's true talent level. If we can filter out these bits of luck and random chance, we can figure out which teams are really more likely to play better for the rest of the season, or even in the following season.

It turned out that I wasn't the only person out there who loved football and really wanted to know what made teams win and lose. Professional football is America's most popular sport, and one of the things that makes it so great is that it can be enjoyed on so many different levels: as spectacle, as sport, as gladiator contest, or as chess game. Until Football Outsiders came along, the football as chess game audience was underserved. As the work began to spread around the Internet, people came out of the woodwork. Not only did fans want to read intelligent analysis of football, but some of them had plenty of intelligent analysis to contribute themselves. Gradually, a Web site that started as me and a couple of college buddies had expanded with a number of writers who were exploring the game in all kinds of interesting ways.

None of the four editions of *Pro Football Prospectus* would be possible without that group of writers, but that's never been quite as true as it is this year. More than our first three books, *Pro Football Prospectus 2008* is a collaborative project. My name may remain on the front cover, and I may still be hammering out all the statistics, but nearly every essay in this book first sprung from the mind of one of the talented writers that we've attracted to our staff over the past five years. Past just the writing, a number of guys in the FO crew went above and beyond the call of duty to help shepherd this book along and make sure it was the best edition of *PFP* yet.

We still feel like we've only scratched the surface of what we can learn about the game. Some of the things we want to know can't even be touched until we have more years of data from the Football Outsiders game charting project, our venture where a cadre of football-obsessed volunteers track things that don't appear in standard NFL play-by-play, like when teams are blitzing or using play-action. Other things require historical data, which requires scanning and typing play-by-play from the pre-Internet era—a project that began this past winter when we added 1995, the final season before NFL.com had play-by-play, into our database.

As football analysis expands, our goal is to focus as much as possible on "why" and "how," not just "which team is better." Every new statistic we create fills in part of the explanation for a team's wins and losses, whether it's Adjusted Line Yards, defensive back Success Rate, or something new like Speed Score (introduced in "Five Seconds Can Be a Lifetime") or Adjusted Games Lost (introduced in "The Injury Effect").

There are a number of objective computerized power rating systems out there, and they all rank teams in a fairly similar order. You didn't need overall team DVOA or any other objective power rating to tell you that the Patriots should be heavy favorites over the Giants in Super Bowl XLII. After an upset like that, we want to do more than just say, "Hey, what an upset, the team that was better during the season lost." Through a mixture of scouting and stats, we want to dig deeper, to find out why the Giants were able to keep that game close, and what changed during their astonishing postseason run. Did Eli Manning really get better? If he did, was it improvement on the deep ball? Short passes? Third downs? The Giants chapter in this book looks at a play-by-play breakdown of Manning's performance to answer just that very question.

The general feel of our work will be familiar to those who also read our partners at Baseball Prospectus. For new readers, the essay "Pregame Show" introduces the most important research that we've done in our first two books and our first three years online. In "Statistical Toolbox," we present our new statistics, what they mean, and how they are derived. "The Year in Quotes," frequently requested by readers, preserves for posterity some of the most prescient and/or ridiculous things said about the NFL over the past 12 months.

Each team chapter features an essay that covers what happened in 2007 and projects that team's prospects for the upcoming season. Are there reasons to believe that the team was actually better or worse than its record last year? What did the team do in the offseason, and what does that mean for the team's chances to win in 2008? Several chapters also include primary research on a subject related to the team.

Later in each team chapter, you'll find a number of team statistics as well as individual offensive and defensive numbers. Some of these are stats you know, like interceptions or touchdowns; others are unique to our book. We have stats derived from the play-by-play, such as Stop Rate, which measures how often a tackle stops the offense before what we consider a successful play. We also have stats that come from the Football Outsiders game charting project, including measures of defensive coverage and pass pressure. We also present some unique numbers which examine team strategies. How often does this team run or pass? How often does the offense like to run play-action, or use specific formations? How aggressive is the head coach on fourth down? Mixed in with all these stats is detailed commentary on each of the major units of the team: offensive line, defensive front seven, defensive secondary, special teams, and coaching staff.

You'll notice the phrase "skill players" missing from that paragraph. That is because skill players get their own section in the back of the book, where we list the major players at each position alphabetically, along with commentary and a 2008 KUBIAK projection that will help you win your fantasy football league. We also have the most accurate projections anywhere for two fantasy football positions that people wrongly consider impossible to predict: kickers and team defense.

Our last section features a number of research essays. We analyze what injuries say about teams improving and declining in the future, and for the first time, we rank the medical staffs of all 32 teams. Our second annual Top 25 Prospect list looks not at the best college prospects, but instead at the best young players sitting on NFL benches, waiting to explode into stardom. This year we also re-evaluate the infamous draft value chart and new methods to predict the success of young running backs and wide receivers, among other topics.

In each of our books, we've expanded our analysis to cover new elements of the game. This year, we expand our analysis to cover a different part of the weekend. For the first time, *PFP 2008* features a forecast of the top 40 teams in college football to go with our annual review of the best college games in the season to come. This is another step towards our goal of expanded college football coverage, both in this book and on our Web site.

Speaking of our Web site, that's how this all started, so we invite those of you who enjoy this book to become regular visitors at FootballOutsiders.com. Each week, you'll find updated DVOA and DYAR ratings as well as regular columns on the NFL and college football. Each of our articles includes a discussion thread featuring the kind of intelligent conversation about the game that you won't find at a site where readers spell "rules" with five Z's at the end. Readers can also discuss the most important news and best articles from around the Web at our Extra Points blog. This summer, you can buy a downloadable spreadsheet of our KUBIAK fantasy football projections, customizable to your league's rules and constantly updated with preseason news and injuries. And for a yearly fee, you can get access to the Football Outsiders premium stat database, featuring access to 13 years of DVOA splits and, beginning this year, weekly DVOA-based picks against the spread.

Whether you randomly picked up *Pro Football Prospectus* in your local bookstore, had it recommended to you by a friend, or have been reading Football Outsiders since it was just me and my buddies from Brown, we thank you again for buying this book. The traditional fifth anniversary present is wood, so if you don't mind, we're going to keep choppin' it.

Pregame Show

Aaron Schatz

This is the fourth edition of *Pro Football Prospectus*, and our Web site, FootballOutsiders.com, has been online for four seasons. During that time, we've done a lot of primary research on the National Football League, and we reference that research in many of the articles and comments in *Pro Football Prospectus 2008*.

New readers may come across an offhand comment in a team chapter about, for example, the idea that fumble recovery is not a skill, and wonder what in the heck we are talking about. We can't repeat all our research in every new edition of the book, so we wanted to start this year's *Pro Football Prospectus* with a basic look at some of the most important precepts that have emerged during four years of Football Outsiders research. You will see these issues come up again and again throughout the book.

You can also find this introduction online at www.footballoutsiders.com/pregame.php, along with links to the original research whenever the research appeared online instead of (or as well as) in print.

You run when you win, not win when you run.

If we could only share one piece of anticonventional wisdom with you before you read the rest of our book, this would be it. The first article ever written for Football Outsiders was devoted to debunking the myth of "establishing the run." There is no correlation whatsoever between giving your running backs a lot of carries early in the game and winning the game. Just running the ball is not going to help a team score; it has to run successfully.

There are two reasons why nearly every beat writer and television analyst still repeats the tired old school mantra that "establishing the run" is the secret to winning football games. The first problem is confusing cause and effect. There are exceptions—usually involving the Indianapolis Colts without Bob Sanders—but in general, winning teams have a lot of carries because their running backs are running out the clock at the end of wins, not because they are running wild early in games.

The second problem is history. Most of the current crop of NFL analysts came of age or actually played the game during the 1970s. They believe that the run-heavy game of that decade is how football is meant to be, and today's pass-first game is an aberration. As we addressed in an essay in last year's book on the history of NFL stats, it was actually the game of the 1970s that was the aberration. The 1970s were far more slanted toward the run than any other era since the arrival of Paul Brown, Otto Graham, and the Cleveland Browns in 1946. Optimal strategies from 1974 are not optimal strategies for 2008.

A sister statement to "you have to establish the run" is "team X is 5-1 when running back John Doe runs for at least 100 yards." Unless John Doe is ripping off six-yard gains LaDainian Tomlinson–style, the team isn't winning because of his 100-yard games. He's putting up 100-yard games because his team is winning.

A great defense against the run is nothing without a good pass defense.

This is a corollary to the absurdity of "establish the run." If you don't believe us, meet our good friends the Minnesota Vikings. With rare exceptions, teams win or lose with the passing game more than the running game—and by stopping the passing game more than the running game. Ron Jaworski puts it best: "The pass gives you the lead, and the run solidifies it." Teams need a strong run defense in the playoffs not to shut the run down early, but to keep the opponents from icing the clock if they get a lead. You can't mount a comeback if you can't stop the run.

Note that "good pass defense" may mean "good pass rush" rather than "good defensive backs."

Running on third-and-short is more likely to convert than passing on third-and-short.

On average, passing will always gain more yardage than running, with one very important exception: when a team is just one or two yards away from a new set of downs or the goal line. On third-and-1, a run will convert for a new set of downs 36 percent more often than a pass will. Expand that to all third or fourth downs with 1 or 2 yards to go, and the run is successful 40 percent more often. With these percentages, the possibility of a long gain with a pass is not worth the tradeoff of an incomplete that kills a drive.

This is one reason why teams have to be able to both run and pass. The offense also has to keep some semblance of balance so that it can use its play-action fakes and so that the defense doesn't just run its nickel-and-dime packages all game. Balance also means that teams do need to pass occasionally in short-yardage situations; they just need to do it less often than they do now. Teams pass roughly 60 percent of the time on third-and-2, even though runs in that situation convert 20 percent more often than do passes. And teams pass 68 percent of the time on fourth-and-2, even though runs in that situation convert twice as often as passes.

Standard team rankings based on total yardage are inherently flawed.

When you open your newspaper on Sunday morning, you'll see that the little agate-type previews of each game list team rankings by total yardage. This is still how the NFL "officially" ranks teams, but these rankings rarely match up with common sense. That is because total team yardage may be the most context-dependent number in football.

It starts with the basic concept that rate stats are generally more valuable than cumulative stats. Yards per carry says more about a running back's quality than total yardage does, and completion percentage says more than just a quarterback's total number of completions. The same thing holds for teams; in fact, rate stats are even more important because of the way football strategy influences the number of runs and passes in the game plan. Poor teams will give up fewer passing yards and more rushing yards because opponents will stop passing once they have a late-game lead and will run out the clock instead. For winning teams, the opposite is true. Did New Orleans really have a better passing game than Dallas last year? Or did New Orleans have more passing yards because it threw the ball a ridiculous 652 times, 101 more than Dallas and 62 more than any other NFL team?

Total yardage rankings are also skewed because some teams play at a faster pace than other teams. Chicago had more passing yards than Jacksonville last year, but to say Chicago had a better passing game is absurd. Perhaps one reason why Chicago had more passing yards is that it ran 201 offensive drives, the most in the league, while Jacksonville had 159 offensive drives, the third-lowest figure in the league, just ahead of New England and Indianapolis—two other offenses that could have put up bigger numbers if they had an average number of offensive drives. (Yes, the Patriots really could have put up more points. Scary.)

A team will score more when playing a bad defense and will give up more points when playing a good offense.

This sounds absurdly basic, but when people consider team and player stats without looking at strength of schedule, they are ignoring this. In 2004, Carson Palmer and Byron Leftwich had very similar numbers, but Palmer faced a much tougher schedule than Leftwich did. Palmer was better that year and better in the long run. Last year, Oakland running back Justin Fargas had four games with at least 115 rushing yards. Those games came against the teams ranked 31st (Miami), 30th (New York Jets), 29th (Houston), and 26th (Denver) in defensive DVOA against the run. On the other hand, he gained only 41 yards on 15 carries against Green Bay, ranked eighth, and only 58 yards on 22 carries against Minnesota, ranked first. Obviously, because players and teams don't give the same performance every week, this is more of a general law and it doesn't necessarily apply in the short term. (For example, Fargas did have a 100-yard game against Indianapolis, which ranked ninth in defensive DVOA against the run last season.)

If the overall yards per carry of two running backs are equal, the running back who consistently gains yardage on every play is more valuable than a boom-and-bust running back who is frequently stuffed at the line but occasionally breaks a long, highlight-worthy run.

Our brethren at Baseball Prospectus believe that the most precious commodity in baseball is outs. Since teams get only 27 of them per game, you can't afford to give one up for very little return. So imagine if there were a new rule that gave a baseball team a way to earn another three outs in the middle of the inning. That would be pretty useful, right?

That's the way football works. You may start a drive 80 yards away from scoring, but as long as you can earn 10 yards in four chances, you get another four chances. Long gains have plenty of value, but if those long gains are mixed with a lot of short gains, you are going to put the quarterback in a lot of difficult third-and-long situations. That means more punts and more giving the ball back to the other team rather than moving the chains and giving the offense four more plays to work with.

The running back who gains consistent yardage is also going to do a lot more for you late in the game, when the goal of running the ball is not just to gain yardage but to eat clock time. If you are a Chicago Bears fan watching your team with a late lead, you don't want to see three straight Cedric Benson stuffs at the line followed by a punt. You want to see a game-icing first down.

A common historical misconception is that our preference for consistent running backs means that "Football Outsiders believes that Barry Sanders was overrated." Sanders wasn't just any boom-and-bust running back, though; he was the greatest boom-and-bust runner of all time, with bigger booms and fewer busts. Our play-by-play database only goes back to 1995, but Sanders led the league in rushing DYAR for 1996 and was second behind Terrell Davis in 1997.

Rushing depends more on the offensive line than people realize, but pass protection depends more on the quarterback himself than people realize.

Some readers complain that this idea contradicts the previous one. Aren't those consistent running backs just the product of good offensive lines? The truth lies somewhere in between. Certainly, some good running backs, such as Edgerrin James since his move to the Arizona Cardinals, suffer because their offensive lines cannot create consistent holes. Most boom-and-bust running backs, however, contribute to their own problems by hesitating behind the line whenever the hole is unclear, looking for the home run instead of charging forward for the four-yard gain that keeps the offense moving.

As for pass protection, some quarterbacks have better instincts for the rush than others do, and are thus better at getting out of trouble by moving around in the pocket or throwing the ball away. Others will hesitate, hold on to the ball too long, and lose yardage over and over.

Note that "moving around in the pocket" does not necessarily mean scrambling. In fact, a scrambling quarterback will often take more sacks than a pocket quarterback will, because while a scrambler is running around trying to make something happen, a defensive lineman will often catch up with him.

Shotgun formations are generally more efficient than formations with the quarterback under center.

In 2007, offenses gained 5.9 yards per play from shotgun, but just 5.1 yards per play with the quarterback under center. The year before, the difference was even greater, with 6.4 yards per play from shotgun and just under 5.0 yards per play with the quarterback under center. This wide split exists even if you try to weed out statistical biases like teams using shotgun more often on third-and-long, or against prevent defenses in the fourth quarter. Shotgun offense is more efficient if you look only at the first half, on every down, and even if you look only at running back carries rather than at passes and scrambles.

Clearly, NFL teams have figured out the importance of the shotgun for themselves. Last year, for the first time, every team ran at least 8 percent of its plays from shotgun, and the average team used shotgun 27 percent of the time, a huge jump over the 19 percent average of 2006. The Patriots were the first team in our records to use shotgun on more than half of their offensive plays. It is likely that if teams continue to increase their usage of the shotgun, defenses will adapt and the benefit of the formation will become less pronounced.

A running back with 370 or more carries during the regular season will usually suffer either a major injury or a loss of effectiveness the following year, unless he is named Eric Dickerson.

Terrell Davis, Jamal Anderson, and Edgerrin James all blew out their knees. Larry Johnson broke his foot. Earl Campbell and Eddie George went from legendary powerhouses to plodding, replacement-level players. Shaun Alexander broke his foot *and* became a plodding, replacement-level player. This is what happens when a running back is overworked to the point of having at least 370 carries during the regular season.

The Curse of 370, expanded in *Pro Football Prospectus 2005*, now includes seasons with 390 or more carries in regular and postseason play combined. Research also shows that receptions don't cause a problem, only workload on the ground.

Plenty of running backs get injured without hitting 370 carries in a season, but there is a clear difference. On average, running backs with 300 to 369 carries and no postseason appearance will see their total rushing yardage decline by 15 percent the following year and their yards per carry decline by 2 percent. The average running back with 370 or more regular-season carries, or 390 including the postseason, will see his rushing yardage decline by 35 percent and his yards per carry decline by 8 percent.

The question of workload for college running backs is explored in this year's Detroit chapter.

Wide receivers must be judged on both complete and incomplete passes.

We don't yet know enough to precisely parse the blame for incomplete passes, but we know that wide receiver catch rates are as consistent from year to year as quarterback completion percentages. Since 2001, Hines Ward has never caught fewer than 59 percent of intended passes, whether from Kordell Stewart, Tommy Maddox, or Ben Roethlisberger. Plaxico Burress, playing with the same quarterbacks and with Eli Manning, has never caught more than 58 percent of intended passes and, in three years, had a catch rate below 50 percent.

The total quality of an NFL team is three parts offense, three parts defense, and one part special teams.

There are three units on a football team, but they are not of equal importance. Our DVOA ratings provide good evidence for this. The special-teams ratings are turned into DVOA by comparing how often field position on special teams leads to scoring compared with field position and first downs on offense. After figuring out these numbers, the top ratings for special teams are roughly one-third as high as the top ratings for offense or defense.

Offense is more consistent from year to year than defense, and offensive performance is easier to project than defensive performance. Special teams performance is less consistent than either.

Nobody in the NFL understands this concept better than Indianapolis Colts general manager Bill Polian. Both the Super Bowl champion Colts and the four-time AFC champion Buffalo Bills of the early 1990s were built around the idea that if you put together an offense that can dominate the league year after year, eventually you will luck into a year where good health and a few smart decisions will give you a defense good enough to win a championship. (As the Colts learned in 2006, you don't even need a year—just four weeks.) Even the New England Patriots, who are led by a defense-first head coach in Bill Belichick, have been more consistent on offense than on defense since they began their run of success in 2001.

Field-goal percentage is almost entirely random from season to season, whereas kickoff distance is one of the most consistent statistics in football.

This theory, which originally appeared in the *New York Times* in October 2006, is one of the most controversial, but it is hard to argue against the evidence. Measuring every kicker who had at least 10 field-goal attempts in each of two consecutive years from 1999 to 2006, the year-to-year correlation coefficient for field-goal percentage was an insignificant .05. Mike Vanderjagt didn't miss a single field goal in 2003, but his percentage was a below-average 74 percent the year before and 80 percent the year after. Adam Vinatieri, supposedly the best kicker in the game, has never had two straight seasons with accuracy better than last year's NFL average of 83 percent.

On the other hand, the year-to-year correlation coefficient for kickoff distance, over the same 1999-2006 period and with the same minimum of 10 kicks per year, is .61. The same players consistently lead the league in kickoff distance, particularly Neil Rackers, Olindo Mare, Josh Brown, and, for the last two years, Stephen Gostkowski.

Recovery of a fumble, despite being the product of hard work, is almost entirely random.

Stripping the ball is a skill. Holding on to the ball is a skill. Pouncing on the ball as it is bouncing all over the place is not a skill. There is no correlation whatsoever between the percentage of fumbles recovered by a team in one year and the percentage it recovers in the next year. The odds of recovery are based solely on the type of play involved, not the teams or any of their players.

Fans like to insist that specific coaches can teach their teams to recover more fumbles by swarming to the ball. Chicago's Lovie Smith, in particular, is supposed to have this ability. But since Smith took over the Bears, their rate of fumble recovery on defense went from a league-best 76 percent to a league-worst 33 percent in 2005, then back to 67 percent in 2006. Last year, they recovered 57 percent of fumbles, close to the league average.

Fumble recovery is equally erratic on offense. In 2006, the Detroit Lions fumbled 21 times on offense and recovered just four of those fumbles. Last year, the Lions fumbled 29 times on offense—but actually had fewer turnovers because they recovered 16 of those fumbles.

Fumble recovery is a major reason why the public overestimates or underestimates certain teams. Although fumbles are huge, turning-point plays that dramatically affect wins and losses in the past, fumble recovery percentage says absolutely nothing about a team's chances of winning games in the future. With this in mind, Football Outsiders stats treat all fumbles as equal, penalizing them according to the likelihood that each type of fumble (run, pass, sack, etc.) will be recovered by the defense.

Other plays that qualify as nonpredictive events include blocked kicks and touchdowns during turnover returns. These plays are not "lucky," per se, but they have no value whatsoever for predicting future performance.

Field position is fluid.

As discussed in the Statistical Toolbox, every yard line on the field has a value based on how likely a team is to score from that location on the field as opposed to from a yard further back. The change in value from one yard to the next is the same whether the team has the ball or not. The goal of a defense is not just to prevent scoring, but also to hold the opposition so that the offense can get the ball back in the best possible field position. A bad offense will score as many points as a good offense will if the bad offense starts each drive five yards closer to the goal line.

A corollary to this precept: The most underrated aspect of an NFL team's performance is the field position gained or lost on kickoffs and punts. This is part of why Devin Hester has such an impact on the game, even when he isn't returning a kickoff or a punt for a touchdown.

Teams that are strong on first and second down, but weak on third down, will tend to improve the following year. Teams that are weak on first and second down, but strong on third down, will tend to decline the following year.

We discovered this precept when creating our first team projection system in 2004. Our data said that the lowly San Diego Chargers would have one of the best offenses in the league, which seemed a little ridiculous. But looking closer, our projection system treated the previous year's performance on different downs as different variables, and the 2003 Chargers were actually good on first and second down, but terrible on third.

Teams get fewer opportunities on third down, so third-down performance is more volatile—but it's also a bigger part of a team's overall performance than first or second down, because the result is usually either very good (four more downs) or very bad (losing the ball to the other team with a punt). Over time, a team will play as well in those situations as it does in other situations, which will bring the overall offense or defense in line with the offense and defense on first and second down.

This trend is even stronger between seasons. Struggles on third down are a pretty obvious problem, and teams will generally target their off-season moves at improving their third-down performance ... which often leads to an improvement in third-down performance. Teams significantly affected by this trend in 2008 include Pittsburgh and Arizona (offense better on third downs in 2007), Kansas City (defense better on third downs in 2007), and Philadelphia (offense worse on third downs in 2007, but defense better on third downs).

By and large, a team built on depth is better than a team built on stars and scrubs.

The Redskins went into 2007 with a Super Bowl–quality starting lineup and finished 5-11 because they had no depth. You cannot concentrate your salaries on a handful of star players, because there is no such thing as avoiding injuries in the NFL. Every team will suffer injuries; the only question is how many. The game is too fast and the players too strong to build a team based around the idea that "if we can avoid all injuries this year, we'll win." This issue is explored later in the book in an essay titled "The Injury Effect."

Running backs usually decline after age 28, tight ends after age 29, wide receivers after age 30, and quarterbacks after age 32.

This research was originally done by Doug Drinen of footballguys.com in 2000. In recent years, a few players have had huge seasons above these general age limits (most notably Tiki Barber, Tony Gonzalez, and Corey Dillon), but the peak ages Drinen found a few years ago still apply to most players.

As for "nonskill players," research we conducted in 2007 for *ESPN The Magazine* suggested that defensive ends and defensive backs generally begin to decline after age 29, linebackers and offensive linemen after age 30, and defensive tackles after age 31. But because we still have so few statistics on linemen and defensive players, this research should not be considered definitive.

The future NFL success of quarterbacks chosen in the first two rounds of the draft can be projected with a high degree of accuracy by using just two statistics from college: games started and completion percentage.

This theory was introduced in *Pro Football Prospectus 2006* and further refined in *Pro Football Prospectus 2007*. The projection created by these stats is known as the Lewin Career Forecast, after David Lewin, the creator of the theory.

Scouts expected players such as Kyle Boller (48 percent), Jim Druckenmiller (54 percent), and Ryan Leaf (54 percent) to suddenly figure out how to complete passes once they hit the NFL. Not surprisingly, this didn't happen. Having a high completion percentage (above 60 percent or so) is no guarantee of success, especially if the figure came from a small number of games in a fluky system (Tim Couch being a good example), but it is a prerequisite for success. Games started is an important stat, because the more film that exists of a player in game conditions, the easier it is to find weaknesses that might come out against different opponents or different schemes. When scouts have insufficient information, they place too much weight on "measurables" and off-field workouts and make mistakes like Couch (26 starters), Leaf (24 starts), or Akili Smith (19 starts). The Lewin Career Forecast applies only to the first two rounds, because it assumes that with enough game film to judge, scouts can accurately identify players who are "system quarterbacks" and will not succeed in the NFL, and those players appropriately fall on draft day (Colt Brennan being a good example from 2008).

From 1996 to 2005, the worst quarterback drafted in the top two rounds who had 37 or more college starts and a completion rate above 60 percent was Eli Manning. When the worst projection belongs to a quarterback who just led a two-minute drill to finish off a historic Super Bowl upset, that's a good projection system.

Championship teams are generally defined by their ability to dominate inferior opponents, not their ability to win close games.
Football games are often decided by just one or two plays—a missed field goal, a bouncing fumble, the subjective spot of an official on fourth-and-1. One missed assignment by a cornerback or one slightly askew pass that bounces off a receiver's hands and into those of a defensive back five yards away, and the game could be over. In a blowout, however, one lucky bounce isn't going to change things. Championship teams beat their good opponents convincingly and destroy the cupcakes on the schedule. Certainly, the rule has its exceptions, including the past two Super Bowl champions. Unless this becomes a trend that lasts four or five years, it is hard to say that this rule no longer exists.

Statistical Toolbox

Aaron Schatz

Three years ago, *Pro Football Prospectus* introduced a number of new statistics unlike any that had been used to measure the National Football League. Since then we've improved the accuracy of those statistics and introduced some new ones, in particular a number of metrics that would not be possible without the Football Outsiders Game Charting Project, which is explained later in this introduction in the section of the same name. Our statistical palette contains a wide variety of colors with which to paint a picture of the NFL. What follows is an explanation of all the statistics you'll find in this book: how we calculate them, what the numbers mean, and what they tell us about why teams win or lose football games. We've done our best to present these numbers in a way that makes them easy to understand. This explanation is long, so feel free to read some of it, flip around the rest of the book, and then come back.

Veteran readers of FootballOutsiders.com and *Pro Football Prospectus* will be familiar with most of these stats but should note the major change in our individual statistics, which are now stated in terms of yardage rather than points.

DEFENSE-ADJUSTED VALUE OVER AVERAGE (DVOA)

One running back runs for three yards. Another running back runs for three yards. Which is the better run? This sounds like a stupid question, but it isn't. In fact, this question is at the heart of nearly all the analysis in this book.

Several factors can differentiate one three-yard run from another. What is the down and distance? Is it third-and-2, or second-and-15? Where on the field is the ball? Does the player get only three yards because he hits the goal line and scores? Is the player's team up by two touchdowns in the fourth quarter and thus running out the clock, or down by two touchdowns and thus facing a defense that is playing purely against the pass? Is the running back playing against the porous defense of the Raiders or the stalwart defense of the Vikings?

Conventional NFL statistics value plays based solely on their net yardage. The NFL determines the best players by adding all their yards no matter what situations they came in or how many plays it took to get them. Now, why would they do that? Football has one objective—to get to the end zone—and two ways to achieve that, by gaining yards and achieving first downs. These two goals need to be balanced to determine a player's value or a team's performance. All the yards in the world won't help a team win if they all come in eight-yard chunks on third-and-10.

The popularity of fantasy football only exacerbates the problem. Fans have become used to judging players based on how much they help fantasy teams win and lose, not how much they help *real* teams win and lose. Typical fantasy scoring further skews things by counting the yard between the one and the goal line as 61 times more important than all the other yards on the field (each yard worth 0.1 points, a touchdown worth 6). Let's say Anquan Boldin catches a pass on third-and-15 and goes 50 yards but gets tackled two yards from the goal line, and then Edgerrin James takes the ball on 1st-and-goal from the two-yard line and plunges in for the score. Has Edgerrin James done something special? Not really. When an offense gets the ball on 1st-and-goal at the two-yard line, they are going to score a touchdown five out of six times. Edge is getting credit for the work done by the passing game.

Doing a better job of distributing credit for scoring points and winning games is the goal of **DVOA**, or Defense-adjusted Value Over Average. DVOA breaks down every single play of the NFL season, assigning each play a value based on both total yards and yards toward a first down, based on work done by Pete Palmer, Bob Carroll, and John Thorn in their seminal book, *The Hidden Game of Football*. On first down, a play is considered a success if it gains 45 percent of needed yards; on second down, a play needs to gain 60 percent of needed yards; on third or fourth down, only gaining a new first down is considered success.

We then expand on that basic idea with a more complicated system of success points, improved over the past four years with a lot of mathematics and a bit of trial and error. A successful play is worth one point, an unsuccessful play zero points, with fractional points in between (for example, eight yards on third-and-10 is worth 0.54 success points). Extra points are awarded for big plays, gradually increasing to three points for 10 yards (assuming those yards result in a first down), four points for 20 yards, and five points for 40 yards or more. Losing three or more yards is -1 point, an interception is -8 points, and a fumble is worth anywhere from -2.15 to -6.54 points depending on how often a fumble in that situation is lost to the defense—no matter who recovers the fumble. Red zone plays are worth 20 percent more, and there is a bonus given for a touchdown that acknowledges that the goal line is significantly more difficult to cross than the previous 99 yards (this bonus is nowhere near as large as the one used in fantasy football).

Our system is a bit more complex than the one in *Hidden Game* thanks to our subsequent research, which added a larger penalty for turnovers, the fractional points, and a slightly higher baseline for success on first down. The reason why all fumbles are counted, no matter whether they are recovered by the offense or defense, is that fumble recovery is random, as explained in the essay "Pregame Show."

Every single play run in the NFL gets a success value based on this system, and that number gets compared to the average success values of plays in similar situations for all players, adjusted for a number of variables. These variables include down and distance, field location, time remaining in game, and the team's lead or deficit in the game score. Teams are always compared to the overall offensive average, because the team made its own choice whether to pass or rush. When it comes to individual players, however, rushing plays are compared to other rushing plays, passing plays to other passing plays, tight ends to tight ends, and wideouts to wideouts.

Going back to our example of the three-yard rush, if Player A gains three yards under a set of circumstances in which the average NFL running back gains only one yard, Player A has a certain amount of value above others at his position. Likewise, if Player B gains three yards on a play on which, under similar circumstances, an average NFL back gains four yards, that Player B has negative value relative to others at his position. Once we make all our adjustments, we can evaluate the difference between this player's rate of success and the expected success rate of an average running back in the same situation (or between the opposing defense and the average defense in the same situation, and so on). Add every play by a certain team

or player, divide by the total of the various baselines for success in all those situations, and you get VOA, or Value Over Average.

The biggest variable in football is the fact that each team plays a different schedule against teams of disparate quality. By adjusting each play based on the opposing defense's average success in stopping that type of play over the course of a season, we get DVOA. Rushing and passing plays are adjusted based on down and location on the field; passing plays are adjusted also based on how the defense performs against passes to running backs, tight ends, or wide receivers. Defenses are adjusted based on the average success of the *offenses* they are facing. (Yes, technically the defensive stats are offense-adjusted. If it seems weird, think of the *D* in *DVOA* as standing for *opponent-Dependent*.)

The biggest advantage of DVOA is the ability to break teams and players down to find strengths and weaknesses in a variety of situations. In the aggregate, DVOA may not be quite as accurate as some of the other, similar power ratings formulas based on comparing drives rather than individual plays, but unlike those other ratings, DVOA can be separated not only by player but also by down, or by week, or by distance needed for a first down. This can give us a better idea of not just which team is better but why, and what a team has to do to improve itself in the future. You will find DVOA used in this book in a lot of different ways—because it takes every single play into account, it can be used to measure a player' or team's performance in any situation. All Pittsburgh third downs can be compared to how an average team does on third down. Matt Leinart and Kurt Warner can each be compared to how an average quarterback performs in the red zone, or with a lead, or in the second half of the game.

Since it compares each play only to plays with similar circumstances, it gives a more accurate picture of how much better a team really is compared to the league as a whole. The list of top DVOA offenses on third down, for example, is more accurate than the conventional NFL conversion statistic because it takes into account that converting 3rd-and-long is more difficult than converting third-and-short, and that a turnover is worse than an incomplete pass because it eliminates the opportunity to move the other team back with a punt on fourth down.

One of the hardest parts of understanding a new statistic is interpreting its scale, or what numbers represent good performance or bad performance. We've made that easy with DVOA. In all cases, 0% represents the league average. A positive DVOA represents a situation that favors the offense, and a negative DVOA represents a situation that favors the defense. This is why the best offenses have positive DVOA ratings (last year, New England led the league at +52.0%) and the best defenses have negative DVOA ratings (with Tennessee number one at -13.4%). For both teams and starting players, the best and worst ratings tend to be around +/-30%. However, you'll notice that this wasn't the case in 2007, when New England set the all-time record for offensive DVOA, and Tennessee had the worst rating of any defense to rank number one in the 13 years for which we have data. Because league average is determined across multiple years, no single year will average exactly 0%. This gives DVOA the added benefit of being able to show us how the scoring environment has fluctuated from year to year. Last year's total league DVOA was 1.1%, the second-highest season on record behind 2004. The NFL's offensive level was average in 2006 and below 0% in both 2003 and 2005.

Team DVOA totals combine offense and defense by subtracting the latter from the former because the better defenses will have negative DVOA ratings. (Special teams performance is also added, as described later in this essay.)

Does it work? Using correlation coefficients, we can show that only actual points scored are better than DVOA at indicating how many games a team has won (Table 1) and DVOA does a better job of predicting wins in the coming season than either wins or points scored in the previous season (Table 2). (Correlation coefficient is a statistical tool that measures how two variables are related by using a number between 1 and -1. The closer to -1 or 1, the stronger the relationship, but the closer to 0, the weaker the relationship.)

Table 1. Correlation of Various Stats to Wins, 2000-2007

Stat	Offense	Defense	Total
Points Scored/Allowed	.74	-.68	.92
DVOA	.68	-.53	.87
Yards Gained/Allowed	.54	-.42	.67
Yards Gained/Allowed per Play	.51	-.34	.70

Table 2. Correlation of Various Stats to Wins Following Year, 2000-2007

Stat	Correlation
DVOA	.32
Point Differential	.27
Yards per Play Differential	.25
Wins	.25
Yardage Differential	.22

DEFENSE-ADJUSTED YARDS ABOVE REPLACEMENT (DYAR)

After using DVOA for a few months, we came across a strange phenomenon: Well-regarded players, particularly those known for their durability, had DVOA ratings that came out around average. The reason is that DVOA, by virtue of being a percentage or rate statistic, doesn't take into account the cumulative value of having a player producing at a league-average level during an above-average number of plays. By definition, an average level of performance is better than that provided by half of the league and the ability to maintain that level of performance while carrying a heavy work load is valuable indeed. In addition, a player who is involved in a high number of plays can draw the defense's attention away from other parts of the offense, and if that player is a running back, he can take time off the clock with repeated runs.

Let's say you have a running back who carries the ball 300 times in a season. What would happen if you were to remove this player from his team's offense? What would happen to those 300 plays? Those plays don't disappear with the player, though some might be lost to the defense because of the associated loss of first downs. Rather, those plays would have to be distributed among the remaining players in the offense, with the bulk of them being given to a replacement running back. This is where we arrive at the concept of replacement level, borrowed from our partners at Baseball Prospectus. When a player is removed from an offense, he is usually not replaced by a player of similar ability. Nearly every starting player in the NFL is a starter because he is better than the alternative. Those 300 plays will typically be given to a significantly worse player, someone who is the backup because he doesn't have as much experience or talent or both. A player's true value can then be measured by the level of performance he provides above that replacement level baseline, totaled over all of his run or pass attempts.

Of course, the *real* replacement player is different for each team in the NFL. Over the past two years, the second-string running back in Dallas (Marion Barber) had a much higher DVOA than the first-string back (Julius Jones). Ryan Grant started the year as the fifth-string running back for the Giants and ended the year with a 12.4% DVOA for Green Bay. On other teams, the drop from the starter to the backup can be even greater than the general drop to replacement level. Suppose, for example, that Peyton Manning broke his leg. The choice to start an inferior player or to employ a subreplacement level backup, however, falls to the team, not the starter being evaluated. Thus we generalize replacement level for the league as a whole because the ultimate goal is to evaluate players independent of the quality of their teammates.

Originally, we estimated replacement level by simply using a scale similar to the one our partners at Baseball Prospectus use for hitters and pitchers, putting replacement level about three-eighths of the way between average (0%) and the worst starters in the league. For example, since the worst quarterbacks are usually around -35% DVOA, the replacement level was -13.3% DVOA. One of our main projects this past offseason was to rework replacement level to make it more accurate for each position. For quarterbacks, we analyzed situations where two or more quarterbacks had played meaningful snaps for a team in the same season, and then compared the overall DVOA of the original starters to the overall DVOA of the replacements. We did not include situations where the backup was actually a top prospect waiting his turn on the bench, since a first-round pick is by no means a replacement-level player. By comparing the replacement-level quarterbacks to the quarterbacks they replaced, as well as the quarterbacks who played the entire season, we determined that the replacement level for quarterbacks is roughly -12.5% DVOA, fairly similar to what we had before.

The same is not true at other positions. There was no easy way to separate running backs and receivers into starters and replacements, since unlike at quarterback, being the starter doesn't make you the only guy who gets in the game. Instead, we decided to use a simpler method. First, we ranked players at each position in each season by attempts. The players who made up the final 10 percent of passes or runs were split out as replacement players and then compared to the players making up the other 90 percent of plays at that position. This took care of the fact that not every nonstarter at running back or wide receiver is a freely available talent (for example, Jerious Norwood or Anthony Gonzalez). Replacement level is now higher in most ways but by different degrees, and replacement level actually went down for both running back receiving and wide receiver rushing (Table 3).

Once again, the challenge of any new stat is to present it on a scale that is meaningful to those attempting to use it. Saying that Carson Palmer was worth 106.3 success value points over replacement in 2007 has little value without a context to tell us whether 106.3 is a good total or a bad one. For the past four years, we've translated these success values into a number representing actual points scored, with a statistic called Defense-

Table 3. Old and New Replacement-Level DVOA

Measurement	Old	New
Passing	-13.3%	-12.5%
QB rushing	-17.1%	-12.5%
RB rushing	-13.7%	-8.0%
RB receiving	-9.8%	-12.6%
WR receiving	-12.7%	-7.6%
TE receiving	-15.0%	-12.3%
WR/TE rushing	-26.0%	-43.0%

adjusted Points Above Replacement, or DPAR. For example, in 2007 Carson Palmer was worth 51.8 DPAR.

Unfortunately, DPAR wasn't the easiest thing to understand either. The reason is simple: Who refers to player value by how many points they score? I mean, we know touchdowns are six points, and we talk about kickers in terms of points when we talk about fantasy football, but people don't think of football players in terms of *points*. They think in terms of *yards*.

Therefore, along with the new set of replacement baselines comes a new way to think about Football Outsiders' advanced stats for individual players: **DYAR**, or Defense-adjusted Yards Above Replacement. Carson Palmer's season is now worth 1,215 DYAR, which ranked sixth in the NFL last year. By comparison, Jeff Garcia's season was worth 694 DYAR, Rex Grossman's season was worth -168 DYAR (yes, below replacement level), and Tom Brady's season was worth an all-time record 2,788 DYAR. Turning success points into yards was easier than turning success into points, because we happen to have tangible yardage totals for all the players we are measuring.

Besides more accurate replacement levels and the transition to stating our stats in terms of yardage, we made a number of other improvements to the individual player versions of DVOA to bring them more in line with team DVOA. Individual DVOA ratings now use more complicated (and accurate) opponent adjustments. Passing and receiving DVOA now includes defensive pass interference as a positive play, just like team DVOA. Finally, the bonus for plays in the red zone for individual DVOA has been dropped to 10 percent, as opposed to 20 percent for team DVOA, which improved correlation for players from season to season.

PROBLEMS WITH DVOA AND DYAR

Football is a game in which nearly every action requires the work of two or more teammates—in fact, usually 11 teammates all working in unison. Unfortunately, when it comes to individual player ratings, we are still far from the point at which we can determine the value of a player independent from the performance of his teammates. That means that when we say, "In 2007, Earnest Graham had a DVOA of 8.4%," what we are really saying is "In 2007, Earnest Graham, playing in Jon Gruden's offensive system with the Tampa Bay offensive line blocking for him and Jeff Garcia selling the fake when necessary, had a DVOA of 8.4%."

DVOA is limited by what's included in the official NFL play-by-play or tracked by the Football Outsiders game charting project (introduced later). Because we need to have the entire play-by-play of a season to compute DVOA and DYAR, these metrics are not yet ready to compare players of today to players throughout the league's history. As of this writing, we have processed 13 seasons, from 1995 to 2007.

SPECIAL TEAMS

The problem with a system based on measuring both yardage and yardage towards a first down is what to do with plays that don't have the possibility of a first down. Special teams are an important part of football, and we needed a way to add that performance to the team DVOA rankings. Our special teams metric includes five measurements: field goals and extra points, net punting, punt returns, net kickoffs, and kick returns.

The foundation of most of these special teams ratings is the concept that each yard line has a different value based on the likelihood of scoring from that position on the field. In *Hidden Game*, the authors suggested that each additional yard for the offense had equal value, with a team's own goal line being worth -2 points, the 50-yard line, 2 points, and the opposing goal line, 6 points. (-2 points is not only the value of a safety but also reflects the fact that when a team is backed up in its own territory it is likely that its drive will stall, forcing a punt that will give the ball to the other team in good field position. Thus, the negative point value reflects the fact that the defense is more likely to score next.) Our studies have updated this concept to reflect the actual likelihood that the offense or defense will have the next score from a given position on the field based on results from the past few seasons. The line that represents the value of field position is not straight, but curved, with the value of each yard increasing as teams approach either goal line.

Our special teams ratings compare each kick or punt to the league average based on the point value of the position of the kick, catch, and return. We've determined a league average for how far a kick goes based on the line of scrimmage for each kick (almost always the 30-yard line for kickoffs, variable for punts) and a league average for how far a return goes based on both the yard line where the ball is caught and the distance that it traveled in the air.

The kicking or punting team is rated based on net points compared to average, taking into account both the kick and the return, if there is one. Because the average return is always positive, punts that are not returnable (touchbacks, out of bounds, fair catches, and punts downed by the coverage unit) will rate higher than punts of the same distance which are returnable. (This is also true of touchbacks on kickoffs.) There are also separate individual ratings for kickers and punters based on distance and whether the kick is returnable, assuming an average return in order to judge the kicker separate from the coverage.

For the return team, the rating is based on how many points the return is worth compared to average, based on the location of the catch and the distance the ball traveled in the air. Return teams are not judged on the distance of kicks, nor are they judged on kicks that cannot be returned. As explained below, blocked kicks are so rare as to be statistically insignificant as predictors for future performance and are thus ignored. For the kicking team they simply count as missed field goals; for the defense they are gathered with their opponents' other missed field goals in Hidden value (also explained below).

Field goal kicking is measured differently. Measuring kickers by field goal percentage is a bit absurd because it assumes that all field goals are of equal difficulty. In our metric, each field goal is compared to the average number of points scored on all field goal attempts from that distance over the past decade, with adjustments for rule changes such as the introduction of the special-teams-use-only "k-ball" in 1999. The value of a field goal increases as the distance from the goal line increases. Kickoffs, punts, and field goals are then adjusted based on weather and altitude. It will surprise no one to learn that it is easier to kick the ball in Denver or in a dome than it is to kick the ball in Buffalo in December. Because we do not yet have enough data to tailor our adjustments specifically to each stadium, we have one of four categories: Cold, Warm, Dome, and Denver. An additional adjustment drops the value of field goals in Florida (because the warm temperatures allow the ball to carry better) and raises the value of punts in San Francisco (because of those infamous winds).

Once we've totaled how many points above or below average can be attributed to special teams, we translate those points into DVOA so the ratings can be added to offense and defense to get total team DVOA.

Three aspects of special teams affect wins and losses but don't show up in the standard special teams rating because a team has little or no influence on them. The first is the length of kickoffs by the opposing team. The other two are field goals against your team and punt distance against your team. Research shows no indication that teams can influence the accuracy or strength of field-goal kickers and punters, except for blocks. As mentioned, although blocked field goals and punts are skillful plays, they are so rare that they have no correlation to how well teams have played in the past or will play in the future, and thus they are included here as if they were any other missed field goal or botched punt, giving the defense no additional credit for their efforts. The value of these three elements is listed separately as Hidden value.

The 2007 Chicago Bears were an important exception to the general fact that a team has no influence on opposing kickoffs and punts. The 2007 special teams value attempted to correct for this by giving Chicago net value rather than no value on a kickoff that was not returned because it was deliberately kicked short to avoid Devin Hester. We also did this with a handful of kickoffs against Cleveland and the New York Jets. This doesn't fully compensate for the effect of Hester on the kicking game, but it is a more accurate measure of the value Chicago gets out of special teams. Hester's unique place in football history is explored further in an essay in the Chicago chapter.

Special teams ratings also do not include two-point conversions or on-side kick attempts, both of which, like blocks, are so infrequent as to be statistically insignificant in judging future performance.

PYTHAGOREAN PROJECTION

The Pythagorean projection is an approximation of each team's wins based solely on their points scored and allowed. This basic concept was introduced by baseball analyst Bill James, who discovered that the record of a baseball team could be closely approximated by taking the square of team runs scored and dividing it by the sum of the squares of team runs scored and allowed. Statistician Daryl Morey later extended this theorem to professional football, refining the exponent to 2.37 rather than 2.

Pythagorean projections have done a remarkable job of projecting Super Bowl champions. Of the 20 Super Bowls played since the 1987 strike season, 11 were won by the team that led the NFL in Pythagorean wins, but only seven were won by the team with the most actual victories. Super Bowl champions that led the league in Pythagorean wins but not actual wins include the 2004 Patriots, 2000 Ravens, 1999 Rams, and 1997 Broncos. The last two years have provided a dramatic exception to this general rule; the 2006 Colts (9.6) had the fewest Pythagorean wins of any Super Bowl champion in history, and then the Giants (8.6) shattered that mark last year. However, the other conference champion in each of the last two seasons was the team that led its conference in Pythagorean wins, and overall, 22 of the 40 teams to make the Super Bowl over the past 20 years led their conference in Pythagorean wins. (The improbability of New York's Super Bowl victory given the team's Pythagorean projection is explored in an essay in the Giants chapter.)

Teams that win a minimum of one full game more than their Pythagorean projection tend to regress the following year; teams that win a minimum of one full game less than their Pythagorean projection tend to improve the following year, particularly if they were at or above .500 despite their underachieving. The 2006 Jacksonville Jaguars, for example, finished 8-8 but had 10.8 Pythagorean wins, one of the larger differences in recent history. Last year, they improved to 11-5. In the upcoming season, this trend favors a repeat division title from Pittsburgh, which went 10-6 but had 11.4 Pythagorean wins. It also suggests improvement for two 8-8 teams, Philadelphia and Minnesota, that had more than 9.0 Pythagorean wins in 2007.

ADJUSTED LINE YARDS

One of the most difficult goals of statistical analysis in football is isolating the degree to which each of the 22 men on the field is responsible for the result of a given play. Nowhere is this as significant as in the running game, in which one player runs while up to nine other players—including wideouts, tight ends, and a fullback—block in different directions. None of the statistics we use for measuring rushing—yards, touchdowns, yards per carry—differentiate between the contribution of the running back and the contribution of the offensive line. Neither do our advanced metrics DVOA and DYAR.

We do, however, have enough play-by-play data amassed that we can try to separate the effect that the running back has on a particular play from the effects of the offensive line (and other offensive blockers) and the opposing defense. A team might have two running backs in its stable: RB A, who averages 3.0 yards per carry, and RB B, who averages 3.5 yards per carry. Who is the better back? Imagine that RB A doesn't just average 3.0 yards per carry but gets exactly 3 yards on every single carry; RB B has a highly variable yardage output: sometimes 5 yards, sometimes -2 yards, sometimes 20 yards. The difference in variability between the runners can be exploited to determine not only the difference between the runners but the effect the offensive line has on every running play.

At some point in every long running play, the running back passes all of his offensive line blocks as well as additional blocking backs or receivers. From there on, the rest of the play depends on the runner's own speed and elusiveness and the speed and tackling ability of the opposing defense. If Frank Gore breaks through the line for 50 yards, avoiding tacklers all the way to the goal line, his offensive line has done a great job—but they aren't responsible for the majority of the yards gained. The trick is figuring out exactly how much they *are* responsible for.

For each running back carry, we calculated the probability that the back involved would run for the specific yardage on that play based on that back's average yardage per carry and the variability of their yardage from play to play. We also calculated the probability that the offense would get the yardage based on the team's rushing average and variability using all backs *other* than the one involved in the given play, and the probability that the defense would give up the specific amount of yardage based on its average rushing yards allowed per carry and variability. For example, based on his rushing average and variability, the probability in 2004 that Tiki Barber would have a positive carry was 80 percent while the probability that the Giants would have a positive carry without Barber running was only 73 percent.

A regression analysis breaks the value for rushing yardage into the following categories: losses, 0-4 yards, 5-10 yards, and 11+ yards. In general, the offensive line is 20 percent more responsible for lost yardage than it is for positive gains up to four yards, but 50 percent less responsible for additional yardage gained between five and 10 yards, and not at all responsible for additional yardage past 10 yards.

By applying those percentages to every running back carry, we were able to create **Adjusted Line Yards**, a statistic that measured offensive line performance. (We don't include carries by receivers, which are usually based on deception rather than straight blocking, or carries by quarterbacks, which are almost always busted passing plays unless they involve Vince Young.) Next, those numbers are adjusted based on down, distance, and situation as well as opponent (similar to DVOA) and then normalized so that the league average for Adjusted Line Yards per carry is the same as the league average for RB yards per carry (in 2007, 4.17 yards).

The NFL distinguishes between runs made to seven locations on the line: left end, right end, left tackle, right tackle, left guard, right guard, and middle. Further research showed no statistically significant difference between how well a team performed on runs listed as having gone up the middle or past a guard, so we separated runs into just five directions (left end, right end, left tackle, right tackle, and middle). Note that there may not be a statistically significant difference between right tackle and middle/guard either, but pending further research (and for the sake of symmetry) we still list runs behind the right tackle separately. These splits allow us to evaluate subsections of a team's offensive line but not necessarily individual linesmen, because we can't account for blocking assignments or guards who pull towards the opposite side of the line after the snap.

SUCCESS RATE

Success rate is a statistic for running backs that measures how consistently they achieve the yardage necessary for a play to be deemed successful. Some running backs will mix a few long runs with a lot of failed runs of one or two yards; others with similar yards-per-carry averages will consistently gain five yards on first down or as many yards as necessary on third down. This statistic helps us differentiate between the two.

Since Success Rate compares rush attempts to other rush attempts, without consideration of passing, the standard for success on first down is slightly lower than those described previously for DVOA. In addition, the standard for success changes slightly in the fourth quarter when running backs are used to run out the clock. A team with the lead is satisfied with a shorter run as long as it stays in bounds. Conversely, for a team down by a few touchdowns in the fourth quarter, four yards on first down isn't going to be a big help.

The formula for Success Rate is as follows:

- A successful play must gain 40 percent of needed yards on first down, 60 percent of needed yards on second down, and 100 percent of needed yards on third or fourth down.

- If the offense is behind by more than a touchdown in the fourth quarter, the benchmarks switch to 50 percent, 65 percent, and 100 percent, respectively.
- If the offense is ahead by any amount in the fourth quarter, the benchmarks switch to 30 percent, 50 percent, and 100 percent, respectively.

The league-average Success Rate in both 2006 and 2007 was 45.4 percent. Success Rate is not adjusted based on defenses faced and is not calculated for quarterbacks and wide receivers who occasionally carry the ball.

SIMILARITY SCORES

Similarity scores were first introduced by Bill James to compare baseball players to other baseball players from the past. It was only natural that the idea would spread to other sports as statistical analysis spread to other sports. NBA analyst John Hollinger has created his own version to compare basketball players, and we have created a version to compare football players.

Similarity scores have a lot of uses, and we aren't the only football analysts who use them. Doug Drinen of the website Footballguys.com has a system for comparing fantasy football performances. The major goal of our similarity scores is to compare career progressions to try to determine when players have a higher chance of a breakout, a decline, or—due to age or usage—an injury (much like Baseball Prospectus's PECOTA player projection system). Therefore we compare not only numbers such as attempts, yards, and touchdowns but also age and experience. We often are looking not for players who had similar seasons but for players who had similar two- or three-year spans in their careers.

Similarity scores have some important weaknesses. The database for player comparison begins in 1978, the year the 16-game season began and passing rules were liberalized (a reasonable starting point to measure the "modern" NFL), thus the method compares only standard statistics such as yards and attempts, which are subject to all kinds of biases from strength of schedule to quality of receiver corps. For our comparisons, we project full-season statistics for the strike years of 1982 and 1987, although we cannot correct for players who crossed the 1987 picket line to play more than 12 games.

If you are interested in the specific computations behind our similarity scores system, we have listed the standards for each position online at http://www. footballoutsiders.com/stats/similarity.php.

KUBIAK PROJECTION SYSTEM

Most skill position players whom we expect to play a role this season receive a projection of their standard 2008 NFL statistics using the KUBIAK projection system. KUBIAK takes into account a number of factors including expected role, performance over the past two seasons, age, height, weight, historical comparables, and projected team performance on offense and defense. When we named our system KUBIAK, it was a play on the PECOTA system used by our partners at Baseball Prospectus—if they were going to name their system after a longtime eighties backup, we would name our system after a longtime eighties backup. Little did we know that Gary Kubiak would finally get a head coaching job the very next season. After some debate, we decided to keep the name, although discussing projections for Houston players can be a bit awkward.

To clear up a common misconception among our readers, KUBIAK projects only individual player performances, not team performances.

2008 WIN PROJECTION SYSTEM

In this book, each of the 32 NFL teams receives a **2008 Mean Projection** at the beginning of its chapter. These projections stem from three equations that forecast 2008 DVOA for offense, defense, and special teams based on a number of factors including the previous two years of DVOA in various situations, improvement in the second half of 2007, recent draft history, coaching experience, injury history, specific coaching styles, and the combined tenure of the offensive line. Compared to last year's model, the standard error is now 28 percent smaller on offense, 30 percent smaller on defense, and six percent smaller on special teams.

These three equations produce precise numbers representing the most likely outcome but also produce a range of possibilities used to determine the probability of each possible offensive, defensive, and special teams DVOA for each team. This is particularly important when projecting football teams because, with only 16 games in a season, a team's performance may vary wildly from its actual talent level due to a few random bounces of the ball or badly timed injuries. In addition, the economic structure of the NFL allows teams to make sudden jumps or drops in overall ability more often than in other sports.

To project wins, Dr. Benjamin Alamar created a simulation that plays out the entire schedule for each team using random draws of DVOA for each team's offense, defense, and special teams to calculate a final score for each game in each season. The values and frequencies of these DVOA ratings are based on the projection equations described previously. This game-by-game simulation also accounts for home-field advantage, warm-weather or dome-stadium teams playing in the cold after November 1, and several other variables that can affect the outcome of each game. We ran the simulation 10,000 times producing 10,000 unique seasons representing the full range of possibilities for each team in 2008. We then compared the results to the historical probability that a certain win total would be achieved in a 16-game NFL season, adjusting the simulation to produce a more realistic number of 16-, 15-, one-, and zero-win seasons, because these are historically very low probability.

The resulting possible win totals are then separated into five categories:

- On the Clock (0-3 wins)
- Loserville (5-6 wins)
- Mediocrity (7-8 wins)
- Playoff Contender (9-10 wins)
- Super Bowl Contender (11+ wins)

From 2000 to 2007, the projection system explains roughly 65 percent of the change in each team's win total between seasons. That percentage does shift from year to year, because 32 teams isn't a large sample size. Last year, the current system explained 72 percent of the variance in win totals. For 2006, it explained only 57 percent of the variance.

The percentage given for each category is dependent not only on how good we project the team to be in 2008 but the level of variation possible in that projection and the expected performance of the teams on the schedule. Each variable has a different impact on the variability of the projection. For example, offenses that were better through the air in 2007 have more variation in their 2008 projections than offenses that were better on the ground. Defensive improvement in the second half of last season leads to less variation, but a rookie kicker or punter leads to more variation.

In response to reader requests, we also list the mean projection for each team. We do not expect any teams to win the exact number of games in their mean projection, however—particularly since no team can win 0.8 of a game (although it is rumored that the Matt Walsh tapes include footage of Bill Belichick creating a strategy to steal fractional games).

FOOTBALL OUTSIDERS GAME CHARTING PROJECT

Each of the formulas listed above relies primarily on the play-by-play data published by the NFL. When we began to analyze the NFL, that was all we had to work with. Just as a television broadcast has a color commentator who gives more detail to the facts related by the play-by-play announcer, so too we need some color commentary to provide contextual information that breathes life into these plain lines of numbers and text. The Football Outsiders game charting project is our attempt to provide color for the simple play-by-play.

Providing color to 512 hours of football is a daunting task. To put it into perspective, there were over 54,000 lines of play-by-play information in the 2007 NFL season and our goal is to add several layers of detail to nearly all of them. We recruited over 50 volunteers to collectively chart each week's NFL games. Unfortunately, we do not have access to the coaches' film that the NFL provides to the 32 teams. That tape includes sideline and end zone perspectives for each play, and shows all 22 players at all times. Only NFL teams and NFL Films are allowed to have access to the film, and the only place it is ever shown to the public is on NFL Network or ESPN's *NFL Matchup*. Anyone who has watched *Matchup* knows the benefit of watching coaches' film. It is easy to see the type of coverage being run and the cause-and-effect of certain actions taken on the field; the end zone perspective enables the identification of individual linemen.

Without access to coaches' film, we had to chart games using regular broadcast footage. Broadcast footage is not as definitive, but it served our purposes. In the end, we have data on nearly every play from the past three NFL seasons. (In 2007, for the first time, we did not miss a single half of any game.) A handful of plays are missing due to technical difficulties—for example, many games were charted using Direct TV Short Cuts, which would occasionally skip a play to fit the 30-minute window.

Through trial-and-error, we have narrowed our focus to charting things both traceable and definitive. We are limited by the camera angles on standard television broadcasts and the time constraints of our volunteers. Charting a game, and rewinding to make sure mistakes are minimized, can take two to three hours. More than a couple of these per week can be hazardous to one's marriage. Our goal was to provide comprehensive information while understanding that our charters were doing this on a volunteer basis.

We want to emphasize that all data from the charting project is unofficial. (For this reason, we will usually mention the charting project when using this data in comments later in the book.) Other sources for football statistics may keep their own measurements of yards after catch or how teams perform against the blitz. Our data will not necessarily match theirs. However, any other group that is publicly tracking this data is also working from the same television broadcast footage, and thus will run into the same difficulties. No one outside the league can get official game film from the NFL.

This section describes the information that the Football Outsiders game charting project tracks.

Formation

For each play, charters recorded the number of running backs, wide receivers, and tight ends. The formation was recorded in the moment before the snap, so it does not include any presnap motion. Formations have become more fluid in recent years, so these numbers should not be considered gospel. Because television cameras do not always show player numbers, we told our game charters to mark formations based on appearance, not personnel. It can be hard to tell where to draw the distinction between an H-back and an offset fullback, or between a flex tight end and a slot receiver. We did not want a hard-and-fast rule that any tight end standing up off the line becomes a slot receiver because that's not the way defensive coordinators think when they send in their personnel in response.

Rushers and Blockers

Blitz is a ubiquitous word in football, and a standard definition is difficult to nail down. Rather than asking charters to determine when a team was blitzing, we asked them to record the number of blockers and rushers on passing plays. Counting rushers was easy, but counting blockers proved to be an art as much as a science. Offenses base their blocking schemes on how many rushers they expect. A running back or tight end's assignment may depend on how many pass-rushers cross the line at the snap. Therefore, an offensive player was deemed to be a blocker if he engaged in an actual block or there was some hesitation before running a route. A running back that immediately heads out into the flat is not a blocker, but one that waits to verify that the blocking scheme is working and then goes out to the flat would, in fact, be considered a blocker.

Quarterback Action

In passing situations, the charters recorded the movement of the quarterback. This consisted of three items:

- Marking plays which began with a play-action fake, including a fake end-around or a flea flicker.
- Marking when the quarterback left the pocket. Charters marked rollouts and bootlegs. (A rollout has the quarterback moving behind his blockers, whereas a bootleg has the quarterback moving one way and his blockers the other, usually in connection with a play-action fake.) Charters also marked when a quarterback run past the line of scrimmage was a sneak, a draw, or a scramble. We asked the charters to differentiate between designed runs and plays in which the quarterback originally intended to pass, although this is often a judgment call.
- Marking a defender with a hurry if he clearly caused the quarterback to rush his motion or leave the pocket after originally setting up in the pocket to throw. If the quarterback stood tall and delivered the pass with defenders in his face, this was not a hurry. Charters were allowed to list two names if necessary and could also attribute a hurry to Overall Pressure or list a play as a Coverage Scramble when the quarterback wasn't under pressure but ran because there were no open receivers.

Pass Details

We divided all pass yardage into two numbers: distance in the air and yards after catch. You will see much of this information throughout the team chapters and in each of the individual player tables. Distance in the air was based on the distance from the line of scrimmage to the place where the receiver either caught or was supposed to catch the pass. We did not count how far the quarterback was behind the line or horizontal yardage if the quarterback threw across the field. All touchdowns were counted to the goal line, so that distance in the air added to yards after catch always equals the official yardage total kept by the league. Charters also marked screen passes and tried to differentiate between passes to running backs that were standard pass routes, swing passes, or dumpoffs.

Defenders

The NFL play-by-play lists tackles and, occasionally, tipped balls, but it does not definitively list the defender on the play. Charters were asked to determine which defender was primarily responsible for covering either the receiver at the time of the throw or the location to which the pass was thrown, regardless of whether the pass was complete or not.

Every defense in the league plays zone coverage at times, some more than others, which leaves us with the question of how to handle plays without a clear man assigned to that receiver. We gave charters three alternatives:

- We asked charters to mark passes that found the holes in zone coverage as Hole in Zone, rather than straining to assign that pass to an individual defender. We asked the charter to also note the player who appeared to be responsible for that zone, and these defenders are assigned half credit for those passes. Some holes were so large that no defender could be listed along with the Hole in Zone designation.
- Charters were free to list two defenders instead of one. This could be used for actual double coverage or for zone coverage in which the receiver was right between two close defenders rather than sitting in a gaping hole. When two defenders are listed, ratings assign each with half credit.
- Screen passes and dumpoffs are marked as Uncovered unless a defender (normally a linebacker) is obviously shadowing that specific receiver on the other side of the line of scrimmage.

Since we began the charting project three years ago, nothing has changed our analysis more than this information on pass coverage. However, we want to be upfront: It was often the most difficult information to chart. Broadcast camera angles often do not show the setup of the secondary, making it impossible to identify before the play whether there is man coverage. On passes longer than a few yards, the camera won't show the receiver until the pass is in the air. The sideline view of network cameras makes seeing the specific numbers

on some jerseys difficult. (At this point, we would like to give a big shout out to all the defensive backs with dreadlocks that come out of their helmets, making them easier to identify.) Zone coverage makes things even twice as difficult. That being said, reviewing tape kept mistakes to a minimum and, if two cornerbacks might have been confused for one another once or twice, such mistakes tend to cancel out.

Incomplete Passes

Quarterbacks are evaluated based on their ability to complete passes. However, not all incompletes should have the same weight. Throwing a ball away to avoid a sack is actually a valuable incomplete, and a receiver dropping an otherwise quality pass is hardly a reflection on the quarterback. Therefore, our charters marked the reason for every incomplete pass. Possible entries were Overthrown, Underthrown, Thrown Away, Tipped/Batted at Line, Hit in Motion (indicating the quarterback was hit as his arm was coming forward to make a pass), Defensed, Dropped, and a few others. Defensed was listed when the pass was incomplete as the direct result of actions by the defender. That action can include balls tipped or batted in coverage or hard hits that jar a ball loose. For the first time in 2007, we also asked charters to track dropped interceptions by defenders. Terrence McGee of Buffalo led the league with five, followed by Pittsburgh's Ike Taylor with four.

(Note: Our count of passes defensed will be different from the unofficial totals kept by the league, as explained in the section on Defensive Secondary tables.)

Additional Details

Charters marked each quarterback sack with one of the following terms: Blown Block, Coverage Sack, QB Fault, or Blitz/Overall Pressure. Blown Blocks were listed with the name of a specific offensive player who allowed the defender to come through. Coverage Sack denotes when the quarterback has plenty of time to throw but cannot find an open receiver. QB Fault represents self sacks listed without a defender, such as when the quarterback drops back, only to find that the ball slips out of his hands with no pass-rusher touching him.

All draw plays were marked, whether by halfbacks or quarterbacks.

An additional column called Extra Comment allowed the charters to add any description they wanted to the play. These comments might be good blitz pickup by a running back, a missed tackle, a great hit, a description of a pass route, an angry tirade about the poor camera angles of network broadcasts, or a number of other possibilities.

Finally, we asked the game charters to mark when a mistake was made in the official play-by-play. The most common mistake was for an official scorer not to mark a quarterback hit, since that has only been tracked in the official play-by-play for two seasons. Other mistakes included incorrect names on tackles, penalties, or intended receivers, as well as missing direction on runs or passes, or the absence of the scramble designation when a quarterback ran on a play that began as a pass. Thanks to the diligence of our volunteer game charters and a friendly contact at the league office, the NFL corrected over 250 mistakes in the official play-by-play based on the data collected by our game charters.

Acknowledgements

None of this would have been possible without the time spent by all the volunteer game charters. There are some specific acknowledgements at the end of the book, but we want to give a general thank-you here to everyone who has helped collect data over the last two seasons. Without your unpaid time, the task of gathering all this information would have been too time-consuming to yield anything useful.

If you are interested in participating in next year's charting project, e-mail your contact information to charting@footballoutsiders.com. Please make sure to mention where you live, what team you follow, and whether or not you have the Sunday Ticket package.

HOW TO READ THE PROSPECTUS BOX

Here is a rundown of all the tables and stats that appear in the 32 team chapters. Each team chapter begins with a box in the upper-right corner that gives a summary of our statistics for that team, as follows:

2007 Record gives each team's actual win-loss record.

Pythagorean Wins gives the approximate number of wins expected last year based on this team's raw totals of points scored and allowed, along with their NFL rank.

DVOA gives the team's total DVOA rating, with rank. We also give each team's **weighted DVOA**, based on a formula that gives more emphasis to performance in games later in the season. This gives a more accurate picture of where each team stood at the end of the regu-

lar season and is a useful indicator for which teams may improve or decline in 2008 (particularly on defense).

Offense, Defense, and **Special Teams** list the team's DVOA rating in each category, along with NFL rank. Remember that good offenses and special teams have positive DVOA numbers, and a better defense has a negative DVOA, so the lowest defensive DVOA is ranked number one (Tennessee).

Variance measures a team's consistency over the 2007 season. Teams are ranked from most consistent (Cleveland, which had single-game DVOA between -20% and 40% for 15 straight games) to least consistent (32nd-ranked Denver). Longtime readers should note that this is a change from past years, when we ranked teams in the other direction.

2008 Mean Projection gives the average number of wins for this team based on the 2008 Win Projection System described earlier in this chapter. The next few lines give the team's chances of finishing in the five win categories.

Projected Average Opponent gives the team's strength of schedule for 2008 based not on last year's record but on the median projected DVOA for each opponent. A positive schedule is harder and a negative schedule is easier. Teams are ranked from the hardest projected schedule (top-ranked Pittsburgh) to the easiest (32nd-ranked New England). This strength of schedule projection does not take into account which games are home and which are away or the timing of the bye week.

After the Prospectus box, each team gets an essay discussing its 2007 season and prospects for 2008, followed in some chapters by a research essay connected to that team. You'll also find a table with the team's 2008 schedule. A handful of teams have a graph showing their week-to-week performance by single-game DVOA, along with a trendline with a longer-term view of when they were improving and declining. After the essays come statistical tables and comments related to that team and its specific units.

Weekly Performance

The first table gives a quick look at the team's week-to-week performance in 2007. This includes the playoffs for those teams that made the postseason, with the four weeks of playoffs numbered 18 (wild card) through 21 (Super Bowl). All other tables in the team chapters represent only regular-season performance unless otherwise noted.

2007 Bills Stats by Week

Wk	vs.	W-L	PF	PA	YDF	YDA	TO	Total	Off	Def	ST
1	DEN	L	14	15	184	470	0	-32%	-42%	11%	22%
2	@PIT	L	3	26	223	420	+1	-45%	-17%	35%	6%
3	@NE	L	7	38	193	485	-1	-40%	-18%	14%	-8%
4	NYJ	W	17	14	304	347	0	-8%	9%	21%	4%
5	DAL	L	24	25	229	385	+5	40%	-32%	-49%	23%
6	BYE										
7	BAL	W	19	14	242	308	0	14%	0%	8%	22%
8	@NYJ	W	13	3	347	254	+2	34%	-2%	-26%	10%
9	CIN	W	33	21	479	299	0	1%	32%	14%	-17%
10	@MIA	W	13	10	214	269	-1	-30%	-35%	4%	8%
11	NE	L	10	56	229	510	-2	-42%	-7%	37%	2%
12	@JAC	L	14	36	297	416	-2	-18%	-3%	8%	-6%
13	@WAS	W	17	16	357	281	+1	43%	23%	-13%	6%
14	MIA	W	38	17	389	285	+4	61%	31%	-26%	4%
15	@CLE	L	0	8	232	304	0	-35%	-27%	4%	-4%
16	NYG	L	21	38	244	383	0	-16%	-43%	-35%	-8%
17	@PHI	L	9	17	271	391	+2	-7%	-14%	-1%	5%

Looking at the first week for the Buffalo Bills in Week 1, the first five columns are fairly obvious: the Bills lost to Denver at home in Week 1, 15-14. **YDF** and **YDA** are net yards on offense and net yards against the defense, respectively. These numbers do not include penalty yardage or special teams yardage. **TO** represents the turnover margin. Unlike other parts of the book in which we consider all fumbles as equal, this represents only actual turnovers: fumbles lost and interceptions. The Bills forced five more turnovers than Dallas in that famous Week 5 Monday Night game, for example, but turned the ball over two more times than the Patriots in Week 11.

Finally, you'll see DVOA ratings for this game: total **DVOA** first, then offense (**Off**), defense (**Def**), and special teams (**ST**). Note that these are DVOA ratings, adjusted for opponent. This is why the Giants have a much higher DVOA than the Patriots for Super Bowl XLII. If we were using VOA, without opponent adjustments, the two teams would be virtually identical.

Trends and Splits

Next to the week-to-week performance is a table giving DVOA for different portions of a team's performance, on both offense and defense. Each split is listed with the team's rank among the 32 NFL teams. These numbers represent regular season performance only.

Total DVOA gives total offensive and defensive DVOA in all situations. **Unadjusted VOA** represents the breakdown of play-by-play considering situation but not op-

ponent. A team whose offensive DVOA is higher than its offensive VOA played a harder-than-average schedule of opposing defenses; a team with a lower defensive DVOA than defensive VOA played a harder-than-average schedule of opposing offenses.

Weighted Trend lowers the importance of earlier games to give a better idea of how the team was playing at the end of the regular season. The final four weeks of the season are full strength; moving backwards through the season, each week is given less and less weight until the first three weeks of the season, which are not included at all. **Variance** is the same as noted above, with a higher percentage representing less consistency. This is true for both offense and defense: Seattle, for example, had one of the league's *most* consistent offenses (3.1% variance, ranked second) and one of the *least* consistent defenses (10.4% variance, ranked 27th).

Passing and **Rushing** are fairly self-explanatory. Note that rushing includes all rushes, not just those by running backs, including quarterback scrambles that may have begun as pass plays.

The next three lines split out DVOA on **First Down**, **Second Down**, and **Third Down**. Third Down here includes fourth downs on which a team runs a regular offensive play instead of punting or attempting a field goal. **First Half** and **Second Half** represent the first two quarters and last two quarters (plus overtime), not the first eight and last eight games of the regular season. Next comes DVOA in the **Red Zone**, which is any offensive play starting from the defense's 20-yard line through the goal line. The final split is **Late and Close**, which includes any play in the second half or overtime when the teams are within eight points of each other in either direction. (Eight points is the biggest deficit that can be made up with a single score, a touchdown and two-point conversion.)

Five-Year Performance

This table gives each team's performance over the past five seasons. It includes win-loss record, Pythagorean Wins, **Estimated Wins**, points scored and allowed, and turnover margin. Estimated wins are based on a formula that estimates how many games a team would have been expected to win based on 2007 performance in specific situations, normalized to eliminate luck (fumble recoveries, opponents' missed field goals, and so on) and assuming an average schedule strength. The formula emphasizes consistency and overall DVOA as well as DVOA in the most important specific situations: red zone defense, first quarter offense, and performance in the second half when the score is close. The last eight columns of this table give total DVOA along with DVOA for offense, defense, and special teams, and the rank for each among that season's 32 NFL teams.

Individual Offensive Statistics

Each team chapter contains a table giving passing and receiving numbers for any player who either threw five passes or was thrown five passes, along with rushing numbers for any players who carried the ball at least three times. These numbers appear also in the player comments at the end of the book (except for wide receiver rushing attempts). By putting them together in the team chapters we hope we make it easier to compare the performances of different players on the same team.

Players who are no longer on the team are marked with an asterisk. New players who were on a different team in 2006 are in italics. Changes should be accurate through mid-May. Rookies are not included.

All players are listed with DYAR and DVOA. Passing statistics then list total pass plays (**Plays**), net yardage (**NtYds**), and net yards per pass (**Avg**). These numbers include not just passes (and the positive yardage from them) but aborted snaps and sacks (and the negative yardage from them). Then comes average yards after catch (**YAC**) as determined by the game charting project. This average is based on charted receptions, not total pass attempts. The final three numbers are completion percentage (**C%**), which does not include aborted snaps or sacks, passing touchdowns (**TD**), and interceptions (**Int**).

Sample Passing Table

Player	DYAR	DVOA	Plays	NtYds	Avg	YAC	C%	TD	Int
Trent Edwards	57	-7.8%	282	1556	5.5	5.4	56.6%	7	8
J. P. Losman	26	-8.9%	188	1101	5.9	5.2	63.8%	4	6

Rushing statistics start with DYAR and DVOA, then list rushing plays and net yards along with average yards per carry and rushing touchdowns. The final two columns are fumbles (**Fum**)—both those lost to the defense and those recovered by the offense—and Success Rate (**Suc**), explained earlier in this chapter. Fumbles listed in the rushing table include all quarterback fumbles on sacks and aborted snaps as well as running back fumbles on receptions, but not wide receiver fumbles.

Sample Rushing Table

Player	DYAR	DVOA	Plays	Yds	Avg	TD	Fum	Suc
Marion Barber	233	18.0%	203	984	4.8	10	3	49%
Julius Jones*	12	-6.7%	164	603	3.7	2	0	37%
Tony Romo	28	12.4%	22	137	6.2	2	9	—
Tyson Thompson*	-9	-27.8%	14	54	3.9	0	0	21%

Receiving statistics start with DYAR and DVOA and then list the number of passes thrown to this receiver (**Plays**), the number of passes caught (**Catch**), and the total receiving yards (**Yds**). Yards per catch (**Y/C**) includes total yardage per reception, based on standard play-by-play, and yards after catch (**YAC**) is based on information from our game charting project. Finally we list total receiving touchdowns and catch percentage (**C%**), which is the percentage of passes intended for this receiver which were caught.

Sample Receiving Table

Player	DYAR	DVOA	Plays	Catch	Yds	Y/C	YAC	TD	C%
Steve Smith	42	-9.1%	148	86	1002	11.7	5.5	7	58%
Drew Carter*	38	-6.6%	75	38	517	13.6	2.9	4	51%
Keary Colbert*	-122	-34.6%	69	32	332	10.4	3.3	0	46%
Dwayne Jarrett	-34	-49.6%	13	6	73	12.2	0.2	0	46%
Muhsin Muhammad	43	-5.9%	81	40	570	14.3	4.7	4	49%
D. J. Hackett	99	12.8%	47	32	384	12.0	4.3	3	68%

An important note: Individual numbers in the team tables will differ from individual numbers in the player comments. The team tables feature our numbers, which are edited to remove plays such as kneeldowns, Hail Marys, and clock-stopping spikes, and include aborted snaps as passes rather than rush attempts. The tables in the player comment chapters at the end of the book contain the official NFL totals.

Strategic Tendencies

The Strategic Tendencies table presents a mix of information garnered from both the standard play by play and the Football Outsiders game charting project. It gives you an idea of what kind of plays teams run in what situations and with what personnel. Each category is given a league-wide **Rank** from most often (1) to least often (32) except as noted below. The sample table shown here lists the NFL average in each category for 2006.

The first column of strategic tendencies lists how often teams ran in different situations. These ratios are based on the type of play, not the actual result, so quar-

Sample Strategic Tendencies Table

Run/Pass		Rank	Offense		Rank	Defense		Rank	Other		Rank
Runs, all plays	41%	16	3+ WR	52%	16	Rush 3	5.9%	16	2+ RB, Pct Runs	57%	16
Runs, first half	41%	16	4+ WR	12%	16	Rush 4	62.6%	16	1 RB/2 TE, Pct Runs	50%	16
Runs, first down	50%	16	2+ TE	25%	16	Rush 5	22.6%	16	1 RB/3+ WR, Pct Runs	25%	16
Runs, second-long	35%	16	Single back	57%	16	Rush 6+	8.9%	16	CB1 on WR1	45%	16
Runs, power sit.	62%	16	Play action	18%	16	Rush 7+	1.9%	16	Go for it on 4th	1.00	16
Runs, behind 2H	29%	16	Max protect	10%	16	Sacks by LB	31.0%	16	Offensive Pace	30.8	16
Pass, ahead 2H	45%	16	Outside pocket	11%	16	Sacks by DB	6.8%	16	Defensive Pace	30.8	16

terback scrambles count as "passes" while quarterback sneaks and draws count as "runs."

The first three entries are self-evident: **Runs** on **all plays**, in the **first half**, and on **first down**. **Runs, second-and-long** is the percentage of runs on second down with seven or more yards to go, giving you an idea of how teams follow up a failed first down. **Runs, power situations** is the percentage of runs on third or fourth down with 1-2 yards to go, or at the goal line with 1-2 yards to go. **Runs, behind 2H** tells you how often teams ran when they were behind in the second half, generally a passing situation. **Pass, ahead 2H** tells you how often teams passed when they had the lead in the second half, generally a running situation.

In each case, you can determine the percentage of plays that were passes by subtracting the run percentage from 100 (the reverse being true for Pass, ahead 2H, of course).

The second column gives information about offensive formations and strategy, as tracked by our game charters.

3+ WR/4+ WR: Plays with three or more wide receivers, and plays with four or more wide receivers. This may include a player normally identified as a tight end or running back lining up as a wide receiver.

2+ TE: Plays with multiple tight ends, including H-backs.

Single back: Plays with only one running back, no matter the mixture of tight ends and wide receivers.

Play action: The percentage of pass plays (including quarterback scrambles) that began with a play-action fake to the running back. This percentage does not include fake end-arounds unless there was also a fake handoff.

Max protect: The percentage of this team's passing plays (including quarterback scrambles) on which blockers outnumber pass rushers by at least two, with a minimum of seven blockers.

Outside pocket: The percentage of this team's passing plays in which the quarterback was listed as leaving the pocket on a rollout, a bootleg, or an unplanned scramble, no matter whether the play ended with a pass attempt, sack, or scramble for positive yardage.

The third column shows strategies used by the **Defense**. We've expanded our listing of various pass-rush strategies compared to our previous books.

Rush 3/Rush 4/Rush 5: The percentage of pass plays (including quarterback scrambles) on which our game charters recorded this team rushing the passer with three or fewer defenders, four defenders, or five defenders. These percentages do not include goal-line plays on the one- or two-yard line.

Rush 6+/Rush 7+: The percentage of pass plays (including quarterback scrambles) on which our game charters recorded this team rushing the passer with six or more defenders, as well as seven or more defenders. These are the only two of the pass-rush categories which overlap—plays included in Rush 7+ are all included in Rush 6+ as well. Again, these percentages do not include goal-line plays.

Sacks by LB/Sacks by DB: The percentage of this team's sacks that came from linebackers and defensive backs. To figure out the percentage of sacks from defensive linemen, simply subtract the sum of these numbers from 100%.

The fourth column has data on run strategies that don't fit in the first column and other assorted statistics.

2+ RB, Pct Runs: When this offense came out with two or three running backs, how often did they run the ball as opposed to passing? Two running backs usually means a fullback and a halfback, but not necessarily. The percentage of runs does not include quarterback scrambles.

1 RB/2 TE, Pct Runs: The percentage of running plays when this offense came out with two tight ends and only one running back.

1 RB/3+ WR, Pct Runs: The percentage of running plays when this offense came out with three or four wide receivers and only one running back.

CB1 on WR1: The percentage of passes targeting the team's number one cornerback that were thrown with the offense's number one receiver as the intended target. Obviously, both of these designations are subjective, but this gives a good idea of how often a defensive coordinator assigned his top corner to shadow a specific receiver. In some cases, different cornerbacks were used for different weeks depending on injuries.

After three years of game charting, we've learned that each team's best cornerback does not necessarily match up against the opponent's best receiver. Most cornerbacks play a particular side of the field and cover a wider range of receivers than we assumed before we saw the charting data.

Go for it on fourth: This is the aggressiveness index (AI) introduced by Jim Armstrong in *Pro Football Prospectus 2006*, which measures how often a team goes for a first down in various fourth down situations compared to the league average. A coach over 1.00 is more aggressive, and one below 1.00 is less aggressive. Coaches are ranked from most aggressive to least aggressive.

Offensive Pace: Situation-neutral pace represents the seconds of game clock per offensive play, with the following restrictions: No drives are included if they start in the fourth quarter or final five minutes of the first half, and drives are included only if the score is within six points or less. Teams are ranked from quickest pace (Indianapolis, 28.3 seconds) to slowest pace (Pittsburgh, 34.4 seconds).

Defensive Pace: Situation-neutral pace based on seconds of game clock per defensive play. This is a representation of how a defense was approached by its opponents, not the strategy of the defense itself (an issue discussed in the Indianapolis chapter of *PFP 2006*). Teams are ranked from quickest pace (Baltimore, 29.3 seconds) to slowest pace (New York Jets, 31.8 seconds).

Following each strategic tendencies table, you'll find a series of comments highlighting interesting data from that team's charting numbers. These comments are primarily written by Bill Moore, coordinator of the game charting project. This includes DVOA ratings split for things such as different formations, draw plays, or play-action passing. Please note that all DVOA ratings given in these comments are standard DVOA with no adjustments for the specific situation being analyzed, and the average DVOA for a specific situation will not necessarily be 0%. For example, the average DVOA on play-action passes in 2006 was 21.8%, and the average DVOA when the quarterback is hurried (but not sacked) is -46.9%.

How to Read the Offensive Line Tables

The offensive line tables list the last three years of Adjusted Line Yards and other statistics for each team.

The first column gives standard yards per carry by each team's running backs (**Yds**). The next two columns give Adjusted Line Yards (**ALY**) followed by rank among the 32 teams.

Then come three other rushing statistics. **Power** gives the percentage of runs in power situations that achieved a first down or touchdown. Those situations include any third or fourth down with one or two yards to go and any runs in goal-to-go situations from the two-yard line or closer. Unlike the other rushing numbers on the Offensive Line table, Power includes quarterbacks.

10+ Yards gives the percentage of a team's rushing yards that came more than 10 yards past the line of scrimmage. A team with a high ranking in Adjusted Line Yards but a low ranking in 10+ Yards depends heavily on its offensive line to make the running game work. A team with a low ranking in Adjusted Line Yards but a high ranking in 10+ Yards depends heavily on its running back breaking long runs to make the running game work, and therefore tends to have a less consistent running attack.

Stuff gives the percentage of runs that are stuffed based on the following parameters:

- On first down, zero or negative gain.
- On other downs, less than one-fourth the yards needed for another first down.
- Since being stuffed is bad, teams are ranked from stuffed least often (1) to most often (32).

The final two numbers on the first part of the table are Adjusted Sack Rate (**ASR**) and its rank among the 32 teams. Some teams allow a lot of sacks because they throw a lot of passes; Adjusted Sack Rate accounts for this by dividing sacks and intentional grounding by total pass plays. It is adjusted also for situation (sacks are much more common on third down, particularly third-and-long) and opponent, all of which makes it a better measurement than raw sack totals. Remember that quarterbacks share responsibility for sacks, and two quarterbacks behind the same line can have very different Adjusted Sack Rates—particularly if one is named Rob Johnson.

The second part of the Offensive Line table gives Adjusted Line Yards in each of the five directions with rank among the 32 teams. Note that the league average is

Offensive Line Sample

Year	Yards	ALY	Rank	Power	Rank	10+ Yds	Rank	Stuff	Rank	Sacks	ASR	Rank
2005	4.84	4.37	10	56%	27	27%	1	25%	16	28	5.3%	8
2006	4.99	4.61	4	71%	6	19%	9	25%	20	25	5.4%	7
2007	4.79	4.62	2	70%	7	20%	8	21%	7	28	5.1%	11

Year	LE	Rank	LT	Rank	Mid	Rank	RT	Rank	RE	Rank
2005	4.44	11	4.62	6	4.31	11	4.42	12	3.99	15
2006	5.27	3	3.69	29	4.45	12	4.65	4	5.46	3
2007	4.84	7	4.38	15	4.70	3	4.46	12	4.87	3

higher on the left than the right. Specifically in 2007, the league average was 4.07 on left end runs (**LE**), 4.35 on left tackle runs (**LT**), 4.15 on runs up the middle (**MID**), 4.23 on right tackle runs (**RT**), and 4.04 on right end runs (**RE**).

How to Read the Defensive Front Seven Tables

Defensive players make plays. Plays aren't just tackles—interceptions and pass deflections change the course of the game, and so does the act of forcing a fumble or beating the offensive players to a fumbled ball. While some plays stop a team on third down and force a punt, others merely stop a receiver after he's caught a 30-yard pass. We still cannot measure each player's opportunities to make a tackle. We can measure a linebacker's opportunities in pass coverage, however, thanks to the Football Outsiders game charting project.

Defensive Linemen

Defensive linemen are listed in the team chapters if they made at least 15 plays during the 2007 season. Players are listed with the following numbers:

Age: The player's age, listed simply as the difference between birth year and 2008. Players born in January and December of the same year will have the same listed age.

Position (**Pos**): The player's position on the line.

Plays (**Plays**): The total defensive plays including tackles, pass deflections, interceptions, fumbles forced, and fumble recoveries. This number comes from the official NFL gamebooks and therefore does not include plays in which the player is listed by the Football Outsiders game charting project as in coverage but does not appear in the standard play-by-play. Special teams tackles are also not included.

Percentage of Team Plays (**TmPct**): The percentage of total team plays involving this defender. The sum of the percentages of team plays for all defenders on a given team will exceed 100 percent, primarily due to shared tackles. This number is adjusted based on games played, so an injured player may be fifth on his team in plays but third in TmPct.

Stops (**Stop**): The total number of plays which prevent a success by the offense (45 percent of needed yards on first down, 60 percent on second down, 100 percent on third or fourth down).

Defeats (**Dfts**): The total number of plays that stop the offense from gaining first down yardage on third or fourth down, stop the offense behind the line of scrimmage, or result in a fumble (regardless of which team recovers) or interception.

Stop Rate (**StpRt**): The percentage of all plays that are Stops.

Average Yards (**AvYds**): The average number of yards gained by the offense when this player is credited with making the play. Note that passes defensed count as zero yards.

Sample Defensive Line Table

Defensive Line	Age	Pos	Plays	TmPct	Rk	Stop	Dfts	Stop%	Rk	AvYd	Rk	Sack	Hit	Hur	Runs	RuStop	RuYd	Pass	PaStop	PaYd
Adewale Ogunleye	31	DE	61	7.3%	21	44	27	72%	58	0.8	21	9.0	11	17	38	68%	1.6	23	78%	-0.5
Alex Brown	29	DE	47	5.6%	45	34	16	72%	57	1.4	33	4.0	8	7	27	63%	2.8	20	85%	-0.5
Tommie Harris	25	DT	35	4.2%	52	29	15	83%	18	0.7	9	7.5	5	8	25	76%	2.7	10	100%	-4.2
Mark Anderson	25	DE	32	4.3%	61	25	11	78%	37	0.0	7	4.5	4	7	25	72%	1.9	7	100%	-7.0

Sack: Standard NFL sack totals.

Hit: A new element added to the official NFL play-by-play in 2006. To qualify as a quarterback hit, the defender must knock the quarterback to the ground in the act of throwing or after the pass is thrown. We have listed hits on all plays, including those cancelled by penalties. (After all, many of the hardest hits come on plays cancelled because the hit itself draws a roughing-the-passer penalty.)

Hurries (Hur): The number of quarterback hurries recorded by the Football Outsiders game charting project. This includes both hurries on standard plays and hurries that force an offensive holding penalty that cancels the play and costs the offense yardage.

Because quarterback hits are a new statistic, some official scorers are not quite as vigilant about recording every one, while other scorers misinterpret the rules and mark some hits that didn't put the quarterback on the ground or favor marking hits for the home team over the visiting team. Similar problems exist with our game charting volunteers because the definition of what qualifies as a quarterback hurry is somewhat subjective. Therefore, both hits and hurries are adjusted based on which official scorer or FO game charter was doing the game in question.

Finally, we split our stats for defensive linemen into **Run** plays and **Pass** plays. Pass plays include sacks, tackles after completions, and pass deflections. We list separate Stop Rate for passes (**PaStp**) and runs (**RuStp**) as well as separate average yards for passes (**PaYds**) and runs (**RuYds**).

Defensive linemen are ranked by percentage of team plays, Stop Rate, and average yards. The lowest number of average yards earns the top rank (negative numbers indicate the average play ending behind the line of scrimmage). Except for pass-rush specialists, most linemen do not have enough pass plays to make separate rankings of pass and run statistics viable. Defensive linemen are ranked if they made 24 or more plays during 2007. There are 77 defensive ends who qualify, and 66 defensive tackles. Each position is ranked separately.

Linebackers

Linebackers are listed in team chapters if they made at least 15 plays during the season. Most of the stats for linebackers are the same as those for defensive linemen. The listings of both total plays and percentage of team plays are based on standard play-by-play. Average yards on the left side of the table are also based on standard play-by-play and give us a good indication of which linebackers play closer to the line of scrimmage and which players drop into coverage.

Linebackers are ranked in percentage of team plays and also in Stop Rate and average yards for running plays specifically. Linebackers are ranked in these standard stats if they made at least 48 plays during the 2006 season. Outside, inside (3-4), and middle (4-3) linebackers are ranked together, with 99 players ranked in total. This does mean a handful of starting linebackers are not ranked, primarily outside linebackers who didn't play a full season.

The final five columns in the linebacker stats come from the Football Outsiders game charting project.

Targets (Tgts): The number of pass players on which our game charters listed this player in coverage.

Success Rate (Suc%): The percentage of plays targeting this player on which the offense did not have a successful play. This means not only incomplete passes and interceptions but also short completions which do not meet our baselines for success (45 percent of needed yards on first down, 60 percent on second down, 100 percent on third or fourth down). This year, unlike in our two previous books, Success Rate is adjusted for the quality of the receiver covered.

Adjusted Yards per Pass (PaYd): The average number of yards gained on plays on which this defender was the listed target, adjusted for the quality of the receiver covered.

These stats are explained in more detail in the section on secondary tables. Plays listed with two defenders or as Hole in Zone with this defender as the closest player count for only half credit in computing both Success Rate and Average Yards per Pass. Eighty-nine line-

Sample Linebackers Table

Linebackers	Age	Pos	Plays	TmPct	Rk	Stop	Dfts	Stop%	AvYd	Sack	Hit	Hur	Runs	RuStop	Rk	RuYd	Rk	Tgts	Suc%	Rk	APaYd	Rk
Scott Fujita	29	OLB	98	13.4%	40	58	11	59%	5.5	3.0	2	5	57	65%	38	4.1	82	41	56%	26	6.1	47
Mark Simoneau	31	MLB	71	9.1%	77	40	8	56%	4.5	2.0	1	1	53	58%	66	3.8	70	21	50%	42	6.3	52
Scott Shanle	29	OLB	67	9.8%	68	36	11	54%	6.0	0.0	1	1	44	59%	63	4.5	92	20	42%	67	9.2	88
Jonathan Vilma	26	MLB	46	12.4%	—	25	6	54%	4.2	0.0	1	0	31	58%	—	3.8	—	14	54%	—	5.3	—

backers are ranked in the charting stats, with a minimum of 16 charted passes. As a result of the different thresholds, some linebackers are ranked in standard stats but not charting stats, or vice versa.

Further Details

Just as we did in the offensive tables, players who are no longer on the team are marked with asterisks and players who were on other teams last year are in italics. Other than the game charting statistics for linebackers, defensive front seven player statistics are not adjusted for opponent.

Numbers for defensive linemen and linebackers unfortunately do not reflect all of the opportunities a player had to make a play, but they do show us which players were most active on the field. A large number of plays could mean a strong defensive performance, or it could mean that the linebacker in question plays behind a poor part of the line. In general, defensive numbers should be taken as information that tells us what happened on the field in 2007 but not as a strict, unassailable judgment of which players are better than others—particularly when the difference between two players is small (for example, players ranked 20th and 30th) instead of large (players ranked 20th and 70th).

After the individual statistics for linemen and linebackers, the Defensive Front Seven section contains a table that looks exactly like the table in the Offensive Line section. The difference is that the numbers here are for all opposing running backs against this team's defensive front. Because we're on the opposite side of the ball, teams are now ranked in the opposite order, so the number one Defensive Front Seven is the one that allows the fewest adjusted line yards and the lowest percentage in Power situations and has the highest Adjusted Sack Rate. Directions for Adjusted Line Yards are given from the offense's perspective, so runs left end and left tackle are aimed at the right defensive end and (assuming the tight end is on the other side) weak side linebacker.

How to Read the Secondary Tables

The first few columns in the secondary tables are based on standard play-by-play, not game charting. Age, Total Plays, Percentage of Team Plays, Stops, and Defeats are computed as they are for other defensive players, so that the secondary can be compared to the defensive line and linebackers. That means that Total Plays here includes passes defensed, sacks, tackles after receptions, tipped passes, and interceptions, but not pass plays on which this player was in coverage but was not given a tackle or pass defensed by the NFL's official scorer.

(We are proud to report that the official scorers in Philadelphia, perhaps chastened by an essay in *PFP 2006*, tracked passes defensed in 2007 by the same guidelines as everyone else. Passes defensed at Lincoln Financial Field no longer count for half-credit.)

The middle four columns address each defensive back's role in stopping the run. Average Yardage and Stop Rate for running plays is computed in the same manner as for defensive linemen and linebackers.

The third section of statistics represents data from the game charting project as follows.

Targets (**Trgt**): The number of pass plays on which our game charters listed this player in coverage. This number gives full credit to all passes, including those on which two defenders are listed and those listed as Hole in Zone with this player as the closest zone defender (both of those count as half credit in the other stats below). We do not count pass plays on which this player was in coverage, but the incomplete was listed as Thrown Away, Tipped at Line, or Hit in Motion.

Target Percentage (**Tgt%**): The number of plays on which this player was targeted divided by the total number of charted passes against his defense, not including plays listed as Uncovered. Like Percentage of Team Plays, this metric is adjusted based on number of games played.

Distance (**Dist**): The average distance in the air beyond the line of scrimmage of all passes targeted at this defender. It does not include yards after catch and is

Sample of Individual Statistics for Defensive Secondary

Secondary	Age	Pos	Plays	TmPct	Rk	Stop	Dfts	RuYd	Rk	RuStop	Rk	Tgts	Tgt%	Rk	Dist	Suc%	Rk	APaYd	Rk	PaYd	PD	Int
Champ Bailey	30	CB	93	12.3%	8	47	18	5.6	29	50%	34	67	19%	33	11.9	59%	7	6.7	25	6.7	10	3
Dre' Bly	31	CB	66	8.2%	56	32	13	8.4	59	52%	31	81	21%	20	11.5	45%	62	8.5	64	8.9	14	5
John Lynch	37	FS	61	9.3%	41	29	8	4.6	8	55%	13	15	5%	73	11.3	25%	83	10.3	69	10.7	2	0
Nick Ferguson*	34	SS	54	8.9%	47	20	5	5.9	27	43%	43	19	6%	51	14.0	38%	70	11.9	79	12.6	1	0

Sample of Team Statistics for Defensive Secondary

Year	Pass D Rank	vs. #1 WR	Rk	vs. #2 WR	Rk	vs. Other WR	Rk	vs. TE	Rk	vs. RB	Rk
2005	27	16.7%	22	4.2%	25	23.7%	31	1.7%	19	21.3%	30
2006	5	-23.6%	2	28.6%	30	-20.2%	7	-2.8%	17	-18.9%	10
2007	11	-32.3%	1	30.6%	31	-6.9%	18	-5.0%	7	7.7%	25

useful for seeing which defenders were covering receivers deeper or shorter.

Success Rate (**Suc%**): The percentage of plays targeting this player on which the offense did not have a successful play. This means not only incomplete passes and interceptions but also short completions which do not meet our baselines for success (45 percent of needed yards on first down, 60 percent on second down, 100 percent on third or fourth down). Defensive pass interference is counted as a failure for the defensive player, similar to a completion of equal yardage (and a new first down).

Average Yards per Pass (**PaYd**): The average number of yards gained on plays on which this defender was the listed target.

Passes Defensed (**PD**): This is our count of passes defensed, and will differ from the total found in NFL gamebooks. Our count includes

- All passes listed by our charters as Defensed.
- All interceptions, or tipped passes leading to interceptions.
- All passes defensed listed in the NFL gamebooks for games which remain uncharted.
- Any pass where the defender is given a pass defensed by the official scorer, and the game charter listed a reason for incomplete that can be hard to differentiate from a pass defensed, including: Dropped, Miscommunication, Alligator Arms, and Catch Out of Bounds.

Our count of passes defensed does not include passes marked as defensed in the official gamebooks but listed by our charters as Overthrown, Underthrown, or Thrown Away. It also does not include passes tipped in the act of rushing the passer.

Interceptions (**Int**): Standard NFL interception total.

Cornerbacks need 45 charted passes or eight games started to be ranked in the defensive stats, with 81 cornerbacks ranked in total. (We actually had to change the minimum this year in order to make sure Oakland's Nnamdi Asomugha was ranked, because offenses tried so hard to avoid him that he had only 38 charted passes despite playing 15 games.) Safeties are ranked in charting stats if they had either 16 charted passes or 24 tackles on running plays, with 83 safeties ranked in total. (Strong safeties and free safeties are ranked together.)

Just like the front seven, the secondary has a table of team statistics following the individual numbers. This table gives DVOA figured against different types of receivers. Each offense's wide receivers have had one receiver designated as number one and another as number two. (Occasionally this is difficult, due to injury or an amorphous wide receiver corps such as last year's Vikings, but it's usually pretty obvious.) The other receivers form a third category, with tight ends and running backs as fourth and fifth categories. The defense is then judged on the performance of each receiver based on the standard DVOA method, with each rating adjusted based on strength of schedule. (Opponents with Randy Moss and Chad Johnson as top receivers, for example, are tougher than an opponent with Marty Booker as its number one receiver.) **Pass D Rank** is the total ranking of the pass defense, as seen before in the Trends and Splits table, and combines all five categories plus sacks and passes with no intended target.

The defensive secondary table should be used to analyze the defense as a whole rather than individual players. The ratings against types of receivers are generally based on defensive schemes, not specific cornerbacks—although there are exceptions, such as the team in our sample, the Oakland Raiders—and the ratings against tight ends and running backs are in large part due to the performance of linebackers.

How to Read the Special Teams Tables

The special teams tables list the last three years of kick, punt, and return numbers for each team.

The first two columns list total special teams DVOA and rank among the 32 teams. The next two columns list the value in actual points of field goals and extra points (**FG/XP**) when compared to how a league aver-

Special Teams Sample

Year	DVOA	Rank	FG/XP	Rank	Net Punt	Rank	Punt Ret	Rank	Net Kick	Rank	Kick Ret	Rank	Hidden	Rank
2005	7.2%	1	3.6	11	7.5	5	0.4	12	3.8	12	27.2	1	8.9	4
2006	5.9%	2	8.5	4	16.1	1	6.6	3	-2.0	25	5.5	6	-2.2	16
2007	4.1%	6	5.9	4	7.2	4	11.3	3	-2.2	19	2.1	14	-1.4	17

age kicker would do from the same distances, adjusted for weather and altitude, and rank among the 32 teams. Next, we list the estimated value in actual points of field position over or under the league average based on net punting (**Net Punt**), and rank that value among the 32 teams. That is followed by the estimated point values of field position for punt returns (**Punt Ret**), net kickoffs (**Net Kick**), and kick returns (**Kick Ret**) and their respective ranks.

The final two columns represent the value of **Hidden** special teams, plays that throughout the past decade have usually been based on the performance of opponents without this team being able to control the outcome. We combine the opposing team's value on field goals, kickoff distance, and punt distance, adjusted for weather and altitude, and then switch the sign to represent that good special teams by the opponent will cost the listed team points, and bad special teams will effectively hand them points. This year, we have to give the qualifier of *usually* because, as explained previously and again in the Chicago chapter, Devin Hester affects opposing special teams strategy unlike any kick returner in our play-by-play database. Nonetheless, the hidden value is still hidden for most teams, and they are ranked from the most hidden value gained (San Diego, at 13.9 points, was the top team other than Chicago) to the most value lost (St. Louis, -17.9 points). The best and worst individual values for kickers, punters, and returners are listed in the statistical appendix at the end of the book.

ADMINISTRATIVE MINUTIA

Receiving statistics include all passes intended for the receiver in question, including those that are incomplete or intercepted. The word *passes* refers to both complete and incomplete pass attempts. When rating receivers, interceptions are treated as incomplete passes with no penalty.

For the computation of DVOA and DYAR, passing statistics include sacks as well as fumbles on aborted snaps. We do not include kneeldown plays or spikes for the purpose of stopping the clock. Some interceptions which we have determined to be Hail Mary plays that end the first half or game are counted as regular incomplete passes, not turnovers.

All mentions of yards after catch, hurries, hits, blitzes, and screens come from the Football Outsiders game charting project and may be different from totals compiled by other sources.

Unless we say otherwise, when we refer to third-down performance in this book we are referring to a combination of third down and the handful of rushing and passing plays that take place on fourth down (primarily fourth-and-1).

Thank you to Dr. Benjamin Alamar for help with the calculation of the Adjusted Line Yards formula and the 2007 Win Projection System, as well as the explanations for each. Additional thanks to Roland Beech of 82Games.com and TwoMinuteWarning.com, who developed these individual defensive statistics and has allowed us to use them and develop them further.

The Year in Quotes

Compiled by Ben Riley

Most Prescient New York Giants Quote, Malapropos Division

We don't need to make any dramatic changes.
  —**Eli Manning** quoted in *Newsday*, after the Giants started 0-2

Most Prescient New York Giants Quote, Silly Division

He has his team in the position right now; if they win today, they could possibly go on to the Super Bowl and make an appearance there.
  —**Emmitt Smith** on what a win in the NFC Championship game would mean for Eli Manning

Best Quote That Will Make Every New York Giants Fan Smile

If Tom Coughlin had not remained as head coach of the Giants, I might still be in a Giants uniform.
  —**Tiki Barber**, writing in his book, *Tiki: My Life in the Game and Beyond*

Best Quote Involving an Injury

They told me I tweaked my oblique, which is awesome because I didn't know I had any obliques. It's good news, honestly. It's in there somewhere, so I am really happy about that. I'm going to go home and tell my wife.
  —**Matt Hasselbeck**

Worst Quote Involving a Fake Injury Blamed on a Fast Food Wrapper

Its funny because I pride myself on yac [yards after catch] and being one of the toughest players to take down once I have the ball in my hands. So for the next couple of days I'm going to take the time to build my confidence back up after allowing that McDonald's bag to take me down and send me through the entertainment center.
  —Broncos wide receiver **Brandon Marshall,** offering up a lame text-message excuse for injuring his arm in March; Marshall later admitted he was "wrestling" with a family member

Best Quote(s) Involving a Situation That, Should It Come to Pass, Would Virtually Ensure That "The Week in Quotes" Will Write Itself in 2009

If I end up in Dallas, I would just look at which finger I'm gonna put it on. That's it. Ain't no ifs, ands or buts about it.
  —Bengals wide receiver **Chad Johnson**, beginning his public campaign to be traded to the Dallas Cowboys. Presumably, Johnson was referring to a Super Bowl ring, not Jessica Simpson

That'd be a circus.
  — **Johnson,** when asked what it would be like playing with Cowboys wide receiver Terrell Owens

I love throwing to my dogs. They will do anything to get that ball back to me. I mean, they will literally have a heart attack and die before they stop running. I put an 85 jersey on one (dog) and an 84 jersey on the other. They fight over who gets the ball. It really relates well to the football field.
  —Bengals quarterback **Carson Palmer**, offering a canine-based metaphor to explain his relationship with Chad Johnson (no. 85) and fellow Bengals wide receiver T. J. Houshmandzadeh (no. 84)

Best Ill-Advised Mascot-Based Quote from an Owner of an NFL Franchise

We're excited to announce "Steely McBeam" as the name of our new team mascot!
  —Steelers President **Art Rooney II** (McBeam disappeared around Week 4 of the regular season and now lives in San Francisco)

Best List of Alternative Mascot Names from the Football Outsiders Discussion Threads

Packy   McBox?
Viky   McPillage?
Matey   McLoot?
Niny   McGold?
Chargy McInterest Rate?
    —FootballOutsiders.com reader **"Thok"**

The Year in Fred Taylor

It's a dog-eat-dog business. We're living in the belly of the beast, and sometimes that beast has to regurgitate itself.
    —**Fred Taylor**, reacting to the benching
       of Byron Leftwich

Probably some ribs, some chicken.
    —**Taylor**, when asked what quarterback Quinn Gray
       would "bring to the table" for Jacksonville

Best Subtle Burying of Rex Grossman Quote from a Chicago-Area Ten-Year-Old

It's very easy to take snaps: Just open your hands and wait for the ball, and then you close your hands.
    —Chicago area fifth-grader **Jimmy Smolik**, age 10,
       providing some advice to Sexy Rexy

Best Nonsubtle Burying of Rex Grossman Quote

He told us that Rex was kind of a mental midget so you can get into his head and create that doubt.
    —Chargers linebacker **Matt Wilhelm**, describing how
       former Chicago defensive coordinator Ron Rivera
       described Grossman

Best Trent Green Cinematic Allegory Quote

I'm surprised this analogy hasn't come up yet. Can't you see Bill Belichick and Roger Goodell in the office having the conversation, and you picture Roger Goodell as Tom Cruise, and you picture Bill Belichick as Jack Nicholson. And they're sitting in the courtroom, and they're having this discussion, and all of a sudden Goodell is like, "Did you order a code red?!?" And Belichick is sitting there. And you know he's getting peeved because he's even in there, that [Goodell/Cruise] has the audacity to bring him in and question it. That's the analogy and kind of the visual that I have, is that eventually Belichick just kinda snapped and went, "You're darn right I ordered a code red!"
    —**Trent Green**

I don't know, maybe I'm the only one that has that warped perception.
    —**Green**

Best Inspirational Quote from One of the Triplets

I wanted to stand in front of my boys and say, "Do it like your dad, like any proud dad would want to. Why must I go through so much?" At that moment a voice came over me and said, "Look up, get up, and don't ever give up. You tell everyone or anyone that has ever doubted, thought they did not measure up or wanted to quit, you tell them to look up, get up and don't ever give up."
    —**Michael Irvin**, during his NFL Hall of Fame
       acceptance speech

Worst Inspirational Quote from One of the Triplets

That makes me feel like a real sissy.
    —**Troy Aikman**, reacting to seeing scantily clad women
       in Green Bay in January

Best Quote and Headline Combination Submitted by an FO Reader

People are throwing us underneath the radar.
    —Giants linebacker **Antonio Pierce** during the
       preseason. This quote prompted FO reader Gerry D.
       to ask, "Perhaps the radar is on the bus?"

The Year in Roy Williams

He's real quiet … he's a good athlete, he's big as hell, he's Megatron.
    —Lions wide receiver **Roy Williams**,
       describing his teammate Calvin Johnson

I always try to find the little guy, but there wasn't a little guy. I wouldn't bring my little guy here, either.
    —**Williams** on Oakland's Black Hole

I just got involved in orchestra and band when I was a kid. I was tall, so basically I was the only one who was tall enough to hold the bass in orchestra. So I played bass and picked up other instruments along the way. I taught myself on the piano. I was in band or orchestra right up to high school. They used to call me the "Orch Dork."

> —**Williams** on being in the band

It's that cherry syrup that you can put into drinks. It's the greatest stuff ever made. Sprite. Tea. Orange juice and pineapple juice. I can drink it in anything.

> —**Williams** on the magical elixir known as grenadine

I'm good at everything we do. If we had a bowling champion, I'd be the bowling champ. If we had a cooking champ I'd be the cooking champ. I'm good at everything.

> —**Williams** on being the champ

The pizza man knows when he comes to my address, he's coming for free. But I am real polite and I say, "Thank you, sir."

> —**Williams** on tipping

Roy is here. Look at my eyes— he's staying here … When you are a beautiful girl, people will keep knocking on the door and asking for dates— but the old dad has to keep coming out and saying "Nope."

> —Lions head coach **Rod Marinelli**, denying offseason rumors that Williams was on the trading block

Best Quote to Suggest That the Rams Might Want to Consider a New Head Coach

Logic isn't always the answer, for a number of reasons.

> —**Scott Linehan**, struggling to explain why he was continuing to play a clearly injured Marc Bulger during midseason

Best Quote on a Topic That Got a Little Too Much Attention This Year and Single-handedly Destroyed Our Online Discussion Threads

When you lose a guy like me, you're going to do whatever it takes to get the edge to win.

> —49ers linebacker (and former Patriot) **Tully Banta-Cain**, offering his explanation for the signal-taping scandal

Best Quote to Remind You That Not Everyone in the NFL Lives the Life of Tom Brady

The day before I got called by the Seahawks, I got pooped on by a cow.

> —Seattle long snapper **Jared Retkofsky**, who had been working on a ranch in Texas prior to being signed

The Year in Herm

You drive by that Krispy Kreme, you see that sign that says "Hot," you pull your car in there and you get me a dozen glazed donuts and you make sure they are on my desk on Saturday morning. I don't care about anything else. And the sign gotta say … and the sign gotta say … gotta say "Hot," gotta say "Hot."

> —**Herm Edwards**, hazing Chiefs rookie wide receiver Dwayne Bowe in the preseason

What we've done well is we survived. We got into that [0-2] wreck again, but we had our seat belts on, and we got out of the car, took it to the auto shop, knocked out the dents, and we're starting to roll again.

> —**Herm** in Week 4, when the Chiefs sat at 2-2 and had just beaten the San Diego Chargers on the road; the Chiefs finished at 4-12

I go with my gut. Your gut always tells you what's right.

> —**Herm**; perhaps this explains why the Chiefs finished 4-12

It would be nice if we could run the football.

> —**Herm**

It's a bad box to be in, because eventually I'm going to run you out of here.

> —**Herm**, describing his "tolerance box"

I'm a very patient man. But I'm also patient in the fact there are two sides of me. I'm patient with you, and then I put you in the tolerance category. When you get put in the tolerance category, I'll tolerate you until I can replace you.

> —**Herm**

Be a pro, stay out of bad places where bad things happen.

> —**Herm**

We have more three-and-outs than anybody in football. We have more negative plays than anybody in football. It's hard playing that way.

—**Herm**

There are a lot of things other teams are doing that we'd like to do.

—**Herm**

Would we like to do some different things? Sure. If I'm somebody else, then maybe I do it differently. But I know what I am right now.

—**Herm**

When you play the game, the players have to make plays.

—**Herm**

The coaches will take their share of the blame, but the players have a part of it, too. They get in the game, and they've got to go make plays.

—**Herm**

That's how you end up winning.

—**Herm**

People aren't used to this [losing] in Kansas City. Get over it, it happens, it's called life.

—**Herm**

Am I glad it's over? Yes, I'm glad it's over.

—**Herm**, after the season finally ended

Best Quote by a Kicker

I had the trifecta done on me.

—Broncos punter **Todd Sauerbrun**, who had a punt returned by Devin Hester for a touchdown, a kickoff returned by Hester for a touchdown, and a punt blocked, all in one game

Most Prescient Quote from an NFL Agent That Sounded Really Dubious During the Preseason

If he can be healthy, stay healthy, I think he's going to be a great teammate for everybody.

—**Tim DiPiero**, Randy Moss's agent

Least Prescient Quote from an NFL Head Coach

I'm going to be back.

—Former Ravens head coach **Brian Billick**

Best Quote About a Neck Beard

Certainly with the wind, it was cold, but I have a beard so that helps out a little bit. It's kind of warm in this area.

—Bears quarterback **Kyle Orton**

Best Post–Super Bowl Quote (Retired Players Who Are Relevant One Day Each Year Division)

People now will get an idea that the only way you can go undefeated is to win every game.

—Former Miami running back **Mercury Morris**, explaining the hidden secret of the 1972 Dolphins

Best Unheeded Advice from an NFL Owner to His Tail-Chasing Quarterback

I tell you this, Tony. Sometimes they can smell fresh cash.

—**Jerry Jones**, warning Tony Romo about partying with Britney Spears

The Bill Walsh Memorial Lifetime Achievement Quote

He knew me well before I knew myself.

—**Steve Young**

Quote of the Year (NCAA Edition)

That's why I don't read the newspaper! Because it's GARBAGE! And the EDITOR who let it come out is GARBAGE! Attacking an amateur athlete for doing everything right! Are you KIDDING ME? Where are we at in society today? COME AFTER ME! I'M A MAN! I'M 40! I'M NOT A KID! Write something about ME!

—Oklahoma State head coach **Mike Gundy**

Quote of the Year (Misinterpreted by Those with No Sense of "Humor" Edition)

I couldn't find London on a map if they didn't have the names of the countries. I swear to God. I don't know what nothing is. I know Italy looks like a boot. I learned that. I know (Washington Redskins linebacker) London Fletcher. We did a football camp together. So I know him. That's the closest thing I know to London. He's black, so I'm sure he's not from London. I'm sure that's a coincidental name.

> —Dolphins linebacker **Channing Crowder**, who faced an absurd amount of undue criticism for this quote

Quote of the Year (Roy Williams Edition)

I am on my fantasy team. I think I'm gonna bench myself.

> —**Roy Williams**

Quote of the Year (NFL Fan Edition)

It's almost like the son I never had. Except that I do have a son.

> —Buffalo Bills superfan **Ken Johnson**, describing his bowling ball on *Inside the NFL* while his (human) son looked on

Herm of the Year

Here's the concern: In our society now, so many things come up on Web sites and Internet. First of all, I don't even have the Internet. I wouldn't even know how to use it.

> —**Herm**

Quote of the Year

Don't quit. Don't even quit.

> —**Emmitt Smith**

Arizona Cardinals

The Arizona Cardinals are a popular pick to be a surprise playoff team in 2008. The same was true last year, and the year before that, and the year before that. At this point, the only thing that would surprise fans is a preseason in which nobody picked the Cardinals to surprise.

In the past, preseason Cardinals hype has been driven by big-name acquisitions—signing Edgerrin James, drafting Larry Fitzgerald or Matt Leinart. This year's preseason Cardinals hype, however, is driven by the opposite circumstance: continuity. The Cardinals are banking on a number of young talents maturing together, with the help of a well-regarded coaching staff that has spent a year remaking the franchise.

In a strange turn of events, the Cardinals now lead their division in head coach job security. In his first year at the helm, Ken Whisenhunt led the team to an 8-8 record, the Cardinals' best season since 1998. Now look around the rest of the NFC West. In Seattle, Mike Holmgren has declared this is his last year, which means loyalties could split between him and presumptive successor Jim Mora. Employees of Donald Trump have more job security than Rams coach Scott Linehan, and everybody believes the team will soon be sold. San Francisco's Mike Nolan barely survived getting the big haircut after his team regressed to 5-11 last year, and he was so desperate to improve the league's worst offense that he hired the brash and tempestuous Mike Martz as his fourth offensive coordinator in as many years. The resulting ego battles could make Ultimate Fighting look like a friendly cribbage match.

In Arizona, meanwhile, the coaching staff is getting along and working in harmony. Offensive coordinator Todd Haley was given a lucrative three-year extension after Miami showed interest in him as a head coach. Defensive coordinator Clancy Pendergast puts his players in the right position to succeed by running abnormal defensive schemes (like a 3-3-5 nickel with an extra safety) that will maximize their strengths. The staff also sports two other coaches, running backs coach Maurice Carthon and linebackers coach Billy Davis, who have been coordinators. And, of course, the star of the coaching show is offensive line and assistant head coach Russ Grimm, often considered a head coaching candidate himself. Good offensive line coaches can make a huge difference. When Tom Cable blew into Oakland last year, the Raiders went from 29th to 16th in Adjusted Line Yards, while their Adjusted Sack Rate improved from 12.4 percent to 8.5 percent. One former Cardinals scout told us that the offensive line and secondary coaches are the most valued people on any staff.

Arizona's offensive line will return the same five starters for the first time since 1997, and only the second time since the Cardinals moved to the desert in 1988. Of course, in the past the Cardinals never actually *wanted* to return their entire offensive line. If one problem has emblemized the Cardinals' 13 seasons of dou-

---

CARDINALS PROSPECTUS

2007 Record: 8-8

Pythagorean Wins: 8.1 (16th)

DVOA: -9.4% total (23rd), -11.4% weighted (22nd)

Offense: -0.4% (18th)

Defense: 5.3% (20th)

Special Teams: -3.6% (26th)

Variance: 19.4% (25th)

2007: The Cardinals' best season in a decade, even though Matt Leinart didn't develop and Adrian Wilson got hurt.

2008: Don't be surprised if it is defense, not offense, that finally leads Arizona to the postseason.

2008 Mean Projection: 7.5 wins

On the Clock (0-3): 8%

Loserville (4-6): 32%

Mediocrity (7-8): 23%

Playoff Contender (9-10): 23%

Super Bowl Contender (11+): 14%

Projected Average Opponent: 1.8% (13th in NFL)

2008 Cardinals Schedule

Week	Opp.	Week	Opp.	Week	Opp.
1	at SF	7	BYE	13	at PHI (Thu.)
2	MIA	8	at CAR	14	STL
3	at WAS	9	at STL	15	MIN
4	at NYJ	10	SF (Mon.)	16	at NE
5	BUF	11	at SEA	17	SEA (Mon.)
6	DAL	12	NYG		

ble-digit losses in 20 years in Arizona, it is their consistently dreadful offensive-line play.

The most vivid illustration is how quickly the Cardinals took the edge off Edgerrin James. In 2005, James's last year in Indy, he ranked third in DYAR, behind Shaun Alexander and Larry Johnson. He led running backs in Success Rate at 62 percent. The next season in Arizona, he plunged to 43rd in DYAR and his Success Rate dropped to 45 percent. Last year, at least his DYAR rebounded a bit, ranking 21st out of 49 running backs with at least 100 carries.

James is also backed up by plodders. Marcel Shipp weighs 232 pounds and ran a 4.62 40-yard dash—eight years ago. The quick running back is J. J. Arrington, who himself admitted he ran "soft" his rookie season and is now primarily used as a third-down back. Arizona did take a running back in the fifth round of this year's draft, Richmond's Tim Hightower, but as running backs go, he doesn't go fast enough. He clocked a Shipp-shape 4.62 40-time.

The Cardinals wanted to get a quick running back earlier in the draft, but the players they wanted (Curtis Johnson and Jamaal Charles) didn't fall to them and Arizona didn't want to reach to take either player too early. That's a problem for Whisenhunt, who would really rather run the offense that he took to the Super Bowl with the 2005 Steelers. Last year, the Cardinals ran 38 percent of the time, 24th in the NFL, including 49 percent of first downs (which ranked 17th). In 2005, Whisenhunt's Steelers ran on 56 percent of downs, including 66 percent of first downs. Both figures are the highest in the NFL over the past three seasons.

Yet other NFL coaches would salivate at the prospect of running a pass-heavy offense with Arizona's talent. The team sports the best wide receiver tandem in the game, with team leader and franchise face Anquan Boldin alongside explosive deep threat Larry Fitzgerald. Bryant Johnson, the 2003 first-rounder, was supposed to make this a trio; he's a phenomenal athlete with a

great stride, faster than either Johnson or Fitzgerald. Unfortunately, his lack of passion for the game turned him into an adequate third receiver and nothing more. The Cardinals made little effort to keep him from free agency, where he signed with the 49ers.

The Cardinals will replace Johnson with LSU receiver Early Doucet, who dropped into their laps in the third round. Doucet was targeted by some as a first-round prospect, but he ran a disappointing 4.59 40-yard dash at his Pro Day on March 26, after missing Scouting Combine workouts with a leg pull. He's also fathered two children by two mothers, a red flag these days in Roger Goodell's NFL.

Nevertheless, Arizona likes Doucet's quickness and his 210-pound frame. The Arizona coaches believe he can be an improvement on Johnson, not just a replacement.

Of course, this all leads up to the leading question: Who's going to be the leading man? Despite 27 touchdown passes by veteran Kurt Warner, the second most in franchise history, Whisenhunt has stated that Matt Leinart will begin 2008 as Arizona's starting quarterback.

Whisenhunt is going with Leinart despite the player's lax work habits and his propensity for getting photographed with a beer bong in a hot tub with young coeds. Leinart obviously still believes he's very much on scholarship. But the quarterback and the team continue to maintain that he's really a diligent, dedicated worker—a Wallace Cleaver sort who shuns the high life.

Leinart's legion of handlers and the Cardinals have it all wrong. Why not cast Leinart as the next Ken Stabler, another feckless, free-wheeling lefty? If he got the Cardinals into a fraction of the 12 playoff games that the Snake got the Raiders into, Leinart would be the biggest hero ever for this original NFL franchise. Of course, Stabler never shuddered in the pocket or threw wildly just to keep from getting leveled. Leinart was lost and clearly intimidated in last year's loss to Baltimore, leaving the impeccably prepared Warner to try to rescue him. It led to an awkward sharing of duties between the two quarterbacks until Leinart's season ended with a broken collarbone.

The Cardinals simply don't protect their quarterbacks the same way players do at USC, and receivers don't get as open as they do in the Pac-10. But even with his lack of mobility and slow delivery, the Cardinals believe Leinart is the answer. Or at least they believe he can avoid messing things up too badly, so the defense and the receivers can win the game for him.

Warner's no bargain. In his later years, he's been channeling Steve DeBerg—a player who posted strong numbers but was known for throwing game-turning (and stomach-turning) interceptions in the fourth quarter. And even in the losing lore of the Cardinals, a quarterback fumbling in his own end zone in overtime—as Warner did to fall to the hapless 49ers at home in Week 12—is new territory.

The passing game will improve if Grimm can attempt to reproduce the Hogs out West. On the left side, tackle Mike Gandy was surprisingly effective in his first year with the Cardinals, and guard Reggie Wells is consistent against the pass rush (although he struggles against the run). The right side has Pro Bowl potential with second-year man Levi Brown protecting Leinart's blind side and the chippy but uneven Deuce Lutui at guard.

Grimm and Whisenhunt will not only try to develop the line and the offense, but also try to increase the team's football IQ. The Cardinals led the league with a whopping 157 penalties (including declined and offsetting penalties), 19 more than the second-place Raiders. They spread the flags around, ranking second in special-teams penalties, second in offensive penalties, and fourth in defensive penalties. Ten infractions were slapped on tight end Leonard Pope, who tied for the team lead with Gandy. At six foot eight, Pope was supposed to help the Cardinals in the red zone; instead, his boneheaded false starts in scoring territory denied the team shots at the end zone.

The penalties should drop a bit with the move of cornerback Antrel Rolle to free safety. Including special-teams penalties, Rolle has drawn 22 flags over the last two seasons, third in the NFL behind Alex Barron and Robert Gallery. Those penalties include 10 for either defensive pass interference or illegal contact. Rolle was always overmatched as a pure corner. He won't have to play as close to the receivers as a safety, and he'll be more free to use his ball-hawking skills, the ones that helped him pick off five passes over the second half of the season. Teaming Rolle with strong safety Adrian Wilson, who's returning from heel surgery, provides the Cardinals with spectacular talent in the heart of their secondary. Wilson may be the best safety in the game. He can cover a slot receiver, play linebacker in the nickel, cover the deep half, or roam center field, depending on Arizona's needs.

The team wants first-round pick Domnique Rodgers-Cromartie to win the job at one cornerback spot and then have Roderick Hood and Eric Green battle for the other. The long, lean Rodgers-Cromartie has terrific quickness for a man with his frame and projects to be a pure cover man. He'll leave the tackling to the safeties, but if he must, Rodgers-Cromartie will wrestle his man to the turf.

The front seven on defense might be the strength of the team. Darnell Dockett is the team's sack master, with 8.5 last year, but with the drafting of three defensive ends, including Miami's Calais Campbell in the second round, Whisenhunt hopes to establish a greater rotation for his 3-4 defense. Last year, Dockett wore out, getting only one sack in the second half of the season. The Cardinals lost linebacker Calvin Pace in free agency, but there's a reasonable chance his phenomenal 2007 was an unrepeatable career year. They still have the talented Karlos Dansby, they get veteran Chike Okeafor back from the torn biceps tendon that cost him the 2007 season, and they've added free agent Clark Haggans from Pittsburgh.

Overall, the Cardinals do seem to be changing. They seem less afraid to spend money and have increased their value with consistent sellouts in their new stadium. Their drafts, once viewed as a joke, have checked out the last five seasons by filling the roster with 23 players, including 15 starters and two Pro Bowlers.

In other ways, the Cardinals remain the Cardinals. They're still woefully undermanned in the personnel department, which can lead to some major errors (who remembers linebacker Buster Davis in the third round last year?). Whisenhunt is still learning to be a head coach; he had some time-management gaffes last year, and those penalty totals were alarming. And vestiges of the Cardinals' chintzy past remain. The team badly needs a practice bubble to shield players from the oppressive heat, but higher-ups won't pay for it.

Cardinals fans have spent years waiting for the talent on the field to finally overshadow the club's history of widespread ineptitude. Things are definitely improving—particularly on defense, which projects better than the offense, according to our numbers. Whisenhunt seems to have truly changed the culture in Arizona, but that doesn't mean we should fall for another year of preseason hype. The chances this team will be as good as Seattle are small. Another 8-8 season is not a disappointment if it consolidates the gains the Cardinals made last year and prepares the team to be actual playoff contenders—not just an overhyped pick to surprise—in 2009.

Kevin Lynch

2007 Cardinals Stats by Week

Wk	vs.	W-L	PF	PA	YDF	YDA	TO	Total	Off	Def	ST
1	@SF	L	17	20	261	194	-1	-37%	-22%	5%	-10%
2	SEA	W	23	20	431	362	0	34%	44%	14%	5%
3	@BAL	L	23	26	364	381	0	-24%	23%	31%	-16%
4	PIT	W	21	14	301	282	0	93%	18%	-54%	20%
5	@STL	W	34	31	383	375	+1	-49%	-13%	26%	-10%
6	CAR	L	10	25	255	374	-5	-67%	-50%	27%	10%
7	@WAS	L	19	21	364	160	-2	-7%	-14%	-32%	-24%
8	BYE										
9	@TB	L	10	17	195	350	-2	-27%	-15%	13%	2%
10	DET	W	31	21	319	247	+1	51%	-4%	-40%	14%
11	@CIN	W	35	27	247	396	+5	12%	10%	-30%	-29%
12	SF	L	31	37	552	374	-4	-66%	4%	45%	-25%
13	CLE	W	27	21	302	379	+3	-6%	-8%	-2%	0%
14	@SEA	L	21	42	355	349	-5	-38%	-2%	27%	-9%
15	@NO	L	24	31	317	421	0	-35%	-9%	35%	9%
16	ATL	W	30	27	437	405	+1	-9%	16%	26%	2%
17	STL	W	48	19	422	234	+1	33%	5%	-28%	0%

Trends and Splits

	Offense	Rank	Defense	Rank
Total DVOA	-0.4%	18	5.3%	23
Unadjusted VOA	3.0%	14	0.4%	17
Weighted trend	-2.9%	18	4.7%	23
Variance	4.6%	6	9.7%	25
Average opponent	3.4%	29	-5.3%	31
Passing	9.1%	14	10.3%	19
Rushing	-13.8%	27	-1.4%	21
First down	-11.8%	26	-3.4%	13
Second down	3.4%	14	14.6%	28
Third down	17.0%	11	7.3%	21
First half	4.2%	20	4.8%	22
Second half	3.3%	14	5.8%	23
Red Zone	28.8%	3	8.5%	19
Late and close	-6.1%	23	5.0%	21

Five-Year Performance

Year	W-L	Pyth Wins	Est Wins	PF	PA	TO	Total	Rank	Off	Rank	Def	Rank	ST	Rank
2003	4-12	2.6	3.5	225	452	-13	-42.8%	32	-22.2%	32	18.6%	32	-1.9%	25
2004	6-10	6.8	5.0	284	322	+1	-21.6%	29	-22.5%	30	-2.3%	15	-1.4%	21
2005	5-11	6.0	6.3	311	387	-11	-12.3%	22	11.5%	23	-1.5%	17	-2.3%	26
2006	5-11	6.0	6.2	314	399	+3	-17.6%	26	-7.5%	21	5.4%	23	-4.8%	32
2007	8-8	8.1	6.3	404	399	-7	-9.4%	23	-0.4%	18	5.3%	20	-3.6%	26

Strategic Tendencies

Run/Pass		Rank	Offense		Rank	Defense		Rank	Other		Rank
Runs, all plays	38%	24	3+ WR	54%	10	Rush 3	13.7%	2	2+ RB, Pct Runs	56%	19
Runs, first half	38%	24	4+ WR	23%	3	Rush 4	55.1%	25	1 RB/2 TE, Pct Runs	50%	15
Runs, first down	49%	17	2+ TE	20%	22	Rush 5	24.4%	11	1 RB/3+ WR, Pct runs	19%	23
Runs, second-long	30%	25	Single back	52%	19	Rush 6+	6.8%	21	CB1 on WR1	45%	15
Runs, power sit.	47%	29	Play action	10%	30	Rush 7+	1.0%	24	Go for it on 4th	1.29	10
Runs, behind 2H	29%	14	Max protect	9%	23	Sacks by LB	48.6%	6	Offensive Pace	30.3	10
Pass, ahead 2H	55%	3	Outside pocket	8%	25	Sacks by DB	0.0%	30	Defensive Pace	30.6	12

Even with a new coaching regime, Arizona was near the bottom of the league in using play-action fakes for the second straight season. ⌀ Arizona lined up in four- and five-wide sets in short-yardage situations (five yards or less to go) more often than any team other than the Lions. ⌀ The Cardinals ran the highest proportion of screen passes on third down. One out of 17 third-down plays was a screen pass. ⌀ Arizona was most effective in calling a screen pass against the blitz, with almost half of its screen plays run against five or more rushers. ⌀ Arizona quarterbacks were hit in the process of throwing (but not sacked) more often than those of any other team. ⌀ Arizona trailed only New England and Jacksonville in passing DVOA in the fourth quarter, but ranked 27th in rushing DVOA in the same period. ⌀ Although Kurt Warner had a higher passing DVOA than Matt Leinart overall, Leinart (15.8%) had a significantly higher DVOA under pressure (five or more rushers) compared with Warner

(-2.9%). ⌀ Charters marked hurries twice as often when Leinart was playing than when Warner was playing. ⌀ Arizona had the league's best defense against screen passes. Only three out of 21 screens resulted in a first down. ⌀ Arizona's defense ranked third against passes up the middle, trailing only Indianapolis and Seattle. ⌀ Arizona opponents threw to their tight ends on only 14 percent of passes, the lowest percentage in the league. ⌀ The Cardinals' defense was league-average when the opposing quarterback was under center, but ranked 31st in the NFL (ahead of only Miami) when the quarterback was in shotgun. This was the biggest difference in the league, and the Cardinals had a similar split in 2006. Yet Arizona only faced opponents in the shotgun 21 percent of the time, the second-lowest percentage of any defense.

Passing

Player	DYAR	DVOA	Plays	NtYds	Avg	YAC	C%	TD	Int
Kurt Warner	699	11.3%	476	3296	6.9	4.5	62.9%	27	16
Matt Leinart	58	-3.3%	116	624	5.4	4.3	53.6%	2	3
Tim Rattay	3	-9.9%	28	163	5.8	2.3	55.6%	3	2

Rushing

Player	DYAR	DVOA	Plays	Yds	Avg	TD	Fum	Suc
Edgerrin James	101	-1.0%	323	1230	3.8	7	5	46%
J. J. Arrington	-37	-43.4%	26	78	3.0	0	0	27%
Marcel Shipp	-9	-19.9%	15	41	2.7	1	0	40%
Matt Leinart	8	1.0%	10	43	4.3	0	1	—
Kurt Warner	-37	-113.6%	7	8	1.1	1	9	—

Receiving

Player	DYAR	DVOA	Plays	Ctch	Yds	Y/C	YAC	TD	C%
WR									
Larry Fitzgerald	291	9.1%	167	100	1412	14.1	2.7	10	60%
Anquan Boldin	229	16.3%	100	71	854	12.0	5.3	10	71%
Bryant Johnson*	17	-10.2%	88	46	528	11.5	1.8	3	52%
Jerheme Urban	101	22.4%	38	22	329	15.0	3.7	3	58%
Sean Morey	-15	-24.4%	17	8	131	16.4	8.6	0	47%
Steve Breaston	-8	-19.4%	14	8	92	11.5	4.6	0	57%
TE									
Leonard Pope	26	3.6%	34	23	238	10.3	3.4	5	68%
Ben Patrick	15	8.9%	12	7	73	10.4	4.1	2	58%
Troy Bienemann	-8	-17.2%	11	7	46	6.6	1.6	1	64%
RB									
J. J. Arrington	40	5.5%	39	29	241	8.3	9.4	1	74%
Edgerrin James	6	-11.2%	39	25	196	7.8	7.5	0	64%
Marcel Shipp	-33	-60.6%	14	4	25	6.3	7.3	0	29%
Terrelle Smith	15	9.4%	11	7	59	8.4	4.9	0	64%

Offensive Line

Year	Yards	ALY	Rank	Power	Rank	10+ Yds	Rank	Stuff	Rank	Sack	ASR	Rank
2005	3.01	3.26	32	41%	32	11%	29	32%	32	45	6.4%	14
2006	3.34	4.05	23	56%	26	4%	32	25%	25	36	6.2%	14
2007	3.70	4.34	8	65%	14	8%	32	21%	8	24	4.7%	9

Year	LE	Rank	LT	Rank	Mid	Rank	RT	Rank	RE	Rank
2005	3.84	21	2.24	32	3.57	30	3.35	28	3.20	27
2006	4.08	17	3.96	26	4.25	21	3.77	29	3.46	24
2007	3.79	22	4.39	14	4.29	10	4.72	4	4.27	13

The Cardinals offensive line, which has long been the team's tragic flaw, played better than statistics show, and the stats were pretty good. The team made nearly a twofold leap in Adjusted Line Yards from 24th to eighth, and imagine if the line wasn't blocking for Edgerrin James, arguably the slowest starting running back in the league. Arizona also finished in the top 10 in Adjusted Sack Rate despite protecting two statuesque quarterbacks, Matt Leinart and Kurt Warner.

For those reasons, the Cardinals finally have an offensive line they like enough to keep intact from one year to the next. However, this line does have a split personality. The right side is sheer potential with 2007 fifth overall choice Levi Brown protecting lefty Leinart's blind side, and with mauling guard Deuce Lutui, 2006 second-round selection, setting the tone in the run game. Lutui was voted the league's Most Intimidating Lineman in a *Sports Illustrated* poll of the San Francisco 49ers' locker room. The left side, however, will need to be addressed at some point. Mike Gandy is serviceable at tackle, but the Cardinals are his third team in eight years. Valued tackles don't become journeymen. Coaches maintain that left guard Reggie Wells, a 2003 sixth-round choice, was the most consistent member of the line last year, but his play lacked panache.

The line will also have another year of education from well-thought-of position coach Russ Grimm, whose goal will be to limit the line's 36 penalties. The only possible camp battle could ensue between veteran center Al Johnson and second-year man Lyle Sendlein, who made the team as a rookie free agent out of the University of Texas.

Defensive Front Seven

Defensive Line	Age	Pos	Plays	TmPct	Rk	Stop	Dfts	Stop%	Rk	AvYd	Rk	Sack	Hit	Hur	Runs	RuStop	RuYd	Pass	PaStop	PaYd
Darnell Dockett	27	DT	60	7.4%	6	46	26	77%	41	1.0	12	8.5	14	10	38	79%	1.3	22	73%	0.4
Antonio Smith	27	DE	47	5.8%	40	38	18	81%	26	-0.1	4	6.0	5	8	34	76%	0.9	13	92%	-2.9
Gabe Watson	25	DT	36	4.5%	49	26	4	72%	54	3.6	66	0.0	1	1	28	79%	2.4	8	50%	7.5
Bertrand Berry	33	DE	23	5.1%	—	17	8	74%	—	0.1	—	2.5	2	8	15	73%	2.7	5	60%	2.2
Joe Tafoya	30	DE	17	2.6%	—	11	5	65%	—	2.5	—	2.0	1	3	12	67%	2.6	5	60%	2.2
Bryan Robinson	34	DE	22	2.7%	—	19	9	86%	—	0.2	—	1.5	4	3	18	83%	1.1	4	100%	-3.8
Simon Fraser	25	DE	16	1.9%	—	11	5	69%	—	4.1	—	0.0	0	0	14	64%	4.1	2	100%	4.0
Travis LaBoy	27	DE	16	2.5%	—	13	11	81%	—	-2.1	—	6.0	6	10	2	50%	1.0	14	86%	-2.6

Linebackers	Age	Pos	Plays	TmPct	Rk	Stop	Dfts	Stop%	AvYd	Sack	Hit	Hur	Runs	RuStop	Rk	RuYd	Rk	Tgts	Suc%	Rk	APaYd	Rk
Karlos Dansby	27	OLB	107	15.2%	17	57	27	53%	4.4	4.5	0	3	51	61%	54	2.7	20	36	43%	62	6.1	43
Calvin Pace*	28	OLB	100	12.4%	49	67	25	67%	3.3	6.5	4	15	57	65%	37	2.7	18	17	79%	1	3.5	3
Gerald Hayes	28	ILB	100	12.4%	48	56	20	56%	4.4	4.0	0	6	58	64%	44	3.2	43	38	47%	49	7.5	79
Monty Beisel	30	ILB	27	3.3%	—	14	0	52%	4.9	0.0	0	0	20	60%	—	3.4	—	6	67%	—	2.8	—
Clark Haggans	31	OLB	60	8.4%	81	34	11	57%	3.9	4.0	3	12	41	59%	65	3.7	65	22	49%	44	5.6	33

Year	Yards	ALY	Rank	Power	Rank	10+ Yds	Rank	Stuff	Rank	Sack	ASR	Rank
2005	4.07	3.75	8	57%	9	22%	28	29%	1	37	6.8%	19
2006	4.23	4.31	18	66%	17	17%	21	25%	14	38	5.9%	23
2007	3.86	3.97	9	78%	32	16%	15	25%	14	37	6.0%	20

Year	LE	Rank	LT	Rank	Mid	Rank	RT	Rank	RE	Rank
2005	2.49	1	4.37	18	4.36	25	3.67	7	2.33	1
2006	3.30	6	4.56	18	4.76	28	4.39	19	4.34	20
2007	3.61	9	3.45	3	3.89	6	5.13	30	3.84	11

Arizona was among the most injured teams in the league last year, particularly on the defensive line. Pass rusher Chike Okeafor missed the entire year with a torn biceps tendon, and Bertrand Berry's torn triceps tendon landed him on injured reserve for the second half of the season. Berry has finished the season on injured reserve in each of the last three years.

These injuries put pressure on Darnell Dockett, who was the primary pass rush threat from the defensive line. Early in the year, he consistently beat double teams, but late in the year, he clearly got tired, and only one of his nine sacks came in the second half of the season. The Cardinals will reduce his load if Berry and 32-year-old Okeafor can stay healthy. The team will also rotate its front three more often with the drafting of three defensive linemen. Third-round selection Calais Campbell had 19.5 sacks in 25 games started at Miami, but many teams stayed away from him because of his six-foot-eight frame and the fear that his long legs were too much of a target for offensive linemen. Run-defending, fourth-round choice Kenny Iwebema might be lucky to get on the field after two concussions, a broken collarbone, a sprained shoulder, and the triceps tendon damage he sustained in college. Sixth-round choice Chris Harrington is a hard-working type who will have to impress to make the team.

The trio of rookie linemen plus the signing of Titans defensive end Travis LaBoy could make up for the loss of Calvin Pace, who was lured to the Jets with $22 million up front in a six-year deal. Pace isn't just a pass-rusher; he's also surprisingly agile in coverage, with the top Success Rate against the pass among linebackers (albeit with a limited sample size).

One thing the Cardinals have to work on is stopping runs in short-yardage situations. As one of our game charters noted, "for an inside linebacker in the 3-4, Gerald Hayes has far too much trouble with shedding blocks. When a lineman gets in to him, it's over. He might be better suited in a position where he had more protection from the defensive line." The tackles have troubles of their own, however. An offseason knee injury to Gabe Watson will have him out until the end of training camp, while Alan Branch reported to a postdraft minicamp grossly out of shape.

Defensive Secondary

Secondary	Age	Pos	Plays	TmPct	Rk	Stop	Dfts	RuYd	Rk	RuStop	Rk	Tgts	Tgt%	Rk	Dist	Suc%	Rk	APaYd	Rk	PaYd	PD	Int
Roderick Hood	27	CB	78	9.7%	30	35	13	6.5	41	25%	72	113	24%	6	11.3	56%	17	6.6	22	6.3	21	5
Terrence Holt*	28	FS	70	8.7%	51	17	5	8.4	66	43%	42	20	4%	79	12.7	44%	57	11.6	75	11.1	1	0
Antrel Rolle	26	CB	67	8.3%	54	27	15	7.8	51	35%	58	67	14%	67	8.3	40%	73	10.1	79	9.9	9	5
Eric Green	26	CB	59	10.6%	20	21	8	6.1	38	33%	62	76	23%	8	8.8	41%	71	8.3	59	7.9	7	0
Adrian Wilson	29	SS	46	10.1%	33	27	7	6.5	44	69%	3	25	9%	13	13.1	51%	32	8.4	52	7.9	4	2
Aaron Francisco	25	FS	23	4.6%	—	9	3	5.9	—	60%	—	6	2%	—	14.8	27%	—	17.0	—	16.7	0	0
Ralph Brown	25	CB	19	2.2%	—	6	4	7.5	—	0%	—	30	6%	—	9.5	54%	—	6.2	—	5.8	0	0

Year	Pass D Rank	vs. #1 WR	Rk	vs. #2 WR	Rk	vs. Other WR	Rk	vs. TE	Rk	vs. RB	Rk
2005	12	18.2%	23	1.0%	19	-2.4%	15	-18.9%	5	-25.1%	3
2006	26	13.5%	28	1.5%	14	23.7%	27	-5.1%	15	9.3%	24
2007	19	16.4%	26	21.9%	28	-17.6%	9	-15.0%	3	-0.5%	17

Arizona cornerback Roderick Hood was among the most targeted cornerbacks in the league, and the Cardinals struggled against both number one and number two receivers. Scouts feel Hood is clearly more suited to be a nickel back, which is what he was in Philadelphia before Arizona signed him in free agency. Yet Hood was one of the top starting cornerbacks in the NFL, according to our game-charting project. Where is the disconnect?

Apparently, it is between the scouts and our numbers, not between our play-by-play numbers (DVOA) and our game-charting numbers (Success Rate). Yes, Hood occasionally looks like a fool when he tries to jump a route and guesses wrong. (The worst example of the year was probably Vinny Testaverde's 65-yard touchdown pass to Steve Smith in Week 6, when Hood wasn't even facing the right way.) But the Cardinals' team numbers against wide receivers were bad because of Eric Green and Antrel Rolle, not Hood. If our game charters are to be believed, the difference between Hood and the other two cornerbacks was stark:

Player	vs. #1 WR			vs. #2 WR			vs. Other WR		
	Tgts	APaYd	Suc%	Tgts	APaYd	Suc%	Tgts	APaYd	Suc%
Roderick Hood	51	7.5	56%	23	7.3	43%	28	5.5	64%
Eric Green	36	9.0	40%	16	8.2	36%	14	9.1	45%
Antrel Rolle	27	11.9	32%	15	14.7	33%	16	7.8	56%

This analysis doesn't even get to some of the other problems, like Rolle's flag-happy, aggressive style or Green's inexcusable blunders. Last year, in the opener against San Francisco, Green had the opportunity to prevent a tying touchdown by falling on a fumble in the end zone. Instead, he tried to pick the ball up and missed it. The ball was recovered by Darrell Jackson for a 49ers score.

Believing that cornerback was their most ardent defensive need this offseason, the Cardinals addressed the need by using their first-round pick on Dominique Rodgers-Cromartie of Tennessee State. They believe Rodgers-Cromartie has the talent to go straight from Division I-AA to the big leagues, but he needs to replace Green, not Hood, or Arizona will still have a big hole in the lineup at cornerback. Rolle, meanwhile, will move to free safety, where he'll play alongside strong safety Adrian Wilson, one of our *PFP 2007* coverboys. Wilson expects to make a full recovery from heel surgery by the start of training camp. His athleticism and versatility is rivaled only by Baltimore's Ed Reed and Pittsburgh's Troy Polamalu. Wilson has been often used as an extra linebacker, but this year, he will probably spend more time helping the cornerbacks.

Special Teams

Year	DVOA	Rank	FG/XP	Rank	Net Punt	Rank	Punt Ret	Rank	Net Kick	Rank	Kick Ret	Rank	Hidden	Rank
2005	-2.3%	26	20.0	1	-5.7	25	-2.3	20	-20.7	32	-4.7	24	-5.2	21
2006	-4.8%	32	-1.2	19	-20.0	31	-3.8	29	0.5	16	-3.5	22	-8.3	26
2007	-3.6%	26	-6.2	29	-21.8	32	4.7	7	6.8	5	-4.8	24	7.6	8

Once again, the Cardinals were terrible on special teams in 2007. The biggest problem was when the Cardinals had to punt. Arizona lost 21.8 points' worth of field position on punts. Not only was that the worst figure in the league, but it was also nearly twice as bad as the team that ranked 31st, Denver. Ken Whisenhunt inexplicably cut veteran Scott Player—after a decade of service in Arizona and a 44.9 gross yards average in 2006—in the preseason in favor of rookie Mike Barr, who barely averaged 40 yards a punt with no directional ability at all. When Barr (or late-season replacement Mitch Berger) allowed a return, the Cardinals then allowed 13 yards per runback, second to Indianapolis. This year, the Cardinals hope to get better punting out of former Eagle Dirk Johnson, but they better work on the coverage, too. Often, special-teams play is a reflection of how well backups are buying into the team philosophy. If punt coverage was any indication, coach Whisenhunt and special teams coach Kevin Spencer still have some work to do in that area.

As bad as Barr was, that's how good Neil Rackers is when it comes to kickoff distance. Rackers had more kickoff value than any other kicker in the league last year, after finishing second behind Olindo Mare in both 2005 and 2006. Of course, Rackers has been having serious problems with that other part of the kicking job, and his record-setting field goal season in 2005 was clearly one of the greatest fluke seasons ever at a position known for great fluke seasons. Rookie wide receiver Steve Breaston provided the punt return unit with some pop, but the team might want to consider having J. J. Arrington return kickoffs, since he did a better job in 2006 than Breaston did last year.

COACHING STAFF

When was the last time the Cardinals had to step up to prevent a coach from leaving? They did this year, bestowing a lucrative three-year contract on offensive coordinator Todd Haley after his brief dalliance with Miami. It's a reflection on the laudable job done by Ken Whisenhunt, in his first ever role as a head coach at any level. He made some mistakes in both game management (losing late twice to the 49ers) and roster management (cutting Player, for example), and his emphasis on the running game doesn't particularly match the strengths of his offense. But any coach who can coax eight wins out of the Cardinals, particularly in his first season, deserves high praise.

Atlanta Falcons

As difficult as it is to build a great NFL team, futility isn't generally an easy, overnight phenomenon, either. Teams suffering through horrible seasons can often trace their disasters to several different sources. The demise can come when teams hitch their wagons to franchise-killing quarterbacks, such as the 1992 Seahawks (Dan McGwire) and 2000 Chargers (Ryan Leaf). Some teams implode after handing the reins to a college coach who has no business running an NFL franchise: The 1976 Jets (Lou Holtz) and the 2004-2005 Dolphins (Nick Saban) are prime examples. Meddlesome owners who know less about the game than any general manager they could hire, but who insist on making key decisions and crowing about them in the press, or swooping in to take credit for the work of others … well, that's another problem. Just ask Cowboys owner Jerry Jones about the Dave Campo era.

However, if you want to engineer a truly spectacular fall from grace, it's best to avoid subtlety and throw every destructive aspect into the pot at once. This is the story of the 2007 Atlanta Falcons, who experienced as confounding and embarrassing a season as any Falcons club. And given the franchise's 29 losing seasons since joining the NFL in 1966, that's saying something.

The tale actually began innocently enough with a December 2006 appearance by then-Falcons coach Jim Mora on Seattle radio station KJR. On the phone with host Dave Mahler and Mora's college roommate, former NFL quarterback Hugh Millen, Mora said that if the head coaching position at the University of Washington (his alma mater) ever came open, "you'll find me at the head of the line with my résumé in hand ready to take that job." His comment quickly made the rounds. Mora claimed he was joking on the air when he issued a public apology the next day, but time was not on his side. The PR embarrassment, though it now seems quite small in retrospect, sealed Mora's fate. On January 1, 2007, a day after the club's third straight defeat ended a 7-9 season, Falcons owner Arthur Blank handed Mora his walking papers, just two years after the coach led Atlanta to the NFC Championship game and the first consecutive nonlosing seasons in franchise history.

Within a week, Blank had replaced Mora with one of college football's hottest young head coaches: Louisville's Bobby Petrino. Petrino went 41-9 in his four years with the Cardinals, and he felt that the time was right for a new challenge. He briefly said good-bye to his players in Louisville and headed to Atlanta, ostensibly to provide the kind of offensive scheme that could lead quarterback Michael Vick to a more consistent level of production. At the time, Vick was the face of the franchise. In December 2004, he had signed what was then the richest contract in league history, a 10-year, $130 million deal with $37 million in bonuses. In 2006, he became the only quarterback in NFL history to rush for 1,000 yards in a season. Now freed from former offensive coordinator Greg Knapp's more restrictive style, Vick would learn enough from Petrino and the accompanying offense full of

---

FALCONS PROSPECTUS

2007 Record: 4-12

Pythagorean Wins: 4.0 (29th)

DVOA: -22.7% total (28th), -23.8% weighted (26th)

Offense: -10.7% DVOA (24th)

Defense: 12.0% DVOA (29th)

Special Teams: 0.0% DVOA (14th)

Variance: 15.9 % (18th)

2007: *Nightmare on Peachtree Street*, starring Michael Vick and Bobby Petrino.

2008: In this year's sequel, the Falcons hope their nightmares are confined to the football field.

2008 Mean Projection: 3.5 wins

On the Clock (0-3): 52%

Loserville (4-6): 39%

Mediocrity (7-8): 8%

Playoff Contender (9-10): 1%

Super Bowl Contender (11+): 0%

Projected Average Opponent: 3.1% DVOA (10th in NFL)

| \multicolumn{6}{c}{2008 Falcons Schedule} | | | | | |
Week	Opp.	Week	Opp.	Week	Opp.
1	DET	7	BYE	13	at PHI
2	at TB	8	at PHI	14	STL
3	KC	9	at OAK	15	MIN
4	at CAR	10	NO	16	at NE
5	at GB	11	DEN	17	SEA
6	CHI	12	CAR		

options to take his game over the top. Well, at least that was the hope.

During a drug raid just a few days before the 2007 NFL draft, officials discovered that a home owned by Vick in Surry County, Virginia, was part of a dogfighting operation. Sixty-six dogs and all the equipment required to train the animals in this barbaric practice were found on the property. Vick's first response was to say that he wasn't aware of the operation and that family members had taken advantage. Over the next four months, as more and more evidence was uncovered—all of it extremely disturbing and a great deal of it tying Vick to the operation—the quarterback's NFL future and public persona irrevocably changed. Nike suspended him without pay from its lucrative ad campaign, Donruss pulled his likeness from packs of football cards, and Reebok made the unprecedented move to stop selling his jersey. NFL Commissioner Roger Goodell told Vick to stay away from the team's training camp in late July, and Vick pled guilty to dogfighting charges in August to avoid a federal trial. He was suspended from the NFL indefinitely on August 24, the same day his plea was filed in federal court. He received a 23-month sentence in December. Having lied about his role in the operation, Vick was denied an "acceptance of responsibility" credit that would have reduced his sentence. For the Falcons, denial of responsibility would become a common theme.

While all this was happening, Petrino was back at Falcons headquarters in Flowery Branch, trying to put together an NFL team for the first time. Former Lions and Dolphins quarterback Joey Harrington had signed on to be the backup, but Vick's suspension made him Atlanta's new starter. Harrington eventually started the season's first 12 games, though he was pulled in the fourth quarter of a Week 5 loss to the Titans after throwing 16 completions in 31 attempts for 87 yards. Two quarterbacks were behind Harrington on the depth chart: Chris Redman, a onetime Petrino protégé who

had not played an NFL game in four years, and Byron Leftwich, signed by the Falcons after Jacksonville released him on the eve of the regular season. Instead of going with Redman, who knew the offense from his days in Louisville, Petrino threw an unprepared Leftwich into the middle of a close game. Leftwich was completely lost—in less than a month, he had barely learned the Atlanta offensive terminology—and his late interception prevented the Falcons from rallying from a 20-13 deficit in Nashville. It was the beginning of the end for everyone involved.

After the game, tight end Alge Crumpler expressed his displeasure with his coach and the team's situation, accusing Petrino of shoddy play-calling. "They keep telling us to trust them, but right now we are one and four," Crumpler said after the game. Petrino's ironic response? "There's one agenda here with our coaching staff, and that's to win every week. That's it. [Crumpler] understands that I don't like to put things like that out there in the press. *I would rather he walk in my office if he has something to say*."

The Falcons also lost left tackle Wayne Gandy for the season to a knee injury in that game. Gandy's replacement, undrafted rookie free agent Renardo Foster, lasted one game before his own knee injury ended *his* season. The Falcons ended up using four left tackles in 2007, but none of them fit, because Petrino thought he could switch the effective zone-blocking scheme of previous offensive line coach Alex Gibbs to a power-blocking attack without changing personnel. The results were predictable. The Falcons finished last in the league in Adjusted Line Yards after ranking sixth, seventh and 13th under Gibbs from 2004 through 2006.

This rigidity, as much as anything, was symptomatic of the in-season problems that plagued the Falcons throughout Petrino's brief reign. Petrino was uncommunicative and autocratic. He alienated team leaders and treated Harrington miserably. Petrino's hubris is typical of the college coach who busts supremely in the NFL. This kind of coach is used to having complete control, the ability to run his schemes with relative success, and players who end every sentence with "sir." NFL teams are partnerships between coaches and players; even the most control-freak NFL masterminds have to dial it down at certain times and deal with different players in certain ways. Petrino was used to having his own way, and when things went so drastically wrong in Atlanta, he started to look for a way out.

The University of Arkansas provided his escape hatch. Blank received a December call from Jerry Jones, an Arkansas alum and longtime booster, informing Blank that there were people at the university who wanted to talk to Petrino about the school's head coaching position. Blank turned this over to team president Rich McKay, who told Jones that the team would not extend permission to Arkansas to talk to Petrino. After telling Blank and McKay that he wasn't interested in heading back to college, Petrino met with McKay on December 11—the day after a 20-point loss to the Saints on Monday Night Football and the same day that Vick was sentenced. Petrino then called Blank to say that he was, indeed, departing. Yet leaving his Falcons players with nothing but a four-sentence note on their lockers wasn't even the final insult. That was saved for the press conference announcing his acceptance of the Arkansas job, when Petrino helped lead the Razorbacks' "Pig, sooey!" chant from the podium. It painted Petrino as a man totally unconcerned with the fate of the team he left hanging, a cowardly opportunist with no integrity whatsoever.

The Falcons tried to put their best face on a wrecked season that still had three games to go. Defensive backs coach Emmitt Thomas took over as interim head coach. Redman, who'd started the last game of Petrino's time in Atlanta, finished the season as starter. He ended the year ranked 23rd in DYAR and signed a two-year, $5 million contract in February. In the end, Redman may wind up the only positive element Petrino brought to Atlanta.

After the 4-12 season was over, Blank rearranged the deck chairs. He started by stripping McKay of his GM title but retaining him as team president, and hiring former Patriots director of college scouting Thomas Dimitroff as McKay's replacement. Of course, nothing could be simple with this team. The Dimitroff hire came after Bill Parcells agreed in principle to run the Falcons in late December, only to back out and join the 1-15 Dolphins as their executive vice president of football operations. After dancing with USC coach Pete Carroll, Ravens defensive coordinator Rex Ryan, and Vikings defensive coordinator Leslie Frazier, the team decided on Jaguars defensive coordinator Mike Smith as Petrino's permanent replacement.

The next step was to start rebuilding the team on the field. Dimitroff started in mid-February by releasing seven veterans, including Gandy, Leftwich, Crumpler, and defensive tackle Rod Coleman. Aging running back Warrick Dunn was cut in March, one day after the Falcons signed former San Diego backup Michael Turner to a six-year, $34.5 million contract. Turner showed starting-level talent playing behind LaDainian Tomlinson, but as detailed later in this chapter, Atlanta may have paid a lot for something it already had.

Dimitroff's biggest move came March 20, when the Oakland Raiders agreed to a trade for cornerback DeAngelo Hall. Selected with the Falcons' eighth overall pick in the 2004 draft, Hall never quite lived up to his promise in Atlanta, and his very public—and frequently expressed—dissatisfaction with the franchise pretty much sealed his fate. There are not yet definite replacements for big-ticket players like Crumpler and Hall, and reinforcements for the substandard offensive and defensive lines have been slow in coming, but the truth is that those personnel issues are secondary. The Falcons' lead story does not reside on the field.

Mike Smith is an enthusiastic coach with a deep college and NFL background, and Dimitroff's résumé is certainly impressive. But in the end, this team's ability to resurface from its recent string of disasters in any meaningful fashion is reliant on Blank's realization that he must stay away from areas that he is not qualified to run. The decisions that led to the horrid 2007 have Blank as their common denominator, and his openness to the idea of another college coach in Carroll after the Petrino debacle is unsettling, to say the least—especially since Carroll's NFL history was less than spectacular. More disturbing, Blank won't close the book on Vick, even after the Falcons selected Boston College quarterback Matt Ryan with the third overall pick in the 2008 draft. As recently as early April 2008, Blank and Vick, who is incarcerated in the United States Penitentiary in Leavenworth, Kansas, have continued to correspond.

"I just try to be supportive and as understanding as I can be," Blank told the *New York Daily News*. "He talks about the process he is going through and what he has learned, the lessons of life, how he's going to come out a different person. He's sorry he has affected so many people in a negative way—the league, our club, our fans. He feels awful about that. The letters sound quite sincere to me. From a mental standpoint, he sounds good." Blank also told CNNSI's Peter King that he's disappointed that he never received any sort of apology from Petrino. Conventional wisdom says that he shouldn't hold his breath.

It's all well and good to extend a belief in the positive qualities of those who have betrayed you, but the Atlanta Falcons franchise isn't just a football team or a group of friends—it's a multimillion-dollar business whose fate is inexorably tied to 31 other multimillion-dollar businesses. Fans in Atlanta are apathetic, season ticket sales are down, and Blank himself has become little more than a punchline. Until he trusts the people in his charge to make the choices he is not qualified to make (certainly, the character decisions should be made by someone else), Blank will continue to fail, and the results promise to be quite embarrassing for the Falcons.

It's the perfect recipe for futility.

Doug Farrar

Michael Turner and the "Breather Effect"

During the NFL Network's 2008 Scouting Combine coverage, future Hall of Fame running back Marshall Faulk was asked about the impact that Arkansas' Felix Jones will have at the NFL level. Jones, who benefited from having Darren McFadden as his battery-mate, averaged 7.7 yards per carry in three years at Arkansas, including 8.7 yards per carry as a junior in 2007. Jones finished his college career with the second-best career rushing average in NCAA history, behind only the 8.3 yards per carry amassed by Glenn Davis of Army from 1943 to 1946. And while Faulk didn't dismiss Jones's contributions in any way, he brought up a very interesting premise.

"I like Felix Jones," Faulk said. "The question was … when you play behind a guy like McFadden, there's something I call the 'take a breather [effect]' when he comes out of the game. The defense breathes a sigh of relief because McFadden's out, and Felix would rip off these incredible yards per carry [totals]. To see him run a great time and do the other things he did proved to me that he's worthy of being taken in the first round."

The "breather effect," as we'll call it, has allowed certain running backs to turn into sample-size superstars by playing behind elite backs or by producing in certain situational roles. One of the primary members of this club is former Chargers running back Michael Turner, who put up 1,257 rushing yards on 228 carries for an average of 5.5 yards per carry over four years in San Diego. Turner eventually was regarded as one of the NFL's best-kept secrets because he was toiling behind 2006 MVP LaDainian Tomlinson. Trade rumors had circulated around Turner for the last couple of years, but the Chargers held on to him until he became a free agent after the 2007 season.

The Falcons made Turner their biggest free-agency splash of the offseason, offering the Northern Illinois alum a six-year, $34.5 million contract with $15 million guaranteed. The decision was made despite his small résumé and despite the fact that few teams have ever found more value in two-back sets than Atlanta has in recent years. Another consideration is the presence of Jerious Norwood, who has put up his own impressive part-time numbers. In 2007, Norwood had the highest DVOA rating of any running back with at least 100 carries; in 2006, he would have ranked first, except that he only carried the ball 99 times. Unless you believe that Turner's production as a role player in San Diego correlates to full-time success with a different team, the contract seems like a gross overpayment and an uncharacteristic inability to recognize the bargains possible with the two-back system.

Since the start of the 16-game season in 1978, there have been 84 instances of a running back's gaining at least five yards per carry on 50-150 carries in a season while playing in at least eight games. Seventy-two players have accomplished this feat; 10 backs, including both Turner and Norwood, have done it at least twice, and Napoleon Kaufman of the Raiders did it three times (Table 1).

Table 1. Multiple Seasons of Five Yards per Carry with 50-150 Carries

Name	Team	Year 1					Year 2					Career High in Yards		
		Year	G	Runs	Yds	Yd/R	Year	G	Runs	Yds	Yd/R	Year	Runs	Yds
Bruce Harper	NYJ	1978	16	58	303	5.2	1983	9	51	354	6.9	1981	81	393
Tony Nathan	MIA	1980	16	60	327	5.5	1981	13	147	782	5.3	1981	147	782
Hokie Gajan	NO	1983	16	81	415	5.1	1984	14	102	615	6.0	1984	102	615
Stump Mitchell	ARI	1983	15	68	373	5.5	1984	16	81	434	5.4	1985	183	1006
Ronnie Harmon	SD	1990	16	66	363	5.5	1991	16	89	544	6.1	1991	89	544
Kimble Anders	KC	1995	16	58	398	6.9	1997	15	79	397	5.0	1995	58	398
Charlie Garner	PHI	1995	15	108	588	5.4	1996	15	66	346	5.2	1999	241	1229
Napoleon Kaufman*	OAK	1996	16	150	874	5.8	1999	16	138	714	5.2	1997	272	1294
Najeh Davenport	GB	2003	15	77	420	5.5	2004	11	71	359	5.1	2003	77	420
Michael Turner	SD	2005	16	57	335	5.9	2006	13	80	502	6.3	2006	80	502
Jerious Norwood	ATL	2006	14	99	633	6.4	2007	15	103	613	6.0	2006	99	633

*Kaufman accomplished this feat in a third season (2000) as well, with 93 carries for 499 yards in 14 games (5.4 yards per carry).

Table 2. Five Yards per Carry with 50-150 Carries, Highest Yards per Carry over Team's Leading Rusher

Team	Year	Part-Time Back					Leading Rusher					Dif
		Name	G	Runs	Yds	Yd/R	Name	G	Runs	Yds	Yd/R	
NYJ	1983	Bruce Harper	9	51	354	6.9	Freeman McNeil	9	160	654	4.1	2.8
ATL	1997	Byron Hanspard	16	53	335	6.3	Jamal Anderson	16	290	1002	3.5	2.8
ATL	2007	Jerious Norwood	15	103	613	6	Warrick Dunn	16	227	720	3.2	2.8
KC	1995	Kimble Anders	13	58	398	6.9	Marcus Allen	16	207	890	4.3	2.6
CLE	1984	Earnest Byner	16	72	426	5.9	Boyce Green	16	202	673	3.3	2.6
PIT	1999	Richard Huntley	16	93	567	6.1	Jerome Bettis	16	299	1091	3.6	2.5
ATL	2006	Jerious Norwood	14	99	633	6.4	Warrick Dunn	16	286	1140	4	2.4
NO	1984	Hokie Gajan	14	102	615	6	George Rogers	16	239	914	3.8	2.2
LARM	1980	Jewerl Thomas	16	65	427	6.6	Cullen Bryant	16	183	806	4.4	2.2
SD	2004	Jesse Chatman	15	65	392	6	LaDainian Tomlinson	15	339	1335	3.8	2.2

When we look at these 11 running backs, however, we find that consistent success in situational roles does not specifically lead to greater production. Kaufman had two excellent years as the starter in Oakland, but this occurred before two of the three part-time seasons referenced in this study. Only three of the other eight backs before Turner and Norwood eventually had a 1,000-yard season, and only Charlie Garner eventually became a regular starter.

How do we determine when the breather effect is in play? We can start by looking at the biggest differences in yards per carry between running backs who led their team in yardage and those backs whose smaller bursts of productivity outshone their more popular colleagues the most (Table 2). Only one of the top 10 backs on this list eventually had a breakout season: Earnest Byner, six years later, and with a different team. Richard Huntley got to be the leading rusher for the 2001 Panthers, but 665 yards for one of the worst teams of all time doesn't really qualify as breakout. Bruce Harper, Hokie Gajan, and Byron Hanspard each played only one more season in the NFL. (Hanspard at least had a good excuse; a training-camp injury wrecked his knee in 1998.) Jewerl

Thomas played four more years but never had more than 120 yards in a season again. The only running back to appear in the top 10 twice is Jerious Norwood; this grand performance earned him the opportunity to … split time with Michael Turner.

So far, there is little indication that short bursts of production in situational roles are harbingers of big things to come. In fact, it's just as likely that we're dealing with players who catch fire in small doses and enjoy career years. This is also clear when we look at the biggest gaps in rushing yardage between the feature back and the secondary back when the secondary back has at least five yards per carry (Table 3). This list primarily contains running backs from recent years; again, Charlie Garner is the only one who went on to have sustained success as a starter. The other nine running backs on the list have combined for a grand total of one season over 600 rushing yards, and in that season, LaMont Jordan (with the 2005 Raiders) gained less than four yards per carry.

Of course, not all the seasons that qualify for this study provide a good comparison with Turner and Norwood. For example, when Michael Pittman gained 6.2

Table 3. Backs With Five Yards per Carry with 50-150 Carries, Most Yards Behind Leading Rusher

Team	Year	Part-Time Back				Leading Rusher				Dif
		Name	G	Runs	Yds	Name	G	Runs	Yds	
GB	2003	Najeh Davenport	15	77	420	Ahman Green	16	355	1883	1463
SD	2006	Michael Turner	13	80	502	LaDainian Tomlinson	16	348	1815	1313
NYJ	2004	LaMont Jordan	16	93	479	Curtis Martin	16	371	1697	1218
SD	2005	Michael Turner	16	57	335	LaDainian Tomlinson	16	339	1462	1127
PHI	1996	Charlie Garner	15	66	346	Ricky Watters	16	353	1411	1065
PHI	2007	Correll Buckhalter	15	65	392	Brian Westbrook	15	278	1333	1020
MIA	1978	Gary Davis	14	62	313	Delvin Williams	16	272	1258	945
CHI	2005	Adrian Peterson	16	76	391	Thomas Jones	15	314	1335	944
SD	2004	Jesse Chatman	15	65	392	LaDainian Tomlinson	15	339	1335	943
STL	2001	Trung Canidate	16	78	441	Marshall Faulk	14	260	1382	941

Table 4. Part-Time Stars Who Eventually Gained More Than 750 Yards

Player	Great Part-Time Year							Career High				Height	Weight	BMI
	Year	Team	G	Runs	Yds	Yd/R	Rec	Year	Team	Runs	Yds			
Ted McKnight	1978	KC	16	104	627	6.0	14	1979	KC	153	755	6-1	209	27.6
Don Calhoun	1978	NE	14	76	391	5.1	3	1980	NE	200	787	6-0	206	27.9
Tony Nathan	1980	MIA	16	60	327	5.5	57	1981	MIA	147	782	6-0	206	27.9
Stump Mitchell	1984	STL	16	81	434	5.4	26	1985	STL	183	1006	5-9	188	27.8
Earnest Byner	1984	CLE	16	72	426	5.9	11	1990	WAS	297	1219	5-10	215	30.8
Darrin Nelson	1984	MIN	15	80	406	5.1	27	1985	MIN	200	893	5-9	184	27.2
Barry Foster	1991	PIT	10	96	488	5.1	9	1992	PIT	390	1690	5-10	223	32.0
Charlie Garner	1995	PHI	15	108	588	5.4	10	1999	SF	241	1229	5-9	187	27.6
Napoleon Kaufman	1996	OAK	16	150	874	5.8	22	1997	OAK	272	1294	5-9	185	27.3
Priest Holmes	1999	BAL	8	89	506	5.7	13	2002	KC	313	1615	5-9	205	30.3
Troy Hambrick	2001	DAL	16	113	579	5.1	4	2003	DAL	275	972	6-1	235	31.0
Amos Zereoue	2001	PIT	14	85	441	5.2	13	2002	PIT	193	762	5-10	200	28.7
Brian Westbrook	2003	PHI	15	117	613	5.2	37	2007	PHI	278	1333	5-8	200	30.4
Steven Jackson	2004	STL	14	134	673	5.0	19	2006	STL	346	1528	6-2	233	29.9
LaMont Jordan	2004	NYJ	16	93	479	5.2	15	2005	OAK	272	1025	5-10	235	33.7
Tatum Bell	2004	DEN	14	75	396	5.3	5	2006	DEN	233	1025	5-11	213	29.7

yards per carry for the 2005 Buccaneers, he was 30 years old. If we want to see how backs will develop, we need to limit ourselves to just the younger players.

Fifty-seven players in this study had five years of experience or less when they had a season with five yards per carry on 50-150 carries. More than half—33 players—went on to have at least one season with more yardage. That sounds good, but a "better season" could mean something like the 499 yards Najeh Davenport had for last year's Steelers. That's not what the Falcons are looking for from Michael Turner.

Of those 33 players, 16 went on to set a career high with at least 750 rushing yards, and 11 would eventually gain 1,000 yards in a season (Table 4). Most of the backs who eventually succeeded have something surprising in common: small size. The average height of the 16 players is five foot ten and one-half, the average weight is 208 pounds, and the average Body Mass Index (BMI) is 29.4. Only LaMont Jordan has a BMI above 32.

Now look at the Atlanta Falcons' running backs. Jerious Norwood is six feet tall and weighs 203 pounds, for a BMI of 27.5. Michael Turner stands five foot ten and weighs 237 pounds, for a BMI of 34.0. Turner also differs from the great sample-size backs who went on to success in another way, as receivers. Most of these backs were useful in the passing game. In four seasons, Turner had only 11 catches for 71 yards. Eleven of these 16 backs had more receptions in their great part-time season than Turner has had for his entire career.

There's another possible reason that Turner is particularly deserving of his large new contract. Perhaps he is

especially talented at gaining tough yards late in close games or in other crucial situations. Unfortunately, we have no idea whether this is the case, since almost all those carries in San Diego have gone to LaDainian Tomlinson. Norwood has more carries in those situations than Turner does, since Norwood has been part of Atlanta's longtime two-back system.

So the answer to the question about indicators and correlations seems to be that there are no predictors you can really hang your hat on. The few indicators we can find are fairly weak and suggest that Michael Turner is not likely to become a long-term success as a starter. If you're telling Turner that he's worth elite running-back money, it's much more a scouting decision than a sabermetric one.

And that's where things get inexplicable. Isolating Turner and Norwood gets us back to the original point—not whether Turner can be a great NFL running back, but whether paying him X amount of money over X number of years makes sense under the Falcons' current conditions.

By almost any standard, the Falcons already had their sample-size superstar on board before signing Turner. With needs all over the roster, an unbelievable draft class of running backs, a surplus of picks after the DeAngelo Hall trade, and a salary cap imbalance between Turner ($3.75 million cap charge in 2007) and Norwood ($631,166), the move seems to make little sense.

Jerious Norwood led the league in DVOA and gained six yards per carry, despite playing on a team in complete turmoil and running behind an offensive line that finished last in Adjusted Line Yards. The slight indicators that do exist suggest that he is a better candidate for future success as a starting running back. Down the road, are the Falcons ever going to reward Jerious Nor-

wood for doing what Michael Turner has done—and then some?

Doug Farrar
Aaron Schatz

2007 Falcons Stats by Week

Wk	vs.	W-L	PF	PA	YDF	YDA	TO	Total	Off	Def	ST
1	@MIN	L	3	24	265	302	-1	-51%	-38%	7%	-6%
2	@JAC	L	7	13	248	364	0	7%	7%	-15%	-15%
3	CAR	L	20	27	442	313	-2	-18%	35%	52%	-2%
4	HOU	W	26	16	304	398	+2	9%	6%	-3%	0%
5	@TEN	L	13	20	198	249	+3	-34%	-58%	-27%	-2%
6	NYG	L	10	31	284	491	+2	-50%	-4%	41%	-4%
7	@NO	L	16	22	334	310	+1	-34%	-19%	19%	3%
8	BYE										
9	SF	W	20	16	286	251	+3	1%	-15%	-10%	5%
10	@CAR	W	20	13	277	235	+1	34%	3%	-30%	1%
11	TB	L	7	31	265	305	-2	-58%	-30%	25%	-3%
12	IND	L	13	31	250	365	-1	-16%	-18%	1%	3%
13	@STL	L	16	28	435	409	-1	-50%	-15%	43%	7%
14	NO	L	14	34	323	473	0	-43%	-19%	39%	14%
15	@TB	L	3	37	133	285	-3	-111%	-86%	-1%	-25%
16	@ARI	L	27	30	405	437	-1	-7%	12%	27%	8%
17	SEA	W	44	41	364	501	+3	55%	53%	16%	18%

Trends and Splits

	Offense	Rank	Defense	Rank
Total DVOA	-10.7%	24	12.0%	29
Unadjusted VOA	-10.2%	23	12.2%	24
Weighted trend	-11.3%	23	14.8%	31
Variance	11.2%	31	6.4%	16
Average opponent	0.6%	13	0.8%	19
Passing	-6.9%	22	18.8%	26
Rushing	-15.6%	29	4.6%	28
First down	-11.8%	26	10.1%	27
Second down	-14.6%	27	14.6%	27
Third down	-11.1%	22	11.5%	25
First half	-5.9%	22	14.0%	27
Second half	-15.9%	28	9.3%	26
Red Zone	-6.6%	21	17.3%	25
Late and close	-16.7%	28	-1.2%	15

Five-Year Performance

Year	W-L	Pyth Wins	Est Wins	PF	PA	TO	Total	Rank	Off	Rank	Def	Rank	ST	Rank
2003	5-11	4.9	5.5	299	422	0	-17.4%	26	-9.9%	23	9.9%	26	1.5%	13
2004	11-5	8.1	8.0	340	337	+2	-2.7%	17	-6.2%	23	0.5%	17	4.0%	6
2005	8-8	8.3	7.0	351	341	0	-3.5%	17	5.1%	11	10.9%	28	2.3%	5
2006	7-9	6.9	7.4	292	328	+6	-8.3%	21	-2.1%	16	2.4%	17	-3.8%	28
2007	4-12	8.1	6.3	259	414	+4	-9.4%	22	-0.4%	18	5.3%	20	-3.6%	26

Strategic Tendencies

Run/Pass		Rank	Offense		Rank	Defense		Rank	Other		Rank
Runs, all plays	37%	27	3+ WR	66%	5	Rush 3	1.4%	30	2+ RB, Pct Runs	57%	16
Runs, first half	40%	21	4+ WR	14%	10	Rush 4	61.4%	18	1 RB/2 TE, Pct Runs	45%	18
Runs, first down	43%	28	2+ TE	15%	29	Rush 5	20.9%	18	1 RB/3+ WR, pct runs	26%	13
Runs, second-long	33%	19	Single back	61%	11	Rush 6+	16.1%	2	CB1 on WR1	42%	21
Runs, power sit.	69%	6	Play action	11%	27	Rush 7+	3.1%	7	Go for it on 4th	0.82	22
Runs, behind 2H	27%	19	Max protect	7%	27	Sacks by LB	24.0%	17	Offensive Pace	30.0	9
Pass, ahead 2H	43%	20	Outside pocket	10%	21	Sacks by DB	4.0%	26	Defensive Pace	29.8	2

In general, NFL offenses put up higher DVOA ratings when using four- and five-wide sets. However, the difference for Atlanta was far more dramatic than it was for the league as a whole.

Formation	NFL DVOA	NFL Yd/Play	ATL DVOA	ATL Yd/Play
0-1 WR	-2.0%	4.0	-26.1%	3.5
2 WR	-3.4%	5.2	-18.5%	4.7
3 WR	3.2%	5.6	-16.4%	4.9
4-5 WR	12.8%	6.1	30.6%	6.1

One big reason for the DVOA gap: Atlanta quarterbacks threw just one interception with more than three wide receivers on the field, an end-of-half Hail Mary against the Giants. ⌀ Bobby Petrino dramatically altered Atlanta's use of play-action fakes. The Falcons led the league in 2006, using play-action on 27 percent of pass plays. Last year, that percentage was cut by more than half. ⌀ The Falcons led the league in draw plays as a percentage of all runs, with league-average results. ⌀ Although only ranked 25th in number of screen passes thrown, Atlanta was ranked first in DVOA on screen passes. Running-back screen passes were split evenly between Warrick Dunn and Jerious Norwood, but Norwood's DVOA significantly outpaced that of Dunn. In fact, less than half of the screen passes set up for Dunn were completed, and Dunn dropped three of them. ⌀ Only 14 percent of Atlanta passes went deep (16 or more yards through the air), the lowest percentage in the league. ⌀ Roddy White was Atlanta's most targeted receiver on third down, but Michael Jenkins was more effective: 15 of his 28 passes on third down were completed for a first down or a touchdown. ⌀ Atlanta's first-quarter defense was the worst among all NFL teams. ⌀ DeAngelo Hall covered the opponent's number one wide receiver almost twice as often as Chris Houston did. ⌀ Atlanta ranked 30th in defensive DVOA against teams using four or five wide receivers. No team faced more runs from a four-wide set; when opponents spread the field against Atlanta, one out of every four plays was a run.

Passing

Player	DYAR	DVOA	Plays	NtYds	Avg	YAC	C%	TD	Int
Joey Harrington	124	-5.8%	382	2071	5.4	5.2	61.8%	7	7
Chris Redman	163	5.5%	160	1099	6.9	5.4	60.1%	10	5
Byron Leftwich*	-215	-65.0%	64	244	3.8	3.8	55.2%	1	2

Rushing

Player	DYAR	DVOA	Plays	Yds	Avg	TD	Fum	Suc
Warrick Dunn*	-108	-20.0%	227	721	3.2	4	2	37%
Jerious Norwood	133	24.5%	103	613	6.0	1	0	48%
Jason Snelling	9	3.0%	13	43	3.3	1	0	54%
Joey Harrington	0	-12.4%	9	37	4.1	0	1	—
Ovie Mughelli	-5	-20.9%	6	7	1.2	1	0	50%
Chris Redman	-20	-79.7%	6	18	3.0	0	3	—
Artose Pinner*	-6	-26.4%	5	46	9.2	0	0	40%
Byron Leftwich*	-37	-137.7%	5	-3	-0.6	0	6	—
Michael Turner	-52	-27.4%	71	316	4.5	1	1	28%

Receiving

Player	DYAR	DVOA	Plays	Ctch	Yds	Y/C	YAC	TD	C%
WR									
Roddy White	148	1.2%	137	83	1204	14.5	5.5	6	61%
Michael Jenkins	85	0.5%	85	53	532	10.0	3.5	8	62%
Laurent Robinson	-98	-29.5%	74	37	437	11.8	3.5	1	50%
Joe Horn	-79	-32.1%	52	27	243	9.0	1.9	1	52%
Adam Jennings	37	69.3%	6	6	62	10.3	3.2	1	100%
TE									
Alge Crumpler*	35	0.4%	70	42	444	10.6	6.2	5	60%
Martrez Milner	-6	-18.6%	9	9	50	5.6	2.8	0	100%
Dwayne Blakley*	-6	-18.6%	9	7	48	6.9	3.4	0	78%
Ben Hartsock	0	-7.5%	19	12	138	11.5	5.9	0	63%
RB									
Warrick Dunn*	-48	-29.6%	59	37	238	6.4	6.5	0	63%
Jerious Norwood	73	21.6%	39	28	277	9.9	10.3	0	72%
Ovie Mughelli	-14	-38.2%	10	6	36	6.0	4.5	0	60%
Michael Turner	-19	-60.5%	7	4	16	4.0	6.0	0	57%

Offensive Line

Year	Yards	ALY	Rank	Power	Rank	10+ Yds	Rank	Stuff	Rank	Sack	ASR	Rank
2005	4.49	4.47	7	65%	14	20%	12	21%	5	39	8.1%	25
2006	4.64	4.30	13	59%	23	23%	4	25%	24	47	10.4%	31
2007	4.04	3.55	32	62%	17	24%	5	32%	32	47	7.9%	23

Year	LE	Rank	LT	Rank	Mid	Rank	RT	Rank	RE	Rank
2005	5.17	4	4.75	4	3.97	20	4.75	4	5.06	2
2006	4.53	10	3.71	28	4.50	11	4.27	12	4.67	9
2007	3.40	26	3.79	25	3.40	32	3.20	32	4.38	11

Like every other aspect of the Bobby Petrino regime in Atlanta, the attempt to establish a power running game was a complete failure. Things were consistent in the middle of the line, where center Todd McClure started every game, but they got shakier to the outside. Left guard Justin Blalock and right guard Kynan Forney each missed a pair of games. Starting tackles Todd Weiner and Wayne Gandy started only seven and five games, respectively. When all was said and done, six different players started at tackle, including backup guard Quinn Ojinaka (three starts at tackle) and undrafted journeymen like D'Anthony Batiste (four starts), Renardo Foster (two), and Tyson Clabo (11). The result was the worst run-blocking line in the league, after great results with the previous regime under offensive line coach Alex Gibbs. The Falcons ranked dead last in Adjusted Line Yards and Stuff Percentage. Curiously, the motley crew that combined to play tackle outperformed the regulars in the middle of the line; Atlanta ranked dead last in runs up the middle and over right tackle, while they were merely very bad at runs to left end and left tackle, and a surprising ninth on runs around right end.

Blalock, McClure, Forney, and Weiner are all returning for 2008. Still recovering from surgery, Weiner missed the Falcons' predraft minicamp and might not be ready for Week 1. The Falcons released the 37-year-old Gandy and will replace him at left tackle with rookie Sam Baker out of USC. Atlanta may have felt compelled to trade up for Baker after a first-round run that saw four tackles chosen in an eight-pick stretch, so it sent two second-round picks to Washington for the 21st overall selection and grabbed Baker. That's a hefty price to pay, but after the Falcons made Matt Ryan the third overall selection, they had to get him more protection, no matter the cost.

Defensive Front Seven

Defensive Line	Age	Pos	Plays	TmPct	Rk	Stop	Dfts	Stop%	Rk	AvYd	Rk	Sack	Hit	Hur	Runs	RuStop	RuYd	Pass	PaStop	PaYd
Jonathan Babineaux	27	DT	49	6.6%	13	40	16	82%	23	1.1	14	3.0	3	8	35	77%	1.4	14	93%	0.3
John Abraham	30	DE	36	4.3%	62	27	19	75%	46	0.8	19	10.0	12	19	16	69%	2.5	20	80%	-0.6
Jamaal Anderson	22	DE	33	3.9%	67	24	1	73%	56	2.4	58	0.0	4	9	29	69%	2.4	4	100%	1.8
Chauncey Davis	25	DE	32	3.8%	71	19	9	59%	76	2.0	49	2.0	3	4	28	54%	3.1	4	100%	-5.3
Montavious Stanley	27	DT	31	4.2%	51	21	5	68%	65	2.6	60	0.0	0	3	28	64%	3.3	3	100%	-3.3
Grady Jackson	35	DT	29	7.9%	5	24	10	83%	20	1.0	13	1.0	0	3	28	82%	1.3	1	100%	-5.0
Trey Lewis	23	DT	19	4.0%	—	16	4	84%	—	2.5	—	0.0	0	2	18	83%	2.6	1	100%	0.0
Kindal Moorehead	30	DT	19	2.3%	—	15	6	79%	—	0.9	—	2.0	1	2	17	76%	1.6	2	100%	-5.5

Linebackers	Age	Pos	Plays	TmPct	Rk	Stop	Dfts	Stop%	AvYd	Sack	Hit	Hur	Runs	RuStop	Rk	RuYd	Rk	Tgts	Suc%	Rk	APaYd	Rk
Keith Brooking	33	MLB	115	13.6%	38	59	14	51%	5.1	2.0	2	4	73	58%	73	4.0	79	36	53%	33	5.3	26
Michael Boley	26	OLB	109	12.9%	45	60	30	55%	5.3	3.0	7	8	55	53%	92	5.7	98	44	51%	41	6.1	46
Demorrio Williams*	28	OLB	78	9.3%	75	40	12	51%	5.5	0.0	0	2	45	60%	58	3.0	34	23	46%	55	7.4	78
Stephen Nicholas	25	OLB	29	4.2%	—	13	1	45%	5.0	1.0	0	0	19	47%	—	4.6	—	8	14%	—	6.2	—

Year	Yards	ALY	Rank	Power	Rank	10+ Yds	Rank	Stuff	Rank	Sack	ASR	Rank
2005	4.88	4.76	32	67%	21	20%	23	27%	6	37	7.1%	17
2006	3.84	4.15	12	56%	6	12%	4	25%	11	38	7.8%	8
2007	4.40	4.47	28	62%	15	16%	16	21%	26	25	6.0%	21

Year	LE	Rank	LT	Rank	Mid	Rank	RT	Rank	RE	Rank
2005	4.86	25	5.03	31	4.73	32	4.41	25	4.73	23
2006	5.07	28	3.55	8	4.21	15	3.59	10	4.98	29
2007	5.02	27	4.74	24	4.42	27	3.91	11	4.91	28

Defensive tackle Grady Jackson's arrival in 2006 gave the team a significant boost. In a controversial move, however, he was released seven weeks into the season, and the results were disastrous. Atlanta ranked 22nd in run defense in the first half of the season, and 29th in the second half. The other projected starter, Rod Coleman, played only five games in the middle of the season. He was released at the end of the year. This left the Falcons with a tackle crew of 2005 second-rounder Jonathan Babineaux, Montavious Stanley, and Trey Lewis. The team added Kindal Moorehead from Carolina over the offseason. He's slated to start alongside Babineaux in 2008. Those two are listed at the same height (six foot two) and virtually the same weight—which is unfortunate, because both are undersized (285 pounds for Moorehead, 286 for Babineaux). Expect teams to run up the gut against Atlanta again this year, and don't be surprised if you see more of the 308-pound Stanley in an attempt to prevent it.

Right end John Abraham quietly had a very good 2007, starting all 16 games for just the second time of his career, notching his fourth 10-sack season, and tying for third in the league in hurries. Abraham recorded either a sack or a hurry in every game but one. Left end Jamaal Anderson offered durability and run support, but he recorded zero sacks, zero stuffs, and only one forced fumble. On the plus side, he tied Gaines Adams for most hurries among rookies. A slight improvement in his pass-rush technique could lead to a much larger improvement in the results.

Linebacker Michael Boley was perhaps the Falcons' best player in 2007, but he spent his offseason dealing with a battery charge after his wife accused him of getting "physical" during an argument. He's still expected to start at strong-side linebacker. Keith Brooking played his 11th season of mediocre football in 2007, again playing out of position at middle linebacker. The team drafted inside linebacker Curtis Lofton out of Oklahoma in the second round, and the sooner he's ready to take over the middle, the better. That would allow Brooking to finish his career on the outside, where he belongs. For now, Brooking is listed as the starter in the middle, with second-year player Stephan Nicholas playing on the weak side. Whatever happens, Atlanta will have a new starter at that position; Demorrio Williams left as a free agent, signing with the Chiefs.

Defensive Secondary

Secondary	Age	Pos	Plays	TmPct	Rk	Stop	Dfts	RuYd	Rk	RuStop	Rk	Tgts	Tgt%	Rk	Dist	Suc%	Rk	APaYd	Rk	PaYd	PD	Int
Lawyer Milloy	35	SS	98	11.6%	17	35	8	5.1	15	42%	47	24	5%	65	12.0	50%	36	7.0	36	6.7	5	2
DeAngelo Hall*	25	CB	87	10.3%	26	34	18	5.4	26	46%	47	92	21%	22	11.7	52%	32	7.2	35	7.2	16	5
Chris Crocker*	28	FS	67	9.1%	45	28	12	8.8	72	31%	69	42	11%	6	9.9	49%	41	6.6	31	6.4	10	3
Chris Houston	23	CB	64	7.6%	61	26	9	3.4	6	57%	20	78	17%	45	11.9	48%	45	9.4	74	9.4	8	0
Lewis Sanders*	30	CB	36	4.9%	—	10	8	4.1	—	40%	—	42	11%	—	9.0	31%	—	9.1	—	9.1	2	0
Jimmy Williams	29	CB	16	2.2%	—	5	3	8.0	—	33%	—	11	3%	—	13.2	73%	—	6.0	—	5.9	2	1
Von Hutchins	27	FS	100	12.2%	12	24	13	9.5	76	32%	63	59	12%	3	10.1	30%	82	9.8	68	9.9	7	1
Erik Coleman	26	SS	41	5.2%	77	10	3	5.7	24	30%	75	9	2%	83	6.6	41%	66	9.3	63	8.8	0	0

Year	Pass D Rank	vs. #1 WR	Rk	vs. #2 WR	Rk	vs. Other WR	Rk	vs. TE	Rk	vs. RB	Rk
2005	20	7.6%	16	-2.4%	17	4.6%	19	25.1%	28	-1.7%	16
2006	20	35.5%	32	32.4%	31	-5.8%	16	1.2%	21	-37.4%	2
2007	26	-0.4%	14	32.5%	32	10.8%	25	23.9%	28	-5.2%	12

Say what you will about DeAngelo Hall—he's been called overrated, overpaid, overhyped—but he was the best cornerback in Atlanta by leaps and bounds. Hall's relationship with the team had soured, however, forcing a trade that left its defensive backfield hanging in shreds. One starter will be Chris Houston, a second-year player out of Arkansas, who was seen chasing opposing receivers into the end zone in a number of highlight clips in his rookie year. On the other side will be Von Hutchins, who played for the Texans last season. Houston's backfield may have been worse than Atlanta's last year, and the Texans didn't put up much of an effort to re-sign Hutchins, which should tell you all you need to know about him. The nickel back will probably be 2007 sixth-rounder David Irons, who saw limited action in 15 games last season, recording just 13 tackles with no interceptions or passes defensed.

Wily veteran Lawyer Milloy returns for his 13th NFL campaign at strong safety. He's still remarkably productive, ranking among the league leaders in tackles on run plays and average gain on run. At free safety, Chris Crocker left for the Dolphins; his spot will be filled by former Jet Erik Coleman. Coleman went without an interception or pass defensed last year, which means the Falcons have the same problem with Milloy and Coleman that they had with Milloy and Crocker—two safeties much better against the run than against the pass. If you are looking for a good receiver pickup in fantasy football this year, go with anyone playing Atlanta that week.

Special Teams

Year	DVOA	Rank	FG/XP	Rank	Net Punt	Rank	Punt Ret	Rank	Net Kick	Rank	Kick Ret	Rank	Hidden	Rank
2005	2.4%	5	4.2	9	7.6	4	-4.5	27	15.9	1	-9.2	26	-14.4	32
2006	-3.8%	28	-14.8	32	-11.1	30	-0.7	16	12.4	3	-8.0	27	-3.8	21
2007	0.0%	14	-12.6	32	11.2	2	-3.3	20	1.9	13	2.9	12	-10.1	29

One of the Falcons' biggest weaknesses in 2007 went virtually unnoticed: They ranked dead last in kicking for extra points and field goals. This has less to do with kicker Morten Andersen (25 for 28 on the year, and perfect within 40 yards) and more to do with punter Michael Koenen (who missed both of his 50-plus-yard attempts) and Matt Prater, who opened the season as the Falcons' kicker. Prater missed three of four field goals in the first two games and was promptly cut. The team wanted to go younger than the 48-year-old Anderson, and it achieved that goal by a decade, with 38-year-old Jason Elam. A member of the Broncos for 15 years, Elam returns to his home state; he graduated from Brookwood High School in Snellville, Georgia. Elam has been above average on field goals four times in the past five seasons. Ironically, the leading candidate to replace Elam in Denver is Matt Prater.

Koenen enters his fourth year as the Falcons' punter and will probably still kick off as well. He was solid again in 2007 after a calamitous sophomore campaign that saw a series of big returns and blocks. The team still views Jerious Norwood as a part-time running back and uses him primarily to return kickoffs, but he's been merely adequate. Backup wide receiver Adam Jennings will be returning punts again this season.

COACHING STAFF

After watching a season go down the tubes under a two-faced, authoritarian offensive coach, the Falcons needed a trustworthy, reliable defensive coach the players would respect, and that appears to be what they've landed in Mike Smith. Smith was defensive coordinator for the Jacksonville Jaguars from 2003 through last year, and his defense ranked in the top 10 in DVOA four times in that span. If his Falcons defense looks anything like those Jaguars defenses, expect a steady diet of four-man rushes; Jacksonville rushed five or more men on only 26 percent of all pass plays last season, 26th in the NFL. Before he ran the defense in Jacksonville, Smith coached defensive line and linebackers for the great Ravens teams of the early 2000s. In both Baltimore and Jacksonville, however, he had something he definitely does not in Atlanta: great defensive talent, and massive defensive tackles in particular.

Running the offense will be Mike Mularkey, who begins his third stint as offensive coordinator. His first regime was 2001 to 2003 in Pittsburgh, where he started hot in his first year (fourth in DVOA), regressed in year two (14th), and utterly collapsed in year three (22nd). In his one season in Miami in 2006, the offense was even worse (28th). He's known for his love of trick plays. In his three years and 48 games in Pittsburgh, wide receivers ran the ball 73 times and threw 13 passes.

Baltimore Ravens

In the first year of their existence in Baltimore, the Ravens had the best offense in football. No, really. With Vinny Testaverde slinging the ball all over the field and the running-back tandem of Earnest Byner and Bam Morris providing consistent production on the ground, the 1996 Ravens posted a clean sweep of our offensive ratings, coming in first in DVOA, first in weighted DVOA, first in passing DVOA, and first in rushing DVOA. The Ravens couldn't win many games, thanks to a dreadful defense and a propensity for ill-timed turnovers, but Baltimore could move the ball and put up points with the best of them. The difficulty in even remembering the 1996 season tells you all you need to know about what went wrong during the Brian Billick era, which ended less than one day after the Ravens concluded a disappointing 5-11 campaign.

Imagine for a moment how Billick's tenure would be remembered if he had come to Baltimore as a hot-shot defensive coordinator instead of as the architect of Minnesota's 556-point scoring machine. After all, Billick posted an 80-64 record in his nine seasons as head coach of the Ravens. His .556 winning percentage is good for ninth among active coaches, and like four of the coaches ahead of him on that list, Billick has a Super Bowl title to his credit. His record would compare favorably with fellow Minnesota coordinator Tony Dungy, who went 54-42 in his stint with Tampa Bay. But Billick came with the promise of installing a high-flying offense, and though he won plenty of games, he was

never able to shake the perception that he was winning the wrong way.

Billick adapted to his personnel, which is the mark of a good coach, but that shouldn't obscure the fact that his failure to ever get the offense functioning at a high level put a cap on the team's championship potential. In every one of Billick's nine seasons, the Ravens defense finished in the top 10 in DVOA, and in seven of those seasons, the defense was a top five unit. Over that same stretch of time, the Ravens managed to generate a positive DVOA on offense just once, in 2006, when free agent signing Steve McNair pushed the offense into the black with a modest 2.6 percent DVOA. With that Ravens defense, a 2.6 percent DVOA translated into a 13-3 record, which shows just how wide a window of opportunity was squandered by inept offense.

The offensive struggles can be tied directly to the failure to find an answer at quarterback. Since the team chased Testaverde out of town a good four to five years before his expiration date, it has burned through one quarterback after another—Eric Zeier, Jim Harbaugh, Stoney Case, Tony Banks, Scott Mitchell, Trent Dilfer, Eric Grbac, Randall Cunningham, Jeff Blake, Chris Redman, Anthony Wright, and Kyle Boller—trying to find an adequate replacement. McNair's last hurrah stopped the merry-go-round for one year, but the hope that Baltimore could get more than one healthy season out of the brittle veteran was dashed in the first game of 2007, when McNair fumbled three times and threw a

RAVENS PROSPECTUS

2007 Record: 5-11

Pythagorean Wins: 5.0 (25th)

DVOA: -6.7% total (22nd), -13.5% weighted (24th)

Offense: -12.9% DVOA (26th)

Defense: -6.1% DVOA (9th)

Special Teams: 0.1% DVOA (13th)

Variance: 15.3 % (16th)

2007: The Brian Billick era ends with injuries, disappointment, and a nuclear meltdown on Monday Night Football.

2008: The defense should return to excellence, but the offense … yikes!

2008 Mean Projection: 8.5 wins

On the Clock (0-3): 1%

Loserville (4-6): 15%

Mediocrity (7-8): 36%

Playoff Contender (9-10): 33%

Super Bowl Contender (11+): 15%

Projected Average Opponent: 0.1% DVOA (17th in NFL)

2008 Ravens Schedule

Week	Opp.	Week	Opp.	Week	Opp.
1	CIN	7	at MIA	13	at CIN
2	at HOU	8	OAK	14	WAS
3	CLE	9	at CLE	15	PIT
4	at PIT (Mon.)	10	BYE	16	at DAL (Sat.)
5	TEN	11	at NYG	17	JAC
6	at IND	12	PHI		

pick before limping to the sidelines with a strained groin.

He would play only six games all season and never came close to replicating the steady production of his first year in Baltimore. The team played out the string with Boller and rookie Troy Smith taking the snaps. Meanwhile, Baltimore castoff Derek Anderson was polishing up his Pro Bowl credentials in Cleveland, tossing his 29th touchdown, and leading the rival Browns to a 10-win season. Indeed, you can argue that Anderson's big year was the final nail in Billick's coffin, as it was proof that the supposed quarterback guru was unable to spot talent even when it was sitting right there on the roster.

New head coach John Harbaugh (brother of former quarterback Jim) has a special-teams background, but his long-term success is going to be directly tied to his doing a better job of uncovering quarterback talent than his predecessor did. McNair announced his retirement in April, putting pressure on general manager Ozzie Newsome to use the draft to find a replacement. Newsome tried to trade up to acquire Boston College signal caller Matt Ryan, and when those efforts failed, he manipulated the draft, trading down to 26 and then back up to 18 in order to select Delaware phenom Joe Flacco. Footage of Flacco winning the college all-star distance throw will undoubtedly give Ravens fans flashbacks of Kyle Boller throwing a football through the goal posts while down on one knee, but in reality, Boller and Flacco couldn't be more different. Boller started 40 games at Cal and couldn't crack a 50 percent career completion percentage, so there was plenty of evidence out there that he was not an accurate passer, but NFL scouts simply refused to see it. It also turned out that throwing a football as far as you can from a kneeling position isn't a very good way to measure arm strength, and Boller's functional velocity wasn't anything special.

Flacco is a different sort of animal entirely. In strictly physical ability, Flacco compares favorably to any recent number one overall pick. He's got great size, he's athletic enough that Delaware used him to run the option in the red zone, and his arm … well, let's just say that if you were going to reprogram the Terminator to play quarterback, he would throw the ball like Joe Flacco. But there are concerns. According to the Lewin Career Forecast, the two best statistical indicators of pro success are career starts and career completion percentage. Flacco only started 25 games after transferring from Pitt to Delaware, and while completing 63.4 percent of his passes is good, the quality of Flacco's competition needs to be taken into account. Flacco looked comfortable at the Senior Bowl, but the onus is on him to show he can handle the jump in speed from Division I-AA to the NFL (something his predecessor McNair certainly did back when he was chosen out of Alcorn State). Some scouts also expressed concern that Flacco might be a bit too big for his own good. Just as there are minimum heights to be effective, there are also maximum heights, and quarterbacks who are six foot six or bigger often don't have the foot speed to get quickly set up in the pocket before the rush arrives, which means they make too many of their throws under duress. Flacco is considered mobile for his size, but after spending most of his time in the shotgun at Delaware, his technique is going to need a lot of work.

Any hope for immediate offensive improvement rests not with the quarterbacks but with the new offensive coordinator. Cam Cameron was brought in after his failed one-year stint as head coach in Miami, and he should do a better job of utilizing the talents of the players on the Baltimore roster. He can begin at running back, where last year Willis McGahee was forced into a style of play that negated his strengths. When the trade for McGahee went through, Brian Billick suggested he now had a back who could diversify the team's running attack, but once it was time to call the plays, Billick simply jammed his thoroughbred into the middle of the line over and over as if he were another Jamal Lewis. The Ravens ran between the guards 63 percent of the time, the second-highest percentage in the league, but their Adjusted Line Yards on those runs were just 3.94—only Atlanta was worse. Cameron has shown he knows how to use explosive backs to attack inside and out, and he will take better advantage of McGahee's speed and cutback ability. Together, McGahee and two-time Pro Bowl tight end Todd Heap should be capable of executing many of the plays that worked so well with LaDainian Tomlinson and Antonio Gates, but the rest of the parts that made the San Diego offense go are missing. There's some young talent, both on the offensive line and at the skill positions, but it needs to develop.

While the offense goes through its growing pains, the team will again lean heavily on its defense, which, despite some encroaching age, remains one of the best in the league. Still, last year revealed some disturbing cracks in the armor, and none was bigger than the first-down pass defense. In 2006, the Ravens were second in the league defending the run on first down and seventh against the pass. The run defense slid back slightly in 2007, but in the offense-dominated environment of 2007, the Ravens still registered as the league's best. The pass defense, however, collapsed—Baltimore's 46.9 percent DVOA against the pass on first down was the worst in the league by a significant margin.

The problem was one part scheme and two parts personnel, as the aging cornerback pair of Chris McAlister and Samari Rolle spent much of the season either playing hurt or sitting on the sideline. Defensive coordinator Rex Ryan has never been shy about leaving his corners in single coverage, but reserve players like Corey Ivy and Derrick Martin weren't able to hold up. Ivy allowed 9.8 adjusted yards per pass, which ranked 77th among 81 cornerbacks with at least 45 charted passes. Martin allowed 9.5 adjusted yards per pass; if he had enough passes to rank, he would have been 75th.

Even when McAlister and Rolle were on the field, the Ravens showed vulnerability on first-down pass plays, particularly those involving play action. A 78-yard bomb Derek Anderson lofted to Braylon Edwards in Week 4 was typical. Baltimore put eight in the box, and when the ball was snapped, Ray Lewis came hard on a run blitz. Anderson executed a play-action fake that froze both Ed Reed and Chris McAlister so badly that Edwards got a good five yards behind the coverage, allowing Anderson to make an easy read and throw for the Cleveland score. Ryan is a master of situational defense, and the Ravens were among the best units in the league at just about every other down and distance, but on too many first downs, opponents were able to put the ball in the air and exploit the defense's aggressive tendencies.

The Ravens didn't have a lot of cap room to address their pass defense, but they were equally reactive and proactive. The first thing they did was to franchise Terrell Suggs, ensuring that they didn't lose their best pass rusher in free agency for the second year in a row. Suggs filed a grievance against the team for tendering him as a linebacker rather than as a defensive end, a move that saves the team over $800,000, but the dispute should be resolved in the form of a long-term contract using Calvin Pace's blockbuster free agent deal with the Jets as the baseline. The second move was to make a draft-day trade for Oakland cornerback Fabian Washington. This former first-rounder, who was rendered expendable when the Raiders traded for DeAngelo Hall, adds speed and youth to a secondary that didn't have enough of either in 2007. At worst, he'll take over nickel duties, but ideally, Washington would put Samari Rolle on the bench. The team also drafted Notre Dame standout Tom Zbikowski and Cincinnati thumper Haruki Nakamura to augment the depth at safety.

While the offseason moves are little more than tweaks, the Ravens don't need much to get back to being the premier defense in football. The first key is for Ryan to identify what he was tipping off with his first-down defense and to correct it. The unit's success on just about every other down and distance indicates that even if McAllister and Rolle can't stay healthy, he can make the defense work with some minor schematic adjustments. Ryan may want to lessen his emphasis on shutting down the run on first down in favor of putting the safeties in more two-deep coverage. The other key to defensive improvement is better luck, and this year, they're likely to get it. The Ravens were seventh in the league in yards allowed per drive, but 23rd in points allowed per drive. The fault rested with an offense that was spectacularly inept at recovering fumbles. Last season, the Ravens fumbled the ball 25 times and recovered only five, which was by far the worst recovery percentage in the league. As a result, Ray Lewis and company had to defend far too many short fields. Fumble recovery is essentially random, and teams that manage it as poorly as Baltimore did tend to rebound the following season. So even if the offense is as low-octane as ever, it should at the very least give the defense more field to work with.

Hiring a new coach usually implies a shift in team identity, but these Ravens figure to look a whole lot like Brian Billick's old ones. No, the offense won't be good, and for the first time in franchise history, Jonathan Ogden will not be protecting the quarterback's blind side. Nonetheless, if the team can stay healthy in the secondary, there is no reason to think Baltimore won't field one of the top two or three defenses in football. Harbaugh's emphasis on special teams should nudge the coverage teams back to respectability. It's a formula that has worked in the past, and if it results in a surprising run at another AFC North title, Ravens fans will happily take it—knowing that, thanks to Joe Flacco and a developing young line, there is better offense to come in 2009.

Sean McCormick

2007 Ravens Stats by Week

Wk	vs.	W-L	PF	PA	YDF	YDA	TO	Total	Off	Def	ST
1	@CIN	L	20	27	314	236	-4	-6%	-57%	-22%	30%
2	NYJ	W	20	13	303	304	+2	35%	9%	-25%	1%
3	ARI	W	26	23	381	364	0	6%	16%	27%	17%
4	@CLE	L	13	27	418	303	-1	1%	10%	-12%	-21%
5	@SF	W	9	7	315	163	+1	22%	-2%	-22%	3%
6	STL	W	22	3	248	264	+4	7%	-49%	-42%	15%
7	@BUF	L	14	19	308	242	0	-22%	-8%	-1%	-14%
8	BYE										
9	@PIT	L	7	38	104	291	-3	-79%	-75%	-2%	-6%
10	CIN	L	7	21	272	326	-6	-36%	-50%	-22%	-8%
11	CLE	L	30	33	368	380	-2	-36%	-20%	-2%	-17%
12	@SD	L	14	32	210	332	-2	-12%	4%	18%	2%
13	NE	L	24	27	376	326	-1	77%	36%	-36%	5%
14	IND	L	20	44	243	334	-5	-70%	-38%	42%	10%
15	@MIA	L	16	22	345	360	-1	-33%	0%	19%	-14%
16	@SEA	L	6	27	293	336	-1	-17%	-18%	-4%	-3%
17	PIT	W	27	21	334	264	+2	26%	21%	-3%	3%

Trends and Splits

	Offense	Rank	Defense	Rank
Total DVOA	-12.9%	26	-6.1%	9
Unadjusted VOA	-15.2%	28	-1.8%	14
Weighted trend	-14.3%	27	-3.4%	14
Variance	10.1%	29	5.4%	10
Average opponent	2.1%	26	3.4%	10
Passing	-12.8%	25	12.5%	22
Rushing	-13.0%	26	-25.6%	1
First down	-7.8%	24	3.9%	22
Second down	-21.0%	30	-14.9%	5
Third down	-10.0%	20	-10.2%	7
First half	-15.8%	28	-7.9%	9
Second half	-10.0%	24	4.3%	12
Red Zone	-35.1%	32	-23.0%	3
Late and close	-13.7%	26	-0.4%	16

Five-Year Performance

Year	W-L	Pyth Wins	Est Wins	PF	PA	TO	Total	Rank	Off	Rank	Def	Rank	ST	Rank
2003	10-6	11.0	10.2	391	281	+3	18.5%	6	-12.7%	26	-28.4%	1	2.8%	6
2004	9-7	9.6	10.0	317	268	+11	16.8%	9	-5.4%	20	-19.3%	2	3.0%	8
2005	6-10	6.9	7.3	265	299	-10	-5.2%	19	-16.7%	27	-11.1%	5	0.4%	13
2006	13-3	12.7	0.0	353	201	+17	31.8%	1	2.6%	15	-25.8%	1	3.5%	4
2007	5-11	5.0	6.9	275	384	-17	-6.7%	22	-15.9%	29	-10.6%	4	-3.6%	27

Strategic Tendencies

Run/Pass		Rank	Offense		Rank	Defense		Rank	Other		Rank
Runs, all plays	40%	17	3+ WR	46%	19	Rush 3	12.3%	4	2+ RB, Pct Runs	56%	18
Runs, first half	43%	10	4+ WR	10%	19	Rush 4	50.5%	28	1 RB/2 TE, Pct runs	57%	7
Runs, first down	53%	11	2+ TE	19%	24	Rush 5	28.8%	7	1 RB/3+ WR, pct runs	18%	28
Runs, second-long	35%	14	Single back	49%	25	Rush 6+	8.4%	16	CB1 on WR1	51%	9
Runs, power sit.	42%	31	Play action	16%	20	Rush 7+	2.1%	11	Go for it on 4th	1.05	18
Runs, behind 2H	28%	17	Max protect	14%	5	Sacks by LB	45.2%	9	Offensive Pace	31.5	22
Pass, ahead 2H	50%	9	Outside pocket	10%	17	Sacks by DB	19.4%	2	Defensive Pace	29.3	1

Baltimore's use of two tight-end sets dropped almost in half, primarily because of the injury to Todd Heap. The Ravens went from using two or three tight ends on 36 percent of plays in 2006 (third in the NFL) to just 19 percent last year (24th). ⌀ The Ravens ran the lowest number of screen passes in the NFL. They've thrown only one screen pass on third down over the past two seasons combined. ⌀ Derrick Mason was thrown more passes on third and fourth down than any other receiver in the NFL. Baltimore threw to Mason on third down more often than it did to Mark Clayton and Demetrius Williams combined. ⌀ The Ravens' offense had the worst DVOA in the NFL when using play action. Steve McNair's performance was similar with and without the play fake, but Kyle Boller was much worse using play action (4.8 net yards per pass attempt, -33.6% DVOA) than he was without it (5.7 net yards per pass attempt, -4.1% DVOA). ⌀ Baltimore had the league's worst rushing DVOA in the fourth quarter, and only the 49ers were less effective running the ball in the first quarter. The defense showed almost the same pattern, leading the league in defense against the run in both the first and fourth quarters. ⌀ Baltimore opponents only used play-action on 7 percent of plays, the lowest figure in the league for the second straight season. The difference is that in 2006, this strategy made sense because the Ravens ranked third in DVOA against play fakes. In 2007, with a battered secondary, the Ravens were a below-average defense against play fakes. ⌀ Baltimore's aggressive pass-rushing tendencies did not leave it susceptible to draw plays. It ranked fifth in DVOA against draws, close to its number one ranking against runs overall.

Passing

Player	DYAR	DVOA	Plays	NtYds	Avg	YAC	C%	TD	Int
Kyle Boller	-9	-11.6%	298	1652	5.5	3.3	62.0%	9	10
Steve McNair*	-187	-24.4%	217	1040	4.8	4.0	65.2%	2	4
Troy Smith	85	5.2%	80	421	5.3	4.3	53.3%	2	0

Rushing

Player	DYAR	DVOA	Plays	Yds	Avg	TD	Fum	Suc
Willis McGahee	5	-8.2%	294	1207	4.1	7	4	42%
Musa Smith*	-31	-19.2%	75	264	3.5	2	1	29%
Kyle Boller	25	13.1%	18	96	5.3	0	6	—
Mike Anderson*	-8	-22.3%	15	62	4.1	0	1	40%
Cory Ross	27	54.2%	12	72	6.0	1	0	25%
Troy Smith	15	17.5%	9	56	6.2	1	5	—
Le'Ron McClain	-7	-29.3%	8	18	2.30	0	25%	
Steve McNair*	-25	-63.3%	8	31	3.9	0	8	—

Receiving

Player	DYAR	DVOA	Plays	Ctch	Yds	Y/C	YAC	TD	C%
WR									
Derrick Mason	88	-6.0%	164	103	1087	10.6	2.9	6	63%
Mark Clayton	-41	-18.4%	89	48	531	11.1	2.2	0	54%
Demetrius Williams	-63	-28.9%	47	20	290	14.5	1.5	0	43%
Devard Darling*	53	4.3%	39	18	326	18.1	4.4	3	46%
TE									
Quinn Sypniewski	-63	-25.3%	52	34	246	7.2	2.7	1	65%
Todd Heap	25	3.2%	34	23	239	10.4	2.9	1	68%
Daniel Wilcox	-43	-59.8%	11	6	18	3.0	0.0	1	55%
Lee Vickers	-34	-85.5%	5	2	4	2.0	3.0	0	40%
RB									
Willis McGahee	29	-2.8%	49	43	231	5.4	7.1	1	88%
Musa Smith*	30	1.8%	34	27	192	7.1	6.8	0	79%
Le'Ron McClain	-15	-33.1%	13	9	55	6.1	6.0	1	69%

Offensive Line

Year	Yards	ALY	Rank	Power	Rank	10+ Yds	Rank	Stuff	Rank	Sack	ASR	Rank
2005	3.55	3.67	28	76%	4	13%	24	25%	22	42	7.5%	20
2006	3.78	4.22	19	59%	24	14%	24	23%	10	17	3.6%	2
2007	4.02	3.83	27	68%	11	18%	14	25%	19	39	7.6%	22

Year	LE	Rank	LT	Rank	Mid	Rank	RT	Rank	RE	Rank
2005	4.50	9	3.72	25	3.74	27	2.68	31	4.93	5
2006	3.09	26	4.69	9	4.33	20	4.12	19	4.02	17
2007	4.81	8	4.13	21	3.69	30	4.33	16	2.87	32

It's not very often that a franchise's most celebrated offensive player is a lineman, but that's been the situation in Baltimore, where for the last 11 seasons, Jonathan Ogden has provided most of the star power and nearly all the Pro Bowl selections. Ogden limped through 10 games with a hyperextended toe that robbed him of his ability to push off and generate power, and the frustration of playing below his accustomed level clearly got to him as the season went along. Ogden has often said that he would rather hang up his cleats than keep going as his level of play diminished, and after the season, he informed general manager Ozzie Newsome to proceed as if he were retiring. Newsome has done just that, drafting Oniel Cousins and David Hale to provide depth on the right side. This frees up Marshall Yanda to compete with Adam Terry for the pivotal left tackle spot.

Terry was drafted as the heir apparent three years ago, but he has bounced around between left and right tackle without ever settling in. The knock on Terry coming out of Syracuse was that he didn't have the mental toughness to match his physical ability, and to this point, he's done nothing to prove otherwise. Still, Terry is the player with the quick feet to mirror edge rushers, so he remains the odds-on favorite to take over for Ogden. This would allow Yanda to stay at right tackle, where he started 12 games as a rookie and performed respectably. Ben Grubbs, last year's first-round pick out of Auburn, also started 12 games at right guard, and he'll team up with Jason Brown and center Chris Chester to make a talented young trio of interior linemen. Our research suggests that drafting offensive linemen high often results in a short-term decline in production as the rookies adjust to the pro game. This observation proved true in Baltimore, where the run blocking up the middle was among the worst in the league. Still, there is every reason to think that this group will get better with more experience.

Defensive Front Seven

Defensive Line	Age	Pos	Plays	TmPct	Rk	Stop	Dfts	Stop%	Rk	AvYd	Rk	Sack	Hit	Hur	Runs	RuStop	RuYd	Pass	PaStop	PaYd
Kelly Gregg	32	DT	88	11.2%	1	68	17	77%	38	1.8	43	3.0	2	5	78	74%	2.3	10	100%	-1.7
Haloti Ngata	24	DE	64	8.2%	11	51	15	80%	30	1.6	35	3.0	8	8	59	80%	1.8	5	80%	-1.0
Dwan Edwards	27	DE	43	5.5%	47	35	5	81%	23	2.7	66	1.0	2	2	37	84%	2.9	6	67%	2.0
Justin Bannan	29	DT	30	4.1%	53	24	8	80%	27	1.4	21	2.0	0	2	28	79%	1.7	2	100%	-2.0
Trevor Pryce	33	DE	15	6.1%	—	12	7	80%	—	0.7	—	2.0	0	2	11	73%	1.6	4	100%	-2.0

Linebackers	Age	Pos	Plays	TmPct	Rk	Stop	Dfts	Stop%	AvYd	Sack	Hit	Hur	Runs	RuStop	Rk	RuYd	Rk	Tgts	Suc%	Rk	APaYd	Rk
Ray Lewis	33	ILB	132	19.2%	3	81	26	61%	4.4	2.0	0	1	80	61%	51	3.4	52	44	57%	18	6.4	57
Bart Scott	28	ILB	97	12.4%	51	70	23	72%	3.0	1.0	7	7	73	82%	6	1.8	4	22	41%	72	9.0	87
Terrell Suggs	26	OLB	82	10.4%	65	70	24	85%	1.2	5.0	12	16	62	85%	2	1.5	2	9	66%	—	5.3	—
Jarret Johnson	27	OLB	58	7.4%	91	41	11	71%	2.7	2.0	9	6	40	88%	1	1.7	3	17	38%	77	5.3	25
Nick Greisen	29	OLB	24	3.5%	—	13	4	54%	4.9	0.0	0	0	13	77%	—	1.2	—	6	18%	—	7.1	—

Year	Yards	ALY	Rank	Power	Rank	10+ Yds	Rank	Stuff	Rank	Sack	ASR	Rank
2005	3.91	3.91	12	50%	2	19%	22	24%	21	41	7.3%	16
2006	3.26	3.42	2	56%	8	14%	9	25%	12	60	9.3%	2
2007	3.03	3.35	1	56%	8	12%	6	30%	2	32	6.9%	14

Year	LE	Rank	LT	Rank	Mid	Rank	RT	Rank	RE	Rank
2005	4.32	20	3.15	2	4.18	19	4.14	19	3.01	4
2006	2.79	4	3.07	3	3.78	2	3.50	7	2.25	1
2007	2.77	3	2.86	1	3.54	2	3.44	3	2.49	2

Rex Ryan's defense came by its number one ranking against the run honestly, ranking in the top three in Adjusted Line Yardage in all five of the directions we measure. In addition to holding up at the point of attack, Kelly Gregg and Haloti Ngata were incredibly active, placing first and 11th, respectively, in plays made by position. Those are very impressive numbers, though the Ravens do run more of a hybrid than a traditional base 3-4, and the shifting fronts open up more opportunities for the frontline defenders. The concern is that Price and Gregg are both entering the point in their careers where either a decline or injury problems are inevitable, and the depth behind them isn't good. Fortunately, having a talent like Ngata on the roster provides some flexibility, as he can easily move inside to nose tackle, allowing Justin Bannon or Dwan Edwards to play at end.

Ray Lewis's looming contract situation represents as much of an organizational challenge as does Jonathan Ogden's retirement. Like Ogden, Lewis is still playing well, though not at the Hall of Fame level of previous years. His run-stop numbers stick out like a sore thumb compared with the rest of the Ravens linebackers. With Lewis entering the final year of his contract, Ozzie Newsome has to carefully consider how much Lewis figures to contribute going forward and how much of a premium the GM is willing to pay for his star's past service and his value as a team leader. The rest of the linebacker corps is top notch, with Bart Scott playing alongside Lewis and Jarrett Johnson and Terrell Suggs manning the outside. Even coming off a down year, Suggs is by far the best pass rusher on the team, and the team would be wise to get his contract resolved as quickly as possible.

Defensive Secondary

Secondary	Age	Pos	Plays	TmPct	Rk	Stop	Dfts	RuYd	Rk	RuStop	Rk	Tgts	Tgt%	Rk	Dist	Suc%	Rk	APaYd	Rk	PaYd	PD	Int
Dawan Landry	26	SS	85	10.8%	26	30	9	5.3	17	41%	48	42	10%	8	10.6	51%	33	7.3	41	7.4	6	0
Corey Ivy	31	CB	68	8.7%	50	34	16	6.4	40	56%	24	76	19%	34	12.3	45%	63	9.9	77	9.8	10	1
Ed Reed	30	FS	52	6.6%	72	24	13	7.9	61	50%	24	29	7%	37	9.5	37%	73	8.0	47	7.7	12	7
Derrick Martin	23	CB	35	4.5%	—	14	7	6.2	—	45%	—	30	7%	—	13.0	53%	—	9.5	—	9.3	6	2
Chris McAlister	31	CB	28	7.1%	64	10	4	14.3	80	33%	64	43	21%	21	12.9	49%	44	7.8	52	7.6	9	1
Samari Rolle	32	CB	26	8.8%	—	16	6	1.4	—	100%	—	34	22%	—	11.7	50%	—	8.4	—	8.5	5	1
Jim Leonhard	26	SS	54	7.8%	—	7	4	11.2	—	11%	—	12	3%	—	14.5	13%	—	15.1	—	15.2	2	2
Fabian Washington	25	CB	44	6.1%	72	14	3	11.8	76	20%	79	50	14%	65	11.2	46%	55	9.3	71	9.6	8	1

Year	Pass D Rank	vs. #1 WR	Rk	vs. #2 WR	Rk	vs. Other WR	Rk	vs. TE	Rk	vs. RB	Rk
2005	10	2.0%	13	-8.5%	11	6.3%	21	-3.5%	15	-9.6%	10
2006	1	-4.2%	11	-25.4%	3	-6.5%	14	-16.9%	6	-24.3%	7
2007	22	-11.8%	7	25.7%	30	-9.1%	15	7.9%	17	9.1%	26

The Ravens got a glimpse of life without Chris McAlister and Samari Rolle, and it surely had to make them nervous. Their longtime starting duo combined to play only 14 games, and in their absence, fringe players like Corey Ivy and Derrick Martin were pressed into service with distinctly un-Ravens-like results. Only the Raiders were worse defending number two receivers, and while Ed Reed and Dawan Landry had their regular solid seasons, the team's ability to cover tight ends and running backs coming out of the backfield declined drastically as the safeties were caught out of position trying to compensate for the struggling cornerbacks.

With the ever-present threat of more Corey Ivy sightings and no cap room to add free agents, Ozzie Newsome needed to find other ways to improve the talent. He passed on the chance to take a top corner like Leodis McKelvin or Dominique Rodgers-Cromartie in the first round; instead, he worked a trade with Oakland, giving up a fourth-round pick for Fabian Washington. Washington was a first-round disappointment in Oakland, but he has excellent speed and is a willing tackler. At the very least, he represents a major upgrade at nickel back. Instead of corners, Newsome drafted safeties, selecting Notre Dame's Tom Zbikowski and Cincinnati's Haruki Nakamura. Both players are excellent hitters who will help on special teams, but they don't figure to provide much immediate coverage help.

Special Teams

Year	DVOA	Rank	FG/XP	Rank	Net Punt	Rank	Punt Ret	Rank	Net Kick	Rank	Kick Ret	Rank	Hidden	Rank
2005	0.4%	14	4.3	8	-8.0	29	8.4	2	1.1	15	-3.4	20	-11.2	31
2006	3.5%	4	9.0	2	5.3	10	-2.1	20	4.6	12	3.6	8	-4.8	23
2007	0.1%	13	0.2	18	-6.1	26	4.3	8	-0.5	15	2.6	13	-8.6	28

New special teams coach Jerry Rosburg will look to repair a unit that faded badly over the second half of the season; although the Ravens ranked 13th in special teams for the entire season, they were 25th after their bye week. Matt Stover was perfect inside of 40 yards, but his range is starting to decline. The coverage units were a mixed bag, with the above-average kickoff unit being overshadowed by the terrible punt unit. Sam Koch averaged 43.6 yards per punt, but he had to watch the coverage team give more than seven yards of it right back; his net of 36.0 yards was 30th in the league. Baltimore's return game is in better shape. Ozzie Newsome drafted Kansas State speedster Ya-mon Figurs in the third round of last year's draft to replace B. J. Sams as the primary returner, and the move paid off. Figurs consistently generated good yardage, with a touchdown on a kick return and another on a punt return. He does have to work on his ball security, however, as he fumbled four times, losing one.

COACHING STAFF

John Harbaugh was brought in to change up an atmosphere that had grown stale after nine seasons of Brian Billick. (Fox viewers can enjoy Billick's special brand of staleness this fall. Good times.) The players seem energized by Harbaugh; Terrell Suggs took time out from his contract dispute to come to minicamp so that he could show his support for the new head coach. Harbaugh served as the defensive backs coach in Philadelphia last year, but he cut his chops coaching up the Eagles special teams for nine years. Defensive coordinator Rex Ryan was a runner-up for the top job, despite commanding the support of much of the locker room. Ryan interviewed for two head coaching jobs and was a hot candidate for several defensive coordinator openings, and it was touch and go before he decided to return. Harbaugh and Ryan spent a year together on the staff at the University of Cincinnati, and that relationship, along with a promotion to assistant head coach, was enough to keep Ryan in Baltimore.

After being let go in Miami, Cam Cameron was highly sought after, thanks to his five years of solid work as the Chargers' offensive coordinator. What made Cameron especially attractive was his work developing both Drew Brees and Philip Rivers, and the hope is that he will get Joe Flacco quickly acclimated to the pro level. In a bit of trivia that is sure to be beaten into the ground during Ravens telecasts, Cameron started his coaching career at Michigan tutoring John Harbaugh's younger brother Jim. Jerry Rosburg, who was in Atlanta last season, will handle the special-teams duties.

Buffalo Bills

To the optimist, the Bills are a team on the rise. They spent the last two years drafting wisely while prudently trimming overpriced veterans from the roster. Their director of college scouting is one of the most respected executives in the game, and they avoided off-season turmoil by promoting from within when Marv Levy retired. Their quarterback and running back were All-Rookie selections last year, and there's exciting young talent at every position on the roster. Off the field, the franchise is addressing its small-market financial problems by aggressively expanding its fan base across international borders.

To the pessimist, the Bills are football's answer to the Montreal Expos, except the football team is trying to cross the border in the other direction. The Bills are a shoestring franchise in receivership, a glorified farm team that develops young talent and sells it to richer clubs. They no longer have in-house legend Levy, the visionary who built the team into near contenders last season, and with him gone, the team will return to the treadmill of mediocre drafts and free-agent defections. The team's flirtations with Toronto are a desperate attempt to escape a market too small and economically depressed to support the NFL.

It's too early to tell who's right. We'll learn a lot in 2008. The Bills could take the next step toward becoming contenders, but they could just as easily fold their tents, pose for their passport photos, and prepare for a trip across the St. Lawrence River. And what happens

on the field may be less relevant to the team's long-term fortunes than what happens in the front office.

In his two seasons as team president, Levy supervised a brutal salary cap bloodletting. The team allowed most of its recognizable players to leave town. Willis McGahee, Nate Clemens, Takeo Spikes, Eric Moulds, London Fletcher, Sam Adams, and others left Buffalo on Levy's watch; a few of them (most notably McGahee) said good riddance to the fiscally distressed team and region on their way out. Levy avoided the free-agent market as if it were a shark tank; guard Derrick Dockery was his only big-ticket addition in two years. By the start of the 2007 season, the Bills were the most anonymous team in the NFL. Lee Evans was their biggest offensive star; Aaron Schobel and Chris Kelsay were the "big names" on defense. Television promos of Bills games sounded almost comical. "Watch Tom Brady and Randy Moss of the Patriots take on … um … J. P. Losman and the Bills!"

For the Bills, wild spending isn't an option. While revenue sharing and the salary cap creates a relatively level playing field for basic revenues and costs, owners need large amounts of liquid cash to offer the huge signing bonuses top free agents demand. That money often comes from ancillary sources, including luxury box revenues, local radio broadcast rights, and the owner's own fortune. The Bills are stuck in an antiquated stadium in an economically depressed region, and the team is the Wilson family's most significant as-

---

BILLS PROSPECTUS

2007 Record: 7-9

Pythagorean Wins: 4.9 (26th)

DVOA: -3.5% total (19th), 0.8% weighted (19th)

Offense: -7.5% DVOA (22nd)

Defense: 0.1% DVOA (18th)

Special Teams: 4.1% DVOA (6th)

Variance: 11.6 % (5th)

2007: Within a sea of mediocrity, some good young talent begins to develop.

2008: To challenge for the playoffs, the Bills need improvement on defense. Or, better yet, defence.

2008 Mean Projection: 7.2 wins

On the Clock (0-3): 3%

Loserville (4-6): 31%

Mediocrity (7-8): 41%

Playoff Contender (9-10): 22%

Super Bowl Contender (11+): 4%

Projected Average Opponent: -4.3% DVOA (28th in NFL)

2008 Bills Schedule

Week	Opp.	Week	Opp.	Week	Opp.
1	SEA	7	SD	13	SF
2	at JAC	8	at MIA	14	MIA
3	OAK	9	NYJ	15	at NYJ
4	at STL	10	at NE	16	at DEN
5	at ARI	11	CLE (Mon.)	17	NE
6	BYE	12	at KC		

set. It takes some financial maneuvering for the Bills to cough up millions of dollars in signing bonuses, so it's logical that they do so sparingly. Still, the Bills have operated far below the salary cap in the last two years and could have afforded to spend a few more dollars without putting the Wilsons into the street.

While money flowed one-way out of Buffalo, talent didn't. Levy presided over excellent drafts in 2006 and 2007. Scouting director Tom Modrak, who came to Buffalo in 2001, has always been a top talent evaluator. The Bills, however, took too many undue risks when Modrak ran the draft with former general manager Tom Donahoe. The Toms whiffed badly on offensive tackle Mike Williams, then drafted the injured McGahee in the first round, and then traded away their top 2004 pick to select Losman. On Levy's watch, the Bills stopped swinging for the fences and started hitting for a higher average. Starters Donte Whitner, Ashton Youboty, Ko Simpson, Brad Butler, and Keith Ellison entered the fold in 2006; Trent Edwards, Marshawn Lynch, and Paul Posluszny came aboard last year. Modrak found productive role players like running back Fred Jackson and linebacker John DiGiorgio as undrafted free agents. Nearly all of the Bills' 2007 starters came to the team as rookies in the last three years, and while the youngsters weren't household names, they played about as well as the high-priced veterans they replaced.

That doesn't mean the Bills were very good. Their 7-9 record was bolstered by two close wins that they eked out over the Ravens and Redskins that featured clock mismanagement by the opposing coach. They went 4-0 against the comic relief at the bottom of the AFC East. They played the Cowboys close early in the year, forcing Tony Romo to turn the ball over six times, yet Buffalo somehow managed to blow an 11-point lead in the fourth quarter. Late-season thumpings by the Jaguars and Patriots demonstrated how far the Bills really were from the genuine conference contenders.

Still, the Bills were in the wild-card chase until Week 15, an impressive accomplishment for a team with no stars and an all-rookie backfield. Compare their nickel-squeezing roster strategy to that of the veteran-addicted Dolphins, and the Bills' approach makes sense. If the youngsters stay in Buffalo and develop as expected, the Bills should stay competitive and within their means for several years, battling for a wild-card berth this year and then challenging the Patriots for the division in 2009. That last sentence starts with a very big "if."

The Bills have an impressive young core, but will it develop? And will the players who do develop stay in town? The team has a habit of cutting to the quick, releasing players the moment they become too expensive. Many of the players Levy was wise to cut loose were old-timers like Moulds and Drew Bledsoe, but McGahee was 26 when he was traded, and Nate Clements was 28 when the team let him walk via free agency. Losman, still just 27, will give way to Edwards this season and may be traded in camp. The Bills are in a *Logan's Run* predicament that is already yielding diminishing returns. Buffalo released more veterans this offseason, but there were no more big names to cut. Consequently, the Bills bid farewell to specialists like safety Coy Wire, reserve cornerback Kiwaukee Thomas, and special-teams standout Sam Aiken. A team that started the offseason $25 million under the cap shouldn't have to cut its veteran depth, but the Bills felt the need to make their bench even younger.

Despite the cuts, March offered some indicators that the Bills weren't ready to become the NFL's version of a AAA team. For the first time in years, more veteran talent entered Buffalo than left. Defensive tackle Marcus Stroud, acquired in a trade with the Jaguars, is damaged goods with a performance enhancement suspension on his résumé. But if he can play like he did from 2002 to 2005, he's a steal. Linebacker Kawika Mitchell is an effective blitzer who fits coordinator Perry Fewell's scheme and adds needed depth and playmaking ability. The team aggressively sought free-agent solutions to its tight-end problem, auditioning half the players on the market before signing Courtney Anderson. It wasn't a spending spree, but it was a sign that the Bills are at least as interested in winning as in saving money.

Modrak and new chief operations officer Russ Brandon then added another bumper crop of rookies. Leodis McKelvin fills an immediate need at cornerback and will challenge Ashton Youboty as the starter opposite Terrence McGee. The Bills stayed out of the Chad Johnson and Larry Fitzgerald talks but landed a much-needed big receiver in six-foot-six rookie James Hardy. Midround picks like cornerback Reggie Corner and tight end Derek Fine could grow into starters but will fill the special-teams void left by Wire and Aiken in the meantime.

With their solid veteran and rookie additions, the 2008 Bills will be slightly better than last year's team. New offensive coordinator Turk Schonert replaces Steve Fairchild, whose desire to run a Mike Martz–flavored offense never meshed with the available talent. Schonert plans to feature Lynch and Jackson in both the running and the passing games while playing to the strengths of Edwards, who is a much better short passer than bomb-and-scramble specialist Losman. The low-risk, low-yield approach should work with the additions of Kelly and the maturation of Edwards and the backs. Defensively, Fewell now has the pieces in place to run his system. Fewell likes to run a Marvin Lewis–flavored Cover-2, with lots of blitzes mixed in with the more conservative two-deep zones, but he was forced to scale down the scheme after losing his best linebacker and several safeties to injuries last year. The Bills won't finish 31st in the league in Adjusted Sack Rate with Mitchell blitzing and Stroud eating double teams. The returns of Simpson and Posluszny will help both the rush and pass defense, and the team finally has enough depth in the secondary to survive an injury or two. Special-teams coordinator Robert April has enough warm bodies to compensate for the departures of Wire and Aiken, and the team's kicking and return specialists will all be back.

What happens after 2008 depends primarily on the success of the Toronto experiment. A deep-pocketed group of Canadian investors led by Paul Godfrey (Blue Jays), Larry Tanenbaum (Maple Leafs), and communications mogul Ted Rogers will host six regular season and three preseason Bills games at the Rogers Centre over the next six years. The so-called Toronto Series promises to inject millions of dollars into the Bills orga-nization while serving as a feasibility study for a potential franchise move. If the Toronto Series is a financial success, it will give the Bills more short-term spending money and long-term stability. Theoretically, the Wilson family would then sell the Bills to the Godfrey conglomerate, which could move the team a mere 60 miles across the border without alienating existing Bills fans. Early returns on the Toronto Series are encouraging; Rogers Communications reported that over 100,000 fans joined the waiting list for the December 7 Dolphins-Bills game in the great white north.

If the Toronto Series fizzles, the Bills will be stuck in a holding pattern. Godfrey and friends may discover that once the novelty wears off, Toronto isn't a viable NFL market. That will leave the Wilson family short on cash and searching for suitors. Brandon would again be forced to clip coupons while Modrak tried to work miracle upon miracle in the draft to keep the Bills competitive. Three years from now, the Bills would again be 7-9, with Lynch, Poz, and Whitner scattered around the league while a new crop of rookies keeps the dream alive. Brandon and the Wilsons are still hedging toward this possibility. Even as the Rogers team offered Canadian streets paved with gold, the Bills played hardball in contract negotiations with Lee Evans. Think of Evans as the groundhog: if he restructures his deal and stays in Buffalo, sunny fiscal weather is in the forecast.

Even if Evans stays, Bills fans will have to keep their fingers crossed all season long. The team needs a pumped-up sellout crowd at the Rogers Centre on December 7 more than it needs a big year from Edwards or Lynch or a 9-7 finish. The best chance fans in northern New York have to save their franchise is to let it move north to a slightly better neighborhood. The Bills have accomplished as much as a cash-strapped team can. To stay competitive, they need dollars, or at the very least, loonies.

Mike Tanier

2007 Bills Stats by Week

Wk	vs.	W-L	PF	PA	YDF	YDA	TO	Total	Off	Def	ST
1	DEN	L	14	15	184	470	0	-32%	-42%	11%	22%
2	@PIT	L	3	26	223	420	+1	-45%	-17%	35%	6%
3	@NE	L	7	38	193	485	-1	-40%	-18%	14%	-8%
4	NYJ	W	17	14	304	347	0	-8%	9%	21%	4%
5	DAL	L	24	25	229	385	+5	40%	-32%	-49%	23%
6	BYE										
7	BAL	W	19	14	242	308	0	14%	0%	8%	22%
8	@NYJ	W	13	3	347	254	+2	34%	-2%	-26%	10%
9	CIN	W	33	21	479	299	0	1%	32%	14%	-17%
10	@MIA	W	13	10	214	269	-1	-30%	-35%	4%	8%
11	NE	L	10	56	229	510	-2	-42%	-7%	37%	2%
12	@JAC	L	14	36	297	416	-2	-18%	-3%	8%	-6%
13	@WAS	W	17	16	357	281	+1	43%	23%	-13%	6%
14	MIA	W	38	17	389	285	+4	61%	31%	-26%	4%
15	@CLE	L	0	8	232	304	0	-35%	-27%	4%	-4%
16	NYG	L	21	38	244	383	0	-16%	-43%	-35%	-8%
17	@PHI	L	9	17	271	391	+2	-7%	-14%	-1%	5%

Trends and Splits

	Offense	Rank	Defense	Rank
Total DVOA	-7.5%	22	0.1%	18
Unadjusted VOA	-6.4%	22	5.9%	23
Weighted trend	-4.5%	20	-3.3%	15
Variance	5.8%	11	5.8%	12
Average opponent	1.6%	22	7.1%	1
Passing	-6.7%	21	5.4%	16
Rushing	-8.2%	19	-6.0%	13
First down	-5.1%	19	-5.1%	11
Second down	-2.9%	15	-0.4%	14
Third down	-18.8%	28	10.0%	24
First half	-6.4%	23	-4.3%	13
Second half	-8.6%	23	4.3%	21
Red Zone	-23.8%	29	-19.9%	5
Late and close	-5.4%	21	-11.0%	10

Five-Year Performance

Year	W-L	Pyth Wins	Est Wins	PF	PA	TO	Total	Rank	Off	Rank	Def	Rank	ST	Rank
2003	6-10	6.7	6.7	243	279	-16	-7.7%	22	-18.8%	29	-12.8%	7	-1.7%	24
2004	9-7	11.0	11.6	395	284	+10	29.8%	4	-5.8%	22	-28.1%	1	7.5%	1
2005	5-11	5.2	5.5	271	367	+4	-20.4%	28	-18.6%	30	8.9%	26	7.2%	1
2006	7-9	7.7	7.9	300	311	-11	-2.1%	16	-8.7%	24	-0.7%	15	5.9%	2
2007	7-9	4.9	8.3	252	354	+9	-3.5%	19	-7.5%	22	0.1%	18	4.1%	6

Strategic Tendencies

Run/Pass		Rank	Offense		Rank	Defense		Rank	Other		Rank
Runs, all plays	46%	6	3+ WR	45%	23	Rush 3	6.1%	13	2+ RB, Pct Runs	40%	32
Runs, first half	46%	6	4+ WR	13%	13	Rush 4	67.1%	11	1 RB/2 TE, Pct runs	73%	1
Runs, first down	57%	4	2+ TE	39%	3	Rush 5	18.1%	22	1 RB/3+ WR, pct runs	32%	4
Runs, second-long	35%	18	Single back	65%	4	Rush 6+	8.7%	13	CB1 on WR1	47%	13
Runs, power sit.	67%	12	Play action	13%	26	Rush 7+	1.5%	17	Go for it on 4th	0.88	21
Runs, behind 2H	39%	1	Max protect	19%	2	Sacks by LB	25.0%	15	Offensive Pace	32.6	31
Pass, ahead 2H	36%	27	Outside pocket	10%	19	Sacks by DB	4.2%	25	Defensive Pace	31.7	30

For at least the second year in a row, Buffalo never ran a five-wide set all season. It also used an empty backfield less often than any other offense did. ⊘ Buffalo ran the fewest number of draw plays both in absolute terms and as a percentage of all running plays. ⊘ Buffalo had the fewest dropped passes in the league (both by total and by percentage). Tight end Michael Gaines was second on the team with five drops, half of all the incomplete passes with Gaines as the intended receiver. Oddly, Robert Royal, the other tight end, did not drop a single pass, despite having 13 drops the previous two seasons. ⊘ In two-receiver, two-tight-end sets, Buffalo ran the ball 71 percent of the time, the highest of any team. ⊘ The Bills spread the ball around on third down, with Lee Evans and Josh Reed thrown an equal number of passes and Roscoe Parrish not far behind. ⊘ Trent Edwards threw to the tight end at a rate almost twice that of J. P. Losman. ⊘ If you went to a Buffalo game, you were going to see a screen pass. The Bills ran the most screen passes of any NFL team, at a rate almost double the league average. Buffalo's defense also led the league in screen passes by opponents. The offense was average when using the screen, but the defense was terrible stopping them.   ⊘   The Bills' defense was above average in the first, second, and fourth quarters, but ranked 27th in the third quarter.   ⊘   Buffalo opponents used shotgun 35 percent of the time, the highest percentage in the AFC. It was a good strategy, as Buffalo's defense was much better against plays under center (-8.6% DVOA, ninth) than against plays from shotgun (18.3% DVOA, 26th).   ⊘   In a related stat, Buffalo's pass defense ranked 31st against three-wide-receiver sets, ahead of only Miami.

Passing

Player	DYAR	DVOA	Plays	NtYds	Avg	YAC	C%	TD	Int
Trent Edwards	57	-7.8%	282	1556	5.5	5.4	56.6%	7	8
J. P. Losman	26	-8.9%	188	1101	5.9	5.2	63.8%	4	6

Rushing

Player	DYAR	DVOA	Plays	Yds	Avg	TD	Fum	Suc
Marshawn Lynch	42	-5.0%	280	1115	4.0	7	2	45%
Fred Jackson	64	19.7%	58	300	5.2	0	0	47%
Anthony Thomas*	-32	-28.6%	36	89	2.5	0	0	44%
Dwayne Wright	5	-5.0%	29	94	3.2	0	0	45%
J. P. Losman	1	-10.7%	18	112	6.2	0	2	—
Trent Edwards	12	11.3%	10	52	5.2	0	4	—
Josh Reed	0	-38.5%	4	10	2.5	0	0	—
Roscoe Parrish	7	5.4%	3	19	6.3	1	0	—

Receiving

Player	DYAR	DVOA	Plays	Ctch	Yds	Y/C	YAC	TD	C%
WR									
Lee Evans	21	-10.3%	113	55	849	15.4	3.5	6	49%
Josh Reed	36	-7.3%	87	51	578	11.3	4.0	1	59%
Roscoe Parrish	-4	-13.5%	58	35	352	10.1	3.6	1	60%
Peerless Price*	-4	-16.5%	13	7	68	9.7	2.3	0	54%
TE									
Robert Royal	-18	-14.7%	38	25	249	10.0	5.9	3	66%
Michael Gaines*	32	5.9%	35	25	215	8.6	6.7	2	71%
RB									
Fred Jackson	34	9.1%	29	21	183	8.7	8.9	0	72%
Marshawn Lynch	41	14.1%	26	18	184	10.2	10.9	0	69%
Anthony Thomas*	18	5.1%	20	15	95	6.3	7.1	1	75%

Offensive Line

Year	Yards	ALY	Rank	Power	Rank	10+ Yds	Rank	Stuff	Rank	Sack	ASR	Rank
2005	3.80	4.09	16	63%	18	12%	25	18%	1	43	8.9%	27
2006	3.74	3.94	26	69%	11	13%	26	24%	16	47	9.4%	29
2007	3.97	3.98	25	51%	28	16%	17	23%	13	26	5.4%	13

Year	LE	Rank	LT	Rank	Mid	Rank	RT	Rank	RE	Rank
2005	3.32	26	4.07	23	4.07	17	4.34	13	4.78	6
2006	4.57	8	4.36	14	3.73	30	3.92	27	3.42	27
2007	2.80	29	3.91	23	4.02	20	4.65	6	3.48	27

The Bills are starting five returns intact: Jason Peters, Derrick Dockery, Melvin Fowler, Brad Butler, and Langston Walker. All five are locked into contracts that will keep them in Buffalo for at least two more years. Peters started his career as a converted tight end who only played in goal-line packages. Last season, he made the Pro Bowl at left tackle. Peters is just a wall-off guy when run blocking, but he's a nimble pass protector who makes few mistakes. When Peters got hurt against the Giants, Kirk Chambers entered the game and Trent Edwards spent the rest of the day under siege.

Dockery, the team's lone expensive acquisition of the Marv Levy era, played mistake-free but unspectacular football last year. Walker, a perennial disappointment in Oakland, allowed just three sacks last year and appears to have settled in at right tackle. Butler, a third-year pro, was the best run blocker on the line and drew just two penalties all season. Many experts thought the Bills would draft a center to challenge Fowler, but the team didn't select any offensive linemen. Rookie free agent Robert Felton, a top run blocker for Darren McFadden at Arkansas, will join Chambers and all-purpose backup Duke Preston on the bench.

Defensive Front Seven

Defensive Line	Age	Pos	Plays	TmPct	Rk	Stop	Dfts	Stop%	Rk	AvYd	Rk	Sack	Hit	Hur	Runs	RuStop	RuYd	Pass	PaStop	PaYd
Aaron Schobel	31	DE	62	7.3%	20	50	28	81%	27	2.1	51	6.5	9	14	41	76%	2.1	21	90%	2.0
Chris Kelsay	29	DE	46	6.2%	32	30	15	65%	72	2.9	68	2.5	7	8	34	65%	3.1	12	67%	2.2
Larry Tripplett*	29	DT	41	4.8%	37	34	14	83%	17	1.6	30	1.5	7	7	32	78%	1.7	9	100%	1.2
Kyle Williams	25	DT	39	4.6%	43	28	11	72%	56	2.0	47	1.5	3	5	31	77%	1.9	8	50%	2.5
John McCargo	25	DT	33	3.9%	57	25	12	76%	43	0.6	4	2.5	0	2	26	69%	1.3	7	100%	-2.1
Ryan Denney	31	DE	28	7.5%	16	23	5	82%	19	1.6	37	1.0	0	4	24	88%	1.7	4	50%	1.0
Anthony Hargrove	25	DE	21	3.3%	—	13	6	62%	—	2.7	—	1.5	5	8	15	67%	2.7	6	50%	2.8
Marcus Stroud	30	DT	25	5.9%	25	15	8	60%	66	2.6	59	3.0	3	3	18	44%	4.0	7	100%	-1.0
Spencer Johnson	27	DT	24	2.8%	66	19	9	79%	28	1.8	37	3.0	3	5	13	77%	2.1	11	82%	1.4

Linebackers	Age	Pos	Plays	TmPct	Rk	Stop	Dfts	Stop%	AvYd	Sack	Hit	Hur	Runs	RuStop	Rk	RuYd	Rk	Tgts	Suc%	Rk	APaYd	Rk
Angelo Crowell	27	OLB	131	15.4%	15	65	22	50%	5.5	2.0	1	10	64	58%	71	3.9	71	46	44%	59	6.2	51
John DiGiorgio	26	MLB	120	14.2%	28	65	25	54%	4.6	2.0	1	6	74	57%	79	3.8	68	27	52%	35	5.4	29
Keith Ellison	24	OLB	43	6.8%	—	23	8	53%	4.1	1.0	0	0	23	70%	—	3.3	—	19	43%	64	3.8	7
Paul Posluszny	23	MLB	25	15.7%	—	11	2	44%	5.8	0.0	0	0	20	50%	—	4.4	—	3	40%	—	13.7	—
Kawika Mitchell	29	OLB	82	10.5%	64	54	18	66%	3.7	3.5	1	1	44	75%	11	2.8	21	32	57%	16	4.4	12

Year	Yards	ALY	Rank	Power	Rank	10+ Yds	Rank	Stuff	Rank	Sack	ASR	Rank
2005	4.59	4.46	26	76%	29	19%	19	22%	25	38	7.8%	9
2006	4.83	4.76	29	69%	22	18%	24	20%	29	40	8.1%	6
2007	4.59	4.16	15	50%	2	21%	25	26%	10	26	4.7%	31

Year	LE	Rank	LT	Rank	Mid	Rank	RT	Rank	RE	Rank
2005	3.68	10	4.38	19	4.44	26	4.60	28	5.93	32
2006	5.28	30	5.11	28	4.84	30	4.15	15	4.11	17
2007	1.50	1	4.10	12	4.19	17	4.40	21	5.75	32

Under Levy, the Bills let most of their veteran free agents leave town, but the team did sign defensive ends Aaron Schobel and Chris Kelsay to lucrative extensions last year. Unfortunately, the duo provided few sacks, in part because there was little pressure up the middle. Schobel is an underappreciated all-purpose defender who stops a lot of runs in the backfield. His sack totals will go up if Marcus Stroud fills the middle as expected. Kelsay had a quiet year except for his end-zone sack of Cleo Lemon, which resulted in a safety against the Dolphins. Run stuffers John McCargo and Kyle Williams will rotate with Stroud. Former Vikings tackle Spencer Johnson, who had three sacks and six hurries in limited action, provides some pass-rush presence on the inside. Fewell experimented with a 5-2 defense at times last season and may look for ways to get three big tackles in the game against run-oriented opponents like the Jets. Ryan Denney missed all but six games with a broken foot; outside linebacker Kawika Mitchell (who comes over from the Giants as a free agent) or Virginia Tech rookie Chris Ellis could eat into his playing time as a rotation end.

Rookie middle linebacker Paul Posluszny earned a starting job in camp, and for the first two weeks of the season, it looked as if he would challenge Patrick Willis for Defensive Rookie of the Year honors. Unfortunately, Poz landed on injured reserve after breaking his forearm in Week 3. Second-year pro John DiGiorgio stepped in and played well, registering 113 tackles, but DiGiorgio is undersized and fits best as a weakside linebacker or nickel defender. Angelo Crowell led the team in tackles and finished third in the league in pass plays by a linebacker, but he also led the league in "unsuccessful" pass plays, meaning that he did a lot more cleaning up than attacking. Mitchell is at his best when attacking the line of scrimmage as a run stopper and blitzer. Look for coordinator Perry Fewell to mix and match his linebackers, using Poz and Mitchell as run-down defenders, then putting Mitchell's hand in the dirt and making Crowell and DiGeorgio handle coverage duties.

Defensive Secondary

Secondary	Age	Pos	Plays	TmPct	Rk	Stop	Dfts	RuYd	Rk	RuStop	Rk	Tgts	Tgt%	Rk	Dist	Suc%	Rk	APaYd	Rk	PaYd	PD	Int
Terrence McGee	28	CB	98	12.3%	7	44	15	5.7	33	48%	42	105	25%	2	11.0	52%	33	6.1	12	5.9	20	4
Donte Whitner	23	SS	90	11.3%	21	35	16	5.5	23	57%	9	43	10%	9	10.5	43%	59	6.8	34	6.8	3	1
Jabari Greer	26	CB	59	7.0%	66	28	13	2.9	3	57%	19	77	17%	52	12.0	56%	15	7.5	45	7.6	16	2
Jim Leonhard*	26	SS	54	7.8%	—	7	4	11.2	—	11%	—	12	3%	—	14.5	13%	—	15.1	—	15.2	2	2
George Wilson	27	FS	41	6.4%	73	8	3	8.3	65	16%	81	16	5%	75	15.6	50%	37	7.1	39	7.4	2	2
Kiwaukee Thomas*	31	CB	35	7.3%	—	11	5	4.5	—	55%	—	22	9%	—	6.7	40%	—	6.9	—	7.1	3	1
Bryan Scott	27	SS	26	3.3%	—	15	6	1.9	—	78%	—	10	2%	—	9.5	59%	—	10.3	—	10.7	1	0
Ashton Youboty	24	CB	22	3.8%	—	6	3	7.6	—	40%	—	18	6%	—	10.3	42%	—	8.6	—	9.3	1	1
Jerametrius Butler*	30	CB	15	4.0%	—	4	1	0.0	—	0%	—	15	7%	—	7.5	42%	—	8.6	—	8.9	1	0
William James	29	CB	32	4.8%	80	9	3	7.8	52	60%	17	46	12%	77	14.8	55%	19	9.8	76	10.0	2	1

Year	Pass D Rank	vs. #1 WR	Rk	vs. #2 WR	Rk	vs. Other WR	Rk	vs. TE	Rk	vs. RB	Rk
2005	15	7.9%	17	1.5%	20	11.8%	26	-4.8%	14	2.6%	19
2006	6	-25.6%	1	24.2%	29	-2.9%	19	-3.8%	16	0.8%	18
2007	16	-8.7%	9	23.3%	29	-14.2%	10	-13.2%	4	2.1%	22

The Bills' secondary took its lumps last year, but there was really only one major trouble spot. When free safety Ko Simpson broke his leg in the season opener, coordinator Perry Fewell turned to third-year pro Jim Leonhard. Leonhard made a few big plays in pass coverage, but he was so mistake-prone that the Bills' cornerbacks couldn't count on deep support. Fewell stopped blitzing, which left the cornerbacks isolated on receivers with no pass rush or deep help. Fewell tried to replace Leonhard with converted wide receiver George Wilson, but Wilson broke two ribs and Leonhard returned to the lineup. Eventually, Bryan Scott, who wasn't with the team at the start of camp, took over as the starter. Simpson may not be ready for the start of camp, but Scott and Wilson are now around to provide insurance. Leonhard signed with the Ravens.

Under the circumstances, Bills cornerbacks fared well. Terrence McGee let a lot of catches occur in front of him but didn't allow many yards after the catch or deep balls. Jabari Greer replaced injured Jason Webster early in the year and had several big games, earning Defensive Player of the Week honors in Week 4. Greer is great in coverage, but at five foot nine, he's a liability against big receivers. Like former Bills cornerback Antoine Winfield, Greer is a pint-sized tough guy in run support. Top draft pick Leodis McKelvin is an electrifying return man with the tools to be a shutdown corner. He has great speed, lateral quickness, and awareness in coverage, but he's making the leap from a mid-major (Troy) and has a tendency to knock down passes he could easily intercept. Ashton Youboty, who started a few games before getting hurt last season, is also in the mix. Veteran free agent William James may get a tryout as cornerback depth who could also play nickel safety.

The one sure thing in the Bills' secondary is strong safety Donte Whitner. Whitner emerged as a defensive leader last season when the players around him were dropping like flies. Whitner is a hug-the-line safety in the Adrian Wilson mold; if the Bills find a free safety, Fewell will unleash Whitner as a blitzer more often.

Special Teams

Year	DVOA	Rank	FG/XP	Rank	Net Punt	Rank	Punt Ret	Rank	Net Kick	Rank	Kick Ret	Rank	Hidden	Rank
2005	7.2%	1	3.6	11	7.5	5	0.4	12	3.8	12	27.2	1	8.9	4
2006	5.9%	2	8.5	4	16.1	1	6.6	3	-2.0	25	5.5	6	-2.2	16
2007	4.1%	6	5.9	4	7.2	4	11.3	3	-2.2	19	2.1	14	-1.4	17

Every year, the Bills' special teams are excellent, and every year, we point out in this space that the Bills' consistency is amazing, because special teams statistics usually vary wildly from year to year. Coordinator Robert April and scouting director Tom Modrak are the two biggest reasons why the Bills always have an edge in the kicking game. April develops excellent blocking and tackling units and deals well with personnel transitions. Modrak keeps the bottom of the Bills' roster flush with guys who can run down the field on kicks and punts. April lost several of his best gunners, including Sam Aiken and Coy Wire, in the offseason, but he should get back some players who were forced into the starting lineup and less available to play special teams in 2007, such as George Wilson and John Di-Giorgio.

Punter Brad Moorman still has one of the league's strongest, most consistent legs. Kicker Ryan Lindell is reliable if unspectacular. Terrence McGee and Roscoe Parrish are both dynamic return men aided by excellent blocking units. Only Devin Hester added more value on punt returns than Parrish did last season.

COACHING STAFF

The Bills' offense will look very different under new coordinator Turk Schonert. Steve Fairchild preferred single-set-back, H-back formations, but Schonert will re-incorportate the fullback into the Bills' offense. He also plans to get Marshawn Lynch and the other backs more involved in the passing game, and Trent Edwards (or possibly J. P. Losman) will get more opportunities to take three-step drops and release the ball quickly. Schonert is steeped in the West Coast Offense, but head coach Dick Jauron will make sure that the offense doesn't become too pass-happy. "We have to run it, and we have to run it to throw it," Jauron said in April. "We have to use play action. We have two good young quarterbacks with live arms. They can get the ball out quick and be accurate and get it down the field. We have some speed. So we have to take advantage of all those things."

Dick Jauron is the kind of guy who sets his stereo equalization sliders smack dab in the middle. He's not a tactical mastermind or a master motivator, and he's had only one winning season in 7½ years of coaching. Still, his straight-arrow approach works well with a young roster full of developing players. Jauron might want to shake things up—some strategic razzle-dazzle, maybe a little more clubhouse brimstone—if the team is close to contention this year. Being the Great Delegator is just dandy when your team is 12-4, but if the team is stuck at 7-9, a guy like Jauron just looks replaceable.

Carolina Panthers

Is it easier to right the wrongs of others or to fix your own mistakes? That's the question facing the brain trust that runs the Carolina Panthers.

At the end of the 2001 season, the Panthers were in freefall, going 1-15 in George Siefert's third season as their head coach. They lost 15 straight games after beating the Vikings, 24-13, in the opener. One of the few highlights of that year was the 93-yard kick return touchdown by rookie receiver Steve Smith on Minnesota's opening kickoff. It was the first time Smith ever got his hands on a football in an NFL game. More telling was the 15-start season of rookie quarterback Chris Wienke and Richard Huntley's leading the team with 665 rushing yards. Siefert was fired after the season and replaced by former Giants defensive coordinator John Fox. Former salary cap administrator Marty Hurney was promoted to general manager. Fox and Hurney were charged with a Herculean task: get one of the worst teams in recent memory back on track.

Two years later, the Carolina Panthers were two kicks away from a Super Bowl championship. Jake Delhomme's touchdown pass to Ricky Proehl left Super Bowl XXXVIII locked in a 29-29 tie with 1:08 left in regulation. Then Panthers kicker John Kasay sent the subsequent kickoff out of bounds, which gave New England the ball at its own 40-yard line. That field position gift left the Patriots just a couple of first downs away from a 41-yard game-winning field goal by Adam Vinatieri. The Panthers lost their shot at

immortality, but they were seen by many as a contender that could challenge the upper echelon for years to come. It was one of the greatest turnarounds in history, and the Hurney/Fox combo could take a great deal of credit. Hurney's early drafts produced Julius Peppers, Will Witherspoon, Jordan Gross, Travelle Wharton, Ricky Manning, and several other key pieces of the puzzle. Fox was able to motivate the team he inherited and the one Hurney had started to build.

But with the sole exception of the 2005 season, when the Panthers lost the NFC Championship game to the Seattle Seahawks, this franchise has not been able to extend that line of success. The Panthers have missed the playoffs three times and have struggled mightily on offense the last two seasons. More worrisome in 2007 was how the defense, once Carolina's mainstay, began to free-fall. The Panthers couldn't break .500, despite residence in the league's worst division.

The reason for their decline is no mystery. The Panthers have failed to address recent positional needs in free agency, and they've started to fall behind in providing depth through the draft. All eight of the team's 2007 draft picks made the roster, but first-round selection Jon Beason was the only top-flight choice out of the box. He set a team record for tackles and challenged San Francisco's Patrick Willis and New York's David Harris for the title of best rookie linebacker. At the other end of the spectrum was receiver Dwayne Jarrett, who struggled to pick up

---

PANTHERS PROSPECTUS

2007 Record: 7-9

Pythagorean Wins: 5.6 (23rd)

DVOA: -21.1% total (27th), -19.3% weighted (25th)

Offense: -15.2% DVOA (27th)

Defense: 1.0% DVOA (19th)

Special Teams: -4.9% DVOA (30th)

Variance: 16.0 % (19th)

2007: We finally discover what it takes to shut down Steve Smith: four quarterbacks.

2008: Our numbers suggest the defense will return to prominence; if not, it's time to tear down and start over.

2008 Mean Projection: 9.5 wins

On the Clock (0-3): 0%

Loserville (4-6): 9%

Mediocrity (7-8): 23%

Playoff Contender (9-10): 34%

Super Bowl Contender (11+): 34%

Projected Average Opponent: -2.4% DVOA (21st in NFL)

2008 Panthers Schedule

Week	Opp.	Week	Opp.	Week	Opp.
1	at SD	7	NO	13	at GB
2	CHI	8	ARI	14	TB (Mon.)
3	at MIN	9	BYE	15	DEN
4	ATL	10	at OAK	16	at NYG
5	KC	11	DET	17	at NO
6	at TB	12	at ATL		

the playbook. Reporters questioned his work ethic and ability to handle his life off the field. In training camp, Jarrett was competing for the starting job opposite Steve Smith. By the end of the season, Carolina's most productive rookie receiver ended up being tight end Dante Rosario, who caught six passes for 108 yards and two touchdowns in the season's last five games.

The 2006 draft class was led by running back DeAngelo Williams, but the Panthers seem to have no idea how to use him. Williams ranked 19th in DYAR to DeShaun Foster's 46th, but even though both backs were available for every game, Foster got 103 more carries despite gaining 1.5 fewer yards per attempt. Cornerback Richard Marshall and tight end Jeff King were later-round finds in 2006, but the 2005 draft produced linebacker Thomas Davis and little else.

The two clearest areas of concern have been at wide receiver and on the defensive line. The Panthers ranked in the top 10 in defensive Adjusted Line Yards and Adjusted Sack Rate in 2005 and 2006. The 2007 Panthers remained strong against the run (10th in ALY), but Carolina's sack total plummeted from 41 in 2006 to 23 last year. Only the Cincinnati Bengals had fewer quarterback takedowns. The primary responsibility for the drop can be laid at the feet of Julius Peppers, the one-time elite pass rusher who put up 2.5 sacks in 2007 after averaging 11.5 over the previous three seasons. Peppers also dropped from 32 hurries and eight hits in 2006 to 10 hurries and three hits in 2007. That kind of pass-rush deficit will always affect a secondary, and the Panthers finished 17th in DVOA against the pass, their first time out of the top 10 since 2003.

Fox was unable to pinpoint the reason for the Peppers slide, though it's been blamed on everything from injury to some sort of worm, to his supposed desire to leave the team after 2008, the final year of his current contract. And while the Panthers try to fix Peppers, the rest of the line is in transition, starting from the inside.

Defensive tackle Kris Jenkins was traded to the Jets, and free agent Kindal Moorehead was signed by the Falcons. End Mike Rucker retired after a nine-year NFL career. At this point, the Panthers' defense is led by its linebackers, especially Beason. This is a fairly large paradigm shift, and the selection of Dan Connor, the Bednarik Award winner from Penn State and an absolute steal in the third round, makes that unit even stronger. Carolina signed stopgap tackles Darwin Walker and Ian Scott and are left hoping that's enough up front. If not, it doesn't much matter how good Connor and Beason are.

The receiver position has been a problem since Muhsin Muhammad was signed away by the Chicago Bears after the 2004 season. Since then, Carolina's receiver corps has consisted of Steve Smith, Steve Smith, and Steve Smith. This isn't breaking news, but even Smith's production fell off after catching passes from four different quarterbacks in 2007. The Panthers have tried a few fixes, and none have done the trick. Smith finished first in DYAR for receivers in 2005, and Ricky Proehl was next for the Panthers at 36th. In 2006, Smith ranked sixth, and Keyshawn Johnson was next at 47th. Smith dropped to 63rd last year; perhaps the weight of the world became a bit much.

The erosion of the defensive line and the inability to find a reliable second receiver are both by-products of those personnel misses in the draft and free agency. The last defensive lineman of any note drafted by the Panthers was tackle Jovan Haye in 2005. Haye put up six sacks last year, but unfortunately, he did it for the Buccaneers. Young wide receivers Drew Carter and Keary Colbert never developed, either. Colbert's 2007 was especially unproductive—among receivers targeted more than 50 times, only San Francisco's Darrell Jackson and Arnaz Battle finished lower in DYAR. Colbert and Carter have since signed with Oakland and Denver, respectively. Carolina upgraded with perennial breakout prospect D. J. Hackett, whose potential was undercut by injuries in Seattle.

Of course, last year's primary cause of roster upheaval was the quarterback situation. After Jake Delhomme's hot start was shot down in the third game by a season-ending elbow injury, Carolina turned to former Houston Texans punching bag David Carr. Carr started the next two games, then injured his back, forcing the Panthers to coax 43-year-old Vinny Testaverde out of retirement. Testaverde showed up at Carolina's practice facility on Wednesday and, four days later, became the oldest quarterback in NFL history to start and win a game, when the Panthers beat Arizona, 25-10. In the next game, however, Testaverde injured his right

Achilles tendon, and Carr was pressed back into service. Carr started against Tennessee in Week 9 and was sacked seven times by the Titans' brutal pass rush.

Undrafted rookie free agent Matt Moore was brought in at the end of that game, though Testaverde got the next two starts. A sore back sidelined Testaverde against the Saints—in Carolina, back pain is apparently more contagious than MRSA infections in Cleveland—so the Panthers stuck Carr on the field yet again. They then benched him after two interceptions and let Moore mop up in a 31-6 loss. Testaverde was healthy enough to start the next two games, but Moore finally got a chance to start against the Seahawks in Week 15, an ugly win in which neither team scored through three quarters. The Panthers finished 2-1 with Moore as their starter, and though quarterback starts and wins have a flimsy correlation at best, the Panthers' offense is ready to hold on to any reason for optimism it can find.

Mike Ditka could tell John Fox a few things about four-quarterback seasons: Da Coach presided over four teams for which four different quarterbacks started at least one game. The first two teams, the 1984 and 1986 Bears, bookended Ditka's renowned Super Bowl champion with Walter Payton and a killer defense, and finished with winning records. The final two, the 1997 and 1998 Saints, didn't—proving that while rotating so many quarterbacks needn't doom a franchise to failure, the rest of the team does have to step up. Due to an inconsistent running game and declining defense, last year's Panthers did not.

DeShaun Foster, the poster child for the inconsistent running game, has toddled off to San Francisco, leaving DeAngelo Williams as the incumbent starter. Last season, the Panthers were one of three NFC South teams (the Saints and Falcons being the others) that inexplicably gave more carries to the back who proved less effective over time. Foster has always been a boom-and-bust runner, but his -72 DYAR in 2007—tied with Reggie Bush for third-worst among running backs with at least 75 rushes—makes Williams's underutilization all the more curious. The Panthers added power to Williams's speed in the first round of the 2008 draft with Oregon's Jonathan Stewart, a 235-pound monster with sub-4.5 speed who could do some real damage if his college injury history doesn't transfer to the pros. They also moved up to take mammoth Pitt tackle Jeff Otah. With Otah, Travelle Wharton, and Gross, the Panthers have three elite linemen, none of whom project positively at left tackle at this point. Otah gave up 8.5 sacks in his senior season, the Panthers wanted to move Wharton inside anyway, and Gross is a better fit on the right side.

The question is whether the Panthers are in need of a few tweaks or a complete overhaul. If Delhomme recovers from his 2007 injury, if Hackett proves the complement to Smith that the Panthers haven't had since Muhammad, if Muhammad himself still has enough left in the tank as a third receiver, and if the Stewart/Williams combo provides the Steelers-esque two-pronged attack the team has wanted for a long time, then the Panthers have enough to make some waves and get the offense back up to league average. At the very least, they'll give opposing defenses some Excedrin headaches with their power-running focus.

The defensive outlook is a bit harder to forecast. Peppers's 2008 cap hit stands at more than $14 million, and unless he has the contract year to end all contract years, the Panthers won't get their money's worth. The interior line is a problem that will require more fixing than the Band-Aids applied in the offseason, and there are questions in the secondary, despite the presence of strong safety Chris Harris and his eight forced fumbles. On the other hand, our projection system likes the Panthers' chances to rebound on defense. Defenses that struggle on third down but play well on first and second down tend to improve. So do defenses that play worse in the red zone than on the rest of the field. There is continuity in the coaching staff and plenty of young talent at linebacker.

If the defense doesn't rebound, that continuity on the coaching staff may come to an end. In the modern NFL, there are very few coaches like Jeff Fisher and Bill Cowher, who stay with a team through several reconstruction projects. We know that Fox and Hurney can fix a stagnant franchise, because they've done it before. Then again, when Fox and Hurney fixed the Panthers after 2001, they were fixing someone else's mistakes. Fixing your own mistakes is a bit harder because first you have to recognize them.

Doug Farrar

Panthers 2007 Stats by Week

Wk	vs.	W-L	PF	PA	YDF	YDA	TO	Total	Off	Def	ST
1	@STL	W	27	13	385	238	0	-16%	7%	9%	-13%
2	HOU	L	21	34	353	346	-2	-56%	-16%	21%	-19%
3	@ATL	W	27	20	313	442	+2	-15%	28%	45%	2%
4	TB	L	7	20	236	365	-1	-40%	-25%	8%	-7%
5	@NO	W	16	13	243	341	+1	-17%	-33%	-13%	4%
6	@ARI	W	25	10	374	255	+5	52%	6%	-49%	-3%
7	BYE										
8	IND	L	7	31	293	395	-2	-33%	-6%	11%	-16%
9	@TEN	L	7	20	191	236	+2	-44%	-45%	-18%	-17%
10	ATL	L	13	20	235	277	-1	-64%	-55%	12%	3%
11	@GB	L	17	31	382	317	-3	-57%	-10%	19%	-28%
12	NO	L	6	31	195	373	-3	-86%	-65%	18%	-3%
13	SF	W	31	14	323	195	+4	28%	-10%	-47%	-9%
14	@JAC	L	6	37	149	427	-1	-54%	-51%	4%	2%
15	SEA	W	13	10	322	282	+1	10%	2%	-7%	1%
16	DAL	L	13	20	216	405	0	-5%	-14%	1%	10%
17	@TB	W	31	23	349	303	-1	44%	23%	-10%	11%

Trends and Splits

	Offense	Rank	Defense	Rank
Total DVOA	-15.2%	27	1.0%	19
Unadjusted VOA	-13.9%	27	3.9%	21
Weighted trend	-19.3%	31	-3.5%	13
Variance	7.6%	19	5.9%	13
Average opponent	1.7%	23	3.6%	9
Passing	-18.9%	30	6.4%	18
Rushing	-10.9%	24	-5.1%	17
First down	-11.8%	27	-5.5%	10
Second down	-8.5%	26	-1.1%	11
Third down	-30.3%	31	16.2%	27
First half	-18.9%	30	-1.4%	15
Second half	-12.2%	25	3.8%	20
Red Zone	-13.7%	27	14.9%	24
Late and close	5.0%	11	-1.4%	14

Five-Year Performance

Year	W-L	Pyth Wins	Est Wins	PF	PA	TO	Total	Rank	Off	Rank	Def	Rank	ST	Rank
2003	11-5	8.6	7.9	325	304	-5	0.4%	17	-7.2%	18	-7.1%	12	0.6%	16
2004	7-9	8.4	8.6	355	339	+12	2.3%	12	0.8%	13	-3.8%	13	-2.3%	23
2005	11-5	11.6	9.9	391	259	+16	14.0%	11	-3.2%	15	-14.9%	3	2.3%	6
2006	8-8	6.9	7.9	270	305	-5	2.9%	14	-4.3%	19	-10.0%	5	-2.8%	24
2007	7-9	8.1	6.3	267	347	+1	9.4%	27	-0.4%	18	1.0%	20	-3.6%	26

Strategic Tendencies

Run/Pass		Rank	Offense		Rank	Defense		Rank	Other		Rank
Runs, all plays	43%	9	3+ WR	42%	27	Rush 3	7.0%	11	2+ RB, Pct Runs	61%	12
Runs, first half	43%	11	4+ WR	13%	12	Rush 4	63.3%	16	1 RB/2 TE, Pct Runs	55%	10
Runs, first down	50%	15	2+ TE	28%	11	Rush 5	20.7%	19	1 RB/3+ WR, pct runs	16%	31
Runs, second-long	56%	1	Single back	51%	21	Rush 6+	9.0%	12	CB1 on WR1	41%	22
Runs, power sit.	50%	27	Play action	14%	24	Rush 7+	1.2%	19	Go for it on 4th	0.70	27
Runs, behind 2H	32%	9	Max protect	10%	14	Sacks by LB	28.3%	13	Offensive Pace	30.8	17
Pass, ahead 2H	27%	32	Outside pocket	10%	20	Sacks by DB	8.7%	11	Defensive Pace	31.3	24

Conservative Carolina may have run more often than any other team on second-and-long, but that doesn't mean the Panthers were particularly good at it. Carolina ranked 26th in DVOA in these situations, gaining just 3.6 yards per carry. Barely one-third of these runs made it even halfway to a new set of downs. ✐ The Panthers used two tight-end sets more than twice as often as they did in 2006. ✐ Carolina was one of six offenses that used shotgun formations less than 20 percent of the time, and with good reason—it ranked 31st in offensive DVOA from shotgun, behind everyone except San Francisco. ✐ The Panthers threw almost half of all their screen passes on third down, the highest percentage in the league. ✐ In general, NFL teams had a higher DVOA with four or five wide receivers on the field. Carolina was the opposite. Although its offense was league-average with one or two wide receivers, it was 31st with three wideouts (-42.0% DVOA) and 26th with four or five wideouts (-14.5% DVOA). ✐ On first down, the Panthers threw to Steve Smith more than twice as often as they threw to every other wide receiver combined. Targets were much more evenly distributed on second and third down. ⌀ The Carolina defense was below average in the first three quarters, but ranked seventh in the fourth quarter. ⌀ Only two teams saw opponents run fewer screens than the Panthers did.

Passing

Player	DYAR	DVOA	Plays	NtYds	Avg	YAC	C%	TD	Int
Vinny Testaverde	-214	-28.6%	183	942	5.1	5.1	54.7%	5	6
David Carr*	-171	-29.1%	152	599	3.9	3.9	53.7%	3	5
Matt Moore	66	-2.8%	118	686	5.8	4.1	56.8%	3	4
Jake Delhomme	175	17.7%	92	649	7.1	5.7	64.7%	8	1

Rushing

Player	DYAR	DVOA	Plays	Yds	Avg	TD	Fum	Suc
DeShaun Foster*	-72	-15.8%	247	893	3.6	3	7	43%
DeAngelo Williams	104	11.9%	144	717	5.0	4	1	41%
David Carr*	2	-9.9%	14	60	4.3	0	1	—
Brad Hoover	9	7.3%	12	39	3.3	0	0	50%
Steve Smith	44	58.5%	9	66	7.3	0	0	—
Vinny Testaverde	-3	-24.6%	5	26	5.2	0	3	—
Jake Delhomme	2	-4.9%	4	27	6.8	0	1	—
Alex Haynes	-9	-112.4%	3	3	1.0	0	0	33%
LaBrandon Toefield	-17	-34.4%	13	27	2.1	1	0	23%

Receiving

Player	DYAR	DVOA	Plays	Ctch	Yds	Y/C	YAC	TD	C%
WR									
Steve Smith	42	-9.1%	148	86	1002	11.7	5.5	7	58%
Drew Carter*	38	-6.6%	75	38	517	13.6	2.9	4	51%
Keary Colbert*	-122	-34.6%	69	32	332	10.4	3.3	0	46%
Dwayne Jarrett	-34	-49.6%	13	6	73	12.2	0.2	0	46%
Ryne Robinson	-16	-37.5%	8	4	35	8.8	4.3	0	50%
Muhsin Muhammad	43	-5.9%	81	40	570	14.3	4.7	4	49%
D. J. Hackett	99	12.8%	47	32	384	12.0	4.3	3	68%
TE									
Jeff King	-68	-20.1%	80	46	406	8.8	3.0	2	58%
Dante Rosario	54	88.4%	7	6	108	18.0	6.0	2	86%
Christian Fauria	33	63.1%	6	5	39	7.8	1.6	2	83%
RB									
DeAngelo Williams	-25	-25.9%	38	24	175	7.3	8.9	1	63%
DeShaun Foster*	-22	-24.4%	36	25	180	7.2	7.1	1	69%
Brad Hoover	6	-7.3%	14	10	58	5.8	5.1	1	71%

Offensive Line

Year	Yards	ALY	Rank	Power	Rank	10+ Yds	Rank	Stuff	Rank	Sack	ASR	Rank
2005	3.62	4.17	13	60%	22	12%	26	24%	13	27	5.6%	9
2006	3.98	4.02	24	50%	31	17%	12	25%	26	32	6.4%	16
2007	4.07	4.11	20	63%	16	14%	20	25%	22	33	6.4%	15

Year	LE	Rank	LT	Rank	Mid	Rank	RT	Rank	RE	Rank
2005	3.72	23	4.62	7	4.07	18	3.96	21	4.41	10
2006	4.64	5	4.32	16	4.12	22	4.41	9	2.43	32
2007	5.26	3	3.78	26	3.86	23	4.16	19	4.43	8

Carolina's offense was an unmitigated disaster in 2007, but if there was a bright spot, it was the offensive line. Their numbers are average, but that's actually impressive given the poor skill players that surrounded them. After implementing zone blocking techniques to overcome personnel deficiencies in 2007, Carolina plans to return to its preferred power-blocking scheme next year. That's going to require some changes. The first one was the release of left guard Mike Wahle, a veteran who is still effective but fits better in a line requiring more athleticism and less raw strength. After failing in attempts to trade center Justin Hartwig, Carolina released the seven-year veteran. Second-year man Ryan Kalil will take Hartwig's place. Right tackle Jordan Gross, the best of the Panthers' linemen, will move from right to left in the short term. Gross was given the franchise tag in March. The team would like to move Travelle Wharton, last year's left tackle, inside to guard. Wharton received a new six-year deal in February.

The man who may someday be the long-term left tackle is Pitt's Jeff Otah, a massive but inexperienced player who will require some finishing work before he's a worthy adversary for the best the NFL has to offer. Otah gave up 8.5 sacks in his senior season, and Gross will probably be the stopgap on the left side. The Panthers' line basically has three players who *can* play its most demanding position, but who are better suited to other spots at this time. This is not unusual for power-blocking lines, but there is such a thing as taking the power angle too far and winding up with a bunch of grinders who can't fan out against speed rushers, or get to the second level against any defense.

Defensive Front Seven

Defensive Line	Age	Pos	Plays	TmPct	Rk	Stop	Dfts	Stop%	Rk	AvYd	Rk	Sack	Hit	Hur	Runs	RuStop	RuYd	Pass	PaStop	PaYd
Mike Rucker*	33	DE	51	6.1%	36	43	16	84%	10	1.0	27	3.0	4	10	43	81%	1.6	8	100%	-1.9
Maake Kemoeatu	29	DT	50	6.0%	22	36	9	72%	55	2.2	54	0.0	1	3	45	71%	2.3	5	80%	1.0
Julius Peppers	28	DE	41	5.6%	44	29	9	71%	64	2.5	61	2.5	3	10	26	69%	3.3	15	73%	1.0
Kris Jenkins*	29	DT	38	4.6%	44	34	15	89%	4	0.7	8	2.5	6	3	33	88%	1.5	5	100%	-4.4
Damione Lewis	30	DT	31	4.0%	55	26	12	84%	15	1.5	27	3.5	3	5	24	79%	2.3	7	100%	-0.9
Kindal Moorehead*	30	DT	19	2.3%	—	15	6	79%	—	0.9	—	2.0	1	2	17	76%	1.6	2	100%	-5.5
Darwin Walker	31	DT	16	2.8%	—	13	6	81%	—	0.7	—	1.5	0	2	14	79%	2.2	2	100%	-10.0

Linebackers	Age	Pos	Plays	TmPct	Rk	Stop	Dfts	Stop%	AvYd	Sack	Hit	Hur	Runs	RuStop	Rk	RuYd	Rk	Tgts	Suc%	Rk	APaYd	Rk
Jon Beason	23	MLB	145	17.4%	6	77	22	53%	5.1	0.0	0	1	91	62%	50	3.8	69	54	60%	10	4.3	11
Thomas Davis	25	OLB	91	10.9%	61	53	25	58%	4.7	3.0	6	6	46	72%	20	2.5	12	42	42%	66	7.2	70
Na'il Diggs	30	OLB	52	6.3%	93	33	13	63%	2.3	3.5	0	2	34	62%	49	2.4	11	18	59%	13	5.6	32
Dan Morgan*	30	MLB	23	14.7%	—	12	6	52%	7.3	0.0	0	2	9	67%	—	5.8	—	11	49%	—	6.6	—
Landon Johnson	27	MLB	110	13.3%	41	52	13	47%	5.4	1.0	3	4	63	59%	64	3.5	55	34	40%	73	7.3	72

Year	Yards	ALY	Rank	Power	Rank	10+ Yds	Rank	Stuff	Rank	Sack	ASR	Rank
2005	3.52	3.68	7	46%	1	13%	6	24%	20	45	7.5%	12
2006	3.97	4.03	9	48%	2	16%	17	28%	3	41	8.0%	7
2007	3.85	3.99	10	53%	3	16%	14	25%	15	23	4.8%	30

Year	LE	Rank	LT	Rank	Mid	Rank	RT	Rank	RE	Rank
2005	3.93	14	3.42	5	3.85	11	3.40	2	3.13	6
2006	3.55	10	4.67	20	4.02	7	4.53	21	3.51	10
2007	2.39	2	4.10	13	4.21	18	3.53	5	4.80	26

From 2002 through 2006, Carolina's defensive front four was the cornerstone of the franchise and consistently one of the NFL's best. That changed drastically in 2007. Only Cincinnati sacked the quarterback less often, and the Panthers' sack total fell nearly in half, compared with 2006. Although the defense's Adjusted Line Yards stats didn't change much, Kris Jenkins was the only Panthers tackle with an acceptable Stop Rate, and he was traded to the Jets after weight and contract issues cemented his departure.

End Mike Rucker has been a leader in the Carolina locker room for years, but he retired in a tearful press conference after nine seasons. And Julius Peppers, the resident sack master and star of the show, suffered a shocking decline in quarterback takedowns: from 13.0 to 2.5. Unless he can rebound fully to his pre-2007 level of performance, Peppers is now a financial albatross around the team's neck—he has a salary cap charge of over $14 million in 2008, the final year of his contract. Peppers was placed on injured reserve with a sprained medial collateral ligament (MCL) in late December, but there is no clear explanation for the downturn in his 14 games. Offseason trade rumors were false, and the team finds itself over a barrel—it could extend his contract to decrease the 2008 cap hit, but what do you pay for that production, especially when a move to the right side is being considered? The Panthers have been slow in replacing their formerly elite defenders. Reserve tackle Damione Lewis signed a three-year, $14 million contract, but little was done in the draft and the cupboard could really be bare next year if Peppers signs elsewhere. Tackles Darwin Walker and Ian Scott were signed as placeholders. The Panthers were expected to address their defensive-line deficiency in the draft, but they stood pat until the sixth round, when they took Wisconsin tackle Nick Nayden. Hayden and Scott are the only Panthers defensive linemen under the age of 28.

Things are much better when it comes to the linebackers. Rookie Jon Beason took Dan Morgan's starting spot in the middle and set a franchise record for tackles. He proved apt in every aspect of the game and should cement his position for years to come. The question is, which position will he be cementing? Beason was mostly a weak-side linebacker at Miami, and the Panthers greatly fortified the unit when they picked up Penn State's Dan Connor with an absolute steal pick in the third round. Connor projects best in the middle, though some teams talked to him at the Combine about playing outside. The Panthers will be pretty thrilled if Connor, this year's Bednarik Award winner as best collegiate defensive player, has a career as strong as the Bednarik winners from 2000 and 2001: Morgan and Peppers. With Na'il Diggs back in the fold and Thomas Davis continuing to develop, Carolina's linebackers have replaced its line as the squad that opposing offenses must worry about.

Defensive Secondary

Secondary	Age	Pos	Plays	TmPct	Rk	Stop	Dfts	RuYd	Rk	RuStop	Rk	Tgts	Tgt%	Rk	Dist	Suc%	Rk	APaYd	Rk	PaYd	PD	Int
Chris Harris	26	SS	99	12.7%	7	43	14	5.9	28	47%	31	30	7%	42	9.1	46%	50	9.0	59	9.2	4	1
Richard Marshall	24	CB	86	10.3%	25	47	27	6.0	36	63%	10	71	15%	59	10.0	60%	4	7.0	30	7.1	12	3
Ken Lucas	29	CB	77	9.3%	37	35	16	4.9	20	54%	28	82	18%	43	11.1	47%	51	7.6	47	8.0	12	2
Deke Cooper	31	FS	62	7.8%	61	17	5	6.1	36	31%	65	22	6%	57	8.5	52%	27	5.5	14	6.0	4	3
Chris Gamble	25	CB	53	6.8%	68	26	9	8.0	56	50%	37	61	14%	68	11.4	56%	12	7.1	33	7.5	7	1
Marquand Manuel*	29	SS	15	1.8%	—	5	4	6.8	—	20%	—	5	1%	—	21.5	29%	—	18.4	—	18.2	2	1
Terrence Holt	28	FS	70	8.7%	51	17	5	8.4	66	43%	42	20	4%	79	12.7	44%	57	11.6	75	11.1	1	0

Year	Pass D Rank	vs. #1 WR	Rk	vs. #2 WR	Rk	vs. Other WR	Rk	vs. TE	Rk	vs. RB	Rk
2005	2	-14.5%	3	-28.9%	3	6.1%	20	-3.0%	16	-4.8%	12
2006	9	-16.4%	6	7.3%	21	-17.0%	9	16.5%	29	-21.0%	9
2007	18	14.7%	24	-2.8%	12	-11.9%	12	13.6%	22	-19.6%	5

Carolina's secondary was severely tested by the defense's inability to provide consistent quarterback pressure. Not only were the Panthers' sack numbers alarming, but the pass rushers also proved to be average in the number of hurries that affected opposing quarterbacks. No Panthers player registered an interception until the fifth game of the season, when they encountered New Orleans quarterback Drew Brees at the end of his pick-happy streak. The Panthers' 14 interceptions ranked among the NFL's lowest, despite their three solid cornerbacks, Ken Lucas, Richard Marshall, and Chris Gamble. Although Lucas and Gamble started for most of last season, Marshall may be the best of the trio. Gamble has some consistency issues, but overall this is a good group in nickel coverage.

The Panthers had a big hole at safety a year ago; now they have a surplus at the position. Strong safety Chris Harris came over from Chicago in a trade right before the season began and ended up starting 15 games with a team-record eight forced fumbles. He's a dynamic hitter who also finished second on the team in tackles. Deke Cooper and Terrence Holt fill out the roster from a veteran perspective, but the really interesting player here is third-round pick Charles Godfrey. A cornerback at the University of Iowa, Godfrey was projected as an NFL safety from the word go because of his ability to play the run and his physical nature—he's better playing back than man-on-man, and he could surprise his way into serious starting time.

Special Teams

Year	DVOA	Rank	FG/XP	Rank	Net Punt	Rank	Punt Ret	Rank	Net Kick	Rank	Kick Ret	Rank	Hidden	Rank
2005	2.4%	6	0.7	15	7.3	6	6.4	6	7.5	4	-8.0	25	-4.4	20
2006	-2.8%	24	11.5	1	0.8	18	-15.3	32	-1.8	23	-11.6	30	-2.6	18
2007	-4.9%	30	2.5	13	-9.0	27	-4.0	21	-5.6	24	-12.7	30	1.7	13

The Panthers now have two kickers. Joining veteran John Kasay on the roster is English kickoff specialist Rhys Lloyd, signed by the team in time to put up as many touchbacks in the season finale as Kasay did all year. Carolina signed Lloyd to a two-year contract in the offseason. Kasay put in his second straight good season after a horrible 2005, booting 24 field goals in 28 attempts and making eight of 11 from 40 yards and longer. Punter Jason Baker has seen his net average drop every year since 2005, but that may be a function of wear and tear—Carolina's third-down conversion rate of 36.2 was among the league's worst. Second-year receiver Ryne Robinson was an average return man last year, but has potential for growth. Last year he handled punts for the whole year and kickoffs for the second half, after Nick Goings and DeAngelo Williams struggled returning kickoffs in the first few weeks.

COACHING STAFF

Going from 1-15 to the Super Bowl gets a young head coach a lot of respect, but missing the playoffs in three of the following four years can tarnish the glow of past accomplishments. For the first time in John Fox's tenure, there are rumblings that a downturn in wins might be the precursor to a change at the top. That may not be entirely fair, in that Fox has been at the mercy of injuries and some very iffy personnel decisions, but this is the coaching life.

The assistant coach on the hot seat is offensive coordinator Jeff Davidson. Fans gave him a mulligan when he had to try to win with four quarterbacks in his first season, but now the Panthers are counting on Davidson to guide the transformation back to a power offense. Defensive coordinator Mike Trgovac is an extension of Fox, and the two men have worked closely together since Fox first came to Carolina. His challenge will be to find new ways to put pressure on quarterbacks despite a defensive line that barely resembles the one he benefited from in previous years. You'll also find a familiar name a little lower on the coaching roster—defensive quality control assistant Sam Mills III, son of the late, great Panthers linebacker. The younger Mills played defensive back at Montclair State, his father's alma mater, and has been with the Panthers since 2005.

Chicago Bears

The triumph of defense over offense has long been the story of the Chicago Bears franchise. Since the AFL-NFL merger in 1970, the Bears have allowed an average of just 288 points per season, in a tie with Dallas for the lowest average of any NFC franchise. The Bears have also scored just 283 points per season, the lowest average of any nonexpansion franchise. As head coach for the past four years, Lovie Smith has stuck to the kind of football that defines the City of Big Shoulders and even bigger linebackers.

Plenty of teams in recent years have fielded strong defenses and poor offenses, and on first glance, this portends good things for the Bears in 2008. Ten teams since 1995 have finished in the top five in defensive DVOA but the bottom five in offensive DVOA, a list the Bears made two years ago and just missed making this past season. On average, teams with bottom-five offenses and top-five defenses won 9.4 games the following season, up from 6.8 (Table 1). However, there's a difference between these teams that improved and the current Chicago Bears: The other teams used the offseason to acquire impact offensive players. The Raiders signed Rich Gannon after 1998 and won 41 games the following four years. The Panthers inked Jake Delhomme after 2001, and two years later were in the Super Bowl. The 2000 Ravens drafted Jamal Lewis to rush the ball nearly 20 times a game during their title run. Bears offseason acquisitions Marty Booker and Brandon Lloyd don't qualify as impact offensive players. Most importantly, neither one is a quarterback.

Rex Grossman was Chicago's first-round pick in 2003, and during his career he has been one of three things: injured, maddeningly inconsistent, or on the bench. It took nearly five years for Smith to decide that maybe Grossman wasn't an NFL starting quarterback, but then the organization resigned him to a one-year contract this offseason with the understanding that he would be given the opportunity to win the job in training camp. In addition to Grossman, there is Kyle Orton, a 2005 fourth-rounder who started 15 games as a rookie after Grossman broke his ankle and proceeded to lead the team to 11 wins. And by "lead," we mean "not completely throw up on himself," because Orton completed just 51.9 percent of his passes, tossed nine touchdowns to 13 interceptions, and ranked 45th out of 46 quarterbacks in our DYAR metric.

The Bears have decided to let Grossman and Orton battle it out for the starting gig, and the best quarterback on the roster last season, Brian Griese, is now in Tampa Bay. Griese didn't even put up replacement-level numbers in 2007, and at 33, he was nothing more than a stopgap while the younger quarterbacks developed. Now that he's gone, and with no experienced backup on the roster, Chicago is stuck with Grossman and Orton.

While the guys throwing the ball are frequent targets of the fans' ire, those tasked with catching it haven't exactly been facilitating the Bears' offensive renaissance. This becomes something of a chicken-and-egg problem (do really bad quarterbacks trump good wide receivers?) complicated by the fact that last year's two

Table 1. Teams with Bottom 5 Offense and Top 5 Defense in DVOA, 1995-2007

Year	Team	Offense DVOA	Rank	Defense DVOA	Rank	W-L	Next Year W-L
1995	PHI	-12.6%	26	-13.4%	3	10-6	10-6
1995	CAR	-23.8%	29	-11.5%	5	7-9	12-4
1998	OAK	-24.9%	28	-18.1%	2	8-8	8-8
1998	SD	-26.7%	29	-17.4%	3	4-5	5-11
1999	BAL	-18.8%	27	-21.5%	2	8-8	12-4
2001	CLE	-22.7%	30	-18.0%	3	7-9	9-7
2002	CAR	-22.9%	31	-13.8%	3	1-15	7-9
2004	WAS	-17.0%	28	-15.0%	4	6-10	10-6
2005	CHI	-16.8%	28	-21.8%	1	11-5	13-3
2006	MIN	-15.9%	29	-10.6%	4	6-10	8-8

2008 Bears Schedule

Week	Opp.	Week	Opp.	Week	Opp.
1	at IND	7	MIN	13	at MIN
2	at CAR	8	BYE	14	JAC
3	TB	9	DET	15	NO (Thu.)
4	PHI	10	TEN	16	GB (Mon.)
5	at DET	11	at GB	17	at HOU
6	at ATL	12	at STL		

starting wideouts are no longer with the team. Muhsin Muhammad arrived in Chicago as a legitimate pass catcher after several productive seasons in Carolina. In 2004, his last with the Panthers, he ranked second in DYAR and had a catch rate of 58 percent; last season, he ranked 62nd and sported a 49 percent catch rate. Known for great route running and even better hands, Muhammad displayed neither during his three years with the Bears. Following his release in Chicago, he returned to Carolina for a two-year deal. Bernard Berrian played opposite Muhammad and put up relatively impressive numbers last season: 71 catches, 951 yards, and five touchdowns. He ranked just 60th in DYAR, but he served as the Bears' only proper deep threat, something the team now lacks after choosing not to re-sign Berrian this offseason.

The team plans to have Devin Hester, the game-changing return man, assume Berrian's duties. That is partly because Hester has blinding speed and the Bears would like to get him involved outside special teams, but it's also because the depth chart includes names such as Mark Bradley, Rashied Davis, and the aforementioned Booker and Lloyd. Even if it is the case that good wideouts make up for bad quarterbacks, Chicago's roster is currently light on one and heavy on the other.

These concerns could be mitigated by a reliable running game. Unfortunately for Chicago, the running game is in worse shape than the passing game. The passing game at least finished 30th in DVOA; the running game finished dead last.

Undeniably, some of the blame belongs to one-time fourth overall pick Cedric Benson; before Thomas Jones was traded last spring, the running game ranked ninth (2006) and 15th (2005). But Jones also ran behind a better-blocking offensive line. Just like quarterbacks and wide receivers, running backs and offensive lines have

a symbiotic relationship; the performance of one relies on the performance of the other. Olin Kreutz is still one of the NFC's best centers, and Chicago, as in previous seasons, rushed the majority of the time behind him with some success. Because the guards have been so inconsistent, however, defenses had little trouble stuffing the run. Chicago ranked 29th in Adjusted Line Yards between the guards and was just as ineffective going to the left. The Bears' first-round pick, tackle Chris Williams, will get every opportunity to win the left tackle job, allowing 33-year-old Jon Tait to move to right tackle. The internal options at left guard, however, are iffy. Perhaps nobody informed the Bears that Alan Faneca was an unrestricted free agent this offseason.

Chicago's decision to sit idly by as the quickly fading playoff window slams shut is mystifying. Sometimes the best strategy is to do nothing, but unlike, say, the New England Patriots or the New York Giants, the Bears have gaping holes at almost every offensive position. If there were ever a time to err on the side of being too active in free agency, it was this offseason. To its credit, the organization addressed several needs in the draft, selecting Williams and running back Matt Forte with its first two picks. Both should see plenty of playing time, but if the Bears are going to a running-back-by-committee, they might still be one back short.

Now that we've painted a sufficiently bleak picture, some less depressing news: Hester will still return kicks and punts. As the second essay in this chapter details, there has never been a return man who affected opposing kick-punt numbers like Hester. According to our metrics, the Bears had the best punt return team in the NFL by a large margin, despite teams intentionally punting the ball out of bounds to avoid the implausible touchdown that would inevitably follow. (Well, unless you're Mike Shanahan; then you kick to Hester and watch him sprint past you on his way to the end zone. Twice.) Opponents will hope (and pray) that Hester's double-duty as a full-time wide receiver affects his special teams productivity, although there's no evidence to suggest such a relationship exists.

In addition to special teams, the defense should be improved next season. Injuries were this unit's downfall a season ago. Starting cornerback Nathan Vasher missed 12 weeks with a pulled groin, and safeties Mike Brown, Kevin Payne, and Adam Archuleta missed time with various ailments. (A case can be made that Archuleta didn't miss *enough* time, which probably had something to do with why he was released in May.) In part due to these injuries, the Bears struggled early, but over the course of the year, the defense returned to its proper place as one of the league's best. The Bears ranked seventh in defensive DVOA but second in our weighted formula, which gives more strength to late-season games. As long as the defense remains healthy, the Bears will be competitive.

And yet, because of their lethargic approach to off-season player acquisition, Chicago will put the offense in the not-so-capable hands of Grossman or Orton, two players perfectly suited as NFL backups. Things are no different when it comes to the pass catchers, ball carriers, and blockers. Other than center Olin Kreutz and tight ends Desmond Clark and Greg Olsen, who on the Chicago offense really brings anything to the table? Perhaps offensive coordinator Ron Turner can petition the league to let the Bears feature two quarterbacks at a time. Knowing this group, it would probably just lead to twice as many sacks without an increase in production.

As has been the case since Lovie Smith arrived in Chicago four summers ago, the team's best chance to make it to the postseason will lie with the defense. Plenty of Hester touchdown returns couldn't hurt, either.

Ryan Wilson

Devin Hester:
The Kicking Game's Gordian Knot

The Gordian Knot, a mythological metaphor for an impossible problem solved by cutting through conventional strategy and "squaring the circle," was Alexander the Great's key to the kingdom of what is now Asia. When King Gordius, a peasant turned monarch, tied his fabled ox-cart to Zeus with the mother of all knots, he posed a problem so difficult that the one to solve the knot would be named ruler. After endless attempts by others to solve the puzzle logically, the ambitious Alexander simply utilized his sword to sever the knot. That he cut the knot as opposed to weaving through to a solution was irrelevant to those who presented him with his rightful reward.

In today's NFL, the closest thing to an insoluble perplexity is return man Devin Hester of the Chicago Bears. To this point, the circle has not been squared, and Gordius is laughing all the way to the bank.

Selected out of Miami in the second round of the 2006 draft, Hester became a feared returner from his first regular-season game, when he became the first Chicago rookie to take a return to the house in his debut game in 51 years. His ability to make cuts, his patience in allowing blocking schemes to be established, and his sheer speed quickly turned him into a household name. Opposing teams were forced to create a game plan on how to kick to him, if at all. The strategies varied from avoiding him altogether, to keeping the ball on the ground, to challenging him directly. Every Chicago NFL broadcast was almost certain to include the announcers uttering the phrase, "We talked to coach [fill in name] yesterday, and he said his special team unit would [fill in tactic] on kicks to Devin Hester." Unless your name was Lane Kiffin or Wade Phillips, your response was generally some variation about how you planned to avoid Hester as much as possible. Broncos coach Mike Shanahan famously changed his strategy midgame, directing Todd Sauerbrun to both punt and kick the ball to Hester in the second half of Chicago's November 25 victory over Denver, a 37-34 overtime thriller. Hester scored on a punt *and* a kickoff return during a 10-minute span in the third quarter, the Broncos were basically out of the playoffs at 5-6, and Shanahan and Sauerbrun both looked like fools. Broncos' cornerback Dré Bly put it succinctly after the game: "I feel like we single-handedly got beat [sic] by one guy."

Hester's six touchdown returns in 2007 eclipsed the NFL mark he set the previous year as a rookie and places him within two of the NFL career record held by Brian Mitchell. Mitchell took the ball to the house 13 times over 223 games. Hester's 11 touchdowns have come in just 32 games. To quote our own Michael David Smith, "The guy is absolutely ridiculous."

Hester has scored a touchdown every 13.5 returns, which currently ranks as the greatest touchdown-per-return rate in NFL history. The all-time leader in kick return average, Bears' Hall of Fame legend Gale Sayers, is second in touchdown rate at 14.8. Mitchell scored once every 82.3 returns. Other notable return men include Deion Sanders (40.8), Dante Hall (47.8), Desmond Howard (75.4), and career punt return touchdown leader Eric Metcalf (52.6).

The amazing fact about Hester's 2007 performance was not necessarily that he scored more often than he did as a rookie, but that he did it despite a decreasing number of opportunities. Eleven percent of kickoffs to the Bears sailed out of bounds, compared to two percent league-wide. Opposing teams decided that handing the ball to Rex Grossman or Kyle Orton at the 40-yard line was more palpable than giving Hester open field running options. A further 58 percent of kickoffs were either squibbed or otherwise intentionally short. Essentially, Hester saw a clean kickoff only three out of every 10 kicks. Nevertheless, he took three all the way to the end zone last season—although one was called back on a holding penalty—and almost broke away for a fourth.

It is easier to come up with a strategy for punting to Hester than it is for kicking to him, since punting out of bounds doesn't earn a penalty. If they are in Chicago territory, most punters can kick a deliberate touchback that starts the Bears' offense on the 20-yard line. In addition, an NFL punter can vary how high and where the ball is kicked to coordinate a certain coverage package. Last year, 34 percent of punts to Hester were kicked either out of bounds or into the end zone, compared to 20 percent league-wide. In a Week 6 game at Soldier Field, Minnesota punter Chris Kluwe kicked the ball so far out of bounds that it landed in the stands. An additional 19 percent of all punts to Hester were kicked high and short enough that they were either downed by the special teams unit or a fair catch was forced. Given Hester's ability to break a scoring return from any point on the field and the fact that so many punts were angled out of bounds, Chicago only fair-caught four percent of punts, compared to 18 percent among the rest of the teams. Consequently, Hester had the opportunity to return roughly the same percentage of punts as the average return man. Opponents expanded the Hester avoidance strategies by focusing on not only how deep a ball was kicked but also where it landed. The most common practice appears to have been an attempt to place the ball between the numbers and the sideline, but it was met with mixed results.

Clearly the most dangerous spot to kick to Hester is in the middle of the field, where he has options to either side. Hester is particularly adept at waiting for his blocking to develop, finding open lanes, and outrunning flanking gunners. It helps that Chicago uses a seemingly unique NFL strategy: double-covering the gunners on almost every punt. Approximately one out of every six kicks to Hester (both kickoffs and punts) were received between the hashmarks. Three of those kicks bounced before they got to Hester. Hester ended up in the end zone on three of the remaining 12 kicks down the middle, and was one defender short of scor-

ing on a fourth. Two of these returns were against Denver in the aforementioned Week 12 contest. Ironically, up to that point in the game, Shanahan had chosen to squib-kick to Hester. Deviating from that strategy cost the Broncos dearly.

So if we know where kickers shouldn't place the ball, can we figure out specifically where they *should* try to place it? Not really. Considering Hester's success between the hashmarks, it would be logical to assume that a ball kicked near the sideline would yield the best results. Such a strategy risks the ball going out of bounds, but it also narrows the field, and thus Hester's opportunities. In fact, a number of special teams coaches sought to box Hester in by kicking between the numbers and the sidelines and using the weakside gunners to flank any cross-field maneuvers. In a number of instances it worked, and worked well. Dallas's punting unit in Week 3 was particularly effective. With little room to run after catching the ball, Hester was wedged into a path that led him out of bounds. However, the results were not consistent week to week. Three of Hester's six touchdowns came when the opponent kicked the ball between the numbers and the sideline (one kickoff, two punts) including a great run against Minnesota. Kluwe booted a 54-yarder away from Hester to the 11-yard line. Hester caught it and patiently waited on the 8-yard line while the blocking scheme developed. He proceeded to cut parallel to the goal line, outrunning the flankers and taking it 91 yards to the house. Kluwe could not have kicked it any better. It was a perfect coffin corner punt, away from the returner, but it still resulted in 6 points.

If directional kicking is not the answer, distance may be. A widely used strategy to combat a highly effective returner is to kick the ball short, and opponents used it against the Bears quite often, so that they could get their coverage team to Hester as quickly as possible. Thirty of the 75 kickoffs by Chicago opponents were squib kicks. A total of 34 kickoffs didn't reach the 20-yard line (including nine that went out of bounds and thus, by rule, put the ball on the 40). Not counting onside attempts, the average kickoff to Chicago traveled only 54.3 yards. That's the lowest average since 1995 by more than four yards (Table 2). Only two teams are within five yards of last year's Bears. More than 200 teams are within five yards of the team in second place, the 2000 Bengals.

Hypothetically, short kicks should be effective in limiting average return yardage. However, when the shorter distance of the kick is factored in, the benefit is lost (Table 3). For instance, kickoffs against Chicago that traveled beyond the 10-yard line saw an average

Table 2. Shortest Average Kickoff Distance by Receiving Team, 1995-2007

Rank	Team	Avg Yds
1	2007 Bears	54.3
2	2000 Bengals	58.5
3	1995 Bears	59.3
4	2001 Browns	59.8
5	2004 Browns	59.9
6	2003 Patriots	60.2
7	2001 Jets	60.3
8	1995 Jets	60.4
9	2005 Browns	60.4
10	2003 Steelers	60.4

Last year's Jets are tied for 11th place at 60.5 average yards.

Table 3. Chicago Opponents' Average Net Kickoff by Average Kick Distance, 2007

Kickoff Distance	Net Kick Distance
End Zone	54.5
Goal line to 10-yard line	39.0
10- to 20-yard line	36.9
Beyond 20-yard line	32.1

return of 24.6 yards, whereas kickoffs that failed to make it to the 10-yard line saw an average return of 19.3 yards. The benefit of five yards is negated by the fact that the ball is kicked ten or more yards shorter.

The risk and reward of punting is a bit different. As with kickoffs, the average net kicking distance between long punts with long returns and short punts with short or no returns was basically the same due to the lack of distance on the punt itself. However, the key word in this case is *average*. Hester's returns on long-distance punts had a high variance with a mixture of no yardage as well as long open-spaced runs. On punts that flew at least 45 yards, Hester returned four for touchdowns but also had 13 punt returns that generated zero, or even negative, return yardage. On the other hand, all but one kick less than 35 yards either went out of bounds or was downed. The remainder of punts kicked between 35 yards and 45 yards averaged 40.5 yards with an average return of less than four yards.

But short punts didn't penalize opposing teams the way kickoffs did. Average net yards in punts by Chicago's opponents were indifferent between punts specifically marked in the charting process as "short kicks" versus not, both at 31.5 yards. Although these punts were considerably below the league average of 37.3 net yards, it is noteworthy that Hester did not re-

turn a punt or a kick that traveled shorter than 46 yards. Booming a punt deep may result in excellent field position; the risk of kicking it long is high. It is better to punt the ball short and take Hester out of the equation as much as possible, removing the variability of returns. That is why not only Hester's abilities but the mere threat of them gave the Bears the NFL's best average starting field position in 2007, with an average start just short of their own 34-yard line.

There is one glaring negative to Hester's game, and teams have sought ways to exploit it. Although Hester has great legs, the one-time cornerback does not have the best hands. He fumbled (including muffs) a league leading seven times, although the Bears were fortunate to lose possession only once. Baltimore's Yamon Figurs and Tennessee's Chris Davis tied for second in the NFL with five fumbled returns. Hester also led the league in 2006 with eight fumbles and has more than twice as many fumbles on kickoffs and punts than any other player over the past two seasons combined. There does not appear to be a secret recipe for manipulating Hester into a fumble, but a common strategy was to put the ball on the ground. In kickoffs to Chicago, 32 out of 65 hit the ground. Of those kicks, 15 made it to Hester; he fumbled one of them and did not take a single one all the way. Twenty out of 45 punts that didn't go out of bounds hit the ground. Hester had an opportunity to return only four of those, and he fumbled twice. Although probably not statistically significant, it will likely lead to more bouncing punts in the future. Not all Hester's fumbles came on bouncing balls—in fact, the majority did not. Yet the common thread is keeping Hester off-balance. Two of the other four fumbled balls were kicked over his head, causing him to backpedal. Another fumble came on a punt that was wobbly and may have been partially blocked.

When Hester fields a kick comfortably, that is a major risk for the opposing special teams unit. Whether through short kicks, bouncing balls, or off-balance catches, opponents will continue to seek ways to disrupt Hester's effect on the game. He has only two years under his belt, and there are many adjustments to be made. Hester may not hold the career touchdown rate record when his career is said and done, and his abilities may diminish over time, but the NFL is a "here and now" league. No team has yet emerged with Alexander's sword in hand, but they will keep looking. In the meantime, Hester remains the kicking game's Gordian Knot.

Bill Moore

2007 Bears Stats by Week

Wk	vs.	W-L	PF	PA	YDF	YDA	TO	Total	Off	Def	ST
1	@SD	L	3	14	202	263	-2	-24%	-39%	-16%	-1%
2	KC	W	20	10	239	281	-1	2%	-34%	-10%	26%
3	DAL	L	10	34	239	431	-3	-76%	-42%	21%	-13%
4	@DET	L	27	37	303	310	-1	-41%	-62%	3%	24%
5	@GB	W	27	20	285	439	+4	-4%	-6%	4%	5%
6	MIN	L	31	34	458	444	-4	8%	-4%	3%	15%
7	@PHI	W	19	16	386	334	0	14%	28%	17%	3%
8	DET	L	7	16	255	365	-3	-54%	-49%	11%	6%
9	BYE										
10	@OAK	W	17	6	295	193	+3	-2%	-19%	-21%	-4%
11	@SEA	L	23	30	345	425	0	-2%	3%	18%	13%
12	DEN	W	37	34	293	430	-2	25%	-30%	-9%	45%
13	NYG	L	16	21	312	356	+4	30%	3%	-24%	3%
14	@WAS	L	16	24	356	345	-1	-19%	-15%	-1%	-5%
15	@MIN	L	13	20	209	372	+3	-4%	-25%	-13%	8%
16	GB	W	35	7	240	274	+2	92%	8%	-79%	5%
17	NO	W	33	25	275	413	0	11%	-39%	-23%	27%

Trends and Splits

	Offense	Rank	Defense	Rank
Total DVOA	-20.4%	31	-6.9%	7
Unadjusted VOA	-18.5%	31	-3.7%	12
Weighted Trend	-13.7%	25	-11.2%	2
Variance	5.9%	12	5.8%	11
Average Opponent	1.0%	18	3.6%	8
Passing	-18.8%	29	0.4%	13
Rushing	-22.4%	32	-14.4%	4
First Down	-27.2%	30	-3.3%	14
Second Down	-15.2%	28	1.5%	16
Third Down	-16.0%	26	-26.3%	2
First Half	-13.6%	27	11.2%	6
Second Half	-27.9%	31	-3.0%	14
Red Zone	-12.5%	26	-20.9%	4
Late and Close	-16.7%	29	5.5%	22

Five-Year Performance

Year	W-L	Pyth Wins	Est Wins	PF	PA	TO	Total	Rank	Off	Rank	Def	Rank	ST	Rank
2003	7-9	6.1	6.2	283	346	-9	-17.8%	27	-20.3%	29	0.4%	18	2.9%	5
2004	5-11	4.8	4.4	231	331	-8	-30.2%	31	-36.5%	32	-4.5%	10	1.9%	11
2005	11-5	10.3	8.5	260	202	+6	2.3%	14	-16.8%	28	-21.8%	1	-2.7%	27
2006	13-3	12.4	10.8	427	255	+8	24.0%	4	-4.2%	18	-20.6%	2	7.6%	1
2007	7-9	7.6	7.5	334	348	-1	-4.1%	20	-20.4%	31	-6.9%	7	9.3%	1

Strategic Tendencies

Run/Pass		Rank	Offense		Rank	Defense		Rank	Other		Rank
Runs, all plays	39%	21	3+ WR	49%	15	Rush 3	0.7%	32	2+ RB, Pct Runs	66%	5
Runs, first half	41%	18	4+ WR	8%	22	Rush 4	71.2%	7	1 RB/2 TE, Pct Runs	35%	28
Runs, first down	46%	25	2+ TE	22%	20	Rush 5	22.4%	16	1 RB/3+ WR, Pct Runs	17%	29
Runs, second-long	36%	13	Single back	57%	14	Rush 6+	5.7%	25	CB1 on WR1	38%	28
Runs, power sit.	68%	9	Play action	13%	25	Rush 7+	1.0%	22	Go for it on 4th	1.00	20
Runs, behind 2H	23%	28	Max protect	10%	15	Sacks by LB	20.0%	20	Offensive Pace	28.8	3
Pass, ahead 2H	45%	18	Outside pocket	8%	24	Sacks by DB	10.0%	7	Defensive Pace	31.4	26

In the first quarter, Chicago's offense ranked 11th in rushing DVOA. The Bears ranked 28th or lower in quarters two, three, and four and had the worst rushing DVOA in the league if quarters two through four are combined. ✑ Only Buffalo ran fewer draw plays than Chicago, and with good reason. The Bears had a -94.3% DVOA on draw plays, the lowest in the league. The Bears also ran very few draw plays in 2006—they ranked dead last—but actually had the league's *highest* DVOA on the rare occasions they ran a draw. ✑ Chicago was one of a number of teams that dramatically increased the usage of shotgun formations in 2007. The Bears used shotgun 21 percent of the time, after using it only six times in 2006. No, not six percent. Six plays, period. ✑ After using play action, no team threw back to the running back more often than the Bears. ✑ Over the first three quarters, the Bears' defense was ranked third in DVOA. In the fourth quarter, it collapsed to 25th. Even if you remove the Week 4 game in which the Lions scored 34 points in the fourth quarter, Chicago's fourth-quarter defense still ranks just 19th. ✑ Chicago ranked 31st in DVOA against the screen pass, allowing an average of 9.2 yards on screens. This was a dramatic change from 2006, when the Bears ranked fifth in DVOA and averaged just 5.3 yards allowed on screen passes. Chicago schemes effectively disguised the blitz; only St. Louis had more sacks marked as "Rusher Untouched."

Passing

Player	DYAR	DVOA	Plays	NtYds	Avg	YAC	C%	TD	Int
Brian Griese*	-62	-15.0%	276	1687	6.1	5.6	62.4%	9	12
Rex Grossman	-168	-21.8%	248	1221	4.9	4.6	55.2%	4	7
Kyle Orton	-73	-25.0%	83	444	5.3	6.6	53.8%	3	2

Rushing

Player	DYAR	DVOA	Plays	Yds	Avg	TD	Fum	Suc
Cedric Benson	-67	-17.0%	197	673	3.4	4	4	40%
Adrian Peterson	-30	-13.5%	151	511	3.4	3	5	38%
Garrett Wolfe	-34	-40.8%	31	85	2.7	0	1	23%
Brian Griese*	4	-3.7%	8	30	3.8	0	5	—
Rex Grossman	-7	-28.2%	8	38	4.8	0	5	—
Devin Hester	-29	-124.9%	7	-10	-1.4	0	0	—
Jason McKie	2	-2.5%	6	17	2.8	1	1	67%

Receiving

Player	DYAR	DVOA	Plays	Ctch	Yds	Y/C	YAC	TD	C%
WR									
Bernard Berrian*	58	-6.9%	128	71	951	13.4	3.5	5	55%
Muhsin Muhammad*	43	-5.9%	81	40	570	14.3	4.7	4	49%
Devin Hester	-27	-21.1%	39	20	299	15.0	6.4	2	51%
Rashied Davis	-26	-24.1%	31	17	165	9.7	3.3	0	55%
Mark Bradley	-45	-44.9%	17	6	71	11.8	3.3	1	35%
Marty Booker	-122	-27.3%	105	50	556	11.1	2.6	1	48%
Brandon Lloyd	-59	-85.3%	11	2	14	7.0	8.0	0	18%
TE									
Desmond Clark	99	16.1%	66	44	545	12.4	5.3	4	67%
Greg Olsen	-9	-9.4%	66	39	391	10.0	3.8	2	59%
John Gilmore*	-23	-54.5%	7	3	14	4.7	3.0	0	43%
RB									
Adrian Peterson	70	7.2%	65	51	420	8.2	8.4	0	78%
Cedric Benson	-10	-20.7%	27	17	123	7.2	7.3	0	63%
Jason McKie	-37	-50.6%	15	9	33	3.7	4.4	0	60%
Garrett Wolfe	12	4.8%	13	9	117	13.0	14.7	0	69%

Offensive Line

Year	Yards	ALY	Rank	Power	Rank	10+ Yds	Rank	Stuff	Rank	Sack	ASR	Rank
2005	4.41	4.12	15	55%	28	23%	4	28%	27	31	7.7%	21
2006	4.07	4.46	9	71%	7	12%	27	21%	6	25	4.6%	6
2007	3.34	3.71	30	75%	3	9%	29	25%	20	43	7.1%	18

Year	LE	Rank	LT	Rank	Mid	Rank	RT	Rank	RE	Rank
2005	4.06	19	4.33	17	4.28	12	4.05	18	3.21	26
2006	3.65	22	4.71	8	4.80	1	4.11	21	4.28	13
2007	2.83	28	3.62	29	3.69	31	4.43	14	3.74	24

The Bears headed into the offseason with myriad needs, the offensive line chief among them. Two veteran starters, left guard Ruben Brown and right tackle Fred Miller, are gone. Left tackle John Tait will likely relocate to the right side, where he'll be joined by two other returning starters, center Olin Kreutz and right guard Roberto Garza. The team's 2008 first-round pick, Chris Williams out of Vanderbilt, will have every opportunity to win the left tackle job in training camp. He should immediately be an upgrade as a pass blocker; unfortunately, Williams struggles in the running game, and scouts questioned his ability to get to the second level and sustain downfield blocks. This would be good news for the to-be-named quarterback—except there are no receivers to speak of—and is bad news for an already moribund running attack.

Many of us wondered why the Bears chose not to pursue left guard Alan Faneca when there was an obvious need for his services. Instead, the battle for Brown's spot will be between 30-year-old career backup Terrence Metcalf and Josh Beekman, a second-year player from Boston College. Beekman, a fourth-round pick a year ago, should be the favorite. He was a disappointment in limited playing time as a rookie, but now that he has a year of experience in Chicago's system, his talent should earn him the starting nod over Metcalf. If 2006 sixth-rounder Tyler Reed or 2008 seventh-rounder Chester Adams show even a glimpse of NFL potential, the underachieving Metcalf could be released, even if the line already has tenuous depth issues.

Defensive Front Seven

Defensive Line	Age	Pos	Plays	TmPct	Rk	Stop	Dfts	Stop%	Rk	AvYd	Rk	Sack	Hit	Hur	Runs	RuStop	RuYd	Pass	PaStop	PaYd
Adewale Ogunleye	31	DE	61	7.3%	21	44	27	72%	58	0.8	21	9.0	11	17	38	68%	1.6	23	78%	-0.5
Alex Brown	29	DE	47	5.6%	45	34	16	72%	57	1.4	33	4.0	8	7	27	63%	2.8	20	85%	-0.5
Tommie Harris	25	DT	35	4.2%	52	29	15	83%	18	0.7	9	7.5	5	8	25	76%	2.7	10	100%	-4.2
Mark Anderson	25	DE	32	4.3%	61	25	11	78%	37	0.0	7	4.5	4	7	25	72%	1.9	7	100%	-7.0
Anthony Adams	28	DT	27	4.7%	41	19	7	70%	59	1.6	28	0.5	0	1	24	71%	2.0	3	67%	-2.0
Israel Idonije	28	DE	23	2.7%	—	18	7	78%	—	3.9	—	0.5	0	1	16	81%	2.0	7	71%	8.1
Darwin Walker*	31	DT	16	2.8%	—	13	6	81%	—	0.7	—	1.5	0	2	14	79%	2.2	2	100%	-10.0

Linebackers	Age	Pos	Plays	TmPct	Rk	Stop	Dfts	Stop%	AvYd	Sack	Hit	Hur	Runs	RuStop	Rk	RuYd	Rk	Tgts	Suc%	Rk	APaYd	Rk
Brian Urlacher	30	MLB	137	16.3%	11	75	30	55%	5.0	5.0	2	3	74	57%	80	4.2	88	44	71%	3	3.9	8
Lance Briggs	28	OLB	105	14.3%	25	66	32	63%	4.1	2.0	5	4	53	83%	5	1.3	1	43	42%	68	6.4	58
Hunter Hillenmeyer	28	OLB	81	9.6%	71	39	11	48%	5.8	0.0	6	4	47	60%	62	3.6	60	27	47%	50	5.7	34
Jamar Williams	24	OLB	24	2.9%	—	11	4	46%	4.8	1.0	0	0	14	50%	—	4.9	—	3	42%	—	3.3	—

Year	Yards	ALY	Rank	Power	Rank	10+ Yds	Rank	Stuff	Rank	Sack	ASR	Rank
2005	3.93	3.67	6	59%	12	20%	25	27%	7	40	7.3%	14
2006	4.21	3.85	4	63%	15	22%	28	29%	2	40	6.5%	16
2007	4.55	3.93	7	57%	10	28%	32	30%	4	41	7.6%	5

Year	LE	Rank	LT	Rank	Mid	Rank	RT	Rank	RE	Rank
2005	3.08	5	3.29	4	4.09	16	3.70	9	2.92	3
2006	4.09	16	3.52	7	3.99	5	4.18	17	3.09	6
2007	4.80	25	3.40	2	3.91	7	3.92	12	3.93	12

Like the offensive line, the defensive line lacks depth. In fact, just as curious as the Bears' decision not to try to sign Alan Faneca was their decision not to make serious inquiries when Jacksonville put Marcus Stroud on the trading block. Injuries plagued the defensive tackles last season. Dusty Dvoracek had an outstanding preseason only to be lost for the year after a serious knee injury in Week 1, and Tommie Harris played on a sprained knee for most of the season. Darwin Walker, acquired from the Bills during training camp, was released this spring after one ineffective season. He will be replaced on the depth chart by third-round rookie Marcus Harrison, a four-year starter at Arkansas. Harrison suffered a serious knee injury during the spring of his junior season, but when healthy, he should be an upgrade over Walker. On the outside, defensive end Mark Anderson was a pass-rushing demon as a rookie in 2006, registering 12 sacks in limited duty. As a starter last season, he was uneven. Anderson did manage five sacks in 14 starts, but he struggled to hold the point of attack in running situations, which helps explain why the Bears had a lot of trouble against runs around the offense's left end. In February, the Bears extended the contract of Alex Brown, Anderson's backup last season, and the Bears may do more to rotate the two, thus allowing Anderson to specialize in passing situations.

Adewale Ogunleye will man the other defensive end spot, and he shows no signs of slowing as he enters his eighth season. The Bears used their 2007 second-round pick on Central Michigan defensive end Dan Bazuin because the team was coming off a Super Bowl appearance, seemingly had few needs, and he was the best player available. Now Bazuin could be playing for his roster spot this summer after missing his rookie season with, you guessed it, a knee injury. Competing for Bazuin's spot is fifth-rounder Kellen Davis, an interesting prospect who was a super-sized Mike Vrabel as a combined tight end and defensive end at Michigan State.

Middle linebacker Brian Urlacher is the face of the team, and he has finally shaken the "overrated" label. A converted college safety, Urlacher's freakish combination of size and speed make him a perfect fit in Smith's cover-2 defense. One of the knocks early in his career was his inability to shed blockers and stop running plays coming right at him. According to our advanced statistics, it's no longer an issue: Opponents rushed between the guards only 41 percent of the time, far below the league average of 50 percent, and the Bears have been in the top 10 of Adjusted Line Yards on runs up the middle for two straight seasons. Urlacher's contract runs through 2011, but he is looking to renegotiate. Early offseason threats could mean nothing—last year, Lance Briggs reported to training camp after threatening for months that he would hold out—but any troubles with Urlacher could erase the razor-thin margin for error the Bears will face on a weekly basis in 2008. More likely, Urlacher and the organization will work through their differences, and he will team with Briggs and Hunter Hillenmeyer to solidify the middle of Chicago's defense. Jamar Williams was drafted in 2006 with the idea that he could grow into Briggs's weakside spot if Briggs eventually left in free agency. Briggs signed a long-term deal this offseason, but Williams remains as the top option off the bench.

Defensive Secondary

Secondary	Age	Pos	Plays	TmPct	Rk	Stop	Dfts	RuYd	Rk	RuStop	Rk	Tgts	Tgt%	Rk	Dist	Suc%	Rk	APaYd	Rk	PaYd	PD	Int
Charles Tillman	27	CB	89	11.3%	15	35	18	11.5	74	50%	38	93	23%	11	10.3	52%	31	5.9	6	5.9	12	3
Danieal Manning	26	FS	84	10.0%	37	19	6	11.8	83	15%	82	39	9%	16	10.8	46%	49	9.7	67	10.1	5	2
Brandon McGowan	25	SS	64	8.7%	50	28	12	4.8	10	55%	12	21	5%	63	10.5	41%	68	9.1	60	9.3	5	2
Adam Archuleta*	31	SS	59	7.5%	66	25	11	4.9	12	58%	8	21	5%	70	19.3	36%	75	14.2	82	14.8	2	1
Trumaine McBride	22	CB	43	5.1%	78	13	4	5.4	27	71%	6	56	13%	73	10.0	50%	41	7.1	31	7.1	5	0
Ricky Manning	28	CB	42	5.0%	—	18	9	4.6	—	62%	—	35	8%	—	6.9	50%	—	7.4	—	8.0	1	0

Year	Pass D Rank	vs. #1 WR	Rk	vs. #2 WR	Rk	vs. Other WR	Rk	vs. TE	Rk	vs. RB	Rk
2005	1	-3.9%	10	-8.8%	10	-50.0%	1	-34.7%	2	-17.9%	5
2006	2	-2.3%	13	-24.7%	4	-20.1%	8	-41.5%	1	-29.3%	4
2007	13	-26.3%	2	8.9%	21	-8.7%	16	5.3%	15	27.7%	31

Mike Brown is to the defensive backfield what Brian Urlacher is to the linebacker corps. Brown missed 15 games last season and the secondary suffered. Adam Archuleta was abysmal as his replacement and has since been released. Unfortunately, Brown can't be counted on to stay healthy. Since 2004, he's started just 17 games, with only seven in the last two seasons. Chicago's 2006 fifth-round pick, Kevin Payne, could emerge as Brown's successor; that could come as early as September, assuming Payne is fully recovered from a broken arm that saw him miss virtually all of 2007. Danieal Manning is penciled in at free safety, and although generally considered a very good all-around player, he sometimes blows assignments, which is a big problem when you are the last line of defense in the Tampa-2.

Rookie fourth-round pick Craig Steltz will provide depth at safety, but his greatest contribution will come on special teams. At cornerback, the Bears have counted on the talented tandem of Charles Tillman and Nathan Vasher for a few years. Tillman had a very strong season in 2007—notice that the Bears were extremely strong against the opposition's top receivers—but Vasher missed 12 games with a pulled groin, which created a big hole on the other side of the field. Ricky Manning, originally signed as a nickel back, was hugely disappointing, although two rookies—Corey Graham and Trumaine McBride—played surprisingly well in spot duty.

Special Teams

Year	DVOA	Rank	FG/XP	Rank	Net Punt	Rank	Punt Ret	Rank	Net Kick	Rank	Kick Ret	Rank	Hidden	Rank
2005	-2.6%	27	-12.0	32	-2.5	20	-2.3	19	5.2	10	-3.9	21	14.9	1
2006	7.6%	1	8.8	3	2.0	16	11.7	2	18.9	1	3.4	9	11.0	3
2007	9.4%	1	6.5	3	10.6	3	18.0	1	6.0	8	14.1	4	33.7	1

Thanks primarily to Devin Hester, the Bears own two of the top-five special teams DVOA ratings since our stats begin in 1995. (That doesn't even count the "Hidden" rating, which for the 2007 Bears is more of a "Hester" rating.) The top spot still belongs to the 2002 New Orleans Saints, who had a fine return man in Michael Lewis, spectacular kickoff and punt coverage, and John Carney going 11-for-13 on field goals of 40 or more yards. Like the 2002 Saints, the Bears' success on special teams has been about more than just touchdown returns. In particular, the coverage teams are outstanding. Last year, only the Chargers were better at preventing kickoff returns, and only the Bills were better at preventing punt returns. In fact, when looking solely at kick distance, Robbie Gould's kickoffs and Brad Maynard's punts were below average according to our measurements. The Bears' value came entirely from coverage. Given these numbers—and the general inconsistency of field goal kickers—we have to wonder whether the Bears made a good choice handing out special teams contracts. The team rewarded Gould with a five-year, $15.5 million extension but lost special teams captain Brendon Ayanbadejo, who has made two consecutive Pro Bowls as a blocking and coverage specialist. He signed a free agent contract with Baltimore for four years and $4.9 million.

COACHING STAFF

Lovie Smith enters his fifth year as the Bears' head coach. He made it to the Super Bowl two years ago, but this Chicago team is closer to a top-10 selection in next year's draft than a postseason berth. Smith ascended the coaching ranks from the defensive side of the ball, but the anemic offense could be his downfall with the Bears. He replaced defensive coordinator Ron Rivera with Bob Babich last offseason, and the unit, despite numerous injuries, was a bright spot in a season devoid of them.

Offensive coordinator Ron Turner is the obvious scapegoat for the team's struggles, but he has also been handicapped by the uncertainties at quarterback. Even when healthy, Rex Grossman has had issues with confidence stemming from a seemingly inexplicable knack for misreading coverages and making extremely poor decisions. More generally, in the four years that Turner has been in the job, the Bears have had four different quarterbacks lead the team in passing. Turner isn't blameless, but it's much easier to coordinate an offense when the most important position on the field is settled. There's no reason to think one more season will change things (for either Grossman or Orton), which could be bad news for Smith and, by extension, his coaching staff.

Cincinnati Bengals

At its heart, DVOA relies on a comparison—how did this team (or player) do compared with a league-average team (or player) faced with the same situation? To this end, Football Outsiders has analyzed the success or otherwise of every play since 1995, averaging together the results to provide a measure of a team's performance over a full season. In all that time, offense, defense and special teams, no team has been so close to the league average as the 2007 Cincinnati Bengals, who were just one part in a thousand removed from the standard for comparison.

Of course, a single figure like Cincinnati's 0.1% DVOA can hide many things, and while the team was average overall, some parts of the team were good—even very good—while others were very much not. As Bengals fans have come to expect, the passing offense excelled. T. J. Houshmandzadeh tied for the league lead in receptions. Chad Johnson finished third in receiving yards, behind Randy Moss and Reggie Wayne, who happened to play for the two most prolific offenses in the league. Carson Palmer threw for over 4,000 yards for the second year running.

Unfortunately, the pass defense was as bad as the pass offense was good. Sporting a pair of young cornerbacks still growing into their jobs, the Bengals needed a strong performance from the pass rush to prevent the secondary's inexperience from showing. They didn't get it. Cincinnati was a distant last in Adjusted Sack Rate and only middle-of-the-pack in terms of hurries, giving opposing quarterbacks the leisure time to pick apart the Bengals' defense.

Many call the NFL a copycat league, and Cincinnati is not the first franchise attempting to build around a high-powered passing game. The logic is sound. Since offense generally varies from year to year less than defense does, it makes sense to construct a high-scoring offense that will keep the team in contention year-in, year-out. Eventually, the defense will have a strong year, and the team will get a good shot to win the Super Bowl. This template was constructed by Bill Polian, whose Bills and Colts squads lit up the league and made the playoffs regularly, with the Colts eventually winning the title two years ago.

The core of Polian's method is to locate a franchise quarterback and then concentrate the team's resources in the areas most important to his performance: pass protection and receivers. The Bengals definitely are following this part of the playbook. Indianapolis had the good fortune to be picking first when Peyton Manning came out of college (and the wisdom not to draft Ryan Leaf); Cincinnati was likewise lucky to go 2-14 during Carson Palmer's senior year at USC. Though he doesn't have Manning's consistency (no one does), Palmer is clearly in the league's upper echelon of quarterbacks and capable of carrying the team with his right arm. The Bengals poured resources into pass protection, using first-round picks and lucrative extensions to acquire and then keep tackles Levi Jones and Willie Anderson. This year, they used the franchise tag to help retain highly regarded prospect Stacy Andrews, who was a regular starter for the first time in 2007.

BENGALS PROSPECTUS

2007 Record: 7-9

Pythagorean Wins: 7.9 (17th)

DVOA: -0.1% total (16th), 0.7% weighted (20th)

Offense: 11.0% DVOA (6th)

Defense: 10.3% DVOA (24th)

Special Teams: -0.7% DVOA (19th)

Variance: 8.4 % (2nd)

2007: Bengals enjoy the most average season of all time.

2008: Whither Ocho Cinco?

2008 Mean Projection: 6.8 wins

On the Clock (0-3): 2%

Loserville (4-6): 45%

Mediocrity (7-8): 34%

Playoff Contender (9-10): 16%

Super Bowl Contender (11+): 2%

Projected Average Opponent: 4.1% DVOA (8th in NFL)

2008 Bengals Schedule

Week	Opp.	Week	Opp.	Week	Opp.
1	at BAL	7	PIT	13	BAL
2	TEN	8	BYE	14	at IND
3	at NYG	9	JAC	15	WAS
4	CLE	10	at HOU	16	at CLE
5	at DAL	11	PHI	17	KC
6	at NYJ	12	at PIT (Thu.)		

There's been little news out of Cincinnati about progress on an extension for Andrews, which is confusing, because franchising a 26-year-old prospect with his best years ahead of him makes little sense if it isn't a prelude to a longer deal. Cincinnati might be waiting another year to be more confident in what it has in Andrews, but the delay is likely to make him significantly more expensive to sign if he's the elite tackle prospect the Bengals think they have. Or perhaps Cincinnati is just trying to ride out a particularly uncertain period in franchise history.

The cause of that uncertainty, of course, is the other position crucial to the Polian model of offense: wide receiver. Johnson has been a reliable 1,000-yard receiver since his sophomore year, and after Houshmandzadeh's breakout 2004, the Bengals had a pair of starting receivers to rival any in the league. With receivers, linemen, and quarterback all in place, Cincinnati's passing offense flourished, recording DVOA in excess of 20% each of the last three years. 2007 showed a slight downturn, and that along with a handful of highly visible mistakes was enough for some to pin the majority of the blame for the Bengals' 7-9 season on the passing game and its most visible member, Johnson.

Not surprisingly, he took this criticism poorly. It did not help that the blame was mostly unwarranted—Johnson ended the year sixth in DYAR, after leading the league in 2006. But even had Johnson been suffering from a loss of form, it is unlikely he would have been happy at being singled out. Considering his high-strung, adulation-driven personality, which has been visible enough during the past several years, his poor response to the criticism (much of it from the same sources as the previous unbounded praise) shouldn't shock anyone.

It isn't uncommon for a player or even a unit (such as Denver's offensive line) to feud with the media. If you're the 2007 Patriots, your entire team may end up fighting with the media. Properly managed by the head coach, these feuds create a siege mentality that can benefit a team. The Bengals, however, didn't even try to support their star wideout. Rumors of dust-ups with Marvin Lewis and Carson Palmer raged unchecked. Johnson felt abandoned, and being Chad Johnson, he said so. What began as a couple of misrun routes and the odd sideline argument—a common sight when teams lose close games—turned into a battle of wills between coach and player. Soon Johnson and agent Drew Rosenhaus were publicly linking him with other teams and Marvin Lewis was daring him to sit the year out. There seemed little concern that Cincinnati's offense depended on having Pro Bowl receivers for Palmer to throw to. By the time the Bengals rejected Washington's trade offer that packaged this year's 21st overall selection with a conditional 2009 pick no lower than the third round, common sense had long departed. Washington's offer would have been a good one for a motivated Johnson: Despite his ranking as sixth-best receiver in the league, a trade of two high draft picks for a 30-year-old is good value, and all the more so when he doesn't want to play for you next year.

Things got worse when Chris Henry, the backup plan in case of a Johnson holdout, went and got himself arrested for the sixth time. Cincinnati finally gave up on Henry's legal problems and cut the talented deep threat. Now Cincinnati, previously reliant on the passing game, looks forward to a season with just one receiver with 10 career starts to his name—T. J. Houshmandzadeh, who happens to be in the final year of his contract. (This is assuming that Johnson either eventually forces a trade or goes through with an extended holdout; at press time, the situation is unresolved.) Wisely, the Bengals took three receivers in the draft, but this strategy usually takes some time to pay off. Since 2000, second-round rookie receivers (such as Jerome Simpson) have averaged 27 catches for 355 yards. Third-round rookie receivers (such as Andre Caldwell) have averaged 16 catches for 207 yards. Cincinnati's aerial attack will probably be fine long term, but a step backward for 2008 looks likely.

The Bengals hope improvements to the ground game will make up for the question marks at wide receiver. Last year, injuries to workhorse tailback Rudi Johnson enabled backup Kenny Watson to emerge as an above-average starter in his own right. It's unlikely that Johnson can return to his former glories—he's 28, which is traditionally the age at which running backs begin to decline—but he and Watson will provide a solid one-two combination that gives the Bengals more options than they have had in the past. Third-stringer DeDe Dorsey, who racked up 183 yards on just 21 carries last year, might make a good third-down back, although that role could also go to former first-round pick Chris Perry, who is finally supposed to be healthy after a severely broken ankle cost him the end of 2006 and all of 2007. More continuity among the young offensive linemen should improve the blocking as well.

Cincinnati has definitely followed the offensive section of the Indianapolis template, but defense is another matter. Like the Colts, the Bengals hired a coach from a team with a highly respected defensive pedigree—Marvin Lewis from Baltimore. Indianapolis hired Tony Dungy to create a simple defense that could perform consistently despite a roster with continuous turnover because most of the team's resources were being spent elsewhere. Marvin Lewis and the Bengals have the continuous turnover down pat, but are still struggling with the performance part. Part of Lewis's problem is that the defensive concepts he learned in Pittsburgh and Baltimore are intrinsically ill suited to high roster turnover—both the Ravens and the Steelers franchises emphasize continuity. Another problem is that despite a defensive scheme that relies on opportunism more heavily than most other teams do, Cincinnati has no obvious defensive playmakers. It's clearly a fault that the Bengals themselves recognize, as their last four first-round picks have all been spent on defenders. USC's Keith Rivers joins cornerbacks Leon Hall and Johnathan Joseph in attempting to give Lewis some star talent to build his defense around. (The fourth player, linebacker David Pollack, retired after a tragic 2006 neck fracture.)

Neither Hall nor Joseph showed much sign in 2007 that they were ready to be that player, but since both have yet to reach their 25th birthday, they still have plenty of time to grow into this role. Bengals fans probably have many memories of watching one or the other of these cornerbacks be beaten for big plays and touchdowns, but pass defense is a function of both secondary and pass rush, and Cincinnati's pass rush was the worst in the league by a considerable margin. Under the circumstances, it's hard to assess the performance of the secondary and even harder to work out what to expect from it next year, given the natural progression expected from young players. Most top cornerbacks, such as Rashean Mathis and Nnamdi Asomugha, didn't blossom until their third or fourth season in the NFL.

The other problem on defense was the cavalcade of injuries at linebacker. The Bengals started with Odell Thurman suspended for the year for violating the league's substance-abuse policy. A preseason leg injury took out Rashad Jeanty for the first six weeks of the year, Ahmad Brooks and Lemar Marshall were lost for the season in Week 3, and Caleb Miller dropped out in Week 4. At that point, defensive end Robert Geathers and safety Chinedum Ndukwe were taking snaps at linebacker, and the Bengals grabbed Dhani Jones, who had been discarded by the Saints and Eagles, just to have enough healthy linebackers to take the field.

The rest of the defense had enough upheaval this offseason to match what happened to the linebackers during the season. Lewis fired coordinator Chuck Bresnahan and replaced him with former Cowboys defensive coordinator Mike Zimmer. The Bengals lost Justin Smith, Madieu Williams, and Landon Johnson in free agency and signed former Titans defensive end Antwan Odom. Thurman was reinstated (and then released in May for missing voluntary workouts), Brooks was moved to the outside, and Geathers prepared to return to playing defensive end full-time. Then the Bengals drafted Rivers and defensive tackle Pat Sims, both of whom will have a good chance to start as rookies.

With so much disruption, it is likely that Cincinnati's defense will get worse before it gets better. Wholesale change is probably a good thing in the long run, since things were clearly stagnating and the Bengals were wasting the potential of their offense. For this season, though, the new players will have to get used to, or reacquainted with, their teammates; the returning players will become accustomed to the new ones; and their new defensive coordinator's schemes—however similar to the old ones they might be—won't be the same. On offense, Carson Palmer will be introducing two new wideouts plus tight end Ben Utecht to the Bengals' passing schemes. Although Cincinnati has a good track record at evaluating receiver talent, even Chad Johnson took until his sophomore year to be highly productive. The AFC North faces the two best divisions in football in the fixture rotation, and the in-division opponents look strong as well. Add up all these uncertainties, and you get the dreaded phrase "rebuilding season."

Stuart Fraser

2007 Bengals Stats by Week

Wk	vs.	W-L	PF	PA	YDF	YDA	TO	Total	Off	Def	ST
1	BAL	W	27	20	236	314	+4	-3%	-6%	-37%	-34%
2	@CLE	L	45	51	531	554	-2	-15%	39%	44%	-10%
3	@SEA	L	21	24	412	340	-2	7%	19%	-1%	-12%
4	NE	L	13	34	283	404	-1	-8%	3%	13%	2%
5	BYE										
6	@KC	L	20	27	373	354	-1	-38%	-14%	24%	0%
7	NYJ	W	38	31	395	342	+1	1%	27%	23%	-2%
8	PIT	L	13	24	296	390	0	-10%	20%	35%	6%
9	@BUF	L	21	33	299	479	0	-9%	24%	49%	16%
10	@BAL	W	21	7	326	272	+6	35%	0%	-26%	9%
11	ARI	L	27	35	396	247	-5	-33%	-23%	20%	9%
12	TEN	W	35	6	426	305	+1	74%	58%	-19%	-3%
13	@PIT	L	10	24	249	285	+3	2%	0%	-10%	-8%
14	STL	W	19	10	370	241	0	30%	-9%	-21%	18%
15	@SF	L	13	20	313	337	0	-45%	19%	59%	-6%
16	CLE	W	19	14	270	380	+1	0%	-22%	-20%	1%
17	@MIA	W	38	25	393	336	0	-6%	21%	29%	2%

Trends and Splits

	Offense	Rank	Defense	Rank
Total DVOA	11.0%	6	10.3%	24
Unadjusted VOA	11.2%	6	2.5%	19
Weighted trend	8.1%	11	10.7%	28
Variance	5.0%	8	8.8%	22
Average opponent	0.5%	11	-3.1%	29
Passing	22.4%	6	24.1%	31
Rushing	-4.0%	15	-5.4%	16
First down	18.5%	5	8.7%	26
Second down	-4.1%	20	23.2%	30
Third down	20.3%	9	-7.0%	8
First half	16.6%	6	19.8%	29
Second half	5.8%	10	0.4%	16
Red Zone	11.5%	10	-15.4%	8
Late and close	1.5%	15	2.2%	19

Five-Year Performance

Year	W-L	Pyth Wins	Est Wins	PF	PA	TO	Total	Rank	Off	Rank	Def	Rank	ST	Rank
2003	8-8	7.0	7.6	346	384	+2	-5.7%	21	5.9%	10	12.7%	31	1.1%	15
2004	8-8	8.1	9.4	384	372	+4	11.5%	10	4.7%	11	-2.9%	14	3.9%	7
2005	11-5	9.7	10.3	421	350	+24	18.9%	9	19.6%	5	1.0%	20	0.4%	14
2006	8-8	9.1	8.6	373	331	+7	8.8%	11	14.6%	4	7.1%	25	1.3%	12
2007	7-9	7.9	8.5	380	385	+5	.0.1	16	11.0%	6	10.3%	24	-0.7%	19

Strategic Tendencies

	Run/Pass	Rank		Offense	Rank		Defense	Rank		Other		Rank
Runs, all plays	40%	20	3+ WR	65%	6	Rush 3	2.8%	25	2+ RB, Pct Runs	51%		26
Runs, first half	40%	20	4+ WR	9%	21	Rush 4	57.1%	24	1 RB/2 TE, Pct runs	38%		25
Runs, first down	48%	19	2+ TE	7%	32	Rush 5	25.1%	10	1 RB/3+ WR, pct runs	23%		19
Runs, second-long	39%	9	Single back	40%	32	Rush 6+	15.0%	4	CB1 on WR1	44%		17
Runs, power sit.	55%	26	Play action	9%	32	Rush 7+	3.5%	5	Go for it on 4th	0.72		26
Runs, behind 2H	29%	11	Max protect	9%	22	Sacks by LB	40.0%	10	Offensive Pace	30.4		12
Pass, ahead 2H	45%	17	Outside pocket	4%	31	Sacks by DB	20.0%	1	Defensive Pace	31.1		20

Never let it be said that Cincinnati offensive coordinator Bob Bratkowski is not a creature of habit. The Bengals ranked sixth in using three or more wideouts and 21st in using four or more wideouts for the second straight season. Cincinnati has now ranked 31st or 32nd in using two-tight-end sets or single-back sets for three straight seasons. Cincinnati also ranked last in using play-action fakes after ranking 31st a year ago. ✑ Despite using play fakes infrequently, the Bengals ranked sixth in DVOA on play-action passes. ✑ The Bengals had the league's best DVOA in four-wide sets but were one of four teams that never ran a draw from a four-wide set. ✑ Cincinnati converted third-and-10 or more yards into a first down (or a touchdown) a league-leading 35 percent. The league average was 22 percent. ✑ Only Detroit threw to tight ends less often than Cincinnati. ✑ Thirty percent of Cincinnati's passes were thrown to T. J. Houshmandzadeh. No other team threw more than 25 percent of its passes to the number-two receiver. New England (Wes Welker) ranked second. ✑ Houston and Seattle were the only teams to use the shotgun less often than the Bengals. ⬭ Cincinnati's defense allowed an average of just 3.7 yards after catch, second in the league behind Pittsburgh. Cleveland ranked sixth at 4.2 yards after catch, but not every AFC North defense excelled in this area; Baltimore allowed 5.5 yards after catch, which ranked 28th. ⬭ Cincinnati was one of only two defenses in the NFL whose opponents threw to the number-one receiver over 30 percent of the time. (St. Louis was the other.) On the other hand, only 11 percent of passes against the Bengals' defense were thrown to nonstarting wide receivers, the lowest percentage in the league.

Passing

Player	DYAR	DVOA	Plays	NtYds	Avg	YAC	C%	TD	Int
Carson Palmer	1215	20.1%	595	4075	6.8	4.1	65.3%	26	19

Rushing

Player	DYAR	DVOA	Plays	Yds	Avg	TD	Fum	Suc
Kenny Watson	162	13.0%	178	763	4.3	7	3	56%
Rudi Johnson	-71	-18.5%	170	497	2.9	3	3	39%
DeDe Dorsey	70	68.9%	21	183	8.7	0	0	62%
Jeremi Johnson	-2	-13.7%	7	25	3.6	0	0	14%
Carson Palmer	-3	-17.8%	7	25	3.6	0	8	—
Chad Johnson	24	32.8%	6	47	7.8	0	0	—
T. J. Houshmandzadeh	3	-25.9%	4	15	3.8	0	0	—

Receiving

Player	DYAR	DVOA	Plays	Ctch	Yds	Y/C	YAC	TD	C%
WR									
T. J. Houshmandzadeh	238	5.1%	170	113	1150	10.2	3.1	14	66%
Chad Johnson	305	10.9%	161	93	1441	15.5	3.2	9	58%
Chris Henry	56	5.9%	38	21	343	16.3	3.0	2	55%
Antonio Chatman	2	-11.9%	29	19	149	7.8	3.5	1	66%
Glenn Holt	46	9.3%	23	16	143	8.9	3.1	1	70%
Tab Perry*	-27	-75.3%	5	1	7	7.0	0.0	0	20%
TE									
Reggie Kelly	25	8.5%	27	20	211	10.6	2.5	0	74%
Daniel Coats	39	33.8%	16	12	122	10.2	4.2	0	75%
Ben Utecht	100	33.6%	37	31	364	11.7	5.3	1	84%
RB									
Kenny Watson	32	-4.7%	67	52	374	7.2	8.1	0	78%
Rudi Johnson	39	32.0%	16	13	110	8.5	9.0	1	81%
Jeremi Johnson	14	10.1%	7	6	32	5.3	3.3	1	86%
DeDe Dorsey	-5	-29.4%	6	4	19	4.8	7.5	0	67%

Offensive Line

Year	Yards	ALY	Rank	Power	Rank	10+ Yds	Rank	Stuff	Rank	Sack	ASR	Rank
2005	4.30	4.52	4	70%	8	14%	21	23%	8	21	3.9%	2
2006	3.97	4.43	10	72%	5	9%	29	25%	27	36	5.9%	12
2007	3.90	4.25	12	73%	5	10%	27	23%	16	17	3.2%	2

Year	LE	Rank	LT	Rank	Mid	Rank	RT	Rank	RE	Rank
2005	3.26	28	4.57	10	4.65	3	4.77	3	4.34	12
2006	4.19	16	4.44	13	4.34	18	5.29	1	3.89	18
2007	4.09	16	4.20	20	4.60	6	3.24	31	4.80	4

After using their franchise tag on the promising Stacy Andrews, the Bengals will have two of the 10 highest-paid offensive linemen in the league in 2008. Andrews had only three career starts before this year, but he played 14 games at both tackle slots and guard while filling in for absent players along the line. With both left tackle Levi Jones and right tackle Willie Anderson slowed by injuries, Andrews looked like the Bengals' best pass protector this year—and in time a very solid replacement for the 32-year-old Anderson. One might wonder why the Bengals are giving a huge single-year contract to a player at a position where they currently have two solid starters. It might indicate that Cincinnati lacks confidence in one or both tackles; Jones especially struggled on occasion, "leading" the Bengals with five blown blocks that led to sacks. That said, Cincinnati doesn't struggle in pass protection—even if some of the credit for their low Adjusted Sack Rate must be given to Carson Palmer. The Bengals are still above average if hurries rather than sacks are used as the measuring stick. But still, why not sign Andrews to a longer deal?

On the ground, the Bengals apparently haven't suffered much from the loss of left guard Eric Steinbach, losing a little performance at runs over left tackle but gaining it back up the gut. That reflects well on Steinbach's replacement, Andrew Whitworth. Whitworth was not only a positive contributor at guard but also slid out to left tackle without seeming out of place—even handling Jared Allen after the All-Pro defensive end had destroyed Levi Jones. Center Eric Ghiaciuc missed three early-season games with thumb and neck injuries and ended the year on injured reserve after a foot sprain in Week 16, but he'll be fine going forward. Veteran right guard Bobbie Williams started every game without attracting special notice, which is always good at a position that's mostly visible in failure.

Defensive Front Seven

Defensive Line	Age	Pos	Plays	TmPct	Rk	Stop	Dfts	Stop%	Rk	AvYd	Rk	Sack	Hit	Hur	Runs	RuStop	RuYd	Pass	PaStop	PaYd
Justin Smith*	29	DE	81	9.8%	3	51	14	63%	74	3.2	71	2.0	6	18	72	61%	3.4	9	78%	1.1
Domata Peko	24	DT	54	6.5%	14	42	9	78%	34	2.1	52	1.5	5	3	45	80%	2.2	9	67%	2.0
Michael Myers	32	DT	35	4.5%	45	27	8	77%	40	2.1	51	1.0	2	3	29	72%	2.3	6	100%	1.0
John Thornton	32	DT	34	4.7%	39	24	8	71%	58	2.4	55	1.0	2	3	28	75%	2.2	6	50%	3.2
Bryan Robinson*	34	DE	22	2.7%	—	19	9	86%	—	0.2	—	1.5	4	3	18	83%	1.1	4	100%	-3.8
Antwan Odom	27	DE	28	3.6%	74	25	15	89%	1	-1.3	1	8.0	14	19	12	83%	0.7	16	94%	-2.8

Linebackers	Age	Pos	Plays	TmPct	Rk	Stop	Dfts	Stop%	AvYd	Sack	Hit	Hur	Runs	RuStop	Rk	RuYd	Rk	Tgts	Suc%	Rk	APaYd	Rk
Landon Johnson*	27	MLB	110	13.3%	41	52	13	47%	5.4	1.0	3	4	63	59%	64	3.5	55	34	40%	73	7.3	72
Dhani Jones	30	OLB	89	12.3%	52	47	13	53%	4.5	1.0	1	2	46	57%	82	3.7	61	33	36%	83	6.4	56
Robert Geathers	25	OLB	51	6.2%	94	38	11	75%	1.8	4.0	11	19	39	74%	14	2.8	24	8	21%	—	10.1	—
Rashad Jeanty	25	OLB	34	6.6%	—	24	4	71%	3.6	0.0	0	1	23	83%	—	2.7	—	8	40%	—	5.7	—
Anthony Schlegel*	27	MLB	29	4.3%	—	17	6	59%	3.2	0.0	1	0	26	62%	—	2.7	—	4	55%	—	6.6	—

Year	Yards	ALY	Rank	Power	Rank	10+ Yds	Rank	Stuff	Rank	Sack	ASR	Rank
2005	4.46	4.56	29	64%	19	16%	13	22%	23	28	5.1%	30
2006	4.03	4.24	16	56%	7	16%	18	26%	10	35	6.1%	22
2007	4.49	4.21	20	54%	5	23%	29	22%	24	22	3.7%	32

Year	LE	Rank	LT	Rank	Mid	Rank	RT	Rank	RE	Rank
2005	5.59	32	4.47	23	4.53	28	4.13	18	4.34	19
2006	3.41	8	4.55	17	4.68	27	3.57	9	3.46	9
2007	3.26	7	4.86	27	4.03	12	5.00	29	4.31	20

All change! The Bengals have undertaken a near-complete rebuild of the front seven, hoping to reinvigorate a unit that couldn't get to the quarterback in 2007. Does that mean the Bengals had no pass rush at all? Not necessarily. According to our game charters, the Bengals hurried opposing quarterbacks on 13.5 percent of pass plays, which is higher than the NFL average. Justin Smith was tied for seventh in the league with 18 hurries. He's now gone to San Francisco and has been replaced by Antwan Odom, who was tied with John Abraham, DeMarcus Ware, and new teammate Robert Geathers for third in the league with 19 hurries. Odom was the best free agent available at defensive end, but how will he fare without Albert Haynesworth and Kyle Vanden Bosch to concentrate attention elsewhere? Instead, Odom and Geathers get to benefit from each other's presence. Geathers will start on the other side, returning to defensive end after he was pressed into emergency service as linebacker last year. Third-round rookie Pat Sims of Auburn will hope to crack the starting lineup at defensive tackle, which may not be too hard given the poor production from the current tackles.

Marvin Lewis raved about top pick Keith Rivers after rookie minicamp, and he's likely to start as weakside linebacker. Rivers's greatest strength is pass coverage—to the extent that he played some safety as well as linebacker at USC—but he's a solid tackler as well. After the Bengals' first offseason practices, Ahmad Brooks told Cincinnati-area beat reporters he'd been moved to strongside linebacker, a sign that the returning Odell Thurman would be playing in the middle. Then, right before *PFP 2008* went to press, the Bengals released Thurman, supposedly for missing voluntary workouts when he didn't return from Georgia immediately after his grandmother's funeral. If the idea of a player being released for missing so-called voluntary workouts sounds strange to you, you have something in common with the NFLPA. By the time you are reading this, Thurman may be pursuing a grievance against the Bengals for violating the Collective Bargaining Agreement. As for what the departure of Thurman means for the Bengals' starting linebackers, our guess is that Brooks will return to the middle with Rashad Jeanty remaining as the starter on the strong side. As of mid-May, the Bengals' website listed Dhani Jones as the starting middle linebacker, which is an excellent strategy if the linebacker that Cincinnati really wants is named Rey Maualuga or James Laurinitis.

Defensive Secondary

Secondary	Age	Pos	Plays	TmPct	Rk	Stop	Dfts	RuYd	Rk	RuStop	Rk	Tgts	Tgt%	Rk	Dist	Suc%	Rk	APaYd	Rk	PaYd	PD	Int
Madieu Williams*	27	FS	78	11.6%	18	35	12	7.8	60	53%	16	28	8%	30	12.5	45%	51	9.6	65	9.4	6	2
Dexter Jackson	31	SS	76	10.5%	29	33	13	6.1	37	56%	10	31	8%	28	12.2	44%	56	10.4	70	10.1	5	2
Leon Hall	23	CB	72	8.7%	48	26	14	5.9	35	36%	56	76	17%	51	10.7	31%	80	9.3	70	8.7	10	5
Johnathan Joseph	24	CB	72	9.3%	35	23	12	10.0	68	25%	74	95	23%	10	11.2	42%	70	7.6	46	7.4	12	4
Deltha O'Neal	31	CB	62	7.5%	62	21	10	9.6	67	71%	7	72	16%	56	11.4	48%	46	5.9	8	5.8	8	1
Chinedum Ndukwe	23	SS	42	5.8%	75	16	11	7.5	57	31%	68	22	6%	61	6.6	31%	81	7.4	44	7.1	6	3
Marvin White	24	FS	17	2.2%	—	8	3	12.9	—	43%	—	13	3%	—	11.9	53%	—	7.7	—	8.1	1	0

Year	Pass D Rank	vs. #1 WR	Rk	vs. #2 WR	Rk	vs. Other WR	Rk	vs. TE	Rk	vs. RB	Rk
2005	13	-23.8%	1	3.4%	24	-15.5%	8	23.3%	26	-38.0%	1
2006	27	12.1%	26	-15.3%	6	31.2%	30	-6.3%	13	23.2%	31
2007	31	20.8%	29	14.7%	24	-21.3%	7	9.8%	20	-9.5%	9

It was a season to chalk up to experience for Leon Hall and Johnathan Joseph, who between them allowed 77 first downs and touchdowns and 1,377 passing yards, one of the worst results in the league for a pair of starting corners. In their defense, those results are not unusual for rookie cornerbacks, who generally take three to four years to blossom. Joseph is entering his third year and Hall, his second, and the Bengals are hoping to see them both take a big step forward. Eighth-year veteran Deltha O'Neal will stick around as a reliable nickel back. Safety Madieu Williams left in free agency, which leaves the Bengals thin at that position, especially given that Dexter Jackson is now the wrong side of 30. In the words of one Football Outsiders game charter, Jackson now has two specialties: blitzing and getting beat deep. That's a reasonable assessment given that he had more sacks, hits, and hurries than Troy Polamalu or Adrian Wilson but gave up over 10 yards per pass. Chinedum Ndukwe is the immediate replacement for Williams and is growing into the job.

The Bengals drafted Appalachian State safety Corey Lynch in the sixth round, but he's likely to be more of a special teams contributor this season. Cincinnati's mostly young secondary remains more potential than production, but we may see the beginnings of an upturn this year—as long as Cincinnati doesn't release anyone for missing an optional meeting or coming home late from the grocery store or something.

Special Teams

Year	DVOA	Rank	FG/XP	Rank	Net Punt	Rank	Punt Ret	Rank	Net Kick	Rank	Kick Ret	Rank	Hidden	Rank
2005	0.4%	15	5.3	6	-4.9	24	-2.8	21	1.0	16	3.6	11	-10.6	30
2006	1.3%	12	2.2	11	9.7	5	-3.4	28	7.4	8	-8.0	28	2.4	13
2007	-0.7%	19	4.6	8	1.6	13	-6.0	26	-2.4	21	-1.8	20	4.6	10

Special teams were almost as average as the franchise as a whole. Kicker Shayne Graham is a reliable performer who so far has been more consistent on field goals than most of his kicker brethren. He's also good but never great on kickoffs. Punter Kyle Larson is basically average. Both were let down in 2007 by their coverage teams, which were significantly worse than in 2006. When the ball is coming the other way, the Bengals have some issues. They tried several kick returners before finally settling on Glenn Holt, who was steady if unspectacular; neither Antonio Chatman nor Skyler Green reached even that level of performance when returning punts.

COACHING STAFF

Marvin Lewis may be running out of time. Having raised expectations with a division title in 2005, the 8-8 and 7-9 seasons that followed were a letdown. Even those Bengals' fans who remember the long years of futility wonder whether this group of players could be doing better. Lewis is vulnerable to the same lines of criticism that took down his former boss, Brian Billick, in Baltimore. Lewis's team is weak in his area of expertise but strong on the other side of the ball, and his players show questionable discipline (though more off the field than on the field as was the case in Baltimore). Lewis switched defensive coordinators this offseason, replacing Chuck Bresnahan with Mike Zimmer. Zimmer was the defensive coordinator of the Atlanta Falcons, one of the few defenses distinguished by being worse than the Bengals in 2007. (To be fair, Cincinnati didn't have to deal with Bobby Petrino alienating the team's best corner and cutting its best defensive tackle.) He does have a history of success in Dallas, and the fairly significant roster turnover this year means less upheaval than normal in switching to a new coach.

Offensive coordinator Bob Bratkowski is largely responsible for the Bengals' pass-based offense. He is credited with having convinced the Bengals to take the Oregon State pair of Johnson and Houshmandzadeh in the 2001 draft, so he knows a thing or two about receiver talent. Bengals' fans will be hoping he can work the same magic on Jerome Simpson and Andre Caldwell.

Cleveland Browns

One week into the regular season, the Cleveland Browns looked dead in the water. The torpedo came in the form of the archrival Pittsburgh Steelers, who blasted the Browns 34-7 in a game that was if anything more lopsided than the score suggested. Charlie Frye, the opening-day starter by default, was so inept that he wasn't simply benched after the game; he was traded away to Seattle. It was the first time since the NFL/AFL merger in 1970 that a quarterback went from being a starter on one team to a backup on another in the space of a week. Fortunately, the Browns had the solution already on their roster, having traded up into the first round to nab Notre Dame star Brady Quinn. With the season in the balance, Romeo Crennel decided to hand the reins over to his quarterback of the future.

Wait a minute, is that really what happened? Actually, no. Quinn was a lengthy training-camp holdout and wasn't up to speed on the offense, so former Baltimore sixth-round pick Derek Anderson got the nod instead. Anderson promptly worked over the Cincinnati secondary to the tune of 328 yards and five touchdowns, started the rest of the year, led the Browns to 10 wins, and turned in the best performance of any Cleveland quarterback since Bernie Kosar. Quinn, the supposed franchise savior, threw eight passes on the season, all in the meaningless finale. You'd like to think that Quinn's story would act as a cautionary tale for the next first-round quarterback who

holds out on the advice of his agent, but it probably won't.

Quinn's homecoming was upstaged by one of the most unforeseeable breakout seasons in recent memory. Even with the benefit of hindsight, it's hard to know what to make of Derek Anderson. How could the same player who threw for more than 3,500 yards and 29 touchdowns not make the cut in Baltimore? How could he lose a training-camp battle to Charlie Frye? Is Anderson another of those late-round gems in the mold of Tom Brady or Matt Hasselbeck, a big, strong-armed quarterback who simply needed the right opportunity to show what he could do? Or was Anderson's performance primarily a product of circumstances—an emerging Braylon Edwards, a healthy Kellen Winslow, and an offensive line that was so good it could protect him with one hand while using the other to pull the pitchfork out of Jamal Lewis's back and prod him in the general direction of the end zone?

Can we learn anything from other quarterbacks who broke out in their third seasons after playing very little in their first two? The two players whose three-year similarity scores are closest to Anderson's are Ken O'Brien 1983-1985 and Aaron Brooks 1999-2001. No one else even comes close. When you just look at single-season comparisons, you get an eclectic list that somehow manages to include both Dan Marino's 1985 masterpiece and 1982 vintage Scott Brunner, with some

---

BROWNS PROSPECTUS

2007 Record: 10-6

Pythagorean Wins: 8.5 (14th)

DVOA: 6.2% total (13th), 15.0% weighted (7th)

Offense: 6.9% DVOA (11th)

Defense: 7.6% DVOA (22nd)

Special Teams: 6.9% DVOA (2nd)

Variance: 6.2 % (1st)

2007: The young quarterback leads Cleveland to a winning season—it just wasn't the young quarterback everyone expected.

2008: The one step back that comes after the two steps forward.

2008 Mean Projection: 6.3 wins

On the Clock (0-3): 8%

Loserville (4-6): 47%

Mediocrity (7-8): 31%

Playoff Contender (9-10): 13%

Super Bowl Contender (11+): 2%

Projected Average Opponent: 5.6% DVOA (4th in NFL)

2008 Browns Schedule

Week	Opp.	Week	Opp.	Week	Opp.
1	DAL	7	at WAS	13	IND
2	PIT	8	at JAC	14	at TEN
3	at BAL	9	BAL	15	at PHI (Mon.)
4	at CIN	10	DEN (Thu.)	16	CIN
5	BYE	11	at BUF (Mon.)	17	at PIT
6	NYG (Mon.)	12	HOU		

Jim Zorn and Jeff Blake thrown in for good measure. That's a long way of saying that Anderson could be a stud, could be a backup masquerading as a starter, or could be anything in between.

Bum Philips used to say that if you have two quarterbacks, you really don't have any. Bum was wrong on that one, as a quick perusal of the 1990 San Francisco 49ers roster can attest, but in the salary-cap era, it's safe to say that even if you have two quarterbacks, you won't for long, because you can only pay one of them. While it's not uncommon to sit a first-round quarterback pick anywhere up to a year, it's rare to see a first-rounder stuck on the bench any longer than that. The nightmare situation for general manager Phil Savage and Romeo Crennel would be something like what happened in San Diego when the Chargers engineered a draft-day deal for North Carolina State's Philip Rivers to replace Drew Brees. If Rivers had gotten to camp on time, he probably would have been the starter, but he held out (stop me if this sounds familiar), and by the time he was signed, Brees had a stranglehold on the starting job. The logjam meant that the Chargers eventually had to get rid of a Pro Bowl quarterback because they had too much money tied up in his replacement.

To keep that from happening, Cleveland signed Anderson to a three-year, $24 million contract with $14 million in guarantees—nearly twice the guaranteed money that Quinn signed for. In an offseason where Tony Romo and David Garrard were rewarded with six- and seven-year extensions in the neighborhood of $60 million on the basis of one or two productive seasons, Anderson was probably hoping for better. In fact, the deal may be nothing more than a one-year placeholder, as a looming $5 million roster bonus before the 2009 season means that the quarterback status will be reevaluated at that time. If Anderson stumbles, the team can cut him before the roster bonus is due and plug Quinn into the starting role. If Anderson plays well

again, he'll probably get a lengthier extension, and Quinn will become trade bait.

No matter who plays quarterback, they're going to have clean uniforms most Sundays, because the Browns have put together an elite offensive line for the first time since returning to the league. The line jumped from 31st to third in Adjusted Line Yards, their stuff rate improved from 28 percent to 20 percent, and the Adjusted Sack Rate more than halved, dropping from 9.1 percent to 4.2 percent. Part of the improvement in pass protection came from replacing the sack machine that is Charlie Frye with Derek Anderson, but much of the credit belongs to the front five.

Over the last eight years, no team juggled its linemen more than the Browns. In 2006 alone, Cleveland used nine starters on the line and turned over four of the five starters again prior to 2007. Our research suggests that the key to achieving quality line play is to maintain continuity and that it is often better to trot out the same five players game after game than to constantly tinker with the lineup in an attempt to achieve incremental improvements. Tinkering can also be the difference between incremental improvements and swapping out ground chuck for filet mignon, which is what the Browns did when they signed left guard Eric Steinbach away from Cincinnati and selected Wisconsin tackle Joe Thomas with the third pick in the draft. Thomas, if anything, outplayed his draft spot, starting all 16 games and earning a Pro Bowl berth in his rookie season. No team ran better behind left tackle than Cleveland, and Thomas was dominant in protection to the point that many defenders stopped trying late in games. With Thomas and Steinbach anchoring the left side, Kevin Shaffer could move over to the right side, with Ryan Tucker kicked inside to guard. And just like that, the merry-go-round that had plagued the team since its rebirth was over. Four of the Browns' five starters on the line played all 16 games at the same position.

The bad news is that continuity, once achieved, is difficult to sustain, and teams that go injury-free in one year tend to regress toward the mean in the next. The Browns may be going into 2008 intending to play the same offensive line, but that doesn't mean they'll be able to do so. And any injuries, particularly on the left side, could cause a significant backslide in effectiveness. Even if they stay healthy, recent history says that the line is likely to regress somewhat. Cleveland is one of eight teams since 2001 to see its Adjusted Line Yards figure increase by 0.8 or more. Every one of the other teams regressed somewhat the following season, with only two still ranking in the top 10 (Table 1).

Table 1. Top Year-to-Year Improvement in Adjusted Line Yards, 2001-2007

Team	Years	Y1 ALY	Rank	Y2 ALY	Rank	Change	Y3 ALY	Rank	Change
DEN	2002	4.11	11	5.06	1	0.96	4.37	9	-0.69
MIA	2002	3.48	30	4.42	7	0.94	3.74	28	-0.68
MIA	2005	3.41	32	4.33	11	0.92	4.22	20	-0.12
CLE	2007	3.70	31	4.62	3	0.92	--	--	--
PIT	2004	3.82	26	4.69	4	0.86	4.28	12	-0.40
SF	2006	3.63	29	4.48	7	0.85	4.28	11	-0.20
JAC	2006	3.83	25	4.66	2	0.84	4.14	17	-0.53
PHI	2006	3.79	27	4.62	3	0.83	4.53	4	-0.09

The threat of declining performance extends beyond the offensive line and into the skill positions as well, as the Browns milked career years out of a number of players with significant injury or reliability issues. Jamal Lewis put together a 1,300-yard season by pointing himself at the backs of his linemen and running straight into them, but he has logged a ton of carries in his career and is due for a decline. Joe Jurevicius, at 34, is still recovering from one of those staph infections that they hand out like party favors in Cleveland's training room, though he should be recovered in time for training camp. The plan is to reduce the wear on Jurevicius by moving him into the slot, but Donté Stallworth, who was signed to take over the number two role, comes with both a bad set of hands and a lengthy injury history of his own. The two centerpieces of the Browns' passing game are Edwards and Winslow, and while no one questions their talent, both players suffered injury-plagued campaigns in 2005 and 2006 before playing full seasons in 2007, and it is unlikely that they'll each play 16 games again this year.

If the offense regresses, Crennel will be forced to lean on his defense, a unit that wasn't very good last year. The defensive linemen struggled to hold up at the point of attack unless they knew exactly what was coming—they were best in the league in power situations, but 30th overall in Adjusted Line Yards. Quality defensive tackles who fit the 3-4 defense have become something of a rarity in the college ranks, and with no attractive draft options, Phil Savage decided to take advantage of a brisk trade market by double-dipping. He began by sending a second-round pick to Green Bay in exchange for franchised tackle Corey Williams. Williams blossomed last year in the Packers' gap control scheme, and

he injects some much needed youth into the Browns' front line. Savage then took advantage when a potential deal between Detroit and division-rival Cincinnati for disgruntled tackle Shaun Rogers fell through; Savage hurriedly put together a package of cornerback Leigh Bodden and a third-round pick to bring Rogers to Cleveland. Rogers has the body to excel at nose tackle, and the hope is he'll play more like the Rogers of 2005, who single-handedly made Detroit's interior run defense one of the best in football, and less like the Rogers of last season, who mailed in the last eight games so egregiously that the Lions finished dead last in the league against runs up the middle.

The cost of attaining Rogers was steep. Not only did Savage have to give away the team's last remaining first-day pick, but he also had to use Bodden to sweeten the pot. Bodden is one of the most underrated players in football and a perennial Football Outsiders favorite, although he has recurring injury problems and did not play up to his standards in 2007. If Savage detected the beginning of a decline, he was wise to pull the trigger; however, if Bodden returns to form, and if Rogers disappoints, the deal could look ugly. With Bodden gone, second-year man Eric Wright will assume the number one corner role. Wright has rare skills and helped the Browns rank sixth in the league at defending number two wide receivers, so there is reason to think that he can be effective at taking away opponents' primary receivers. Still, the depth in the secondary is lacking. If the defense is going to improve against the pass, the responsibility will fall heavily on the front seven to generate pass rush, something they were unable to do with much regularity last year.

The most optimistic scenario is that the offensive line maintains continuity, the receivers stay healthy, Derek Anderson proves he was no fluke, and the sudden infusion of 700 pounds of beef allows Crennel to scheme the defense into at least an average unit. If all that happens, you can pencil the Browns in as AFC North champions. More likely, Anderson comes back to earth a little bit, the offense takes a step back, and the defense manages only incremental improvement. The Browns are still headed in the right direction, but after the promise of last season, 2008 might not feel like progress at all.

Sean McCormick

2007 Browns Stats by Week

Wk	vs.	W-L	PF	PA	YDF	YDA	TO	Total	Off	Def	ST
1	PIT	L	7	34	221	365	-4	-66%	-54%	6%	-5%
2	CIN	W	51	45	554	531	+2	20%	43%	35%	12%
3	@OAK	L	24	26	312	396	0	-2%	-7%	17%	22%
4	BAL	W	27	13	303	418	+1	-8%	10%	30%	13%
5	@NE	L	17	34	353	412	-4	-12%	-17%	-5%	0%
6	MIA	W	41	31	384	356	+1	23%	39%	21%	5%
7	BYE										
8	@STL	W	27	20	368	393	+1	18%	41%	34%	11%
9	SEA	W	33	30	428	423	+1	-2%	28%	12%	-18%
10	@PIT	L	28	31	163	401	0	38%	2%	-6%	31%
11	@BAL	W	33	30	380	368	+2	32%	12%	0%	21%
12	HOU	W	27	17	397	314	+2	12%	13%	1%	-1%
13	@ARI	L	21	27	379	302	-3	2%	1%	0%	1%
14	@NYJ	W	24	18	337	387	+1	29%	18%	-6%	5%
15	BUF	W	8	0	304	232	0	16%	10%	-10%	-3%
16	@CIN	L	14	19	380	270	-1	-1%	-23%	-25%	-3%
17	SF	W	20	7	358	185	-1	29%	0%	-3%	26%

Trends and Splits

	Offense	Rank	Defense	Rank
Total DVOA	6.9%	11	7.6%	22
Unadjusted VOA	8.5%	10	5.1%	22
Weighted Trend	9.1%	9	1.0%	19
Variance	6.4%	15	3.0%	2
Average Opponent	3.1%	28	-1.8%	26
Passing	10.5%	13	16.1%	24
Rushing	2.8%	10	-2.1%	20
First Down	-1.0%	15	-0.8%	17
Second Down	10.3%	10	20.2%	29
Third Down	17.9%	10	4.3%	18
First Half	-5.4%	21	1.4%	17
Second Half	19.9%	5	13.1%	28
Red Zone	10.6%	12	-13.7%	10
Late and Close	26.6%	4	9.8%	26

Five-Year Performance

Year	W-L	Pyth Wins	Est Wins	PF	PA	TO	Total	Rank	Off	Rank	Def	Rank	ST	Rank
2003	5-11	5.8	6.6	254	322	-11	-9.8%	23	-12.6%	25	-2.7%	1	0.1%	20
2004	4-12	4.9	5.5	276	390	-12	-19.0%	27	12.5%	27	8.4%	23	1.9%	12
2005	6-10	5.6	6.3	232	301	-7	-17.1%	24	-13.5%	26	5.4%	24	1.7%	8
2006	4-12	4.4	4.8	238	356	-15	-21.3%	30	-18.5%	31	5.0%	21	2.3%	10
2007	10-6	8.5	8.9	402	382	-2	6.2%	13	6.9%	11	7.6%	22	6.9%	2

Strategic Tendencies

Run/Pass		Rank	Offense		Rank	Defense		Rank	Other			Rank
Runs, all plays	42%	14	3+ WR	39%	30	Rush 3	10.7%	6	2+ RB, Pct Runs	56%		17
Runs, first half	41%	16	4+ WR	10%	18	Rush 4	57.8%	23	1 RB/2 TE, Pct Runs	53%		11
Runs, first down	52%	13	2+ TE	28%	12	Rush 5	23.0%	14	1 RB/3+ WR, Pct Runs	12%		32
Runs, second-long	35%	16	Single back	48%	27	Rush 6+	8.6%	15	CB1 on WR1	51%		8
Runs, power sit.	63%	19	Play action	18%	16	Rush 7+	1.1%	20	Go for it on 4th	1.28		11
Runs, behind 2H	24%	27	Max protect	5%	32	Sacks by LB	66.7%	4	Offensive Pace	30.8		15
Pass, ahead 2H	42%	21	Outside pocket	7%	28	Sacks by DB	5.6%	18	Defensive Pace	30.9		18

Cleveland led the league in DVOA on passes to the left side of the field but ranked 31st on passes to the right side and 29th on passes up the middle (although they had a good DVOA on deep passes up the middle). ⌀ The Browns rarely threw a screen pass, ranking 30th in the league in frequency of screens. They threw only one screen pass on first down all season, and only three on third down. ⌀ When Cleveland lined up with only one wide receiver, they ran the ball more than three-quarters of the time, but when they threw, they threw most often to Kellen Winslow. ⌀ Of course, Winslow was the most targeted receiver on the team overall. All those throws to the tight end have to come from somewhere, and the Browns ranked last in the league in the percentage of throws that went to nonstarting wide receivers. ⌀ Only Seattle's offense had a lower percentage of its passes defensed by the opposition. ⌀ Cleveland's opponents used four or more wide receivers on 16 percent of plays, ranking the Browns' defense third behind Jacksonville and Pittsburgh. One reason why: It worked. Cleveland ranked 28th in DVOA against four or five wideouts. ⌀ The front seven ranked fourth in passes tipped at the line of scrimmage. ⌀ Cleveland was one of two defenses whose opponents threw up the middle less than 20 percent of the time. (Seattle was the other.) ⌀ Only Miami faced fewer screens than the Browns.

Passing

Player	DYAR	DVOA	Plays	NtYds	Avg	YAC	C%	TD	Int
Derek Anderson	797	12.3%	539	3727	6.9	5.0	57.5%	29	19
Charlie Frye*	-105	-123.0%	15	3	0.2	2.8	40.0%	0	1
Brady Quinn	7	3.2%	8	45	5.6	6.0	37.5%	0	0

Rushing

Player	DYAR	DVOA	Plays	Yds	Avg	TD	Fum	Suc
Jamal Lewis	125	1.5%	298	1304	4.4	9	4	45%
Jason Wright	37	5.6%	60	277	4.6	1	1	50%
Jerome Harrison	45	40.4%	23	142	6.2	0	0	74%
Derek Anderson	50	34.2%	17	83	4.9	3	4	—
Lawrence Vickers	15	5.5%	15	43	2.9	0	0	73%
Josh Cribbs	25	25.9%	8	50	6.3	0	0	—

Receiving

Player	DYAR	DVOA	Plays	Ctch	Yds	Y/C	YAC	TD	C%
WR									
Braylon Edwards	189	3.3%	153	80	1289	16.1	4.0	16	52%
Joe Jurevicius	112	4.6%	81	50	614	12.3	4.7	4	62%
Tim Carter	-19	-23.7%	22	8	117	14.6	2.4	2	36%
Josh Cribbs	-10	-32.6%	6	4	48	12.0	9.5	0	67%
Donté Stallworth	150	12.2%	74	46	697	15.2	6.8	3	62%
TE									
Kellen Winslow	75	0.5%	148	82	1111	13.5	4.4	5	55%
Steve Heiden	-35	-34.1%	21	12	104	8.7	2.5	0	57%
RB									
Jamal Lewis	99	33.3%	39	30	248	8.3	7.8	2	77%
Jason Wright	63	16.5%	37	24	233	9.7	7.7	0	65%
Lawrence Vickers	25	2.3%	24	13	91	7.0	5.6	2	54%

Offensive Line

Year	Yards	ALY	Rank	Power	Rank	10+ Yds	Rank	Stuff	Rank	Sack	ASR	Rank
2005	3.86	3.88	21	48%	31	17%	16	19%	4	45	8.0%	24
2006	3.29	3.70	31	74%	3	7%	31	28%	31	54	9.1%	27
2007	4.46	4.62	3	64%	15	17%	15	20%	3	19	4.2%	5

Year	LE	Rank	LT	Rank	Mid	Rank	RT	Rank	RE	Rank
2005	3.05	29	4.18	19	3.87	23	4.12	16	4.13	14
2006	0.06	32	4.27	18	3.54	32	4.26	13	3.59	23
2007	6.10	1	5.14	3	4.35	8	4.73	3	5.04	2

For the first time since the franchise returned to Cleveland, the Browns want to bring back the same offensive line. According to our game charters, no team had fewer blown blocks that led to sacks. That's a major contrast with 2006, when the Browns ranked 26th in the league. The Browns surrendered only 19 sacks on the season, and five of those came in the first half of the opening game, when Charlie Frye impersonated a starting quarterback. The jewel of this group is left tackle Joe Thomas, who stepped out of the 2007 draft (or off a fishing boat, more precisely) and into the starting lineup as the anchor of the line. Adrian Peterson of the Vikings may have received all the attention, but Thomas was the real rookie of the year. He'll have to settle for being named Rookie of the Month in November and being selected to the first of what figures to be many Pro Bowls. Joining Thomas as a Pro Bowl alternate was guard Eric Steinbach, who did not disappoint after signing a seven-year, $49 million contract in free agency. Between the two, the Browns are set on the left side for years to come.

The right side features two displaced tackles, as Kevin Shaffer moved over from the left side and Ryan Tucker moved inside to guard. Both moves clicked. Shaffer, who is six foot five and 320 pounds, proved to be a mauling-run blocker, and the Browns were in the top three in the league for Adjusted Line Yards on runs off right tackle and right end. Tucker was suspended for the first four games of the season after he tested positive for steroids, but once he returned he quickly beat out Seth McKinney for the starting job. Tucker may have to fight for his spot again this season, because the team signed Rex Hadnot to a two-year, $7 million deal. Hadnot had the distinction of being one of the few functioning parts on Miami's line, and he has the flexibility to play both guard and center. He won't be competing for the starting center spot because the Browns have committed to Hank Fraley, who has started every game for the past two seasons. Fraley signed a four-year extension before the start of last season, and although he isn't the kind of elite player the Browns thought they were getting after landing LeCharles Bentley in free agency, he does have two working knees. Speaking of Bentley, the star-crossed Cleveland native is expected to finally be ready to play after four separate operations to repair the knee he injured on the very first play of training camp in 2006 (not to mention the staph infections that followed). For now, Bentley is fighting for a roster spot, but he could quickly climb the depth chart if he is truly healthy.

Defensive Front Seven

Defensive Line	Age	Pos	Plays	TmPct	Rk	Stop	Dfts	Stop%	Rk	AvYd	Rk	Sack	Hit	Hur	Runs	RuStop	RuYd	Pass	PaStop	PaYd
Shaun Smith	27	DT	64	8.1%	4	48	7	75%	48	2.1	53	2.0	2	5	59	73%	2.7	5	100%	-4.0
Robaire Smith	31	DE	58	6.9%	26	49	11	84%	8	2.0	47	4.0	3	5	48	85%	2.2	10	80%	0.9
Orpheus Roye*	35	DE	37	5.4%	50	30	3	81%	25	3.1	69	0.5	1	2	33	82%	2.9	4	75%	4.3
Ethan Kelley	28	DT	24	3.5%	63	19	2	79%	29	3.3	65	1.0	2	3	21	86%	2.9	3	33%	6.7
Simon Fraser*	25	DE	16	1.9%	—	11	5	69%	—	4.1	—	0.0	0	0	14	64%	4.1	2	100%	4.0
Shaun Rogers	29	DT	45	5.2%	33	37	15	82%	22	-0.5	1	7.0	12	14	31	77%	1.8	14	93%	-5.5
Corey Williams	28	DT	35	4.5%	47	29	14	83%	19	1.3	18	7.0	7	3	25	80%	2.2	10	90%	-0.9

Linebackers	Age	Pos	Plays	TmPct	Rk	Stop	Dfts	Stop%	AvYd	Sack	Hit	Hur	Runs	RuStop	Rk	RuYd	Rk	Tgts	Suc%	Rk	APaYd	Rk
D'Qwell Jackson	25	ILB	105	14.2%	27	55	15	52%	5.5	1.0	0	2	72	58%	67	4.3	89	33	41%	71	6.8	67
Leon Williams	25	ILB	83	9.8%	69	42	11	51%	5.2	4.0	1	3	45	60%	59	3.1	36	36	36%	84	9.7	89
Andra Davis	30	ILB	70	8.3%	82	46	14	66%	3.4	0.0	2	5	55	76%	10	2.1	6	14	43%	—	7.1	—
Kamerion Wimbley	25	OLB	51	6.0%	96	29	11	57%	3.5	5.0	14	17	36	56%	86	3.1	38	8	24%	—	8.6	—
Willie McGinest	37	OLB	36	5.2%	—	26	8	72%	2.2	3.0	1	8	22	68%	—	2.9	—	10	60%	—	6.4	—
Antwan Peek	29	OLB	24	3.2%	—	18	9	75%	2.0	4.0	7	10	11	64%	—	3.9	—	7	65%	—	5.9	—
Chaun Thompson*	28	OLB	15	1.8%	—	9	7	60%	2.1	1.0	1	2	10	40%	—	4.1	—	2	28%	—	7.3	—

Year	Yards	ALY	Rank	Power	Rank	10+ Yds	Rank	Stuff	Rank	Sack	ASR	Rank
2005	4.40	4.48	28	70%	25	16%	15	21%	28	23	5.5%	28
2006	4.73	4.71	27	58%	9	20%	26	21%	24	28	5.1%	30
2007	4.38	4.51	30	48%	1	15%	9	22%	21	28	4.8%	29

Year	LE	Rank	LT	Rank	Mid	Rank	RT	Rank	RE	Rank
2005	3.80	13	4.92	30	4.65	31	3.52	3	4.87	27
2006	5.00	26	5.03	27	4.60	22	4.54	22	5.48	32
2007	4.16	18	5.13	29	4.39	24	4.46	22	4.82	27

There was no doubt that Phil Savage would try to upgrade the defensive line in the offseason; the only question was how effectively he could do so. The answer turned out to be "very effectively" because half a dozen general managers with quality defensive tackles surprisingly decided to put them up for sale. The key acquisition is Shaun Rogers, who has the size and strength to be a dominant nose tackle in a 3-4 front. Rogers very nearly had more sacks last year than the entire Browns' line put together, but in this scheme he's going to be asked to occupy blockers and free up the linebackers to make plays. Rogers was on his way to Cincinnati, but when the deal fell through, Savage jumped in and offered a better package, thus keeping the two-time Pro Bowler away from a division rival. (That's a net difference of 680 pounds in the Battle of Ohio, for those keeping track.) Rogers will combine with Robaire Smith and ex-Packer Corey Williams to give the team a much stronger, younger, and more athletic line than last year. Sixth-round pick Ahatyba Rubin gets this year's Babtunde Oshinowo Award as the defensive tackle prospect with the complicated name who slipped to Cleveland in the draft. The Browns hope he's better than Oshinowo was.

Second-year outside linebacker Kamerion Wimbley found out how hard it can be to fight through double and triple teams, as offensive coordinators made sure that someone else would beat them. Although Wimbley registered only five sacks after notching 11 his rookie season, he was still fighting his way to the quarterback, as evidenced by his excellent hit and hurry numbers. With the new defensive linemen soaking up blockers in front of him, Wimbley could be poised for another double-digit sack total. On the other side, Willie McGinest would appear to be well past his due date, but he posted a respectable 72 percent Stop Rate while splitting snaps with Antwan Peek and Chaun Thompson. In May, McGinest announced that he would retire after the upcoming season.

D'Qwell Jackson made too many tackles five yards down the field, which is one reason why the Browns traded up in the fourth round for UNLV thumper Beau Bell. Bell has the kind of thick frame that Romeo Crennel relishes in an inside linebacker, and he has a real chance to contribute on first and second downs. Beau could be a terror against the run when teamed with Andra Davis, who was one of the top run-stopping linebackers in the league for the second straight year.

Defensive Secondary

Secondary	Age	Pos	Plays	TmPct	Rk	Stop	Dfts	RuYd	Rk	RuStop	Rk	Tgts	Tgt%	Rk	Dist	Suc%	Rk	APaYd	Rk	PaYd	PD	Int
Leigh Bodden*	27	CB	106	12.5%	5	42	22	7.9	53	35%	61	101	21%	23	11.1	54%	22	7.3	40	7.1	16	6
Sean Jones	26	SS	106	12.5%	9	45	21	7.0	55	42%	45	40	8%	24	13.2	47%	46	8.1	48	7.9	9	5
Eric Wright	23	CB	82	11.1%	16	34	14	7.3	49	52%	30	88	20%	24	11.4	51%	38	7.4	42	7.1	13	1
Brodney Pool	24	FS	64	7.6%	65	22	11	8.5	70	34%	58	21	4%	77	13.2	43%	62	9.2	62	9.1	5	2
Daven Holly	26	CB	55	6.9%	67	19	7	4.0	9	75%	5	58	13%	74	11.9	42%	69	7.4	43	7.2	8	0
Brandon McDonald	23	CB	23	2.7%	—	14	9	11.0	—	0%	—	32	7%	—	13.5	67%	—	5.8	—	5.6	8	2
Ralph Brown	30	CB	19	2.2%	—	6	4	7.5	—	0%	—	30	6%	—	9.5	54%	—	6.2	—	5.8	1	1

Year	Pass D Rank	vs. #1 WR	Rk	vs. #2 WR	Rk	vs.Other WR	Rk	vs.TE	Rk	vs.RB	Rk
2005	23	0.5%	12	-28.0%	4	49.5%	32	-18.6%	6	9.3%	24
2006	16	-15.7%	7	-4.2%	11	-2.5%	20	-25.1%	4	-16.1%	11
2007	24	1.0%	17	-16.8%	6	15.3%	29	19.4%	26	-8.8%	10

We've been high on Leigh Bodden for years, and it's nice to see that other teams recognized his ability enough to want to trade for him, even though he had an injury-riddled 2007. The Browns were willing to part with Bodden because they have a talented pair of young corners, Eric Wright and Brandon McDonald. Wright, the UNLV man with the silky-smooth backpedal, is the heir apparent to Bodden's throne. He was drafted with the idea of being a shutdown corner, and Cleveland's DVOA against number-two receivers suggests that he's on his way. McDonald split his time with third-year man Daven Holly in nickel-and-dime situations, and they'll compete to be the other starter in 2008. McDonald should have the clear edge because he gave up fewer yards per pass and sported a higher success rate than anyone in the secondary (albeit with a small sample size). Oft-injured veteran Gary Baxter re-signed for a one-year deal, but it's doubtful he has much left in the tank.

Sean Jones was one of the busiest safeties in the league according to our game charters, participating in 106 plays, but don't let his five interceptions fool you—he wasn't that effective in coverage. Where Jones excels is down in the box, and he proved it with game-clinching fourth-down stops in back-to-back weeks against the Rams and Seahawks. Coverage is supposed to be free safety Brodney Poole's forte, but his pass defense numbers were mediocre across the board. Depth comes from two free agents signed a year ago: former 49ers starter Mike Adams and special teams standout Nick Sorenson.

Special Teams

Year	DVOA	Rank	FG/XP	Rank	Net Punt	Rank	Punt Ret	Rank	Net Kick	Rank	Kick Ret	Rank	Hidden	Rank
2005	1.7%	8	3.7	10	-6.2	26	7.9	3	2.6	14	2.3	14	5.0	10
2006	2.3%	10	-5.2	27	6.9	8	2.2	9	-0.2	20	9.7	4	4.2	10
2007	6.9%	2	-1.1	22	-5.5	24	9.2	4	6.6	6	31.2	1	-3.8	22

Joshua Cribbs went to the Pro Bowl after averaging a whopping 30.7 yards per kickoff return—and 13.5 yards per punt return, with three touchdowns. Our methods say Cribbs, not Devin Hester, was the most valuable kickoff returner in the league last year. (Hester was superior to Cribbs on punts.) By year's end, some teams were even starting to squib the ball to Cribbs, just like they did all year with Hester.

Phil Dawson's bang-it-off-the-crossbar-but-good 51-yard field goal against the Ravens was one of the most memorable plays of the year, but otherwise Dawson's season was ordinary. The Browns had good value on net kickoffs thanks to strong coverage. The coverage was not as good on punts, and Cleveland had 25 penalties on kickoffs or punts, making it third in the league behind Arizona and Atlanta. Poor coverage was only half the reason why the Browns ranked 24th in net punt value. Punter Dave Zastudil also had an injury-plagued and inconsistent season. Zastudil is a master at dropping the ball inside the 20, but he managed the trick only 14 times last year after 28 successful pins in 2006.

COACHING STAFF

What a difference a year makes. In January, Romeo Crennel officially climbed down off the hot seat and signed a two-year extension worth $4 million that will keep him in Cleveland through 2011. He tinkered with his staff, promoting Mel Tucker to the defensive coordinator spot after three seasons serving as the Browns' defensive backs coach. Tucker's job is to restore some of the confidence that was lost under previous coordinator Todd Grantham, who was fired after a minirevolt from players and assistant coaches. Grantham repeatedly refused to listen to input from his players, and there were whispers that he tried to get Crennel fired during the bye week so he could be named interim head coach. Offensive coordinator Rob Chudzinski put himself on the short list of head coach prospects after developing Derek Anderson and getting Braylon Edwards and Kellen Winslow performing up to their abilities. New special teams coach Ted Daisher spent the last two seasons in Oakland, but his prior work as special teams quality control coach in Philadelphia recommended him.

Dallas Cowboys

The Dallas Cowboys entered the 2007 season with a number of question marks against their name. The mainstream questioned whether they'd be able to recover from a crushing playoff loss, if Tony Romo would ever live down his failed hold, and what the effects would be of losing Bill Parcells. Our projection for the Cowboys in *Pro Football Prospectus 2007* was pessimistic as well. The real issue with Romo was a December slump, not a missed hold. The spectacular health record of the 2006 Cowboys was unlikely to repeat itself in 2007, and the extraordinary third-down performance of the offense was bound to come back to earth.

Instead, the Cowboys ducked all those concerns en route to an excellent season, albeit one spoiled by the archrival Giants in the NFC playoffs. Romo maintained his gaudy numbers of the previous season while seeing a slight rise in his DVOA. The effects of losing Bill Parcells were overblown by the media to begin with (Table 1), as the first three post-Parcells teams all finished within 1.5 wins of their expected performance.

The issue isn't that Parcells-led teams aren't lost after he leaves, but instead that the Tuna usually departs at a high-water mark. Simply put, there's not much higher to go than 13 wins. We calculated the average number of wins a team with a given number of wins in one season has in the next ("expected wins") and compared it to the number of wins that teams had in the year after Parcells departed and found that it was nothing out of

---

COWBOYS PROSPECTUS

2007 Record: 13-3

Pythagorean Wins: 11.0 (6th)

DVOA: 24.3% total (3rd), 17.4% weighted (6th)

Offense: 19.0% DVOA (4th)

Defense: -5.8% DVOA (10th)

Special Teams: -0.6% DVOA (18th)

Variance: 24.0 % (30th)

2007: The young guns take a huge step forward, only to collapse in a shocking playoff loss.

2008: Terrell Owens and Pac-Man Jones in the same locker room. What could go wrong?

2008 Mean Projection: 8.1 wins

On the Clock (0-3): 0%

Loserville (4-6): 22%

Mediocrity (7-8): 36%

Playoff Contender (9-10): 30%

Super Bowl Contender (11+): 12%

Projected Average Opponent: 5.2% DVOA (5th in NFL)

---

the ordinary. The 2007 Cowboys were the first team in which a post-Parcells team's expected wins differed from their actual wins by two or more—and the Cowboys got better, not worse. In general, the Parcells effect is merely the Tuna leaving good teams when they're still good.

Our apprehensions about the Silver and Blue were based on probabilities, not regurgitated media hype, but the Cowboys handily defied the odds. On third downs in 2006, the Cowboys' offensive DVOA was second despite being only 13th on first down and 11th on second down. Instead of seeing their third-down performance regress, as most teams do, the Cowboys improved their first- and second-down performance to match third down. The 2007 Cowboys ranked third in the league on first downs, ninth on second downs, and sixth on third downs. That's a much more sustainable split and a positive indicator for the Cowboys in the future.

What was more surprising was the ability of the Cowboys to avoid the injury bug, a bite they've eluded since 2003. Over the past five years, the Cowboys have been the healthiest team in football by a significant margin (Table 2). The second-place team, Houston, is closer to 12th than it is to Dallas. (For more details on how we calculate injuries and how "adjusted value" works, check out "The Injury Effect.")

What's remarkable is that the Cowboys have managed to stay so healthy despite retaining only eight players throughout that timespan—one of whom,

Table 1. Winning After Tuna

Team	Last Parcells Year	Next Year	Expected Wins
1990-1991 Giants	13-3	8-8	9.5
1996-1997 Patriots	11-5	10-6	9.0
1999-2000 Jets	8-8	9-7	8.0
2006-2007 Cowboys	9-7	13-3	8.1

Table 2. Healthiest Teams by Adjusted Games Lost, All Players, 2003-2007

Team	2003	2004	2005	2006	2007	Average
DAL	1	3	8	1	5	3.6
HOU	7	1	2	6	25	8.2
PIT	4	11	9	24	2	10.0
BUF	2	4	11	4	32	10.6
DEN	13	10	1	10	22	11.2
WAS	23	6	20	3	4	11.2
NYJ	8	7	28	7	7	11.4
SEA	9	19	6	16	9	11.8

wideout Terry Glenn, lost almost all of 2007 due to a chronic knee injury. Glenn and nose tackle Jason Ferguson were the only two significant Cowboys to miss more than three weeks in 2007, and they were ably replaced by Patrick Crayton and Jay Ratliff, respectively, both mid-to late-round draft selections from the Parcells era.

The Cowboys' continued health raises several important questions. First, how are the Cowboys avoiding injuries? They have always been a bit ahead of the curve when it comes to health issues, but their focus for the past few seasons has been a shift from cardio and weight room skills to functional fitness. Squatting a truck and flipping tires looks good on TV, but no one asked what helped football players play football until strength and conditioning coach Jim Juraszak took a hard look at the tools and methods. Instead of the commonplace weight room and blocking sled, Juraszek's methods use everything from parachutes to medicine balls and trampolines. While this is becoming common, Juraszek was doing this a few years ago and his functional, preventative approach began paying off, leaving the Cowboys as a team of injury extremes. Dallas players suffer traumatic season-ending injuries or take one-game "vacations," but there are rarely extended three- and four-game stretches of missed time. A great medical staff also deserves some credit here.

Second, how can and do the Cowboys use this to their advantage? In a league in which teams will attempt to find an edge at any cost, the Cowboys have a huge swath of player real estate that's opened up to

them if they can shop in the damaged goods department and heal the product. A perfect example is right tackle Marc Colombo, a talented offensive lineman who missed 30 of his first 48 games after being drafted by the Bears in the first round of the 2002 draft. The Bears gave up on him early in the 2005 season; the Cowboys signed him and allowed him to slowly mend over the rest of that season. He has rewarded Dallas by answering the bell 32 consecutive times. That's the definition of freely available talent.

Picking up freely available talent matters only if you have some stars for them to play alongside, and the Cowboys have done a superb job of building a team to their specifications and hitting on their key draft picks. The standout player is outside linebacker DeMarcus Ware, who was arguably the best defensive player in the NFC last year. What makes Ware such a threat is his ability to rush the passer while maintaining his responsibilities against the run, an issue that the Dwight Freeney-style pass rushers of the league shirk.

The version of the 3-4 defense that Wade Phillips installed when he came over from San Diego places more emphasis on getting to the passer than the version that Bill Parcells and Mike Zimmer had used. This was borne out in the team's performance: The Cowboys' Adjusted Sack Rate rose from 6.5 percent in 2006 to 7.2 percent in 2007. Some of that increase has to do with the return of outside linebacker Greg Ellis to health (he was the lone Cowboy who missed significant time in 2006); Ellis had an impressive 12.5 sacks in only 13 games. Behind him is 2006 first-round pick Anthony Spencer, who could replace Ellis at the first sign of a slip.

The other benefit to Phillips's 3-4 being more aggressive in the pass rush is that it mitigates some concerns about the Cowboys' ability to cover. A huge disconnect exists between Pro Bowl voters, who put three Cowboys defensive backs in the Pro Bowl, and reality. This is most obvious in the case of strong safety Roy Williams, who has gone from star safety to sieve in two years.

2008 Cowboys Schedule

Week	Opp.	Week	Opp.	Week	Opp.
1	at CLE	7	at STL	13	SEA (Thurs.)
2	PHI (Mon.)	8	TB	14	at PIT
3	at GB	9	at NYG	15	NYG
4	WAS	10	BYE	16	BAL (Sat.)
5	CIN	11	at WAS	17	at PHI
6	at ARI	12	SF		

Williams is such a liability in coverage that teams coming in to face the Cowboys have specific plays designed to isolate Williams against whoever they can. And when we say "whoever," we really mean *anybody*. Sure, Brian Westbrook split out against Williams is an obvious mismatch that drew an immediate throw from Donovan McNabb upon snapping the ball, but the Eagles ran the same play with Brent Celek. Yes, third-string tight end Brent Celek. Williams's struggles are a huge reason why the Cowboys ranked 30th in the league in DVOA against tight ends last year. Although he is still a big hitter, Williams seemed hesitant last year in moving toward the line of scrimmage, fearful of the play-action pass and being forced to drop back.

One solution might be to make Williams an inside linebacker. He has great instincts, takes good routes to the ball, and has superb timing at getting to the line and fighting his way through trash quickly when called upon to blitz. Sure, he will still have to cover, but not as frequently nor as far downfield. He is probably too small at 230 pounds, but with 20 more pounds of bulk, Williams could be a valuable linebacker as opposed to a glorified mini-linebacker playing safety.

The rest of the secondary was much better, particularly free safety Ken Hamlin, who had to cover for Williams all those times he got lost. Terence Newman won't ever be an elite cornerback, but he's a very good one and has been for three years now; the hole comes on the other side of the secondary, where Anthony Henry was picked on throughout the season. Henry isn't awful; he's slightly above average. The Cowboys made an attempt to replace him in the offseason with Pac-Man Jones, who at this point is neither Shadow, Speedy, Bashful, nor Pokey. (Okay, maybe Pokey.) Jones was among the best cornerbacks in the league in 2006, but that was two years and a CW teenage serial-level of drama ago. Jones's talents remain somewhere, but your guess is as good as ours whether they'll ever see the light of day in Dallas. The team also added Mike Jenkins with their second first-round pick; the USF product will likely serve as a nickel corner in the slot his rookie year.

Much like the defense, the offense has lost only one marginal contributor: running back Julius Jones, whose Thanksgiving Day 2004 halo lasted approximately three seasons before Cowboys' fans insisted on getting more Marion Barber III. Barber got his first start of the season in the playoffs, a sign that the Cowboys' future at tailback was squarely in the hands of MB3.

The commonly held assumption among fans in explaining why Barber wasn't a full-time back was based on usage patterns or blocking, but in our observations that hasn't been the case. Barber's not a great blocker, but he's certainly a decent blocker with the strength to handle anyone who comes at him. He looked better than Jones, who seemed to get lost more in the backfield when locating rushers. The Cowboys split their usage more or less by series as opposed to by particular situations. Barber got 53 percent of the carries on first down and 54 percent on second down, but on third down he ran the ball 73 percent of the time that the Cowboys chose to do so. Even in 2006, when Jones carried the ball the majority of the time on first and second down, Barber got 38 of the 41 third-down carries. Expect Barber to hold onto the bulk of the third-down carries again this year.

Replacing Julius Jones is Arkansas tailback Felix Jones, chosen with Dallas's first-round pick. Warning signs surround Jones: He played as the lesser back in a two-back rotation in college, relied somewhat on a gimmick offense, and at 207 pounds his 4.47 in the Combine 40-yard dash yielded only a 103.7 Speed Score, below the 112-point average for a first-round pick. (Speed Score is introduced later in the book in "Five Seconds Can Be a Lifetime.") Although everyone agrees that Jones plays fast, a lot of questions remain about how he will do in the NFL. This year, Cowboys' fans shouldn't expect him to be more than an above-average kick returner and change-of-pace back.

The Cowboys success in 2008 depends on their continued ability to buck the odds. They will need to survive the spectacle that is a Terrell Owens contract year as well as the spectacle that surrounds Pac-Man Jones at all times. They have a hard schedule and play in a division where no team had a losing record last year. The offensive line—the second oldest in the league, with All-Pro left tackle Flozell Adams now 33 and only one starter below 30—has to stave off the effects of age. Most importantly, the Cowboys must hope that their core can remain historically healthy for another season.

With nearly the entire starting lineup back, it seems absurd to suggest that the Cowboys may not be Super Bowl contenders again. The problem is that if the Dallas injury report ceases to be much smaller than the others in the league, the entire starting lineup *won't* be back. An injury to Romo, Owens, Adams, Ware, or Newman could turn the Cowboys overnight from a contender into a flawed team with a huge hole, and that's reflected in our pessimistic projection. It will take another season with an empty trainer's room for Dallas to live up to the standard of 2007.

Bill Barnwell

2007 Cowboys Stats by Week

Wk	vs.	W-L	PF	PA	YDF	YDA	TO	Total	Off	Def	ST
1	NYG	W	45	35	478	438	-1	58%	89%	36%	4%
2	@MIA	W	37	20	352	334	+5	24%	9%	-8%	7%
3	@CHI	W	34	10	431	239	+3	72%	46%	-25%	1%
4	STL	W	35	7	502	187	0	48%	48%	-18%	-18%
5	@BUF	W	25	24	385	229	-5	-12%	-31%	-27%	-8%
6	NE	L	27	48	285	448	0	47%	23%	-18%	6%
7	MIN	W	24	14	381	196	-1	40%	16%	-22%	2%
8	BYE										
9	@PHI	W	38	17	434	316	+2	92%	64%	-22%	6%
10	@NYG	W	31	20	323	300	+1	21%	25%	5%	1%
11	WAS	W	28	23	362	423	+1	19%	43%	12%	-11%
12	NYJ	W	34	3	344	180	+1	56%	14%	-38%	4%
13	GB	W	37	27	414	357	+1	92%	64%	-15%	14%
14	@DET	W	28	27	368	390	-1	-11%	14%	24%	-2%
15	PHI	L	6	10	240	315	-2	-63%	-75%	-7%	4%
16	@CAR	W	20	13	405	216	0	7%	16%	-4%	-13%
17	@WAS	L	6	27	147	354	+1	-78%	-66%	7%	-5%
18	BYE										
19	NYG	L	17	21	336	230	-1	-18%	20%	34%	-4%

Trends and Splits

	Offense	Rank	Defense	Rank
Total DVOA	19.0%	4	-5.8%	10
Unadjusted VOA	22.7%	3	-5.4%	9
Weighted trend	12.7%	6	-5.1%	10
Variance	19.9%	32	4.0%	4
Average opponent	0.7%	16	-0.2%	21
Passing	29.9%	4	-6.0%	9
Rushing	5.3%	8	-5.6%	15
First down	19.6%	3	1.4%	20
Second down	12.6%	9	-22.5%	2
Third down	28.1%	6	5.5%	20
First half	9.5%	10	-4.7%	11
Second half	28.9%	2	-7.0%	8
Red zone	14.3%	8	-6.9%	12
Late and close	32.9%	2	-14.6%	5

Five-Year Performance

Year	W-L	Pyth Wins	Est Wins	PF	PA	TO	Total	Rank	Off	Rank	Def	Rank	ST	Rank
2003	10-6	9.0	8.2	289	260	-4	4.2%	14	-8.6%	21	-13.7%	6	-0.8%	21
2004	6-10	5.1	6.6	293	405	-15	14.3%	24	-2.8%	17	12.8%	25	1.3%	13
2005	9-7	8.5	8.2	325	208	-5	1.7%	15	-3.0%	14	-5.4%	13	-0.7%	22
2006	9-7	9.8	8.6	425	350	+1	9.7%	10	9.9%	8	5.0%	16	-0.2%	20
2007	13-3	11.0	10.8	455	325	+5	24.3%	3	19.0%	4	5.8%	10	-0.6%	18

Strategic Tendencies

Run/Pass		Rank	Offense		Rank	Defense		Rank	Other		Rank
Runs, all plays	40%	18	3+ WR	41%	29	Rush 3	1.7%	29	2+ RB, Pct runs	57%	15
Runs, first half	36%	29	4+ WR	3%	31	Rush 4	58.9%	20	1 RB/2 TE, Pct runs	32%	31
Runs, first down	48%	20	2+ TE	33%	5	Rush 5	35.4%	3	1 RB/3+ WR, Pct runs	20%	22
Runs, second long	38%	10	Single back	52%	18	Rush 6+	3.9%	29	CB1 on WR1	50%	10
Runs, power sit.	76%	2	Play action	21%	8	Rush 7+	0.2%	32	Go for it on 4th	1.62	4
Runs, behind 2H	26%	24	Max protect	10%	18	Sacks by LB	70.7%	3	Offensive pace	31.4	21
Pass, ahead 2H	42%	22	Outside pocket	11%	14	Sacks by DB	2.2%	28	Defensive pace	30.4	9

The Cowboys have an inexplicable problem scoring in the first quarter. They ranked 25th in offensive DVOA in the first quarter and then third (and first in the NFC) for the rest of the game combined. This was a problem in 2006 as well, when Dallas ranked 23rd in offensive DVOA for the first quarter and then sixth for the rest of the game combined. ⌀ Although they were one of the league's top five offenses overall, Dallas went three-and-out on 24 percent of drives, which ranked 22nd in the NFL. Two-thirds of all Dallas drives ended in a score or a three-and-out. ⌀ The Cowboys had an above-average passing DVOA in all formations, but their most efficient passing came in formations with just one wide receiver (125.3% DVOA). ⌀ Dallas ran a league average number of draw plays but had 84.8% DVOA on those plays, the highest in the NFL. ⬭ Only three teams used fewer screen passes than Dallas, and they had the league's worst DVOA at -72.5%. Screens may have been the only type of play in which Julius Jones was better than Marion Barber; Jones had a positive DVOA on his screen passes and Marion Barber was notably negative, losing yardage on three of his eight screens and fumbling a fourth. ⬭ New England was the only offense with a higher DVOA when using play-action fakes. ⬭ On defense, the Cowboys ranked seventh in DVOA against the play-fake. In a major change from 2006, Dallas was one of the five defenses that saw the fewest percentage of play-fakes. Two years ago, the Cowboys saw more play-fakes than any team except the Giants. ⬭ Dallas had above-average defensive DVOA against the run from every formation except one: four wide-receiver sets, where they ranked 20th. ⬭ Dallas hurried the quarterback as often with four rushers as with five. ⬭ The defense ranked fifth in DVOA against the screen pass.

Passing

Player	DYAR	DVOA	Plays	NtYds	Avg	YAC	C%	TD	Int
Tony Romo	1297	25.5%	551	4173	7.6	5.0	64.6%	36	19
Brad Johnson	-2	-13.8%	12	70	5.8	7.6	63.6%	0	0

Rushing

Player	DYAR	DVOA	Plays	Yds	Avg	TD	Fum	Suc
Marion Barber	233	18.0%	203	984	4.8	10	3	49%
Julius Jones*	12	-6.7%	164	603	3.7	2	0	37%
Tony Romo	28	12.4%	22	137	6.2	2	9	—
Tyson Thompson*	-9	-27.8%	14	54	3.9	0	0	21%

Receiving

Player	DYAR	DVOA	Plays	Ctch	Yds	Y/C	YAC	TD	C%
WR									
Terrell Owens	449	28.2%	141	81	1355	16.7	4.3	15	57%
Patrick Crayton	205	19.6%	81	50	697	13.9	5.7	7	62%
Sam Hurd	64	9.0%	37	19	314	16.5	5.2	1	51%
Miles Austin	44	34.0%	10	5	76	15.2	8.6	0	50%
TE									
Jason Witten	256	21.1%	141	96	1145	11.9	3.9	8	68%
Anthony Fasano*	7	-2.5%	21	14	143	10.2	3.9	1	67%
RB									
Marion Barber	4	-12.6%	55	45	273	6.1	5.7	2	82%
Julius Jones*	75	38.2%	26	23	203	8.8	9.4	0	88%
Deon Anderson	29	62.5%	6	6	55	9.2	6.8	0	100%

Offensive Line

Year	Yards	ALY	Rank	Power	Rank	10+ Yds	Rank	Stuff	Rank	Sack	ASR	Rank
2005	3.76	3.88	22	60%	23	14%	19	25%	21	50	9.7%	28
2006	4.21	4.47	8	63%	17	15%	20	23%	11	37	7.9%	25
2007	4.31	4.22	15	68%	12	20%	11	25%	23	25	4.5%	7

Year	LE	Rank	LT	Rank	Mid	Rank	RT	Rank	RE	Rank
2005	3.31	27	3.62	26	4.33	10	4.02	19	3.14	29
2006	3.66	21	5.57	1	4.37	16	4.12	20	4.78	7
2007	2.71	31	4.61	9	3.79	27	4.95	2	5.14	1

Dallas's $49 million gamble was whether Leonard Davis, a mediocre tackle and decent right guard in Arizona, would make an elite right guard in Dallas' offense. So far, the gamble has paid off. Davis deserved his Pro Bowl selection last year; the 354-pound ex-Longhorn was simply a force of nature on the interior. Saying that he sometimes took over games would not be an understatement. His only misstep was an unnecessary roughness penalty in the playoffs that killed a Cowboys' drive. Both Davis and left tackle Flozell Adams were second-team All-Pros, but Adams was less deserving. He did a good job in handling the murderers' row of pass rushers that he went up against in 2007, but his 14 penalties led the team. The 33-year-old received a new six-year, $42 million contract in the offseason; he's not likely to see it end. The Cowboys drafted former Boston College tackle James Marten in 2006 with the idea that he would eventually replace Adams, but Marten wasn't ready to take over before Adams's contract expired, leading to the extension. Instead, Marten and right tackle Marc Colombo just room together and reminisce about their favorite Chestnut Hill bars.

Colombo has stayed remarkably healthy since arriving in Dallas and has lived up to his first-round pedigree. He did particularly well against Michael Strahan last year, allowing the Giants star only one sack in three games despite being placed on an island against him for most snaps. Center Andre Gurode made it to the Pro Bowl for the second straight year, but he struggled for consistency with his shotgun snaps throughout the season. Left guard Kyle Kosier is the weakest link on the line, but he gets by as a technician surrounded by great athletes. He also looks disturbingly similar to Ricky Gervais. Depth along the line is thin, with Pat McQuistan the likely first man in if someone goes down with an injury. It was a surprise that the Cowboys did not elect to take at least one offensive lineman on the second day of this year's draft.

Defensive Front Seven

Defensive Line	Age	Pos	Plays	TmPct	Rk	Stop	Dfts	Stop%	Rk	AvYd	Rk	Sack	Hit	Hur	Runs	RuStop	RuYd	Pass	PaStop	PaYd
Chris Canty	26	DE	46	5.9%	38	36	14	78%	35	0.3	14	3.5	3	2	39	74%	1.3	7	100%	-5.1
Jay Ratliff	27	DT	34	4.6%	42	26	12	76%	42	0.6	5	3.0	5	7	23	65%	2.2	11	100%	-2.7
Marcus Spears	25	DE	33	4.2%	63	27	8	82%	20	1.6	39	2.0	0	4	26	81%	2.2	7	86%	-0.6
Jason Hatcher	26	DE	27	3.4%	76	21	9	78%	40	1.1	28	2.0	4	7	23	74%	2.0	4	100%	-4.5

Linebackers	Age	Pos	Plays	TmPct	Rk	Stop	Dfts	Stop%	AvYd	Sack	Hit	Hur	Runs	RuStop	Rk	RuYd	Rk	Tgts	Suc%	Rk	APaYd	Rk
Bradie James	27	ILB	104	13.2%	43	65	15	63%	4.1	3.0	1	4	72	72%	19	3.4	53	22	55%	28	6.3	54
DeMarcus Ware	26	OLB	86	11.0%	60	63	34	73%	1.1	14.0	14	19	57	70%	22	2.3	8	8	46%	—	5.0	—
Akin Ayodele*	29	ILB	59	7.5%	90	36	3	61%	3.7	0.0	0	1	43	70%	24	2.8	23	15	35%	—	9.0	—
Kevin Burnett	26	OLB	41	5.2%	—	22	12	54%	5.9	0.0	4	5	13	54%	—	2.6	—	22	51%	38	5.3	23
Greg Ellis	33	OLB	33	5.2%	—	28	15	85%	-0.7	12.5	1	8	14	71%	—	3.4	—	10	65%	—	3.7	—
Anthony Spencer	24	OLB	26	3.3%	—	19	8	73%	2.0	3.0	4	8	19	79%	—	1.8	—	6	55%	—	4.8	—
Zach Thomas	35	ILB	54	21.7%	1	32	7	59%	3.9	1.0	0	0	41	68%	28	3.1	35	14	37%	—	8.7	—

Year	Yards	ALY	Rank	Power	Rank	10+ Yds	Rank	Stuff	Rank	Sack	ASR	Rank
2005	4.16	4.64	30	74%	27	12%	3	23%	22	37	8.2%	6
2006	3.81	4.37	20	60%	10	11%	3	21%	22	34	7.2%	12
2007	4.01	3.93	8	67%	21	19%	22	28%	6	46	7.8%	4

Year	LE	Rank	LT	Rank	Mid	Rank	RT	Rank	RE	Rank
2005	4.49	23	4.22	16	4.60	30	5.47	31	4.78	26
2006	5.42	31	4.22	14	4.11	10	4.87	29	3.98	14
2007	2.96	5	3.78	9	4.09	13	4.06	16	4.13	16

Although the Cowboys are nominally a 3-4 team, they often line up with outside linebackers DeMarcus Ware and Greg Ellis on the line of scrimmage, giving them a five-man front, similar to what Wade Phillips did in San Diego. The look forces an offense to declare its protection presnap, creates confusion amongst those protectors, and prevents offensive linemen from chipping another player before getting to their own. Ware is the ideal player for the system because his ability to rush the passer while maintaining his gap responsibilities makes him a rare commodity and, arguably, the best all-around linebacker in football. Ellis had an excellent rebound season following a torn Achilles tendon in 2006, racking up 12.5 sacks in only 13 games en route to the Comeback Player of the Year award. He will likely give away some snaps this year to 2006 first-rounder Anthony Spencer, the eventual starter on the strong side. In the middle, Akin Ayodele was dealt to Miami before the draft, opening up a spot for either new signing Zach Thomas, Kevin Burnett, or another former first-rounder, Bobby Carpenter. The Cowboys' training staff hopes to work its magic on the 35-year-old Thomas; otherwise, Thomas's continued physical breakdown will leave Burnett and Carpenter competing for the bulk of the playing time. Then again, if the Cowboys had serious faith in either one, they would not have brought in Thomas. Burnett is better in coverage, so he's likely to win the job. Defensive leader Bradie James, at this point, is your basic fundamentally sound middle linebacker. Teams take advantage of his tendency to get lost in deeper zone packages, but he is perfectly acceptable in coverage.

The surprise package for the Cowboys last year was defensive tackle Jay Ratliff, who stepped in following Jason Ferguson's season-ending injury and didn't miss a beat. The 298-pound Ratliff is likely suited to be an end in the long run, which may be connected to the end of Marcus Spears's Cowboys career. The left end fired parting shots at Bill Parcells's style of defense after the Tuna left, but after a year with two sacks and little in the way of pressure, rumors around the draft had Spears leaving the Cowboys after his rookie contract expires next year (and don't bet on him following the Tuna to Miami). Lineman Jason Hatcher would move into the starting lineup on Spears's departure, with Ratliff moving to end; Hatcher's athletic ability and incredible upper-body strength allow him to play anywhere on the line, and Ratliff has the quickness to play on the outside. Right end Chris Canty is a tough player with the vaunted huge motor that never quits.

Defensive Secondary

Secondary	Age	Pos	Plays	TmPct	Rk	Stop	Dfts	RuYd	Rk	RuStop	Rk	Tgts	Tgt%	Rk	Dist	Suc%	Rk	APaYd	Rk	PaYd	PD	Int
Roy Williams	28	SS	95	12.9%	6	37	13	6.0	35	53%	17	59	13%	2	9.1	37%	72	8.1	49	8.2	6	2
Ken Hamlin	27	FS	76	9.7%	40	27	14	9.5	77	31%	67	35	7%	35	13.2	45%	53	6.2	23	6.1	13	5
Jacques Reeves*	26	CB	68	8.7%	51	22	6	10.8	70	17%	80	107	22%	13	13.2	47%	53	8.1	56	7.7	12	1
Terence Newman	30	CB	62	9.7%	29	28	12	13.7	79	50%	41	68	17%	44	8.3	47%	52	6.9	29	7.0	12	4
Anthony Henry	32	CB	49	7.7%	60	19	10	17.7	81	33%	65	78	20%	27	13.2	56%	16	6.0	11	5.9	15	6
Pat Watkins	26	FS	22	3.2%	—	6	4	10.3	—	0%	—	10	2%	—	14.5	74%	—	4.6	—	4.2	3	1
Nate Jones*	26	CB	15	2.0%	—	9	3	5.0	—	50%	—	13	3%	—	7.1	54%	—	9.6	—	10.0	0	0
Pac-Man Jones ('06)	25	CB	75	9.2%	40	36	15	10.0	67	35%	55	69	16%	53	12.3	63%	2	5.4	1	5.4	14	4

Year	Pass D Rank	vs. #1 WR	Rk	vs. #2 WR	Rk	vs. Other WR	Rk	vs. TE	Rk	vs. RB	Rk
2005	7	13.0%	19	-62.0%	1	-23.1%	4	39.5%	31	-7.8%	11
2006	24	1.7%	14	1.7%	15	27.9%	29	-13.6%	8	6.6%	21
2007	9	5.2%	20	-27.0%	4	-13.2%	11	24.7%	30	5.2%	24

We covered Roy Williams earlier in this chapter, but only briefly touched on free safety Ken Hamlin, who made the Pro Bowl alongside Williams. Hamlin's role all year was to be behind the last receiver, with one eye on him and the other on Williams's man. While Hamlin's a competent run-stopper, it won't be his role on the team as long as Williams is the strong safety. Most teams avoided Terence Newman all year, preferring to attack Anthony Henry or Jacques Reeves. To live up to his huge offseason contract, Newman will need to ascend from being merely very good to being elite, while remaining healthy for whole seasons. That contract makes the selection of Mike Jenkins with the Cowboys' second first-round pick seem a little strange; Jenkins is a speedy cover guy who needs to work on his strength to be a cornerback on the line of scrimmage at this level. He'll likely serve as the slot corner in nickel packages in 2008, though.

The unknown quantity is Pac-Man Jones, whose 2006 performance (listed above) placed him among the best cornerbacks in football. Of course, the problem is getting Pac-Man onto the field. If he's reinstated, Jones might take a few weeks to learn the Cowboys' playbook and get back into the swing of things, but by the end of the year, the combination of Jones and Newman could be the best corner combination in football. (Actually, he may not even need to know the playbook; in Tennessee, he was known for freelancing, but his speed and sharp instincts allowed him to make plays even if he wasn't where the coaches expected him to be.) With Newman and Jenkins locked in for the future, Jones is realistically competing against Anthony Henry for a long-term roster spot.

Special Teams

Year	DVOA	Rank	FG/XP	Rank	Net Punt	Rank	Punt Ret	Rank	Net Kick	Rank	Kick Ret	Rank	Hidden	Rank
2005	-0.7%	22	-9.4	31	5.7	7	-7.3	32	4.8	11	1.8	15	-6.6	24
2006	-0.2%	20	-7.3	30	-2.8	22	1.8	11	6.5	9	0.5	13	-3.3	19
2007	-0.6%	18	2.6	12	-0.6	19	-1.0	17	-3.6	23	-0.6	17	-5.9	24

The Cowboys had both Miles Austin and Tyson Thompson split time on returns in 2007, but each had their own strength. Austin (3.5 points of value) was significantly better than Thompson (-2.4) on kick returns, but the opposite was true on punts, with Thompson worth 2.0 points to Austin's 0.1. Thompson was not tendered a contract this off-season, and Felix Jones's arrival in Big D means that the former first-team All-SEC kick returner will see some action at least on kickoff returns. High-profile skill-position players coming out of college, such as Reggie Bush, usually don't see their return skills carry over to the professional level for a variety of reasons; primarily, their teams are afraid that they're going to get hurt, so they keep them away from special teams. Bush didn't have a single return last year, after being an average kickoff returner and only taking three punts in 2006; Jones could follow the same path.

Punter Mat McBriar has a huge leg and often outpunts his coverage unit, but he was roughly as effective last year as he was during his Pro Bowl season in 2006. Meanwhile, a season-ending injury suffered by Martin Gramatica opened up a spot for rookie Nick Folk, who showed off a strong leg in a solid rookie year. He will follow in the steps of Chris Boniol and Billy Cundiff as Cowboys kickers who perform on a rookie salary before moving on elsewhere.

COACHING STAFF

A 13-win season quieted the talk that Wade Phillips was the coaching equivalent of the "Quadruple-A" ballplayer: too good to be a coordinator but not good enough to be a head coach. Phillips's biggest impact was naturally on the Cowboys' defense, where his 3-4 scheme was a better fit than the Bill Parcells 3-4 for this club's talent. Phillips also kept a team with its fair share of egos calm for a year, which may have been the result of being a docile human being following the taciturn Tuna.

Jason Garrett got a significant amount of hype as the team's offensive coordinator in his first year, turning down offers from the Dolphins and Falcons so he could sign a $3 million-a-year deal to remain with the Cowboys. The contract comes with the understanding that he'll eventually replace Phillips as head coach. Although that sort of arrangement is comfortable in Indianapolis, where Tony Dungy is revered, one bad year from Phillips—on the heels of the disappointing playoff loss to the Giants—could see calls for his head coming faster than they would otherwise. Garrett's offense did a good job of allowing Tony Romo to improvise and get out of the pocket, using two tight-end sets to occupy linebackers. Some think the loss of Tony Sparano may cause development stagnation on the offensive line, but the only homegrown Cowboys lineman under Sparano's tenure to become a successful starter was Gurode.

Denver Broncos

On December 3, 2006, Jay Cutler replaced Jake Plummer as quarterback of the Denver Broncos. The Broncos were 7-4 at that point, but lost three of their next five games to finish 9-7 and out of the play-offs for the first time since 2002. Last season, they finished 7-9, the second-worst record of the Mike Shanahan era. It was only the Broncos' fourth losing season since drafting John Elway in 1983.

During these two down years, the highest-profile move in Denver has been the switch to Cutler at quarterback. This switch, however, is far from the reason for the team's losing ways. Instead, while Cutler develops at a rate typical of a first-round quarterback, the team's once-celebrated running attack has fallen apart, and their defense has regressed to mediocrity.

The talent from the 2005 Denver squad that made the AFC Championship game has steadily eroded over the past two seasons. Both offense and defense were hurt by key injuries, and the replacements were not up to the task. This lack of depth was largely attributable to a series of poor drafts between 2002 and 2004. Out of 28 players selected by Denver, only one, linebacker D. J. Williams, was starting for the Broncos last year. The Broncos were not exactly lining other people's teams with talents, as only Clinton Portis was a starter on another team.

The recent draft woes have led some to question the continued carte blanche on personnel matters given to head coach Mike Shanahan. Those woes may have led Shanahan to fire general manager Ted Sundquist this offseason. Sundquist was promoted to the GM position in 2002. The truth, however, is that the Broncos have never drafted well during the Shanahan era. The 2002-2004 period was particularly lean, but rarely has Shanahan enjoyed a draft where the Broncos gained more than one or two solid contributors.

Given this poor draft record, Denver's run of post-Elway success is fairly impressive. The franchise is 83-61 since its icon rode off into the sunset; its record was largely sustained by shrewd acquisitions outside the draft and the ability to cobble an effective running attack out of late-round and undrafted rookies.

The question is whether this strategy for roster-building is tenable in the current NFL. The vastly rising salary cap effectively means that any team can afford to keep what it deems its top players. As a result, less talent is reaching the free-agent market every year. To build a team around free agents, therefore, effectively requires a team to turn another team's castoffs into its own building blocks.

When the Broncos went 13-3 and made the AFC Championship game in 2005, only 10 starters were originally drafted by Denver, and only nine by Shanahan. (The ageless Tom Nalen was drafted by Denver in 1994, the year before Shanahan took over the reins.) For comparison's sake, the Steelers started 16 of their own draft picks. The only draft that yielded two or more starters for Denver was 2000. A number of players, however, were acquired either through trades or veteran free agency, including Bailey, Plummer, safeties John Lynch

---

BRONCOS PROSPECTUS

2007 Record: 7-9

Pythagorean Wins: 5.7 (21st)

DVOA: -3.2% total (18th), 1.9% weighted (17th)

Offense: 7.6% DVOA (10th)

Defense: 6.3% DVOA (21st)

Special Teams: -4.5% DVOA (28th)

Variance: 34.1 % (32nd)

2007: The last gasp of the post-Elway Broncos.

2008: The first gasp of the post-post-Elway Broncos?

2008 Mean Projection: 8.7 wins

On the Clock (0-3): 0%

Loserville (4-6): 13%

Mediocrity (7-8): 30%

Playoff Contender (9-10): 36%

Super Bowl Contender (11+): 20%

Projected Average Opponent: -4.5% DVOA (29th in NFL)

2008 Broncos Schedule

Week	Opp.	Week	Opp.	Week	Opp.
1	at OAK (Mon.)	7	at NE (Mon.)	13	at NYJ
2	SD	8	BYE	14	KC
3	NO	9	MIA	15	at CAR
4	at KC	10	at CLE (Thu.)	16	BUF
5	TB	11	at ATL	17	at SD
6	JAC	12	OAK		

and Nick Ferguson, tight end Stephen Alexander, and defensive linemen Michael Myers, Courtney Brown, and Gerard Warren.

The homegrown Broncos were largely key components of the running game. All five starting offensive linemen plus running back Mike Anderson had played only for the Broncos. The running game under Shanahan developed mythic status for its ability to put any runner into the system and watch him gain 1,000 yards. Until this past season, all these runners were either Broncos draft picks or rookie free-agent signings.

In 2006, the tandem of Anderson and Tatum Bell struggled to run the ball effectively. The Broncos had their worst rushing DVOA since Shanahan arrived. Clearly troubled, Shanahan made two moves. First, he shipped Bell and offensive tackle George Foster to Detroit for cornerback Dre' Bly. He then signed journeyman running back Travis Henry to a contract guaranteeing at least $12 million. Henry had been a below-average back in Buffalo for a number of years before one mediocre season in Tennessee. He seemed like the type of player whom Denver would use to inflate his value and then trade, like Clinton Portis (a back far superior to Henry) or Tatum Bell. Instead, he was guaranteed a big contract.

The offensive line was also reshuffled. Denver signed veteran free-agent guard Montrae Holland from New Orleans. An injury to Ben Hamilton thrust Chris Myers into the lineup at guard. Erik Pears, who started at left tackle when Matt Lepsis was injured in 2006, shifted to right tackle to fill the void left by Foster. Maybe these moves would have worked, but the line never gelled. A year removed from ACL surgery, Lepsis was a shell of his former self. Further complicating matters was a season-ending injury to Nalen after Week 5.

The reshuffled running game was only mildly improved over 2006 and still below average. Henry in particular was a disaster. He battled nagging injuries

throughout the season and struggled mightily after a hot start. Predictably, the Broncos found a diamond in the rough at running back, undrafted free agent Selvin Young. The undersized rookie from Texas was impressive when on the field, although concerns about durability limited his carries.

Denver's other forays into the free-agent market worked no better than importing Henry. Defensive tackle Sam Adams was an unmitigated disaster, and tight end Daniel Graham did little to warrant his sizable contract. Simeon Rice was a short-lived desperate move. Other recent signees, such as defensive end John Engelberger and linebacker Nate Wayne, provided little. Safety John Lynch, a major asset the previous two seasons, was injured and a step slow.

Surrounded by mediocre veterans, Denver's best players are primarily recent draft picks: Cutler, wide receiver Brandon Marshall, and defensive end Elvis Dumervil. They represent the possibility that Denver has improved in the draft over the past several seasons. The 2006 draft, in particular, was a massive haul. The Broncos acquired Cutler, Marshall, Dumervil, and tight end Tony Scheffler. The draft is already the team's best since at least 2000, and a fifth player, Chris Kuper, will probably replace Nalen when he retires. The 2005 draft pales in comparison but still netted the late Darrent Williams, a solid cornerback, nickel back Domonique Foxworth, and Myers, who was traded to Houston for a sixth-round pick. The 2007 draft is still a mystery: Denver had only four picks, and defensive lineman Jarvis Moss and offensive lineman Ryan Harris missed most of the season due to injury. Defensive linemen Tim Crowder and Marcus Thomas showed promise as rookies.

After years of playing with mediocre free agents on the defensive line, the Broncos successfully acquired defensive linemen in the draft. Now they have holes at linebacker and safety, but rather than working through the draft, they again dove headfirst into free agency and inked some mediocre veterans: safeties Marquand Manuel and Marlon McCree, plus linebackers Boss Bailey and Niko Koutouvides. Instead of waiting for their 2007 draft to develop, they traded the Jets for the underachieving defensive tackle Dewayne Robertson.

Even with the mediocre veteran free agents, the Broncos should be markedly better defensively if they insert Koutouvides at middle linebacker and shift D. J. Williams outside. The talented Williams is too small at the point of attack, but his speed plays well on the outside. A combination of Lynch and McCree will fortify the run defense from one safety spot, even if one of the veterans goes down. Still, the Broncos failed to add a single defensive player in the draft until the fourth round. In the second round, they selected kick returner and project wide receiver Eddie Royal over a playmaking linebacker or another young defensive lineman.

On offense, the offseason was potentially even crazier. Marshall suffered a serious forearm injury in an off-the-field accident, while Javon Walker signed with Oakland. To add depth, the Broncos played wide-receiver grab bag. They signed Darrell Jackson, Keary Colbert, and Samie Parker. Jackson has not been good for several years, and the other two were never good. If Marshall is ineffective or inactive due to injury, all the Samie Parkers in the world will not save this offense.

The fruit of all these machinations is a team with potential to be an elite unit in a couple years if the team has the patience to go .500 this year. The young players need to play and develop. Clady replaces Lepsis, who retired, at left tackle, and the team has to stick with him through his inevitable early-season struggles. Engelberger needs to be benched for either Moss or Crowder, while Alvin McKinley should yield to Marcus Thomas. Henry needs to spell Young to limit the rookie's carries, not vice versa.

Rebuilding should not mean that the Broncos are stuck with a 5-11 season. While they remain behind the Chargers in terms of talent, they certainly are good enough to get a couple breaks and make the playoffs.

They already got one break, courtesy of an easy schedule, with games against the mediocre NFC South and the sub-Pats weaklings of the AFC East. The young players were more talented than the veterans last year and should be even better this year, even if they make the occasional mental mistake.

In the end, the Broncos' chances of returning to the playoffs may depend on whether Cutler moves from promising talent to outright star. The quarterback's second season was unquestionably a success. With supposed top wideout Walker battling injuries, Cutler turned to the unproven Marshall for repeated big plays. Cutler's second receiver, Brandon Stokley, turned in a rare healthy season and continued his career trend of making big plays when he can stay on the field. Cutler's success came without the usual Denver threat of a potent running attack.

Cutler is not a finished product—right now he throws too many interceptions based on poor decisions—but his first two years have shown enormous promise. A heavier dose of Young and a healthy Henry should make the running game adequate, and with defensive improvement, the Broncos should be on the fringe of the wild-card race. Another fruitful draft, and the Broncos may return to their rightful place as perennial playoff contenders.

Ned Macey

2007 Broncos Stats by Week

Wk	vs.	W-L	PF	PA	YDF	YDA	TO	Total	Off	Def	ST
1	@BUF	W	15	14	470	184	0	9%	19%	-27%	-37%
2	OAK	W	23	20	441	253	+1	28%	5%	-28%	-5%
3	JAC	L	14	23	265	326	-1	0%	1%	-8%	-8%
4	@IND	L	20	38	354	419	-2	-40%	22%	58%	-4%
5	SD	L	3	41	296	484	-3	-84%	-1%	71%	-12%
6	BYE										
7	PIT	W	31	28	324	379	+1	11%	15%	9%	5%
8	GB	L	13	19	332	430	-1	-7%	16%	30%	6%
9	@DET	L	7	44	303	376	-3	-58%	-34%	25%	0%
10	@KC	W	27	11	327	284	+3	34%	-4%	-29%	8%
11	TEN	W	34	20	359	423	+2	101%	74%	-1%	26%
12	@CHI	L	34	37	430	293	+2	-46%	6%	-1%	-53%
13	@OAK	L	20	34	292	372	-3	-64%	-27%	32%	-4%
14	KC	W	41	7	453	129	+3	123%	74%	-50%	-1%
15	@HOU	L	13	31	308	358	+1	-45%	-7%	38%	1%
16	@SD	L	3	23	225	334	-2	-47%	-40%	6%	0%
17	MIN	W	22	19	362	332	+3	40%	21%	-16%	3%

Trends and Splits

	Offense	Rank	Defense	Rank
Total DVOA	7.6%	10	6.3%	21
Unadjusted VOA	6.5%	13	2.8%	20
Weighted trend	7.6%	12	4.2%	21
Variance	10.1%	30	11.2%	30
Average opponent	-1.5%	2	-0.6%	22
Passing	16.7%	10	10.4%	20
Rushing	-2.9%	14	2.6%	26
First down	-2.1%	17	5.9%	24
Second down	17.5%	5	6.0%	20
Third down	11.3%	13	7.7%	22
First half	16.2%	7	5.6%	23
Second half	0.2%	20	7.1%	24
Red Zone	7.6%	14	24.7%	28
Late and close	15.5%	6	19.8%	30

Five-Year Performance

Year	W-L	Pyth Wins	Est Wins	PF	PA	TO	Total	Rank	Off	Rank	Def	Rank	ST	Rank
2003	10-6	10.2	9.8	381	301	-4	14.5%	8	8.6%	8	-7.1%	11	-1.2%	22
2004	10-6	10.1	10.6	381	304	-9	22.6%	7	11.3%	10	13.7%	5	-2.4%	24
2005	13-3	11.7	11.7	395	258	+20	30.7%	2	23.4%	4	-10.5%	6	-3.2%	28
2006	9-7	8.4	7.0	319	305	0	-3.9%	18	-8.3%	23	3.7%	12	0.7%	15
2007	7-9	5.7	7.3	320	409	+1	-3.2%	18	7.6%	10	6.3%	21	-4.5%	28

Strategic Tendencies

Run/Pass		Rank	Offense		Rank	Defense		Rank	Other		Rank
Runs, all plays	41%	15	3+ WR	42%	28	Rush 3	10.5%	7	2+ RB, Pct runs	57%	14
Runs, first half	45%	7	4+ WR	4%	28	Rush 4	63.3%	15	1 RB/2 TE, pct runs	37%	27
Runs, first down	53%	10	2+ TE	32%	7	Rush 5	15.8%	27	1 RB/3+ WR, pct runs	22%	20
Runs, second-long	33%	20	Single back	50%	23	Rush 6+	10.4%	11	CB1 on WR1	27%	32
Runs, power sit.	61%	21	Play action	21%	13	Rush 7+	3.3%	6	Go for it on 4th	1.33	8
Runs, behind 2H	33%	7	Max protect	16%	4	Sacks by LB	10.0%	27	Offensive Pace	29.9	8
Pass, ahead 2H	52%	5	Outside pocket	13%	9	Sacks by DB	5.7%	16	Defensive Pace	31.2	23

Jay Cutler was hurried on just 9.2 percent of pass plays, the lowest percentage of any starting quarterback in the league. His DVOA when hurried ranked third behind Ben Roethlisberger and Marc Bulger. ⊘ The Broncos were the AFC's most aggressive team with five or fewer yards to go. They threw the ball 10 or more yards 22.4 percent of the time, which ranked them second behind Arizona. They threw it 20 or more yards 6.8 percent of the time, which ranked fifth. ⊘ Denver rarely lined up in four-wide sets on first down, doing so only six times all season. ⊘ The Broncos' passing attack was most efficient with one wide receiver (78.7% DVOA) and least efficient with four wide receivers (-47.7% DVOA). ⊘ Denver threw the ball from two tight-end sets more often than any offense except Philadelphia. ⊘ Broncos' opponents led the league in using four or more wide receivers on downs with five or less yards to go. ⊘ Only Buffalo saw more screens run against them than Denver did. ⊘ Denver's defense ranked fifth in percentage of play-action passes run against them and 30th in DVOA against the play-action pass. The Broncos allowed 8.8 yards per play after a play-fake but only 5.6 yards on the average pass play without a fake. ⊘ Denver's run defense changed dramatically depending on the presence of a fullback. Against single-back sets, Denver had the league's worst DVOA (27.1%) and allowed 5.8 yards per carry. Every other team except St. Louis gave up less than five yards per carry against single-back sets. Against two-back sets, Denver allowed just 3.7 yards per carry and ranked fourth in the NFL with a -21.6% DVOA.

Passing

Player	DYAR	DVOA	Plays	NtYds	Avg	YAC	C%	TD	Int
Jay Cutler	972	19.4%	501	3403	6.8	5.2	64.0%	20	14
Patrick Ramsey	-41	-24.5%	51	269	5.3	2.9	61.7%	1	1

Rushing

Player	DYAR	DVOA	Plays	Yds	Avg	TD	Fum	Suc
Travis Henry	40	-2.9%	167	691	4.1	4	3	46%
Selvin Young	92	8.4%	140	759	5.4	1	2	43%
Andre Hall	7	-4.9%	44	213	4.8	2	1	39%
Jay Cutler	38	9.3%	30	208	6.9	1	7	—
Cecil Sapp	14	8.8%	18	59	3.3	2	0	44%
Mike Bell	-24	-110.1%	6	3	0.5	0	1	33%
Brandon Marshall	48	124.0%	5	57	11.4	0	0	—

Receiving

Player	DYAR	DVOA	Plays	Ctch	Yds	Y/C	YAC	TD	C%
WR									
Brandon Marshall	152	-1.3%	170	102	1325	13.0	5.2	7	60%
Brandon Stokley	219	25.7%	71	40	635	15.9	3.0	5	56%
Javon Walker*	-66	-30.2%	50	26	287	11.0	4.5	1	52%
Glenn Martinez	19	-2.0%	24	14	165	11.8	2.9	0	58%
Brian Clark*	-25	-79.9%	5	4	23	5.8	2.5	0	80%
Darrell Jackson	-126	-27.9%	104	46	495	10.8	1.9	5	44%
Keary Colbert	-122	-34.6%	69	32	332	10.4	3.3	0	46%
Samie Parker	62	6.9%	39	24	272	11.3	3.8	2	62%
Taylor Jacobs	3	-8.1%	9	3	40	13.3	1.3	2	33%
TE									
Tony Scheffler	149	26.1%	65	49	549	11.2	4.1	5	75%
Daniel Graham	54	16.3%	33	24	246	10.3	4.3	2	73%
Chad Mustard	20	37.8%	7	5	62	12.4	7.4	0	71%
RB									
Selvin Young	14	-7.7%	43	35	231	6.6	7.6	1	81%
Cecil Sapp	-35	-40.7%	20	14	51	3.6	3.4	1	70%
Travis Henry	-7	-23.2%	14	7	65	9.3	9.9	0	50%

Offensive Line

Year	Yards	ALY	Rank	Power	Rank	10+ Yds	Rank	Stuff	Rank	Sack	ASR	Rank
2005	4.71	4.62	2	68%	9	23%	5	19%	3	23	4.9%	4
2006	4.44	4.23	18	63%	16	21%	7	25%	19	31	5.7%	9
2007	4.60	4.23	14	49%	32	23%	6	25%	21	32	5.9%	14

Year	LE	Rank	LT	Rank	Mid	Rank	RT	Rank	RE	Rank
2005	5.28	1	4.40	13	4.84	1	4.45	11	3.29	25
2006	2.65	30	4.04	24	4.64	6	4.46	8	3.44	25
2007	4.88	5	4.77	8	3.83	25	3.81	26	4.72	5

The decline of the offensive line is the single largest reason why the Broncos missed the playoffs two straight seasons. Left tackle Matt Lepsis was not himself on his return to the field from a torn ACL, and the Broncos were not able to stretch out to the left. After center Tom Nalen left the lineup with a torn biceps, teams were able to get immediate penetration and blow up some of Denver's slower developing plays. The Broncos also got no push in the middle of their line. The good news is that much of the line is different from those who played last year. Rookie Ryan Clady takes over at left tackle for the retiring Lepsis, although that may be a short-term downgrade. Nalen returns at center, flanked at left guard by old standby Ben Hamilton, who missed all of last year with post-concussion syndrome.

The right side of the line remains a question mark. Tackle Erik Pears is inconsistent and can be beaten on the outside, while guard Montrae Holland is merely adequate. Second-year player Ryan Harris could compete for either spot, although replacing the older Holland is the more likely outcome. The Broncos feature good depth in the interior with free agent Casey Wiegmann, Chris Kuper, and third-round pick Kory Lichtensteiger. Given Nalen and Hamilton's recent injuries, the Broncos may need all the depth they can find.

Defensive Front Seven

Defensive Line	Age	Pos	Plays	TmPct	Rk	Stop	Dfts	Stop%	Rk	AvYd	Rk	Sack	Hit	Hur	Runs	RuStop	RuYd	Pass	PaStop	PaYd
Elvis Dumervil	24	DE	44	5.5%	48	31	17	70%	65	1.5	34	12.5	10	14	22	55%	4.8	22	86%	-1.7
John Engelberger	32	DE	42	5.2%	52	32	5	76%	43	3.4	74	1.0	2	5	40	75%	3.8	2	100%	-4.0
Gerard Warren	30	DT	23	3.8%	—	15	9	65%	—	0.9	—	4.0	2	2	14	57%	2.2	9	78%	-1.1
Marcus Thomas	22	DT	22	2.7%	—	14	8	64%	—	3.4	—	0.0	0	2	19	68%	2.9	3	33%	6.3
Tim Crowder	23	DE	18	2.7%	—	16	8	89%	—	-1.3	—	4.0	0	3	11	82%	2.5	7	100%	-7.3
Josh Mallard	28	DE	16	4.0%	—	12	7	75%	—	1.9	—	3.5	4	5	9	78%	3.2	7	71%	0.1
Dewayne Robertson	27	DT	58	6.9%	11	41	13	71%	57	1.8	41	4.0	4	3	49	67%	2.7	9	89%	-3.0

Linebackers	Age	Pos	Plays	TmPct	Rk	Stop	Dfts	Stop%	AvYd	Sack	Hit	Hur	Runs	RuStop	Rk	RuYd	Rk	Tgts	Suc%	Rk	APaYd	Rk
D. J. Williams	26	MLB	147	18.2%	4	93	26	63%	4.3	1.0	0	4	111	68%	25	3.2	45	36	59%	11	6.3	53
Nate Webster	31	OLB	89	11.0%	59	55	13	62%	4.2	0.0	0	3	63	70%	23	3.1	40	21	52%	36	6.8	66
Ian Gold*	30	OLB	78	11.1%	58	42	14	54%	6.5	2.0	1	1	44	57%	77	6.3	99	42	52%	34	6.0	41
Jamie Winborn	29	OLB	24	3.4%	—	17	5	71%	4.9	0.5	1	2	13	77%	—	3.5	—	8	62%	—	7.1	—
Boss Bailey	29	OLB	49	6.0%	97	23	9	47%	4.7	3.5	0	0	25	52%	94	4.1	83	21	38%	78	5.8	36

Year	Yards	ALY	Rank	Power	Rank	10+ Yds	Rank	Stuff	Rank	Sack	ASR	Rank
2005	3.89	4.07	17	70%	24	13%	8	22%	26	28	5.0%	31
2006	4.18	4.42	22	76%	29	13%	5	22%	20	35	5.6%	27
2007	4.69	4.42	27	59%	12	21%	27	23%	20	33	6.1%	18

Year	LE	Rank	LT	Rank	Mid	Rank	RT	Rank	RE	Rank
2005	5.51	31	3.86	10	3.96	13	3.96	13	3.50	8
2006	5.06	27	4.60	19	4.38	18	4.10	13	3.75	12
2007	4.45	22	4.46	21	4.18	16	5.27	32	4.03	14

The Broncos were weak across the board at the point of attack on running plays. Teams had a field day going up the middle. Tackles Gerard Warren and Marcus Thomas got little to no push, while middle linebacker D. J. Williams struggled to shed blockers. The Broncos attempted to solve this problem by importing oversized and underachieving defensive tackle Dewayne Robertson; he should be an improvement, but he won't be a star. The biggest weakness of the poor run defense, however, was defensive end Elvis Dumervil. This pass-rusher extraordinaire made his average tackle on running plays 4.8 yards downfield, the worst of any defensive end in football. The Broncos have to consider putting second-year defensive end Tim Crowder into the lineup and using John Engelberger to spell Dumervil on obvious running downs. Such a move will no doubt hamper the Denver pass rush. Good first-down run defense, however, will put opponents in long-yardage situations in which Dumervil could amass double-digit sacks—even if he were to play in nothing but nickel situations.

One plan to improve the run defense is to return Williams to outside linebacker; Williams is devastating at knifing through the line if he is allowed to roam free. The rest of the linebackers are average. Niko Koutouvides has the skill-set—but no real experience—to be a solid middle linebacker. Nate Wayne is mostly filler at this point, and Detroit import Boss Bailey is alternately injured or ineffective. Come back Al Wilson: All is forgiven.

Defensive Secondary

Secondary	Age	Pos	Plays	TmPct	Rk	Stop	Dfts	RuYd	Rk	RuStop	Rk	Tgts	Tgt%	Rk	Dist	Suc%	Rk	APaYd	Rk	PaYd	PD	Int
Champ Bailey	30	CB	93	12.3%	8	47	18	5.6	29	50%	34	67	19%	33	11.9	59%	7	6.7	25	6.7	10	3
Dre' Bly	31	CB	66	8.2%	56	32	13	8.4	59	52%	31	81	21%	20	11.5	45%	62	8.5	64	8.9	14	5
John Lynch	37	FS	61	9.3%	41	29	8	4.6	8	55%	13	15	5%	73	11.3	25%	83	10.3	69	10.7	2	0
Nick Ferguson*	34	SS	54	8.9%	47	20	5	5.9	27	43%	43	19	6%	51	14.0	38%	70	11.9	79	12.6	1	0
Hamza Abdullah	25	SS	51	9.2%	44	13	5	9.4	74	29%	76	16	6%	58	11.6	48%	43	5.1	9	4.8	4	0
Domonique Foxworth	25	CB	41	5.8%	—	10	4	11.1	—	23%	—	30	9%	—	9.9	45%	—	7.3	—	7.4	3	0
Karl Paymah	26	CB	19	2.5%	—	7	5	10.0	—	0%	—	33	9%	—	13.2	58%	—	5.3	—	5.0	5	2
Marlon McCree	31	FS	72	8.6%	52	19	8	8.5	68	30%	73	26	6%	62	14.2	43%	58	8.9	58	9.3	4	3
Marquand Manuel	29	SS	15	1.8%	—	5	4	6.8	—	20%	—	5	1%	—	21.5	29%	—	18.4	—	18.2	2	1

Year	Pass D Rank	vs. #1 WR	Rk	vs. #2 WR	Rk	vs. Other WR	Rk	vs. TE	Rk	vs. RB	Rk
2005	5	-2.0%	11	-11.2%	9	-32.8%	3	-46.7%	1	13.4%	28
2006	10	-17.0%	5	-15.2%	7	-21.1%	5	2.1%	22	8.8%	23
2007	20	0.4%	15	-1.7%	14	8.1%	23	44.7%	32	-26.1%	2

Champ Bailey and Dré Bly were touted before the season as the top starting cornerback duo in football. They both gave up huge pass plays in a prime-time loss to Green Bay, and Denver struggled against the pass all season, so people assume that they were overhyped. Bly was merely average, but Bailey remains among the top five cornerbacks in football. The real problems for the Broncos were their extra cornerbacks and safeties. Safety Nick Ferguson has been dismissed but John Lynch remains and no longer has good coverage skills. Nickel back Domonique Foxworth was more or less replaced by Karl Paymah, who played better over the course of the season. Fourth-round rookie cornerback Jack Williams is undersized but has good coverage skills. The Broncos signed safeties Marlon McCree and Marquand Manuel, who both will improve the run defense but do little in pass coverage. Their weakness in pass coverage means the Broncos may continue to struggle against tight ends. They were worst in the league defending tight ends, even after we adjust for playing Tony Gonzalez and Antonio Gates two times each.

Quite simply, teams that spread out the field with multiple receivers and athletic tight ends will find openings against the deeper parts of the Broncos' secondary, and Champ Bailey can cover only one guy. As a result, Denver played an inordinate amount of zone, somewhat wasting the talents of their two highly paid cornerbacks. In 2006, the opposition's top receiver was the intended target for 54 percent of passes where our game charters listed Champ Bailey in coverage; last year, that dropped in half.

Special Teams

Year	DVOA	Rank	FG/XP	Rank	Net Punt	Rank	Punt Ret	Rank	Net Kick	Rank	Kick Ret	Rank	Hidden	Rank
2005	-3.1%	28	-6.8	26	1.0	16	-3.8	24	-4.3	23	-4.4	22	2.9	12
2006	0.7%	15	6.0	7	3.1	14	-1.7	17	-0.1	19	-3.4	20	-13.5	30
2007	-4.5%	28	1.5	15	-11.1	31	0.4	12	-2.7	22	-14.7	31	-7.8	27

The Jason Elam era has ended after a long and distinguished career in Denver. The venerable kicker's conventional stats were always inflated by his mile-high home, but he was reliable at a generally inconsistent position. His replacement will be determined in a training camp battle between Matt Prater, a flop in Atlanta last year, and rookie free agent Garrett Hartley. Prater is the definite favorite, but Hartley showed a big leg while kicking for Oklahoma. Kickers are generally interchangeable, and the Broncos made the right decision to let the aging Elam leave for the big money, particularly since he was no longer trusted to do kickoffs. Still, the new kicker will be under enormous pressure due to his predecessor. A few early misses could lead to a midseason change for a "proven veteran" waiting at home for the phone to ring.

The rest of the Broncos' special teams are a mess. Punter Todd Sauerbrun was past his expiration date and had a woeful (for altitude) 36.1 yards net, plus his infamous third quarter in Chicago against Devin Hester. The punter position in Denver remains even more open than the kicker position. The early favorite may be Sam Paulescu, who signed and punted well in Week 17 last season. He will be challenged by Danny Baugher, a University of Arizona alum whose promising leg has gotten him numerous tryouts but no game experience. Rookie free agent Brett Kern out of the University of Toledo will also be in the running.

Glenn Martinez was an adequate punt returner but weaker in kickoff returns. Andre Hall was the best of a bad bunch at kick returner. Both will be fighting to retain return duties after the drafting of Eddie Royal in the second round. The speedy wide receiver was taken so high largely for his abilities in the return game, and he should get a chance to win both the kickoff and punt return duties.

COACHING STAFF

The Broncos are Mike Shanahan's team, and his imprint is all over the offense, which is always interesting to watch from a play-design perspective. Shanahan will go entire drives running different plays out of the same formation. The creative flourishes, however, are less effective since former offensive coordinator Gary Kubiak departed two years ago to coach the Houston Texans. New coordinator Rick Dennison has been with Shanahan a long time but the results have been two relatively poor offensive seasons, despite an improved quarterback. The biggest problem has been the inability to generate a consistent running game. The running game was excellent in 2005, after the departure of much-admired offensive line coach Alex Gibbs. This past season, they were unable to run the football even with a heavy reliance on two tight-end formations. Perhaps the team is in need of some new ideas.

Defensive coordinator Jim Bates never meshed with the Broncos. He tried to force his scheme on personnel not up to the task. New coordinator Bob Slowik has a weak résumé in several previous stints as a defensive coordinator but should be more attuned to current personnel.

Detroit Lions

History will remember the Lions' 2007 season as just another sub-.500 campaign, part of an unbroken string that started in 2001 and may not end until the polar ice caps melt. History doesn't dwell on details, and in the rush to tell the tale of the Giants and Patriots, Michael Vick and Spygate, it will soon forget how unique last season was in the Motor City. The Lions started the year 6-2. They were in the playoff hunt until the final week of the season. Jon Kitna's preseason 11-win prediction, which sounded like a hollow boast at the time, seemed a foregone conclusion for a few weeks in October. The Lions, for too brief and too early a period, were contenders. Then the weather turned, reality rebooted, and the team thudded to a 1-7 finish that left them in their permanently furnished townhouse at the bottom of the NFC North.

The team's 6-2 start, which culminated with a 44-7 rout of the Broncos in Week 9, was the high-water mark of the Matt Millen era. Few teams in modern professional sports have been so bad for so long that a two-month hot streak could produce a mix of euphoria and trepidation. "This is uncharted territory for us," center Dominic Raiola said a week before the Broncos blowout, after the team completed a season sweep of the Bears. It speaks volumes about the Millen epoch when a seven-year Lions vet refers to five early autumn wins as "uncharted territory." When told the Lions hadn't started a season 5-2 since 2000, Roy Williams asked if that meant 2,000 years. After beating the Broncos, the Lions led the NFL in takeaways and were seventh in passing yards per game. Their résumé wasn't sparkling—their two losses came by a combined 90-24 score—but they appeared to be a legitimate wild card in the weak NFC.

Unfortunately, the tide was already rising on Millen's latest sand castle. An ugly loss to the Cardinals immediately followed the Broncos rout. Lions running backs carried the ball just six times against Arizona, and the team set a modern record with -18 rushing yards to complement five turnovers, 11 penalties, and enough missed tackles to fill a Tecmo Super Bowl clip on YouTube. Losses to the Giants and Packers (on Thanksgiving) brought the Lions quickly back to charted territory. A 44-10 loss to the Vikings on December 2 marked the end of the fleeting Detroit Renaissance. The Lions did what they do best in the season's final weeks: They folded tents, pointed fingers, and spoke wistfully of the "intensity" and "winning attitude" that somehow abandoned them in the second half of the season.

It's easy to pinpoint why the Lions had early success but collapsed late in the season. Millen the Magnificent may have assembled a pretty good offense for coordinator Mike Martz to conduct (that'll happen when you draft a receiver or running back in the first round five years out of six), but he built an awful defense featuring one of the worst secondaries in recent history. Millen let cornerbacks Dre' Bly and Terrence Holt leave via free agency and expected Daniel Bullocks and Stanley Wil-

---

LIONS PROSPECTUS

2007 Record: 7-9

Pythagorean Wins: 5.7 (22nd)

DVOA: -19.9% total (24th), -25.0% weighted (28th)

Offense: -3.1% DVOA (20th)

Defense: 13.8% DVOA (31st)

Special Teams: -3.0% DVOA (23rd)

Variance: 18.5 % (23rd)

2007: The Lions were surprising contenders early, but it was back to business as usual after midseason.

2008: Sure, they may revert to their previous 4-12 form, but they'll win those four games with character and integrity, gosh darn it.

2008 Mean Projection: 4.3 wins

On the Clock (0-3): 40%

Loserville (4-6): 46%

Mediocrity (7-8): 9%

Playoff Contender (9-10): 5%

Super Bowl Contender (11+): 0%

Projected Average Opponent: 5.8% DVOA (3rd in NFL)

2008 Lions Schedule					
Week	Opp.	Week	Opp.	Week	Opp.
1	at ATL	7	at HOU	13	TEN (Thurs.)
2	GB	8	WAS	14	MIN
3	at SF	9	at CHI	15	at IND
4	BYE	10	JAC	16	NO
5	CHI	11	at CAR	17	GB
6	at Min	12	TB		

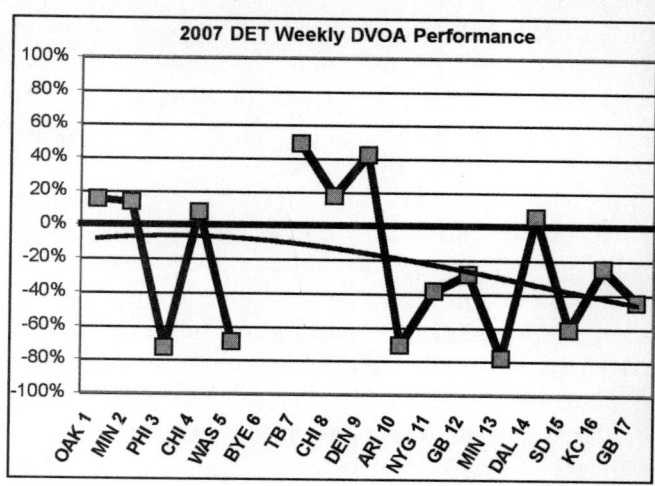

Figure 1

son to replace them. Bullocks got hurt in camp, and Wilson was a walking disaster before getting benched, then injured. That left aging Fernando Bryant and awful Travis Fisher at cornerback, with journeyman Kenoy Kennedy and rookie Gerald Alexander at safety. The team also lacked quality coverage linebackers, a big problem for Rod Marinelli's Cover-2 defense. With no quality cornerbacks, no depth, and no help underneath, the Lions finished 25th in the league in DVOA against number one receivers, 26th against number two receivers, and dead last against running backs. Their figures against slot receivers and tight ends were better, but then there are only so many balls to go around.

The Lions' secondary deficiency wasn't immediately obvious. In the first half of the season, they faced few competent quarterbacks, and those they did face (like Donovan McNabb) racked up silly stats (381 yards, with an 81 percent completion rate and four touchdowns). The Lions fattened up on a steady diet of Brian Griese, Josh McCown, Tarvaris Jackson, and Patrick Ramsey during their 6-2 start. Jeff Garcia, the one truly good quarterback they beat, threw for 316 yards and completed 18 straight passes, but the Lions won on a blocked punt, an end-around touchdown, and other oddities. In the second half of the year, the Lions faced fewer McCowns, Grieses, and Ramseys and more Romos, Favres, and Mannings. Opponents figured out the Lions' defense, the front four grew fatigued, and 20-17 wins over mediocre teams in September became 52-14 losses to good teams in December.

The Lions certainly got worse in the second half of the season. Injuries to Kevin Jones and Roy Williams slowed the offense, fatigue set in on defense, and opponents used film of the Eagles' and Redskins' blowouts to find easy-to-exploit weaknesses. The Lions' worst second-half losses match those early season defeats statistically (Figure 1). Still, it doesn't take a hard drive full of stats and game tapes to see that the Lions faced just two playoff teams in the first half but five in the second half.

Detroit's back-loaded schedule made the late-season slide seem more catastrophic. They were a .500-caliber team that caught some early breaks but no late ones.

Millen didn't recognize the 2007 season for what it was: a small step in the right direction. Instead, he saw a missed opportunity. This was the best team he had ever assembled, but instead of consolidating his gains, Millen embarked on an offseason clubhouse cleansing to rid the team of the bad feng shui that ruined the second half.

Martz left the team immediately after the season. Depending on who you believe, he was fired, left to pursue the Niners job, or disappeared in a poof of acrid smoke and brimstone. The Martz dismissal was justifiable. He had a doghouse as big and crowded as a Tokyo subway station, and his six-carry game plans put an awful lot of pressure on Jon Kitna. At the same time, his offense was the team's most effective unit, finishing a respectable 20th in the league in DVOA, the Lions' highest ranking in six years. Martz's personality conflicts were no doubt conflagrated by Millen and Marinelli, who are no strangers to clubhouse politics. And Martz knew that his game plans were too one-dimensional; in April, he explained that he felt forced to compensate for the team's terrible defense. "When you have to throw the football to win, that's not a good thing," he said after joining the Niners.

Marinelli replaced Martz with Jim Colletto, a veteran offensive line coach who mentioned "simplicity" and "balance" in every offseason interview he gave. The Lions won't rush for -18 yards in a game anymore, but Colletto's back-to-basics approach may backfire against the solid run defenses of the NFC North.

With Martz gone, the Lions began an aggressive roster overhaul. Millen dealt defensive tackle Shaun

Rogers, the hero of the blowout of the Broncos and one of the Lions' best defenders, to the Browns for great-when-healthy cornerback Leigh Bodden and a draft pick. Like Martz's dismissal, the Rogers trade was defensible. Rogers battled weight issues throughout his Lions career, and he wore down during the losing streak. Bodden patches a big hole in the secondary if he can stay in the lineup. But Millen opened one hole to plug another, and Rogers's conditioning, like Martz's people skills, was an organization-exacerbated problem. Rogers gained weight in the 2006 offseason, but Millen opted not to fine him, because he was rehabbing an injury. Instead of disciplining and possibly motivating Rogers, Millen waited for his play to deteriorate, then traded him when his value was low.

A small army followed Rogers out the door. Linebackers Teddy Lehman and Boss Bailey and left tackle Damien Woody left via free agency. Defensive end Kalimba Edwards and cornerback Fernando Bryant were waived. In mid-March, the team released Kevin Jones, a talented running back recovering from an ACL tear. Marinelli said that the team couldn't risk waiting for him to return. Many of the expatriates, like Rogers, were recent first-day draft choices, the types of players who should form the nucleus of a successful team. Most were disappointments, due to injuries or stunted development, but players like Bailey, Lehman, and Jones were still viable NFL starters in their primes. The Lions suddenly had no use for them.

Millen and Marinelli replaced their outgoing free agents with a parade of ex-Buccaneers. Marinelli unapologetically gobbled up players he knows from his days as a defensive assistant in Tampa: safety Dwight Smith, cornerback Brian Kelly, tackle Chartric Darby, and safety Kalvin Pearson. The veteran journeymen, along with Bodden, should upgrade the woeful Lions secondary. But Darby is no substitute for Rogers, and the Lions' linebacker corps is dangerously thin despite the addition of rookie Jordon Dizon. On offense, Detroit's main addition was hard-blocking tight end Michael Gaines. The plan appears to be to run the ball behind Gaines and rookie tackle Gosder Cherilus while the talented backup wideouts who Martz developed (Mike Furrey and Shaun McDonald) twiddle their thumbs on the sidelines. With Jones gone, Tatum Bell and rookie Kevin Smith will do the running. Bell is a slasher who doesn't fit a power running scheme. Smith was overused at Central Florida (901 total carries, including an NCAA record 450 last season) and has lots of mileage for a 215-pounder. This does not sound like a formula for success.

Taken as a whole, the Lions' offseason moves are clearly personality driven. Millen and Marinelli spent the spring replacing talent with character. They purged players and coaches perceived as injury cases, egomaniacs, or loafers, replacing them with Howling Commandos and good company men. Marinelli and Millen share an obsession with intangibles like character, competitiveness, and chemistry. "The strength of a team is the chemistry of a team," Marinelli told the *Detroit Free Press* in March. Marinelli called the team's mass defection of former high draft picks "addition by subtraction," then claimed that he was building the Lions for "five to 10 years down the road," a quote that warmed the hearts of Lions fans who've already been on the road far too long.

Of course, winning usually breeds chemistry, not the other way around. The 2007 Lions didn't lose because they didn't try hard enough, or because there weren't enough firebrands in the locker room, or because Martz was a jerk who wouldn't hand off. They lost because their secondary couldn't cover anybody and their offense produced too many sacks and three-and-outs. Their problems were very tangible and fixable. While the Lions took some reasonable steps to fix some of their problems, all their moves were tinged with that strange Millen baggage of disappointment and resentment. The Lions gave up far more than they got in the offseason, which was exactly the wrong way to go after a near-.500 finish.

In a February interview, Millen accepted blame for the team's decade of ineptitude. It was a big step for an exec who has always seemed to be in denial about his shortcomings. He admitted that he made bad coaching choices, that his revolving-door staffs never established continuity, that his scouts were trying to hit a moving target while offensive and defensive philosophies kept shifting. "It's awful. It's beyond awful," he said of his record as team president. The interview occurred just weeks after he fired his sixth offensive coordinator in eight years. Even when Millen admits his mistakes, he seems determined to repeat them. Once again, the Lions are changing philosophies. Once again, scouts are adapting on the fly, acquiring power-and-zone blocking personnel to replace Martz's run-and-shoot players, grabbing Tampa-2 defenders straight from Tampa.

It's all wasted motion. The 2008 Lions will be less talented and less creative than last year's team, and their schedule will be harder. Marinelli's head will hit the chopping block, and the cycle will restart. The Lions will be very bad, again. We'll strain our memories to recall those few weeks in uncharted territory, the time they looked kinda good.

Mike Tanier

Curse of 370: The College Years

I think it's actually a positive because he has already shown himself to be durable. I think it would be a bigger issue if he'd stayed and did it again as a senior. He won't get 450 in the NFL anytime soon, so in a way he saved some wear and tear already in my opinion.

—KYLE HIGHTOWER, *Orlando Sentinel,*
writing about Detroit third-round pick
Kevin Smith

The "Curse of 370" has long been one of the staple theories of Football Outsiders. The basic idea, expounded further in the "Pregame Show" chapter at the start of the book, is that running backs who get more than 370 carries in the regular season (or 390 carries, including the postseason) tend to break down, declining in effectiveness, suffering injury, or both. Over the past three seasons, the Curse for 370 is three-for-three. Curtis Martin's 371 carries in 2004 basically ended his career. So did Shaun Alexander's 370 carries (430, including the playoffs) in 2005. Larry Johnson set an NFL record with 416 carries in 2006; last year, his average dropped to 3.5 yards per carry and his season ended after eight games.

So it was with great interest that we watched the University of Central Florida beat running back Kevin Smith into the ground during the 2007 college season. Smith ended the regular season with 415 carries in 13 games. A few minutes into the third quarter of the Liberty Bowl on December 29, Smith took the ball for a seven-yard gain and broke Marcus Allen's 26-year-old Division I record for most carries in a season. Smith finished the Liberty Bowl with 450 carries for the year. It was his eighth game with 33 or more carries. By comparison, when Larry Johnson broke the NFL record for carries in 2006, he carried the ball 33 or more times in only three games.

Smith's ridiculous workload brings up the question: Does the Curse of 370 apply in college football? The differences between the college game and the pro game mean that the answer to that question is not an obvious "yes." College running backs who carry a large workload are generally taking less punishment from smaller defensive players. Most of the Conference USA defensive linemen and linebackers that went after Smith last

year won't be plying their trade in the NFL someday. In the current college game, many backs run through larger holes thanks to the trend towards spread offenses. The schedule is also different, with more rest, particularly before bowl games. Smith had a month off before his final 35 carries.

It's also difficult to track the effects of overuse on college running backs because they all don't necessarily do the same thing in the following season. All NFL running backs who carried the ball over 370 times were back in the NFL the next year, with the exception of Ricky Williams after his so-called retirement in 2004. Sixteen running backs have carried the ball 370 or more times in Division I since 1968. Six of them were in the NFL the following year, and two more will be in 2008 (Smith and Ray Rice of Rutgers). Five of them returned to college football. The final three were seniors who went undrafted and never played in the NFL (coincidentally, all were from the MAC: Shawn Faulkner was the highest of the three, with 394 carries for Western Michigan in 1983).

There is simply no way to produce an easy number that says "overworked college running backs will average X fewer yards per carry in the NFL." Nonetheless, by looking at the history of overworked college running backs, we can get a sense of whether a Curse of 370 exists for college football. We've lowered the threshold a bit to get more data. Table 1 lists all running backs who carried the ball over 330 times in a season in college and were eventually drafted by the NFL. Players are listed only once, although some carried the ball over 330 times in two seasons.

There is no doubt that many of the players with high collegiate workloads became superstars. Marcus Allen, who previously had the record for carries, played 16 years in the NFL, made six Pro Bowls, and was elected to the Pro Football Hall of Fame. So were Barry Sanders, O. J. Simpson, and Tony Dorsett. If LaDainian Tomlinson isn't the best running back in the game today, Adrian Peterson is.

On the other hand, this list includes a number of top picks who either started their careers slowly or were out-and-out busts. Ricky Bell's career was shortened by a disease that cost him his life in 1984, but he struggled even when he was healthy. He gained less than three yards per carry as a rookie and had only one season where he ran for more than 700 yards. Thomas Jones was horrible in Arizona for three years, had a good part-time year in Tampa Bay, and then finally became a starter in his fifth season, 2004. Lorenzo White was also considered a failure until he broke out in his fifth season. Charles White played nine years in the NFL and had

Table 1. College Running Backs with Over 330 Carries in a Season, with NFL Stats

Player	Year	College	Att	Yds	2nd Season	Dft Yr	Team	Round	Overall	G	Runs	RuYd	Yd/At
Kevin Smith*	2007	Central Florida	450	2567		2008	DET	3	64	—	—	—	—
Marcus Allen	1981	USC	433	2427	354 carries, 1980	1982	OAK	1	10	222	3022	12243	4.1
Lorenzo White	1985	Michigan State	419	2066	357 carries, 1987	1988	HOU	1	22	107	1062	4242	4.0
Troy Davis	1996	Iowa State	402	2185	345 carries, 1995	1997	NO	3	62	46	150	446	3.0
Craig Heyward	1987	Pittsburgh	387	1791		1988	NO	1	24	149	1031	4301	4.2
Darnell Autry	1995	Northwestern	387	1785		1997	CHI	4	105	24	224	653	2.9
Ricky Bell	1975	USC	385	1957		1977	TB	1	1	64	822	3063	3.7
Herschel Walker	1981	Georgia	385	1891	335 carries, 1982	1985	DAL	5	114	187	1954	8225	4.2
O. J. Simpson	1968	USC	383	1880		1969	BUF	1	1	135	2404	11236	4.7
Charles Alexander	1978	LSU	381	1172		1979	CIN	1	12	102	748	2645	3.5
Ray Rice*	2007	Rutgers	380	2012	335 carries, 2006	2008	BAL	2	55	—	—	—	—
Charles White	1978	USC	374	1859	332 carries, 1979	1980	CLE	1	27	108	780	3075	3.9
Tony Dorsett	1976	Pittsburgh	370	2150		1977	DAL	1	2	173	2936	12739	4.3
LaDainian Tomlinson*	2000	TCU	369	2158		2001	SD	1	5	111	2365	10650	4.5
Travis Prentice	1998	Miami (OH)	365	1787	354 carries, 1999	2000	CLE	3	63	30	187	525	2.8
Vaughn Dunbar	1991	Indiana	364	1805		1992	NO	1	21	39	267	935	3.5
Steve Bartalo	1986	Colorado State	362	1419	338 carries, 1985	1987	TB	6	143	9	9	30	3.3
Ricky Williams*	1998	Texas	361	2124		1999	NO	1	5	83	1763	7112	4.0
Matt Forte*	2007	Tulane	361	2127		2008	CHI	2	44	—	—	—	—
Steve Owens	1969	Oklahoma	358	1523	357 carries, 1968	1970	DET	1	19	53	635	2451	3.9
Anthony Thompson	1989	Indiana	358	1793	355 carries, 1988	1990	ARI	2	31	37	251	831	3.3
Ernest Anderson	1982	Oklahoma State	353	1877		1984	DET	3	74	0	0	0	0.0
Steven Jackson*	2003	Oregon State	350	1545		2004	STL	1	24	57	971	4249	4.4
Brian Calhoun*	2005	Wisconsin	348	1636		2006	DET	3	74	11	14	54	3.9
Paul Palmer	1986	Temple	346	1866		1987	KC	1	19	41	270	1053	3.9
Barry Sanders	1988	Oklahoma State	344	2628		1989	DET	1	3	153	3062	15269	5.0
Charlester Crumpler	1972	East Carolina	340	1309		1974	BUF	4	95	0	0	0	0.0
Adrian Peterson*	2004	Oklahoma	339	1925		2007	MIN	1	7	14	238	1341	5.6
Byron Hanspard	1996	Texas Tech	339	2084		1997	ATL	2	41	28	189	718	3.8
Chris Perry*	2003	Michigan	338	1674		2004	CIN	1	26	22	73	337	4.6
Michael Turner*	2002	Northern Illinois	338	1915		2004	SD	5	154	59	228	1257	5.5
Ron Dayne*	1999	Wisconsin	337	2034		2000	NYG	1	11	96	983	3722	3.8
Keith Byars	1984	Ohio State	336	1764		1986	PHI	1	10	189	865	3109	3.6
Thomas Jones*	1999	Virginia	334	1798		2000	ARI	1	7	116	1659	6503	3.9

*Still active

more than 100 carries only once, in 1987. Vaughn Dunbar blew out his knee in his second NFL season during training camp, and Chris Perry can't stay healthy either.

Each of these players just mentioned was a first-round pick. Move down the draft, however, and players with high college workloads begin to look less like a mixed bag and more like a flaming one left on your doorstep as a high school prank.

Prior to 2008, only two of these high-workload backs had been chosen in the second round. Anthony Thompson played only three seasons in the NFL, averaging 3.3 yards per carry. Byron Hanspard, like Dunbar, blew out his knee during training camp of his second season.

Kevin Smith is the seventh high-workload back to be chosen in the third or fourth round. Three of the six

washed out of the NFL quickly, and a fourth, Brian Calhoun, is about to do the same. The other two backs didn't even make it to their first regular season. Earnest Anderson, chosen by the Lions in the third round of the 1984 draft, is the highest-drafted running back since 1978 who never played an NFL game. (The fourth-rounder who never took the field, Charlester Crumpler, eventually lived his NFL dream vicariously through his kids, Titans tight end Alge and former Seahawks tight end Carlester.)

That leaves three other high-workload backs who were drafted in later rounds. Herschel Walker was spectacular in the USFL and excellent in the NFL as well, but he wasn't your normal fifth-round draft pick. Michael Turner has played very well in his limited time in San

Diego, and we'll see this year if he can carry the starting job in Atlanta. Steve Bartalo was a scrub with just nine career carries.

Overall, the average running back chosen in the first round between 1978 and 2004 played 93 NFL games with 1,058 carries and 4.1 yards per carry. The average among our high-workload first-rounders is actually higher: 102 NFL games, nearly 1,300 carries, and 4.2 yards per carry.

However, the average running back chosen in the second or third round between 1978 and 2004 went on to play 71 games with 530 carries for 4.0 yards per carry. The average for high-workload backs taken in the second or third round—not including the three chosen in this year's draft—is 25 NFL games, 132 carries, and 3.3 yards per carry.

A blanket statement can't be made here; the sample size is small and each of these players had numerous other factors that contributed to their NFL success or lack thereof. Nonetheless, it is hard to get away from this clear fact: Other than Herschel Walker, who was only a fifth-round pick because he was playing in a competing pro league, no post-first-round running

back with a college season over 330 carries has ever had a successful career as an NFL starter. Michael Turner could become the first. So could Kevin Smith, or Ray Rice, or Matt Forte, but as of right now, there are none.

From the looks of things, there is no reason to stay away from a top prospect with a high college workload. Tell any NFL general manager that his first-round pick has a 50 percent chance of becoming Marcus Allen or Adrian Peterson and a 50 percent chance of becoming Vaughn Dunbar or Lorenzo White, and he'll happily take those odds. However, teams need to think twice before taking a midlevel prospect who was worked hard in his college years. These numbers should worry the Ravens, the Bears, and especially the Lions. Smith not only had far more carries in 2007 than either Rice or Forte, he is also the only one of the three entering training camp as the clear starter. No other rookie running back—not even Darren McFadden—is likely to get as many carries in his first NFL season. Then again, Smith won't lead this year's rookies in carries if he lands on injured reserve halfway through the year.

Aaron Schatz

2007 Lions Stats by Week

Wk	vs.	W-L	PF	PA	YDF	YDA	TO	Total	Off	Def	ST
1	@OAK	W	36	21	392	375	+1	15%	21%	19%	13%
2	MIN	W	20	17	415	313	0	13%	3%	-21%	-11%
3	@PHI	L	21	56	432	536	-1	-73%	-2%	66%	-5%
4	CHI	W	37	27	310	303	+1	7%	7%	-29%	-28%
5	@WAS	L	3	34	144	366	-1	-69%	-56%	19%	6%
6	BYE										
7	TB	W	23	16	278	422	+2	49%	58%	17%	7%
8	@CHI	W	16	7	365	255	+3	17%	14%	-16%	-12%
9	DEN	W	44	7	376	303	+3	42%	12%	-28%	1%
10	@ARI	L	21	31	247	319	-1	-71%	-51%	8%	-11%
11	NYG	L	10	16	376	341	-2	-39%	-22%	6%	-11%
12	GB	L	26	37	331	481	0	-29%	7%	44%	8%
13	@MIN	L	10	42	253	443	0	-79%	-10%	57%	-12%
14	DAL	L	27	28	390	368	+1	5%	27%	11%	-11%
15	@SD	L	14	51	328	416	-6	-61%	-21%	31%	-10%
16	KC	W	25	20	236	407	0	-25%	-14%	28%	17%
17	@GB	L	13	34	293	394	-1	-45%	-29%	26%	9%

Trends and Splits

	Offense	Rank	Defense	Rank
Total DVOA	-3.1%	20	13.8%	31
Unadjusted VOA	-4.4%	21	11.2%	27
Weighted Trend	-5.2%	21	17.4%	32
Variance	8.4%	24	7.9%	20
Average Opponent	-2.3%	1	0.9%	18
Passing	0.1%	18	22.0%	30
Rushing	-8.7%	20	2.7%	27
First Down	9.3%	9	19.6%	31
Second Down	-6.1%	23	12.2%	24
Third Down	-26.5%	30	5.1%	19
First Half	-2.7%	18	32.2%	32
Second Half	-3.5%	22	-6.1%	9
Red Zone	-11.8%	25	27.1%	31
Late and Close	3.6%	14	-14.7%	4

Five-Year Performance

Year	W-L	Pyth Wins	Est Wins	PF	PA	TO	Total	Rank	Off	Rank	Def	Rank	ST	Rank
2003	5-11	4.9	5.6	270	379	0	-24.6%	31	-22.1%	31	5.8%	23	3.3%	4
2004	6-10	6.4	7.7	296	350	+4	-5.0%	19	-4.5%	19	4.9%	20	4.4%	5
2005	5-11	5.2	5.8	254	345	+1	-19.3%	26	-13.1%	24	1.8%	21	-4.3%	32
2006	3-13	5.6	5.6	305	398	-9	-20.6%	29	-9.2%	25	14.2%	30	2.8%	6
2007	7-9	5.7	6.3	346	444	-1	-19.9%	24	-3.1%	20	13.8%	31	-3.0%	23

Strategic Tendencies

Run/Pass		Rank	Offense		Rank	Defense		Rank	Other		Rank
Runs, all plays	31%	32	3+ WR	68%	4	Rush 3	2.9%	23	2+ RB, Pct Runs	54%	23
Runs, first half	33%	32	4+ WR	32%	1	Rush 4	70.5%	8	1 RB/2 TE, Pct Runs	48%	17
Runs, first down	39%	32	2+ TE	16%	27	Rush 5	20.3%	20	1 RB/3+ WR, Pct Runs	18%	27
Runs, second-long	22%	32	Single back	64%	6	Rush 6+	6.3%	23	CB1 on WR1	40%	24
Runs, power sit.	49%	28	Play action	11%	28	Rush 7+	1.1%	21	Go for it on 4th	0.66	30
Runs, behind 2H	17%	32	Max protect	11%	12	Sacks by LB	16.5%	24	Offensive Pace	30.3	11
Pass, ahead 2H	49%	11	Outside pocket	11%	15	Sacks by DB	5.1%	20	Defensive Pace	31.3	25

The Lions went four- or five-wide on first down 28 percent of the time; no other team was above 20 percent. Even with five yards or less to go, the Lions trotted out spread sets one-third of the time. ⊘ The Lions ranked sixth in the number of draw plays run but trailed only Chicago with a dreadful -60.0% DVOA on draws. ⊘ The Lions were the only NFL team to throw over 30 percent of passes to nonstarting wide receivers, and they ranked last in percentage of passes to tight ends. ⊘ For the second straight season, the Lions' offense led the league in sacks marked by our charters as coverage sacks. ⊘ When the Lions did not hurry the quarterback, they had the worst pass defense in the league (38.0% DVOA). When they did hurry the quarterback, they had the *best* pass defense in the league (-104.5% DVOA). The Lions allowed 7.0 yards per play without a hurry, and only 2.7 yards per play with a hurry. Unfortunately, they hurried the quarterback on only 11.2 percent of pass plays, which ranked them 23rd in the league. ⊘ Excluding screen plays, where we do not typically list a defender, Detroit's defense had the most passes listed as uncovered—25 percent more than Minnesota, which ranked second. The Lions had particular difficulty keeping track of running backs slipping out of the backfield. These stats are even more remarkable when we consider that a dumpoff to the running back often comes on a play where the defense gets a quarterback hurry. More than a quarter of passes against the Lions (26 percent) were to running backs, second in the league behind Tampa Bay. ⊘ Detroit was the only NFC defense that faced four or more wide receivers on less than 10 percent of plays.

Passing

Player	DYAR	DVOA	Plays	NtYds	Avg	YAC	C%	TD	Int
Jon Kitna	387	-1.2%	616	3840	6.2	4.3	63.4%	18	20
J. T. O'Sullivan*	-18	-21.5%	30	126	4.2	6.2	50.0%	1	2

Rushing

Player	DYAR	DVOA	Plays	Yds	Avg	TD	Fum	Suc
Kevin Jones*	40	-2.7%	153	581	3.8	8	2	47%
T. J. Duckett*	56	12.2%	65	335	5.2	3	1	38%
Tatum Bell	6	-5.5%	44	182	4.1	1	1	50%
Jon Kitna	-15	-31.7%	17	68	4.0	0	12	—
Aveion Cason	-9	-28.4%	11	38	3.5	0	0	55%
Brian Calhoun	10	24.7%	7	35	5.0	0	0	43%
Jon Bradley	-22	-65.5%	5	9	1.8	0	1	60%
Calvin Johnson	43	154.8%	4	52	13.0	1	0	—
Shaun McDonald	-22	-163.9%	4	2	0.5	0	1	—

Receiving

Player	DYAR	DVOA	Plays	Ctch	Yds	Y/C	YAC	TD	C%
WR									
Shaun McDonald	108	-1.6%	126	79	947	12.0	3.2	6	63%
Roy Williams	115	1.1%	105	64	840	13.1	4.6	5	61%
Calvin Johnson	90	-0.3%	93	48	756	15.8	3.4	4	52%
Mike Furrey	136	6.5%	91	61	664	10.9	3.0	2	67%
Troy Walters	44	42.1%	10	9	101	11.2	2.2	1	90%
Brandon Middleton	34	27.7%	10	8	70	8.8	3.1	1	80%
TE									
Sean McHugh	10	-2.6%	29	17	252	14.8	8.6	0	59%
Casey Fitzsimmons	34	39.5%	10	8	85	10.6	6.3	1	80%
Michael Gaines	32	5.9%	35	25	215	8.6	6.7	2	71%
RB									
Kevin Jones*	4	-12.3%	44	32	197	6.2	6.1	1	73%
Tatum Bell	-35	-46.5%	21	14	63	4.5	5.1	0	67%
Aveion Cason	22	16.4%	16	14	129	9.2	7.4	0	88%
T. J. Duckett*	26	47.7%	7	4	54	13.5	16.3	0	57%
Brian Calhoun	16	32.9%	5	5	35	7.0	4.6	0	100%

Offensive Line

Year	Yards	ALY	Rank	Power	Rank	10+ Yds	Rank	Stuff	Rank	Sack	ASR	Rank
2005	3.71	4.15	14	61%	20	14%	22	28%	29	30	5.7%	10
2006	3.62	3.66	32	37%	32	18%	11	29%	32	63	9.8%	30
2007	4.14	4.03	23	50%	29	20%	9	26%	24	54	8.3%	26

Year	LE	Rank	LT	Rank	Mid	Rank	RT	Rank	RE	Rank
2005	4.24	15	4.39	15	3.86	24	4.68	5	3.93	17
2006	3.57	23	3.90	27	3.83	29	4.18	17	2.91	30
2007	4.24	13	4.31	17	3.82	26	3.98	23	3.86	20

Most early-round Lions draft picks are injury-plagued underachievers, but left tackle Jeff Backus and center Dominic Raiola are exceptions to the rule. Both are capable starters, and neither has missed a game since 2002. Both players are holdovers from Matt Millen's first—and most successful—draft back in 2001, the draft that also produced Shaun Rogers. Backus is one of the highest-paid left tackles in the league. He's overpriced, but the Lions are willing to pay a premium for durability at such a critical position.

First-round pick Gosder Cherilus may eventually unseat Backus. For now, he'll replace Damien Woody at right tackle. Cherilus was an excellent right tackle at Boston College from 2004 to 2006, but he played poorly when he moved across the line as a senior. He has a reputation as a competitive, gritty guy who sometimes makes catastrophically poor football decisions. In other words, a mini-Millen. George Foster started the first half of last season at right tackle but was benched at midseason after committing 10 penalties. He has an outside chance of returning to the lineup until Cherilus is ready. Left guard Edwin Mulitalo will be 34 on opening day but is still effective. Right guard Stephen Peterman earned a starting job in 2007 after three seasons on the Cowboys' and Lions' benches. He's a road-grader type who will be happy in the new offense.

It's hard to evaluate the Lions' line based on last year's tape and statistics. Adjusted Line Yards account for the number of third-and-long situations the team faced, but it's hard to quantify the fact that opponents knew the Lions would run the ball only once or twice per quarter.

Defensive Front Seven

Defensive Line	Age	Pos	Plays	TmPct	Rk	Stop	Dfts	Stop%	Rk	AvYd	Rk	Sack	Hit	Hur	Runs	RuStop	RuYd	Pass	PaStop	PaYd
James Hall	31	DE	54	6.6%	28	43	15	80%	31	2.2	54	2.5	7	11	48	77%	3.0	6	100%	-4.3
DeWayne White	29	DE	47	6.2%	33	37	17	79%	32	1.2	29	6.5	9	10	30	77%	3.1	17	82%	-2.1
Shaun Rogers*	29	DT	45	5.2%	33	37	15	82%	22	-0.5	1	7.0	12	14	31	77%	1.8	14	93%	-5.5
Cory Redding	28	DE	40	4.6%	59	33	21	83%	15	1.6	38	1.0	9	7	32	88%	0.3	8	63%	6.8
Jared DeVries	32	DE	29	3.8%	70	24	15	83%	13	0.7	18	6.5	11	4	18	78%	2.9	11	91%	-3.0
Langston Moore	27	DT	23	2.6%	—	18	7	78%	—	1.0	—	2.0	1	1	17	71%	2.2	6	100%	-2.7
Kalimba Edwards*	29	DE	18	4.1%	—	13	7	72%	—	1.6	—	3.0	5	4	10	80%	2.9	8	63%	0.0
Corey Smith	29	DE	17	1.9%	—	13	8	76%	—	0.4	—	2.5	2	3	13	77%	1.3	4	75%	-2.8
Shaun Cody	25	DT	17	2.1%	—	11	4	65%	—	3.1	—	0.0	0	3	14	71%	2.4	3	33%	6.0

Linebackers	Age	Pos	Plays	TmPct	Rk	Stop	Dfts	Stop%	AvYd	Sack	Hit	Hur	Runs	RuStop	Rk	RuYd	Rk	Tgts	Suc%	Rk	APaYd	Rk
Ernie Sims	24	OLB	136	15.6%	13	57	19	42%	6.1	1.0	5	3	64	56%	83	3.7	62	60	39%	75	5.7	35
Paris Lenon	31	MLB	117	13.4%	39	45	17	38%	5.5	2.0	5	4	63	51%	96	3.9	73	37	35%	85	6.9	68
Boss Bailey*	29	OLB	49	6.0%	97	23	9	47%	4.7	3.5	0	0	25	52%	94	4.1	83	21	38%	78	5.8	36
Teddy Lehman*	27	MLB	21	2.4%	—	10	3	48%	7.0	0.0	0	1	12	67%	—	3.6	—	3	36%	—	8.5	—
Alex Lewis	27	OLB	15	2.0%	—	5	1	33%	8.5	0.0	0	0	5	60%	—	3.2	—	7	18%	—	16.2	—

Year	Yards	ALY	Rank	Power	Rank	10+ Yds	Rank	Stuff	Rank	Sack	ASR	Rank
2005	4.23	4.07	15	63%	16	18%	18	29%	3	31	6.0%	26
2006	4.23	4.50	24	71%	27	16%	15	20%	30	30	5.8%	24
2007	4.59	4.33	23	67%	22	21%	26	22%	23	37	6.3%	16

Year	LE	Rank	LT	Rank	Mid	Rank	RT	Rank	RE	Rank
2005	3.68	12	4.83	28	3.65	4	4.06	16	4.63	22
2006	3.88	14	5.59	32	4.60	23	4.05	12	4.48	21
2007	4.08	16	4.44	20	5.08	32	4.25	19	3.73	9

When Shaun Rogers was playing to his potential at the start of last year, the Lions' front four generated a lot of pressure. Once Rogers wore down, the entire line slipped. Former Seahawks' defensive tackle Chartric Darby and rookie Andre Fluellen will try to fill the void left by Rogers. Darby was a well-regarded run defender early in his career, but he is now 32 and coming off a knee injury. Fluellen battled injuries in his senior season at Florida State and produced few sacks but has great athleticism and pass-rush potential. Cory Redding is a solid three-technique tackle against the run but leaves the field on passing downs. He may have the highest motor on the defense. Neither starting defensive end can apply much pressure without interior help. All but one of DeWayne White's 6.5 sacks came in the Lions' first eight games (before Rogers fizzled). Jared DeVries was quiet except for a three-sack game against the Bears.

Ernie Sims led all NFL linebackers in pass plays, but he was playing Little Dutch Boy: He had 49 tackles on successful pass plays for the offense, which is the second highest total in the league. Sims is fast and hustles, but the Lions need him to be more than a glorified mop-up man for their leaky defensive line. Middle linebacker Paris Lenon's interception return touchdown was the highlight of the Lions' win over Kansas City in Week 16. Like Sims, he registered a lot of high-calorie, low-protein tackles seven yards downfield. Rookie Jordon Dizon is an undersized speedster who led the NCAA in tackles last year. He's the kind of competitor that the Lions crave, but he needed halftime IVs to get through most games at Colorado. Former Colts starter Gilbert Gardner gives the Lions yet another small, fast linebacker with little big-play potential. Long time high-potential, high-injury-rate linebackers Teddy Lehman and Boss Bailey moved on to other teams in free agency.

Defensive Secondary

Secondary	Age	Pos	Plays	TmPct	Rk	Stop	Dfts	RuYd	Rk	RuStop	Rk	Tgts	Tgt%	Rk	Dist	Suc%	Rk	APaYd	Rk	PaYd	PD	Int
Kenoy Kennedy*	31	SS	93	10.7%	27	26	9	5.9	31	33%	60	31	7%	49	11.3	47%	48	5.7	18	5.8	6	2
Gerald Alexander	24	FS	89	10.2%	32	26	13	8.5	69	31%	66	18	4%	81	8.5	34%	79	7.0	37	7.2	5	2
Fernando Bryant*	31	CB	81	9.3%	36	29	12	4.7	17	50%	32	85	18%	39	9.1	45%	61	6.7	24	6.7	11	2
Travis Fisher	29	CB	79	9.0%	43	26	10	9.6	66	57%	21	66	14%	66	7.5	33%	79	8.3	58	8.6	4	2
Keith Smith	28	CB	48	5.9%	76	11	9	9.5	65	33%	63	47	11%	79	10.6	43%	67	5.8	5	6.0	8	3
Stanley Wilson	26	CB	37	6.8%	69	9	4	5.5	28	50%	33	45	15%	58	11.8	28%	81	10.9	80	10.8	2	0
Dovonte Edwards	26	CB	18	6.6%	—	6	1	5.5	—	0%	—	15	10%	—	14.3	52%	—	8.3	—	8.8	3	0
Idrees Bashir	30	FS	18	3.7%	—	7	4	5.3	—	50%	—	5	2%	—	1.9	22%	—	2.3	—	2.8	1	1
Leigh Bodden	27	CB	106	12.5%	5	42	22	7.9	53	35%	61	101	21%	23	11.1	54%	22	7.3	40	7.1	16	6
Dwight Smith	30	FS	61	8.2%	56	31	10	5.0	13	70%	2	33	7%	34	10.8	54%	21	6.8	33	7.0	9	4
Brian Kelly	32	CB	29	5.3%	—	15	8	4.2	—	67%	—	34	12%	—	8.7	55%	—	4.8	—	4.3	6	2

Year	Pass D Rank	vs.#1 WR	Rk	vs.#2 WR	Rk	vs.Other WR	Rk	vs.TE	Rk	vs.RB	Rk
2005	17	20.9%	25	-6.7%	12	-19.4%	6	-1.9%	18	3.4%	20
2006	30	-22.2%	3	34.5%	32	31.9%	31	15.6%	28	8.3%	22
2007	30	15.0%	25	19.7%	26	1.6%	21	0.7%	10	36.7%	32

Leigh Bodden lost a total of 10 games to injuries in 2005 and 2006 for Cleveland, but our charting data revealed that he was one of the best cornerbacks in the league when healthy in those seasons. (He ranked 11th in Success Rate in 2005 and 10th in 2006.) Last year Bodden was able to stay on the field for 16 games, but he still dealt with some nagging injuries and graded out as just another solid cornerback, not a shut-down guy. Opponents threw a lot of passes against the Browns last season, and Bodden was often in the crosshairs against receivers such as Chad Johnson. As a result, he allowed a lot of completions but also picked off five passes and was rarely toasted deep. Compared to the stumblebums who played cornerback in Detroit last season, Bodden will look like Ronnie Lott.

The other starting cornerback position is up for grabs. Stanley Wilson was a disaster last season, but he's young enough to improve and signed a one-year deal to stay with the team. Travis Fisher was only slightly better than Wilson, but the team re-signed him to a three-year deal. He can play nickel back without embarrassing himself. Brian Kelly is a 32-year-old Tampa Bay castoff who knows the scheme and may still have enough veteran savvy to contribute.

Like Kelly, free safety Dwight Smith played for the Bucs during their glory years and knows his role in the Tampa-2. Smith is a good zone defender who can anticipate the quarterback and pick off a pass. He may move into underneath zone coverage in nickel situations so second-year pro Gerald Alexander can play deep. Alexander was another burn victim in the Lions' secondary last season, but he's fast and has room to grow. Hard-hitting strong safety Dan Bullocks will return after missing last season with an ACL tear.

Special Teams

Year	DVOA	Rank	FG/XP	Rank	Net Punt	Rank	Punt Ret	Rank	Net Kick	Rank	Kick Ret	Rank	Hidden	Rank
2005	-4.3%	32	-2.7	22	-8.6	30	0.3	13	-11.2	30	-3.2	19	6.6	9
2006	2.8%	6	8.3	5	4.0	13	1.5	12	5.9	10	-3.5	21	-7.0	24
2007	-3.0%	23	0.7	17	4.3	11	-2.6	19	-15.7	30	-4.1	22	9.4	7

Jason Hanson is now 38 years old and started kicking for the Lions when Rodney Peete was the quarterback and Wayne Fontes used a run-and-shoot offense. Hanson posted his highest scoring total since those pass-happy days of yesteryear, topping 120 points for the first time since 1995. Hanson can still nail 50-yard field goals and is consistent on kickoffs. He is in the final year of his contract, but he looks like the kind of kicker who will still be in the league when he's 44, so expect him to push for one more deal.

Hanson is the lone bright spot on Detroit's special teams. The kick coverage units allowed two touchdowns last season and gave up an estimated 17.2 points worth of field position overall. (Hanson's kickoffs on their own were actually worth 1.5 points of positive value according to our measurements.) Mike Furrey and Troy Walters combined to return just 18 punts while calling for 20 fair catches (Lions opponents didn't have to punt very often). Punter Nick Harris and kickoff returner Aveion Cason did their jobs but didn't shine. Fifth-round pick Kenneth Moore will get a chance to make an impact as a return man. The team signed former Buccaneers safety Kalvin Pearson to improve the coverage units, but Pearson was accused of a violent crime in April and may no longer be in the team's plans.

The Hidden special teams rating did a lot to drive Detroit's early success last season. In the first eight games of the year, Detroit's opponents were a mind-boggling 5-for-14 on field-goal attempts (although two of those misses were Detroit blocks). In the second half of the year, things went back to normal, and opposing field-goal kickers were 12-for-13.

COACHING STAFF

Offensive coordinator Jim Colletto stresses simplicity and balance so often that he sounds like a transcendental philosopher. He plans to run-run-run the ball, of course, but he is also installing a zone blocking system on the offensive line. *Zone blocking* has been the cool NFL buzzword for about two years and is already getting stale the way *zone blitz* and *Cover-2* did. All teams use zone blocking to some degree in the running game, but Mike Martz used it sparingly, so Colletto is probably making real changes to the blocking assignments and not just blowing smoke up the media's collective tuchus. The Lions promoted Kippy Brown from receivers coach to passing game coordinator to reassure fans that the football would be thrown occasionally.

It's easy to spot the Tampa-2 teams when you study the Strategic Tendencies table: the Rush 4 percentage must be high, and all other percentages (particularly Rush 7+) must be very low. Defensive coordinator Mike Barry, like Rod Marinelli, learned the scheme at the feet of Monte Kiffin. Barry showed at the start of last year that he can prepare and install a sound defensive game plan if he has a few pieces to work with.

Green Bay Packers

Take a deep breath, cheeseheads. Everything is going to be just fine. The Packers are going to be very good. Aaron Rodgers is going to be okay: not great, not a bust, but good enough to win a bunch of games. If you've huddled in the back room since the day Brett Favre retired, waiting for a sign from heaven, this is your mighty wind. Life goes on without Favre. The Packers are still contenders.

We understand your fear and skepticism. It has been 16 years since someone other than Favre started at quarterback for the Packers. He made the Packers competitive, then made them champions, then helped them stay in the playoff hunt for a full decade. His skills slipped in the last few seasons, but he provided one final glimpse of greatness in 2007, and the team responded with its best season since 1996. As usual, Packers coverage revolved around Favre last year, so it was hard to see what else went right for the team. The young offensive line meshed into one of the best units in the conference. New skill position weapons came of age. The defensive front seven played very well. Coach Mike McCarthy established himself as one of the league's most creative schemers. Even the rookie kicker turned heads. All those elements will be back in 2008, and because the overall roster is so young, the Packers have the potential to get even better.

After years of salvation from, by, and through Favre, it's tempting to place caveats on all analysis of the Packers' offense. The offensive line allowed just 19 sacks, *in part* because of Favre's decisiveness and ability to es-

cape trouble. Donald Driver, Greg Jennings, and James Jones had great years, *in part* because Favre delivered such accurate passes. Ryan Grant emerged from nowhere to provide the Packers with a running game, *in part* because defenses were on their heels to stop Favre. McCarthy's schemes worked *in part* because of Favre's experience and leadership. You get the idea. All the caveats are true to an extent: Every successful offense is enhanced by the play of the quarterback. But Favre's impact on the Packers (and all of our lives) is often exaggerated, and after years of Favrocentric thought, it is easy to imagine the whole house of cards folding without the king at its center.

Luckily for the Packers, the team's success wasn't just a by-product of Favre's brilliance. Their offensive line led the league in Adjusted Sack Rate because the players were good and the system was better. Tackles Chad Clifton and Mark Tauscher are reliable veterans who make few mistakes. Interior linemen Scott Wells, Jason Spitz, and Darren Colledge are young players on the rise. McCarthy placed special emphasis on pass protection, creating formations that put fullbacks and tight ends in a specialized blocking back position just behind the guard. When McCarthy had to turn to his bench, he found Junius Colston and Tony Moll, two subs with the right mix of youth and experience. Yes, Favre razzle-dazzled or quick-thought his way out of trouble a few times, but all quarterbacks do so, now that Drew Bledsoe is retired. The Packers' line is very good, no matter the quarterback.

PACKERS PROSPECTUS

2007 Record: 13-3

Pythagorean Wins: 11.5 (3rd)

DVOA: 21.2% total (5th), 19.5% weighted (5th)

Offense: 17.3% DVOA (5th)

Defense: -1.3% DVOA (15th)

Special Teams: 2.6% DVOA (8th)

Variance: 21.6 % (27th)

2007: Brett Favre goes out a winner. Hey ... that sounds awfully familiar for some reason.

2008: No Favre, no problem, thanks to young talent up and down the depth chart.

2008 Mean Projection: 11.4 wins

On the Clock (0-3): 0%

Loserville (4-6): 2%

Mediocrity (7-8): 7%

Playoff Contender (9-10): 23%

Super Bowl Contender (11+): 68%

Projected Average Opponent: 1.8% DVOA (13th in NFL)

2008 Packers Schedule

Week	Opp.	Week	Opp.	Week	Opp.
1	MIN (Mon.)	7	IND	13	CAR
2	at DET	8	BYE	14	HOU
3	DAL	9	at TEN	15	at JAC
4	at TB	10	at MIN	16	at CHI (Mon.)
5	ATL	11	CHI	17	DET
6	at SEA	12	at NO (Mon.)		

Similarly, the team's receiving corps is full of exciting young players capable of making things happen without help from His Grizzled Greatness. The Packers led the NFL in yards after catch last season (Table 1). The Packers' YAC totals aren't distorted by screens and dump-offs to running backs; as the table shows, the team also led the NFL in YAC by wide receivers. Again, some of those YAC resulted from great reads and throws by Favre, but that argument takes on water quickly. A quick review of the game tape shows Driver, Jennings, and others spinning and juking to create big plays. And the Colts finished in the bottom half of the league in YAC: If anyone is generating YAC by his tremendous cerebral skills, shouldn't it be Peyton Manning?

Table 1. Top Offenses in Yards After Catch, 2007

Team	YAC	YAC by WR
GB	5.7	5.5
CHI	5.4	4.1
TB	5.3	5.4
MIN	5.3	3.3
BUF	5.3	3.6
ATL	5.1	4.1
NE	5.1	4.8
DAL	5.0	5.0
DEN	5.0	4.4
CLE	5.0	4.3

Offensively, all the pieces are in place for a smooth transition to a world without Favre. The Packers can replace a living legend with an average quarterback and still win the NFC North handily. But some Packers fans may be worried that the team doesn't have an average quarterback. The line, receivers, defense, three-headed sophomore backfield, and coaching won't get the team anywhere unless Aaron Rodgers can deliver. And Rodgers is the biggest enigma in the league entering the 2008 season.

There's scant hard data available about Rodgers. What we know offers mixed signals. He was a product of the Jeff Tedford pipeline at Cal, which places him in the dubious company of David Carr, Akili Smith, Kyle Boller, Joey Harrington, and A. J. Feeley. Rodgers completed 66.1 percent of his passes and threw 24 touchdowns at Cal in 2004, but the system was quarterback friendly, and Pro Football Weekly's Prospect Preview said in 2005 that he was "not as physically gifted as Boller." NFL scouts were wise to Tedford's ability to coach-up marginal prospects by 2005, so Rodgers slid until the end of the first round, then found a seat on the Packers' bench.

Rodgers saw nothing but garbage duty as a rookie. When the Packers needed him to replace an injured Favre in 2006, he threw just 12 passes before breaking his foot. For two seasons, rumors filtered out of Green Bay that the team was dissatisfied with Rodgers. General Manager Ted Thompson hedged his bets by drafting Ingle Martin in 2006. Rodgers tore up the league in preseason, throwing six touchdowns and one interception in 2006 and 2007 exhibitions, but there's a wide gap between August and September football. Our own Lewin Career Forecast suggests that Rodgers will have a Brian Griese–caliber career, which isn't exactly a ringing endorsement. Rodgers started just 22 games at Cal; among first-round quarterbacks this decade, the only players with fewer college starts were Michael Vick and Akili Smith.

With all the questions surrounding Rodgers, it was shocking to see him replace the injured Favre against the Cowboys in Week 13 and play outstanding football. Rodgers completed 18 of 26 passes for 201 yards and a touchdown. He scrambled five times for 30 yards. He faced down a heavy pass rush, improvised, and appeared cool under fire in the first meaningful action of his pro career. The Cowboys game offers us the only recent game film on Rodgers that's worth scouting, and the evidence is encouraging.

That Cowboys game taught us that Rodgers is capable of thriving within the Packers' system. It demonstrated that the Packers' offense wasn't just riding Favre's shoulders. The receivers could turn Rodgers's slants into long gains. The line could protect Rodgers, and Rodgers could help his cause by buying time. McCarthy's wide-open system, like Tedford's, is quarterback friendly, but when Green Bay has a lead, McCarthy can put snow tires on his playbook and grind out wins using power running and a full-house backfield. It's a great system to grow up in.

The Packers can even survive a complete Rodgers

meltdown. Brian Brohm and Matt Flynn arrived on draft day to provide extra inoculation against Post-Favre Stress Disorder. Brohm is similar to Rodgers in many ways: He was a top prospect whose college coach (Bobby Petrino) inspired suspicion in pro circles, so he slipped down the draft board despite great college production and good scouting reports. Like Rodgers, he gets high marks for effort but average grades for his arm and athleticism. Flynn is a big-armed scrambler who starred in the state of Louisiana; naturally, the Packers were intrigued. Neither youngster is a real threat to Rodgers in training camp (though the talk shows will surely drum up a controversy), but Brohm is relatively polished and the Louisville product should be ready if called upon in midseason.

Pencil in an average quarterback, and the Packers still have the best offense in the NFC North and one of the best in the conference. Defensively, most of the key pieces—end Aaron Kampman, linebackers A. J. Hawk and Nick Barnett, pass rusher Kabeer Gbaja-Biamila—are still in place. The team traded away defensive tackle Corey Williams but upgraded its linebacking corps by signing Brandon Chillar, who replaces weak link Brady Poppinga. The entire projected front seven is still under 30 years old. In the secondary, however, there are con-

cerns. Cornerbacks Al Harris and Charles Woodson are old starters on a young team, and Harris's play has slipped in the last two seasons. Rookie Patrick Lee is a Harris clone, a big bump-and-run guy who hits like a safety, but he's too raw to be anything more than a dime defender this season. Safety is another trouble spot, though sophomore Aaron Rouse could improve the unit by unseating Atari Bigby. The Packers will try to get through one more season with Harris and Woodson, knowing that with Mike Martz out of Detroit, there's no pass offense in the division that will pose much of a threat.

So take heart, Packers faithful. Your team is young and deep everywhere but in the secondary. The organization itself is strong. Thompson has proven himself as a drafter and a cap manager. Recent drafts have produced a bonanza of young talent, and the team that was always scraping by early in the decade now has the cap room to lock up its young stars (think Ryan Grant). McCarthy and his staff are stable and seasoned. The division is ripe for the plucking. There will be plenty of exciting football in Green Bay this year.

Oh, and if Favre has un-retired by the time you read this, the Packers will still be pretty good.

Mike Tanier

2007 Packers Stats by Week

Wk	vs.	W-L	PF	PA	YDF	YDA	TO	Total	Off	Def	ST
1	PHI	W	16	13	215	283	+1	15%	-31%	-27%	19%
2	@NYG	W	35	13	368	325	+1	34%	41%	0%	-6%
3	SD	W	31	24	405	364	+1	41%	50%	17%	9%
4	@MIN	W	23	16	384	382	0	21%	7%	-8%	6%
5	CHI	L	20	27	439	285	-4	9%	26%	14%	-3%
6	WAS	W	17	14	225	304	+1	-12%	-26%	-41%	-27%
7	BYE										
8	@DEN	W	19	13	430	332	+1	26%	38%	7%	-5%
9	@KC	W	33	22	432	234	0	13%	6%	5%	12%
10	MIN	W	34	0	488	247	+1	85%	50%	-35%	0%
11	CAR	W	31	17	317	382	+3	53%	33%	3%	23%
12	@DET	W	37	26	481	331	0	35%	42%	9%	2%
13	@DAL	L	27	37	357	414	-1	-37%	5%	45%	2%
14	OAK	W	38	7	445	233	+2	59%	29%	-14%	17%
15	@STL	W	33	14	277	364	-1	20%	-8%	4%	33%
16	@CHI	L	7	35	274	240	-2	-116%	-51%	23%	-43%
17	DET	W	34	13	394	293	+1	60%	30%	-24%	5%
18	BYE										
19	SEA	W	42	20	408	200	-1	88%	65%	-22%	1%
20	NYG	L	20	23	264	377	-1	-40%	-25%	12%	-3%

Trends and Splits

	Offense	Rank	Defense	Rank
Total DVOA	17.3%	5	-1.3%	15
Unadjusted VOA	18.7%	5	-6.3%	8
Weighted trend	16.7%	4	-0.4%	16
Variance	9.5%	27	5.1%	8
Average opponent	0.7%	15	-4.2%	30
Passing	26.1%	5	6.0%	17
Rushing	3.5%	9	-9.7%	8
First down	-1.6%	16	-0.1%	18
Second down	33.5%	3	3.4%	18
Third down	29.5%	5	-10.8%	6
First half	20.6%	3	7.7%	25
Second half	13.9%	6	-10.5%	4
Red Zone	18.6%	7	-16.4%	7
Late and close	14.3%	7	-19.2%	3

Five-Year Performance

Year	W-L	Pyth Wins	Est Wins	PF	PA	TO	Total	Rank	Off	Rank	Def	Rank	ST	Rank
2003	10-6	11.3	10.2	442	307	0	21.8%	4	10.5%	7	-9.5%	8	1.9%	10
2004	10-6	9.0	8.4	424	380	-14	1.6%	13	17.1%	7	16.4%	29	0.9%	14
2005	4-12	6.7	6.0	298	344	-24	-12.9%	23	-7.0%	20	2.1%	22	-3.8%	30
2006	8-8	6.2	7.7	301	366	0	-0.6%	15	-5.9%	20	-9.3%	6	-3.9%	29
2007	13-3	11.5	11.1	435	291	+4	21.2%	5	17.3%	5	-1.3%	15	2.6%	8

Strategic Tendencies

Run/Pass		Rank	Offense		Rank	Defense		Rank	Other		Rank
Runs, all plays	37%	28	3+ WR	59%	8	Rush 3	2.6%	26	2+ RB, Pct Runs	64%	7
Runs, first half	36%	28	4+ WR	19%	6	Rush 4	76.0%	5	1 RB/2 TE, Pct runs	42%	21
Runs, first down	46%	24	2+ TE	17%	26	Rush 5	16.0%	26	1 RB/3+ WR, pct runs	19%	26
Runs, second-long	31%	24	Single back	44%	30	Rush 6+	5.5%	26	CB1 on WR1	53%	4
Runs, power sit.	39%	32	Play action	15%	23	Rush 7+	0.2%	30	Go for it on 4th	1.11	14
Runs, behind 2H	23%	29	Max protect	6%	31	Sacks by LB	12.5%	26	Offensive Pace	30.8	18
Pass, ahead 2H	54%	4	Outside pocket	7%	27	Sacks by DB	0.0%	30	Defensive Pace	31.1	21

Green Bay threw the ball to the middle of the field more often than any other team and threw to the left side less often than any other team. That split is even more interesting when you consider that the official scorer at Lambeau Field marked passes as "middle" at a rate far below the league average. The Packers actually were above average on passes to the left side, and were below average on passes to the right side. ∅ For the second straight season, the Packers used shotgun formations more often than any other NFC team and had a much higher DVOA on these plays. ∅ The Packers dropped from fourth in the league using max protect (17 percent of plays in 2006) to 31st. ∅ The Packers had the highest percentage of first downs from passing plays at 77.4 percent, versus the league average of 68.5 percent. ∅ Ryan Grant was one of the league's top 10 screen targets, but he was among the worst running backs in DVOA on screens. Only two of his 15 screens gained a new set of downs, and only three in total got at least half of the needed yardage for a first down. The Packers were significantly more effective throwing screens to Vernand Morency. ∅ The Packers like to take their chances in short-yardage situations. When it was third down in Green Bay territory with less than five yards to go, the Packers threw the ball 20 or more yards 11.4 percent of the time; this is the highest figure in the league and more than twice the league average. ∅ Green Bay ranked second in rushing DVOA in the first half of games but 27th in rushing DVOA after halftime. ∅ Green Bay had an empty backfield more often than any team in the league; they went empty 30 percent more often than the team in second place, New Orleans. ∅ The Packers led the league in yards after catch not only on offense but also on defense. ∅ Passes caught behind the line of scrimmage against Green Bay gained an average of 6.6 yards, which is the highest figure in the NFL. ∅ As you might expect—given their preference for man coverage—Green Bay's defense had the fewest plays marked Hole in Zone by our game charters. ∅ The opposition threw to their top receiver on only 15 percent of passes; every other defense was above 20 percent. ∅ Green Bay was one of the five defenses that saw screen passes most often, and rightly so, because they had the league's worst DVOA and allowed more first downs on screens than any other team. ∅ Green Bay was one of the 10 worst teams against play-action passes, and their opponents ran play-action more often than the league average. ∅ Only two teams saw a greater number of opponents' passes dropped. ∅ One product of Green Bay's aversion to the blitz is that only one Packers sack all season was marked Rusher Untouched. ∅ Only Tennessee got a higher percentage of sacks from defensive linemen.

Passing

Player	DYAR	DVOA	Plays	NtYds	Avg	YAC	C%	TD	Int
Brett Favre*	1438	28.0%	556	4151	7.5	5.7	66.9%	28	14
Aaron Rodgers	84	31.7%	30	194	6.5	6.3	74.1%	1	0
Craig Nall*	-39	-44.6%	18	75	4.2	5.7	46.7%	1	0

Rushing

Player	DYAR	DVOA	Plays	Yds	Avg	TD	Fum	Suc
Ryan Grant	161	12.3%	188	956	5.1	8	1	47%
Brandon Jackson	-3	-9.4%	75	267	3.6	1	0	44%
DeShawn Wynn	45	13.4%	50	203	4.1	4	0	36%
Vernand Morency	1	-7.5%	29	108	3.7	0	1	34%
Brett Favre*	-26	-61.3%	9	24	2.7	0	8	—
Aaron Rodgers	10	27.8%	5	30	6.0	0	0	—

Receiving

Player	DYAR	DVOA	Plays	Catch	Yds	Y/C	YAC	TD	C%
WR									
Donald Driver	224	10.2%	122	82	1048	12.8	4.8	3	67%
Greg Jennings	302	31.5%	84	53	920	17.4	7.7	12	63%
James Jones	17	-10.0%	80	47	676	14.4	4.7	2	59%
Koren Robinson*	-8	-15.7%	34	21	241	11.5	5.7	1	62%
Ruvell Martin	88	22.2%	28	16	242	15.1	3.8	4	57%
TE									
Donald Lee	164	30.2%	63	48	575	12.0	5.6	6	76%
Bubba Franks*	-24	-18.2%	32	18	132	7.3	2.7	3	56%
RB									
Vernand Morency	-8	-17.6%	39	30	199	6.6	7.5	0	77%
Ryan Grant	-38	-31.8%	37	30	145	4.8	5.7	0	81%
Brandon Jackson	12	-3.8%	22	16	130	8.1	8.4	0	73%
DeShawn Wynn	18	11.4%	14	9	73	8.1	9.3	0	64%
Korey Hall	6	-4.0%	11	8	49	6.1	4.0	0	73%

Offensive Line

Year	Yards	ALY	Rank	Power	Rank	10+ Yds	Rank	Stuff	Rank	Sack	ASR	Rank
2005	3.41	3.59	30	67%	13	14%	18	24%	9	27	4.9%	5
2006	4.11	4.27	16	63%	18	15%	19	24%	17	24	3.7%	3
2007	4.49	3.95	26	50%	30	27%	3	24%	17	19	3.1%	1

Year	LE	Rank	LT	Rank	Mid	Rank	RT	Rank	RE	Rank
2005	2.88	30	4.44	11	3.34	31	4.06	17	3.79	19
2006	4.63	6	4.84	7	4.02	26	4.28	11	3.43	26
2007	3.98	18	3.98	22	4.10	17	4.23	17	3.46	28

Mark Tauscher and Chad Clifton have been the bookend tackles in Green Bay since 2002. Their personalities are different—Clifton is quiet and Tauscher is a practical joker with his own talk show—but they get similar results on the field. Tauscher is in a contract year, and the Packers may replace him in 2009 with Tony Moll or rookie Breno Giacomini, a nice Irish kid. Clifton's not going anywhere if Mike McCarthy can help it. "If you ever had to play without a left tackle that is not very good at pass protection, you appreciate Chad Clifton," McCarthy said in January. "Chad Clifton makes my job as a play-caller very easy." Daryn Colledge, Scott Wells, and Jason Spitz round out a line that came into its own late in the season. Scott Wells is the oldest of the interior linemen at 27. Moll, with 13 starts in two seasons, is the first lineman off the bench.

The Packers' low ranking in Adjusted Line Yards is a good example of how our attempts to separate blocking from the running back are useful but not perfect. Green Bay had 3.58 ALY per carry though Week 5. After Ryan Grant became the main back in Week 6, that improved to 4.09 ALY per carry. However, the line's main weakness did not change when Grant became the lead back: The Packers need to work on getting better push in short-yardage situations.

Defensive Front Seven

Defensive Line	Age	Pos	Plays	TmPct	Rk	Stop	Dfts	Stop%	Rk	AvYd	Rk	Sack	Hit	Hur	Runs	RuStop	RuYd	Pass	PaStop	PaYd
Aaron Kampman	29	DE	63	8.6%	8	48	22	76%	42	0.9	26	12.0	20	21	45	67%	2.6	18	100%	-3.3
Cullen Jenkins	27	DT	50	6.4%	15	39	18	78%	33	1.9	46	1.0	6	11	40	75%	2.0	10	90%	1.5
Ryan Pickett	29	DT	41	6.0%	23	31	8	76%	44	2.7	61	1.0	0	2	35	77%	2.4	6	67%	4.5
Corey Williams*	28	DT	35	4.5%	47	29	14	83%	19	1.3	18	7.0	7	3	25	80%	2.2	10	90%	-0.9
Kabeer Gbaja-Biamila	31	DE	27	3.7%	72	21	15	78%	39	0.9	24	9.5	7	14	14	64%	3.2	13	92%	-1.6
Johnny Jolly	25	DT	26	5.3%	29	19	7	73%	52	2.9	62	1.0	1	0	17	71%	3.4	9	78%	1.9
Mike Montgomery	25	DE	17	3.9%	—	11	3	65%	—	2.8	—	0.0	1	0	16	63%	2.8	1	100%	2.0
Justin Harrell	24	DT	16	4.7%	—	12	1	75%	—	3.5	—	0.0	0	0	14	86%	2.4	2	0%	11.0

Linebackers	Age	Pos	Plays	TmPct	Rk	Stop	Dfts	Stop%	AvYd	Sack	Hit	Hur	Runs	RuStop	Rk	RuYd	Rk	Tgts	Suc%	Rk	APaYd	Rk
Nick Barnett	27	MLB	136	17.4%	5	72	24	53%	5.0	3.5	5	9	93	58%	68	4.2	84	45	51%	39	4.9	20
A. J. Hawk	24	OLB	108	13.8%	31	56	19	52%	5.3	1.0	2	3	65	55%	87	4.2	87	52	62%	8	4.8	19
Brady Poppinga	29	OLB	47	6.0%	—	32	9	68%	3.2	0.0	2	2	36	75%	—	2.2	—	21	43%	63	7.1	69
Brandon Chillar	26	OLB	65	8.7%	80	39	17	60%	4.4	2.5	5	4	38	68%	27	3.2	41	26	43%	61	6.8	65

Year	Yards	ALY	Rank	Power	Rank	10+ Yds	Rank	Stuff	Rank	Sack	ASR	Rank
2005	3.95	4.35	24	64%	18	13%	9	26%	12	35	7.3%	15
2006	4.17	4.50	23	53%	4	14%	7	21%	26	46	8.1%	5
2007	4.04	4.19	18	65%	18	15%	10	21%	25	36	6.0%	22

Year	LE	Rank	LT	Rank	Mid	Rank	RT	Rank	RE	Rank
2005	4.14	17	5.10	32	4.27	21	4.01	14	4.45	20
2006	4.60	23	4.82	24	4.68	26	3.66	11	4.28	19
2007	4.83	26	4.74	25	3.92	8	4.70	25	2.86	6

Middle linebacker Nick Barnett finished sixth among NFL linebackers in successful tackles on running plays, and he's grown into one of the best all-purpose linebackers in the league. Barnett blitzes well and has improved in coverage over the last two years. A. J. Hawk also made strides in coverage in his sophomore season and uses his open-field tackling ability to neutralize screens and flat passes. Hawk's tackle totals were down from his rookie year, but that's a statistical illusion. Tackle statistics have a lot of noise, and when a team improves, tackle totals often drop because opponents execute fewer plays (particularly running plays) against them. Barnett and Hawk combined to make the same percentage of team tackles in 2007 as in 2006, so they were performing at about the same level or maybe better. Brady Poppinga is an outstanding special teamer and adequate point-of-attack defender who lacks range and coverage skills. Free agent Brandon Chillar is more of a playmaker who could also be used as a situational pass rusher. Abdul Hodge missed all of his sophomore season with a knee injury. He still has potential and could work his way into the Poppinga-Chillar mix.

Defensive end Aaron Kampman led the NFL in hurries and finished second to Tennessee's Kyle Vanden Bosch in quarterback hits. Kampman registered eight sacks in his first eight games and just four in his last eight, but he applied plenty of pressure all season long. Kampman is one of the best three-down linemen in the league and makes plenty of stops in the running game, although they don't always come so close to the line. Cullen Jenkins's sack total doesn't accurately reflect his value. He's a disruptive run defender who often stays at home on passing downs, chasing down screens and scrambling quarterbacks. Kabeer Gbaja-Biamila is still an effective designated pass rusher. His production comes in bunches: five sacks in two games against the Vikings and a two-sack game against the Chiefs but 10 games with no sacks and little other production.

Tackle Ryan Pickett never lived up to his potential in St. Louis but has reinvented himself as a sturdy run stuffer. Johnny Jolly started seven games last season before injuring his shoulder and giving way to Corey Williams. With Williams gone, Jolly should get his job back. Like Pickett, he's a massive run stopper.

Defensive Secondary

Secondary	Age	Pos	Plays	TmPct	Rk	Stop	Dfts	RuYd	Rk	RuStop	Rk	Tgts	Tgt%	Rk	Dist	Suc%	Rk	APaYd	Rk	PaYd	PD	Int
Atari Bigby	27	SS	93	11.9%	14	33	13	4.9	11	45%	38	47	11%	7	12.1	37%	71	8.4	51	8.4	9	5
Charles Woodson	32	CB	73	10.7%	19	34	18	5.2	22	55%	27	62	16%	55	10.9	58%	8	7.7	50	7.4	10	4
Nick Collins	25	FS	51	8.0%	59	16	4	11.0	82	33%	62	27	8%	31	12.8	65%	4	7.1	38	7.2	4	0
Al Harris	34	CB	46	5.9%	73	18	6	3.3	5	75%	4	74	17%	53	14.0	40%	74	9.4	73	9.1	8	2
Jarrett Bush	24	CB	30	4.4%	81	12	4	12.0	78	50%	40	56	14%	64	14.7	56%	13	6.9	28	6.7	7	0
Aaron Rouse	24	FS	27	5.0%	—	11	4	6.9	—	25%	—	11	3%	—	8.2	50%	—	5.8	—	5.4	5	2

Year	Pass D Rank	vs. #1 WR	Rk	vs. #2 WR	Rk	vs. Other WR	Rk	vs. TE	Rk	vs. RB	Rk
2005	22	-4.2%	9	8.9%	28	8.8%	22	25.6%	29	7.3%	23
2006	4	-7.6%	10	-28.5%	2	-12.0%	11	-31.2%	3	14.7%	28
2007	17	-24.3%	3	-1.4%	16	26.4%	32	5.3%	14	-15.5%	6

The Packers led the NFL with 13 pass interference penalties last season, all by defensive backs. Cornerbacks Al Harris and Charles Woodson were among the most penalized defenders in the NFL. Woodson incurred 12 penalties, three for pass interference and nine for holding or illegal contact. Harris, who was a penalty factory early in his career, drew 11 flags: two for interference, the rest for a gumbo of holds, facemasks, and a delay of game. Atari Bigby added eight penalties, Jarrett Bush seven, and the four combined to allow 186 yards on pass interference flags alone.

All of the clutching and bumping would be excusable if the Packers were shutting down receivers, but only Woodson graded out as an above-average defender. Harris almost always draws the opponents' top receiver, but he wasn't up to the task last season. His Pro Bowl selection was a lifetime achievement award. Harris is 33, but he's been incredibly durable (160 consecutive games played) and could find a way to bounce back. Patrick Lee will get a chance to make an immediate impact, and it's too early to give up on Bush, a third-year pro with the skills to handle nickel duty.

Safety Aaron Rouse earned a handful of midseason starts and graded out well in limited action. He could push the mistake-prone Bigby, who is a hard hitter against the run but extremely undisciplined. Nick Collins is an adequate free safety with job security for another year.

Special Teams

Year	DVOA	Rank	FG/XP	Rank	Net Punt	Rank	Punt Ret	Rank	Net Kick	Rank	Kick Ret	Rank	Hidden	Rank
2005	-3.8%	30	-8.7	29	-6.2	27	7.9	4	-3.1	21	-12.1	30	-8.6	27
2006	-3.9%	29	-5.9	29	-4.9	23	-2.3	22	3.4	14	-13.5	31	-14.4	31
2007	2.5%	8	1.1	16	-3.7	22	12.3	2	7.1	4	-2.2	21	-7.7	26

Mason Crosby twice led the NCAA in 50-plus-yard field goals, but it was easy to write off his accomplishments to the thin air at the University of Colorado. This turns out not to be the case; he proved his big leg was no high-altitude fluke by going 3-of-5 on 50-plus-yard field goals and nailing 14 touchbacks as a rookie in Green Bay. Crosby led the NFL in scoring thanks to a lot of extra points and midrange field goals, and he showed he could kick in poor conditions. Cowboys kicker Nick Folk went to Honolulu, but Crosby would have been the better choice for the NFC.

Punter Jon Ryan will be challenged by undrafted rookie Ken DeBauche, a four-year starter at Wisconsin. Rookie receiver Jordy Nelson returned five punts for touchdowns at Kansas State and will battle Tramon Williams to replace Charles Woodson as the Packers' punt returner. Nelson could also get a look on kickoffs, where Williams was nothing special. The Packers are flush with young running backs such as DeShawn Wynn and Brandon Jackson, so they should find a capable kick returner somewhere.

Long snapper Rob Davis retired after 11 seasons with Green Bay. Fortunately, we didn't have to endure two months of unretirement rumors like the ones about a certain teammate. Undrafted rookie J. J. Jansen will battle practice squader Thomas Gafford for the job.

COACHING STAFF

The strategic tendency tables above show that Mike McCarthy and coordinator Jim Philbin are aggressive in their use of multi-wideout sets. They don't show how creative they are at designing and implementing formations. The Packers use three-back formations more than any other team in the league. Against the Seahawks in the snow, they used the full-house backfield to turn their offense into an ATV, overpowering the Seahawks with isolation plays that seemed ripped from Walter Camp's playbook. The full-house backfield became a favorite passing formation for McCarthy as the Packers entered the red zone. Eight defenders usually crowded the line to counter the full-house attack, leaving Donald Driver or Greg Jennings one-on-one for a slant or a fade in the end zone. In shotgun formations, McCarthy would often deploy a tight end to stand two yards behind the right or left guard, like the blocking back in a single-wing offense. The strategy worked very well against opponents such as the Bears, who liked to blitz up the middle. Defensive coordinator Bob Sanders favors man coverage more than most of the Cover-2 automatons coaching in the NFL right now, but he's still a conservative blitzer. Mike Stock has been coaching special teams in the NFL on-and-off since 1987.

Houston Texans

In Space City, it is perhaps fitting that a team that has improved by small steps the past two years could be ready to make one giant leap—into the postseason.

Houston's professional football team no longer plays in a venue named for the space program, but the Texans could be ready for launch if the slow, steady improvement of the offense is matched by a defense that has been bolstered by a couple of strong drafts. Gary Kubiak was brought in to coach the Houston Texans in 2006 because the team's offense had been putrid since its inception. In the franchise's first five seasons—including Kubiak's debut campaign—the offense never ranked better than 21st in yards gained, never better than 19th in points scored. Last year, Kubiak's second at the helm, those numbers improved to 12th and 14th, respectively. The Texans gained over 5,300 yards, scored 43 touchdowns, and finished 8-8, the best win total in their history. The offensive success came despite the fact that prize acquisition Matt Schaub missed five games under center, while top receiver Andre Johnson missed seven with a knee injury.

Traditional statistics tell a nice story about the offense, but advanced metrics are our forte. DVOA shows a more modest improvement, but the trend is likewise positive. Houston's offense ranked 29th in 2005 before improving to 17th and 13th in Kubiak's first two seasons. If our projections are correct, the Texans will take another small step on offense in 2008. But Houston's ability to make the playoffs in the rugged AFC South will probably be determined on the other side of the ball.

You want to talk about small steps? Despite a number of headline-grabbing young talents on defense, the Texans have finished 32nd, 31st, and 30th in overall defensive DVOA the last three years. They'll have to accelerate the pace of improvement if they want to be a contender before their home state's oil wells run dry. Still, even a casual football observer would be hard-pressed to miss the talent Houston has amassed on that side of the ball. In the space of a single year, former first-overall selection Mario Williams went from looking like a bust to making everyone in Houston stop grumbling about Reggie Bush. Fourteen sacks will do that for a player. Rookie teammate Amobi Okoye, still too young to celebrate with a postgame beer, chipped in with six sacks and is still growing into his 300-pound body. Add in 2006 defensive rookie of the year DeMeco Ryans, and the reasons for optimism in the Texans' defensive meeting room are obvious.

One of the main reasons why our projections like the Texans this season is the presence of that young defensive core. Our research has shown that when teams spend multiple high picks on defense in consecutive years, as Houston did in taking defensive players with its first selection in four consecutive drafts from 2003 to 2006, those young talents often blossom all at the same time.

TEXANS PROSPECTUS

2007 Record: 8-8

Pythagorean Wins: 7.9 (18th)

DVOA: -2.0% total (17th), 1.1% weighted (18th)

Offense: 5.6% DVOA (13th)

Defense: 13.4% DVOA (30th)

Special Teams: 5.7% DVOA (3rd)

Variance: 13.7 % (11th)

2007: Houston, we have liftoff ... liftoff of an honest-to-goodness NFL offense.

2008: Now if the defense would just follow suit we might have ourselves a playoff team.

2008 Mean Projection: 8.9 wins

On the Clock (0-3): 1%

Loserville (4-6): 10%

Mediocrity (7-8): 31%

Playoff Contender (9-10): 39%

Super Bowl Contender (11+): 20%

Projected Average Opponent: 1.0% DVOA (15th in NFL)

2008 Texans Schedule

Week	Opp.	Week	Opp.	Week	Opp.
1	at PIT	7	DET	13	JAC (Mon.)
2	BAL	8	BYE	14	at GB
3	at TEN	9	at MIN	15	TEN
4	at JAC	10	CIN	16	at OAK
5	IND	11	at IND	17	CHI
6	MIA	12	at CLE		

There are some concerns. In a division that includes Indianapolis and Jacksonville, a team can never have enough corners, but Houston's best one, Dunta Robinson, is coming off a combined hamstring/knee injury that could keep him out until midseason and prevent him from fully regaining his prior form. Houston attempted to address the secondary in free agency, where the team's biggest signing was cornerback Jacques Reeves, formerly of the Cowboys. The Texans believe Reeves will fare better lined head up on receivers than he did in Dallas's softer zones, and they thought enough of him cross-state to hand Reeves a four-year, $20 million deal with a $4 million signing bonus. Even if Reeves is successful in Houston, however, it doesn't change the fact that Texans safeties are subpar and the secondary has little depth.

The success or failure of Reeves and his secondary mates will have a lot to do with Williams, Okoye, and the men up front. Nothing can make a good secondary look average and an average one look great like the absence or presence of a consistent pass rush from the front four. Houston would appear to have the tools to achieve just that, particularly if fifth-round pick Frank Okam, a player many believed to have first-round talent, can contribute to a rotation at defensive tackle.

Still, the Texans' biggest acquisition this past offseason may not have been a player at all. Heralded offensive-line guru Alex Gibbs was lured out of semiretirement to rejoin Kubiak as assistant head coach/offense. It was at then-Denver offensive coordinator Kubiak's side, with the Broncos in the late 1990s, that Gibbs and his zone-blocking scheme enjoyed its greatest success.

In Denver, Gibbs molded a group of undersized, mobile linemen and a stable of little-known running backs into a cut-blocking, yardage-producing rushing machine that won two Super Bowls. Denver's rushing DVOA ranked in the top six in the league seven times from 1995 to 2003. One of the two down years was 1999,

the year Terrell Davis blew out his knee, and yet the Broncos still ranked 11th in rushing. The ultra-intense Gibbs has not had a full-time coaching position since his initial retirement from the Broncos following the 2004 campaign. He served two years as a consultant with the Falcons before sitting out last year, but if the Texans' 2008 draft was any indication, he intends to stick around a while in Houston.

Many draft observers felt the Texans could have found the long-term answer to their case of running-back-by-very-average-committee in the first round. Rashard Mendenhall of Illinois was still on the board when the Texans' turn to pick arrived at number 18. Houston fans no doubt groaned at the way things were shaping up. The franchise tackles—another significant need in Houston—were already gone, and then the Texans passed on a possible solution to their running-back morass. But Gibbs's fingerprints were all over Houston's move. It traded down eight spots, to number 26, and selected Virginia Tech offensive tackle Duane Brown. The pick was quickly labeled a reach by many in the media, but Brown is a former tight end who is mobile and appears to be a perfect fit for Gibbs's ideal offensive line. He was the fastest offensive tackle at this year's NFL Scouting Combine. Gibbs loves mobile linemen; one of his mainstays in Denver was left tackle Matt Lepsis, who played his entire college career at tight end.

If Brown ends up being the answer at left tackle, it will solve a problem that has plagued the franchise literally since its birth. The Texans' first-ever player was left tackle Tony Boselli, who had been instrumental in turning the Jacksonville Jaguars into instant contenders in the late 1990s. Injuries and an enormous salary led Jacksonville to expose Boselli in the 2002 expansion draft, where Houston took him with its first pick. Shoulder injuries prevented him from ever playing a down with his new team, putting the Texans behind the eight ball both at a critical position on the field and with the salary cap from day one.

Further help for the line arrived in the form of center Chris Myers. The former Bronco is already familiar with the Gibbs system, which is still used in Denver.

Perhaps Houston can now put a respectable line together for the first time in franchise history. Its inability to do so in the early days of the franchise helped doom the career of quarterback David Carr, who had been taken with the first pick in the 2002 college draft. Playing behind a Swiss-cheese line, Carr spent more time on his back than he did scanning defenses, and his entire Houston tenure no doubt proved a boon to local chiropractors.

It isn't just the line that's getting an overhaul. Houston's most intriguing selection in the draft was running back Steve Slaton of West Virginia, taken in the third round. Slaton put up incredible numbers as a freshman and sophomore in a spread-option offense before injuries derailed his junior season. The college spread option bears little resemblance to most NFL offenses, except as it applies to Gibbs's approach to the running game. Gibbs has always preached the "one-cut" approach. He wants his linemen to cut the man in front of them to create seams, and he has his backs make a single cut and get upfield as quickly as possible. Rich Rodriguez's staff at West Virginia admitted to copying Gibbs's approach wholesale. Slaton is undersized, but very fast and a home-run threat in space. He's probably not going to be an every-down back, but could be dangerous if Gibbs's line in Houston can create some of the same seams he saw in college. At the very least, he should be add some lightning to the not exactly scintillating trio of Ron Dayne, Ahman Green, and Chris Brown, the latter signed away from Tennessee in the offseason.

Houston's running game was successful last year, but it lacked the big-play threat, as our offensive-line ratings show. The Texans led the league in not getting stuffed and ranked in the top 10 in power rushing, but were just 22nd in runs of 10 yards or more. If Kubiak can effectively utilize the talents of all his backs, Houston has the makings of a truly dangerous rushing attack.

By almost any measure, the Texans are significantly improved over the past two seasons. In most NFL divisions, they might be seen as an obvious, trendy playoff pick. But the AFC South is not like most divisions. Its other three members all qualified for the playoffs last year. Indianapolis and Jacksonville are elite teams, while Tennessee could again contend for the postseason.

We are cautiously optimistic about the Texans in 2008. The team is certainly on a positive trend, but if the Texans backslide or make only another modest improvement, they are at risk of becoming the NFL's version of the Tampa Bay Rays: loaded with young talent, improving slowly, but destined for perennial also-ran status behind their division's superpowers. With the Colts and Jaguars playing the role of the Yankees and Red Sox, Houston could be better than it was a year ago and still finish last. It's a devilish quandary.

Another last-place finish could spell doom for Kubiak, whose owner, Bob McNair, may be getting impatient considering his initial $800 million investment has yielded just a single .500 season in six campaigns. That would certainly be the owner's right, but he might want to think twice about shifting gears just when this perennially disorganized team finally appears to be following a plan.

As we suggested in last year's book, Houston was a rudderless ship in recent years when it came to roster management. Kubiak initially pledged loyalty to Carr before dumping him a year later in favor of Schaub. There was the odd signing of the aging Green and the failure to find a proper complement for Johnson at wide receiver. But the 2008 free-agency period was devoid of any real head-scratchers by Houston, and it was followed by a draft in which the Texans selected players who, on paper, at least, were perfect fits for their scheme.

McNair's model for building his franchise appears to have been the Jaguars, a team that enjoyed a meteoric rise to the AFC title game in just its second season, but never got over the hump and has only now been rebuilt into a contender. Thanks to some early missteps, the Texans never even got near the hump in their first five years.

In year seven, this is changing. With a potentially potent offense and defense that has the talent, if not yet the results, the Texans could indeed be ready for launch.

Russell Levine

2007 Texans Stats by Week

Wk	vs.	W-L	PF	PA	YDF	YDA	TO	Total	Off	Def	ST
1	KC	W	20	3	315	219	+2	20%	5%	-13%	2%
2	@CAR	W	34	21	346	353	+2	37%	26%	11%	21%
3	IND	L	24	30	254	362	-2	-7%	-25%	7%	25%
4	@ATL	L	16	26	398	304	-2	-41%	-6%	31%	-5%
5	MIA	W	22	19	352	285	-1	-20%	-19%	14%	13%
6	@JAC	L	17	37	390	457	0	-12%	8%	23%	3%
7	TEN	L	36	38	333	422	-4	-29%	-4%	21%	-3%
8	@SD	L	10	35	367	237	-5	-73%	-7%	38%	-28%
9	@OAK	W	24	17	359	310	+2	14%	25%	1%	-9%
10	BYE										
11	NO	W	23	10	390	327	+1	47%	11%	-33%	3%
12	@CLE	L	17	27	314	397	-2	-26%	-3%	18%	-5%
13	@TEN	L	20	28	315	382	-1	-29%	3%	35%	2%
14	TB	W	28	14	257	305	0	24%	13%	3%	15%
15	DEN	W	31	13	358	308	-1	44%	35%	-3%	6%
16	@IND	L	15	38	299	458	-2	-24%	9%	37%	4%
17	JAC	W	42	28	290	381	0	58%	33%	26%	51%

Trends and Splits

	Offense	Rank	Defense	Rank
Total DVOA	5.6%	13	13.4%	30
Unadjusted VOA	1.9%	16	16.2%	31
Weighted trend	10.3%	7	14.3%	29
Variance	3.0%	1	3.7%	3
Average opponent	-0.7%	5	3.7%	7
Passing	14.3%	11	20.1%	28
Rushing	-4.5%	16	5.1%	29
First down	-7.7%	23	11.2%	28
Second down	7.9%	12	10.5%	23
Third down	26.7%	7	22.5%	29
First half	4.4%	13	14.5%	26
Second half	6.8%	9	12.1%	27
Red Zone	3.6%	15	26.8%	30
Late and close	6.6%	9	19.7%	29

Five-Year Performance

Year	W-L	Pyth Wins	Est Wins	PF	PA	TO	Total	Rank	Off	Rank	Def	Rank	ST	Rank
2003	5-11	4.5	5.8	255	380	-5	-21.1%	29	-12.9%	27	10.6%	28	2.3%	8
2004	7-9	7.1	7.6	309	339	+5	-4.0%	18	0.4%	15	0.8%	18	-3.7%	29
2005	2-14	3.7	3.6	260	431	-8	-34.8%	31	-17.3%	29	21.2%	32	-3.7%	3
2006	6-10	5.1	5.8	267	366	-3	-20.1%	28	-2.5%	17	15.5%	31	-2.1%	23
2007	8-8	7.9	7.7	379	384	-13	-2.0%	17	5.6%	13	13.4%	30	5.7%	30

Strategic Tendencies

Run/Pass		Rank	Offense		Rank	Defense		Rank	Other		Rank
Runs, all plays	41%	16	3+ WR	45%	24	Rush 3	6.1%	12	2+ RB, Pct Runs	56%	20
Runs, first half	41%	19	4+ WR	11%	17	Rush 4	71.4%	6	1 RB/2 TE, Pct runs	51%	13
Runs, first down	48%	21	2+ TE	26%	17	Rush 5	16.0%	25	1 RB/3+ WR, pct runs	24%	16
Runs, second-long	29%	27	Single back	47%	29	Rush 6+	6.5%	22	CB1 on WR1	44%	16
Runs, power sit.	72%	3	Play action	21%	12	Rush 7+	1.4%	18	Go for it on 4th	1.09	16
Runs, behind 2H	27%	20	Max protect	6%	30	Sacks by LB	17.7%	23	Offensive Pace	31.0	19
Pass, ahead 2H	37%	25	Outside pocket	13%	10	Sacks by DB	1.6%	29	Defensive Pace	30.1	7

Houston was one of only two offenses to use shotgun on fewer than 10 percent of plays (the other was Seattle). The Texans were much worse in shotgun than with the quarterback under center—only Carolina had a larger negative difference in DVOA. ✐ In formations with two wide receivers, the Texans both threw and ran the ball equally. However, they ranked third in DVOA when passing, and 20th when rushing. ✐ The Texans faced a league-low number of third downs with 10 or more yards to go. They converted 30 percent of those situations, much better than the league average of 21 percent. ✐ Houston called an average number of screens, and ranked in the top 10 of DVOA. Oddly, although screen passes tend to be most effective against the blitz, Houston actually ranked last in screen plays called against five or more rushers. ✐ Only Buffalo had a lower percentage of passes dropped. ✐ Houston threw only 31 percent of passes to the right side, the lowest percentage in the league, and 33 percent of passes up the middle, more than any other offense except Green Bay. ✍ Houston had the fewest number of non-screen passes to a receiver listed as uncovered. ✍ Although the Texans ranked 23rd in Adjusted Sack Rate, they ranked 30th in quarterback hurries per pass. ✍ Houston's defense saw a below average number of draw plays, but ranked 10th in DVOA on such plays.

Passing

Player	DYAR	DVOA	Plays	NtYds	Avg	YAC	C%	TD	Int
Matt Schaub	381	8.2%	303	2132	7.0	4.0	67.4%	9	9
Sage Rosenfels	599	24.3%	246	1647	6.7	3.8	64.4%	15	12
Quinn Gray	302	20.9%	155	932	6.0	4.4	55.6%	10	4

Rushing

Player	DYAR	DVOA	Plays	Yds	Avg	TD	Fum	Suc
Ron Dayne	34	-4.6%	195	771	4.0	6	2	48%
Ahman Green	33	3.2%	70	260	3.7	2	0	41%
Darius Walker	46	10.7%	58	264	4.6	1	0	48%
Adi Echemandu*	-14	-25.5%	20	85	4.3	0	1	30%
Samkon Gado*	-12	-20.7%	18	46	2.6	1	0	44%
Matt Schaub	3	-8.2%	14	54	3.9	0	8	—
Sage Rosenfels	30	41.5%	10	61	6.1	1	4	—
Jameel Cook	-10	-35.5%	8	24	3.0	0	0	25%
Kevin Walter	23	36.9%	5	30	6.0	0	0	—
Jacoby Jones	-2	-53.1%	3	-1	-0.3	0	0	—
Chris Brown	100	13.8%	102	463	4.5	5	1	57%
Quinn Gray	20	22.2%	9	63	7.0	0	2	—

Receiving

Player	DYAR	DVOA	Plays	Ctch	Yds	Y/C	YAC	TD	C%
WR									
Kevin Walter	182	8.9%	106	65	800	12.3	2.6	5	61%
Andre Johnson	288	29.9%	86	60	851	14.2	4.2	8	70%
André Davis	75	2.5%	63	33	583	17.7	3.1	3	52%
Jacoby Jones	-12	-19.0%	24	15	147	9.8	3.6	0	63%
David Anderson	43	18.8%	17	12	131	10.9	1.8	1	71%
TE									
Owen Daniels	127	12.7%	94	63	773	12.3	3.3	3	67%
Jeb Putzier*	-2	-10.5%	10	6	39	6.5	2.8	1	60%
Joel Dreessen	33	70.0%	6	4	55	13.8	2.0	2	67%
RB									
Vonta Leach	-37	-30.9%	33	25	108	4.3	3.9	2	76%
Ron Dayne	-4	-16.8%	26	17	112	6.6	7.1	0	65%
Ahman Green	4	-9.7%	18	14	123	8.8	9.3	0	78%
Darius Walker	37	25.0%	15	13	81	6.2	5.4	0	87%
Jameel Cook	10	3.7%	8	8	40	5.0	2.9	0	100%
Samkon Gado*	2	-9.9%	8	8	59	7.4	7.1	0	100%
Chris Brown	33	14.7%	21	19	128	6.7	6.4	0	90%

Offensive Line

Year	Yards	ALY	Rank	Power	Rank	10+ Yds	Rank	Stuff	Rank	Sack	ASR	Rank
2005	4.06	4.43	8	50%	30	12%	27	24%	10	68	13.0%	32
2006	4.00	4.18	21	71%	8	14%	22	20%	2	43	9.3%	28
2007	3.91	4.33	10	69%	10	13%	22	18%	1	22	4.8%	10

Year	LE	Rank	LT	Rank	Mid	Rank	RT	Rank	RE	Rank
2005	4.24	16	4.14	22	4.61	4	3.75	23	4.32	13
2006	4.23	15	2.66	32	4.41	14	4.25	14	4.20	14
2007	4.92	4	4.46	12	4.18	14	4.67	5	4.11	15

As noted earlier in this chapter, the biggest change to the Houston offensive line is on the coaching staff, where Alex Gibbs will remake the unit in his preferred cut-blocking mode. To that end, the Texans have done a good job acquiring the type of mobile, athletic linemen that Gibbs prefers. In addition to first-rounder Duane Brown, who is expected to immediately challenge the incumbent Ephraim Salaam for the starting spot at left tackle, center Chris Myers was acquired from Denver. The right tackle spot is already manned by a Gibbs-type lineman: Eric Winston, who is yet another former tight end. Both of last year's starting guards, Chester Pitts and Fred Weary, are back. The Texans re-signed Weary in the offseason, which suggests the team was not overly concerned about the broken leg he suffered last season. The same cannot be said for former starting left tackle Charles Spencer. A year and a half after suffering a gruesome broken leg, Spencer was a limited participant in spring drills, and hopes to be fully ready for training camp, but his odds of getting back into the starting lineup are long.

It will be interesting to watch the development of the offensive line under Gibbs's tutelage in 2008, because this unit, long an Achilles' heel for the Texans, had begun to make strides in 2007. The most notable improvement was in pass protection, where Matt Schaub and Sage Rosenfels were able to remain upright far more consistently than David Carr ever had. The Texans used max protect less than half as often as they did in 2006, and their NFL rank dropped from ninth to 30th. Last year in this space we speculated that Texans fans would learn in 2007 just how much of the sack parade was Carr's fault. Given that major improvement in this area was accomplished without a major change in offensive line personnel, the answer looks like "a lot."

Defensive Front Seven

Defensive Line	Age	Pos	Plays	TmPct	Rk	Stop	Dfts	Stop%	Rk	AvYd	Rk	Sack	Hit	Hur	Runs	RuStop	RuYd	Pass	PaStop	PaYd
Mario Williams	23	DE	61	7.5%	18	48	25	79%	33	0.9	25	14.0	4	11	40	75%	1.9	21	86%	-1.0
Travis Johnson	26	DT	44	5.7%	27	32	8	73%	53	2.6	58	0.0	1	2	32	75%	2.3	12	67%	3.4
Anthony Weaver	28	DE	41	5.3%	51	29	6	71%	63	2.4	59	0.0	0	2	34	76%	1.7	7	43%	6.0
Amobi Okoye	21	DT	32	3.9%	56	24	10	75%	47	1.6	31	5.0	3	5	22	64%	3.1	10	100%	-1.6
Earl Cochran	27	DE	30	3.9%	68	19	7	63%	73	4.0	76	1.0	0	3	21	57%	4.0	9	78%	4.2
Anthony Maddox	30	DT	17	2.1%	—	12	3	71%	—	2.4	—	2.0	0	5	10	70%	2.9	7	71%	1.6
Jeff Zgonina	38	DT	17	2.1%	—	10	3	59%	—	2.5	—	0.0	2	5	17	59%	2.5	0	0%	0.0

Linebackers	Age	Pos	Plays	TmPct	Rk	Stop	Dfts	Stop%	AvYd	Sack	Hit	Hur	Runs	RuStop	Rk	RuYd	Rk	Tgts	Suc%	Rk	APaYd	Rk
DeMeco Ryans	24	MLB	135	16.5%	9	69	17	51%	4.9	2.0	1	4	80	60%	61	4.2	86	44	45%	57	7.3	75
Morlon Greenwood	30	OLB	123	15.0%	18	49	11	40%	6.3	1.0	1	3	64	45%	99	4.7	96	54	38%	80	6.7	64
Danny Clark*	31	OLB	44	6.6%	—	23	4	52%	4.3	0.0	1	4	28	64%	—	2.9	—	16	57%	17	4.6	15
Charlie Anderson*	27	OLB	25	3.1%	—	12	5	48%	4.2	2.0	1	3	12	58%	—	4.2	—	12	48%	—	4.9	—
Kevin Bentley	29	OLB	17	2.4%	—	8	1	47%	5.8	0.0	0	1	13	46%	—	5.2	—	5	48%	—	8.9	—
Chaun Thompson	28	OLB	15	1.8%	—	9	7	60%	2.1	1.0	1	2	10	40%	—	4.1	—	2	28%	—	7.3	—

Year	Yards	ALY	Rank	Power	Rank	10+ Yds	Rank	Stuff	Rank	Sack	ASR	Rank
2005	4.66	4.73	31	67%	23	16%	12	19%	32	37	8.2%	5
2006	4.32	4.36	19	77%	30	15%	13	21%	25	28	5.6%	26
2007	4.33	4.36	25	76%	29	17%	18	20%	27	31	6.0%	23

Year	LE	Rank	LT	Rank	Mid	Rank	RT	Rank	RE	Rank
2005	4.88	27	4.89	29	4.51	27	6.18	32	3.72	15
2006	5.45	32	4.12	10	4.02	8	4.75	25	4.72	25
2007	4.51	24	4.73	23	4.40	25	3.67	7	4.31	19

The cornerstones are now in place for Houston to turn this area of weakness into a team strength. Mario Williams is poised for a monster year after making "the leap" in 2007, or more accurately, sometime around the team's Week 10 bye. After compiling four sacks in the first nine games, he had 10 in his next six to finish with 14. Williams's opposite, Anthony Weaver, is serviceable enough and the Texans upgraded their defensive tackle situation by drafting 20-year-old Amobi Okoye last year. It is possible Houston may have found another gem in this year's draft by taking Frank Okam of Texas in the fifth round. Okam had the talent to go much higher, but not always the desire. If Kubiak and his staff can motivate him, he could eventually compete for a starting spot next to Okoye, creating an Okam-Okoye duo to torment announcers and offenses alike.

The Texans are set at middle linebacker with DeMeco Ryans, but the players on either side of him have been a concern. Here, Houston attempted to upgrade without breaking the bank by bringing in a pair of moderately-priced free agents, Kevin Bentley (Seattle) and Chaun Thompson (Cleveland). Both could challenge for starting spots against the likes of Morlon Greenwood and Zac Diles. Fourth-round pick Xavier Adibi of Virginia Tech is like Okam in that he was a very productive college player who fell in the draft, but he fell for different reasons. Adibi has a high motor and motivation is not an issue, but he's small and, considering that speed is supposed to be his strength, had a less-than-stellar time in the 40-yard dash at the scouting combine.

Defensive Secondary

Secondary	Age	Pos	Plays	TmPct	Rk	Stop	Dfts	RuYd	Rk	RuStop	Rk	Tgts	Tgt%	Rk	Dist	Suc%	Rk	APaYd	Rk	PaYd	PD	Int
Von Hutchins*	27	FS	100	12.2%	12	24	13	9.5	76	32%	63	59	12%	3	10.1	30%	82	9.8	68	9.9	7	1
C. C. Brown	25	SS	93	11.4%	20	37	13	6.0	32	45%	39	39	8%	25	13.7	54%	23	7.3	43	7.2	6	1
Fred Bennett	24	CB	69	9.6%	31	36	14	9.3	64	54%	29	63	15%	62	9.2	61%	2	4.4	1	4.8	17	3
Will Demps	29	FS	53	6.9%	70	21	7	6.8	51	46%	35	24	5%	66	10.3	45%	52	8.6	53	8.7	3	0
Demarcus Faggins	29	CB	48	5.9%	75	15	6	11.2	72	20%	78	58	12%	76	11.2	44%	65	9.1	69	8.9	3	0
Dunta Robinson	26	CB	42	9.1%	42	20	10	4.4	13	55%	25	37	14%	70	8.7	57%	9	7.7	51	7.7	10	2
Jamar Fletcher	29	CB	15	2.9%	—	7	3	9.0	—	0%	—	20	7%	—	9.9	40%	—	12.8	—	12.3	4	0
Jacques Reeves	26	CB	68	8.7%	51	22	6	10.8	70	17%	80	107	22%	13	13.2	47%	53	8.1	56	7.7	12	1
Nick Ferguson	34	SS	54	8.9%	47	20	5	5.9	27	43%	43	19	6%	51	14.0	38%	70	11.9	79	12.6	1	0

Year	Pass D Rank	vs. #1 WR	Rk	vs. #2 WR	Rk	vs. Other WR	Rk	vs.TE	Rk	vs.RB	Rk
2005	30	29.7%	31	24.9%	31	13.0%	28	26.1%	30	-3.9%	14
2006	31	8.8%	23	-6.3%	10	26.2%	28	-0.9%	18	30.0%	32
2007	28	21.2%	30	-1.4%	15	11.4%	26	18.0%	25	-2.3%	16

Sometimes an injury—even to a key player—can have a silver lining. Such was the case with cornerback Dunta Robinson. The blow from his midseason injury was greatly softened by the wholly astonishing play of rookie Fred Bennett. Stepping into the starting lineup for Robinson in Week 9, Bennett not only outplayed the former first-round pick he replaced—he outplayed most every corner in the league. Bennett led the league in Adjusted Yards per Pass and was second in Success Rate. He was at his best when covering the opposition's top receiver, allowing 4.0 Adjusted Yards per Pass with a 63 percent Success Rate (compared to 7.8 and 61 percent for Robinson, or 10.4 and 36 percent for Demarcus Faggins). He wasn't perfect—he needs to improve his tackling—but if Bennett's rookie performance is for real, and Robinson is able to return to full effectiveness in the second half of the season, the Texans will turn a historical weakness into a team strength. Free-agent signee Jacques Reeves should provide some stability opposite Bennett while Robinson is recovering. Third-round pick Antwaun Molden out of Eastern Kentucky could see the field plenty as a rookie as well. Molden is a great athlete—he ran a sub-4.4 40 and led all corners in bench-press repetitions at the combine—and probably would have gone a lot higher had he come from a BCS-conference school. He has good size and the speed to run with receivers, and should develop into a starter after some seasoning.

The picture at safety isn't as rosy. Will Demps is a serviceable pro, but C. C. Brown was not a favorite of our game charters, who noted his tendency to get lost in zone coverage and his poor tackling form in run support—the latter being his supposed strength. Still, Houston can be effective enough to win with this group, even in a pass-happy division, if Williams and Okoye are able to bring heat on opposing quarterbacks without blitzing.

Special Teams

Year	DVOA	Rank	FG/XP	Rank	Net Punt	Rank	Punt Ret	Rank	Net Kick	Rank	Kick Ret	Rank	Hidden	Rank
2005	3.6%	3	-8.2	28	-0.4	18	-4.8	29	11.9	2	22.9	2	8.2	5
2006	-2.1%	23	-0.8	18	-6.1	27	3.0	6	-2.6	26	-6.1	26	-7.5	25
2007	5.7%	3	4.6	7	0.7	17	-1.0	16	7.9	1	21.2	2	-0.1	16

Houston got back on the right track in the special teams department last year, recovering nicely from a drop-off suffered by its kickoff return and coverage teams in 2006. André Davis led a stunning improvement for the return team by finishing as the league's second-most-effective kickoff returner behind Cleveland's Joshua Cribbs. Davis was worth 19.3 points of field position better than average, better than Jerome Mathis had been even in 2005 when he led a stellar return unit. The kick coverage unit had a similar rebound, while veteran punter Matt Turk proved to be a replacement-level upgrade over Chad Stanley. Kris Brown remains one of the game's better kickers.

Across the board, special teams are the Texans' biggest strength. The coverage units should again be solid with the additions at linebacker providing depth.

COACHING STAFF

Other than the addition of assistant head coach Alex Gibbs, the biggest change to Houston's coaching staff in head coach Gary Kubiak's third season is the elevation of Kyle Shanahan to offensive coordinator. Shanahan, 28, became the NFL's youngest coordinator when Mike Sherman departed for the head job at Texas A&M. Shanahan has the family name, but his rise up the coaching ranks is not just a case of nepotism. As Houston's receivers coach in 2006, he was credited with helping Andre Johnson to his finest season, and last year he worked closely with Kubiak on a passing game that was much improved despite losing starting quarterback Matt Schaub for much of the season's second half.

In his second year as Houston's defensive coordinator, Richard Smith dramatically changed the way his defense rushed the passer. In 2006, the Texans were one of the top 10 teams sending six or more pass rushers; last year, they fell to 22nd.

Indianapolis Colts

Can we just fast-forward past the 2008 regular season and pencil in Colts-Patriots for the AFC Championship in January? That will obviously sound like blasphemy to Chargers fans, not to mention the fans of most other AFC teams. Nevertheless, the AFC in recent years has felt like the Patriots, the Colts, and everyone else—much as the NFC in the 1990s once seemed like the Cowboys, the 49ers, and everyone else. Yes, predicting a conference championship is an inaccurate science, but the Patriots still look like the best team in the NFL, and if we had to pick one team to challenge them, it would have to be the Colts.

Taking September through February as a whole, the Colts were every bit as good a team in 2007-2008 as they were in 2006-2007. But we usually remember football teams for how well they play in the playoffs, not the regular season. So last year's Colts were a disappointment and the previous year's Colts were a success.

And this year's Colts? They'll probably be a lot like the Colts of the past four years: one of the best teams in the league, good enough so that if things break right in January, they could win the Super Bowl, but also capable of losing in the first week of the playoffs. Reading between the lines, we can safely assume that the Colts front office agrees with that assessment because the club's offseason philosophy was to keep the players it has, refrain from big changes, and head into the 2008 season with almost the same starting lineup it had in 2007.

COLTS PROSPECTUS

2007 Record: 13-3

Pythagorean Wins: 12.5 (2nd)

DVOA: 33.1% total (2nd), 22.4% weighted (4th)

Offense: 28.3% DVOA (2nd)

Defense: -10.7% DVOA (3rd)

Special Teams: -5.9% DVOA (32nd)

Variance: 16.3 % (20th)

2007: As great as ever, except when the only healthy receivers were Reggie Wayne and some random dudes with funny names.

2008: The less things change, the more they stay the same.

2008 Mean Projection: 9.9 wins

On the Clock (0-3): 0%

Loserville (4-6): 2%

Mediocrity (7-8): 18%

Playoff Contender (9-10): 45%

Super Bowl Contender (11+): 35%

Projected Average Opponent: 7.4% DVOA (2nd in NFL)

According to our injury value chart (see "The Injury Effect"), the Colts had more injuries to their starting lineup than any other team in the NFL (Table 1). In fact, the difference between Indianapolis and number two Miami was larger than the difference between Miami and the 12th-ranked team, Cincinnati. The list of injured players only starts with big names like Marvin Harrison and Dwight Freeney, who each missed most of the season. The Colts also played the whole year without nose tackle Booger McFarland, lost much of their depth at linebacker, and had a few games in which Peyton Manning was just passing to Reggie Wayne and some guys off the street.

If the Colts are no longer unlucky with injuries and rebound to just average health in 2008, they should win their fifth straight AFC South title and challenge for a second Lombardi Trophy. But if the breaks go against them, especially if safety Bob Sanders can't replicate his healthy 2007, it won't be a Super Bowl season in Indianapolis.

Health is a good place to start talking about the Colts because of the ridiculous way they handled Harrison's injury. When he suffered a knee injury in Week 4 against the Broncos, the Colts claimed the injury was minor— "a bruise" was the term coming out of Indianapolis. Then ESPN's Ed Werder reported that the injury was serious, potentially threatening Harrison's season or even his career, and the Colts released a statement denouncing Werder's report. They then put Harrison on the field

Table 1. 2007 Adjusted Games Lost to Injuries, Starters

Rank	Team	Off	Rank	Def	Rank	Total
1	IND	18.8	17	53.9	1	72.7
2	MIA	26.2	8	34.8	4	61.0
3	STL	40.0	1	19.7	11	59.6
4	BAL	24.4	10	35.0	3	59.4
5	CHI	19.7	14	39.7	2	59.4
6	WAS	38.4	2	19.1	12	57.4
7	HOU	26.0	9	29.8	7	55.8
8	BUF	21.9	12	32.1	5	54.0
9	ARI	27.5	7	23.2	9	50.7
10	OAK	31.2	5	18.3	13	49.6

for a game against the Jacksonville Jaguars in October—a game he clearly wasn't ready to play—and sat him down for the rest of the regular season. Come playoff time, they put him on the field again for a game he still wasn't ready to play, and Harrison was terrible, losing a crucial fumble on one of the two passes he caught and feeling too much pain to go in late in the game, when the Colts desperately needed their passing game firing on all cylinders. We still don't know the severity of Harrison's injury (the Colts shed a little more light on it late in the season by calling it a "minor sprain" and a "burst bursa sac"), but we do know that the Colts should have just put Harrison on injured reserve in October.

Will Harrison be healthy in 2008? Who knows? The Colts just aren't disclosing any information about him, so there's really no way to say whether his injury is likely to affect him in 2008. What we can say is that looking back on Werder's report during the 2007 season now, it sure seems as if the ESPN man had solid sources, and Werder reported that knee pain would be Harrison's constant companion for the rest of his career. It's hard to believe that Harrison is ever going to be close to the same again.

Then again, if Harrison doesn't see the field in 2008, it may have nothing to do with his knee whatsoever. Football fans were shocked in May when Harrison was accused of being involved in a shooting in his hometown of Philadelphia, an accusation that couldn't have been more at odds with the public perception of him. As of press time, we do not know Harrison's legal status.

But here's the thing about Harrison: He really doesn't matter. That may sound like an awfully harsh assessment of a future Hall of Famer, but the fact is, the Colts still had the second-best offense in the league in 2007, even though Harrison played only five games. Even in the small sample size of passes that were thrown his way, Harrison's DVOA was far below that of the Colts' starting wide receivers, Anthony Gonzalez and Reggie Wayne.

Gonzalez and Wayne are very good. They're faster than Harrison, and although they don't seem to have the ability to read the mind of quarterback Peyton Manning like Harrison always has, they both fit very well in the Colts' passing game. Wayne had the best season of his career in 2007 and is still in his prime, and Gonzalez clearly improved as the year went along. Manning doesn't have anything to worry about at wide receiver.

We also consider Dallas Clark more of a third wide receiver than a first tight end, based on the way the Colts use him in their offense. Officially he's a tight end, and while labeling him as such might seem like semantics, it could have had real-world consequences. In February 2008, the Colts slapped Clark with the franchise tag, meaning he had a standing one-year contract offer, with a salary equal to the average of the five highest-paid tight ends in the league, or $4.5 million. If he had been considered a wide receiver, the franchise tender offer would have been $7.8 million. It would have been interesting to see what would have happened if Clark and his agent had tried to challenge the franchise tender and said Clark was really a wide receiver, but it became a moot point when the team and the player came to a long-term contract agreement. That's the Colts' modus operandi: They spend their first-round picks wisely (Clark was their first-rounder in 2003) and reward them handsomely when the players become free agents. Clark will be back in 2008 as the same-as-always over-the-middle threat.

The bottom line: The Colts have one of the greatest quarterbacks in NFL history throwing passes to a more experienced Gonzalez and the same Wayne and Clark whom they've had the last few years. Anything they get from Harrison is gravy. There's no reason to think this passing game won't be better than it was last year.

And the running game? Joseph Addai was the same player in 2007 that he was in 2006, and he'll be that same player again in 2008: Count on him for a little over 1,000 rushing yards, somewhere between four and five yards a carry, about 40 catches for somewhere between 300 and 400 receiving yards, and very few mistakes. He rarely misses his blocks when he's supposed to pick up the blitz, and he has only two fumbles in 568 career touches. Bonus: Backup running back Kenton Keith was surprisingly effective when coming in off the bench, meaning the Colts don't need to burden Addai with more than 15 or 20 carries a game. Throw in sixth-round draft pick Mike Hart and veteran Dominic Rhodes, the latter returning from a year of exile in Oakland, and the Colts have at running back something that they don't have anywhere else on offense: depth.

2008 Colts Schedule

Week	Opp.	Week	Opp.	Week	Opp.
1	CHI	7	at GB	13	at CLE
2	at MIN	8	at TEN (Mon.)	14	CIN
3	JAC	9	NE	15	DET
4	BYE	10	at PIT	16	at JAC (Thu.)
5	at HOU	11	HOU	17	TEN
6	BAL	12	at SD		

The Colts' offensive line always comes out looking good in our metrics, and there's no reason to believe it won't again this year. For starters, Manning is so good at making opposing defenses pay for it when they blitz, that as long as he is the quarterback, the Colts will be one of the top teams in the league in Adjusted Sack Rate. But also give the offensive line credit: The no-huddle and the stretch—the staples of the Colts' offense—aren't easy for 300-pounders, but the 300-pounders up front for the Colts run that offense to perfection.

One of the strengths of the offensive line has been its consistency and continuity, which is why it's a bit of a worry that guard Jake Scott, who started all 16 games each of the last three years for the Colts, has left as a free agent for the Titans. But the personnel should still be fine up front. Center Jeff Saturday, the reliable leader of the line, is still going strong. They should have a solid pair of guards with Ryan Lilja on one side and the other side to be determined by a training-camp battle between Charlie Johnson and second-round draft pick Mike Pollak. Ryan Diem is a good if not overpowering right tackle. And then there's the guy who got the most attention on the Colts offensive line last year.

Left tackle Tony Ugoh should be better in 2008 than he was as a rookie in 2007. When the Colts drafted him, general manager Bill Polian thought that Ugoh would spend his rookie year on the bench behind Tarik Glenn and that the rookie would be ready to shine in 2009. As it happened, Glenn retired and Ugoh had to play earlier than expected. While he wasn't quite as good as Glenn, he was fine. The Colts don't need to be too worried about Manning's blind side.

Add it all up, and there's every reason to believe that the Colts are going to continue to have not just a good offense, but a great one. Our 2008 projections show two offenses far ahead of the other 30. If you guessed that these two offenses belong to the Patriots and Colts, you are correct and a master of the obvious.

Something else makes the Colts similar to their archrivals in New England: It is hard to predict what the teams will get out of their defense. The Colts' unit was pathetic in 2006, ranking 27th in the league in DVOA, but it stiffened in the playoffs and the Colts won the Super Bowl. Things were quite different a year later. Despite the loss of Freeney and McFarland, as well as the numerous injuries at linebacker, the defense was excellent throughout the regular season and finished third in DVOA. Then the Colts lost their first playoff game as the defense allowed four touchdown drives of more than 70 yards to a Chargers team that played most of the game without LaDainian Tomlinson.

That playoff loss was the first time all year that the Colts really looked as if they missed the pass rushing off the edge that Dwight Freeney usually provides. Freeney's grand total of nine sacks in the last two years and the Colts' ability to do just fine without him in the regular season suggest that he doesn't make a big difference to the defense. But Freeney provides a lot of pressure even on the plays when he doesn't record a sack, and in that playoff loss, when Philip Rivers and Billy Volek took their sweet time in the pocket and combined to average 13.6 yards per pass, Colts fans were reminded why their team made Freeney the highest-paid defensive player in the league last year.

So it's good news in Indianapolis that Freeney should be fine in time for training camp. His Lisfranc injury is a serious one, but it's also one that players have come back from and played at a high level again. And although it feels as if Freeney has been around forever, he just turned 28, so his injury doesn't signal the beginning of the end, the way Harrison's does.

Although Freeney is important, the real heart and soul of the defense is Sanders, the injury-prone safety who surprisingly missed only one game in 2007. Sanders is one of the hardest hitters in the league. He's effective against both the run and the pass, and his importance to the defense is evident in the simple observation that when he's healthy (2005, playoffs after 2006, 2007), the Colts' defense is good, and when he's not healthy (2004 and 2006 regular season), the Colts defense is bad.

Linebacker has not been the Colts' strong suit; they tend to look for young, low-cost players and not hold on to them beyond their rookie contracts. Veteran Rob Morris was cut, as was Rocky Boiman, who started seven games after Morris went on injured reserve with a knee injury, and signed with Philadelphia as a free agent. Tyjuan Hagler and Freddie Keiaho will probably be the starters on the outside in 2008.

Gary Brackett started all 16 games in the middle last year and will start there again this year. Brackett isn't a great player, but for a guy who isn't very fast and is generously listed at five foot eleven and 235 pounds, he's making a pretty good career for himself as an NFL linebacker. Brackett is known as one of the most respected players inside the locker room; when the Colts chose team captains last year, the players elected Brackett and Manning.

The Colts have an enormous, glaring weakness, the same enormous, glaring weakness they always have: special teams. It's not so much that the Colts don't care about special teams as that they're just nowhere near as good at assembling special-teams talent as they are at assembling talent on offense and defense.

Indianapolis gave kicker Adam Vinatieri a huge (for a kicker) free-agent contract in 2006, and he's been below average in two years with the Colts. Last season, he was the only regular kicker in the league who never made a field goal of at least 45 yards. For that matter, Vinatieri never even made one from 40 yards. He still gets decent length on his kickoffs, but the low trajectory of his kicks leads to long returns. Vinatieri is not the only problem, either; the Colts finished last in the league in special teams DVOA and were below average in every area except punt returns.

Despite the special-teams soft spot, the Colts offense looks so good that it should make the problems on special teams more a minor annoyance than a fatal flaw. Indianapolis is again on the short list of Super Bowl favorites.

Michael David Smith

2007 Colts Stats by Week

Wk	vs.	W-L	PF	PA	YDF	YDA	TO	Total	Off	Def	ST
1	NO	W	41	10	452	293	+2	80%	43%	-37%	0%
2	@TEN	W	22	20	381	313	+1	12%	39%	16%	-11%
3	@HOU	W	30	24	362	254	+2	44%	25%	-44%	-25%
4	DEN	W	38	20	419	354	+2	71%	73%	7%	5%
5	TB	W	33	14	400	177	0	64%	64%	-2%	-3%
6	BYE										
7	@JAC	W	29	7	384	226	+2	63%	20%	-42%	2%
8	@CAR	W	31	7	395	293	+2	51%	35%	-4%	12%
9	NE	L	20	24	329	342	0	23%	19%	-16%	-12%
10	@SD	L	21	23	386	177	-3	-21%	-16%	-46%	-52%
11	KC	W	13	10	216	234	+1	-57%	-31%	15%	-12%
12	@ATL	W	31	13	365	250	+1	37%	17%	-19%	1%
13	JAC	W	28	25	342	411	+1	22%	38%	19%	3%
14	@BAL	W	44	20	334	243	+5	97%	81%	-37%	-21%
15	@OAK	W	21	14	322	253	-1	4%	-8%	0%	12%
16	HOU	W	38	15	458	299	+2	52%	48%	-7%	-3%
17	TEN	L	10	16	194	356	+1	-5%	17%	25%	3%
18	BYE										
19	SD	L	24	28	446	411	-2	-16%	28%	50%	6%

Trends and Splits

	Offense	Rank	Defense	Rank
Total DVOA	28.3%	2	-10.7%	3
Unadjusted VOA	27.0%	2	-9.5%	4
Weighted trend	20.1%	3	-8.2%	4
Variance	9.4%	26	5.9%	14
Average opponent	0.0%	7	2.8%	11
Passing	43.4%	2	-12.0%	3
Rushing	11.0%	4	-9.5%	9
First down	18.0%	6	-21.9%	1
Second down	39.4%	2	-6.9%	7
Third down	30.6%	4	2.2%	15
First half	29.6%	2	-8.1%	8
Second half	26.4%	3	-13.1%	2
Red Zone	25.3%	5	-14.8%	9
Late and close	29.4%	3	-25.7%	1

Five-Year Performance

Year	W-L	Pyth Wins	Est Wins	PF	PA	TO	Total	Rank	Off	Rank	Def	Rank	ST	Rank
2003	12-4	10.6	10.5	447	336	+10	19.8%	5	17.3%	2	-1.3%	15	1.3%	14
2004	12-4	11.5	12.0	522	351	+19	22.8%	3	39.9%	1	3.5%	19	-2.5%	25
2005	14-2	12.7	12.7	439	247	+12	33.5%	1	26.9%	1	-8.8%	8	-2.2%	25
2006	12-4	9.6	10.6	427	360	+7	19.5%	7	33.7%	1	11.3%	27	-2.9%	25
2007	13-3	12.5	12.4	450	262	+18	31.6%	2	28.3%	2	-10.7%	3	-5.9%	32

Strategic Tendencies

Run/Pass		Rank		Offense		Rank		Defense		Rank		Other		Rank
Runs, all plays	42%	11		3+ WR	73%	1		Rush 3	2.9%	24		2+ RB, Pct Runs	42%	31
Runs, first half	37%	25		4+ WR	6%	26		Rush 4	84.8%	1		1 RB/2 TE, Pct runs	63%	3
Runs, first down	52%	14		2+ TE	24%	19		Rush 5	8.6%	32		1 RB/3+ WR, pct runs	36%	2
Runs, second-long	29%	28		Single back	91%	1		Rush 6+	3.8%	30		CB1 on WR1	34%	30
Runs, power sit.	66%	14		Play action	21%	9		Rush 7+	0.5%	27		Go for it on 4th	1.16	13
Runs, behind 2H	33%	8		Max protect	7%	28		Sacks by LB	7.4%	30		Offensive Pace	28.3	1
Pass, ahead 2H	49%	10		Outside pocket	6%	29		Sacks by DB	14.8%	5		Defensive Pace	31.7	31

Indianapolis is not a team that changes its offense very often. This was the third straight season the Colts ranked first in single-back sets and first in using three or more wide receivers (including Dallas Clark split out) but 26th or lower in using four or more wide receivers. ✐ The Colts lined up with a single wide receiver on first down once all season. Other than the Jets with five, no other team lined up with such a formation less than 12 times. ✐ Indianapolis ran the ball out of four-wide sets 40 percent of the time, the highest percentage in the league, and did so quite effectively with a 28.3% DVOA. ✐ The Colts ranked 24th in number of draw plays, but recorded the second highest DVOA on such plays, behind only Dallas. As you might expect, the Colts ran the NFL's highest percentage of draw plays out of four-wide sets. ✐ Peyton Manning did not throw a single interception on the right side of the field. ✐ Only Buffalo ran the ball more often in two-wide receiver, two-tight end sets. ✐ For the second straight season, Indianapolis faced more draw plays than any other defense. Nevertheless, the Colts ranked in the top 10 for defensive DVOA against draw plays. ✐ The Colts also improved dramatically against play-action fakes in 2007. Two years ago, the Colts ranked 28th in defensive DVOA against play-action. Last year, they ranked seventh. The yardage allowed by Indianapolis on non-play-action passes remained constant, but average yards allowed on passes with play-action dropped from 7.6 to 6.0. Only three defenses faced play-action on a higher percentage of pass plays. ✐ The Colts had the league's best defensive DVOA in the third quarter. ✐ Only three teams allowed a greater percentage of passes into a hole in the zone, but the Colts gave up the third fewest yards on such plays. ✐ The Colts only tipped seven passes at the line of scrimmage, ranking 27th in the NFL. ✐ The Colts were the only defense that had no sacks marked "Rusher Untouched." ✐ Even though they were often passing in the second half in an attempt to catch up, Colts opponents used four or more receivers on only six percent of plays, the lowest percentage in the league. ✐ The Colts had the league's best defensive DVOA against deep passes (over 15 yards through the air) and ranked second against short or midrange passes in the middle of the field. ✐ The Colts had the league's biggest discrepancy between defense at home and defense on the road. On the road, they had the league's top defensive DVOA, but at home they were league average.

Passing

Player	DYAR	DVOA	Plays	NtYds	Avg	YAC	C%	TD	Int
Peyton Manning	1841	40.6%	542	4033	7.4	4.5	65.4%	31	13
Jim Sorgi	20	-1.9%	38	117	3.1	4.2	50.0%	1	0

Rushing

Player	DYAR	DVOA	Plays	Yds	Avg	TD	Fum	Suc
Joseph Addai	222	11.1%	261	1072	4.1	12	0	54%
Kenton Keith	125	14.0%	121	533	4.4	3	1	58%
Clifton Dawson	-26	-31.0%	30	64	2.1	1	0	40%
Peyton Manning	16	17.3%	6	12	2.0	3	7	—
Luke Lawton	-5	-28.8%	5	13	2.6	0	0	60%

Receiving

Player	DYAR	DVOA	Plays	Ctch	Yds	Y/C	YAC	TD	C%
WR									
Reggie Wayne	443	22.5%	156	104	1515	14.6	3.8	10	67%
Anthony Gonzalez	239	43.5%	51	37	576	15.6	5.4	3	73%
Marvin Harrison	40	2.3%	32	20	247	12.4	2.0	1	63%
Aaron Moorehead	-54	-44.7%	22	8	65	8.1	0.8	0	36%
Craphonso Thorpe	-28	-30.3%	20	12	70	5.8	1.4	1	60%
Devin Aromashodu	-15	-24.0%	17	7	96	13.7	5.6	0	41%
TE									
Dallas Clark	107	0.6%	101	58	616	10.6	3.7	11	57%
Ben Utecht*	100	33.6%	37	31	364	11.7	5.3	1	84%
Bryan Fletcher*	-8	-12.0%	27	18	143	7.9	2.3	0	67%
RB									
Joseph Addai	150	43.7%	49	41	364	8.9	8.4	3	84%
Kenton Keith	13	-1.9%	23	13	77	5.9	5.7	1	57%
Clifton Dawson	-13	-45.2%	9	2	15	7.5	8.0	0	22%

Offensive Line

Year	Yards	ALY	Rank	Power	Rank	10+ Yds	Rank	Stuff	Rank	Sack	ASR	Rank
2005	3.95	4.71	1	54%	29	9%	32	19%	2	20	3.7%	1
2006	4.13	4.56	5	60%	22	10%	28	20%	4	15	3.4%	1
2007	4.03	4.52	5	78%	1	9%	31	19%	2	23	4.2%	6

Year	LE	Rank	LT	Rank	Mid	Rank	RT	Rank	RE	Rank
2005	5.28	2	4.75	5	4.45	5	5.23	1	4.58	9
2006	4.56	9	5.45	2	4.72	5	4.56	5	3.64	21
2007	3.70	24	5.85	2	4.63	5	4.18	18	4.53	7

When left tackle Tony Ugoh missed five games in the middle of the season, Charlie Johnson stepped into his role in the starting lineup. Ugoh's return coincided with the departure of Ryan Diem, and Johnson just slipped over to the right side. In 2008, Johnson won't be filling in for Ugoh and Diem, he'll be lining up with them, taking over at right guard for Jake Scott, who left for division rival Tennessee in free agency. Game charters had some decidedly mixed things to say about Johnson. The Colts trust that he can take over as a starter, but there is no doubt that his second season was not as smooth as his appearance in Super Bowl XLI.

This is one of the league's best lines, and that should remain a constant. There are no changes besides Johnson along the line, with left guard Ryan Lilja and center Jeff Saturday both returning. Lilja made a surprising number of mistakes last season that cost the Colts chunks of yards, but Saturday is coming off an All-Pro season. He's far from retirement, but the Colts have his replacement lined up: rookie Mike Pollack from Arizona State, who can also play guard. The Colts had no first-round pick in the 2008 draft (it was lost in a 2007 trade with the 49ers to acquire Ugoh), but they still managed to snare the top center coming out of college. Saturday is the only Colts starting lineman over 30 and his contract expires at the end of the season, when he and the team will have decisions to make. Until then, Pollack will sit, unless he can win Johnson's position in training camp.

Defensive Front Seven

Defensive Line	Age	Pos	Plays	TmPct	Rk	Stop	Dfts	Stop%	Rk	AvYd	Rk	Sack	Hit	Hur	Runs	RuStop	RuYd	Pass	PaStop	PaYd
Ed Johnson	24	DT	41	5.0%	34	28	7	68%	64	2.9	63	1.0	4	7	36	72%	2.7	5	40%	4.2
Raheem Brock	30	DT	35	6.2%	17	27	13	77%	39	0.7	6	2.5	1	7	26	73%	1.9	9	89%	-3.0
Robert Mathis	27	DE	32	4.8%	57	27	12	84%	9	0.9	23	6.5	4	13	24	83%	3.1	8	88%	-5.9
Josh Thomas	27	DE	32	4.2%	65	19	6	59%	77	2.5	62	1.0	3	8	27	52%	3.3	5	100%	-1.6
Jeff Charleston	25	DE	26	3.9%	69	19	7	73%	54	2.2	53	1.0	1	4	21	71%	2.8	5	80%	-0.6
Keyunta Dawson	22	DE	22	2.7%	—	13	5	59%	—	2.7	—	1.0	3	2	19	53%	4.4	3	100%	-7.7
Dwight Freeney	28	DE	21	4.5%	—	17	10	81%	—	0.0	—	4.0	10	7	16	75%	2.3	5	100%	-7.2
Quinn Pitcock	24	DT	18	3.9%	—	12	5	67%	—	1.9	—	1.5	1	1	14	64%	2.8	4	75%	-1.0

Linebackers	Age	Pos	Plays	TmPct	Rk	Stop	Dfts	Stop%	AvYd	Sack	Hit	Hur	Runs	RuStop	Rk	RuYd	Rk	Tgts	Suc%	Rk	APaYd	Rk
Gary Brackett	28	MLB	125	15.2%	16	60	20	48%	4.7	0.5	0	1	72	57%	76	3.6	58	39	57%	20	3.7	4
Freddie Keiaho	26	OLB	81	14.3%	24	41	14	51%	4.0	0.5	2	0	54	61%	53	3.4	49	21	41%	70	4.4	13
Tyjuan Hagler	27	OLB	51	8.3%	84	27	10	53%	3.3	1.0	0	1	33	64%	45	2.3	9	11	49%	—	4.3	—
Rocky Boiman*	28	OLB	49	6.0%	98	22	6	45%	4.7	0.0	0	1	25	64%	43	2.9	29	25	46%	53	4.1	9
Clint Session	23	OLB	21	3.1%	—	10	7	48%	4.2	0.0	0	0	10	70%	—	1.1	—	7	28%	—	5.3	—

Year	Yards	ALY	Rank	Power	Rank	10+ Yds	Rank	Stuff	Rank	Sack	ASR	Rank
2005	4.45	4.19	20	60%	14	19%	20	25%	17	46	8.6%	2
2006	5.37	4.80	31	81%	32	23%	30	21%	21	25	6.1%	21
2007	3.80	4.01	12	71%	26	11%	4	25%	13	28	6.1%	19

Year	LE	Rank	LT	Rank	Mid	Rank	RT	Rank	RE	Rank
2005	4.91	28	4.49	25	4.07	15	4.40	23	3.90	17
2006	1.87	1	4.96	26	4.99	32	5.71	32	3.22	8
2007	3.83	14	3.50	4	4.16	15	4.78	26	3.27	7

When Booger McFarland was placed on injured reserve before the 2007 season began, things looked bleak for the Colts. Enter Ed Johnson, an undrafted rookie free agent from Penn State. Johnson made an immediate impact in the season opener against New Orleans, collecting three tackles including one that stuffed Reggie Bush behind the line. Johnson stayed in the starting lineup for the rest of the year. The Colts run defense actually improved under Johnson, though it was much worse in short-yardage scenarios.

This year, Indianapolis expects only one new starter on defense: Tyjuan Hagler, who will take over at outside linebacker for Rocky Boiman, who left for Philadelphia. The transition should be smooth: Hagler started seven games in 2007 when Boiman was injured. This is how the Colts do business: They draft for need before the need arrives, and they are always prepared for any injury or departure. Not one projected starter for the Colts defense has ever played a game for another NFL team. That stability has been the key to the team's string of playoff appearances. Well, that and Peyton Manning.

Defensive Secondary

Secondary	Age	Pos	Plays	TmPct	Rk	Stop	Dfts	RuYd	Rk	RuStop	Rk	Tgts	Tgt%	Rk	Dist	Suc%	Rk	APaYd	Rk	PaYd	PD	Int
Bob Sanders	27	SS	103	13.4%	4	45	21	5.5	21	47%	32	30	8%	27	9.1	52%	29	5.9	22	5.8	8	2
Kelvin Hayden	25	CB	94	11.4%	13	33	13	6.6	42	32%	66	71	17%	48	8.8	44%	64	6.0	10	6.2	10	3
Marlin Jackson	25	CB	93	11.3%	14	37	17	4.9	19	56%	23	62	15%	60	6.6	45%	60	6.2	13	6.6	4	1
Antoine Bethea	24	FS	70	10.5%	30	27	13	7.6	58	44%	41	23	7%	39	17.7	34%	77	9.1	61	9.5	7	4
Tim Jennings	25	CB	24	4.2%	—	12	8	3.3	—	33%	—	35	12%	—	10.2	51%	—	6.0	—	6.3	6	0
Matt Giordano	26	SS	21	3.4%	—	6	4	9.3	—	0%	—	9	3%	—	11.1	36%	—	5.5	—	5.2	4	2
T. J. Rushing	25	CB	19	2.6%	—	6	2	1.0	—	100%	—	25	7%	—	11.6	31%	—	7.7	—	7.9	1	0

Year	Pass D Rank		vs. #1 WR	Rk	vs. #2 WR	Rk	vs. Other WR	Rk	vs. TE	Rk	vs. RB	Rk
2005	4		-7.4%	6	-15.5%	7	-2.0%	16	-2.4%	17	-4.0%	13
2006	19		11.7%	25	15.1%	24	-13.8%	10	-8.4%	12	4.7%	20
2007	3		-21.3%	4	4.4%	17	-35.4%	1	-21.7%	2	4.3%	23

Let it be known that a team that sees Bob Sanders return to health will improve drastically in pass defense. Cornerback Jason David's departure to New Orleans caused a domino effect in the Colts line-up: Nickel back and backup safety Marlin Jackson moved into David's cornerback position; Antoine Bethea, who played strong and free safety in 2006, settled in at free; and Sanders returned to play strong safety. Jackson had a lower Success Rate than David did in 2006, but he also allowed fewer yards per pass, so that switch basically balanced out. Kelvin Hayden took over at the other corner for Nick Harper, who left for the Titans. He was less consistent than Harper, though he still prevented big plays.

In an offseason interview with FootballOutsiders.com, we asked Bill Polian which of his players had improved the most since they were first acquired, and his answer was Kelvin Hayden. Colts defensive backs also offer solid run support. Sanders gets all the headlines and awards, but it was Jackson who placed among the leaders in average yards per tackle on run plays. Dante Hughes, a 2007 second-rounder, plays nickel back, although the Colts rarely use that position: The four starting defensive backs all had at least 47 tackles in 2007. The next highest total among Colts defensive backs belonged to Melvin Bullitt, with just 17.

Special Teams

Year	DVOA	Rank	FG/XP	Rank	Net Punt	Rank	Punt Ret	Rank	Net Kick	Rank	Kick Ret	Rank	Hidden	Rank
2005	-2.2%	25	5.3	7	3.8	12	-2.2	18	-9.7	29	-9.9	28	10.0	2
2006	-2.9%	25	4.8	8	-9.7	29	2.5	8	-15.2	30	0.5	14	10.0	4
2007	-5.9%	32	-12.4	31	-9.5	28	7.3	6	-15.5	29	-4.7	23	4.5	11

It's hard to believe that a team so strongly based in depth and stability up and down the roster would be so bad at special teams each and every year, but the Colts actually got worse in 2007. Let's start with the positives: T. J. Rushing, though nothing special returning kickoffs, was a quality punt returner, tying a franchise record with a 90-yard touchdown against Oakland. Thus endeth the positives. The signing of Adam Vinatieri has been a disaster. He was fine placekicking in 2006 before crashing and burning last season. His kickoffs were just fine in 2007, slightly above average, but they were wasted when his coverage unit kept giving up big returns; the Colts kickoff coverage, ignoring the kick itself, were third-worst in the league. It was a similar story when the Colts punted: Hunter Smith's punts were slightly below average, but the coverage team was fourth-worst in the league. The coverage units were also bad the year before. In the past two seasons, the Colts have allowed five kickoffs and two punts to be returned for touchdowns, effectively turning all opponents into Devin Hester.

COACHING STAFF

Here's what we know about the Colts coaching situation: Tony Dungy will be the head coach in 2008. At some point after that, he will retire, and when he does, associate head coach Jim Caldwell will take the reigns of the team. Whether that transition takes place in 2009 or 2010 or 2015, it should be smooth as glass. Caldwell joined the Colts with Dungy in 2002, first as quarterbacks coach before a promotion to his current position. For his entire tenure, he has worked very closely with Peyton Manning and one of the great offenses in NFL history, and that is a boat that needs no rocking.

On the other side of the ball, the Colts have never come close to that level of success, but once again they offer consistency up top. Ron Meeks has been Dungy's defensive coordinator in Indianapolis for seven seasons. Whoever is head coach next season, it's hard to believe that Meeks won't still be in charge of the defense.

And then there is Dungy. Since he first became a head coach in 1996, he has won 127 games with Tampa Bay and Indianapolis, the most in the NFL for any coach in that time frame. For his career, he has won 62 more games than he has lost; no active coach can match that number. In his 12 seasons, he has led his team to the playoffs 10 times, and despite the unfair reputation his teams have of failing in the postseason, he has actually gone .500 in the playoffs (9-9). He has a realistic chance of winning a second Super Bowl this year. You won't find any coach more beloved by his current and former players. And while Dungy himself is a product of the Marty Schottenheimer coaching tree, he also has a tree of his own, helping to start the careers of Herm Edwards, Lovie Smith, Rod Marinelli, and Mike Tomlin. Jim Caldwell will be the fifth name on that list, and Minnesota defensive coordinator Leslie Frazier, a former member of Dungy's Indianapolis staff, may be the sixth someday. Whenever Dungy decides to retire, he will be dearly missed, but his touch on the game will be felt for years to come.

Jacksonville Jaguars

The 2007 training-camp season was bracketed by a pair of stunning quarterback changes, with dramatically different results.

In Atlanta, Michael Vick's legal woes came to a head on the eve of camp, wrecking the Falcons' season before the first practice. Six weeks later and a few hundred miles southeast, Jacksonville coach Jack Del Rio shocked NFL observers by not only naming David Garrard his starter, but also releasing incumbent Byron Leftwich a week before the dawn of the new regular season.

Atlanta had no choice regarding its quarterback situation, but Del Rio certainly did, and he chose to act boldly and against popular opinion. It was certainly not a risk-averse move for an as-yet unproven coach of a team with playoff aspirations.

The decision to release Leftwich as opposed to leaving him on the roster as a backup and hedge against Garrard's performance may have had as much to do with the salary cap as with locker-room politics, but regardless of the motive, it set the tone for the Jaguars' season. To say we were bullish on the Jaguars' move would be about as accurate as any further comparisons between Leftwich and Vick. According to our metrics, Leftwich was the better player, so the locker-room politics aside, Jacksonville appeared to have taken a step back, talent-wise, at the game's most important position.

But a funny thing happened. Given the chance to shed the label of "NFL's best backup," Garrard improved

dramatically over his past performances, which included 15 starts over the past two seasons while Leftwich was injured. Garrard sustained his high level of play for the entire season, and had his team knocking on the door of truly elite status in January. Winning a road playoff game in Pittsburgh—where, granted, Garrard did not play particularly well—and taking undefeated New England to the wire (while playing brilliantly) will do that for a quarterback's, and a team's, reputation. As the 2008 season opens, the Jaguars have to be viewed as a serious AFC title contender.

So what facets of Garrard's game did Del Rio know about that the rest of us didn't? Many pundits pointed to his mobility as a deciding factor over Leftwich, but though that's the easy answer, it's also the incorrect one. Yes, Garrard is niftier on his feet than Leftwich will ever be, but Adjusted Sack Rate actually shows that Leftwich was more effective at avoiding sacks. The biggest problem with Leftwich was arm speed, not foot speed. He is burdened with a painfully slow windup that makes him look like Satchel Paige in some grainy black-and-white baseball film. Leftwich has tremendous arm strength, but it often gets lost in the three- and five-step drops that make up the majority of almost every modern passing offense. With Garrard under center, the Jaguars had a quarterback who was much more in rhythm with his receivers on the short- and medium-length passes. On three- and five-step drops, Garrard's right arm was

2008 Jaguars Schedule

Week	Opp.	Week	Opp.	Week	Opp.
1	at TEN	7	BYE	13	at HOU (Mon.)
2	BUF	8	CLE	14	at CHI
3	at IND	9	at CIN	15	GB
4	HOU	10	at DET	16	IND (Thu.)
5	PIT	11	TEN	17	at BAL
6	at DEN	12	MIN		

usually moving forward to deliver the ball the second he planted his back foot, and the result was usually an accurate pass that hit a receiver in the hands.

Hitting Jacksonville receivers accurately is important because collectively, they haven't exactly been a bunch of Cris Carters in the hands department. As a group, the Jacksonville receivers and tight ends possess a single dominant quality: size. Receivers Ernest Wilford, Reggie Williams, and Matt Jones are all between six foot three and six foot six, and the four tight ends who caught passes in 2007 averaged six foot seven. None of the group is known for route-running skills—although Williams did enjoy his finest year and appears to be shedding the "bust" label—but any player with a half-foot height advantage on the defender covering him can be effective running a seven-yard slant. Though Wilford departed via free agency, Jacksonville brought in another big receiver, Jerry Porter, to replace him.

One trend that is likely to continue for the Jacksonville offense in 2008 is the increased use of the tight end. As the season wore on, Garrard tossed more passes in the direction of his huge tight ends, particularly the athletic Marcedes Lewis, who could be on the verge of a breakout year after catching 15 balls over a four-week stretch in the season's second half.

While Jacksonville didn't substantially alter its approach to the passing game, Garrard's quick release and improved accuracy allowed the Jaguars to throw fewer short passes and more midrange balls. In 10 starts in 2006, 45 percent of Garrard's passes were short (up to five yards in the air), and 32 percent were midrange (6-15 yards). Last year, those numbers were 39 percent and 40 percent, respectively. This change enabled the Jaguars to have a much more effective passing game even as Garrard's yards after catch (YAC) figure dropped substantially, from sixth in the NFL in 2006 to 25th in 2007.

It helps to have the threat of a running game to open up those longer-range passes, and in the resurrected Fred Taylor and Maurice Jones-Drew, the Jaguars have just that: a dangerous running game, but an inconsistent one. Taylor and Jones-Drew put up lots of long runs, but also left Garrard and his subpar receivers in lots of third-and-longs. Further evidence of Garrard's exceptional play and dramatic improvement comes from the fact that the running game was also dangerous in 2006 (third in DVOA, versus sixth last season), when Garrard was merely average.

The knock on Garrard earlier in his career was consistency. He clearly had ability, but struggled with consistent mechanics. Enter a pair of exiled college coaches who were new to the Jacksonville staff in 2007: offensive coordinator Dirk Koetter and quarterbacks coach Mike Shula. The former head coaches at Arizona State and Alabama, respectively, Koetter and Shula worked with Garrard to correct flaws in his footwork and delivery. By the end of training camp, the staff had seen enough. The Garrard with whom they would entrust their season, and their professional livelihood, was not the same player from 2006.

After a few early struggles—the Jaguars' offensive DVOA was negative in four of the team's first eight games—Jacksonville improved rapidly on that side of the ball. Over the season's second half, the offense was on fire, registering positive DVOA over 20% in every contest, despite facing four playoff teams. In Week 13, Jacksonville proved it could hang with division rival Indianapolis in a 28-25 loss at the RCA Dome. The Garrard-led offense finished that game with a DVOA figure of 47.8%, its second-best outing of the season. By season's end, Jacksonville had the league's third-best offense according to DVOA and, perhaps just as important, the league's third-most consistent offense as measured by variance. That was in stark contrast to 2006, when Jacksonville had an above-average offense, but a wildly inconsistent one.

Merely hanging with the Colts won't be enough for Jacksonville to take the next step. The Jaguars have finished second to the Colts in the AFC South four years running, going 2-6 against the Colts during that time. While Garrard injured an ankle and missed much of the big Week 7 loss to Indianapolis last season, the Week 13 game, along with Jacksonville's season-long performance on offense, would seem to suggest that the Jaguars can compete with Indianapolis. Our projections, however, tell a different story. We see an offensive decline for Jacksonville—an observation based in part on a regression to the mean. (Even if Garrard has another superb year, he's going to throw more than three interceptions.) Our research also shows other areas in which the 2007 Jaguars excelled but that usually fail to hold up year after year. These include the team's performance in late-and-close situations, as well as its high number of 10-plus yard runs—indicating a boom-and-bust rushing attack. Jacksonville was also slightly better on third down than it was on first and second, another indicator of a possible drop-off in 2008.

Still, if there's an area Jacksonville needs to concentrate on improving in order to catch up to the Colts in the AFC South, it isn't offense. It's defense. The Jaguars have been primarily a defensive club during Del Rio's tenure, but in 2007, they were much better on offense. Jacksonville fell out of the top 10 in defensive DVOA (12th, -3.3%) for the first time since 2003.

The drop-off was most notable up front. The Jaguars are generally thought to have one of the best defensive lines in football, led by run-stuffing tackles Marcus Stroud and John Henderson. In 2007, that perception was no longer a reality. With Stroud missing games due to injury and suspension, Jacksonville fell to 24th in Adjusted Line Yards. It was better in short-yardage situations and at preventing long runs, but the overall ranking indicates a unit that could be run upon with consistency.

Jacksonville was not the pass-rushing force it once was, either. Though the Jaguars managed to rank 10th in Adjusted Sack Rate, they rarely were able to generate any consistent pressure with the front four. The defense hit its nadir in Week 9 at New Orleans, when Saints quarterback Drew Brees had time to drop back, scan the field, polish off some beignets, dust the powdered sugar off the FieldTurf, and then pick which of several open receivers to throw to. Jacksonville tried rushing three and dropping a lineman in zone coverage, they tried rushing four, and they tried blitzing. Nothing worked. Brees threw for 339 yards in the first half, and the Saints rolled up 438 total yards (435 passing) while giving up just a single sack in a 41-24 victory.

Given the struggles of the line, it was not surprising that the Jaguars did what would have once been unthinkable: They dealt Stroud in the offseason. Jacksonville did well to get third- and fifth-round picks from Buffalo for an at-times dominant tackle who could no longer be counted on, especially after missing four games due to a failed drug test for performance-enhancing substances. Run-stuffing tackle Grady Jackson was also released, though he still may be brought back before training camp.

Even though the offseason left the Jaguars thin at tackle, they chose to address the pass rush by selecting a pair of defensive ends in the first two rounds of the draft. In the copycat NFL, every team is trying to follow the model the Giants used to upset the Patriots in Super Bowl XLII. For Jacksonville, this means being able to harass Peyton Manning with the front four. Using some of the extra picks they acquired for Stroud, they traded up in each of the first two rounds to select a pair of defensive ends: Florida's Derrick Harvey in the first round, eighth overall, and Auburn's Quentin Groves in the second round. Most draftniks felt the Harvey pick was a reach, as the Jaguars gave up three picks for a player who was not always dominant in college. Still, the Jacksonville brain trust should be commended for managing to move up 18 spots in the first round without parting with next year's top pick, and the Jaguars won't mind if Harvey develops into a disrupting edge-rusher in the mold of a Terrell Suggs.

While the Harvey pick got most of the attention, Groves could turn out to be the better player. He fell on many draft boards due to injuries and off-field concerns, but was one of the best defensive linemen in the SEC as a junior. Both he and Harvey are expected to join the rotation at end, where Paul Spicer is a solid, but aging, player and Reggie Hayward has struggled to return from an Achilles injury. Groves could also move to outside linebacker.

The job of getting more out of the pass rush will fall to new defensive coordinator Gregg Williams, who held the same position in Washington the past four seasons. Williams was known for his blitz-happy schemes in Washington, and under his direction, Jacksonville is likely to become more aggressive as well, putting pressure on a secondary that struggled to contain receivers when the rush didn't get home.

No matter what Jacksonville gets from its defense in 2008, the Jaguars are now Garrard's team and will largely sink or swim on his performance. Management reinforced that idea by signing Garrard to a $60 million extension in the offseason, marking as complete his transition from question mark to unquestioned leader of his team. Hard to believe that just a year ago, Garrard was locked in a battle with Leftwich to win the starting job. What a difference a year makes. Just ask Leftwich—late of the Falcons, where he failed in an attempt to replace Michael Vick.

Russell Levine

2007 Jaguars Stats by Week

Wk	vs.	W-L	PF	PA	YDF	YDA	TO	Total	Off	Def	ST
1	TEN	L	10	13	272	350	+1	6%	11%	6%	1%
2	ATL	W	13	7	364	248	0	-22%	-5%	17%	0%
3	@DEN	W	23	14	326	265	+1	18%	2%	-9%	7%
4	BYE										
5	@KC	W	17	7	357	271	+1	40%	34%	0%	5%
6	HOU	W	37	17	457	390	0	25%	30%	-4%	-9%
7	IND	L	7	29	226	384	-2	7%	-9%	-10%	6%
8	@TB	W	24	23	219	385	+3	18%	-9%	-27%	0%
9	@NO	L	24	41	432	538	-2	-30%	0%	49%	20%
10	@TEN	W	28	13	262	292	+2	46%	20%	-32%	-6%
11	SD	W	24	17	311	388	+2	29%	35%	13%	8%
12	BUF	W	36	14	416	297	+2	37%	29%	0%	8%
13	@IND	L	25	28	411	342	-1	33%	48%	11%	-4%
14	CAR	W	37	6	427	149	+1	66%	25%	-38%	3%
15	@PIT	W	29	22	421	217	-1	46%	34%	-24%	-11%
16	OAK	W	49	11	437	215	+2	119%	53%	-47%	18%
17	@HOU	L	28	42	381	290	0	-49%	34%	32%	-50%
18	@PIT	W	31	29	239	340	+2	34%	-2%	-29%	7%
19	@NE	L	20	31	350	403	-2	-12%	17%	27%	-2%

Trends and Splits

	Offense	Rank	Defense	Rank
Total DVOA	20.7%	3	-3.2%	13
Unadjusted VOA	19.1%	4	-2.6%	13
Weighted trend	26.6%	2	-6.5%	6
Variance	4.0%	3	6.6%	17
Average opponent	-0.9%	3	1.9%	15
Passing	37.1%	3	-6.7%	8
Rushing	6.8%	6	1.1%	22
First down	15.4%	7	-11.0%	6
Second down	16.0%	6	2.5%	17
Third down	35.8%	3	2.3%	16
First half	19.7%	4	2.7%	19
Second half	21.8%	4	-9.1%	6
Red Zone	11.1%	11	0.2%	13
Late and close	19.5%	5	-13.8%	6

Five-Year Performance

Year	W-L	Pyth Wins	Est Wins	PF	PA	TO	Total	Rank	Off	Rank	Def	Rank	ST	Rank
2003	5-11	6.3	8.2	276	331	-4	1.2%	16	-1.4%	15	-7.6%	10	-5.0%	29
2004	9-7	7.3	8.6	261	280	+6	0.4%	14	-3.7%	18	-4.5%	9	-0.5%	17
2005	12-4	10.7	10.3	361	269	+11	17.0%	10	6.6%	10	-10.2%	7	0.3%	15
2006	8-8	10.8	9.6	371	274	+1	22.0%	6	4.3%	12	-17.9%	3	-0.2%	19
2007	11-5	10.7	11.4	411	304	+9	23.9%	4	20.7%	3	-3.2%	13	-0.1%	15

Strategic Tendencies

	Run/Pass	Rank		Offense	Rank		Defense	Rank		Other		Rank
Runs, all plays	47%	2	3+ WR	36%	31	Rush 3	4.8%	17	2+ RB, Pct runs	63%	10
Runs, first half	48%	3	4+ WR	4%	30	Rush 4	69.4%	9	1 RB/2 TE, pct runs	50%	14
Runs, first down	55%	8	2+ TE	42%	1	Rush 5	18.2%	21	1 RB/3+ WR, pct runs	28%	9
Runs, second-long	40%	7	Single back	61%	12	Rush 6+	7.6%	18	CB1 on WR1	40%	23
Runs, power sit.	72%	4	Play action	24%	3	Rush 7+	2.1%	9	Go for it on 4th	1.47	5
Runs, behind 2H	34%	6	Max protect	12%	9	Sacks by LB	15.3%	25	Offensive Pace	30.8	16
Pass, ahead 2H	46%	14	Outside pocket	16%	6	Sacks by DB	5.6%	18	Defensive Pace	30.8	14

The Jaguars used shotgun only 18 percent of the time, below the NFL average, even though they had the league's best offense in plays from the shotgun (58.7% DVOA, slightly ahead of New England). ⌀ Only Cincinnati posted better passing DVOA than Jacksonville in four-wide sets; however, when they ran the ball from four-wide, only two teams recorded a worse DVOA. ⌀ Maurice Jones-Drew was third in screen passes, only behind Brian Westbrook and Clinton Portis. ⌀ The Jaguars offensive line had only one sack noted as "rusher untouched," the fewest in the league. ⌀ One reason the Jaguars ran more often than most teams on second-and-long: they ranked third in both DVOA and yards per carry on these runs, behind Minnesota and Seattle. ⌀ The Jaguars had the NFL's best offensive DVOA on passes to the middle of the field. ⊘ Jacksonville ranked fifth in the league in terms of using bootlegs and rollouts, and David Garrard's mobility was effective: the Jaguars ranked sixth in converting a first down (or touchdown) when Garrard left the pocket. ⊘ Jacksonville's defense saw more formations with four or five wide receivers than any other team, and it was the only formation where the Jaguars had a below-average defensive DVOA. ⊘ The Jaguars ranked third in defensive DVOA against passes thrown on the offense's left side, but were average against passes up the middle or to the right.

Passing

Player	DYAR	DVOA	Plays	NtYds	Avg	YAC	C%	TD	Int
David Garrard	1086	37.4%	350	2442	7.0	4.6	64.2%	18	3
Quinn Gray*	302	20.9%	155	932	6.0	4.4	55.6%	10	4
Cleo Lemon	-91	-15.5%	337	1625	4.8	4.8	56.4%	6	6

Rushing

Player	DYAR	DVOA	Plays	Yds	Avg	TD	Fum	Suc
Fred Taylor	171	11.1%	223	1225	5.5	5	2	45%
Maurice Jones-Drew	81	2.1%	167	770	4.6	9	2	46%
Greg Jones	4	-6.3%	42	119	2.8	2	0	48%
David Garrard	58	13.3%	37	199	5.4	1	7	—
LaBrandon Toefield*	-17	-34.4%	13	27	2.1	1	0	23%
Quinn Gray*	20	22.2%	9	63	7.0	0	2	—
Dennis Northcutt	23	59.3%	6	27	4.5	0	0	—
Cleo Lemon	62	24.5%	28	103	3.7	4	7	—

Receiving

Player	DYAR	DVOA	Plays	Ctch	Yds	Y/C	YAC	TD	C%
WR									
Ernest Wilford*	136	10.2%	74	45	518	11.5	2.2	4	61%
Dennis Northcutt	132	11.1%	73	44	601	13.7	2.9	4	60%
Reggie Williams	183	25.6%	60	38	630	16.6	5.8	10	63%
Matt Jones	15	-8.6%	50	24	317	13.2	3.5	4	48%
John Broussard	5	-7.7%	12	4	126	31.5	1.0	1	33%
Jerry Porter	16	-10.7%	102	44	705	16.0	4.3	6	43%
Troy Williamson	-21	-19.5%	38	18	236	13.1	2.8	1	47%
TE									
Marcedes Lewis	28	0.0%	57	37	391	10.6	3.3	2	65%
George Wrighster	-15	-15.8%	24	17	123	7.2	4.3	1	71%
Greg Estandia	24	16.5%	16	9	136	15.1	4.1	0	56%
Richard Angulo	28	33.7%	9	8	81	10.1	1.8	1	89%
RB									
Maurice Jones-Drew	142	32.0%	55	40	407	10.2	9.4	0	73%
Greg Jones	34	11.5%	19	11	99	9.0	8.7	2	58%
Fred Taylor	-3	-17.9%	14	9	58	6.4	6.0	0	64%

Offensive Line

Year	Yards	ALY	Rank	Power	Rank	10+ Yds	Rank	Stuff	Rank	Sack	ASR	Rank
2005	3.94	3.83	25	61%	21	19%	13	24%	12	32	5.8%	11
2006	5.13	4.66	2	65%	14	23%	5	22%	9	30	7.0%	19
2007	4.81	4.14	17	61%	18	28%	2	27%	25	31	6.9%	17

Year	LE	Rank	LT	Rank	Mid	Rank	RT	Rank	RE	Rank
2005	3.70	24	4.14	21	4.16	15	2.44	32	1.79	32
2006	4.60	7	5.22	3	4.72	4	3.92	26	4.42	11
2007	4.85	6	3.73	27	4.13	15	5.06	1	3.27	31

The Jacksonville line returns virtually intact from last season, as all five regular starters are expected to man the same positions in 2008. That continuity should serve the Jaguars well, for after tinkering with the line-up throughout 2007, the five men who performed most effectively are returning (from left to right): Khalif Barnes, Vince Manuwai, Brad Meester, Maurice Williams, and Tony Pashos. As a whole, the unit's run-blocking performance dropped significantly from 2006, but the line was at its best with those five starting over the season's second half. With Brad Meester out for the first five weeks, Jacksonville's Adjusted Line Yards figure was 3.96. With Meester back in the line-up Weeks 6-8, that improved to 4.12. When Maurice Williams replaced Chris Naeole at right guard Weeks 9-17, it improved to 4.21. Unfortunately, our directional data is skewed for the Jaguars because the official scorer in Jacksonville persists in only marking runs as left end, right end, or middle. Thus, the only "tackle" runs come on the road, and the team's rankings are all over the map: Jacksonville rated tops in the league on runs over right tackle, but next-to-last on plays around right end. They ranked sixth at left end, but 27th at left tackle. You get the picture.

In pass protection, the unit is just average, posting only a slight improvement despite moving from a statue (Byron Leftwich) to a very mobile quarterback in David Garrard. Of course, Garrard's mobility also leads to some sacks, as he'll keep a play alive long enough to get sacked, whereas Leftwich might have decided earlier to throw the ball away.

The coaching staff has perpetual concerns about the inconsistent left tackle Barnes, and he could see a challenge from Richard Collier, a talented but raw tackle from Valdosta State who was signed as an undrafted free agent in 2006. Collier is six foot seven, 358 pounds, and can play either tackle spot. At right tackle, Pashos was solid, if unspectacular, but he was among the league leaders with 6.5 blown blocks. Left guard Manuwai might be the best player on the line, though he is occasionally beaten by lesser opponents. Meester is getting on in years, and the Jaguars appear to be grooming Uche Nwaneri, a second-year player from Purdue, to replace him. Overall, this is a solid group that will benefit from having played together last year, and Jacksonville's running backs and quarterback are good fits for its strengths.

Defensive Front Seven

Defensive Line	Age	Pos	Plays	TmPct	Rk	Stop	Dfts	Stop%	Rk	AvYd	Rk	Sack	Hit	Hur	Runs	RuStop	RuYd	Pass	PaStop	PaYd
John Henderson	29	DT	41	5.8%	26	32	12	78%	32	1.3	17	2.0	3	3	34	76%	2.0	7	86%	-2.3
Paul Spicer	33	DE	34	4.8%	56	28	16	82%	16	-1.1	2	7.5	9	11	25	76%	1.1	9	100%	-7.3
Rob Meier	31	DT	27	3.6%	60	26	10	96%	1	-0.5	2	4.0	2	4	21	95%	1.0	6	100%	-5.8
Marcus Stroud*	30	DT	25	5.9%	25	15	8	60%	66	2.6	59	3.0	3	3	18	44%	4.0	7	100%	-1.0
Bobby McCray*	27	DE	19	2.9%	—	14	8	74%	—	1.5	—	3.0	7	13	11	64%	3.1	8	88%	-0.8
Reggie Hayward	29	DE	19	3.4%	—	17	8	89%	—	0.1	—	3.5	3	6	14	86%	1.7	5	100%	-4.6

Linebackers	Age	Pos	Plays	TmPct	Rk	Stop	Dfts	Stop%	AvYd	Sack	Hit	Hur	Runs	RuStop	Rk	RuYd	Rk	Tgts	Suc%	Rk	APaYd	Rk
Daryl Smith	26	OLB	77	10.9%	62	43	18	56%	4.9	1.5	1	3	35	60%	60	4.0	78	38	67%	6	5.3	27
Mike Peterson	32	MLB	74	15.7%	12	37	11	50%	5.7	2.0	2	2	43	53%	90	3.9	72	25	42%	65	8.3	84
Justin Durant	22	OLB	48	7.8%	87	30	9	63%	3.2	1.0	2	8	34	68%	32	2.7	17	24	64%	7	4.7	18
Clint Ingram	25	OLB	33	5.4%	—	13	3	39%	4.9	1.0	0	1	20	30%	—	4.5	—	19	71%	2	2.5	1

Year	Yards	ALY	Rank	Power	Rank	10+ Yds	Rank	Stuff	Rank	Sack	ASR	Rank
2005	3.97	4.10	18	59%	10	13%	7	22%	24	47	8.9%	1
2006	3.52	3.65	3	69%	25	15%	12	27%	6	35	7.2%	13
2007	4.20	4.35	24	57%	9	14%	7	23%	19	37	7.2%	10

Year	LE	Rank	LT	Rank	Mid	Rank	RT	Rank	RE	Rank
2005	3.66	8	4.28	17	4.33	23	3.78	11	3.82	16
2006	3.12	5	3.12	4	4.00	6	2.90	4	4.12	18
2007	4.02	15	4.43	19	4.46	29	4.85	28	4.01	13

Credit the Jacksonville front office for pulling the trigger on the trade that sent Marcus Stroud to Buffalo for third- and fifth-round picks. It's never easy to pull the plug on a prominent player, and Stroud was believed by some to be the best defensive tackle in the game as recently as 2005. The team simply could not count on him to remain in the line-up—he missed time due to both injury and suspension in 2007—and even when he did play they weren't getting enough pressure on the quarterback. Jacksonville turned those extra picks into a pair of pass-rushing ends, Derrick Harvey of Florida and Quentin Groves of Auburn, who should put a jolt in the pass rush as they work in rotation with the still-outstanding Paul Spicer. Up the middle, the Jaguars still have John Henderson (and, presumably, a coach to slap him in the face before every game) and feel that Rob Meier can be a more-than-adequate replacement for Stroud. Meier has never been able to crack the starting line-up full time in his eight seasons in Jacksonville, but he's no scrub. He led the league in Stop Rate in limited duty last season, and the Jaguars signed him to a four-year extension in May.

Age and injuries may be catching up to middle linebacker Mike Peterson, but Jacksonville has depth at the second level. On the outside, Daryl Smith is a versatile player who moved inside when Peterson was hurt, allowing rookie Justin Durant to see the field. Durant showed enough that he could challenge both Smith and the other starter on the outside, Clint Ingram, for playing time this season. Ingram was impressive as a rookie in 2006 but struggled last season to get off blocks. He can run and make plays in space, but needs to get stronger. If there was a noticeable weakness among the linebackers, it happened in pass coverage. When the Jaguars weren't generating pressure with the front four, the linebackers tended to get lost in coverage against tight ends and receivers, leading to some big plays off short passes.

Defensive Secondary

Secondary	Age	Pos	Plays	TmPct	Rk	Stop	Dfts	RuYd	Rk	RuStop	Rk	Tgts	Tgt%	Rk	Dist	Suc%	Rk	APaYd	Rk	PaYd	PD	Int
Sammy Knight*	33	SS	104	13.8%	3	43	18	5.3	16	48%	30	46	10%	10	10.1	47%	47	6.8	32	6.9	11	4
Brian Williams	29	CB	77	11.7%	12	38	14	4.6	14	63%	11	83	20%	26	11.6	54%	21	6.7	23	6.8	12	3
Reggie Nelson	24	FS	66	8.8%	48	17	11	10.7	81	11%	83	55	12%	4	17.5	55%	20	8.8	54	9.2	11	5
Rashean Mathis	28	CB	65	9.9%	27	19	9	4.7	18	40%	52	61	15%	61	13.6	47%	49	6.5	21	7.1	5	1
Terry Cousin*	33	CB	45	6.0%	—	20	12	6.8	—	40%	—	41	9%	—	7.9	53%	—	7.4	—	7.3	4	1
Aaron Glenn*	36	CB	16	6.8%	—	5	3	10.3	—	0%	—	20	14%	—	13.3	58%	—	6.5	—	7.4	1	1
Drayton Florence	28	CB	73	8.7%	47	26	11	9.1	62	38%	54	77	16%	54	8.9	44%	66	9.3	72	9.6	10	2
Pierson Prioleau	31	FS	37	4.9%	78	12	5	4.2	6	42%	46	23	5%	72	7.1	34%	78	8.9	57	9.0	1	0

Year	Pass D Rank		vs. #1 WR	Rk	vs. #2 WR	Rk	vs. Other WR	Rk	vs. TE	Rk	vs. RB	Rk
2005	9		-5.6%	7	-12.4%	8	11.1%	25	-19.0%	4	1.5%	18
2006	3		-7.7%	9	-38.1%	1	-32.3%	3	0.8%	20	-1.7%	17
2007	8		-7.6%	12	-32.8%	3	-3.1%	19	4.9%	13	-6.2%	11

Jacksonville entered the 2007 offseason with a gaping hole at safety, but they hit the jackpot in the first round of the draft with Florida's Reggie Nelson, an undersized free safety who nevertheless hits a ton and who has cornerback coverage skills. The strong safety who was supposed to play next to Nelson, Gerald Sensabaugh, had his season wrecked by shoulder injuries, but the Jaguars picked up veteran Sammy Knight on a make-good, one-year contract and he was all over the field making plays. Now he's gone to the Giants, and Sensabaugh will be back to fulfill the promise he showed in 2005 and 2006.

At corner, the Jaguars are set on one side with Rashean Mathis, whom they hope can return to the form that made him a Pro Bowl starter two seasons ago after he battled injuries throughout 2007. On the other side, Drayton Florence was lured away from San Diego with a six-year, $36 million contract, ostensibly to upgrade the other corner. The contract means he'll start ahead of Brian Williams, but Jacksonville might want to reconsider. Based on our numbers, Williams was better than Florence across the board last season. He had a higher Success Rate, made plays closer to the line of scrimmage, and was better in run support. Still, Jacksonville spends more than 60 percent of its plays in nickel, so regardless of who is named the starter, Williams and Florence will both spend plenty of time on the field. The Jaguars also added some depth in the draft. Fifth-round pick Trae Williams of South Florida could battle for playing time as a rookie. This unit needs help from up front to be outstanding, but if Jacksonville's reconfigured front four can get to the quarterback, look for the secondary to have a big year.

Special Teams

Year	DVOA	Rank	FG/XP	Rank	Net Punt	Rank	Punt Ret	Rank	Net Kick	Rank	Kick Ret	Rank	Hidden	Rank
2005	0.6%	13	-6.6	24	-3.3	23	0.2	14	6.8	6	6.2	7	7.7	8
2006	-0.2%	19	1.4	12	-21.2	32	-2.5	23	12.9	2	8.1	5	12.3	2
2007	-0.1%	15	-3.9	25	-2.1	20	0.0	14	4.9	11	0.3	15	-3.2	20

Jacksonville's special teams got off to a lousy start when outstanding kicker Josh Scobee injured his quadriceps warming up for the season opener. Jacksonville was forced to sign the aged John Carney, and their performance on field goals and kickoffs suffered as a result. With Scobee healthy again, those numbers should rise again this season. The return units are solid, but not spectacular, and you have to wonder how much longer Jacksonville will employ Maurice Jones-Drew as a kick returner. He's as explosive as anyone not named "Hester," but he is also going to be counted on to carry an increasing share of the load in the run game if Fred Taylor ever decides to start acting his age. Dennis Northcutt is a decent, but hardly spectacular, punt returner. If Jacksonville wants to give him a rest, they could give rookie cornerback Trae Williams a look. Williams was great in the open field returning interceptions at South Florida, averaging 27 yards on six returns a year ago. Adam Podlesh was an upgrade over Chris "Choppin' Wood" Hanson, but the team's punting is still below average and the Jaguars still made a mistake taking Podlesh ahead of Daniel Sepulveda.

COACHING STAFF

A year ago, Jack Del Rio made the biggest decision of his coaching career, casting aside Byron Leftwich in favor of David Garrard. Del Rio seemed to gain confidence as the year went on and his move was proven correct, and he enters 2008 on much more solid footing than he did a year ago. The successful handling of the quarterback situation may have emboldened Del Rio to address Marcus Stroud this offseason without fear of backlash. He'll be in for some heat if the draft moves to select Derrick Harvey and Quentin Groves don't upgrade the pass rush. Another sign of Del Rio's growing confidence: he wasn't afraid to bring in a big-name defensive coordinator to replace the departed Mike Smith, now the head coach in Atlanta. Gregg Williams was supposed to be the heir apparent to Joe Gibbs in Washington, but when the Redskins opted to go in a different direction, Del Rio snatched him up in Jacksonville. His primary task is to tune up the pass rush. Williams has always been enamored with the blitz, but it will be interesting to see if he gives the front four the chance to get the job done by themselves, especially with the investment the team made in that area on draft day.

Kansas City Chiefs

The following are signs that your team needs to rebuild:

1. A poor win-loss record.
2. An aging core of players past their prime.
3. Little to no reason to expect a competitive team the next season.
4. A young quarterback not ready to play consistently at a high level.

The Chiefs came out of the 2007 season a perfect four-for-four, and as a result, the 2008 offseason was dedicated to shredding talent and stockpiling draft picks. Just one year after a playoff berth, the Chiefs have shed almost all the vestiges of the high-octane Dick Vermeil era. The plan is being executed soundly on a number of fronts, but a very questionable quarterback situation could hold the Chiefs back.

The Chiefs' 4-12 record was the team's worst since 1978. They finished the season with nine straight losses, a futile run that forced the team to rebuild. Kansas City fans probably did not enjoy much about those nine games, but the fate of the franchise is better off because of that disturbing slide. Had the Chiefs sneaked out some close wins and finished near .500, they may have foolishly believed that a return to health by running back Larry Johnson would be enough to get them back in the playoffs.

The decision to rebuild is not undertaken easily. It requires a teamwide commitment to improving for several years down the road. This goal sometimes runs contrary to the team's goal of winning each week. In 2006, the Chiefs were clearly aging at important positions, but their playoff chase led to the disastrous decision to run Johnson into the ground. Johnson carried the ball an absurd 416 times on the season, the sole offense for a flawed playoff team.

The wear and tear predictably led to an injury this past season, an injury that undid the Chiefs' season but allowed the franchise to realize how flawed it was. Johnson's actual output was extremely mediocre, but he constantly faced eight or nine men in the box, allowing the weak Kansas City passing attack to approach competency. With the threat of Johnson removed, the Chiefs were able to see the teamwide mediocrity that had infected the club. The team was 4-4 with Johnson and 0-8 without him.

The late-season fade was also the result of a surprising breakdown in defensive performance. The defense was above average in nine of Kansas City's first 10 games; after Week 11, the Chiefs ranked fifth in defensive DVOA (-10.1%). In the final six games, they were above average only twice and absolutely dreadful in three of the other four games. From Weeks 12 to 17, the Chiefs' defensive DVOA of 25.4% was the second-worst in the NFL, ahead of only Detroit. Opponents eventually figured out that you could hold in additional blockers and find openings in the secondary. Also, running backs increasingly found big holes

---

CHIEFS PROSPECTUS

2007 Record: 4-12

Pythagorean Wins: 4.5 (28th)

DVOA: -20.9% total (26th), -24.8% weighted (27th)

Offense: -18.0% DVOA (29th)

Defense: -0.4% DVOA (16th)

Special Teams: -3.3% DVOA (24th)

Variance: 21.5 % (26th)

2007: Larry Johnson breaks down. Golly, who would have expected that?

2008: A strong draft kicks off a massive rebuilding project... that has a big, gaping hole at quarterback.

2008 Mean Projection: 6.6 wins

On the Clock (0-3): 6%

Loserville (4-6): 44%

Mediocrity (7-8): 31%

Playoff Contender (9-10): 17%

Super Bowl Contender (11+): 2%

Projected Average Opponent: -3.3% DVOA (25th in NFL)

2008 Chiefs Schedule

Week	Opp.	Week	Opp.	Week	Opp.
1	at NE	7	TEN	13	at OAK
2	OAK	8	at NYJ	14	at DEN
3	at ATL	9	TB	15	SD
4	DEN	10	at SD	16	MIA
5	at CAR	11	NO	17	at CIN
6	BYE	12	BUF		

once they burst through the defensive line, with young safeties Bernard Pollard and Jarrad Page sometimes getting lost in the shuffle.

Of course, the defense is not the unit that has recently carried the Chiefs. This team was built on offense since the start of the decade, and the 2007 offense was a far cry from its predecessors. The 2002-2005 Chiefs had one of the greatest offensive runs of any team in NFL history. Trent Green, Priest Holmes, and Tony Gonzalez got the press clippings, but the team sported as fine an offensive line as has been assembled in recent years. The line was anchored by the great left tackle Willie Roaf, but also received exceptional play from guards Brian Waters and Will Shields and center Casey Wiegmann. Of this core four, who all played from 2002-2005, all but Waters were well past their prime in 2005. Roaf retired before the 2006 season, and the team's offense trended heavily back towards league-average. Shields moved on before last season, and by this point the offensive line was in disarray.

Kansas City's inability to maintain offensive line dominance was undone by its strategy to get over the hump. Perhaps recognizing the age of their offensive core, the Chiefs consistently supplemented the roster with aging veteran free agents. On the offensive line, this meant that Damion McIntosh, John Welbourn, Chris Terry, and Kyle Turley all were counted on last season, despite being at least 30 and all being unwanted by a previous team. Predictably, they struggled.

Defensively, the team stacked its ranks with retreads and former stars. The Chiefs acquired mediocrities like middle linebacker Napoleon Harris, who was in his presumptive prime, to combine with the 2002 AFC Pro Bowl roster of cornerbacks Ty Law and Patrick Surtain and linebacker Donnie Edwards.

The reliance on veteran free agents was in part an attempt to win now, but was also a necessity, given the abysmal drafting by the Chiefs in the early part of the decade. Only one Kansas City draft pick from 2000 to

2003 remained in the starting lineup in 2007: Larry Johnson. The best player the team drafted and let go to another team is linebacker Scott Fujita, a league-average starter in New Orleans. Kansas City's draft prowess was no better from 1997 to 1999, with only three players (Tony Gonzalez, John Tait, and Gary Stills) remaining in the NFL.

The good news is that the team has made dramatically better decisions in recent drafts: 2004 yielded All-Pro defensive end Jared Allen, 2005 gave them the underrated linebacker Derrick Johnson, and 2006 produced defensive end Tamba Hali and safety Bernard Pollard. It's too soon to tell how most of last year's draft picks will develop, but wide receiver Dwayne Bowe was exceptional in his first season.

Successful drafting allowed the Chiefs to jettison some of the aging starters who would have served as stopgaps on the way to respectable 8-8 mediocrity, but it also would have blocked the young players whose development is essential if the Chiefs want to be winners again. The front office let Wiegmann, fullback Kris Wilson, and receiver Samie Parker leave in free agency. Then, it got serious, releasing Law, Welbourn, wide receiver Eddie Kennison, linebacker Kendrell Bell, and tight end Jason Dunn. The Chiefs' offseason additions were all players with five years or less of NFL experience.

These moves were enough to start the Chiefs on a serious rebuilding project, but the predraft trade of Allen to the Minnesota Vikings was the ultimate admission that the Chiefs are not serious about competing in 2008. Allen was Kansas City's best player last season and among the top 10 defensive players in all of football. An unrestricted free agent, Allen was franchised by the Chiefs, but talks stalled in negotiating a long-term deal. Allen has twice been arrested for drunk driving and is one strike away from a potentially serious league-mandated suspension. Perhaps the Chiefs felt that a long-term investment was too risky. Either way, their decision to send him to Minnesota was a bold move.

The good news is that the Chiefs got an impressive haul of draft picks in return, a rate commensurate with Allen's immense skill. The 2008 draft then worked out perfectly for Kansas City. Potentially dominant defensive tackle Glenn Dorsey fell to Kansas City at the fifth selection. With Minnesota's pick, the Chiefs added uber-talented Brandon Albert to play offensive line, potentially at left tackle. They added the technically proficient Brandon Flowers to play cornerback, a third likely starter in one draft.

Before these players see the field, it is a little tough to assume they are stars, but Dorsey, in particular, appears to be a "can't miss" prospect. Combine him with Johnson, Hali, and second-year defensive linemen Turk McBride and Tank Tyler, and the Chiefs definitely have the pieces for a developing defense. Offensively, Albert, Bowe, and Johnson are the start of a developing core.

The key to the offense will be the development of Croyle as the signal-caller. Croyle's season was disappointing from start to finish. He was given every opportunity to win the starting quarterback job but failed to beat out Damon Huard. When Huard moved to the bench, first with injury and then because the Chiefs were out of playoff contention, Croyle's performance was eminently forgettable. He performed below replacement level in our advanced stats. He averaged a paltry 5.5 yards per attempt, comfortably last in the NFL among qualifying quarterbacks.

The only way to have confidence in Croyle is to just assume that he is young and therefore will improve into a competent player. A pure exercise in wishful thinking would look at the similar case of Derek Anderson, who also struggled as a second-year starter but emerged as a Pro Bowler in his third season.

The Anderson example is extremely rare. Croyle is one of 25 quarterbacks since 1995 who have attempted 100 passes for the first time in their second season. Even though these players have no previous NFL experience, most quarterbacks show their true colors immediately. Only five quarterbacks had an above-average DVOA during their first season of playing time: Daunte Culpepper, Carson Palmer, Aaron Brooks, Steve McNair, and Tom Brady. The only other great quarterback on the list, Drew Brees, was just below average and had the fourth highest DYAR of the group.

Croyle is very near the middle of this group, ranking 16th in DYAR and 14th in DVOA. The surrounding company is not all that impressive (Table 1). The only players who offer any hope, if it can be considered that, are Anderson and Trent Dilfer. Anderson, of course, is a one-year wonder to date, but his 2007 was an outstanding season. Time will tell if he is for real. Dilfer did win a Super Bowl, but he only had a positive DYAR three times while playing over a decade in the NFL. Dilfer's best season was his second full year as a starter. So for 2008, Dilfer and Anderson show that a solid season from Croyle is not impossible.

It is, however, about as far from being realistic as the Chiefs are from being a contender. These numbers indicate that Croyle would be bucking recent history to become a successful quarterback. For another place to lack faith, consider Croyle's draft position. Croyle was the 85th player taken in the 2006 draft. Between 1990 and 2005, 51 quarterbacks were drafted between the

Table 1. Quarterbacks with First Season of 100 Pass Attempts in Second Year, 1995-2007

Player	Team	Year	DYAR	DVOA
Daunte Culpepper	MIN	2000	1263	27.3%
Carson Palmer	CIN	2004	429	3.8%
Aaron Brooks	NO	2000	183	2.8%
Steve McNair	HOU	1996	133	2.8%
Tom Brady	NE	2001	339	0.3%
Jason Campbell	WAS	2006	141	-0.7%
Gus Frerotte	WAS	1995	257	-1.3%
Drew Brees	SD	2002	336	-1.5%
Brian Griese	DEN	1999	185	-5.2%
Tarvaris Jackson	MIN	2007	107	-5.8%
Bobby Hoying	PHI	1997	23	-9.6%
Koy Detmer	PHI	1998	6	-10.6%
Danny Kanell	NYG	1997	-87	-15.7%
Brodie Croyle	KC	2007	-111	-18.5%
Kellen Clemens	NYJ	2007	-136	-18.9%
Derek Anderson	CLE	2006	-93	-22.8%
Brock Huard	SEA	2000	-106	-28.0%
Trent Dilfer	TB	1995	-523	-29.7%
Todd Collins	BUF	1996	-162	-36.1%
Josh McCown	ARI	2003	-401	-43.2%
J. P. Losman	BUF	2005	-482	-43.3%
Danny Wuerffel	NO	1998	-272	-44.2%
Andrew Walter	OAK	2006	-629	-44.2%
Kurt Kittner	ATL	2003	-336	-57.3%
Spergon Wynn	MIN	2000	-422	-75.1%

50th and 120th selection. Of those 51, only Mark Brunell was a consistently high-level performer. The 51 players have a combined six Pro Bowl appearances: three for Brunell, and one each for Neil O'Donnell, Brian Griese, and Kordell Stewart. The only other quality player is David Garrard, who so far has had only one very good season.

No, the only reason to project Croyle as a competent NFL starter is hope and faith. At least last year's poor performance was partly attributable to a weak supporting cast. The offensive line was a disaster, and Croyle played primarily without Larry Johnson. This year, however, he'll have no such excuse. While not the league's most talented group, Croyle's skill position players this year include Tony Gonzalez, Bowe, and Johnson. That core compares favorably to the skill position players featured by the New York Giants on the way to the Super Bowl.

The problem with Croyle's lack of progress is that when he almost inevitably struggles this season, the Chiefs will again have to address their quarterback position. At that point, they face the prospect of either grabbing a short-term stopgap or going with another rookie.

Given the team's probable sub-.500 record, the Chiefs will probably go the rookie route, and the team's rebuilding timeline will be set back another two years, while this newest quarterback does or does not develop.

As a result, the Chiefs have started on a successful, teamwide rebuilding process that may be undone because their plan at the quarterback position is based on coordinating a citywide finger-crossing campaign. Even without Allen, the defense could quickly develop into a respectable unit, led by a talented front seven. However, the young players in the secondary still have a lot to learn, so that improvement is unlikely to get past league-average in 2007.

The team is still very much rebuilding the offensive line; as currently constructed, the roster is dedicated to wasting the considerable talent of Johnson and the twilight of Gonzalez's Hall of Fame career. Eight-man fronts will be the order of the day, and nothing about Croyle indicates an ability to make opposing defenses pay. You have to respect the Chiefs for acknowledging the obvious need to tear it down and start over, but the struggles of Croyle are likely to mean a long-term rebuilding project rather than a two-year turnaround plan.

Ned Macey

2007 Chiefs Stats by Week

Wk	vs.	W-L	PF	PA	YDF	YDA	TO	Total	Off	Def	ST
1	@HOU	L	3	20	219	315	-2	-58%	-47%	-1%	-12%
2	@CHI	L	10	20	281	239	+1	-41%	-21%	-15%	-35%
3	MIN	W	13	10	251	256	0	12%	-9%	-12%	9%
4	@SD	W	30	16	390	333	+2	29%	15%	-16%	-2%
5	JAC	L	7	17	271	357	-1	-32%	-14%	12%	-7%
6	CIN	W	27	20	354	373	+1	27%	-6%	-21%	12%
7	@OAK	W	12	10	290	268	+1	-5%	-20%	-16%	-1%
8	BYE										
9	GB	L	22	33	234	432	0	-7%	-13%	-10%	-3%
10	DEN	L	11	27	284	327	-3	-41%	-51%	-11%	-1%
11	@IND	L	10	13	234	216	-1	51%	10%	-59%	-18%
12	OAK	L	17	20	292	312	0	-66%	-18%	44%	-3%
13	SD	L	10	24	268	330	-3	-4%	-29%	-12%	12%
14	@DEN	L	7	41	129	453	-3	-147%	-76%	71%	0%
15	TEN	L	17	26	306	327	-3	-23%	20%	38%	-5%
16	@DET	L	20	25	407	236	0	-8%	-5%	-8%	-12%
17	@NYJ	L	10	13	219	337	0	-26%	-24%	12%	10%

Trends and Splits

	Offense	Rank	Defense	Rank
Total DVOA	-18.0%	29	-0.4%	16
Unadjusted VOA	-17.9%	30	1.7%	18
Weighted trend	-19.0%	30	4.5%	22
Variance	6.1%	13	9.3%	24
Average opponent	1.4%	21	2.6%	12
Passing	-15.5%	27	-2.9%	10
Rushing	-21.4%	31	1.9%	24
First down	-24.7%	29	15.1%	29
Second down	-19.8%	29	-1.2%	10
Third down	-3.8%	18	-29.7%	1
First half	-13.0%	26	-4.2%	14
Second half	-22.8%	30	3.4%	19
Red Zone	-16.7%	28	12.6%	23
Late and close	-3.2%	17	9.5%	25

Five-Year Performance

Year	W-L	Pyth Wins	Est Wins	PF	PA	TO	Total	Rank	Off	Rank	Def	Rank	ST	Rank
2003	13-3	11.4	10.4	484	332	+19	25.9%	1	27.0%	1	6.7%	24	5.5%	1
2004	7-9	9.0	9.3	483	435	-6	11.4%	11	28.7%	2	16.7%	30	-0.5%	18
2005	10-6	10.0	11.1	403	325	+8	27.5%	4	23.7%	2	-5.7%	12	-2.0%	23
2006	9-7	8.5	8.4	331	315	+4	3.4%	13	4.8%	11	2.8%	18	1.3%	13
2007	4-12	4.5	5.1	226	335	-11	-20.9%	26	-18.0%	29	-0.4%	16	-3.3%	24

Strategic Tendencies

Run/Pass		Rank	Offense		Rank	Defense		Rank	Other		Rank
Runs, all plays	37%	25	3+ WR	45%	21	Rush 3	4.9%	16	2+ RB, Pct Runs	54%	24
Runs, first half	44%	8	4+ WR	13%	14	Rush 4	65.2%	14	1 RB/2 TE, Pct runs	38%	26
Runs, first down	45%	26	2+ TE	33%	6	Rush 5	23.8%	13	1 RB/3+ WR, pct runs	24%	15
Runs, second-long	33%	22	Single back	60%	13	Rush 6+	6.1%	24	CB1 on WR1	52%	6
Runs, power sit.	67%	11	Play action	21%	11	Rush 7+	0.4%	28	Go for it on 4th	1.37	7
Runs, behind 2H	25%	26	Max protect	9%	20	Sacks by LB	21.6%	18	Offensive Pace	31.1	20
Pass, ahead 2H	51%	8	Outside pocket	8%	23	Sacks by DB	2.7%	27	Defensive Pace	30.0	6

The Chiefs faced the most third downs with 10 or more yards to go. ✐ With 11 different intended receivers, Kansas City had the widest variety of screen pass targets, but their DVOA on screen passes dropped significantly after Larry Johnson's injury in Week 9. ✐ Think Tony Gonzalez is Kansas City's easy outlet on third downs? Think again. Gonzalez was thrown 50 percent more passes than Dwayne Bowe on first and second down, but Bowe was actually Kansas City's most frequent target on third down. ✐ The Chiefs ranked seventh in DVOA on passes thrown to the left, but 30th on passes to the right and 31st on passes up the middle. ✐ Kansas City threw 23 percent of its passes behind the line of scrimmage, second in the league to New Orleans. Ironically, the defense faced the highest percentage of passes behind the line of scrimmage, 22 percent. At least they had some experience facing that stuff in practice. ✐ Another place where the Chiefs offense matched their defense: Kansas City running backs had the league's worst rushing DVOA with a fullback in the game, and averaged less than three yards per carry. They were a yard per carry better from single-back sets. On defense, the Chiefs were *also* a yard per carry better without a fullback in the game. They allowed 3.9 yards per carry with one back (-18.9% DVOA, fourth) and 4.9 yards per carry with two backs (10.5% DVOA, 30th). The Chiefs had the league's biggest discrepancy on both sides of the ball. ✐ Kansas City hurried the opposing quarterbacks on a higher percentage of passes than any other defense, but it didn't help them as much as you might expect—they ranked 29th in defensive DVOA when the quarterback was hurried. ✐ The front seven also ranked second in passes tipped at the line of scrimmage. ✐ Only the Raiders and Jets faced play-action fakes more often, and only the Saints had a worse defensive DVOA when the offense used play-action. ✐ The Kansas City defense only benefited from 25 dropped passes, the fewest in the NFL.

Passing

Player	DYAR	DVOA	Plays	NtYds	Avg	YAC	C%	TD	Int
Damon Huard	-13	-11.8%	370	2119	5.7	4.6	62.2%	11	13
Brodie Croyle	-111	-18.5%	240	1115	4.6	4.2	57.0%	6	6
Tyler Thigpen	-29	-80.5%	8	43	5.4	14.0	33.3%	0	1

Rushing

Player	DYAR	DVOA	Plays	Yds	Avg	TD	Fum	Suc
Larry Johnson	-35	-14.0%	158	559	3.5	3	1	41%
Kolby Smith	25	-3.4%	112	407	3.6	2	0	49%
Priest Holmes*	-30	-25.6%	46	137	3.0	0	0	37%
Michael Bennett*	-14	-29.4%	20	52	2.6	0	2	25%
Jackie Battle	10	8.6%	14	47	3.4	1	0	43%
Gilbert Harris	-54	-132.6%	9	9	1.0	0	1	11%
Brodie Croyle	-7	-38.5%	5	20	4.0	0	6	—
Kris Wilson*	-6	-37.9%	3	7	2.3	0	2	33%
Damon Huard	-13	-86.7%	3	5	1.7	0	6	—

Receiving

Player	DYAR	DVOA	Plays	Ctch	Yds	Y/C	YAC	TD	C%
WR									
Dwayne Bowe	207	10.0%	118	70	995	14.2	5.2	5	59%
Jeff Webb	-115	-39.6%	57	28	313	11.2	2.0	1	49%
Samie Parker*	62	6.9%	39	24	272	11.3	3.8	2	62%
Eddie Kennison	-49	-36.8%	26	13	101	7.8	1.8	0	50%
Devard Darling	53	4.3%	39	18	326	18.1	4.4	3	46%
TE									
Tony Gonzalez	206	14.1%	154	99	1172	11.8	2.8	6	64%
RB									
Kris Wilson*	-59	-35.0%	50	24	222	9.3	4.9	1	48%
Larry Johnson	-12	-19.2%	42	30	186	6.2	7.7	1	71%
Kolby Smith	7	-8.7%	29	22	148	6.7	6.9	0	76%
Michael Bennett*	-41	-88.2%	13	10	49	4.9	6.2	0	77%
Priest Holmes*	-13	-40.3%	10	5	17	3.4	8.0	1	50%
Jackie Battle	-25	-97.0%	5	1	4	4.0	5.0	0	20%

Offensive Line

Year	Yards	ALY	Rank	Power	Rank	10+ Yds	Rank	Stuff	Rank	Sack	ASR	Rank
2005	4.79	4.62	3	68%	10	21%	7	21%	6	32	6.6%	15
2006	4.34	4.24	17	74%	2	21%	8	24%	15	41	7.5%	21
2007	3.37	3.61	31	61%	20	12%	24	28%	29	55	9.1%	29

Year	LE	Rank	LT	Rank	Mid	Rank	RT	Rank	RE	Rank
2005	5.18	3	4.59	9	4.44	6	4.25	14	4.63	8
2006	3.53	24	4.58	12	4.57	8	2.57	32	4.69	8
2007	2.30	32	4.30	18	4.01	21	3.42	30	3.31	30

Guard Brian Waters must have thought last year that he had awoken in the middle of a bad dream. After years of playing on one of the best offensive lines in football, he was still performing at a Pro Bowl level for the same team, but suddenly he was surrounded by players flat-out overmatched as starters in the NFL. Kansas City led the league in blown blocks as tracked by our game charting project. The team decided to unload underperforming veterans Chris Terry, Kyle Turley, and John Welbourn, as well as center Casey Wiegmann, who was still adequate. Instead, the Chiefs are going with unproven youngsters. The only player besides Waters to survive the purge is tackle Damion McIntosh, who was not an embarrassment but is below-average on the left side. First-round pick Branden Albert was a guard in college but has been projected to left tackle in the NFL. If he can play there and move McIntosh to the right side, the team would be upgrading two positions.

Center and right guard are very uncertain positions. Some combination of Will Svitek, Adrian Jones, and Rudy Niswanger will likely man the two spots, unless Albert stays at guard, pushing someone else to right tackle. If Albert impresses, along with Waters and McIntosh, the line could be decent. If he transitions slowly, then the Chiefs running game will stall again, and Brodie Croyle will finish a number of plays enjoying the delicious taste of freshly mowed grass.

Defensive Front Seven

Defensive Line	Age	Pos	Plays	TmPct	Rk	Stop	Dfts	Stop%	Rk	AvYd	Rk	Sack	Hit	Hur	Runs	RuStop	RuYd	Pass	PaStop	PaYd
Jared Allen*	26	DE	75	10.7%	1	62	32	83%	14	0.1	9	15.5	8	17	41	78%	1.5	34	88%	-1.6
Tamba Hali	25	DE	61	7.6%	15	40	21	66%	71	2.1	52	7.0	4	15	46	59%	3.5	15	87%	-2.2
Alfonso Boone	32	DT	32	4.3%	50	24	11	75%	49	3.1	64	1.0	2	13	23	70%	3.3	9	89%	2.6
Ron Edwards	29	DT	28	3.5%	62	21	8	75%	46	1.6	29	3.0	2	2	22	68%	3.2	6	100%	-4.3

Linebackers	Age	Pos	Plays	TmPct	Rk	Stop	Dfts	Stop%	AvYd	Sack	Hit	Hur	Runs	RuStop	Rk	RuYd	Rk	Tgts	Suc%	Rk	APaYd	Rk
Napoleon Harris	29	MLB	118	14.8%	21	60	16	51%	5.2	2.0	0	2	81	57%	78	4.0	77	20	38%	79	7.3	73
Donnie Edwards	35	OLB	110	13.8%	34	54	22	49%	5.6	2.0	2	4	59	64%	41	3.2	46	29	34%	86	8.7	86
Derrick Johnson	26	OLB	99	12.4%	50	63	35	64%	3.9	4.0	3	11	53	68%	31	3.2	42	48	56%	25	5.5	31
Demorrio Williams	28	OLB	78	9.3%	75	40	12	51%	5.5	0.0	0	2	45	60%	58	3.0	34	23	46%	55	7.4	78

Year	Yards	ALY	Rank	Power	Rank	10+ Yds	Rank	Stuff	Rank	Sack	ASR	Rank
2005	4.10	3.87	10	65%	20	21%	27	21%	29	28	5.1%	29
2006	4.15	4.23	15	63%	13	17%	22	28%	5	32	5.6%	28
2007	4.56	4.03	13	60%	14	22%	28	26%	12	37	7.9%	3

Year	LE	Rank	LT	Rank	Mid	Rank	RT	Rank	RE	Rank
2005	3.37	7	3.68	8	3.99	14	3.69	8	4.48	21
2006	4.43	19	4.18	12	3.92	3	4.77	27	5.01	30
2007	3.66	10	3.53	5	3.96	9	3.92	13	5.18	31

This group was among the best in the league last year, thanks in large part to Jared Allen. The right defensive end excelled against both the run and the pass and demanded a double team much of the time. Even with their superstar gone to Minnesota, the front seven remains the Chiefs' strength. The run defense should be solid this year, as rookie Glenn Dorsey, Alfonso Boone, Ron Edwards, and Tank Tyler form an excellent defensive tackle rotation.

Linebacker Derrick Johnson is one of the most underrated players in the league, one of the best and most versatile linebackers in football. Middle linebacker Napoleon Harris is a veteran who knows his limitations and generally makes the plays he should, but he rarely makes an impact. Donnie Edwards is older and can get exploited in coverage, which likely accounts for the acquisition of the younger and faster Demorrio Williams. The big question following Allen's departure is the pass rush. The 2007 second-round pick Turk McBride steps in for Allen and should be solid in run defense, but he is not known as a fierce pass rusher—he played tackle, not end, in college at Tennessee. Tamba Hali was rarely double-teamed at left defensive end last year, yet he only had seven sacks.

Defensive Secondary

Secondary	Age	Pos	Plays	TmPct	Rk	Stop	Dfts	RuYd	Rk	RuStop	Rk	Tgts	Tgt%	Rk	Dist	Suc%	Rk	APaYd	Rk	PaYd	PD	Int
Bernard Pollard	24	SS	96	12.0%	13	31	16	7.9	62	30%	72	32	9%	20	15.5	49%	42	11.6	76	11.8	6	2
Patrick Surtain	32	CB	65	8.1%	57	26	10	6.7	44	48%	44	66	18%	42	9.1	43%	68	8.4	62	8.6	8	2
Jarrad Page	24	FS	61	7.6%	63	30	15	6.4	42	56%	11	26	7%	41	16.3	53%	25	9.7	66	10.0	6	3
Ty Law*	34	CB	60	7.5%	63	28	13	5.7	32	50%	36	73	20%	31	11.1	55%	18	6.9	27	6.9	12	2
Benny Sapp*	27	CB	34	4.9%	—	18	9	5.8	—	67%	—	35	11%	—	9.3	51%	—	6.5	—	6.9	4	1
Greg Wesley	30	SS	29	3.9%	82	10	3	6.8	50	43%	44	19	5%	64	17.6	50%	39	9.5	64	10.0	3	0
Tyron Brackenridge	24	CB	17	2.6%	—	12	5	4.0	—	80%	—	6	2%	—	3.7	75%	—	6.8	—	7.0	0	0

Year	Pass D Rank	vs. #1 WR	Rk	vs. #2 WR	Rk	vs. Other WR	Rk	vs. TE	Rk	vs. RB	Rk
2005	16	-5.3%	8	1.6%	22	-42.2%	2	20.2%	25	10.8%	26
2006	22	-19.3%	4	16.0%	25	42.0%	32	-15.5%	7	-3.7%	15
2007	10	14.3%	23	-21.6%	5	-34.1%	2	30.0%	31	-14.7%	7

A much neglected part of the Chiefs' recent draft history, the cornerback position was filled by grizzled veterans Ty Law and Patrick Surtain last season. Law actually outplayed Surtain in almost all of our metrics, but he was the one released. Of course, Surtain outperformed Law in both 2005 and 2006, and he is two years younger than Law. Also, Surtain generally played the defense with more integrity, allowing plays to develop underneath but preventing bigger plays. To replace Law, the Chiefs drafted Brandon Flowers, a potentially very solid Tampa-2 style cornerback who is a sound tackler and smart cover man. His primary weakness is his speed. He'll compete for playing time with Benny Sapp and Tyron Brackenridge. Sapp is more proven, but Brackenridge offers more upside.

At safety, the Chiefs actually featured youth in Bernard Pollard and Jarrad Page. Pollard spent most of the season cleaning up plays way downfield, while Page exhibited some potential to be an impact safety. Veteran Jon McGraw can be exploited in coverage, but he has been in a Tampa-2 system both in Detroit and Kansas City and provides some depth at safety.

Special Teams

Year	DVOA	Rank	FG/XP	Rank	Net Punt	Rank	Punt Ret	Rank	Net Kick	Rank	Kick Ret	Rank	Hidden	Rank
2005	-2.0%	24	-0.6	20	1.0	15	-2.9	22	-14.1	31	4.9	8	2.8	13
2006	1.3%	13	-3.6	24	14.4	2	2.2	10	-3.2	27	-2.2	16	7.9	6
2007	-3.3%	24	-10.2	30	5.9	8	-6.3	28	6.2	7	-14.9	32	-15.9	31

If you spend a third-round pick on a punter, as Kansas City did in 2005, he better be good. At least Dustin Colquitt is that. Son of Craig Colquitt, punter for the championship Steelers in the 1970s, he was comfortably above average for the second year in a row with the Chiefs. Then again, if you spend a fifth-round pick on a placekicker, he better actually make it past Week 1. Justin Medlock did not; the Chiefs cut him after he missed a 30-yarder against Houston, and signed former Indianapolis kickoff specialist Dave Rayner. As usual, Rayner had a strong leg on kickoffs but struggled to put the ball between the uprights. The Chiefs are currently planning on a training camp battle to determine their kicker for 2008, with mediocrities Billy Cundiff and Nick Novak playing a prominent role. Given the rebuilding across the rest of the roster, it seems silly for the Chiefs to recycle another veteran instead of giving a shot to some undrafted youngster like Arthur Carmody, Alexis Serna, or Jeremy Ito. In the return game, the Chiefs were awful a year ago, with specialist Eddie Drummond among the league's worst punt returners. The early favorite for kick return duties is receiver Jeff Webb, who has been adequate in limited opportunities to return kickoffs. Webb should see competition from rookie running back Jamaal Charles, who has breakaway speed.

COACHING STAFF

Herm Edwards is certainly the most entertaining coach in the NFL, and he provides approximately 35 percent of our weekly *The Week in Quotes* compilation. He is easy to mock for his odd statements, clock mismanagement, and propensity for wearing out his feature running backs. The latter two are legitimate complaints, but they overlook Edwards's gifts for motivation, teaching, and preparation. Effectively, Edwards is an average coach. He wins when he has talent and loses when he does not. The most important coach on the staff will be Chan Gailey, who replaces Mike Solari as offensive coordinator. Gailey had success at his two previous stops with run-heavy offenses and unproven quarterbacks, so while not an innovative genius, he is a good match for what Edwards wants to do. Gailey coaxed adequate to above-average performance out of Mike Tomczak and Kordell Stewart in Pittsburgh and Jay Fiedler in Miami. Fiedler ranked eighth in DYAR during Gailey's second and final year as his coordinator.

The next season of Brodie Croyle's development will be overseen by quarterbacks coach Dick Curl. Curl is an odd choice in that before being appointed in 2005, his only previous experience with quarterbacks was when he played the position himself at the University of Richmond from 1958 to 1962. Gunther Cunningham is still on board as defensive coordinator; he is a solid veteran coach who tends to get the most out of his players, and he's seamlessly transitioned from the blitz-heavy style of his earlier years to a style more in line with the Tampa-2 principles espoused by Edwards.

Miami Dolphins

It took seven years of mismanagement to create a team as awful as the 2007 Dolphins. It will take Bill Parcells a few seasons to turn them into a professional football franchise again.

The Dolphins' long slide into oblivion began with the retirement of head coach Jimmy Johnson, one day after the 1999 regular season ended. The Dolphins spent the next eight years wandering in the desert, lurching from would-be savior to would-be savior. Dave Wannstedt, Johnson's top lieutenant, shepherded the team through several winning seasons, but Wannstedt lacked Johnson's personnel acumen, and each year, the Dolphins shed a little more of their talent base. Wannstedt imported Rick Speilman, the personnel guru who helped him through his Bears tenure, but Speilman added little new talent to the roster. After the 2003 season, owner Wayne Huizenga scoured the league for a personnel mastermind. Inexplicably, he decided upon ex-quarterback and HBO analyst Dan Marino. Marino knew a boondoggle when he saw it, and his tenure as team president lasted just a few days. Huizenga then promoted Speilman over Wannstedt, leaving the coach to twist in the wind before firing him late in the 2004 season.

Nick Saban replaced Wannstedt. Speilman presided over one draft before Huizenga (with Saban's input) replaced him. Enter Randy Mueller, a well-regarded exec who helped build the Seahawks into a contender. Mueller and Saban were supposed to work hand in glove, but the Dolphins were Saban's team right up until the moment he quit to take the Alabama job after the 2006 season. Mueller stayed behind, assuming more personnel control as coach Cam Cameron arrived to turn the Dolphins into the East Coast Chargers.

That's a lot of regime changes in seven years: Wannstedt, Wannstedt-Speilman, Marino for a week, Speilman-Wannstedt, Speilman-Saban, Saban-Mueller, Mueller-Cameron. The names changed—or at least the positions of power did—but the sins remained. No matter who made the decisions in Miami, the team made the same critical mistakes.

The Dolphins lacked a clear front-office voice. The Dolphins kept changing coaches and general managers, but never at the same time. The new guy inevitably had to play nice-nice with holdovers from the old regime: Saban with Speilman, Mueller with Saban, Cameron with Mueller. It's hard to clean house when you are working with the previous architect, and the Dolphins could never commit to a rebuilding timetable. It was often hard to tell who was calling the final shots in Miami, and philosophies shifted annually. The constant change led to a win-now mentality, because there's no reason to think about the future when the team has already hired your next challenger/replacement. That win-now mentality led to the next two blunders.

The Dolphins never developed a post-Marino quarterback. Marino retired a few weeks after the 1999 season. Most teams would have drafted a high-round quarterback that season or the next, but the Dolphins never did. In fact, the Dolphins drafted just one quar-

DOLPHINS PROSPECTUS

2007 Record: 1-15

Pythagorean Wins: 3.8 (30th)

DVOA: -27.6% total (29th), -30.7% weighted (31st)

Offense: -8.5% DVOA (23rd)

Defense: 16.8% DVOA (32nd)

Special Teams: -2.3% DVOA (22nd)

Variance: 12.6 % (9th)

2007: The sputtering Dolphins end up one Greg Camarillo touchdown away from 0-16.

2008: The very definition of a rebuilding season.

2008 Mean Projection: 5.5 wins

On the Clock (0-3): 14%

Loserville (4-6): 58%

Mediocrity (7-8): 21%

Playoff Contender (9-10): 7%

Super Bowl Contender (11+): 0%

Projected Average Opponent: -1.5% DVOA (19th in NFL)

2008 Dolphins Schedule

Week	Opp.	Week	Opp.	Week	Opp.
1	NYJ	7	BAL	13	at STL
2	at ARI	8	BUF	14	at BUF
3	at NE	9	at DEN	15	SF
4	BYE	10	SEA	16	at KC
5	SD	11	OAK	17	at NYJ
6	at HOU	12	NE		

terback between 1999 and 2006: Josh Heupel, a sixth-rounder in 2001.

The Dolphins signed journeymen Damon Huard and Jay Fiedler to replace Marino in 2000. Fiedler provided several seasons of credible leadership, but he was 29 when the team signed him. Instead of drafting a top prospect to learn under the heady Fiedler, the Dolphins tried to outsmart the league. They became a retread center for other teams' second-tier prospects, granting extended tryouts to A. J. Feeley, Ray Lucas, Sage Rosenfels, and Cleo Lemon. They made reclamation projects of damaged goods like Trent Green and Daunte Culpepper. When they finally invested a second-round pick in a quarterback last year, they chose John Beck, already 25 years old as a rookie. Beck got his chance when Green and Lemon were hurt last season; the rookie looked dreadful. He still has potential, but he's just a few months younger than Eli Manning, so he doesn't have much time to shake the rookie lumps.

The Dolphins treated draft picks like arcade tokens. When the Dolphins traded two first-round picks to acquire Ricky Williams, it was a defensible move by a team that appeared to be one running back away from a Super Bowl run. But soon, the Dolphins were throwing draft picks away for near-replacement-level veteran talent. A. J. Feeley cost the team a second-round pick. Lamar Gordon, acquired in a panic-button move when Williams "retired" rather than face a drug suspension, cost a third-round pick. To get Lemon, the Dolphins packaged Feeley with a sixth-rounder. Culpepper cost the team a second-round pick in 2006. The Dolphins also traded up when they couldn't afford to, squandering a fourth-round pick in 2004 to move up a single spot and take Vernon Carey.

From 1999 to 2003, the Dolphins selected just one player in the first round: defensive back Jamar Fletcher, who was gone after three years. They lacked second-round picks in 2002, 2004, and 2006. Their batting aver-

age on the picks they made was poor, with lots of busts like Fletcher and Eddie Moore mixed in with a few hits like Ronnie Brown. Throw in some first-round reaches—Carey, Jason Allen, Ted Ginn—and the Dolphins have very little to show for six years of drafting.

After years of revolving-door leadership, poor drafts, and bad decisions at quarterback, a season like 2007 was inevitable. Last year, the Dolphins' two best defenders, Taylor and Thomas, were holdovers from the Johnson era. All the team had to show for the years 2000-2006 were Ronnie Brown, Chris Chambers, and a handful of average starters. The rest of the lineup consisted of rookies, fringe-caliber holdovers from recent drafts, and creaky veterans like Trent Green, Marty Booker, and Vonnie Holliday. The Dolphins had become a glorified expansion team.

By midseason, they were worse than an expansion team. The early losses were sloppy but competitive, marred by careless penalties and blooper-reel mistakes (Green's fumble during a fake-spike play leaps to mind). The Dolphins always seemed to commit back-to-back penalties when they entered the red zone, and every punt was a misadventure, but three of their first five losses were by three-point margins. Then, one by one, their few capable veterans got hurt. Once Green, Brown, Thomas, and Taylor were on the sidelines and Chambers was traded, the 40-13 and 38-17 losses began. It was time for a real regime change, not the kind of halfhearted, hedged-bet front-office reshuffling that Huizenga supervised so many times in the last eight years.

Parcells arrived in late December after Huizenga bested Falcons owner Arthur Blank in a bidding war for his services. Parcells knew sweeping changes were necessary. Cameron had proven personally and strategically overmatched as a head coach. The closest thing to a young franchise player was Brown, a running back who couldn't stay healthy. Parcells watched the Dolphins' final game from the owner's box, looking like a man who wanted to start issuing pink slips midway through the second quarter.

As soon as the season ended, he fired Mueller and Cameron, then set about re-creating the front office he had built in Dallas. Parcells hired Cowboys scouting director Jeff Ireland as general manager, then Cowboys offensive assistant Tony Sporano as head coach. Ireland and Parcells oversaw several productive drafts in Dallas. Sporano, an offensive line coach and running game coordinator in Dallas, helped make coordinators Sean Payton and Jason Garrett two of the league's hottest young offensive minds. Sporano imported every former

Parcells coach he could sneak out of Dallas when Jerry Jones's back was turned, including defensive coaches Paul Pasqualoni and Todd Bowles.

Immediately, Parcells corrected the Dolphins' biggest problem. Gone were the days when Dolphins coaches and general managers came from different hiring cycles and didn't have a clear division of duties. Now, the hierarchy from Sporano to Ireland to Parcells is clear, and the three principals in Team Tuna know each other and their roles. Parcells's staff is realistic about the team's needs and isn't afraid of a rebuilding cycle, another welcome change after years of quick fixes and sudden philosophical lurches.

Parcells began his roster rebuild in February, when he released Thomas, Booker, Green, and several other Dolphins veterans. The cuts were harsh but necessary: The players Parcells released were on the decline, and while Thomas was a Miami institution, he wouldn't be around to help the team when it became good again. The cuts erased some bad draft choices (Anthony Alibi), short-sighted free agent signings (L. T. Shelton), and old-timers with no place on a rebuilding team (Keith Traylor). Jason Taylor survived the axe, but Team Tuna worked through the winter to trade him or ease him into retirement. Ultimately, Taylor decided to remain in Miami after a stint in reality television.

The Dolphins' toe-dips into free agency confirmed that Parcells is taking a slow and steady approach to roster recycling. Veterans like receiver Ernest Wilford and defenders Keith Davis, Reggie Torbor, and Charlie Anderson will do little more than fill vacancies while the new brain trust sifts through the rubble of the roster for real players. Few returning players will get the benefit of the doubt, though the team did re-sign defensive backs Michael Lehan and Yeremiah Bell, and even Ricky Williams will get a chance to make his case to the new regime in training camp.

Just before the draft began, Team Tuna started acquiring real building blocks. Michigan tackle Jake Long signed with Miami days before the start of the draft; his early signing was another reminder that uber-professionalism now reigned in the Dolphins' front office. Once the draft started, the Dolphins picked up an all-purpose defensive end with Pro Bowl potential (Philip Merling) and a bona fide young prospect at quarterback (Chad Henne). Miami traded one of its draft choices for veterans, just as it did too often in the past, but this time, it didn't get magic beans in return. For the price of a fourth-round pick, Parcells raided the Cowboys one last time, acquiring tight end Anthony Fasano and linebacker Akin Ayodele. Ayodele is another veteran space-holder, but Fasano is a perfect fit in Sporano's system and is better than all but one or two of the tight ends available in the draft.

Long and Merling are excellent prospects. They join Brown and Samson Satele as potential great players for a playoff-bound Dolphins team in the future. There are a few other decent young players on the roster—Ted Ginn, Will Allen, Channing Crowder, Fasano, Carey—but there are still far more questions than answers. Henne could leapfrog Beck by the end of training camp, but free agent Josh McCown could open the season at quarterback. Taylor remained the subject of trade rumors in the offseason. Joey Porter, a free agent failure last year, could thrive in the new 3-4 defense, or Parcells could make an example of him the first time he skips a practice. There are lots of third-tier veteran free agents vying for roster spots, and any of them could be supplanted by an undrafted rookie who catches the boss's eye.

Parcells is doing the same thing in Miami that he did in Dallas in 2003. He's taking over a once-proud franchise that fell on hard times in the years since Jimmy Johnson left. He's rebuilding a team that drafted poorly and got too cute at quarterback, a team with an unprofessional front office made worse by a meddling or misguided owner. Parcells left before the job was done in Dallas, just as he did with the Patriots and Jets, but he always leaves infrastructure in his wake. The Cowboys finished 13-3 last season because of the players and coaches Parcells acquired and developed. Over the next few years, Parcells will install similar architecture in Miami. When he leaves, Ireland or some other well-prepared exec will take over a well-run machine. If Huizenga decides to sell the Dolphins (he shopped them aggressively in 2007), he'll be able to woo suitors with a respectable professional football operation to go with a strong media market and an established name brand.

For now, all Parcells has is Ireland, Sporano, and a handful of decent players. By next year, he'll have more bricks and mortar; by 2010, we might be able to talk seriously about the Dolphins as contenders. It's a long wait, but there's a lot of planning and demolition to be done before the building can begin.

Mike Tanier

2007 Dolphins Stats by Week

Wk	vs.	W-L	PF	PA	YDF	YDA	TO	Total	Off	Def	ST
1	@WAS	L	13	16	273	400	+1	8%	5%	-1%	2%
2	DAL	L	20	37	334	352	-5	-23%	-16%	11%	3%
3	@NYJ	L	28	31	424	256	-1	-34%	35%	45%	-24%
4	OAK	L	17	35	278	369	-1	-66%	-14%	57%	6%
5	@HOU	L	19	22	285	352	+1	10%	-8%	-6%	11%
6	@CLE	L	31	41	356	384	-1	-46%	3%	49%	0%
7	NE	L	28	49	382	443	-1	-41%	22%	45%	-18%
8	NYG	L	10	13	245	238	-1	-23%	-14%	0%	-9%
9	BYE										
10	BUF	L	10	13	269	214	+1	-2%	-2%	-9%	-9%
11	@PHI	L	7	17	186	352	+3	-13%	-27%	-3%	11%
12	@PIT	L	0	3	159	216	-1	1%	-28%	-36%	-7%
13	NYJ	L	13	40	187	372	-3	-100%	-76%	27%	4%
14	@BUF	L	17	38	285	389	-4	-106%	-43%	55%	-8%
15	BAL	W	22	16	360	345	+1	-16%	13%	34%	5%
16	@NE	L	7	28	241	400	+4	5%	-12%	-22%	-6%
17	CIN	L	25	38	336	393	0	-18%	7%	26%	1%

Trends and Splits

	Offense	Rank	Defense	Rank
Total DVOA	-8.5%	23	16.8%	32
Unadjusted VOA	-11.6%	25	21.2%	32
Weighted trend	14.2%	26	14.4%	30
Variance	7.0%	18	8.5%	21
Average opponent	0.7%	14	4.9%	3
Passing	-15.0%	26	20.0%	27
Rushing	-0.7%	12	14.4%	31
First down	-4.8%	18	19.1%	30
Second down	-6.2%	24	6.0%	21
Third down	-18.5%	27	29.8%	31
First half	20.0%	31	19.8%	30
Second half	1.7%	17	13.4%	29
Red Zone	-2.5%	18	43.7%	32
Late and close	-4.3%	20	24.6%	32

Five-Year Performance

Year	W-L	Pyth Wins	Est Wins	PF	PA	TO	Total	Rank	Off	Rank	Def	Rank	ST	Rank
2003	10-6	9.6	9.6	311	261	+2	12.5%	10	-8.0%	20	-18.1%	4	2.5%	7
2004	4-12	5.7	6.6	275	354	-17	-14.0%	23	-28.9%	31	-9.8%	7	5.0%	4
2005	9-7	8.0	8.8	318	317	+1	3.2%	13	-7.5%	21	-7.9%	10	2.8%	4
2006	6-10	7.2	7.2	260	283	+2	-3.9%	17	12.2%	28	-8.9%	7	-0.7%	21
2007	1-15	3.8	4.2	267	437	-7	-27.6%	29	-8.5%	23	16.8%	32	-2.3%	22

Strategic Tendencies

Run/Pass		Rank	Offense		Rank	Defense		Rank	Other		Rank
Runs, all plays	37%	26	3+ WR	46%	20	Rush 3	7.1%	10	2+ RB, Pct Runs	44%	30
Runs, first half	43%	12	4+ WR	9%	20	Rush 4	65.3%	13	1 RB/2 TE, Pct runs	39%	22
Runs, first down	47%	22	2+ TE	30%	9	Rush 5	24.1%	12	1 RB/3+ WR, pct runs	27%	10
Runs, second-long	25%	31	Single back	51%	20	Rush 6+	3.4%	32	CB1 on WR1	39%	26
Runs, power sit.	69%	7	Play action	26%	1	Rush 7+	0.2%	29	Go for it on 4th	2.10	1
Runs, behind 2H	29%	12	Max protect	18%	3	Sacks by LB	21.2%	19	Offensive Pace	31.6	24
Pass, ahead 2H	51%	7	Outside pocket	12%	13	Sacks by DB	9.1%	9	Defensive Pace	31.6	28

Miami quarterbacks used a play-action fake on one out of every four pass attempts, the highest percentage in the league; however, only Baltimore had a worse DVOA on plays using play action. ⊘ The Dolphins threw the ball more often than they ran it from a two-tight end set, yet they ranked sixth in DVOA on runs from two-tight end formations, and 26th on passes. ⊘ Facing one or two yards to go in non-goal-line situations, the Dolphins ran the ball 78 percent of the time, and threw it 10 or more yards only once. ⊘ The Dolphins kept Cleo Lemon on the move. They ranked sixth in designed bootlegs and rollouts despite the fact that Trent Green almost never left the pocket. ⊘ Miami's defense was middle of the pack against four or more wide receivers, but one of the four worst in the league against all other formations, and the absolute worst against three-receiver sets. ⊘ The Dolphins saw the fewest screen passes of any NFL team, even though only two defenses were worse against the screen. ⊘

Only St. Louis had a worse defensive DVOA in the fourth quarter. ✑ The official scorer at Dolphins Stadium is not very popular with Democrats; no matter whether the Dolphins were on offense or defense, he marked passes as "right" 50 percent more often than he marked them as "left."

Passing

Player	DYAR	DVOA	Plays	Nt Yds	Avg	YAC	C%	TD	Int
Cleo Lemon*	-91	-15.5%	337	1625	4.8	4.8	56.4%	6	6
Trent Green*	174	7.8%	149	958	6.4	5.4	61.6%	5	7
John Beck	-303	-51.7%	118	486	4.1	3.5	57.5%	1	3
Josh McCown	-236	-29.1%	207	1088	5.3	4.9	58.4%	10	10

Rushing

Player	DYAR	DVOA	Plays	Yds	Avg	TD	Fum	Suc
Jesse Chatman*	6	-7.5%	128	515	4.0	1	1	41%
Ronnie Brown	156	21.2%	119	602	5.1	4	0	51%
Samkon Gado*	14	1.2%	35	104	3.0	3	0	29%
Cleo Lemon*	62	24.5%	28	103	3.7	4	7	—
Patrick Cobbs	10	7.8%	15	47	3.1	1	0	47%
Ricky Williams	-16	-66.7%	6	15	2.5	0	1	50%
John Beck	10	12.0%	6	13	2.2	1	6	—
Trent Green*	-7	-34.7%	5	19	3.8	0	2	—
Reagan Mauia	-17	-84.1%	4	5	1.3	0	0	0%
Ted Ginn	-8	-79.3%	4	3	0.8	0	0	—
Josh McCown	1	-11.4%	25	143	5.7	0	11	—

Receiving

Player	DYAR	DVOA	Plays	Ctch	Yds	Y/C	YAC	TD	C%
WR									
Marty Booker*	-122	-27.3%	105	50	556	11.1	2.6	1	48%
Ted Ginn	-71	-25.9%	71	34	420	12.4	5.1	2	48%
Chris Chambers*	6	-11.5%	66	31	415	13.4	2.8	0	47%
Derek Hagan	29	-6.3%	59	29	373	12.9	2.3	2	49%
Greg Camarillo	72	82.1%	10	8	160	20.0	8.4	2	80%
Tab Perry	-27	-75.3%	5	1	7	7.0	0.0	0	20%
Ernest Wilford	136	10.2%	74	45	518	11.5	2.2	4	61%
TE									
David Martin	-7	-9.3%	50	34	303	8.9	2.3	2	68%
Justin Peelle	-40	-19.7%	47	29	228	7.9	5.4	2	62%
Anthony Fasano	7	-2.5%	21	14	143	10.2	3.9	1	67%
Sean Ryan	-1	-11.1%	5	3	46	15.3	2.7	0	60%
RB									
Ronnie Brown	160	52.0%	46	39	389	10.0	9.6	1	85%
Jesse Chatman*	-28	-26.6%	37	27	161	6.0	4.9	0	73%
Lorenzo Booker*	85	26.7%	36	28	237	8.5	6.2	0	78%
Patrick Cobbs	-1	-15.5%	6	3	24	8.0	3.3	0	50%
Samkon Gado*	11	27.5%	5	4	47	11.8	12.3	0	80%

Offensive Line

Year	Yards	ALY	Rank	Power	Rank	10+ Yds	Rank	Stuff	Rank	Sack	ASR	Rank
2005	4.35	4.33	11	71%	6	19%	14	25%	20	26	4.9%	6
2006	4.18	4.22	20	70%	9	19%	10	25%	18	41	7.0%	20
2007	4.22	4.09	22	70%	8	17%	16	24%	18	42	7.4%	20

Year	LE	Rank	LT	Rank	Mid	Rank	RT	Rank	RE	Rank
2005	5.01	6	5.12	1	4.21	14	4.21	15	3.94	16
2006	3.43	25	4.66	10	4.05	24	4.76	2	4.91	6
2007	3.86	21	5.05	4	3.86	24	3.84	24	4.63	6

Left tackle Jake Long and center Samson Satele could develop into the nucleus of a great offensive line. Long is a two-time Big Ten Offensive Lineman of the Year with great power, toughness, and work habits. He just needs to re-fine his technique. Satele was the team's best rookie last year and its best offensive player after Ronnie Brown was hurt. Satele excels at climbing out to the second level on inside runs and at open-field blocking on screens. Both linemen avoid mistakes: Satele drew just two holding penalties in his rookie season, and Long was only penalized three times in his entire college career. Right tackle Vernon Carey was a reach as a number one pick in 2002 but is solid and durable. Right guard Rex Hadnot signed with the Browns, leaving recent Edmonton Eskimo Trey Darilek to compete with rookie Shawn Murphy at the position. Murphy, the son of former Braves outfielder Dale Murphy, spent three years in Brazil on a Mormon mission and entered this year's draft as a 25-year-old rookie. Justin Smiley, a free agent from the Niners, will start at left guard.

Defensive Front Seven

Defensive Line	Age	Pos	Plays	Tm Pct	Rk	Stop	Dfts	Stop%	Rk	AvYd	Rk	Sack	Hit	Hur	Runs	RuStop	RuYd	Pass	PaStop	PaYd
Jason Taylor	34	DE	60	7.5%	17	44	24	73%	53	2.5	60	11.0	8	16	40	68%	3.6	20	85%	0.2
Kevin Carter	35	DE	46	5.8%	42	36	11	78%	36	1.7	41	3.0	5	10	37	81%	2.4	9	67%	-1.0
Keith Traylor*	39	DT	45	6.0%	21	34	5	76%	45	1.9	45	1.0	2	1	43	74%	2.0	2	100%	0.0
Matt Roth	26	DE	43	6.6%	27	31	9	72%	59	2.5	63	3.0	3	5	37	70%	3.0	6	83%	-0.5
Vonnie Holliday	33	DT	43	7.2%	8	32	14	74%	50	1.7	34	2.0	4	8	38	76%	1.9	5	60%	0.0
Rodrique Wright	24	DT	40	6.2%	18	31	7	78%	36	1.8	39	1.5	1	4	34	76%	2.1	6	83%	0.0
Randy Starks	25	DT	18	2.6%	—	14	5	78%	—	1.6	—	0.0	1	2	14	79%	1.6	4	75%	1.8

Linebackers	Age	Pos	Plays	TmPct	Rk	Stop	Dfts	Stop%	AvYd	Sack	Hit	Hur	Runs	RuStop	Rk	RuYd	Rk	Tgts	Suc%	Rk	APaYd	Rk
Channing Crowder	25	OLB	77	14.1%	30	35	9	45%	4.8	0.5	3	6	63	49%	97	4.1	80	15	33%	—	7.4	—
Joey Porter	31	OLB	71	8.9%	78	48	22	68%	3.7	5.5	3	5	44	68%	30	3.3	48	26	54%	29	6.6	63
Derrick Pope*	26	MLB	61	7.7%	89	32	11	52%	3.9	0.0	1	0	51	55%	88	3.1	37	10	52%	—	5.0	—
Zach Thomas*	35	MLB	54	21.7%	1	32	7	59%	3.9	1.0	0	0	41	68%	28	3.1	35	14	37%	—	8.7	—
Donnie Spragan	32	OLB	31	3.9%	—	14	3	45%	5.6	0.0	0	0	26	46%	—	5.3	—	5	79%	—	4.9	—
Akin Ayodele	29	ILB	59	7.5%	90	36	3	61%	3.7	0.0	0	1	43	70%	24	2.8	23	15	35%	—	9.0	—
Reggie Torbor	27	OLB	32	4.1%	—	18	4	56%	4.8	1.0	2	1	18	72%	—	2.6	—	10	36%	—	11.2	—
Charlie Anderson	27	OLB	25	3.1%	—	12	5	48%	4.2	2.0	1	3	12	58%	—	4.2	—	12	48%	—	4.9	—

Year	Yards	ALY	Rank	Power	Rank	10+ Yds	Rank	Stuff	Rank	Sack	ASR	Rank
2005	3.70	3.64	3	54%	3	19%	21	25%	14	49	8.4%	3
2006	3.55	3.87	6	66%	16	11%	2	24%	17	47	8.4%	4
2007	4.58	4.57	31	70%	24	18%	19	20%	30	30	7.3%	8

Year	LE	Rank	LT	Rank	Mid	Rank	RT	Rank	RE	Rank
2005	2.88	4	4.04	13	3.44	1	4.41	24	3.62	12
2006	3.68	12	4.47	16	4.03	9	3.24	5	3.07	5
2007	5.55	31	5.33	30	4.26	21	4.62	23	4.34	21

Jason Taylor was one of the most penalized players in the NFL last season, drawing 11 flags: five for jumping offside, four for various types of roughness, and two for holding. The offside penalties are a sign that Taylor has lost some burst and is trying to beat the snap count. Penalties aside, Taylor is still disruptive, and he should help rookie Philip Merling develop into a solid starter at defensive end. Merling, a second-rounder out of Clemson, is a great size-speed-motor prospect who hasn't matured as a pass-rusher yet. If Taylor teaches him the tricks of the trade, Merling can be special.

With Zach Thomas gone, Channing Crowder will have to assume a leadership role on defense. Crowder is an adequate run defender who never developed as a big play threat or as a coverage linebacker. He'll play inside in the new system. Reggie Torbor and Akin Ayodele will compete for a starting job next to Crowder. Ayodele, acquired in a draft day trade with the Cowboys, has the advantage of knowing the system.

Beyond Crowder, Taylor, and Merling, there are few certainties as the Dolphins switch to a hybrid 3-4 defense. Outside linebackers will have to be versatile enough to play with their hands in the dirt in the new scheme, which mixes three-, four-, and five-man fronts. Incumbents Matt Roth and Vonnie Holiday will battle new arrivals Merling and Randy Starks (signed as a free agent from Tennessee) for the end positions. Taylor will drift from end to outside linebacker. Jason Ferguson, who missed most of 2007 with a torn biceps, is another Parcells guy who will get a long look at nose tackle. If Ferguson's tank is empty, undrafted rookie Anthony Toribio will get a chance to make the team. Toribio, a 315-pounder from Carson Newman, drew praise from the Tuna himself during May minicamp. Joey Porter notched four sacks in his final five games and should thrive in the new system, but the new regime won't tolerate his me-first antics.

Defensive Secondary

Secondary	Age	Pos	Plays	TmPct	Rk	Stop	Dfts	RuYd	Rk	RuStop	Rk	Tgts	Tgt%	Rk	Dist	Suc%	Rk	APaYd	Rk	PaYd	PD	Int
Will Allen	30	CB	73	9.2%	40	35	16	5.3	24	36%	55	74	21%	19	12.2	56%	14	5.9	7	5.8	11	1
Michael Lehan	29	CB	65	8.7%	49	18	10	8.2	58	27%	71	56	17%	47	13.2	50%	39	7.9	54	7.9	7	1
Jason Allen	25	FS	56	7.0%	68	12	5	9.5	78	24%	80	14	4%	80	15.3	43%	61	12.3	81	12.6	3	3
*Cameron Worrell	29	SS	51	8.5%	53	16	5	4.5	7	46%	34	13	5%	69	16.7	35%	76	16.1	83	16.1	1	0
*Lance Schulters	33	SS	37	10.6%	28	17	2	5.4	19	50%	22	12	8%	29	13.1	42%	65	11.8	78	11.8	2	0
Renaldo Hill	30	FS	34	9.8%	—	13	4	5.7	—	47%	—	15	10%	—	10.3	43%	—	8.4	—	9.0	2	1
Travis Daniels	26	CB	31	3.9%	—	12	6	7.4	—	43%	—	37	11%	—	16.5	52%	—	9.5	—	10.2	2	1
André Goodman	30	CB	24	3.7%	—	11	7	8.0	—	60%	—	34	12%	—	11.0	30%	—	8.8	—	9.1	4	2
Chris Crocker	28	FS	67	9.1%	45	28	12	8.8	72	31%	69	42	11%	6	9.9	49%	41	6.6	31	6.4	10	3
Nate Jones	26	CB	15	2.0%	—	9	3	5.0	—	50%	—	13	3%	—	7.1	54%	—	9.6	—	10.0	0	0

Year	Pass D Rank	vs. #1 WR	Rk	vs. #2 WR	Rk	vs. Other WR	Rk	vs. TE	Rk	vs. RB	Rk
2005	11	21.2%	27	5.2%	26	-20.0%	5	-5.1%	13	-14.9%	8
2006	12	7.8%	22	2.2%	17	9.0%	23	0.7%	19	-25.9%	5
2007	27	11.9%	22	21.0%	27	17.3%	30	0.7%	11	-4.0%	13

Will Allen graded out as one of the best cornerbacks in the league according to our metrics, but he's not as good as his numbers: opponents didn't need to challenge him very often. Allen is a good bump-and-run defender who does well in run support and on corner blitzes. Michael Lehan emerged as a starter last year; he gave up a few big plays but showed the new staff enough to earn a one-year contract. Like Allen, Lehan is solid in run support. The Dolphins lack a true nickel corner: they keep flopping Travis Daniels from cornerback to safety, but he's ineffective at both positions. Daniels was a Nick Saban favorite who is now two regimes removed from his primary benefactor, so he's down to his last shot.

Strong safety Yeremiah Bell opened eyes with a strong 2006 season, but he tore his Achilles tendon in the season opener last year. He's a capable run defender with some big play ability. Jason Allen started the second half of last season and intercepted three passes, but he was a better cherry picker than defender and made a lot of mistakes in deep coverage. Free safety Renaldo Hill is on the mend from an October ACL tear. He's a useful nickel/dime player when healthy. Veteran Chris Crocker, a free agent from Atlanta, is a serviceable center fielder-type who expects to compete for a starting job.

Special Teams

Year	DVOA	Rank	FG/XP	Rank	Net Punt	Rank	Punt Ret	Rank	Net Kick	Rank	Kick Ret	Rank	Hidden	Rank
2005	3.1%	4	0.3	16	10.1	2	-0.9	16	7.8	3	1.0	16	-10.1	29
2006	-0.7%	21	-10.6	31	2.3	15	-1.7	18	10.3	5	-4.3	23	-4.0	22
2007	-2.3%	22	5.3	5	1.0	14	0.0	13	-18.6	32	-1.0	18	-7.4	25

Ted Ginn Jr. flashed potential as a return man with a touchdown against the Eagles and a handful of long kickoff returns. There's a lot of room for improvement: Ginn must improve his ball security (he muffed two punts against the Bills), and he called 15 fair catches on just 39 punts. His greatest attribute is his long speed, but it takes him a while to gather up speed, making him a better long-term prospect as a kickoff returner than a punt returner.

Jay Feely had a quiet year in 2007 because the Dolphins were rarely in scoring position. He's an accurate short kicker but one of the worst kickoff men in the league, so the Dolphins signed Dave Rayner as a possible kickoff specialist. Rayner is above average in the role and can kick field goals in a pinch, so he may replace Feely on the roster altogether. Punter Brandon Fields was involved in several punting misadventures, including the mud-sinker punt against the Steelers and a low line drive against the Redskins in Week 1, but he graded out as an average overall performer.

COACHING STAFF

Tony Sporano is a former offensive line coach, and offensive coordinator Dan Henning is known for his smash-mouth tactics. They're sure to dial up a steady dose of power runs, which will suit the Big Tuna just fine. The most important assistant on Sporano's staff is quarterbacks coach David Lee, who helped facilitate the Rise of Romo during his Dallas tenure. Lee must turn either Josh Beck or Chad Henne into a quarterback of the future. In May rookie camp, Lee, Sporano, and Henning threw the entire playbook at Henne in four days, confusing the rookie so badly that he couldn't remember his snap counts and was forced to run punishment laps. "We wanted to see exactly how much sticks," Sporano said of the full-immersion baptism.

Longtime Syracuse head coach Paul Pasqualoni is the Dolphins defensive coordinator. He spent the last three seasons in Dallas (imagine that), coaching linebackers and tight ends. He's expected to run a system similar to Wade Philips's 3-4 scheme. It's a 3-4 in name only: one or both of the outside linebackers will line up with a hand in the dirt on about 70 percent of defensive snaps.

Minnesota Vikings

The Vikings held the seventh overall pick in the 2007 NFL Draft, and teams generally don't find themselves in that position without having myriad needs. Minnesota, 6-10 the season before, was no exception. Former first-round wide receiver Troy Williamson had struggled as Randy Moss's replacement, hauling in just 61 passes and averaging a sub-50 percent catch rate in two seasons. A pass-rushing defensive end was also on the wish list, as was adding depth in the secondary and along the offensive line.

Despite so many holes in their pass offense and pass defense, the Vikings ended up using that seventh overall pick on a player at a position where they seemed set: running back. As it turns out, this was not a bad move. Adrian Peterson ran for more than 1,300 yards, averaging 5.6 yards per carry and breaking the all-time single-game yardage record with 296 against San Diego in only his eighth professional game.

Yet Minnesota's biggest need heading into the 2007 draft was arguably one it had already tried to address the year before: quarterback. In 2006, the Vikings traded up into the second round of the draft to take Tarvaris Jackson, who was long on athleticism and short on polish. The Vikings wanted to give Jackson time on the bench to develop into an NFL-caliber quarterback, but that time ended up lasting just 12 weeks before he made his first NFL appearance. Jackson went on to play in three more games (and start two) as a rookie. During the stint, he tossed two touchdowns and four interceptions, fumbled four more times, and took eight sacks.

Jackson started 12 games in his sophomore season (he was injured the other four weeks). Despite facing defenses entirely devoted to stopping the dynamic Peterson, Jackson completed just 58 percent of his passes, with nine touchdowns, 12 interceptions, and five fumbles. Sometimes he was throwing bullets that showed why the Vikings had put so much faith in him. Most of the time, however, he was throwing off his back foot, throwing into coverage, and skipping balls to his receivers. Ron Jaworski spent all of Week 15's Monday Night Football broadcast picking on Jackson's mechanics.

The Vikings seemed unconcerned about Jackson in the short term; there was speculation they could draft a quarterback on the first day of the draft, but Minnesota instead took USC's John David Booty in the fifth round. He's considered a heady player who has to rely on guile to make up for mediocre physical skills. In many ways, Booty is a younger version of Kelly Holcomb, the backup quarterback Minnesota released earlier in the offseason.

As for Jackson's long-term outlook, we can use similarity scores to compare him to other quarterbacks in their second NFL season to get a rough sketch of how his career might unfold. Here are the most similar second-year quarterbacks since 1980:

- David Carr, 2003 Texans
- Jim McMahon, 1983 Bears
- Don Majikowski, 1988 Packers

VIKINGS PROSPECTUS

2007 Record: 8-8

Pythagorean Wins: 9.5 (10th)

DVOA: 5.5% total (14th), 6.9% weighted (13th)

Offense: 3.5% DVOA (16th)

Defense: 0.1% DVOA (17th)

Special Teams: 2.1% DVOA (9th)

Variance: 19.3 % (24th)

2007: The Vikings finally decide to address their woeful passing game by drafting Adrian Peterson.

2008: Peterson and Jared Allen could march into the playoffs, dragging Tarvaris Jackson behind them.

2008 Mean Projection: 10.1 wins

On the Clock (0-3): 0%

Loserville (4-6): 5%

Mediocrity (7-8): 16%

Playoff Contender (9-10): 36%

Super Bowl Contender (11+): 44%

Projected Average Opponent: 2.6% DVOA (11th in NFL)

2008 Vikings Schedule

Week	Opp.	Week	Opp.	Week	Opp.
1	at GB (Mon.)	7	at CHI	13	CHI
2	IND	8	BYE	14	at DET
3	CAR	9	HOU	15	at ARI
4	at TEN	10	GB	16	ATL
5	at NO (Mon.)	11	at TB	17	NYG
6	DET	12	at JAC		

- Steve Fuller, 1980 Chiefs
- David Klingler, 1993 Bengals
- Neil O'Donnell, 1991 Steelers
- Chris Simms, 2005 Buccaneers
- Charlie Batch, 1999 Lions
- Cade McNown, 2000 Bears
- Rodney Peete, 1990 Lions

That list is a jumble of high-round draft busts and slightly-above-replacement-level starters who had quality NFL careers. We're working from basically one year of data, so the results are highly variable, but the bottom line is seemingly clear: Jackson's development, while nice, doesn't automatically assume that the Vikings' offense will be magically transported to those halcyon days of Culpepper-to-Moss. That doesn't mean the team will deemphasize the passing game because of Jackson's inconsistencies and Peterson's emergence. Just the opposite. Minnesota traded Williamson, who never seemed comfortable in Moss's shadow, and signed Bernard Berrian this offseason to give Jackson a legitimate deep threat, something he could certainly use. Last season, Jackson ranked last among NFL starters on completions of more than 20 yards (he had just 15; the NFL's best, Tom Brady, had 56). That was partly because of Jackson's struggles with accuracy and also due to a roster full of second and third receivers. Second-year wideout Sidney Rice could eventually evolve into the player Williamson never did, but Berrian will be tasked with that responsibility next season.

A franchise quarterback isn't a necessary condition for winning regularly, especially when an offense has a dominating running game. It's the ideal but not a requirement; just look at the 2006 Chicago Bears for the most recent example or the 2000 Baltimore Ravens as the standard-bearer for successful offensive-less football. Both teams featured starting quarterbacks among the worst in the NFL, but they also relied on a solid run-

ning game and, perhaps more importantly, menacing defenses.

Brad Childress has yet to make the playoffs since Minnesota hired him three years ago. Although his background is on offense, he has taken a keen interest in improving the defense. One of his first moves after getting the Vikings job was to hire Buccaneers defensive backs coach Mike Tomlin as his defensive coordinator. In one year, Tomlin took the defense from 19th in DVOA to fourth. The once-porous front seven became impossible to run against, finishing as the league's best rushing defense in 2006. A season later, Tomlin was in Pittsburgh as head coach, but Minnesota continued its run-stuffing ways under new coordinator Leslie Frazier. Unfortunately, the pass defense lagged behind the rush defense, and opponents opted for the path of least resistance to the end zone. An absentee pass rush and suspect coverage skills among linebackers and the secondary exacerbated the imbalance.

It's easy to point to the defensive backfield and lay the blame at their feet, but the Vikings recorded only 38 sacks last year and ranked 28th in Adjusted Sack Rate. A secondary full of cover corners sans a consistent pass rush would meet the same fate as the 2007 Minnesota defense.

That's why the Vikings pulled off a predraft trade that could prove to be the difference between another 8-8 season and a deep postseason run. Minnesota sent its 2008 first-round pick (17th overall) and two third-rounders to Kansas City for defensive end Jared Allen. At first glance, it seems like a steep price to pay for a defensive end who missed four games last season for violating the league's substance abuse policy. But Allen brings the pass-rushing skills that the Vikings were looking for when they used consecutive first-round picks on defensive ends Kenechi Udeze and Erasmus James starting in 2004. Allen registered 15.5 sacks last season, exceeding the total for the Vikings' top three sack leaders combined: Ben Leber, Ray Edwards, and Udeze had just five sacks apiece. Allen's presence makes it easier for Frazier to eschew the blitz and drop extra bodies into coverage.

Typically, the Cover-2 defense relies on four defensive linemen generating a pass rush with linebackers and defensive backs dropping into coverage. The scheme is designed to avoid big plays, but that's contingent on pressuring the quarterback. The Vikings' front four were inconsistent, which is why Frazier frequently blitzed linebackers and cornerbacks. The results weren't pretty and help explain why Minnesota was so active this offseason.

Allen fills an obvious need—even if the Vikings had to fork over almost $74 million ($31 guaranteed) over six years—but there are still myriad concerns along the defensive line, primarily related to quality depth. Udeze is out for the 2008 season after being diagnosed with leukemia, and James's immediate future is unclear after he tore his left ACL near the end of last season. It was the same knee he injured in 2006, and over the past two years, James has as many knee surgeries as he does games started: three. Ray Edwards filled in for James most of 2007 before serving a four-game suspension for violating the league's substance-abuse policy and will play opposite Allen when the season starts. Pass-rush specialist Brian Robison will spell Edwards again in 2008, just as he did last year as a rookie.

The linebackers have improved since Minnesota opted to let Napoleon Harris walk after the 2006 season. The addition of Allen, coupled with a full year to digest Frazier's defense, should mean fewer blown coverages and missed assignments in 2008. Last season, E. J. Henderson replaced Harris as middle linebacker, Chad Greenway, the team's 2006 first-rounder, fully recovered from a knee injury to fill the void left by Henderson on the weak side, and offseason acquisition Ben Leber bolstered the strong side.

The Vikings' secondary ranked in the bottom third of the league against opposing wide receivers, which had everything to do with the club signing free agent safety Madieu Williams. Williams, a college cornerback, will replace Dwight Smith, whose off-field issues had as much to do with his departure as his on-field production. (Smith was arrested for indecent conduct a month after signing with the Vikings in 2006; he was then cited for marijuana possession last December, although that charge was later dropped.) Williams will team with veteran Darren Sharper, and his coverage skills should immediately upgrade the unit. He's also good in run support, though that is less of a priority in this defense. Antoine Winfield and Cedric Griffin were more susceptible to big plays in 2007 than the season before, but again, some of the blame lies with the front four, who were unable to pressure the quarterback.

Adrian Peterson and the strong run defense get this team into the postseason conversation, but professional football is still driven by the passing game. Ultimately, the Vikings' fate rests with Jackson's ability to minimize turnovers and improve his decision making and the defense becoming just as effective against the pass as it has been against the run. With one of those developments, the Vikings should be able to snag a playoff spot. With both developments, they become a leading Super Bowl contender. The former seems more likely than the latter.

Ryan Wilson

2007 Vikings Stats by Week

Wk	vs.	W-L	PF	PA	YDF	YDA	TO	Total	Off	Def	ST
1	ATL	W	24	3	302	265	+1	37%	0%	-30%	7%
2	@DET	L	17	20	313	415	0	-35%	-30%	8%	2%
3	@KC	L	10	13	256	251	0	-13%	-8%	9%	4%
4	GB	L	16	23	382	384	0	9%	-9%	-9%	9%
5	BYE										
6	@CHI	W	34	31	444	458	+4	-9%	19%	16%	-13%
7	@DAL	L	14	24	196	381	+1	-16%	-16%	-3%	-3%
8	PHI	L	16	23	256	385	0	-18%	2%	22%	2%
9	SD	W	35	17	528	229	0	111%	63%	-50%	-1%
10	@GB	L	0	34	247	488	-1	-72%	-37%	33%	-2%
11	OAK	W	29	22	478	372	-3	14%	12%	3%	4%
12	@NYG	W	41	17	251	309	+4	44%	3%	-31%	9%
13	DET	W	42	10	443	253	0	69%	49%	-3%	17%
14	@SF	W	27	7	280	282	+4	9%	-4%	-12%	1%
15	CHI	W	20	13	372	209	-3	-5%	-3%	-4%	-6%
16	WAS	L	21	32	299	367	-3	-26%	8%	30%	-4%
17	@DEN	L	19	22	332	362	-3	-23%	-19%	12%	9%

Trends and Splits

	Offense	Rank	Defense	Rank
Total DVOA	3.5%	16	0.1%	17
Unadjusted VOA	1.1%	17	-3.8%	11
Weighted Trend	7.4%	13	2.2%	20
Variance	6.6%	16	5.1%	9
Average Opponent	1.2%	20	-2.9%	28
Passing	-5.3%	19	14.8%	23
Rushing	11.1%	3	-23.1%	2
First Down	-6.5%	21	-1.0%	16
Second Down	22.9%	4	-4.0%	9
Third Down	-5.8%	19	8.4%	23
First Half	2.3%	15	-1.3%	16
Second Half	4.6%	13	1.6%	17
Red Zone	19.0%	6	-17.4%	6
Late and Close	3.7%	13	-2.0%	13

Five-Year Performance

Year	W-L	Pyth Wins	Est Wins	PF	PA	TO	Total	Rank	Off	Rank	Def	Rank	ST	Rank
2003	9-7	9.5	8.9	416	352	+11	7.7%	13	15.9%	3	3.0%	21	-5.2%	31
2004	8-8	8.2	8.6	405	395	+1	-0.5%	15	26.3%	3	23.8%	32	-3.1%	27
2005	9-7	6.9	7.8	306	344	+5	-7.2%	21	-5.9%	17	0.6%	19	-0.6%	20
2006	6-10	6.6	7.9	282	327	+4	-9.0%	22	-15.9%	29	-10.6%	4	-3.6%	27
2007	8-8	9.5	8.9	365	311	+1	5.5%	14	3.5%	16	0.1%	17	2.1%	9

Strategic Tendencies

Run/Pass		Rank	Offense		Rank	Defense		Rank	Other		Rank
Runs, all plays	47%	3	3+ WR	44%	25	Rush 3	3.3%	22	2+ RB, Pct Runs	59%	13
Runs, first half	50%	1	4+ WR	5%	27	Rush 4	62.4%	17	1 RB/2 TE, Pct Runs	58%	6
Runs, first down	57%	5	2+ TE	37%	4	Rush 5	22.3%	17	1 RB/3+ WR, Pct Runs	31%	5
Runs, second-long	43%	5	Single back	63%	7	Rush 6+	12.0%	9	CB1 on WR1	39%	25
Runs, power sit.	69%	8	Play action	22%	6	Rush 7+	1.7%	15	Go for it on 4th	1.29	9
Runs, behind 2H	27%	18	Max protect	11%	11	Sacks by LB	26.4%	14	Offensive Pace	32.2	29
Pass, ahead 2H	36%	26	Outside pocket	17%	5	Sacks by DB	0.0%	30	Defensive Pace	29.9	3

The Vikings ran a lot on second-and-long because it worked—they had 7.9 yards per carry in these situations, with a 55.6% DVOA. Seattle was the only other offense to gain more than 5.2 yards per carry on second-and-long. ⊘ Of Minnesota's first downs, 43 percent came on runs, well above the league average of 31.5 percent. ⊘ Only one team threw to the left side of the field less often than the Vikings, and for good reason, since they ranked 27th in DVOA on passes thrown left. In addition, 57 percent of Minnesota's interceptions came on that side. ⊘ Only the Giants had a lower DVOA in four-wide sets. ⊘ The Vikings ranked 28th in number of screens thrown but rated second in DVOA on screen passes. Chester Taylor saw the bulk of the screens, with more than 60 percent going for first downs and half going for double-digit gains, including a 50-yarder. ⊘ Minnesota had the highest rushing DVOA of any team in the fourth quarter. ⊘ The Vikings were one of just three teams that never tested the opposing defense with a pass over 20 yards when it was third-and-short on their own half of the field. ⊘ Minnesota's quarterbacks ranked third in hurries per pass play, behind Pittsburgh and Tampa Bay. ⊘ Although Kansas City's opponents dropped the fewest passes, Minnesota's opponents dropped the fewest passes as a percentage of all throws. ⊘ The Vikings defense faced shotgun on 37 percent of plays, the highest percentage in the league. ⊘ Although the Vikings had a hard time getting to the quarterback, they made their sacks count. Minnesota had a 9.8 percent Adjusted Sack Rate when the opposing offense was within 40 yards of the end zone, better than every defense except the Giants and the Dolphins. ⊘ The Vikings also managed to get their hands on the ball even if they didn't get their hands on the quarterback, trailing only San Diego and Kansas City in passes tipped or batted down. ⊘ Only Denver saw fewer four- and five-wide receiver sets, but only two teams saw more formations with only one wide receiver.

Passing

Player	DYAR	DVOA	Plays	NtYds	Avg	YAC	C%	TD	Int
Tarvaris Jackson	107	-5.8%	308	1852	6.0	4.9	59.7%	9	12
Kelly Holcomb*	-25	-15.5%	96	422	4.4	5.3	51.2%	2	1
Brooks Bollinger	28	-3.3%	57	355	6.2	6.0	67.3%	1	1
Gus Frerotte	-176	-26.2%	179	992	5.5	3.6	56.6%	7	12

Rushing

Player	DYAR	DVOA	Plays	Yds	Avg	TD	Fum	Suc
Adrian Peterson	228	16.4%	238	1344	5.6	12	5	45%
Chester Taylor	101	8.0%	157	848	5.4	7	5	46%
Tarvaris Jackson	80	25.4%	41	260	6.3	3	5	—
Mewelde Moore*	25	31.5%	20	114	5.7	0	1	50%
Tony Richardson*	5	3.8%	7	13	1.9	0	0	57%
Naufahu Tahi	-13	-60.9%	6	15	2.5	0	0	17%
Brooks Bollinger	6	49.4%	3	19	6.3	0	1	—
Maurice Hicks	0	-8.7%	21	117	5.6	1	1	33%
Thomas Tapeh	-3	-15.2%	5	18	3.6	0	0	60%
Gus Frerotte	-13	-53.2%	4	1	0.3	0	2	—

Receiving

Player	DYAR	DVOA	Plays	Ctch	Yds	Y/C	YAC	TD	C%
WR									
Bobby Wade	133	8.5%	83	54	655	12.1	3.0	3	65%
Robert Ferguson	-26	-17.9%	62	32	391	12.2	3.8	1	52%
Sidney Rice	100	11.5%	53	31	396	12.8	3.0	4	58%
Troy Williamson*	-21	-19.5%	38	18	236	13.1	2.8	1	47%
Aundrae Allison	-33	-35.6%	18	8	113	14.1	6.0	0	44%
Bernard Berrian	58	-6.9%	128	71	951	13.4	3.5	5	55%
TE									
Visanthe Shiancoe	3	-6.0%	43	27	324	12.0	4.6	1	63%
Jimmy Kleinsasser	-11	-23.5%	10	4	43	10.8	4.5	1	40%
Jeff Dugan	-19	-43.0%	8	7	58	8.3	6.6	0	88%
RB									
Chester Taylor	64	15.7%	43	29	281	9.7	8.3	0	67%
Adrian Peterson	97	43.5%	29	20	267	13.4	14.1	1	69%
Tony Richardson*	9	-3.2%	16	11	89	8.1	6.6	0	69%
Mewelde Moore*	2	-7.8%	8	6	48	8.0	6.5	0	75%
Maurice Hicks	14	2.6%	16	14	86	6.1	4.6	0	88%

Offensive Line

Year	Yards	ALY	Rank	Power	Rank	10+ Yds	Rank	Stuff	Rank	Sack	ASR	Rank
2005	3.75	3.55	31	63%	17	21%	9	26%	23	55	10.1%	30
2006	4.20	4.30	14	68%	12	16%	14	24%	13	43	7.6%	22
2007	5.44	4.23	13	76%	2	32%	1	27%	26	38	8.6%	28

Year	LE	Rank	LT	Rank	Mid	Rank	RT	Rank	RE	Rank
2005	4.84	7	5.09	2	3.09	32	2.72	30	3.74	20
2006	3.00	27	4.85	6	4.33	19	4.54	6	5.15	5
2007	4.68	9	4.21	19	4.32	9	4.09	21	3.49	26

Minnesota's offensive line has its good points and its bad points when it comes to performance and personnel. The Vikings have been much better run blocking than pass blocking over the last two seasons, although some of the high Adjusted Sack Rate is the fault of the quarterbacks. Bryant McKinnie is an upper-echelon left tackle, but his off-field issues (the latest is a felony assault charge) could lead to an NFL-mandated suspension—and the Vikings have no clear replacement. Marcus Johnson and Artis Hicks both have starting experience but inconsistent play at less demanding positions—right tackle and guard, respectively—pushed both players to the bench. There's no reason to think that either would suddenly be a viable option should McKinnie be forced out of action.

Next to McKinnie, Steve Hutchinson continues to be arguably the NFL's best guard. In addition to dominating in the running game—he's extremely agile in space—Hutchinson is a reliable pass blocker. Center Matt Birk is entering his 11th season, and it could be his last in Minnesota. The Vikings have a history of replacing seemingly irreplaceable centers—Birk made his way into the starting lineup after the team decided Jeff Christy wasn't worth paying—and John Sullivan, drafted in the sixth round out of Notre Dame, could be his successor. If the Vikings choose to extend Birk, Sullivan will serve as his backup; he could also get some work at right guard, currently the weakest position on the unit. Hicks lost his job to Anthony Herrera last season, but neither is considered anything more than adequate. Right tackle Ryan Cook is a converted college center. He was handed the starting job last year and fared well. He also provides emergency depth at center should Birk go down or Sullivan struggle.

Defensive Front Seven

Defensive Line	Age	Pos	Plays	TmPct	Rk	Stop	Dfts	Stop%	Rk	AvYd	Rk	Sack	Hit	Hur	Runs	RuStop	RuYd	Pass	PaStop	PaYd
Pat Williams	36	DT	69	8.2%	3	59	21	86%	9	0.9	11	2.0	1	4	59	85%	1.2	10	90%	-0.3
Kenechi Udeze*	25	DE	49	5.8%	41	35	16	71%	62	1.8	45	5.0	11	16	35	69%	2.3	14	79%	0.8
Kevin Williams	28	DT	45	5.3%	30	31	13	69%	62	1.8	38	3.0	6	8	28	68%	2.1	17	71%	1.2
Ray Edwards	23	DE	33	5.2%	53	29	15	88%	5	0.4	15	5.0	4	11	23	83%	1.8	10	100%	-2.8
Spencer Johnson*	27	DT	24	2.8%	66	19	9	79%	28	1.8	37	3.0	3	5	13	77%	2.1	11	82%	1.4
Brian Robison	25	DE	23	2.7%	—	16	13	70%	—	2.5	—	4.5	0	9	16	63%	3.9	7	86%	-0.7
Jared Allen	26	DE	75	10.7%	1	62	32	83%	14	0.1	9	15.5	8	17	41	78%	1.5	34	88%	-1.6

Linebackers	Age	Pos	Plays	TmPct	Rk	Stop	Dfts	Stop%	AvYd	Sack	Hit	Hur	Runs	RuStop	Rk	RuYd	Rk	Tgts	Suc%	Rk	APaYd	Rk
E. J. Henderson	28	MLB	125	14.8%	20	59	30	47%	5.2	4.5	7	10	63	63%	47	2.6	14	45	38%	76	8.3	85
Chad Greenway	25	OLB	106	12.5%	47	40	18	38%	5.8	0.0	4	2	43	56%	85	3.1	39	57	33%	89	8.0	81
Ben Leber	30	OLB	70	8.3%	83	43	24	61%	3.2	5.0	7	4	35	66%	36	2.6	13	30	37%	82	6.5	61
Derrick Pope	26	MLB	61	7.7%	89	32	11	52%	3.9	0.0	1	0	51	55%	88	3.1	37	10	52%	—	5.0	—

Year	Yards	ALY	Rank	Power	Rank	10+ Yds	Rank	Stuff	Rank	Sack	ASR	Rank
2005	3.93	4.07	16	72%	26	17%	17	25%	15	33	6.5%	21
2006	2.97	2.78	1	47%	1	23%	29	40%	1	30	4.8%	31
2007	3.25	3.36	2	54%	6	12%	5	33%	1	38	5.5%	28

Year	LE	Rank	LT	Rank	Mid	Rank	RT	Rank	RE	Rank
2005	4.44	22	4.05	14	4.14	17	4.18	20	3.06	5
2006	2.08	3	2.56	1	2.95	1	2.84	3	3.10	7
2007	2.80	4	4.19	16	2.89	1	4.17	18	4.50	24

Before the blockbuster deal that sent Jared Allen from Kansas City to Minnesota, the biggest Vikings-related story of the offseason was defensive end Kenechi Udeze being diagnosed with leukemia. Fortunately, the disease is in remission, although Udeze won't see the field until 2009 at the earliest. The Allen deal means that one of the league's premiere pass rushers will join two of the NFL's best defensive tackles, the unrelated Pat and Kevin Williams. In recent seasons, the Vikings' defense has been impenetrable against the run, but Allen could go a long way in upgrading the pass defense. The other defensive end spot is a bit up in the air. Erasmus James, coming off his second serious knee surgery, failed a physical in May and was subsequently released—which means neither of Minnesota's two first-round picks from the 2005 draft (the other: wide receiver Troy Williamson) are still with the team.

The linebackers have improved since Minnesota chose not to re-sign Napoleon Harris before the 2007 season. They moved E. J. Henderson from the weak side to the middle, Chad Greenway, the team's 2006 first-rounder, graduated to the weak-side slot, and Ben Leber upgraded to the strong-side position. Greenway and Leber accounted for three of the team's 15 interceptions, but perhaps the pass-defense issues have less to do with personnel and more to do with scheme. Leber told the *Minneapolis Star Tribune* that "I think that's more of a product of just not having a lot of time during the season. We would play some coverages and we would play them well. But now [during the offseason] we really get to break down just the nuances of them. . . . It's not that we were doing anything wrong; it's just more detailed. So we've got to use this time to focus in and sharpen up those . . . coverages." Depth at outside linebacker is an issue. Dontarrious Thomas is now with the 49ers, and the only free-agent acquisition, Derrick Pope (ex-Miami), is a better fit at middle linebacker. Heath Farwell and Vinny Ciurciu are listed as linebackers but are primarily special teamers.

Defensive Secondary

Secondary	Age	Pos	Plays	TmPct	Rk	Stop	Dfts	RuYd	Rk	RuStop	Rk	Tgts	Tgt%	Rk	Dist	Suc%	Rk	APaYd	Rk	PaYd	PD	Int
Cedric Griffin	26	CB	99	11.7%	11	39	17	5.9	34	48%	43	97	19%	32	10.7	39%	75	9.7	75	9.7	12	0
Antoine Winfield	31	CB	75	14.2%	1	36	17	2.6	2	84%	2	69	21%	18	10.3	52%	30	6.5	19	6.2	8	1
Darren Sharper	33	SS	70	8.3%	55	23	9	7.2	56	38%	56	38	7%	32	14.9	58%	15	6.2	25	6.2	6	1
Marcus McCauley	24	CB	68	8.0%	59	21	7	10.5	69	20%	77	79	15%	57	12.4	41%	72	8.5	65	8.6	6	4
Dwight Smith*	30	FS	61	8.2%	56	31	10	5.0	13	70%	2	33	7%	34	10.8	54%	21	6.8	33	7.0	8	0
Charles Gordon	24	CB	34	4.0%	—	17	9	2.0	—	80%	—	28	5%	—	7.2	57%	—	7.6	—	7.5	9	4
Madieu Williams	27	FS	78	11.6%	18	35	12	7.8	60	53%	16	28	8%	30	12.5	45%	51	9.6	65	9.4	5	1
Benny Sapp	27	CB	34	4.9%	—	18	9	5.8	—	67%	—	35	11%	—	9.3	51%	—	6.5	—	6.9	6	2

Year	Pass D Rank	vs.#1 WR	Rk	vs.#2 WR	Rk	vs.Other WR	Rk	vs.TE	Rk	vs.RB	Rk
2005	19	4.9%	14	-24.6%	5	-3.3%	14	24.8%	27	19.9%	29
2006	15	16.7%	29	-13.1%	8	18.8%	26	10.7%	25	17.9%	29
2007	23	23.2%	31	16.9%	25	26.4%	31	-12.1%	5	1.7%	20

The Vikings signed safety Madieu Williams away from Cincinnati to replace Dwight Smith. As a former college cornerback, he will be an upgrade in coverage, but he also plays well near the line of scrimmage. Free safety Darren Sharper continues to play at a high level, although at 32 his career is winding down. The team is high on second-round pick Tyrell Johnson of Arkansas (he was the 17th-best player on Minnesota's draft board) and he will eventually take over for Sharper. Cedric Griffin earned the starting cornerback job over Fred Smoot as a rookie in 2006, and although he gave up more big plays last season, he's firmly entrenched in the lineup. Antoine Winfield, like Griffin, struggled with balls thrown down the field, but he's still the team's most physical cornerback, solid in coverage and stout against the run. The addition of Jared Allen should allow the secondary to be more aggressive in passing situations, mitigating the big-play threat. Marcus MacCauley, 2007 third-round pick, plays the nickel; although he looked overwhelmed at times as a rookie last season, often finding himself out of position, he's a smart player with a strong ability to quickly assimilate information, and he should improve in his second year.

Special Teams

Year	DVOA	Rank	FG/XP	Rank	Net Punt	Rank	Punt Ret	Rank	Net Kick	Rank	Kick Ret	Rank	Hidden	Rank
2005	-0.6%	21	-8.8	30	-9.4	31	4.4	8	6.7	7	3.4	12	-1.2	17
2006	-3.6%	27	-3.4	23	-5.3	24	2.7	7	-12.8	29	-2.6	17	-3.8	20
2007	2.1%	9	5.2	6	0.9	15	-4.9	24	5.1	10	6.3	7	-12.0	30

The Vikings' special teams improved significantly last season, primarily due to huge improvements on kickoffs. Kicker Ryan Longwell averaged almost 63 yards per kickoff, his best effort since his rookie season in 1997 and 3.6 yards per kickoff more than in 2006, his first year with the Vikings. The coverage itself was also better; the Vikings allowed 5.5 points' worth of field position over average on returns in 2006 but were 4.1 points below average in 2007. Rookie Aundrae Allison averaged 28.7 yards per kick return, including a 104-yard touchdown in a victory over the Lions, and was a marked upgrade over the since-released Bethel Johnson. Vikings' punt returners were again average last season, but Mewelde Moore, the primary returner, is now in Pittsburgh. Sixth-round pick Jaymar Johnson will have every chance to win the job in training camp. The Vikings thought enough of punter Chris Kluwe to sign him to a six-year, $8.3 million extension last October. He ranked 10th in the league in punt average (44.7), and his 34 punts downed inside the 20-yard line were third behind San Francisco's Andy Lee and San Diego's Mike Scifres.

COACHING STAFF

Brad Childress enters his third season and still has questions about his quarterback. The running game is one of the best in the league, the offensive line is above average, and the pass catchers are young and improving. But the quarterback position could determine not only how far Minnesota goes in the postseason but Childress' long-term future with the team. Before coming to Minnesota, Childress spent the 2002-2005 seasons as the Eagles' offensive coordinator and had the opposite problem: an elite quarterback without much of a running game. Philadelphia was 41-23 over that stretch, including a Super Bowl appearance, and much of the team's success could be attributed to limiting turnovers. Now Darrell Bevell, entering his third season as offensive coordinator, will be tasked with helping Jackson improve his decision making and minimize interceptions. Bevell has plenty of experience to draw on: He served as the Packers' quarterback coach from 2003 to 2005. Given the quality of Minnesota's running game, it is also worth Eric Bieniemy, who spent nine years in the NFL and five years coaching in college before Minnesota hired him as running backs coach in 2006.

Current Steelers head coach Mike Tomlin spent one year as the Vikings' defensive coordinator before getting the big promotion. Leslie Frazier, who replaced Tomlin before the 2007 season, has already interviewed for head coaching positions with the Falcons and Dolphins. Frazier played on the 1985 Bears' historic defense and led the franchise in interceptions from 1983 through their Super Bowl Shuffle season. Last season the Vikings featured the same smothering run defense but the pass defense languished. However, that had more to do with injuries and players needing time to absorb Frazier's system.

New England Patriots

The Patriots played two seasons in 2007, one super-imposed on the other.

Their surface season, the On-Field Season, was a magnificent, historic 16-0 run filled with shattered records and, ultimately, shattered hopes. The season began with an offensive explosion unlike any the NFL has ever seen and a series of almost embarrassing blowouts. It then settled into a succession of tight, dramatic wins against highly motivated foes, a trend that continued through the playoffs and into the Super Bowl. The Patriots failed in their bid to become the Best Team Ever, but they became the Best Non-Champion Ever, a booby prize that's easier to stomach on a team whose many veterans can already play multiple choice when searching their jewelry boxes for Super Bowl rings.

New England's season off the field, however, was far from perfect. There was Spygate, the signal-stealing scandal that threatened everything the Patriots ever accomplished. There were allegations of poor sportsmanship after lopsided Patriots wins. There was tabloid drama surrounding Tom Brady's personal life and a late-season Randy Moss battery charge. This Off-Field Season played out on a gridiron of television studios, league offices, Greenwich Village hotels (where Brady foolishly stayed in the pre–Super Bowl off-week), the floor of Congress, and in the cacophonous blogosphere echo-chamber. At times, the Off-Field Patriots ripped the spotlight away from the On-Field Patriots, no mean feat as the team chased the 1972 Dolphins.

PATRIOTS PROSPECTUS

2007 Record: 16-0

Pythagorean Wins: 13.8 (1st)

DVOA: 52.0% total (1st), 40.9% weighted (1st)

Offense: 42.6% DVOA (1st)

Defense: -6.4% DVOA (8th)

Special Teams: 3.0% DVOA (7th)

Variance: 14.6 % (13th)

2007: 39 seconds short of perfection.

2008: Still making plenty of noise when on the field, and hopefully a lot less noise when off.

2008 Mean Projection: 12.8 wins

On the Clock (0-3): 0%

Loserville (4-6): 0%

Mediocrity (7-8): 1%

Playoff Contender (9-10): 10%

Super Bowl Contender (11+): 89%

Projected Average Opponent: -8.9% DVOA (32nd in NFL)

It's impossible to write about the team without addressing both seasons, but they are best discussed separately. The Off-Field Patriots had little to do with the On-Field Patriots. Even the critics who cast Bill Belichick as a Nixon-like manipulator with a microphone in every flower pot must admit that the 2007 Patriots won (and ultimately lost) on merit, not because of some illegal competitive edge. After all, the Spygate story broke after the Patriots beat the Jets handily in Week 1, and Commissioner Roger Goodell punished the team before it even took the field against San Diego for its second game. Even if Belichick dared defy the commish after that, every coach in the NFL knew to change his signals and frisk suspicious photographers before Patriots games.

The 2007 On-Field Patriots fielded the greatest offense in NFL history. They posted the highest DVOA of any team for which we have data (Tables 1 and 2). They established new all-time highs in points scored, yards gained, touchdowns, and so on. They also fielded one of the best defenses in the league and rock-solid special teams units, but it was their offense that separated them from the league and from past Patriots teams.

Belichick and team VP Scott Pioli built the mighty offense through a series of prudent signings and calculated risks. When the team acquired Randy Moss, Wes Welker, Donté Stallworth, and Kelley Washington in the 2007 offseason, it seemed to be overreacting to its failure to cobble together a receiving corps from Jabar

2008 Patriots Schedule

Week	Opp.	Week	Opp.	Week	Opp.
1	KC	7	DEN (Mon.)	13	PIT
2	at NYJ	8	STL	14	at SEA
3	MIA	9	at IND	15	at OAK
4	BYE	10	BUF	16	ARI
5	at SF	11	NYJ (Thu.)	17	at BUF
6	at SD	12	at MIA		

Table 1. Top Teams in Total DVOA, 1995-2007

Year	Team	W-L	DVOA	Result
2007	NE	16-0	52.0%	lost Super Bowl
1999	STL	13-3	45.8%	won Super Bowl
1995	SF	11-5	41.0%	lost divisional round
1996	GB	13-3	40.6%	won Super Bowl
2001	STL	14-2	38.5%	lost Super Bowl
2000	TEN	13-3	37.4%	lost divisional round
2004	NE	14-2	35.7%	won Super Bowl
2004	PIT	15-1	34.8%	lost AFC Championship
1999	JAC	14-2	34.8%	lost AFC Championship
2002	TB	12-4	34.0%	won Super Bowl

Table 2. Top Teams in Offensive DVOA, 1995-2007

Year	Team	W-L	DVOA	Result
2007	NE	16-0	42.6%	lost Super Bowl
2004	IND	12-4	39.9%	lost divisional round
2006	IND	12-4	33.7%	won Super Bowl
2002	KC	8-8	33.3%	missed playoffs
2000	STL	10-6	31.7%	lost wild-card round
2000	IND	10-6	30.1%	lost wild-card round
2004	KC	7-9	28.7%	missed playoffs
1995	DAL	12-4	28.6%	won Super Bowl
2007	IND	13-3	28.3%	lost divisional round
1998	DEN	14-2	28.0%	won Super Bowl

Gaffney, Reche Caldwell, and Troy Brown the previous year. Belichick and Pioli risked receiver overkill and all that comes with it: players who don't fit or adapt to the scheme, guys clamoring for the football, Moss-related freakouts. In late August, rumors circulated that the team would cut Moss, who barely participated in the preseason.

We all know how it worked out. Moss was a model employee for most of the year. Receivers accepted their roles, and coordinator Josh McDaniels retooled the offense into a wide-open attack with plenty of passes to

go around. In their championship seasons, the Patriots fielded a balanced offense that scored plenty of points but didn't quicken the pulse. McDaniels, now two years removed from the influence of former coordinator Charlie Weis, stomped on the accelerator and refused to ease up. The Patriots scored 38 points in each of their first three games, then 34 in each of their next two, and then got even better.

In hindsight, the brilliance of the team's multireceiver gambit was obvious. Moss arrived at a bargain rate. Welker, a great route runner trapped in a bad organization that didn't recognize his talents, was worth the modest price of a second-round pick. Stallworth, an injury-prone burner miscast as a number one receiver in Philly, was a perfect fit as the scariest third wideout in the league. Gaffney outperformed Washington and became an important part of four-wide sets, while Washington earned his keep as a special-teams ace. Factor in homegrown talent like Benjamin Watson, Laurence Maroney, Kevin Faulk, and of course Brady, and the Patriots possessed the deepest corps of skill position players in league history. The Patriots played a five-game midseason stretch in which they averaged 45.8 points, 445.8 offensive yards, and 27.2 first downs per game. They did that against legit competition: Three of their five opponents during that span would reach the playoffs. The 1999 Rams set most standards for offensive dominance, but the Patriots put St. Louis's best five-week stretch (38 points, 324.6 yards per game from Weeks 4 to 8) to shame.

Even molten lava eventually cools, and the Patriots couldn't sustain that pace forever (Figure 1). When the Eagles held the Patriots to 31 points (24 if you discount a defensive touchdown by New England), experts speculated that the league finally figured the Patriots out. Opponents found small chinks in the Patriots' armor, particularly at right tackle and on the interior offensive line, and began devising exotic defensive game plans to exploit those weaknesses. Moss's intensity began to wane; Ron Jaworski caught him dogging it through several plays on *NFL Matchup*, and opposing defenders suddenly found him easier to cover. The Patriots' defense was also slipping. Linebacker Rosevelt Colvin was injured in the Eagles game, and his aging fellow linebackers (Tedy Bruschi and Junior Seau) began to fade down the stretch. Opponents threw into the flats and used screens to isolate Bruschi and Seau in coverage. Still, all the scheming amounted to just modest success. Only the Jets held the Patriots under 27 points in the regular season, and the New Yorkers had help from sloppy conditions and 25-mile-per-hour wind gusts.

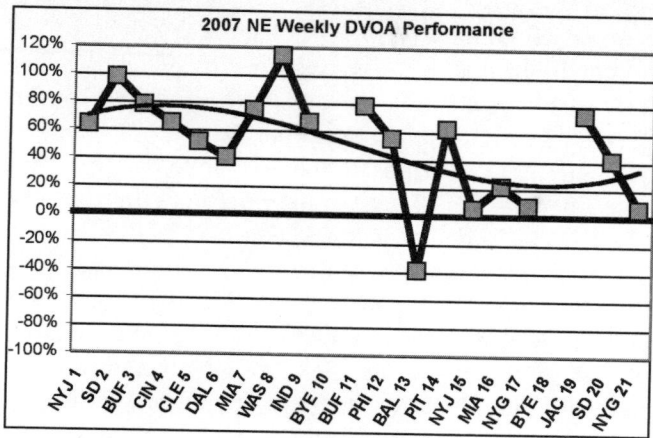

Figure 1

Without actually beating them, late-season opponents demonstrated that the Patriots were beatable. That trend continued into the playoffs. The Jaguars proved that offenses could dink-and-dunk their way to success against the Patriots' defense, but the Jaguars' defense couldn't stop Brady from having one of the greatest games in playoff history (26-of-28, 262 yards, three touchdowns). The Chargers forced some uncharacteristic Brady mistakes and were able to move the ball from 20 to 20, but turned into red zone pumpkins. The Patriots were prohibitive Super Bowl favorites, having beaten the Giants just a month earlier (though New England had to rally in the fourth quarter to do it). To win the Super Bowl, the Giants would need a performance for the ages from their defensive line, an uncharacteristically predictable Patriots game plan, and a few miracle plays from their offense.

They got all three. In an inversion of the national media cliché, spunky underdogs from New York beat a success-bloated team from Boston. It was stunning and exhilarating, Super Bowl III redux, mixed with a healthy dollop of Yankees–Red Sox. So ended the story of the On-Field Patriots.

It would take a whole other book to tell the full story of the Off-Field Patriots—and a few of them will surely be written—but we'll try to squeeze it all into a few paragraphs. During the season opener against the Jets, Jets coach Eric Mangini (a former Belichick assistant who knew where the shovels were buried) confiscated a video camera used by Patriots employee Matt Estrella. Mangini accused Belichick of using surveillance equipment to steal defensive signals. Belichick apologized for "misinterpreting" a league rule, Goodell launched an investigation, and Spygate was born.

A Category 5 media maelstrom followed: confessions, accusations, condemnations, and harsh rhetoric that grew shriller by the hour. Terrell Davis said the Patriots should be banned from the postseason for two years. Major media columnists bit down on the story and refused to let go. Snippets of insight slowly came to light amid all the shouting and posturing. We learned that signal stealing is common, but the use of video equipment is forbidden. Coaches like Jimmy Johnson said that they experimented with video surveillance but didn't inhale: It took too much effort to gain too small an edge. We discovered that lots of coaches bend the rules, but Belichick was probably the most egregious offender, the guy weaving through traffic at 90 miles per hour while everyone else does 70 in a 55 zone. After three days of investigation, Goodell handed down a penalty—a $500,000 fine for Belichick, a $250,000 fine for the team, and a lost first-round pick—that was harsher than any in league history but not severe enough by half to satisfy conspiracy theorists who wanted the Patriots stripped of their rings. Goodell then destroyed the evidence, giving the black helicopter brigade something else to howl about.

After the fine, Spygate moved to the back burner in favor of another controversy. As scores grew more lopsided, opponents and observers grumbled that the Patriots were running up the score. The whispers started when Brady and Moss connected on a 45-yard touchdown bomb in the fourth quarter of Week 3 against the Bills. The touchdown made the score 38-7 and seemed a little gratuitous against an opponent already pinned to the mat. The grumbles grew louder as the Patriots produced a series of Michigan-versus-Mercyhurst-type blowouts: 34-13 over the Bengals, 52-7 over the Redskins, and 56-10 in the Bills rematch.

Here, the On-Field and Off-Field seasons briefly converged: To the ever-growing legions of Patriots haters, Belichick the cheater was thumbing his nose at the league (and at the rules of sportsmanship that we hold sacred) to protest his Spygate punishment. Sportsmanship is a slippery concept, particularly in reference to professional athletes rather than Pop Warner kids or beer league softball players, so it's impossible to argue about whether the Patriots were good sports or poor ones during their steamroller period. Ultimately, the facts get in the way of a good story: Backup quarterback Matt Cassel and other irregulars typically entered the game in the first full series of the fourth quarter of blowout wins, a typical NFL stratagem. Brady only stayed in later than that against dangerous opponents like the Chargers and Bengals. The fact that the Patriots sometimes rolled up 42-7 halftime leads made Cassel's entrances seem belated, but it's hard to argue that any NFL team should begin resting its starters at halftime.

Just as the Patriots stopped blowing out opponents, Spygate reemerged. In the week before the Super Bowl, Senator Arlen Specter of Pennsylvania—whose Eagles had been denied in Super Bowl XXXIX by Belichick & Co.—stated that he might call a congressional hearing on the spying allegations. Meanwhile, the *Boston Herald* reported that a former Patriots assistant named Matt Walsh taped Rams practices in the days leading up to Super Bowl XXXVI. The Off-Field Patriots were now a three-ring circus. A controversial senator held court in the center ring. A shadowy Deep Throat informant, sequestered in Hawaiian exile, occupied the second ring. The New York media turned the hotel room of Brady and girlfriend Gisele Bundschen into a third ring, snapping photos of the couple, reporting on their dinner choices, and printing salacious cheap shots about Brady's ex and his out-of-wedlock child. And don't forget "Brady's boot"—a walking cast for a mysterious injury on the quarterback's right foot when he was spied in New York the day after clinching the AFC title—which drew more attention than any supermodel.

When these vilified, scandal-tainted Patriots fell to the Giants in the Super Bowl, most of America cheered. After the season, we learned that Walsh had no evidence to back his claims, that firsthand witnesses didn't even remember a Rams walkthrough on the date in question, and that Belichick's cloak-and-dagger tactics had become a running joke among veteran coaches like Herm Edwards, who wrote it all off as irrelevant gamesmanship. By then, it was too late to save the majesty and agony of the Patriots' 2007 season from the taint of scandal.

Both the On-Field and the Off-Field Patriots will look different in 2008. Erosion took its toll on the team as soon as free agency began. Asante Samuel, the team's best cornerback, signed a six-year, $57-million deal with the Eagles. Fellow cornerback Randall Gay, safety Eugene Wilson, linebacker Rosevelt Colvin, and receiver Donté Stallworth left town a few days later. The Patriots will easily absorb the loss of Stallworth, who can be replaced by Washington or former top prospect Chad Jackson. But the team will miss its elite defenders. Veterans like Tank Williams, Fernando Bryant, Jason Webster, and Lewis Sanders arrived to shore up the secondary, but these were Dumpster dive acquisitions. Bryant had a reasonable Yards per Pass figure in Detroit's Cover-2, but ranked 61st among cornerbacks in Success Rate last year. Sanders just missed our requirements to be ranked among cornerbacks; if we did rank

him, he would have been 79th in Success Rate and 71st in Adjusted Yards per Pass. Webster missed nearly all of 2007 with a broken arm, but in 2006, he ranked 79th in Success Rate and 78th in Yards per Pass.

Belichick has tried to make chicken soup from chicken scratch in the secondary before. When Ty Law left in 2005, Belichick signed veterans Chad Scott and Duane Starks and tried to plug them into regular roles. Both were terrible, but Samuel developed, Gay and Ellis Hobbs became serviceable, and Belichick's system (which made Otis Smith look like a viable starter five years after every other team gave up on him) concealed the most glaring weaknesses. Belichick may be hoping for similar results here: Brandon Meriweather could develop into a Samuel-like superstar at cornerback or free safety, and the veterans should be able to hold down the fort until rookie Terrence Wheatley develops. Belichick and Pioli insured their investment by hiring Dom Capers as secondary coach. Capers, a mad blitzer as a coordinator, often asked his cornerbacks to cover deep zones with little safety help. He should be able to teach veterans like Bryant and Sanders how to minimize toastings.

The Patriots used the draft to offset their losses in the secondary and get younger at linebacker. Wheatley intercepted 11 passes at Colorado, but his best attribute may be his intelligence, a must for a defender in the league's most complex defense. Jerod Mayo and Shawn Crable were the first linebackers drafted by the Patriots in the first four rounds since Andy Katzenmoyer back in the pre-Belichick era. Mayo is a top pass-rusher whose versatility allowed him to switch between the inside and outside at Tennessee. Michigan's Crable draws comparisons to Carl Banks. Both are good system fits.

Despite the additions and defections, most of the major pieces of the Patriots machine remain the same. After two weeks of February drama, Moss re-signed with the Patriots, turning down comparable offers elsewhere because he wanted to stay with a winner. Bruschi, aging but still effective in his role, also re-upped, as did Gaffney, who was already gradually moving into Stallworth's role by the postseason. The Patriots are still AFC favorites, but without Samuel and with a merely mortal receiving corps, they are no longer 1-to-3 favorites.

Moss's return also ensures that the Off-Field Patriots will be back, albeit in a muted form. His mercurial personality and penchant for controversy guarantee that there will be plenty of temperature-taking after every Patriots loss or subpar performance. Goodell worked hard to sweep Spygate under the carpet in the offseason, soothing Specter and creating new rules governing franchise behavior. A $100 million lawsuit against the Patriots by a former Rams player sprouted and disappeared in early March; principal anti-Patriot witness Walsh seems more like Frankie Five Angels or Kato Kaelin than a reliable source of information. Still, this story has legs, not to mention Barry Sanders's calves. Reporters will crack open the bait pail every time the Patriots face the Jets or an opponent from Specter's Keystone State. The Patriots remain great tabloid fare: Brady is still a *GQ* guy with a supermodel girlfriend, while Belichick is still gruff, socially awkward, secretive, and easy to demonize.

In the minds of many fans, and in dimly lit corners of the Internet, this team will always be the Cheatriots, clandestine operatives who stole opponents' secrets, celebrated too long after meaningless touchdowns, and trampled through the league with a hubris that flattened them in the final minutes of the Super Bowl. This season, the off-field din may fade, allowing the On-Field excellence to reclaim the spotlight. The On-Field Patriots look like just another 12-4 playoff team. After the two-seasons-in-one that was last year, they may even prefer being run-of-the-mill.

Mike Tanier

2007 Patriots Stats by Week

Wk	vs.	W-L	PF	PA	YDF	YDA	TO	Total	Off	Def	ST
1	@NYJ	W	38	14	431	227	0	64%	52%	6%	18%
2	SD	W	38	14	407	201	+1	98%	63%	-48%	-14%
3	BUF	W	38	7	485	193	+1	78%	49%	-18%	10%
4	@CIN	W	34	13	404	283	+1	65%	42%	-16%	6%
5	CLE	W	34	17	412	353	+4	51%	26%	-30%	-4%
6	@DAL	W	48	27	448	285	0	41%	32%	-7%	3%
7	@MIA	W	49	28	443	382	+1	75%	71%	23%	27%
8	WAS	W	52	7	486	224	+3	114%	73%	-36%	5%
9	@IND	W	24	20	342	329	0	66%	37%	-15%	15%
10	BYE										
11	@BUF	W	56	10	510	229	+2	78%	76%	-4%	-2%
12	PHI	W	31	28	410	391	+3	55%	45%	-4%	5%
13	@BAL	W	27	24	326	376	+1	-39%	6%	41%	-4%
14	PIT	W	34	13	421	349	+1	62%	63%	1%	0%
15	NYJ	W	20	10	265	234	+1	5%	-7%	-31%	-19%
16	MIA	W	28	7	400	241	-4	21%	1%	-8%	13%
17	@NYG	W	38	35	390	316	+1	7%	55%	37%	-10%
18	BYE										
19	JAC	W	31	20	403	350	+2	73%	62%	-10%	1%
20	SD	W	21	12	347	311	-1	41%	18%	-14%	9%
21	NYG	L	14	17	274	338	0	6%	10%	3%	-1%

Trends and Splits

	Offense	Rank	Defense	Rank
Total DVOA	42.6%	1	-6.4%	8
Unadjusted VOA	43.6%	1	-7.1%	7
Weighted trend	39.0%	1	-0.1%	18
Variance	6.7%	17	6.2%	15
Average opponent	0.9%	17	1.2%	17
Passing	61.8%	1	-7.0%	6
Rushing	18.1%	1	-5.8%	14
First down	30.9%	1	-7.4%	9
Second down	52.1%	1	4.7%	19
Third down	49.5%	1	-22.0%	3
First half	47.0%	1	-15.2%	4
Second half	37.8%	1	1.6%	18
Red Zone	39.5%	1	3.2%	16
Late and close	38.1%	1	0.0%	17

Five-Year Performance

Year	W-L	Pyth Wins	Est Wins	PF	PA	TO	Total	Rank	Off	Rank	Def	Rank	ST	Rank
2003	14-2	11.4	11.6	348	238	+17	22.8%	3	0.4%	14	-22.0%	2	0.4%	17
2004	14-2	12.4	13.1	437	260	+9	35.7%	1	24.2%	4	-11.3%	6	0.2%	16
2005	10-6	9.1	8.9	379	338	-6	3.4%	12	12.8%	7	10.5%	27	1.1%	12
2006	12-4	12.2	11.0	385	237	+8	23.2%	5	12.3%	6	-8.4%	9	2.5%	8
2007	16-0	13.8	14.2	589	274	+16	52.0%	1	42.6%	1	-6.4%	8	3.0%	7

Strategic Tendencies

Run/Pass		Rank	Offense		Rank	Defense		Rank	Other		Rank
Runs, all plays	40%	19	3+ WR	72%	2	Rush 3	17.7%	1	2+ RB, Pct Runs	72%	1
Runs, first half	37%	27	4+ WR	22%	5	Rush 4	46.7%	30	1 RB/2 TE, Pct runs	66%	2
Runs, first down	47%	23	2+ TE	26%	15	Rush 5	28.0%	8	1 RB/3+ WR, pct runs	29%	8
Runs, second-long	26%	30	Single back	77%	2	Rush 6+	7.6%	19	CB1 on WR1	43%	19
Runs, power sit.	55%	25	Play action	16%	21	Rush 7+	2.0%	13	Go for it on 4th	1.81	2
Runs, behind 2H	26%	23	Max protect	7%	26	Sacks by LB	60.0%	5	Offensive Pace	29.7	5
Pass, ahead 2H	52%	6	Outside pocket	4%	30	Sacks by DB	6.7%	15	Defensive Pace	31.2	22

The Patriots dropped from the team running the most two-tight end sets in 2006 to the middle of the pack in 2007, and instead were one of the teams running the most three- and four-wide sets. The Patriots lined up five-wide more than twice as often as any other team.   ∅   New England was the first offense in the 21st century to use the shotgun on more than 50 percent of offensive plays. The Patriots had the best DVOA in the league with the quarterback under center (30.2%) and the second-best DVOA with the quarterback in shotgun (56.9%). The Patriots ran 190 plays from the shotgun with a lead of more than a touchdown. The Colts were second with just 73.   ∅   Although they used it infrequently, the Patriots' DVOA with two wide receivers was the best in the league.   ∅   The Patriots ran in 82 percent of power situations in 2006, which led the league; last year they barely ran half the time in these situations. On third-and-short from their own half of the field, Tom Brady threw deeper than ten yards 27.5 percent of the time, nearly twice the league average.   ∅   New England tied with Atlanta for the second highest number of draw plays, behind only the Jets.   ∅   No team threw more wide receiver screens, and Wes Welker had the league's highest DVOA on screen passes.   ∅   New England was effective in timing its screens, ranking second in screens against five or more pass rushers.   ∅   An abundance of targets meant New England only threw to a running back only 14 percent of the time, last in the league.   ∅   No quarterback ran fewer designed rolls from the pocket than Brady. When unplanned scrambles are factored in, only Carson Palmer and Marc Bulger left the pocket less often.   ∅   The Patriots defense ranked second in hurries per pass play, trailing only the Chiefs. They also ranked second in sacks listed as "blown blocks" by the opposing offense.   ∅   Teams threw left against the Patriots more often than they did against any other team, generally trying to avoid Asante Samuel.   ∅   Does Bill Belichick need work on halftime adjustments? New England's defense was above average in each quarter except the third, where it ranked 29th. On offense, the Patriots had the highest DVOA in the league except in the third quarter, when they ranked fourth.   ∅   The Patriots were reluctant to blitz on first down, but ranked fourth and third in blitzing on second and third down, respectively.

Passing

Player	DYAR	DVOA	Plays	NtYds	Avg	YAC	C%	TD	Int
Tom Brady	2788	56.9%	606	4760	7.9	5.1	68.9%	50	8
Matt Cassel	-35	-80.6%	7	38	5.4	4.0	57.1%	0	1

Rushing

Player	DYAR	DVOA	Plays	Yds	Avg	TD	Fum	Suc
Laurence Maroney	199	16.7%	185	835	4.5	6	0	58%
Sammy Morris	92	15.3%	85	384	4.5	3	0	54%
Kevin Faulk	63	15.2%	62	265	4.3	0	1	56%
Heath Evans	48	16.9%	34	121	3.6	3	0	68%
Kyle Eckel	-16	-19.3%	33	90	2.7	2	0	33%
Tom Brady	25	3.7%	24	112	4.7	2	4	—
Wes Welker	14	18.1%	4	34	8.5	0	0	—

Receiving

Player	DYAR	DVOA	Plays	Ctch	Yds	Y/C	YAC	TD	C%
WR									
Randy Moss	569	29.3%	160	98	1482	15.1	3.3	23	61%
Wes Welker	384	21.3%	145	112	1175	10.5	5.7	9	77%
Donté Stallworth*	150	12.2%	74	46	697	15.2	6.8	3	62%
Jabar Gaffney	144	22.5%	50	36	449	12.5	3.3	5	72%
TE									
Benjamin Watson	104	23.0%	49	36	389	10.8	3.2	6	73%
Kyle Brady*	-2	-8.8%	16	9	70	7.8	2.7	2	56%
Marcus Pollard	82	25.8%	35	28	273	9.8	4.6	2	80%
RB									
Kevin Faulk	146	31.0%	59	47	383	8.1	7.3	1	80%
Laurence Maroney	42	87.4%	8	4	116	29.0	26.0	0	50%
Sammy Morris	-3	-20.2%	8	6	35	5.8	5.5	0	75%
Heath Evans	12	19.4%	6	4	43	10.8	10.3	0	67%

Offensive Line

Year	Yards	ALY	Rank	Power	Rank	10+ Yds	Rank	Stuff	Rank	Sack	ASR	Rank
2005	3.53	3.79	26	77%	3	10%	31	28%	25	28	4.9%	7
2006	4.22	4.37	12	82%	1	16%	13	21%	7	29	5.6%	8
2007	4.25	4.73	1	70%	9	11%	26	20%	4	21	4.1%	4

Year	LE	Rank	LT	Rank	Mid	Rank	RT	Rank	RE	Rank
2005	4.09	18	2.40	31	3.83	25	4.53	8	3.57	22
2006	5.05	4	4.23	20	4.55	10	3.75	30	2.82	31
2007	4.48	11	4.99	5	4.75	2	4.65	7	4.39	10

For the first half of the year, it seemed like Tom Brady could take a snap, drop back, survey the field, go through his progressions, knit a baby blanket for his young son, and then throw a 50-yard touchdown to Randy Moss without a defensive lineman so much as breathing on him. That ended in the second half of the season, however, as opponents began attacking the right side of the Patriots line when guard Stephen Neal was out with a shoulder injury. Backup Ross Hochstein wasn't in Neal's class, and right tackle Nick Kaczur is the line's weakest pass protector. Some opponents dropped a defensive tackle into coverage while rushing a linebacker from outside Kaczur's right shoulder. Others lined a defensive end over Hochstein and a linebacker directly over Kaczur, forcing the two linemen to block quicker defenders one-on-one. The tactics had some success: Kaczur finished ninth in the league with seven blown blocks, though that number is slightly inflated by the amount of passes the Patriots threw.

Neal is still rehabbing his shoulder and may have to play through pain this season, just as he did in the playoffs. If he can't answer the bell, Hochstein or longtime Patriots practice squad body Billy Yates will be pressed into service. The rest of the offensive line is set, with Matt Light, Logan Mankins, Dan Koppen, and Kaczur entrenched as starters. Most experts thought the Patriots would target a lineman like Brandon Albert in the draft, but they're satisfied with little-used reserves Wesley Britt and Ryan O'Callaghan at tackle.

Although the Patriots are good at both run-blocking and pass-blocking, they are *not* the best run-blocking line in the league. That top rank in Adjusted Line Yards comes in part from the fact that defenses facing New England were completely concentrated on stopping the pass. The Patriots probably faced five in the box more often than they faced eight.

Defensive Front Seven

Defensive Line	Age	Pos	Plays	TmPct	Rk	Stop	Dfts	Stop%	Rk	AvYd	Rk	Sack	Hit	Hur	Runs	RuStop	RuYd	Pass	PaStop	PaYd
Ty Warren	27	DE	56	7.7%	14	46	12	82%	18	0.9	22	4.0	12	13	46	80%	2.4	10	90%	-6.2
Vince Wilfork	27	DT	51	7.0%	10	41	8	80%	26	1.4	20	2.0	5	3	43	81%	1.9	8	75%	-1.6
Jarvis Green	29	DE	40	5.5%	46	31	19	78%	41	-0.1	5	7.0	5	17	26	69%	2.3	14	93%	-4.6
Richard Seymour	29	DE	24	5.8%	39	18	11	75%	47	1.4	30	1.5	7	5	20	75%	2.4	4	75%	-3.8

Linebackers	Age	Pos	Plays	TmPct	Rk	Stop	Dfts	Stop%	AvYd	Sack	Hit	Hur	Runs	RuStop	Rk	RuYd	Rk	Tgts	Suc%	Rk	APaYd	Rk
Tedy Bruschi	35	ILB	94	12.9%	46	45	10	48%	4.4	2.0	2	1	59	56%	84	3.2	47	27	33%	87	7.3	74
Adalius Thomas	31	ILB	87	11.9%	56	49	24	56%	4.1	6.5	4	7	45	64%	40	3.4	51	33	40%	74	6.1	44
Junior Seau	39	ILB	77	10.5%	63	46	21	60%	3.3	3.5	2	5	51	61%	55	3.2	44	17	53%	32	6.2	49
Mike Vrabel	33	OLB	75	10.3%	66	53	19	71%	2.3	11.0	8	15	41	71%	21	3.0	33	13	78%	—	3.8	—
Rosevelt Colvin*	31	OLB	31	6.2%	—	22	13	71%	1.2	4.0	3	12	17	71%	—	2.5	—	11	48%	—	5.5	—
Victor Hobson	28	OLB	67	7.9%	86	29	9	43%	4.6	2.0	7	4	37	49%	98	3.9	74	22	57%	22	4.6	14

Year	Yards	ALY	Rank	Power	Rank	10+ Yds	Rank	Stuff	Rank	Sack	ASR	Rank
2005	3.73	4.30	22	76%	28	9%	1	21%	30	33	6.0%	25
2006	3.91	3.99	8	68%	21	17%	20	24%	18	44	7.8%	10
2007	4.40	4.20	19	68%	23	17%	17	20%	28	47	8.4%	2

Year	LE	Rank	LT	Rank	Mid	Rank	RT	Rank	RE	Rank
2005	4.29	19	4.41	20	4.20	20	4.52	26	4.77	25
2006	3.30	7	4.33	15	4.15	12	2.83	2	4.05	16
2007	4.21	19	4.22	17	4.26	20	4.83	27	2.71	4

The average age of the Patriots four starting linebackers in the Super Bowl was 33.8. The old-timers played well against the Giants, but teams with great pass-catching running backs (like the Jaguars and Chargers, the Patriots' playoff opponents) were able to isolate backs against graybeards and rack up large chunks of yardage. Bill Belichick is excellent at defining roles and picking spots for old linebackers, but last season he had to do too much spot-picking and role-defining. Adalius Thomas, the youngster of the group at 30, was the only linebacker who could handle coverage, blitz, and run responsibilities without risking a mismatch.

The Patriots hedged their bets at linebacker in the offseason, signing Tedy Bruschi to a new contract while also signing Victor Hobson from the Jets and drafting three rookies. Top pick Jerod Mayo should slip into Junior Seau's spot next to Bruschi on the inside. He'll add speed in the middle, but he'll have to prove that he won't bite on every play-action fake, which was one of his major shortcomings at the University of Tennessee. Shaun Crable, who notched 28.5 tackles for a loss at Michigan last season, will learn from Mike Vrabel, while sixth-rounder Bo Ruud (brother of Tampa Bay's Barrett) will provide depth. Hobson is a Vrabel-like player who can rush the passer and defend the point-of-attack but can be exploited in coverage. Undrafted rookie Gary Guyton was a productive tackler at Georgia Tech and has great speed and work habits. He could be the next Larry Izzo.

The Patriots will once again field one of the best defensive lines in the NFL. Vince Wilfork must be double-teamed on every play and makes far more tackles at the line of scrimmage than the typical nose tackle. Ty Warren is a productive run defender who can shed blocks and pursue plays along the line. A knee injury limited Richard Seymour to nine games last year, and he wasn't at full speed when he did play. When healthy, he's a Pro Bowl end. Jarvis Green played very well in Warren's absence and provides a pass rush boost off the bench.

At press time, Seau was on the mend from offseason shoulder surgery. He didn't sound like he was in any hurry to return to the football field. "I have a choice of playing or a choice of surfing. Those are great choices to have." Don't count Seau out: he can still fill a role as a run-down inside linebacker, and he's retired and un-retired before.

Defensive Secondary

Secondary	Age	Pos	Plays	TmPct	Rk	Stop	Dfts	RuYd	Rk	RuStop	Rk	Tgts	Tgt%	Rk	Dist	Suc%	Rk	APaYd	Rk	PaYd	PD	Int
Ellis Hobbs	25	CB	77	10.5%	23	24	12	8.0	55	25%	73	89	20%	29	13.6	47%	50	8.6	67	8.5	14	1
Rodney Harrison	36	SS	73	13.3%	5	29	13	5.5	22	31%	64	39	11%	5	9.0	52%	28	5.5	13	5.4	7	1
James Sanders	25	FS	69	10.1%	34	23	12	8.0	63	31%	71	22	5%	67	9.0	62%	7	5.4	11	4.9	6	2
Asante Samuel*	27	CB	64	8.8%	46	27	15	12.0	77	44%	49	81	18%	41	11.4	51%	34	6.3	14	6.0	17	6
Randall Gay*	26	CB	43	5.9%	74	19	12	11.3	73	0%	81	47	10%	80	10.4	59%	5	7.2	34	7.1	10	3
Eugene Wilson*	28	FS	35	7.0%	69	12	5	9.3	73	31%	70	23	7%	33	10.1	52%	30	7.4	45	7.3	2	1
Brandon Meriweather	24	FS	18	2.5%	—	10	4	5.3	—	50%	—	11	2%	—	12.7	58%	—	5.8	—	5.2	1	0
Fernando Bryant	31	CB	81	9.3%	36	29	12	4.7	17	50%	32	85	18%	39	9.1	45%	61	6.7	24	6.7	11	2
Lewis Sanders	30	CB	36	4.9%	—	10	8	4.1	—	40%	—	42	11%	—	9.0	31%	—	9.1	—	9.1	2	0

Year	Pass D Rank		vs. #1 WR	Rk		vs. #2 WR	Rk		vs. Other WR	Rk		vs. TE	Rk		vs. RB	Rk
2005	29		20.2%	24		18.8%	30		12.3%	27		10.7%	23		4.6%	21
2006	7		-3.7%	12		22.2%	28		-9.2%	13		-31.5%	2		13.9%	27
2007	6		1.1%	18		-10.2%	9		-10.2%	14		9.9%	21		0.0%	18

Expect fierce competition at cornerback in training camp. Ellis Hobbs, the lone returning starter, is a dynamic return man who covers small receivers well but matches up poorly against taller receivers (see the Super Bowl for evidence). Free agent Fernando Bryant is one of the league's greatest philanthropists, having won Man of the Year awards in Jacksonville and Detroit. But he's on the downside of his career and played through a foot injury last year. Rookie Terrence Wheatley is small and fast like Hobbs and smart and injury prone like Bryant. Veteran free agents Jason Webster and Lewis Sanders are also in the mix. Sanders has the size to match up with bigger receivers but is limited athletically; Webster is 31 years old and coming off a major arm injury. Coaches liked what they saw of Mike Richardson last season before he suffered a hand injury at the end of camp. Richardson, a 2007 sixth-rounder out of Notre Dame, is strong in run support and zone defense but must prove he can run with fast receivers.

Rodney Harrison is in the final year of his contract and may retire after the season. He's still a big hitter and gambler who will make a few big plays, get beaten in the open field occasionally, and miss four to six games with nagging injuries. Brandon Meriweather, last year's top pick, will get a long look at free safety. Meriweather has the talent to take over Eugene Wilson's role as the deep safety who doubles as a dime cornerback. Incumbent starter James Sanders will battle Meriweather, while Lewis Sanders (no relation) could also move to free safety to ease the glut at cornerback.

Special Teams

Year	DVOA	Rank	FG/XP	Rank	Net Punt	Rank	Punt Ret	Rank	Net Kick	Rank	Kick Ret	Rank	Hidden	Rank
2005	1.1%	12	0.1	17	-0.4	19	1.7	10	0.6	17	4.7	9	-6.2	23
2006	2.5%	8	-5.5	28	-5.9	25	4.9	4	4.9	11	16.6	1	3.7	11
2007	3.0%	7	-0.2	19	0.8	16	-1.1	18	7.3	3	11.0	5	1.7	14

Under Bill Belichick and Scott Pioli, the Patriots have always spent extra money and resources on role players and specialists. The extra attention has usually paid off. They refused to get lured into an Adam Vinatieri bidding war two years ago, but they did invest a fourth-round pick on Steve Gostkowski. Gostkowski will miss a few medium-range field goals, but he has one of the most powerful kickoff legs in the league. During their wide receiver splurge last offseason, the team traded a second-round pick for Wes Welker and signed Kelley Washington, who seemed destined to only play in 12-wideout formations. Welker provides reliability and ball security as a return man, while Washington made 16 tackles and blocked a kick last season. Izzo is back, and newcomer Sam Aiken was a first-class gunner in Buffalo. The bench is loaded with players like Sammy Morris and Kyle Eckel who can block and shag down kicks, while players like Faulk and Laurence Maroney give the Patriots multiple options in the return game. Punter Chris Hanson arrived from the Jaguars last year and did next to nothing, punting just four times in September and six times in November before a 20-punt December flurry. If he wasn't the placekick holder, Hanson would have been forced to give a quarter of his paycheck back.

COACHING STAFF

When the team hired ex-Panthers and Texans skipper Dom Capers as defensive backs coach, conspiracy bloggers leapt into action. Their reasoning: Capers was insurance against Bill Belichick's impending suspension. Capers was a candidate for the Patriots head coaching job in 2000, and with Matt Walsh hiding behind a coconut tree with a shoebox full of signal-stealing footage, the Patriots front office had to ready themselves for whatever hit the fan. While the Walsh/taping story will never die, it appears that Capers was hired because he's an expert in the 3-4 defense who can help Belichick and defensive coordinator Dean Pees get the rebuilt secondary quickly up to speed with their assignments. Capers is also a well-respected coach who draws rave reviews from veterans: free agent Fernando Bryant cited Capers as one of the reasons he chose the Patriots. Of course, if Walsh produces video of Belichick selling weapons-grade plutonium to our nation's enemies and Capers takes over as head coach, we'll send the conspiracy nuts a letter of apology.

Offensive coordinator Josh McDaniels has shown great versatility in his short career. In 2006, he built an offense around power running and short passes to tight ends. Last year, he created a spread offense that used screens, draws, and short passes to set up home run throws to Randy Moss. McDaniels will soon become a hot head coaching candidate, either in the NFL or at a college seeking the next Urban Meyer.

New Orleans Saints

As a quick-turnaround artist, Bill Parcells stands alone among NFL coaches. He has taken the playbook for four franchises in his illustrious career, and each team has experienced a dramatic reversal of fortune. From the New York Giants of the 1980s, who personified his toughness, to the new Dallas Cowboys, one of the most impressive examples of team-building in recent memory, Parcells knows how to take a sad song and make it better.

He also knows how to teach others to do it. Tom Coughlin, his receivers coach with the old Giants, made the new Giants defending Super Bowl champions a decade after taking the expansion Jacksonville Jaguars to the AFC Championship game in their second season. Bill Belichick worked with Parcells before and after a no-win situation in Cleveland and finally got it really, really right with the Patriots. Eric Mangini was a defensive assistant and quality control coach from 1997 to 1999 with the Jets; after following Belichick to New England in 2000 and staying for six seasons, he returned to the Jets and orchestrated a six-win upswing. It was the second-most impressive turnaround of the 2006 season. Another Parcells acolyte did his old boss and all the apostles one better and wrote the greatest comeback story in NFL history.

We all know the details: The 2005 Saints were nomads in the wake of Hurricane Katrina. The Superdome wasn't home for them because it was a temporary shelter for thousands as the city tried to recover. They played home games in San Antonio and at LSU's Tiger Stadium and finished 3-13 under Jim Haslett. The Saints went into the 2006 season with little more than hope that they could return to life as normal.

New head coach Sean Payton, who had worked under Parcells in Dallas from 2003 to 2005 as his quarterbacks coach and passing game coordinator, threw the standard recovery timetable in the garbage and built from the ground up. Eleven new starters later, the Saints shocked the world with a 10-6 season that ended with a loss in the NFC Championship game. It was the season that inspired a city that had been on its knees.

At the 2008 owners' meetings, Payton discussed what he learned about franchise recuperation from Parcells. "He's someone that really taught you all the dynamics inside the building and how to be successful," Payton said. "In other words, it wasn't so much the football scheme on offense or defense but what we're looking for in players, how he wants the training room to function, what he thinks the offseason program should consist of, what's important in his coaching staff. Things that are a little bit broader than the football game itself. . . . We tried to simulate the same thing in New Orleans because having three good years of watching it in Dallas, I'm a big believer in that program."

For Payton in 2007, one question was left: How do you follow a miracle? The answer? "About as expected." In *Pro Football Prospectus 2007*, we ran a chart of the 12 teams since 1972 that have won four or fewer games in one season and 10 or more the next. In the season fol-

---

SAINTS PROSPECTUS

2007 Record: 7-9

Pythagorean Wins: 7.8 (19th)

DVOA: -4.9% total (21st), 4.1% weighted (15th)

Offense: 10.1% DVOA (8th)

Defense: 11.4% DVOA (27th)

Special Teams: -3.6% DVOA (25th)

Variance: 13.5 % (10th)

2007: Miracle of New Orleans II: The sequel is never as good as the original.

2008: A long-term plan for success is in place, but a few immediate repairs must be made.

2008 Mean Projection: 8.3 wins

On the Clock (0-3): 0%

Loserville (4-6): 20%

Mediocrity (7-8): 32%

Playoff Contender (9-10): 31%

Super Bowl Contender (11+): 17%

Projected Average Opponent: -3.8% DVOA (26th in NFL)

2008 Saints Schedule

Week	Opp.	Week	Opp.	Week	Opp.
1	TB	7	at CAR	13	at TB
2	at WAS	8	SD	14	ATL
3	at DEN	9	BYE	15	at CHI (Thu.)
4	SF	10	at ATL	16	at DET
5	MIN (Mon.)	11	at KC	17	CAR
6	OAK	12	GB (Mon.)		

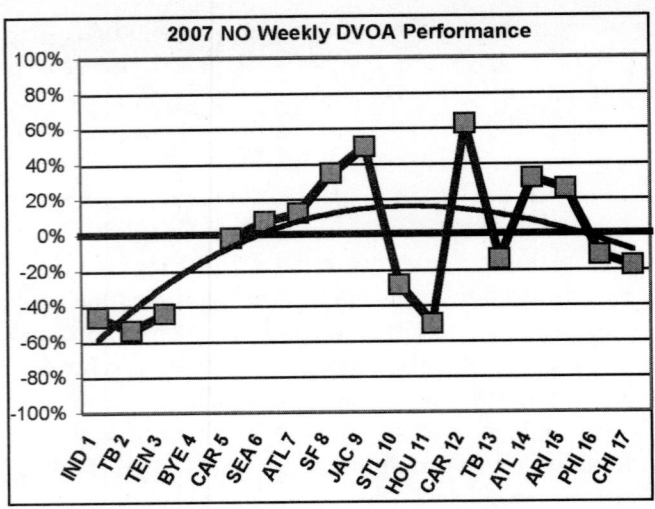

Figure 1

lowing their ascents, those teams averaged a decline of 2.7 wins, which put the Saints with a projection of 7-9; exactly where they ended up in 2007 (Mangini's Jets sunk back to 4-12). The surprise was not the final record but how the 2007 season started and how emblematic that beginning was of the problems that would plague the team through the year.

The Saints opened the NFL season against the Super Bowl Champion Colts on a Thursday night at the RCA Dome. Cornerback Jason David, signed to a lucrative free agent contract and facing his former team, played the goat in the first quarter by getting torched on a Marvin Harrison touchdown. He redeemed himself in the second quarter by returning a fumble for a touchdown, but that balance wouldn't remain for long. David was burned for two more touchdowns in the game—both passes from Peyton Manning to Reggie Wayne—and the Saints began to get the idea that converting a cornerback from Tampa-2 to man-on-man isn't a smooth process.

Meanwhile, on the offensive side of the ball, quarterback Drew Brees alternated between running away from constant pressure and forcing throws into microscopic areas with questionable timing. Brees had finished second in quarterback DYAR the year before, behind only Peyton Manning; now he found it impossible to set his feet and make his reads. Through the first four games of 2007, all losses, Brees threw nine interceptions and one touchdown pass. In the third game, a disastrous loss to the Titans, running back Deuce McAllister—already the victim of a season-ending right ACL injury in 2005—tore his left ACL on a short pass and was lost for the season again. Brees threw four picks in the game, Vince Young continued the trend of opposing quarterbacks demolishing the Saints' secondary at will, and it looked as if the team that had inspired so many a year before was taking the elevator back to the basement.

Payton and his staff made adjustments. Brees worked with shorter drops and more four-receiver sets. The running game, problematic without McAllister as its fulcrum, became more of a short passing game as the Saints led the NFL in passing attempts and running back Reggie Bush joined Philadelphia's Brian Westbrook as the only running back in 2007 to finish in the NFL's top 25 in receptions. The fourth straight loss was a 16-13 nail-biter to the Panthers, which is when things started to turn around. The Saints traveled to Seattle for a Sunday night game where they finally put it all together. Brees threw his first interceptionless game, Bush was everything his multidimensional talent promised, and the defense finally managed a string of consistent stops. Four straight wins followed those four consecutive losses; halfway through the season, the Saints had returned to square one.

And that is when they found out what kind of team they really were—a .500 squad at root, requiring considerable progress at certain positions before anything great was going to happen. The offensive line may have allowed an NFL-low 16 sacks in 2007, but the linemen were the real beneficiaries of Brees's ability to make quick throws under pressure. His inefficiency was the side effect of this mythical pass protection. This is fairly common even among elite quarterbacks. In 2005, Brett Favre lost both of his starting guards to free agency, but the Packers finished third in Adjusted Sack Rate. Problem solved, right? Not if you look behind the statistical mask to find Favre's 29 interceptions, the most he ever threw in a single season. The Packers recommitted to their line and Favre threw a total of 33 picks in his last two seasons. It's time for the Saints to do the same thing. New Orleans was the best offense in the NFL at running up the middle, but they lost center Jeff Faine to the Buccaneers in free agency. Tackles Jammal Brown and Jon Stinchcomb, generally solid players, were disturbingly vulnerable to speed rushers last season, and Brown suffered knee and calf injuries.

Brees led the NFL in pass attempts and set a league record for completions in a season, but that didn't help when defenses caught up with the ineffective New Orleans running game around midseason. In Weeks 10-13, the Saints barely registered a pulse on the ground, never gaining more than 64 yards. With the Saints sitting at 5-7, Bush was lost for the season with a torn knee ligament. Backup Aaron Stecker and undrafted rookie Pierre Thomas were left to grind it out over the last quarter of the year, and the Saints engineered their second four-game turnaround of the season. There was a late, hopeful playoff shot, but the dream was over.

The secondary was the most obvious problem. New Orleans gave up 54 pass plays of 20 yards or more and it was distressingly easy to throw long bombs downfield because the front seven found it difficult to exert the same kind of pressure that Brees was facing on offense. The Saints ranked in the top 10 among defenses that sent six or more defenders, but those defenders were decidedly middle-of-the-pack in sacks, hits, and hurries. Ends Will Smith and Charles Grant saw their sack totals plummet from a combined 16.5 in 2006 to 9.5 last season. The defense was better against the run, but they weren't facing the run all that often with such an awful secondary.

Offseason defensive reinforcements came from all over. The biggest name is middle linebacker Jonathan Vilma, who will dramatically improve the Saints' defense if he can overcome a 2007 knee injury. Vilma was a Pro Bowl linebacker and one of the top playmakers in the league before the Jets' drastic switch to the 3-4 defense left him out of place. The Saints also added former Jacksonville defensive end Bobby McCray, a tall pass rusher who put up 10 sacks in 2006. The interior line will get a huge boost from first-round draft pick and Senior Bowl star Sedrick Ellis. If David isn't careful, second-round pick Tracy Porter, a lightning-quick but tackling-impaired cornerback with man coverage skills, could easily unseat him. The uncertainty surrounding Mike McKenzie's age and ACL surgery recovery is somewhat mitigated by the potential displayed by second-year cornerback Usama Young as well as the depth provided by 10-year veteran Jason Craft and offseason signings Randall Gay and Aaron Glenn. After stinking up the universe in 2007, New Orleans's defensive backfield has surprising potential going forward.

Our projections for the Saints center right around 8-8, and everything about this team seems like an *if*. If Brees isn't forced to get rid of the ball and is allowed to read through his progressions; *if* Pierre Thomas lives up to that out-of-the-blue rookie season; *if* Sean Payton can keep thinking up new ways to use Reggie Bush; *if* the Saints' other receivers step up and keep Marques Colston from becoming a one-man show; *if* a defense that played too frequently behind, out of gas, and moving backward can turn it around and at least hit respectable status; if these *if*s become realities, something great could happen. The NFC South is rife with low-hanging fruit, and the Saints could easily return to the top of the division, but the offseason attempts to fix this team's biggest holes don't necessarily inspire great confidence.

Having performed his miracle turnaround and then confronting the harsh realities that followed, what is Payton left with now? A team that's much better than the moribund unit he inherited but still falls short in key areas. After a dizzying trip from low to high, the Saints must now deal with life in the middle. For some teams, that's the toughest place to be.

Doug Farrar

2007 Saints Stats by Week

Wk	vs.	W-L	PF	PA	YDF	YDA	TO	Total	Off	Def	ST
1	@IND	L	10	41	293	452	-2	-46%	-16%	26%	-5%
2	@TB	L	14	31	343	330	-2	-54%	-6%	35%	-13%
3	TEN	L	14	31	252	284	-4	-45%	-27%	11%	-6%
4	BYE										
5	CAR	L	13	16	341	243	-1	-2%	-5%	-15%	-11%
6	@SEA	W	28	17	367	425	+1	7%	21%	13%	-1%
7	ATL	W	22	16	310	334	-1	12%	13%	8%	6%
8	@SF	W	31	10	438	260	0	34%	46%	15%	3%
9	JAC	W	41	24	538	432	+2	49%	68%	-10%	-28%
10	STL	L	29	37	299	409	-2	-29%	13%	48%	6%
11	@HOU	L	10	23	327	390	-1	-51%	-37%	17%	2%
12	@CAR	W	31	6	373	195	+3	62%	22%	-41%	-1%
13	TB	L	23	27	246	466	0	-15%	6%	22%	1%
14	@ATL	W	34	14	473	323	0	31%	36%	5%	1%
15	ARI	W	31	24	421	317	0	25%	38%	3%	-9%
16	PHI	L	23	38	346	435	0	-12%	15%	37%	10%
17	@CHI	L	25	33	413	275	0	-18%	-10%	-8%	-17%

Trends and Splits

	Offense	Rank	Defense	Rank
Total DVOA	10.1%	8	11.4%	27
Unadjusted VOA	9.8%	8	11.5%	28
Weighted trend	16.5%	5	10.3%	27
Variance	7.7%	20	4.8%	6
Average opponent	0.2%	9	-2.5%	27
Passing	20.3%	8	28.6%	32
Rushing	-6.0%	18	-10.3%	6
First down	19.3%	4	7.5%	25
Second down	-4.3%	21	12.3%	25
Third down	14.7%	12	17.5%	28
First half	12.6%	8	17.4%	28
Second half	7.6%	8	5.3%	22
Red zone	26.3%	4	17.7%	26
Late and close	-1.6%	16	1.5%	18

Five-Year Performance

Year	W-L	Pyth Wins	Est Wins	PF	PA	TO	Total	Rank	Off	Rank	Def	Rank	ST	Rank
2003	8-8	8.4	8.1	340	326	-1	-1.2%	18	4.2%	12	4.1%	22	-1.2%	23
2004	8-8	6.6	6.1	348	405	+7	-17.3%	26	-7.8%	26	15.2%	27	5.7%	3
2005	3-13	3.6	5.4	235	398	-24	-23.0%	30	-13.4%	25	7.6%	25	-2.0%	24
2006	10-6	10.3	9.1	413	322	-4	11.0%	9	13.4%	5	3.2%	19	0.7%	14
2007	7-9	7.8	7.6	379	388	-7	-4.9%	21	10.1%	8	11.4%	27	-3.6%	25

Strategic Tendencies

	Run/Pass	Rank		Offense	Rank		Defense	Rank		Other		Rank
Runs, all plays	35%	31	3+ WR	57%	9	Rush 3	2.3%	27	2+ RB, Pct runs	48%	29
Runs, first half	35%	30	4+ WR	23%	4	Rush 4	69.1%	10	1 RB/2 TE, Pct runs	32%	30
Runs, first down	40%	31	2+ TE	19%	23	Rush 5	15.0%	28	1 RB/3+ WR, Pct runs	30%	7
Runs, second-long	35%	17	Single back	49%	24	Rush 6+	13.6%	6	CB1 on WR1	34%	31
Runs, power sit.	56%	24	Play action	24%	4	Rush 7+	2.5%	8	Go for it on 4th	1.74	3
Runs, behind 2H	21%	30	Max protect	10%	16	Sacks by LB	18.8%	22	Offensive pace	29.1	4
Pass, ahead 2H	49%	12	Outside pocket	8%	26	Sacks by DB	15.6%	4	Defensive pace	30.6	11

New Orleans ran the ball from four-wide sets a quarter of the time, more than any team except Indianapolis, but did so ineffectively with a negative DVOA. ⚬ The Saints went empty backfield more often than any team other than Green Bay. ⚬ Only the Buccaneers threw more often to their running backs, and no team threw a higher percentage of passes behind the line of scrimmage. ⚬ The Saints were second in wide receiver screen passes behind only the Patriots, although a quarter of those passes were to running backs lined up in a wide receiver position. ⚬ Drew Brees ranked eighth in designed rolls out of the pocket, but 30th in number of scrambles. ⚬ The Saints had the second highest percentage of passes dropped, behind only the Giants. ⚬ Brees had more passes tipped at the line of scrimmage than any other quarterback. ⚬ The Saints ranked 11th in rushing DVOA for the first half, but 25th in the second half. ⚬ The Lions had the only defense worse than the Saints against four-wide receiver sets

⌀ The Saints defense led the league in facing passes to non-starting receivers (25 percent) and was second behind Indianapolis facing passes to tight ends (23 percent). ⌀ The Saints had five sacks from defensive backs, after just one in 2006.

Passing

Player	DYAR	DVOA	Plays	NtYds	Avg	YAC	C%	TD	Int
Drew Brees	1285	17.0%	673	4362	6.5	4.7	67.8%	28	17

Rushing

Player	DYAR	DVOA	Plays	Yds	Avg	TD	Fum	Suc
Reggie Bush	-72	-19.4%	157	569	3.6	4	7	46%
Aaron Stecker	64	4.1%	114	444	3.9	5	1	50%
Pierre Thomas	87	33.5%	50	251	5.0	1	0	60%
Deuce McAllister	-12	-21.1%	24	92	3.8	0	1	42%
Drew Brees	23	14.2%	13	60	4.6	1	9	—
Mike Karney	-3	-12.8%	11	17	1.5	2	0	45%

Receiving

Player	DYAR	DVOA	Plays	Ctch	Yds	Y/C	YAC	TD	C%
WR									
Marques Colston	351	16.8%	144	98	1202	12.3	4.1	11	68%
David Patten	136	6.6%	88	54	792	14.7	4.6	4	61%
Lance Moore	76	6.3%	50	32	302	9.4	1.8	3	64%
Devery Henderson	78	9.7%	43	20	409	20.5	3.8	3	47%
Terrance Copper	27	4.2%	21	15	126	8.4	3.9	2	71%
TE									
Eric Johnson	18	-3.2%	63	48	380	7.9	3.1	2	76%
Billy Miller	79	21.8%	38	27	328	12.1	7.0	2	71%
RB									
Reggie Bush	25	-9.6%	98	73	417	5.7	5.6	2	74%
Aaron Stecker	49	5.0%	43	37	215	5.8	6.6	0	86%
Pierre Thomas	53	25.5%	23	19	152	8.0	8.4	1	83%
Mike Karney	6	-8.9%	19	13	78	6.0	4.9	0	68%
Deuce McAllister	-4	-26.5%	5	4	15	3.8	3.8	0	80%

Offensive Line

Year	Yards	ALY	Rank	Power	Rank	10+ Yds	Rank	Stuff	Rank	Sack	ASR	Rank
2005	3.78	4.01	18	57%	25	14%	20	24%	11	41	7.3%	18
2006	3.99	4.37	11	54%	30	13%	25	22%	8	23	4.1%	4
2007	3.86	4.39	7	66%	13	9%	30	21%	6	16	3.6%	3

Year	LE	Rank	LT	Rank	Mid	Rank	RT	Rank	RE	Rank
2005	2.17	31	3.20	28	4.41	7	3.71	24	3.83	18
2006	4.38	12	4.12	21	4.55	9	3.91	28	4.43	10
2007	4.04	17	3.47	30	4.98	1	3.98	22	3.79	22

The advanced statistics in *Pro Football Prospectus* do a lot to isolate individual performances in the ultimate team sport, but they are still far from perfect. Adjusted Sack Rate, for example, can often be a bit deceiving when the quarterback has a very quick release. Drew Brees's first four games of 2007 showed just how much impact a quarterback has on his own sack totals. Under pressure almost constantly in those first four games, Brees was only sacked four times, but he threw nine interceptions to one touchdown. Against the Tennessee Titans and their outstanding front seven in a Week 3 loss, Brees was sacked just once, but he threw four interceptions. As the season progressed and the offense went to more short, quick passing strikes, the line became a beneficiary of the game plan, not the other way around.

One thing the line had going for it in 2007 was continuity—left guard Jamar Nesbit, right guard Jahri Evans, and right tackle Jon Stinchcomb started all 16 games at their positions. Center Jeff Faine and left tackle Jammal Brown missed only three games between them. However, Brown struggled with knee and calf injuries through the season, and he's not yet lived up to his potential as an elite pass protector. Stinchcomb and Nesbit are decent veterans, and Evans has been a great story since being drafted in the fourth round in 2006 out of Division II Bloomsburg in 2006, but the Saints suffered a big loss when Faine signed an enormous contract with the Buccaneers in the offseason. As much as the pass protection numbers were better for the line than they should have been, that line took too much heat for New Orleans' dismal running game. The Saints ranked first in Adjusted Line Yards up the middle, and their stats would be even better if not for Reggie Bush's predilection for going sideways instead of forwards. (The Saints had 4.66 ALY on Bush runs up the middle, 5.20 ALY when someone else was carrying the ball.) Taking Faine's place is Jonathan Goodwin, who signed a three-year, $8.5 million extension in the offseason but has only started 15 games in six NFL seasons with the Jets and Saints. The Saints have some interesting depth linemen: Nebraska tackle Carl Nicks could be a fifth-round steal if he overcomes the character concerns that dropped him a good three rounds, while 2007 third-round guard Andy Alleman has a great work ethic but is still learning the position because he spent his first two years in college as a defensive end.

Defensive Front Seven

Defensive Line	Age	Pos	Plays	TmPct	Rk	Stop	Dfts	Stop%	Rk	AvYd	Rk	Sack	Hit	Hur	Runs	RuStop	RuYd	Pass	PaStop	PaYd
Will Smith	27	DE	71	9.1%	7	51	22	72%	60	1.8	43	7.0	12	13	52	73%	2.5	19	68%	-0.2
Hollis Thomas	34	DT	50	6.4%	16	42	12	84%	14	2.0	49	3.0	0	5	42	86%	1.8	8	75%	3.1
Charles Grant	30	DE	49	7.2%	22	40	15	82%	21	1.4	32	2.5	5	13	40	80%	1.4	9	89%	1.6
Antwan Lake	29	DT	20	2.7%	—	13	7	65%	—	2.9	—	1.0	1	7	16	56%	3.0	4	100%	2.5
Brian Young	31	DE	19	4.3%	—	16	4	84%	—	0.9	—	3.0	3	10	15	80%	2.1	4	100%	-3.5
Kendrick Clancy	30	DT	15	2.2%	—	14	5	93%	—	1.5	—	0.5	1	2	13	92%	1.8	2	100%	0.0
Bobby McCray	27	DE	19	2.9%	—	14	8	74%	—	1.5	—	3.0	7	13	11	64%	3.1	8	88%	-0.8

Linebackers	Age	Pos	Plays	TmPct	Rk	Stop	Dfts	Stop%	AvYd	Sack	Hit	Hur	Runs	RuStop	Rk	RuYd	Rk	Tgts	Suc%	Rk	APaYd	Rk
Scott Fujita	29	OLB	98	13.4%	40	58	11	59%	5.5	3.0	2	5	57	65%	38	4.1	82	41	56%	26	6.1	47
Mark Simoneau	31	MLB	71	9.1%	77	40	8	56%	4.5	2.0	1	1	53	58%	66	3.8	70	21	50%	42	6.3	52
Scott Shanle	29	OLB	67	9.8%	68	36	11	54%	6.0	0.0	1	1	44	59%	63	4.5	92	20	42%	67	9.2	88
Brian Simmons*	33	MLB	18	2.3%	—	13	4	72%	3.3	1.0	0	0	12	92%	—	1.1	—	5	35%	—	9.9	—
Jonathan Vilma	26	MLB	46	12.4%	—	25	6	54%	4.2	0.0	1	0	31	58%	—	3.8	—	14	54%	—	5.3	—

Year	Yards	ALY	Rank	Power	Rank	10+ Yds	Rank	Stuff	Rank	Sack	ASR	Rank
2005	4.34	4.11	19	78%	31	24%	30	25%	16	26	6.1%	24
2006	4.59	4.25	17	48%	3	23%	31	28%	4	38	7.8%	9
2007	3.99	4.16	16	62%	16	15%	11	22%	22	32	5.6%	27

Year	LE	Rank	LT	Rank	Mid	Rank	RT	Rank	RE	Rank
2005	3.19	6	4.51	26	4.31	22	4.03	15	3.61	11
2006	4.59	22	4.89	25	4.20	14	3.51	8	4.03	15
2007	5.39	29	4.18	15	3.96	10	3.60	6	4.72	25

After nice improvement in 2006, the Saints' Adjusted Sack Rate fell back to previously feeble levels in 2007. The early season was especially troubling, with only one sack in the first four games. Ends Will Smith and Charles Grant saw their combined sack totals cut in half. That lack of consistent quarterback pressure made an already vulnerable secondary downright feeble. However, Smith and Grant did have plenty of hits and hurries, so another rebound towards league-average is likely in 2008. The addition of former Jaguars end Bobby McCray, who had 10 sacks in 2006, can only help, especially if Grant has to miss any time due to legal issues. (In May, Grant was indicted on a charge of involuntary manslaughter, based on his alleged role in a February nightclub fight. Grant, who was stabbed in the neck in the altercation, has posted bond and pled not guilty.)

The interior line is led by veteran and longtime NFL Films comedy star Hollis Thomas. Brian Young earned a three-year deal in the offseason despite landing on injured reserve with a rare form of pneumonia in December. Thomas and Young are good players, but the big keg of dynamite is the addition of first-round draft pick Sedrick Ellis, a terrifying pass rusher with a motor that simply doesn't turn off. (Perhaps he ate the keys.) From the double teams he demolished in his senior season, to his amazing performance in the Senior Bowl, to his Combine, Pro Day, and private workouts with NFL teams, Ellis never failed to impress. Where he lands—nose or three-technique—will decide who starts around him. It's not often that a rookie is the linchpin of a front four, but Ellis, like Glenn Dorsey in Kansas City, possesses that kind of potential.

Scott Fujita was once again the star of New Orleans' linebacker corps, improving his numbers against the run and keeping his pass defense above average. Scott Shanle did well on the weak side against the pass, but his numbers against the run are not impressive. His below-average Stop Rate is actually an improvement over 2006, when he ranked 89th among linebackers with a Stop Rate of 53 percent on running plays. Mark Simoneau and Brian Simmons combined for average results in the middle, and the Saints dealt a conditional fourth-round choice to the Jets for former first-round pick Jonathan Vilma. Recovering from a season-ending knee injury and misplaced in New York's 3-4 defense, Vilma could be a lifesaver in the middle if he can return to the form that won him the 2004 Defensive Rookie of the Year award and allowed him to lead the NFL in tackles in 2005. The Saints also signed former Panthers linebacker Dan Morgan to a one-year contract in the offseason, but Morgan's concussion history, and other injuries, hastened his retirement.

Defensive Secondary

Secondary	Age	Pos	Plays	TmPct	Rk	Stop	Dfts	RuYd	Rk	RuStop	Rk	Tgts	Tgt%	Rk	Dist	Suc%	Rk	APaYd	Rk	PaYd	PD	Int
Roman Harper	26	SS	90	11.5%	19	40	22	7.6	59	45%	40	28	6%	53	11.4	50%	38	6.9	35	6.6	5	3
Josh Bullocks	25	FS	85	12.5%	10	29	9	8.7	71	40%	52	27	7%	43	15.8	42%	64	12.0	80	12.1	5	2
Mike McKenzie	32	CB	69	9.4%	33	32	13	4.3	12	60%	16	72	17%	46	13.6	59%	6	6.3	15	6.2	16	3
Jason Craft	32	CB	63	8.1%	58	19	12	9.2	63	27%	70	82	18%	37	11.8	46%	54	7.1	32	6.8	11	2
Jason David	26	CB	62	9.8%	28	25	7	5.7	31	50%	35	82	23%	9	12.0	37%	77	12.1	81	12.4	15	3
Kevin Kaesviharn	32	FS	37	4.7%	79	23	10	3.1	1	58%	6	23	5%	68	8.6	77%	1	3.5	4	3.1	7	0
Randall Gay	26	CB	43	5.9%	74	19	12	11.3	73	0%	81	47	10%	80	10.4	59%	5	7.2	34	7.1	10	3
Aaron Glenn	36	CB	16	6.8%	—	5	3	10.3	—	0%	—	20	14%	—	13.3	58%	—	6.5	—	7.4	1	1

Year	Pass D Rank	vs. #1 WR	Rk	vs. #2 WR	Rk	vs. Other WR	Rk	vs. TE	Rk	vs. RB	Rk
2005	26	25.2%	29	12.5%	29	-4.7%	13	10.1%	22	6.8%	22
2006	21	27.8%	31	8.0%	22	-37.9%	2	-12.3%	10	-34.0%	3
2007	32	59.2%	32	-8.9%	11	12.4%	27	16.5%	24	9.5%	27

When the Saints signed Colts restricted free agent Jason David to a four-year, $16.5 million offer sheet in April of 2007, they did not expect the second coming of Champ Bailey. All they wanted was an upgrade on former starting cornerback Fred Thomas, who was burnt repeatedly in the second half of 2006. Instead, what they got was a cornerback who was toasted so often that he had to have his crusts cut off after the season. David won the first official Football Outsiders Reverse Triple Crown by allowing the most total passing yards (1,051), yards after catch (321), and passing touchdowns (11) of any defender in 2007, despite missing three games with a forearm injury. David allowed 12.1 yards per pass, even after adjusting for his opponents. Plays where our game charters marked "Hole in Zone" gained 11.6 yards per pass, meaning that last year David was actually worse than empty space. He will forever reign as a cautionary tale, teaching the lesson that when you sign a zone corner to play man defense, you'd better know he can play receivers without the same kind of safety help.

Veteran Mike McKenzie provided valuable (actually, desperately needed) acumen on the left side, but he tore his right ACL in the second-to-last game of the season, and he probably won't be ready to go until at least training camp, possibly later. He'll enter this season at age 32, which is not an encouraging number for anyone asked to go step-for-step with NFL receivers nine months after knee surgery. The Saints do have a lot of depth behind McKenzie and David, although it generally comes with question marks. Second-round draft pick Tracy Porter from Indiana is a fast corner with suspect tackling ability that the Saints likely don't care about—they need man coverage speed, and Porter has it. With the team's secondary situation, Porter might be learning on the job. If that's the case, look for alternating head-shaking mistakes and eye-popping plays. Some people think 2007 third-round pick Usama Young is Kent State's finest defensive product since some guy by the name of Lambert terrorized opposing offenses 35 years ago. Like Porter, he's known more for his speed than his tackling ability. The Saints also brought former New England cornerback Randall Gay back home to Louisiana, where he starred at Brusly High School and LSU. Gay had pretty good numbers with the Patriots, but he is injury-prone and was generally used in zone coverage. Uh-oh.

Strong safety Roman Harper had his ups and downs, and there were inklings that he might be replaced by Kevin Kaesviharn late in the season, but he's got real potential. The Saints would do well to be patient and let Harper and young free safety Josh Bullocks develop over time—especially with the mess that surrounds them in the defensive backfield.

Special Teams

Year	DVOA	Rank	FG/XP	Rank	Net Punt	Rank	Punt Ret	Rank	Net Kick	Rank	Kick Ret	Rank	Hidden	Rank
2005	-2.0%	23	-6.7	25	10.0	3	-0.6	15	0.1	18	-14.5	32	-7.0	25
2006	0.7%	14	2.7	10	6.3	9	-1.9	19	0.4	17	-3.3	19	12.8	1
2007	-3.6%	25	-5.3	27	-2.3	21	-4.3	23	-1.7	18	-7.5	27	-3.3	21

Olindo Mare had a disappointing season—seriously, how do you miss five of 13 field goals indoors?—and lost the last three games of the year to a hip injury. The Saints cut bait on Mare and used a sixth-round pick on Wisconsin's Taylor Mehlhaff, universally regarded as the best kicker in this draft class. Not only is Mehlhaff incredibly reliable and consistent—he never missed a field goal inside the 30-yard line in his collegiate career, and made three of four from outside the 50 in his last two seasons—he also has amazing leg strength on kickoffs. He registered 50 touchbacks in 2007, despite the NCAA's decision to move kickoffs back to the kicking team's 30-yard line. It's hard to imagine Mehlhaff losing a training camp battle with Martin Grammatica, who had replaced Mare for the final three games of 2007. The rest of this unit is fairly stable but unexciting. Punter Steve Weatherford and long snapper Kevin Houser are a solid combination (Houser has been with the team since 2000). Pierre Thomas and Lance Moore should continue to be the primary return men unless Thomas gets too many reps as a starter in the Saints' two-back set.

COACHING STAFF

Asking Sean Payton to follow his miracle 2006 season was going to be difficult at best. How do you top the *Are You Experienced* of coaching debuts? The only satisfactory sequel would have been a Super Bowl victory, and that wasn't going to happen with injuries and personnel deficits all around. Still, Payton had his troops in the playoff hunt in a mediocre division and abysmal conference until the very end, and there's no reason to think that with a few lucky breaks, he won't have his Saints there again. For the first time since the Jim Mora era of the late 1980s and early 1990s, this franchise is expected to contend for a playoff berth every year, and that's an important development when your team's history is so full of disappointment and every bit of civic pride helps your fans to rebuild. Defensive coordinator Gary Gibbs is the one with the challenges ahead—it's going to get hot under his collar if the Saints' defense keeps the team out of the playoffs again. Gibbs was Bill Parcells' linebackers coach in Dallas when Payton was also on the staff.

Speaking of lineages, offensive assistant Joe Lombardi has a very impressive family tree—he's Vince Lombardi's grandson. A graduate of the Air Force Academy in 1994, the younger Lombardi previously coached with several small colleges, the New York/New Jersey Hitmen of the XFL, and the Atlanta Falcons. 2008 will be his second season with the Saints.

General Manager Mickey Loomis is just as important to the Saints organization as Payton. Over the last few years, Loomis has been especially adept at bringing successful low draft picks and undrafted players to the team. In 2006, he hit big on guard Jahri Evans and receiver Marques Colston. Running back Pierre Thomas, an undrafted rookie free agent in 2007, was a very pleasant surprise. This front office team is poised for consistent success over time.

New York Giants

Week 14: David Akers lines up for a 57-yard field-goal attempt that would tie a game between the 5-7 Eagles and 8-4 Giants at 16. The kick hits the upright and bounces out; if it bounces in, and the Eagles go on to win in overtime, the resulting three-game Eagles' winning streak pushes them, not the Giants, into the playoffs by virtue of a tiebreaker.

NFC Championship Game: Eli Manning drops back to pass in the first quarter, with the score 3-0, but he is pressured and forces a throw at the last moment. It strikes Packers' defensive end Cullen Jenkins, with an open field and blockers in front of him, square in the hands and falls harmlessly to the ground.

Super Bowl XLII: The Giants are on their final drive of the fourth quarter, down 14-10. Manning drops back to pass but is once again forced to hurry his throw. He steps up and throws an out pattern but misses badly with the throw. It's only after the throw is out that he sees Patriots' All-Pro cornerback Asante Samuel, lurking underneath in zone coverage, doing his best to success-fully lure Manning into making an ill-advised pass. Samuel takes several steps back, settles himself, leaps . . . and has the uncontested ball, the interception that would seal the game, the perfect season, his huge free agent deal, a lifetime of endorsements and fame, the pinnacle of his career, his legacy . . . run right through his fingertips and out of bounds. On the very next play, Manning somehow escapes several New England rushers and hits David Tyree on one of the most famous plays in Super Bowl history.

It's easy to create a narrative in which players take huge, permanent leaps forward in skill in the light of an improbable run to victory. It's even easier when Eli Manning plays significantly better at a time of huge importance. Assigning him traits and spells based upon outcomes that existed because previously poor processes and decisions ended up avoiding danger, though? That's lazy journalism. Eli Manning isn't a better player because Asante Samuel didn't catch that duck. He's not a better player because David Tyree made a miraculous catch. He's not worse because he threw three interceptions that were returned for touchdowns against Minnesota 10 weeks before. The same quarterback made all those throws. Some outcomes were more fortunate than others. Judging Manning's ability based on those outcomes is like crediting your neighbor for buying the one house in the neighborhood that has oil underneath it.

In a media cycle that demands immediate explanation and judgment of events, however, those are the sort of storylines that get pushed out—especially when something unforeseen takes place, like the worst team to make the postseason (according to regular-season DVOA) ending the year as Super Bowl champions. This kind of thing is not exclusive to Eli Manning, mind you; how much of Tom Brady's clutch mythology has to do with the Rams throwing out a prevent defense for eight consecutive plays, or John Kasay kicking a ball out of bounds? Mistakes and poor performances are ignored if they don't match the best-fit narrative, and once a

---

GIANTS PROSPECTUS

2007 Record: 10-6

Pythagorean Wins: 8.6 (13th)

DVOA: 0.0% total (15th), -1.1% weighted (21st)

Offense: -2.3% DVOA (19th)

Defense: -3.1% DVOA (14th)

Special Teams: -0.8% DVOA (20th)

Variance: 8.6 % (3rd)

2007: Perhaps the most improbable championship run in the history of American professional sports.

2008: They should be better than the regular-season Giants and not as good as the postseason ones.

2008 Mean Projection: 9.6 wins

On the Clock (0-3): 0%

Loserville (4-6): 8%

Mediocrity (7-8): 22%

Playoff Contender (9-10): 38%

Super Bowl Contender (11+): 32%

Projected Average Opponent: 2.7% DVOA (12th in NFL)

2008 Giants Schedule

Week	Opp.	Week	Opp.	Week	Opp.
1	WAS (Thu.)	7	SF	13	at WAS
2	at STL	8	at PIT	14	PHI
3	CIN	9	DAL	15	at DAL
4	BYE	10	at PHI	16	CAR
5	SEA	11	BAL	17	at MIN
6	at CLE (Mon.)	12	at ARI		

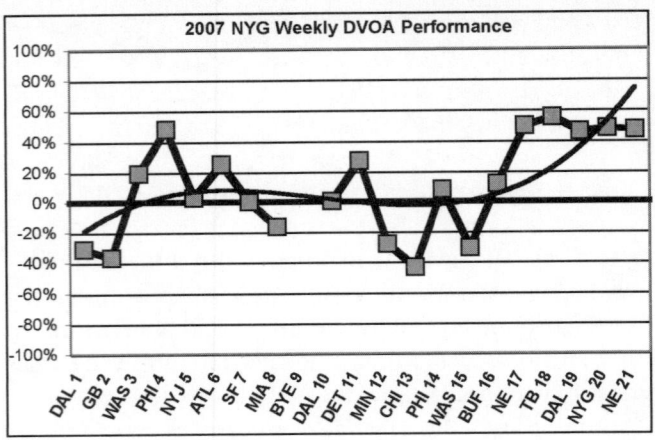

Figure 1

player has obtained his label, he's got it until defini-tively proven otherwise. It's inherent to deadline jour-nalism. More often than not, results are used to justify the validity of the events that preceded them, regard-less of actual probabilities.

By looking at what conventional wisdom says about the Giants' extraordinary postseason run and analyzing the processes that created those storylines, we can best understand how the Giants managed to shock the world and how likely those events are to recur in 2008.

ELI MANNING MATURED AND LED HIS TEAM TO THE SUPER BOWL

This one is a self-fulfilling prophecy. Let's be honest: Manning won the Super Bowl MVP because he was the most prominent skill-position player on the winning team. Simply stating that he is now a top quarterback "because he owns a Super Bowl MVP award" is falla-cious. A look at Manning's 2007 performance reveals that he is no different than he was before the post-season: a talented player with flaws that prevent him from being a consistently elite quarterback.

Remember that before the Patriots' game in Week 17, Eli Manning was playing so poorly that writers in New York were questioning whether he would be the team's starting quarterback in 2008. After the Giants' 41-17 loss at home against the Vikings in Week 12, the first game in a horrific five-game stretch for Manning, Har-vey Araton of the *New York Times* wrote:

It appears to be that time of year again, when the Meadowlands wind starts whipping and the leaves are almost done falling, and Tom Cough-lin's jaw starts dropping as he watches Eli Man-ning throw incomprehensible pass after pass and wonders, Is this all there is?

During that five-game stretch, Manning's perfor-mance (Table 1) was not below average. It was not even abysmal. It was downright grotesque. Manning's com-pletion percentage over the five-game span was the second-worst for any quarterback throwing 15 or more attempts in a given five-game span over the DVOA era (1995-2007). Manning's defenders blamed it on the weather, but opposing quarterbacks performed signifi-cantly better than he did under the same conditions and those quarterbacks weren't exactly a murderer's row: Tarvaris Jackson, Rex Grossman, Donovan Mc-Nabb, Todd Collins, and Trent Edwards.

Table 1. Eli Manning vs. Opposing Quarterbacks, Weeks 12-16

	Att	Comp	C%	Yds	Yd/Pa	TD	INT
Manning	175	79	45.1%	982	5.61	4	8
Opponents	148	72	48.6%	931	6.29	5	3

So, of course, it was a minor miracle when Manning's performance dramatically improved in the four playoff games. Even during the playoffs, Manning still one-hopped and two-hopped too many throws, particularly on checkdowns. A fair number of his important comple-tions were also poor throws. The wounded duck to Steve Smith that kept the two-minute drill alive at the end of the first half of the Cowboys' game comes to mind. So does the lob to Amani Toomer in the first quarter of the Super Bowl. Manning should be given credit for some of the great throws he made in big situations, such as his howitzer-like touchdown pass to Tyree to give the Giants an early fourth quarter lead in the Super Bowl. Nonethe-less, it isn't logical to assign him much credit for, say, Toomer's touchdown catch against the Cowboys, where the receiver juked out one Cowboys defensive back and had Ken Hamlin and Roy Williams run into each other while attempting to make a tackle.

What Manning should be given credit for is his improved accuracy in the playoffs on short and intermediate routes (Table 2). Manning's footwork in 2008 was significantly better than in previous years, and he was concise in the playoffs at setting up at the right depths relative to his protection and picking apart zone defenses. That should stick around in 2008; expecting a quarterback who led the league in interceptions to throw just one every four games, on the other hand, is wishcasting based on unlikely outcomes.

Table 2. Eli Manning by Pass Distance

	Short (6 Yds)	Medium (6-15 Yds)	Deep (16+ Yds)
Pass distribution, Weeks 1-16	47%	32%	21%
Pass distribution, Weeks 17-21	36%	46%	18%
Completion percentage, Weeks 1-16	63%	56%	37%
Completion percentage, Weeks 17-21	74%	67%	37%

THE DEFENSIVE LINE SUFFOCATED QUARTERBACKS

No one disputes that the Giants' defensive line, particularly Michael Strahan and Justin Tuck, dominated the Patriots' offensive line in Super Bowl XLII. In particular, Tuck's abuse of Patriots' Pro Bowl left guard Logan Mankins in the first half was downright Tecmo Bowl. It's another overly easy narrative to claim that the Giants' pass rush carried them to and through the Super Bowl, but realistically, that wasn't the case.

The Giants' defensive line dominated parts of the first three playoff games, but they were held in check for most of those games. Against Tampa Bay, the Giants pressured Jeff Garcia heavily in the first half, particularly with Michael Strahan abusing Tampa Bay right tackle Jeremy Trueblood. As the game went on and Tampa Bay went to more max protect schemes, the Giants weren't able to get to Garcia.

For the first three quarters of the Cowboys game, the Giants defensive line was silent. Although they did a reliable job against the run, it wasn't until the first Cowboys possession of the fourth quarter that the Giants front seven even sniffed Romo. In fact, when they pressured Romo into two incomplete passes on second and third down, FOX announcer Joe Buck flat-out said, "That whole series, the Giants *finally* got pressure on Romo." From that point forward, the Giants pass rush was fantastic, but it was strictly a fourth-quarter phenomenon.

Against the Packers, the pressure was barely there; Brett Favre wasn't sacked once and was barely touched all game. His poor performance was due to simply being inaccurate, something which was accredited to the -1°F weather and . . .

COREY WEBSTER BECAME A SHUTDOWN CORNER

Webster started the year as the Giants' number-two cornerback. After two and a half games and some of the worst run support you'll ever see, Webster was benched. He fell off the active roster in Week 10 and alternated between being inactive and playing just special teams for four weeks, slowly working his way back into rotation. Then, when Sam Madison went down with an injury in Week 17, Webster suddenly became the guy that the Giants were relying on to guard the other team's top wideout.

Amazingly, it mostly worked. Webster was hailed as a new man following four games in which he spent most of his time against legitimately elite receivers in man coverage, intercepted two passes, and recovered a fumble.

Analyzing Webster on a play-by-play basis, though, reveals that while Webster was far better than at the beginning of the season, he was also playing with fire for most of the playoffs. Tampa Bay went right after Webster, but Jeff Garcia's throws were erratic at best, particularly down the field, and Webster capitalized with an interception on an awful Garcia pass into good coverage.

Dallas saw him matched up against Terrell Owens with a healthy quarterback in Tony Romo, and Webster's day was far less impressive. Owens beat him on a lob pass for the Cowboys' first score, and it was only the start for Owens, who consistently got open all afternoon. Webster had a chance to make a big play when a Romo pass to Terry Glenn hit him right in the hands, but he bobbled it away. On back-to-back plays, Owens badly beat Webster on a hitch-and-go—only to drop a pass that went through his hands—and then Patrick Crayton went up one-on-one against Webster and caught a jump ball for a first down. On the Cowboys' final drive, Webster took a penalty against Owens for a Dallas first down, and on the penultimate play of the game, Crayton beat him to the end zone, only to have Romo overthrow him. Webster's play against the Cowboys was uneven at best.

He was better in Green Bay, but two dramatic plays stand out. He lost his footing against Donald Driver when trying to jam him at the line, and the result was a 90-yard touchdown. On the flip side, his interception in overtime gave the Giants a chance to kick the game-winning field goal. Giving the credit for the play to Webster would be, again, disingenuous: Webster was beat on the play, and Favre threw the wrong route. As Clark Judge of cbssportsline.com noted in his postgame report:

> Driver had three steps on his defender and was wide open for the delivery. Only the delivery was three steps behind, hitting Webster between the 2 and 3 of his white jersey. "I just didn't throw it outside enough. I just didn't get it out far enough," a somber Favre said afterward.

Webster had an impressive Super Bowl, but backdating that performance to the entire postseason is simply inaccurate.

THE GIANTS WERE ROAD WARRIORS

The Giants came into the playoffs with only a 3-5 home record, supplemented by a 7-1 road record that would be 11-1 by the time the playoffs were over. From 1983 to 2006, only 11 teams had a regular season road record two or more games better than their home record (Table 3). Those teams went a combined 1-5 on the road in the playoffs and were only 3-6 overall. The road warrior phenomenon simply doesn't exist.

Furthermore, in a sobering thought for Giants fans, the good-on-the-road thing appears to be a fluke. Teams that fit this criteria were an average of two games worse on the road than at home the year before the road warrior year and were a half-game worse on the road than they were at home the next year. The average NFL team over the same time span was 1.28 games better at home than they were on the road. That's classic regression to the mean. All in all, those 11 teams averaged nearly two fewer wins the year after their road warrior season, with only the 3-13 Redskins improving by more than a game.

Not everything that was written about the Giants' playoff run was untrue. The most prominent piece of correct conventional wisdom has to do with a draft that broke two media clichés into pieces. Although the media will forget this story as soon as the next veteran-laden, playoff-experienced, Old Spice-commercial-spouting team rolls around, the Giants got major contributions in all four postseason games from a bunch of rookies who had no NFL experience before last year, let alone any NFL playoff experience. For what it's worth, every year we write an article on Football-Outsiders.com compiling the draft grades of the "experts" and looking at which drafts were most praised, most criticized, or caused the most disagreement. When we wrote this article after the 2007 draft, the Giants' consensus rank among the experts was 22nd in the league.

First-round pick Aaron Ross emerged as the team's best cornerback despite separating his shoulder and missing most of the Cowboys game, while Steve Smith developed as a zone-buster in the vein of Bobby En-

Table 3. Why Don't We Do It on the Road? Teams Far Better Away from Home, 1983-2007

Year	Team	That Year			Prior Year			Next Year			Total Change in Wins Next Year
		Home Wins	Road Wins	Dif	Home Wins	Road Wins	Dif	Home Wins	Road Wins	Dif	
2007	CAR	2	5	3	4	4	0	—	—	—	—
2007	NYG	3	7	4	3	5	2	—	—	—	—
2002	CLE	3	6	3	4	3	-1	2	3	1	-4
2001	NYJ	3	7	4	5	4	-1	5	4	-1	-1
2001	PHI	4	7	3	5	6	1	7	5	-2	1
2000	NO	3	7	4	3	0	-3	3	4	1	-3
1997	CAR	2	5	3	8	4	-4	2	2	0	-3
1996	HOU	2	6	4	3	4	1	6	2	-4	0
1994	WAS	0	3	3	3	1	-2	4	2	-2	3
1987	SF	5	8	3	6*	4	-2	4	6	2	-3
1986	ATL	2*	5	2	3	1	-2	2	1	-1	-4
1986	DET	1	4	3	6	1	-5	1	3	2	-1
1986	NE	4	7	3	7	5	-2	5	3	-2	-3
Non-2007 Averages			3.2			-2.0			-0.5		-1.7

*In 1986, the Falcons and 49ers played a tie in Atlanta, included in the averages as half a win.

gram, which is high praise. Jay Alford was a fearsome pass-rusher on the interior, Zak DeOssie was a valuable special teams contributor, and Michael Johnson started five games as a league-average safety. Tight end Kevin Boss played so well that fans started calling for the head of injured tight end Jeremy Shockey in a classic "correlation simply *has* to be causation" move. Shockey is a much better blocker than Boss and runs deeper routes than the younger, slower tight end, who's limited to running the crossing patterns and ins that Manning is simply better at throwing.

The most prominent contributor, though, was seventh-round halfback Ahmad Bradshaw, who emerged in the playoffs as the proverbial lightning to Brandon Jacobs's thunder. Bradshaw got his chance after beating out Ryan Grant for a roster spot in training camp (with Grant getting dealt to Green Bay and having his career take off in the process), but it took an injury to the also impressive Derrick Ward and a strong whiff of Reuben Droughns before Bradshaw got his shot. Bradshaw's quick cuts and vicious attacking of holes made him an immediate fan favorite, and in the playoffs he was the Giants' cooler back, taking over in the fourth quarter and seemingly picking up successful run after successful run. Bradshaw's still got a ways to go on improving his pass blocking and receiving out of the backfield, but he's an intelligent player—unfortunately, he's not subtle, which came into play during the win over the Patriots, when he casually batted a fumbled ball forward to Steve Smith for what would have been a Giants first down but was, instead, a penalty.

Speaking of which, one of the most prominent—but unspoken—forces behind the Giants' Super Bowl victory was fumble recovery. As we've written many times, forcing fumbles is a skill. Recovering fumbles is luck, plain and simple. The Giants forced three fumbles and recovered two; they themselves fumbled seven times and lost only one. Furthermore, several of these fumble recoveries came in huge, game-changing situations (Table 4).

The other factor that emerged as a real motivator for the Giants' success was the mellowing of Tom Coughlin. The team had quit on Coughlin at points in both 2005 and 2006, struggling dramatically under a militant style that grew tiresome by the end of each season. Even if the Giants had failed to make the playoffs this year, Coughlin deserved to retain his job by being willing to change a style that obviously didn't fit a team with strong veteran leadership.

The win projections in *Pro Football Prospectus 2007* predicted the Giants to win roughly seven games, and some of our writers expected them to be even worse because of the intangibles our statistics don't see. We pegged Coughlin to be a lame-duck coach, anticipated that Strahan would be halfhearted after nearly retiring in preseason, and didn't think utility lineman David Diehl was good enough to start at left tackle. Instead, Coughlin radically changed the way he related to his players, Strahan had a fantastic year, and Diehl was good enough on running plays to mitigate his league-leading 11 sacks allowed. The Giants' line as a whole was the second-healthiest in football in 2007. The Giants finished 10-6, but DVOA pegged their performance during the season to be worth, with a normal level of luck, 8.0 wins. Our subjective predictions about the Giants were way off, but the empirical forecast in the book really was not. The Giants were an average team . . . until January.

Our 2008 projection for the Giants sees them splitting the difference between the mediocrity of the regular season and the strong, well-balanced squad that beat three of the best teams in the league during the playoffs. Even without any knowledge of his playoff performance, KUBIAK projects Manning to have the best season of his career. The team will get back several injured players who missed the playoff run, including

Table 4. Giants' Fumble Luck in Playoffs

Opp	Fumble Situation	Score	Result
TB	Garcia fumbles after Strahan sack	7-6	Garcia falls on it, Buccaneers punt
TB	Spurlock fumbles opening kickoff of 2nd half	14-7	Giants recover on TB 32 and kick eventual GW FG
GB	Burress fumbles on GB 17 after 21-yard gain	3-0	Ball rolls out of bounds at GB 12; kick FG
GB	O'Hara fumbles snap on NYG 5	6-7	Manning recovers and throws incomplete pass
GB	Jacobs fumbles on GB 1	6-7	Boss recovers; Jacobs scores TD three plays later
GB	McQuarters fumbles on NYG 19 following INT	20-17	Tauscher recovers; Packers kick FG to tie game
GB	McQuarters fumbles punt on GB 38 with 2:30 left	20-20	Jarrett Bush has hands on ball and tries to advance but fails; Domenik Hixon recovers; Giants eventually miss FG
NE	Jacobs fumbles handoff on NYG 32	3-7	Pierre Woods immediately falls on it but Bradshaw grabs it away in pile; Giants eventually punt
NE	Manning stripped from behind	3-7	Bradshaw bats ball to Smith for first down but is called for illegal batting; Giants punt
NE	Brady stripped by Tuck	3-7	Giants recover and stop Pats drive; throw two incomplete passes to end half

Shockey, running back Derrick Ward, and linebacker Mathias Kiwanuka. They lost only two starters, linebacker Kawika Mitchell and safety Gibril Wilson, the latter of whom should be replaced immediately by first-round pick Kenny Phillips. As we go to press, Strahan is considering retirement for the second offseason in a row; losing their defensive leader would cause the Giants' projection to drop about half a win.

The team projection system knows that the Giants have continuity on the offensive line and that Amani Toomer and Shaun O'Hara are the only offensive starters not in their prime. It knows that Manning was better on first and second down than he was on third down, a sign that he will improve this year. However, the projection system also sees those well-timed fumble recoveries, the unusually healthy offensive line, the outperforming of Pythagoras, and the unlikely performance on the road. It doesn't factor these things into a positive projection because they're not likely to recur. Without them, the Giants are a good team but not the world-beaters of the postseason.

If David Akers's kick bounces in and Philadelphia winds up in the playoffs instead of New York, the Giants would have undoubtedly fired Tom Coughlin and Giants fans would have slammed Eli Manning as a failure for ending the season on such a sour note. Wholesale changes would have ensued and the 2007 Giants would be seen as a failure, not a champion. Would the Giants have been any less talented had that field-goal attempt bounced in? Of course not. Should they be lauded for their incredible playoff run? Most certainly, but it's that tiny margin, that little lucky bounce that the Giants got, that represents the reason why we at Football Outsiders look at the process of how a team performed during the year, not just the outcome.

Bill Barnwell

How Improbable Was the Giants' Championship?

When Tampa Bay lost to the Giants in the wild card game, fans were surprised. When Dallas went down a week later, fans were startled. When Green Bay fell in the NFC Championship game, fans were shocked. And when the unbeatable Patriots were finally beaten, fans were gobsmacked, floored, ambushed, struck dumb, and astonished.

Except for the Giants themselves and their most optimistic fans, no one saw this coming. During the 2007 regular season, no other team that eventually made the

playoffs outscored its opponents by a smaller amount or lost the turnover battle by a larger one. What are the odds that New York would have beaten Tampa Bay, Dallas, Green Bay, and New England? What are the odds that any team would pull off that four-game sweep?

To a degree, we can answer that question with two tools: the Pythagorean theorem and the log5 method. Like many other sports statistics, these were both developed by baseball statistician Bill James. The Pythagorean theorem projects a team's winning percentage based on points scored and allowed (and is introduced with more detail in the "Statistical Toolbox" earlier in the book). The log5 method predicts the odds of one team defeating another, taking the strength of both teams into account. (More on the log5 method can be found in this article at Diamond Mind Baseball: http://www.diamond-mind.com/articles/playoff2002. htm.)

The difficulty of the Giants' playoff slate can be determined in two ways. We can estimate the odds of the Giants running the table, but the Giants finished the regular season with a Pythagorean projection of only .536, the lowest of any Super Bowl champion. Unless they had faced an extremely weak playoff field, the log5 method would naturally assume that the Giants' four-game winning streak was the least likely of any Super Bowl champion.

Instead, we'll measure each Super Bowl winner's playoff schedule in two ways: the odds of that particular team running the table and the odds of a "typical" Super Bowl champion with a .750 Pythagorean winning percentage pulling off the same feat. (The average Pythagorean projection for a Super Bowl champion is .757 and the median is .759.) Plenty of factors could throw this number off—injuries, home-field advantage, strength of schedule, overall league strength—but it should be fairly accurate for most teams. Table 5 gives us a look at the Giants' four opponents, along with the odds of winning for both the Giants and our .750 typical Super Bowl champion.

Table 5. New York's 2007 Postseason Chances

Team	Pyth%	2007 Giants	"Typical" Odds
Tampa Bay	.623	41.1%	64.5%
Dallas	.689	34.2%	57.5%
Green Bay	.722	30.8%	53.6%
New England	.860	15.8%	32.8%

These numbers were calculated using the Giants' regular-season record alone. We could add the results of each progressive playoff game, but the numbers would change very little and we're going to compare New York to other Super Bowl winners, whose ratings would also improve as the playoffs progressed.

Multiplying the four percentages leaves us with a very small number; the log5 method gives the Giants merely a 0.7 percent chance of reaching and winning the Super Bowl against that schedule. That is not a typo: If they faced that schedule 1,000 times, log5 would expect them to win the Super Bowl only seven times. These are the lowest odds out of any of the 42 Super Bowl champions. The fact that the Giants *did* win the Super Bowl does not necessarily mean they were lucky to do so. It means that faced with a longer and more difficult road than any Super Bowl winner before them, they still emerged triumphant and should be celebrated for that.

Our typical Super Bowl champion, facing that same schedule, would have about a 6.5 percent chance of winning the Super Bowl. That makes this a difficult slate but not the most difficult of all time. That honor goes to John Madden, Ken Stabler, and the rest of the 1976 Oakland Raiders, which is all the more remarkable given that the Raiders played only three playoff games.

The Raiders began their postseason run with a 24-21 win over the Steve Grogan-Sam Cunningham Patriots (Pythagorean: .751) in the divisional round, the infamous "Sugar Bear Hamilton Roughing the Passer Game." Next, the Raiders squared off against the Pittsburgh Steelers, whose Steel Curtain defense was at its absolute peak. The defending champion Steelers had won their final nine regular-season games, and only once in those nine games did they allow seven or more points. They pitched five shutouts, including three in a row, and finished with a Pythagorean projection of .896. That is not only higher than the 2007 Patriots but the highest of any team since the AFL-NFL merger. The Steelers whipped the Baltimore Colts 40-14 in the opening round of the playoffs but in the process lost both of their leading rushers, Franco Harris and Rocky Bleier, to injury. Without their ground game, they were no match for the Raiders, who won the AFC Championship 24-7. Oakland then finished off the Minnesota Vikings (Pythagorean: .786) to win Super Bowl XI. The typical champion, facing this schedule, would have just a 5.8 percent chance of taking home the Lombardi trophy. Table 6 shows the 10 most unlikely Super Bowl champions, ranked by the odds of that particular team winning the Super Bowl against that particular schedule. (For a complete table with all 42 Super Bowl champions, visit http://www.footballoutsiders.com/2008/02/12/ramblings/stat-analysis/6101/.)

The last three Super Bowl winners have each been among the five least likely champions of all time. All

Table 6. Against All Odds: The 10 Most Unlikely Super Bowl Champions

Team	Year	Pyth%	Games	Specific Team Odds	"Typical" Odds
NYG	2007	.536	4	0.7%	6.5%
IND	2006	.600	4	1.3%	6.2%
OAK	1980	.601	4	3.5%	12.9%
OAK	1976	.716	3	4.2%	5.8%
PIT	2005	.726	4	5.5%	7.1%
GB	1967	.694	3	5.6%	8.2%
SF	1988	.631	3	5.9%	14.6%
NYJ	1968	.722	2	6.5%	8.0%
NE	2001	.676	3	7.2%	12.8%
BAL	2000	.766	4	9.0%	7.7%

three teams faced difficult schedules. The Giants and Steelers had to beat teams that flirted with perfection, while the Colts beat three teams—the Ravens, Patriots, and Bears—with Pythagorean winning percentages above .750. Five of the 10 most unlikely Super Bowl winners had to win four playoff games; most Super Bowl champions had to win only three. That does make their schedules more difficult, but it's not the deciding factor.

If we ignore the wild card round and look only at each team's chances of winning their final three playoff games, the Giants and Colts still rank 1-2 and the Steelers are still in the top 10 (Table 7).

Table 7. Three the Hard Way: The 10 Most Unlikely Playoff Streaks, Post-Wild Card

Team	Year	Pyth%	Games	Specific Team Odds	"Typical" Odds
NYG	2007	.536	3	1.7%	10.1%
IND	2006	.600	3	2.2%	8.4%
OAK	1976	.716	3	4.2%	5.8%
GB	1967	.694	3	5.6%	8.2%
SF	1988	.631	3	5.9%	14.6%
NYJ	1968	.722	2	6.5%	8.0%
OAK	1980	.601	3	6.9%	19.2%
NE	2001	.676	3	7.2%	12.8%
PIT	2005	.726	3	8.7%	10.7%
LA RAI	1983	.654	3	13.6%	24.3%

At the other end of the spectrum are the 1979 Pittsburgh Steelers, the Super Bowl champion with the easiest postseason schedule based on the Pythagorean projection of a typical Super Bowl winner. Their first playoff opponents, the Miami Dolphins, were their most difficult, with a Pythagorean projection of .662. They then beat two mediocre teams—the Houston Oilers (.553) and the Los Angeles Rams (.526)—to win the

Super Bowl. The next easiest playoff slates belong to the 1995 Cowboys and the 1999 Rams.

If the Giants were the most surprising Super Bowl champion ever, those 1999 Rams were the least surprising. Considering not only the opponents they faced but also how good the Rams were themselves, they came out with a 52.8 percent chance of beating the Vikings (.602), Buccaneers (.582), and Titans (.611). Only one other Super Bowl champion had at least a 50 percent chance of sweeping their postseason foes: the 1985 Chicago Bears. The lesson here is that winning the Super Bowl is really, really hard. Here we have two great teams, one with a historically great offense and the other with a historically great defense, each facing relatively weak competition. Yet each was basically an even-money bet to not win the Super Bowl. (Last year's Patriots would have been the third such team. Things didn't work out that way.)

New England fans can take some solace in the fact that two teams with even higher Pythagorean projections than the 2007 Patriots have also lost Super Bowls: the 1969 Minnesota Vikings (.923) and the 1968 Baltimore Colts (.919). The fact that both teams lost to oppo-

nents from the so-called inferior AFL gives us some good evidence that public perception of the difference between the AFL and NFL before the merger was *really* off.

The Patriots, it turns out, aren't even the first team to see an undefeated season spoiled by the Giants in the championship game. In 1934, three full decades before the first Super Bowl, the 8-5 Giants (.680) beat the 13-0 Chicago Bears (.945) in the NFL Championship. This became known as "The Sneakers Game." Freezing rain overnight left the playing surface at the Polo Grounds as slick as a hockey rink. Trailing 10-3 at halftime, Giants' head coach Steve Owen frantically acquired sneakers for his team to wear instead of their football cleats. The extra traction proved to be a huge boost, and Chicago head coach George Halas was never able to adjust. The Giants scored four touchdowns in the second half, winning by a final score of 30-13. The log5 method predicts that the Giants had just an 11.0 percent chance of winning that game—proof that you never know who'll win until you lace 'em up.

Vince Verhei

2007 Giants Stats by Week

Wk	vs.	W-L	PF	PA	YDF	YDA	TO	Total	Off	Def	ST
1	@DAL	L	35	45	438	478	+1	-31%	36%	68%	1%
2	GB	L	13	35	325	368	-1	-37%	-8%	22%	-7%
3	@WAS	W	24	17	315	260	-2	19%	2%	-25%	-8%
4	PHI	W	16	3	212	190	0	48%	0%	-52%	-4%
5	NYJ	W	35	24	374	277	+1	3%	4%	-20%	-21%
6	@ATL	W	31	10	491	284	-2	25%	27%	3%	1%
7	SF	W	33	15	279	267	+3	0%	2%	-3%	-5%
8	@MIA	W	13	10	238	245	+1	-17%	-18%	-8%	-7%
9	BYE										
10	DAL	L	20	31	300	323	-1	0%	6%	5%	0%
11	@DET	W	16	10	341	376	+2	27%	-12%	-24%	14%
12	MIN	L	17	41	309	251	-4	-28%	-41%	-9%	4%
13	@CHI	W	21	16	356	312	-4	-44%	-19%	20%	-5%
14	@PHI	W	16	13	318	306	-1	8%	-4%	-4%	8%
15	WAS	L	10	22	307	309	-1	-31%	-16%	11%	-4%
16	@BUF	W	38	21	383	244	0	11%	-29%	-38%	2%
17	NE	L	35	38	316	390	-1	50%	40%	6%	16%
18	@TB	W	24	14	277	271	+3	55%	43%	-5%	7%
19	@DAL	W	21	17	230	336	+1	46%	34%	0%	11%
20	@GB	W	23	20	377	264	+1	48%	10%	-46%	-9%
21	@NE	W	17	14	338	274	0	47%	6%	-43%	-2%

Trends and Splits

	Offense	Rank	Defense	Rank
Total DVOA	-2.3%	19	-3.1%	14
Unadjusted VOA	-3.5%	19	-1.0%	15
Weighted Trend	-7.5%	22	-4.2%	11
Variance	4.8%	7	7.6%	19
Average Opponent	1.1%	19	2.0%	14
Passing	-10.0%	24	1.3%	15
Rushing	5.7%	7	-8.5%	10
First Down	3.2%	12	-4.5%	12
Second Down	-3.3%	17	-1.0%	12
Third Down	-11.1%	23	3.6%	9
First Half	-3.1%	19	2.0%	18
Second Half	-1.6%	21	-8.4%	7
Red Zone	3.6%	16	22.3%	27
Late and Close	-3.2%	18	-12.1%	8

Five-Year Performance

Year	W-L	Pyth Wins	Est Wins	PF	PA	TO	Total	Rank	Off	Rank	Def	Rank	ST	Rank
2003	4-12	4.0	5.6	243	387	-16	-21.1%	30	-13.8%	28	2.3%	20	-5.1%	30
2004	6-10	6.7	6.4	303	347	+4	12.1%	22	-6.8%	25	5.9%	21	0.7%	15
2005	11-5	10.7	10.4	422	314	+12	20.3%	8	9.0%	9	-6.9%	11	4.4%	2
2006	8-8	7.8	9.0	355	362	0	11.1%	8	8.6%	9	-2.1%	13	0.4%	16
2007	10-6	8.6	8.0	373	351	-9	0.0%	15	-2.3%	19	-3.1%	14	-0.8%	20

Strategic Tendencies

Run/Pass		Rank	Offense		Rank	Defense		Rank	Other		Rank
Runs, all plays	43%	10	3+ WR	49%	16	Rush 3	7.9%	8	2+ RB, Pct Runs	63%	9
Runs, first half	41%	15	4+ WR	3%	32	Rush 4	54.4%	26	1 RB/2 TE, Pct Runs	52%	12
Runs, first down	49%	18	2+ TE	20%	21	Rush 5	27.2%	9	1 RB/3+ WR, Pct Runs	23%	17
Runs, second-long	43%	4	Single back	56%	16	Rush 6+	10.6%	10	CB1 on WR1	62%	2
Runs, power sit.	78%	1	Play action	23%	5	Rush 7+	2.1%	12	Go for it on 4th	1.00	19
Runs, behind 2H	38%	2	Max protect	10%	13	Sacks by LB	19.2%	21	Offensive Pace	31.6	23
Pass, ahead 2H	44%	19	Outside pocket	10%	18	Sacks by DB	4.8%	21	Defensive Pace	30.6	13

The Giants' only positive passing DVOA came on three-wide receiver sets. ✏ The Giants spread the ball across the field quite evenly, throwing a third of their passes each to the left, middle, and right. In 2006, they threw to the left less than any other team. ✏ No team had a lower offensive DVOA with four or five wide receivers, and only one team ran fewer four- and five-wide sets in short-yardage situations. ✏ The Giants ranked fifth in use of the draw but never ran one from a four-wide set. No team ran more draw plays on third down with 10 or more yards to go. ✏ Eli Manning was hurried on a below-average percentage of pass plays, but when he was hurried—during the regular season, at least—he had the worst DVOA of any quarterback with at least 30 passes under pressure. ✏ The Giants led the league in percentage of dropped passes. ✏ The Giants big-blitzed far more often than they did in 2006, sending six or more pass rushers on more than three times as many plays. ✏ The Giants blitzed on first and third downs more often than on second downs. ✏ Not only did the Giants lead the league in Adjusted Sack Rate overall, but their ASR of 12.6 percent on third down was more than three percentage points higher than any other NFL defense. ✏ No team did more to keep their best cornerback (Sam Madison) on the opposition's top receiver. Because of this, charters listed Madison in coverage for an equal number of passes on the left and right sides. By comparison, Al Harris was on the left more than twice as often as he was on the right, Sheldon Brown was on the left four times as often as he was on the right, and Asante Samuel was on the right *15 times* as often as he was on the left.

Passing

Player	DYAR	DVOA	Plays	NtYds	Avg	YAC	C%	TD	Int
Eli Manning	-70	-13.1%	560	3161	5.6	4.4	56.4%	23	19
Jared Lorenzen	-21	-42.4%	9	23	2.6	1.5	50.0%	0	0
Anthony Wright	0	-11.4%	7	12	1.7	9.0	14.3%	0	0
David Carr	-171	-29.1%	152	599	3.9	3.9	53.7%	3	5

Rushing

Player	DYAR	DVOA	Plays	Yds	Avg	TD	Fum	Suc
Brandon Jacobs	220	18.3%	201	1017	5.1	4	5	57%
Derrick Ward	112	13.0%	125	598	4.8	3	2	46%
Reuben Droughns	-9	-10.6%	85	274	3.2	6	1	47%
Ahmad Bradshaw	59	50.5%	23	190	8.3	1	0	61%
Eli Manning	11	-0.9%	16	83	5.2	1	11	—
David Carr	2	-9.9%	14	60	4.3	0	1	—

Receiving

Player	DYAR	DVOA	Plays	Ctch	Yds	Y/C	YAC	TD	C%
WR									
Plaxico Burress	139	-0.6%	141	70	1025	14.6	4.0	12	50%
Amani Toomer	133	3.1%	104	59	760	12.9	3.5	3	57%
Sinorice Moss	-39	-26.2%	37	21	225	10.7	3.4	0	57%
Steve Smith	-4	-15.8%	14	8	63	7.9	2.5	0	57%
Anthony Mix*	6	4.6%	5	3	39	13.0	5.7	0	60%
David Tyree	-2	-17.1%	5	4	35	8.8	4.5	0	80%
TE									
Jeremy Shockey	63	3.0%	93	57	619	10.9	4.1	6	61%
Kevin Boss	48	43.9%	14	9	118	13.1	3.7	2	64%
Michael Matthews	-47	-60.8%	13	6	28	4.7	2.2	0	46%
RB									
Derrick Ward	-15	-20.4%	40	26	179	6.9	7.0	1	65%
Brandon Jacobs	-17	-21.6%	38	23	174	7.6	7.9	2	61%
Reuben Droughns	-28	-52.4%	15	7	49	7.0	5.6	0	47%
Madison Hedgecock	-7	-24.8%	11	6	45	7.5	5.3	0	55%
Ahmad Bradshaw	-14	-62.8%	5	2	12	6.0	2.0	0	40%

Offensive Line

Year	Yards	ALY	Rank	Power	Rank	10+ Yds	Rank	Stuff	Rank	Sack	ASR	Rank
2005	4.84	4.37	10	56%	27	27%	1	25%	16	28	5.3%	8
2006	4.99	4.61	4	71%	6	19%	9	25%	20	25	5.4%	7
2007	4.79	4.62	2	70%	7	20%	8	21%	7	28	5.1%	11

Year	LE	Rank	LT	Rank	Mid	Rank	RT	Rank	RE	Rank
2005	4.44	11	4.62	6	4.31	11	4.42	12	3.99	15
2006	5.27	3	3.69	29	4.45	12	4.65	4	5.46	3
2007	4.84	7	4.38	15	4.70	3	4.46	12	4.87	3

The question mark on the line coming into the season was left tackle David Diehl, who was making the rare move from utility lineman to the most difficult spot on the line. Diehl allowed 11 sacks and had a team-high eight penalties; his biggest problem was against bull rushers who would simply get underneath his pads and push him backwards into Manning. Diehl made up for it by being an effective run blocker, using his agility to get outside and seal the corner for Giants runners. The weak link of the line was left guard Rich Seubert, who's solid enough when asked to simply block the rusher in front of him but struggles mightily when pulling to either side, far too frequently failing to complete his assignment on the edge. The Giants' rushing offense revolves around the guards being able to successfully pull to either side on sweeps and tosses, which is why Seubert may not be long for a starting job despite signing a new contract in the offseason.

Right guard Chris Snee had a Pro Bowl-caliber year; Tom Coughlin's son-in-law stayed healthy and showed consistency in all facets of his game. He's particularly adept at getting a quick chip in, getting to the second level, and taking whichever linebacker he's matched up against out of the play. Center Shaun O'Hara also had an excellent season, highlighted by his pancake of Vince Wilfork on a fourth-and-1 on the Giants' final possession in the Super Bowl. Right tackle Kareem McKenzie is a solid run blocker but has difficulty with speed rushers and takes too many plays off when they're not in his direction; that can be a serious hindrance when Ahmad Bradshaw is in the game and looking for a cut back. Center/guard Grey Ruegamer is the team's utility interior lineman, and he's about as skilled as you would expect your backup guard to be. Tackle Guy Whimper was the developmental prospect who was supposed to move in at left tackle as soon as possible, but it's hard to see where Whimper fits in with Diehl and

Seubert both signing long-term contracts in the offseason. Since the terms of Seubert's contract are unknown, the likeliest scenario would see Diehl move inside to left guard and Whimper take over at left tackle.

Defensive Front Seven

Defensive Line	Age	Pos	Plays	TmPct	Rk	Stop	Dfts	Stop%	Rk	AvYd	Rk	Sack	Hit	Hur	Runs	RuStop	RuYd	Pass	PaStop	PaYd
Justin Tuck	25	DE	64	8.2%	10	55	29	86%	7	0.1	10	10.0	11	9	46	83%	1.2	18	94%	-2.7
Michael Strahan	37	DE	58	7.4%	19	48	23	83%	12	0.2	11	9.0	10	15	43	81%	1.5	15	87%	-3.7
Osi Umenyiora	28	DE	54	6.9%	25	38	20	70%	67	1.8	44	13.0	11	13	36	67%	3.7	18	78%	-1.9
Fred Robbins	31	DT	42	5.4%	28	36	12	86%	8	1.3	19	5.5	5	7	32	84%	1.9	10	90%	-0.6
Barry Cofield	24	DT	35	4.5%	48	26	7	74%	51	1.8	42	1.0	1	5	31	74%	1.9	4	75%	1.3

Linebackers	Age	Pos	Plays	TmPct	Rk	Stop	Dfts	Stop%	AvYd	Sack	Hit	Hur	Runs	RuStop	Rk	RuYd	Rk	Tgts	Suc%	Rk	APaYd	Rk
Antonio Pierce	30	MLB	108	13.8%	32	60	18	56%	5.6	1.0	3	4	62	66%	35	3.0	30	42	48%	49	6.6	62
Kawika Mitchell*	29	OLB	82	10.5%	64	54	18	66%	3.7	3.5	1	1	44	75%	11	2.8	21	32	57%	16	4.4	12
Mathias Kiwanuka	25	OLB	47	9.6%	—	30	13	64%	3.1	4.5	5	4	29	66%	—	3.0	—	10	46%	—	8.7	—
Reggie Torbor*	27	OLB	32	4.1%	—	18	4	56%	4.8	1.0	2	1	18	72%	—	2.6	—	10	36%	—	11.2	—
Danny Clark	31	OLB	44	6.6%	—	23	4	52%	4.3	0.0	1	4	28	64%	—	2.9	—	16	57%	17	4.6	15

Year	Yards	ALY	Rank	Power	Rank	10+ Yds	Rank	Stuff	Rank	Sack	ASR	Rank
2005	3.88	3.76	9	59%	13	20%	24	24%	19	41	6.5%	22
2006	3.74	3.85	5	70%	26	17%	19	26%	9	32	6.2%	19
2007	4.01	3.83	4	63%	17	20%	23	28%	7	53	8.8%	1

Year	LE	Rank	LT	Rank	Mid	Rank	RT	Rank	RE	Rank
2005	5.18	29	3.28	3	3.79	8	2.92	1	3.67	13
2006	3.55	9	3.00	2	4.25	16	2.82	1	4.84	27
2007	2.98	6	4.61	22	3.72	3	3.46	4	4.45	23

Everything here starts on the edges, where Michael Strahan and Osi Umenyiora serve as three-down ends who do everything well. Umenyiora actually had only an average year as a pass-rusher; remember, six of his 13 sacks came in one game. Strahan is arguably the best defensive lineman who ever lived when you consider his longevity, the quality of the talent he had to face, the rules he played under, and his ability against both the run and the pass. Although he had an incredible Super Bowl, his best playoff game was the divisional win over Tampa Bay, when he made the right side of the Buccaneers line look silly on a play-by-play basis. Justin Tuck emerged in 2007; at 274 pounds, he's ideally an end but serves as a defensive tackle on obvious passing downs, where isolated guards struggle with his speed. The regular rotation tackles, Barry Cofield, Fred Robbins, and Jay Alford, didn't see a double team all year. Their primary function is to play the run, but each has the ability to get to the passer if an offensive lineman tries to take a play off.

If Strahan retires, the Giants could choose to move Tuck to defensive end full-time or insert the fourth member of the team's "Four Aces" package, hybrid end Mathias Kiwanuka. Kiwanuka's elite athleticism and the logjam of talent on the line caused the Giants to move him to linebacker before the season, but he still ended up playing every spot on the defensive line at some point before breaking his leg against Detroit in Week 11. The problem with Kiwanuka as a linebacker is that he doesn't have the instincts yet to be anything more than a target in coverage. That could have been hidden on a team with a great cover linebacker on the outside, but Kawika Mitchell started the season looking like Kiwanuka without the athletic ability. Mitchell got better as the season went along, but his departure to Buffalo will not affect the Giants dramatically. Middle linebacker Antonio Pierce is the team's defensive leader and a film junkie, but he had only an average year considering the talent in front of him. That said, his play in fighting off three Packers linemen to make an open-field tackle on a screen pass in the second quarter of the NFC Championship game was one of the more impressive individual plays you'll ever see a linebacker make. Gerris Wilkinson will step in for Mitchell on the weak side, while Kiwanuka will likely return as the team's SAM linebacker . . . for now.

Defensive Secondary

Secondary	Age	Pos	Plays	TmPct	Rk	Stop	Dfts	RuYd	Rk	RuStop	Rk	Tgts	Tgt%	Rk	Dist	Suc%	Rk	APaYd	Rk	PaYd	PD	Int
Gibril Wilson*	27	FS	92	14.5%	1	35	13	6.0	33	49%	26	31	9%	18	11.9	51%	34	7.2	40	7.7	5	4
Sam Madison	34	CB	83	10.6%	21	34	18	7.0	45	47%	46	102	24%	5	13.2	51%	35	7.3	39	7.2	18	4
James Butler	26	SS	66	10.4%	31	28	8	6.3	40	52%	18	24	7%	45	17.1	51%	31	10.5	72	10.6	5	1
Aaron Ross	25	CB	51	7.0%	65	24	15	7.3	48	42%	51	51	13%	72	10.5	47%	47	8.3	60	8.4	8	3
Kevin Dockery	24	CB	48	7.6%	—	19	10	3.3	—	50%	—	44	13%	—	13.6	50%	—	7.2	—	7.0	7	0
Michael Johnson	24	SS	24	3.1%	—	12	3	4.8	—	53%	—	10	2%	—	15.1	85%	—	1.0	—	0.3	2	0
Corey Webster	26	CB	17	2.5%	—	6	4	6.5	—	50%	—	19	5%	—	15.8	50%	—	11.3	—	11.5	5	1
R. W. McQuarters	32	CB	15	1.9%	—	5	2	7.7	—	33%	—	21	5%	—	8.0	56%	—	8.2	—	8.2	1	0
Sammy Knight	33	SS	104	13.8%	3	43	18	5.3	16	48%	30	46	10%	10	10.1	47%	47	6.8	32	6.9	11	4

Year	Pass D Rank	vs. #1 WR	Rk	vs. #2 WR	Rk	vs. Other WR	Rk	vs. TE	Rk	vs. RB	Rk
2005	18	5.7%	15	-6.1%	13	1.7%	17	-31.5%	3	-0.1%	17
2006	13	-9.9%	8	-1.4%	12	6.0%	22	20.1%	31	-1.9%	16
2007	15	9.2%	21	-15.8%	7	-21.3%	8	24.7%	29	11.9%	29

The relationship between pass rush and coverage is symbiotic, which made the Giants' group of defensive backs look significantly better than their actual level of ability at many points during the 2007 season. The team's most impressive cornerback was first-round pick Aaron Ross, who was exactly what he was purported to be coming out of Texas: an NFL-ready cornerback capable of stepping in virtually immediately as a starter but not likely to become a shutdown corner. Ross is capable, has good technique and strength in his jamming, and anticipates throws well. Veteran Sam Madison has lost several steps since his glory days in Miami, but his performance was underrated when you consider how often he was in single coverage against the opposing team's top wideout. Corey Webster was covered at length in the team chapter; to be a starting cornerback, he'll need to improve his tackling and consistency. Gibril Wilson left in the offseason for one of the Raiders' silly money offers; he's an unquestionably talented player but is also injury-prone and subject to basic mistakes that veterans shouldn't make. Wilson will be replaced by Miami safety Kenny Phillips, the Giants' first-round pick. James Butler will start at the other safety spot but will be pushed by Michael Johnson; both have enough missteps to necessitate keeping the other close by. Both are physical, better against the run, occasionally get caught looking into the backfield, and take the occasional Magellan route to the ballcarrier. Butler's a better tackler and slightly better in coverage. The Giants also added veteran Sammy Knight, who played in Jacksonville last year. He could compete at either safety spot.

Special Teams

Year	DVOA	Rank	FG/XP	Rank	Net Punt	Rank	Punt Ret	Rank	Net Kick	Rank	Kick Ret	Rank	Hidden	Rank
2005	4.4%	2	7.0	4	0.5	17	6.2	7	3.8	13	8.5	5	2.5	14
2006	0.4%	16	0.8	13	11.3	3	-2.3	21	3.1	15	-10.5	29	-1.3	15
2007	-0.8%	20	-2.9	24	5.2	10	-4.3	22	-6.0	26	3.5	10	5.7	9

Lawrence Tynes ran the gamut of emotions during the NFC Championship game, missing a game-winning field goal from 36 yards at the end of regulation only to hit a 47-yarder in overtime. He's your average NFL kicker, but because of his newfound prominence, he'll have a job somewhere or another for as long as he wants it. Punter Jeff Feagles won his first Super Bowl in his 20th NFL season; a deadly accurate punter with his coffin-corner style, he can continue to do this for as long as *he* wants to. The team strangely used Reuben Droughns as a kickoff returner for half the year; Droughns, who probably won't even make the 2008 roster, simply isn't effective in that role. Expect to see Ahmad Bradshaw return kicks in 2008, while R. W. McQuarters, nearly the goat of the NFC Championship Game alongside Tynes, will return punts again. The Giants' coverage units were mediocre at best last year, despite featuring a Pro Bowl-caliber special teams leader in Chase Blackburn.

COACHING STAFF

Although it was Tom Coughlin's mellowing-out that helped steer the team in the right direction, all the talk following the season was about defensive coordinator Steve Spagnuolo. His game plan for beating the Patriots was talked about incessantly but never really explained. Spagnuolo dropped his linebackers deep into coverage on most plays, anywhere from 10 to 13 yards behind the line of scrimmage. The idea was to keep Wes Welker in front of the linebackers, who wouldn't be able to cover him anyway, while preventing the Patriots from running curl patterns. That allowed the Giants' cornerbacks to shade the Patriots' receivers deep while still enjoying safety support across the field. This forced the Patriots to run deeper patterns, which—here comes the brilliance—allowed the Giants' front four more time to get to Tom Brady. Of course, if Spagnuolo's game plan also specifically called for Justin Tuck to embarrass Logan Mankins on a play-by-play basis, it really was genius. Spagnuolo turned down the Redskins' advances to re-up as the highest-paid defensive coordinator in football.

Offensive coordinator Kevin Gilbride improved Eli Manning's footwork while eventually integrating Bradshaw and a healthy Steve Smith into his lineup during the playoffs. His next act will be to find touches for all the skill-position players in his lineup. As for Coughlin, very little changed about him on Sundays. He still runs in power situations and is right around league average when it comes to being aggressive. He's gone from a group of players who clearly disliked and didn't respect him to a group that seems to adore him. In these uncharted waters, it will be interesting to see how the new, cuddlier Coughlin handles his team after victory. Remember that Bill Cowher left his team a year after their Super Bowl win and Tony Dungy had to be talked into staying; it's possible that a mediocre season could see Coughlin step into the sunset.

New York Jets

Remember ManGenius? Just a year ago, Jets coach Eric Mangini was the toast of the NFL. He won AFC Coach of the Year honors, guest-starred on *The Sopranos*, and earned a premature Mensa coronation by the hyperbolic Gotham media. Mangini morphed into Man-Genius after making chicken salad from a chicken scratch roster, using smoke-and-mirror strategies on both sides of the ball to transform the 4-12 Jets of 2005 into a 10-6 wild-card team in 2006.

Alas, one wild-card berth does not a genius make. Start with NFL parity, add a soft schedule and a few close wins, sprinkle in a few high-impact rookies, and it's possible to stumble into a 10-6 record without doing anything brilliant. Take away the tomato can schedule and even out the late-game luck, and a team that stuns the league one year can crash to earth the next. That's precisely what happened to the Jets. They faced the league's toughest schedule in 2007 after cruising through the 12th easiest in 2006, and they finished 3-7 in games decided by a touchdown or less after going 5-3 in close games in 2006. Suddenly, the genius was back in the bottle.

The Jets have ridden the salt shaker since 2002, oscillating between nine- to 10-win seasons and losing records each year. The Jets have been consistently mediocre over the last five years (their truly good 2004 team being the exception), but they've been propelled up and down the standings by competitive balance, fumble luck, and the health of their quarterback. The

team's 10-6 record two years ago was just another spin on the merry-go-round; the Jets finished 19th in DVOA, 26th in defensive DVOA, and last in defensive Adjusted Line Yards that year. Fans and *New York Post* headline writers can be excused for their overenthusiasm entering last season. Mangini and GM Mike Tannenbaum don't get off the hook so easily. They mistook the mirage for an oasis, and they entered 2007 firmly believing their own hype.

Mangini and Tannenbaum assumed that they could build on their 2006 success by fostering roster continuity and making very modest upgrades. Last summer, they proudly announced that the Jets would return 21 of their 22 starters from the previous season. The only new face was free-agent running back Thomas Jones, signed to fix the team's most obvious problem. Their assessment of the previous year's roster was overoptimistic, but not loopy. Youngsters like D'Brickishaw Ferguson, Nick Mangold, Kerry Rhodes, and Jerrico Cotchery appeared ready to grow into stars, and if Jones stabilized the running game and Chad Pennington stayed healthy, it wasn't ridiculous to imagine the Jets gaining a game or so in the standings.

Unfortunately, the 2006 roster needed more than a quick patch. Many of the retained starters were adequate at best, and there was little depth anywhere. The depth issue struck the team before the season started, when Mangini and Tannenbaum made their biggest mistake: underestimating the impact of Pete Kendall, a

---

JETS PROSPECTUS

2007 Record: 4-12

Pythagorean Wins: 5.4 (24th)

DVOA: -20.7% total (25th), -12.5% weighted (23rd)

Offense: -11.1% DVOA (25th)

Defense: 10.9% DVOA (25th)

Special Teams: 1.2% DVOA (10th)

Variance: 11.7 % (6th)

2007: We go back and forth and back and forth and back and forth and back.

2008: With an actual living, breathing left guard and a season divisible by two, the Jets return to wild card contention.

2008 Mean Projection: 7.2 wins

On the Clock (0-3): 1%

Loserville (4-6): 36%

Mediocrity (7-8): 37%

Playoff Contender (9-10): 23%

Super Bowl Contender (11+): 4%

Projected Average Opponent: -5.4% DVOA (30th in NFL)

2008 Jets Schedule

Week	Opp.	Week	Opp.	Week	Opp.
1	at MIA	7	at OAK	13	DEN
2	NE	8	KC	14	at SF
3	at SD (Mon.)	9	at BUF	15	BUF
4	ARI	10	STL	16	at SEA
5	BYE	11	at NE (Thu.)	17	MIA
6	CIN	12	at TEN		

33-year-old veteran who in 2006 manned what is usually one of the least important positions on the field.

Kendall had been an NFL starter since 1996 and spent three seasons as the Jets' left guard and emergency center. Before the 2006 season, he restructured his contract to remain with the team, and he had arguably his finest season. Kendall started between rookies Mangold and Ferguson and became a stabilizing force on the Jets' offensive line. After the season, Kendall asked for a raise, claiming that he had a verbal agreement to earn a $1 million bonus after a successful season. The team refused to pay Kendall, who skipped all offseason programs and became an outspoken critic of the organization. In August, the Jets shipped him off to the Redskins, their favorite trading partners, in exchange for some magic beans (or, as Adam Schefter might call them, conditional second-day draft picks).

The favorites to replace Kendall were Adrien Clarke, an all-purpose lineman who spent 2006 on the inactive list, and Jacob Bender, the sixth-round pick from McNeese State. Bender appeared to win the starting job in camp, but after he got roughed up by the Giants in an exhibition game, Mangini turned to the bigger, more experienced Clarke.

Clarke started 14 games and was a walking disaster. The Jets finished 31st in the league in Adjusted Line Yards for runs off left tackle, plays where Clarke and Ferguson had primary blocking responsibilities. Clarke's blown blocks led to just four sacks, but Chad Pennington was knocked down (by either a sack or a quarterback hit) on 18.4 percent of dropbacks, the highest percentage in the league for a quarterback with over 150 attempts. Ferguson's and Mangold's performances slipped; instead of relying on Kendall to cover their mistakes, they were forced to cover for Clarke's, and the sophomores combined to allow eight sacks, plus several miscommunication sacks for which no single lineman could be blamed.

After Richard Seymour tossed Clarke aside and nearly decapitated Kellen Clemens in Week 14, Mangini deactivated Clarke in favor of undrafted rookie Will Montgomery. His first start came against the sack-happy Titans' defense. Pennington compared the situation to Vinny Testaverde's starting debut against the 1985 Bears. Pennington endured six sacks; veteran right guard Brandon Moore rolled his eyes after the game when asked to explain Mangini's offensive line strategy.

The Kendall-Clarke situation wasn't Mangini and Tannenbaum's only misstep, but it was the biggest, and it demonstrated that organizational hubris set in quickly after one successful season. Defensively, Mangini stuck with his blitz-happy 3-4 scheme despite the fact that it was still a poor fit with his personnel. The undersized Jets front three quickly wore down, grinding down undersized linebacker Jonathan Vilma in the process. Linebacker David Harris had an outstanding rookie season after replacing Vilma in the starting lineup, but he spent most of his time chasing down running backs after seven-yard gains as the Jets finished dead last in the league in defensive Adjusted Line Yards for a second straight year.

Offensively, Pennington tried in vain to duplicate his crafty junkballer success of 2006 while the blocking in front of him crumbled. Mangini eventually turned the reins over to an overmatched Clemens, who wasn't ready to play behind a spaghetti strainer line. Coordinator Brian Schottenheimer's formations and shifts didn't fool defenses as they did the previous year, and the Jets' offense deteriorated into a series of off-tackle runs by Jones and flat routes by the receivers. When Clemens got slammed by Seymour in Week 15, Mangini initially left Pennington on the bench and sent "slash" receiver Brad Smith onto the field. Smith ran an ineffective series of quarterback draws and option plays. It looked more like desperation than creativity.

The Jets' front office got the message after last year's debacle. It takes more than Mangini pixie dust to turn a sputtering organization around. The team had been conservative in free agency since the start of the Herm Edwards/Terry Bradway era in 2001. Its overall draft record has been solid but unspectacular, with busts like Dewayne Robertson and dumb choices like Mike Nugent offsetting fine selections like Mangold, Vilma, and Rhodes. The team slowly lost talent from 2002 to 2007: Curtis Martin retired, John Abraham left, Kendall defected, Pennington's arm turned to mush. First Edwards's motivational skills and then Mangini's schemes kept the Jets competitive, but they needed a dose of veteran talent—not just to stay out of the cellar, but also to keep young players like Clemens and Ferguson from developing bad habits.

Tannenbaum started by adding two new faces to the coaching staff: assistant head coach Bill Callahan and special teams coordinator Kevin O'Dea. Callahan spent four embattled seasons as head coach of the University of Nebraska after coaching the Raiders to Super Bowl XXXVIII. Callahan's head coaching record is spotty: His Super Bowl team was built by Jon Gruden, and his Nebraska teams fielded awful defenses as he struggled to install his systems. But as an assistant, he's a valuable asset with deep roots in the West Coast offense and an intimate knowledge of the running game. He'll help Schottenheimer develop the ball-control offense the coordinator has been trying to install over the last two seasons. O'Dea replaces special teams guru Mike Westhoff, who stepped down for health reasons. O'Dea worked with Devin Hester in Chicago and inherits another dangerous return weapon in Leon Washington.

Tannenbaum then upgraded the roster, starting with the offensive line. Alan Faneca slides into that gaping void between Mangold and Ferguson, while Damien Woody replaces disappointing Anthony Clement at right tackle. Faneca, a seven-time Pro Bowler, is a mammoth upgrade over Clarke and Montgomery. Woody isn't in Faneca's class, but he's a reliable veteran who only allowed one sack on the Lions' porous line, according to our game charters. With Callahan around to define roles and integrate the veterans, the Jets should have one of the best offensive lines in the AFC. That line will get extra blocking support from two more veteran free agents: fullback Tony Richardson and tight end Bubba Franks.

The Jets also made major changes on defense, acquiring tackle Kris Jenkins and linebacker Calvin Pace while trading disappointing tackle Robertson and square-peg linebacker Vilma. Jenkins is injury-prone and has weight problems, but he's the type of two-down run stuffer that Mangini needs to make his defense work. Pace is a tweener who can provide pass rush as a down lineman or linebacker. There's a lot of young talent on defense—Harris, safety Kerry Rhodes, corrnerback Darrelle Revis, rookie end Vernon Gholston, and others—and the Jets can get a lot better if Jenkins provides a few stuffs and the offense sustains a few more drives.

Assuming every free agent meets expectations and the young players keep advancing, the Jets will have a punishing running game and an improved defense. They could be this year's Vikings, though with better passing and less dominant run defense. They could be just good enough to miss the playoffs or sneak in as a wild card, which will buy the brain trust some job security. Getting back to 8-8 or 9-7 should be easy for a team that's accustomed to on-again, off-again success. To earn back his ManGenius label, Mangini (and Tannenbaum) must figure out what to do next.

The future of the Jets ultimately belongs to Clemens, Mangold, Ferguson, Harris, Revis, Gholston, plus other youngsters like Bender and Brad Smith, all of whom could still improve into useful players. In the long term, this year's free-agent acquisitions will only help the Jets if the veterans contribute to the development of the young players. Faneca's arrival should help Mangold and Ferguson while keeping Clemens alive, so he was worth $32 million. But some of the other vets may actually impede the progress of the younger players. Unless the team plays contract hardball with Chris Baker, Franks's presence will limit rookie Justin Keller's playing time. Jenkins's contract is cap-smart (almost nothing is guaranteed beyond this year), but a defender who must be weighed 10 times per year to stay under 400 pounds will probably bring diminishing returns. In 2009, the Jets may again be stuck with a hole at defensive tackle and a shortage of offensive playmakers, continuing their great merry-go-round ride.

Our 2008 projection for the Jets may look optimistic, but our 2009 forecast won't be so rosy if the team is dragged down by its veterans through this season. Hovering near .500 won't do this season. The Jets must get Clemens into the lineup. Ferguson and Mangold must make real strides. The run defense must stiffen, and some playmakers must emerge on the front seven. Mangini and Tannenbaum spent a lot of remodeling money to avoid a wholesale rebuilding project. A few of their signings were inspired, but some look like a quick fix. The Jets could very well remain in a holding pattern. But if the Faneca-Woody-Jenkins gambit succeeds in reinforcing and improving the young nucleus, than Mangini really will look like a genius.

Mike Tanier

2007 Jets Stats by Week

Wk	vs.	W-L	PF	PA	YDF	YDA	TO	Total	Off	Def	ST
1	NE	L	14	38	227	431	0	-54%	-5%	27%	-22%
2	@BAL	L	13	20	304	303	-2	-68%	-31%	32%	-5%
3	MIA	W	31	28	256	424	+1	-11%	16%	53%	26%
4	@BUF	L	14	17	347	304	0	-20%	11%	24%	-6%
5	@NYG	L	24	35	277	374	-1	-24%	-31%	17%	24%
6	PHI	L	9	16	267	413	0	-22%	-6%	19%	4%
7	@CIN	L	31	38	342	395	-1	-23%	3%	31%	5%
8	BUF	L	3	13	254	347	-2	-60%	-34%	16%	-9%
9	WAS	L	20	23	338	431	0	16%	20%	22%	18%
10	BYE										
11	PIT	W	19	16	297	263	+1	31%	4%	-18%	9%
12	@DAL	L	3	34	180	344	-1	-63%	-46%	11%	-6%
13	@MIA	W	40	13	372	187	+3	55%	-4%	-56%	3%
14	CLE	L	18	24	387	337	-1	-40%	-22%	19%	2%
15	@NE	L	10	20	234	265	-1	-17%	-37%	-36%	-15%
16	@TEN	L	6	10	296	273	0	-35%	-27%	1%	-6%
17	KC	W	13	10	337	219	0	-2%	0%	3%	1%

Trends and Splits

	Offense	Rank	Defense	Rank
Total DVOA	-11.1%	25	10.9%	25
Unadjusted VOA	-10.9%	24	12.5%	30
Weighted trend	-13.1%	24	-0.4%	17
Variance	4.3%	4	7.3%	18
Average opponent	-0.8%	4	4.4%	5
Passing	-8.3%	23	10.4%	21
Rushing	-14.0%	28	11.3%	30
First down	1.9%	13	4.0%	23
Second down	-26.6%	31	26.2%	31
Third down	-10.4%	21	-1.5%	13
First half	-7.3%	24	3.4%	21
Second half	-14.4%	27	18.2%	31
Red Zone	-33.5%	31	24.7%	29
Late and close	-27.4%	31	19.2%	27

Five-Year Performance

Year	W-L	Pyth Wins	Est Wins	PF	PA	TO	Total	Rank	Off	Rank	Def	Rank	ST	Rank
2003	6-10	7.5	7.6	283	299	0	-5.6%	20	4.8%	11	12.2%	29	1.9%	11
2004	10-6	10.2	11.3	333	261	+17	26.4%	5	20.0%	5	-4.1%	11	2.3%	9
2005	4-12	4.5	5.2	240	355	-6	-20.0%	27	-19.3%	31	0.6%	18	-0.1%	18
2006	10-6	8.7	7.7	316	295	0	-4.3%	19	2.8%	14	10.3%	26	3.2%	5
2007	4-12	5.4	5.0	268	355	-4	-20.7%	25	-11.1%	25	10.9%	25	1.2%	10

Strategic Tendencies

Run/Pass		Rank	Offense		Rank	Defense		Rank	Other		Rank
Runs, all plays	42%	12	3+ WR	72%	3	Rush 3	12.7%	3	2+ RB, pct runs	72%	2
Runs, first half	46%	5	4+ WR	25%	2	Rush 4	43.2%	31	1 RB/2 TE, pct runs	60%	5
Runs, first down	58%	3	2+ TE	11%	30	Rush 5	30.5%	5	1 RB/3+ WR, pct runs	32%	3
Runs, second-long	27%	29	Single back	77%	3	Rush 6+	13.7%	5	CB1 on WR1	38%	27
Runs, power sit.	65%	17	Play action	10%	31	Rush 7+	2.1%	10	Go for it on 4th	1.06	17
Runs, behind 2H	28%	15	Max protect	6%	29	Sacks by LB	48.3%	8	Offensive Pace	32.3	30
Pass, ahead 2H	40%	23	Outside pocket	10%	22	Sacks by DB	6.9%	14	Defensive Pace	31.8	32

Only the Bengals used play action less often than the Jets, but when they used play action they were hugely successful. The Jets ranked fourth in DVOA when using a play-fake and were the only team to average more than twice as many yards with play-action (10.3) compared to without (5.0). ⊘ The Jets threw the ball to the left side more often than any other offense. ⊘ The Jets ran the ball more than any other team out of formations with two wide receivers, over two-thirds of all plays. ⊘ The Jets led the league in draw plays. ⊘ The Jets offense collapsed in the fourth quarter, ranking 27th in offensive DVOA after ranking near league average in the first three quarters. ⊘ Only Cincinnati ran fewer formations with only one wide receiver. ⊘ How much difference does it make to put the quarterback in shotgun? A lot, if you are facing the Jets. Although offenses are generally much more successful in shotgun, the opposite was the case when playing the Jets. New York had the league's worst defense against formations with the quarterback under center (18.6% DVOA) but ranked second on defense behind Kansas City when facing shotgun formations (-18.4% DVOA). Perhaps the Jets were good against the shotgun because they always saw it in practice; their offense used shotgun formations more often than any team except for New England. ⊘ The Jets defense ranked 21st in Adjusted Sack Rate on first down and 31st on second down, but only the crosstown Giants could beat their 9.5 percent Adjusted Sack Rate on third down. ⊘ The Jets secondary had 11.5 percent of all passes thrown against them listed as "defensed," the highest percentage in the league. ⊘ The Jets defense ranked second in sacks listed as "rusher untouched." ⊘ After spending 2006 in the middle of the pack, the Jets were back to their old, slow ways in 2007. It was the fifth time in seven years that the Jets were one of the NFL's five slowest offenses by situation-neutral pace, and the second time in three years that the Jets faced the league's slowest pace on defense.

Passing

Player	DYAR	DVOA	Plays	NtYds	Avg	YAC	C%	TD	Int
Chad Pennington	140	-3.6%	286	1599	5.6	3.6	69.4%	10	9
Kellen Clemens	-136	-18.9%	278	1474	5.3	5.1	52.8%	5	9

Rushing

Player	DYAR	DVOA	Plays	Yds	Avg	TD	Fum	Suc
Thomas Jones	-36	-11.3%	310	1126	3.6	1	2	43%
Leon Washington	30	2.3%	71	353	5.0	3	1	37%
Kellen Clemens	16	-1.0%	25	112	4.5	1	6	—
Chad Pennington	-21	-30.3%	15	33	2.2	1	3	—
Brad Smith	-15	-62.7%	12	39	3.3	0	1	—
Jerricho Cotchery	18	16.2%	5	38	7.6	0	0	—
Jesse Chatman	6	-7.5%	128	515	4.0	1	0	1
Tony Richardson	5	3.8%	7	13	1.9	0	0	57%

Receiving

Player	DYAR	DVOA	Plays	Ctch	Yds	Y/C	YAC	TD	C%
WR									
Jerricho Cotchery	240	11.6%	127	82	1130	13.8	4.9	4	65%
Laveranues Coles	130	5.7%	89	55	646	11.7	2.6	7	62%
Brad Smith	-57	-23.7%	67	32	325	10.2	3.8	3	48%
Justin McCareins*	-42	-23.6%	46	19	232	12.2	2.0	0	41%
Wallace Wright	4	-7.7%	11	6	87	14.5	5.5	0	55%
TE									
Chris Baker	69	9.0%	61	41	409	10.0	3.5	3	67%
Joe Kowalewski	-22	-41.1%	9	5	18	3.6	1.8	1	56%
Sean Ryan*	-1	-11.1%	5	3	46	15.3	2.7	0	60%
Bubba Franks	-24	-18.2%	32	18	132	7.3	2.7	3	56%
RB									
Leon Washington	10	-10.4%	51	36	213	5.9	5.4	0	71%
Thomas Jones	80	34.4%	34	28	217	7.8	7.7	1	82%
Jesse Chatman	-28	-26.6%	37	27	161	6.0	4.9	0	73%
Tony Richardson	9	-3.2%	16	11	89	8.1	6.6	0	69%

Offensive Line

Year	Yards	ALY	Rank	Power	Rank	10+ Yds	Rank	Stuff	Rank	Sack	ASR	Rank
2005	3.46	3.86	24	71%	7	11%	30	25%	17	53	10.3%	31
2006	3.40	3.96	25	56%	27	8%	30	25%	23	34	6.6%	17
2007	3.88	4.10	21	50%	31	12%	25	22%	10	53	9.3%	30

Year	LE	Rank	LT	Rank	Mid	Rank	RT	Rank	RE	Rank
2005	2.15	32	4.17	20	3.79	26	4.65	6	4.37	11
2006	2.77	29	4.65	11	3.94	27	4.72	3	3.76	20
2007	3.48	25	3.30	31	4.22	12	4.38	15	4.05	18

The Jets allowed 13 sacks by untouched defenders, tying them with the Seahawks for the second highest figure in the league (and the Jets threw far fewer passes). Some of those sacks were the result of jailbreak blitzes, but others were caused by miscommunication on the offensive line. Left guard Pete Kendall was the leader of this unit and a former center who helped inexperienced Nick Mangold make adjustments and calls. When he left before the 2007 season, the Jets lacked a stabilizing presence on the line. Right guard Brandon Moore tried his best to fill Kendall's shoes. He became more vocal on the sidelines and helped Mangold make adjustments. Moore became the Jets' most dependable lineman last year, and his presence will help the coaching staff integrate young incumbents (Nick Mangold and D'Brickashaw Ferguson) with veteran newcomers (Damien Woody and Alan Faneca).

Defensive Front Seven

Defensive Line	Age	Pos	Plays	TmPct	Rk	Stop	Dfts	Stop%	Rk	AvYd	Rk	Sack	Hit	Hur	Runs	RuStop	RuYd	Pass	PaStop	PaYd
Kenyon Coleman	29	DE	83	9.8%	2	52	5	63%	75	3.4	73	1.5	0	1	80	63%	3.5	3	67%	0.3
Dewayne Robertson*	27	DT	58	6.9%	11	41	13	71%	57	1.8	41	4.0	4	3	49	67%	2.7	9	89%	-3.0
Shaun Ellis	31	DE	48	5.7%	43	32	9	67%	70	2.8	67	5.0	3	10	35	71%	3.1	13	54%	1.8
Sione Pouha	29	DT	41	4.9%	36	35	2	85%	11	2.4	56	0.0	0	0	40	85%	2.5	1	100%	0.0
Eric Hicks	32	DE	17	2.9%	—	10	1	59%	—	3.3	—	0.0	1	1	17	59%	3.3	0	0%	0.0
C. J. Mosley	25	DT	15	2.0%	—	10	6	67%	—	2.5	—	2.5	1	1	11	64%	3.7	4	75%	-1.0
Kris Jenkins	29	DT	38	4.6%	44	34	15	89%	4	0.7	8	2.5	6	3	33	88%	1.5	5	100%	-4.4

Linebackers	Age	Pos	Plays	TmPct	Rk	Stop	Dfts	Stop%	AvYd	Sack	Hit	Hur	Runs	RuStop	Rk	RuYd	Rk	Tgts	Suc%	Rk	APaYd	Rk
David Harris	24	ILB	124	14.7%	22	67	17	54%	4.5	5.0	2	5	90	52%	93	4.5	93	25	61%	9	4.6	16
Eric Barton	31	ILB	75	8.9%	79	48	9	64%	3.9	2.0	2	5	59	64%	42	3.7	64	13	50%	—	6.4	—
Victor Hobson*	28	OLB	67	7.9%	86	29	9	43%	4.6	2.0	7	4	37	49%	98	3.9	74	22	57%	22	4.6	14
Bryan Thomas	29	OLB	48	5.7%	99	34	11	71%	3.3	2.5	2	5	30	83%	4	2.7	19	10	40%	—	6.6	—
Jonathan Vilma*	26	ILB	46	12.4%	—	25	6	54%	4.2	0.0	1	0	31	58%	—	3.8	—	14	54%	—	5.3	—
David Bowens	31	OLB	19	2.2%	—	15	8	79%	1.7	2.5	2	2	12	67%	—	3.1	—	3	91%	—	2.5	—
Brad Kassell	28	ILB	15	1.8%	—	11	1	73%	3.4	0.0	0	0	13	77%	—	3.2	—	4	48%	—	5.7	—
Calvin Pace	28	OLB	100	12.4%	49	67	25	67%	3.3	6.5	4	15	57	65%	37	2.7	18	17	77%	1	3.5	3

Year	Yards	ALY	Rank	Power	Rank	10+ Yds	Rank	Stuff	Rank	Sack	ASR	Rank
2005	4.04	4.47	27	83%	32	12%	4	20%	31	30	6.7%	20
2006	4.65	4.99	32	67%	18	14%	8	16%	32	35	6.3%	18
2007	4.32	4.88	32	78%	30	9%	2	15%	32	29	6.6%	15

Year	LE	Rank	LT	Rank	Mid	Rank	RT	Rank	RE	Rank
2005	4.82	24	4.63	27	4.35	24	5.02	29	3.55	9
2006	5.12	29	5.30	30	4.61	24	5.67	31	4.54	22
2007	5.12	28	5.39	31	4.52	30	5.25	31	4.93	29

Vernon Gholston recorded 14 sacks at Ohio State in 2007 and overpowered Jake Long several times during the Buckeyes' victory over Michigan. Gholston was a defensive end in college, but he is perfectly suited to outside linebacker in a 3-4 scheme because of his speed and ability to drop into zone coverage when not blitzing. He is incredibly strong and should prove to be a dominant point-of-attack defender, but he will also have to improve his pass rush technique. Free agent Calvin Pace is a king-sized end/linebacker hybrid at 270 pounds. Like Gholston, he anchors well as a run defender. He also was excellent last year when Arizona asked him to drop into coverage, plus he led the Cardinals in hurries and was second in sacks. However, it is hard to tell whether Pace's 2007 performance was a talented player finally developing or a player having a career year when he was about to hit free agency. Bryan Thomas, yet another converted end, started 14 games last season but recorded just 2.5 sacks. His role will diminish this season.

Nose tackle Kris Jenkins has battled weight problems, alcoholism, and depression throughout his career. He conquered most of his demons, but his contract with the Jets calls for ten weigh-ins per year. When healthy and fit, he's still a force in the middle of the line. Buccaneers coach Jon Gruden was happy when the Jets acquired Jenkins, taking him out of Gruden's NFC South. "I gave Eric Mangini the biggest hug I've ever given a coach and told him, 'Thank you. Good God, do we appreciate you taking that guy out of our division,'" Gruden said during the winter owner's meetings.

Rookie inside linebacker David Harris recorded 41 tackles in two games after Jonathan Vilma was injured and demonstrated some pass rush ability. Harris is a big, stout defender who fits the system well, but he's limited in pass coverage and isn't the budding superstar suggested by his sack totals.

Kenyon Coleman led all defensive linemen in rushing tackles, but he produced few big plays and left the field in nickel situations. He's pretty good, but his stats are padded by the sheer number of times opponents ran against the Jets. The rest of the Jets front seven is filled out by veterans like Eric Barton, David Bowens, and Shawn Ellis, guys who won't kill you but don't do anything to close the gap with the Patriots.

Defensive Secondary

Secondary	Age	Pos	Plays	TmPct	Rk	Stop	Dfts	RuYd	Rk	RuStop	Rk	Tgts	Tgt%	Rk	Dist	Suc%	Rk	APaYd	Rk	PaYd	PD	Int
Darrelle Revis	23	CB	105	12.4%	6	41	17	6.6	43	35%	59	89	22%	12	12.6	45%	56	8.3	61	8.1	13	3
Kerry Rhodes	26	FS	78	9.2%	42	26	14	6.9	53	34%	59	28	7%	38	12.3	43%	60	6.4	28	6.1	10	5
David Barrett	31	CB	70	8.3%	55	18	7	6.4	39	36%	57	68	17%	49	10.8	45%	58	8.8	68	8.5	9	1
Abram Elam	27	SS	52	7.6%	64	23	4	5.1	14	52%	19	10	3%	82	7.1	55%	19	6.6	30	6.9	2	0
Hank Poteat	31	CB	43	5.1%	79	22	8	5.4	25	61%	14	35	9%	81	11.5	45%	57	7.9	53	7.5	6	2
Erik Coleman*	26	SS	41	5.2%	77	10	3	5.7	24	30%	75	9	2%	83	6.6	41%	66	9.3	63	8.8	0	0
Eric Smith	25	FS	35	4.4%	80	14	7	6.3	39	47%	33	19	5%	71	11.9	58%	13	5.6	17	5.4	5	0
Andre Dyson*	29	CB	15	3.2%	—	6	2	13.0	—	0%	—	22	10%	—	13.4	50%	—	12.2	—	12.0	6	1

Year	Pass D Rank	vs. #1 WR	Rk	vs. #2 WR	Rk	vs. Other WR	Rk	vs. TE	Rk	vs. RB	Rk
2005	8	15.1%	21	-40.2%	2	-18.4%	7	12.2%	24	-20.9%	4
2006	18	2.8%	17	6.1%	18	5.8%	21	-11.9%	11	2.3%	19
2007	21	20.8%	28	-9.2%	10	-11.2%	13	7.3%	16	16.5%	30

Cornerback Darrelle Revis had a tremendous rookie season. His stats don't look great—he was one of the ten cornerbacks with the most first downs plus touchdowns allowed—but his performance was very strong for a number-one cornerback who had to cover Randy Moss twice, Lee Evans twice, Terrell Owens, Braylon Edwards, and so on. Revis is entrenched as the top cornerback, but there's competition for the other starting job. Justin Miller suffered a serious knee injury in Week 2 and may not be back in time for training camp. Miller is a fine return man and nickel corner who never developed into a starter. Veterans Hank Poteat and David Barrett are back to compete for playing time, but neither distinguished himself last season. Rookie fourth-rounder Dwight Lowery led the NCAA in interceptions at San Jose State in 2006 but lacks top speed and athleticism. He projects as a nickel or dime corner. Free safety Kerry Rhodes signed a five-year contract extension in the offseason making him one of the league's highest-paid safeties. He's a ballhawk who can pick off passes and will force some fumbles. Strong safety Abram Elam was waived by the Cowboys at the start of last season but worked his way into the Jets starting lineup. He's a high-motor guy who excels at special teams but is just an adequate starting defender. The man he replaced in the starting lineup, Eric Coleman, departed for Atlanta. Eric Smith, a third-year player who started four games last season, is an Eric Mangini favorite. He'll push Elam and play in dime packages.

Special Teams

Year	DVOA	Rank	FG/XP	Rank	Net Punt	Rank	Punt Ret	Rank	Net Kick	Rank	Kick Ret	Rank	Hidden	Rank
2005	0.0%	18	-2.4	21	4.8	9	-4.5	28	-6.7	26	8.5	4	-9.0	28
2006	3.2%	5	0.4	15	7.9	7	-2.6	24	-1.1	21	14.3	2	6.7	8
2007	1.2%	10	-2.7	23	0.5	18	-0.2	15	-6.7	27	16.3	3	0.7	15

Leon Washington is one of the best kickoff returners in the NFL, and like Cleveland's Joshua Cribbs, he was getting the Devin Hester squib treatment at times last season. However, Washington is nothing special as a punt returner, so several players may push him for that job, including rookies Marcus Henry and Danny Woodhead. Henry, a sixth-round pick from Kansas, has a return man's skill set but lacks experience. Woodhead, undrafted out of Chadron State, was the Division II player of the year. At five foot eight, he resembles Darren Sproles of the Chargers. Justin Miller was also an excellent kickoff return man before his injury, and while it is hard to see him taking back the kickoff job from Washington, the Jets will want to find some way to take advantage of his speed on special teams. Kicker Mike Nugent is average on kickoffs, was just 1-of-4 on 50-yard field goals, and sometimes shanks attempts inside 40 yards. Punter Ben Graham had some busy days in 2007, including an eight-punt, 361-yard performance in the season finale, but he's just a league average performer. Both players are entering their fourth seasons, and neither figures to get much better.

COACHING STAFF

Offensive coordinator Brian Schottenheimer appeared to be doing his best Al Saunders impression last season. Like the former Redskins and Chiefs assistant, Schottenheimer often dressed up the most basic off-tackle runs with gimmicky formations and motion packages. The motion fooled some opponents in 2006, but last season, with the offensive line in shambles, it was all wasted energy. Schottenheimer may lose some of the window dressing this season, but his offense will be as power-oriented as ever now that the team has loaded up with veteran run blockers.

Eric Mangini and defensive coordinator Bob Sutton are extremists: some teams use more six-man blitzes, and other teams use more eight-man coverage schemes, but no team uses both as often as the Jets. Just as the offensive motion lost effectiveness last year, the defensive gadgetry stopped fooling opponents. Most teams were able to pick up the big blitzes while taking what was offered by the eight-man zones. Mangini and Sutton, like Schottenheimer, may choose to opt for a simplified approach in 2008.

Oakland Raiders

When Al Davis, the despotic ruler of the Oakland Raiders, capitulates, it's news. When Davis abandons his own theory of running and adopts the rushing philosophy of an avowed enemy, it's time to interrupt network broadcasting.

Losing can do strange things to people, and no team has lost more games (61) than the Raiders over the last five years. So when new head coach Lane Kiffin hired offensive line coach Tom Cable and running backs coach Tom Rathman with the idea of going to a zone-blocking running game, Davis, shockingly, didn't object. That's stunning because the Denver Broncos popularized the scheme in the 1990s under Mike Shanahan and line coach Alex Gibbs. Ever since Davis bounced Shanahan as his head coach after a 7-9 record in 1988 and a 1-3 start in 1989, the two have despised each other. Shanahan threatened to sue Davis for back pay, until the two decided to give the disputed thousands to charity, but a high level of red-hot hatred still remains.

Davis probably looked the other way while Cable, who coached with Gibbs in Atlanta before his hiring in Oakland, installed the Denver running game right in front of him. It turned out to be among the best decisions Davis has made over the last five years. With a few personnel shifts on the offensive line—and despite getting limited production from two of their top three running backs—the Raiders' running game went from 29th in Adjusted Line Yards to 16th. In doing so, they found a peg on which to hang their offensive hat. That peg got bigger when they chose

Arkansas speedster Darren McFadden with the fourth overall choice in April's draft.

McFadden figures to be perfectly suited for the Raiders' zone-blocking scheme, which calls upon the running back to make a quick cut before squaring his shoulders and exploding into the secondary.

"You talk about running to a spot, putting a foot down and accelerating, that's what he is," Rathman said after watching his prized prospect in the team's first minicamp in May. Rathman emerged from another organization abhorred in Raiderland, the 49ers. He was a Super Bowl–winning fullback with San Francisco, and then coached their running backs until co-owner John York fired him along with Steve Mariucci and the rest of the staff after the 49ers' last playoff appearance in 2002. Rathman was reared on a running system developed by the late Bobb McKittrick, the 49ers' longtime offensive line coach. McKittrick's system of sweeps, traps, and counters is somewhat similar to Denver's zone-blocking scheme in its employment of light, athletic linemen who can cut block. The 49ers and Broncos competed for the lightest line in the league throughout the 1990s, but the Broncos took over that designation after the 49ers changed their running philosophy following Mariucci's firing.

The Raiders, meanwhile, stuck with Davis's bludgeoning offensive lines throughout the last several decades. They also featured some of the bigger running backs in the league, from Marv Hubbard and Mark van Eeghen in the 70s up through Bo Jackson, Roger Craig,

---

RAIDERS PROSPECTUS

2007 Record: 4-12

Pythagorean Wins: 4.9 (27th)

DVOA: -28.3% total (30th), -26.7% weighted (29th)

Offense: -15.4% DVOA (28th)

Defense: 8.3% DVOA (23rd)

Special Teams: -4.6% DVOA (29th)

Variance: 18.2 % (21st)

2007: The Raiders learn how to run but forget how to stop the run.

2008: Holes on the offensive and defensive lines will not be filled by running back Darren McFadden.

2008 Mean Projection: 3.9 wins

On the Clock (0-3): 47%

Loserville (4-6): 41%

Mediocrity (7-8): 8%

Playoff Contender (9-10): 4%

Super Bowl Contender (11+): 0%

Projected Average Opponent: 1.0% DVOA (16th in NFL)

2008 Raiders Schedule

Week	Opp.	Week	Opp.	Week	Opp.
1	DEN (Mon.)	7	NYJ	13	KC
2	at KC	8	at BAL	14	at SD (Thu.)
3	at BUF	9	ATL	15	NE
4	SD	10	CAR	16	HOU
5	BYE	11	at MIA	17	at TB
6	at NO	12	at DEN		

Harvey Williams, and Tyrone Wheatley. Hubbard said that the running was so tough that he stuffed cardboard into his thigh pads for extra protection. The slender-hipped Marcus Allen and the relatively diminutive Napoleon Kaufman were exceptions to the Raider rules.

To convert to a zone-blocking team last year, the Raiders moved six-foot-seven, 325-pound former first-round pick Robert Gallery inside to guard. Gallery struggled mightily as a pass-protector, but has the athletic ability to cut block and get to the second level as a guard. The Raiders then signed what previously was an anomaly for them, an offensive lineman weighing less than 300 pounds, when they lured guard Cooper Carlisle from Denver in free agency. He became the team's best and most consistent lineman last year. It also helped when former 49ers center Jeremy Newberry recovered from his myriad knee injuries and won the job as the starting center. Like Rathman, Newberry learned McKitrick's system after nine years in San Francisco.

The Raiders then grabbed a zone-blocking runner, former Colt Dominic Rhodes, in free agency. Rhodes slipped into a Randy Moss-like malaise while in Oakland and never emerged as a running threat. The same malady struck starter LaMont Jordan. The Raiders cut Rhodes and may do the same with Jordan.

Justin Fargas grabbed the starting job and became only the second Raiders runner in the last eight seasons to rush for more than 1,000 yards. The switch in systems brought the offensive line a modicum of respectability after the 2006 Raiders put up one of the worst O-line performances in recent memory. The improvement didn't come only in the running game. The 2006 Raiders yielded a league-high 72 sacks with a league-worst 12.4 percent Adjusted Sack Rate. Those numbers reduced to 41 and 8.5 percent, respectively, last season.

The team continued their conversion to zone blocking this offseason by releasing tackle Barry Simms and signing former 49ers tackle Kwame Harris to play on the left side. Anyone who has watched Harris struggle in San Francisco has one piece of advice for quarterback JaMarcus Russell: "Look out!" After the 49ers drafted Joe Staley in the first round of the 2006 draft, they moved Harris from left tackle to right tackle and finally to the bench. It appeared as if Harris, a former number-one pick himself, would go elsewhere in a backup role until the Raiders called and handed him the left tackle spot and a $14 million, three-year deal.

The move reveals not only how much money the Raiders are willing to spend on a left tackle who can't pass protect but also how committed Oakland is to the running game. The athletic Harris is a superb run blocker and can reach the second level. The belief in Oakland is that when the Raiders run to the right, Harris will create a bigger cutback lane for runners in the zone-blocking scheme. As far as pass protection, Harris will get lots of help from backs and tight ends.

The Raiders aren't planning anything elaborate for Russell in his first year as a starter. They basically want him to avoid game-killing turnovers while he hands the ball to McFadden and Fargas. How well that sits with Davis bears watching. Not only has Davis favored a powerful running game, but he also likes a deep passing game. From 1985 to 1991, Davis's Raiders led the league in yards per pass completion, and he probably tapped the strong-armed Russell in an effort to revive the "mad bomber" years. How much patience will Davis have watching his strapping $61 million quarterback throw hitches and dumpoffs before he starts barking into the sideline phone from the owner's box? The Raiders, possibly in a nod to Davis, have cleared the decks for last year's first overall pick. Veterans Daunte Culpepper and Josh McCown are gone, leaving the limited Andrew Walter as the lone veteran backup.

According to some writers, Russell prepared for his season as the unquestioned starter by locking himself in the pantry. Offseason rumors had Russell weighing 300 pounds, up from his playing weight of 270. The Raiders say Russell reported to minicamp notably lighter compared to last year, and Russell himself said he weighed 269 pounds. The Raiders deflected the reports about the ballooning Russell by saying he was big-boned and that he was impressing offensive coordinator Greg Knapp with his knowledge of the offense.

The Raiders' mediocre wide receiver corps gives Russell another reason to hand off the ball. The once-productive Jerry Porter followed Randy Moss out the door. Oakland hopes to revive Javon Walker, who has spent the majority of the past three years in the trainer's room. The team is hopeful Ronald Curry can rebound off a horrible year, but he underwent foot surgery in

May and may not be able to start training camp. There are some quiet rumblings behind the signing of former Carolina deep threat Drew Carter. Carter's first season was wiped out by a knee injury, and in his second season he couldn't get on the field. In his third, he caught 38 passes for 517 yards while amassing 28 first downs. He's just the type of receiver Davis salivates over.

No one in Oakland salivated over last year's defense. In the disastrous two-win 2006 campaign, the defense played heroically. Despite being on the field constantly, they finished eighth in DVOA in 2006 at -8.6%, and were even better on third down with a seventh-ranked -12.2%. FootballOutsiders.com readers voted Rob Ryan coordinator of the year in our postseason awards balloting, and the performance even got him an interview for the head job before Davis hired Kiffin.

Going into last year, the Raiders figured that if they could improve their offensive time of possession, the defense could shine. The offense held up its end, tying for seventh in possession time, but the defense faltered. The team fell from eighth in DVOA to 25th, mainly because they couldn't tackle. The rush defense finished last in DVOA. Ten different running backs rushed for more than 100 yards over the cleat-marked defenders.

The middle of the defensive line collapsed frequently, in spite of (or maybe due to) nose tackle Terdell Sands and the big contract he won the year before. Sands struggled with personal problems, including the loss of his mother, and the Raiders expect the six-foot-seven, 335-pounder to once again man the middle. Warren Sapp's weight loss before 2007 apparently sapped his strength for the run game, and linebackers Thomas Howard and Kirk Morrison struggled getting off blocks.

The secondary was no help, with one exception. Cornerback Nnamdi Asomugha harkens to the Raiders' glorious past, when Willie Brown, Lester Hayes, and Mike Haynes provided zip-lock coverage. Unfortunately, Asomugha can't zip-lock the field from sideline to sideline, and opposing quarterbacks simply threw the ball everywhere Asomugha was not. Cornerback Fabian Washington never lived up to his first-round status the way Asomugha did, so he's been sent off to Baltimore. Strong safety and former first-round pick Michael Huff doesn't bring the wood, so he's been switched to free safety. As is Davis's way, the Raiders hope a few aging players can shore up the defense. The hard-hitting Gibril Wilson was signed for seven years and $16 million up front. Mercurial cornerback DeAngelo Hall, fetched in a trade with Atlanta, is not particularly big, but he's not averse to hitting people. His coverage skills are overrated, but his speed most certainly is not.

As usual, dysfunction simmers just below the surface with the Raiders. Kiffin was stripped of much of his authority in the offseason. Lacking tact, the kid coach apparently went to tell Davis what was wrong with his team after the 4-12 season. Davis didn't take kindly after giving the 31-year-old Kiffin a chance, and there's a feeling Kiffin could be fired if the Raiders stumble early.

Then there's the signing of defensive tackle Tommy Kelly. He signed a seven-year, $50.5 million deal with $18.25 million up front—a contract so absurd Profootballtalk.com thought the numbers were wrong. It made Kelly the highest paid defensive lineman in the league. Kelly has 13 career sacks in four years and missed nine games last year with a knee injury. It was further evidence that the Raiders are one of the looniest organizations in sports.

But apparently nothing is impossible with Al Davis calling the shots. And that includes the adoption of a running game from his most fierce and hated rival.

Kevin Lynch

Adding a Rookie Defensive Tackle

The Oakland Raiders' selection of Darren McFadden with the fourth overall pick was not a curious one because of McFadden's ability, but it did raise a few eyebrows because defensive tackle Glenn Dorsey was still available. Dorsey is a vaunted three-technique tackle, which means he lines up between the guard and tackle and shoots the B-gap between them play after play. The preeminent three-technique tackle of the last 15 years was also a Raider last year, but Warren Sapp had become a bizarre shell of the player he once was. His desire to run around blockers helped the Raiders put up the worst rush defense DVOA in the league in 2007. Instead of opting for the LSU defensive tackle, Oakland passed and grabbed Florida State defensive tackle Mario Henderson in the third round.

Of course, the question remains whether Dorsey would have improved the team's performance. Although it seems logical that drafting a potentially elite defensive tackle would improve a team's rush defense, what happens in reality hasn't been studied until now.

For each college defensive tackle drafted from 1998 through 2006, we recorded a variety of metrics and statistics, particularly in the first two years of a player's career. They include the following:

- **OTS:** Original Team Seasons, or the number of years a draftee played with the team that selected him.
- **OT%:** The percentage of seasons since the player was drafted in which he has played for the team that selected him, regardless of whether he was in the league or not.
- **2GP:** The number of games a player played in his first two seasons with the club that selected him. We also tracked GP, which are the total number of games he's played amongst all teams over the course of his career.
- **2GS:** The number of games a player started in his first two seasons with that club; we also tracked a player's games started, or GS, for his career with all teams.
- **ALY:** Adjusted Line Yards, our metric that attempts to isolate defensive line play.
- **DVOA:** In this case we're referring specifically to defensive rush DVOA.

To measure a rookie defensive tackle's impact, we noted the Adjusted Line Yards of his team the year before his selection and then calculated the average of his team's Adjusted Line Yards in the two years following his selection. We limited the player pool to those players who participated in at least 20 games for the team that selected them over their first two seasons; that eliminates the likes of Raheem Brock, who was cut by the Eagles before playing a single game for them.

Table 1, which separates the players by the round they were selected in, reveals a mix of both common-sense conclusions and utterly baffling surprises. Players who get drafted earlier play more seasons, both for their original team and in general; they play more games and start more. The only problem is that they don't help the run defense seemingly at all. The teams

saw their Adjusted Line Yards fall all of -.01 yards and their rushing DVOA decline less than 0.5%, a pittance considering the expense. Furthermore, Day Two players actually had more of an effect on their teams than Day One picks (rounds one through three in this time-frame); although the difference is negligible, it implies that there's little difference in performance between the two.

The effects of the players were negligible; no one is shelling out $24 million in guaranteed money to see their Adjusted Line Yards drop .01 yards. There is no trend indicating that Day One players, or even first-round picks, are better than late-round selections in directly influencing Adjusted Line Yards or defensive rush DVOA.

Furthermore, by comparing the number of players who fit into the criteria for each of the two tables, we can see how likely a player is to make a contribution to the team that picked him (Table 2). We define success, in this case, as playing at least 20 games in the two seasons following the draft.

Table 2. Successful DT by Round, 1998-2006

Round	Total	Success	Pct
1	29	29	100.0%
2	19	15	78.9%
3	18	6	33.3%
4	26	14	53.8%
5	16	4	25.0%
6	37	8	21.6%
7	39	9	23.1%

The third round has been a disaster area for defensive tackles for many reasons. Some guys made their name after being cut (Darwin Walker), some players struggled with injury (Dusty Dvoracek), and some were plain old busts (Donnell Washington and Atiyyah Elli-

Table 1. Effect of Drafting a Defensive Tackle, 1998-2006*

Round	Num	OTs	OT%	2GP	GP	2GS	GS	ALY Y-1	ALY Avg	Dif	DVOA Y-1	DVOA Avg	Dif
1	29	4.3	82.2%	28.0	67.2	19.0	52.1	4.12	4.10	-0.03	-2.48%	-3.07%	-0.58%
2	15	3.9	68.3%	28.1	70.4	12.8	45.9	4.10	4.05	-0.04	-1.33%	-2.53%	-1.20%
3	6	4.2	73.9%	26.5	64.8	12.0	32.8	3.93	4.10	0.16	-4.22%	-0.10%	4.12%
4	14	3.7	68.2%	27.6	64.3	7.9	26.1	4.15	4.08	-0.07	-1.84%	-3.49%	-1.65%
5	4	2.5	79.2%	28.0	41.0	16.0	18.3	4.31	4.43	0.12	4.94%	2.39%	-2.54%
6	8	2.9	66.2%	24.5	43.4	5.0	8.4	4.20	4.19	0.00	-2.73%	-1.90%	0.83%
7	9	3.3	51.5%	28.9	52.4	2.2	11.7	4.00	4.01	0.01	-4.39%	-3.76%	0.63%
Day 1	50	4.2	77.0%	27.9	67.9	16.3	47.9	4.09	4.08	-0.01	-2.35%	-2.55%	-0.20%
Total	85	3.8	71.9%	27.6	62.1	12.3	35.4	4.11	4.10	-0.01	-2.17%	-2.54%	-0.37%

*Includes all defensive tackles who played at least 20 games in their first two seasons.

Table 3. Effect of Drafting a Starting-Quality Defensive Tackle, 1998-2006*

Num	OTs	OT%	2GP	GP	2GS	GS	ALY Y-1	ALY Avg	Dif	DVOA Y-1	DVOA Avg	Dif
24	4.5	86.0%	30.5	72.5	26.7	63.8	4.19	4.10	-0.09	-1.32%	-4.01%	-2.69%

*Includes all defensive tackles who started at least 20 games in their first two seasons.

Table 4. Effect of Drafting a Defensive Tackle, by Conference, 1998-2006*

Conference	Num	OTs	OT%	2GP	GP	2GS	GS	ALY Y-1	ALY AVG	Dif	DVOA Y-1	DVOA AVG	Dif
ACC	15	3.9	70.1%	28.1	68.3	13.3	39.2	4.08	4.09	0.01	-2.76%	-3.57%	-0.81%
Big Ten	12	3.1	86.3%	27.2	41.3	12.7	20.8	4.13	4.19	0.06	-4.54%	1.19%	5.73%
Big 12	11	4.5	77.0%	27.9	65.7	15.0	40.8	4.21	4.17	-0.04	-2.97%	-2.40%	0.57%
Pac-10	12	3.8	73.5%	27.8	62.0	10.9	28.7	4.10	3.98	-0.11	-2.80%	-6.47%	-3.67%
SEC	23	4.0	70.4%	27.2	63.1	13.2	41.8	4.16	4.08	-0.07	-0.67%	-2.92%	-2.25%

*Includes all defensive tackles who played at least 20 games in their first two seasons.

son, neither of whom ever played an NFL game). We're dealing with small samples, but the downward trend is evident across the board; of course, teams are more likely to play a first-round defensive tackle than they are a fifth-rounder, so there's some selection bias here.

The inherent issue with games played is that it takes only one snap to qualify. What if we break down the issue further and analyze only players who *started* 20 or more games for the team that drafted them? Only 24 defensive tackles in our timeframe fit that bill (Table 3), but they were the only ones to exhibit any sort of effect on their team's Adjusted Line Yards or defensive rush DVOA.

Defensive tackles good enough to pick up 20 starts in their first two seasons helped their teams drop .09 yards per carry over the course of two years and saw their team's defensive rush DVOA drop nearly three percentage points. Although .09 yards per carry doesn't sound like much, an average estimate would peg that at around 360 yards for an entire season.

So then, we have an idea that a defensive tackle good enough to step almost immediately into the lineup can affect a team's run defense. Of course, if every team could find defensive tackles good enough to step in immediately, we wouldn't need to write this essay. The next logical step is to attempt to find a common thread among those successful defensive tackles.

In the past, we've written online about the strong record of first-round defensive tackles from the SEC. When the players in question include Richard Seymour, John Henderson, Marcus Stroud, and Albert Haynesworth, we're going to look smart in saying that. The last few years, however, have begun to see that trend turn around. Gerard Warren has now washed out of two cities, and a poorly timed belly flop from Johnathan

Sullivan could drown two others. Dewayne Robertson has also done little to stand out as a premiere defensive tackle. That shift is borne out by an analysis of the effectiveness of defensive tackles from specific college conferences who play 20 or more games in their first two seasons (Table 4).

The SEC has still given the NFL more defensive tackles than the other big conferences, but those tackles haven't been any more effective than those coming out of the Big 12 or Pac-10. What's even more surprising is just how poor Big Ten tackles have been; their teams went up nearly six percentage points in rush defense DVOA. Outside of Luis Castillo, the best defensive tackle produced by the conference over this timeframe is Barry Cofield or Jared DeVries, and high-profile busts include Wendell Bryant and Jimmy Kennedy. Perhaps Big Ten defensive tackles aren't the best investment these days. That's a premise backed perhaps unknowingly by scouts; Big Ten defensive tackle Alan Branch saw his stock drop into the second round following the 2007 college season, and SEC defensive tackle Justin Harrell rose into the late first round, where the Packers chose him.

The results of our research are simple at first glance: Drafting a successful defensive tackle helps, but drafting an average one doesn't. Looking at the numbers more closely, though, reveals several factors that could aid NFL teams in their personnel decisions. Stud defensive tackles have a real effect, but nonelite defensive tackles are relatively interchangeable. Defensive tackles who don't break out early in their career are unlikely to mature into impact players; the same goes for tackles from the Big Ten. A smart team incorporates this into their valuation of players both before and during the draft, transcending the traditional draft value chart methodology by incorporating a more tier-based system into their selection process. It's easy to point at the Raiders and make caveman sounds while implying that they get impressed by shiny things, but considering McFadden's rarified air in the Speed Score metric intro-duced later in the book in the essay "Five Seconds Can Be a Lifetime", more may be going on in Oakland than meets the eye.

Bill Barnwell

2007 Raiders Stats by Week

Wk	vs.	W-L	PF	PA	YDF	YDA	TO	Total	Off	Def	ST
1	DET	L	21	36	375	392	-1	-64%	-15%	30%	-19%
2	@DEN	L	20	23	253	441	-1	-57%	-48%	9%	-1%
3	CLE	W	26	24	396	312	0	-12%	-2%	-11%	-22%
4	@MIA	W	35	17	369	278	+1	23%	30%	4%	-4%
5	BYE										
6	@SD	L	14	28	245	362	-2	-72%	-28%	33%	-11%
7	KC	L	10	12	268	290	-1	-43%	-31%	8%	-4%
8	@TEN	L	9	13	235	218	-2	-23%	-40%	-6%	12%
9	HOU	L	17	24	310	359	-2	-51%	-21%	31%	1%
10	CHI	L	6	17	193	295	-3	-29%	-29%	10%	10%
11	@MIN	L	22	29	372	478	+3	-39%	-18%	23%	2%
12	@KC	W	20	17	312	292	0	24%	28%	11%	8%
13	DEN	W	34	20	372	292	+3	36%	9%	-26%	0%
14	@GB	L	7	38	233	445	-2	-87%	-29%	25%	-33%
15	IND	L	14	21	253	322	+1	19%	-4%	-33%	-10%
16	@JAC	L	11	49	215	437	-2	-106%	-61%	41%	-4%
17	SD	L	17	30	316	253	-3	3%	1%	-6%	-4%

Trends and Splits

	Offense	Rank	Defense	Rank
Total DVOA	-15.4%	28	8.3%	23
Unadjusted VOA	-13.4%	26	10.4%	25
Weighted Trend	-16.3%	28	7.5%	25
Variance	6.4%	14	4.6%	5
Average Opponent	0.5%	12	2.2%	13
Passing	-21.6%	31	-0.9%	11
Rushing	-10.3%	22	16.7%	32
First Down	-32.5%	32	4.0%	23
Second Down	-3.2%	16	26.2%	31
Third Down	-3.4%	17	-1.5%	13
First Half	-18.5%	29	3.4%	21
Second Half	-12.2%	26	18.2%	31
Red Zone	11.7%	24	9.2%	20
Late and Close	-16.0%	27	22.7%	31

Five-Year Performance

Year	W-L	Pyth Wins	Est Wins	PF	PA	TO	Total	Rank	Off	Rank	Def	Rank	ST	Rank
2003	4-12	4.9	5.8	270	379	-1	-17.9%	28	-11.1%	24	8.4%	25	1.7%	12
2004	5-11	5.1	6.2	320	442	-17	-16.3%	25	0.1%	16	14.7%	26	-1.8%	22
2005	4-12	5.5	7.4	290	383	-4	-6.0%	20	0.1%	13	2.4%	23	-3.5%	29
2006	2-14	2.7	3.9	168	332	-23	-30.0%	32	-35.6%	32	-8.6%	8	-3.0%	26
2007	4-12	4.9	4.1	283	398	-11	-28.3%	30	-15.4%	28	8.3%	23	-4.6%	29

Strategic Tendencies

Run/Pass		Rank	Offense		Rank	Defense		Rank	Other		Rank
Runs, all plays	47%	5	3+ WR	45%	22	Rush 3	6.1%	14	2+ RB, Pct Runs	63%	8
Runs, first half	49%	2	4+ WR	4%	29	Rush 4	76.8%	4	1 RB/2 TE, Pct Runs	43%	19
Runs, first down	52%	12	2+ TE	15%	28	Rush 5	12.3%	29	1 RB/3+ WR, Pct Runs	27%	11
Runs, second-long	50%	2	Single back	47%	28	Rush 6+	4.8%	27	CB1 on WR1	46%	14
Runs, power sit.	66%	16	Play action	26%	2	Rush 7+	0.8%	25	Go for it on 4th	1.40	6
Runs, behind 2H	38%	3	Max protect	13%	7	Sacks by LB	8.7%	28	Offensive Pace	32.1	28
Pass, ahead 2H	37%	24	Outside pocket	26%	1	Sacks by DB	4.3%	24	Defensive Pace	30.8	16

Only Miami used play action more often than Oakland, but while the Dolphins saw little benefit, the Raiders saw a ton. Only four teams had a greater difference in DVOA on play-action and non-play-action passes. ⌀ When Oakland used play action, they threw it back to the running back more than a quarter of the time. ⌀ Oakland's only positive passing DVOA came on four- and five-wide receiver sets.   ⊘   The Raiders kept their quarterback on the move. No team designed more plays to roll their quarterback out of the pocket, and no team had more quarterback scrambles.   ⊘   Teams threw right against Oakland's defense more often than against any other team. Can you guess which side Nnamdi Asomugha was on?   ⊘   Opposing offenses ran more play action against Oakland than any other team, even though their defense against it ranked sixth in the league.   ⊘   No team blitzed less often on third down.   ⊘   The Raiders were third in DVOA against formations with three wideouts, but 31st against formations with two.   ⊘   The Raiders allowed an average of 5.5 yards after catch, the worst in the AFC.

Passing

Player	DYAR	DVOA	Plays	NtYds	Avg	YAC	C%	TD	Int
Daunte Culpepper*	76	-4.9%	210	1181	5.6	5.0	58.1%	5	5
Josh McCown*	-236	-29.1%	207	1088	5.3	4.9	58.4%	10	10
JaMarcus Russell	-144	-42.7%	75	341	4.5	4.3	54.5%	2	4
Andrew Walter	0	-11.5%	8	38	4.8	5.0	62.5%	0	0

Rushing

Player	DYAR	DVOA	Plays	Yds	Avg	TD	Fum	Suc
Justin Fargas	92	1.6%	222	1009	4.5	4	3	46%
LaMont Jordan	-32	-14.0%	145	549	3.8	3	1	37%
Dominic Rhodes*	21	-2.0%	75	302	4.0	1	1	51%
Josh McCown*	1	-11.4%	25	143	5.7	0	11	—
Daunte Culpepper*	0	-11.9%	15	38	2.5	3	6	—
Justin Griffith	-2	-19.3%	7	27	3.9	0	0	43%
JaMarcus Russell	-3	-36.2%	3	11	3.7	0	5	—
Adi Echemandu	-14	-25.5%	20	85	4.3	0	1	30%

Receiving

Player	DYAR	DVOA	Plays	Ctch	Yds	Y/C	YAC	TD	C%
WR									
Jerry Porter*	16	-10.7%	102	44	705	16.0	4.3	6	43%
Ronald Curry	106	1.0%	97	55	717	13.0	4.0	4	57%
Mike Williams*	-59	-56.4%	20	7	90	12.9	4.0	0	100%
Tim Dwight*	7	-6.1%	15	6	98	16.3	1.2	2	40%
Johnnie Lee Higgins	-4	-21.3%	8	6	47	7.8	0.3	0	75%
Drew Carter	38	-6.6%	75	38	517	13.6	2.9	4	51%
Javon Walker	-66	-30.2%	50	26	287	11.0	4.5	1	52%
TE									
Zach Miller	5	-6.1%	69	44	444	10.1	3.3	3	64%
John Madsen	22	20.2%	12	8	102	12.8	4.3	1	67%
RB									
Justin Griffith	34	1.8%	36	26	165	6.3	4.3	1	72%
LaMont Jordan	65	19.6%	34	28	247	8.8	9.2	0	82%
Justin Fargas	58	22.0%	32	23	188	8.2	8.0	0	72%
Dominic Rhodes*	-21	-36.9%	18	11	70	6.4	6.3	0	61%

Offensive Line

Year	Yards	ALY	Rank	Power	Rank	10+ Yds	Rank	Stuff	Rank	Sack	ASR	Rank
2005	3.75	4.06	17	64%	15	11%	28	25%	15	44	7.8%	23
2006	3.74	3.84	29	58%	25	15%	18	28%	30	72	12.4%	32
2007	4.20	4.16	16	55%	25	16%	18	27%	27	41	8.5%	27

Year	LE	Rank	LT	Rank	Mid	Rank	RT	Rank	RE	Rank
2005	4.31	13	4.41	12	4.12	16	3.59	26	3.50	24
2006	4.37	13	3.65	30	3.89	28	4.39	10	3.09	28
2007	3.71	23	4.53	11	4.02	19	4.44	13	4.18	14

The Raiders are still on the road back from the nightmare of 2006, one of the worst offensive line performances in NFL history. That line ruined careers. Quarterback Aaron Brooks hasn't been heard from since. Randy Moss was left for dead until Tom Brady and Bill Belichick gave him football-to-end-zone resuscitation. Backup quarterback Andrew Walter may never recover from the memories of that season, and former starting running back LaMont Jordan remains on the trading block.

Now the Raiders have a real offensive line coach in Tom Cable and a zone run-blocking scheme that makes sense for them. They've also revamped the line, moving Robert Gallery to guard, releasing tackle Barry Sims, and signing another veteran center (John Wade, ex-Tampa Bay) to possibly replace the unsigned Jeremy Newberry, who played center a year ago.

The Raiders can't help but make progress with another year under Cable, but there are red flags. Their two tackles, Cornell Green and Kwame Harris, are pedestrian at best. Green has knocked around the league for 10 seasons but has only 18 starts and is coming off a knee injury. Harris became one of the most criticized players in 49ers annals with his inability to pass protect. He will man the left side and will get lots of help from guards, backs, and tight ends in pass protection. If injuries strike the line, they could return to the nightmare of 2006, which features names such as Jake Grove and Paul McQuistan.

Defensive Front Seven

Defensive Line	Age	Pos	Plays	TmPct	Rk	Stop	Dfts	Stop%	Rk	AvYd	Rk	Sack	Hit	Hur	Runs	RuStop	RuYd	Pass	PaStop	PaYd
Warren Sapp*	36	DT	53	6.9%	12	41	17	77%	37	1.7	36	2.0	6	9	44	80%	2.0	9	67%	0.7
Derrick Burgess	30	DE	43	6.4%	30	38	16	88%	4	0.6	16	8.0	9	20	33	85%	2.2	10	100%	-4.9
Jay Richardson	24	DE	34	4.4%	60	25	6	74%	52	3.3	72	1.0	1	0	30	73%	3.5	4	75%	2.3
Tommy Kelly	28	DE	31	9.2%	6	25	7	81%	28	4.1	77	1.0	1	6	28	82%	4.5	3	67%	-0.3
Terdell Sands	29	DT	24	3.1%	65	20	5	83%	16	1.5	22	0.0	0	1	22	82%	1.6	2	100%	0.0
Chris Clemons*	26	DE	19	2.5%	—	16	13	84%	—	-3.1	—	8.0	6	5	8	63%	0.9	11	100%	-5.9
Kalimba Edwards	29	DE	18	4.1%	—	13	7	72%	—	1.6	—	3.0	5	4	10	80%	2.9	8	63%	0.0

Linebackers	Age	Pos	Plays	TmPct	Rk	Stop	Dfts	Stop%	AvYd	Sack	Hit	Hur	Runs	RuStop	Rk	RuYd	Rk	Tgts	Suc%	Rk	APaYd	Rk
Kirk Morrison	26	MLB	132	17.1%	8	86	32	65%	4.0	1.0	0	1	88	68%	29	2.8	22	37	69%	4	4.1	10
Thomas Howard	25	OLB	106	13.7%	35	58	30	55%	5.3	1.0	0	2	55	55%	89	4.5	91	57	56%	23	5.9	38
Robert Thomas	28	OLB	62	9.2%	76	38	7	61%	4.2	0.0	0	0	51	65%	39	3.7	67	12	54%	—	5.4	—
Sam Williams	28	OLB	15	2.8%	—	12	2	80%	2.4	0.0	0	0	10	80%	—	1.6	—	6	80%	—	2.9	—

Year	Yards	ALY	Rank	Power	Rank	10+ Yds	Rank	Stuff	Rank	Sack	ASR	Rank
2005	4.11	4.42	25	63%	17	16%	16	24%	18	35	7.3%	13
2006	4.06	4.11	11	61%	11	16%	16	25%	13	34	7.4%	11
2007	5.06	4.41	26	72%	27	25%	31	23%	18	27	5.8%	24

Year	LE	Rank	LT	Rank	Mid	Rank	RT	Rank	RE	Rank
2005	3.68	9	4.43	22	4.55	29	4.24	21	5.05	28
2006	3.94	15	3.38	5	4.14	11	4.63	23	4.59	23
2007	4.48	23	5.07	28	4.43	28	3.91	10	4.28	18

No team was pushed around last year more than the Raiders. They will now try to balance their pass rush with a little more run defense. Part of the problem was the lack of stoutness from huge nose tackle Terdell Sands, who was fresh off a new contract. Sands had some personal problems last season involving the loss of a family member, and the Raiders believe he'll rebound this year.

Oakland is also banking—and we do mean banking—on defensive tackle Tommy Kelly, who received a contract worthy of a 15-sack season. Kelly had one sack last year and is coming off a knee injury, but Oakland believes he can be a dynamic presence at the three-technique. He will slide in for the retiring Warren Sapp, who was never a great run player. The Raiders apparently can't do without a former Tampa Bay D-lineman, so they signed 34-year-old Greg Spires to play right end.

The team, as is Al Davis's custom, will rely on older players to bring some stoutness. Former Ravens linebacker Ed Hartwell was signed after sitting out a year recovering from an Achilles injury. It is hard to tell how much tread is left on Hartwell's tires. The Raiders believed former Jaguars safety Donovan Darius would add some toughness last year, but he never made it out of training camp.

Outside linebackers Robert Thomas and Thomas Howard have ability but neither is a real thumper capable of flattening a pulling guard and then tearing down a running back. Middle linebacker Kirk Morrison is a bit of an enigma. Scouts generally say he is similar to Thomas and Howard, a quick, darting player who gets blocked from the play far too often. Our numbers say he may be the most underrated middle linebacker in the league, strong against the run and ranked in the top ten for two straight seasons in both Success Rate and adjusted yards allowed per pass. The truth is probably somewhere in between, but it is hard to argue with the idea that he's the best player in this front seven.

Defensive Secondary

Secondary	Age	Pos	Plays	TmPct	Rk	Stop	Dfts	RuYd	Rk	RuStop	Rk	Tgts	Tgt%	Rk	Dist	Suc%	Rk	APaYd	Rk	PaYd	PD	Int
Michael Huff	25	SS	97	12.5%	8	48	15	4.2	5	62%	5	58	15%	1	11.8	48%	45	8.9	55	9.4	10	1
Stuart Schweigert*	27	FS	59	8.1%	58	14	6	10.2	80	24%	79	22	6%	54	13.1	42%	63	11.8	77	12.0	5	2
Stanford Routt	25	CB	48	6.2%	71	11	7	8.4	60	29%	68	55	15%	63	12.6	37%	76	10.1	78	10.1	5	3
Fabian Washington*	25	CB	44	6.1%	72	14	3	11.8	76	20%	79	50	14%	65	11.2	46%	55	9.3	71	9.6	8	1
Nnamdi Asomugha	27	CB	41	5.7%	77	19	5	11.8	75	50%	39	38	11%	78	14.9	61%	3	5.8	4	5.8	7	1
Chris Carr*	25	CB	29	3.8%	—	12	10	5.7	—	67%	—	18	5%	—	11.4	44%	—	11.2	—	11.0	1	0
Hiram Eugene	28	SS	27	3.5%	—	7	0	8.1	—	33%	—	2	1%	—	9.0	56%	—	11.7	—	12.0	0	0
Gibril Wilson	27	SS	92	14.5%	1	35	13	6.0	33	49%	26	31	9%	18	11.9	51%	34	7.2	40	7.7	5	4
DeAngelo Hall	25	CB	87	10.3%	26	34	18	5.4	26	46%	47	92	21%	22	11.7	52%	32	7.2	35	7.2	16	5

Year	Pass D Rank	vs. #1 WR	Rk	vs. #2 WR	Rk	vs.Other WR	Rk	vs.TE	Rk	vs.RB	Rk
2005	27	16.7%	22	4.2%	25	23.7%	31	1.7%	19	21.3%	30
2006	5	-23.6%	2	28.6%	30	-20.2%	7	-2.8%	17	-18.9%	10
2007	11	-32.3%	1	30.6%	31	-6.9%	18	-5.0%	7	7.7%	25

How awesome is Nnamdi Asomugha? Opposing quarterbacks tried so hard to avoid him in coverage that we had to change the minimum standards in our defensive back stats so that we could rank him with the league's other 63 starting cornerbacks. Asomugha has also won the Byron "Whizzer" White award recognizing the NFL player who does the most charity work for *three straight years*. Asomugha's new partner, DeAngelo Hall, is a good player who many people (including Hall himself) mistakenly think is a great player. The Raiders believe they can revive the career of the disgruntled former Falcon, and he should help narrow the wide disparity between the coverage statistics against first and second receivers. If nothing else, he may lead the league in interceptions because of quarterbacks desperate to stay away from Asomugha.

Speaking of interceptions, perhaps former top-round pick Michael Huff will finally make a few now that he's moving to free safety. He has only one in his last two years as a starter. Taking Huff's old role as strong safety is Gibril Wilson, who was given bucketfuls of money to leave the Giants. Wilson is one of the best blitzing safeties in the league, so perhaps Rob Ryan will do a little more blitzing next season. Wilson's signing knocked Stuart Schweigert from the starting lineup, and the Raiders cut him. He savaged the Raiders after his release, saying that no one in the NFL plays eight in the box and man "zero" coverage. Of course, if Schweigert tackled better he would be crushing sour grapes. The team is high enough on Hiram Eugene (a third-year undrafted free agent out of Louisiana Tech) that Schweigert was expendable.

Special Teams

Year	DVOA	Rank	FG/XP	Rank	Net Punt	Rank	Punt Ret	Rank	Net Kick	Rank	Kick Ret	Rank	Hidden	Rank
2005	-3.5%	29	-8.0	27	-7.8	28	-6.1	31	-7.5	27	8.7	3	-5.4	22
2006	-3.0%	26	-0.6	17	-8.1	28	-3.0	26	-15.9	31	9.8	3	2.2	14
2007	-4.6%	29	2.9	10	-5.8	25	-17.2	32	0.8	14	-7.6	29	13.2	3

Sebastian Janikowski and Shane Lechler might be the most powerful kicker-punter combination in the game. No kicker had more touchbacks than Janikowski's 22, and that was kicking half the time in the squishy turf—or worse, from the dirt infield—of the Coliseum. Janikowski also got some help, as the Raiders' kickoff coverage, which gave up the most value in returns in 2006, improved significantly in 2007. The same can't be said for the punt coverage. Once again, Lechler had the best net punting average in the league, but as usual, the Raiders gave up plenty of yards on punt returns. According to our measurements, Lechler's punts were worth 9.9 points of field position more than average, third in the league, but the Raiders gave up 8.3 points worth of field position on returns, worse than any team except Arizona. (The numbers don't quite add to the net punting value above because of the way nonreturned punts are measured in different ways on punt and net.) The Raiders used four different punt returners (Nnamdi Asomugha, Chris Carr, Tim Dwight, and Johnnie Lee Higgins) and none of them were adequate. No one returned more kickoffs than Chris Carr's 67, but the best return he could muster was 43 yards.

COACHING STAFF

Coaching in Oakland might be the hardest job in the NFL. Al Davis has never been a coach's owner, and players know that they always have Al as a back channel if they don't like the coach.

If the Raiders start slowly, Lane Kiffin could be the first Oakland head coach since Mike Shanahan in 1989 to be bounced during the season. At least Raiders fans should be happy that Kiffin brought in competent assistant coaches after the one-year disaster of Art Shell. Offensive line coach Tom Cable is renowned, as is offensive coordinator Greg Knapp and running backs coach Tom Rathman. Quarterbacks coach John DeFilippo is considered to be an up-and-comer.

If Samson (of Samson and Delilah fame) had ever reached middle age and started drinking a lot of ale, he might have gained a protruding boiler and his flowing locks might have turned gray. In other words, he would have looked like Raiders defensive coordinator Rob Ryan. Hair flying, Ryan's red-eyed, spit-splattering tirades made the Raiders more watchable on the sidelines than on the field. But now the mane is gone. Ryan buzzed his 10-inch strands and donated them to "Locks of Love," an organization that provides hairpieces to kids who lose their hair because of medical reasons. Ryan's buzz cut won't last. He plans on another 18-month barber-less vigil.

Philadelphia Eagles

L ong-time readers of *Pro Football Prospectus* are as-suredly well aware that our projection systems consistently forecast success for the Philadelphia Eagles. Over the past three years, the Eagles have not quite lived up to our expectations. Before the 2007 season, it was easy to point to fluke incidents such as Matt Bryant's game-winning 62-yard field goal and note the unlikelihood that they would recur. In 2007, however, although the Eagles' losses were close, they weren't particularly unfair or unlikely. Week 1 saw the Packers win with a last-second field goal in a game in which two fumbles on punt returns led to 10 of the 16 Green Bay points. In Week 7, the Bears came back in the fourth quarter and scored on the next-to-last play of the game. The Eagles lost to the Giants in Week 14 when a last-second David Akers field goal attempt hit the upright. If that field goal had gone through and the Eagles had gone on to an overtime victory, both teams would have finished the year 9-7 and the Eagles would have won the tiebreaker with the Giants and made the playoffs.

Regardless, does DVOA look at the Eagles with rose-colored glasses? Although DVOA has certainly seen them to be a better team than their record indicated over the past three seasons, that wasn't always the case (Table 1). (Note that in the table, expected wins is not the preseason projection but how many wins a team with the Eagles' DVOA in specific important situations would be expected to win in a season in which the team had average luck and an average schedule.) Much as

anyone could have said that the Eagles were underrated by DVOA from 2002 to 2004, they have been overrated over the last three years. It just so happens that those three were the ones in which we've released books.

EAGLES PROSPECTUS

2007 Record: 8-8

Pythagorean Wins: 9.1 (11th)

DVOA: 8.5% total (11th), 7.9% weighted (11th)

Offense: 10.2% DVOA (7th)

Defense: -3.7% DVOA (12th)

Special Teams: -5.4% DVOA (31st)

Variance: 15.0 % (14th)

2007: We said they were the favorites in the NFC East, but they ended up the only team in the division to miss the postseason.

2008: We're saying they are the favorites in the NFC East. Yes, again.

2008 Mean Projection: 11.7 wins

On the Clock (0-3): 0%

Loserville (4-6): 1%

Mediocrity (7-8): 2%

Playoff Contender (9-10): 21%

Super Bowl Contender (11+): 77%

Projected Average Opponent: -4.0% DVOA (27th in NFL)

Table 1. Eagles Under Andy Reid

	Actual Wins	Pythagorean Wins	DVOA Expected Wins
1999	5	5.5	7.1
2000	11	11.2	10.8
2001	11	12.3	11.1
2002	12	12.5	10.7
2003	12	10.4	10.3
2004	13	11.5	11.4
2005	6	5.9	7.4
2006	10	9.8	11.6
2007	8	9.1	9.6
Avg	9.8	9.8	10.0

The man inextricably linked to Andy Reid's career with the Eagles is Donovan McNabb, the quarterback Reid chose with his first pick in his first draft. McNabb's torn ACL during the 2006 season opened up a spot for Jeff Garcia, who went 5-1 and helped earn the Eagles a playoff spot. When the team followed that by using their first 2007 draft pick on Lewin Career Forecast darling Kevin Kolb, McNabb was in the unenviable position of having to prove that he was still capable of playing championship-caliber quarterback while recovering from his knee injury.

The conventional wisdom about McNabb, and indeed most players returning from severe knee injuries, is that a player returning from a torn ACL gets better as the season goes along. Troy Aikman, for one, has said that a quarterback requires a full season before returning to 100 percent. Although that may or may not be true, it's not borne out by McNabb's performance in

2008 Eagles Schedule

Week	Opp.	Week	Opp.	Week	Opp.
1	STL	7	BYE	13	ARI (Thu.)
2	at DAL (Mon.)	8	ATL	14	at NYG
3	PIT	9	at SEA	15	CLE (Mon.)
4	at CHI	10	NYG	16	at WAS
5	WAS	11	at CIN	17	DAL
6	at SF	12	at BAL		

2007 (Table 2). On the surface, it looks like McNabb played his best football in the final four weeks because of his gaudy completion percentage and higher touchdown-to-interception ratio. However, he was also completing those passes for less yardage while eating more sacks than he had since the disastrous Week 4 game, in which backup left tackle Winston Justice was put on an island against Osi Umenyiora and was taken for six sacks while McNabb went down 12 times altogether.

Table 2. Donovan McNabb Game Splits

	Comp	Att	C%	Yds	Y/Att	TD	Int	Sacks	ASR
Weeks 1-4	79	136	58.1%	943	6.9	5	1	17	12.3%
Weeks 6-9	93	151	61.6%	1101	7.3	4	3	11	6.4%
Weeks 10-13	23	39	59.0%	285	7.3	4	2	2	2.7%
Weeks 14-17	96	147	65.3%	995	6.8	6	1	14	8.6%

Overall, McNabb's 2007 season was right around his career averages, with a slightly higher completion percentage and yards per attempt balanced out by a higher sack rate and a lower touchdown percentage. As easy as it is to lay the blame at his feet, Donovan McNabb was not the problem with the 2007 Philadelphia Eagles.

Another player who certainly wasn't the problem was Brian Westbrook, who would have been a legitimate MVP candidate had the Patriots not fielded the best offense in NFL history. Westbrook led the team in rushing yards and receptions, topped the NFL in yards from scrimmage, and was the first running back since Marshall Faulk in 2000 to lead the league in both rushing and receiving DYAR. Westbrook didn't play significantly better than he had in previous years; instead, he stayed on the field more and set career highs in every counting statistic in 2007. Comparisons have been made between the career paths of Westbrook and Tiki Barber, who was constantly told that he was too small to hold up to a huge workload until he pulled it off at the end of his career. The difference is that Barber spent virtually his entire career without missing time due to

injury, while Westbrook has missed time each year. Westbrook is not a back who should be going over 300 carries, which means some of the workload will have to fall on Correll Buckhalter and the newly acquired Lorenzo Booker.

Although we can point to a number of individuals whose performance wasn't up to scratch in 2007, such as wideout Reggie Brown and defensive ends Darren Howard and Jevon Kearse, the Eagles' performance has dramatically shifted since the glory days of 2000-2004 in only two major ways: their performance on special teams and the difficulty of their schedule (Table 3).

Table 3. The Big Shift

	ST Rank	Schedule Rank
1999	15	7
2000	5	31
2001	1	20
2002	5	32
2003	2	23
2004	2	22
2005	17	5
2006	22	18
2007	31	6

The degradation of the Eagles' special teams has been steady and multifaceted. The departure of special teams standouts such as Ike Reese has caused Philadelphia's coverage units to dramatically decline, an effect compounded by the performance of kicker David Akers and punters Dirk Johnson (through 2006) and Saverio Rocca (2007).

Akers was once the best kicker in football but those days are gone. The Eagles attempted to do more directional kicking in 2007, but Akers's performance on kickoffs was still far below his peak levels. Meanwhile, although Rocca is a tough guy and has a huge leg, he struggled to harness it in his rookie year, a problem that was again perpetuated by poor coverage. The sheer value of Rocca's punts from the actual punt alone was 29th in football, but the coverage on those punts was dead last. Buckhalter checked in as the fourth-worst kick returner in football, and Reno Mahe was the ninth-worst among regular punt returners. Second-round pick DeSean Jackson should shoulder some of this load, but the coverage units simply need to be better across all situations.

New Ravens head coach John Harbaugh served as the special teams coordinator from 1999 to 2006, with Rory Segrest taking over last year. Segrest's only previous experience coaching special teams was one year doing quality control with the Eagles and, before that, four years as the special teams coordinator with Sanford University. Segrest will need to halt an alarming trend. Having linebacker Akeem Jordan healthy for the entire season will help because Jordan excelled when available. Free agent acquisition Rocky Boiman has been a valuable special teams contributor throughout his six-year career. Odds are that the Eagles will improve in this area because it would be hard for them to drop any further in the league rank.

On the brighter side for Eagles fans, a strong relationship exists between the difficulty of the Eagles' schedule and their number of wins, something we expect will continue this year. A good chunk of DVOA's fuzzy feelings when it comes to the Eagles in 2007 has to do with a nondivision schedule that is projected to be the easiest in football. That's not enough to push a team into the playoffs—last year, the projection system pegged the 49ers to have the easiest schedule in football, and although their schedule ended up being the fifth easiest, it still couldn't help them from offensive implosion. However, an easy schedule is enough to make aging players look like they're in the midst of a renaissance. Getting to play against the AFC North and the NFC West more than mitigates the strain of having to play in the NFC East.

Since the Eagles elected to take an overwhelming offer from the Panthers for their first-round pick, acquiring an extra second- and fourth-round pick while swapping their 2008 first-round pick for Carolina's same pick in 2009, the impetus for change will have to come from their big free agent signing, former Patriots cornerback Asante Samuel. The 2007 All-Pro signed a front-loaded six-year, $57 million deal to join Philadel-

phia. Samuel represents the latest Pro Bowl defensive back to switch teams, a move that has seen mixed results for both sellers and buyers. Before Samuel, 12 Pro Bowl defensive backs had switched teams since 1995. On average, their new teams watched their DVOA ratings on pass defense improve by 8.8%. However, the teams that lost these Pro Bowl defensive backs also saw their DVOA on pass defense improve—by an average of 8.5%. It remains to be seen if the Eagles will benefit from Samuel's addition any more than they would have by improving a pass rush that consisted almost solely of Trent Cole in 2007. What we do know is that last year the Eagles had a huge hole in their secondary by the name of William James; replacing James as the nickel corner with former starter Sheldon Brown and replacing Brown with Samuel should dramatically upgrade the Eagles' secondary, assuming opposite corner Lito Sheppard wants to play and is healthy enough to do so. Samuel and Sheppard would make up the most fearsome corner combination in the NFC immediately, and although both are considered gamblers who challenge quarterbacks to throw the ball, better coverage should give the front seven more time to get home on defensive coordinator Jim Johnson's exotic blitz packages.

The 2008 Eagles have endless built-in excuses to fail. Andy Reid is distracted by family issues. Donovan McNabb is old and past his prime. Brian Dawkins is past where McNabb is. If our projection is right, these things won't matter. If our projection is wrong, these three men will see the end of their run in the City of Brotherly Love.

Bill Barnwell

2007 Eagles Stats by Week

Wk	vs.	W-L	PF	PA	YDF	YDA	TO	Total	Off	Def	ST
1	@GB	L	13	16	283	215	-1	28%	-17%	-59%	-14%
2	WAS	L	12	20	340	337	+1	-2%	11%	18%	5%
3	DET	W	56	21	536	432	+1	73%	65%	-4%	3%
4	@NYG	L	3	16	190	212	0	-44%	-40%	0%	-5%
5	BYE										
6	@NYJ	W	16	9	413	267	0	1%	18%	0%	-17%
7	CHI	L	16	19	334	386	0	-16%	33%	42%	-7%
8	@MIN	W	23	16	385	256	0	38%	33%	-4%	0%
9	DAL	L	17	38	316	434	-2	-59%	-10%	46%	-4%
10	@WAS	W	33	25	379	361	0	14%	47%	25%	-8%
11	MIA	W	17	7	352	186	-2	-6%	-9%	-22%	-19%
12	@NE	L	28	31	391	410	0	5%	12%	-6%	-13%
13	SEA	L	24	28	363	311	-2	-9%	-30%	-8%	13%
14	NYG	L	13	16	306	318	+1	9%	10%	-5%	-6%
15	@DAL	W	10	6	315	240	+2	98%	8%	-101%	-10%
16	@NO	W	38	23	435	346	0	28%	35%	1%	-6%
17	BUF	W	17	9	391	271	-2	14%	7%	-10%	-2%

Trends and Splits

	Offense	Rank	Defense	Rank
Total DVOA	10.2%	7	-3.7%	12
Unadjusted VOA	8.2%	11	0.6%	16
Weighted trend	10.3%	8	-3.9%	12
Variance	7.8%	22	12.4%	32
Average opponent	0.0%	8	4.0%	6
Passing	5.8%	17	-0.9%	12
Rushing	16.1%	2	-7.1%	12
First down	22.4%	2	2.5%	21
Second down	4.5%	13	-0.6%	13
Third down	-2.9%	16	-18.9%	4
First half	17.2%	5	3.2%	20
Second half	2.4%	16	-10.4%	5
Red zone	-5.4%	19	-25.7%	2
Late and close	6.2%	10	-12.0%	9

Five-Year Performance

Year	W-L	Pyth Wins	Est Wins	PF	PA	TO	Total	Rank	Off	Rank	Def	Rank	ST	Rank
2003	12-4	10.4	10.3	374	287	+4	15.6%	7	11.1%	6	0.1%	17	4.7%	2
2004	13-3	11.5	11.4	386	260	+6	22.9%	6	14.8%	9	-2.2%	16	5.9%	2
2005	6-10	5.9	7.4	310	388	-7	-4.7%	18	-9.2%	22	-4.6%	14	0.0%	17
2006	10-6	9.8	11.6	398	328	+5	24.3%	3	19.8%	3	-6.4%	11	-1.9%	22
2007	8-8	9.1	9.6	336	300	-8	8.5%	11	10.2%	7	-3.7%	12	-5.4%	31

Strategic Tendencies

Run/Pass		Rank	Offense		Rank	Defense		Rank	Other		Rank
Runs, all plays	36%	29	3+ WR	53%	11	Rush 3	3.9%	20	2+ RB, Pct runs	49%	28
Runs, first half	37%	26	4+ WR	14%	11	Rush 4	58.5%	22	1 RB/2 TE, Pct runs	34%	29
Runs, first down	42%	29	2+ TE	18%	25	Rush 5	22.4%	15	1 RB/3+ WR, Pct runs	27%	12
Runs, second-long	33%	21	Single back	53%	17	Rush 6+	15.2%	3	CB1 on WR1	42%	20
Runs, power sit.	68%	10	Play action	21%	10	Rush 7+	4.5%	2	Go for it on 4th	0.62	32
Runs, behind 2H	28%	16	Max protect	13%	6	Sacks by LB	8.6%	29	Offensive pace	29.8	6
Pass, ahead 2H	59%	1	Outside pocket	14%	7	Sacks by DB	5.7%	16	Defensive pace	30.0	4

The Eagles are tied with the Redskins for the most running back screen passes with 40, but they threw only a few screens to wide receivers so they ranked tenth in total screen passes. Brian Westbrook led the league in screen passes with 33. ∅ Philadelphia was significantly more efficient throwing with two wide receivers (29.4% DVOA) than with four (-11.2% DVOA). ∅ No team passes more often from two tight-end sets. ∅ The Philadelphia defense allowed an average of 5.5 yards after catch, second in the league behind Green Bay. ∅ The Eagles led the league in defensive DVOA in the fourth quarter after ranking 21st during the first three quarters combined. ∅ Philadelphia hurried quarterbacks more often than any other NFC defense, narrowly ahead of Minnesota and the New York Giants. ∅ The Eagles' defense trailed only the Chargers in DVOA on passes thrown to the left; however, they ranked 25th and 23rd on passes to the middle and right, respectively. ∅ Only three teams blitzed more often on third down than the Eagles.   ⊘   Philadelphia's defense ranked second in DVOA on the road (-14.7%) but 25th at home (7.6%).   ⊘   The Eagles were significantly better at stopping the run when the offense used just one running back (3.3 yards per carry, -23.2% DVOA) instead of two (4.3 yards per carry, -4.0% DVOA).

Passing

Player	DYAR	DVOA	Plays	NtYds	Avg	YAC	C%	TD	Int
Donovan McNabb	659	8.2%	520	3150	6.1	5.2	61.8%	19	7
A. J. Feeley	-31	-15.6%	107	686	6.4	4.1	57.3%	5	8

Rushing

Player	DYAR	DVOA	Plays	Yds	Avg	TD	Fum	Suc
Brian Westbrook	334	19.9%	278	1333	4.8	7	1	53%
Correll Buckhalter	81	21.9%	62	313	5.0	4	0	48%
Donovan McNabb	29	3.3%	37	238	6.4	0	7	—
Tony Hunt	9	6.5%	10	16	1.6	1	0	60%
A. J. Feeley	0	-11.6%	7	23	3.3	0	1	—
Thomas Tapeh*	-3	-15.2%	5	18	3.6	0	0	60%
Reggie Brown	28	70.8%	5	36	7.2	0	0	—
Lorenzo Booker	34	16.3%	28	125	4.5	0	0	54%
Kris Wilson	-6	-37.9%	3	7	2.3	0	2	33%

Receiving

Player	DYAR	DVOA	Plays	Ctch	Yds	Y/C	YAC	TD	C%
WR									
Kevin Curtis	195	5.1%	135	77	1110	14.4	4.6	6	57%
Reggie Brown	47	-7.3%	111	61	780	12.8	2.8	4	55%
Jason Avant	85	20.1%	33	23	267	11.6	2.3	2	70%
Greg Lewis	85	31.8%	23	13	265	20.4	4.0	3	57%
Hank Baskett	17	-2.5%	22	16	142	8.9	2.4	1	73%
TE									
L. J. Smith	-52	-24.2%	44	22	236	10.7	3.2	1	50%
Brent Celek	45	23.3%	22	16	178	11.1	4.5	1	73%
Matt Schobel	-11	-14.5%	21	11	108	9.8	2.4	1	52%
RB									
Brian Westbrook	189	12.5%	120	90	771	8.6	8.5	6	75%
Correll Buckhalter	6	-8.6%	21	12	87	7.3	6.9	0	57%
Thomas Tapeh*	-4	-20.6%	11	8	50	6.3	6.3	0	73%
Kris Wilson	-59	-35.0%	50	24	222	9.3	4.9	1	48%
Lorenzo Booker	85	26.7%	36	28	237	8.5	6.2	0	78%

Offensive Line

Year	Yards	ALY	Rank	Power	Rank	10+ Yds	Rank	Stuff	Rank	Sack	ASR	Rank
2005	4.12	3.79	27	68%	11	20%	10	28%	30	42	6.7%	16
2006	4.68	4.62	3	62%	21	16%	17	20%	3	28	5.9%	11
2007	4.73	4.53	4	74%	4	19%	12	23%	12	49	7.6%	21

Year	LE	Rank	LT	Rank	Mid	Rank	RT	Rank	RE	Rank
2005	4.27	14	4.39	14	3.64	29	3.68	25	3.52	23
2006	4.49	11	4.25	19	4.72	3	4.21	16	5.48	2
2007	5.31	2	6.00	1	4.20	13	4.58	10	3.65	25

Any talk about the Eagles offensive line has to start with a discussion of backup tackle Winston Justice, whose figurative defenestration at the hands of Osi Umenyiora in Week 4 almost single-handedly cost the Eagles a game in which they were otherwise competitive. Justice was previously seen as a long-term replacement for left tackle Tra Thomas, but Eagles fans are going to howl the second they see Justice lining up again on the left side. With the 34-year-old Thomas manning McNabb's blind side and the 35-year-old Jon Runyan on the right, the Eagles will need to commit more resources to replacing them in the future or bite the bullet and hope that Justice's disaster was simply a bad game. Thomas and Runyan are still good enough to hold up on the ends, but each had nagging injuries last year that could easily turn into something worse.

Right guard Shaun Andrews, arguably the best interior lineman in football in 2006, wasn't quite as good in 2007, perhaps owing to a knee injury that caused him to publicly voice fears that it would force him to retire. Andrews was still among the best guards in football, particularly when pulling and smothering linebackers, and the Eagles expect him to be even better in 2008. Center Jamaal Jackson is unquestionably talented but struggles for consistency. Andrews and Jackson sometimes can take over the game, and when the two are in full swing, the Eagles pretty much have a permanent hall pass to pick up five yards at a time up the middle. Left guard Todd Herremans also had an uneven season in 2008, and young Max Jean-Gilles showed off rare power in the time he spent filling in on the line last year. They enter training camp in a competition that invariably, in Eagles' camp, seems to end with the younger guy winning. New depth is provided by strong-but-slow fourth-round pick Mike McGlynn out of Pitt, a hard worker who is best at guard but can also fill in at center, tackle, and even long-snapper. Seventh-round pick King Dunlap has a first-round name, third-round talent, and a 47th-round work ethic.

Defensive Front Seven

Defensive Line	Age	Pos	Plays	TmPct	Rk	Stop	Dfts	Stop%	Rk	AvYd	Rk	Sack	Hit	Hur	Runs	RuStop	RuYd	Pass	PaStop	PaYd
Trent Cole	26	DE	71	9.4%	4	57	32	80%	29	-0.1	6	12.5	7	11	51	75%	1.5	20	95%	-4.1
Mike Patterson	25	DT	67	8.8%	2	52	16	78%	35	1.7	32	4.0	3	7	57	79%	2.1	10	70%	-0.9
Juqua Thomas	30	DE	39	5.1%	54	29	9	74%	50	3.4	75	5.0	4	10	23	83%	2.7	16	63%	4.4
Brodrick Bunkley	25	DT	32	4.5%	46	22	12	69%	63	1.5	25	3.0	1	2	25	68%	2.4	7	71%	-1.4
Chris Clemons	26	DE	19	2.5%	—	16	13	84%	—	-3.1	—	8.0	6	5	8	63%	0.9	11	100%	-5.9

Linebackers	Age	Pos	Plays	TmPct	Rk	Stop	Dfts	Stop%	AvYd	Sack	Hit	Hur	Runs	RuStop	Rk	RuYd	Rk	Tgts	Suc%	Rk	APaYd	Rk
Omar Gaither	24	MLB	108	14.2%	26	64	21	59%	5.1	0.0	5	1	63	75%	12	3.4	50	44	54%	31	5.3	24
Takeo Spikes*	32	OLB	88	13.3%	42	48	13	55%	5.3	1.0	1	4	57	58%	70	4.1	81	35	54%	30	5.9	39
Chris Gocong	25	OLB	55	7.3%	92	26	8	47%	5.1	1.0	0	6	36	61%	52	2.7	16	23	46%	52	6.1	45
Rocky Boiman	28	OLB	49	6.0%	98	22	6	45%	4.7	0.0	0	1	25	64%	43	2.9	29	25	46%	53	4.1	9

Year	Yards	ALY	Rank	Power	Rank	10+ Yds	Rank	Stuff	Rank	Sack	ASR	Rank
2005	3.77	3.65	4	56%	7	20%	26	28%	4	29	5.8%	27
2006	4.28	4.41	21	53%	5	13%	6	24%	16	40	9.3%	1
2007	3.89	4.00	11	59%	11	18%	20	28%	5	37	7.4%	6

Year	LE	Rank	LT	Rank	Mid	Rank	RT	Rank	RE	Rank
2005	2.78	3	4.11	15	3.66	6	3.83	12	3.98	18
2006	4.19	17	5.27	29	4.57	21	4.81	28	3.03	3
2007	3.82	13	3.59	6	4.22	19	3.93	14	4.06	15

Although the Eagles' plan in 2007 was to build their defense around an incredibly deep defensive line, that depth was of little use. The star man was defensive end Trent Cole, who picked up 12.5 sacks despite being the Eagles' only consistent pass rusher. Cole is a disciplined two-way end adept at getting quickly off blocks with handwork, so when teams attempted to neutralize his pass-rushing ability by running straight at him, he was able to shed blockers and make tackles. Across from him was Juqua Thomas, who had an uneven year despite having one-on-one matchups against offensive linemen on most snaps. He could be pushed this year by 2007 second-round pick Victor Abiamiri, who lined up as the first-team starter at defensive end in June minicamp despite playing only six games in his rookie year. Abiamiri and Thomas will rotate out on passing downs to allow Chris Clemons to rush the passer; the former Raider isn't much against the run but has the potential to pick up seven to ten sacks with teams keying on Cole. Darren Howard will back up Cole, but the former Saints standout spends his time on the sidelines trying to find all the steps he misplaced.

The Eagles used their first draft pick on Notre Dame defensive tackle Trevor Laws, the fourth time in six years the Eagles have used their first draft pick on a defensive lineman. The first of those, Jerome McDougle, missed all of 2007 with an injury and may not play much in what is likely his final year with the team. Laws will rotate inside behind starting tackles Mike Patterson and Brodrick Bunkley. Both struggled some with endurance in their rookie years but are maturing into stout three-down tackles. There's not much between them as far as ability goes, but Bunkley seems to get double-teamed more frequently.

Omar Gaither was moved to middle linebacker in training camp when the team decided to cut Jeremiah Trotter, but Gaither's skill set is more suited to the outside; he'll start on the weak side in 2008, which should allow him to show off his range in coverage while limiting his run responsibilities. Moving into the middle, it appears, will be second-year man Stewart Bradley, who entered the starting lineup in Week 16 and impressed Jim Johnson. Bradley was originally drafted to play on the strong side, and his limitations in coverage at Nebraska were such that the team avoided using nickel packages strictly to keep Bradley on the field; in other words, he wasn't good enough to be in nickel packages there. He'll be in them for the Eagles if he maintains the role, which is still up in the air. Bradley replaced Takeo Spikes, who was cut following an inconsistent year and looks set to retire. If Bradley struggles, the team would have to move Gaither back inside or use another inexperienced player, 2007 undrafted free agent Pago Togafau out of Idaho State. Chris Gocong is an inoffensive starter at strong linebacker, while Rocky Boiman was signed to provide depth and special teams support. The struggles of the Eagles' linebackers were evidenced in their dramatic fall in defending passes to running backs. The team's DVOA in the category was in the top six from 2004 through 2006 but 26th in 2007.

Defensive Secondary

Secondary	Age	Pos	Plays	TmPct	Rk	Stop	Dfts	RuYd	Rk	RuStop	Rk	Tgts	Tgt%	Rk	Dist	Suc%	Rk	APaYd	Rk	PaYd	PD	Int
Sheldon Brown	29	CB	83	10.9%	17	36	16	5.7	30	45%	48	83	19%	35	13.5	53%	25	7.4	41	7.6	16	3
Quintin Mikell	28	SS	75	11.3%	22	33	15	5.4	20	54%	14	34	9%	19	9.1	64%	6	4.0	5	3.8	6	1
Lito Sheppard	27	CB	56	10.7%	18	9	4	8.0	54	20%	76	61	20%	30	12.0	36%	78	8.5	66	8.9	7	2
Joselio Hanson	27	CB	48	6.3%	—	17	10	11.4	—	21%	—	38	8%	—	5.9	67%	—	5.7	—	6.0	2	0
Brian Dawkins	35	FS	43	9.1%	46	15	7	6.8	52	39%	55	25	9%	15	15.5	65%	5	3.4	3	4.0	6	1
Sean Considine	27	SS	38	10.0%	36	17	4	6.2	38	54%	15	14	6%	55	13.0	56%	17	5.9	21	6.4	4	1
William James*	29	CB	32	4.8%	80	9	3	7.8	52	60%	17	46	12%	77	14.8	55%	19	9.8	76	10.0	2	1
J. R. Reed	26	SS	24	3.4%	—	10	7	5.9	—	29%	—	9	2%	—	6.4	45%	—	5.4	—	5.7	2	0
Asante Samuel	27	CB	64	8.8%	46	27	15	12.0	77	44%	49	81	18%	41	11.4	51%	34	6.3	14	6.0	17	6

Year	Pass D Rank	vs. #1 WR	Rk	vs. #2 WR	Rk	vs. Other WR	Rk	vs. TE	Rk	vs. RB	Rk
2005	24	21.0%	26	-4.8%	15	20.0%	29	-13.8%	7	-16.8%	6
2006	8	2.0%	15	18.9%	26	-29.7%	4	-5.9%	14	-6.2%	14
2007	12	-10.1%	8	6.2%	19	3.0%	22	-10.9%	6	1.7%	21

The Eagles spent their entire offseason debating what to do with Lito Sheppard, who had a poor year in 2007. Sheppard struggled with a knee injury early on and performed better as the season went along, but his daring style of play wasn't up to scratch. Sheppard is more talented than his good friend Sheldon Brown, but Brown was a more consistent cornerback last year and might see more snaps during the season. In fact, Sheppard's inconsistency is pretty remarkable. In 2005, he had a miserable Success Rate of 42 percent, one of the worst in the NFL, and allowed 10.4 yards per pass. In 2006, he was in the top ten among cornerbacks with a Success Rate of 60 percent while allowing just 6.6 yards per pass. Then last year, his Success Rate was even worse than it was in 2005. According to official play-by-play, 30 percent of passes against the Eagles were on the offensive left side, manned by Brown, and 44 percent were on the right, manned by Sheppard or William James. The only defense with a larger split between left and right was Oakland, which was caused by teams avoiding Nnamdi Asomugha. Sheppard's injury-prone nature would seemingly best lend itself to an arrangement in which the two corners split time on the outside and Brown serves as the slot corner in a nickel arrangement.

Asante Samuel will definitely be starting at one corner. His role should be relatively similar to the one he played in New England, as both teams use their top cornerback in the same sort of style. He will have the opportunity to pick up a few more interceptions by virtue of the Eagles' pass rush, but teams won't be throwing as frequently against a team that isn't 16-0, so it should even out in the wash. Joselio Hanson will be the dime corner, and although he's no great shakes, he's good enough to be able to shake the "Toastolio" monicker that was thrust upon him. All the adjectives we thought of to describe William James's performance in 2007 were unprintable; his play was analogous to Willis McGahee's view of the women of Buffalo, which is where James will play in 2008.

Quinton Mikell will be the starting strong safety. He's not as good as those game charting numbers suggest, but his talents are a good fit for his role in the scheme. He is an active run defender who times blitzes well, can take on linebackers and win, and doesn't often get beat deep. His size and slight frame limit his durability, so the Eagles have likely already seen his best year. Sean Considine was the original starter last season at strong safety before getting injured and losing his job; it's also possible that the Eagles could choose to move the physical Brown to strong safety in an attempt to get their four best defensive backs on the field for as many snaps as possible.

Last year was the first sign that Brian Dawkins had lost a step, particularly against the run; this view was backed by his game charting numbers. You won't see that in a downfield chase because Dawkins is still an intelligent player who takes great angles to the ball in the open field. Instead, it comes out in more subtle ways; Dawkins cheated more in 2007 when rushing to the line of scrimmage, attempting to go around blockers more frequently instead of going through them to get a better angle at the ballcarrier. That's "cheating," and although it allowed him to avoid contact more frequently and kept him healthier, it cost his team a yard or two at times. Dawkins's last step is also less explosive so he's getting worse angles on his tackles and seeing some tackles he'd make becoming whiffs. He's still a valuable player at this level, but his performance bears watching early in 2008. Eagles' fans hoping for improvement from the group this year can take heart in the fact that the team's pass defense was 20th in the league through Week 9 but sixth in the season's final eight weeks.

Special Teams

Year	DVOA	Rank	FG/XP	Rank	Net Punt	Rank	Punt Ret	Rank	Net Kick	Rank	Kick Ret	Rank	Hidden	Rank
2005	0.0%	17	-0.2	19	5.5	8	-0.9	17	-1.4	19	-3.1	18	-1.4	18
2006	-1.9%	22	-5.1	26	-6.0	26	-2.7	25	7.9	7	-5.4	25	-15.2	32
2007	-5.4%	31	-4.1	26	-10.3	30	-7.5	30	-2.4	20	-7.1	26	10.8	6

We spoke about the importance of an improvement in the Eagles' special teams play in 2008 in this chapter. Adding DeSean Jackson is a noble idea, but shouldn't affect things unless the coverage improves significantly. That's on the coaching staff but also on players such as Akeem Jordan, Considine, Mikell, J. R. Reed, and Hank Baskett, players whose value to the team and justification for maintaining a roster spot is tied up at least partly in the idea that they will contribute on special teams. Having Rocky Boiman around should help. Kicker David Akers should bounce back some after going 2-for-10 from beyond 40 yards last year. He is a fantasy sleeper inasmuch as a kicker can be a fantasy sleeper. Sav Rocca was a disappointment in his first year as the punter.

COACHING STAFF

The plight of Andy Reid's sons and Reid's departures to deal with their situation was given as an excuse for the Eagles' poor play in 2007, but it's not as though the Eagles were showing up to games underprepared or making obvious mental errors. Reid has a core of coaches around him that he trusts, and he delegates a good portion of weekly planning to them. Offensive coordinator Marty Mornhinweg calls the plays on the offensive side, and Jim Johnson does the same defensively. Reid, presumably, handles the coin toss. Although we often consider the Eagles to be at the forefront of statistical analysis and proactive management among NFL teams, and we also read study after study that say teams should go for it more on fourth-and-1, the Eagles were the least likely team to try and convert on fourth down in 2007, a year after being the sixth most likely team to do so in 2006. It will be interesting to see whether the shift is an aberration or a trend.

Pittsburgh Steelers

Momentum is an overused word in football analysis. Clichés such as "season of two halves" and "backed into the playoffs" are bandied around freely when writing about teams that declined during the season. Many of those teams didn't really get worse. They suffered a few injuries at key positions, had a particularly difficult section in their schedule, or saw a few important bounces go the other way.

When a team's play actually does drop off significantly in the middle of a season, other root causes must be reviewed. The 2007 Pittsburgh Steelers were such a team. Following their Week 9 victory over the Baltimore Ravens, the 6-2 Steelers ranked fourth in the Football Outsiders DVOA ratings at 36.1%. In the 13 years of DVOA, going back to 1995, the 2007 Steelers are one of the top 20 teams ever through Week 9. It just so happens that three other teams playing last year—the Patriots, Colts, and Cowboys—are among the top seven teams ever through Week 9, so the Steelers weren't getting too much attention from the national media.

Over the remainder of the season, the Steelers did not manage to turn in a single performance of that level on either side of the ball. They became a below-average team, with a -3.8% DVOA that ranked 18th in the NFL from Week 10 through Week 17. Normally when a team declines like this, the process is gradual; but for Pittsburgh the descent was steep and sudden (Figure 1). The team lurched onto a division championship at 10-6 before Jacksonville came in to Pittsburgh and beat the

Steelers in the first round of the playoffs. It could hardly be called an upset loss, since the 11-5 Jaguars had already beaten the Steelers at Heinz Field during the regular season.

Pittsburgh collapsed for a number of reasons, starting with injuries. Free safety Ryan Clark is an underrated player whose presence in the backfield allows Troy Polamalu to play with more freedom. But when the Steelers went to Denver in Week 8, playing in the altitude activated Clark's dormant sickle-cell trait, causing his red blood cells to sickle and leading to an infection that, due to an initial misdiagnosis, cost him his gall bladder and spleen before being brought under control. Needless to say, it also ended Clark's season. As for Polamalu, he missed Weeks 12-14 with a knee sprain, forcing Pittsburgh to face New England's aerial assault without either starting safety. Defensive end Aaron Smith was lost for the season in the New England game, and Fred Taylor and Maurice Jones-Drew took full advantage of that the next week. On the other side of the ball, left tackle Marvel Smith missed four of the last seven games of the regular season, and starting wideouts Santonio Holmes and Hines Ward both struggled with nagging injuries.

Other teams had a similar number of second-half injuries, and not one matched the Steelers' decline. This speaks ill of Pittsburgh's depth at several positions. The Steelers didn't need to have both safeties injured to watch the defensive backfield struggle. Ryan Clark's backup, free safety Anthony Smith, came into the sea-

---

STEELERS PROSPECTUS

2007 Record: 10-6

Pythagorean Wins: 11.4 (4th)

DVOA: 17.7% total (8th), 5.8% weighted (14th)

Offense: 6.8% DVOA (12th)

Defense: -12.3% DVOA (2nd)

Special Teams: -1.4% DVOA (21st)

Variance: 22.6 % (29th)

2007: The Steelers were apparently unaware that the season continues after Week 10.

2008: The schedule and the offensive line compete to derail the playoff challenge.

2008 Mean Projection: 7.2 wins

On the Clock (0-3): 3%

Loserville (4-6): 38%

Mediocrity (7-8): 28%

Playoff Contender (9-10): 22%

Super Bowl Contender (11+): 8%

Projected Average Opponent: 8.2% DVOA (1st in NFL)

2008 Steelers Schedule

Week	Opp.	Week	Opp.	Week	Opp.
1	HOU	7	at CIN	13	at NE
2	at CLE	8	NYG	14	DAL
3	at PHI	9	at WAS (Mon.)	15	at BAL
4	BAL (Mon.)	10	IND	16	at TEN
5	at JAC	11	SD	17	CLE
6	BYE	12	CIN (Thu.)		

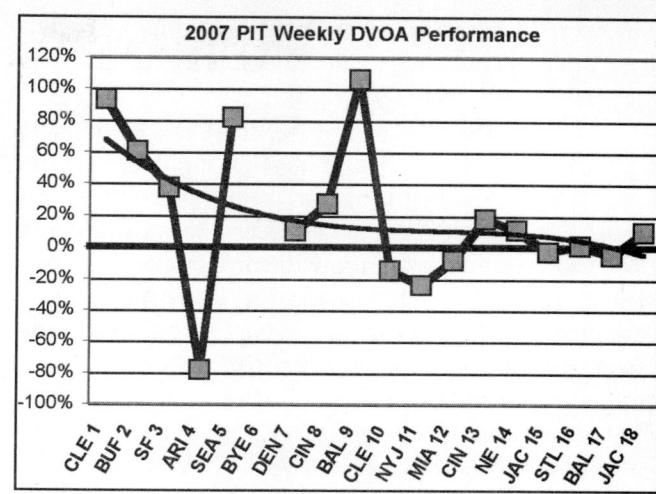

Figure 1

son as a highly touted prospect. Expected to win the starting job in training camp, he lost out to the incumbent Clark. Smith was promoted after Clark went down, and it rapidly became apparent why he hadn't been made the starter. As only a third-year player, Smith still has plenty of potential, especially as most of his problems seem to be in terms of mindset. Smith has the physical tools to play the last line of defense, which is the proper role of the free safety in Dick LeBeau's scheme, but he wants to make the big play instead—and as a result often ends up out of position. Theoretically, you can teach a player how to follow the system more easily than you can teach him physical skills. Since Pittsburgh waited until its final pick of the 2008 draft to select a safety, it seems the Steelers have confidence in Clark's continued health (he's regained fitness and is working out with the team, but further sickle-cell-related problems are a possibility). Polamalu's ability to stay healthy despite his reckless playing style must also be a concern, but clearly the Steelers are willing to trust their depth at safety to Anthony Smith's continuing development

The defensive line looks similarly thin. After end Aaron Smith was lost for the season, Pittsburgh's run defense collapsed, with their opponents averaging over five yards per carry in the next three weeks. They recovered slightly in the wild card game, but it's hard to say whether a single match is indicative of an improvement. Pittsburgh re-signed backups Travis Kirschke and Nick Eason in the off-season rather than look elsewhere for answers, so once again the franchise seems to be happy with its depth. Another backup the Steelers re-signed (via the transition tag) was Max Starks. Starks replaced Marvel Smith when the starting left tackle was sidelined with a back injury for four games. Pittsburgh didn't fare significantly worse in pass protection when Starks was in, but then they were already so bad that "didn't fare significantly worse" is faint praise indeed.

The reasons for Pittsburgh's decline go beyond simple injuries. The Steelers weren't the only team to have a rocky second half in 2007. Pittsburgh heads the list of largest drops in DVOA between weeks 1-9 and 10-17 for a 10-plus-win team, but four other squads from last year join them in the top 10 (Table 1). This suggests that at least part of whatever it was that caused the Steelers to fall apart applied league-wide or at least to the best teams. Some of it may be due to a relative lack of competition in this year's AFC. The Patriots, Colts, and Steelers had their division titles all but decided by Week 10, and it was fairly apparent that the first-round byes were going to New England and Indianapolis. It wouldn't be surprising if the effort levels were a little lower or if coordinators decided to hold new schemes and plays back for the playoffs. The bad news for the Steelers is that, historically, winning teams that went

Table 1. Top Second Half Declines in DVOA, 10 or More Wins, 1995-2007

Team	Year	DVOA Weeks 1-9	DVOA Weeks 10-17	Change
PIT	2007	40.3%	-1.1%	-41.3%
IND	2007	56.3%	21.1%	-35.1%
PHI	2001	35.9%	1.0%	-34.9%
NE	2007	64.0%	30.0%	-34.0%
DAL	2007	40.8%	8.6%	-32.2%
DAL	1996	32.9%	2.2%	-30.7%
TEN	2007	25.5%	-4.5%	-30.0%
SF	2002	31.4%	4.3%	-27.1%
DEN	1996	42.6%	16.6%	-25.9%
GB	2002	23.6%	-0.4%	-24.0%
CIN	2005	29.1%	5.2%	-23.9%
GB	1996	46.3%	22.5%	-23.7%

through this sort of decline tended to play nearer to their post-decline level than their early-season performances the following season.

Going forward, the biggest problem for the Steelers is the offensive line. The standard of line play in Pittsburgh has been dropping for a few years now and should bottom out in 2008. Left guard Alan Faneca, the team's best lineman, signed with the Jets; the Steelers were unable or unwilling to accommodate his contract demands. Faneca grumbled his way through training camp, presenting Mike Tomlin with his first locker room crisis in the process, but once the season started he quieted down and played hard. Whether that was the result of Tomlin's skill as a motivator, Faneca's enlightened self-interest, or an undertaking from the front office not to use the franchise tag is unclear. Faneca's departure, coupled with the failure of free agent Sean Mahan to fill Jeff Hartings's boots at center, leaves Pittsburgh's interior line a shambles. The Steelers had another go at finding a center in free agency, signing Justin Hartwig. The Steelers might have wanted to draft an offensive lineman high as well, but a run on tackles in the first round saw seven (including Virginia guard/tackle Branden Albert) leave the board before Pittsburgh picked. This left the Steelers with no sensible offensive line pick and a clear best player available in Rashard Mendenhall. Mendenhall might seem a strange pick with Willie Parker on the roster, but Parker is an inconsistent runner ill-suited to the role of feature back. His value comes in his breakaway speed and ability to make long runs, but last year the Steelers tried to turn their racehorse into a workhorse. It didn't work—the heavy workload caused Parker to tire more quickly, losing some of his top-end speed, and as a result the Steelers fell from third in long runs (of 10 yards or more) to 13th. Parker was exhausted by the closing weeks of the season, and Parker himself recognized that, telling the *Pittsburgh Post-Gazette* before the draft, "If they bring somebody else in here, I'm all for it."

It is not Parker's career that Mendenhall has been brought in to extend, though; it is the length of Pittsburgh's offensive drives. Mendenhall has been compared to a "bigger, faster Edgerrin James" by Steelers' offensive coordinator Bruce Arians. He's a reliable runner who will have fewer 20-yard runs than Parker but also fewer runs for no gain. That will, in turn, help Pittsburgh's pass protection by reducing the number of second- and third-and-long situations where the Steelers turn to Ben Roethlisberger to bail them out and the opposing defenses can tee off on Big Ben because they know he has to pass. Roethlisberger performed miracles there last year—Pittsburgh's DVOA in third-and-

long situations was an unlikely-to-be-sustained 102.6%—but putting him in such scenarios greatly increases the likelihood of injury.

Something else that might help the Steelers avoid those third-and-long situations would be a shift in offensive play-calling. Although Pittsburgh's line is somewhat better at run blocking than it is in pass protection, the Steelers overall are better equipped as a passing team than as a running one. Quarterback Ben Roethlisberger has shown a remarkable capacity for being productive despite being sacked repeatedly, and Pittsburgh's receiving corps—Santonio Holmes, Hines Ward, Nate Washington, the newly drafted Limas Sweed, and tight end Heath Miller—is well above average and skilled at improvising plays after the pocket collapses. The Steelers ranked seventh in passing DVOA and 17th in rushing. Plenty of other teams had a similar split—Arizona, Cincinnati, and Seattle—but those teams didn't keep running the football like Pittsburgh did. Pittsburgh had 69 more runs than pass attempts; the only offense that was more slanted in favor of the ground game was Tennessee. Franchise traditions are all very well, but Herm Edwards put it best: You play to win the game. The Steelers' best chance of winning games comes when they put the ball in the hands of their franchise quarterback. It's not a tremendously popular idea in Pittsburgh, as the reaction to the team's loss in Denver revealed. To be fair, Pittsburgh's game plan—on a cold night against a poor run defense—was too pass-heavy (Willie Parker had only three carries at the half). However, offense wasn't the Steelers' problem in that game, as the 31-28 final score showed. Offensive coordinator Bruce Arians was excoriated for being too pass happy and the demand was great for a return to "Steeler Football." Yes, the Steelers were the best team of the historically run-heavy 1970s, and under Bill Cowher the presence of Jerome Bettis and the absence of a reliable quarterback dictated a certain reliance on the run, but the league's current offensive climate is a passing one and the Steelers have perhaps the best young quarterback-receiver tandem in the league in Roethlisberger and Holmes. It's time to let them live up to their promise.

The Steelers also need to deal with their gaping holes on special teams, or more precisely, their punt and kick coverage. The Steelers have been in the bottom third of the league in these areas for two seasons now, and on more than one occasion a long runback became a decisive turning point in a Pittsburgh loss. Mike Tomlin supposedly made special teams a priority in his first training camp as head coach, but the results are limited. To improve in this area, Pittsburgh might need to shift their evaluation of backup players, emphasizing special teams value over the ability to move into the starting lineup when necessary.

Overall, the Pittsburgh Steelers are a talented team with flaws rather than a flawed team with some talent. The defense is capable of suffocating performances when at full strength and rarely drops below average even when dealing with multiple injuries. The future success of the offense largely depends on Roethlisberger continuing to succeed despite the state of the offensive line—which includes managing to stay healthy—and on the willingness of the team to trust in him.

The success of the Steelers? This year, that may well be a function of the schedule. The NFL's rotation has given them the NFC East and the AFC South as opponents in 2008, two divisions that between them in 2007 had no losing teams. By virtue of last year's division title, the Steelers get to round out the schedule with New England and San Diego. Baltimore and Cincinnati are the only two teams on Pittsburgh's schedule that had losing records in 2007. A wild card seems out of the question, so the Steelers have to win the AFC North. With Cleveland stacking the roster for the short term and Baltimore poised for a rebound, it will be a challenge.

Stuart Fraser

Win Expectancy after a Hot Start

Although the Pittsburgh Steelers couldn't complain too loudly about an AFC North title and home playoff game in Mike Tomlin's first year as coach, the distinct reality exists that the team could have done so much more. It's hard to end your season with a home playoff loss by less than a field goal, but the bigger issue may be Pittsburgh's regular season performance. The Steelers saw their winning streaks broken at the hands of the Cardinals, Broncos, and Jets—teams that should be slumpbusters, not slumpstarters.

Did the Steelers underachieve in 2007? That question can be asked in two ways. First, how many wins should we expect from a team that over the course of the season plays at the same level as the Steelers but with average luck and timing? Metrics such as the Pythagorean theorem and DVOA help us analyze that in a theoretical fashion. But another way to underachieve is not playing better than your record overall but failing even though you were in the right position to succeed. That's the question we need to ask about the Steelers, who began

the season 7-2 and then crashed and burned and lost in the first round of the playoffs. We can track the Steelers' progress, see how the losses affected them, and try to find out where they peaked by looking at a "dumb" win model.

The way this model predicts wins is simple: It tracks the game-by-game winning percentages of every team it's fed and spits out expectations based on history. In this scenario, we're going to compare the 2007 Steelers to every team since 1990, when the now-standard 17-week schedule was introduced. We're excluding 1993 because of its two-by-week schedule setup that made the regular season 18 weeks long.

First, how likely were the Steelers to be at a certain place at a certain time? Table 2 displays the percentage of teams that had a certain number of wins at any given game during the regular season. So then, when the Steelers started 4-1, they were in the 95th percentile of all teams, with only 4.3 percent of teams starting the year 5-0. This would end up being the peak point of the Steelers' season, the highest percentile-ranking they would share during the year.

Another interesting way to tease out that data is to analyze the win expectations the Steelers had after each win or loss during the regular season (Table 3). In more colloquial terms, how good is the average 3-1 team end up after 16 games? The answer: Teams that start 3-1 will win, on average, 9.8 games.

According to this methodology, the Steelers peaked after their 12th game, a 24-10 defeat of the Bengals that pushed the Steelers to 9-3. That moved their expected win total for the season up to 11.6 wins (Figure 2).

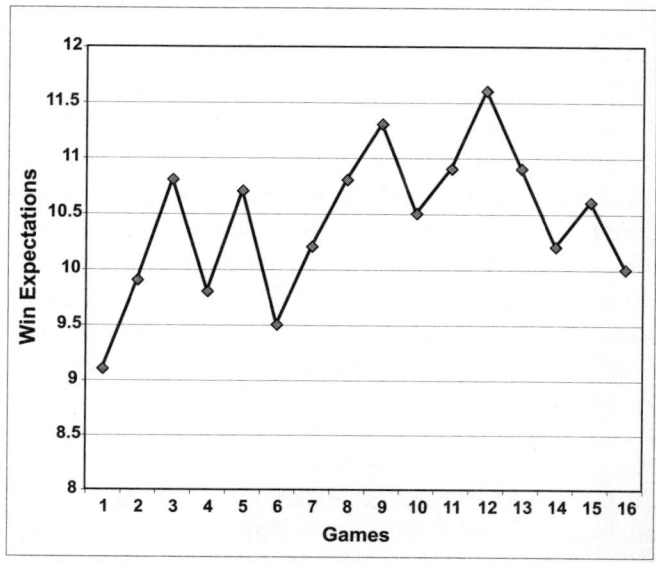

Figure 2. Steelers Win Expectations by Week

Table 2. NFL Distribution of Wins by Week

Wins	1	2	3	4	5	6	7	8	9	10	11	12	13	14	15	16
0	50.0%	27.1%	16.6%	11.0%	6.4%	3.7%	3.1%	2.1%	1.2%	0.8%	0.6%	0.4%	0.2%	0.0%	0.0%	0.0%
1	50.0%	46.2%	33.3%	23.8%	16.2%	11.8%	8.1%	6.0%	4.8%	3.3%	2.7%	2.1%	1.9%	1.7%	1.5%	1.2%
2		26.7%	33.1%	28.6%	27.9%	24.6%	18.4%	13.0%	9.7%	8.7%	6.4%	5.2%	4.1%	3.5%	2.3%	1.7%
3			17.0%	26.9%	25.1%	20.3%	20.1%	19.5%	16.2%	12.0%	10.1%	8.5%	7.4%	6.2%	5.6%	4.1%
4				9.7%	19.0%	23.2%	19.3%	19.5%	18.2%	18.6%	15.9%	11.2%	10.1%	8.7%	7.4%	7.5%
5					5.4%	12.2%	19.9%	17.0%	19.1%	15.5%	15.1%	16.2%	12.4%	9.7%	8.5%	7.9%
6						4.3%	8.3%	14.9%	12.8%	15.5%	13.5%	13.5%	13.2%	12.8%	11.0%	10.1%
7							2.7%	6.4%	11.4%	12.0%	15.1%	13.2%	13.5%	13.7%	14.1%	11.0%
8								1.5%	4.6%	8.9%	9.5%	11.8%	13.5%	12.0%	10.4%	11.2%
9									1.5%	3.3%	7.0%	9.1%	9.5%	12.4%	12.6%	11.6%
10										1.2%	2.7%	5.0%	6.4%	6.6%	9.3%	10.4%
11											0.8%	1.9%	4.6%	6.2%	7.2%	8.5%
12												0.6%	1.5%	3.7%	4.1%	6.0%
13													0.6%	1.5%	4.1%	4.8%
14														0.2%	0.6%	2.1%
15															0.2%	0.4%
16																0.2%

Table 3. Average Wins at Particular Win/Game State

Wins	1	2	3	4	5	6	7	8	9	10	11	12	13	14	15	16
0	6.9	5.9	5.0	4.4	3.7	2.7	2.6	2.1	1.7	1.8	1.3	1.5	1.0			
1	9.1	8.1	7.0	6.4	5.6	4.8	4.3	3.8	3.1	2.4	2.2	1.7	1.6	1.3	1.3	1.0
2		9.9	9.1	7.8	7.0	6.4	5.7	5.2	4.6	4.1	3.7	3.3	3.0	2.8	2.4	2.0
3			10.8	9.8	8.8	8.1	7.3	6.5	6.1	5.5	4.8	4.4	4.1	3.8	3.4	3.0
4				11.5	10.7	9.5	8.6	7.9	7.0	6.6	6.2	5.6	5.1	4.7	4.3	4.0
5					12.4	11.2	10.2	9.6	8.9	8.1	7.4	6.8	6.3	5.8	5.3	5.0
6						12.7	11.8	10.8	10.0	9.4	8.8	8.1	7.4	6.9	6.4	6.0
7							13.3	12.3	11.3	10.5	9.8	9.3	8.6	8.0	7.5	7.0
8								13.8	12.9	11.9	10.9	10.2	9.7	9.2	8.6	8.0
9									13.8	13.0	12.5	11.6	10.9	10.2	9.6	9.0
10										14.2	13.4	12.8	12.0	11.3	10.6	10.0
11											14.5	13.8	13.0	12.3	11.6	11.0
12												14.7	14.0	13.3	12.7	12.0
13													14.7	14.1	13.5	13.0
14														16.0	14.7	14.0
15															16.0	15.0
16																16.0

Twelve wins would have given the Steelers a first-round game with the Titans instead of the Jaguars, and that would have been a much better matchup for Pittsburgh. Of course, the model doesn't know that the Patriots and Jaguars were the next two opponents on the Steelers' schedule; on the other hand, the Steelers still got to play the Rams and Ravens, losing to the latter, so it wasn't as if their final four games were *all* tough.

The Steelers' win expectancy was above their final 10-6 record for most of the season, including every week from Week 7 through the end of the year. They were realistically safe at 9-3, but you can see how much each loss hurt the Steelers; the most painful one was the Week 6 defeat at the hands of Denver, which took them off the path of a 10.7-win team and dropped them all the way down to 9.5.

Of course, what does a 9.8-6.2 record mean when it comes to making the playoffs? Table 4 details what percentage of teams with a given record at a given time in the regular season got to play extra football. Using this methodology, the Steelers' playoff chances peaked in Week 12. Not a single team in the timeframe of this research started the season 9-3 and ended up missing the playoffs.

Table 4. Likelihood of Making the Playoffs

Wins	1	2	3	4	5	6	7	8	9	10	11	12	13	14	15	16
0	24.7%	11.4%	3.5%	1.8%	0.0%	0.0%	0.0%	0.0%	0.0%	0.0%	0.0%	0.0%	0.0%			
1	54.3%	41.0%	22.7%	14.6%	6.0%	0.0%	0.0%	0.0%	0.0%	0.0%	0.0%	0.0%	0.0%		0.0%	0.0%
2		65.2%	53.8%	33.1%	19.4%	8.7%	3.2%	1.5%	0.0%	0.0%	0.0%	0.0%	0.0%	0.0%	0.0%	0.0%
3			79.5%	66.2%	50.0%	40.0%	20.2%	4.0%	3.6%	1.6%	0.0%	0.0%	0.0%	0.0%	0.0%	0.0%
4				88.0%	80.6%	62.5%	49.0%	34.7%	10.6%	5.2%	3.7%	0.0%	0.0%	0.0%	0.0%	0.0%
5					96.4%	87.3%	76.7%	69.3%	54.5%	30.0%	10.3%	4.8%	0.0%	0.0%	0.0%	0.0%
6						95.5%	88.4%	81.8%	74.2%	66.3%	50.0%	28.6%	10.3%	3.0%	0.0%	0.0%
7							100.0%	97.0%	91.5%	82.3%	71.8%	60.3%	42.9%	21.1%	6.8%	0.0%
8								100.0%	100.0%	97.8%	93.9%	82.0%	71.4%	54.8%	37.0%	12.1%
9									100.0%	100.0%	100.0%	100.0%	93.9%	87.5%	69.2%	51.7%
10										100.0%	100.0%	100.0%	100.0%	100.0%	100.0%	90.7%
11											100.0%	100.0%	100.0%	100.0%	100.0%	100.0%
12												100.0%	100.0%	100.0%	100.0%	100.0%
13													100.0%	100.0%	100.0%	100.0%
14														100.0%	100.0%	100.0%
15															100.0%	100.0%
16																100.0%

What also makes Table 3 interesting is that, using its percentages for making the playoffs, you can analyze which games are the most important in football by finding the most dramatic differences between one game/win state and another. For example, a team that's 3-1 after four games (66.2 percent) is twice as likely to make the playoffs as a team that's 2-2 (33.1 percent). The difference between winning and losing the game would increase or decrease the team's odds of making the playoffs a full 100 percent.

It came as a surprise even to us that the most important game in football, measured by its effect on a team's chance of making the postseason, takes place nine games into the season. A team that enters its ninth game with a record of 4-4 has a 54.5 percent chance of making the playoffs if they win and go to 5-4 but only a 10.6 percent chance of getting to the postseason if they start 4-5 instead. More intuitively, two of the five most important games occur in the season's final week: the last game for a team that is 9-6 and the last game for a team that is 10-5. (The other two games in the top five are the 11th game for a 5-5 team and the tenth game for a 5-4 team.)

The issue for the Steelers after their 9-3 start wasn't whether they'd make the playoffs but what they'd do when they got there. Instead of reverting to the form that led the team to 9-3, they played more like the team that finished 1-3. If 2008 doesn't prove to be particularly kind to Steelers' fans, they might find themselves ruing the underperformance shown by the team last season.

Bill Barnwell

2007 Steelers Stats by Week

Wk	vs.	W-L	PF	PA	YDF	YDA	TO	Total	Off	Def	ST
1	@CLE	W	34	7	365	221	+4	93%	10%	-75%	8%
2	BUF	W	26	3	420	223	-1	61%	43%	-19%	-2%
3	SF	W	37	16	350	289	0	37%	31%	18%	24%
4	@ARI	L	14	21	282	301	0	-78%	-50%	5%	-23%
5	SEA	W	21	0	342	144	+1	82%	30%	-60%	-8%
6	BYE										
7	@DEN	L	28	31	379	324	-1	10%	10%	-4%	-4%
8	@CIN	W	24	13	390	296	0	27%	31%	-1%	-5%
9	BAL	W	38	7	291	104	+3	106%	24%	-74%	8%
10	CLE	W	31	28	401	163	0	-15%	-5%	-21%	-31%
11	@NYJ	L	16	19	263	297	-1	-24%	-22%	4%	1%
12	MIA	W	3	0	216	159	+1	-8%	-44%	-33%	3%
13	CIN	W	24	10	285	249	-3	18%	-10%	-28%	1%
14	@NE	L	13	34	349	421	-1	11%	16%	5%	-1%
15	JAC	L	22	29	217	421	+1	-3%	-6%	3%	6%
16	@STL	W	41	24	425	316	+2	1%	38%	33%	-4%
17	@BAL	L	21	27	264	334	-2	-5%	9%	17%	3%
18	JAC	L	29	31	340	239	-2	10%	-15%	-36%	-11%

Trends and Splits

	Offense	Rank	Defense	Rank
Total DVOA	6.8%	12	-12.3%	2
Unadjusted VOA	10.6%	7	-10.9%	3
Weighted Trend	2.4%	17	-5.9%	8
Variance	7.8%	21	10.6%	28
Average Opponent	4.4%	32	0.6%	20
Passing	20.5%	7	-8.7%	5
Rushing	-4.8%	17	-17.3%	3
First Down	-5.6%	20	-8.9%	8
Second Down	-3.6%	18	-25.4%	1
Third Down	47.0%	2	1.7%	14
First Half	3.5%	14	-13.2%	5
Second Half	10.0%	7	-11.5%	3
Red Zone	10.1%	13	-10.4%	11
Late and Close	-5.4%	22	-2.9%	12

Five-Year Performance

Year	W-L	Pyth Wins	Est Wins	PF	PA	TO	Total	Rank	Off	Rank	Def	Rank	ST	Rank
2003	6-10	7.2	7.6	300	327	-3	-2.0%	19	-9.3%	22	-3.8%	13	3.5%	3
2004	15-1	11.5	12.1	372	251	+11	34.8%	2	15.0%	8	-17.6%	3	2.3%	10
2005	11-5	11.6	11.6	398	258	+7	28.1%	3	11.5%	8	-15.1%	2	1.4%	9
2006	8-8	9.1	8.5	353	315	-8	7.5%	12	5.2%	10	-6.5%	10	-4.2%	30
2007	10-6	11.4	9.3	393	269	+3	17.7%	8	6.8%	12	-12.3%	2	-1.4%	21

Strategic Tendencies

Run/Pass		Rank	Offense		Rank	Defense		Rank	Other		Rank
Runs, all plays	48%	1	3+ WR	49%	17	Rush 3	10.8%	5	2+ RB, Pct Runs	66%	4
Runs, first half	42%	14	4+ WR	16%	8	Rush 4	41.2%	32	1 RB/2 TE, Pct Runs	62%	4
Runs, first down	60%	1	2+ TE	40%	2	Rush 5	40.8%	2	1 RB/3+ WR, Pct Runs	30%	6
Runs, second-long	44%	3	Single back	65%	5	Rush 6+	7.1%	20	CB1 on WR1	52%	7
Runs, power sit.	63%	20	Play action	16%	18	Rush 7+	1.9%	14	Go for it on 4th	0.64	31
Runs, behind 2H	36%	4	Max protect	9%	19	Sacks by LB	72.2%	1	Offensive Pace	34.4	32
Pass, ahead 2H	32%	30	Outside pocket	22%	3	Sacks by DB	6.9%	13	Defensive Pace	30.4	8

Ben Roethlisberger was the most hurried quarterback in the league, but he also was the best quarterback in the league when hurried (36.9% DVOA). Roethlisberger had to scramble on 15 percent of pass plays, more than any other quarterback and more than twice the league average of seven percent. ✐ The Steelers had the greatest discrepancy between their offensive efficiency in the shotgun (41.0% DVOA) and with the quarterback under center (-3.4% DVOA). Their usage of shotgun dropped from 33 percent of plays in 2006 to 28 percent of plays in 2007, even though league-wide usage of the shotgun ballooned from 19 percent of plays in 2006 to 27 percent of plays in 2007. ✐ Pittsburgh was significantly more efficient when they went three-wide (39.4% DVOA) or four-wide (38.1% DVOA) compared to the conventional two wide receivers (-20.9% DVOA). ✐ Only Tampa Bay had a higher percentage of plays with only one wide receiver in the formation. ✐ The Pittsburgh offense was last in the league with only six tipped passes. ⊘ Pittsburgh averaged 5.7 yards when using a play-fake but 6.6 yards without play action. That's the largest yardage discrepancy of any team that was better without play-action, although three teams had wider gaps when measured by DVOA rather than yards. ⊘ Pittsburgh allowed an average of just 3.6 yards after catch, the lowest figure in the league. One of the reasons: Steelers' opponents threw to their running backs less often than against any other defense. However, the Steelers also led the league in preventing yards after catch if we consider only passes beyond the line of scrimmage. ⊘ Bill Cowher was among the most aggressive coaches of the past decade on fourth down, but Mike Tomlin was extremely conservative in his first season.

Passing

Player	DYAR	DVOA	Plays	NtYds	Avg	YAC	C%	TD	Int
Ben Roethlisberger	743	15.5%	449	2821	6.3	4.0	65.9%	32	11
Charlie Batch	29	0.5%	37	270	7.3	6.2	47.2%	2	3

Rushing

Player	DYAR	DVOA	Plays	Yds	Avg	TD	Fum	Suc
Willie Parker	-27	-10.8%	321	1317	4.1	2	4	42%
Najeh Davenport	118	15.1%	107	500	4.7	5	1	52%
Ben Roethlisberger	65	24.6%	30	204	6.8	2	9	—
Carey Davis	-4	-16.8%	17	68	4.0	0	0	29%
Gary Russell	6	10.7%	7	21	3.0	0	0	43%
Santonio Holmes	-17	-101.4%	5	17	3.4	0	1	—
Mewelde Moore	25	31.5%	20	114	5.7	0	1	50%

Receiving

Player	DYAR	DVOA	Plays	Ctch	Yds	Y/C	YAC	TD	C%
WR									
Hines Ward	124	1.8%	113	72	736	10.2	3.1	7	64%
Santonio Holmes	259	26.2%	85	52	952	18.3	4.9	8	61%
Nate Washington	124	16.5%	56	29	450	15.5	2.5	5	52%
Cedrick Wilson*	33	1.9%	30	18	207	11.5	2.4	1	60%
Willie Reid	3	-4.9%	6	4	54	13.5	13.0	0	67%
TE									
Heath Miller	194	38.9%	61	47	566	12.0	4.4	7	77%
Matt Spaeth	35	70.2%	6	5	34	6.8	2.8	3	83%
RB									
Willie Parker	29	3.2%	31	23	164	7.1	6.0	0	74%
Najeh Davenport	51	25.5%	27	18	184	10.2	6.4	2	67%
Carey Davis	-7	-23.8%	14	12	49	4.1	4.0	0	86%
Mewelde Moore	2	-7.8%	8	6	48	8.0	6.5	0	75%

Offensive Line

Year	Yards	ALY	Rank	Power	Rank	10+ Yds	Rank	Stuff	Rank	Sack	ASR	Rank
2005	4.18	4.28	12	68%	12	18%	15	25%	18	32	7.8%	22
2006	4.38	4.16	22	63%	19	24%	3	25%	22	49	7.9%	24
2007	4.21	4.12	19	60%	21	19%	13	23%	15	47	10.1%	31

Year	LE	Rank	LT	Rank	Mid	Rank	RT	Rank	RE	Rank
2005	5.05	5	2.71	30	4.41	8	4.48	10	4.95	4
2006	4.02	19	4.05	23	4.43	13	3.66	31	4.05	16
2007	4.66	10	4.59	10	3.73	28	4.54	11	4.33	12

To say that the Steelers' offensive line could do with an overhaul is an understatement, but the biggest change will be negative: the departure of veteran left guard Alan Faneca. After that, the changes made were rather timid, signing center Justin Hartwig away from the Panthers and drafting Texas tackle Tony Hills. Hills, a first-day talent who dropped to the fourth round because of a broken fibula, might have been the first tackle the Steelers thought was good value after the early run on linemen. He came back from a much worse injury (a severe knee injury in high school that threatened his ability to walk) to be a star at Texas, so the Steelers appear to have picked up a solid contributor. Hills will probably back up left tackle Marvel Smith, the best lineman remaining on Pittsburgh's roster after Faneca's departure. Smith missed four games with a back injury in 2007, which will have the Steelers concerned, but the 30-year-old probably has several productive seasons left. He's likely to be the only point of stability as the Steelers shuffle players around in the hope that the resulting structure will be less flimsy. Chris Kemoeatu will get the first chance to replace Faneca; his career currently extends to two starts, so it's a bit much asking him to replace a regular Pro Bowler without a drop-off in performance. Another possibility is center Sean Mahan, who was awful at that position in 2007 but had more success as a guard in Tampa. Hartwig is likely to take over snapping duties, holding the edge over Mahan and second-year player Darnell Stapleton going into training camp.

Right guard Kendall Simmons was another reason why the Steelers had trouble running up the middle and keeping the interior rush away from Ben Roethlisberger. Simmons had seven blown blocks leading to sacks, as many as Cleveland's entire offensive line combined. Right tackle Willie Colon maintained consistent incompetence throughout the season. Colon might move inside to replace Simmons at right guard, with Max Starks regaining the position he lost last year at right tackle. Simmons could end up playing center or even left guard. The normal result of all this chopping and changing would be deterioration in the quality of the line's play, though Steelers' fans could be forgiven for wondering how it could get any worse.

Defensive Front Seven

Defensive Line	Age	Pos	Plays	TmPct	Rk	Stop	Dfts	Stop%	Rk	AvYd	Rk	Sack	Hit	Hur	Runs	RuStop	RuYd	Pass	PaStop	PaYd
Brett Keisel	30	DE	44	6.1%	34	31	9	70%	66	2.7	65	2.0	5	12	30	73%	2.9	14	64%	2.4
Aaron Smith	32	DE	32	6.5%	29	25	9	78%	38	0.7	17	2.5	4	3	26	77%	1.7	6	83%	-3.8
Casey Hampton	31	DT	32	4.8%	38	27	7	84%	13	1.2	16	0.5	0	3	31	84%	1.5	1	100%	-9.0
Travis Kirschke	34	DE	26	3.6%	73	23	7	88%	3	1.4	31	2.0	1	2	23	87%	2.1	3	100%	-4.3

Linebackers	Age	Pos	Plays	TmPct	Rk	Stop	Dfts	Stop%	AvYd	Sack	Hit	Hur	Runs	RuStop	Rk	RuYd	Rk	Tgts	Suc%	Rk	APaYd	Rk
James Farrior	33	ILB	101	14.1%	29	63	26	62%	3.4	6.5	9	17	57	68%	26	3.0	32	39	46%	54	5.5	30
James Harrison	30	OLB	88	12.3%	53	67	29	76%	2.1	8.5	10	8	55	82%	7	2.3	10	19	55%	27	6.2	50
Larry Foote	28	ILB	84	11.7%	57	56	18	67%	3.1	3.0	2	12	59	75%	13	2.6	15	25	51%	40	3.8	6
Clark Haggans*	31	OLB	60	8.4%	81	34	11	57%	3.9	4.0	3	12	41	59%	65	3.7	65	22	48%	48	5.6	33

Year	Yards	ALY	Rank	Power	Rank	10+ Yds	Rank	Stuff	Rank	Sack	ASR	Rank
2005	3.41	3.65	5	56%	6	12%	5	26%	10	47	8.3%	4
2006	3.31	3.92	7	63%	14	10%	1	26%	8	39	6.9%	15
2007	3.84	3.91	5	55%	7	16%	13	26%	11	36	7.2%	11

Year	LE	Rank	LT	Rank	Mid	Rank	RT	Rank	RE	Rank
2005	4.20	18	3.47	6	3.61	3	3.66	6	3.67	14
2006	2.00	2	4.77	22	3.94	4	4.11	14	4.68	24
2007	5.72	32	3.68	8	4.15	14	3.39	2	2.34	1

The Steelers have a solid core of high-quality veterans both on the defensive line and at linebacker, though they look thin beyond those players. Nose tackle Casey Hampton may be the best 3-4 tackle in the league; San Diego's Jamal Williams and New England's Vince Wilfork are his main rivals. Hampton's backup, Chris Hoke, lacks the former Longhorn's raw physical presence against the run and ability to occupy blockers—something that can be said also of Travis Kirschke and Nick Eason, the primary backups at defensive end. The Steelers thus struggled to adjust to the loss of Aaron Smith, an end who doesn't get media attention but has no less skill than the sack artists who play end in 4-3 alignments. There was an attempt last year to convert Brett Keisel into more of a hybrid end/linebacker, but it met with limited success at best and Keisel's play suffered. If Pittsburgh is sensible, he'll go back to being a pure end, and probably a more successful one, in 2008.

The Steelers have a rich tradition at linebacker, and the current starters are worthy heirs. James Harrison stepped into Joey Porter's shoes and walked all the way to Hawaii in them, establishing himself as a pass-rushing force and a hard-hitting tackler. Across from him, Clark Haggans was the weak link, failing to provide penetration or much in the way of pass coverage. Pittsburgh made no attempt to re-sign him in the off-season (he's now in Arizona), and he will be replaced by sophomore LaMarr Woodley, who had as many sacks as Haggans in far fewer plays. (Woodley isn't listed on our tables because he made only 13 tackles, but he did have four sacks along with two hits and three hurries.) Woodley's fellow sophomore Lawrence Timmons will be attempting to dislodge Larry Foote at inside linebacker, pitting his speed against the incumbent's greater experience. In the long run though, it's likely that Timmons will be the replacement for James Farrior—still an outstanding linebacker at 32, and probably at 33 as well, but for how much longer?

Defensive Secondary

Secondary	Age	Pos	Plays	TmPct	Rk	Stop	Dfts	RuYd	Rk	RuStop	Rk	Tgts	Tgt%	Rk	Dist	Suc%	Rk	APaYd	Rk	PaYd	PD	Int
Ike Taylor	28	CB	95	13.3%	2	44	16	4.0	8	63%	12	111	23%	7	11.4	53%	26	7.2	36	7.0	18	3
Troy Polamalu	27	SS	68	13.8%	2	35	16	5.7	25	49%	28	32	10%	12	8.4	61%	9	4.9	8	4.5	9	0
Deshea Townsend	33	CB	67	9.4%	34	35	14	3.2	4	69%	8	86	18%	40	11.0	55%	20	5.5	2	5.1	15	2
Anthony Smith	25	FS	66	9.2%	43	14	6	9.4	75	30%	74	33	7%	44	21.8	54%	22	11.0	74	11.1	2	2
Tyrone Carter	32	SS	55	7.7%	62	25	8	6.6	46	58%	7	21	4%	78	9.0	61%	8	5.5	16	5.0	1	0
Bryant McFadden	27	CB	26	4.5%	—	8	4	7.7	—	33%	—	41	11%	—	11.0	69%	—	4.4	—	4.1	3	1
Ryan Clark	29	FS	23	8.6%	—	8	4	5.5	—	38%	—	13	7%	—	13.8	74%	—	2.6	—	3.1	3	0

Year	Pass D Rank	vs. #1 WR	Rk	vs. #2 WR	Rk	vs.Other WR	Rk	vs.TE	Rk	vs.RB	Rk
2005	6	-13.1%	4	-5.7%	14	-10.9%	10	-6.5%	12	21.8%	31
2006	14	18.3%	30	20.5%	27	-42.6%	1	8.8%	24	-40.5%	1
2007	5	-8.5%	10	7.4%	20	-32.6%	3	7.9%	18	-30.5%	1

The Steelers made Troy Polamalu the highest-paid safety in the league before this season, and in another exceptional season he proved it was money well spent. The loss of Ryan Clark somewhat limited Polamalu's normal risk-taking, freewheeling style because Anthony Smith proved much less capable of covering for him. As a result, his numbers in our individual defensive statistics aren't as impressive as they've been in previous years; he had less license to attack the line of scrimmage—although different responsibilities allowed him to show he's not just a ball-hawk but also reliable in pass coverage.

At cornerback, Ike Taylor was again one of the most targeted players in the NFL, but he played much better than he did the year before, ranking in the top five in passes defensed and improving a Success Rate that ranked a dismal 70th in 2006. Taylor and fellow starter DeShea Townsend also proved invaluable in run support. Townsend will once again have to hold off his advancing years, Bryant McFadden, and William Gay to retain his position, and there has been talk of a move to safety given the spotty injury history of the starters and Anthony Smith's questionable performance as a backup.

Special Teams

Year	DVOA	Rank	FG/XP	Rank	Net Punt	Rank	Punt Ret	Rank	Net Kick	Rank	Kick Ret	Rank	Hidden	Rank
2005	1.4%	10	0.9	14	-3.2	22	12.4	1	-1.6	20	-0.1	17	0.9	15
2006	-4.2%	30	-4.4	25	0.5	19	-5.4	30	-10.2	28	-5.0	24	-2.5	17
2007	-1.4%	21	6.9	2	2.8	12	-10.8	31	-7.5	28	0.3	16	4.4	12

Mike Tomlin fired the coordinator, spent a fourth-round pick on a punter, re-signed coverage specialist Chidi Iwouma, dedicated several training camp practices to special teams, and still couldn't get Pittsburgh's most dysfunctional unit to a point where Steelers fans don't hold their breath every time a kicker or punter enters the game. There were definite signs of improvement—rookie punter Daniel Sepulveda was an immediate upgrade over Chris Gardocki, while Jeff Reed made over 90 percent of his field goals and was roughly average in terms of kick distance. Unfortunately, field goal percentage is a highly volatile aspect of kicker performance, and Reed is no exception as you can see from Pittsburgh's numbers over the last three years. Coverage and return teams, meanwhile, were just as bad as ever. The coverage teams gave up long runbacks all year long, including one on a 100-yard touchdown on a bouncing kickoff that Cleveland's Joshua Cribbs would not have even tried to return if it had not stopped slightly before the end zone. The signing of former Kansas City linebacker Keyaron Fox should help, but a full solution to the problem will take more than just one free agent. Allen Rossum took on most of the return duties; he had three fumbles and generally failed to provide any value as a punt returner, though he did better as a kick returner with a touchdown in Week 3. Rossum is now in San Francisco, and Pittsburgh's search for the heir to Antwaan Randle El continues.

COACHING STAFF

Mike Tomlin has emerged from Bill Cowher's shadow in a single year, and that's an impressive achievement. All of his assistants return for another season in the Steel City. For some, such as defensive coordinator Dick LeBeau, their job may be for life, or at least as long as they want it. When your players start campaigning to get you enshrined in Canton—as several Steelers veterans did, wearing LeBeau's old #44 Lions jersey before Pittsburgh's participation in the Hall of Fame game last season—you're probably fairing well as a motivator. Offensive coordinator Bruce Arians has become something of a favored whipping boy for sections of the Pittsburgh media, but both Tomlin and Roethlisberger seem to like him and the franchise has been perfectly happy ignoring calls for change from the direction of the press for decades. Arians is more traditional than most people think; Steelers fans will be surprised to learn that if you count only planned runs, not quarterback scrambles, Pittsburgh had the highest percentage of running plays in the league after ranking in the middle of the pack in 2006. Tomlin and his staff did seem to make several rookie mistakes, such as their overuse of Willie Parker and a maddening refusal to adjust game plans on-the-fly when they clearly weren't working. There were also some very strange play calls, such as a quarterback draw on third-and-6 against Jacksonville in the wild card game, and handing the ball to Hines Ward on a slow-developing sweep when it was fourth-and-goal against New England.

St. Louis Rams

Bubonic plague swept through Europe in the 14th century. First breaking out in Asia, it then swept west. It is believed that the disease first entered Europe from a fleet of trading vessels that docked in Sicily. It quickly spread northward through France, Spain, and England, then east into Germany and Scandinavia. Experts estimate that the Black Death wiped out more than half the population of the continent. Entire villages succumbed to the plague. It was a time of misery. It was a time of despair. It was a time of woe. It was not entirely unlike what happened to the offensive line of the St. Louis Rams in 2007.

To fully appreciate the havoc and devastation that struck the St. Louis line in 2007, we must start at the beginning and move through the season one crisis at a time. The Rams planned to start future Hall of Famer Orlando Pace at left tackle, Mark Setterstrom at left guard, Brett Romberg at center, Richie Incognito at right guard, and Alex Barron at right tackle. That unit would never see the field together.

The trouble began in the preseason, when Incognito suffered a high ankle sprain. He would miss the season's first four games. His backup, Todd Steussie, would miss the first 10 games with a broken foot. Incognito's spot in the season opener against Carolina was filled by Milford Brown. Late in the first half of that game, Pace tore a labrum and rotator cuff in his shoulder and was lost for the season. This after a torn triceps cost him half the 2006 campaign.

In Week 2, against San Francisco, the Rams moved Barron to left tackle, where he would remain for the rest of the year. Brown moved into the right tackle spot, with Claude Terrell stepping up to play right guard. There was a new right tackle for the Rams in their Week 3 contest with Tampa Bay, with Adam Goldberg taking over for Brown. In that game, Setterstrom hurt his knee and was lost for the year. Terrell started in Setterstrom's place in Week 4, against Dallas, with Brown playing at left guard. In that game, right tackle Adam Goldberg hurt his knee; his season was also over.

In four games, the Rams had lost three players for the season, but the parade of pain was just beginning. In their Week 5 game against the Cardinals, the Rams shifted Brown back over to right tackle and put Andy McCollum at left guard. Remarkably, all would survive the game and play the next week against Baltimore. It marked the first game all season in which the Rams were not forced to start a new offensive lineman. They came out of that game healthy as well and that group started again in Week 7 against Seattle.

That is where the streak ended. Romberg sprained not one but two ankles against the Seahawks; he would play in only two more games the rest of the year. Two days later, another lineman was lost for the season, though this time injuries had nothing to do with it. The Rams released Terrell after he was arrested for assaulting his wife.

RAMS PROSPECTUS

2007 Record: 3-13

Pythagorean Wins: 3.7 (32nd)

DVOA: -33.5% total (31st), -30.4% weighted (30th)

Offense: -18.7% DVOA (30th)

Defense: 10.9% DVOA (26th)

Special Teams: -3.9% DVOA (27th)

Variance: 9.6 % (4th)

2007: Offensive linemen fall like dominoes. Big, fat dominoes.

2008: A healthier line means the Rams should rebound in fantasy football, but in real football, improvement requires a defense.

2008 Mean Projection: 5.1 wins

On the Clock (0-3): 25%

Loserville (4-6): 49%

Mediocrity (7-8): 17%

Playoff Contender (9-10): 9%

Super Bowl Contender (11+): 1%

Projected Average Opponent: -2.4% DVOA (22nd in NFL)

2008 Rams Schedule

Week	Opp.	Week	Opp.	Week	Opp.
1	at PHI	7	DAL	13	MIA
2	NYG	8	at NE	14	at ARI
3	at SEA	9	ARI	15	SEA
4	BUF	10	at NYJ	16	SF
5	BYE	11	at SF	17	at ATL
6	at WAS	12	CHI		

With Romberg unavailable for the team's Week 8 game against Cleveland, McCollum was moved to center and Brown was placed at left guard, where he would remain for the rest of the season. The new right tackle was Brandon Gorin, who won two Super Bowls with the Patriots and started 10 games for the 2004 championship team. He had been traded to Arizona in 2006, but he never played for the Cardinals that year and was cut just before the 2007 season. The Rams signed him after Pace was hurt in the opener, and Gorin ended up starting eight games at right tackle. Needless to say, in his first start, one of his teammates went down. Incognito hurt his kneecap against Cleveland and was—yes—lost for the season.

After a much needed bye week, the Rams debuted a new right guard, Nick Leckey, a former Cardinals center who joined the team a month into the season. Leckey made his first start against New Orleans in Week 10. He must have carried some good luck with him, because the Rams beat the Saints for their first win of the year, and they even managed to do so without losing another lineman. The same crew started the next week against San Francisco in Week 11, and they won again.

In Week 12, against Seattle, the Rams made three more changes. Two of those changes were positive, with Romberg returning to play center and Steussie coming back to play right guard. The third change was Rob Petitti, another player picked off the unemployment line. He became the fifth player to start at right tackle for the Rams and the third player to start on the line after beginning the season without a job. Petitti started 16 games for Dallas as a rookie in 2005 but was waived just before the start of the 2006 season. He played one game that year for the Saints. The Rams signed him shortly after Terrell was released. In Petitti's one start, he squared off against Pro Bowl defensive end Patrick Kerney, who pitilessly feasted on his overmatched foe, collecting three sacks on the day.

Then things stabilized, with Barron, Brown, McCollum, Steussie, and Gorin starting every game, save for Romberg's final appearance against Pittsburgh. When the season came to its merciful end, the numbers were gruesome. This was carnage like no team had seen in this century. In last year's edition of *PFP*, Jason McKinley introduced a method of measuring offensive line continuity, using the number of players who started a game, the number of games in which at least one change was made in the starting lineup, and the longest streak of any group of five players. Dating back to the 2000 season, he found three teams tied for the lowest continuity score, all from the 2003 season: the 49ers, the Chargers, and the Raiders each posted a score of 21 that year.

In 2007, 13 different men started on the St. Louis line. No five-man unit started more than three games in a row. In 10 games, the Rams made at least one change. Plugging those numbers into McKinley's formula gives us a continuity score of only 17. The Rams didn't just set a record for chaos, they lapped the field.

The only semblance of stability on the line was Alex Barron. He was the only player to register 16 starts, although 15 were out of position. And what did Barron contribute to the Rams' offense? Sixteen penalties, more than any other lineman in the league except for Oakland's Robert Gallery. This is nothing new; over the past three seasons, Barron has been flagged 50 times, by far the most of any player in the NFL (the distant second is 38 penalties).

Perhaps the most remarkable note about all this is that the Rams did not have the worst line in the league; the Kansas City Chiefs ranked below the Rams in both Adjusted Line Yards (3.75 to 3.61) and Adjusted Sack Rate (8.1 percent to 9.1 percent).

Still, the devastation ruined the season for the Rams' passing and running attacks. Marc Bulger has been on the team for six years and Stephen Jackson for four, and both posted career lows in DVOA in 2007. Injuries along the line lead to injuries in the backfield; Bulger and Jackson missed four games each.

A closer look at the numbers suggests that it was indeed the line and not Bulger and Jackson at fault. In 2007, Bulger's top two receivers, Torry Holt and Isaac Bruce, posted DVOAs of 13.2% and 3.7%, respectively. Those numbers are not unprecedented. Bruce was worse in 2003 and 2005; Holt was worse in 2002, 2005, and 2006. DVOA for quarterbacks includes sacks and passes thrown with no intended receiver because of pressure. Wide receiver DVOA does not, so it looks like when Bulger did have time to pass, he was reasonably successful. Meanwhile, the team ranked only 28th in Adjusted Line Yards, but seventh in percentage of rushing yards gained 10 yards or more downfield. In other words, on the odd occasion that the patchwork line managed to open any rushing lanes, Jackson was able to zip through for big gains.

It's virtually guaranteed that the health of the Rams' line will improve in 2008, because it certainly can't get any worse. Pace, Romberg, Incognito, and Barron are all returning, joined by Jacob Bell, a free agent from the Titans who will take over at left guard. Although the health of these men is questionable (particularly Pace, who is now 32 years old and has a history of tricep tears), as a unit they should see more playing time together than anything the Rams could put together in 2007. That means Bulger and Jackson should both bounce back in 2008.

The only other change to the offense is at wide receiver, where Drew Bennett takes over for Isaac Bruce. Although that seems like a downgrade—Bruce has had a higher DVOA than Bennett each of the past four seasons—remember that Bruce will be 36 years old in November. The list of wide receivers who have been productive at that age is very short, and a change would have been necessary at some point. The Rams were also the first team to choose a wide receiver in this year's draft: lightning-fast Donnie Avery from the University of Houston. He should be able to step into the slot right away.

Put it all together, and it seems like the offense should bounce back to some degree this season. Unfortunately for the Rams, they were nearly as bad without the ball as they were with it. That can't be blamed on a barrage of injuries because nine Rams' defenders started at least 12 games. To be fair, none of those nine were Leonard Little. The team's most accomplished pass rusher, Little underwent surgery on his big toe in November and missed the final nine games of the season. However, Little notched only one sack in the seven games he did play, so his presence may not have helped. All told, St. Louis defensive ends managed only 5.5 sacks in 2007.

Hoping to fix that problem, the team chose Chris Long, son of Howie, with the second overall pick in the draft. Long by himself notched 14 sacks last season at Virginia, so he should boost the St. Louis pass rush from day one. After the draft, Long was listed as a backup to James Hall at right defensive end, but it wouldn't be surprising to see him in the starting lineup on opening day. If so, he'll be lining up alongside Adam Carriker, last year's top draft pick and one of the few players on the Rams who didn't have a completely lost season in 2007. He showed a knack for getting into the backfield and for standing his ground in short-yardage situations; the Rams ranked fourth in the league in such scenarios. If Carriker continues to develop and Long is the player the Rams think he will be, the right side of the St. Louis defensive line is going to be intimidating down the road.

Since his defensive ends couldn't rush the passer, defensive coordinator Jim Haslett had to blitz his linebackers a lot; only the Steelers, Chargers, and Jets rushed five or more men more often than the Rams. Because the team rushed five as often as the top 3-4 defenses, it makes sense that Linehan experimented with switching the Rams' 4-3 alignment to a 3-4 towards the end of 2007. He reportedly wants to try it again in 2008. We wonder how their personnel will fit into that scheme. Carriker usually lines up at nose tackle, even in a 4-3 front, so he would remain there, with ageless veteran La'Roi Glover moving out to one end position. The other end would then be Hall or Long, both of whom weigh about 280 each, which is on the small side for a 3-4 end. The Rams certainly have enough quality linebackers to make the formation work, but then what do they do with Leonard Little? Will the 263-pounder become an enormous linebacker, moving out to the flat to cover tight ends? Isn't that a little like signing Barry Bonds and asking him to bunt?

It's ironic that while the St. Louis offense steadies itself as its linemen return to health, the defense enters a state of flux. To a degree, those changes will offset each other in 2008. The Rams will take baby steps forward, though they are still years away from playoff contention. If they can catch the 49ers and Cardinals for second place in the division, it would have to be considered a successful year.

Vince Verhei

2007 Rams Stats by Week

Wk	vs.	W-L	PF	PA	YDF	YDA	TO	Total	Off	Def	ST
1	CAR	L	13	27	238	385	0	-31%	-9%	32%	11%
2	SF	L	16	17	392	186	-1	-14%	-11%	-6%	-9%
3	@TB	L	3	24	245	322	-2	-104%	-42%	38%	-24%
4	@DAL	L	7	35	187	502	0	-46%	-28%	39%	21%
5	ARI	L	31	34	375	383	-1	16%	4%	-3%	8%
6	@BAL	L	3	22	264	248	-4	-39%	-54%	-23%	-8%
7	@SEA	L	6	33	221	289	-4	-66%	-49%	-7%	-24%
8	CLE	L	20	27	393	368	-1	-42%	10%	46%	-6%
9	BYE										
10	@NO	W	37	29	409	299	+2	15%	22%	6%	-2%
11	@SF	W	13	9	207	244	+2	-39%	-34%	9%	4%
12	SEA	L	19	24	265	302	0	-57%	-52%	-6%	-10%
13	ATL	W	28	16	409	435	+1	0%	14%	8%	-6%
14	@CIN	L	10	19	241	370	0	-48%	-43%	-6%	-11%
15	GB	L	14	33	364	277	+1	-28%	-12%	-15%	-31%
16	PIT	L	24	41	316	425	-2	-7%	30%	45%	8%
17	@ARI	L	19	48	234	422	-1	-49%	-49%	14%	14%

Trends and Splits

	Offense	Rank	Defense	Rank
Total DVOA	-18.7%	30	10.9%	26
Unadjusted VOA	-16.9%	29	10.7%	26
Weighted Trend	-18.1%	29	7.3%	24
Variance	8.2%	23	5.1%	7
Average Opponent	1.8%	24	-0.7%	23
Passing	-17.9%	28	18.6%	25
Rushing	-19.7%	30	2.5%	25
First Down	-24.1%	28	-0.1%	19
Second Down	-8.3%	25	13.9%	26
Third Down	-24.1%	29	30.4%	32
First Half	-2.6%	17	5.7%	24
Second Half	-34.7%	32	16.3%	30
Red Zone	-28.8%	30	10.3%	22
Late and Close	-45.7%	30	19.4%	28

Five-Year Performance

Year	W-L	Pyth Wins	Est Wins	PF	PA	TO	Total	Rank	Off	Rank	Def	Rank	ST	Rank
2003	12-4	10.8	9.2	447	328	+7	9.0%	12	-3.2%	16	-14.4%	5	-2.2%	26
2004	8-8	6.1	5.6	319	392	-24	-23.0%	30	0.7%	14	16.1%	28	-7.5%	32
2005	6-10	6.4	5.1	363	429	-10	-21.8%	29	-3.6%	16	14.0%	29	-4.1%	31
2006	8-8	7.6	7.4	367	381	+14	-5.0%	20	12.3%	7	12.9%	29	-4.4%	31
2007	3-13	3.7	3.7	263	438	-10	-33.5%	31	-18.7%	30	10.9%	26	-3.9%	27

Strategic Tendencies

Run/Pass		Rank	Offense		Rank	Defense		Rank	Other		Rank
Runs, all plays	38%	22	3+ WR	47%	18	Rush 3	3.9%	19	2+ RB, Pct Runs	49%	27
Runs, first half	43%	13	4+ WR	12%	15	Rush 4	52.6%	27	1 RB/2 TE, Pct Runs	56%	8
Runs, first down	50%	16	2+ TE	26%	14	Rush 5	31.3%	4	1 RB/3+ WR, Pct Runs	19%	24
Runs, second-long	35%	15	Single back	56%	15	Rush 6+	12.3%	8	CB1 on WR1	49%	12
Runs, power sit.	60%	22	Play action	16%	21	Rush 7+	4.3%	3	Go for it on 4th	0.78	23
Runs, behind 2H	30%	10	Max protect	12%	8	Sacks by LB	36.8%	11	Offensive Pace	30.7	14
Pass, ahead 2H	56%	2	Outside pocket	4%	32	Sacks by DB	15.8%	3	Defensive Pace	31.4	27

In the fourth quarter, the Rams ranked last in the league in both offense and defense. ⌀ Remember when the Rams offense was all about hitting receivers in stride? Not anymore—the Rams were last in the league with an average of just 3.6 yards after catch. ⌀ The Rams were second to last behind Baltimore in number of screen passes, and ranked 31st in DVOA on screens. ⌀ St. Louis quarterbacks had the highest percentage of their passes defensed. ⌀ Only Kansas City allowed more sacks listed as "blown blocks." ⌀ Bulger is a true pocket passer. No quarterback remained in the pocket more often. ⌀ Torry Holt was the most targeted receiver overall by more than 50 percent, except on third down, when the ball was spread more evenly among Holt, Issac Bruce, and Drew Bennett. ⌀ The Rams running game ranked ninth in DVOA in the first quarter, then ranked 31st in the last three quarters combined, ahead of only Chicago. ⌀ The Rams gained 4.5 yards per carry with two running backs in the game, but only 3.2 yards per carry with one back in the game, the largest discrepancy in the league. ⌀ The Rams also preferred two running backs when they were on defense. St. Louis gave up 5.4 yards per carry when running backs took the ball in single-back sets (20.3% DVOA) but only 3.8 yards per carry when there was a fullback in the game (-6.9% DVOA). ∅ The Rams defense led the league in sacks marked "rusher untouched." ∅ The St. Louis defense was in the top six in blitzes on each down. ∅ The Rams ranked third in defense against screen passes. ∅ St. Louis was one of only two defenses in the NFL whose opponents threw to the number-one receiver over 30 percent of the time (Cincinnati was the other.) ∅ The Rams allowed scores on 41 percent of drives, worse than any team except Miami. However, they also stopped opponents three-and-out on 25 percent of drives, which ranked seventh in the NFL. Two-thirds of all drives against the Rams defense ended either in a score or a three-and-out.

Passing

Player	DYAR	DVOA	Plays	NtYds	Avg	YAC	C%	TD	Int
Marc Bulger	-142	-16.5%	419	2224	5.3	3.7	58.8%	11	13
Gus Frerotte*	-176	-26.2%	179	992	5.5	3.6	56.6%	7	12
Brock Berlin	-19	-22.6%	28	153	5.5	3.9	60.7%	0	1
Trent Green	174	7.8%	149	958	6.4	5.4	61.6%	5	7

Rushing

Player	DYAR	DVOA	Plays	Yds	Avg	TD	Fum	Suc
Steven Jackson	11	-7.4%	238	1000	4.2	5	6	43%
Brian Leonard	12	-5.1%	86	303	3.5	0	0	41%
Antonio Pittman	0	-8.7%	38	139	3.7	0	1	34%
Travis Minor	16	19.0%	17	68	4.0	0	0	29%
Gus Frerotte*	-13	-53.2%	4	1	0.3	0	2	—
Dante Hall	18	83.2%	3	18	6.0	0	0	—
Brock Berlin	-39	-266.8%	3	-12	-4.0	0	2	—
Trent Green	-7	-34.7%	5	19	3.8	0	2	—

Receiving

Player	DYAR	DVOA	Plays	Ctch	Yds	Y/C	YAC	TD	C%
WR									
Torry Holt	244	7.9%	149	93	1193	12.8	2.3	8	62%
Isaac Bruce*	110	0.9%	101	55	733	13.3	2.5	4	54%
Drew Bennett	-68	-24.5%	73	33	375	11.4	2.8	4	45%
Marques Hagans	5	-8.2%	15	8	101	12.6	2.8	0	53%
Dane Looker	-33	-42.7%	14	6	38	6.3	1.8	1	43%
Dante Hall	-37	-55.1%	12	5	27	5.4	3.6	0	42%
Reche Caldwell	22	-0.7%	22	15	141	9.4	1.4	0	68%
TE									
Randy McMichael	72	8.9%	67	39	429	11.0	3.7	4	58%
Dominique Byrd	15	49.4%	5	4	44	11.0	5.0	0	80%
Anthony Becht	2	-4.1%	7	5	20	4.0	2.0	2	71%
RB									
Steven Jackson	-4	-15.4%	52	38	271	7.1	7.3	1	73%
Brian Leonard	13	-7.7%	39	30	183	6.1	4.8	0	77%
Travis Minor	17	5.9%	17	12	86	7.2	6.0	0	71%
Antonio Pittman	-39	-87.0%	9	3	15	5.0	5.0	0	33%

Offensive Line

Year	Yards	ALY	Rank	Power	Rank	10+ Yds	Rank	Stuff	Rank	Sack	ASR	Rank
2005	4.13	3.88	23	57%	26	21%	8	30%	31	46	7.4%	19
2006	4.36	4.50	6	63%	20	16%	15	25%	21	49	7.9%	23
2007	3.98	3.75	28	54%	26	22%	7	27%	28	48	8.1%	25

Year	LE	Rank	LT	Rank	Mid	Rank	RT	Rank	RE	Rank
2005	3.52	25	4.19	18	4.23	13	3.08	29	3.66	21
2006	2.44	31	4.34	15	4.76	2	4.11	22	5.35	4
2007	2.75	30	3.22	32	4.04	18	3.68	28	4.03	19

There's nowhere to go but up for a unit that just went through the most catastrophic season an offensive line ever saw. The big question mark is Orlando Pace, who has missed 23 games the past two seasons with arm and shoulder injuries. He's hopeful to be back in time for training camp. "When you've been injured the past year and a half or so, there's a different desire or hunger or purpose for playing," Pace says. He'll be joined in the starting lineup by Brett Romberg and Richie Incognito, refugees from last season's biblical injury list, plus Alex "The Human Penalty" Barron. The fifth lineman will be left guard Jacob Bell, signed in free agency from the Titans. The Rams tried to build up their depth in the draft, using a third-round pick on Toledo tackle John Greco (whose excellent Senior Bowl boosted his draft stock) and a fifth-round pick on Oregon State guard Roy Schuening.

Defensive Front Seven

Defensive Line	Age	Pos	Plays	TmPct	Rk	Stop	Dfts	Stop%	Rk	AvYd	Rk	Sack	Hit	Hur	Runs	RuStop	RuYd	Pass	PaStop	PaYd
La'Roi Glover	34	DT	39	4.9%	35	33	17	85%	12	0.7	7	6.0	12	7	29	83%	2.0	10	90%	-3.2
Adam Carriker	24	DT	32	4.0%	54	29	10	91%	2	1.2	15	2.0	1	5	26	88%	1.5	6	100%	-0.2
Victor Adeyanju	25	DE	31	4.2%	64	23	6	74%	51	2.6	64	0.0	3	8	27	74%	2.3	4	75%	4.5
Clifton Ryan	24	DT	30	3.8%	58	26	6	87%	6	0.7	10	2.0	1	2	27	85%	1.3	3	100%	-4.3
Leonard Little	34	DE	19	5.5%	—	16	8	84%	—	1.3	—	1.0	6	4	15	80%	2.1	4	100%	-1.8

Linebackers	Age	Pos	Plays	TmPct	Rk	Stop	Dfts	Stop%	AvYd	Sack	Hit	Hur	Runs	RuStop	Rk	RuYd	Rk	Tgts	Suc%	Rk	APaYd	Rk
Will Witherspoon	28	MLB	119	14.9%	19	75	31	63%	3.6	7.0	6	8	79	63%	48	3.5	56	34	44%	60	7.5	80
Brandon Chillar*	26	OLB	65	8.7%	80	39	17	60%	4.4	2.5	5	4	38	68%	27	3.2	41	26	43%	61	6.8	65
Chris Draft	32	OLB	49	6.2%	95	34	8	69%	3.6	1.0	1	1	24	79%	8	2.0	5	18	59%	14	5.9	40
Pisa Tinoisamoa	27	OLB	40	8.9%	—	23	10	58%	7.4	0.0	0	1	20	75%	—	4.4	—	22	59%	15	4.7	17

Year	Yards	ALY	Rank	Power	Rank	10+ Yds	Rank	Stuff	Rank	Sack	ASR	Rank
2005	4.90	4.27	21	77%	30	27%	31	27%	5	41	7.6%	10
2006	4.94	4.73	28	67%	20	21%	27	19%	31	34	6.5%	17
2007	4.34	4.22	21	54%	4	21%	24	27%	8	31	6.2%	17

Year	LE	Rank	LT	Rank	Mid	Rank	RT	Rank	RE	Rank
2005	3.68	11	4.41	21	4.15	18	4.38	22	5.49	31
2006	4.97	25	4.79	23	4.89	31	4.48	20	3.61	11
2007	3.70	11	4.15	14	4.35	23	3.88	9	5.17	30

The line is highlighted by tackle Adam Carriker, last year's top rookie, and end Chris Long, this year's top rookie. Carriker was one of the few highlights of the team last season. Long will open training camp as a backup to James Hall, but should be a starter sooner rather than later. Assuming the team sticks with a 4-3 set, defensive end Leonard Little will return to the starting lineup after missing nine games last year. Whether he'll return to his top form is another question, since he'll be 34 in October. He had only one sack in the seven games he did play last year, although he was getting to the quarterback enough to post some hits and hurries. Still, it isn't like two years ago, when Little was fifth in the NFL in sacks, third in hits, and fourth in hurries. Ironman La'Roi Glover will man the other tackle spot. He hasn't missed a game in 10 years, and with 39 tackles and 6 sacks last year, he's still going strong.

The linebackers were unquestionably the strength of the team in 2007. Will Witherspoon led the team in tackles, which is not abnormal for a middle linebacker. But he also led the team in sacks, which is pretty rare. His pass coverage numbers look bad, but that's most likely because if he was dropping back in coverage, there was nobody else who could put much pressure on opposing quarterbacks. Quinton Culberson, an undrafted second-year player out of Mississippi State, will take over at strong-side linebacker for Brandon Chillar, who moved on to Green Bay. Culberson actually started as a cornerback in college before bulking up to 236 pounds, but he'll surely be targeted by opposing offenses. On the other side, Pisa Tinoisamoa and Chris Draft virtually split time, and ended the year with very similar numbers. Tinoisamoa is definitely the starter, but Draft provides good depth at the position. When they weren't rushing the passer, Rams linebackers were effectively covering running backs, ranking 16th in defending passes to backs.

Defensive Secondary

Secondary	Age	Pos	Plays	TmPct	Rk	Stop	Dfts	RuYd	Rk	RuStop	Rk	Tgts	Tgt%	Rk	Dist	Suc%	Rk	APaYd	Rk	PaYd	PD	Int
O. J. Atogwe	27	FS	87	10.9%	25	30	10	8.4	67	40%	51	30	7%	46	13.1	36%	74	7.7	46	7.7	12	8
Corey Chavous	32	SS	77	11.1%	23	29	8	6.4	43	49%	27	34	9%	17	13.2	32%	80	10.4	71	10.0	4	0
Ronald Bartell	26	CB	73	9.2%	39	27	13	7.4	50	35%	60	61	14%	69	12.3	45%	59	8.5	63	8.6	10	2
Fakhir Brown	31	CB	62	10.4%	24	30	13	10.9	71	63%	13	92	28%	1	12.9	56%	11	7.5	44	7.6	17	4
Tye Hill	26	CB	42	10.6%	22	13	8	7.0	46	20%	75	47	21%	17	11.4	53%	24	6.4	18	5.9	9	1
Jonathan Wade	24	CB	20	2.5%	—	5	4	8.0	—	0%	—	21	5%	—	10.3	33%	—	9.7	—	10.8	2	1

Year	Pass D Rank	vs. #1 WR	Rk	vs. #2 WR	Rk	vs.Other WR	Rk	vs.TE	Rk	vs.RB	Rk
2005	28	35.3%	32	3.2%	23	10.7%	24	-7.2%	10	-15.6%	7
2006	25	10.8%	24	6.6%	20	-20.8%	6	8.4%	23	-7.4%	13
2007	25	19.1%	27	11.8%	22	-22.6%	6	1.1%	12	-3.3%	14

Let's be blunt: The game charting numbers for the Rams secondary do not make sense. The Rams had one of the worst pass defenses in the league, and they were poor against both number-one and number-two receivers. How on earth can their two main cornerbacks, Fakhir Brown and Tye Hill, be ranked so high in Success Rate and adjusted yards per pass? The answer starts with the colossal gap between Brown and Hill's performance covering top receivers, and their performance covering other receivers. Compared to the average of the NFL's top 64 cornerbacks, Hill and Brown are worse against number-ones, and far better against everyone else (Table 1).

Table 1. Rams Starting Cornerbacks vs. Average Starting Cornerbacks

vs. Position	Brown/Hill APYd	Brown/Hill Suc%	NFL CB APYd	NFL CB Suc%
#1 WR	9.9	45%	8.0	49%
#2 WR	5.3	60%	7.4	50%
Other WR	3.2	75%	7.0	53%
TE	2.7	70%	5.3	56%

On top of this, our game charters list Brown and Hill in coverage much less than the starting cornerbacks on other poor pass defenses. Fakhir Brown missed the first four games of the year with a drug suspension, and Tye Hill dealt with injuries. From Week 6 on, once Brown and Hill are both in the lineup, less than half the passes to number-one receivers are marked with Brown and Hill as the defender. Compare that to 67 percent of passes to number-one receivers covered by Nate Clements and Walt Harris in San Francisco, or 59 percent covered by Mike McKenzie and Jason David in New Orleans. Most of the worst pass plays against St. Louis are listed not with the main cornerbacks in coverage, or even nickelback Ron Bartell, but with safeties Corey Chavous and O. J. Atogwe in coverage, or linebacker Will Witherspoon, or the cornerbacks down on the depth chart like Lenny Walls and Jonathan Wade (who were both awful). In addition, Brown and Hill are listed as covering tight ends twice as often as the average cornerback, while safeties Chavous and Atogwe are listed as covering tight ends about half as often as the average safety. Since tight ends generally gain less yardage than wide receivers, that helps the cornerback numbers and hurts the safety numbers.

Are Brown and Hill better than most people think, or are our numbers completely off? Are these discrepancies related to the Rams' scheme? Do they show mistakes by our charters who did Rams games? Or are they related to the limitations inherent in any attempt to chart defensive statistics using inadequate television camera angles? Unfortunately, there are no clear answers to these questions. Whatever the individual numbers, this much is clear: as a team effort, the Rams pass defense has ranked 25th or lower in DVOA for four straight seasons, and since everyone is coming back this year, there's no reason to believe it will be significantly better in 2008.

Special Teams

Year	DVOA	Rank	FG/XP	Rank	Net Punt	Rank	Punt Ret	Rank	Net Kick	Rank	Kick Ret	Rank	Hidden	Rank
2005	-4.1%	31	8.9	3	-13.4	32	-3.5	23	-6.1	25	-10.2	29	7.9	6
2006	-4.4%	31	4.1	9	0.0	20	-0.1	14	-16.0	32	-13.7	32	-11.5	28
2007	-3.9%	27	-5.3	28	6.1	7	2.5	11	-18.4	31	-7.6	28	-17.9	32

The Rams signed Josh Brown away from division rival Seattle. After excelling in Qwest Field for years, he'll likely look even better in a dome. Nevertheless, the Rams will still have issues with kickoffs, because Jeff Wilkins wasn't the problem last year—the problem was his coverage unit, fourth worst in the league. Donnie Jones returns as the punter. He's got good leg strength (third in the league in gross average) but poor directional ability (third in the league in ratio of touchbacks to punts downed inside the 20). Like Wilkins, Jones had to work with a poor coverage unit, but he was the league's sixth most valuable punter last year when we measure only punt distance assuming an average return on any returnable punt. Dante Hall remains the main return man. Someday he'll slow down, but that day has not yet come. He averaged 15.1 yards per punt return last season, which would have ranked third in the league if the Rams defense had forced enough punts for Hall to qualify for that title. On kickoffs, the Rams split things between Hall, who had positive value, and wide receivers Brandon Williams and Derek Stanley, who each had negative value. The Rams also suffered due to "hidden" special teams they could not control. Their opponents averaged 68.3 yards per kickoff, the highest in the league, and missed only one field goal under 46 yards.

COACHING STAFF

Head coach Scott Linehan has a tendency to get excessively cute at times (witness the end-around he called on second-and-goal against the 49ers in Week 2), so a partnership with Al Saunders, the master of the backfield-crossing triple-fake screen pass, should be fairly interesting. After chafing for two years under ultra-conservative Redskins coach Joe Gibbs, Saunders is looking forward to digging deep into his patented phonebook-as-playbook in his second stint as Rams offensive coordinator. Another former head coach, Saunders studied under Don Coryell in San Diego and took over the Chargers when Coryell left, lasting three seasons. He was the wide receivers coach for the Greatest Show on Turf Rams in 1999 and 2000, then was named offensive coordinator in Kansas City, where the Chiefs' offense was first or second in DVOA for four straight years. Things in Washington didn't go quite as well.

Jim Haslett returns as defensive coordinator and should have a lot of fun with the new toy the Rams grabbed for him in the first round. He'll also be the one to decide whether or not the team switches to a 3-4 look. Haslett coached the Saints for six years starting in 2000. He is one of two former Saints head coaches on the Rams staff. Rick Venturi, whose official title is "Assistant Head Coach/Linebackers," took over for eight games in New Orleans after Jim Mora was fired in 1996.

San Diego Chargers

The San Diego Chargers fired head coach Marty Schottenheimer after he failed to back up a 14-2 season with a playoff win. Schottenheimer has the sixth most wins in NFL history. His replacement, Norv Turner, had a career record of 58-82 in two previous head coaching stops. One year later, the Chargers were in their first AFC Championship game since the 1994 season. Schottenheimer's departure was largely the result of a personality clash with general manager A. J. Smith. The Chargers were backed into a difficult corner but made the right choice to keep Smith rather than Schottenheimer. The talent Smith has built should be able to win with almost any competent coach, but no coach can win without sufficient talent.

After this unprecedented move of firing a coach who went 14-2, the team's fortunes last year were viewed largely as a referendum on the two head coaches. When the Chargers struggled to a 5-5 start, Turner was ridiculed in the national media and questioned in his own locker room. When the team rebounded to win its last six regular season games and its first two playoff games in more than a decade, Turner was suddenly just the coach the Chargers needed.

Given his previous track record, the idea that Turner was a magic panacea borders on absurd. A look at history shows that we should not have been surprised by San Diego's continued success, because a new head coach—no matter his past performance—is likely to be successful with a very talented team. It may be time to

consider the possibility that the conventional media overrates NFL head coaches.

Nobody doubts that an NFL coach has more control over his team's success than a baseball manager or an NBA coach. Creating a true measure of a coach's ability is almost impossible. Right now, the only metric used is win-loss record. Wins and losses, however, are largely related to the talent on the field.

Consider the case of Jon Gruden. Five years ago, he was widely considered one of the top two or three coaches in the NFL. He had just won a Super Bowl for a franchise that could not get over the hump under his well-respected predecessor, Tony Dungy. Nobody thought to consider that his former team, the Raiders, got to the Super Bowl under the incompetent Bill Callahan after years of falling short with Gruden. Furthermore, as the talent on that Tampa team has eroded, so has Gruden's record. Since 2002, Tampa Bay is 38-44.

For further proof of how talent and coaching are hard to separate, look at situations similar to San Diego's first season under Turner. Successful teams that change coaches do not see a great deal of regression (Table 1). Since 1988, 13 teams have changed coaches a year after they won at least 10 games. Of those 13 teams, only three (23 percent) finished 8-8 or worse the next season and none won fewer than seven games. For comparison's sake, 174 teams over the past 20 years won 10 games and did not change coaches. Of those, 71 (41 percent) went 8-8 or worse and 34 (20 percent) won fewer than seven games

---

CHARGERS PROSPECTUS

2007 Record: 11-5

Pythagorean Wins: 11.3 (5th)

DVOA: 19.1% total (6th), 27.3% weighted (3rd)

Offense: 4.9% DVOA (15th)

Defense: -9.8% DVOA (5th)

Special Teams: 4.5% DVOA (5th)

Variance: 24.8 % (31st)

2007: Surprise! The Chargers still win with Norv as head coach.

2008: The same personnel takes another shot at the Super Bowl.

2008 Mean Projection: 11.0 wins

On the Clock (0-3): 0%

Loserville (4-6): 1%

Mediocrity (7-8): 8%

Playoff Contender (9-10): 29%

Super Bowl Contender (11+): 62%

Projected Average Opponent: -6.2% DVOA (31st in NFL)

2008 Chargers Schedule

Week	Opp.	Week	Opp.	Week	Opp.
1	CAR	7	at BUF	13	ATL
2	at DEN	8	at NO	14	OAK (Thu.)
3	at NYJ (Mon.)	9	BYE	15	at KC
4	at OAK	10	KC	16	at TB
5	at MIA	11	at PIT	17	DEN
6	NE	12	IND		

the next season. The teams that replaced their successful coach declined by 1.1 wins the next season, while 10-win teams over the past 20 seasons who have kept their coach declined by 2.2 wins.

Table 1. Ten-Win Teams That Have Changed Coaches Since 1988

Team	Year	Old Coach	W-L	New Coach	W-L
Cleveland	1989	Schottenheimer	10-6	Carson	9-6
San Francisco	1989	Walsh	10-6	Seifert	14-2
New York Giants	1991	Parcells	13-3	Handley	8-8
Philadelphia	1991	Ryan	10-6	Kotite	10-6
Dallas	1994	Johnson	12-4	Switzer	12-4
New England	1997	Parcells	11-5	Carroll	10-6
San Francisco	1997	Seifert	12-4	Mariucci	13-3
Green Bay	1999	Holmgren	11-5	Rhodes	8-8
St. Louis	2000	Vermeil	13-3	Martz	10-6
Oakland	2002	Gruden	10-6	Callahan	11-5
San Francisco	2003	Mariucci	10-6	Erickson	7-9
Kansas City	2005	Vermeil	10-6	Edwards	9-7
San Diego	2007	Schottenheimer	14-2	Turner	11-5

Conventional wisdom may stress the importance of head coaches, but the free market seems to understand their limited impact. Bill Belichick is universally considered the best head coach in football. His reported 2007 salary was $4.2 million. The Cowboys last season paid $7 million per season for the underachieving Leonard Davis to play guard, the least important position on the offensive line. Davis was signed in a market that has a salary cap that deflates salaries. Teams are entitled to spend whatever they want on coaches, yet the best coach in football earns only 65 percent of Leonard Davis's contract.

Of course, Turner had proven at two previous stops that he was not capable of turning poor to mediocre talent into championship-caliber teams. Fortunately for him, he now works for Smith, a general manager capable of building a deep and flexible team.

Although Turner's season is often measured directly against Schottenheimer's, the truth is that the 2007 team was different from the 2006 squad in several ways. First, Schottenheimer's departure followed the defection of his two coordinators to head coach other teams. Offensive coordinator Cam Cameron went to Miami and defensive coordinator Wade Phillips took over Dallas (where he won more games with a similar roster than Hall-of-Famer-to-be Bill Parcells). Cameron was replaced by Clarence Shelmon, but Turner became the designer of the offense and the main play-caller.

On defense, Ted Cottrell replaced Phillips. Cottrell has a solid reputation but few would consider him the equal of Phillips. Cottrell, however, had a new toy that Phillips never enjoyed at full strength, cornerback Antonio Cromartie. Cromartie was chosen in the first round of the 2006 draft after missing his entire final season at Florida State with a torn ACL. It was a high-risk, high-reward pick, and it paid huge dividends in 2007. Cromartie earned a Pro Bowl bid with his league-leading 10 interceptions. Our game-charting project does not think he is quite an elite level cornerback, but he certainly had a great year for a second-year cornerback. More importantly, he solidified the back end of a defense that had been far too reliant on its impressive front seven over the previous several seasons.

The book on attacking the Chargers under Phillips's regime was pretty simple. Find a way to protect your quarterback, and holes in the secondary will appear. The task was at times easier said than done because the Chargers featured dominant outside linebackers Shawne Merriman and Shaun Philips. Cottrell frustrated his team by responding to this weakness with a much more conservative approach at the beginning of the season. The blitzes were fewer and less aggressive. Merriman suddenly was facing constant double teams, and no additional rusher was taking advantage by coming free. Through 10 games, Merriman had only 5.5 sacks.

The low point for the defense came in Week 9, when the Chargers gave up an NFL-record 296 yards to running back Adrian Peterson. The Vikings presented a limited passing threat, but Cottrell still refused to trust his improved secondary and devote all his resources to stopping the run. A few missed tackles on the outside gave Peterson the opening he needed to scamper his way into the record book.

The next week, Cromartie replaced Drayton Florence in the starting lineup and proceeded to intercept Peyton Manning three times. As Cottrell realized what he had in the freakishly athletic Cromartie, he began to dial up a more aggressive defense. Over his last five games of the season (he missed one game due to injury), Merriman racked up seven sacks. The improvement in the secondary and corresponding unleashed pass rush made San Diego a dominant defense. They were comfortably the best defense in the NFL over the second half of the season and downright dominant down the stretch. The Chargers did not lose again until the AFC Championship game.

While the defense was carrying the weight, the offense was nothing near the exceptional unit of the year before. Turner's offensive reputation has lost some luster since his days as the offensive coordinator for Jimmy Johnson's Cowboys. Opposing defenses stacked the box against Tomlinson and forced Philip Rivers to beat them. They blitzed Rivers consistently, and the young quarterback struggled to make plays when the pocket collapsed.

The Chargers were susceptible to these tactics because they were down both of their starting receivers from 2006. Keenan McCardell was let go due to his advanced age. Eric Parker suffered a toe injury and missed the season. That left Rivers with the incomparable Gates but no established receivers on the outside. The talented Vincent Jackson was not sufficiently consistent to provide the outside threat Rivers needed to beat single coverage.

To remedy this situation, Smith acquired Chris Chambers from the Dolphins for a second-round pick in October. Chambers's production never matched his reputation in Miami, thanks in large part to a low catch rate. As the Dolphins' primary receiver, however, he often faced double coverage. In San Diego, opposing defenses geared up to stop Tomlinson first and Gates second. Suddenly Chambers was in single coverage and quite productive. The reduced pressure on Jackson allowed him to develop, and by the playoffs they were a quality duo on the outside. The effects of the trade were felt mostly in the team's three playoff games, as the offense remained inconsistent throughout the regular season.

The amazing thing about San Diego's solid season is that the most negative aspect of the team was Turner's supposed specialty: the development of his young quarterback. Rivers clearly appeared to take a step back throughout the season. He exhibited streaks of wild inaccuracy, an inability to stand in against a pass rush, and a propensity to drop the ball (he fumbled 10 times). He still was solidly above average but was not the burgeoning superstar he appeared to be in 2006. Rivers dropped from fifth to 16th in DVOA among quarterbacks.

Rivers remained an excellent quarterback on second and third down, but he was downright Grossmanesque on first down. He should excel on first down, where

teams frequently stack eight in the box to take away Tomlinson. Turner thwarted this possibility with his play-calling mix, an odd combination of short dump-offs and low percentage deep passes. The result was that Rivers completed only 53.3 percent of his first-down passes. Rivers had no such first-down trouble the year before, and if Turner calls more favorable plays on first down, Rivers's overall numbers should improve.

Rivers's play will continue to be under the microscope because the rest of the team appears beyond reproach. Smith has built an exceedingly talented, extremely young team. The oldest expected starters are nose tackle Jamal Williams and guard Mike Goff, who are both 32 years old this season. The defense is expected to regress according to our projection system, but our system may not adequately account for the massive improvement that came about because of a single personnel move, the insertion of Cromartie. The defense's only change is Eric Weddle at safety to replace Marlon McCree, who was released primarily because Weddle is the better player.

Offensively, a healthy Tomlinson and Gates (and both should be recovered from their injuries of a year ago) almost guarantee a solid team. The offensive line from the playoffs remains intact, and both tackles, Marcus McNeil and Jeromey Cleary, are entering their prime. The Chargers even have depth at receiver with Parker's return and the continued development of 2007 draft picks Craig Davis and Legedu Naanee.

The question mark is Rivers, who had surgery to repair his ACL after the AFC Championship game. Rivers will be ready for the start of the season, but quarterbacks Carson Palmer and Donovan McNabb struggled early in their first season back from ACL surgery. The Chargers should be equipped to stay afloat through their running game and defense until Rivers becomes fully healthy.

The only other potential problem for the Chargers is Turner's continued presence as the head coach, but perhaps we overstated that concern a year ago. Norv may not be the best coach in football, and he may eventually cost them a playoff game through his mistakes, but he seems unlikely to keep the Chargers out of the playoffs due to his mediocrity. Remember, Barry Switzer averaged over 11 wins a season and won a Super Bowl in his first three seasons after Jimmy Johnson left. The 49ers won for years after Bill Walsh was replaced by George Seifert and for two more after Steve Mariucci replaced Seifert. Only when the 49ers' mismanagement of the salary cap gutted the talent did the 49ers suffer through a few bad seasons.

The talent should remain plentiful in San Diego with

Smith at the helm. He has drafted consistently well, stole Gates on the rookie free agent market, signed appropriate free agents, and managed the salary cap exceptionally well. In three years, this core of players will begin to exit their prime. If Smith is an extraordinary general manager, he will be able to rebuild on-the-fly.

He has proved that he is good enough to build a talented core and surround them with enough complementary players to make the playoffs an annual expectation—even with Norv Turner as the head coach.

Ned Macey

2007 Chargers Stats by Week

Wk	vs.	W-L	PF	PA	YDF	YDA	TO	Total	Off	Def	ST
1	CHI	W	14	3	263	202	+2	21%	0%	-29%	-8%
2	@NE	L	14	38	201	407	-1	-47%	-38%	15%	6%
3	@GB	L	24	31	364	405	-1	3%	20%	21%	4%
4	KC	L	16	30	333	390	-2	-35%	-18%	25%	8%
5	@DEN	W	41	3	484	296	+3	100%	74%	-18%	8%
6	OAK	W	28	14	362	245	+2	45%	30%	-23%	-9%
7	BYE										
8	HOU	W	35	10	237	367	+5	61%	33%	-20%	8%
9	@MIN	L	17	35	229	528	0	-93%	-47%	50%	4%
10	IND	W	23	21	177	386	+3	60%	-32%	-57%	35%
11	@JAC	L	17	24	388	311	-2	8%	24%	10%	-6%
12	BAL	W	32	14	332	210	+2	28%	28%	6%	5%
13	@KC	W	24	10	330	268	+3	8%	-4%	-22%	-10%
14	@TEN	W	23	17	341	240	-1	15%	-3%	-16%	2%
15	DET	W	51	14	416	328	+6	76%	31%	-33%	13%
16	DEN	W	23	3	334	225	+2	67%	4%	-60%	3%
17	@OAK	W	30	17	253	316	+3	-5%	-10%	8%	13%
18	TEN	W	17	6	350	248	+1	38%	27%	-8%	3%
19	@IND	W	28	24	411	446	+2	64%	62%	-12%	-9%
20	@NE	L	12	21	311	347	+1	21%	-6%	-29%	-2%

Trends and Splits

	Offense	Rank	Defense	Rank
Total DVOA	4.9%	15	-9.8%	5
Unadjusted VOA	2.8%	15	-9.3%	6
Weighted trend	5.9%	14	-15.9%	1
Variance	9.8%	28	9.0%	23
Average opponent	0.5%	10	1.6%	16
Passing	7.9%	15	-15.2%	2
Rushing	2.0%	11	-3.1%	19
First down	11.5%	25	-2.3%	15
Second down	13.6%	8	-16.5%	4
Third down	22.2%	8	-13.7%	5
First half	4.5%	12	-19.7%	2
Second half	5.2%	11	0.1%	15
Red zone	31.3%	2	-27.1%	1
Late and close	-10.4%	25	7.9%	24

Five-Year Performance

Year	W-L	Pyth Wins	Est Wins	PF	PA	TO	Total	Rank	Off	Rank	Def	Rank	ST	Rank
2003	4-12	4.9	6.1	313	441	-11	-14.8%	24	0.8%	13	12.2%	30	-3.4%	27
2004	12-4	11.2	10.7	446	313	+15	19.9%	8	19.0%	6	-3.9%	12	-3.0%	26
2005	9-7	10.7	10.9	418	312	-8	21.5%	6	18.1%	6	-3.1%	16	0.2%	16
2006	14-2	12.1	12.0	492	303	+13	29.0%	2	24.0%	2	-1.5%	14	4.4%	3
2007	11-5	11.3	9.6	412	284	+24	19.1%	6	4.9%	15	-9.8%	5	4.5%	5

Strategic Tendencies

Run/Pass		Rank	Offense		Rank	Defense		Rank	Other		Rank
Runs, all plays	47%	4	3+ WR	33%	32	Rush 3	2.0%	28	2+ RB, Pct Runs	61%	11
Runs, first half	47%	4	4+ WR	6%	24	Rush 4	49.8%	29	1 RB/2 TE, Pct runs	38%	24
Runs, first down	60%	2	2+ TE	30%	10	Rush 5	44.7%	1	1 RB/3+ WR, Pct runs	21%	21
Runs, second-long	36%	12	Single back	40%	31	Rush 6+	3.6%	31	CB1 on WR1	54%	3
Runs, power sit.	66%	15	Play action	19%	15	Rush 7+	0.2%	31	Go for it on 4th	0.75	25
Runs, behind 2H	21%	31	Max protect	10%	17	Sacks by LB	71.4%	2	Offensive pace	30.6	13
Pass, ahead 2H	34%	28	Outside pocket	12%	12	Sacks by DB	4.8%	22	Defensive pace	30.9	17

Phillip Rivers was ranked sixth among quarterbacks in hurries per pass play and had the fifth lowest DVOA when hurried. ✏ San Diego's offensive line led the league in sacks marked "rusher untouched." ✏ San Diego had a -12.9% DVOA when using play-action, which ranked 30th in the league. The Chargers' spread of DVOA between play-action and non-play-action passes was the widest of any team other than Washington. ✏ After play action, the Chargers threw it back to a running back 30 percent of the time, the most of any team other than Chicago. ✏ The Chargers threw only 42 percent of passes to wide receivers, the lowest percentage in the league. ✏ The Chargers offense was above average in each of the first three quarters, including ranking second in DVOA in the third quarter. However, only two teams had a worse DVOA in the fourth quarter. The weakness came from the passing game, since the Chargers ranked third in fourth-quarter rushing. This weakness is even stranger than you might think, because the Chargers had the league's *best* fourth-quarter DVOA in 2006. Two years ago, they had no fumbles and just one interception in the fourth quarter; last year, they had six fumbles and five interceptions. ✏ Think the Chargers have a ferocious pass rush? Perhaps not. San Diego was the only defense other than Washington to hurry the quarterback on less than 10 percent of all pass plays. However, the Chargers did lead the league in passes tipped or batted down at the line of scrimmage. ✏ San Diego's defense ranked third in Adjusted Sack Rate on first down, fifth on second down, but just 29th on third down. ✏ San Diego's defense led the league in passes marked "Hole in Zone." ✏ Only Arizona was more effective at covering screen passes than San Diego. ✏ SD faced 62 empty backfields, far more than any other team. ✏ San Diego had the league's biggest defensive advantage at home last year, ranking first in defensive DVOA at home (-25.8%) but 20th on the road (5.8%).

Passing

Player	DYAR	DVOA	Plays	NtYds	Avg	YAC	C%	TD	Int
Philip Rivers	552	6.9%	490	3038	6.2	4.6	60.2%	21	15
Billy Volek	-122	-167.3%	12	-1	-0.1	1.7	30.0%	0	1

Rushing

Player	DYAR	DVOA	Plays	Yds	Avg	TD	Fum	Suc
LaDainian Tomlinson	287	13.6%	315	1474	4.7	15	0	45%
Michael Turner*	-52	-27.4%	71	316	4.5	1	1	28%
Darren Sproles	13	0.9%	37	164	4.4	2	0	41%
Philip Rivers	-12	-23.6%	17	41	2.4	1	11	—
Lorenzo Neal*	-9	-19.7%	13	32	2.5	0	1	54%
Andrew Pinnock	-13	-133.2%	4	1	0.3	0	0	0%
Craig Davis	1	-29.6%	3	9	3.0	0	0	—

Receiving

Player	DYAR	DVOA	Plays	Ctch	Yds	Y/C	YAC	TD	C%
WR									
Vincent Jackson	68	-1.8%	81	41	623	15.2	2.7	4	51%
Chris Chambers	80	3.6%	63	35	555	15.9	1.9	4	56%
Craig Davis	35	-0.3%	34	20	188	9.4	3.7	1	59%
Malcom Floyd	9	-3.8%	13	7	97	13.9	1.3	1	54%
Legedu Naanee	-17	-30.1%	13	8	69	8.6	6.6	0	62%
TE									
Antonio Gates	278	30.0%	117	75	984	13.1	3.5	9	64%
Brandon Manumaleuna	-2	-9.0%	15	10	86	8.6	5.1	1	67%
RB									
LaDainian Tomlinson	113	10.7%	86	60	475	7.9	9.0	3	70%
Darren Sproles	-21	-46.2%	12	10	31	3.1	5.9	0	83%
Lorenzo Neal*	-25	-53.0%	11	8	23	2.9	2.8	1	73%
Michael Turner*	-19	-60.5%	7	4	16	4.0	6.0	0	57%

Offensive Line

Year	Yards	ALY	Rank	Power	Rank	10+ Yds	Rank	Stuff	Rank	Sack	ASR	Rank
2005	4.49	4.39	9	78%	2	20%	11	25%	19	30	5.9%	13
2006	5.38	4.82	1	73%	4	29%	1	18%	1	28	6.3%	15
2007	4.52	3.98	24	61%	19	26%	4	29%	30	24	4.7%	8

Year	LE	Rank	LT	Rank	Mid	Rank	RT	Rank	RE	Rank
2005	4.39	12	4.86	3	4.05	19	4.52	9	5.44	1
2006	5.90	2	5.08	4	4.34	17	4.48	7	5.81	1
2007	4.36	12	3.67	28	3.97	22	3.60	29	4.39	9

The decline in the Chargers' offensive performance can largely traced to a decline in the offensive line. A season ago, the Chargers seemed set for years to come at the tackle position with Marcus McNeil and Shane Olivea. McNeil had a sophomore slump and was merely solid. Olivea was a disaster, eventually benched for unknown Jeromey Clary and later released. Center Nick Hardwick missed four games with injuries, including two of the Chargers' three worst offensive games. That highlights the biggest weakness, which is a complete lack of depth. The Chargers tried to address this by signing veteran tackle L. J. Shelton. On the interior, Cory Withrow struggled to replace Hardwick, and Shelton would probably take over if either guard, Mike Goff or Kris Dielman, were to go down. Hardwick may miss the beginning of this season recovering from off-season foot surgery. The good news is that the line remained very good at pass protection. They struggled at times in identifying all-out blitzes, but other than the departed Olivea, they mostly held their own against conventional rushes.

Defensive Front Seven

Defensive Line	Age	Pos	Plays	TmPct	Rk	Stop	Dfts	Stop%	Rk	AvYd	Rk	Sack	Hit	Hur	Runs	RuStop	RuYd	Pass	PaStop	PaYd
Igor Olshansky	26	DE	50	6.0%	37	38	11	76%	44	2.3	55	3.5	7	6	42	71%	3.1	8	100%	-2.0
Jamal Williams	32	DT	41	6.0%	20	35	6	85%	10	2.1	50	0.0	0	0	38	84%	2.3	3	100%	-1.3
Jacques Cesaire	28	DE	40	4.8%	58	28	8	70%	69	2.0	48	2.5	2	7	32	63%	3.0	8	100%	-2.0
Ryon Bingham	27	DT	39	4.7%	40	27	5	69%	61	2.0	48	1.5	4	2	34	65%	2.6	5	100%	-1.6
Luis Castillo	25	DE	32	6.1%	35	24	11	75%	48	1.6	40	2.5	1	3	25	72%	2.6	7	86%	-1.7
Brandon McKinney	25	DT	22	3.0%	—	19	1	86%	—	2.6	—	0.0	0	0	17	88%	2.4	5	80%	3.2

Linebackers	Age	Pos	Plays	TmPct	Rk	Stop	Dfts	Stop%	AvYd	Sack	Hit	Hur	Runs	RuStop	Rk	RuYd	Rk	Tgts	Suc%	Rk	APaYd	Rk
Stephen Cooper	29	ILB	114	13.7%	37	47	17	41%	6.1	2.0	2	3	59	51%	95	4.7	95	41	50%	43	6.0	42
Matt Wilhelm	27	ILB	101	13.8%	33	49	10	49%	5.3	1.0	3	2	67	57%	81	4.8	97	37	46%	51	6.4	59
Shawne Merriman	24	OLB	73	9.3%	73	58	30	79%	1.0	12.5	9	7	42	74%	15	2.9	27	4	89%	—	2.8	—
Shaun Phillips	27	OLB	73	9.3%	74	46	21	63%	3.1	8.5	3	6	40	58%	74	4.6	94	6	56%	—	5.6	—
Derek Smith	33	ILB	82	10.0%	67	46	9	56%	4.5	0.0	2	1	55	64%	46	3.5	54	22	33%	88	6.3	55

Year	Yards	ALY	Rank	Power	Rank	10+ Yds	Rank	Stuff	Rank	Sack	ASR	Rank
2005	3.60	3.92	14	67%	22	14%	11	26%	9	46	8.2%	7
2006	4.05	4.20	13	78%	31	15%	11	23%	19	61	9.0%	3
2007	4.25	4.49	29	65%	19	16%	12	20%	29	42	7.0%	12

Year	LE	Rank	LT	Rank	Mid	Rank	RT	Rank	RE	Rank
2005	5.25	30	3.86	9	3.80	9	3.74	10	3.59	10
2006	4.52	20	4.18	13	4.30	17	4.31	18	3.06	4
2007	5.41	30	6.02	32	4.30	22	3.81	8	3.83	10

Shawne Merriman gets the headlines and has the dance moves, but the defense is anchored by nose tackle Jamal Williams. He constantly demands a double team and collapses opposing offensive lines. Ends Igor Olshansky and Luis Castillo are also very good run defenders. The defense weakened when Castillo missed six games with knee and ankle sprains, as Jacque Cesaire is not his equal in run defense. Still, Cesaire is a solid backup, and along with Ryon

Bingham and nose tackle Brandon McKinney provides support for what is one of the league's deeper three-man lines.

At linebacker, Merriman continues to terrorize opposing quarterbacks, but he struggles at containing outside runs and never really plays in coverage. Merriman plays close to the line, so when he does make plays in the running game, they are usually after short gains, but he too often gets blocked out of the play. Shaun Phillips is not Merriman's match as a pass rusher, but he's pretty good in his own right, and he's the more complete outside linebacker. Inside linebacker Matt Wilhelm is probably the front seven's weak link, but the Chargers have provided stiff competition with veteran free agent Derek Smith, formerly of San Francisco. Smith will first be used to spell tackling machine Stephen Cooper who is suspended for four games for use of performance-enhancing substances. And yes, that does make it now three players in the Chargers' starting front seven who have been caught using steroids at some point in their careers.

Defensive Secondary

Secondary	Age	Pos	Plays	TmPct	Rk	Stop	Dfts	RuYd	Rk	RuStop	Rk	Tgts	Tgt%	Rk	Dist	Suc%	Rk	APaYd	Rk	PaYd	PD	Int
Clinton Hart	31	SS	92	11.0%	24	41	18	4.7	9	49%	25	43	9%	14	8.4	51%	35	5.2	10	5.4	8	5
Drayton Florence*	28	CB	73	8.7%	47	26	11	9.1	62	38%	54	77	16%	54	8.9	44%	66	9.3	72	9.6	10	2
Quentin Jammer	29	CB	72	9.2%	38	21	8	4.3	11	58%	18	81	18%	38	11.9	53%	28	6.4	17	6.6	13	1
Marlon McCree*	31	FS	72	8.6%	52	19	8	8.5	68	30%	73	26	6%	62	14.2	43%	58	8.9	58	9.3	4	3
Antonio Cromartie	24	CB	55	6.6%	70	25	17	8.0	57	43%	50	57	12%	75	13.8	50%	40	8.2	57	8.5	18	10
Eric Weddle	23	FS	54	6.9%	71	20	16	5.4	18	45%	37	35	8%	26	10.3	48%	44	5.9	20	6.2	5	1

Year	Pass D Rank	vs. #1 WR	Rk	vs. #2 WR	Rk	vs. Other WR	Rk	vs. TE	Rk	vs. RB	Rk
2005	21	11.7%	18	-1.1%	18	10.3%	23	-9.6%	9	12.4%	27
2006	11	12.4%	27	-0.4%	13	-5.8%	17	-13.4%	9	12.4%	26
2007	2	-8.2%	11	-72.1%	1	12.8%	28	9.7%	19	-11.7%	8

The weak link of the recent Chargers is suddenly a strength. Antonio Cromartie's insertion into the lineup completely changed the dynamic of the Chargers' defense. Cromartie's ten interceptions are impressive, but he is not yet an elite cornerback, as he will still gamble and get beat at times. Despite these minor limitations, he was a massive upgrade on Drayton Florence, who was not re-signed this offseason. The more surprising development was the continued improvement of Quentin Jammer. Jammer has grown into a complete cornerback who continues to excel in run support but also greatly improved his coverage skills. Cromartie is more talented and may be the better player as soon as this year, but last year, Jammer was the better cornerback. The Chargers knew this and assigned Jammer the task of shutting down Randy Moss in the AFC Championship game, a task Jammer completed with skill.

At safety, the Chargers made their only personnel change, cutting Marlon McCree in favor of Eric Weddle. McCree was on the down slope of his career, and Weddle is already a much better pass defender. Clinton Hart is the no-name of the defense, but he is a stout run defender in the box at the other safety position. The departures of Florence and McCree could test the depth, but the Chargers used their first-round pick on cornerback Antoine Cason, and he should step in immediately as the third cornerback. Cletis Gordon is the fourth corner. At safety, Paul Oliver was acquired in the supplemental draft and will be shifted from cornerback. He should support Weddle with his coverage ability, but the Chargers really have no answer if Hart goes down.

Special Teams

Year	DVOA	Rank	FG/XP	Rank	Net Punt	Rank	Punt Ret	Rank	Net Kick	Rank	Kick Ret	Rank	Hidden	Rank
2005	0.2%	16	6.0	5	4.5	10	-4.4	26	-8.7	28	4.1	10	9.7	3
2006	4.4%	3	7.8	6	10.8	4	-3.4	27	8.4	6	2.4	10	-12.4	29
2007	4.5%	5	2.6	11	6.8	5	3.4	9	7.3	2	6.2	8	13.9	2

One of the underrated reasons for the Chargers' success the past two years has been their very solid special teams. Probably the most important player last year was Darren Sproles, who is solidly above average as both a kick and punt returner. Sproles is super quick and has the speed to make the big play. What may be most impressive is his ability to always gain positive yards. Sproles only called for a fair catch twice all year. Chargers opponents were fair-catch happy thanks to the excellent hang time of punter Mike Scifres. Nate Kaeding also had an excellent season, and after struggling in his first four career playoff games (he was just 2-for-6) he hit all four field goals in the AFC Championship game. His kickoffs are only adequate, hampered in part last year by a broken left leg, but fortunately he has outstanding kick coverage. The ace of both punt and kickoff coverage is Kassim Osgood, who deservedly earned a second trip to Hawaii as the Pro Bowl special teamer. Rumors abounded about using Antonio Cromartie sometimes as a punt returner, but the Chargers dismissed them. If Sproles gets injured, the team would likely turn to Craig "Buster" Davis.

COACHING STAFF

The playoffs sure looked like a vindication for Norv Turner. Not only did they win where Marty Schottenheimer had lost twice before, but they won thanks to a downfield passing attack that Turner worked to implement. Before we completely rethink Turner, however, it is worth noting that at midseason his entire team doubted him. The season was saved by two things, one of which was completely out of Turner's control: the improved defense after Cromartie was inserted into the starting lineup, and the fact that the rest of the AFC West spent 2007 as the gang that couldn't shoot straight. The offense remained highly inconsistent throughout the season, the offensive line regressed markedly, and Philip Rivers failed to take the proverbial next step. Defensively, Ted Cottrell had a nice season once he gained confidence in his secondary. This year, he will have better coverage players at safety and nickelback, so he should be even more aggressive. Offensive coordinator Clarence Shelmon is sort of the de facto running game coordinator, while Turner handles the passing game. Shelmon will be crucial in helping complete the transition from a two-back to a one-back offense and the impact that has on their most important player, LaDainian Tomlinson. Also of note is secondary coach Bill Bradley, who in his first season oversaw massive improvement by Jammer and the development of Cromartie.

San Francisco 49ers

If San Francisco was an 18th-century European village, a mob would have arrived at the doorstep of head coach Mike Nolan last December, carrying torches and pitch forks.

After a highly touted draft and the signing of five starters through free agency, expectations for the 49ers were high. Mike Nolan himself said the team should make the playoffs. The 49ers were so confident that the season would go well that they dealt their 2008 top-round pick—which they figured would be the middle of the draft or lower—to the Patriots for a pick near the bottom of the first round in 2007. Even we gave the 49ers the best forecast of any team in the NFC West in *Pro Football Prospectus 2007*, although the mean projection of 8.1 wins wasn't exactly calling for a return to greatness.

When the time came to actually play the 2007 season, the 49ers couldn't even return to mediocrity. Instead, San Francisco finished 5-11 after bumbling through an eight-game losing streak. For the second time in three years, the 49ers finished last in DVOA. Nolan seems to consistently coach his teams to close wins that leave them with better records than the numbers would otherwise suggest—the 49ers have outperformed both their Pythagorean Wins and DVOA Estimated Wins for three straight years—but that's a fragile consolation, seeing as Nolan put the team together.

The 2007 49ers labored under a dark cloud the entire season. Linchpin left tackle Jonas Jennings left the team for a week to tend to his ailing mother and niece, who

---

49ERS PROSPECTUS

2007 Record: 5-11

Pythagorean Wins: 3.7 (31st)

DVOA: -37.5% total (32nd), -31.8% weighted (32nd)

Offense: -30.5% DVOA (32nd)

Defense: 11.5% DVOA (28th)

Special Teams: 4.5% DVOA (4th)

Variance: 11.7 % (7th)

2007: The best laid plans of mice and men oft go astray.

2008: Yes, but what of the best laid plans of mice and Martz?

2008 Mean Projection: 5.3 wins

On the Clock (0-3): 18%

Loserville (4-6): 55%

Mediocrity (7-8): 18%

Playoff Contender (9-10): 7%

Super Bowl Contender (11+): 0%

Projected Average Opponent: -1.7% DVOA (20th in NFL)

---

was injured in a car accident. Nolan lost his father, Dick, to Alzheimer's during the season. The team's lone offensive threat, Frank Gore, lost his mother to kidney disease, and he was stunned when good friend and former Miami Hurricane teammate Sean Taylor was shot to death. Defensive coordinator Greg Manusky and running backs coach Bishop Harris both lost parents.

The team often played in a funk and coached in one too. In his first two years, Nolan benched and then shipped out established players such as linebacker Jamie Winborn and cornerback Ahmad Plummer. He dealt malcontents such as running back Kevan Barlow and wide receiver Brandon Lloyd. None of those players regained starting jobs with their new teams.

But last season, Nolan lost all his prescience. He couldn't see that quarterback Alex Smith's shoulder injury was limiting his effectiveness, despite Smith telling him so. Nolan figured that the 23-year-old needed to learn to play through injury, and Smith didn't help by initially saying he could play four weeks after the injury. Nolan then stuck with backup Trent Dilfer too long and refused to bench struggling linebacker Derek Smith for Brandon Moore, a talented player who also happened to be one of the most popular guys in the locker room.

Nolan's first bad decision, however, came long before the season started when he replaced offensive coordinator Norv Turner with quarterbacks coach Jim Hostler. The 49ers were left with few options after Turner deserted very late in the coach-hiring process to take over

2008 49ers Schedule

Week	Opp.	Week	Opp.	Week	Opp.
1	ARI	7	at NYG	13	at BUF
2	at SEA	8	SEA	14	NYJ
3	DET	9	BYE	15	at MIA
4	at NO	10	at ARI (Mon.)	16	at STL
5	NE	11	STL	17	WAS
6	PHI	12	at DAL		

the San Diego Chargers and they wanted to keep Turner's digital offensive system. Nolan chose relative neophyte Hostler over receivers coach Jerry Sullivan, offensive line coach George Warhop, and tight ends coach Pete Hoener. All three had significant turns as coordinators at either the pro or major college level.

When the offense flailed, however, Hostler shouldered an inordinate amount of blame, and he didn't have the authority to keep the conservative Nolan out of offensive meetings. Hostler's game plans were generally good and he called a game similar to Turner. But he lacked Turner's authority and gravitas and players didn't believe in him. The 49ers finished last in points, yards, first downs, third-down efficiency, passing rate, sacks per play, and several other categories.

The far more significant factor in the offensive woes was the collapse of the offensive line. Lapses by individual linemen led to losses. Guard Justin Smiley, a terrific pass blocker in 2007, kept overstriding in a Week 4 loss where Seattle held the 49ers to just three points. Rookie right tackle Joe Staley played well for most of the season but was schooled by Michael Strahan in an October 21 loss to the Giants. Jennings clashed with Warhop and then once again ended his season shelved after undergoing ankle surgery that probably could have waited until after the season. Left guard Larry Allen will someday have his bust in the Hall of Fame, but last year it looked like that inanimate sculpture had replaced the flesh-and-blood Allen on the field. The 49ers finished last in Adjusted Sack Rate and couldn't open holes for Gore to charge through.

The failure to protect and run block instigated a series of events that led to the team's demise. The team exposed its vulnerability to pick up blitzes most acutely in the aforementioned Seattle game. In the first quarter, Allen and center Eric Heitmann fixated on a Seahawks linebacker looping around on a mock blitz. Meanwhile, 300-pound defensive tackle Rocky Bernard slipped between them, slammed into Smith, and landed on Smith's right shoulder with the brunt of his girth. Bones in Smith's shoulder separated faster than Buzz Bissinger and reality.

Within four weeks, Smith returned against New Orleans. Smith was knocked around and after every series he slumped to the bench dragging his right arm. After the 31-10 thumping, Nolan was vilified in the press for playing Smith. Nolan responded by turning a blind eye to Smith's injury for the rest of the season, which led to public sniping between player and coach. Just before undergoing season-ending shoulder surgery, Smith was quoted as saying that Nolan had undermined him in a team meeting.

Meanwhile, with still no protection from the opposing pass rush, the quarterback injuries came fast and furious. Dilfer (concussion) and third-stringer Shaun Hill (back injury) finished the season on the bench and the team started Chris Weinke in the season-ending loss in Cleveland.

Nolan was nearly fired at the end of the season. His final say over the roster was shifted to vice president of personnel Scot McCloughan, who was promoted to general manager. Nolan retained control of his coaching staff and made a startling move: He hired the explosive Mike Martz as the offensive coordinator. The brash and pass-happy Martz will signal the third shift in offensive systems for the 49ers, but nevertheless it was a brilliant move by Nolan. The head coach knew he had to dramatically improve the offense or he'd be ousted, and no one can resuscitate an offense better than Martz.

The 49ers might not have a quarterback to run Martz's complex, pass-dominated offense. His quarterbacks often lead the league in pass attempts or come close (Jon Kitna finished fifth last year, second in 2006) and also take a lot of sacks (Kitna led the league the last two seasons). Martz must discover whether he has a quarterback who can handle and ultimately succeed with that kind of workload. Martz can alienate his coworkers, but so far this offseason, he has been a uniter, not a divider.

First, Martz smoothed things over with McCloughan, who didn't want him initially. McCloughan responded by fetching Martz a few of his favorites in free agency, journeyman quarterback J. T. O'Sullivan and Rams veteran wide receiver (and salary cap casualty) Isaac Bruce. Martz also raved about Smith, which seemed to paper over the rift between Nolan and his quarterback.

The dreadful offense and the stunning play of rookie linebacker Patrick Willis hid a porous defense. No one made more tackles than the active Willis, who never seemed to hit the rookie wall, never seemed to miss a tackle, and played much of the season with a cast covering his right hand after breaking his wrist.

Willis wouldn't have experienced such an explosive year if he had received more help from his fellow tacklers. Nevertheless, he might not have been the busiest member of the 49ers' defense. Nate Clements might have taken on more responsibility than any other cornerback in the league. And why not after an $80 million contract? Clements took the opposition's best receiver a league-high half the time and often with no help behind him. In fact, that's one reason the 49ers took Oklahoma cornerback Reggie Smith in the third round of the draft. Smith is a tough press corner, and that's what the 49ers want because the cover man opposite Clements will likely get safety help.

The 49ers boasted Willis at the linebacker level and Clements in their secondary. But the defense sorely needed a pass-rush linebacker to terrorize quarterbacks out of Mike Nolan's New England-fashioned 3-4 defense. No one emerged in that role, despite the signing of Patriots free agent Tully Banta-Cain. After signing his deal last season, Banta-Cain reported to training camp 20 pounds overweight. Predictably, he sustained an injury (sprained ankle) and wasn't effective. The team still pins hope on his pass-rush abilities and helped him out by drafting defensive lineman Kentwan Balmer. By improving the line, the 49ers hope to free up Banta-Cain, who came to minicamp in mean shape, to go after the quarterback. The 49ers are also looking closely at a fourth-round choice from last year, Jay Moore, as a pass-rush specialist.

In the front office, incompetence continues to be a theme, with the stadium issue as a glowing example. The Yorks, who own the team, pulled out of San Francisco and the city said they still don't know why. The 49ers have shifted their attention to Santa Clara, which is the site of team headquarters. But problems loom: to build a stadium in Santa Clara requires the expensive relocation of an electrical station and the passing of a bond issue that will go to the voters in November. Meanwhile, the 49ers are also courting the city of Brisbane, which owns the open space across Highway 101 from Candlestick (Monster) Park, and San Francisco is trying to lure the York family back into negotiations. The city has brought in Senator Dianne Feinstein and former Mayor Willie Brown as part of the effort.

The 49ers also got Roger Goodell's attention by tampering with Bears linebacker Lance Briggs (the team professed its innocence) and were stripped of a fifth-round pick. A contract error reportedly cost the 49ers $7 million in cap space this year, although it will be restored in 2009. Support staff seems to constantly change, all adding up to the question: Can the Yorks field a winning organization? If they can't, that roving band of 18th-century villagers will set up permanent camp outside the Yorks' doorstep.

Kevin Lynch

2007 49ers Stats by Week

Wk	vs.	W-L	PF	PA	YDF	YDA	TO	Total	Off	Def	ST
1	ARI	W	20	17	194	261	+1	-10%	-28%	-10%	8%
2	@STL	W	17	16	186	392	+1	-53%	-42%	18%	7%
3	@PIT	L	16	37	289	350	0	-48%	-2%	33%	-13%
4	SEA	L	3	23	184	371	-2	-83%	-81%	8%	6%
5	BAL	L	7	9	163	315	-1	-60%	-42%	25%	7%
6	BYE										
7	@NYG	L	15	33	267	279	-3	-43%	-34%	12%	3%
8	NO	L	10	31	260	438	0	-69%	-30%	46%	6%
9	@ATL	L	16	20	251	286	-3	-55%	-51%	7%	3%
10	@SEA	L	0	24	173	380	0	-54%	-51%	17%	13%
11	STL	L	9	13	244	207	-2	-26%	-37%	-2%	8%
12	@ARI	W	37	31	374	552	+4	17%	15%	13%	14%
13	@CAR	L	14	31	195	323	-4	-87%	-83%	10%	6%
14	MIN	L	7	27	282	280	-4	-40%	-45%	6%	11%
15	CIN	W	20	13	337	313	0	24%	32%	15%	7%
16	TB	W	21	19	213	434	0	11%	-16%	-12%	16%
17	@CLE	L	7	20	185	358	+1	-65%	-34%	4%	-26%

Trends and Splits

	Offense	Rank	Defense	Rank
Total DVOA	-30.5%	32	11.5%	28
Unadjusted VOA	-29.3%	32	7.3%	24
Weighted Trend	-27.4%	32	9.7%	26
Variance	9.1%	25	2.1%	1
Average Opponent	2.0%	25	-1.4%	24
Passing	-43.9%	32	20.5%	29
Rushing	-11.1%	25	1.5%	23
First Down	-27.4%	31	-10.6%	7
Second Down	-26.9%	32	26.3%	32
Third Down	-40.0%	32	28.5%	30
First Half	-40.5%	32	24.4%	31
Second Half	-21.9%	29	-3.2%	13
Red Zone	-8.7%	23	9.9%	21
Late and Close	-21.9%	30	-5.5%	11

Five-Year Performance

Year	W-L	Pyth Wins	Est Wins	PF	PA	TO	Total	Rank	Off	Rank	Def	Rank	ST	Rank
2003	7-9	9.2	7.5	384	337	+12	2.0%	15	8.3%	9	1.4%	19	-5.0%	28
2004	2-14	3.4	2.3	259	452	-19	-46.1%	32	-22.3%	29	22.9%	31	-0.9%	19
2005	4-12	3.2	1.6	239	428	-9	-56.6%	32	-39.8%	32	18.0%	31	1.3%	11
2006	7-9	5.1	6.2	298	412	-5	-19.8%	27	-7.8%	22	12.1%	28	0.1%	18
2007	5-11	3.7	4.0	219	364	-12	-37.5%	32	-30.5%	32	11.5%	28	4.5%	4

Strategic Tendencies

Run/Pass		Rank	Offense		Rank	Defense		Rank	Other		Rank
Runs, all plays	36%	30	3+ WR	52%	14	Rush 3	3.7%	21	2+ RB, Pct Runs	54%	22
Runs, first half	39%	22	4+ WR	8%	23	Rush 4	58.5%	21	1 RB/2 TE, Pct Runs	48%	16
Runs, first down	41%	30	2+ TE	25%	18	Rush 5	29.2%	6	1 RB/3+ WR, Pct Runs	19%	25
Runs, second-long	42%	6	Single back	63%	8	Rush 6+	8.6%	14	CB1 on WR1	63%	1
Runs, power sit.	47%	30	Play action	11%	29	Rush 7+	1.5%	16	Go for it on 4th	1.18	12
Runs, behind 2H	29%	13	Max protect	9%	24	Sacks by LB	48.4%	7	Offensive Pace	31.6	25
Pass, ahead 2H	46%	15	Outside pocket	14%	8	Sacks by DB	10.9%	6	Defensive Pace	30.5	10

After a strong performance in 2006, fullback Moran Norris was a major disappointment last year. Frank Gore and Maurice Hicks gained 4.7 yards per carry from single-back sets, but just 3.6 yards per carry with a fullback in the game. ⌀ The 49ers had the worst rushing offense in the first quarter (-42.6% DVOA) but ranked 14th over the rest of the game. ⌀ The 49ers ranked 21st in their use of screen passes, and only Dallas was less effective on screens. ⌀ Only three teams used play action less often than the 49ers. Although the 49ers were one of only six teams with a negative DVOA on play-action passes (-0.6%) it was far better than their DVOA the rest of the time (-45.9%). ⌀ The 49ers' defense was also better against play action than against standard plays, ranking last in defense without play action (24.3% DVOA) but 11th in defense against play action (9.9% DVOA). ⌀ Unexplainable stat of the year: San Francisco's defensive DVOA from quarter to quarter ranked 24th, 31st, second, and 28th. Indianapolis was the only defense with a better DVOA in the third quarter. ⌀ Opponents did not run a lot of screen passes against the 49ers (they ranked 25th), but they were one of the five worst defenses against the screen. ⌀ San Francisco was the only defense in the league to allow a positive DVOA even when it hurried the quarterback. The 49ers gave up an average of 6.6 yards on these plays; no other team gave up an average of more than 5.4 yards.

Passing

Player	DYAR	DVOA	Plays	NtYds	Avg	YAC	C%	TD	Int
Trent Dilfer*	-632	-52.2%	245	1000	4.1	4.4	52.6%	7	11
Alex Smith	-509	-49.4%	209	789	3.8	3.4	49.2%	2	4
Shaun Hill	101	6.0%	84	458	5.5	4.6	69.2%	5	1
Chris Weinke	-66	-48.4%	27	73	2.7	5.8	59.1%	1	0
J.T. O'Sullivan	-18	-21.5%	30	126	4.2	6.2	50.0%	1	2

Rushing

Player	DYAR	DVOA	Plays	Yds	Avg	TD	Fum	Suc
Frank Gore	130	4.3%	260	1102	4.2	5	4	42%
Michael Robinson	-20	-27.4%	26	121	4.7	0	1	38%
Maurice Hicks*	0	-8.7%	21	117	5.6	1	1	33%
Alex Smith	24	35.6%	9	92	10.2	0	10	—
Moran Norris	5	3.9%	7	17	2.4	0	0	57%
Trent Dilfer*	-22	-98.6%	6	14	2.3	0	6	—
Shaun Hill	6	8.1%	5	21	4.2	1	2	—
Arnaz Battle	-9	-67.3%	4	7	1.8	1	1	—
DeShaun Foster	-72	-15.8%	247	893	3.6	3	7	43%

Receiving

Player	DYAR	DVOA	Plays	Ctch	Yds	Y/C	YAC	TD	C%
WR									
Darrell Jackson*	-126	-27.9%	104	46	495	10.8	1.9	5	44%
Arnaz Battle	-151	-31.3%	104	50	600	12.0	3.1	5	48%
Ashley Lelie	-82	-52.7%	26	10	115	11.5	1.3	0	38%
Bryan Gilmore*	-18	-25.3%	19	7	111	15.9	3.0	0	37%
Taylor Jacobs*	3	-8.1%	9	3	40	13.3	1.3	2	33%
Isaac Bruce	110	0.9%	101	55	733	13.3	2.5	4	54%
Bryant Johnson	17	-10.2%	88	46	528	11.5	1.8	3	52%
TE									
Vernon Davis	-7	-8.6%	85	52	509	9.8	3.4	4	61%
Delanie Walker	-90	-39.4%	42	21	174	8.3	5.6	1	50%
RB									
Frank Gore	110	14.3%	69	53	436	8.2	7.7	1	77%
Maurice Hicks*	14	2.6%	16	14	86	6.1	4.6	0	88%
Michael Robinson	26	28.1%	13	11	73	6.6	6.2	0	85%
Moran Norris	-12	-32.3%	11	6	38	6.3	4.5	0	55%
DeShaun Foster	-22	-24.4%	36	25	180	7.2	7.1	1	69%

Offensive Line

Year	Yards	ALY	Rank	Power	Rank	10+ Yds	Rank	Stuff	Rank	Sack	ASR	Rank
2005	4.11	3.63	29	58%	24	24%	3	24%	14	48	10.1%	29
2006	4.99	4.48	7	55%	28	26%	2	21%	5	35	6.8%	18
2007	4.31	4.28	11	57%	24	15%	19	22%	11	55	10.3%	32

Year	LE	Rank	LT	Rank	Mid	Rank	RT	Rank	RE	Rank
2005	3.93	20	3.17	29	3.70	28	3.93	22	3.18	28
2006	6.01	1	4.30	17	4.40	15	4.04	23	4.34	12
2007	3.27	27	4.34	16	4.27	11	4.60	9	4.08	16

The offensive linemen deserve their share of the blame for the lack of run production last year, but so also do Frank Gore and the receivers, who couldn't make the downfield blocks needed to maintain Gore's status as a breakaway runner. When the 49ers released Antonio Bryant and traded for Darrell Jackson, they lost a big downfield blocker. The offensive line was in disarray for most of last season, and other teams noticed. The 49ers' offense faced a ton of blitzes, and miscommunication was a problem all season long. They hoped to address the issue by signing former Ravens line coach Chris Foerster to share the O-line coaching duties with the embattled George Warhop. The line will also undergo major changes with the expected retirement of guard Larry Allen and the switch of tackles Joe Staley and Jonas Jennings. These changes break up a left side that had been nearly unstoppable when it was manned by Allen and Jennings. The 49ers will also be without guard David Baas until the end of training camp; he tore a pectoral muscle working out in the offseason. The team showed little interest in re-signing pass-protecting demon Justin Smiley, who moved on to Miami.

The Smiley departure and the Baas injury could open an opportunity for second-round choice Chilo Rachal, a guard out of USC who has been compared to Allen. The line is very thin at tackle, and surprisingly, the 49ers didn't address the issue with their six-member draft class or in the 11 rookie free agents they signed in the offseason. Jennings has missed 16 of his last 32 starts and has never played a full 16-game season. Should he get injured again, the team will likely move short-armed guard Adam Snyder out to tackle. Behind Snyder is a former practice-squad defensive lineman, Damane Duckett.

Defensive Front Seven

Defensive Line	Age	Pos	Plays	TmPct	Rk	Stop	Dfts	Stop%	Rk	AvYd	Rk	Sack	Hit	Hur	Runs	RuStop	RuYd	Pass	PaStop	PaYd
Marques Douglas*	31	DE	75	8.6%	9	59	23	79%	34	1.7	42	3.0	1	6	59	81%	1.7	16	69%	1.9
Bryant Young*	36	DE	36	4.1%	66	31	14	86%	6	0.2	12	6.5	7	12	27	81%	1.6	9	100%	-3.9
Aubrayo Franklin	28	DT	27	3.5%	61	19	8	70%	60	2.6	57	0.0	1	2	25	72%	2.3	2	50%	5.5
Isaac Sopoaga	27	DT	21	2.4%	—	19	6	90%	—	1.0	—	1.5	1	1	17	88%	2.1	4	100%	-3.3
Ronald Fields	27	DT	21	2.4%	—	13	2	62%	—	2.4	—	1.0	0	1	20	60%	2.7	1	100%	-3.0
Justin Smith	29	DE	81	9.8%	3	51	14	63%	74	3.2	71	2.0	6	18	72	61%	3.4	9	78%	1.1

Linebackers	Age	Pos	Plays	TmPct	Rk	Stop	Dfts	Stop%	AvYd	Sack	Hit	Hur	Runs	RuStop	Rk	RuYd	Rk	Tgts	Suc%	Rk	APaYd	Rk
Patrick Willis	23	ILB	180	20.6%	2	98	30	54%	5.6	4.0	3	4	114	58%	69	4.0	76	48	49%	47	6.5	60
Derek Smith*	33	ILB	82	10.0%	67	46	9	56%	4.5	0.0	2	1	55	64%	46	3.5	54	22	33%	88	6.3	55
Tully Banta-Cain	28	OLB	44	5.0%	—	32	16	73%	2.5	3.5	3	10	31	77%	—	1.9	—	4	26%	—	10.4	—
Parys Haralson	24	OLB	34	3.9%	—	24	9	71%	2.1	2.5	2	3	26	69%	—	3.2	—	6	55%	—	8.9	—
Jeff Ulbrich	31	ILB	31	3.5%	—	16	4	52%	5.2	0.0	0	1	23	52%	—	4.5	—	7	51%	—	6.3	—
Brandon Moore	29	OLB	18	2.1%	—	15	8	83%	0.7	2.5	1	2	12	83%	—	1.6	—	2	22%	—	9.4	—

Year	Yards	ALY	Rank	Power	Rank	10+ Yds	Rank	Stuff	Rank	Sack	ASR	Rank
2005	4.04	4.30	23	60%	15	16%	14	29%	2	28	5.0%	32
2006	4.33	4.64	26	67%	19	15%	10	21%	27	34	6.2%	20
2007	3.88	4.10	14	70%	25	14%	8	24%	16	31	5.7%	25

Year	LE	Rank	LT	Rank	Mid	Rank	RT	Rank	RE	Rank
2005	4.87	26	3.60	7	3.90	12	5.11	30	5.05	29
2006	4.23	18	4.13	11	4.80	29	4.73	24	4.93	28
2007	3.74	12	4.00	11	4.41	26	4.13	17	2.78	5

Is it a 3-4, or a 4-3? The 49ers won't say. Since Mike Nolan's arrival, the 49ers have toggled back and forth, and that's likely to continue this year. Nolan loves the flexibility and disguise ability of the 3-4, but even he admits a good 3-4 is fueled by a pair of terrorizing pass-rushing outside linebackers, and the 49ers don't even have one. They hoped former Patriot Tully Banta-Cain would bring that element last year when they signed him to a free-agent deal, but it didn't happen. Banta-Cain reported to training camp out of shape, then sprained his ankle in the fifth game of the season and never became a consistent outside threat. His lack of coverage ability also hurt the team. Hope comes from two younger players: 2006 first-rounder Manny Lawson, who is back after tearing his ACL in practice during the third week of the season, and fellow outside linebacker Jay Moore, a fourth-round selection from last year.

Rookie linebacker Patrick Willis's rundown of Cardinals receiver Sean Morey to save a touchdown in overtime still draws "wows" from the 49ers' faithful. The play wasn't the game-saver most think it was—if Willis hadn't tackled Morey, safety Michael Lewis would have—but watching an inside linebacker chase down a receiver was something to behold. Asked about Willis after the season, position coach Mike Singletary didn't rave about his young charge. Instead, Singletary, who's not prone to bombast, simply said, "He's only scratching the surface." Yikes. Willis can improve in his pass coverage, particularly in the red zone, where he was drawn in by play-action too often, and he needs to make tackles closer to the line of scrimmage. The Morey play shows he has the hustle and ability to make plays down the field, but his tackles came after an average gain of 5.6 yards per carry, which is a tad high.

The team tried desperately to find an inside linebacker to pair with Willis, but Atlanta stole Oklahoma's Curtis Lofton two picks before San Francisco was set to choose him in the second round. They also wanted to sign Takeo Spikes in the offseason but his contract demands were too high. Brandon Moore wasn't getting looks as the starting inside linebacker in a May minicamp, but the 49ers might be reserving him for pass-rush duty.

The defensive line is undergoing an overhaul. After 14 seasons, Bryant Young retired and the team showed no interest in re-signing Marques Douglas, a terrific run-stopper. Moving in is the team's big free agent signing, former Bengal Justin Smith. He'll be moved around the defensive line and will even be used as a stand-up pass rusher. The team looks to get some juice out of first-round pick Kentwan Balmer and hopes Ron Fields and Isaac Sopoaga will take the next step after flip-flopping positions (Fields is now an end and Sopoaga is a nose tackle).

Defensive Secondary

Secondary	Age	Pos	Plays	TmPct	Rk	Stop	Dfts	RuYd	Rk	RuStop	Rk	Tgts	Tgt%	Rk	Dist	Suc%	Rk	APaYd	Rk	PaYd	PD	Int
Michael Lewis	28	SS	108	12.4%	11	34	17	6.6	45	28%	77	39	9%	21	9.9	58%	12	5.4	12	5.2	6	2
Nate Clements	29	CB	106	12.1%	10	53	26	4.6	15	56%	22	109	24%	4	10.2	50%	42	8.0	55	8.1	16	4
Walt Harris	34	CB	70	8.5%	52	32	15	5.3	23	47%	45	73	17%	50	13.2	53%	27	7.7	49	7.7	13	4
Mark Roman	31	FS	68	7.8%	60	22	9	6.7	48	41%	49	32	7%	40	9.9	45%	54	8.3	50	8.4	3	0
Donald Strickland	28	CB	33	4.6%	—	14	6	5.8	—	45%	—	20	5%	—	7.5	37%	—	8.4	—	8.6	4	0
Shawntae Spencer	26	CB	27	4.5%	—	11	8	6.5	—	50%	—	34	11%	—	13.8	56%	—	7.4	—	7.2	3	1
Marcus Hudson	26	FS	21	3.5%	83	9	6	6.7	47	33%	61	21	7%	47	7.2	57%	16	5.5	15	4.7	2	0
Mike Adams	27	FS	15	1.8%	—	5	3	8.8	—	20%	—	4	1%	—	16.0	86%	—	7.4	—	7.0	2	0

Year	Pass D Rank	vs. #1 WR	Rk	vs. #2 WR	Rk	vs.Other WR	Rk	vs.TE	Rk	vs.RB	Rk
2005	31	22.9%	28	-15.8%	6	-5.9%	12	52.6%	32	10.1%	25
2006	29	3.0%	18	-10.2%	9	-4.6%	18	36.4%	32	18.5%	30
2007	29	0.7%	16	13.6%	23	0.4%	20	23.2%	27	-2.5%	15

The defense hopes to see more benefits from the Nate Clements signing of 2007. His eight-season, $80 million contract with $22 million in guaranteed cash has stood for more than a year as the richest cornerback contract in the league. The idea was that Clements could take the opposition's best receiver by himself, freeing up another player to rush the passer. Clements did his job for the most part, but the free blitzer rarely got home.

While Clements's spot is nailed down, a competition could ensue for the other cornerback slot and will certainly ensue for the nickel back role. After a ball-thieving 2006, Walt Harris suddenly realized he was 33. Harris devotes most of his offseason to workouts in Arizona, so he could possibly rebound. Otherwise, he'll have to fend off third-round pick Reggie Smith and last year's fifth-rounder, Tarrell Brown, who is coming off a knee injury. Shawntae Spencer is also a possibility. The 49ers are solid in the middle with the versatile Mark Roman at free safety and last year's free agent find Michael Lewis on the strong side. It might be difficult to keep Dashon Goldson out of the lineup. Last year's fourth-round pick seems to make a play every day in practice.

If the 49ers get any semblance of a pass rush, they could move out of the pass defense doldrums. For the last four years the pass defense DVOA has ranked 32nd, 31st, 29th, and 29th.

Special Teams

Year	DVOA	Rank	FG/XP	Rank	Net Punt	Rank	Punt Ret	Rank	Net Kick	Rank	Kick Ret	Rank	Hidden	Rank
2005	1.3%	11	12.8	2	2.0	14	0.8	11	5.9	9	-13.9	31	7.7	7
2006	0.1%	18	-0.1	16	1.8	17	-0.3	15	-1.4	22	0.2	15	-11.4	27
2007	4.5%	4	4.6	9	18.1	1	3.3	10	2.1	12	-1.5	19	-5.1	23

Even in the leanest of years, the 49ers have been decent on special teams, probably for the same reason that players never gave up on their coaches, Dennis Erickson, and his staff. The team has consistently drafted high-character personalities and players who simply love the game and will play through any circumstance. (This is good proof that morality and a strong work ethic do not, on their own, lead to a winning ballclub.) Last season, the high character met a drill sergeant of a coach and a superb motivator in special teams coach Al Everest. His straightforward game plans and Saturday night speeches got the team ready for Sunday. It also helped that the team had a Pro Bowl punter in Andy Lee and proven special teams standouts such as Michael Robinson and Brandon Moore. Joe Nedney's a pretty good kicker too, when the 49ers manage to get him into field-goal range. With Maurice Hicks gone to Minnesota, 11-year veteran Allen Rossum was signed to return kicks and punts. According to our metrics, Rossum was average returning kickoffs for Pittsburgh last year, but he was the worst punt returner in the league, costing his team 9.1 points worth of field position compared to an average return man.

COACHING STAFF

After a disappointing 2007, the edict was clear for Mike Nolan: either find some offense and win some games, or look for work. So Nolan did something no one anticipated, hiring the pass-oriented and sometimes abrasive Mike Martz to run his offense. The entire organization seemed to bristle, but Martz has so far turned out to be a marvel. He has helped diffuse the tension between Nolan and quarterback Alex Smith, ingratiated himself to resistant general manager Scot McCloughan, and made players excited about the offense for the first time since Steve Mariucci left. But obstacles remain. Can he find a quarterback among Alex Smith, Shaun Hill, and J. T. O'Sullivan? Can the wildly aggressive Martz and the frightfully conservative Nolan actually manage the game together on Sunday? With drama like this, who says the 49ers don't belong in Los Angeles?

Seattle Seahawks

Last year was the penultimate campaign for Seattle Seahawks head coach Mike Holmgren. During the offseason, Seahawks general manager Tim Ruskell confirmed that secondary-coach Jim Mora will take over in the 2009 season. The Seahawks won their fourth consecutive NFC West title last year, and over the past five years, only the Patriots and the Colts have won more total games, so it seems strange that Holmgren would choose to retire now. But he and Ruskell have never shared the same vision for the franchise, and if Holmgren's offseason remarks are any indication, it's pretty clear that he is ready to leave football for good.

"I've always wanted to buy a bookstore," Holmgren said in an interview with the *Seattle Post-Intelligencer*, just before announcing that he'd be back for one final year as head coach. "You know, sell some of those muffins and a little coffee."

Sure, it may *sound* less stressful selling paperbacks and lattes than coaching an NFL team, but remember that the corporate headquarters for Starbucks and Amazon.com are in Seattle too. And one has to wonder if Holmgren's decision results in part from his frustration watching his once-dominant offense slowly decline into mediocrity. Unlike two years ago, when the team suffered a rash of injuries to seemingly every skill-position player and offensive lineman on the roster, the Seahawks' offense was relatively healthy in 2007 yet they posted an offensive DVOA of just 5.6%, 14th in the NFL.

The problem was simple: The Seahawks could not run the football. Over the first eight games of the sea-

son, Seattle's ground game tallied a pathetic 22.3% DVOA, which was second to last in the league. Need we even make the obligatory Shaun-Alexander-as-Poster-Child-for-the-Curse-of-370 reference here? Things improved (relatively) after Alexander succumbed to a series of self-described "boo-boos" and missed three games in early November, which forced Holmgren to use backup running back Maurice Morris and fullback Leonard Weaver. The Seahawks' offense immediately improved to a rushing DVOA of -4.3% over this period and managed to inch into positive territory for the final five weeks of the season.

Despite the anemic ground game, the Seahawks managed to win 10 games in the regular season. This was partly the result of an extraordinarily soft schedule, even by NFC West standards. It helps to play four games against the Rams and the 49ers, the two worst teams in DVOA last year, but it *really* helps when you have to play only four teams with a positive DVOA the entire season. Seattle's opening week victory over Tampa Bay was their only regular-season win over a team that would finish 2007 with a winning record. Seahawks' fans may complain about the lack of media attention paid to their team, but they seem to have a mole inside the NFL's scheduling department.

The easy schedule helped, but the real reason the Seahawks remained competitive was the defense, led by their outstanding linebacker trio of Lofa Tatupu, Julian Peterson, and Leroy Hill. Tatupu and Peterson both went to the Pro Bowl, and rightly so, but Hill is perhaps the most underrated linebacker in the league. Hill

---

SEAHAWKS PROSPECTUS

2007 Record: 10-6

Pythagorean Wins: 10.7 (8th)

DVOA: 12.1% total (9th), 14.2% weighted (8th)

Offense: 5.6% DVOA (14th)

Defense: -5.5% DVOA (11th)

Special Teams: 1.0% DVOA (11th)

Variance: 12.1 % (8th)

2007: Another year, another NFC West title.

2008: Another year, another NFC West title—the Atlanta Braves of the NFL!

2008 Mean Projection: 10.5 wins

On the Clock (0-3): 0%

Loserville (4-6): 2%

Mediocrity (7-8): 10%

Playoff Contender (9-10): 40%

Super Bowl Contender (11+): 48%

Projected Average Opponent: -2.8% DVOA (24th in NFL)

2008 Seahawks Schedule

Week	Opp.	Week	Opp.	Week	Opp.
1	at BUF	7	at TB	13	at DAL (Thu.)
2	SF	8	at SF	14	NE
3	STL	9	PHI	15	at STL
4	BYE	10	at MIA	16	NYJ
5	at NYG	11	ARI	17	at ARI
6	GB	12	WAS		

ranked third in run stops (with an excellent 85 percent Stop Rate) and vastly improved his previously suspect pass coverage skills (ranking fifth in yards per pass according to our game charting stats). Combine those linebackers with a deep defensive line rotation, and you get a front seven that ranked third in Adjusted Line Yards and seventh in Adjusted Sack Rate.

Just three years ago, the Super Bowl Seahawks were an offense-first team, ranking third in offensive DVOA and 15th in defensive DVOA. There's little mystery as to how this change came about. Over the past three years, Tim Ruskell has patiently and methodologically built up the defense through a series of astute decisions in drafting and free agency. Yet every savvy decision he's made on defense seems to be offset by a mistaken signing on offense. Consider the following hypothetical starting lineup (Table 1), using only defensive players acquired during Ruskell's tenure as general manager (prior to 2008).

Table 1. Best Ruskell-Era Players, Defense

Player	Pos	Acquired	Year	Notes
Brandon Mebane	DT	Drafted (3rd)	2007	87% Stop Rate in rookie season, will start this year
Bryce Fisher	DT	Free agency	2005	Played 32 games before being traded to Tennessee
Patrick Kerney	DE	Free agency	2007	14.5 sacks + 9 hits + 17 hurries = Pro Bowl
Darryl Tapp	DE	Drafted (2nd)	2006	Seven sacks last year, expected to start in 2008
Lofa Tatupu	LB	Drafted (2nd)	2005	Three Pro Bowls
Julian Peterson	LB	Free agency	2006	Two Pro Bowls, 19.5 sacks over two years
Leroy Hill	LB	Drafted (4th)	2005	See gushing paragraph above
Kelly Jennings	CB	Drafted (1st)	2006	Full-time starter in second season
Andre Dyson	CB	Free agency	2005	Solid contributor for Seattle in 2005, less so for Jets
Deon Grant	FS	Free agency	2007	Top-ranked safety in Run Stop Rate last year (72%)
Brian Russell	SS	Free agency	2007	Didn't impress in Seattle but Cleveland fans would love to have him back.

By contrast, here is the All-Ruskell Team on offense (Table 2).

Table 2. Best Ruskell-Era Players, Offense

Player	Pos	Acquired	Year	Notes
Chris Spencer	C	Drafted (1st)	2005	Could not make line calls last year
Rob Sims	OL	Drafted (4th)	2006	Fighting to hold onto starting job
Tom Ashworth	OL	Free agency	2006	Horrific in spot appearance, cut in February
Ray Willis	OL	Drafted (4th)	2005	Never seen
Mansfield Wrotto	OL	Drafted (4th)	2007	Equally invisible
Marcus Pollard	TE	Free agency	2007	Last seen dropping passes in Green Bay
Deion Branch	WR	Traded for 1st	2006	Ranked 50th in DYAR before tearing his ACL
Nate Burleson	WR	Traded for 3rd	2005	Ranked 48th in DYAR and wildly inconsistent
Joe Jurevicius	WR	Free agency	2005	Played well before leaving for Cleveland
Alvin Pearman	RB	Traded (5th)	2007	Out of league
David Greene	QB	Drafted (3rd)	2005	Currently buried on Chiefs' practice squad
Charlie Frye	QB	Traded (6th)	2007	Still breathing

The pattern is unmistakable, which is why Ruskell's most recent free agency acquisitions on offense should be viewed with some caution. That said, the signing of former Panthers guard Mike Wahle, a two-time Pro Bowler, should improve the Seahawks' pathetic 3.74 adjusted-line yards last year (29th in the NFL). And although on most teams the addition of former Cowboys' running back Julius Jones and former Lions' bowling ball T. J. Duckett would constitute a downgrade, the Jones-Duckett combo can't be worse than watching Shaun Alexander dance sideways and spin around three times before falling down in the backfield for a two-yard loss.

The most important addition to the Seahawks' running game, however, may be the hiring of new offensive line coach Mike Solari from the Kansas City Chiefs. Solari coached the Chiefs offensive line for nine years before his recent (and failed) stint as their offensive coordinator, and he is considered one of the premier line technique coaches in the NFL. Although it's too soon to know how Seattle's blocking schemes will change this year, Solari's emphasis on power running should fit perfectly with the new, smashmouth brand of running game that the Seahawks seem to be moving toward. (Make sure to keep an eye on rookie fullback Owen "Runaway Beertruck" Schmitt, a fifth-round draft choice out of West Virginia who broke 11 helmet facemasks in college.) It will also be interesting to see whether Solari is able to coax anything out of Ray Willis and Mansfield Wrotto, the forgotten gigantic-but-clueless guards who thus far have failed to master the intricacies of blocking at the professional level—you may insert your own "size doesn't matter" joke here.

Although the running game will improve, there are questions regarding wide receivers. The Seahawks lost D. J. Hackett to the Carolina Panthers in free agency, Branch is coming off surgery that will likely keep him sidelined until the start of the season (if not longer), and as much as we love the guy, there's no way Bobby Engram can repeat his career-best performance of last year. The Seahawks are hoping that underachieving Nate Burleson will start at flanker, but he is inconsistent. Seattle's other receiver options are limited to Ruskell's quartet of late-round draft fliers: Courtney Taylor (sixth round), Jordan Kent (sixth round), Ben Obamanu (seventh round), and Logan Payne (undrafted). We are also contractually obligated at this stage to once again urge the Seahawks to consider moving backup quarterback Seneca Wallace to wide receiver.

Despite all these questions, the Seahawks' offense should improve this year. Quarterback Matt Hasselbeck managed to throw for nearly 4,000 yards in 2007, despite the lack of a ground game to take the pressure off him. He also has a new weapon in rookie tight end John Carlson (from Notre Dame), who will be a definite upgrade over the aged Marcus Pollard. All of this assumes that the starting offensive line stays healthy; if it

doesn't, the Seahawks may suffer a St. Louis Rams-like implosion due to their lack of depth.

As for the defense, Seattle will go into 2008 with high hopes. First-round draft pick Lawrence Jackson, a defensive end from USC, should be another solid contributor to the defensive line, and the team may have gotten a steal in their fourth-round selection of defensive tackle Red Bryant from Texas A&M. True, the Seahawks are thin at linebackers after backup Niko Koutouvides left to join the Denver Broncos, and they need another safety (or two), but these are minor quibbles. Ruskell has built a defense that is poised to become one of the league's elite.

The one lingering question is the coaching staff. Although he's never figured out clock management, Holmgren is one of the league's best coaches, and his control over his players is not in doubt. Still, it's somewhat unusual that his successor-in-waiting is on his own coaching staff, and you have to wonder how the players will react to the seeming division of authority between him and Mora. Provided Holmgren doesn't start daydreaming about java blends and new translations of *Remembrances of Things Past*, the Seahawks should send him off into retirement with another NFC West title—and possibly much more.

Ben Riley

2007 Seahawks Stats by Week

Wk	vs.	W-L	PF	PA	YDF	YDA	TO	Total	Off	Def	ST
1	TB	W	20	6	343	284	+1	55%	18%	-31%	6%
2	@ARI	L	20	23	362	431	0	-28%	10%	39%	2%
3	CIN	W	24	21	340	412	+2	2%	-9%	4%	15%
4	@SF	W	23	3	371	184	+2	51%	-7%	-57%	1%
5	@PIT	L	0	21	144	342	-1	-49%	-38%	18%	7%
6	NO	L	17	28	425	367	-1	-16%	7%	8%	-16%
7	STL	W	33	6	289	221	+4	57%	-15%	-37%	34%
8	BYE										
9	@CLE	L	30	33	423	428	-1	8%	12%	17%	14%
10	SF	W	24	0	380	173	0	27%	14%	-24%	-10%
11	CHI	W	30	23	425	345	0	2%	31%	17%	-13%
12	@STL	W	24	19	302	265	0	33%	-8%	-40%	1%
13	@PHI	W	28	24	311	363	+2	21%	3%	-45%	-28%
14	ARI	W	42	21	349	355	+5	41%	33%	-10%	-2%
15	@CAR	L	10	13	282	322	-1	-6%	4%	10%	0%
16	BAL	W	27	6	336	293	+1	28%	3%	-12%	13%
17	@ATL	L	41	44	501	364	-3	-53%	14%	58%	-8%
18	WAS	W	35	14	304	319	0	18%	1%	-16%	0%
19	@GB	L	20	42	200	408	+1	-64%	-15%	48%	-1%

Trends and Splits

	Offense	Rank	Defense	Rank
Total DVOA	5.6%	14	-5.5%	11
Unadjusted VOA	7.7%	12	-12.4%	2
Weighted trend	9.1%	10	-7.0%	5
Variance	3.1%	2	10.4%	27
Average opponent	3.7%	30	-6.6%	32
Passing	17.3%	9	0.2%	14
Rushing	-10.0%	21	-12.9%	5
First down	7.3%	10	-17.3%	4
Second down	14.4%	7	6.8%	22
Third down	-11.2%	24	-2.1%	11
First half	8.6%	11	-5.0%	10
Second half	2.5%	15	-5.9%	10
Red zone	13.3%	9	3.8%	17
Late and close	3.7%	12	3.8%	20

Five-Year Performance

Year	W-L	Pyth Wins	Est Wins	PF	PA	TO	Total	Rank	Off	Rank	Def	Rank	ST	Rank
2003	10-6	10.0	10.0	404	327	-1	14.4%	9	13.3%	5	-0.9%	16	0.2%	18
2004	9-7	7.9	7.6	371	373	+8	-5.0%	20	3.6%	12	6.3%	22	-1.3%	20
2005	13-3	12.3	11.7	452	271	+10	26.2%	5	23.4%	3	-3.5%	15	-0.6%	21
2006	9-7	7.8	6.3	335	341	-8	-13.1%	25	-11.7%	27	4.1%	20	2.6%	7
2007	10-6	10.7	9.1	393	291	+10	12.1%	9	5.6%	14	-5.5%	11	1.0%	11

Strategic Tendencies

Run/Pass		Rank	Offense		Rank	Defense		Rank	Other		Rank
Runs, all plays	38%	23	3+ WR	63%	7	Rush 3	4.1%	18	2+ RB, Pct runs	52%	25
Runs, first half	33%	31	4+ WR	17%	7	Rush 4	65.9%	12	1 RB/2 TE, Pct runs	39%	23
Runs, first down	43%	27	2+ TE	10%	31	Rush 5	16.7%	24	1 RB/3+ WR, Pct runs	23%	18
Runs, second-long	29%	26	Single back	49%	26	Rush 6+	13.2%	7	CB1 on WR1	49%	11
Runs, power sit.	69%	5	Play action	18%	17	Rush 7+	3.9%	4	Go for it on 4th	0.68	28
Runs, behind 2H	26%	25	Max protect	8%	25	Sacks by LB	30.0%	12	Offensive pace	28.7	2
Pass, ahead 2H	47%	13	Outside pocket	13%	11	Sacks by DB	4.4%	23	Defensive pace	30.8	15

Seattle used shotgun on only eight percent of plays, the lowest percentage of any offense in the league but the highest percentage of any season since Mike Holmgren took over the team. (Overall, league usage of shotgun rose by 50 percent last year.) The Seahawks had a 45.8% DVOA in shotgun, best in the NFC, but only a 2.7% DVOA on plays with the quarterback under center. ⊘ For the second straight year, the Seahawks threw to the right side of the field more often than any other team. They were the only team to throw over half their passes in one direction, which made them a bottom three offense in both passes to the left and passes up the middle. Despite this, seven of Matt Hasselbeck's 12 interceptions were thrown to the left side of the field. Seattle was the only offense with no interceptions in the middle of the field. ⊘ Seattle ranked in the bottom ten in use of the screen pass. Half of all Seattle's screens came on first down. Only Green Bay's screen game was skewed more towards first down. ⊘ The Seahawks kept Hasselbeck (and occasionally Seneca Wallace) on the move. Only two teams designed plays to roll out their quarterback more often. ⊘ Seattle didn't run as much as other teams on second-and-long, but when they did run, they were successful at it. The Seahawks gained 6.5 yards per carry in these situations, second to Minnesota. ⊘ The Seahawks dramatically boosted their blitzing from 2006 to 2007, going from 26th in rushing six or more and 28th in rushing seven or more to the top ten in both categories. ⊘ Seattle led the league in defensive DVOA in the first quarter. ⊘ Seattle's defense led the league in sacks marked as blown blocks. ⊘ The Seattle defense was 31st in DVOA against passes thrown to the (offense's) left, but second against passes up the middle and third against passes to the right. ⊘ Seattle was one of two defenses whose opponents threw up the middle less than 20 percent of the time. (Cleveland was the other.)

Passing

Player	DYAR	DVOA	Plays	NtYds	Avg	YAC	C%	TD	Int
Matt Hasselbeck	937	12.8%	599	3824	6.4	4.7	63.0%	28	12
Seneca Wallace	-8	-14.6%	32	207	6.5	6.1	67.9%	2	1

Rushing

Player	DYAR	DVOA	Plays	Yds	Avg	TD	Fum	Suc
Shaun Alexander*	-74	-17.3%	207	716	3.5	4	2	38%
Maurice Morris	57	0.7%	141	629	4.5	4	2	51%
Leonard Weaver	40	16.0%	33	146	4.4	1	0	61%
Matt Hasselbeck	-3	-14.9%	22	104	4.7	0	6	—
Mack Strong*	-4	-37.4%	4	19	4.8	0	0	25%
Seneca Wallace	8	27.5%	4	17	4.3	0	1	—
T. J. Duckett	56	12.2%	65	335	5.2	3	1	38%
Julius Jones	12	-6.7%	164	603	3.7	2	0	37%

Receiving

Player	DYAR	DVOA	Plays	Ctch	Yds	Y/C	YAC	TD	C%
WR									
Bobby Engram	270	12.9%	134	94	1151	12.2	3.9	6	70%
Nate Burleson	107	1.2%	95	50	694	13.9	3.9	9	53%
Deion Branch	97	1.8%	85	49	661	13.5	4.2	4	58%
D. J. Hackett*	99	12.8%	47	32	384	12.0	4.3	3	68%
Ben Obomanu	-30	-25.5%	29	12	180	15.0	4.5	1	41%
Courtney Taylor	4	-5.0%	6	5	38	7.6	2.8	0	83%
TE									
Marcus Pollard*	82	25.8%	35	28	273	9.8	4.6	2	80%
Will Heller	-36	-26.7%	26	13	82	6.3	3.7	3	50%
Jeb Putzier	-2	-10.5%	10	6	39	6.5	2.8	1	60%
RB									
Leonard Weaver	87	17.3%	52	39	313	8.0	8.6	0	75%
Maurice Morris	55	17.0%	32	23	213	9.3	7.5	1	72%
Shaun Alexander*	-30	-36.4%	25	14	76	5.4	5.4	1	56%
Mack Strong*	33	32.4%	12	9	72	8.0	5.8	0	75%
T. J. Duckett	26	47.7%	7	4	54	13.5	16.3	0	57%
Julius Jones	75	38.2%	26	23	203	8.8	9.4	0	88%

Offensive Line

Year	Yards	ALY	Rank	Power	Rank	10+ Yds	Rank	Stuff	Rank	Sack	ASR	Rank
2005	4.92	4.49	6	81%	1	25%	2	26%	24	27	5.9%	12
2006	3.70	3.81	30	70%	10	14%	23	26%	28	49	8.7%	26
2007	3.92	3.73	29	52%	27	20%	10	31%	31	37	7.1%	19

Year	LE	Rank	LT	Rank	Mid	Rank	RT	Rank	RE	Rank
2005	4.21	17	3.77	24	4.65	2	5.22	2	4.70	7
2006	4.29	14	4.00	25	3.66	31	3.93	25	2.97	29
2007	3.95	19	3.86	24	3.70	29	3.84	25	3.32	29

When Steve Hutchinson left Seattle to join the Minnesota Vikings, the Seahawks' offensive line didn't just lose the best left guard in the league. It also lost its identity. Enter Mike Wahle, a free agent signing from Carolina who will take over at left guard this season. Although he's entering his 11th season, Wahle is aging well—he made his first Pro Bowl appearance in 2006. He's one of the better pass blockers in the league and has always been strong pulling on running plays. Wahle's arrival also means that Rob Sims can move over to his more natural position of right guard so that the ancient Chris Gray may finally be taken out to pasture.

With Walter Jones and Sean Locklear manning the tackles, the only question is at center. In four years, general manager Tim Ruskell has drafted only one offensive player in the first round, but Chris Spencer is about to enter his fourth season and the lightbulb still hasn't turned on. Last year, the Seahawks were forced to rely on Gray to make line adjustments due to Spencer's inability to react to disguised coverage schemes, although part of the problem may be that he was forced to play guard for most of 2006. In any event, Spencer has yet to show any run- or pass-blocking ability that justifies his first-round selection, so the Seahawks are hoping that new offensive line coach Mike Solari will manage to unearth the talent Spencer displayed at the University of Mississippi.

Seattle continues to play with fire when it comes to offensive line depth. Floyd Womack remains on the team (possibly for salary-cap purposes only), guards Ray Willis and Mansfield Wrotto are buried on the practice squad, and Tom Ashworth is preparing for his new career in insurance sales. If any of the starters get injured, it could easily lead to a domino effect on the line that will culminate in quarterback Matt Hasselbeck getting pounded into the turf. In a draft year stocked with offensive line talent, Ruskell's decision to trade away the Seahawks third-round pick may come back to haunt him.

Defensive Front Seven

Defensive Line	Age	Pos	Plays	TmPct	Rk	Stop	Dfts	Stop%	Rk	AvYd	Rk	Sack	Hit	Hur	Runs	RuStop	RuYd	Pass	PaStop	PaYd
Patrick Kerney	32	DE	64	7.8%	13	52	26	81%	24	0.8	20	14.5	9	17	43	77%	2.7	21	90%	-3.2
Darryl Tapp	24	DE	58	7.1%	23	48	22	83%	11	0.0	8	7.0	8	12	37	81%	1.1	21	86%	-1.9
Rocky Bernard	29	DT	37	5.2%	32	29	13	78%	31	1.5	24	3.5	4	8	29	79%	2.0	8	75%	-0.5
Brandon Mebane	23	DT	30	3.7%	59	26	8	87%	7	1.7	35	2.0	0	2	26	88%	1.6	4	75%	2.5
Craig Terrill	28	DT	26	3.2%	64	21	7	81%	25	1.8	40	0.0	1	5	24	79%	1.8	2	100%	2.5

Linebackers	Age	Pos	Plays	TmPct	Rk	Stop	Dfts	Stop%	AvYd	Sack	Hit	Hur	Runs	RuStop	Rk	RuYd	Rk	Tgts	Suc%	Rk	APaYd	Rk
Lofa Tatupu	26	MLB	117	14.3%	23	77	30	66%	4.2	1.0	5	4	66	73%	18	2.2	7	36	59%	12	5.1	22
Leroy Hill	26	OLB	86	12.0%	55	65	25	76%	3.2	3.0	2	5	54	85%	3	2.9	26	31	68%	5	3.7	5
Julian Peterson	30	OLB	78	9.6%	72	42	23	54%	4.6	9.5	3	12	38	61%	56	3.6	57	24	41%	69	8.0	83
Kevin Bentley*	29	OLB	17	2.4%	—	8	1	47%	5.8	0.0	0	1	13	46%	—	5.2	—	5	48%	—	8.9	—

Year	Yards	ALY	Rank	Power	Rank	10+ Yds	Rank	Stuff	Rank	Sack	ASR	Rank
2005	3.47	3.55	1	54%	4	14%	10	27%	8	50	7.9%	8
2006	4.73	4.03	10	69%	23	29%	32	27%	7	41	7.1%	14
2007	4.11	3.83	3	60%	13	24%	30	30%	3	45	7.3%	7

Year	LE	Rank	LT	Rank	Mid	Rank	RT	Rank	RE	Rank
2005	4.11	16	4.02	12	3.66	5	3.53	4	2.45	2
2006	3.81	13	4.77	21	4.17	13	3.38	6	2.92	2
2007	4.32	20	3.79	10	3.88	5	3.98	15	2.52	3

Is it safe to say that Patrick Kerney was an upgrade over Grant Wistrom? At the time of his signing last year, Kerney seemed like a poor consolation prize after the Seahawks failed to land Chargers guard Kris Dielman or current Broncos tight end Daniel Graham in free agency. The Seahawks were consoled to the tune of 14.5 sacks, second in the league. Kerney's performance against the Washington Redskins in the playoffs was among the finest individual defensive efforts of any player last season; he disrupted or drew a double-team on virtually every play he was involved in.

Kerney wasn't the only happy surprise for Seattle in 2008. Rookie defensive tackle Brandon Mebane, a third-round pick out of Cal, was a big reason why the Seahawks' run defense rebounded after a poor 2006. Mebane is also further proof that general manager Tim Ruskell's draft strategy of targeting players who slide because of size concerns can yield positive returns. The Seahawks are counting on Mebane to be a full-time starter this year because they know they can't rely on Marcus "Bionic Knee" Tubbs, who is coming off reconstructive surgery to his right knee after suffering yet another season-ending injury last year. Some have suggested that this most recent injury may actually be a good thing for Tubbs, insofar as it has given his *left* knee more time to recover from microfracture surgery in 2006. Don't believe the hype: It will be near-miraculous if Tubbs sees any significant playing time this year.

You may, however, believe all the hype you want about the Seahawks starting linebackers. Lofa Tatupu is one of the smartest players in the league, as evidenced by an interception of a pass by former USC teammate Matt Leinart in Week 4. Tatupu read Leinart's eyes at the line of scrimmage and sprinted downfield 30 yards to make the pick. Julian Peterson is a pass-rushing beast (albeit a beast who is prone to disappear every fourth game or so). Leroy Hill was already one of the league's best run-stoppers, and with his improved play in pass coverage, he may just become the league's highest paid linebacker when he becomes a free agent in 2009. Seattle will be in trouble if one of the starters gets hurt and misses significant time. Will Herring, a second-year player out of Auburn, is primarily a pass defender, and Launce Laury is an undrafted free agent who's spent the past two years honing his special-teams skills.

Defensive Secondary

Secondary	Age	Pos	Plays	TmPct	Rk	Stop	Dfts	RuYd	Rk	RuStop	Rk	Tgts	Tgt%	Rk	Dist	Suc%	Rk	APaYd	Rk	PaYd	PD	Int
Marcus Trufant	28	CB	100	12.3%	9	40	18	6.0	37	38%	53	113	24%	3	12.9	53%	29	6.8	26	6.5	19	7
Deon Grant	29	SS	82	10.0%	35	47	7	3.8	3	72%	1	39	8%	22	11.5	39%	69	7.3	42	7.1	10	3
Brian Russell	30	FS	71	8.7%	49	23	6	9.9	79	39%	54	27	6%	60	15.8	56%	18	5.8	19	5.7	3	1
Kelly Jennings	26	CB	68	8.3%	53	29	17	3.4	7	78%	3	101	21%	16	13.4	54%	23	7.6	48	7.4	14	0
Jordan Babineaux	26	SS	58	7.1%	67	24	11	3.9	4	50%	21	46	10%	11	7.1	41%	67	8.9	56	8.1	4	1

Year	Pass D Rank	vs. #1 WR	Rk	vs. #2 WR	Rk	vs. Other WR	Rk	vs. TE	Rk	vs. RB	Rk
2005	25	14.7%	20	7.4%	27	4.5%	18	5.3%	20	-11.0%	9
2006	23	4.9%	19	-24.2%	5	16.7%	25	11.5%	27	-25.1%	6
2007	14	-13.8%	6	5.3%	18	10.2%	24	13.9%	23	-23.6%	3

Two things helped Seattle's pass coverage improve in 2007. First, cornerback Marcus Trufant moved back to the left side of the field. Although the shift may seem subtle, the change allowed Trufant to be more aggressive in pass coverage—hence his jump in interceptions. And in a year where the Eagles and the Raiders raised the bar on cornerback salaries, Seattle's decision to re-sign Trufant to a six-year, $50.2 million contract extension already looks like a bargain.

Second, the Seahawks swapped Ken Hamlin for Deon Grant at free safety. Like almost everyone on the Cowboys last year, Hamlin made the Pro Bowl, but astute Dallas fans may now realize why the Seahawks did not make a concerted effort to re-sign him: Yes, Hamlin hits hard when he's in position but there are plenty of times when he takes the wrong angle and lets his assigned receiver burn him deep. That never happens with Grant, although he must get frustrated watching his backfield companion Brian Russell whiff on tackles so frequently. (Backup C. J. Wallace is probably a better option at this point.) Nonetheless, credit should be given to soon-to-be-head-coach Jim Mora for Seattle's resurgence in the secondary.

With that said, this is still the weaker part of the Seahawks defense, and it's here where Tim Ruskell's "size doesn't matter" approach to football starts to cause problems. Kelly Jennings played fairly well in his second full year in the league, but he's only five foot eleven, and nickel back Josh Wilson is two inches shorter than that. As a result, the Seahawks' struggle whenever they are forced to cover two or more tall wide receivers—during Week 3's contest against the Bengals, six-foot-one T. J. Houshmanzadeh got open at will and was filmed laughing on the sideline. Expect this to be the soft spot that offensive coordinators continue to attack this year.

Special Teams

Year	DVOA	Rank	FG/XP	Rank	Net Punt	Rank	Punt Ret	Rank	Net Kick	Rank	Kick Ret	Rank	Hidden	Rank
2005	-0.6%	20	2.6	12	-3.1	21	-4.9	30	6.5	8	-4.7	23	-7.6	26
2006	2.6%	7	0.6	14	8.6	6	0.4	13	4.0	13	1.8	11	5.8	9
2007	1.0%	11	1.7	14	-9.8	29	8.6	5	-1.5	17	6.8	6	-2.5	19

Long snapper Boone Stutz was so unbelievably bad that he actually received two percent of the vote in Football Outsiders' annual "Keep Choppin' Wood Award" for the player who most hurt his team in 2007. *As a long snapper.* Thus, even though they were widely ridiculed on draft day, the Seahawks were smart to use a sixth-round draft pick to select Tyler Schmitt out of San Diego State. Schmitt claims to have been long snapping since he was in fifth grade, which not coincidentally is probably the last time anyone ever drafted a long snapper. The problems at snapper go a long way toward explaining the regression of punter Ryan Plackemeier, who dropped 12 points in field position value because he spent most of the year making sure the ball did not sail over his head.

The other major shakeup in the kicking game is the loss of former franchise-designee kicker Josh Brown to the St. Louis Rams, who apparently were tired of losing to Seattle due to his game-winning field goals. The current plan is to have washed-up veteran Olindo Mare—who was a disaster in New Orleans last year—compete with seventh-round draft pick Brandon "Who do the voodoo that you do?" Coutu from Georgia. The smart money and the Seahawks special teams DVOA is betting on Coutu winning the job.

Although he remains a disappointment in the receiving game, Nate Burleson remains one of the great unheralded punt returners of our time. He returned a whopping 58 punts last year, the third most in NFL history, which goes a long way toward explaining his league-leading 658 yards in punt returns. (By way of comparison, Devin Hester totaled 651 punt-return yards, albeit on 16 fewer returns.) But given their lack of depth at receiver, the Seahawks cannot afford an injury to Burleson. Do not be surprised if punt return duties are turned over to kick returner Josh Wilson, the diminutive but speedy cornerback, or rookie seventh-round draft pick Justin Forsett out of Cal, who is equally diminutive and speedy.

COACHING STAFF

There is a precedent in a head coaching legend naming his own successor before retirement—Bill Walsh begat George Seifert, Bill Parcells begat Bill Belichick—but the actual retirement date is typically not known with any certainty. That's not the case for the Seahawks: Mike Holmgren is definitely retiring at the end of 2008, and he's already started to focus on losing weight so he can travel with his wife and kids (seriously, he's lost 35 pounds using Jenny Craig). Given Tim Ruskell's focus on defense, defensive backs coach Jim Mora may be a better fit for the current Seahawks team anyway, although Seahawks' fans may be haunted by memories of the younger Mora sniffing smelling salts and making sideline cell phone calls while head coach of the Falcons.

Gil Haskell remains the nominal offensive coordinator—Holmgren will continue to call all the plays on offense—but virtually every other coach on the offensive staff has changed, in part to allow Mora to build a coaching tree of his own. The most significant loss is quarterbacks coach Jim Zorn, who ended up becoming head coach of the Redskins after initially being hired to be their offensive coordinator. Perhaps Daniel Snyder is tired of getting stomped by the Seahawks in the first round of the playoffs. Bill Lazor will take over for Zorn and continue Seattle's tradition of only hiring quarterback coaches with the letter z in their name. Also gone are running backs coach Stump Mitchell (now on Zorn's staff), wide receivers coach Nolan Cromwell (the new offensive coordinator for Texas A&M under Mike Sherman), and quality control coach Gary Reynolds (also with the Aggies). The Seahawks will replace them with Kasey Dunn, Keith Gilbertson, and Chris Beake, respectively. Beake served as quality control coach under Jim Mora in Atlanta and may have a shot at becoming the Seahawks' offensive coordinator in 2009. In addition, new offensive line coach Mike Solari hired Mike DeBord, the offensive coordinator at Michigan for the last three years, to be his assistant offensive line coach. Got all that? Mercifully, John Marshall is still the defensive coordinator and the defensive assistants are unchanged.

Tampa Bay Buccaneers

Six seasons in and five years after he won the franchise's only Super Bowl, it's time to ask the question: Has Jon Gruden's tenure in Tampa Bay been not only successful as a whole but more successful than the six seasons that preceded it?

Those seasons under Tony Dungy took the pathetic Buccaneers, who had suffered 15 straight losing seasons, and set them up for what was to come with Gruden at the helm. With a new commitment to scouting and building from within, the Dungy Bucs established one of the greatest defenses of the modern era. Dungy had only one losing season in Tampa Bay, and that was his first. Rich McKay's front office was convinced that the draft was the best way to build, as opposed to taking chances on expensive free agents, and one of the NFL's best scouting departments built a team with a vicious defense and a highly effective running game.

It was good enough to get to the NFC Championship game in 1999, but after two straight early playoff exits at the hands of the Philadelphia Eagles in 2000 and 2001, Dungy was fired by an ownership group that found the team's offense painful to watch. (The presence of Mike Shula as offensive coordinator through Dungy's first four seasons probably didn't help matters.) Dungy went on to Indianapolis, winning Super Bowl XLI with, ironically, a transcendent offense and one of the worst-run defenses in NFL history.

With a new coach came a change in philosophy, and it was instant. When Tampa Bay sent two first-round

---

BUCCANEERS PROSPECTUS

2007 Record: 9-7

Pythagorean Wins: 10.0 (9th)

DVOA: 18.1% total (7th), 13.7% weighted (9th)

Offense: 7.7% DVOA (9th)

Defense: -10.2% DVOA (4th)

Special Teams: 0.2% DVOA (12th)

Variance: 22.0 % (28th)

2007: A team with aging stars and a rebuilt engine wins half a battle by taking a weak division.

2008: Jon Gruden and Bruce Allen look to put their stamp on a team built more by their own hand than by the castoffs of others.

2008 Mean Projection: 10.3 wins

On the Clock (0-3): 0%

Loserville (4-6): 5%

Mediocrity (7-8): 12%

Playoff Contender (9-10): 33%

Super Bowl Contender (11+): 50%

Projected Average Opponent: -2.6% DVOA (23rd in NFL)

---

and two second-round picks to the Oakland Raiders for Jon Gruden's services, they sent a clear message: The future is now, if not yesterday. Gruden brought the West Coast offense he learned from Mike Holmgren as an assistant in San Francisco and Green Bay, and for a time it was the perfect match. The mercurial Gruden benefited greatly from the defense he inherited, and he pushed the offense over the hump. In Super Bowl XXXVII, he beat a Raiders team that was still carrying enough of his playbook that the coach himself played the opposing quarterback in practice and the Bucs defense called plays before they even happened. The Buccaneers' 48-21 win over Oakland was the culmination of a long uphill road.

In the five years since that championship season, Gruden has posted a 36-44 record (contrast this with the 48-32 record Dungy put up in his final five years in Tampa Bay). He has presided over two fewer winning seasons than Dungy, with the same postseason record Dungy had after that NFC Championship loss in 1999: 0-2. He has had five primary starting quarterbacks, spent a mint on free agents, and suffered the inevitable effects of some questionable drafts. When Gruden was joined by ex-Raiders general manager Bruce Allen in 2004, it was a clean break from the old way of doing things. Tampa Bay was now far less about scouting long-term prospects and far more about finding quick free agent fixes. In the NFL, free agency is rarely a panacea in the larger sense—teams that cobble to-

2008 Buccaneers Schedule

Week	Opp.	Week	Opp.	Week	Opp.
1	at NO	7	SEA	13	NO
2	ATL	8	at DAL	14	at CAR (Mon.)
3	at CHI	9	at KC	15	at ATL
4	GB	10	BYE	16	SD
5	at DEN	11	MIN	17	OAK
6	CAR	12	at DET		

gether a roster of veterans rather than develop their own young players are doing little more than spackling their own crumbling houses. That was particularly true given the general approach Gruden and Allen took to free agency, signing a number of veterans and guys coming off injury to one-year make-good deals rather than investing huge dollars in one or two big names.

The Buccaneers finished the 2006 season with a 4-12 record, lost quarterback Chris Simms to a Week 3 spleen injury that he is still recovering from, and didn't put out much hope for the near future. The offense was a dismal 31st in DVOA, but an even more worrisome sign was the defense finishing 21st in DVOA after being in the top 10 every year since 1996.

Despite adding veteran Jeff Garcia, a quarterback who had played in a number of Bill Walsh-influenced offenses similar to Tampa Bay's, the Bucs began the 2007 season looking much like the nonstarters they had been in 2006. Garcia and running back Cadillac Williams were knocked out of a 20-6 loss to Seattle, although Garcia returned later. Williams, the 2005 Offensive Rookie of the Year, was lost for the season in the fourth game, but it didn't matter because Earnest Graham came out of nowhere and gained 898 yards in relief. Garcia had seemingly ended Gruden's long search for a reliable quarterback, showing impressive efficiency and proving to be one of the NFL's toughest to intercept. Receiver Joey Galloway continued his ageless trend, finishing one of the best three-year runs for any player in his mid-30s.

Garcia and Galloway hooked up for two touchdowns in the season's second contest, a 31-14 win over the Saints to start a three-game winning streak. Tampa Bay was winning in other ways as well. Against the Rams and Panthers, it was defense and the running game. Against the Titans, it was kicker Matt Bryant and Garcia's ability to drive his team against a great defense. Against the Cardinals, it was safeties Jermaine Phillips

and Tanard Jackson who surprised and impressed. Against Washington, the defense recovered four fumbles in the span of 16 offensive plays. The team's two season-ending losses to the 49ers and Panthers were basically the product of Gruden's desire to rest most of his starters as much as possible after the Bucs wrapped up the NFC South. This decision was questioned at the time and certainly after a 24-14 first-round playoff exit at the hands of the Giants, but it's indicative of the fact that this could have easily been an 11-5 team. Defense led the way and the offense outperformed expectations, but the real story is how the front office is starting to rebuild the team, using a scouting focus to inject young blood where it's greatly needed.

General manager Bruce Allen's father, George, put together the Redskins' *Over the Hill Gang* in the early 1970s, and Tampa Bay's aging skill position players seem to indicate that the apple didn't fall far from the tree. However, the perception that the Tampa Bay franchise is teetering with geriatrics is overblown. The Bucs fielded the youngest offensive line in football in 2007, and that unit got younger this offseason when the team signed former Saints center Jeff Faine (age 27) to replace 10-year veteran John Wade (age 33). Of Tampa Bay's 33 regular-season sacks, 30 came from the front four, and 15.5 of those came by way of players in their first year with the team. Linebackers Cato June and Barrett Ruud have helped to define a new Tampa Bay defense that may not be at the level of the Super Bowl XXXVII unit, but the Bucs have regained a stronghold as one of the league's best.

Tampa Bay's 2007 draft was exceptional, perhaps the best of the Gruden era. First-round pick Gaines Adams replaced Simeon Rice on the defensive line, starting the last eight games at right defensive end, and he could be the team's next great quarterback mauler. Second-round pick Arron Sears started all 16 games at left guard, helping the line finish sixth in Adjusted Line Yards. Fourth-rounder Tanard Jackson moved from cornerback to free safety, started every game there, and led the team in average yards per pass target. The 2008 draft included Kansas cornerback Aqib Talib, Appalachian State receiver Dexter Jackson, and Rutgers tackle Jeremy Zuttah, three players who could see major starting time sooner rather than later.

In late January, both Gruden and Allen were rewarded with three-year contract extensions. Barring a complete collapse, they'll chart the Buccaneers' course through the 2011 season. Although the defensive refortification has been impressive, the brain trust must turn its attention to the offensive skill positions. Cadillac Williams's knee injury, a torn patellar tendon, was severe enough that the 2008 season (and possibly his career) is in doubt. Garcia could see a rerun of his great season, but he's 38 years old, and Tampa Bay's line gave up too many hits last season. Galloway appears to be as good as he's ever been—he led the NFC last year with a 17.8 yards per catch average—but he's 36 and his shoulder injury in the playoff loss to New York proved how vulnerable that offense is when he's not in top condition. Michael Pittman is 33, and so is Warrick Dunn, who returns from Atlanta as another placeholder and change-of-pace back. Ike Hilliard is 32. While Tampa Bay builds with youth along the lines, their skill position players have morphed into the cast of *Cocoon*.

The Buccaneers are a few bad breaks away from disaster and could turn into the 2003 Raiders, imploding as their best players simultaneously succumb to the power of age. Then again, the old guys could just keep on rockin' like the Van Halen reunion tour, with Graham taking the place of Eddie's son Wolfgang as the token youngster.

Our projections say that the Bucs will get another shot at the postseason in 2008. We like their coaching continuity and their offensive continuity (as long as the old guys hold up). Another easy schedule is on the books, and there's no reason to believe that the defense can't be even better this year. The concerns, and how they will be addressed, will define the next phase of the Gruden-Allen tenure. To make this team a Super Bowl success again, they'll have to keep going back to the future—not with free agent hand-me-downs but with a continued belief in the power of team-building over time.

Doug Farrar

2007 Buccaneers Stats by Week

Wk	vs.	W-L	PF	PA	YDF	YDA	TO	Total	Off	Def	ST
1	@SEA	L	6	20	284	343	-1	-32%	-19%	10%	-3%
2	NO	W	31	14	330	343	+2	74%	41%	-25%	8%
3	STL	W	24	3	322	245	+2	82%	39%	-37%	7%
4	@CAR	W	20	7	365	236	+1	46%	21%	-20%	6%
5	@IND	L	14	33	177	400	0	-12%	15%	26%	-1%
6	TEN	W	13	10	304	317	+2	42%	43%	3%	2%
7	@DET	L	16	23	422	278	-2	-56%	12%	52%	-16%
8	JAC	L	23	24	385	219	-3	22%	-14%	-33%	3%
9	ARI	W	17	10	350	195	+2	36%	15%	-30%	-9%
10	BYE										
11	@ATL	W	31	7	305	265	+2	49%	20%	-31%	-2%
12	WAS	W	19	13	192	412	+6	24%	-6%	-28%	2%
13	@NO	W	27	23	466	246	0	26%	21%	-11%	-6%
14	@HOU	L	14	28	305	257	0	-18%	-5%	1%	-13%
15	ATL	W	37	3	285	133	+3	111%	-6%	-85%	32%
16	@SF	L	19	21	434	213	0	-22%	-21%	-1%	-3%
17	CAR	L	23	31	303	349	+1	-33%	-3%	26%	-4%
18	NYG	L	14	24	271	277	-3	-37%	5%	36%	-6%

Trends and Splits

	Offense	Rank	Defense	Rank
Total DVOA	7.7%	9	-10.2%	4
Unadjusted VOA	8.7%	9	-12.8%	1
Weighted Trend	3.2%	16	-11.0%	3
Variance	4.4%	5	10.4%	26
Average Opponent	4.0%	31	-1.7%	25
Passing	7.8%	16	-10.6%	4
Rushing	7.6%	5	-9.8%	7
First Down	11.7%	8	-18.0%	3
Second Down	8.9%	11	-6.8%	8
Third Down	-1.6%	15	-2.4%	10
First Half	10.4%	9	-15.6%	3
Second Half	5.0%	12	-4.9%	11
Red Zone	-0.5%	17	1.1%	14
Late and Close	-3.4%	19	-12.5%	7

Five-Year Performance

Year	W-L	Pyth Wins	Est Wins	PF	PA	TO	Total	Rank	Off	Rank	Def	Rank	ST	Rank
2003	7-9	9.2	9.4	301	264	+2	11.2%	11	-4.6%	17	-21.3%	3	-5.4%	32
2004	5-11	7.9	7.9	301	304	-9	-2.3%	16	-5.6%	21	-7.0%	8	-3.6%	28
2005	11-5	8.9	8.1	300	274	+7	1.3%	16	-6.9%	19	-8.7%	9	-0.6%	19
2006	4-12	3.6	5.1	211	353	-12	-23.0%	31	-18.0%	30	5.1%	22	0.1%	17
2007	9-7	10.0	10.1	334	270	+15	18.1%	7	7.7%	9	-10.2%	4	0.2%	12

Strategic Tendencies

Run/Pass		Rank	Offense		Rank	Defense		Rank	Other		Rank
Runs, all plays	42%	13	3+ WR	43%	26	Rush 3	7.9%	9	2+ RB, Pct Runs	64%	6
Runs, first half	39%	23	4+ WR	6%	25	Rush 4	79.1%	3	1 RB/2 TE, Pct Runs	31%	32
Runs, first down	55%	7	2+ TE	32%	8	Rush 5	9.2%	31	1 RB/3+ WR, Pct Runs	17%	30
Runs, second-long	32%	23	Single back	50%	22	Rush 6+	3.9%	28	CB1 on WR1	36%	29
Runs, power sit.	65%	18	Play action	16%	19	Rush 7+	0.6%	26	Go for it on 4th	1.10	15
Runs, behind 2H	27%	21	Max protect	9%	21	Sacks by LB	3.2%	31	Offensive Pace	32.1	27
Pass, ahead 2H	31%	31	Outside pocket	19%	4	Sacks by DB	9.7%	8	Defensive Pace	31.7	29

The classic Bill Walsh offense doesn't use the shotgun, but as the league has moved towards using the formation more and more, so have the Walsh disciples. In *Pro Football Prospectus 2007*, we wrote about Jon Gruden's decision to begin using the shotgun, and the Bucs did in fact use it on 25 percent of plays after not running it a single time in 2006. Ironically, the Bucs ended up playing worse in shotgun (-0.6% DVOA) than with the quarterback under center (10.0% DVOA). ⊘ Tampa Bay's quarterbacks were second in the league in hurries per pass play. Jeff Garcia was hurried more often than Luke McCown, but both were above the league average. ⊘ Tampa Bay threw to running backs 31 percent of the time, the highest percentage in the league. ⊘ No team lined up more often with only one wide receiver. ⊘ Tampa Bay's offense had the lowest percentage of passes listed as defensed, and the highest percentage of passes listed as Hole in Zone rather than with a specific defender in coverage. ⊘ The Bucs gained 10.5 yards per pass with a play-action fake (76.3% DVOA) but only 5.7 yards on the average play without play action (-2.6% DVOA). Only New England and Dallas had higher DVOA with play action, and only the Jets had a larger DVOA advantage when using a play fake. ⊘ Tampa Bay was just as strong sniffing out play-action fakes, ranking second behind Tennessee with a -20.1% DVOA. ⊘ The Tampa Bay defense faced fewer passes to number-two receivers than any other team. ⊘ Tampa Bay's defense got progressively better the more receivers there were on the field, except in rarely used five-wide sets, where only two teams had a worse DVOA than the Buccaneers. ⊘ The Bucs ranked just 28th in quarterback hurries per pass play and ranked 31st in defense when they had a quarterback hurry, ahead of only San Francisco.

Passing

Player	DYAR	DVOA	Plays	NtYds	Avg	YAC	C%	TD	Int
Jeff Garcia	694	19.5%	346	2356	6.8	5.5	64.9%	13	4
Luke McCown	-28	-13.9%	154	915	5.9	5.3	68.6%	5	3
Bruce Gradkowski	-30	-30.2%	25	106	4.2	2.9	56.5%	0	1
Brian Griese	-62	-15.0%	276	1687	6.1	5.6	62.4%	9	12

Rushing

Player	DYAR	DVOA	Plays	Yds	Avg	TD	Fum	Suc
Earnest Graham	162	8.4%	222	898	4.0	10	1	50%
Michael Pittman*	10	-4.6%	68	286	4.2	0	1	44%
Cadillac Williams	44	10.6%	54	208	3.9	3	2	52%
Michael Bennett	22	4.0%	41	189	4.6	1	2	49%
Jeff Garcia	17	1.0%	22	121	5.5	1	3	—
Luke McCown	52	86.7%	10	118	11.8	0	3	—
Michael Clayton	5	-22.5%	5	22	4.4	1	1	—
Warrick Dunn	-108	-20.0%	227	721	3.2	4	2	37%
Brian Griese	4	-3.7%	8	30	3.8	0	5	—

Receiving

Player	DYAR	DVOA	Plays	Ctch	Yds	Y/C	YAC	TD	C%
WR									
Joey Galloway	230	16.4%	98	57	1014	17.8	6.6	8	58%
Ike Hilliard	122	5.8%	86	62	724	11.7	5.0	1	72%
Michael Clayton	-5	-14.3%	40	22	301	13.7	5.7	0	55%
Maurice Stovall	20	7.6%	13	10	86	8.6	2.3	1	77%
Chad Lucas	34	69.5%	5	5	82	16.4	1.4	0	100%
Brian Clark	-25	-79.9%	5	4	23	5.8	2.5	0	80%
TE									
Alex Smith	34	2.3%	53	32	385	12.0	4.3	3	60%
Jerramy Stevens	88	53.5%	21	18	189	10.5	2.7	4	86%
Anthony Becht*	2	-4.1%	7	5	20	4.0	2.0	2	71%
Ben Troupe	-16	-30.6%	9	5	47	9.4	7.4	0	56%
John Gilmore	-23	-54.5%	7	3	14	4.7	3.0	0	43%
RB									
Earnest Graham	-10	-16.5%	69	49	324	6.6	5.7	0	71%
Michael Pittman*	-24	-24.4%	39	26	191	7.3	5.8	0	67%
B. J. Askew	86	64.0%	20	18	175	9.7	8.3	0	90%
Michael Bennett	23	32.1%	9	5	54	10.8	10.0	1	56%
Cadillac Williams	-24	-108.4%	5	3	17	5.7	2.3	0	60%
Warrick Dunn	-48	-29.6%	59	37	238	6.4	6.5	0	63%

Offensive Line

Year	Yards	ALY	Rank	Power	Rank	10+ Yds	Rank	Stuff	Rank	Sack	ASR	Rank
2005	4.21	4.00	19	75%	5	22%	6	28%	28	41	8.3%	26
2006	3.68	3.88	28	64%	15	14%	21	26%	29	33	5.8%	10
2007	4.10	4.49	6	59%	23	13%	21	20%	5	36	7.9%	24

Year	LE	Rank	LT	Rank	Mid	Rank	RT	Rank	RE	Rank
2005	4.46	10	4.61	8	3.92	21	3.48	27	2.73	31
2006	2.97	28	4.06	22	4.02	25	4.14	18	4.11	15
2007	4.10	15	4.42	13	4.63	4	4.65	8	4.05	17

As noted in the main essay, the Bucs' offensive line was the youngest in the league. Of the 80 starts logged by Tampa Bay linemen, exactly three-quarters went to players in their first or second year. One of those youngsters, rookie left tackle Donald Penn will move to the bench in 2008 as veteran Luke Petitgout returns from a torn ACL. Given Petitgout's recent injury history (he missed 19 games in 2006 and 2007), Penn will provide a valuable and necessary Plan B. The other three youngsters—rookie left guard Arron Sears and right guard Davin Joseph and right tackle Jeremy Trueblood, both in their second year—will all return. Those three players were all drafted in the first or second rounds in 2006 and 2007, and the payoff for that investment has been an underreported story across the league. Joining the line at center will be Jeff Faine, formerly of the Saints, who were the best team in the league at running up the middle last season. The Buccaneers ranked much higher in run blocking than they did at pass blocking, though some of that is no doubt due to Jeff Garcia scrambling around to make a play rather than throwing the ball away. This will be one of the league's top units this season if everyone can stay healthy. Depth is a particular concern at center; they don't even have a backup at the position listed on their depth chart.

Defensive Front Seven

Defensive Line	Age	Pos	Plays	TmPct	Rk	Stop	Dfts	Stop%	Rk	AvYd	Rk	Sack	Hit	Hur	Runs	RuStop	RuYd	Pass	PaStop	PaYd
Jovan Haye	26	DE	74	9.3%	5	53	13	72%	61	2.0	50	6.0	7	6	56	73%	2.7	18	67%	0.0
Chris Hovan	30	DT	49	6.1%	19	40	7	82%	24	1.8	44	1.5	2	0	43	81%	2.3	6	83%	-1.8
Gaines Adams	25	DE	39	4.9%	55	29	12	74%	49	2.0	46	6.0	8	9	29	69%	3.7	10	90%	-3.1
Greg White	29	DE	28	3.5%	75	25	17	89%	2	-0.8	3	8.0	10	8	17	82%	2.8	11	100%	-6.4
Greg Spires*	34	DE	27	5.4%	49	22	5	81%	22	2.3	57	3.0	1	2	21	86%	2.9	6	67%	0.2
Ryan Sims	28	DT	16	3.6%	—	13	5	81%	—	1.1	—	1.0	0	0	15	80%	1.4	1	100%	-3.0
Marques Douglas	31	DT	75	8.6%	9	59	23	79%	34	1.7	42	3.0	1	6	59	81%	1.7	16	69%	1.9

Linebackers	Age	Pos	Plays	TmPct	Rk	Stop	Dfts	Stop%	AvYd	Sack	Hit	Hur	Runs	RuStop	Rk	RuYd	Rk	Tgts	Suc%	Rk	APaYd	Rk
Barrett Ruud	25	MLB	116	15.5%	14	73	20	63%	4.7	0.0	2	2	82	78%	9	3.0	31	33	49%	46	8.0	82
Derrick Brooks	35	OLB	109	13.7%	36	66	19	61%	5.1	0.0	1	2	68	68%	33	3.6	59	42	56%	24	7.3	77
Cato June	29	OLB	77	9.6%	70	41	12	53%	5.5	0.0	0	0	43	67%	34	4.2	85	31	57%	21	4.9	21
Teddy Lehman	27	MLB	21	2.4%	—	10	3	48%	7.0	0.0	0	1	12	67%	—	3.6	—	3	36%	—	8.5	—

Year	Yards	ALY	Rank	Power	Rank	10+ Yds	Rank	Stuff	Rank	Sack	ASR	Rank
2005	3.29	3.63	2	59%	11	10%	2	26%	11	36	7.0%	18
2006	3.92	4.21	14	74%	28	15%	14	24%	15	25	5.4%	29
2007	3.88	4.28	22	73%	28	11%	3	19%	31	33	7.0%	13

Year	LE	Rank	LT	Rank	Mid	Rank	RT	Rank	RE	Rank
2005	2.70	2	4.47	24	3.47	2	3.66	5	4.76	24
2006	3.63	11	3.44	6	4.47	19	5.02	30	3.87	13
2007	4.16	17	3.65	7	4.58	31	4.68	24	3.35	8

Six of the starting positions are set here. Cato June, Barrett Ruud, and future Hall of Famer Derrick Brooks all return at linebacker. Although the 34-year-old Brooks still has great speed, he is starting to miss tackles, which can lead to big plays by backs catching passes out of the backfield. The Hovan-Jovan Connection of Chris Hovan and Jovan Haye returns at defensive tackle. Gaines Adams, who led all rookies in sacks and hurries, will take over full-time at right defensive end. That leaves the left end position, left vacant by Greg Spires's departure to Oakland. Three veterans will compete for the starting role. The first candidate is Marques Douglas, new to the Buccaneers and formerly of the Saints, Ravens, and 49ers. He offers durability and run support, collecting 16 starts and at least 58 tackles each of the last five seasons, but little in the way of pass-rushing; he has just seven sacks in the last three seasons combined. This is fairly typical of 3-4 ends, which is what Douglas was in his last two stops. He'll be an option to move inside on passing downs. The second candidate is Greg White, an undrafted rookie who graduated from Jay Gruden's Orlando Predators to older brother Jon's Buccaneers and led the team with eight sacks. He made some noise in the offseason about a new contract, wanting to be paid like an elite sacker instead of an Arena League castoff. The third candidate is Kevin Carter, a former star with the Rams and Titans who was released after his first season in Tampa Bay. He re-signed with the team, however, turning down more money to follow Spires to Oakland. "In the end, he realized he's never been happier playing football," Carter's agent Harold Lewis told the *St. Petersburg Times*. Whoever wins the job, the other two will provide elite depth at the position. The shallowest position is outside linebacker. Should injury befall June or Brooks, the backups are a pair 2007 draft picks: third-rounder Quincy Black and sixth-rounder Adam Hayward.

Defensive Secondary

Secondary	Age	Pos	Plays	TmPct	Rk	Stop	Dfts	RuYd	Rk	RuStop	Rk	Tgts	Tgt%	Rk	Dist	Suc%	Rk	APaYd	Rk	PaYd	PD	Int
Jermaine Phillips	29	SS	88	11.8%	16	37	15	5.9	29	51%	20	27	7%	36	9.7	49%	40	6.4	27	6.2	8	4
Ronde Barber	33	CB	72	9.0%	44	37	14	4.2	10	63%	9	53	13%	71	7.3	47%	48	6.5	20	6.5	11	2
Phillip Buchanon	28	CB	70	8.8%	45	27	9	4.6	16	55%	26	82	20%	25	10.9	51%	36	6.4	16	6.3	11	3
Tanard Jackson	23	FS	65	8.1%	57	23	7	8.0	64	26%	78	33	8%	23	12.8	60%	10	4.8	7	5.0	11	2
Brian Kelly*	32	CB	29	5.3%	—	15	8	4.2	—	67%	—	34	12%	—	8.7	55%	—	4.8	—	4.3	6	2
Sammy Davis	28	CB	18	2.6%	—	3	2	7.5	—	50%	—	23	6%	—	14.1	47%	—	8.2	—	7.9	1	0
Eugene Wilson	28	FS	35	7.0%	69	12	5	9.3	73	31%	70	23	7%	33	10.1	52%	30	7.4	45	7.3	2	1

Year	Pass D Rank	vs. #1 WR	Rk	vs. #2 WR	Rk	vs.Other WR	Rk	vs.TE	Rk	vs.RB	Rk
2005	14	-10.4%	5	-4.5%	16	20.0%	30	-7.1%	11	-1.7%	15
2006	28	5.9%	20	6.5%	19	-9.3%	12	11.4%	26	-10.4%	12
2007	4	-20.0%	5	-11.7%	8	-8.0%	17	-1.1%	9	0.8%	19

Buccaneers fans will be happy to see this starting lineup return intact. Tampa Bay ranked fourth in pass defense in 2007, and most of the credit must go to cornerbacks Ronde Barber and Phillip Buchanon, strong safety Jermaine Phillips, and free safety Tanard Jackson. Buchanon is the inverse Jason David, in a way—less spectacular in man coverage with the Raiders and Texans from 2002 through 2005, he has fit like a glove in the Tampa 2 over the last two seasons. Jackson's primary role is pass coverage, not run support, but in either case he was noted for punishing ball-carriers with his tackles. The most well-known member of the group is Barber, an iron man who has started every game for the past 10 seasons, all while playing physical run support in the Tampa-2 defense. At 33, however, the end of his career is in sight, so for the first time since 1986 the team drafted a defensive back in the first round, selecting Kansas cornerback Aqib Talib with the 20th overall pick. Talib told reporters that his first name was a Muslim word meaning "last to come" (he is the youngest of four children), but he didn't know the meaning of his last name. Bucs coach Jon Gruden suggested it translates to "good corner." Talib is a big cornerback at six feet one, 209 pounds, and he fits this defense very well. Tampa Bay goes to their nickel defense much less often than most teams, but with Brian Kelly opting out of his Tampa Bay contract to re-join Rod Marinelli in Detroit and Buchanon in the last year of his current contract, Talib may be asked to hit the ground running. Eugene Wilson participated in the NFL's run on ex-Patriots defensive backs and signed a one-year deal; he'll switch from safety to play nickel back.

Phillips and Jackson are the linchpins of the secondary now. Phillips enjoyed a rebound season in 2007, leading the team in interceptions. Jackson had a fabulous rookie year, finishing top ten in Success Rate and average passing yards per play. Backing them up will be veteran Will Allen, who started 16 games for the team in 2006, and one of the greatest names in the NFL, Sabatino Carmine Piscitelli, Jr. ("Sabby" to his friends), a second-round pick out of Oregon State in 2007. Piscitelli didn't see the field much in his rookie year. He played on special teams for three games until going on injured reserve with a foot fracture.

Special Teams

Year	DVOA	Rank	FG/XP	Rank	Net Punt	Rank	Punt Ret	Rank	Net Kick	Rank	Kick Ret	Rank	Hidden	Rank
2005	-0.3%	19	1.6	13	4.2	11	6.7	5	-5.0	24	-9.3	27	-1.1	16
2006	0.1%	17	-1.6	21	-1.5	21	-5.6	31	12.2	4	-3.0	18	6.8	7
2007	0.2%	12	-0.3	20	5.7	9	-6.1	27	-1.3	16	3.2	11	-1.4	18

The first 1,865 kickoff returns in Tampa Bay history produced a grand total of zero touchdowns, but as they say, the 1,866th time's the charm. Michael Spurlock's 90-yard return for a touchdown against Atlanta was a footnote in history, a trivial play that had little effect on the Bucs' 37-3 win, but it was enough to earn Spurlock the job again in 2008. Rumors of a statue of Spurlock being erected at Raymond James Stadium remain unconfirmed. (This really is a great idea. They could give him a hook and eye patch and throw him in the big pirate boat.) The team was much less successful on punt returns, roughly split between Buchanon and receivers Ike Hilliard and Mark Jones. Jones was most productive, but Hilliard goes into 2008 as the favorite to win the job. The kickers remain constant. Matt Bryant will handle placekicking and kickoffs for the fourth straight season. He has been remarkably average kicking for points and remarkably erratic on kickoffs. Josh Bidwell returns as Bucs punter for his fifth season; at his best, he has been above average. Both Bryant and Bidwell benefited from strong coverage teams in 2007.

COACHING STAFF

The titles of the Tampa Bay coaching staff read like an ancient scroll of Norwegian runes: baffling, mysterious, and almost indecipherable. There's an associate head coach, an assistant head coach, an offensive assistant coach, a defensive quality control coach, an assistant to the head coach/football operations, and an offensive coordinator/offensive line coach. The only two titles that have mattered in recent years are head coach (Jon Gruden, who runs the offense) and defensive coordinator (Monte Kiffin, who runs the defense). The strategic tendencies of both men are well known: The defense will rush four, drop back in zone coverage, take away the deep pass and make all their tackles to keep the short stuff short. The offense will use an efficient short passing game to build a lead, and then grind out the clock with their running game in the second half, often motioning wide receivers inside to block. The Buccaneers will focus on preventing big plays on both sides of the ball and rely on the execution of their athletes to win games, and it will usually work.

In 2007, another name was added to the roll of Those You Need to Know: new defensive backs coach Raheem Morris, who worked under predecessor Mike Tomlin from 2002 to 2005. Morris has not only helped mold Tampa Bay's post-Super Bowl secondary but has also been instrumental in its recent turnaround. Morris is one of the most well-respected assistants in the league, and don't be surprised if he soon follows Tomlin and Herm Edwards from his current position through the NFL coaching pipeline.

Tennessee Titans

If someone had told you before the 2007 season that the Titans would be a playoff team, you would have assumed that meant Vince Young would take a big step forward and emerge as one of the league's best quarterbacks. As it turned out, Young didn't take a step forward at all. But the defense did take a step forward—about a thousand steps forward, actually—with Albert Haynesworth's phenomenal season more than making up for the year-long suspension of Pac-Man Jones. The Titans only outscored their opponents by four points, but they won their final three games, and when the smoke cleared on the regular season, there the Titans were, playing in January.

Will they be playing in January again this season? If they are going to have a chance to get back to the playoffs, Young really will need to take a step forward this time; it's unrealistic to expect the defense to be as good in 2008 as it was in 2007.

No matter how well the defense plays, the first topic of conversation when it comes to the Tennessee Titans will always be Vince Young. The second-year quarterback turned in a disappointing season but did not, contrary to popular belief, play worse than he did as a rookie. The problem is that highly drafted quarterbacks tend to improve in their second seasons, and Young didn't do that, either. Offensive coordinator Norm Chow had Young playing a more cautious brand of football in 2007 than he had in 2006. It resulted in an improved completion percentage (from 51.5 percent to 62.3 percent) but fewer big plays (from 33 completions

of 20 or more yards to 24). The net result was about the same.

Titans coach Jeff Fisher wanted his quarterback to do more than just stand still, so he fired Chow and brought back Mike Heimerdinger, the offensive coordinator in Tennessee until he left for the Jets in 2004. Many people in Tennessee are saying that Heimerdinger could get Young to play the way Steve McNair played in 2003, when he was named league MVP playing in Heimerdinger's offense. But don't believe that talk. The 2003 version of McNair was an experienced, accurate pocket passer who rarely took off and ran. Heimerdinger knows he doesn't have a pocket passer on his hands in Young, and the offense he calls in Tennessee in 2008 won't be the offense he called in Tennessee in 2003.

So what offense will Heimerdinger call? If things go as planned, an offense with a heavy reliance on the running game. The Titans have the right offensive line for that approach. Michael Roos and David Stewart are a good pair of starting tackles, and both of them are just 25 years old, meaning they should only get better. Center Kevin Mawae isn't the player he was five or 10 years ago, but he's still a solid drive blocker and a great team leader. The Titans struggled to find a good pair of guards last season, but they should have one this year. Eugene Amano, who entered the starting lineup late in the season, showed promise, and Tennessee beefed up by signing free-agent guard Jake Scott, formerly of the Colts, to a four-year contract that pays about $5 million a year. That's an awful lot of

TITANS PROSPECTUS

2007 Record: 10-6

Pythagorean Wins: 8.1 (15th)

DVOA: 9.0% total (10th), 2.4% weighted (16th)

Offense: -4.1% DVOA (21st)

Defense: -13.4% DVOA (1st)

Special Teams: -0.4% DVOA (17th)

Variance: 18.3 % (22nd)

2007: An Albert Haynesworth-led defense gets the Titans to the playoffs.

2008: The defense will decline, and they look like the bottom-dwellers in the AFC South.

2008 Mean Projection: 6.7 wins

On the Clock (0-3): 5%

Loserville (4-6): 45%

Mediocrity (7-8): 30%

Playoff Contender (9-10): 17%

Super Bowl Contender (11+): 4%

Projected Average Opponent: 5.1% DVOA (6th in NFL)

2008 Titans Schedule

Week	Opp.	Week	Opp.	Week	Opp.
1	JAC	7	at KC	13	at DET (Thu.)
2	at CIN	8	IND (Mon.)	14	CLE
3	HOU	9	GB	15	at HOU
4	MIN	10	at CHI	16	PIT
5	at BAL	11	at JAC	17	at IND
6	BYE	12	NYJ		

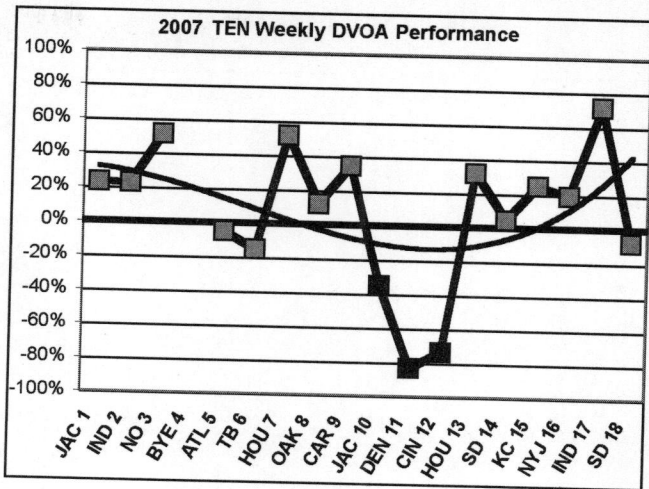

Figure 1

money for a player who has been a consistent lineman but rarely a dominant one, but Scott, who has started the last 55 games for the Colts, will make the Titans better. It just may not be $5-million-a-year better.

There are some questions about how the Titans will divvy up carries for the backs who will run behind that line. Chris Brown was a solid if not spectacular player during his five-year career with the Titans, but last year it became clear that the coaching staff was phasing him out. He carried 102 times for 462 yards last season, and when he became a free agent after the year was over, the Titans made almost no effort to re-sign him. He ended up in Houston, where he'll get two chances a year to make the Titans regret not keeping him.

Once Brown left, the Titans appeared perfectly happy to let LenDale White carry even more of the load in 2008 than he did in 2007, when he had 303 rushes for 1,110 yards. As of March, the plan was clearly to let White be a workhorse in 2008, with last year's second-round pick "The Other, Non-Criminal" Chris Henry backing him up.

But then Tennessee selected a running back, East Carolina's Chris Johnson, in the first round of the draft. Johnson was the fastest player at the scouting combine and will act as lightning to White's thunder, but it was surprising that the Titans decided to devote even more draft resources to running backs. The Titans have now used a top 50 draft pick on a running back for three straight years. They're a long way off from equaling Matt Millen's unhealthy obsession with wide receivers, but the Titans are going back to the running back well again and again while other positions are overlooked.

Actually, the Titans could use a little bit of Millen's wide receiver obsession right about now, because that happens to be the most significant position being overlooked in Tennessee. Yes, in March the Titans signed wide receiver Justin McCareins, who returns to the team that dealt him to the Jets in 2003. But McCareins, who had some costly drops and fell out of favor in New

York in 2007, is a decent number three receiver, not a number one. That makes him a lot like the Titans' incumbent starters, Justin Gage and Roydell Williams. The Titans don't have a top-notch wide receiver, something that would be an awfully nice asset if they ever want Young to become a top-notch quarterback.

It's open to debate whether they have a top-notch tight end. Alge Crumpler, who signed with the Titans after spending the first seven years of his career in Atlanta, was once one of the top tight ends in the league. But he's now 30 years old, and he's coming off a 444-yard season, the worst total since his rookie year. Still, Crumpler's 3.4% DVOA wasn't bad for a guy playing in that terrible Falcons offense, and he's an experienced presence who should help Young develop.

Overall, the Titans' offense looks as if it should be a little better than it was a year ago. The defense, however, won't be. For starters, top defenses just don't stay top defenses very often: Defense is more inconsistent than offense from year to year, and it's not at all unusual for top defenses to decline significantly. And the Titans' defense came out of nowhere last year, going from 24th in DVOA in 2006 to first in 2007. There's bound to be a bit of regression to the mean.

How far the defense declines will largely depend on Albert Haynesworth, who was the best defensive player in football last season when he was healthy. Tennessee got off to a 6-2 start behind an absolutely dominant defense in the first half of the season. The media were so busy watching the Patriots set offensive records that the Titans' stifling pass rush barely got any attention. In the 13 seasons for which we have DVOA statistics, only four teams had better defensive performance than the 2007 Titans over the first half of the season (Table 1).

Table 1. Top Teams in Defensive DVOA Through Week 9, 1995-2007

Year	Team	DVOA Wk 1-9	DVOA Wk 10-17	Rank Wk 10-17
2002	TB	-41.2%	-27.4%	1
1996	GB	-38.4%	-10.2%	11
1998	OAK	-32.7%	-3.1%	14
1999	JAC	-31.3%	-0.4%	17
2007	TEN	-30.7%	1.8%	18
1997	SF	-29.9%	-15.7%	5
1995	SF	-29.1%	-19.8%	2
2006	BAL	-29.0%	-30.6%	2
1996	DEN	-28.7%	-11.7%	8
2000	BAL	-27.1%	-24.0%	1

Then Haynesworth suffered a hamstring injury that forced him to miss Week 10 through Week 12, and the Titans lost three straight by scores of 28-13, 34-20, and 35-6. Haynesworth returned and the defense got better, but the hamstring was still sore; Haynesworth missed much of practice and didn't play at 100 percent the rest of the year.

Even if he's healthy, Haynesworth probably won't be as dominant as he was in 2007, which seemed like a one-year improvement motivated in part by his impending free agency. (As of press time, he has not signed the franchise tender.) And the Tennessee defensive line took a hit when Antwan Odom, who started all 16 games at defensive end last year and recorded eight sacks, signed with the Bengals as a free agent. To replace him, the Titans signed Jevon Kearse, who was once among the league's best pass rushers and earned three trips to the Pro Bowl with the Titans before leaving for the Eagles and a record-setting contract in 2003, but Kearse now has no gas left in the tank. Tennessee also drafted Eastern Michigan's Jason Jones in the second round. Look for Jones, a gifted athlete who started college as a tight end and also played some defensive tackle, to win the starting job, but not to play as well as Odom did.

Even without Odom, a starting defensive line of Haynesworth, Jones, Tony Brown, and Kyle Vanden Bosch should be a good one. Vanden Bosch, in particular, has been a perfect fit in coordinator Jim Schwartz's defense since signing with Tennessee as a free agent in 2005. After starting only 20 games in four injury-plagued seasons with the Cardinals, Vanden Bosch has started every game and recorded 31 sacks in three years with the Titans.

The Titans were the best team in the league at defending passes to tight ends and the third-best at stopping passes to running backs, which says a lot about the team's speedy linebackers. In David Thornton and Keith Bulluck, Tennessee has one of the league's best outside linebacker pairs. Ryan Fowler was a first-year starter in the middle last season and was more effective than the Titans could have hoped when they signed him as a free agent from Dallas, although he's far from an elite player.

You'd think the season-long suspension of cornerback Pac-Man Jones, one of the league's most talented cornerbacks, would have created big problems with the defense. And maybe it did, a little—stopping number one receivers was the weakness of the Tennessee pass defense. But Cortland Finnegan and Nick Harper, the Titans' new pair of starting corners, played well, for the most part. The Titans didn't look like they missed Jones, and they were happy to trade him to the Cowboys for a fourth-round draft pick.

Where the Titans did miss Jones last year—and will continue to this year—is in punt returns. They went from the best punt-returning team in the league in 2006 (yes, even better than the Bears) to significantly below average in 2007. In fact, the Titans basically had one good special-teams player, kicker Rob Bironas. He was the best kicker in football last season, with an unmatched combination of kickoff distance, field goal distance, and field goal accuracy. But the Titans struggled in all other phases of special teams, and unless Johnson is a great return man as a rookie, they will have problems in that area again this year.

Overall, 2008 is shaping up as a season in which the Titans may struggle in a lot of places. It's not that the Titans are a bad team so much as they're a team with just one clear strength: the front seven, in particular the defensive line. As good as players like Haynesworth and Bulluck are, they can't fully compensate for holes elsewhere on the roster—especially playing in what looks like the toughest division in the NFL. Aside from the front seven, the Titans are mediocre just about everywhere, and the passing game is dismal. Unless Young takes that big step forward this season, the Titans won't return to the playoffs.

Michael David Smith

2007 Titans Stats by Week

Wk	vs.	W-L	PF	PA	YDF	YDA	TO	Total	Off	Def	ST
1	@JAC	W	13	10	350	272	-1	23%	2%	-25%	-5%
2	IND	L	20	22	313	381	-1	23%	21%	-5%	-3%
3	@NO	W	31	14	284	252	+4	51%	2%	-50%	0%
4	BYE										
5	ATL	W	20	13	249	198	-3	-5%	-42%	-59%	-22%
6	@TB	L	10	13	317	304	-2	-15%	7%	19%	-3%
7	@HOU	W	38	36	422	333	+4	52%	3%	-30%	18%
8	OAK	W	13	9	218	235	+2	12%	-21%	-36%	-3%
9	CAR	W	20	7	236	191	-2	35%	-21%	-44%	11%
10	JAC	L	13	28	292	262	-2	-35%	-33%	-3%	-6%
11	@DEN	L	20	34	423	359	-2	-83%	-13%	56%	-14%
12	@CIN	L	6	35	305	426	-1	-74%	-32%	37%	-4%
13	HOU	W	28	20	382	315	+1	32%	19%	-13%	-1%
14	SD	L	17	23	240	341	+1	4%	-13%	-20%	-2%
15	@KC	W	26	17	327	306	+3	25%	33%	25%	17%
16	NYJ	W	10	6	273	296	0	19%	-15%	-28%	6%
17	@IND	W	16	10	356	194	-1	71%	33%	-33%	5%
18	@SD	L	6	17	248	350	-1	-8%	-4%	5%	1%

Trends and Splits

	Offense	Rank	Defense	Rank
Total DVOA	-4.1%	21	-13.4%	1
Unadjusted VOA	-4.1%	20	-7.2%	6
Weighted trend	-4.3%	19	-5.5%	9
Variance	5.4%	9	10.7%	29
Average opponent	2.4%	27	5.0%	2
Passing	-5.5%	20	-19.1%	1
Rushing	-2.8%	13	-4.9%	18
First down	1.4%	14	-20.6%	2
Second down	-3.6%	19	-17.1%	3
Third down	-15.2%	25	3.8%	17
First half	-9.6%	25	-10.8%	7
Second half	1.6%	18	-15.8%	1
Red Zone	-6.3%	20	3.9%	18
Late and close	8.1%	8	19.7%	2

Five-Year Performance

Year	W-L	Pyth Wins	Est Wins	PF	PA	TO	Total	Rank	Off	Rank	Def	Rank	ST	Rank
2003	12-4	10.7	10.6	435	324	+13	23.3%	2	14.3%	4	-8.9%	9	0.1%	19
2004	5-11	5.8	5.4	344	439	-1	-21.1%	28	-6.7%	24	10.6%	24	-3.9%	30
2005	4-12	4.9	5.3	299	421	-6	-18.6%	25	-6.2%	18	14.3%	30	1.9%	7
2006	8-8	6.0	6.8	324	400	+2	-13.0%	24	-9.3%	26	6.2%	24	2.4%	9
2007	10-6	8.1	9.2	301	297	0	9.0%	10	-4.1%	21	-13.4%	1	-0.4%	17

Strategic Tendencies

Run/Pass		Rank	Offense		Rank	Defense		Rank	Other		Rank
Runs, all plays	46%	7	3+ WR	52%	13	Rush 3	1.0%	31	2+ RB, Pct runs	67%	3
Runs, first half	41%	17	4+ WR	11%	16	Rush 4	79.7%	2	1 RB/2 TE, pct runs	56%	9
Runs, first down	57%	6	2+ TE	27%	13	Rush 5	11.5%	30	1 RB/3+ WR, pct runs	25%	14
Runs, second-long	40%	8	Single back	63%	9	Rush 6+	7.8%	17	CB1 on WR1	53%	5
Runs, power sit.	59%	23	Play action	22%	7	Rush 7+	1.0%	23	Go for it on 4th	0.67	29
Runs, behind 2H	35%	5	Max protect	21%	1	Sacks by LB	2.5%	32	Offensive Pace	32.0	26
Pass, ahead 2H	34%	29	Outside pocket	22%	2	Sacks by DB	7.5%	12	Defensive Pace	31.0	19

The Titans would rank first in run/pass ratio if we included quarterback scrambles as runs rather than passes. ✍ Not surprisingly, Tennessee ranked second in designed plays that rolled Young out of the pocket. However, he did limit his improvisation, ranking only fifth in unplanned scrambles. Combined, Young left the pocket on nearly one out of every five pass plays, nearly twice the league average. ✍ Tennessee ranked seventh in DVOA on runs from two tight-end sets, but last in passes from the same formation. ✍ Tennessee ranked dead last in rushing during the first half, but was fifth in the second half. ✍ The Titans ranked seventh in use of play action, but 22nd in DVOA on such plays. ✍ The Titans were one of three defenses to hurry the opposing quarterback on more than 15 percent of pass plays. ✍ In Titans hurries, 65 percent came with only four rushers. Only Indianapolis had a higher percentage. ✍ Tennessee opponents threw 21 percent of their passes behind the line of scrimmage, second in the league behind Kansas City, but the Titans allowed an average of just 6.2 yards after catch on passes thrown behind the line of scrimmage, the lowest figure in the league.   ◎   Tennessee had the league's top defense against play-action passes.   ◎   Tennessee got 90 percent of its sacks from defensive linemen, the highest percentage in the league.   ◎   In 2006, only two defenses rushed three more often than Tennessee; in 2007, only one defense rushed three less often.   ◎   We hope Titans fans don't really like scoring. At home, Tennessee ranked 28th in offense (-12.9% DVOA) and second in defense (-24.7% DVOA). On the road, Tennessee ranked 12th in offense (4.1% DVOA) and 12th in defense (-0.5% DVOA).

Passing

Player	DYAR	DVOA	Plays	NtYds	Avg	YAC	C%	TD	Int
Vince Young	74	-8.4%	411	2433	5.9	4.6	62.5%	9	17
Kerry Collins	148	15.3%	88	513	5.8	4.3	61.0%	0	0

Rushing

Player	DYAR	DVOA	Plays	Yds	Avg	TD	Fum	Suc
LenDale White	26	-6.5%	303	1115	3.7	7	5	46%
Chris Brown*	100	13.8%	102	463	4.5	5	1	57%
Vince Young	9	-9.7%	75	401	5.3	3	8	—
Chris Henry	-6	-13.5%	31	119	3.8	2	0	32%

Receiving

Player	DYAR	DVOA	Plays	Ctch	Yds	Y/C	YAC	TD	C%
WR									
Roydell Williams	85	-1.1%	93	55	719	13.1	3.9	4	59%
Justin Gage	189	14.5%	85	55	748	13.6	4.3	2	65%
Eric Moulds*	35	-4.2%	52	32	342	10.7	3.7	0	62%
Brandon Jones	24	-4.0%	34	21	248	11.8	3.2	2	62%
Chris Davis	-49	-84.0%	9	5	39	7.8	5.0	0	56%
Justin McCareins	-42	-23.6%	46	19	232	12.2	2.0	0	41%
Mike Williams	-59	-56.4%	20	7	90	12.9	4.0	0	100%
TE									
Bo Scaife	-80	-22.8%	78	46	421	9.2	3.2	1	59%
Ben Hartsock*	0	-7.5%	19	12	138	11.5	5.9	0	63%
Ben Troupe*	-16	-30.6%	9	5	47	9.4	7.4	0	56%
Alge Crumpler	35	0.4%	70	42	444	10.6	6.2	5	60%
Dwayne Blakley	-6	-18.6%	9	7	48	6.9	3.4	0	78%
RB									
LenDale White	-6	-17.4%	31	20	114	5.7	6.3	0	65%
Chris Brown*	33	14.7%	21	19	128	6.7	6.4	0	90%
Ahmard Hall	6	-3.7%	12	9	60	6.7	5.9	0	75%
Chris Henry	22	50.4%	7	6	53	8.8	12.0	0	86%

Offensive Line

Year	Yards	ALY	Rank	Power	Rank	10+ Yds	Rank	Stuff	Rank	Sack	ASR	Rank
2005	3.78	3.92	20	62%	19	13%	23	28%	26	31	4.7%	3
2006	4.29	3.93	27	67%	13	22%	6	24%	14	29	6.0%	13
2007	3.90	4.33	9	71%	6	12%	23	21%	9	30	6.6%	16

Year	LE	Rank	LT	Rank	Mid	Rank	RT	Rank	RE	Rank
2005	3.77	22	3.61	27	3.91	22	4.65	7	2.80	30
2006	3.82	20	3.37	31	4.08	23	4.24	15	3.61	22
2007	3.88	20	4.92	6	4.45	7	3.73	27	3.85	21

The Titans will open the season with a pair of new guards. Right guard Benji Olson, a rock on the line for 10 seasons, finally stepped into retirement. Injuries and age were starting to take their toll on Olson; after missing just one start in seven years, he missed one in 2006 and four more last year, including the playoff loss to San Diego. Meanwhile, left guard Jacob Bell signed with the Rams in free agency, so Tennessee went out and signed their own free agent: Jake Scott, formerly of the Colts. The Titans were excellent on run blocking to left tackle and up the middle last season, but the Colts were even better, and Scott's acquisition carries the extra benefit of chipping away at the reigning division champs. The returning starters bring a mix of experience and youth. The youth is on the outside, where left tackle Michael Roos and right tackle David Stewart will be entering their fourth seasons. Stewart struggled with an ankle injury last year, notably against Jacksonville in Week 10. The experience lies in the middle with former All-Pro Kevin Mawae, now entering his 15th season. He's still a top-notch road grader, but he had problems last year getting the ball back to the quarterback, which is not a good problem for a center to have. After the front five, there is no depth of any kind to speak of here. Only one backup lineman on the team has ever started an NFL game: Eugene Amano, a center/guard, has a whopping total of eight starts. In the past three seasons, the team has drafted only two offensive linemen, both in 2007: third-round center Leroy Harris and seventh-round tackle Michael Otto.

Defensive Front Seven

Defensive Line	Age	Pos	Plays	TmPct	Rk	Stop	Dfts	Stop%	Rk	AvYd	Rk	Sack	Hit	Hur	Runs	RuStop	RuYd	Pass	PaStop	PaYd
Kyle Vanden Bosch	30	DE	62	7.9%	12	47	24	76%	45	2.3	56	12.0	22	18	41	73%	3.3	21	81%	0.3
Tony Brown	28	DT	57	7.3%	7	47	12	82%	21	1.5	26	4.0	8	10	45	78%	2.2	12	100%	-1.0
Albert Haynesworth	27	DT	45	7.1%	9	40	20	89%	5	0.4	3	6.0	9	14	29	93%	0.6	16	81%	0.1
Antwan Odom*	27	DE	28	3.6%	74	25	15	89%	1	-1.3	1	8.0	14	19	12	83%	0.7	16	94%	-2.8
Randy Starks*	25	DT	18	2.6%	—	14	5	78%	—	1.6	—	0.0	1	2	14	79%	1.6	4	75%	1.8
Travis LaBoy*	27	DE	16	2.5%	—	13	11	81%	—	-2.1	—	6.0	6	10	2	50%	1.0	14	86%	-2.6

Linebackers	Age	Pos	Plays	TmPct	Rk	Stop	Dfts	Stop%	AvYd	Sack	Hit	Hur	Runs	RuStop	Rk	RuYd	Rk	Tgts	Suc%	Rk	APaYd	Rk
David Thornton	30	OLB	129	16.5%	10	77	24	60%	4.4	1.0	0	4	61	74%	16	2.9	28	53	49%	45	5.8	37
Keith Bulluck	31	OLB	96	12.2%	54	48	20	50%	5.0	0.0	3	3	51	53%	91	4.4	90	35	50%	44	3.5	2
Ryan Fowler	26	MLB	53	7.7%	88	29	7	55%	4.2	0.0	1	1	37	73%	17	2.9	25	17	45%	56	5.4	28
Stephen Tulloch	23	MLB	35	4.5%	—	19	3	54%	4.6	0.0	0	0	23	70%	—	2.6	—	4	33%	—	4.9	—

Year	Yards	ALY	Rank	Power	Rank	10+ Yds	Rank	Stuff	Rank	Sack	ASR	Rank
2005	4.38	3.91	13	54%	5	24%	29	22%	27	41	7.5%	11
2006	4.47	4.57	25	69%	24	18%	25	20%	28	26	5.7%	25
2007	4.11	3.91	6	78%	31	18%	21	27%	9	40	7.2%	9

Year	LE	Rank	LT	Rank	Mid	Rank	RT	Rank	RE	Rank
2005	4.08	15	2.25	1	3.85	10	4.55	27	5.12	30
2006	4.94	24	4.00	9	4.51	20	4.16	16	5.26	31
2007	3.33	8	4.42	18	3.99	11	2.95	1	4.45	22

The long-term status of Albert Haynesworth is up in the air. The Titans named Haynesworth their franchise player (and rarely has that moniker fit so well) to stop him from leaving in free agency, but as of mid-May he had not signed a tender offer and was not participating in the team's organized team activities. "I'm not really worried about it," he said. "I guess I'll have a job next year." Get your season tickets now, Titans fans! The NFL owners' decision to end their agreement with the players' union shouldn't affect Haynesworth's negotiations. "It just throws a few different dynamics in there that you have to think about moving forward," Haynesworth's agent Chad Speck told *The Tennesseean*, "but I don't think it changes things at all. It certainly doesn't change the fact Albert wants to remain a Titan and would like to execute a long-term contract."

Right end Kyle Vanden Bosch particularly benefits from the attention Haynesworth's presence draws. In the past two seasons, Vanden Bosch has averaged 0.7 sacks per game in the 22 games that Haynesworth has started. The ten times Haynesworth wasn't in the starting lineup, however, Vanden Bosch averaged only 0.3 sacks per game. When he was isolated against tackles one-on-one, though, Vanden Bosch often abused them, including Ephraim Salaam and Marcus McNeil. The Titans' other tackle, Tony Brown, was clearly Haynesworth's inferior in almost every measure except for one: penalties. Haynesworth's nine penalties were fourth among NFL defenders; Brown had eight penalties, which placed him in a huge tie for fifth. Apparently, the game plan in Tennessee is, if you can't beat 'em, cheat 'em. At least Haynesworth didn't step on anyone's face last year.

The Titans' linebackers are fast and excel in pass coverage and sure tackling. All three primary linebackers ranked higher in yards per pass allowed than they did in success rate. That means running backs could get open for short plays, but David Thornton, Keith Bulluck, and Ryan Fowler made sure they ended up on the ground quickly and couldn't turn short gains into big plays. Stephen Tulloch, who backs up Fowler, is a promising young player as well.

Defensive Secondary

Secondary	Age	Pos	Plays	TmPct	Rk	Stop	Dfts	RuYd	Rk	RuStop	Rk	Tgts	Tgt%	Rk	Dist	Suc%	Rk	APaYd	Rk	PaYd	PD	Int
Cortland Finnegan	24	CB	104	13.3%	3	39	13	7.1	47	31%	67	99	22%	15	11.7	51%	37	7.2	37	7.2	13	1
Nick Harper	34	CB	90	13.1%	4	41	17	5.0	21	61%	15	89	22%	14	11.8	49%	43	7.2	38	7.7	11	3
Calvin Lowry	25	SS	66	8.4%	54	24	5	6.3	41	46%	36	28	6%	59	15.3	44%	55	10.6	73	11.1	9	2
Chris Hope	28	SS	53	9.8%	39	27	7	5.7	26	48%	29	21	7%	48	12.8	66%	3	6.4	26	6.4	2	2
Michael Griffin	23	FS	49	6.3%	74	21	9	7.0	54	40%	50	30	6%	52	10.2	58%	14	3.0	2	3.3	7	3
Vincent Fuller	26	FS	32	4.1%	81	15	13	6.0	34	50%	23	30	7%	50	7.6	53%	24	6.2	24	5.9	4	2
Chris Carr	25	CB	29	3.8%	—	12	10	5.7	—	67%	—	18	5%	—	11.4	44%	—	11.2	—	11.0	1	0

Year	Pass D Rank		vs. #1 WR	Rk		vs. #2 WR	Rk		vs. Other WR	Rk		vs. TE	Rk		vs. RB	Rk
2005	32		29.6%	30		41.4%	32		-11.4%	9		9.3%	21		38.2%	32
2006	17		7.6%	21		1.9%	16		-6.2%	15		-24.0%	5		11.5%	25
2007	1		-4.0%	13		-2.3%	13		-32.0%	4		-28.9%	1		-21.0%	4

Tennessee had the league's top pass defense last season, but the specter of Pac-Man Jones still haunts the team. Rafael Little, an undrafted rookie running back from Kentucky, wore Jones's old 32 jersey onto the field for a mini-camp session, but coach Jeff Fisher quickly put a stop to that. "He's not going to be wearing that," Fisher said to the *Daily News Journal* of Murfreesboro. "We had discussed it this morning and for some reason someone told him to get dressed and come out. But that won't be his number. . . . He'd prefer to wear a different number than 32 and you can read into it all you want." When asked if he was retiring or exorcising the number, Fisher replied, "I'm sending it to Dallas." Pac-Man may be gone, but the actual 2007 starters are not: once again, Cortland Finnegan and Nick Harper will man the corners, with Chris Hope at strong safety and Michael Griffin at free safety. Finnegan was a seventh-round steal in the 2006 draft and one of the most successful members of our first annual "Top 25 Prospects" list in *Pro Football Prospectus 2007,* although he does better in zone coverage than when he plays man. Harper started his career in Indianapolis, where the team demands that corners play the run, and he still offers superb run support, but he will turn 34 just after the season starts. Depth is a concern here. Calvin Lowry struggled mightily filling in for both Hope and Griffin last season, and Reynaldo Hill, the nickel corner, was regularly abused in the limited time he saw in 2007.

Special Teams

Year	DVOA	Rank	FG/XP	Rank	Net Punt	Rank	Punt Ret	Rank	Net Kick	Rank	Kick Ret	Rank	Hidden	Rank
2005	2.0%	7	-3.2	23	2.6	13	2.7	9	7.1	5	2.5	13	4.1	11
2006	2.4%	9	-1.4	20	4.2	12	12.4	1	-1.9	24	1.1	12	9.4	5
2007	-0.4%	17	8.7	1	-4.4	23	-5.7	25	5.9	9	-6.7	25	13.0	4

With the retirement of Benji Olson, punter Craig Hentrich remains the last player on the Titans roster from the Super Bowl year of 1999 (unless you count Jevon Kearse, who left but has returned). His numbers were down last year, but in eight of his ten seasons with the club, the Titans have been above average in punting. Wide receiver Chris Davis heads into training camp with his punt returner job intact, and kick returns are split between running back Chris Henry and safety Michael Griffin, who were both below average last year. Finally, there is Rob Bironas, one of the best kickers in football. Last year, Tennessee topped our stats for field goal value, and Bironas kicked an NFL-record eight field goals in a 38-36 win over Houston in October. The Titans also ranked tenth in kickoffs, and Bironas himself was actually better than that—his kickoffs alone were third in the league, but his coverage unit ranked just 26th. Bironas signed a one-year, $1.47 million deal to stay with the team in February.

COACHING STAFF

Entering his 15th season, all with the Tennessee Titans/Houston Oilers franchise, Jeff Fisher remains one of the most underrated coaches in all of sports. With the retirement of Joe Gibbs, Fisher ranks fifth among active coaches with 115 wins. Mike Holmgren will retire at the end of the year, and if Tony Dungy does as well, Fisher will leap into third place. He will still trail Bill Belichick and Mike Shanahan, but he's also six years younger than those men and may pass them before all is said and done. Critics will point out that Fisher is the only coach in this paragraph who has never won a Super Bowl, while supporters will point out that he is one of only two coaches in this paragraph who always had someone else picking his players. (Dungy is the other.) Offensive coordinator Norm Chow was shown the door in January; taking his place will be Mike Heimerdinger, who filled the same role with this team from 2000 to 2004. The Titans' offense was top 10 in DVOA three times in that span. Most recently he was working with Jay Cutler in Denver, where he protected the young quarterback with a minimum of multiple-receiver sets and a lot of maximum protection passes. (Denver ranked 29th in usage of three or more wide receivers, seventh in usage of two tight ends, and fourth in max protect.) Expect the same treatment for Vince Young, particularly given the Titans' scarcity of quality receivers. Jim Schwartz will run the Titans defense for the seventh straight season. Improved depth and a career year from Albert Haynesworth freed him up to run a more aggressive defense, and the Titans finished first in DVOA after they had been in the bottom ten from 2004 through 2006.

Washington Redskins

The Washington Redskins ran an emotional gamut in 2007 that will long remain in the minds of both players and fans. The stunning, senseless death of safety Sean Taylor in an attempted robbery won't show up in a record book or in their DVOA ratings, and its effect upon the team is obviously unquantifiable. It presents a significant challenge in both analyzing what happened with this team in 2007 and projecting how they might perform in 2008.

The tragedy took place the morning after the Redskins' Week 12 loss to the Buccaneers, which left the team 5-6 on the season. The team mourned Taylor throughout the week and had a memorable memorial for him when they sent out just 10 players on defense for the first play of their Week 13 home game against the Bills. They lost the game when head coach Joe Gibbs called an illegal second consecutive timeout to attempt to ice kicker Rian Lindell. The flag turned a 51-yard field goal attempt into a much easier 36-yarder, which Lindell hit to sink the Redskins and push them back to 5-7.

Taylor's funeral was the next morning. The team flew to Miami, attended the services, and returned with only three days to prepare for their next game, a Thursday night tilt against the Chicago Bears. During the game, quarterback Jason Campbell went down with a knee injury that would cost him the rest of his season. He was replaced by backup Todd Collins, who went on to lead the Redskins to victory. For the next three weeks, Collins—who had not started a game in 10 years—was

one of the best quarterbacks in the NFL. The Redskins finished with a four-game winning streak and snuck into the playoffs on the last day of the season.

As writers who focus so frequently on quantifying ideas by working with data, it is not our forte to attempt to analyze the effects of emotion. We know the effects are there and can't ignore them, but because they're not remotely measurable, it's a story better left to beat writers and people around the team. What we can take out of the final four games of the Redskins' season are the statistical changes that help explain why things turned around.

First, the performance of the Washington pass defense changed dramatically over the course of the season (Table 1). One possible reason may have been the spotting of LaRon Landry in Taylor's center field role as free safety. Taylor occupied that role for the first eight games of the year. In the three weeks that Taylor was injured—he was expected to return later in the year—Landry played some center field, but he spent most of his time in his previous role as strong safety, near the line. After Taylor's murder, Landry moved full-time into the free safety role, even though Reed Doughty was listed as the free safety in the lineup. Landry excelled in that spot, which is a good sign for the Redskins' pass defense come 2008.

The other huge factor, as mentioned, was the play of Collins. Collins was the primary backup, rather than the more talented Mark Brunell, because of his familiarity

---

REDSKINS PROSPECTUS

2007 Record: 9-7

Pythagorean Wins: 8.7 (12th)

DVOA: 7.9% total (12th), 10.4% weighted (10th)

Offense: 1.0% DVOA (17th)

Defense: -7.2% DVOA (6th)

Special Teams: -0.3% DVOA (16th)

Variance: 15.1 % (15th)

2007: The tragedy of Sean Taylor's death pushed Washington on an emotional run to the playoffs.

2008: Goodbye complex triple-fake end arounds; hello slants and flats.

2008 Mean Projection: 6.9 wins

On the Clock (0-3): 3%

Loserville (4-6): 40%

Mediocrity (7-8): 35%

Playoff Contender (9-10): 18%

Super Bowl Contender (11+): 4%

Projected Average Opponent: 1.4% DVOA (14th in NFL)

Table 1. 2007 Redskins Defensive Pass Splits

Split	DVOA	Rank
Weeks 1-9 (Taylor in lineup)	-11.4%	5
Weeks 10-12 (Taylor injured)	15.8%	25
Weeks 13-17 (after Taylor's death)	-10.2%	9

2008 Redskins Schedule

Week	Opp.	Week	Opp.	Week	Opp.
1	at NYG (Thu.)	7	CLE	13	NYG
2	NO	8	at DET	14	at BAL
3	ARI	9	PIT (Mon.)	15	at CIN
4	at DAL	10	BYE	16	PHI
5	at PHI	11	DAL	17	at SF
6	STL	12	at SEA		

with offensive coordinator Al Saunders's passing offense from their days together in Kansas City. Collins put up an impressive 49.1% DVOA in the regular season, but a healthy amount of luck went into his performance. Rare is the quarterback who throws zero interceptions in 113 attempts; even rarer is the backup quarterback who suddenly acquires that skill after holding a clipboard for most of the decade. Collins had been anointed with game manager oils heading into the Redskins' playoff game against Seattle, but two interceptions and an ugly performance later, Collins had fallen back to earth. Without Saunders and his familiar system around, there's no reason Collins should be given consideration as the starting quarterback this year.

The departure of Saunders happened along with that of Joe Gibbs and the rest of his expensively assembled retirement community of assistant coaches, except for offensive line coach Joe Bugel. Although Gibbs's blunder against the Bills was presented as evidence that he was ill-prepared for the modern game, the more telling evidence was how his coordinators, particularly Saunders, failed to apply their extensive playbooks and complicated schemes to the teams they faced.

Under Saunders, the Washington offense consisted mostly of a variety of screen passes and chicanery. The quick hitch was Saunders's version of the Colts' stretch play or the Lombardi Packers' off-tackle sweep. What made the offense maddening was its stubborn resistance to attack its opponent's weaknesses. In Week 3, the eventual Super Bowl champion Giants were 0-2 with a clear glaring weakness: At the time, to an almost comical extent, they could not defend tight ends or passes over the middle. Despite this, the Redskins had only one possession all game where they threw to tight end Chris Cooley. After completing two quick passes to Cooley in succession, the Giants pushed their safeties up to assist overmatched linebacker Kawika Mitchell in coverage; in response, the Redskins sent Santana Moss deep, and the star wideout picked up 49 yards. Three plays later, Cooley caught an eight-yard touchdown pass. He didn't see the ball again the rest of the game, and when the Giants held on a fourth-and-goal late in the game, they won the game and saved their season. The rest is history.

After Gibbs chose to re-retire, the search for a new coach became a farce. The first leading candidate was just-fired "assistant head coach for defense" Gregg Williams, who was then quickly supplanted by Jim Fassel, who was so close to having the job that tickers were reporting the story and press conferences were arranged. Before Fassel's potential appointment, though, Snyder and Cerrato hired Seahawks quarterback coach Jim Zorn to be the team's offensive coordinator in 2008, while promoting defensive line coach (although he'd had the title of defensive coordinator since 2004) Greg Blache to manage the defense. Hiring a head coach's coordinators for him is an extremely peculiar move, one that may have been enough to prevent Fassel or Giants defensive coordinator Steve Spagnuolo from taking the position.

After further waffling regarding the position, it was decided that Zorn himself would be the head coach as well as the offensive coordinator. It will be Zorn's first time with either role at the NFL level; in our coaching database, which goes back to 1987, there has never been a man hired to be both a head coach and a coordinator at the same time who was never a coordinator at the NFL level or a head coach in college previously. It's a marker of how much faith the Redskins have in Zorn— or the mess they've gotten themselves into.

Zorn will install Seattle's West Coast offense in Washington, a move that dramatically changes the way the team will run and pass relative to Saunders's scheme. One benefit Zorn will likely enjoy that Saunders did not was the right side of his offensive line. Right tackle Jon Jansen broke his ankle in the opening game of the year, and Randy Thomas tore a triceps muscle a week later. Both missed the remainder of the season, and the Redskins spent the rest of the campaign patching holes across their line. The run blocking was roughly as effective as it had been in 2006, but the pass blocking clearly suffered.

Although there was talk that Campbell will be entering 2008 in a battle for his job against Collins, it's just that: chatter. Jason Campbell is ready. Statistically, he performed well last year, ranking 17th in DYAR and 22nd in DVOA. Many have debated whether Campbell is a good fit for Zorn's version of the West Coast offense. On one hand, his arm strength won't have the same benefit in a system with fewer downfield throws, and he'll need to work on his ability to hit receivers in stride. On the other hand, his mechanics as a pro have been extremely consistent, with throws coming as his back foot completes his dropback. That level of consistency is essential to a system relying so heavily on timing. Campbell played in a Bill Walsh-style offense in his senior year at Auburn and completed nearly 70 percent of his passes.

Some have been concerned about Campbell's ability to waggle and the sacks he takes as a result, but there's a hidden benefit to Campbell's comfort in the pocket: At six foot five, Campbell can see over most linemen and make last-second plays that other smaller quarterbacks simply cannot. The cost of an extra sack or two is mitigated by the benefit of Campbell being able to stay properly set up in the pocket and pass when other quarterbacks would run out of the pocket, trying to make something out of a broken play.

Campbell will need an improved performance from his receivers to take his game to the next level in 2008. Although Antwaan Randle El enjoyed a surprising resurgence as a wideout last year, Santana Moss was incredibly disappointing. Moss played through injuries most of the season, but that does not excuse a number of crucial drops. In the playoff game against Seattle, Moss famously gave up on a Collins pass that Marcus Trufant picked off and returned for a touchdown. It remains to be seen whether Moss or Randle El are the caliber of route runners needed to successfully use the West Coast offense in Washington, which led to the Redskins spending their top three picks on receivers. Each of these rookies has a different skill set and level of NFL-readiness. Devin Thomas had one big year in college, his final season at Michigan State. He has the build and raw talent of an elite wideout but still needs to develop his technique. On the other hand, wide receiver Malcolm Kelly is as NFL-ready as any wide receiver in the draft; the six-foot-four behemoth runs excellent routes and has great hands, which is exactly what the doctor ordered for Campbell.

Tight end Fred Davis's role in the offense will be understated because he'll be used primarily as an in-line blocker, but he could be hugely important regarding the effect he could have on Cooley. If Davis succeeds as a blocker, Cooley can match himself up in the slot against linebackers and nickel backs all day; if not, Campbell loses arguably his best underneath receiver because he needs to stay upright.

Halfback Clinton Portis is the other current Redskins star who is a perfect fit for the new offensive scheme. Portis quietly racked up 1,262 rushing yards last year, but what makes him the ideal West Coast back is his ability to both catch balls in the flat and pass block, two things he does as well as any running back in football. Portis's role in the offense, assuming he can stay healthy, should be reminiscent of Roger Craig on the late-1980s 49ers. If Portis can't stay on the field, the running game might be safe in the hands of Ladell Betts but the offense as a whole would be weakened.

Of course, in typical Redskins fashion, the situation nearly ended up entirely different. Draft-day reports had the Redskins offering the Bengals a 2008 first-round pick and a third-rounder that could have escalated to a first-rounder in 2009 in return for disgruntled wide receiver Chad Johnson. The move would have cost a shallow team dramatically, though giving them a vaunted receiver for Campbell.

Outside of that attempt, things have changed in Washington. There's no (real) quarterback controversy. There's no rich, experienced head coach. There's no huge free agent signing. The Redskins have to prove that the level of play they showed in the final four games is more representative than what they displayed in a 5-7 start. Their plan: Progress in, progress out.

Bill Barnwell

Do Head Coaches Have an Age Limit?

The second Joe Gibbs era was not a roaring success for a number of reasons. The team that Gibbs inherited was below average. The NFL salary cap had altered the league he dominated at times during his first run. Owner Daniel Snyder could not change his spending habits. These issues were oft-reported in the aftermath of Gibbs's re-retirement from the Redskins, but one important difference that received less play was that Gibbs had simply grown older.

The aging pattern of players is a serious part of any discussion of NFL transactions. We know that most NFL players are in their prime during their middle to late 20s. Is it possible that coaches also have a prime age?

ESPN.com columnist Bill Simmons, in a piece that came out in the wake of Bill Parcells's last playoff loss with the Cowboys after the 2006 season, floated the idea that old coaches struggle. In his patented style, Simmons introduced his "Speed Limit Coaching Corollary," which basically holds that coaches 55 and older are a dangerous proposition. (The original article is at http://sports.espn.go.com/espn/page2/story?page=simmons/070112.)

Simmons writes thousands of words a week and seemingly one-quarter of them are devoted to some new theory that may or may not have factual support. His anecdotal evidence to support the aging coach theory, however, was particularly interesting, so we crunched some numbers to see whether coaches see decreased results at a certain age.

Measuring coaching performance is, quite frankly, a near-impossible task. The coach is merely working with the talent he has. The currency for coaches remains win-loss record, which is an unsatisfactory solution for measuring an individual coach. Over a sample of dozens of coaches, however, the randomness that affects a team in a single season will generally even out.

With this in mind, we looked at every coach since the NFL liberalized passing rules and went to a 16-game season in 1978. Over the past 30 years, the youngest coach in the NFL was Lane Kiffin at age 32. The oldest was Marv Levy at age 72. For this study, we considered ages 39 through 65. At each age in this span, various men have coached at least 100 NFL games since 1978.

A look at winning percentage by age lends some credence to Simmons's theory that coaches tend to do better before they hit their late 50s. Simmons's choice of 55 is a little off, but coaches above the age of 57 have a combined record of 1,041-1,171, which works out to a .471 winning percentage. (Unfortunately, the actual age limit does not lend itself to a catchy sobriquet, unless our theory was to apply only to the Pittsburgh Steelers.)

One puzzle piece that Simmons may have missed is that young coaches are not particularly successful either. Coaches aged 41 or younger are a combined 484-569. At age 42, however, coaches seem to hit their stride. They are a combined 214-194, and seven of the 10 best ages for coaches (100 games minimum) are the nine years from 42 to 50. The absolute peak seasons, in terms of winning percentage, are ages 44 and 45 (Figure 1).

In Gibbs's case, however, the issue was not only that he struggled with a 30-34 record but that it was so much worse than his previous performance. To account for this phenomenon, we can compare a coach's given performance in a particular year to his overall career

Figure 1. Head Coach Winning Percentage by Age

performance. For example, Gibbs has a career winning percentage of .621, which translates to 9.94 wins out of 16. We can then compare the expected wins to his actual total in any given year. For instance, his nine wins last season at the age of 67 gives him a -.94 win differential for that season.

Win differential shows us how a coach at any given age did compared to his career as a whole. In this way, we are comparing Rich Kotite to Rich Kotite and Jimmy Johnson to Jimmy Johnson. A positive win differential for a given season means that coaches of that age outperformed their own career winning percentage.

Win differential shows a younger coaching prime than pure win-loss record. The overall win differential is positive from age 42 through 51 and then negative for age 52 and older for any age with at least 100 games coached (Figure 2). The very youngest coaches also

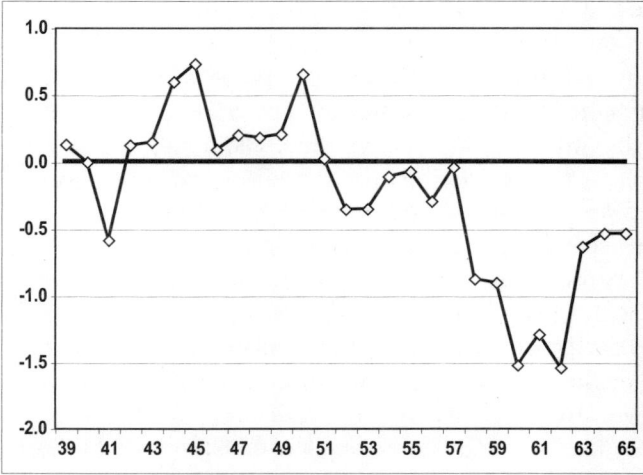

Figure 2. Head Coach Win Differential per 16 Games by Age

struggle in win differential. The total win differential for ages 32-41 is a net negative.

A closer look at win differential probably explains Simmons's perception of the problems with age. In many instances, proven coaches no longer were winning at the same consistent level. The six worst ages for win differential on a per game basis are 58-63. The worst by a substantial margin are ages 60-62. A number of all-time great coaches had losing teams at age 60, including Don Coryell, Mike Ditka, Chuck Knox, and Marty Schottenheimer.

These numbers pretty clearly demonstrate that coaches peak in their late 40s and then decline in their mid- to late 50s, but how much of an impact does the age of a coach have on any given team? Remember that these are general trends, not absolutes. Two of the most successful coaches last season were Romeo Crennel and Wade Phillips, both of whom were 60 years old. The Super Bowl Champion Giants were led by 61-year-old Tom Coughlin. Further, Marv Levy was making annual trips to the Super Bowl with the Bills after he was eligible to start receiving Social Security.

Still, while the difference between most ages is not huge, the advantages can be substantial given the narrow margin necessary to make the playoffs. The most successful age for coaches in win differential is 45 years old, where coaches add on average .72 wins over the course of a 16-game season. Coaches aged 60-62 show a win differential deficit of over one game per season. In a league where 10 wins is enough to make the playoffs, a half a win is important. The difference between the two poles, age 45 and 62, is a total of over two wins.

Finding a discrepancy is not the same thing as finding a reason for the discrepancy. Simmons's primary thesis—that the demands of the job are too tough as people get older—makes as much sense as any other theory. He also argues that coaches lack motivation after making money and that players respect older coaches less because they are unlikely to be around for the long haul. Another possible explanation could be the difficulty keeping up with the constantly innovating game of the NFL; plays and strategies that dominated one era are effectively countered 10 years later.

Some of the difference is coaches who were successful at earlier stops getting hired by struggling franchises, such as Ditka in New Orleans, George Seifert in Carolina, or the Gibbs rehiring in Washington. However, this is only one piece, because coaches such as Tom Landry and Chuck Noll stayed with the same team they had coached. Landry's last three seasons were a combined 17-30, and Noll went 51-60 after turning 53.

Gibbs's career almost exactly parallels the overall trends. He was hired at age 41 and went 8-8. Between the ages of 42 and 52 he had only one losing season. He was rehired at age 64 and suddenly was a sub-.500 coach. Of course, Gibbs coached in two very different organizations, even if both were called the Redskins. The lower performance of older head coaches could be a result of poor management in the front office. Some organizations rely on a retread because they are unable to unearth their own hidden gem; other teams grow stale at the end of a successful run.

The bad news is that Gibbs's replacement, Jim Zorn, joins the same dysfunctional organization and is no spring chicken himself. He is already 55 years old, past his coaching prime. Not many people get their first head coaching opportunity at this age, and the results of Zorn's predecessors could charitably be described as mixed. Only four coaches in the past 20 years—Rich Brooks, Al Groh, Richie Petitbon, and Nick Saban—coached a full season for the first time between the ages of 54 and 56. The four are a total of 14 games under .500, and none coached longer than two years. The only "successful" coaches who have received first NFL head coaching jobs later than Zorn are Jerry Burns, Bobby Ross, and Barry Switzer. All three had previously been head coaches in the collegiate ranks.

Zorn's future is still very much in doubt, as his age is only one factor in the equation. Still, Daniel Snyder apparently did not seem to learn from the age of his previous three hires, all of whom finished their tenure .500 or below and were older than even Zorn when hired. Since Snyder bought the team before the 1999 season, the only coach with a winning record was the incumbent Norv Turner, who went 17-12 for Snyder at the ages of 47 and 48.

No matter what the cause, Simmons's intuition that older coaches struggle certainly seems to be correct. The most successful coaches are generally in their 40s, and as coaches move into their mid- to late 50s, they begin to perform worse. Nobody is suggesting that the Patriots should fire 56-year-old Bill Belichick, but if a franchise has two finalists, one in his 50s and one in his 40s, the one in his 40s appears more likely to be successful. If general managers continue to hire older retreads as head coaches, maybe owners will have to consider employing an ESPN.com columnist as a general manager. We would be happy to be hired to test his more interesting theories.

Ned Macey

2007 Redskins Stats by Week

Wk	vs.	W-L	PF	PA	YDF	YDA	TO	Total	Off	Def	ST
1	MIA	W	16	13	400	273	-1	-23%	-19%	7%	3%
2	@PHI	W	20	12	337	340	-1	23%	23%	-4%	-4%
3	NYG	L	17	24	260	315	+2	-16%	-19%	-1%	2%
4	BYE										
5	DET	W	34	3	366	144	+1	65%	9%	-61%	-5%
6	@GB	L	14	17	304	225	-1	26%	-37%	-55%	9%
7	ARI	W	21	19	160	364	+2	-11%	-36%	-23%	3%
8	@NE	L	7	52	224	486	-3	-46%	-19%	28%	0%
9	@NYJ	W	23	20	431	338	0	-25%	8%	23%	-10%
10	PHI	L	25	33	361	379	0	-1%	28%	29%	0%
11	@DAL	L	23	28	423	362	-1	15%	26%	19%	7%
12	@TB	L	13	19	412	192	-6	7%	-18%	-21%	4%
13	BUF	L	16	17	281	357	-1	-31%	-12%	23%	4%
14	CHI	W	24	16	345	356	+1	0%	10%	-7%	-17%
15	@NYG	W	22	10	309	307	+1	33%	14%	-17%	2%
16	@MIN	W	32	21	367	299	+3	33%	36%	-2%	-5%
17	DAL	W	27	6	354	147	-1	108%	13%	-92%	2%
18	@SEA	L	14	35	319	304	0	3%	-8%	-14%	-4%

Trends and Splits

	Offense	Rank	Defense	Rank
Total DVOA	1.0%	17	-7.2%	6
Unadjusted VOA	-3.0%	18	-4.5%	11
Weighted trend	4.2%	15	-6.4%	7
Variance	5.4%	10	12.1%	31
Average opponent	-0.2%	6	4.6%	4
Passing	12.7%	12	-6.9%	7
Rushing	-10.3%	23	-7.6%	11
First down	6.3%	11	-11.8%	5
Second down	-5.0%	22	-14.0%	6
Third down	0.8%	14	11.9%	26
First half	0.9%	16	-23.8%	1
Second half	1.2%	19	8.2%	25
Red zone	-7.1%	22	1.5%	15
Late and close	-9.0%	24	7.8%	23

Five-Year Performance

Year	W-L	Pyth Wins	Est Wins	PF	PA	TO	Total	Rank	Off	Rank	Def	Rank	ST	Rank
2003	5-11	5.6	5.6	287	372	+2	-15.6%	25	-7.2%	19	10.3%	27	1.9%	9
2004	6-10	7.1	6.8	240	265	-1	-5.8%	21	-17.0%	28	-15.0%	4	-3.9%	31
2005	10-6	9.9	10.4	359	293	+1	20.9%	7	5.1%	12	-14.4%	4	1.4%	10
2006	5-11	6.1	6.8	307	376	-5	-11.6%	23	4.2%	13	17.6%	32	1.7%	11
2007	9-7	8.7	8.3	334	310	-5	7.9%	12	1.0%	17	-7.2%	6	-0.3%	16

Strategic Tendencies

Run/Pass	Rank	Offense		Rank	Defense		Rank	Other		Rank	
Runs, all plays	44%	8	3+ WR	53%	12	Rush 3	5.4%	15	2+ RB, Pct Runs	54%	21
Runs, first half	43%	9	4+ WR	15%	9	Rush 4	60.2%	19	1 RB/2 TE, Pct runs	42%	20
Runs, first down	55%	9	2+ TE	26%	16	Rush 5	17.0%	23	1 RB/3+ WR, Pct runs	37%	1
Runs, second-long	37%	11	Single back	62%	10	Rush 6+	17.3%	1	CB1 on WR1	43%	18
Runs, power sit.	67%	12	Play action	20%	14	Rush 7+	5.9%	1	Go for it on 4th	0.77	24
Runs, behind 2H	26%	22	Max protect	11%	10	Sacks by LB	24.2%	16	Offensive pace	29.9	7
Pass, ahead 2H	46%	16	Outside pocket	11%	16	Sacks by DB	9.1%	9	Defensive pace	30.0	5

Washington was substantially more efficient with three wide receivers (30.4% DVOA) than with four (9.2% DVOA). ⌀ The Redskins ranked third in number of screen passes thrown, but ranked 24th in DVOA. Although no single player stood out on the positive side, Chris Cooley's four screen passes for a combined four yards don't help the aggregate value. Clinton Portis was a mix of feast and famine, but was second only behind Brian Westbrook in the total number of screen passes. ⌀ Facing short yardage on their own half of the field, the Redskins rarely aired it out. Only Atlanta threw the ball at least ten yards less often with five or less yards to go. ⌀ Washington hurried the opposing quarterback on less than nine percent of all pass plays, the lowest percentage in the NFL. ⌀ Washington's defense posted above average DVOA in all formations except three-wide receiver sets, where they ranked 24th. ⌀ Washington's defense ranked last in the league in hurries per pass play, just 8.4 percent. ⌀ Washington's offense had the lowest Adjusted Sack Rate in the league on first down, but was roughly league-average on second and third downs. ⌀   The Redskins ranked fourth in DVOA against play-action passes. ⌀   Only Indianapolis faced more draw plays, but the Redskins ranked sixth in defensive DVOA against draws, allowing only six first downs all season. ⌀   The Washington defense benefited from 47 dropped passes, the most in the NFL. ⌀   The Redskins had one of the top five defensive DVOA ratings in the first and second quarter, but were in the bottom ten for both the third and fourth quarter.

Passing

Player	DYAR	DVOA	Plays	NtYds	Avg	YAC	C%	TD	Int
Jason Campbell	433	4.4%	437	2596	5.9	4.7	60.5%	12	11
Todd Collins	311	31.6%	115	854	7.4	5.4	63.8%	5	0

Rushing

Player	DYAR	DVOA	Plays	Yds	Avg	TD	Fum	Suc
Clinton Portis	75	-3.0%	325	1252	3.9	11	6	46%
Ladell Betts	-21	-13.9%	93	335	3.6	1	1	45%
Jason Campbell	0	-12.3%	30	183	6.1	1	11	—
Mike Sellers	7	-4.1%	26	78	3.0	2	1	62%
Antwaan Randle El	-14	-116.1%	4	-3	-0.8	0	0	—
Santana Moss	-15	-142.4%	3	13	4.3	0	1	—

Receiving

Player	DYAR	DVOA	Plays	Ctch	Yds	Y/C	YAC	TD	C%
WR									
Santana Moss	25	-9.9%	115	61	808	13.2	3.1	3	53%
Antwaan Randle El	179	16.9%	77	51	728	14.3	3.6	1	66%
Keenan McCardell	88	24.0%	31	22	256	11.6	2.6	1	71%
Reche Caldwell*	22	-0.7%	22	15	141	9.4	1.4	0	68%
James Thrash	13	-3.5%	18	9	107	11.9	3.3	2	50%
Brandon Lloyd*	-59	-85.3%	11	2	14	7.0	8.0	0	18%
Anthony Mix	6	4.6%	5	3	39	13.0	5.7	0	60%
TE									
Chris Cooley	121	9.4%	110	66	786	11.9	4.3	8	60%
Todd Yoder	21	20.9%	12	7	97	13.9	7.9	1	58%
RB									
Clinton Portis	96	15.4%	58	47	389	8.3	9.6	0	81%
Ladell Betts	14	-6.3%	32	21	174	8.3	9.1	1	66%
Mike Sellers	-4	-16.7%	24	17	117	6.9	3.8	1	71%

Offensive Line

Year	Yards	ALY	Rank	Power	Rank	10+ Yds	Rank	Stuff	Rank	Sack	ASR	Rank
2005	4.39	4.51	5	63%	16	16%	17	22%	7	31	6.9%	17
2006	4.41	4.28	15	55%	29	16%	16	24%	12	19	4.4%	5
2007	3.73	4.14	18	60%	22	10%	28	23%	14	29	5.1%	12

Year	LE	Rank	LT	Rank	Mid	Rank	RT	Rank	RE	Rank
2005	4.51	8	4.36	16	4.39	9	4.01	20	5.06	3
2006	4.05	18	4.95	5	4.58	7	3.94	24	3.86	19
2007	4.12	14	4.83	7	4.11	16	4.11	20	3.75	23

While the Redskins have invested significant resources into their offensive line, the nature of the salary cap and the construction of their team means that each year, the team will send out a great starting five and hope that they stay healthy. In 2007, that plan was in shambles after two weeks. First, right tackle Jon Jansen broke his ankle in Week 1; the problem was exacerbated when right guard Randy Thomas tore his triceps a week later, meaning that the Redskins were out one whole side of their line until Thomas returned in Week 14. The result had a dramatic effect upon the team: Washington's protections were all shifted to the right side, so left tackle Chris Samuels and new left guard Pete Kendall were often left in one-on-one matchups literally for every snap. Under those circumstances, Samuels and Kendall did a rather admirable job. Because of his pass-blocking abilities, Clinton Portis saw more snaps than his injury history should have dictated. The Redskins went from ranking 30th in usage of max protect schemes in 2006 to ranking tenth in 2007.

The Redskins replaced Jansen and Thomas with a variety of players depending upon their health and abilities, with Jason Fabini seeing time on the inside and both Todd Wade and Stephon Heyer appearing on the outside.

Heyer is your standard-issue mammoth developmental tackle prospect, Fabini is your standard-issue aging tackle becoming a utility lineman, and Wade is your standard-issue failed developmental tackle prospect. Center Casey Rabach struggled with a groin injury for a number of weeks in 2007; as a technician who already gets the maximum out of his talent, he is a player who can't particularly afford to get hurt.

Defensive Front Seven

Defensive Line	Age	Pos	Plays	TmPct	Rk	Stop	Dfts	Stop%	Rk	AvYd	Rk	Sack	Hit	Hur	Runs	RuStop	RuYd	Pass	PaStop	PaYd
Andre Carter	29	DE	56	6.9%	24	46	20	82%	17	0.2	13	10.5	14	6	36	78%	1.9	20	90%	-2.9
Phillip Daniels	35	DE	48	6.3%	31	35	14	73%	55	1.6	36	2.5	0	4	33	61%	2.8	15	100%	-1.1
Anthony Montgomery	24	DT	48	5.9%	24	43	10	90%	3	1.5	23	0.5	4	2	39	92%	1.6	9	78%	0.9
Cornelius Griffin	32	DT	42	5.2%	31	33	9	79%	30	1.7	33	2.5	7	5	36	81%	1.8	6	67%	1.2
Demetric Evans	29	DE	27	3.3%	77	19	9	70%	68	3.1	70	1.0	2	5	15	60%	3.7	12	83%	2.4

Linebackers	Age	Pos	Plays	TmPct	Rk	Stop	Dfts	Stop%	AvYd	Sack	Hit	Hur	Runs	RuStop	Rk	RuYd	Rk	Tgts	Suc%	Rk	APaYd	Rk
London Fletcher	33	MLB	140	17.3%	7	74	22	53%	5.0	0.0	1	1	81	60%	57	3.7	66	39	57%	19	7.2	71
Rocky McIntosh	26	OLB	93	13.1%	44	46	11	49%	6.4	3.0	2	3	35	57%	75	3.9	75	48	52%	37	7.3	76
Marcus Washington	31	OLB	49	8.1%	85	26	11	53%	3.7	5.0	0	1	26	58%	72	3.7	63	21	37%	81	6.2	48
Randall Godfrey	35	OLB	31	5.6%	—	22	3	71%	3.1	0.0	2	2	23	74%	—	2.7	—	8	72%	—	3.0	—

Year	Yards	ALY	Rank	Power	Rank	10+ Yds	Rank	Stuff	Rank	Sack	ASR	Rank
2005	4.23	3.88	11	57%	8	27%	32	26%	13	35	6.4%	23
2006	4.71	4.78	30	62%	12	18%	23	21%	23	19	4.6%	32
2007	3.67	4.19	17	65%	20	8%	1	24%	17	33	5.7%	26

Year	LE	Rank	LT	Rank	Mid	Rank	RT	Rank	RE	Rank
2005	4.44	21	3.94	11	3.74	7	4.10	17	3.13	7
2006	4.52	21	5.42	31	4.62	25	4.76	26	4.75	26
2007	4.37	21	4.80	26	3.88	4	4.39	20	4.14	17

The revelation of the defensive line was defensive tackle Anthony Montgomery, a 2006 fifth-round pick who took over from Joe Salave'a on the interior and emerged as a huge difference-maker in one-on-one situations. Playing alongside the criminally underrated Cornelius Griffin, who stayed healthy for all 16 games for the first time since he came to Washington, Montgomery was excellent at consistently holding his ground against bigger offensive linemen, particularly earlier in the season. Defensive linemen who get significant playing time early in their career tend to stick around for a long time, so Montgomery's going to have a role on one team or another for the next ten years if he can stay healthy. Remember the name. Matthias Askew and Kedric Golston are the primary backups here.

Right end Andre Carter was every bit the player the Redskins hoped he would be when they signed him to a big deal in free agency in 2006, but it took him a year to get comfortable in the team's scheme. He picked up 10.5 sacks in 2007 despite having most opposing protection schemes shifted towards his side of the line. Left end Philip Daniels is 36 and plays as such; he's a heady player who gets by on his technique and guile. The odds of him starting 15 games again are slim, which is why many draftniks were calling for the Redskins to take an end early in the draft, but the Skins only took Rob Jackson, a project, in the sixth round. Demetric Evans is a competent backup, but there's little behind him. There's also no specialization of roles with the backups; in other words, there's no situational pass rusher or heavy-duty run guy coming off the bench, just guys who aren't talented enough to start.

The addition of London Fletcher in the offseason had to be considered a success, as Fletcher stayed healthy for the whole year and put on a performance similar to the job he did in Buffalo. He's slipping in coverage, so the Redskins might end up giving him a few more third downs off this year, with former Pittsburgh star H. B. Blades taking his spot. Marcus Washington struggled with a hamstring injury and had a relatively abysmal year by his standards. Linebackers don't shed injury very easily, even on a year-to-year basis, so expect a reoccurrence of the injury at some point in 2008. Washington's backup was Randall Godfrey, who is to the linebackers what Daniels is to the ends. Rocky McIntosh is the weakside backer; while McIntosh was improving in 2007, he tore his ACL in December and had reconstructive knee surgery. McIntosh needs to improve in coverage to become the linebacker the team envisioned when they drafted him; reconstructive knee surgeries, from what we can remember, don't help you improve in coverage. If there's one spot in the lineup where the Redskins could find themselves in a disaster scenario, it's at outside linebacker.

Defensive Secondary

Secondary	Age	Pos	Plays	TmPct	Rk	Stop	Dfts	RuYd	Rk	RuStop	Rk	Tgts	Tgt%	Rk	Dist	Suc%	Rk	APaYd	Rk	PaYd	PD	Int
LaRon Landry	23	FS	96	11.9%	15	35	14	5.9	30	40%	53	23	5%	76	12.9	59%	11	4.4	6	4.9	7	0
Shawn Springs	33	CB	77	9.5%	32	39	15	8.9	61	29%	69	94	18%	36	10.8	62%	1	6.0	9	6.1	13	4
Fred Smoot	29	CB	60	9.1%	41	32	14	2.1	1	90%	1	83	20%	28	9.7	57%	10	5.6	3	5.3	9	1
Reed Doughty	26	SS	46	5.7%	76	24	8	3.8	2	68%	4	24	5%	74	11.2	53%	26	6.6	29	6.6	2	0
Sean Taylor*	25	FS	45	9.9%	38	17	9	6.8	49	38%	57	18	6%	56	19.1	68%	2	2.7	1	2.7	8	5
Pierson Prioleau*	31	FS	37	4.9%	78	12	5	4.2	6	42%	46	23	5%	72	7.1	34%	78	8.9	57	9.0	1	0
Leigh Torrence	26	CB	33	4.1%	—	12	9	7.9	—	29%	—	31	6%	—	7.9	45%	—	6.9	—	6.9	1	0
Carlos Rogers	27	CB	27	7.6%	—	15	7	6.6	—	40%	—	37	16%	—	14.6	66%	—	5.7	—	6.0	8	1

Year	Pass D Rank	vs. #1 WR	Rk	vs. #2 WR	Rk	vs. Other WR	Rk	vs. TE	Rk	vs. RB	Rk
2005	3	-14.5%	2	1.6%	21	-7.7%	11	-13.6%	8	-31.8%	2
2006	32	2.5%	16	9.1%	23	15.0%	24	18.6%	30	-24.0%	8
2007	7	3.5%	19	-39.6%	2	-28.4%	5	-3.9%	8	10.0%	28

The changes in the secondary were discussed at length in the chapter, but the other absence that affected the team was that of cornerback Carlos Rogers, who showed signs of being an elite corner in the first half of the year, but missed the second half of the season with a knee injury. That forced Fred Smoot into a starting role; he rebounded from his struggles in Minnesota and once again was a surprisingly effective corner. Leigh Torrence was pushed into regular duty, and he looked lost at times out there. Not lost in the "He doesn't know his assignment" sense, but lost in the "He ended up in a football stadium by accident and needs to find his way home" sense. Shawn Springs continued his late-career resurgence by leading all cornerbacks in Success Rate and finishing ninth in adjusted yards per pass. If Springs had been healthier early in his career, he'd have the reputation that his play deserves. The Redskins will likely roll out Reed Doughty at strong safety and LaRon Landry at free safety to start off 2008, with their roles changing some because of the departure of Gregg Williams. Landry should end up in the centerfield role he occupied at the end of the year, with Doughty plugging gaps closer to the line.

Special Teams

Year	DVOA	Rank	FG/XP	Rank	Net Punt	Rank	Punt Ret	Rank	Net Kick	Rank	Kick Ret	Rank	Hidden	Rank
2005	1.4%	9	-0.1	18	10.1	1	-4.3	25	-3.5	22	6.2	6	-1.8	19
2006	1.7%	11	-2.9	22	4.4	11	3.7	5	0.0	18	5.1	7	3.0	12
2007	-0.3%	16	-1.1	21	6.1	6	-7.0	29	-6.0	25	6.1	9	11.9	5

Kicker Shaun Suisham went from being average across the board in 2006 to uncomfortably mediocre across the board in 2007. According to our metrics, his kickoffs (without considering returns) were worth 6.1 points of field position worse than average, the worst figure in the league. His contract was renewed, but he should be on a short leash this year. Punter Derrick Frost was also below average, but strong punt coverage helped the Redskins end up ahead on net punting. With Randle El assuming a larger role within the offense, Rock Cartwright became the full-time returner and excelled, outperforming Randle El in both categories compared to 2006. Still, expect Randle El to assume more return duties again this year.

COACHING STAFF

Jim Zorn's huge leap to head coach comes with more questions than answers. The theme of his first minicamp involved the newcomers to the team, himself included, having to prove themselves to the veterans. Rookies got logoless helmets. Zorn's opening speech to the team was part auto-biography. The core of veterans who control the locker room in Washington aren't stupid; they know Zorn is inexperienced, wasn't the team's first choice, and doesn't have anywhere near the pedigree that any of their previous coaches have had. If everything goes wrong in the first half of the season, there exists the distinct possibility that this could be a one-and-done head coaching career. That's not to say it's likely, but it's possible. Sherman Smith is listed as the offensive coordinator, but expect Zorn to do the playcalling. Greg Blache was promoted to be the new defensive coordinator; he will retain Gregg Williams' scheme, but odds are that he'll undoubtedly open up the jail cells a little less frequently; the Redskins rushed both six and seven guys more often than anyone in football. Part of that had to do with the opposition's fear of going over the middle and meeting Sean Taylor, whose role Landry will now have to play in 2008. The only assistant coach retained by Zorn in the same role was offensive line guru Joe Bugel.

Quarterbacks

2007 revealed just how dramatically a quarterback's performance can change by virtue of the players around him. Although Tom Brady had settled into a pretty consistent statistical pattern before last season, the addition of Randy Moss and Wes Welker, along with the improvement of an offensive line that gave Brady eons to throw, resulted in a dramatic rise that saw Brady put up one of the best seasons in fantasy football history. Brady's fantasy points increased by an incredible 76 percent last year—among quarterbacks who threw 500 attempts in back-to-back seasons for the same teams, the highest previous increase was 49 percent, by Brett Favre in 1994.

The rise represents the dramatic differences in player value that ensue from shifts in both system and personnel, something that affects almost every top offense this year. Favre is gone—unless he changes his mind again—to be replaced by either Aaron Rodgers or Brian Brohm. Indianapolis is likely phasing Marvin Harrison out of the starting lineup to open a spot for Anthony Gonzalez. Dallas has handed their starting running back spot over to Marion Barber. Cincinnati could be without Chad Johnson this year and T. J. Houshmandzadeh next. It's adapting to these changes and accounting for the effects they'll have on a team's offensive abilities that make projecting NFL performance an incredibly difficult process on a year-to-year basis.

In this section of the book, we give the last three years' worth of numbers for the top two quarterbacks on each team's depth chart, as well as a few other quarterbacks who may prove to be important in 2008. Each quarterback also gets a projection from our KUBIAK fantasy football projection system, based on a complicated regression analysis that takes into account numerous variables including projected role, performance over the past two years, performance on third down versus all downs, experience of the projected offensive line, historical comparables, collegiate stats, height, age, and strength of schedule.

It is difficult to accurately project statistics for a 162-game baseball season, but it is exponentially more difficult to accurately project statistics for a 16-game football season because of the small size of the data samples involved. With that in mind, consider our pro-jections not predictions of exact numbers but the mean of a range of possible performances. What's important is not so much the exact number of yards and touchdowns we project, but whether or not we're projecting a given player to improve or decline. Along those same lines, rookie projections will not be as accurate as veteran projections due to lack of data.

Our quarterback projections look a bit different than our projections for the other skill positions. At running back and wide receiver, second stringers see plenty of action, but at quarterback, either a player starts or he does not start. We recognize that when a starting quarterback gets injured in Week 8, you don't want to grab your *Pro Football Prospectus* to find out whether his backup is any good only to find that we've projected that the guy will throw 12 passes this year. Therefore, like we did last year, we have projected all quarterbacks to start all 16 games. If Matt Hasselbeck goes down in November, you can look up Seneca Wallace or Charlie Frye, divide the stats by 16, and get an idea of what we think each player will do in an average week.

HOW TO READ THE QUARTERBACK STATISTICS TABLE

The first line contains biographical data—each player's name, height, weight, college, draft position, birth date, and age. **Height** and **weight** are the best data we could find; weight, of course, can fluctuate during the off-season. **Age** is simple: the number of years between the player's birth year and 2008, but birth date is provided if you want to figure out the exact age.

Draft position gives draft year and round, with the overall pick number with which the player was taken in parentheses. In the sample table, it says that Peyton Manning was chosen in the 1998 draft in the first round with the first overall pick. Undrafted free agents are listed as FA with the year they came into the league, even if they were only in training camp or on a practice squad.

To the far right of the first line is the player's **Risk** for fantasy football in 2008. A player's Risk level indicates the likelihood that he will fall short of his listed KUBIAK projection no matter what the reason—injury, a change

Quarterback Statistics Sample

Peyton Manning   Height: 6-5   Weight: 230   College: Tennessee   Draft: 1998/1 (1)   Born: 24-Mar-1976   Age: 32   Risk: Green

Year	Team	G	Att	Comp	C%	Yds	TD	INT	FUM	ASR	NY/P	Rk	DVOA	Rk	DYAR	Rk	YAR	Runs	Yds	TD	DVOA	DYAR
2005	IND	16	453	305	67.3%	3747	28	10	4	3.6%	7.8	1	40.4%	1	1598	1	1781	33	45	0	-56.3%	-40
2006	IND	16	557	362	65.0%	4397	31	9	3	3.3%	7.8	4	51.0%	1	2308	1	2287	23	36	4	48.2%	42
2007	IND	16	515	337	65.4%	4040	31	14	7	4.2%	7.3	5	40.6%	2	1841	2	1679	20	-5	3	17.3%	16
2008	IND		553	369	66.6%	4359	38	13			7.6		42.3%					14	19	1	22.4%	

2007:   45% Short   34% Mid   12% Deep   9% Bomb   YAC: 4.5 (31)   2006:   43% Short   35% Mid   13% Deep   9% Bomb   YAC: 3.9 (40)

in playing time, decline of skills, decline of overall team offense, and so on. Instead of giving you some sort of estimated risk percentage statistic, we have borrowed an idea from the preseason "Team Health Reports" on BaseballProspectus.com by listing each player's Risk as Green, Yellow, or Red. In addition, there is an extra color of Risk for quarterbacks only. The five projected backup quarterbacks who are most likely to meet their KUBIAK projections if they become starters are listed as Orange.

Next we give the last three years of player stats. The majority of these statistics are passing numbers, though the final five columns on the right are the quarterback's rushing statistics.

The first few columns after the year and team the player played for are standard numbers: games (**G**), pass attempts (**Att**), pass completions (**Comp**), completion percentage (**C%**), passing yards (**Yds**), passing touchdowns (**TD**), and interceptions (**INT**). These numbers are official NFL totals and therefore include plays we leave out of our own metrics, such as clock-stopping spikes, and omit plays we include in our metrics, such as sacks and aborted snaps. Note that the games total includes all games the player appeared in, not just games started, which is why a backup quarterback who holds on field goals will often be listed with 16 games played.

The next column is fumbles (**FUM**), which adds all fumbles by this player, whether turned over to the defense or recovered by the offense (explained in the essay "Pregame Show"). Even though this fumble total is listed among the passing numbers, it includes all fumbles, including those on sacks, aborted snaps, and rushing attempts. By listing fumbles and interceptions next to one another, we hope to give a general idea of how many total turnovers the player was responsible for.

Next comes Adjusted Sack Rate (**ASR**). This is the same statistic you'll find in the team chapters, only here it is specific to the individual quarterback. It represents sacks and intentional groundings per pass play (total pass plays = pass attempts + sacks) adjusted based on down, distance, and strength of schedule. For reference, the NFL average over the past three seasons is 6.8 percent.

The next two columns are Net Yards per Pass (**NY/P**), a standard stat but a particularly good one, and the player's rank (**Rk**) in Net Yards per Pass for that season. Consider the inclusion of this number our tribute to the godfather of football stats, Bud Goode. It consists of passing yards minus yards lost on sacks, divided by total pass plays.

The five columns remaining in passing stats give our advanced metrics: DVOA (Defense-Adjusted Value Over Average), DYAR (Defense-Adjusted Yards Above Replacement), and YAR (Yards Above Replacement), along with the player's rank in both DVOA and DYAR. These metrics compare each quarterback's passing performance to league-average or replacement-level baselines based on the game situations that quarterback faced. DVOA and DYAR are also adjusted based on the opposing defense. The methods used to compute these numbers are described in detail in the "Statistical Toolbox" introduction in the front of the book. The important distinctions between them follow:

- DVOA is a rate statistic, and DYAR is a cumulative statistic. Thus, a higher DVOA means more value per pass play, and a higher DYAR means more aggregate value over the entire season.
- Because DYAR is defense adjusted and YAR is not, a player whose DYAR is higher than his YAR faced a harder-than-average schedule. A player whose DYAR is lower than his YAR faced an easier-than-average schedule.

To qualify for a ranking in Net Yards per Pass, passing DVOA, and passing DYAR in a given season, a quarterback must have had 100 pass plays in that season.

There are 51 quarterbacks ranked for 2007, 45 quarterbacks for 2006, and 46 quarterbacks for 2005.

The final five shaded columns contain rushing statistics, starting with **Runs**, rushing yards (**Yds**), and rushing touchdowns (**TD**). Once again, these are official NFL totals and include kneeldowns, which means you get to enjoy statistics such as Charlie Batch running 12 times for a loss of seven yards. The final two columns give **DYAR** and **DVOA** for quarterback rushing, which are calculated separately from passing. Rankings for these statistics, as well as numbers that are not adjusted for defense (YAR and VOA), can be found on our website, FootballOutsiders.com.

The italicized row of statistics for the 2008 season is our 2008 KUBIAK projection, as detailed previously. This year, for the first time, we have projected some of our advanced metrics along with conventional statistics. Again, in the interest of producing relevant projections for fantasy football, all quarterbacks are projected to start a full 16-game season, regardless of the likelihood of them actually doing so.

The final line represents data from the Football Outsiders game charting project. First, we break down charted passes based on distance: **Short** (5 yards or less), **Mid** (6-15 yards), **Deep** (16-25 yards), and **Bomb** (26 or more yards). These numbers are based on distance in the air only and include both complete and incomplete passes. Passes thrown away or tipped at the line are not included, nor are passes where the quarterback's arm was hit by a defender while in motion. We also give Yards after Catch (**YAC**) with the Rank in parentheses for the 51 quarterbacks who qualify.

A number of third- and fourth-string quarterbacks are briefly discussed at the end of the chapter in a section we call "Going Deep."

Top 20 QB by Passing DYAR (Total Value), 2007

Rank	Player	Team	DYAR
1	Tom Brady	NE	2788
2	Peyton Manning	IND	1841
3	Brett Favre	GB	1438
4	Tony Romo	DAL	1297
5	Drew Brees	NO	1285
6	Carson Palmer	CIN	1215
7	David Garrard	JAC	1086
8	Jay Cutler	DEN	972
9	Matt Hasselbeck	SEA	937
10	Derek Anderson	CLE	797
11	Ben Roethlisberger	PIT	743
12	Kurt Warner	ARI	699
13	Jeff Garcia	TB	694
14	Donovan McNabb	PHI	659
15	Sage Rosenfels	HOU	599
16	Philip Rivers	SD	552
17	Jason Campbell	WAS	433
18	Jon Kitna	DET	387
19	Matt Schaub	HOU	381
20	Todd Collins	WAS	311

Top 20 QB by Passing DVOA (Value per Pass), 2007

Rank	Player	Team	DVOA
1	Tom Brady	NE	56.9%
2	Peyton Manning	IND	40.6%
3	David Garrard	JAC	37.4%
4	Todd Collins	WAS	31.6%
5	Brett Favre	GB	28.0%
6	Tony Romo	DAL	25.5%
7	Sage Rosenfels	HOU	24.3%
8	Quinn Gray	JAC	20.9%
9	Carson Palmer	CIN	20.1%
10	Jeff Garcia	TB	19.5%
11	Jay Cutler	DEN	19.4%
12	Drew Brees	NO	17.0%
13	Ben Roethlisberger	PIT	15.5%
14	Matt Hasselbeck	SEA	12.8%
15	Derek Anderson	CLE	12.3%
16	Kurt Warner	ARI	11.3%
17	Matt Schaub	HOU	8.2%
18	Donovan McNabb	PHI	8.2%
19	Trent Green	MIA	7.8%
20	Philip Rivers	SD	6.9%

Derek Anderson

Height: 6-6   Weight: 239   College: Oregon State   Draft: 2005/6 (213)   Born: 15-Jun-1983   Age: 25   Risk: Green

Year	Team	G	Att	Comp	C%	Yds	TD	INT	FUM	ASR	NY/P	Rk	DVOA	Rk	DYAR	Rk	YAR	Runs	Yds	TD	DVOA	DYAR
2006	CLE	5	117	66	56.4%	793	5	8	1	6.0%	6.3	24	-22.8%	39	-93	34	-120	4	47	0	34.4%	7
2007	CLE	16	527	298	56.5%	3787	29	19	4	3.5%	7.0	9	12.3%	15	797	10	888	32	70	3	34.2%	50
2008	CLE		495	295	59.6%	3365	26	19			6.0		1.3%					26	51	2	24.7%	

2007: 43% Short 36% Mid 17% Deep 4% Bomb YAC: 5.0 (17)   2006: 36% Short 43% Mid 18% Deep 3% Bomb YAC: 6.3 (3)

If the Browns knew how good Derek Anderson was, they might have saved themselves a first-round pick. Still, it's not a given that he's the team's long-term answer. There were a few red flags during his otherwise sparkling season. When you look at the top quarterback performances of 2007, Anderson's 56.5 percent completion percentage sticks out like a sore thumb. Anderson ran hot and cold all season—he had three games where he completed more than 68 percent of his passes and three games where he completed well under half of them. Anderson's accuracy issues go back to his college days at Oregon State, so there's no reason to think he can readily improve this part of his game. Anderson also faded after a hot start, throwing nine touchdowns and 10 interceptions in his final five games after racking up 20 touchdowns and nine interceptions in his first 10 games. The three-year, $24-million contract Anderson signed in the offseason guarantees that he is the unquestioned starter come training camp, but it shouldn't be viewed as a long- or even medium-term commitment. The $9 million roster bonus due in March of 2009 means that Anderson effectively has one year to prove himself a better option than Brady Quinn. If he can duplicate last season's effort, he'll be rewarded with a long-term deal. If he falters, he'll be playing somewhere else.

Charlie Batch

Height: 6-2   Weight: 220   College: Eastern Michigan   Draft: 1998/2 (60)   Born: 5-Dec-1974   Age: 34   Risk: Red

Year	Team	G	Att	Comp	C%	Yds	TD	INT	FUM	ASR	NY/P	Rk	DVOA	Rk	DYAR	Rk	YAR	Runs	Yds	TD	DVOA	DYAR
2005	PIT	4	36	23	63.9%	246	1	1	1	3.7%	6.7	—	25.6%	—	91	—	102	11	30	1	12.8%	9
2006	PIT	8	53	31	58.5%	492	5	0	1	3.6%	9.0	—	64.6%	—	278	—	262	13	15	0	-134.2%	-20
2007	PIT	7	36	17	47.2%	232	2	3	0	2.9%	6.6	—	0.5%	—	29	—	33	12	-7	0	—	—
2008	PIT		406	227	55.9%	3025	22	20			6.0		-14.4%					33	52	2	-13.3%	

2007: 38% Short 35% Mid 6% Deep 21% Bomb YAC: 6.2 (—)   2006: 35% Short 35% Mid 18% Deep 12% Bomb YAC: 7.4 (—)

A disappointing performance in Week 17 against the Ravens—Batch's only 2007 outing—is tempered by the knowledge that the Steelers were locked into the AFC's fourth seed and were primarily trying to avoid injuries. Batch is now at an age where quarterbacks begin to decline, and playing behind Pittsburgh's offensive line could well accelerate that process should he be called on. He is better than the average backup quarterback, but as Pittsburgh's offense grows more dependent on Roethlisberger it becomes increasingly unlikely that Batch could save their season were Big Ben to go down.

John Beck

Height: 6-2   Weight: 215   College: BYU   Draft: 2007/2 (40)   Born: 21-Aug-1981   Age: 27   Risk: Red

Year	Team	G	Att	Comp	C%	Yds	TD	INT	FUM	ASR	NY/P	Rk	DVOA	Rk	DYAR	Rk	YAR	Runs	Yds	TD	DVOA	DYAR
2007	MIA	5	107	60	56.1%	559	1	3	6	8.7%	4.3	48	-51.7%	50	-303	49	-304	9	12	1	12.0%	10
2008	MIA		490	292	59.6%	2818	16	13			5.1		-19.3%					30	62	2	14.1%	

2007: 58% Short 25% Mid 14% Deep 4% Bomb YAC: 3.5 (49)

Take out Beck's Week 17 garbage time production (13-of-21, 135 yards and a touchdown; the score was 28-10 when he entered the game) and you have a rookie season ugly enough to meet Ryan Leaf/Alex Smith quality standards. Beck had no feel for the pass rush, demonstrated little athletic ability, and made the kinds of rookie decisions that would be more excusable if he wasn't four months older than Philip Rivers. Granted, he had no weapons and played for one of the most miserable teams in NFL history, but it's hard to project him as more than a career backup. Chad Henne will leapfrog him on the depth chart sooner rather than later.

Brock Berlin

Height: 6-1 Weight: 215 College: Miami   Draft: 2007/FA   Born: 14-Jul-1981   Age: 27   Risk: Red

Year	Team	G	Att	Comp	C%	Yds	TD	INT	FUM	ASR	NY/P	Rk	DVOA	Rk	DYAR	Rk	YAR	Runs	Yds	TD	DVOA	DYAR
2007	STL	1	28	17	60.7%	153	0	1	1	1.7%	5.5	—	-22.6%	—	-19	—	2	3	-16	0	-266.8%	-39
2008	STL		455	271	59.5%	2612	14	20			4.9		-27.3%					40	71	0	-34.8%	

2007: 50% Short 29% Mid 13% Deep 8% Bomb   YAC: 3.9 (—)

The story of Brock Berlin's NFL career is pretty boring—undrafted free agent, third on the depth chart, threw 28 passes for a bad team, yee-haw. His collegiate career, however, is fascinating. Berlin started at Florida but couldn't take the quarterback job away from Rex Grossman. (That, in hindsight, seems like a clear sign that Berlin was never meant to be an NFL passer.) He transferred to Miami, where in his first home game he led his team to a furious 38-33 comeback victory over Grossman and the Gators. It wasn't all halcyon days at Miami though; at one point Berlin was benched for someone named Derrick Crudup. Crudup, who is black, once suggested that Berlin was named starter because of a racial bias in Miami's coaching staff. The fact that Berlin is in the NFL while Crudup is quarterbacking the Stockton Lightning of af2, the minor league of the Arena League, indicates that skin color had nothing to do with it. Berlin's NFL career, however, is tenuous at best. His coach has little confidence in him. "Regardless of whether we drafted one or signed a free agent that could be competing with Brock (Berlin), that would be fine, too," Scott Linehan said to the *Belleville News-Democrat*. When the head coach hopes he can find a guy on the street who can do your job better than you, that's bad.

Kyle Boller

Height: 6-3 Weight: 220 College: California   Draft: 2003/1 (19) Born: 17-Jun-1981   Age: 27   Risk: Red

Year	Team	G	Att	Comp	C%	Yds	TD	INT	FUM	ASR	NY/P	Rk	DVOA	Rk	DYAR	Rk	YAR	Runs	Yds	TD	DVOA	DYAR
2005	BAL	9	293	171	58.4%	1799	11	12	6	8.0%	5.3	35	-10.0%	28	23	28	-24	23	66	1	-31.6%	-23
2006	BAL	5	55	33	60.0%	485	5	2	2	5.1%	8.3	—	19.9%	—	118	—	95	22	34	0	-40.4%	-16
2007	BAL	12	275	168	61.1%	1743	9	10	6	8.6%	5.3	38	-11.6%	33	-9	33	1	19	89	0	13.1%	25
2008	BAL		478	281	58.8%	2605	11	20			4.2		-36.4%					36	130	3	-42.3%	

2007: 44% Short 32% Mid 16% Deep 8% Bomb   YAC: 3.3 (51)   2006: 37% Short 41% Mid 12% Deep 10% Bomb   YAC: 6.2 (—)

Boller has been making incremental progress as a quarterback; by the time he's 35, he might be a pretty good starter for someone. It doesn't look like it's going to happen in Baltimore, however, where in five years Boller has gone from being the next big thing to being the seat warmer for the new big thing, Joe Flacco. Boller still has the physical tools to be a good player, but he is a robotic decision-maker who struggles in the red zone where quick decisions are necessary. Boller has received a majority of the snaps in minicamp and is the favorite to be the Week 1 starter, but he's going to have to pull a Drew Brees-style breakout to hold onto the job past midseason.

Brooks Bollinger

Height: 6-0 Weight: 205 College: Wisconsin   Draft: 2003/6 (200) Born: 15-Nov-1979   Age: 29   Risk: Red

Year	Team	G	Att	Comp	C%	Yds	TD	INT	FUM	ASR	NY/P	Rk	DVOA	Rk	DYAR	Rk	YAR	Runs	Yds	TD	DVOA	DYAR
2005	NYJ	11	266	150	56.4%	1558	7	6	3	11.3%	4.6	42	-26.3%	38	-295	41	-218	35	135	0	-14.1%	-4
2006	MIN	2	18	13	72.2%	146	0	1	1	24.6%	5.8	—	7.7%	—	27	—	3	0	0	0	—	—
2007	MIN	5	50	33	66.0%	391	1	1	1	12.0%	6.3	—	-3.3%	—	28	—	25	5	18	0	49.4%	6
2008	MIN		455	283	62.1%	3224	14	14			5.6		-8.3%					33	77	0	2.5%	

2007: 53% Short 34% Mid 6% Deep 6% Bomb   YAC: 6.0 (—)   2006: 59% Short 29% Mid 6% Deep 6% Bomb   YAC: 8.0 (—)

When the Vikings traded up in the fifth round to select USC quarterback John David Booty, they likely incited a string of profanity in the Bollinger household. NFL teams rarely carry four quarterbacks, particularly when the fourth is a 28-year-old career journeyman. To keep his job, Bollinger will have to beat out Gus Frerotte in training camp or hope somebody gets injured. If he can't pull it off . . . well, any quarterback who can't stick on the Vikings roster should probably consider a move to Canada or a career change.

John David Booty

Height: 6-3 Weight: 213 College: USC   Draft: 2008/6 (186)   Born: 3-Jan-1985   Age: 23   Risk: Red

Year	Team	G	Att	Comp	C%	Yds	TD	INT	FUM	ASR	NY/P	Rk	DVOA	Rk	DYAR	Rk	YAR	Runs	Yds	TD	DVOA	DYAR
2008	MIN		465	266	57.2%	3348	23	16			6.4		11.4%					33	50	1	-19.4%	

The knock on many USC prospects of the last few seasons is that they are system guys who are propped up by the best program in college football. Take Booty, a two-year starter who helped the Trojans win two Rose Bowls, set a record by throwing seven touchdowns in the two Bowl games, and compiled a 9-0 record against Top 25 teams in 2006-2007. Tremendous prospect, right? Well, he doesn't run well, has an average arm, and doesn't make great reads, which is why he was hanging around in the fifth round of the draft. Booty is a fine student and an athletically limited quarterback can win in Brad Childress's system, but Booty is a developmental player, not a guy to challenge Tarvaris Jackson in the short term. That's a shame, because Jackson needs a challenge. However, fortunately for us, booties4booty.com may have a new cause to promote. One warning to future participants: It's slightly colder in Minneapolis than in Westwood.

Tom Brady

Height: 6-4 Weight: 220 College: Michigan   Draft: 2000/6 (199)   Born: 3-Aug-1977   Age: 31   Risk: Red

Year	Team	G	Att	Comp	C%	Yds	TD	INT	FUM	ASR	NY/P	Rk	DVOA	Rk	DYAR	Rk	YAR	Runs	Yds	TD	DVOA	DYAR
2005	NE	16	530	334	63.0%	4110	26	14	4	5.0%	7.1	4	27.8%	5	1378	3	1236	27	89	1	11.8%	36
2006	NE	16	516	319	61.8%	3529	24	12	13	5.2%	6.5	17	17.4%	8	1010	5	953	49	102	0	4.4%	25
2007	NE	16	578	398	68.9%	4806	50	8	4	4.1%	7.8	1	56.9%	1	2788	1	2698	37	98	2	3.7%	25
2008	NE		536	346	64.5%	4415	37	10			7.8		46.5%					26	57	1	-6.1%	
2007:	52% Short	29% Mid	11% Deep	7% Bomb	YAC: 5.1 (14)				2006:	52% Short	27% Mid	14% Deep	7% Bomb	YAC: 5.0 (16)								

The top ten passing seasons in DYAR, from 1995 to 2007:

Player	Team	Year	DYAR
Tom Brady	NE	2007	2,788
Peyton Manning	IND	2004	2,497
Peyton Manning	IND	2006	2,308
Daunte Culpepper	MIN	2004	1,930
Peyton Manning	IND	2007	1,841
Peyton Manning	IND	2000	1,766
Peyton Manning	IND	2003	1,756
Kurt Warner	STL	2001	1,671
Scott Mitchell	DET	1995	1,611
Erik Kramer	CHI	1995	1,603

Sometimes last season the Patriots looked like they were playing a different sport offensively: Arena Football, or basketball with an ellipse, or maybe pinball. The Colts have been playing that kind of offense for years, as the list shows. Other coaches have noticed, and any team that can get its hands on a franchise-caliber quarterback and a few good wide receivers is going to spread the field and wait for the scoreboard to explode. Those who can't get the quarterback and the receivers will try their luck with Joey Harrington and Roddy White. If you hoped the Steelers Super Bowl win two seasons ago would usher in a new era of power running, dream on. The future belongs to Brady and Peyton, the few with the talent to challenge them (Carson Palmer, perhaps Ben Roethlisberger and Tony Romo, a few others) and the generation of youngsters who spend recess emulating them.

Drew Brees

Height: 6-0 Weight: 221 College: Purdue   Draft: 2001/2 (32)   Born: 15-Jan-1979   Age: 29   Risk: Green

Year	Team	G	Att	Comp	C%	Yds	TD	INT	FUM	ASR	NY/P	Rk	DVOA	Rk	DYAR	Rk	YAR	Runs	Yds	TD	DVOA	DYAR
2005	SD	16	500	323	64.6%	3576	24	15	8	5.6%	6.4	12	13.9%	9	838	8	724	21	49	1	3.7%	15
2006	NO	16	554	356	64.3%	4418	26	11	5	3.7%	7.8	3	25.1%	2	1386	2	1458	42	32	0	-72.4%	-51
2007	NO	16	652	440	67.5%	4423	28	18	9	3.6%	6.5	16	17.0%	12	1285	5	1193	23	52	1	14.2%	23
2008	NO		599	378	63.0%	4225	30	19			6.5		11.4%					16	24	0	0.1%	
2007:	55% Short	29% Mid	10% Deep	5% Bomb	YAC: 4.7 (23)				2006:	55% Short	27% Mid	12% Deep	6% Bomb	YAC: 5.5 (6)								

Brees's season started out like a nightmare—he threw one touchdown and nine interceptions in the Saints first four games as the team started the season 0-4. He rebounded with a strong performance against the Seahawks in the first win of the year, but his 2007 was marked by two serious issues. First, there was his tendency to throw head-scratching passes into double coverage when there was still time to make a play. Second, as the season went on, opposing defenses were more able to attack the pocket because New Orleans wasn't running the ball consistently, and everyone knew it. By the end of the season, Brees was relegated to playing in a spread offense, throwing little check-downs on three-step drops to stay alive. Brees rebounded to play well down the stretch, but his league-leading 652 pass attempts and NFL-record 440 completions tell you all you need to know about the team's offensive balance.

Brian Brohm

Height: 6-3 Weight: 227 College: Louisville   Draft: 2008/2 (56) Born: 23-Sep-1985 Age: 23 Risk: Red

Year	Team	G	Att	Comp	C%	Yds	TD	INT	FUM	ASR	NY/P	Rk	DVOA	Rk	DYAR	Rk	YAR	Runs	Yds	TD	DVOA	DYAR
2008	GB		499	298	59.8%	3634	25	13			6.4		14.8%					34	21	1	-8.0%	

Brohm spent the 2007 season traveling up and down various draft boards with Chad Henne and Joe Flacco as the Guys Behind Matt Ryan in the 2008 quarterback draft class. Had he declared for the NFL after his junior year, Brohm would have been an elite prospect. However, injuries and a coaching and scheme change (mark Brohm down as possibly the only football player ever negatively affected by Bobby Petrino's departure from anywhere) facilitated a drop to the middle second round, which is where the Packers got him. Brohm has the intelligence and a variety of short-to-midrange throws that are perfect for Green Bay's offense. If he shows no lingering effects from a fairly extensive list of collegiate injuries, he could start to push Aaron Rodgers right away.

Mark Brunell

Height: 6-1 Weight: 217 College: Washington   Draft: 1993/5 (118) Born: 17-Sep-1970 Age: 38 Risk: Red

Year	Team	G	Att	Comp	C%	Yds	TD	INT	FUM	ASR	NY/P	Rk	DVOA	Rk	DYAR	Rk	YAR	Runs	Yds	TD	DVOA	DYAR
2005	WAS	16	454	262	57.7%	3050	23	10	10	6.6%	6.0	21	4.9%	18	494	14	484	42	111	0	-27.7%	-23
2006	WAS	10	260	162	62.3%	1789	8	4	4	5.5%	6.5	16	10.5%	12	363	16	344	13	34	0	-52.0%	-19
2008	NO		471	283	60.2%	3285	15	20			5.6		-14.7%					15	33	1	-19.3%	
2006:	54% Short	26% Mid	13% Deep	7% Bomb	YAC: 6.1 (4)																	

Brunell is now the veteran insurance policy in New Orleans. When we last saw him (at the end of 2006), he was a rickety junkballer performing a smoke-and-mirrors routine in the Redskins' screen-and-hitch heavy offense. He could do the same if called upon in New Orleans: Sean Payton's system is full of spread formations and short passes. The original backup to Brett Farve needs 399 yards to pass Sonny Jurgenson for 25th on the all-time passing yardage list. Although pursued by other teams that had a greater potential for him to see action (including Green Bay and Atlanta), he announced to all his "friends" on his MySpace page that he signed with New Orleans. I LMAO when my BFF Mike txt me the 411. Aren't there laws against 37-year-old quarterbacks having MySpace pages? Due to his lack of deep accuracy or footspeed, he's unlikely to get past Sonny unless Drew Brees were to get hurt, and even then he'd be most effective in one or two spot starts, not for a large chunk of the season.

Marc Bulger

Height: 6-3 Weight: 215 College: West Virginia   Draft: 2000/6 (168) Born: 5-Apr-1977 Age: 31 Risk: Green

Year	Team	G	Att	Comp	C%	Yds	TD	INT	FUM	ASR	NY/P	Rk	DVOA	Rk	DYAR	Rk	YAR	Runs	Yds	TD	DVOA	DYAR
2005	STL	8	287	192	66.9%	2297	14	9	4	8.4%	6.7	9	13.0%	10	477	16	592	9	29	0	-30.5%	-6
2006	STL	16	588	370	62.9%	4301	24	8	8	8.0%	6.8	11	16.6%	11	1140	4	1274	18	44	0	12.4%	12
2007	STL	12	378	221	58.5%	2392	11	15	5	9.4%	5.2	41	-16.5%	40	-142	42	-81	9	13	0	78.6%	9
2008	STL		502	303	60.4%	3345	26	21			6.0		-6.9%					22	77	1	-2.5%	
2007:	43% Short	34% Mid	17% Deep	6% Bomb	YAC: 3.7 (46)			2006:	50% Short	26% Mid	16% Deep	8% Bomb	YAC: 4.8 (25)								

"We want to just start clean, not look back," Marc Bulger said during May minicamp. While everyone in St. Louis probably echoes those sentiments, nobody else can feel more passionate about them then Bulger. As the blockers in front of him went snap, crackle, and pop game after game, Bulger found himself violently hitting the ground over and over again. All told, combining sacks and quarterback hits, Bulger was knocked down 56 times in 12 games last season; if he had somehow managed to withstand that kind of beating for 16 games, he would have been knocked down about 75 times, which would have been second in the league behind Jon Kitna. Few quarterbacks can survive that sort of abuse, and Bulger is not one of them, having played all 16 games just once in his career. As long as he is given protection, he's still an effective quarterback, but heavy pressure causes him to make mistakes, leading to interceptions.

Jason Campbell

Height: 6-4   Weight: 223   College: Auburn   Draft: 2005/1 (25)   Born: 31-Dec-1981   Age: 26   Risk: Red

Year	Team	G	Att	Comp	C%	Yds	TD	INT	FUM	ASR	NY/P	Rk	DVOA	Rk	DYAR	Rk	YAR	Runs	Yds	TD	DVOA	DYAR
2006	WAS	7	207	110	53.1%	1297	10	6	4	3.3%	6.0	32	-0.7%	17	141	21	159	24	107	0	23.0%	29
2007	WAS	13	417	250	60.0%	2700	12	11	11	4.7%	6.0	25	4.4%	22	433	17	344	36	185	1	-12.3%	0
2008	WAS		530	321	60.6%	3496	19	20			5.6		-12.0%					28	102	0	-6.3%	

2007: 49% Short   30% Mid   13% Deep   9% Bomb   YAC: 4.7 (24)   2006: 42% Short   32% Mid   14% Deep   12% Bomb   YAC: 5.1 (15)

Campbell put up promising numbers in his sophomore year, statistics that would have looked even better had Santana Moss been something more than a shadow of the player he was in 2006. The Auburn grad is the prototypical quarterback, with consistent mechanics, a high release point that allows the ball to get up over even the tallest lineman, and excellent footwork that improves his timing and accuracy. The bad news is that Campbell must master yet another offensive system in 2008, as Jim Zorn brings the West Coast Offense to the nation's capital. His skill set is a great fit for the system; if Malcolm Kelly or Devin Thomas can emerge as a possession receiver to play alongside Moss and Antwaan Randle El, Campbell could finally emerge as a star this season.

David Carr

Height: 6-3   Weight: 223   College: Fresno State   Draft: 2002/1 (1)   Born: 21-Jul-1979   Age: 29   Risk: Red

Year	Team	G	Att	Comp	C%	Yds	TD	INT	FUM	ASR	NY/P	Rk	DVOA	Rk	DYAR	Rk	YAR	Runs	Yds	TD	DVOA	DYAR
2005	HOU	16	423	256	60.5%	2488	14	11	18	13.6%	4.3	45	-29.6%	39	-575	44	-606	56	308	1	4.7%	43
2006	HOU	16	442	302	68.3%	2767	11	12	14	9.6%	5.7	38	-8.6%	28	81	26	-50	54	193	2	-3.0%	20
2007	CAR	6	136	73	53.7%	635	3	5	1	8.7%	3.8	51	-29.1%	47	-171	44	-221	17	59	0	-9.9%	2
2008	NYG		468	273	58.3%	3025	18	14			5.3		-10.2%					61	117	1	12.6%	

2007: 52% Short   27% Mid   10% Deep   10% Bomb   YAC: 3.9 (44)   2006: 62% Short   26% Mid   7% Deep   5% Bomb   YAC: 4.8 (20)

David Carr was asked in the spring of 2008 why his 2007 season went so wrong. "I don't know, man," he said. "I don't worry about things like that. If I tried to do that, I'd be a mess. You just enjoy it, that's what it's all about. That's what I learned two or three years ago; if you get bummed out after every game, let it fester inside you and you don't enjoy the opportunity you've been given, then you're going to look back on it and be angry that you didn't take advantage of what you had, and smile enough and enjoy the game. We're definitely blessed to be in the position we're in. So just enjoy what you got and go on." That's the kind of gutsy, inspiring leadership that will endear Carr to his new Giants teammates. Carr is clearly in the advanced stages of PTBD (Post-Traumatic Blitz Disorder) after getting beaten to a pulp in his first few seasons, and it continued to afflict him in Carolina—Carr had an Adjusted Sack Rate of 8.7 percent compared to 5.5 percent for the other three Panthers quarterbacks combined.

Matt Cassel

Height: 6-4   Weight: 232   College: USC   Draft: 2005/7 (230)   Born: 17-May-1982   Age: 26   Risk: Red

Year	Team	G	Att	Comp	C%	Yds	TD	INT	FUM	ASR	NY/P	Rk	DVOA	Rk	DYAR	Rk	YAR	Runs	Yds	TD	DVOA	DYAR
2005	NE	3	24	13	54.2%	183	2	1	3	2.2%	7.6	—	-1.6%	—	16	—	15	6	12	0	17.4%	8
2006	NE	6	8	5	62.5%	32	0	0	1	27.2%	1.4	—	-90.4%	—	-52	—	-49	2	4	0	20.1%	3
2007	NE	6	7	4	57.1%	38	0	1	0	1.2%	5.4	—	-80.6%	—	-35	—	-35	4	12	1	99.9%	15
2008	NE		478	299	62.5%	3751	27	23			7.5		17.0%					32	71	1	-31.8%	

2007: 71% Short   29% Mid   0% Deep   0% Bomb   YAC: 4.0 (—)   2006: 83% Short   17% Mid   0% Deep   0% Bomb   YAC: 5.0 (—)

The scouting report on Rusher McFumbles hasn't changed: great size, great wheels, knows the system, works cheap. Patriots coaches have exactly zero confidence in him, which is why they hired Vinny Testaverde to caddie for Tom Brady two years ago and allowed Cassel into the game only when the Patriots held 35-point leads last year (then took him out when he turned the ball over). Kevin O'Connell is younger and has more upside, while Matt Gutierrez can do everything Cassel does for the same low, low price. Of course, if Cassel is released, some team might sign him just to learn some sensitive Belichick secrets. Matt: If you see a pinpoint of red light hovering over a vital organ, duck.

Kellen Clemens

Height: 6-2 Weight: 215 College: Oregon   Draft: 2006/2 (49) Born: 6-Jun-1983 Age: 25 Risk: Red

Year	Team	G	Att	Comp	C%	Yds	TD	INT	FUM	ASR	NY/P	Rk	DVOA	Rk	DYAR	Rk	YAR	Runs	Yds	TD	DVOA	DYAR
2006	NYJ	2	1	0	0.0%	0	0	0	1	79.2%	-5.4	—	-99.9%	—	-80	—	-85	2	10	0	-23.4%	-1
2007	NYJ	10	250	130	52.0%	1529	5	10	6	9.6%	5.1	42	-18.9%	42	-136	41	-183	27	111	1	-1.0%	16
2008	NYJ		454	262	57.7%	3099	20	17			6.1		-25.2%					45	178	2	0.2%	
2007:	43% Short	35% Mid	14% Deep	7% Bomb	YAC: 5.1 (15)																	

Clemens was awful in the red zone last season: 13-of-33 (39 percent) for 105 yards, five touchdowns but two interceptions, a DVOA of -62.4%. The red zone can be a rough place for an experienced passer with no go-to possession receiver, no running game, and a bad offensive line. Clemens will get better with experience and with the changes the Jets made, and a few more positive plays near the goal line will go a long way toward turning the offense around. This all assumes that Clemens will get the opportunity to improve: Chad Pennington is still on the roster, and veteran quarterbacks have a way of looking appealing to hot seat coaches in July and August.

Kerry Collins

Height: 6-5 Weight: 240 College: Penn State   Draft: 1995/1 (5) Born: 30-Dec-1972 Age: 35 Risk: Red

Year	Team	G	Att	Comp	C%	Yds	TD	INT	FUM	ASR	NY/P	Rk	DVOA	Rk	DYAR	Rk	YAR	Runs	Yds	TD	DVOA	DYAR
2005	OAK	15	565	302	53.5%	3759	20	12	13	7.2%	5.8	24	-2.0%	22	348	20	320	18	38	1	19.7%	15
2006	TEN	4	90	42	46.7%	549	1	6	0	4.0%	5.9	—	-45.8%	—	-205	—	-201	0	0	0	—	—
2007	TEN	6	82	50	61.0%	531	0	0	1	6.2%	5.7	—	15.3%	—	148	—	170	3	-3	0	—	—
2008	TEN		409	244	59.6%	2504	12	16			4.8		-20.5%					20	24	1	-0.1%	
2007:	54% Short	25% Mid	11% Deep	11% Bomb	YAC: 4.3 (—)			2006:	44% Short	31% Mid	17% Deep	9% Bomb	YAC: 5.1 (—)									

Kerry Collins was better than Vince Young in 2007. A lot better. He was better on first down (0.8% compared to -3.3% DVOA), better on second down (26.2% to -5.2%), and better on third down (65.5% to -13.6%). If Collins had just been a little bit better we could write it off as no big deal that the trusty old veteran outplayed the flashy youngster, but when the backup played a lot better in limited action during the season, and when the team lost a playoff game in which the starter played badly, it does create a problem. No, there's no quarterback controversy in Tennessee, but if the Titans lose games early in the season and Young plays badly, there could be one.

Todd Collins

Height: 6-4 Weight: 219 College: Michigan   Draft: 1995/2 (45) Born: 5-Nov-1971 Age: 37 Risk: Red

Year	Team	G	Att	Comp	C%	Yds	TD	INT	FUM	ASR	NY/P	Rk	DVOA	Rk	DYAR	Rk	YAR	Runs	Yds	TD	DVOA	DYAR
2007	WAS	4	105	67	63.8%	888	5	0	4	5.8%	7.6	2	31.6%	4	311	20	288	8	1	0	19.4%	4
2008	WAS		476	272	57.2%	2885	17	20			5.1		-22.1%					13	33	0	-25.3%	
2007:	50% Short	28% Mid	15% Deep	7% Bomb	YAC: 5.4 (6)																	

Walpole's own Todd Collins stepped in with three-and-a-half superb games after Jason Campbell went down with an injury, winning four straight games to propel the Redskins into the playoffs. Although Collins's DVOA for the four-game stretch was fantastic, the winning streak had more to do with the Redskins' defensive performance: The team went from giving up 21.4 points through their first 12 games to 13.3 points in their final four. Collins, meanwhile, threw no interceptions in 105 attempts, a nifty trick that most backup quarterbacks can't keep going for very long. Sure enough, when Collins went up against the Seahawks in the playoffs, he threw two picks in 50 attempts and looked more like a career backup than a season savior. Collins is now 36; there's every reason to believe that last season was his big send-off.

Brodie Croyle

Height: 6-3 Weight: 205 College: Alabama   Draft: 2006/3 (85) Born: 6-Feb-1983 Age: 25 Risk: Red

Year	Team	G	Att	Comp	C%	Yds	TD	INT	FUM	ASR	NY/P	Rk	DVOA	Rk	DYAR	Rk	YAR	Runs	Yds	TD	DVOA	DYAR
2006	KC	2	7	3	42.9%	23	0	2	1	12.8%	1.6	—	-99.9%	—	-70	—	-71	3	-3	0	—	—
2007	KC	9	224	127	56.7%	1227	6	6	6	7.5%	4.7	47	-18.5%	41	-111	40	-164	7	18	0	-38.5%	-7
2008	KC		522	305	58.4%	2990	22	18			5.2		-23.9%					53	106	3	-5.9%	
2007:	50% Short	33% Mid	11% Deep	6% Bomb	YAC: 4.1 (37)			2006:	14% Short	71% Mid	0% Deep	14% Bomb	YAC: 0.0 (—)									

The most important attribute of a quarterback coming out of college is accuracy. Teams will often overlook second-rate accuracy if the prospect has a cannon arm. With Croyle, the Chiefs overlooked both accuracy and arm strength in favor of moxie. He seems like a tough guy, but when he is throwing wildly and not threatening teams down the field, all the moxie in the world does not help. It is too soon to give up completely on Croyle, and his weak supporting cast must be acknowledged. Still, any assertion that Croyle is going to be great is simply wishing at this point. Most troubling is that Croyle did not appear to improve throughout the season. He has one year to show some talent, or he will go the way of Charlie Frye.

Daunte Culpepper

Height: 6-4 Weight: 264 College: UCF Draft: 1999/1 (11) Born: 28-Jan-1977 Age: 31 Risk: Red

Year	Team	G	Att	Comp	C%	Yds	TD	INT	FUM	ASR	NY/P	Rk	DVOA	Rk	DYAR	Rk	YAR	Runs	Yds	TD	DVOA	DYAR
2005	MIN	7	216	139	64.4%	1564	6	12	5	13.5%	5.7	29	-25.6%	37	-224	40	-265	23	148	1	38.0%	53
2006	MIA	4	134	81	60.4%	929	2	3	3	14.1%	5.9	34	-23.1%	40	-109	36	-77	10	20	1	-8.1%	2
2007	OAK	7	186	108	58.1%	1331	5	5	6	10.4%	5.9	31	-4.9%	27	76	27	-4	20	40	3	-11.9%	0

2007: 49% Short 30% Mid 13% Deep 8% Bomb YAC: 5.0 (16)   2006: 53% Short 29% Mid 11% Deep 7% Bomb YAC: 6.7 (2)

No country for broken men. Daunte Culpepper is a man without a team and has not been the same since his 2005 knee injuries. When talks between New England and Randy Moss stalled, Moss made some noise by talking about the possibility of reuniting with his former quarterback, but the concept ignored one concrete fact: No team is looking to Culpepper to be anything but a backup.

Jay Cutler

Height: 6-4 Weight: 225 College: Vanderbilt Draft: 2006/1 (11) Born: 29-Apr-1983 Age: 25 Risk: Yellow

Year	Team	G	Att	Comp	C%	Yds	TD	INT	FUM	ASR	NY/P	Rk	DVOA	Rk	DYAR	Rk	YAR	Runs	Yds	TD	DVOA	DYAR
2006	DEN	5	137	81	59.1%	1001	9	5	5	7.8%	6.7	13	-12.8%	33	-16	33	68	12	18	0	-159.0%	-65
2007	DEN	16	467	297	63.6%	3497	20	14	7	5.5%	6.8	12	19.4%	11	972	8	809	44	205	1	9.3%	38
2008	DEN		468	296	63.1%	3140	24	20			6.0		0.5%					40	154	3	9.4%	

2007: 45% Short 37% Mid 12% Deep 6% Bomb YAC: 5.2 (9)   2006: 34% Short 40% Mid 11% Deep 15% Bomb YAC: 4.7 (27)

Cutler took enormous steps forward in his second season. Without much help from the running game, Cutler engineered a short passing attack largely featuring Brandon Marshall. As a result, his completion percentage went up while his sack rate went down. Cutler is often compared to Brett Favre (not in these pages, mind you), and sometimes he buys into the gunslinger mentality too much. He will force passes if no one is open and he will occasionally completely misread coverage. His projection is off in part due to concerns about Marshall and an uncertain offensive line situation. He will likely be a better player in 2008, but his stats may hold steady as the players around him struggle.

Jake Delhomme

Height: 6-2 Weight: 205 College: Louisiana-Lafayette Draft: 1998/FA Born: 10-Jan-1975 Age: 33 Risk: Yellow

Year	Team	G	Att	Comp	C%	Yds	TD	INT	FUM	ASR	NY/P	Rk	DVOA	Rk	DYAR	Rk	YAR	Runs	Yds	TD	DVOA	DYAR
2005	CAR	16	435	262	60.2%	3421	24	16	14	5.8%	7.0	7	8.1%	14	583	11	560	24	31	1	-38.4%	-14
2006	CAR	13	431	263	61.0%	2805	17	11	6	5.8%	6.1	28	-0.9%	18	303	18	416	18	12	0	9.0%	4
2007	CAR	3	86	55	64.0%	624	8	1	1	6.6%	6.5	—	17.7%	—	175	—	249	6	26	0	-4.9%	2
2008	CAR		503	315	62.7%	3640	22	14			6.5		15.3%					40	86	0	-14.8%	

2007: 49% Short 36% Mid 6% Deep 9% Bomb YAC: 5.7 (—)   2006: 46% Short 32% Mid 14% Deep 8% Bomb YAC: 4.7 (26)

It was fun while it lasted. In Carolina's first three games, Delhomme passed for eight touchdowns and only one interception, putting up a DYAR of 175 that was by far the best among quarterbacks below 100 passes in 2007. But his season-ending elbow injury, suffered in the third quarter of a Week 3 win over the Falcons, sent the Panthers on a merry-go-round of quarterbacks that doomed the offense. If he fully recovers from Tommy John surgery, Delhomme has all the ingredients for a great season. He still has Steve Smith, free agent D. J. Hackett provides an explosive (if injury-prone) target, and Carolina's commitment to a power running game should divert the attention of enemy defenses. Should Delhomme's season be scuttled by injury or inconsistency, Matt Moore is now in the picture, which makes Delhomme's incumbent status less than airtight.

Trent Dilfer

Height: 6-4 Weight: 225 College: Fresno State   Draft: 1994/1 (6) Born: 13-Mar-1972 Age: 36 Risk: Red

Year	Team	G	Att	Comp	C%	Yds	TD	INT	FUM	ASR	NY/P	Rk	DVOA	Rk	DYAR	Rk	YAR	Runs	Yds	TD	DVOA	DYAR
2005	CLE	11	333	199	59.8%	2321	11	12	7	6.4%	6.1	18	-7.3%	26	89	25	73	20	46	0	-86.9%	-44
2007	SF	7	219	113	51.6%	1166	7	12	6	10.8%	4.1	49	-52.2%	51	-632	51	-612	10	25	0	-98.6%	-22

2007: 50% Short 26% Mid 16% Deep 9% Bomb   YAC: 4.4 (33)

There's a good chance Dilfer will retire. If he is hired, it will probably be more as a coach than a player, possibly for the Raiders, who were expressing interest in Dilfer at press time. Dilfer is known as a great caddie for young quarterbacks, so he might make a support system for JaMarcus Russell. Of course, we said the same thing when he backed up Alex Smith.

Trent Edwards

Height: 6-4 Weight: 231 College: Stanford   Draft: 2007/3 (92) Born: 30-Oct-1983 Age: 25 Risk: Green

Year	Team	G	Att	Comp	C%	Yds	TD	INT	FUM	ASR	NY/P	Rk	DVOA	Rk	DYAR	Rk	YAR	Runs	Yds	TD	DVOA	DYAR
2007	BUF	10	269	151	56.1%	1630	7	8	4	4.1%	5.5	35	-7.8%	30	57	31	42	14	49	0	11.3%	12
2008	BUF		450	269	59.8%	2730	20	18			5.5		-5.6%					32	119	1	4.9%	

2007: 53% Short 31% Mid 9% Deep 7% Bomb   YAC: 5.4 (5)

Edwards's awful three-game stretch to end the season (42.7 completion percentage, two touchdowns, three picks, -178 DYAR) can be interpreted in several ways. One, the league figured out Edwards's dink-and-dunk style after watching seven full games of film. Two, in late December, the weather was bad and the opponents (the Browns, Giants, and Eagles) were better and highly motivated. Three, a combination of one and two. DVOA liked Losman better than Edwards, but the difference is small and the Bills were wise to pick a rookie who played like a rookie over a fourth-year veteran who played like a rookie. Edwards's inability to throw deep has been exaggerated; he's no Losman, but he's no Charlie Frye either.

Brett Favre

Height: 6-2 Weight: 225 College: SMU   Draft: 1991/2 (33) Born: 10-Oct-1969 Age: 39 Risk: Green

Year	Team	G	Att	Comp	C%	Yds	TD	INT	FUM	ASR	NY/P	Rk	DVOA	Rk	DYAR	Rk	YAR	Runs	Yds	TD	DVOA	DYAR
2005	GB	16	607	372	61.3%	3881	20	29	9	4.7%	5.9	22	3.2%	19	590	10	476	18	62	0	-22.9%	-5
2006	GB	16	613	343	56.0%	3885	18	18	7	3.5%	6.1	26	-1.2%	19	406	14	479	23	29	1	-55.4%	-24
2007	GB	16	535	356	66.5%	4155	28	15	8	2.7%	7.5	3	28.0%	5	1438	3	1457	29	12	0	-61.3%	-26
2008	GB?		492	317	64.4%	4032	22	13			7.5		23.6%					20	38	0	-31.2%	

2007: 54% Short 30% Mid 8% Deep 8% Bomb   YAC: 5.7 (1)   2006: 50% Short 30% Mid 11% Deep 9% Bomb   YAC: 5.9 (5)

In zombie movies, the teenager heroes always think the zombie is dead so they turn their backs on the zombie, who rises from the grave to impale them on sharp farm tools. We're smarter than the teenagers in zombie movies, so we won't turn our backs on Favre until he's safely beyond the Michael Jordan Wizards age for a comeback. The KUBIAK projection is based on a return to the Packers; you'll have to check FootballOutsiders.com for more accurate data if Favre is on the Bears or Vikings by August. We hope Favre will find something better to do with his time than play golf and generate comeback rumors. Favre's BFF Peter King suggested a tour of Iraq and Afghanistan, which would certainly be a worthy endeavor. Favre could also do some good here at home: Now that he and Steve McNair are retired, they could do a lot to help families and towns that are still battling back from Hurricane Katrina. Let's hope Favre does something fulfilling and exciting, even if it means a return to the gridiron. Seeing him on a set next to Marshall Faulk and Jamie Dukes would seem unsettling.

A. J. Feeley

Height: 6-3 Weight: 225 College: Oregon   Draft: 2001/5 (155) Born: 16-May-1977 Age: 31 Risk: Orange

Year	Team	G	Att	Comp	C%	Yds	TD	INT	FUM	ASR	NY/P	Rk	DVOA	Rk	DYAR	Rk	YAR	Runs	Yds	TD	DVOA	DYAR
2006	PHI	2	38	26	68.4%	342	3	0	1	5.1%	8.8	—	50.7%	—	153	—	152	1	3	0	-102.5%	-5
2007	PHI	3	103	59	57.3%	681	5	8	1	1.5%	6.3	18	-15.6%	39	-31	36	-64	7	23	0	-11.6%	0
2008	PHI		456	281	61.6%	3240	23	16			6.6		7.0%					23	16	0	-15.2%	

2007: 39% Short 31% Mid 22% Deep 8% Bomb   YAC: 4.1 (40)   2006: 80% Short 20% Mid 0% Deep 0% Bomb   YAC: 4.0 (—)

From about 10 PM on November 25 to about 3:30 PM on December 2, Feeley was popular enough to run for mayor in Philadelphia. You can't find a single Eagles fan today who argued that Feeley was better than McNabb in those days between his three-touchdown heroics against the Patriots and his four-pick meltdown against Seattle, but you couldn't mention the Eagles that week without hearing the conversation. Feeley now goes from folk hero to third-stringer. The downward spiral for forgotten Philadelphia cult heroes isn't pretty—go read an article about Darren Daulton if you want to see what Feeley's future looks like.

Ryan Fitzpatrick

Height: 6-2   Weight: 221   College: Harvard   Draft: 2005/7 (250)   Born: 24-Nov-1982   Age: 26   Risk: Red

Year	Team	G	Att	Comp	C%	Yds	TD	INT	FUM	ASR	NY/P	Rk	DVOA	Rk	DYAR	Rk	YAR	Runs	Yds	TD	DVOA	DYAR
2005	STL	4	135	76	56.3%	777	4	8	2	6.8%	5.1	39	-20.1%	36	-83	32	-58	14	64	2	-2.0%	7
2008	CIN		489	299	61.1%	3499	19	15			5.9		-2.1%					37	111	1	-0.4%	

After watching Doug Johnson complete just half of his passes last preseason with two touchdowns and four interceptions, Marvin Lewis decided he needed a better backup and sent a seventh-round pick to St. Louis for Fitzpatrick. Fitzpatrick hasn't thrown a pass since his rookie year, but preseason stats suggest that he's still a runner (150 yards on 31 exhibition attempts) who throws a pass once in a while for variety.

Joe Flacco

Height: 6-7   Weight: 236   College: Delaware   Draft: 2008/1 (18)   Born: 16-Jan-1985   Age: 23   Risk: Red

Year	Team	G	Att	Comp	C%	Yds	TD	INT	FUM	ASR	NY/P	Rk	DVOA	Rk	DYAR	Rk	YAR	Runs	Yds	TD	DVOA	DYAR
2008	BAL		464	281	60.7%	2729	10	15			5.8		-16.5%					16	42	1	31.8%	

Flacco started his college career at Pitt, but he was trapped behind Tyler Palko and played just one series before transferring to Delaware, where he slowly climbed onto the national radar thanks to his size and his cannon arm. He already has one of the strongest arms in the NFL, and he has the athleticism and the work habits to succeed. It will take a while, though: Flacco played in a shotgun offense against I-AA competition, and his footwork and decision-making need work. ESPN's Ron Jaworski broke down tape of Flacco failing to identify a Villanova zone blitz, and the blitzes will only be faster and more complex when the Steelers come to town. Still, rookie camp reports were encouraging, and Flacco may supplant Kyle Boller or Troy Smith by season's end. He's a stronger-armed version of Derek Anderson, who was drafted by the Ravens in 2005. Here's guessing that the team gives Flacco a little more time to develop.

Gus Frerotte

Height: 6-3   Weight: 225   College: Tulsa   Draft: 1994/7 (197)   Born: 3-Jul-1971   Age: 37   Risk: Orange

Year	Team	G	Att	Comp	C%	Yds	TD	INT	FUM	ASR	NY/P	Rk	DVOA	Rk	DYAR	Rk	YAR	Runs	Yds	TD	DVOA	DYAR
2005	MIA	16	494	257	52.0%	2996	18	13	10	5.3%	5.5	31	-9.1%	27	67	27	170	27	61	0	2.5%	12
2006	STL	1	3	1	33.3%	27	0	0	1	0.7%	9.0	—	3.4%	—	3	—	7	0	0	0	—	—
2007	STL	8	167	94	56.3%	1014	7	12	2	6.2%	5.4	36	-26.2%	45	-176	45	-141	6	3	0	-53.2%	-13
2008	MIN		423	260	61.4%	2780	8	14			5.4		-12.9%					13	3	0	-12.6%	

2007:	39% Short	40% Mid	14% Deep	7% Bomb	YAC: 3.6 (48)		2006:	0% Short	0% Mid	50% Deep	50% Bomb	YAC: 7.0 (—)

It's easy to forget how long Frerotte has been playing, or how successful he's been at times. As recently as 2005, he was starting quarterback for a Miami Dolphins team that went 9-7, throwing 18 touchdowns and only 13 interceptions. (Fumbles and an easy schedule pushed his DVOA down to -11.0%.) For 15 seasons, Frerotte has bounced in and out of the lineups of seven different teams and in the process has thrown for more yards than former Rams teammate Marc Bulger. (Bulger should make up the 509 yards separating the two sometime in September.) Now Frerotte finds himself in Minnesota for a second tour of duty. The Vikings think that Frerotte's mentorship had a lot to do with Daunte Culpepper's success, and they hope he can have the same affect on Tarvaris Jackson. "I know Tarvaris is young and has a lot of raw ability," Frerotte said to the *St. Paul Pioneer Press*. "Hopefully, I can come in and, if he's willing, I can give him ideas, and hopefully he'll listen." In the same interview, he said that the best game of his life came in 2001, when he threw five touchdowns to lead the Denver Broncos to a comeback win over San Diego. On the downside, the Chargers built their big lead due in part to Frerotte's four interceptions.

Charlie Frye

Height: 6-4 Weight: 217 College: Akron Draft: 2005/3 (67) Born: 28-Aug-1981 Age: 27 Risk: Orange

Year	Team	G	Att	Comp	C%	Yds	TD	INT	FUM	ASR	NY/P	Rk	DVOA	Rk	DYAR	Rk	YAR	Runs	Yds	TD	DVOA	DYAR
2005	CLE	7	164	98	59.8%	1002	4	6	6	10.7%	4.8	40	-19.3%	35	-94	34	-143	18	60	1	-6.9%	4
2006	CLE	14	392	252	64.3%	2454	10	17	7	9.8%	5.6	39	-18.7%	37	-215	41	-245	47	215	3	6.7%	42
2007	CLE	1	10	4	40.0%	34	0	1	0	32.8%	0.2	—	-123.0%	—	-105	—	-121	1	1	0	-92.4%	-3
2008	SEA		451	267	59.1%	2948	8	25			4.9		-33.7%					27	254	0	11.0%	

2007: 60% Short 40% Mid 0% Deep 0% Bomb YAC: 2.8 (—) 2006: 50% Short 34% Mid 8% Deep 8% Bomb YAC: 4.5 (31)

It took just one week for Frye to go from the Browns starting lineup to third on the Seahawks depth chart. Mike Holmgren loves reclamation projects, and he'll tinker with Frye in camp, give him lots of third-quarter action in August, say nice things about him, and then cut him. Frye's the answer to a question no one ever asked: How far could a quarterback go if he had everything—speed, size, intangibles—except a decent arm? The limit is probably 19 starts and 14 touchdowns.

Jeff Garcia

Height: 6-1 Weight: 195 College: San Jose State Draft: 1999/FA Born: 24-Feb-1970 Age: 38 Risk: Yellow

Year	Team	G	Att	Comp	C%	Yds	TD	INT	FUM	ASR	NY/P	Rk	DVOA	Rk	DYAR	Rk	YAR	Runs	Yds	TD	DVOA	DYAR
2005	DET	6	173	102	59.0%	937	3	6	2	4.6%	5.1	38	-13.6%	31	-29	31	-37	17	51	1	-10.9%	1
2006	PHI	8	188	116	61.7%	1309	10	2	6	4.2%	6.8	12	17.4%	9	359	17	365	25	87	0	6.2%	17
2007	TB	13	327	209	63.9%	2440	13	4	3	6.2%	6.9	10	19.5%	10	694	13	746	35	116	1	1.0%	17
2008	TB		487	299	61.4%	3582	23	11			6.6		20.1%					38	94	1	-10.1%	

2007: 53% Short 29% Mid 10% Deep 8% Bomb YAC: 5.5 (3) 2006: 50% Short 28% Mid 12% Deep 10% Bomb YAC: 3.9 (41)

The 2007 version of Garcia could be likened to a Geo Metro, souped-up just enough to compete in a version of the Indy 500 that turned into a demolition derby every 50 miles. It was a battle for survival from start to finish, as Tampa Bay ranked third in quarterback knockdowns (hits plus sacks) per pass attempt. In Garcia's first game in Tampa Bay, he was knocked out by Seahawks linebackers Julian Peterson and Leroy Hill on an "Upstairs, Downstairs" hit, and he was attacked mercilessly by the Giants' spectacular front four in the wild card loss that ended Tampa Bay's season. In between, behind the youngest offensive line in the NFL and throwing to one legitimate target in Joey Galloway, Garcia made the best of what he was given. He missed two straight midseason games with a back contusion (another consequence of his risk-reward style), but he also gave Tampa Bay the kind of leadership at quarterback not seen since the (sort of) halcyon days of Brad Johnson. Garcia fits what Jon Gruden wants in a quarterback—he's been playing in variations of the West Coast Offense long enough to know exactly what Gruden means when he says, "West Left Slot, Fox Three Wide, Bingo Z Smash on One," when less experienced quarterbacks have trouble reciting Gruden's verbiage, much less executing it. Garcia will do it again in 2008, and he'll most likely exceed expectations just as he has throughout his career.

David Garrard

Height: 6-1 Weight: 238 College: East Carolina Draft: 2002/4 (108) Born: 14-Feb-1978 Age: 30 Risk: Yellow

Year	Team	G	Att	Comp	C%	Yds	TD	INT	FUM	ASR	NY/P	Rk	DVOA	Rk	DYAR	Rk	YAR	Runs	Yds	TD	DVOA	DYAR
2005	JAC	8	168	98	58.3%	1117	4	1	4	4.6%	6.1	20	11.9%	11	265	21	362	31	172	3	32.3%	58
2006	JAC	11	241	145	60.2%	1735	10	9	6	8.3%	6.6	15	-4.8%	24	107	23	108	47	250	0	17.0%	56
2007	JAC	12	325	208	64.0%	2509	18	3	7	6.9%	7.0	8	37.4%	3	1086	7	986	5	-5	0	13.3%	58
2008	JAC		473	290	61.3%	3898	23	13			7.3		29.1%					40	169	2	2.3%	

2007: 39% Short 40% Mid 15% Deep 6% Bomb YAC: 4.6 (25) 2006: 45% Short 32% Mid 13% Deep 10% Bomb YAC: 5.4 (7)

There may not be another player in the league who improved as much as David Garrard did a year ago. Now signed to a lucrative, long-term extension, he's the unquestioned leader of the Jacksonville offense and knocking on the door of elite status among NFL quarterbacks. To join that club, he'll have to do it for more than one year, but there's no reason to suspect he'll turn into a one-hit wonder—even if it's unlikely he'll repeat his three-interception performance of a year ago (see "Lowest Interception Rate" Table). Garrard's achievements were all that much more impressive due to the cast he had to work with at receiver, where Reggie Williams was the best of a below-average group. If Jerry Porter can continue his career resurrection (and the Jaguars bet a $30 million contract that he can),

Garrard should have more opportunities down the field than he did a year ago, giving him a chance to take advantage of his excellent accuracy.

Lowest Interception Rate Since 1978, Min. 200 Attempts

Player	Year	Team	Att	Int	Int/At	Int Next Year	Int/At Next Year
Damon Huard	2006	KC	244	1	0.4%	13	3.9%
Steve Deberg	1990	KC	444	4	0.9%	14	3.2%
David Garrard	2007	JAC	325	3	0.9%	—	—
Steve Bartkowski	1983	ATL	432	5	1.2%	10	3.7%
Neil O'Donnell	1998	CIN	343	4	1.2%	5	2.6%
Brian Griese	2000	DEN	336	4	1.2%	19	4.2%
Jeff Garcia	2007	TB	327	4	1.2%	—	—
Phil Simms	1990	NYG	311	4	1.3%	4	2.8%
Jim Harbaugh	1997	IND	309	4	1.3%	11	3.8%
Doug Flutie	2000	BUF	231	3	1.3%	18	3.5%
Brad Johnson	2002	TB	451	6	1.3%	21	3.7%
Brad Johnson	2005	MIN	294	4	1.4%	15	3.4%
Marc Bulger	2006	STL	588	8	1.4%	15	4.0%
Tom Brady	2007	NE	578	8	1.4%	—	—
Jeff Hostetler	1991	NYG	285	4	1.4%	3	1.6%

Bruce Gradkowski
Height: 6-2   Weight: 222   College: Toledo   Draft: 2006/6 (194)   Born: 27-Jan-1983   Age: 25   Risk: Red

Year	Team	G	Att	Comp	C%	Yds	TD	INT	FUM	ASR	NY/P	Rk	DVOA	Rk	DYAR	Rk	YAR	Runs	Yds	TD	DVOA	DYAR
2006	TB	14	328	177	54.0%	1661	9	9	11	7.5%	4.7	45	-31.5%	42	-451	44	-443	41	161	0	-6.1%	11
2007	TB	4	24	13	54.2%	130	0	1	0	12.8%	4.8	—	-30.2%	—	-30	—	-47	7	20	0	48.8%	6
2008	TB		480	291	60.5%	3186	14	13			5.7		-5.8%					43	127	0	-3.4%	

2007:   41% Short   36% Mid   18% Deep   5% Bomb   YAC: 2.9 (—)   2006:   55% Short   27% Mid   11% Deep   6% Bomb   YAC: 4.7 (28)

Pressed into service as a rookie after Chris Simms's spleenectomy in 2006, Gradkowski's inexperience was undeniable. Luke McCown beat him out for the second-string slot before the 2007 season, and Gradkowski couldn't move the team when he was given a chance during Garcia's absence. Tampa Bay is carrying enough quarterbacks for two teams this preseason, and Gradkowski could be on the way out.

Quinn Gray
Height: 6-3   Weight: 246   College: Florida A&M   Draft: 2002/FA   Born: 21-May-1979   Age: 29   Risk: Red

Year	Team	G	Att	Comp	C%	Yds	TD	INT	FUM	ASR	NY/P	Rk	DVOA	Rk	DYAR	Rk	YAR	Runs	Yds	TD	DVOA	DYAR
2005	JAC	1	14	8	57.1%	100	2	0	0	4.5%	6.1	—	25.8%	—	30	—	49	3	1	0	32.3%	4
2006	JAC	2	22	13	59.1%	166	0	0	0	4.7%	7.0	—	26.7%	—	50	—	60	2	26	2	206.8%	29
2007	JAC	8	144	80	55.6%	986	10	5	2	6.8%	6.0	26	20.9%	8	302	21	312	19	57	0	22.2%	20
2008	HOU		453	278	61.3%	3284	16	21			5.7		-14.8%					31	87	0	-13.5%	

2007:   36% Short   36% Mid   20% Deep   7% Bomb   YAC: 4.4 (34)

In last year's book, we described Gray as "a prospect with a good arm, good size, and some mobility." Gee, does that remind you of anyone, a former teammate of Gray's perhaps? Gray needs an extended opportunity to play before he can emulate Garrard's success in Jacksonville, which makes his signing in Houston somewhat odd. The Texans already have two quarterbacks with more established credentials on the roster, Matt Schaub and Sage Rosenfels. Then again, Garrard was once buried on the Jaguars depth chart.

Trent Green . Height: 6-3 Weight: 217 College: Indiana Draft: 1993/8 (222) Born: 9-Jul-1970 Age: 38 Risk: Red

Year	Team	G	Att	Comp	C%	Yds	TD	INT	FUM	ASR	NY/P	Rk	DVOA	Rk	DYAR	Rk	YAR	Runs	Yds	TD	DVOA	DYAR
2005	KC	16	507	317	62.5%	4014	17	10	8	6.6%	7.1	3	25.0%	7	1234	5	1263	35	82	0	-5.0%	8
2006	KC	8	198	121	61.1%	1342	7	9	4	9.6%	6.1	27	-2.5%	22	122	22	-15	19	59	0	-8.2%	2
2007	MIA	5	141	85	60.3%	987	5	7	2	5.5%	6.5	15	7.8%	19	174	22	123	7	32	0	-34.7%	-7
2008	STL		405	246	60.7%	2660	14	18			5.4		-22.1%					21	55	1	-24.7%	

2007: 46% Short 35% Mid 17% Deep 2% Bomb YAC: 5.4 (7) 2006: 42% Short 38% Mid 15% Deep 5% Bomb YAC: 4 (38)

Green spent the final weeks of last season working as a player-reporter for the NFL Network. We liked the handsome, articulate, well-coiffed Green much better than the guy we saw strapped to a stretcher after vicious hits in each of the last two seasons. We hope he'll spend all his time in St. Louis carrying a clipboard, gabbing with the offensive coordinator, and golfing with Marc Bulger. Green's skills were deteriorating before his first brush with the toe tag in 2006. There's not much left athletically and little to be gained backing up a veteran quarterback on a bad team. Spartans left the battlefield carrying their shields or carried on them. Green has other options and should explore them.

Brian Griese Height: 6-3 Weight: 215 College: Michigan Draft: 1998/3 (91) Born: 18-Mar-1975 Age: 33 Risk: Red

Year	Team	G	Att	Comp	C%	Yds	TD	INT	FUM	ASR	NY/P	Rk	DVOA	Rk	DYAR	Rk	YAR	Runs	Yds	TD	DVOA	DYAR
2005	TB	6	174	112	64.4%	1136	7	7	2	6.7%	5.7	26	-13.1%	30	-23	30	-4	13	12	0	-62.5%	-15
2006	CHI	6	32	18	56.3%	220	1	2	2	7.6%	6.2	—	-52.4%	—	-84	—	-87	6	-5	0	-254.9%	-12
2007	CHI	7	262	161	61.5%	1803	10	12	5	6.1%	6.2	21	-15.0%	37	-62	37	40	13	28	0	-3.7%	4
2008	TB		500	304	60.9%	3440	18	16			5.7		-2.8%					19	24	0	-18.8%	

2007: 52% Short 28% Mid 14% Deep 5% Bomb YAC: 5.6 (2) 2006: 50% Short 38% Mid 13% Deep 0% Bomb YAC: 2.9 (—)

After riding a quarterback carousel with Rex Grossman and Kyle Orton in Chicago, Griese returns to Tampa Bay to find quarterback bumper cars. Griese will compete with (deep inhale) Jeff Garcia, Chris Simms, Bruce Gradkowski, Luke McCown, and rookie Josh Johnson for practice snaps. Contract squabbles aside, Garcia will be the starter, and everything after that is up in the air. We're not even sure how the Bucs will find time to evaluate all these men. Perhaps Jon Gruden will get them all on the field at the same time and run a mutant version of the Stanford Band Play. Regardless, Griese's second tenure with the Bucs comes with an air of redemption. His last full season as a starter came in Tampa Bay in 2004, when he ranked 11th in DVOA, although the Bucs won only five games. The next season, Griese and the Bucs started 5-1, but he tore knee ligaments playing against the Dolphins and missed the rest of the year. The next offseason, Tampa Bay cut Griese and handed the starter's role to Simms rather than open a competition. "There's no doubt about it that I have unfinished business here," Griese told the *St. Petersburg Times*. "I felt very comfortable and never really wanted to leave here. I really wanted to be here, and so two years later, it's good to be back. I'm off my hiatus and ready to go back to work."

Rex Grossman Height: 6-1 Weight: 222 College: Florida Draft: 2003/1 (22) Born: 23-Aug-1980 Age: 28 Risk: Red

Year	Team	G	Att	Comp	C%	Yds	TD	INT	FUM	ASR	NY/P	Rk	DVOA	Rk	DYAR	Rk	YAR	Runs	Yds	TD	DVOA	DYAR
2005	CHI	2	39	20	51.3%	259	1	2	0	1.6%	6.3	—	-5.3%	—	14	—	20	0	0	0	—	—
2006	CHI	16	480	262	54.6%	3193	23	20	7	4.3%	6.4	21	-9.3%	29	59	29	212	24	2	0	15.4%	9
2007	CHI	8	225	122	54.2%	1411	4	7	5	8.9%	4.9	44	-21.8%	43	-168	43	-262	14	27	0	-28.2%	-7
2008	CHI		490	272	55.5%	3480	12	15			6.1		-5.1%					33	58	1	-1.4%	

2007: 45% Short 30% Mid 18% Deep 8% Bomb YAC: 4.6 (26) 2006: 42% Short 32% Mid 14% Deep 12% Bomb YAC: 4.8 (24)

Trent Dilfer is often touted as the worst quarterback to win a Super Bowl, but you rarely hear anyone argue about the worst quarterback to lose a Super Bowl. If Grossman can't turn his career around—and when coaches announce you'll have to beat out Kyle Orton to win your job, it's a bad sign—he'll likely be the answer to that question. Every quarterback to lose a Super Bowl has led their own team in passing yards for at least three seasons, with the three-timers being Vince Ferragamo, David Woodley, and Tony Eason. To this point, the Bears' 2006 Super Bowl run remains Grossman's only season as his team's leading passer. To avoid lying alone at the bottom of the barrel, he'll need to not only get through 2008 unscathed but be brought back as the team's starter in 2009 and beyond. That's not impossible, but at some point Chicago is going to wake up and fix the quarterback position.

Joey Harrington

Height: 6-4   Weight: 220   College: Oregon   Draft: 2002/1 (3)   Born: 21-Oct-1978   Age: 30   Risk: Red

Year	Team	G	Att	Comp	C%	Yds	TD	INT	FUM	ASR	NY/P	Rk	DVOA	Rk	DYAR	Rk	YAR	Runs	Yds	TD	DVOA	DYAR
2005	DET	13	330	188	57.0%	2021	12	12	7	6.4%	5.3	34	-15.7%	32	-104	35	-206	24	80	0	-24.0%	-12
2006	MIA	11	388	223	57.5%	2236	12	15	5	4.3%	5.5	41	-14.9%	34	-98	35	-241	19	24	0	-33.6%	-19
2007	ATL	12	348	215	61.8%	2215	7	8	1	8.7%	5.3	39	-5.8%	29	124	25	142	14	33	0	-12.4%	0
2008	ATL		509	280	55.1%	2796	18	26			4.2		-46.4%					18	40	1	-13.2%	

2007:   56% Short   31% Mid   8% Deep   5% Bomb   YAC: 5.2 (10)   2006:   46% Short   35% Mid   13% Deep   6% Bomb   YAC: 4 (37)

Because Harrington and David Carr were both taken in the first three picks of the 2002 draft and have followed high prospect praise with strikingly similar (and underwhelming) NFL stats, the temptation is to lump them together as quarterbacks with no current usefulness at the professional level. Although that may be true of Carr, whose understudy status to a guy nicknamed "The Hefty Lefty" in New York is probably the last step down before a broadcasting internship somewhere, Harrington does have nominal value as a league-average, emergency-level backup quarterback. His 10 starts for the Falcons in 2007 came under unreal circumstances—Harrington was the default starter after Michael Vick's legal problems exploded, he was bounced around by Bobby Petrino, and he was eventually usurped by Chris Redman, a quarterback who hadn't taken an NFL snap in three years. His performance wasn't horrible when you consider the conditions, just as his Dolphins performance in 2006 was credible when you factored in the state of their offense. Cut by Atlanta in early March as a cost-saving move, Harrington was re-signed by the team a week later and will sit behind Chris Redman until Matt Ryan passes him on the depth chart, which should be sometime between now and when you reach the section on running backs.

Matt Hasselbeck

Height: 6-4   Weight: 233   College: Boston College   Draft: 1998/6 (187)   Born: 25-Sep-1975   Age: 33   Risk: Green

Year	Team	G	Att	Comp	C%	Yds	TD	INT	FUM	ASR	NY/P	Rk	DVOA	Rk	DYAR	Rk	YAR	Runs	Yds	TD	DVOA	DYAR
2005	SEA	16	449	294	65.5%	3455	24	9	4	5.7%	7.0	6	30.0%	4	1290	4	1403	36	124	1	21.5%	38
2006	SEA	12	371	210	56.6%	2442	18	15	3	8.4%	6.0	31	-10.3%	31	22	30	118	18	110	0	38.6%	33
2007	SEA	16	562	352	62.6%	3966	28	12	6	6.9%	6.4	17	12.8%	14	937	9	1167	39	89	0	-14.9%	-3
2008	SEA		489	313	63.9%	3793	24	14			6.9		22.4%					27	49	0	-6.6%	

2007:   48% Short   32% Mid   14% Deep   6% Bomb   YAC: 4.7 (22)   2006:   36% Short   41% Mid   15% Deep   8% Bomb   YAC: 3.5 (43)

What a difference an offensive line makes. Two years after getting sacked on every other offensive series, Hasselbeck returned to the ranks of the NFC's elite quarterbacks, thanks to the relative health of the Seattle blockers last year. His numbers are more impressive given that defensive coordinators spent the first nine weeks of the season learning how few defenders they needed to put in the box to stop Shaun Alexander (answer: none). This year, Hasselbeck gets an actual running game again, plus a non-ancient, non-insane tight end to throw to, rookie John Carlson. New running backs Julius Jones and T. J. Duckett had excellent receiving numbers with their previous teams; the dumpoff as an escape hatch for Hasselbeck had died along with Shaun Alexander's effectiveness. These changes should mitigate the fact that the Seahawks wide receivers are a mixture of old, injured, enigmatic, and unproven.

Chad Henne

Height: 6-2   Weight: 225   College: Michigan   Draft: 2008/2 (57)   Born: 2-Jul-1985   Age: 23   Risk: Red

Year	Team	G	Att	Comp	C%	Yds	TD	INT	FUM	ASR	NY/P	Rk	DVOA	Rk	DYAR	Rk	YAR	Runs	Yds	TD	DVOA	DYAR
2008	MIA		505	290	57.4%	2979	18	15			5.2		-22.6%					35	37	1	-33.9%	

Nobody among the 2008 draft class of quarterbacks has more divergent scouting reports than Chad Henne. To some, he's a scattershot thrower with major consistency issues and no mobility. To others, he's the most NFL-ready of the rookies, thanks to 47 major-program starts and an extensive postseason resume. As is the case with most left/right reports, the answer lies somewhere in the middle. Henne spent his final three years at Michigan trying to live up to one of the greatest freshman seasons any quarterback has ever enjoyed, and while his sub-60 completion percentage won't blow anyone away as much as his strong arm, he is more mobile in the pocket than he's given credit for. Sometimes he'll hurry throws and make some head-scratching plays. Look for him to have the inside track to start early on over John Beck and Josh McCown—if he doesn't, it's not for lack of interest from Bill Parcells and Tony Sparano. Sparano threw the playbook at Henne in rookie camp, and while Henne ended up so confused that he forgot the snap count, he impressed coaches with his poise and willingness to learn. Perhaps Henne's most important asset is that he's mentally tough enough for the Parcells Quarterback Bootcamp by Proxy.

Shaun Hill Height: 6-3 Weight: 235 College: Maryland Draft: 2002/FA Born: 9-Jan-1980 Age: 28 Risk: Red

Year	Team	G	Att	Comp	C%	Yds	TD	INT	FUM	ASR	NY/P	Rk	DVOA	Rk	DYAR	Rk	YAR	Runs	Yds	TD	DVOA	DYAR
2007	SF	3	79	54	68.4%	501	5	1	2	9.7%	5.7	—	6.0%	—	101	—	129	12	14	1	8.1%	6
2008	SF		519	303	58.5%	3481	15	19			5.3		-19.0%					43	169	1	-8.5%	
2007:	66% Short	28% Mid	5% Deep	0% Bomb	YAC: 4.6 (—)																

Comparisons have already been drawn between Hill and Marc Bulger, a player that new 49ers offensive coordinator Mike Martz developed into a prolific quarterback for the Rams. Hill, like Bulger, doesn't possess a big arm and doesn't move all that well. Unlike Bulger, he never got a chance to play in the regular season until his sixth year in the league. Hill won his first-ever start against the Bengals on a nationally televised Sunday night game last year, completing 21-of-27 passes for 181 yards and a touchdown with a broken finger on his throwing hand. The question for Hill as he competes with J. T. O'Sullivan and Alex Smith will be whether he can throw hard enough to complete the medium range in-routes and comeback patterns that make up much of the Mike Martz offense.

Kelly Holcomb Height: 6-2 Weight: 212 College: Middle Tennessee State Draft: 1996/FA Born: 9-Jul-1973 Age: 35 Risk: Red

Year	Team	G	Att	Comp	C%	Yds	TD	INT	FUM	ASR	NY/P	Rk	DVOA	Rk	DYAR	Rk	YAR	Runs	Yds	TD	DVOA	DYAR
2005	BUF	10	230	155	67.4%	1509	10	8	10	7.8%	5.6	30	-18.6%	34	-124	36	-120	18	11	1	-35.4%	-17
2007	MIN	3	83	42	50.6%	515	2	1	1	13.9%	4.7	—	-15.5%	—	-25	—	-54	0	0	0	—	—
2007:	50% Short	32% Mid	6% Deep	12% Bomb	YAC: 5.1 (—)																

Released by Minnesota and still unsigned in mid-May, Holcomb has likely played his last game. He finished his career with a shockingly high completion percentage (63.3 percent) but below-average yardage (10.5 yards per completion) and a poor TD-INT ratio (39-38). He'll always be remembered for January 5, 2003, his only career playoff game, when he threw for 429 yards and three touchdowns and put his Browns ahead 24-7 early in the third quarter, only to see Tommy Maddox and the Steelers came back to win 36-33. Those who saw it will never forget it; those who missed it will have trouble believing that Kelly Holcomb and Tommy Maddox once engaged in a playoff shootout.

Damon Huard Height: 6-3 Weight: 215 College: Washington Draft: 1997/FA Born: 9-Jul-1973 Age: 35 Risk: Red

Year	Team	G	Att	Comp	C%	Yds	TD	INT	FUM	ASR	NY/P	Rk	DVOA	Rk	DYAR	Rk	YAR	Runs	Yds	TD	DVOA	DYAR
2006	KC	10	244	148	60.7%	1878	11	1	6	5.7%	7.2	7	24.3%	3	584	12	655	9	9	0	-175.4%	-30
2007	KC	11	332	206	62.0%	2257	11	13	6	9.9%	5.6	33	-11.8%	34	-13	34	8	9	-1	0	-86.7%	-13
2008	KC		496	302	60.9%	3002	20	20			5.0		-24.3%					32	85	1	-39.1%	
2007:	43% Short	34% Mid	17% Deep	7% Bomb	YAC: 4.5 (29)			2006:	47% Short	29% Mid	21% Deep	3% Bomb	YAC: 5.3 (9)								

The magic of 2006 was not to be repeated in 2007, but Huard still proved he is a competent NFL quarterback. He outplayed Brodie Croyle, but he returned to the bench for most of the second half of last season with the rebuilding project in full swing. Huard is a testament to what guile and toughness can do for a player with mediocre physical tools, but he also shows the limited upside such a player offers. Huard likely gives the Chiefs a better chance to win in 2008, but they are much more concerned with 2010 right now.

Tarvaris Jackson   Height: 6-2   Weight: 225   College: Alabama State   Draft: 2006/2 (64)   Born: 21-Apr-1983   Age: 25   Risk: Red

Year	Team	G	Att	Comp	C%	Yds	TD	INT	FUM	ASR	NY/P	Rk	DVOA	Rk	DYAR	Rk	YAR	Runs	Yds	TD	DVOA	DYAR
2006	MIN	4	81	47	58.0%	475	2	4	1	8.8%	5.5	—	-52.6%	—	-237	—	-236	15	77	1	-3.7%	6
2007	MIN	12	294	171	58.2%	1911	9	12	5	6.5%	6.0	23	-5.8%	28	107	26	156	54	260	3	25.4%	80
2008	MIN		483	280	57.9%	3376	21	18			5.8		-7.0%					73	343	2	-8.1%	

2007:   45% Short   37% Mid   9% Deep   10% Bomb   YAC: 4.9 (19)   2006:   52% Short   17% Mid   22% Deep   9% Bomb   YAC: 7.2 (—)

Heavy is the head that wears the quarterbacking crown in Minnesota. The Vikings led the league in rushing yards in 2007, and they added one of the league's preeminent pass rushers, Jared Allen. If they miss the playoffs in 2008, the blame will likely lie at the feet of Tarvaris Jackson and the wide receivers. Some observers lost faith in Jackson last year, when his erratic play may have cost the team a playoff berth. Others didn't make it that far; they saw his poor play as a rookie and figured that was enough. And some gave up before he ever played in the NFL, when he failed to beat out Matt Jones for the quarterback job at Arkansas. Still, the Vikings believed in him, trading a pair of third-round picks to draft Jackson at the end of the second round in 2006. Rather than trade for Derek Anderson or acquire a veteran like Daunte Culpepper or Byron Leftwich, they're counting on Jackson to lead them to the promised land. If they do sneak into the playoffs, could Jackson go on a hot streak? Consider this: last year Jackson had more DYAR and a higher DVOA than Eli Manning.

Brad Johnson   Height: 6-5   Weight: 226   College: Florida State   Draft: 1992/9 (227)   Born: 13-Sep-1968   Age: 40   Risk: Red

Year	Team	G	Att	Comp	C%	Yds	TD	INT	FUM	ASR	NY/P	Rk	DVOA	Rk	DYAR	Rk	YAR	Runs	Yds	TD	DVOA	DYAR
2005	MIN	15	294	184	62.6%	1885	12	4	5	7.5%	5.7	28	10.6%	12	418	19	363	18	53	0	18.2%	11
2006	MIN	15	439	270	61.5%	2750	9	15	9	6.7%	5.9	36	-17.9%	36	-203	40	-186	29	82	1	-4.6%	9
2007	DAL	16	11	7	63.6%	79	0	0	0	8.8%	5.8	—	-13.8%	—	-2	—	-7	3	-2	0	-105.6%	-7
2008	DAL		420	257	61.2%	3072	15	18			6.0		-16.6%					20	59	1	1.5%	

2007:   64% Short   18% Mid   9% Deep   9% Bomb   YAC: 7.6 (—)   2006:   36% Short   48% Mid   11% Deep   5% Bomb   YAC: 4.9 (17)

Johnson is interning under Jason Garrett as much as he's backing up Tony Romo. Some teams prefer to have a backup who's similar in style to their starter, but it's hard to imagine a quarterback less similar to Romo than Johnson. Romo's pretty reckless with his body, so while it looks like Johnson is sitting out the string, it wouldn't be surprising to see him in the lineup for a start or two. It's not clear what he has left; he looked rickety in his last action.

Jon Kitna   Height: 6-2   Weight: 220   College: Central Washington   Draft: 1997/FA   Born: 21-Sep-1972   Age: 36   Risk: Green

Year	Team	G	Att	Comp	C%	Yds	TD	INT	FUM	ASR	NY/P	Rk	DVOA	Rk	DYAR	Rk	YAR	Runs	Yds	TD	DVOA	DYAR
2005	CIN	3	29	17	58.6%	99	0	2	0	7.6%	2.9	—	-78.0%	—	-132	—	-140	2	14	0	52.1%	8
2006	DET	16	596	372	62.4%	4208	21	22	9	9.9%	6.4	18	-2.3%	21	369	15	295	34	156	2	-9.2%	4
2007	DET	16	561	355	63.3%	4068	18	20	12	8.2%	6.1	22	-1.2%	23	387	18	293	25	63	0	-31.7%	-15
2008	DET		526	318	60.5%	3128	23	18			5.1		-16.5%					24	75	1	2.2%	

2007:   43% Short   33% Mid   19% Deep   6% Bomb   YAC: 4.3 (35)   2006:   46% Short   31% Mid   17% Deep   6% Bomb   YAC: 4.8 (21)

Kitna starts the season with 26,535 yards, 48th on the all-time passing list. If he throws for a modest 3,000 yards this season, he'll pass Bobby Layne, Joe Namath, Ken Stabler, Ron Jaworski, Terry Bradshaw, and others. If he hangs around as a backup for two or three years after that and racks up, say, an additional 5,000 yards, he'll pass Steve Young, Sonny Jurgensen, Troy Aikman, Ken Anderson, and Y. A. Tittle. Kitna could easily retire among the top 20 passers in NFL history, even assuming that Tom Brady and Donovan McNabb (both hot on his heels right now) pass him before he retires. The all-time passing yardage list isn't a meritocracy; it's filled with recent players who had long careers of 16-game seasons on pass-happy offenses. Kitna is now the best example of this phenomenon.

Kevin Kolb   Height: 6-3   Weight: 218   College: Houston   Draft: 2007/2 (36)   Born: 24-Aug-1984   Age: 24   Risk: Orange

Year	Team	G	Att	Comp	C%	Yds	TD	INT	FUM	ASR	NY/P	Rk	DVOA	Rk	DYAR	Rk	YAR	Runs	Yds	TD	DVOA	DYAR
2007	PHI	1	0	0	0.0%	0	0	0	1	98.7%	-6.5	—	-601.6%	—	-51	—	-49	3	-2	0	—	—
2008	PHI		459	266	58.0%	3130	21	16			5.8		1.7%					18	27	1	-32.7%	

Okay, so it wasn't such a great 2007 for this Lewin Career Forecast darling (50 college games started with a 62 percent completion rate). Kolb's rookie season involved lots of clipboard holding plus some mop-up duty against the Lions, where he was sacked twice and never threw a pass. The period of time before Kolb becomes the Eagles full-time starter is inversely correlated to the number of wins the Eagles have this year, but if McNabb gets hurt, Kolb should be first in line to take his place. The resulting quarterback controversy could form a chasm that swallows Philadelphia whole.

Byron Leftwich

Height: 6-5   Weight: 245   College: Marshall   Draft: 2003/1 (7)   Born: 14-Jan-1980   Age: 28   Risk: Red

Year	Team	G	Att	Comp	C%	Yds	TD	INT	FUM	ASR	NY/P	Rk	DVOA	Rk	DYAR	Rk	YAR	Runs	Yds	TD	DVOA	DYAR
2005	JAC	11	302	175	57.9%	2123	15	5	8	6.6%	6.2	14	17.6%	8	571	12	556	31	67	2	14.0%	29
2006	JAC	6	183	108	59.0%	1159	7	5	5	5.6%	6.0	29	-10.1%	30	13	31	138	25	41	2	-12.3%	0
2007	ATL	3	58	32	55.2%	279	1	2	6	9.4%	3.8	—	-65.0%	—	-215	—	-218	6	7	0	-137.7%	-37

2007: 50% Short   30% Mid   12% Deep   8% Bomb   YAC: 3.8 (—)   2006:   50% Short   31% Mid   15% Deep   4% Bomb   YAC: 5.3 (12)

We had a very high projection for Leftwich in last year's book; he was ranked eighth in fantasy value among quarterbacks, far ahead of Brett Favre or Ben Roethlisberger. However, it should be noted that a large part of Leftwich's projection was actually a projection for "Jacksonville quarterback," whoever that quarterback may have been. (The projection for David Garrard was almost as strong.) Football is a team game, and the KUBIAK projection system takes into account a lot of team-oriented variables. A mediocre quarterback will have a good season if he has a good running game to take the pressure off or has a good offensive line and receivers. A great quarterback won't put up fabulous numbers if he doesn't have the teammates. Ask Peyton Manning about the weeks he had to play with Aaron Moorehead and Craphonoso Thorpe as two of his top three options.

This is what Leftwich's KUBIAK projection looked like last year and what it would have looked like if we had known before publication that Leftwich was playing in Atlanta instead of Jacksonville:

Team	Att	Comp	C%	Yds	Yd/At	TD	INT
JAC	497	315	63.3%	3780	7.6	23	10
ATL	513	313	61.1%	3524	6.9	17	13

At this point, it looks like Leftwich has been consigned to NFL purgatory. No one has come forward with an interest in signing him this offseason. His last two years are so messed up that everyone forgets that his development curve was on a clear upswing through 2005. Byron Leftwich should be remembered as one of the great talent mismanagement stories in NFL history.

Matt Leinart

Height: 6-5   Weight: 225   College: USC   Draft: 2006/1 (10)   Born: 11-May-1983   Age: 25   Risk: Red

Year	Team	G	Att	Comp	C%	Yds	TD	INT	FUM	ASR	NY/P	Rk	DVOA	Rk	DYAR	Rk	YAR	Runs	Yds	TD	DVOA	DYAR
2006	ARI	12	377	214	56.8%	2547	11	12	9	5.7%	6.4	19	-1.2%	20	246	19	215	22	49	2	4.7%	13
2007	ARI	5	112	60	53.6%	647	2	4	1	3.5%	5.4	37	-3.3%	25	58	30	72	11	42	0	1.0%	8
2008	ARI		526	316	60.1%	3526	21	19			5.6		-6.2%					47	128	1	-0.4%	

2007: 43% Short   39% Mid   10% Deep   9% Bomb   YAC: 4.3 (36)   2006:   44% Short   34% Mid   13% Deep   9% Bomb   YAC: 3.7 (42)

Cardinals coach Ken Whisenhunt declared Matt Leinart the starter for 2008 despite an injury-marred and disappointing 2007 season. Leinart's quest is to get himself in good enough shape to take hits and to be a good enough student to decipher defenses and find his talented receivers. Questions still linger about Leinart's work ethic; if you own a computer and have ever read a blog, you probably know what we are talking about. Some scouts believe Arizona whiffed on Leinart, whose shortcomings (deliberate delivery, slow feet) were covered up by his supporting cast at USC. If Leinart doesn't develop, he'll be just another athletically challenged quarterback from a great program, like Ken Dorsey, Andrew Walter, and many others—except that we never saw embarrassing photos of those guys.

Cleo Lemon

| | | Height: 6-2 | Weight: 215 | College: Arkansas State | | | | | Draft: 2001/FA | | Born: 16-Aug-1979 | | Age: 29 | Risk: Red |

Year	Team	G	Att	Comp	C%	Yds	TD	INT	FUM	ASR	NY/P	Rk	DVOA	Rk	DYAR	Rk	YAR	Runs	Yds	TD	DVOA	DYAR
2006	MIA	4	68	38	55.9%	412	2	1	2	7.7%	6.0	—	4.9%	—	73	—	69	3	7	0	-19.2%	-1
2007	MIA	9	309	173	56.0%	1773	6	6	7	7.8%	4.9	45	-15.5%	38	-91	39	-71	49	185	1	24.5%	62
2008	JAC		430	257	59.8%	3063	17	16			6.3		-0.8%					22	83	1	3.9%	

| 2007: | 49% Short | 31% Mid | 13% Deep | 7% Bomb | YAC: 4.8 (21) | | 2006: | 54% Short | 29% Mid | 14% Deep | 4% Bomb | YAC: 4.5 (—) |

The lowlight of the Dolphins season, if we can choose only one, might have been Lemon's safety in the end zone against the Bills in Week 10. Lemon watched for a near eternity as Chris Kelsey hurdled a blocker and closed in for the kill. The quarterback looked like a hapless doe awaiting a collision with a Ford Explorer, except that deer don't try to pump-fake just before getting a face full of fender. Lemon takes too many sacks and bails out too quickly on other plays; the more you see of him, the worse he looks. He's now in Jacksonville, where he'll replace Quinn Gray as the backup who looks like an All-Pro until the moment the ball is snapped.

J. P. Losman

| | | Height: 6-2 | Weight: 217 | College: Tulane | | | | | Draft: 2004/1 (22) | | Born: 12-Mar-1981 | | Age: 27 | Risk: Red |

Year	Team	G	Att	Comp	C%	Yds	TD	INT	FUM	ASR	NY/P	Rk	DVOA	Rk	DYAR	Rk	YAR	Runs	Yds	TD	DVOA	DYAR
2005	BUF	9	228	113	49.6%	1340	8	8	9	10.1%	4.6	43	-43.3%	45	-482	43	-414	31	154	0	3.1%	20
2006	BUF	16	429	268	62.5%	3051	19	14	10	9.5%	6.3	22	-8.3%	27	86	25	12	38	140	1	-25.7%	-24
2007	BUF	8	175	111	63.4%	1204	4	6	2	7.3%	5.9	30	-8.9%	32	26	32	25	20	110	0	-10.7%	1
2008	BUF		410	252	61.4%	2660	11	18			5.1		-27.0%					36	146	0	-4.0%	

| 2007: | 52% Short | 27% Mid | 12% Deep | 9% Bomb | YAC: 5.2 (12) | | 2006: | 44% Short | 34% Mid | 12% Deep | 9% Bomb | YAC: 4.8 (19) |

Losman executed just three bootleg/rollout passes last season. Does that seem like a good use of his skills? The Bills had rollouts in their playbook—Trent Edwards ran 21 of them—but Steve Fairchild didn't dial them up when the speedy Losman was at the helm. Maybe Fairchild was afraid Losman would tuck and run on every play. Losman demanded a trade in January, but the Bills couldn't find any takers. Edwards is hardly entrenched as a starter, and Losman could redeem himself by learning Turk Schonert's system, mastering the short passes that have always bedeviled him and engineering a few wins off the bench.

Eli Manning

| | | Height: 6-4 | Weight: 218 | College: Mississippi | | | | | Draft: 2004/1 (1) | | Born: 3-Jan-1981 | | Age: 27 | Risk: Green |

Year	Team	G	Att	Comp	C%	Yds	TD	INT	FUM	ASR	NY/P	Rk	DVOA	Rk	DYAR	Rk	YAR	Runs	Yds	TD	DVOA	DYAR
2005	NYG	16	557	294	52.8%	3762	24	17	10	5.3%	6.1	19	5.2%	17	604	9	575	29	80	1	23.9%	27
2006	NYG	16	522	301	57.7%	3244	24	18	10	5.5%	5.9	35	3.9%	16	520	13	475	25	21	0	-38.8%	-17
2007	NYG	16	529	297	56.1%	3336	23	20	11	5.1%	5.6	32	-13.1%	35	-70	38	-60	29	69	1	-0.9%	11
2008	NYG		546	326	59.7%	2987	26	15			6.6		13.1%					36	115	0	11.9%	

| 2007: | 46% Short | 32% Mid | 15% Deep | 7% Bomb | YAC: 4.4 (32) | | 2006: | 47% Short | 33% Mid | 13% Deep | 7% Bomb | YAC: 4.5 (30) |

Tiki Barber questioned Eli Manning's leadership at the start of last season, saying that teammates chuckled whenever Eli tried to make a motivational speech. Tiki's comments sounded like raw meat for the WFAN/*New York Post* crowd, but the response of the New York media was surprisingly measured. Many media personalities sided with Eli, or at least reserved judgment, while Tiki took backlash for telling tales out of school. One year later, Eli has a Super Bowl ring and Tiki's football cred has been destroyed by his morning gabfests with Barbara Walters; the leadership comments are horribly dated, an ironic precursor to an amazing season.

At Football Outsiders and within these pages, we often rail against the kind of simplistic logic that brands players as winners or losers based on the fate of their teams. Sometimes, we forget that we're arguing a pretty obvious point. Some semi-informed fans (writers, talk radio hosts) thought Eli was a bum to be run out of Gotham last season, and those same individuals will spend August crowning him as one of New York's greatest champions. But smarter, more attentive fans know that Eli has become a little better, not a lot. They know he will still struggle at times and that no magic spell was cast in the fourth quarter of the Super Bowl. These fans didn't take the bait when Tiki called Eli out last season, and they won't get hooked when Eli is canonized as a star on the Brady/Peyton level. Those fans are the type of people who get to this page of *Pro Football Prospectus;* fans like you. You're in the choir. You've already heard the sermon.

Peyton Manning

Height: 6-5 Weight: 230 College: Tennessee Draft: 1998/1 (1) Born: 24-Mar-1976 Age: 32 Risk: Green

Year	Team	G	Att	Comp	C%	Yds	TD	INT	FUM	ASR	NY/P	Rk	DVOA	Rk	DYAR	Rk	YAR	Runs	Yds	TD	DVOA	DYAR
2005	IND	16	453	305	67.3%	3747	28	10	4	3.6%	7.8	1	40.4%	1	1598	1	1781	33	45	0	-56.3%	-40
2006	IND	16	557	362	65.0%	4397	31	9	3	3.3%	7.8	4	51.0%	1	2308	1	2287	23	36	4	48.2%	42
2007	IND	16	515	337	65.4%	4040	31	14	7	4.2%	7.3	5	40.6%	2	1841	2	1679	20	-5	3	17.3%	16
2008	IND		553	369	66.6%	4359	38	13			7.6		42.3%					14	19	1	22.4%	

2007: 45% Short 34% Mid 12% Deep 9% Bomb YAC: 4.5 (31) 2006: 43% Short 35% Mid 13% Deep 9% Bomb YAC: 3.9 (40)

As Brett Favre ambles into retirement, he sits atop the NFL's passing record throne, the league's all-time leader in pass attempts, completions, yards, touchdowns, and interceptions. How long is he likely to stay there? About five years, give or take. It's inevitable that Peyton Manning will surpass some or all of Favre's marks. As a service to both Packers and Colts fans, we present this handy list estimating the season and game in which Peyton Manning will break each record, in expected chronological order. All figures are based on his career totals and his per-game averages over the last three seasons. Touchdowns: 2013, Game 9. Yards: 2013, Game 15. Completions: 2014, Game 12. Attempts: 2015, Game 10. Interceptions: 2021, Game 4. In other words, Manning would start with the touchdown record at age 37 and finish up with the interception record at age 45. All right, we admit, that last record seems unlikely. There's one mark Brett may keep forever.

Josh McCown

Height: 6-4 Weight: 212 College: Sam Houston State Draft: 2002/3 (81) Born: 4-Jul-1979 Age: 29 Risk: Red

Year	Team	G	Att	Comp	C%	Yds	TD	INT	FUM	ASR	NY/P	Rk	DVOA	Rk	DYAR	Rk	YAR	Runs	Yds	TD	DVOA	DYAR
2005	ARI	9	270	163	60.4%	1836	9	11	4	6.8%	6.2	17	-6.8%	24	80	26	92	29	139	0	-21.7%	-15
2007	OAK	9	190	111	58.4%	1151	10	11	11	6.9%	5.2	40	-29.1%	48	-236	48	-169	29	143	0	-11.4%	1
2008	MIA		475	293	61.6%	3114	13	11			5.7		-5.4%					37	132	0	-22.4%	

2007: 50% Short 26% Mid 12% Deep 11% Bomb YAC: 4.9 (20)

The Dolphins know what they're getting in McCown: a good runner with a decent arm, a gunner's mentality, and a bad fumbling habit (39 fumbles in 31 career starts). McCown's athleticism and willingness to gamble make him an effective relief pitcher who can surprise opponents. His best starts in 2007 came in Week 1 (313 yards, two touchdowns against the Lions) and after returning to the lineup in Week 13 (three touchdowns and a completion rate of 67 percent against the Broncos). In 2005 with the Cardinals, he took over as the starter in Week 4 (385 yards, two touchdowns) and then came off the bench to beat the Eagles in Week 16 (297 yards on 31-of-42 passing). Usually McCown crashes to earth once opponents have a week or two to game plan for him. If McCown wins the opening day starter job, he'll be productive for a few starts. Rest assured that Josh Beck and Chad Henne will be loose in the bullpen at all times.

Luke McCown

Height: 6-3 Weight: 208 College: Louisiana Tech Draft: 2004/4 (106) Born: 12-Jul-1981 Age: 27 Risk: Red

Year	Team	G	Att	Comp	C%	Yds	TD	INT	FUM	ASR	NY/P	Rk	DVOA	Rk	DYAR	Rk	YAR	Runs	Yds	TD	DVOA	DYAR
2007	TB	5	139	94	67.6%	1009	5	3	3	11.0%	6.0	27	-13.9%	36	-28	35	97	12	117	0	86.7%	52
2008	TB		479	299	62.4%	3270	20	13			5.7		-14.7%					30	166	0	7.8%	

2007: 61% Short 22% Mid 14% Deep 4% Bomb YAC: 5.3 (8)

Luke, the younger of the Fighting McCown Boys, started the two games Jeff Garcia missed with a back injury and the season finale in which Jon Gruden rested most of his starters. McCown looked fairly impressive in the win over New Orleans that basically clinched the division for the Bucs. However, it's a bit of a stretch to call him an eventual starter. In college, he enjoyed the same kind of numbers enjoyed by fringe prospects such as Tim Rattay and Ty Detmer, and he shares their NFL fates as good backups who shouldn't be overhyped, despite their occasional (and somewhat startling) NFL hot streaks.

Donovan McNabb   Height: 6-2   Weight: 226   College: Syracuse   Draft: 1999/1 (2)   Born: 25-Jan-1976   Age: 32   Risk: Yellow

Year	Team	G	Att	Comp	C%	Yds	TD	INT	FUM	ASR	NY/P	Rk	DVOA	Rk	DYAR	Rk	YAR	Runs	Yds	TD	DVOA	DYAR
2005	PHI	9	357	211	59.1%	2507	16	9	7	5.8%	6.4	13	9.0%	13	492	15	459	25	55	1	-12.6%	0
2006	PHI	10	316	180	57.0%	2647	18	6	4	7.2%	8.0	2	18.7%	6	658	9	751	32	212	3	58.9%	95
2007	PHI	14	473	291	61.5%	3324	19	7	7	8.5%	6.0	24	8.2%	18	659	14	666	50	236	0	3.3%	29
2008	PHI		507	328	64.8%	3851	29	12			6.6		35.2%					35	134	0	-5.9%	

2007: 49% Short   33% Mid   12% Deep   6% Bomb   YAC: 5.2 (11)   2006: 48% Short   29% Mid   13% Deep   11% Bomb   YAC: 7.4 (1)

McNabb's hate-hate-hate-love-hate relationship with the Philadelphia media and fan base continued this year. Websites constantly manufactured rumors and scenarios about McNabb trades to one locale or another, and sports talk radio sounded like a Feeley-Kolb fan club, even after McNabb's best games. McNabb did show some lingering effects from his torn ACL, but his yearly metrics were all near his career averages, with one exception: Adjusted Sack Rate, which was inflated by Winston Justice's infamous Turnstile Game against the Giants. As usual, McNabb sailed the occasional pass and sometimes didn't step into throws, but he threw only one interception in his last four games. Our McNabb projections, just like our Eagles projections, are often a little too sanguine—it'll take a huge step forward in Reggie Brown's route-running or an unexpectedly ready DeSean Jackson to get McNabb to match KUBIAK's enthusiasm.

Steve McNair   Height: 6-2   Weight: 235   College: Alcorn State   Draft: 1995/1 (3)   Born: 14-Feb-1973   Age: 35   Risk: Red

Year	Team	G	Att	Comp	C%	Yds	TD	INT	FUM	ASR	NY/P	Rk	DVOA	Rk	DYAR	Rk	YAR	Runs	Yds	TD	DVOA	DYAR
2005	TEN	14	476	292	61.3%	3161	16	11	7	3.8%	6.2	15	6.8%	16	570	13	632	32	139	1	9.7%	30
2006	BAL	16	468	295	63.0%	3050	16	12	9	3.5%	6.4	20	9.4%	14	628	10	660	45	119	1	34.4%	55
2007	BAL	6	205	133	64.9%	1113	2	4	8	7.4%	4.8	46	-24.4%	44	-187	46	-63	10	32	0	-63.3%	-25

2007: 56% Short   35% Mid   5% Deep   3% Bomb   YAC: 4 (42)   2006: 49% Short   38% Mid   8% Deep   5% Bomb   YAC: 4.2 (35)

The only quarterbacks in history to throw for over 30,000 yards while rushing for over 3,000 yards are McNair, Steve Young, Fran Tarkenton, and John Elway. McNair was a great runner early in his career, rushing for over 500 yards twice and 400 yards three other times. His top-end athleticism abandoned him in 2003, starting a slow but steady decline punctuated by injuries. McNair is just 35, but there won't be a huge market for his services even if he itches to return: The arm has faded, the legs are gone, and most of the other body parts are past warranty. He had a great, underappreciated career.

Matt Moore   Height: 6-3   Weight: 192   College: Oregon State   Draft: 2007/FA   Born: 9-Aug-1984   Age: 24   Risk: Red

Year	Team	G	Att	Comp	C%	Yds	TD	INT	FUM	ASR	NY/P	Rk	DVOA	Rk	DYAR	Rk	YAR	Runs	Yds	TD	DVOA	DYAR
2007	CAR	9	111	63	56.8%	730	3	5	2	4.3%	5.9	28	-2.8%	24	66	29	20	3	5	0	-82.0%	-4
2008	CAR		450	275	61.1%	3018	17	19			5.6		-5.3%					34	53	0	-41.5%	

2007: 44% Short   35% Mid   9% Deep   12% Bomb   YAC: 4.1 (39)

In 2007, the Carolina offense enjoyed exactly five games with positive offensive DVOA. The first two, in Weeks 1 and 3, were victories authored by Jake Delhomme. The third, in Week 6, came in a win over the Cardinals courtesy of Vinny Testaverde. The last two, wins in Weeks 15 and 17, saved the season from total disaster and established undrafted rookie Matt Moore as a player to watch. Moore was a ramblin' man at the college level, playing for UCLA, transferring to College of the Canyons (!), and winding up at Oregon State for the 2005 and 2006 season. It was there that he put up more passing yards per game than any Pac-10 quarterback other than Matt Leinart in 2005, and threw 161 straight passes without an interception in 2006. In 2007, he's an intriguing potential starter, pending Jake Delhomme's return from Tommy John surgery.

Kevin O'Connell   Height: 6-6   Weight: 228   College: San Diego State   Draft: 2008/3 (94)   Born: 25-May-1985   Age: 23   Risk: Red

Year	Team	G	Att	Comp	C%	Yds	TD	INT	FUM	ASR	NY/P	Rk	DVOA	Rk	DYAR	Rk	YAR	Runs	Yds	TD	DVOA	DYAR
2008	NE		481	310	64.3%	3641	32	13			6.7		30.6%					22	52	1	-23.4%	

Two San Diego-based college quarterbacks were drafted in 2008, having been willing beneficiaries of some real pro-level coaching. USD's Josh Johnson learned the basics of the West Coast Offense from Jim Harbaugh and parlayed that into a fifth-round chip with the Buccaneers. San Diego State's O'Connell learned from former Lions and Rams quarterback Chuck Long, the Aztecs' current head coach. He's a big player with a great arm whose potential slipped under the radar of the general public, but many scouts and experts had him on their sleepers list. O'Connell has great mobility, especially for his size, and a howitzer for an arm. What he needs is more work on the fundamentals—footwork, delivery angle, and ball security. Watching Tom Brady every day won't exactly hurt, and the Patriots now move back behind the Colts in the "how screwed are we if our quarterback goes down" derby.

Kyle Orton

Height: 6-4 Weight: 226 College: Purdue   Draft: 2005/4 (106) Born: 14-Nov-1982 Age: 26 Risk: Red

Year	Team	G	Att	Comp	C%	Yds	TD	INT	FUM	ASR	NY/P	Rk	DVOA	Rk	DYAR	Rk	YAR	Runs	Yds	TD	DVOA	DYAR
2005	CHI	15	368	190	51.6%	1869	9	13	10	8.4%	4.3	44	-33.8%	41	-594	45	-624	24	44	0	-102.1%	-33
2007	CHI	3	80	43	53.8%	478	3	2	2	4.0%	5.7	—	-25.0%	—	-73	—	-6	5	-1	0	-30.3%	-3
2008	CHI		477	258	54.0%	3211	12	17			6.0		-8.5%					43	40	0	-25.7%	

2007: 51% Short 35% Mid 7% Deep 7% Bomb YAC: 6.6 (—)

A mid-May Internet search for Kyle Orton turned up the following headlines: "Orton confident heading into QB duel"; "Orton excited about opportunity"; "Kyle Orton Thinks He Will Be the Starter." The fuel for Orton's confidence, besides the inept play of Rex Grossman, is apparently the 2-1 record Orton produced in the three games he started at the end of last season. That's all well and good, but Orton played horribly in those three games. The Bears lost a 20-13 squeaker to Minnesota in large part because Orton gained only 184 yards on 38 attempts. He played better in the 35-7 win over Green Bay but threw only 14 passes; the Bears won because their defense picked off Brett Favre twice (one returned for a touchdown) and their special teams blocked two punts (one of which was also returned for a score). And in the season finale, a 33-25 win over the Saints, Orton completed fewer than half his passes but was bailed out by Devin Hester, who got open for a 55-yard touchdown bomb and returned a punt for another score. We admire Orton's confidence, but in his only season as a starter in 2005, he almost single-handedly kept a great team out of a Super Bowl. Unless he has improved tremendously since then, he belongs on a bench or in the stands.

J. T. O'Sullivan

Height: 6-2 Weight: 220 College: UC Davis   Draft: 2002/6 (186) Born: 25-Aug-1979 Age: 29 Risk: Red

Year	Team	G	Att	Comp	C%	Yds	TD	INT	FUM	ASR	NY/P	Rk	DVOA	Rk	DYAR	Rk	YAR	Runs	Yds	TD	DVOA	DYAR
2007	DET	4	26	13	50.0%	148	1	2	1	10.2%	4.5	—	-21.5%	—	-18	—	0	4	-10	0	-255.8%	-33
2008	SF		473	277	58.7%	3225	18	17			6.1		-23.3%					29	115	1	3.4%	

2007: 46% Short 33% Mid 4% Deep 17% Bomb YAC: 6.2 (—)

O'Sullivan played fairly well off the bench in Week 2 against the Vikings, but the Lions put Jon Kitna back into the game anyway, even though Kitna's eyes were glassy and he was muttering about being thrown from his horse on the road to Damascus. The Vikings game was the first real action of O'Sullivan's career, but Mike Martz liked him enough to import him to San Francisco, where he'll look over Alex Smith's shoulder while helping Martz install his system. O'Sullivan is just good enough to have an exciting little Damon Huard–type hot streak if he ever gets to start three or four games in a row.

Carson Palmer

Height: 6-5 Weight: 230 College: USC   Draft: 2003/1 (1) Born: 27-Dec-1979 Age: 28 Risk: Yellow

Year	Team	G	Att	Comp	C%	Yds	TD	INT	FUM	ASR	NY/P	Rk	DVOA	Rk	DYAR	Rk	YAR	Runs	Yds	TD	DVOA	DYAR
2005	CIN	16	509	345	67.8%	3836	32	12	6	3.7%	7.1	5	32.5%	3	1509	2	1491	34	41	1	-6.7%	5
2006	CIN	16	520	324	62.3%	4035	28	13	16	6.1%	7.3	6	21.7%	4	1190	3	1007	26	37	0	-9.3%	2
2007	CIN	16	575	373	64.9%	4131	26	20	8	3.2%	6.8	11	20.1%	9	1215	6	1204	24	10	0	-17.8%	-3
2008	CIN		527	338	64.0%	3780	26	13			6.6		19.9%					25	37	0	-2.4%	

2007: 45% Short 32% Mid 16% Deep 7% Bomb YAC: 4.1 (38)   2006: 39% Short 37% Mid 14% Deep 10% Bomb YAC: 4.4 (32)

Some observers thought Palmer struggled occasionally in 2007, with passes sailing on him at inopportune moments. It didn't show in the statistics, where Palmer was his usual productive self. Most Palmer criticism can be written off as "the team is losing so the quarterback must be doing something wrong" logic. His season might be best encapsulated by the Week 2 outing against the Browns, in which Palmer threw for 401 yards and six touchdowns but was still blamed for the Bengals' 51-44 loss due to a last-gasp interception. Our projection sort of splits the difference when it comes to whether or not Chad Johnson will still be around. If he stays, Palmer will likely throw for more yards; if he goes, subtract a few touchdowns.

Chad Pennington

Height: 6-3　Weight: 225　College: Marshall　　　Draft: 2000/1 (18)　Born: 26-Jun-1976　Age: 32　Risk: Red

Year	Team	G	Att	Comp	C%	Yds	TD	INT	FUM	ASR	NY/P	Rk	DVOA	Rk	DYAR	Rk	YAR	Runs	Yds	TD	DVOA	DYAR
2005	NYJ	3	83	49	59.0%	530	2	3	2	9.1%	5.2	—	-27.0%	—	-92	—	-124	6	27	0	78.9%	13
2006	NYJ	16	485	313	64.5%	3352	17	16	6	5.9%	6.7	14	10.4%	13	740	7	595	35	109	0	4.6%	23
2007	NYJ	9	260	179	68.8%	1765	10	9	3	9.1%	5.6	34	-3.6%	26	140	24	77	20	32	1	-30.3%	-21
2008	NYJ		445	278	62.6%	2876	21	16			5.9		-15.6%					39	152	2	-1.2%	

2007:　52% Short　30% Mid　12% Deep　5% Bomb　YAC: 3.6 (47)　　2006:　48% Short　35% Mid　12% Deep　5% Bomb　YAC: 4.7 (29)

Pennington had a bittersweet late-season surge after he replaced the injured Kellen Clemens against the Patriots. He completed 73 percent of his passes in two games, a sign that he's still a dink-and-dunker par excellence, and he engineered a win against the Titans after a near-miss against the Pats. On the down side, he was sacked 11 times and the Jets offense produced just 20 points. The team said they would listen to trade offers in the offseason but heard none, so Pennington will battle Clemens for a starting job in camp. Although he's just 32, Pennington is best compared to players such as Brad Johnson four years ago or Jeff Garcia in 2005-2006: a rickety, crafty curveballer who can still win some games when he plays mistake-free.

Brady Quinn

Height: 6-4　Weight: 232　College: Notre Dame　　　Draft: 2007/1 (22)　Born: 27-Oct-1984　Age: 24　Risk: Red

Year	Team	G	Att	Comp	C%	Yds	TD	INT	FUM	ASR	NY/P	Rk	DVOA	Rk	DYAR	Rk	YAR	Runs	Yds	TD	DVOA	DYAR
2007	CLE	1	8	3	37.5%	45	0	0	0	1.6%	5.6	—	3.2%	—	7	—	8	0	0	0	—	—
2008	CLE		454	257	56.6%	2605	21	14			4.6		-22.1%					18	27	1	-32.5%	

2007:　14% Short　86% Mid　0% Deep　0% Bomb　YAC: 6.0 (—)

If Quinn had gotten into camp on time, there's a good chance he would have been the Week 1 starter. Instead, Quinn had to sit and watch Derek Anderson run the team, and that's probably what he'll have to do this year, too. He can take comfort in the fact that when it is time for him to take over, he'll have the supporting cast to be successful. Quinn still projects as a solid NFL quarterback, and by all accounts the coaching staff loves him, so while the official line is that Cleveland has no quarterback controversy, Quinn could make things interesting if he performs well in training camp and preseason action and then Anderson struggles to start the year.

Patrick Ramsey

Height: 6-2　Weight: 218　College: Tulane　　　Draft: 2002/1 (32)　Born: 14-Feb-1979　Age: 29　Risk: Red

Year	Team	G	Att	Comp	C%	Yds	TD	INT	FUM	ASR	NY/P	Rk	DVOA	Rk	DYAR	Rk	YAR	Runs	Yds	TD	DVOA	DYAR
2005	WAS	4	25	15	60.0%	279	1	1	0	13.2%	8.9	—	9.5%	—	34	—	18	7	3	0	-57.1%	-7
2007	DEN	2	48	29	60.4%	262	1	1	1	6.4%	4.9	—	-24.5%	—	-41	—	14	2	6	0	19.3%	5
2008	DEN		417	260	62.3%	2847	12	19			5.6		-11.8%					29	24	0	-2.8%	

2007:　59% Short　30% Mid　9% Deep　2% Bomb　YAC: 2.9 (—)

Ramsey saw most of his action last season in a blowout loss to the Lions. DVOA wasn't impressed by his counting stats because they came against the Lions mostly in garbage time and include two turnovers and three sacks in limited work. He'll back up Jay Cutler again this year.

Tim Rattay

Height: 6-0 **Weight:** 215 **College:** Louisiana Tech **Draft:** 2000/7 (212) **Born:** 15-Feb-1977 **Age:** 31 **Risk:** Red

Year	Team	G	Att	Comp	C%	Yds	TD	INT	FUM	ASR	NY/P	Rk	DVOA	Rk	DYAR	Rk	YAR	Runs	Yds	TD	DVOA	DYAR
2005	SF	4	97	56	57.7%	667	5	6	3	9.5%	5.7	27	-29.7%	40	-128	37	-140	7	18	0	51.4%	12
2006	TB	4	101	61	60.4%	748	4	2	5	4.2%	7.1	8	17.2%	10	201	20	160	4	3	0	-37.9%	-4
2007	ARI	4	27	15	55.6%	164	3	3	1	2.3%	6.1	—	-9.9%	—	3	—	11	2	5	0	-1566.8%	-16
2008	ARI		455	254	55.7%	3113	13	21			5.5		-28.2%					35	36	1	-34.8%	

2007: 44% Short 24% Mid 12% Deep 20% Bomb YAC: 2.3 (—)   2006: 55% Short 27% Mid 11% Deep 8% Bomb YAC: 5.1 (14)

The one-time 49ers starter is now a third-string quarterback, as he proved last year by throwing three interceptions in relief of Kurt Warner. When Warner's injured hand made a fumbled snap or handoff more likely, Rattay filled an odd role as a "red zone" quarterback, throwing short touchdowns off the bench in three separate games. He and Mike Vrabel should go golfing together.

Chris Redman

Height: 6-3 **Weight:** 223 **College:** Louisville **Draft:** 2000/3 (75) **Born:** 7-Jul-1977 **Age:** 31 **Risk:** Red

Year	Team	G	Att	Comp	C%	Yds	TD	INT	FUM	ASR	NY/P	Rk	DVOA	Rk	DYAR	Rk	YAR	Runs	Yds	TD	DVOA	DYAR
2007	ATL	7	149	89	59.7%	1079	10	5	3	5.7%	6.5	14	5.5%	21	163	23	221	8	16	0	-79.7%	-20
2008	ATL		507	288	56.9%	2721	20	24			4.4		-43.3%					22	35	0	-39.2%	

2007: 48% Short 34% Mid 11% Deep 7% Bomb YAC: 5.4 (4)

It turned out that 2007 was quite a year for Redman, the former Louisville hotshot who washed out with the Ravens, Patriots, and Titans and spent the 2006 season selling insurance. First he signed a contract with the Austin Wranglers of the Arena League in January, and then he got another shot in the NFL from Bobby Petrino, who coached him in college and signed him to the Falcons roster in March. Redman spent the early part of the season on the bench behind Joey Harrington and Byron Leftwich, getting his first real reps in Week 13. He started the season's final four games—ironically, only one of those was under Petrino—and did enough correctly to enter the 2008 season as the ad hoc starter until Matt Ryan is ready to be The Franchise. Redman was the only good thing Petrino brought to Atlanta, and with a new two-year deal, he'll be the only Petrino element to survive the purge.

Philip Rivers

Height: 6-4 **Weight:** 226 **College:** North Carolina State **Draft:** 2004/1 (4) **Born:** 8-Dec-1981 **Age:** 27 **Risk:** Red

Year	Team	G	Att	Comp	C%	Yds	TD	INT	FUM	ASR	NY/P	Rk	DVOA	Rk	DYAR	Rk	YAR	Runs	Yds	TD	DVOA	DYAR
2005	SD	3	22	12	54.5%	115	0	1	0	14.5%	4.0	—	-53.6%	—	-69	—	-85	1	-1	0	—	—
2006	SD	16	460	284	61.7%	3388	22	9	7	6.2%	7.0	9	17.8%	7	903	6	943	48	49	0	-41.7%	-45
2007	SD	16	460	277	60.2%	3152	21	15	11	4.4%	6.2	20	6.9%	20	552	16	450	29	33	1	-23.6%	-12
2008	SD		482	294	61.0%	3667	26	16			6.9		16.8%					32	65	1	-6.9%	

2007: 48% Short 29% Mid 16% Deep 8% Bomb YAC: 4.6 (27)   2006: 45% Short 33% Mid 13% Deep 9% Bomb YAC: 4.8 (23)

The playoffs are interesting. Rivers clearly regressed last season, but a few big games in the playoffs and suddenly he is considered a rising star again. Rivers deserves enormous respect for playing the AFC Championship game with a torn ACL, and while he is on track to play in Week 1, that does not mean he will immediately be 100 percent. Even though he is not the most mobile guy—his biggest weakness remains movement, even in the pocket—a quarterback still needs confidence in his legs. Carson Palmer, another immobile quarterback, started slowly two years ago after tearing his ACL in the previous year's postseason. Of particular note, Palmer was sacked 15 times in his first four games. Rivers will likely have some similar problems adjusting to the surgically prepared knee and could be a sitting duck as a guy who doesn't have a step of speed to spare. Don't be surprised if the Chargers offense (which also will feature a potentially limited Antonio Gates) struggles early.

Aaron Rodgers

Height: 6-2   Weight: 223   College: California   Draft: 2005/1 (24)   Born: 2-Dec-1983   Age: 25   Risk: Red

Year	Team	G	Att	Comp	C%	Yds	TD	INT	FUM	ASR	NY/P	Rk	DVOA	Rk	DYAR	Rk	YAR	Runs	Yds	TD	DVOA	DYAR
2005	GB	3	16	9	56.3%	65	0	1	0	15.0%	2.1	—	-117.6%	—	-133	—	-139	2	7	0	128.5%	6
2006	GB	2	15	6	40.0%	46	0	0	1	15.4%	1.9	—	-59.4%	—	-54	—	-68	2	11	0	25.6%	3
2007	GB	2	28	20	71.4%	218	1	0	0	9.2%	6.5	—	31.7%	—	84	—	68	7	29	0	27.8%	10
2008	GB		497	307	61.8%	3729	25	13			6.4		23.8%					34	79	1	-32.7%	

2007:   58% Short   35% Mid   4% Deep   4% Bomb   YAC: 6.3 (—)   2006:   40% Short   27% Mid   27% Deep   7% Bomb   YAC: 4.2 (—)

As of May minicamp, Rodgers was the unquestioned starter for the Packers. The coaching staff told him the job was his, and he got minicamp votes-of-confidence from important superdelegates such as Donald Driver. At some point in the preseason, he'll have a so-so game, Brian Brohm will throw a touchdown against some fourth-stringers, and trumpets will sound everywhere from Deadspin to Around the Horn. But Rodgers will open the season as the starter, and KUBIAK is certain he'll be pretty darn good. He's a good quarterback in a great situation, and he won't have to look over his shoulder in 2008.

Ben Roethlisberger

Height: 6-4   Weight: 242   College: Miami (Ohio)   Draft: 2004/1 (11)   Born: 2-Mar-1981   Age: 27   Risk: Red

Year	Team	G	Att	Comp	C%	Yds	TD	INT	FUM	ASR	NY/P	Rk	DVOA	Rk	DYAR	Rk	YAR	Runs	Yds	TD	DVOA	DYAR
2005	PIT	13	268	168	62.7%	2385	17	9	4	8.1%	7.8	2	35.1%	2	871	7	905	31	69	3	22.7%	36
2006	PIT	15	469	280	59.7%	3513	18	23	5	8.4%	7.0	10	8.1%	15	617	11	428	32	98	2	-1.9%	15
2007	PIT	15	404	264	65.3%	3154	32	11	9	10.7%	6.3	19	15.5%	13	743	11	850	35	204	2	24.6%	65
2008	PIT		480	289	60.2%	3824	28	15			6.7		3.6%					38	108	3	32.5%	

2007:   36% Short   40% Mid   18% Deep   6% Bomb   YAC: 4 (43)   2006:   36% Short   42% Mid   14% Deep   7% Bomb   YAC: 4.8 (18)

Since 1997, 74 quarterbacks have thrown at least 100 passes in a season with a personal Adjusted Sack Rate of 10 percent or higher. Only 18 of those 74 quarterbacks managed an above-average performance overall (i.e., over 0% DVOA). Roethlisberger ranks second among these quarterbacks in DYAR, behind only Chris Chandler with the 1998 Falcons (853 DYAR). He is one of only two quarterbacks to accomplish this feat since 2001; the other is Tony Banks in 2003, and Banks had just 115 pass attempts.

Roethlisberger's average ASR during his career is 9.2 percent, and his total career average DVOA is 22.9%. Fifty quarterbacks have had a season with an ASR within five-tenths of a point of Roethlisberger's career average. Those quarterbacks averaged -12.8% DVOA. Part of the reason Roethlisberger's sack totals are so high is because he holds onto the ball in search of late-developing plays. Part of his success is due to the improvisational skills of his receivers. Still, his ability to transcend Pittsburgh's awful pass protection is both rare and highly useful. Roethlisberger's amazing ability to accurately throw under pressure or on the run gives Pittsburgh fans hope that their troubled offensive line won't keep them from winning again in 2008.

Tony Romo

Height: 6-2   Weight: 227   College: Eastern Illinois   Draft: 2003/FA   Born: 21-Apr-1980   Age: 28   Risk: Yellow

Year	Team	G	Att	Comp	C%	Yds	TD	INT	FUM	ASR	NY/P	Rk	DVOA	Rk	DYAR	Rk	YAR	Runs	Yds	TD	DVOA	DYAR
2006	DAL	16	337	220	65.3%	2903	19	13	9	6.6%	8.2	1	18.9%	5	696	8	821	34	102	0	0.1%	14
2007	DAL	16	520	335	64.4%	4211	36	19	9	4.4%	7.4	4	25.5%	6	1297	4	1349	31	129	2	12.4%	28
2008	DAL		505	312	61.8%	3926	26	17			7.1		15.1%					23	75	1	6.7%	

2007:   40% Short   42% Mid   12% Deep   7% Bomb   YAC: 5.0 (18)   2006:   37% Short   31% Mid   21% Deep   12% Bomb   YAC: 4.4 (33)

Romo went from being a potential flash in the pan to a franchise quarterback by virtue of both improving his 2006 performance and maintaining it for most of the season, until a small slump in December. Although Romo gets flushed out of his dropback too easily, the difference between him and quarterbacks with happy feet is that Romo has superior footwork and an inherent sense of where he needs to be to get out of a situation. Instead of panicking and running forward towards the line while desperately hoping a receiver will get open, Romo eludes the rush while still scanning the field and is as accurate on the run as he is in the pocket. Since Romo is already 28, he's not likely to get much better than he is now, but until his physical skills start eroding, he will continue to be Brett Favre lite, with all the media attention that comes with the title.

Sage Rosenfels

Height: 6-4 Weight: 218 College: Iowa State Draft: 2001/4 (109) Born: 6-Mar-1978 Age: 30 Risk: Red

Year	Team	G	Att	Comp	C%	Yds	TD	INT	FUM	ASR	NY/P	Rk	DVOA	Rk	DYAR	Rk	YAR	Runs	Yds	TD	DVOA	DYAR
2005	MIA	4	61	34	55.7%	462	4	3	0	2.1%	7.8	—	-4.2%	—	27	—	22	6	15	0	-2.5%	2
2006	HOU	4	39	27	69.2%	265	3	1	0	4.3%	6.9	—	47.3%	—	158	—	156	4	5	0	-49.2%	-5
2007	HOU	9	240	154	64.2%	1684	15	12	4	2.6%	6.7	13	24.3%	7	599	15	373	21	51	1	41.5%	30
2008	HOU		440	283	64.2%	3296	18	16			6.3		4.3%					31	56	0	-0.7%	

2007: 46% Short 35% Mid 13% Deep 7% Bomb YAC: 3.8 (45) | 2006: 53% Short 24% Mid 18% Deep 5% Bomb YAC: 5.3 (—)

Rosenfels made the most of his first opportunity at extended playing time, putting up solid numbers when starter Matt Schaub was lost for the season's final five games with a shoulder injury. The most remarkable thing about Rosenfels's season stats, in fact, are their similarity to Schaub's. For several years, Rosenfels has been caught in the football netherworld between "not good enough to start" and "better-than-average backup," but after last season, Houston coach Gary Kubiak now knows what he has in Rosenfels and will not hesitate to go back to his backup if the need arises. The Texans, having invested heavily in Schaub, have declared him the clear-cut starter, but there isn't much—if any—drop-off to Rosenfels.

JaMarcus Russell

Height: 6-6 Weight: 269 College: LSU Draft: 2007/1 (1) Born: 9-Aug-1985 Age: 23 Risk: Red

Year	Team	G	Att	Comp	C%	Yds	TD	INT	FUM	ASR	NY/P	Rk	DVOA	Rk	DYAR	Rk	YAR	Runs	Yds	TD	DVOA	DYAR
2007	OAK	4	66	36	54.5%	373	2	4	5	8.9%	4.7	—	-42.7%	—	-144	—	-208	5	4	0	-36.2%	-3
2008	OAK		494	295	59.8%	2943	19	20			5.8		-18.8%					43	244	1	6.8%	

2007: 53% Short 29% Mid 10% Deep 8% Bomb YAC: 4.3 (—)

JaMarcus Russell, come on down! The reigns of the Oakland Raiders' offense are now yours. The first overall choice from 2006 will use arguably the most powerful arm in the league primarily to hand the ball off. The Raiders hope Russell can complete short passes and dumpoffs in his first full season as a starter while the running game provides most of the punch. The Raiders have decided to go young, and why not? A parade of older quarterbacks ran through the team's Alameda headquarters in the past few seasons, and none of them did anything to justify a long tenure with the team. After rumors that his weight ballooned to 300 pounds, Russell reported to a May minicamp at a relatively trim 269 pounds, which made many wonder what he really weighed last year. Even at a higher weight his rookie season, Russell had no problem looking relatively nimble on rollouts and bootlegs.

Matt Ryan

Height: 6-5 Weight: 224 College: Boston College Draft: 2008/1 (3) Born: 17-May-1985 Age: 23 Risk: Red

Year	Team	G	Att	Comp	C%	Yds	TD	INT	FUM	ASR	NY/P	Rk	DVOA	Rk	DYAR	Rk	YAR	Runs	Yds	TD	DVOA	DYAR
2008	ATL		515	290	56.3%	3259	18	23			5.6		-35.2%					58	155	1	-14.2%	

Ryan is a mature, tough, poised leader who started 34 of 45 possible games and excelled after a coaching change in 2007, when Jeff Jagodzinski took the helm at Boston College. Not unlike another BC alum named Matt (Hasselbeck), he has good pocket presence, surprising mobility, and a great ability to make all the short-to-medium throws—his finesse in this area is unusual for a rookie. There are legitimate concerns about his 59.3 collegiate completion percentage and 19 interceptions as a senior, but whatever barriers might hold him back from NFL stardom, he'd better get the kinks worked out quickly. Falcons owner Arthur Blank doesn't do anything without a misbegotten marketing campaign in mind, and he'll want to show off the new kid sooner than later. The six-year, $74 million contract Ryan signed, a deal which guarantees $34.75 million right away, has turned Ryan into the poster child for both great expectations and the Unhappy Veterans Guild of the NFLPA before he even takes a professional snap. The Falcons will get better returns from this deal than the last ginormous contract they gave to an alleged franchise quarterback, but Ryan will have to start right away behind a shaky offensive line with a questionable receiver corps and no established tight end. The Steelers successfully used the younger Ben Roethlisberger as a dynamic factor in a dominant running game, but Roethlisberger got the big money in his second contract. This deal, like so many things done under Blank's administration, tilts the playing field out of proportion and away from a winning point of view.

Matt Schaub

Height: 6-5   Weight: 237   College: Virginia   Draft: 2004/3 (90)   Born: 25-Jun-1981   Age: 27   Risk: Yellow

Year	Team	G	Att	Comp	C%	Yds	TD	INT	FUM	ASR	NY/P	Rk	DVOA	Rk	DYAR	Rk	YAR	Runs	Yds	TD	DVOA	DYAR
2005	ATL	16	64	33	51.6%	495	4	0	0	9.2%	6.8	—	11.2%	—	97	—	148	9	76	0	60.9%	28
2006	ATL	16	27	18	66.7%	208	1	2	0	6.3%	7.4	—	47.2%	—	95	—	74	7	21	0	27.6%	8
2007	HOU	11	289	192	66.4%	2241	9	9	8	6.6%	7.1	6	8.2%	17	381	19	377	17	52	0	-8.2%	3
2008	HOU		518	342	66.0%	3917	22	15			6.6		15.5%					27	45	0	-4.8%	

2007:   45% Short   38% Mid   10% Deep   7% Bomb   YAC: 4.0 (41)   2006:   17% Short   50% Mid   17% Deep   17% Bomb   YAC: 3.7 (—)

Entering last season, Schaub was a mystery thanks to a mere 161 regular-season pass attempts. This year, we have slightly more data to go on, including 11 starts before his season ended prematurely due to an injury to his non-throwing shoulder. Schaub did enough to show Houston fans that the team's previous sack problems were more about the quarterback than the line. Schaub isn't going to make any highlight reels with his scrambling, but he has a good feel for the rush and his Adjusted Sack Rate was considerably lower than the career-best 9.1 percent that David Carr posted in his final season. The shoulder injury, which required minor surgery, should be a non-issue by the time camp rolls around. And if Schaub needs a little extra motivation, he can take it from the strong performance of his backup, Sage Rosenfels, during his absence last year.

Chris Simms

Height: 6-4   Weight: 220   College: Texas   Draft: 2003/3 (97)   Born: 29-Aug-1980   Age: 28   Risk: Red

Year	Team	G	Att	Comp	C%	Yds	TD	INT	FUM	ASR	NY/P	Rk	DVOA	Rk	DYAR	Rk	YAR	Runs	Yds	TD	DVOA	DYAR
2005	TB	11	313	191	61.0%	2035	10	7	6	9.3%	5.4	32	-4.7%	23	137	22	136	19	31	0	-12.6%	0
2006	TB	3	106	58	54.7%	585	1	7	1	2.5%	5.3	42	-32.5%	43	-154	38	-215	4	7	1	58.8%	10
2008	TB		516	318	61.6%	3738	17	11			6.4		15.9%					36	-5	0	10.9%	

2006:   56% Short   27% Mid   12% Deep   6% Bomb   YAC: 4.2 (34)

Simms is now in the final stages of a very long comeback from losing his spleen, and nearly his life, in a Week 3 game against Carolina in 2006. Neither Simms nor the Buccaneers seem to know how to go about dealing with this long, strange trip. Simms is currently way down on the depth chart in Tampa Bay's Cavalcade of Quarterbacks, and it's entirely possible that he'll be released. That may be the best thing for all involved. Simms can get a chance with another team in a league with diminishing returns at the quarterback position, and the Bucs can stay with the aged veteran under center, as is Jon Gruden's preference. Simms will turn 28 on August 29. Give him about five years with another team, and he'll be ready for a Bucs-tastic reunion. Don't be surprised to see him knocking on the door sometime in 2012, reciting the password (last week, it was "Swordfish"; this week, it's "I Right, Zebra Trojan, Far West, X Slot, Y Dagger, Z Choice on two") and getting all prodigal as Gruden's latest old-guy reclamation project.

Alex Smith

Height: 6-4   Weight: 212   College: Utah   Draft: 2005/1 (1)   Born: 7-May-1984   Age: 24   Risk: Red

Year	Team	G	Att	Comp	C%	Yds	TD	INT	FUM	ASR	NY/P	Rk	DVOA	Rk	DYAR	Rk	YAR	Runs	Yds	TD	DVOA	DYAR
2005	SF	9	165	84	50.9%	875	1	11	10	13.7%	3.6	46	-89.4%	46	-880	46	-905	30	103	0	-39.9%	-30
2006	SF	16	442	257	58.1%	2890	16	16	10	6.9%	6.1	25	-15.3%	35	-125	37	-119	44	147	2	-10.5%	3
2007	SF	7	193	94	48.7%	914	2	4	10	8.8%	3.8	50	-49.4%	49	-509	50	-429	13	89	0	35.6%	24
2008	SF		529	300	56.6%	3699	17	17			5.9		-13.7%					39	125	0	18.2%	

2007:   45% Short   32% Mid   12% Deep   10% Bomb   YAC: 3.4 (50)   2006:   53% Short   25% Mid   14% Deep   7% Bomb   YAC: 5.4 (8)

Smith seemed on his way to developing into a decent quarterback until September 30, when Seattle defensive tackle Rocky Bernard burst through the heart of the 49ers' offensive line and took him to the turf. Watching the replay, you can see Smith bounce on the turf with the 300-pound Bernard on top of him. At that moment, Smith's shoulder separated, and everything changed. The Niners lost three straight games with Smith out, and the third-year player wanted to get back into the lineup. Coach Mike Nolan wanted him back, too. When he did return nearly a month later, he wasn't the same because his shoulder wasn't responding. Smith told this to Nolan, but the coach believed Smith needed to learn to play through injury. Smith then challenged Nolan in the press, saying that he needed time off and that Nolan wasn't listening. Eventually, Smith went outside the team to Dr. James Andrews to get his shoulder repaired. After the tiff with Nolan and with the abrupt halt of his development from the prior year,

Smith is no longer the golden child of the franchise. The former first overall pick of the 2005 draft will be thrown into a three-way camp competition with two free agent journeymen, Shaun Hill and J. T. O'Sullivan. Offensive coordinator Mike Martz will make the decision on who starts, and his criteria is simple: "Whoever completes the ball the most. Accuracy is the biggest issue." The mostly injured Smith completed less than 50 percent of his passes last year.

Troy Smith

Height: 6-0 Weight: 225 College: Ohio State   Draft: 2007/5 (174) Born: 20-Jul-1984 Age: 24 Risk: Red

Year	Team	G	Att	Comp	C%	Yds	TD	INT	FUM	ASR	NY/P	Rk	DVOA	Rk	DYAR	Rk	YAR	Runs	Yds	TD	DVOA	DYAR
2007	BAL	4	76	40	52.6%	452	2	0	5	4.5%	5.4	—	5.2%	—	85	—	41	12	54	1	17.5%	15
2008	BAL		472	264	56.0%	2589	12	17			4.8		-29.5%					53	272	1	-9.4%	

2007:   34% Short   45% Mid   15% Deep   6% Bomb   YAC: 4.3 (—)

Smith's luck has been bad from the moment he stepped onto the field against Florida in the national championship game. As soon as scouts saw he couldn't get away from NFL-caliber edge rushers such as Jarvis Moss and Derrick Harvey, Smith's stock started to drop. It kept dropping through the Combine and through Ohio State's Pro Day, and as a result he fell into the fifth round. At first it looked like he landed in a perfect situation in Baltimore; he barely got on the field before the Ravens decided to use a first-round pick on Joe Flacco, effectively throwing a giant roadblock between Smith and the starting job. Smith didn't light the world on fire in his limited action, but he split his two starts and was the only Ravens quarterback to post a positive DVOA on the season.

Jim Sorgi

Height: 6-3 Weight: 194 College: Wisconsin   Draft: 2004/6 (193) Born: 3-Dec-1980 Age: 28 Risk: Orange

Year	Team	G	Att	Comp	C%	Yds	TD	INT	FUM	ASR	NY/P	Rk	DVOA	Rk	DYAR	Rk	YAR	Runs	Yds	TD	DVOA	DYAR
2005	IND	5	62	43	69.4%	444	3	1	2	4.3%	6.7	—	21.3%	—	135	—	126	12	1	0	5.5%	3
2007	IND	4	36	18	50.0%	132	1	0	2	4.7%	3.1	—	-1.9%	—	20	—	-8	6	-4	0	-1.9%	1
2008	IND		482	308	64.0%	2674	29	14			5.0		-4.8%					40	24	0	24.4%	

2007:   73% Short   15% Mid   9% Deep   3% Bomb   YAC: 4.2 (—)

In the Peyton Manning comment, we predicted when Manning would break Brett Favre's passing records. We tried to run the same projection for Sorgi. Unfortunately, Microsoft Excel predicts that the universe will collapse on itself before Jim Sorgi approaches any of Favre's benchmarks. We hope Sorgi is content to stand on the sideline, high-five Manning after touchdowns, and play the second half of Week 17; he's signed to fill that role through 2010.

Drew Stanton

Height: 6-3 Weight: 226 College: Michigan State   Draft: 2007/2 (43) Born: 7-May-1984 Age: 24 Risk: Red

Year	Team	G	Att	Comp	C%	Yds	TD	INT	FUM	ASR	NY/P	Rk	DVOA	Rk	DYAR	Rk	YAR	Runs	Yds	TD	DVOA	DYAR
2008	DET		489	276	56.4%	2822	15	18			4.6		-56.5%					66	309	2	10.4%	

Last year's second-round pick from Michigan State, Stanton underwent arthroscopic surgery at the start of camp and missed his entire rookie season. He started practicing again in March and is still in the team's plans. New coordinator Jim Colletto may have scaled down the team's playbook to help Stanton get up to speed, but Stanton still thinks highly of He Who Must Not Be Named in Detroit. "I learned a lot from Coach Martz," Stanton said in an off-season interview. "He's so knowledgeable, and I remember writing down everything that came out of his mouth." Eventually, though, Stanton got bored writing "I'm a genius" over and over again.

Vinny Testaverde

Height: 6-5 Weight: 235 College: Miami   Draft: 1987/1 (1) Born: 13-Nov-1963 Age: 45 Risk: Red

Year	Team	G	Att	Comp	C%	Yds	TD	INT	FUM	ASR	NY/P	Rk	DVOA	Rk	DYAR	Rk	YAR	Runs	Yds	TD	DVOA	DYAR
2005	NYJ	6	106	60	56.6%	777	1	6	8	10.3%	5.8	25	-34.8%	43	-183	38	-187	7	4	2	14.4%	7
2006	NE	3	3	2	66.7%	29	1	0	0	0.0%	9.7	—	186.8%	—	37	—	37	8	-8	0	—	—
2007	CAR	7	172	94	54.7%	952	5	6	3	5.9%	5.0	43	-28.6%	46	-214	47	-203	9	22	0	-24.6%	-3

2007:   60% Short   20% Mid   12% Deep   8% Bomb   YAC: 5.1 (13)

With Vinny's final retirement (we think) it is time to look back and appreciate a career that lasted (probably no more than) 21 seasons and left him in the all-time top 10 in completions, attempts, passing yards, and touchdowns. He's no one's Hall-of-Famer, unless they install a wing in Canton for players who hang around long enough to amass decades of relatively average seasons. Steve DeBerg would make the inaugural speech. Honestly, 21 seasons in a league that disposes of players with alarming regularity is an impressive feat. Farewell, Vinny (unless we meet again).

Tyler Thigpen

Height: 6-3   Weight: 220   College: Coastal Carolina   Draft: 2007/7 (217)   Born: 14-Apr-1984   Age: 24   Risk: Red

Year	Team	G	Att	Comp	C%	Yds	TD	INT	FUM	ASR	NY/P	Rk	DVOA	Rk	DYAR	Rk	YAR	Runs	Yds	TD	DVOA	DYAR
2007	KC	1	6	2	33.3%	41	0	1	0	13.4%	4.6	—	-80.5%	—	-29	—	-38	0	0	0	—	—
2008	KC		493	279	56.7%	2820	17	16			4.5		-32.1%					93	667	4	69.4%	

2007:   14% Short   57% Mid   14% Deep   14% Bomb   YAC: 14.0 (—)

Okay, we sort of made fun of Thigpen in last year's "Going Deep" section. Apparently we didn't know what the Vikings had, and neither did the Vikings. They thought they could pass their unknown seventh-round pick through waivers to the practice squad, but the Chiefs snapped him up, and they think he really could turn into something. He's a top athlete with a strong arm, but he also makes quick decisions. His problem is experience—like a lot of Division I-AA or Division II stars, he relies too much on physical gifts, trying to make plays that worked fine against the lesser athletes he played against in college but will get him destroyed in the NFL. If he can learn his way past that, it isn't like the Chiefs are loaded at the position. In a perfect world, he turns into their version of Derek Anderson.

Billy Volek

Height: 6-2   Weight: 214   College: Fresno State   Draft: 2000/FA   Born: 28-Apr-1976   Age: 32   Risk: Red

Year	Team	G	Att	Comp	C%	Yds	TD	INT	FUM	ASR	NY/P	Rk	DVOA	Rk	DYAR	Rk	YAR	Runs	Yds	TD	DVOA	DYAR
2005	TEN	6	88	50	56.8%	474	4	2	1	9.1%	4.5	—	-30.7%	—	-122	—	-171	1	3	0	-42.7%	-2
2006	SD	1	2	1	50.0%	4	0	0	3	33.1%	-0.7	—	-136.1%	—	-26	—	-23	3	-3	0	—	—
2007	SD	5	10	3	30.0%	6	0	1	2	16.0%	-0.1	—	-167.3%	—	-122	—	-128	11	-7	0	-99.9%	-14
2008	SD		412	244	59.3%	2953	20	17			6.1		-4.2%					23	46	0	-4.6%	

2007:   67% Short   22% Mid   0% Deep   11% Bomb   YAC: 1.7 (—)

In 30 years, Billy Volek will be able to gather his grandchildren around and talk about how he beat the defending Super Bowl champions in the playoffs with a fourth-quarter quarterback sneak. He also will probably be having that conversation in a rather large house thanks to a three-year, $9-million contract that he signed despite having just 10 career starts. Volek is an ideal short-term backup because he has a good arm, some experience, and a fearlessness that allows him to come in and take command of desperate situations. If Volek has to play a game or two, the Chargers will be fine, but if he is pushed into full-time duty, his poor decision-making skills will be exposed.

Seneca Wallace

Height: 5-11   Weight: 196   College: Iowa State   Draft: 2003/4 (110)   Born: 6-Aug-1980   Age: 28   Risk: Red

Year	Team	G	Att	Comp	C%	Yds	TD	INT	FUM	ASR	NY/P	Rk	DVOA	Rk	DYAR	Rk	YAR	Runs	Yds	TD	DVOA	DYAR
2005	SEA	7	25	13	52.0%	173	1	1	3	9.5%	5.5	—	-41.0%	—	-53	—	-37	6	-5	0	—	—
2006	SEA	9	141	82	58.2%	927	8	7	6	9.3%	6.0	30	-28.4%	41	-166	39	-130	12	122	0	30.3%	21
2007	SEA	10	28	19	67.9%	215	2	1	1	10.9%	6.5	—	-14.6%	—	-8	—	7	4	17	0	27.5%	8
2008	SEA		430	268	62.3%	3425	12	14			6.3		3.1%					46	196	2	7.6%	

2007:   54% Short   35% Mid   12% Deep   0% Bomb   YAC: 6.1 (—)   2006:   35% Short   41% Mid   15% Deep   9% Bomb   YAC: 3.5 (44)

For a brief period in Weeks 4-6 last year, Mike Holmgren looked as though he was finally ready to end the "Seneca Wallace, Quarterback" experiment and move Wallace to wide receiver. Three targets and two incomplete passes later, Wallace was gone. Underground. A generation from now, you'll see Wallace mentioned in hushed tones on one of those Top 10 shows on the NFL Network, when they talk about players who might have been. They'll show shots of former Broncos quarterback Marlin Briscoe winning Super Bowl rings as a receiver with the early 1970s Dolphins, and the talking heads will nod knowingly.

Andrew Walter

Height: 6-5   Weight: 234   College: Arizona State   Draft: 2005/3 (69)   Born: 11-May-1982   Age: 26   Risk: Red

Year	Team	G	Att	Comp	C%	Yds	TD	INT	FUM	ASR	NY/P	Rk	DVOA	Rk	DYAR	Rk	YAR	Runs	Yds	TD	DVOA	DYAR
2006	OAK	12	276	147	53.3%	1677	3	13	13	13.6%	5.1	43	-44.2%	45	-629	45	-590	14	30	0	-101.5%	-42
2007	OAK	1	8	5	62.5%	38	0	0	0	-0.4%	4.8	—	-11.5%	—	0	—	1	0	0	0	—	—
2008	OAK		415	251	60.5%	2584	8	20			4.6		-38.1%					19	25	1	-39.3%	

2007: 63% Short 25% Mid 0% Deep 13% Bomb YAC: 5.0 (—)   2006: 46% Short 32% Mid 15% Deep 7% Bomb YAC: 3.4 (45)

Did two seasons behind a dreadful offensive line ruin Andrew Walter or did he never possess the athleticism to make it as a starter? The world may never know. The fact that Walter survived the last two seasons says something about either resilience or masochism. Now that the offense has a running game and the offensive line is approaching mediocre, Walter will go back to the bench, maybe the place where he belongs in the first place.

Kurt Warner

Height: 6-2   Weight: 220   College: Northern Iowa   Draft: 1998/FA   Born: 22-Jun-1971   Age: 37   Risk: Red

Year	Team	G	Att	Comp	C%	Yds	TD	INT	FUM	ASR	NY/P	Rk	DVOA	Rk	DYAR	Rk	YAR	Runs	Yds	TD	DVOA	DYAR
2005	ARI	10	375	242	64.5%	2713	11	9	8	5.6%	6.4	10	6.8%	15	444	18	529	13	28	0	-21.9%	-3
2006	ARI	7	168	108	64.3%	1377	6	5	8	7.4%	7.5	5	-4.8%	23	73	27	154	13	3	0	-63.8%	-16
2007	ARI	14	451	281	62.3%	3417	27	17	9	5.2%	7.0	7	11.3%	16	699	12	878	17	15	1	-113.6%	-37
2008	ARI		488	297	61.0%	3193	22	22			5.6		-11.1%					22	30	1	-37.9%	

2007: 41% Short 39% Mid 14% Deep 5% Bomb YAC: 4.5 (30)   2006: 50% Short 29% Mid 17% Deep 4% Bomb YAC: 5.3 (11)

At the start of the year, Ken Whisenhunt used Warner as a designated no-huddle quarterback. He said he was using the tactic to jump-start the offense, but it was clearly a ploy to motivate Matt Leinart while getting Warner some work. After Leinart broke his collarbone, Warner took over and had some touchdown fun with Anquan Boldin and Larry Fitzgerald. But the late-career Warner has the frustrating habit of throwing game-killing interceptions, and he fumbles too easily when he's hit, sometimes even if he's only hit by the center's backside during the quarterback-center exchange. Arizona rightly sees no upside in starting the well-known, well-worn Warner over the nascent Leinart, despite Leinart's relatively disappointing season last year. Warner's presence helped Marc Bulger and Eli Manning develop into quality starters: Maybe he can work the same magic with Leinart.

Chris Weinke

Height: 6-4   Weight: 232   College: Florida State   Draft: 2001/4 (106)   Born: 31-Jul-1972   Age: 36   Risk: Red

Year	Team	G	Att	Comp	C%	Yds	TD	INT	FUM	ASR	NY/P	Rk	DVOA	Rk	DYAR	Rk	YAR	Runs	Yds	TD	DVOA	DYAR
2005	CAR	3	13	7	53.8%	64	1	0	4	0.6%	4.9	—	24.6%	—	30	—	32	8	-5	0	-113.7%	-12
2006	CAR	3	96	56	58.3%	625	2	4	4	10.3%	5.9	—	-25.7%	—	-100	—	-103	4	16	0	-57.7%	-5
2007	SF	2	22	13	59.1%	104	1	0	0	19.6%	2.7	—	-48.4%	—	-66	—	-51	0	0	0	—	—

2007: 70% Short 15% Mid 10% Deep 5% Bomb YAC: 5.8 (—)

Weinke came in and impressed the 49ers with the game he played in the season finale but not enough for San Francisco to sign him back. With Vinny Testaverde now retired, Weinke becomes the go-to guy for any team that has four injured quarterbacks and needs to call a replacement-level veteran to come in off his couch.

Vince Young

Height: 6-5   Weight: 233   College: Texas   Draft: 2006/1 (3)   Born: 18-May-1983   Age: 25   Risk: Red

Year	Team	G	Att	Comp	C%	Yds	TD	INT	FUM	ASR	NY/P	Rk	DVOA	Rk	DYAR	Rk	YAR	Runs	Yds	TD	DVOA	DYAR
2006	TEN	15	357	184	51.5%	2199	12	13	6	6.5%	5.8	37	-6.9%	25	99	24	9	83	552	7	3.1%	58
2007	TEN	15	382	238	62.3%	2546	9	17	8	6.7%	5.9	29	-8.4%	31	74	28	58	93	395	3	-9.7%	9
2008	TEN		475	290	61.0%	2783	13	15			4.7		-15.3%					71	440	1	7.7%	

2007: 45% Short 34% Mid 12% Deep 8% Bomb YAC: 4.6 (28)   2006: 42% Short 29% Mid 18% Deep 10% Bomb YAC: 4.8 (22)

The problem is not so much that Young got worse in 2007. The problem is that a quarterback chosen at the top of the first round is supposed to spend his second season taking a nice big leap toward being one of the NFL's elite passers, and instead Young didn't take any leap at all. Young has the tools to be an effective quarterback, but he needs to get more comfortable in the pocket and choose the right times to run. Last year he frequently tried to take off when there was no room in front of him. New offensive coordinator Mike Heimerdinger may ask Young to line up in the shotgun more often, where he is clearly more comfortable: The former spread-option quarterback notched a DVOA of 3.8% in 209 shotgun passes, and in 2006 the difference was even greater: 21.9% DVOA from shotgun but -30.5% DVOA under center.

GOING DEEP

Erik Ainge, NYJ: Ainge is more project than prospect at the NFL level; he needs to put some weight on his frame if he's going to withstand the hits he'll get from speed rushers, and his arm strength and mobility raised red flags among many teams. However, he showed a lot in recovering from a finger injury to throw 31 touchdowns in his senior season at Tennessee. This year, he'll be a bystander as Chad Pennington and Kellen Clemens duke it out for starting reps.

Brett Basanez, CAR: The Panthers have been intrigued by Basanez's potential ever since they signed him as an undrafted free agent out of Northwestern in 2006. He displayed good mobility and intelligence in college, and his arm is strong enough to allow Steve Smith to get underneath his throws. Basanez spent 2007 on injured reserve with a hand injury, but the Panthers stuck with him and Matt Moore as backups to Jake Delhomme instead of going after any available free agents.

Colt Brennan, WAS: By any statistical measurement, Brennan was one of the most dominant quarterbacks in college history. Sure, he played in an offense that routinely inflates stats, but there's inflation and then there's throwing for over 13,000 yards, completing 70 percent of your passes, and racking up 131 touchdowns. Brennan doesn't have a strong arm, and he has a sidearm delivery that gets some passes knocked down, but there is no question that he has the accuracy and mobility to play in a West Coast Offense like the one Jim Zorn is installing in Washington. He's a developmental player who must prove that he's big enough for the NFL and can adjust to an offense that doesn't throw 20 screen passes per game. If he proves to be a college system quarterback . . . well, that's why the Lewin Career Forecast applies only to the first two rounds of the draft.

Alex Brink, HOU: The Texans appear to be set at quarterback with Matt Schaub, Sage Rosenfels, and Quinn Gray, but thought enough to take a seventh-round flier on Brink. He had to do something right to become the second-leading passer at a school (Washington State) that has produced a bunch of NFL signal-callers.

Dennis Dixon, PIT: Slash lives again. Before tearing up his knee, Dixon was having a Heisman-caliber senior season at Oregon, completing 67.7 percent of his passes and throwing 20 touchdowns to only five interceptions while rushing for nearly 600 yards. There were enough concerns about his health after ACL surgery that Dixon felt the need to put together a website so teams could track his recovery. Dixon goes to a team with a firmly established starter and a long history of finding things for athletic backups to do, so expect Dixon to make an impact as a jack-of-all trades.

Ken Dorsey, CLE: The fabled Dorsey-to-Winslow connection from the "U" is just two injuries away from recreation re-created. That is the only positive way to spin the lost season that a Ken Dorsey sighting would entail.

Matt Flynn, GB: Although Brian Brohm presents a real threat to Aaron Rodgers's (seemingly earned) starter status, Flynn's more of a project. He was the quarterback for the reigning national champions, but the combination of questionable arm, limited accuracy, and less than optimal mobility doomed him to a late second-day selection. On the other hand, he's one of those "gritty" quarterbacks known for forcing the most from his abilities, which could lead to reams of positive press from a media that always loves that particular attribute.

Matt Gutierrez, NE: Gutierrez attended De La Salle High School in Northern California. His high school principal was Brother Christopher Brady, Tom's uncle. The Gutierrez-Brady connection continued through college: Gutierrez attended Michigan but couldn't wrest a starting job from Chad Henne, just as Brady battled Drew Henson for much of his college career. You get the picture: Gutierrez has a secretary named Lincoln, Brady has a secretary named Kennedy, and so forth. Gutierrez may replace Matt Cassel as Brady's primary backup, and if Brady gets hurt in Week 2, look out! Seriously, though: low-level prospect, career backup material.

Tim Hasselbeck, ARI: See Palmer, Jordan, and then add five years.

Josh Johnson, TB: Forty-three touchdowns and one interception in your senior year is impressive no matter what, right? Well, sort of. Those were Johnson's numbers as a senior for San Diego of the Pioneer League, but intrigue surrounded him because he played under former NFL quarterback Jim Harbaugh for three years. Johnson looked great against stronger competition in the Shrine Game, but back spasms limited his ability to throw accurately at the Combine, and that dropped him down a lot of draft boards. Only the Buccaneers had him in their sights all the way. Personnel executive and former quarterback Doug Williams took Johnson under his wing, spending time with the youngster in San Diego and giving him a sense of what NFL life would be like. Johnson has real potential as a Randall Cunningham-style quarterback, and he couldn't be in a better place to make it happen.

Jared Lorenzen, NYG: J-Load came in when Eli Manning went down with an injury in Week 1, only to suffer an ankle injury which cost him an opportunity to start the next week. He remains a talented athlete with a strong arm, but with the Giants' selection of André Woodson in this year's draft, Lorenzen is likely competing with David Carr for one spot on the roster. (4-for-8, 28 yards and a fumble with -21 DYAR and -42.4% DVOA in limited 2007 action.)

Jamie Martin, NO: The Saints threw the ball more often than any other team, but starter Drew Brees took every snap that led to a pass. This left Martin with little to do, which is what he's had since putting up pedestrian numbers in 2002 and 2005 with the Rams. (Martin's recent stats: 16-29 for 185, 1 TD, 1 INT, -57.3% DVOA, -83 DYAR in 2006.)

Erik Meyer, OAK: Meyer's been in the league for two years and failed to make the Bengals' and Seahawks' rosters. He's one of the 800 quarterbacks in the Raiders' camp, so he likely needs a new agent. If you plug his name into "Alec Eiffel," the song sounds even better. Erik Meyer stands in the archway . . .

Craig Nall, FA: Nall returned to Green Bay after stints in Buffalo and Houston, but his second stint with the team was abruptly cut short by the draft, as the Packers added both Brian Brohm and Matt Flynn. Nall should catch on with some team come training camp, but he's no threat to seeing much playing time.

Jeff Otis, OAK: The former Columbia star was waived by the Raiders in training camp, caught on with the Chiefs, then was re-signed by the Raiders in the offseason. That's a sign that the team was interested in him, and with Daunte Culpepper gone, Otis could be the front-runner for the third-string spot.

Tyler Palko, NO: Promoted from the New Orleans roster from the practice squad in late December, Palko was an undrafted rookie in 2007 who stuck around after being cut in training camp. He's a "try-hard" guy who had a fine career at Pitt, despite a big switch in offense when Dave Wannstedt replaced Walt Harris in 2005. Palko will likely get a few preseason reps and will continue to practice charting plays on the sideline.

Jordan Palmer, CIN: Signed by the Bengals after failing to make Washington's roster, the addition of the former UTEP quarterback allows local Cincinnati media outlets to publicize Bengals intrasquad scrimmages as the "Palmer Bowl." Palmer's a bottom-rung prospect getting by on his brother's reputation.

Jeff Rowe, CIN: Inactive as the Bengals' third quarterback behind Carson Palmer and Ryan Fitzpatrick for the entire 2007 season. Rowe's 2008 is likely to be much the same. There are worse careers than professional clipboard holder, but if Rowe has any greater ambitions, a move to Canada beckons.

Marques Tuiasosopo, OAK: After one year in New York with the Jets, Tuiasosopo returns to Oakland, the team that drafted him. With each passing year, it's getting harder and harder to maintain the fiction that Tuiasosopo is an

NFL-caliber quarterback, but apparently Al Davis likes Tui enough to let him caddy for Jamarcus Russell and Andrew Walter.

Charlie Whitehurst, SD: When a player languishes on the bench several years after being drafted, it becomes difficult to gauge whether he is developing. To figure it out, you have to look for signs of how the team feels about him. A not so subtle sign was the Chargers' decision to re-sign backup quarterback Billy Volek to a three-year extension. Rumors also had Whitehurst on the trading block during the draft. Needless to say, barring two injuries in front of him, Whitehurst is unlikely to see the field as the Chargers' starting quarterback.

André Woodson, NYG: Woodson put up some amazing numbers at Kentucky, throwing for 71 touchdowns in two seasons, leading the SEC in yards and touchdowns in 2007, and setting the conference single-season touchdown record. Unfortunately, he was playing in a scaled-down offense that usually asked him to make only one read, and he has a Byron Leftwich windup that resulted in a few fumbles in college. It will take him time to ramp up to an NFL offense while improving his mechanics, but Woodson has time to develop. Assuming David Carr is the Giants' designated veteran—not a 100 percent safe assumption—Woodson will battle Anthony Wright and fellow Kentucky alum Jared Lorenzen for the third-string job.

Anthony Wright, NYG: Some guys just have a knack for staying in the NFL. Wright is now seven years removed from those epic battles with Ryan Leaf and Quincy Carter for a starting job in Dallas, and three years removed from his seven-game mop-up appearance in Baltimore. He'll compete with David Carr, Jared Lorenzen, and André Woodson for one of two spots behind Eli Manning in New York. Chances are that Wright will land somewhere even if the Giants cut him and we'll still be covering him in "Going Deep" when he's 41. (2006 Bengals: 3-for-3, 31 yards, 97.8% DVOA, 17 DYAR; 2007 Giants: 1-for-7, 12 yards, -11.4% DVOA, 0 DYAR.)

Running Backs

The importance of offensive lines to a running back's success was never more obvious than it was in 2007. Projected rushing leader Frank Gore saw his numbers fall as his offensive line lay in tatters in front of him; meanwhile, rookie Adrian Peterson put up PlayStation numbers behind a great run-blocking line that made Chester Taylor look nearly as good in the process.

Meanwhile, backs that came out of nowhere emerged as viable runners, partly because of the five guys in front of them. Ryan Grant went from fifth on the Giants' depth chart to an upper-echelon starter for the Packers, while the man who beat him out for a roster spot, Ahmad Bradshaw, was a playoff revelation for the World Champions. Earnest Graham took over for the injured Cadillac Williams and put up comparable numbers, while Kenny Watson did the same for an injured Rudi Johnson in Cincinnati.

We're learning that most running backs are more fungible than previously imagined, but that's not true in the world of fantasy football. In first-round picks for fantasy football, picking a running back who stays healthy and effective all year can be the difference between cashing in or giving up after seven weeks. In the following section, we give the last three years' statistics as well as a 2008 KUBIAK projection for every running back who played a significant role in 2007 or who is expected to play a significant role in 2008.

HOW TO READ THE RUNNING BACK STATISTICS TABLE

The first line contains biographical data—each player's name, height, weight, college, draft position, birth date, and age. For height and weight, we used the best data we could find; weight, of course, can fluctuate during the offseason. Age is very simple, the number of years between the player's birth year and 2008, but birth date is provided if you want to figure out exact age.

Draft position gives the draft year and round, with the overall pick number with which the player was taken in parentheses. In the sample table, it says that Marion Barber was chosen in the fourth round of the 2005 draft with the 109th overall pick. Undrafted free agents are listed as "FA" with the year they came into the league, even if they were only in training camp or on a practice squad.

To the far right of the first line is the player's Risk for fantasy football in 2008. The players most likely to match their projected stats in 2008 are marked Green, the players who are riskier but still somewhat dependable are marked Yellow, and everyone else is marked Red. The Risk variable is explained further in the introduction to the Quarterbacks section.

Next, we give the last three years of player stats. The first number is games played (G). This is the official NFL total and may include games in which a player appeared on special teams, but did not carry the ball or catch a pass. The next four columns are familiar: runs, rushing yards (Yds), yards per rush (Yd/R), and rushing touchdowns (TD).

The entry for fumbles (FUM) includes all fumbles by this running back, no matter whether they were recovered by the offense or defense. Holding on to the ball is an identifiable skill; fumbling it so that your own offense can recover it is not. (For more on this issue, see the essay "Pregame Show" in the front of the book.) This entry combines fumbles on both carries and receptions.

Running Back Statistics Sample

Marion Barber   Height: 5-11   Weight: 218   College: Minnesota   Draft: 2005/4 (109)   Born: 10 June 1983   Age: 25   Risk: Red

Year	Team	G	Runs	Yds	Yd/R	TD	FUM	DVOA	Rk	DYAR	Rk	YAR	Suc%	Rec	Pass	Yds	C%	Yd/C	TD	DVOA	Rk	DYAR	Rk
2005	DAL	13	138	538	3.9	5	3	-3.2%	20	31	23	-3	41%	18	25	115	72%	6.4	0	-12.4%	40	2	40
2006	DAL	16	135	654	4.8	14	0	30.5%	1	257	6	250	56%	23	32	196	63%	8.5	2	-19.5%	49	0	45
2007	DAL	16	204	975	4.8	10	3	18.0%	5	233	3	203	49%	44	55	282	82%	6.4	2	-12.6%	40	4	39
2008	DAL		250	1109	4.4	7		3.2%						33	45	231	73%	7.0	2	-10.0%			

The next five columns give our advanced metrics for rushing: DVOA (Defense-Adjusted Value Over Average), DYAR (Defense-Adjusted Yards Above Replacement), and YAR (Yards Above Replacement), along with the player's rank (Rk) in both DVOA and DYAR. These metrics compare every carry by the running back to a league-average baseline based on the game situations in which that running back carried the ball. DVOA and DYAR are also adjusted for the opposing defense. The methods used to compute these numbers are described in detail in the "Statistical Toolbox" introduction in the front of the book. The important distinctions between them are as follows:

- DVOA is a rate statistic, while DYAR is a cumulative statistic. Thus, a higher DVOA means more value per play, while a higher DYAR means more aggregate value over the entire season.
- Because DYAR is defense-adjusted and YAR is not, a player whose DYAR is higher than his YAR faced a harder-than-average schedule. A player whose DYAR is lower than his YAR faced an easier-than-average schedule.

To qualify for ranking in rushing DVOA and DYAR, a running back must have had 100 carries in that season. There are 49 running backs ranked for 2007, 47 for 2006, and 45 for 2005.

The final rushing statistic is Success Rate (Suc%). This number represents running back consistency, measured by successful running plays divided by total running plays. (The definition for success is explained in the "Statistical Toolbox" introduction in the front of the book.) A player with high DVOA and a low Success Rate mixes long runs with plays on which he was stuffed either at or behind the line of scrimmage. A player with low DVOA and a high success rate generally gets the yards needed, but rarely gets more. The league-average Success Rate in 2007 was 45.4 percent. Success Rate is not adjusted for the defenses a player faced.

The 10 columns to the right of Success Rate give data for each running back as a pass receiver. Receptions (Rec) counts passes caught, while Passes (Pass) counts total passes thrown to this player, complete or incomplete. The next four columns list receiving yards (Yds), Catch Rate (C%), yards per catch (Yd/C), and receiving touchdowns (TD).

Our research has shown that receivers bear some responsibility for incomplete passes, even though only their catches are tracked in official statistics. Catch Rate represents receptions divided by all intended passes for this running back. The average NFL running back caught 72.6 percent of passes in 2007.

Finally, we have receiving DVOA and DYAR, which are entirely separate from rushing DVOA and DYAR. To qualify for ranking in receiving DVOA and DYAR, a running back must have 25 passes thrown to him in that season. There are 57 running backs ranked for 2007, 54 for 2006, and 53 for 2005. Numbers without opponent adjustment (YAR and VOA) can be found on our Web site, FootballOutsiders.com.

The italicized row of statistics for the 2008 season is our 2008 KUBIAK projection. This number is based on a complicated regression analysis that takes into account numerous variables, including projected role, performance over the past two years, projected team offense and defense, historical comparables, height, age, experience of the offensive line, and strength of schedule. This year for the first time, we have projected some of our advanced metrics, including DVOA for both rushing and receiving.

It is difficult to accurately project statistics for a 162-game baseball season, but it is exponentially more difficult to accurately project statistics for a 16-game football season, because of the small size of the data samples involved. With that in mind, our projections are not predictions of exact numbers, but the mean of a range of possible performances. What's important is not so much the exact number of yards and touchdowns we project, but whether we're projecting a given player to improve or decline. Actual performance will vary from our projection less for veteran starters and more for rookies and third-stringers. For the latter two groups, we must base our projections on much smaller career statistical samples. Touchdown numbers will vary more than yardage numbers.

The main section for running backs is followed by "Going Deep," in which we briefly discuss lower-round rookies, free-agent veterans, and practice-squad players who may play a role during the 2008 season or beyond. A table with statistics for fullbacks follows, along with comments.

Top 20 RB by Rushing DYAR (Total Value), 2007

Rank	Player	Team	DYAR
1	Brian Westbrook	PHI	334
2	LaDainian Tomlinson	SD	287
3	Marion Barber	DAL	233
4	Adrian Peterson	MIN	228
5	Joseph Addai	IND	222
6	Brandon Jacobs	NYG	220
7	Laurence Maroney	NE	199
8	Fred Taylor	JAC	171
9	Earnest Graham	TB	162
10	Kenny Watson	CIN	162
11	Ryan Grant	GB	161
12	Ronnie Brown	MIA	156
13	Jerious Norwood	ATL	133
14	Frank Gore	SF	130
15	Jamal Lewis	CLE	125
16	Kenton Keith	IND	125
17	Najeh Davenport	PIT	118
18	Derrick Ward	NYG	112
19	DeAngelo Williams	CAR	104
20	Chester Taylor	MIN	101

Top 20 RB by Rushing DVOA (Value per Rush), 2007

Rank	Player	Team	DVOA
1	Jerious Norwood	ATL	24.5%
2	Ronnie Brown	MIA	21.2%
3	Brian Westbrook	PHI	19.9%
4	Brandon Jacobs	NYG	18.3%
5	Marion Barber	DAL	18.0%
6	Laurence Maroney	NE	16.7%
7	Adrian Peterson	MIN	16.4%
8	Najeh Davenport	PIT	15.1%
9	Kenton Keith	IND	14.0%
10	Chris Brown	TEN	13.8%
11	LaDainian Tomlinson	SD	13.6%
12	Kenny Watson	CIN	13.0%
13	Derrick Ward	NYG	13.0%
14	Ryan Grant	GB	12.3%
15	DeAngelo Williams	CAR	11.9%
16	Fred Taylor	JAC	11.1%
17	Joseph Addai	IND	11.1%
18	Earnest Graham	TB	8.4%
19	Selvin Young	DEN	8.4%
20	Chester Taylor	MIN	8.0%

Top 10 RB by Receiving DYAR (Total Value), 2007

Rank	Player	Team	DYAR
1	Brian Westbrook	PHI	189
2	Ronnie Brown	MIA	160
3	Joseph Addai	IND	150
4	Kevin Faulk	NE	146
5	Maurice Jones-Drew	JAC	142
6	LaDainian Tomlinson	SD	113
7	Frank Gore	SF	110
8	Jamal Lewis	CLE	99
9	Adrian Peterson	MIN	97
10	Clinton Portis	WAS	96

Top 10 RB by Receiving DVOA (Value per Pass), 2007

Rank	Player	Team	DVOA
1	Ronnie Brown	MIA	52.0%
2	Joseph Addai	IND	43.7%
3	Adrian Peterson	MIN	43.5%
4	Julius Jones	DAL	38.2%
5	Thomas Jones	NYJ	34.4%
6	Jamal Lewis	CLE	33.3%
7	Maurice Jones-Drew	JAC	32.0%
8	Kevin Faulk	NE	31.0%
9	Lorenzo Booker	MIA	26.7%
10	Najeh Davenport	PIT	25.5%

Joseph Addai

Height: 6-0 | Weight: 205 | College: LSU | Draft: 2006/1 (30) | Born: 3 May 1983 | Age: 25 | Risk: Green

Year	Team	G	Runs	Yds	Yd/R	TD	FUM	DVOA	Rk	DYAR	Rk	YAR	Suc%	Rec	Pass	Yds	C%	Yd/C	TD	DVOA	Rk	DYAR	Rk
2006	IND	16	226	1081	4.8	7	2	18.4%	5	276	4	286	62%	40	50	325	69%	8.1	1	-3.7%	35	28	36
2007	IND	15	261	1072	4.1	12	0	11.1%	17	222	5	257	54%	41	49	364	84%	8.9	3	43.7%	2	150	3
2008	IND		287	1248	4.4	8		12.8%						48	58	391	83%	8.2	1	21.8%			

After leading the league in Success Rate in 2006, Addai slipped to sixth place last year. Still, he has been remarkably consistent; the only other running back to post Success Rates of at least 54 percent in both seasons was Brandon Jacobs. It's obvious that Addai's teammates have as much to do with this as Addai himself; he actually ranked behind teammate Kenton Keith last season, and Edgerrin James lead the league in Success Rate in 2005, his last season in Indianapolis. This is what happens when defenses are terrified that Peyton Manning will throw to Reggie Wayne, Dallas Clark, and the gang: The defense drops defenders to prevent big plays, surrendering chunks of yardage on the ground. Addai fills his role perfectly for Indianapolis, taking what's available, keeping the team out of third-and-long, and catching two or three passes per game. Expect more of the same as long as Addai is in Indy and the offensive core is intact.

Shaun Alexander

Height: 5-11 | Weight: 225 | College: Alabama | Draft: 2000/1 (19) | Born: 30 Aug. 1977 | Age: 31 | Risk: Red

Year	Team	G	Runs	Yds	Yd/R	TD	FUM	DVOA	Rk	DYAR	Rk	YAR	Suc%	Rec	Pass	Yds	C%	Yd/C	TD	DVOA	Rk	DYAR	Rk
2005	SEA	16	370	1880	5.1	27	5	19.3%	3	449	2	502	54%	15	28	78	54%	5.2	1	-21.3%	47	-11	45
2006	SEA	10	252	896	3.6	7	6	-13.8%	44	-53	45	-37	43%	12	16	48	81%	4.0	0	-15.7%	—	1	—
2007	SEA	13	207	716	3.5	4	2	-17.3%	46	-74	48	-91	38%	14	25	76	56%	5.4	1	-36.4%	58	-30	54

Near the end of the first quarter of the Seahawks' wild-card playoff game against the Washington Redskins, Shaun Alexander broke a tackle and rumbled for about 18 yards before hitting the turf and coughing up the football, which was promptly scooped up by Fred Smoot. Instead of chasing after him, Alexander stood in front of the line judge, pointing at his knee and protesting that he was down, before he decided to halfheartedly jog down the sideline watching Smoot bob and weave through traffic. Luckily for the Seahawks, the ruling was overturned on review (his knee was in fact down), but this one play neatly summarizes the arc of Alexander's recent career. Alexander's skills started slipping in 2006, but his effort also started to slip, and he became an easy-way-out runner who hit the ground the moment a defender touched him. The only thing that didn't slip was Alexander's opinion of his skills: He protested to the bitter end that he was a great back victimized by a bad offensive line. The Bengals and Saints had him in for visits, but his future is as an injury replacement at best.

Mike Anderson

Height: 6-0 | Weight: 230 | College: Utah | Draft: 2000/6 (189) | Born: 21 Sept. 1973 | Age: 35 | Risk: Red

Year	Team	G	Runs	Yds	Yd/R	TD	FUM	DVOA	Rk	DYAR	Rk	YAR	Suc%	Rec	Pass	Yds	C%	Yd/C	TD	DVOA	Rk	DYAR	Rk
2005	DEN	15	239	1014	4.2	12	2	20.9%	2	321	7	272	56%	18	21	212	86%	11.8	1	45.4%	—	70	—
2006	BAL	15	39	183	4.7	1	0	3.0%	—	20	—	13	44%	9	14	54	57%	6.0	0	-56.3%	—	-31	—
2007	BAL	8	15	62	4.1	0	1	-22.3%	—	-8	—	-9	40%	4	4	26	100%	6.5	0	38.1%	—	11	—

Released by the Ravens in late February, the 2000 Offensive Rookie of the Year will be remembered as perhaps the best advertisement ever for the ruthless efficiency of the Denver Broncos' running game. After picking up two 1,000-yard seasons with Denver from 2000 to 2005, Anderson did little to distinguish himself in Baltimore. He may have a couple of backup years left, but buyer beware.

J. J. Arrington

Height: 5-9 | Weight: 214 | College: California | Draft: 2005/2 (44) | Born: 23 Jan. 1983 | Age: 25 | Risk: Red

Year	Team	G	Runs	Yds	Yd/R	TD	FUM	DVOA	Rk	DYAR	Rk	YAR	Suc%	Rec	Pass	Yds	C%	Yd/C	TD	DVOA	Rk	DYAR	Rk
2005	ARI	15	112	370	3.3	2	1	-22.2%	41	-62	41	-55	38%	25	33	139	76%	5.6	0	-11.9%	41	3	38
2006	ARI	16	14	19	1.4	0	0	-95.7%	—	-51	—	-49	7%	8	10	58	80%	7.3	0	44.5%	—	30	—
2007	ARI	16	26	78	3.0	0	0	-43.4%	—	-37	—	-37	27%	29	39	241	74%	8.3	1	5.5%	25	40	25
2008	ARI		58	195	3.3	1		-1.6%						24	38	192	63%	8.1	0	-42.2%			

A second-round choice in 2005, Arrington had trouble learning Denny Green's offense and then completely lost his confidence by running into the brick wall of the Cards' offensive line. Now, he remains the only Cardinals runner with speed, but it seems late in the day for Arrington to seriously challenge Edgerrin James, despite an improving Arizona line and Ken Whisenhunt's more run-friendly scheme. Arrington got some opportunities as a receiver last season, with 15 catches in his final six games, and he does have some kickoff return ability. Still, a legit third-down back needs to average more than three yards per carry.

Marion Barber

Height: 5-11 Weight: 218 College: Minnesota   Draft: 2005/4 (109) Born: 10 June 1983 Age: 25 Risk: Red

Year	Team	G	Runs	Yds	Yd/R	TD	FUM	DVOA	Rk	DYAR	Rk	YAR	Suc%	Rec	Pass	Yds	C%	Yd/C	TD	DVOA	Rk	DYAR	Rk
2005	DAL	13	138	538	3.9	5	3	-3.2%	20	31	23	-3	41%	18	25	115	72%	6.4	0	-12.4%	40	2	40
2006	DAL	16	135	654	4.8	14	0	30.5%	1	257	6	250	56%	23	32	196	63%	8.5	2	-19.5%	49	0	45
2007	DAL	16	204	975	4.8	10	3	18.0%	5	233	3	203	49%	44	55	282	82%	6.4	2	-12.6%	40	4	39
2008	DAL		250	1109	4.4	7		3.2%						33	45	231	73%	7.0	2	-10.0%			

Although Barber didn't start a game until the playoffs, he was the top running back in Dallas throughout the 2007 season. While he doesn't possess great breakaway speed, there may not be a back in football who hits the hole harder than Barber, and his lower-body strength allows him to get through trash like he's a Roomba. There was talk that Barber's pass blocking wasn't up to scratch, but he's gotten a majority of the third-down carries each of the last two years, and while he's not the finished product, he's a good help blocker. Although Barber is moving into the starting role in 2007, his workload won't rise more than 30-50 carries or so, with Felix Jones picking up some chunk of the production. The Cowboys gave Barber a seven-year, $45 million deal in this, the last year of his rookie contract. Hopefully, the team will be smart about his extremely physical style and avoid using the big money as a reason to make him a 350-plus carry feature back. The lower-than-expected projection is related to the odds of an overall offensive decline in Dallas, as discussed in the Cowboys chapter, and not to any problem with Barber himself.

Mike Bell

Height: 6-1 Weight: 218 College: Arizona   Draft: 2006/FA Born: 23 April 1983 Age: 25 Risk: Red

Year	Team	G	Runs	Yds	Yd/R	TD	FUM	DVOA	Rk	DYAR	Rk	YAR	Suc%	Rec	Pass	Yds	C%	Yd/C	TD	DVOA	Rk	DYAR	Rk
2006	DEN	15	157	677	4.3	8	1	2.3%	21	77	24	108	51%	20	27	158	67%	7.9	0	7.8%	22	38	30
2007	DEN	5	6	3	0.5	0	1	-110.1	—	-24	—	-22	33%	1		7		7.0	0	—	—	—	—
2008	DEN		37	118	3.2	1		-7.4%						12	20	86	60%	7.3	0	-20.9%			

Nobody ever said Mike Shanahan was not fickle. One year after becoming the darling undrafted free agent du jour, Mike Bell bounced all over the Broncos' depth chart. He suffered a hip injury in training camp, moved to fullback, saw limited action there before suffering a concussion, and then fumbled his one rushing attempt after returning to halfback in Week 12. Shanahan claims Bell has "Pro Bowl potential" at fullback, but Shanny has been trying to trade Bell since last August and would probably say anything to increase the running back's value. Bell will have to fight to stay in the league, but he could change uniforms and get a second chance once other teams' backs start getting hurt in camp.

Tatum Bell

Height: 5-11 Weight: 213 College: Oklahoma State   Draft: 2004/2 (41) Born: 2 March 1981 Age: 27 Risk: Red

Year	Team	G	Runs	Yds	Yd/R	TD	FUM	DVOA	Rk	DYAR	Rk	YAR	Suc%	Rec	Pass	Yds	C%	Yd/C	TD	DVOA	Rk	DYAR	Rk
2005	DEN	15	173	921	5.3	8	3	11.0%	9	144	10	103	43%	18	28	104	64%	5.8	0	-32.5%	48	-29	51
2006	DEN	13	233	1025	4.4	2	5	-4.3%	31	36	30	52	41%	24	31	115	87%	4.8	0	-15.9%	47	0	44
2007	DET	5	44	182	4.1	1	1	-5.5%	—	6	—	5	50%	14	21	63	67%	4.5	0	-46.5%	—	-35	—
2008	DET		148	518	3.5	1		-28.3%						8	11	32	73%	4.0	0	-7.9%			

The Lions traded Dre' Bly to acquire Bell, who saw significant action in the first four games but then disappeared soon after fumbling at the goal line in Week 4. Bell demanded a trade in midseason, but cooled off after Mike Martz and running backs coach Wilbert Montgomery skipped town: In a March interview, Bell claimed that Martz wouldn't speak to him and that Montgomery lied to him. Bell then announced his goals of 1,300 rushing yards and 15 touchdowns for 2008, benchmarks he set at about the same moment that Rob Marinelli was telling every reporter within earshot that running back was the team's greatest need. Bell is a good fit in Jim Colletto's zone-running system, so don't rule out a long stint as the quasi-featured runner, but Kevin Smith will eat into his production.

Michael Bennett

Height: 5-9 **Weight:** 209 **College:** Wisconsin   **Draft:** 2001/1 (27) **Born:** 13 Aug. 1978 **Age:** 30 **Risk:** Red

Year	Team	G	Runs	Yds	Yd/R	TD	FUM	DVOA	Rk	DYAR	Rk	YAR	Suc%	Rec	Pass	Yds	C%	Yd/C	TD	DVOA	Rk	DYAR	Rk
2005	MIN	16	126	473	3.8	3	5	-26.3%	44	-86	42	-92	39%	27	30	124	90%	4.6	2	-7.5%	34	9	36
2006	KC	11	36	200	5.6	0	1	19.2%	—	36	—	34	56%	9	12	77	83%	8.6	0	51.1%	—	54	—
2007	KC	6	20	52	2.6	0	2	-29.4%	—	-14	—	-17	25%	10	13	49	77%	4.9	0	-88.2%	—	-41	—
2007	TB	8	41	189	4.6	1	0	4.0%	—	22	—	20	49%	5	9	54	56%	10.8	1	32.1%	—	23	—
2008	TB		44	155	3.5	2		-9.5%						17	24	132	71%	7.8	0	16.4%			

Bennett signed a three-year contract with the Bucs to be Michael Pittman's replacement as the third man in Tampa Bay's running backs rotation. He's a good receiving option out of the backfield, and his speed will provide a contrast to Earnest Graham's power running style, but look for the team to ask Warrick Dunn to do these things more often.

Cedric Benson

Height: 5-10 **Weight:** 215 **College:** Texas   **Draft:** 2005/1 (4) **Born:** 28 Dec. 1982 **Age:** 25 **Risk:** Yellow

Year	Team	G	Runs	Yds	Yd/R	TD	FUM	DVOA	Rk	DYAR	Rk	YAR	Suc%	Rec	Pass	Yds	C%	Yd/C	TD	DVOA	Rk	DYAR	Rk
2005	CHI	9	67	272	4.1	0	1	-21.4%	—	-34	—	-17	36%	1	1	3	100%	3.0	0	-42.8%	—	-2	—
2006	CHI	15	157	647	4.1	6	0	7.9%	14	104	20	122	47%	8	10	54	78%	6.8	0	22.6%	—	21	—
2007	CHI	11	196	674	3.4	4	4	-17.0%	45	-67	44	-57	40%	17	27	123	63%	7.2	0	-20.7%	48	-10	45
2008	CHI		267	1015	3.8	6		-9.6%						35	50	299	70%	8.6	1	-8.9%			

The events of May 4 on Lake Travis in Texas are murky, so we'll start with what we do know: Benson was drafted fourth overall in 2005, but didn't earn a starting job until his third season, which is virtually unheard-of for a running back picked in the early part of the first round. When he did get to start, he was horrible. Then the Bears spent a second-round draft pick this year on Matt Forte, which showed a lack of faith in Benson. And then came the day on the lake. Officials of the Lower Colorado River Authority say Benson failed a sobriety test and resisted arrest before being hit with pepper spray. Benson says he wasn't drunk and didn't resist arrest. His friends vouch for his story. Although Benson's job was already in jeopardy before his troubles, this incident certainly didn't help things. General manager Jerry Angelo—who supported Tank Johnson and Ricky Manning, Jr., when they were arrested on weapons charges in separate incidents—said he was disappointed "that [Benson] put himself in a position to be the victim. . . . It was a lapse in judgment." That doesn't sound like a vote of confidence.

Ladell Betts

Height: 5-11 **Weight:** 223 **College:** Iowa   **Draft:** 2002/2 (56) **Born:** 27 Aug. 1979 **Age:** 29 **Risk:** Red

Year	Team	G	Runs	Yds	Yd/R	TD	FUM	DVOA	Rk	DYAR	Rk	YAR	Suc%	Rec	Pass	Yds	C%	Yd/C	TD	DVOA	Rk	DYAR	Rk
2005	WAS	12	89	338	3.8	1	2	-11.9%	—	-11	—	-32	39%	10	17	78	59%	7.8	1	-6.3%	—	6	—
2006	WAS	16	245	1154	4.7	4	4	11.6%	9	194	11	178	46%	53	64	445	69%	8.4	1	14.0%	17	148	6
2007	WAS	16	93	335	3.6	1	1	-13.9%	—	-21	—	-21	45%	21	32	174	66%	8.3	1	-6.3%	32	14	34
2008	WAS		118	482	4.1	3		-10.0%						37	59	284	63%	7.7	1	-12.0%			

With Clinton Portis healthy all year, Betts saw his role reduced to pre-2006 levels, and his production went the same way. It's not a surprise that Betts struggled to get on the field—even when Portis isn't running the ball, he's an elite blocker in the backfield, so coaches are loathe to take him out unless absolutely necessary. Portis remains an injury risk, so Betts still has value, but expecting him to reproduce his 2006 campaign would be wishful thinking.

Lorenzo Booker

Height: 5-10 **Weight:** 191 **College:** Florida State   **Draft:** 2007/3 (71) **Born:** 14 June 1984 **Age:** 24 **Risk:** Red

Year	Team	G	Runs	Yds	Yd/R	TD	FUM	DVOA	Rk	DYAR	Rk	YAR	Suc%	Rec	Pass	Yds	C%	Yd/C	TD	DVOA	Rk	DYAR	Rk
2007	MIA	7	28	125	4.5	0	0	16.3%	—	34	—	29	54%	28	36	237	78%	8.5	0	26.7%	9	85	12
2008	PHI		43	205	4.8	1		4.9%						19	29	148	66%	7.8	1	-0.3%			

As last year's third-round pick, Booker looked great at the start of training camp. Unfortunately, his blocking was so bad and his knowledge of the offense so primitive that Cam Cameron limited him to scout team duty while guys like Samkon Gado pretended to be featured runners. Pressed into action as the third-down back in December, Booker responded with several fine games as a receiver. The trick to using guys like Booker is to focus on what they can do (catch passes, fake defenders out), not what they can't do (block). The Eagles traded for Booker during the draft. He'll replace Ryan Moats as the roster's running back least likely to complete a crossword puzzle.

Ahmad Bradshaw

Height: 5-10 Weight: 198 College: Marshall   Draft: 2007/7 (250) Born: 19 March 1986 Age: 22 Risk: Red

Year	Team	G	Runs	Yds	Yd/R	TD	FUM	DVOA	Rk	DYAR	Rk	YAR	Suc%	Rec	Pass	Yds	C%	Yd/C	TD	DVOA	Rk	DYAR	Rk
2007	NYG	12	23	190	8.3	1	0	50.5%	—	59	—	45	61%	2	5	12	40%	6.0	0	-62.8%	—	-14	—
2008	NYG		129	560	4.3	5		8.8%						13	19	135	68%	10.3	1	18.2%			

Bradshaw was one of the jewels in Jerry Reese's Late-Round Bonanza. At five foot ten and 198 pounds, he is frequently categorized as a scatback. Scatbacks, however, generally don't carry defensive tackles on their backs for five yards, as Bradshaw did to New England's Ty Warren in Super Bowl XLII. There were inklings of what could be when Bradshaw gained 177 yards on only 26 carries in the preseason, returned a kickoff 83 yards against the Cowboys (darn those holding penalties!), and put up 151 yards on the ground in a late December win over the Bills. His consistent production through the postseason indicates a bright future, and he could easily exceed our projection if Brandon Jacobs's health remains an issue.

Chris Brown

Height: 6-3 Weight: 219 College: Colorado   Draft: 2003/3 (93) Born: 17 April 1981 Age: 27 Risk: Red

Year	Team	G	Runs	Yds	Yd/R	TD	FUM	DVOA	Rk	DYAR	Rk	YAR	Suc%	Rec	Pass	Yds	C%	Yd/C	TD	DVOA	Rk	DYAR	Rk
2005	TEN	15	224	851	3.8	5	4	-14.5%	40	-54	40	-12	41%	25	36	327	69%	13.1	2	36.8%	4	94	10
2006	TEN	5	41	156	3.8	0	1	-17.5%	—	-15	—	-8	41%	2	9	4	22%	2.0	0	-87.4%	—	-48	—
2007	TEN	12	102	462	4.5	5	1	13.8%	10	100	22	113	57%	19	21	128	90%	6.7	0	14.7%	—	33	—
2008	HOU		183	819	4.5	5		1.4%						29	39	167	74%	5.7	1	-20.9%			

Brown gained 175 yards in the season opener against Jacksonville, but never gained more than 46 yards again. In 2004, he looked like one of the league's up-and-coming young running back stars, but injuries slowed his development. It now appears that he'll never be more than a complementary player. Still, Brown was a solid runner for the Titans last season and should get good playing time for the Texans this year. He offers between-the-tackles power and some rudimentary receiving ability, but zero durability.

Ronnie Brown

Height: 6-0 Weight: 232 College: Auburn   Draft: 2005/1 (2) Born: 12 Dec. 1981 Age: 26 Risk: Red

Year	Team	G	Runs	Yds	Yd/R	TD	FUM	DVOA	Rk	DYAR	Rk	YAR	Suc%	Rec	Pass	Yds	C%	Yd/C	TD	DVOA	Rk	DYAR	Rk
2005	MIA	15	207	907	4.4	4	4	-4.9%	25	31	22	58	46%	32	47	232	68%	7.3	1	-5.0%	35	24	31
2006	MIA	13	241	1008	4.2	5	4	-8.3%	35	3	34	41	46%	33	38	276	63%	8.4	0	2.0%	30	37	32
2007	MIA	7	119	602	5.1	4	0	21.2%	2	156	12	194	51%	39	46	389	85%	10.0	1	52.0%	1	160	2
2008	MIA		256	1150	4.5	6		1.0%						47	63	358	75%	7.6	0	6.4%			

Brown was second among running backs in receiving DYAR, an impressive feat in a league full of guys like Brian Westbrook and Maurice Jones-Drew, and an even more impressive feat given that he did it in only seven games. His 85 percent catch rate was built exclusively on screens, shovels, and dump-offs to the sidelines; unlike a Westbrook or a Kevin Faulk, Brown never ran a route that took him more than five yards upfield before the throw (the lone exception last year came on a Trent Green scramble). The screen game was one of the few working components of the Dolphins' offense last season, and Brown usually had two blockers in front of him and a surprised defense behind him when he caught the ball. Tony Sparano helped get the most out of Marion Barber in Dallas, so he should find creative ways to get Brown the ball as a receiver and a runner. He'll also try to limit Brown's workload so he actually survives a full season, which would provide quite a boost for the Dolphins. When fantasy draft time comes, however, remember that running backs take time to recover from ACL surgery.

Correll Buckhalter

Height: 6-0 Weight: 222 College: Nebraska   Draft: 2001/4 (121) Born: 6 Oct. 1978 Age: 30 Risk: Red

Year	Team	G	Runs	Yds	Yd/R	TD	FUM	DVOA	Rk	DYAR	Rk	YAR	Suc%	Rec	Pass	Yds	C%	Yd/C	TD	DVOA	Rk	DYAR	Rk
2006	PHI	16	83	345	4.2	2	2	5.2%	—	49	—	41	58%	24	28	256	71%	10.7	1	26.4%	5	70	21
2007	PHI	14	62	313	5.0	4	0	21.9%	—	81	—	78	48%	12	21	87	57%	7.3	0	-8.6%	—	6	—
2008	PHI		75	346	4.6	3		15.4%						17	27	124	63%	7.1	0	-7.4%			

Buckhalter stayed relatively healthy (except for a late-season concussion) for two years in a row, a nifty trick he pulled for the first time in his career. He's a remarkably consistent player when he's able to suit up and a smart runner who's a threat catching the ball out of the backfield or split out wide. As a kick returner, he's a backup running back. Buckhalter is likely to keep up this level of performance when healthy and even more likely not to be healthy.

Michael Bush

Height: 6-2 **Weight:** 242 **College:** Louisville   **Draft:** 2007/4 (100) **Born:** 16 June 1984 **Age:** 24 **Risk:** Red

Year	Team	G	Runs	Yds	Yd/R	TD	FUM	DVOA	Rk	DYAR	Rk	YAR	Suc%	Rec	Pass	Yds	C%	Yd/C	TD	DVOA	Rk	DYAR	Rk
2008	OAK		51	160	3.1	0		-10.7%						22	35	153	63%	7.1	0	-0.6%			

Last year, Justin Fargas was where Michael Bush is now. Stacked behind two runners who were more established, Dominic Rhodes and LaMont Jordan, Fargas nevertheless became the starter and gained 1,042 yards. Bush is now behind top-round pick Darren McFadden, Fargas, and possibly Jordan. If Bush shows any verve returning from the leg he broke at Louisville, he could replace Jordan on the depth chart. Tom Rathman demands maximum effort from his backs, and a quick, thorough rehab would endear Bush to his position coach.

Reggie Bush

Height: 6-0 **Weight:** 200 **College:** USC   **Draft:** 2006/1 (2) **Born:** 2 Mar. 1985 **Age:** 23 **Risk:** Red

Year	Team	G	Runs	Yds	Yd/R	TD	FUM	DVOA	Rk	DYAR	Rk	YAR	Suc%	Rec	Pass	Yds	C%	Yd/C	TD	DVOA	Rk	DYAR	Rk
2006	NO	16	155	565	3.6	6	2	-2.4%	27	38	28	8	44%	88	122	742	68%	8.4	2	22.8%	7	306	1
2007	NO	12	157	581	3.7	4	7	-19.4%	48	-72	47	-69	46%	73	98	417	74%	5.7	2	-9.6%	36	25	32
2008	NO		146	677	4.6	5		5.0%						74	109	521	68%	7.1	2	-11.1%			

With all the talk about what Reggie Bush isn't, it's worth outlining what the second overall draft pick in 2006 actually is. He is a fearsome threat to break long gains if he can get outside, and he's even tougher to stop when he cuts back inside, though this is more true with short passes than sweeps or stretch runs. He is as good a slot receiver as any running back in the game, but the talk about switching him full-time to receiver makes as little sense as the idea that he can be a 300-carry feature back. Bush is what he is—a dynamic big-play threat who can be easily limited if he's a primary target too often. When he missed the last four games of the season with a knee injury and the Pierre Thomas/Aaron Stecker combo showed some life, interesting future options emerged, like a Bush/Thomas time-share if Deuce McAllister can't return from his knee injury. For the Saints in 2008, Bush is best thought of as a player, not a running back or receiver. KUBIAK likes him for a third-year breakout, at least when it comes to yards per carry.

Jamaal Charles

Height: 5-11 **Weight:** 200 **College:** Texas   **Draft:** 2008/3 (73) **Born:** 27 Dec. 1986 **Age:** 21 **Risk:** Red

Year	Team	G	Runs	Yds	Yd/R	TD	FUM	DVOA	Rk	DYAR	Rk	YAR	Suc%	Rec	Pass	Yds	C%	Yd/C	TD	DVOA	Rk	DYAR	Rk
2008	KC		52	203	3.9	1		-6.2%						15	18	156	83%	10.7	0	25.4%			

Charles was overlooked in perhaps the deepest draft for running backs in history, but it's also possible that the analysts just couldn't catch up with him. The Texas track star ran a 4.38 40-yard dash at the Combine, and 102 of his collegiate carries went for gains over 10 yards. His size, speed, and receiving ability put him firmly in the "change-of-pace" category—the thunder to someone else's lightning. On a team with an understanding of the importance and historical success of running back rotations, Charles would be in an ideal position. For the Chiefs, and coached up by Herm "Ride 'Em 'Til They're Done!" Edwards, he could just as easily be dramatically overused or lost in the shuffle.

Jesse Chatman

Height: 5-8 **Weight:** 223 **College:** Eastern Washington   **Draft:** 2002/FA **Born:** 22 Sept. 1979 **Age:** 29 **Risk:** Red

Year	Team	G	Runs	Yds	Yd/R	TD	FUM	DVOA	Rk	DYAR	Rk	YAR	Suc%	Rec	Pass	Yds	C%	Yd/C	TD	DVOA	Rk	DYAR	Rk
2007	MIA	14	128	515	4.0	1	1	-7.5%	37	6	37	8	41%	27	37	161	73%	6.0	0	-26.6%	53	-28	53
2008	NYJ		42	177	4.2	2		17.6%						22	29	165	76%	7.6	0	-20.0%			

Chatman nearly ate his way out of the NFL; when the Chargers cut him in 2005, he tipped the scales at nearly 280 pounds. Chatman switched to a diet of oatmeal, stir-fry, and spinach, reportedly working with personal trainers Wilford Brimley, P. F. Chang, and Popeye. The 223-pound model started six games last year, rushing for 348 yards in one four-game stretch before succumbing to an ankle injury. Chatman is now with the Jets, and his one-cut style can help them off the bench if he doesn't rediscover the subtle joys of the White Castle Crave Case.

Tashard Choice

Height: 5-11 Weight: 215 College: Georgia Tech — Draft: 2008/4 (122) Born: 20 Nov. 1984 Age: 24 Risk: Red

Year	Team	G	Runs	Yds	Yd/R	TD	FUM	DVOA	Rk	DYAR	Rk	YAR	Suc%	Rec	Pass	Yds	C%	Yd/C	TD	DVOA	Rk	DYAR	Rk
2008	DAL		40	196	4.9	1		10.8%						8	12	65	67%	7.6	0	-5.7%			

I'm a Ramblin' Wreck from Georgia Tech, and a hell of an Engineer
A Helluva, Helluva, Helluva, Helluva, Helluva Engineer
Like all the jolly good punishing backs, I make my intentions clear.
I'm a Ramblin' Wreck from Georgia Tech and a hell of an Engineer.
If I'm behind Marion Barber, sir, resplendent in blue and gray,
And that violent running style of his makes the ambulance take him away.
If Jerry Jones had drafted me, sir, I'll tell you what he'd say—
"Get that Tashard kid out there!" as I blow the defenders away!
Oh, I wish I had a football in hand, and a depth chart that wasn't so packed
Behind these Jones and Barber guys, they might never see how I attack.
Over 3,000 collegiate yards, and now I'm supposed to say,
"I'm a Ramblin', Gamblin', HELL OF AN ENGI . . . Special teams? Well, okay . . ."

Patrick Cobbs

Height: 5-8 Weight: 210 College: North Texas — Draft: 2006/FA Born: 31 Jan. 1983 Age: 25 Risk: Red

Year	Team	G	Runs	Yds	Yd/R	TD	FUM	DVOA	Rk	DYAR	Rk	YAR	Suc%	Rec	Pass	Yds	C%	Yd/C	TD	DVOA	Rk	DYAR	Rk
2007	MIA	14	15	47	3.1	1	0	7.8%	—	10	—	10	47%	2	6	20	50%	10.0	0	-15.5%	—	-1	—
2008	MIA		39	176	4.5	1		14.8%						26	35	259	74%	10.1	1	23.4%			

Cobbs, the all-time rushing leader at North Texas, led the Patriots and Dolphins in preseason rushing in 2006 and 2007 before earning some real carries in the post–Ronnie Brown, pre–Lorenzo Booker dark ages last year. Cobbs signed a one-year deal with the Dolphins in mid-March and could easily lead them in preseason rushing again this season. Hey, everyone has his niche.

Najeh Davenport

Height: 6-1 Weight: 245 College: Miami — Draft: 2002/4 (135) Born: 8 Feb. 1979 Age: 29 Risk: Red

Year	Team	G	Runs	Yds	Yd/R	TD	FUM	DVOA	Rk	DYAR	Rk	YAR	Suc%	Rec	Pass	Yds	C%	Yd/C	TD	DVOA	Rk	DYAR	Rk
2005	GB	5	30	105	3.5	2	1	-6.0%	—	4	—	8	43%	2	2	3	100%	1.5	0	-75.4%	—	-7	—
2006	PIT	13	60	221	3.7	1	1	-34.5%	—	-71	—	-76	38%	15	21	193	62%	12.9	1	56.8%	—	90	—
2007	PIT	15	107	499	4.7	5	1	15.1%	8	118	17	114	52%	18	27	184	67%	10.2	2	25.5%	—	51	—
2008	PIT		85	321	3.8	3		5.2%						15	23	127	65%	8.5	0	-19.8%			

According to DVOA and DYAR, Davenport outproduced starting tailback Willie Parker handily last year. However, his two performances as starter after Fast Willie broke his leg in Week 16 were thoroughly unspectacular. Davenport is best suited to a change-of-pace role, but unfortunately, so is Parker; it's entirely possible their statistics would have been reversed had their roles been swapped. Despite the impressive performance, there will be no expansion of his role in the new season. Indeed, with Mewelde Moore newly arrived to take on kick-return duty and Rashard Mendenhall around to share carries with Parker, Davenport may struggle to even make the roster. He'll be fighting with Gary Russell for the last spot; the Steelers will have to decide if Davenport's greater versatility (a solid blocker and receiver, he can play fullback as well as halfback) is worth his larger cap charge. If Davenport is cut, he'd be a good pickup for any team in need of a committee or changeup back who can also return kicks.

Ron Dayne

Height: 5-10 Weight: 245 College: Wisconsin — Draft: 2000/1 (11) Born: 14 Mar. 1978 Age: 30 Risk: Red

Year	Team	G	Runs	Yds	Yd/R	TD	FUM	DVOA	Rk	DYAR	Rk	YAR	Suc%	Rec	Pass	Yds	C%	Yd/C	TD	DVOA	Rk	DYAR	Rk
2005	DEN	10	53	270	5.1	1	1	20.0%	—	65	—	47	53%	3	3	17	100%	5.7	0	-166.1%	—	-19	—
2006	HOU	11	151	612	4.1	5	1	5.0%	16	91	23	120	54%	14	18	77	67%	5.5	0	9.1%	—	33	—
2007	HOU	13	194	773	4.0	6	2	-4.6%	32	34	32	69	48%	17	26	112	65%	6.6	0	-16.8%	43	-4	41

Dayne, the former Heisman winner and record-setting college back, has turned himself into enough of a serviceable pro to avoid the "mega-bust" label he wore early in his career. The knock on Dayne was always that for an, ahem, "big" back, he showed remarkably little power. Worse yet, his lack of initial quickness prevents him from getting through some holes and leads to his getting tackled by his own linemen. Nevertheless, he ranked in the top 15 in Success Rate and if Houston opts to bring him back, he could still be good for a few carries per game in a running-back-by-committee situation.

DeDe Dorsey — Height: 5-10 Weight: 194 College: Lindenwood — Draft: 2006/FA — Born: 1 Aug. 1984 — Age: 24 — Risk: Red

Year	Team	G	Runs	Yds	Yd/R	TD	FUM	DVOA	Rk	DYAR	Rk	YAR	Suc%	Rec	Pass	Yds	C%	Yd/C	TD	DVOA	Rk	DYAR	Rk
2006	IND	13	0	0	0.0	0	—	—	—	—	—	—	—	0	—	0	—	0.0	0	—	—	—	—
2007	CIN	12	21	183	8.7	0	0	68.9%	—	70	—	75	62%	4	6	19	67%	4.8	0	-29.4%	—	-5	—
2008	CIN		62	263	4.2	1		1.7%						25	42	221	60%	8.8	0	13.2%			

You don't see many runners averaging 8.7 yards per carry, even on just 21 carries. Dorsey had runs of 45, 21, 19, and 15 yards last season, plus receptions of 19 and 17 yards among his four catches. (He also had one of -7 yards, which helps explain the DVOA rating.) Dorsey was a small-school marvel who rushed for 1,600 yards and earned all-NAIA recognition as a defensive back. That led to a long look with the Colts and last year's trial as a changeup back in Cincinnati. His sample size is small, but we'd like to see a little more of a running back who gains over 15 yards on 24 percent of his touches.

Reuben Droughns — Height: 5-11 Weight: 215 College: Oregon — Draft: 2000/3 (81) — Born: 21 Aug. 1978 — Age: 30 — Risk: Red

Year	Team	G	Runs	Yds	Yd/R	TD	FUM	DVOA	Rk	DYAR	Rk	YAR	Suc%	Rec	Pass	Yds	C%	Yd/C	TD	DVOA	Rk	DYAR	Rk
2005	CLE	16	309	1232	4.0	2	6	-11.6%	37	-39	39	-48	44%	39	56	369	70%	9.5	0	5.2%	17	56	17
2006	CLE	14	220	758	3.4	4	5	-13.8%	45	-45	44	-26	42%	27	34	169	76%	6.3	0	-1.2%	33	23	37
2007	NYG	16	85	275	3.2	6	1	-10.6%	—	-9	—	-17	47%	7	15	49	47%	7.0	0	-52.4%	—	-28	—
2008	NYG		34	118	3.4	2		-14.7%						8	11	56	73%	7.1	0	-24.6%			

Three backs were able to put up above-average DVOA in the Giants offense. The other was Reuben Droughns, who showed little life before being usurped by Derrick Ward and then Ahmad Bradshaw. Miscast as a kickoff returner, Droughns is closer to being out of football than he is to being a full-time back. He has a Super Bowl ring to ease such lament.

T. J. Duckett — Height: 6-0 Weight: 254 College: Michigan State — Draft: 2002/1 (18) — Born: 17 Feb. 1981 — Age: 27 — Risk: Red

Year	Team	G	Runs	Yds	Yd/R	TD	FUM	DVOA	Rk	DYAR	Rk	YAR	Suc%	Rec	Pass	Yds	C%	Yd/C	TD	DVOA	Rk	DYAR	Rk
2005	ATL	14	121	380	3.1	8	2	-12.1%	38	-19	37	-35	39%	6	7	63	86%	10.5	0	56.7%	—	29	—
2006	WAS	11	38	132	3.5	2	1	-18.3%	—	-16	—	-22	37%	2	2	16	50%	8.0	0	-173.3%	—	-19	—
2007	DET	12	65	335	5.2	3	1	12.2%	—	56	—	59	38%	4	7	54	57%	13.5	0	47.7%	—	26	—
2008	SEA		115	494	4.3	5		9.4%						12	15	100	80%	8.4	0	-64.3%			

Duckett causes amnesia. Every year, a team signs him and then forgets that he exists. Exhibit A: In 2006, the Redskins traded for Duckett and then planted him on the bench behind Clinton Portis and Ladell Betts. Exhibit B: The Lions signed him, traded for Tatum Bell, and then gave up completely on their running game for a month before remembering Duckett and giving him some late-season action. Exhibit C: The Seahawks signed him in March and then added Julius Jones to the roster a few days later. Duckett's good enough to fill a role as a 10- to 15-carry power back in a rotation, but for some reason, teams won't even grant him that role. Wait, who were we talking about?

Warrick Dunn — Height: 5-9 Weight: 180 College: Florida State — Draft: 1997/1 (12) — Born: 5 Jan. 1975 — Age: 33 — Risk: Red

Year	Team	G	Runs	Yds	Yd/R	TD	FUM	DVOA	Rk	DYAR	Rk	YAR	Suc%	Rec	Pass	Yds	C%	Yd/C	TD	DVOA	Rk	DYAR	Rk
2005	ATL	16	280	1416	5.1	3	3	18.2%	4	289	8	264	46%	29	37	220	78%	7.6	1	1.4%	29	31	27
2006	ATL	16	286	1140	4.0	4	1	-2.9%	28	66	25	-1	39%	22	27	170	74%	7.7	1	19.9%	9	57	23
2007	ATL	16	227	720	3.2	4	2	-20.0%	49	-108	49	-124	37%	37	59	238	63%	6.4	0	-29.6%	54	-48	57
2008	TB		38	141	3.7	1		-14.9%						19	24	126	79%	6.6	0	-23.4%			

Just as the NFL has seen very few players resembling Dunn in the past, it's entirely possible that his like will never be seen again. When is the next time that a five foot nine, 180-pound running back is going to rush for over 10,000 career yards? Dunn has benefited from several factors throughout his remarkable NFL life. He's always been in situations that allowed him to be a change-of-pace back (no coach was ever stupid enough to run him more than 286 times in a season). He's been adept enough as a receiver to avoid punishment while providing further production for his team. And he was Atlanta's point man in the running game from 2004 through 2006, when Alex Gibbs's blocking schemes and the threat of Michael Vick out of the backfield gave Dunn perhaps his three greatest seasons. Predictably limited by the breakdown in blocking in 2007—the Falcons finished dead last in Adjusted Line Yards—Dunn was cut by Atlanta and returned to Tampa Bay, his first home, where he'll most likely be a backfield receiving threat, a world-champion philanthropist, and little else. Enjoy him while you can, folks. Odds are, you're not getting another Warrick Dunn.

Justin Fargas

Height: 6-1 Weight: 220 College: USC   Draft: 2003/3 (96) Born: 25 Jan. 1980 Age: 28 Risk: Red

Year	Team	G	Runs	Yds	Yd/R	TD	FUM	DVOA	Rk	DYAR	Rk	YAR	Suc%	Rec	Pass	Yds	C%	Yd/C	TD	DVOA	Rk	DYAR	Rk
2005	OAK	14	5	28	5.6	0	0	21.4%	—	7	—	6	40%	1	5	9	20%	9.0	0	-63.5%	—	-16	—
2006	OAK	16	178	659	3.7	1	1	-12.0%	42	-24	40	-6	40%	13	21	91	67%	7.0	0	20.6%	—	61	—
2007	OAK	14	222	1009	4.5	4	3	1.6%	24	92	24	99	46%	23	32	188	72%	8.2	0	22.0%	11	58	20
2008	OAK		179	707	4.0	3		-7.4%						25	33	190	76%	7.7	0	7.4%			

Depending on how quickly Darren McFadden develops, "Snuggly Bear" will either be the main running threat, share the carries, or just relieve the highly touted rookie now and then. Seen as a third-down specialist, Fargas wasn't supposed to see much playing time last year behind established backs LaMont Jordan and Dominic Rhodes. But both those players didn't show the drive needed to satisfy demanding running backs coach Tom Rathman, so Fargas took over. He fit right in to the Raiders' new zone-blocking scheme, and Rathman loved his toughness. Fargas could return to a third-down role, but his deficiency in pass protection limits his usefulness.

Kevin Faulk

Height: 5-8 Weight: 202 College: LSU   Draft: 1999/2 (46) Born: 5 June 1976 Age: 32 Risk: Red

Year	Team	G	Runs	Yds	Yd/R	TD	FUM	DVOA	Rk	DYAR	Rk	YAR	Suc%	Rec	Pass	Yds	C%	Yd/C	TD	DVOA	Rk	DYAR	Rk
2005	NE	8	51	145	2.8	0	3	-35.9%	—	-51	—	-51	33%	29	37	260	78%	9.0	0	3.2%	23	33	26
2006	NE	15	25	123	4.9	1	0	19.7%	—	28	—	27	44%	43	56	356	59%	8.3	2	0.6%	32	38	28
2007	NE	16	62	265	4.3	0	1	15.2%	—	63	—	62	56%	47	59	383	80%	8.1	1	31.0%	8	146	4
2008	NE		31	136	4.4	2		26.1%						31	44	287	70%	9.4	1	16.3			

Faulk's career postseason stats: 17 games, 74 carries, 373 yards, 5.0 yards per carry, 45 receptions, 375 yards, 8.3 yards per catch. It's a fine season unto itself, played in the limelight against the toughest competition in the world. Faulk now has over 5,000 career yards from scrimmage and 4,000 more as a return man; when the Patriots museum opens in Foxboro, Robert Kraft should make him the first curator. Expect a few hundred more scrimmage yards and some third-down goodness from Faulk this season, assuming he stays out of trouble; the normally whistle-clean Faulk got caught with a li'l weed at a Lil Wayne concert in the offseason. Faulk immediately passed a drug test, though conspiracy theorists are certain that the urine he submitted actually belonged to Dwight Schrute.

Matt Forte

Height: 6-2 Weight: 222 College: Tulane   Draft: 2008/2 (44) Born: 10 Dec. 1985 Age: 22 Risk: Red

Year	Team	G	Runs	Yds	Yd/R	TD	FUM	DVOA	Rk	DYAR	Rk	YAR	Suc%	Rec	Pass	Yds	C%	Yd/C	TD	DVOA	Rk	DYAR	Rk
2008	CHI		220	761	3.5	4		-8.7%						31	41	323	76%	10.5	1	26.9%			

Nobody can be happier about Cedric Benson's lack of productivity and various boating escapades than Forte, the MVP of the 2008 Senior Bowl who gained a very under-the-radar 2,007 yards last season for Tulane. Like Benson, Forte is a big power back with decent second-level speed. Unlike Benson, Forte has no known off-field concerns to overcome (Benson had legal and disciplinary issues at Texas). Forte is also a good receiver out of the backfield, so when Chicago's quarterback du jour accidentally throws a dink screen at the back of his head, he might just be able to turn around and catch it.

DeShaun Foster

Height: 6-0   **Weight:** 222   **College:** UCLA   **Draft:** 2002/2 (34)   **Born:** 10 Jan. 1980   **Age:** 28   **Risk:** Red

Year	Team	G	Runs	Yds	Yd/R	TD	FUM	DVOA	Rk	DYAR	Rk	YAR	Suc%	Rec	Pass	Yds	C%	Yd/C	TD	DVOA	Rk	DYAR	Rk
2005	CAR	15	205	879	4.3	2	2	-9.4%	33	-6	33	43	43%	34	48	372	71%	10.9	1	18.6%	15	80	12
2006	CAR	14	227	897	4.0	3	4	-2.0%	26	63	26	14	45%	32	46	159	69%	5.0	0	-3.1%	34	34	34
2007	CAR	16	247	876	3.5	3	7	-15.8%	44	-72	46	-60	43%	25	36	182	69%	7.3	1	-24.4%	50	-22	50
2008	SF		59	195	3.3	2		-11.2%						20	25	145	80%	7.1	0	3.5%			

We're wondering what the Panthers were thinking when they handed Foster the ball 103 more times than they handed it to DeAngelo Williams last season, when Foster trailed Williams in yards per carry, DYAR, DVOA, and touchdowns. Foster had a slight edge in Success Rate, but the only category in which he reigned supreme over Williams was fumbles—Foster had seven in 2007, while Williams had one. Then again, we've been curious about what the Panthers saw in Foster every year since he ranked 41st out of 45 running backs in 2003. Foster is the kind of player who drives our stats to distraction, occasionally productive but unreliable and awful in the red zone. The Panthers finally tired of his boom-or-bust nature and released him in mid-February, a move that saved the team $4.75 million in salary cap space. Signed by the 49ers, he'll probably do very little in the face of the eight-man fronts opponents can endlessly run against Alex Smith.

Samkon Gado

Height: 5-11   **Weight:** 210   **College:** Liberty   **Draft:** 2005/FA   **Born:** 13 Nov. 1982   **Age:** 26   **Risk:** Red

Year	Team	G	Runs	Yds	Yd/R	TD	FUM	DVOA	Rk	DYAR	Rk	YAR	Suc%	Rec	Pass	Yds	C%	Yd/C	TD	DVOA	Rk	DYAR	Rk
2005	GB	8	143	582	4.1	6	4	-7.0%	29	10	29	4	43%	10	12	77	83%	7.7	1	-8.8%	—	4	—
2006	HOU	10	56	210	3.8	1	1	-17.7%	—	-21	—	-28	39%	17	23	85	65%	5.0	0	-18.7%	—	-8	—
2007	HOU	3	18	46	2.6	1	1	-20.7%	—	-12	—	-10	44%	8	8	59	100%	7.4	0	-9.9%	—	2	—
2007	MIA	5	35	104	3.0	3	0	1.2%	—	14	—	-1	29%	4	5	47	80%	11.8	0	27.5%	—	11	—

Gado is assembling an odd little career, changing teams in midseason every year and having a productive game or two before reaffirming his status as bench filler. If history is a guide, he'll sign with San Francisco when Frank Gore gets injured in the preseason, the 49ers will release him in Week 2, he'll sign with the Jets in Week 4, rush for 87 yards in Week 6, and spend the last two months of the year on the inactive list. If you shout "Christian Okoye" across the plains of Nigeria, you hear the faint echo of "Samkon Gado."

Frank Gore

Height: 5-9   **Weight:** 217   **College:** Miami   **Draft:** 2005/3 (65)   **Born:** 14 May 1983   **Age:** 25   **Risk:** Red

Year	Team	G	Runs	Yds	Yd/R	TD	FUM	DVOA	Rk	DYAR	Rk	YAR	Suc%	Rec	Pass	Yds	C%	Yd/C	TD	DVOA	Rk	DYAR	Rk
2005	SF	14	127	608	4.8	3	3	6.6%	14	75	17	77	45%	15	22	131	68%	8.7	0	-15.4%	—	-2	—
2006	SF	16	312	1695	5.4	8	6	10.1%	12	242	8	261	47%	61	86	485	62%	8.0	1	10.9%	19	135	9
2007	SF	15	260	1102	4.2	5	4	4.3%	21	130	14	79	42%	53	69	436	77%	8.2	1	14.3%	19	110	7
2008	SF		233	922	4.0	5		-10.7%						60	78	551	77%	9.1	2	22.0%			

After setting the franchise rushing record with 1,695 yards in 2006, Gore proudly declared he was going for over 2,000 yards in 2007. But that was before his offensive line performed poorly and before training camp, where Gore sustained a broken hand that knocked him out for the entire preseason. After spraining his ankle early in the year, he then had to deal with two deaths, that of his mother and that of his close friend and former college teammate, Redskins safety Sean Taylor. In 2008, Gore will get the opportunity to return to his success from two seasons ago. New offensive coordinator Mike Martz loves him and believes he's a better pure runner than Marshall Faulk. Despite fears that the Niners will only run the ball eight times a month, Martz has stated many times that the offense will run through Gore. The goal is for him to get 20 carries and five receptions a game. Gore is so much better than everybody else on the 49ers' offense that even Martz plans to become more run-oriented. KUBIAK looks at the recent history of Mike Martz running backs and has its doubts.

Earnest Graham

Height: 5-9 Weight: 225 College: Florida Draft: 2004/FA Born: 15 Jan. 1980 Age: 28 Risk: Yellow

Year	Team	G	Runs	Yds	Yd/R	TD	FUM	DVOA	Rk	DYAR	Rk	YAR	Suc%	Rec	Pass	Yds	C%	Yd/C	TD	DVOA	Rk	DYAR	Rk
2005	TB	16	28	83	3.0	0	1	-37.0%	—	-32	—	-36	36%	0	1	0	0%	0.0	0	-106.3%	—	-7	—
2006	TB	16	11	59	5.4	0	0	56.5%	—	26	—	27	45%	1	4	4	75%	4.0	0	67.2%	—	11	—
2007	TB	15	222	898	4.0	10	1	8.4%	18	162	9	175	50%	49	69	324	71%	6.6	0	-16.5%	42	-10	46
2008	TB		273	1230	4.5	6		2.0%						47	59	432	80%	9.2	2	-6.9%			

Raise your hand if you saw this coming. With Cadillac Williams's season-ending knee injury, Graham got a starting shot and took off with it, leading the team in rushing yardage despite the fact that he didn't get serious reps until Week 4. The only clue was Graham's 161 rushing yards in the 2006 preseason, but he was a very pleasant surprise to most observers. With Williams's future in doubt, Graham could extend his time as Tampa Bay's feature back. His DYAR, and a year of development for Tampa Bay's young offensive line, indicates that the future could be very bright.

Ryan Grant

Height: 6-1 Weight: 224 College: Notre Dame Draft: 2005/FA Born: 9 Dec. 1982 Age: 25 Risk: Yellow

Year	Team	G	Runs	Yds	Yd/R	TD	FUM	DVOA	Rk	DYAR	Rk	YAR	Suc%	Rec	Pass	Yds	C%	Yd/C	TD	DVOA	Rk	DYAR	Rk
2007	GB	15	188	956	5.1	8	1	12.3%	14	161	11	152	47%	30	37	145	81%	4.8	0	-31.8%	56	-38	56
2008	GB		290	1296	4.5	9		9.6%						39	58	252	67%	6.5	1	-33.5%			

Grant's performance as a receiver on first downs: -43.8% DVOA, -35 DYAR, and a 95 percent catch rate on 20 passes. How does a player catch 95 percent of the passes thrown to him and still post such a terrible DVOA? Grant lost yardage or was stuffed for no gain five times, then gained one or two yards four times. That's negligible yardage on 45 percent of his first-down passes, and with only two gains of 10-plus yards on first downs, there was little boom to go with a lot of bust. Grant has great ability as an open field runner; he must learn to read his blocks better, and the Packers may want to cut back on those first-down screens. Sometimes, a pass is as good as a long handoff, but sometimes, it's better just to hand the ball off.

Ahman Green

Height: 6-0 Weight: 218 College: Nebraska Draft: 1998/3 (76) Born: 16 Feb. 1977 Age: 31 Risk: Red

Year	Team	G	Runs	Yds	Yd/R	TD	FUM	DVOA	Rk	DYAR	Rk	YAR	Suc%	Rec	Pass	Yds	C%	Yd/C	TD	DVOA	Rk	DYAR	Rk
2005	GB	5	77	255	3.3	0	1	-13.2%	—	-15	—	-19	39%	19	27	147	70%	7.7	0	-1.8%	32	16	34
2006	GB	14	266	1059	4.0	5	4	2.4%	20	116	16	85	43%	46	63	373	70%	8.1	1	-7.2%	39	33	35
2007	HOU	6	70	260	3.7	2	0	3.2%	—	33	—	37	41%	14	18	123	78%	8.8	0	-9.7%	—	4	—
2008	HOU		144	597	4.2	5		3.3%						24	32	132	75%	5.5	0	-9.9%			

Aging running back catches on with new team, looks old, gets hurt. Stop the presses. Green was on a multiyear decline when the Texans picked him up last season. A year older and presumably a little slower after returning from a knee injury, Green will have to fight for his job in camp. If he makes the team, Houston will try to squeeze one more year out of him in a running-back-by-committee timeshare with Chris Brown and Steve Slaton.

Andre Hall

Height: 5-10 Weight: 205 College: USF Draft: 2006/FA Born: 20 Aug. 1982 Age: 26 Risk: Red

Year	Team	G	Runs	Yds	Yd/R	TD	FUM	DVOA	Rk	DYAR	Rk	YAR	Suc%	Rec	Pass	Yds	C%	Yd/C	TD	DVOA	Rk	DYAR	Rk
2007	DEN	10	44	216	4.9	2	1	-4.9%	—	7	—	-10	39%	2	2	69	100%	34.5	0	161.0%	—	23	—
2008	DEN		48	208	4.3	2		6.0%						19	28	143	68%	7.6	1	-10.8%			

Hall has a 4.9-yards-per-carry average, but his DVOA is only -3.3%. Why? One of his 44 carries went for 62 yards. Take that run out, and he averaged 3.6 yards per carry. Even on a depleted Broncos offensive line, it's hard to sustain an NFL career as a running back with so few booms and so many busts. His future is most likely as a kick-return specialist.

Jerome Harrison Height: 5-10 Weight: 200 College: Washington State Draft: 2006/5 (145) Born: 26 Feb. 1983 Age: 25 Risk: Red

Year	Team	G	Runs	Yds	Yd/R	TD	FUM	DVOA	Rk	DYAR	Rk	YAR	Suc%	Rec	Pass	Yds	C%	Yd/C	TD	DVOA	Rk	DYAR	Rk
2006	CLE	10	20	60	3.0	0	1	-46.2%	—	-26	—	-29	30%	9	14	47	79%	5.2	0	-11.8%	—	2	—
2007	CLE	8	23	142	6.2	0	0	40.4%	—	45	—	52	74%	2	2	19	100%	9.5	0	96.3%	—	8	—
2008	CLE		83	343	4.2	1		-5.0%						9	19	111	47%	11.7	1	1.6%			

Harrison only got three more touches in 2007 than he did the year before, but the results were much improved, as he more than doubled his yards per carry and bumped his success rate up from 30 to 74 percent. Harrison is too small to be more than a situational back, and Jason Wright provides more receiving ability and special-teams value. Even so, Harrison should get more playing time in light of how productive he is when he's on the field.

Mike Hart Height: 5-9 Weight: 195 College: Michigan Draft: 2008/6 (202) Born: 9 April 1986 Age: 22 Risk: Red

Year	Team	G	Runs	Yds	Yd/R	TD	FUM	DVOA	Rk	DYAR	Rk	YAR	Suc%	Rec	Pass	Yds	C%	Yd/C	TD	DVOA	Rk	DYAR	Rk
2008	IND		75	305	4.1	2		2.8%						16	25	114	64%	7.1	1	-5.4%			

Hart's a good blocker who carried the ball over 1,000 times in college. Considering that a 4.69 40-yard dash led to an impossibly low Speed Score (introduced in the essay "Five Seconds Can Be a Lifetime"), Hart would need to be the best blocking back in football by a wide margin and an incredible asset out of the backfield to succeed at the NFL level, even in the Colts' system. There's not a single player with a Speed Score under 90, let alone around 85, to have a sustained impact in the pros. Olandis Gary would be the only player who even had a single season of success. (Note that before the advent of electronic timing, Emmitt Smith reportedly ran a 4.71 at the Combine, a figure that would've given him a Speed Score of 89.7.) Hart could potentially stick one day as an undersized fullback, but probably not as a member of the Colts, and he's not going to be a successful running back in the NFL.

Chris Henry Height: 5-11 Weight: 230 College: Arizona Draft: 2007/2 (50) Born: 6 June 1985 Age: 23 Risk: Red

Year	Team	G	Runs	Yds	Yd/R	TD	FUM	DVOA	Rk	DYAR	Rk	YAR	Suc%	Rec	Pass	Yds	C%	Yd/C	TD	DVOA	Rk	DYAR	Rk
2007	TEN	7	31	119	3.8	2	0	-13.5%	—	-6	—	3	32%	6	7	53	86%	8.8	0	50.4%	—	22	—
2008	TEN		79	338	4.3	3		2.3%						11	15	75	73%	7.1	0	-13.6%			

Henry had a couple of good games in the middle of his rookie season, but it's extremely difficult not to be skeptical of a player who shot up draft boards because of a good performance at the Scouting Combine and then served a four-game suspension during the season because of a violation of the NFL's policy on steroids and related substances. Don't expect him to get many carries in 2008.

Travis Henry Height: 5-9 Weight: 215 College: Tennessee Draft: 2001/2 (58) Born: 29 Oct. 1978 Age: 30 Risk: Red

Year	Team	G	Runs	Yds	Yd/R	TD	FUM	DVOA	Rk	DYAR	Rk	YAR	Suc%	Rec	Pass	Yds	C%	Yd/C	TD	DVOA	Rk	DYAR	Rk
2005	TEN	9	88	335	3.8	0	2	-17.8%	—	-30	—	-39	34%	13	20	117	65%	9.0	0	4.9%	—	18	—
2006	TEN	14	270	1211	4.5	7	3	0.9%	23	99	21	105	43%	18	25	78	80%	4.3	0	35.7%	3	78	18
2007	DEN	12	167	691	4.1	4	3	-2.9%	29	40	30	68	46%	7	14	65	50%	9.3	0	-23.2%	—	-7	—
2008	DEN		99	393	4.0	2		-6.2%						12	17	91	71%	7.6	0	1.9%			

Henry had another in a long streak of below-average years, according to our metrics. The party line is that Henry was outstanding early, with three games of 128 or more yards in the first four, before a knee injury slowed him down. Of course, Henry always has lingering injuries, and he has played only 16 games in one season. His pedestrian performance was utterly predictable—he lost most of his big play and receiving capability—but a big surprise was his victory in his appeal of a drug suspension. A two-time offender in the league's banned-substance policy, Henry faced a season-long suspension based on a positive marijuana test in September. Henry's exoneration was the rare example of a player's receiving due process in the NFL. He renegotiated his salary to make it more cap-friendly, but that may not be enough. He'll see a reduction in playing time, and the signing of Michael Pittman as we went to press means Henry may not even make the roster.

Maurice Hicks

Height: 5-10 Weight: 200 College: North Carolina A&T Draft: 2003/FA Born: 22 July 1978 Age: 30 Risk: Red

Year	Team	G	Runs	Yds	Yd/R	TD	FUM	DVOA	Rk	DYAR	Rk	YAR	Suc%	Rec	Pass	Yds	C%	Yd/C	TD	DVOA	Rk	DYAR	Rk
2005	SF	14	59	308	5.2	3	0	17.0%	—	59	—	64	41%	12	16	47	75%	3.9	0	-41.5%	—	-25	—
2006	SF	16	29	82	2.8	0	0	-28.5%	—	-24	—	-17	52%	13	15	137	67%	10.5	1	1.6%	—	14	—
2007	SF	16	21	117	5.6	1	1	-8.7%	—	0	—	0	33%	14	16	86	88%	6.1	0	2.6%	—	14	—
2008	MIN		58	258	4.5	2		2.7%						18	25	162	72%	8.8	0	0.7%			

Hicks does everything well, returning kicks, playing special teams, running, receiving, even pass protecting, but he must be used sparingly because he wears down. The 49ers' linebackers were saddened and pleased he signed a free-agent deal in Minnesota. It means they no longer had to be embarrassed trying to cover him in practice, but it also means the team lost a lethal receiving threat out of the backfield.

Priest Holmes

Height: 5-9 Weight: 213 College: Texas Draft: 1997/FA Born: 7 Oct. 1973 Age: 35 Risk: 0

Year	Team	G	Runs	Yds	Yd/R	TD	FUM	DVOA	Rk	DYAR	Rk	YAR	Suc%	Rec	Pass	Yds	C%	Yd/C	TD	DVOA	Rk	DYAR	Rk
2005	KC	7	119	451	3.8	6	1	7.0%	13	79	16	44	44%	21	32	197	66%	9.4	1	1.6%	30	27	29
2007	KC	4	46	137	3.0	0	0	-25.6%	—	-30	—	-22	37%	5	10	17	50%	3.4	0	-40.3%	—	-13	—

Priest Holmes was one of the greatest signings in the history of NFL free agency when the Chiefs grabbed him from the Super Bowl champion Ravens in 2001. Holmes's three-year run as a full-time starter in Kansas City was absolutely dominant: 960 carries for 4,590 yards and 56 touchdowns to go along with 206 catches at over nine yards per reception. Terrell Davis is going to get serious Hall of Fame consideration, and his three top years totaled 1,106 carries for 5,296 yards and 49 touchdowns with 103 catches. Holmes totaled 1,400 rushing DYAR, compared with 1,342 for Davis. Davis's rookie season totaled 239 DYAR, but Holmes had 273 DYAR in a half-season in 2004 before his hip injury. Davis's Super Bowl rings change the calculus, but as Holmes retires after a recurrence of his neck injury, it is worth remembering that his peak was among the greatest in NFL history.

Tony Hunt

Height: 6-2 Weight: 233 College: Penn State Draft: 2007/3 (90) Born: 24 Nov. 1985 Age: 23 Risk: Red

Year	Team	G	Runs	Yds	Yd/R	TD	FUM	DVOA	Rk	DYAR	Rk	YAR	Suc%	Rec	Pass	Yds	C%	Yd/C	TD	DVOA	Rk	DYAR	Rk
2007	PHI	8	10	16	1.6	1	0	6.5%	—	9	—	9	60%	0	—	0	—	0.0	0	—	—	—	—
2008	PHI		56	274	4.9	1		23.5%						16	23	159	70%	10.0	1	10.4%			

The Eagles' third-round pick failed to learn the fine art of blitz pickup in 2007, which meant that he spent half the year inactive and the other half mostly riding the pine. The Eagles acquired Lorenzo Booker from the Dolphins in the offseason, which appears to be the first nail in Hunt's coffin. He'll need to prove his value as a special-teamer and a short-yardage runner to make the team.

Kenny Irons

Height: 5-11 Weight: 205 College: Auburn Draft: 2007/2 (49) Born: 15 Sept. 1983 Age: 25 Risk: Red

Year	Team	G	Runs	Yds	Yd/R	TD	FUM	DVOA	Rk	DYAR	Rk	YAR	Suc%	Rec	Pass	Yds	C%	Yd/C	TD	DVOA	Rk	DYAR	Rk
2008	CIN		40	207	5.1	1		5.8%						4	7	19	57%	4.8	0	-21.5%			

Irons suffered a torn ACL in his first preseason game, missing his entire rookie season. He'll try to be ready for training camp, though he was 15 pounds below his ideal playing weight of 205 pounds in May of this year, and he's got a long road back. The Bengals would like to see the promise that made Irons the latest in a long line of great Auburn backs, but his only tie to other recent Tigers backs is an inability to overcome rotten luck with injuries.

Brandon Jackson

Height: 5-10 Weight: 210 College: Nebraska Draft: 2007/2 (63) Born: 2 Oct. 1985 Age: 23 Risk: Red

Year	Team	G	Runs	Yds	Yd/R	TD	FUM	DVOA	Rk	DYAR	Rk	YAR	Suc%	Rec	Pass	Yds	C%	Yd/C	TD	DVOA	Rk	DYAR	Rk
2007	GB	11	75	267	3.6	1	0	-9.4%	—	-3	—	-12	44%	16	22	130	73%	8.1	0	-3.8%	—	12	—
2008	GB		93	509	5.4	2		29.2%						21	28	217	75%	10.5	1	34.4%			

The starting job was Jackson's to lose in training camp last season, but his pass blocking was terrible and he ran tentatively. Jackson was useless in some early-season starts but showed some life in the season finale against Detroit

(20 carries, 113 yards). He'll have to prove that he's a special power runner or show some special-teams promise to stick in a crowded backfield. For some reason, KUBIAK really, really likes him—although he wouldn't be projected for 5.4 yards per carry if he was also projected for 200 carries.

Fred Jackson Height: 6-1 Weight: 215 College: Coe Draft: 2007/FA Born: 20 Feb. 1981 Age: 27 Risk: Red

Year	Team	G	Runs	Yds	Yd/R	TD	FUM	DVOA	Rk	DYAR	Rk	YAR	Suc%	Rec	Pass	Yds	C%	Yd/C	TD	DVOA	Rk	DYAR	Rk
2007	BUF	8	58	300	5.2	0	0	19.7%	—	64	—	68	47%	22	29	190	72%	8.6	0	9.1%	23	34	27
2008	BUF		58	253	4.4	1		-7.2%						22	31	189	71%	8.7	1	8.2%			

Jackson (1) earned All America Honors for the D-III Coe College Kohawks in 2003, (2) scored 53 touchdowns for the Sioux City Bandits of the United Indoor Football League to earn MVP honors in 2005, (3) led the Rhein Fire with 731 rushing yards in NFL Europa in 2006, (4) spent a year and a half on the Bills' practice squad, leading the team in rushing in the 2007 preseason, and (5) finally made the Bills' roster when Marshawn Lynch and Anthony Thomas battled injuries last season. On a team full of pleasant surprises, he was the pleasantest, gaining 151 yards from scrimmage against the Redskins and 121 more against the Dolphins. He finished second in the league in DVOA on screen passes, behind Wes Welker. Jackson is fast and has good hands, but he runs upright and takes a lot of hits. He's a very good changeup for Lynch.

Steven Jackson Height: 6-2 Weight: 231 College: Oregon State Draft: 2004/1 (24) Born: 22 July 1983 Age: 25 Risk: Yellow

Year	Team	G	Runs	Yds	Yd/R	TD	FUM	DVOA	Rk	DYAR	Rk	YAR	Suc%	Rec	Pass	Yds	C%	Yd/C	TD	DVOA	Rk	DYAR	Rk
2005	STL	15	254	1046	4.1	8	3	-6.5%	28	21	26	20	42%	43	55	320	78%	7.4	2	23.2%	11	113	7
2006	STL	16	346	1528	4.4	13	2	8.0%	13	243	7	238	48%	90	110	806	63%	9.0	3	5.0%	25	146	7
2007	STL	12	237	1002	4.2	5	6	-7.4%	36	11	36	-5	43%	38	52	271	73%	7.1	1	-15.4%	41	-4	42
2008	STL		289	1246	4.3	8		-4.0%						65	97	539	67%	8.3	2	3.0%			

Even on a lousy team, Jackson looked like a superstar. Some of Jackson's real-life plays looked a lot like that Nike commercial where he goes through team after team on his way to the end zone. New offensive coordinator Al Saunders says Jackson compares favorably with the best backs he has ever coached: "The real good backs that I've been around—Chuck Muncie, Marcus Allen, Marshall Faulk, Priest Holmes, Larry Johnson—have all been three-dimensional backs," Saunders told Mike Sando of ESPN.com. "Steven is in that class. He is a unique player." Saunders specifically noted Jackson's pass-catching and route-running abilities. The 90 passes Jackson caught in 2006 were more than Faulk ever managed in a season, though Faulk gained more yards per reception. Jackson makes up for that on the ground: His 2,334 yards from scrimmage in 2006 were more than Faulk ever had outside the 1999 season. Did we mention that Jackson is in a contract year? If he somehow manages to hit free agency in the summer of 2009 at the age of 26, he's going to be a very rich man.

Brandon Jacobs Height: 6-4 Weight: 256 College: Southern Illinois Draft: 2005/4 (110) Born: 6 July 1982 Age: 26 Risk: Yellow

Year	Team	G	Runs	Yds	Yd/R	TD	FUM	DVOA	Rk	DYAR	Rk	YAR	Suc%	Rec	Pass	Yds	C%	Yd/C	TD	DVOA	Rk	DYAR	Rk
2005	NYG	16	38	99	2.6	7	—	-1.3%	—	20	—	14	61%	0	—	0	—	0.0	0	—	—	—	—
2006	NYG	15	96	423	4.4	9	2	16.4%	—	125	—	115	58%	11	14	149	57%	13.5	0	6.7%	—	29	—
2007	NYG	11	202	1009	5.0	4	5	18.3%	4	220	6	249	57%	23	38	174	61%	7.6	2	-21.6%	49	-17	49
2008	NYG		253	1095	4.3	9		7.6%						21	27	214	78%	10.2	2	16.9%			

The bruising Jacobs wasn't able to withstand the increase in his workload that came with his new starting role. That will happen when you're a big man whose game is built around high-speed collisions. When he was available, Jacobs was the player who Ron Dayne was supposed to be several years ago, the back who can run over linebackers or defensive backs but who is fast enough to cut into and through a gap without getting stuck. Jacobs has the talent to be an elite running back, but he'll need to improve his blocking and receiving. More importantly, he'll need to remain healthy enough to get 275 carries.

Edgerrin James

Height: 6-0 Weight: 214 College: Miami Draft: 1999/1 (4) Born: 1 Aug. 1978 Age: 30 Risk: Green

Year	Team	G	Runs	Yds	Yd/R	TD	FUM	DVOA	Rk	DYAR	Rk	YAR	Suc%	Rec	Pass	Yds	C%	Yd/C	TD	DVOA	Rk	DYAR	Rk
2005	IND	15	360	1506	4.2	13	2	13.0%	8	352	3	373	62%	44	50	337	88%	7.7	1	35.8%	5	143	3
2006	ARI	16	337	1159	3.4	6	3	-10.6%	39	-29	43	15	45%	38	60	217	60%	5.7	0	-8.1%	41	38	31
2007	ARI	16	324	1222	3.8	7	5	-1.0%	27	101	21	74	46%	24	39	204	64%	8.5	0	-11.2%	38	6	38
2008	ARI		285	1061	3.7	6		-11.0%						30	39	204	77%	6.8	0	-4.4%			

James now gets by on guile and vision. He lost his big-play ability after his 2001 ACL tear. When he got to Arizona in 2005, he was stymied by a poor offensive line. James can now count on the powerful right-side combo of Deuce Lutui and Levi Brown to open a few holes for him. The Cardinals could have saved $5 million in cap space by releasing James and drafting a replacement, but fifth-round pick Tim Hightower is a bench player, not a threat.

Chris Johnson

Height: 5-11 Weight: 197 College: East Carolina Draft: 2008/1 (24) Born: 23 Sept. 1985 Age: 23 Risk: Red

Year	Team	G	Runs	Yds	Yd/R	TD	FUM	DVOA	Rk	DYAR	Rk	YAR	Suc%	Rec	Pass	Yds	C%	Yd/C	TD	DVOA	Rk	DYAR	Rk
2008	TEN		179	945	5.1	5		22.8%						53	68	460	78%	8.7	1	18.3%			

Zoom! Johnson's 4.24 40-yard dash at the Combine blew a lot of minds and put this East Carolina back on the national radar. Scouts and NFL personnel execs knew about him because of his ability to chew up yardage in many different ways—his 6,993 all-purpose yards put him second in Conference USA annals behind only DeAngelo Williams of Memphis, and Johnson's 228 all-purpose yards per game in 2007 led the nation. Think of him as Dave Meggett with an extra gear, or perhaps Brian Westbrook if everything plays out right, but Johnson could be the NFL's most versatile rookie weapon in 2008. Titans offensive coordinator Mike Heimerdinger will have a field day with this kid.

Larry Johnson

Height: 6-1 Weight: 230 College: Penn State Draft: 2003/1 (27) Born: 19 Nov. 1979 Age: 29 Risk: Red

Year	Team	G	Runs	Yds	Yd/R	TD	FUM	DVOA	Rk	DYAR	Rk	YAR	Suc%	Rec	Pass	Yds	C%	Yd/C	TD	DVOA	Rk	DYAR	Rk
2005	KC	16	336	1750	5.2	20	5	23.3%	1	468	1	473	55%	33	49	343	67%	10.4	1	23.1%	10	102	8
2006	KC	16	416	1789	4.3	17	2	6.5%	15	257	5	266	45%	41	67	410	67%	10.0	2	17.9%	10	168	3
2007	KC	8	158	559	3.5	3	1	-14.0%	43	-35	42	-41	41%	30	42	186	71%	6.2	1	-19.2%	46	-12	47
2008	KC		310	1170	3.8	9		-5.1%						43	63	288	68%	6.7	0	-19.5%			

Johnson fell victim to the Curse of 370, suffering a foot injury that cost him half the year. He was already struggling through the worst season of his career, averaging a paltry 3.5 yards per carry. Johnson should be fully healed from his injury, but the sledding will be equally tough this season. The Chiefs' offensive line is abysmal, and shaky quarterback play will leave opposing defenses gearing up to stop Johnson. His career is in danger of becoming a gigantic what-if. What if his clash with Dick Vermeil and the presence of Priest Holmes hadn't slowed the start of his career? What if he hadn't been fed to the wolves by Herm Edwards? In between the what-ifs were two amazing seasons when Johnson was probably the best back in the NFL, other than LaDainian Tomlinson. Johnson is now embarking on a series of years in which he will run fruitlessly into a stacked line. By the time the Chiefs are ready to compete, Johnson will be at least 30 and past his prime.

Rudi Johnson

Height: 5-10 Weight: 225 College: Auburn Draft: 2001/4 (100) Born: 1 Oct. 1979 Age: 29 Risk: Red

Year	Team	G	Runs	Yds	Yd/R	TD	FUM	DVOA	Rk	DYAR	Rk	YAR	Suc%	Rec	Pass	Yds	C%	Yd/C	TD	DVOA	Rk	DYAR	Rk
2005	CIN	16	337	1458	4.3	12	1	16.2%	5	341	5	332	52%	23	30	90	77%	3.9	0	-51.9%	53	-62	53
2006	CIN	16	341	1309	3.8	12	6	-1.5%	24	97	22	78	44%	23	31	124	65%	5.4	0	-40.0%	55	-46	54
2007	CIN	11	170	497	2.9	3	3	-18.5%	47	-71	45	-121	39%	13	16	110	81%	8.5	1	32.0%	—	39	—
2008	CIN		201	774	3.8	6		-2.7%						16	22	65	73%	4.0	0	-21.4%			

Cincinnati's reliable workhorse broke down with a series of injuries last year and struggled to match his previous effectiveness even when healthy. Johnson is 29, an age at which it would be unusual for a running back to return to his previous level of play after a season like this. Meanwhile, his injury replacement, Kenny Watson, stepped in and performed at something close to Johnson's former level. While Watson will probably have a larger role this year, Johnson still has a place on the team. He admitted that he did too much dancing last season, and he changed his diet in the offseason, adding 10 pounds of muscle in an effort to return to form as one of the league's best bruisers. The 1,400-yard seasons are over, but Johnson could be the goal-line back. Fantasy owners should keep him on the radar.

Felix Jones

Height: 6-0   Weight: 200   College: Arkansas   Draft: 2008/1 (22)   Born: 8 May 1987   Age: 21   Risk: Red

Year	Team	G	Runs	Yds	Yd/R	TD	FUM	DVOA	Rk	DYAR	Rk	YAR	Suc%	Rec	Pass	Yds	C%	Yd/C	TD	DVOA	Rk	DYAR	Rk
2008	DAL		164	760	4.6	6		31.7%						16	23	156	70%	9.5	1	11.8%			

At Dallas' May minicamp, Jones was tutored on the fine points of the professional running game by none other than Emmitt Smith. It is said that Smith revealed the importance of constatant tremeclity when in the facing of nerbostic habien. Eitherwise, your hoom-afra is going to stuffer a metiflious splunge.

Jones will display his tremeclity, not to mention his speed and agility, as Marion Barber's new backfield-mate. The Cowboys hope he'll develop into the kind of open-field threat that Julius Jones never quite became.

Julius Jones

Height: 5-10   Weight: 211   College: Notre Dame   Draft: 2004/2 (43)   Born: 14 Aug. 1981   Age: 27   Risk: Green

Year	Team	G	Runs	Yds	Yd/R	TD	FUM	DVOA	Rk	DYAR	Rk	YAR	Suc%	Rec	Pass	Yds	C%	Yd/C	TD	DVOA	Rk	DYAR	Rk
2005	DAL	13	257	993	3.9	5	3	-4.7%	24	41	21	-16	39%	35	45	218	78%	6.2	0	-14.1%	43	-1	42
2006	DAL	16	267	1084	4.1	4	1	2.0%	22	112	18	95	45%	9	15	142	53%	15.8	0	27.6%	—	22	—
2007	DAL	16	164	588	3.6	2	0	-6.7%	35	12	35	9	37%	23	26	203	88%	8.8	0	38.2%	4	75	14
2008	SEA		203	859	4.2	7		-0.2%						11	15	47	73%	4.5	1	-25.5%			

Jones finally lost his Thanksgiving Day 2004 scholarship in 2007, and his playing time eroded as the season went along. Although he remained the starter in name, Marion Barber got the bulk of the carries in the second half, and Jones's confidence eroded. Instead of finding his lane and plowing through it, à la Barber, Jones was tentative and seemed to be constantly looking for the perfect hole. In the passing game, Jones is a reliable target whose patience in letting blocks develop is rewarded in the screen game. That might not translate to Seattle, whose offensive line isn't as effective in the open field. Then again, Seahawks linemen had to worry about Shaun Alexander falling asleep on their legs last year. Jones may never achieve the heights that he was expected to in Dallas following his rookie year, but he should be an upgrade on what Seattle rolled out at halfback last year.

Kevin Jones

Height: 5-11   Weight: 221   College: Virginia Tech   Draft: 2004/1 (30)   Born: 21 Aug. 1982   Age: 26   Risk: Red

Year	Team	G	Runs	Yds	Yd/R	TD	FUM	DVOA	Rk	DYAR	Rk	YAR	Suc%	Rec	Pass	Yds	C%	Yd/C	TD	DVOA	Rk	DYAR	Rk
2005	DET	13	186	664	3.6	5	2	-8.2%	31	3	31	-24	43%	20	28	109	71%	5.5	0	-31.5%	52	-27	50
2006	DET	12	181	689	3.8	6	5	-22.1%	46	-109	47	-86	40%	61	78	520	74%	8.5	2	17.5%	12	156	5
2007	DET	13	153	581	3.8	8	2	-2.7%	28	40	31	20	47%	32	44	197	73%	6.2	0	-12.3%	39	4	40

The Lions released Jones in March because they didn't feel they could integrate him into the new offense while he recovered from an ACL tear. (Note: This could well be Lionsspeak for "we've taken a vague dislike to him.") As damaged goods, Jones won't make much of a contribution this season, but he's a great candidate for a Garrison Hearst–like second career if he can get healthy and onto a good team.

Thomas Jones

Height: 5-10   Weight: 220   College: Virginia   Draft: 2000/1 (7)   Born: 19 Aug. 1978   Age: 30   Risk: Green

Year	Team	G	Runs	Yds	Yd/R	TD	FUM	DVOA	Rk	DYAR	Rk	YAR	Suc%	Rec	Pass	Yds	C%	Yd/C	TD	DVOA	Rk	DYAR	Rk
2005	CHI	15	314	1335	4.3	9	2	-3.6%	23	61	20	93	41%	26	39	143	67%	5.5	0	-33.8%	51	-42	52
2006	CHI	16	296	1210	4.1	6	1	3.2%	19	147	14	146	48%	36	47	154	72%	4.3	0	-18.3%	48	-11	49
2007	NYJ	16	310	1119	3.6	1	2	-11.3%	40	-36	43	-43	43%	28	34	217	82%	7.8	1	34.4%	5	80	13
2008	NYJ		292	1149	3.9	6		1.1%						16	21	80	76%	5.1	0	-18.4%			

Welcome to the hotel replacement level. Jones checked in because he was bad on first down (3.62 yards per carry, -21.7% DVOA, 41 percent Success Rate), worse on third downs (2.08, -27.4%, 46 percent), and just miserable in the red zone (one measly touchdown, DVOA of -39.4%). It's hard to fault Jones when two-fifths of the Jets' offensive linemen were incompetent, the quarterbacks were either beat up or inexperienced, and the game plans often demanded 24 carries into the teeth of a good defense. But Jones is now 30, has been worked hard for three straight years, and was never a top-tier goal-line runner.

Maurice Jones-Drew

Height: 5-8 Weight: 205 College: UCLA Draft: 2006/2 (60) Born: 23 March 1985 Age: 23 Risk: Red

Year	Team	G	Runs	Yds	Yd/R	TD	FUM	DVOA	Rk	DYAR	Rk	YAR	Suc%	Rec	Pass	Yds	C%	Yd/C	TD	DVOA	Rk	DYAR	Rk
2006	JAC	16	166	941	5.7	13	1	22.0%	4	217	10	263	51%	46	62	436	66%	9.5	2	17.3%	13	124	10
2007	JAC	15	167	768	4.6	9	2	2.1%	23	81	25	96	46%	40	55	407	73%	10.2	0	32.0%	7	142	5
2008	JAC		230	1032	4.5	11		10.9%						41	62	426	66%	10.4	2	26.6%			

For all the advanced scouting that the NFL employs, it's a wonder that there are certain biases that are still hard to overcome. People see a player who is generously listed at five foot eight and assume he'll be nothing but a bit player at best. Jones-Drew's success in his first two seasons makes you wonder where he would have been drafted had he been three inches taller. After all, it's not as if he didn't succeed at a high level in college. He was a dominant back at UCLA, merited Heisman contention, and was the nation's best punt returner—by a mile—as a senior. What's more, he doesn't play small. Watch Jones-Drew carry tacklers or put Shawne Merriman on his back, and you won't think he's too small to be an every-down back. As long as Fred Taylor is still productive, Jones-Drew is best served splitting time and getting his extra touches on kick returns, where he excels. But he could handle 25 touches per game if called upon.

LaMont Jordan

Height: 5-10 Weight: 230 College: Maryland Draft: 2001/2 (49) Born: 11 Nov. 1978 Age: 30 Risk: Red

Year	Team	G	Runs	Yds	Yd/R	TD	FUM	DVOA	Rk	DYAR	Rk	YAR	Suc%	Rec	Pass	Yds	C%	Yd/C	TD	DVOA	Rk	DYAR	Rk
2005	OAK	14	272	1025	3.8	9	2	1.9%	15	123	11	103	47%	70	103	563	68%	8.0	2	3.0%	25	95	9
2006	OAK	10	114	434	3.8	2	1	-8.2%	34	2	35	-4	34%	10	16	74	63%	7.4	0	-43.1%	—	-28	—
2007	OAK	12	144	549	3.8	3	1	-14.0%	42	-32	41	-8	37%	28	34	247	82%	8.8	0	19.6%	13	65	17
2008	OAK		116	467	4.0	3		-9.5%						26	34	191	76%	7.5	0	-26.7%			

Randy Moss, Jerry Porter, Dominic Rhodes, just to name a few, all had it. It's the Raider malaise, an affliction that can ruin or at least forestall the careers of veterans who sign hefty contracts in Oakland. If players aren't self-motivated, they can find themselves struggling to maintain mediocrity. Jordan has the Raider malaise, and if he doesn't get over it quickly, he may find himself collecting unemployment checks. Jordan may no longer fit in the Raiders' plans after last year's 1,000-yard rushing season by Justin Fargas and the drafting of Arkansas' Darren McFadden. Nor has Jordan seemed to adjust well to the Raiders' zone-blocking scheme: He was more comfortable in the straight-ahead running attack the Jets used.

Kenton Keith

Height: 5-11 Weight: 198 College: New Mexico State Draft: 2007/FA Born: 14 July 1980 Age: 28 Risk: Red

Year	Team	G	Runs	Yds	Yd/R	TD	FUM	DVOA	Rk	DYAR	Rk	YAR	Suc%	Rec	Pass	Yds	C%	Yd/C	TD	DVOA	Rk	DYAR	Rk
2007	IND	16	121	533	4.4	3	1	14.0%	9	125	16	134	58%	13	23	77	57%	5.9	1	-1.9%	—	13	—
2008	IND		56	201	3.6	2		-6.1%						18	23	134	78%	7.6	1	19.1%			

With 500 yards and a top 10 DVOA in 2007, Keith looked as though he had settled in as the change-of-pace runner for a perennial Super Bowl contender. Then came that fateful morning when Keith and his cousin Marquis O'Neal were arrested outside an Indianapolis nightclub after refusing police orders. Apparently, they did not want to go home, nor did they want to get the hell out of there. Police allege that Keith repeatedly tried to tell them he was a Colts player, perhaps thinking this gave him the run of the city. The pair was charged with misdemeanor criminal trespass, a charge that could lead to a year in jail. Keith has pleaded not guilty. The Colts took Mike Hart in the draft and re-signed Dominic Rhodes, so Keith's position on the team may be up in the air.

Brian Leonard

Height: 6-2 Weight: 226 College: Rutgers Draft: 2007/2 (52) Born: 3 Feb. 1984 Age: 24 Risk: Red

Year	Team	G	Runs	Yds	Yd/R	TD	FUM	DVOA	Rk	DYAR	Rk	YAR	Suc%	Rec	Pass	Yds	C%	Yd/C	TD	DVOA	Rk	DYAR	Rk
2007	STL	16	86	303	3.5	0	0	-5.1%	—	12	—	-3	41%	30	39	183	77%	6.1	0	-7.7%	33	13	35
2008	STL		74	255	3.4	1		-19.6%						23	32	192	72%	8.3	0	13.9%			

A jack-of-all-trades, but master of none, Leonard is the utility infielder of the St. Louis Cardinals—er, Rams. He's below average as a runner, but he's not bad. Subpar as a receiver, but not terrible. Adequate as a blocker, not overwhelming. He's also coming off surgery on both shoulders. Rams coach Scott Linehan will try to get the ball into Leonard's hands. "He is going to play fullback for us in certain packages and he'll be a halfback for us in others,"

Linehan told the *Belleville News-Democrat*. "He's got to know both. That's what makes his role so valuable for us. He has to play both, and he has to be good at both." Still, as long as Leonard is playing with Steven Jackson, he's not going to be the team's leading rusher or their top receiver out of the backfield. Leonard is no fool—they don't let just anyone into Rutgers, after all—so he spent his postsurgery time bulking up, adding 10 pounds of muscle in hopes to be a better blocker. Though he has very minimal fantasy value, his versatility will make him a crucial part of the Rams' roster for years to come.

Jamal Lewis

Height: 5-11 Weight: 245 College: Tennessee   Draft: 2000/1 (5) Born: 29 Aug. 1979 Age: 29 Risk: Yellow

Year	Team	G	Runs	Yds	Yd/R	TD	FUM	DVOA	Rk	DYAR	Rk	YAR	Suc%	Rec	Pass	Yds	C%	Yd/C	TD	DVOA	Rk	DYAR	Rk
2005	BAL	15	269	906	3.4	3	6	-23.1%	42	-161	44	-119	41%	32	44	191	73%	6.0	1	-12.5%	39	3	39
2006	BAL	16	314	1132	3.6	9	4	-9.6%	38	-13	38	-5	42%	18	26	115	62%	6.4	0	-20.7%	50	-11	48
2007	CLE	15	298	1304	4.4	9	4	1.5%	25	125	15	88	45%	30	39	248	77%	8.3	2	33.3%	6	99	8
2008	CLE		287	1215	4.2	9		1.1%						23	34	90	68%	4.0	0	-31.6%			

It didn't look like a very significant signing when Browns general manager Phil Savage inked Lewis to a one-year deal, but the former Ravens workhorse proved to be a steal, pounding out 1,300 yards behind Cleveland's rebuilt offensive line. The importance of the line play in Lewis's resurgence can't be understated. Running behind Pro-Bowlers Joe Thomas and Eric Steinbach on the left side, Lewis averaged 5.3 yards per carry. When running behind Kevin Shaffer and the combination of Ross Tucker and Seth McKinney on the right side, Lewis averaged only 3.7 yards per carry.

Marshawn Lynch

Height: 5-11 Weight: 215 College: California   Draft: 2007/1 (12) Born: 22 April 1986 Age: 22 Risk: Yellow

Year	Team	G	Runs	Yds	Yd/R	TD	FUM	DVOA	Rk	DYAR	Rk	YAR	Suc%	Rec	Pass	Yds	C%	Yd/C	TD	DVOA	Rk	DYAR	Rk
2007	BUF	13	280	1115	4.0	7	2	-5.0%	33	42	29	50	45%	18	26	184	69%	10.2	0	14.1%	20	41	24
2008	BUF		330	1438	4.4	9		6.0%						23	32	229	72%	7.3	1	1.4%			

Lynch caught 34 passes in his final season at Cal but just 18 as a rookie. He has fine hands and open field moves, so he deserves a larger role in the passing game; coordinator Turk Schronert plans to get him more involved. Lynch was awful in the red zone last season: 44 rushes, 77 yards, -26.5% DVOA. He has a powerful running style and sometimes dragged defenders into the end zone with him, so his lack of red zone production was more a symptom of the Bills' offense than a cause. Opponents didn't have to worry about a quality possession receiver or tight end in the red zone, and Lee Evans can't catch a bomb from the 10-yard line, so defenders could really key on Lynch. That problem should improve modestly this year.

Laurence Maroney

Height: 5-11 Weight: 205 College: Minnesota   Draft: 2006/1 (21) Born: 5 Feb. 1985 Age: 23 Risk: Red

Year	Team	G	Runs	Yds	Yd/R	TD	FUM	DVOA	Rk	DYAR	Rk	YAR	Suc%	Rec	Pass	Yds	C%	Yd/C	TD	DVOA	Rk	DYAR	Rk
2006	NE	14	175	745	4.3	6	1	-4.5%	32	31	31	58	46%	22	30	194	70%	8.8	1	21.7%	8	83	15
2007	NE	13	185	835	4.5	6	0	16.7%	6	199	7	207	58%	4	8	116	50%	29.0	0	87.4%	—	42	—
2008	NE		234	1092	4.7	11		8.0%						25	42	299	60%	12.0	1	33.4%			

Maroney scouts better than he stats. He has the breakaway speed and raw power to be a superstar, and at his best, he looks like the kind of all-purpose back who should get 30 touches per game. But Maroney hasn't been a featured back since high school (he split time with Marion Barber at Minnesota), battles various aches and pains, disappears from the passing game despite good overall skills, and doesn't make the most of limited touches when the Patriots are in aerial circus mode. Maroney played well late in the season and in the playoffs, so he may be figuring out how to protect his body and make the most of 15-20 touches. Throw in his kick-return ability, and he's a vital cog in the big machine. But he'll frustrate fantasy owners who expect a powerhouse and get three or four six-carry, 18-yard lines per year.

Deuce McAllister

Height: 6-1 Weight: 232 College: Mississippi   Draft: 2001/1 (23) Born: 27 Dec. 1978 Age: 29 Risk: Red

Year	Team	G	Runs	Yds	Yd/R	TD	FUM	DVOA	Rk	DYAR	Rk	YAR	Suc%	Rec	Pass	Yds	C%	Yd/C	TD	DVOA	Rk	DYAR	Rk
2005	NO	5	93	335	3.6	3	0	-6.2%	—	9	—	25	44%	17	18	117	94%	6.9	0	18.5%	—	27	—
2006	NO	15	244	1057	4.3	10	3	11.4%	10	221	9	190	54%	30	36	198	75%	6.6	0	26.0%	6	76	19
2007	NO	3	24	92	3.8	0	1	-21.1%	—	-12	—	-14	42%	4	5	15	80%	3.8	0	-26.5%	—	-4	—
2008	NO		61	239	3.9	3		6.6%						25	36	98	69%	4.0	0	-18.4%			

McAllister had a great 2006 season after missing most of 2005 with a left ACL injury. His powerful style meshed perfectly with Reggie Bush's Shake-and-Bake, and the Saints' rushing attack was the unheralded part of an offensive rebirth. His slow start in 2007 mirrored the team's, and he tore his right ACL in a Week 3 loss to the Titans. McAllister took a pay cut to stay with the Saints, deferring a $1 million roster bonus and reorganizing other payments, but he will still have to beat some serious odds to have a productive NFL future.

Darren McFadden

Height: 6-2 Weight: 210 College: Arkansas   Draft: 2008/1 (4) Born: 27 Aug. 1987 Age: 21 Risk: Red

Year	Team	G	Runs	Yds	Yd/R	TD	FUM	DVOA	Rk	DYAR	Rk	YAR	Suc%	Rec	Pass	Yds	C%	Yd/C	TD	DVOA	Rk	DYAR	Rk
2008	OAK		264	1219	4.6	8		27.9%						34	54	227	63%	6.6	0	9.3%			

The Raiders had to draft Darren McFadden. Al Davis liked him because he's fast and has big hands. Offensive coordinator Greg Knapp liked him because it will give Knapp the opportunity to develop quarterback JaMarcus Russell while the offense relies on McFadden and the zone-blocking running game. Offensive line coach Tom Cable likes him because he fits perfectly in the zone-blocking scheme. McFadden is quick enough to make that one cut needed when the hole opens and then fast enough to blast into the defense. While many scouts vow that McFadden was the most explosive player in the 2008 draft, others will point to his lack of leg drive at contact and his subsequent inability to break tackles. Another question lingers over McFadden—can he catch passes? He didn't do that much receiving at Arkansas, but the Raiders believe he'll be a smooth option out of the backfield. He'll need to contribute as a receiver: The Raiders would rather see Russell swing the ball to McFadden in the flat than zing an interception over the middle, particularly in the fourth quarter.

As for his off-field issues, we know McFadden grew up in the kind of neighborhood 50 Cent would drive through with the doors locked and the windows rolled up. We know the McFadden paternity test was a high school exit exam for many Arkansas girls. And we know that McFadden is no stranger to after-hours incidents at night clubs, making him a prime candidate for a meltdown once the first check clears. But the young man deserves the benefit of the doubt, not another set of clichés about how the Raiders will only encourage or exacerbate his bad-boy behavior.

Willis McGahee

Height: 6-0 Weight: 228 College: Miami   Draft: 2003/1 (23) Born: 20 Oct. 1981 Age: 27 Risk: Green

Year	Team	G	Runs	Yds	Yd/R	TD	FUM	DVOA	Rk	DYAR	Rk	YAR	Suc%	Rec	Pass	Yds	C%	Yd/C	TD	DVOA	Rk	DYAR	Rk
2005	BUF	16	325	1247	3.8	5	1	-2.6%	19	86	14	101	47%	28	37	178	76%	6.4	0	-0.1%	31	26	30
2006	BUF	14	259	990	3.8	6	4	-3.3%	29	57	27	29	45%	18	28	156	61%	8.7	0	-27.0%	53	-21	51
2007	BAL	15	294	1207	4.1	7	4	-8.2%	38	5	38	57	42%	43	49	231	88%	5.4	1	-2.8%	30	29	30
2008	BAL		310	1142	3.7	7		-11.1%						41	55	229	75%	5.6	0	-29.6%			

McGahee's first season in Baltimore was a lot like his last few seasons in Buffalo. He generated impressive raw yardage totals but didn't grade out well in DVOA or DYAR. A lot of that has to do with game situations—McGahee averaged over six yards a carry when Baltimore was trailing by more than eight points, but less than four when the Ravens were within a single touchdown or ahead, so his best production came when defenses were protecting big leads and playing the pass. McGahee has good power, but he also has the cutback ability and acceleration to break big plays on the edges, an asset that was wasted in Brian Billick's offense. The Ravens ran between the guards 63 percent of the time. New offensive coordinator Cam Cameron also likes to run between the guards, but he's more likely to mix in outside runs and to better incorporate McGahee into the passing game. KUBIAK isn't down on McGahee as much as it is down on a Baltimore line without Jonathan Ogden.

Rashard Mendenhall

Height: 5-11 Weight: 210 College: Illinois   Draft: 2008/1 (23) Born: 19 June 1987 Age: 21 Risk: Red

Year	Team	G	Runs	Yds	Yd/R	TD	FUM	DVOA	Rk	DYAR	Rk	YAR	Suc%	Rec	Pass	Yds	C%	Yd/C	TD	DVOA	Rk	DYAR	Rk
2008	PIT		221	1057	4.8	7		19.0%						34	45	279	76%	8.2	1	-23.0%			

Mendenhall was still available with the 23rd pick overall because of what Steelers offensive coordinator Bruce Arians called a "panic attack" on offensive linemen in the middle of the first round. Pittsburgh happily snatched him up. Mendenhall is a great fit for this team, and his physical style of running provides much-needed consistency next to Willie Parker's questionable productivity. The Steelers ran plays from a single-back formation 65 percent of the time in 2007, fifth in the NFL, so don't automatically assume that Mendenhall is there to line up next to, or in front of, Parker. The rookie is another option: as a short-yardage runner, as a receiver out of the backfield, as a pass blocker, though he didn't block much in Illinois' option offense. Sooner than later, Mendenhall could be the better option.

Travis Minor

Height: 5-10 Weight: 203 College: Florida State   Draft: 2001/3 (85) Born: 30 June 1979 Age: 29 Risk: Red

Year	Team	G	Runs	Yds	Yd/R	TD	FUM	DVOA	Rk	DYAR	Rk	YAR	Suc%	Rec	Pass	Yds	C%	Yd/C	TD	DVOA	Rk	DYAR	Rk
2005	MIA	16	5	17	3.4	0	0	-28.4%	—	-4	—	-5	60%	1	1	0	100%	0.0	0	-106.8%	—	-5	—
2006	MIA	16	19	74	3.9	0	0	0.7%	—	7	—	6	47%	3	3	2	33%	0.7	0	-115.2%	—	-27	—
2007	STL	14	17	68	4.0	0	0	19.0%	—	16	—	9	29%	12	17	86	71%	7.2	0	5.9%	—	17	—
2008	STL		67	227	3.4	2		-19.2%						19	39	171	49%	8.8	0	-12.0%			

Travis Minor is, technically speaking, the Rams' number two running back, but that's only because Brian Leonard is listed as the starting fullback. In reality, Minor and Antonio Pittman are battling for the third spot, with the loser looking for a new place of employment. Minor got off to a bad start in the battle; a bum ankle hampered his participation in the team's minicamp, though the injury should have no serious long-term effects. A third-round pick of the Dolphins in 2001, Minor has had seven seasons in the NFL to prove that he is something more than a backup, yet a backup he remains.

Mewelde Moore

Height: 5-11 Weight: 209 College: Tulane   Draft: 2004/4 (119) Born: 24 July 1982 Age: 26 Risk: Red

Year	Team	G	Runs	Yds	Yd/R	TD	FUM	DVOA	Rk	DYAR	Rk	YAR	Suc%	Rec	Pass	Yds	C%	Yd/C	TD	DVOA	Rk	DYAR	Rk
2005	MIN	16	155	662	4.3	1	1	-3.6%	22	30	24	59	43%	37	49	339	76%	9.2	2	31.1%	7	120	5
2006	MIN	16	24	131	5.5	0	0	40.3%	—	32	—	28	33%	46	62	468	69%	10.2	1	13.2%	18	92	12
2007	MIN	12	20	113	5.7	0	1	31.5%	—	25	—	27	50%	6	8	48	75%	8.0	0	-7.8%	—	2	—
2008	PIT		41	219	5.3	1		18.5%						16	28	159	57%	10.0	1	-7.7%			

After spending his entire career in Minnesota, Moore found himself stuck on the bench behind Adrian Peterson and Chester Taylor, and so he opted for free agency. His chosen destination: Pittsburgh, where he thought he would battle Najeh Davenport for second-string and maybe even get a shot to pass Willie Parker for the starting role. Then Rashard Mendenhall slipped in the draft, the Steelers eagerly picked him up, and Moore saw his carries instantly start to shrink. Moore has been outstanding in spot duty the past two seasons: He would have been in the top five in DVOA both years if he had gotten enough carries to qualify. It looks as if he won't qualify in 2008, either. At least Moore will get to return punts and kickoffs for the Steelers, and he was pretty successful doing that in Minnesota.

Vernand Morency

Height: 5-9 Weight: 212 College: Oklahoma State   Draft: 2005/3 (73) Born: 4 Feb. 1980 Age: 28 Risk: Red

Year	Team	G	Runs	Yds	Yd/R	TD	FUM	DVOA	Rk	DYAR	Rk	YAR	Suc%	Rec	Pass	Yds	C%	Yd/C	TD	DVOA	Rk	DYAR	Rk
2005	HOU	13	46	184	4.0	2	0	-0.2%	—	15	—	26	35%	10	15	87	67%	8.7	0	9.2%	—	19	—
2006	GB	15	96	434	4.5	2	2	5.6%	—	56	—	54	40%	17	18	118	78%	6.9	0	18.5%	—	21	—
2007	GB	13	29	108	3.7	0	1	-7.5%	—	1	—	-2	34%	30	39	199	77%	6.6	0	-17.6%	45	-8	44
2008	GB		62	292	4.7	1		6.7%						21	29	226	72%	10.8	1	34.7%			

Morency was injured during 2007 training camp and couldn't compete for a starting job. He got healthy in time to earn a role as a third-down changeup, subbing for various rookies and having a few good games as a receiver. He's nothing special and could be looking for work in September if one of Green Bay's young runners proves dependable in third-down situations.

Maurice Morris

Height: 5-11 Weight: 202 College: Oregon   Draft: 2002/2 (54) Born: 1 Dec. 1979 Age: 29 Risk: Red

Year	Team	G	Runs	Yds	Yd/R	TD	FUM	DVOA	Rk	DYAR	Rk	YAR	Suc%	Rec	Pass	Yds	C%	Yd/C	TD	DVOA	Rk	DYAR	Rk
2005	SEA	16	71	288	4.1	1	0	-1.5%	—	19	—	27	45%	5	6	48	83%	9.6	0	58.2%	—	21	—
2006	SEA	16	161	604	3.8	0	1	-11.3%	40	-17	39	-23	39%	11	20	46	55%	4.2	0	-44.3%	—	-36	—
2007	SEA	14	140	628	4.5	4	2	0.7%	26	57	28	45	51%	23	32	213	72%	9.3	1	17.0%	15	55	21
2008	SEA		70	310	4.4	2		-0.8%						21	29	166	72%	8.0	0	6.5%			

After sputtering for the first half of the season, the Seahawks ground game came alive (relatively) in Week 9, when Morris took over full time for an injured Shaun Alexander. The Seahawks promptly rattled off three straight wins as Morris averaged a respectable 4.1 yards on the ground and actually provided a semblance of a receiving option in the backfield. Mike Holmgren then inexplicably forced Morris to split carries with a battered, indifferent Alexander when he returned in Week 13. During the offseason, Seahawks general manager Tim Ruskell went on a free-agent running-back spending spree. Never let it be said that the life of an NFL backup running back is easy—or fair. Morris probably throws darts at a photo of Michael Turner when he needs to unwind.

Sammy Morris

Height: 6-0 Weight: 218 College: Texas Tech   Draft: 2000/5 (156) Born: 23 Mar. 1977 Age: 31 Risk: Yellow

Year	Team	G	Runs	Yds	Yd/R	TD	FUM	DVOA	Rk	DYAR	Rk	YAR	Suc%	Rec	Pass	Yds	C%	Yd/C	TD	DVOA	Rk	DYAR	Rk
2005	MIA	16	16	58	3.6	1	0	6.3%	—	10	—	12	50%	8	12	54	67%	6.8	0	-23.0%	—	-5	—
2006	MIA	12	92	400	4.3	1	2	-20.0%	—	-46	—	-21	42%	21	35	162	63%	7.7	0	-24.4%	51	-56	55
2007	NE	6	85	384	4.5	3	0	15.3%	—	92	—	97	54%	6	8	35	75%	5.8	0	-20.2%	—	-3	—
2008	NE		166	708	4.3	7		16.3%						26	36	230	72%	8.9	1	12.2%			

Morris, a castoff from Miami, started the 2007 season rotating with Laurence Maroney, played very well, recorded back-to-back 100-yard games when Maroney was hurt, then went on injured reserved with a chest injury. Lessons learned? (1) The Dolphins had no idea how to evaluate the talent on their own roster. (2) When you have a great overall offense, you can plug in any capable runner and get a few 100-yard games, especially against teams like the Bengals. (3) Morris is a great spare part with value as a changeup runner and special-teamer, but he can't handle a 20-carry workload. Lucky for him, the Patriots need spare parts, not workhorses. Morris began working out again in February and should get 5 to 10 carries per game as Maroney's caddie.

Jerious Norwood

Height: 6-0 Weight: 204 College: Mississippi State   Draft: 2006/3 (79) Born: 23 July 1983 Age: 25 Risk: Red

Year	Team	G	Runs	Yds	Yd/R	TD	FUM	DVOA	Rk	DYAR	Rk	YAR	Suc%	Rec	Pass	Yds	C%	Yd/C	TD	DVOA	Rk	DYAR	Rk
2006	ATL	14	99	633	6.4	2	0	35.1%	—	170	—	150	53%	12	15	102	67%	8.5	0	-4.9%	—	-4	—
2007	ATL	15	103	613	6.0	1	0	24.5%	1	133	13	126	48%	28	39	277	72%	9.9	0	21.6%	12	73	15
2008	ATL		133	668	5.0	2		9.0%						47	73	385	64%	8.2	0	-1.6%			

Norwood's underutilization in 2007 was perhaps Falcondom's biggest mystery. And it wasn't as if there weren't other inexplicable things going on in Atlanta. When your offensive line is an unmitigated disaster, your franchise is playing round robin with quarterbacks and coaches, and you still manage six yards per carry and the NFL's best DVOA among running backs . . . well, it makes perfect sense that your team would only hand you the ball 103 times. It makes even more sense that your team would go out and sign LaDainian Tomlinson's longtime backup to a $34.5 million contract when he couldn't post a positive DVOA behind a better offensive line. If you see Norwood and Carolina's DeAngelo Williams commiserating during one of their NFC South matchups this year, they may be establishing a "Who Did I Piss Off?" club.

Willie Parker

Height: 5-10 Weight: 209 College: North Carolina   Draft: 2004/FA Born: 11 Nov. 1980 Age: 28 Risk: Red

Year	Team	G	Runs	Yds	Yd/R	TD	FUM	DVOA	Rk	DYAR	Rk	YAR	Suc%	Rec	Pass	Yds	C%	Yd/C	TD	DVOA	Rk	DYAR	Rk
2005	PIT	15	255	1202	4.7	4	4	-1.5%	17	70	18	99	48%	18	24	218	75%	12.1	1	55.7%	—	93	—
2006	PIT	16	337	1494	4.4	13	6	3.3%	18	165	13	133	45%	31	42	222	67%	7.2	3	-5.1%	36	17	40
2007	PIT	15	321	1316	4.1	2	4	-10.8%	39	-27	39	-13	42%	23	31	164	74%	7.1	0	3.2%	27	29	31
2008	PIT		261	1057	4.0	6		-3.9%						25	34	238	74%	9.7	1	8.6%			

Parker is a better fantasy player than real player. His yardage comes in big chunks—sixes and sevens, sometimes 20s and 30s—but he mixes in too many stuffs at the line. Part of the blame lies with the offensive line, but nonetheless Parker frequently leaves the Steelers in third-and-long. Over half of their third downs had more than seven yards to go, the sixth-highest percentage in the NFL. Parker was close full to speed in April practices, so there should be no aftereffects from the broken fibula he suffered in Week 16. Still, Mike Tomlin knows his back's limitations and no longer plans to ride him "until the wheels come off." Rashard Mendenhall will absorb many of Parker's carries, which will help the Steelers immediately.

Jalen Parmele Height: 6-0 Weight: 222 College: Toledo   Draft: 2008/6 (176) Born: 30 Dec. 1985 Age: 22 Risk: Red

Year	Team	G	Runs	Yds	Yd/R	TD	FUM	DVOA	Rk	DYAR	Rk	YAR	Suc%	Rec	Pass	Yds	C%	Yd/C	TD	DVOA	Rk	DYAR	Rk
2008	MIA		48	202	4.2	1		-2.6%						18	27	151	67%	8.5	0	-17.6%			

Parmele, a big, physical back, gained 2,642 yards in his final two seasons for the Toledo Rockets. He followed that with a solid Combine, which cemented his efforts in the minds of some who would have missed him because of his smaller alma mater. Dolphins general manager Jeff Ireland already has Parmele penciled in as the number three back behind Ronnie Brown and Ricky Williams. In other words, he may be in play sooner than anyone thinks.

Chris Perry Height: 6-0 Weight: 224 College: Michigan   Draft: 2004/1 (26) Born: 27 Dec. 1981 Age: 26 Risk: Red

Year	Team	G	Runs	Yds	Yd/R	TD	FUM	DVOA	Rk	DYAR	Rk	YAR	Suc%	Rec	Pass	Yds	C%	Yd/C	TD	DVOA	Rk	DYAR	Rk
2005	CIN	14	61	279	4.6	0	2	6.1%	—	37	—	40	49%	51	62	328	82%	6.4	2	-16.6%	38	-10	44
2006	CIN	6	10	57	5.7	0	0	27.5%	—	16	—	14	60%	9	11	42	82%	4.7	0	-23.6%	—	-3	
2008	CIN		93	331	3.6	1		-11.2%						11	19	136	58%	12.8	1	61.7%			

When does a first-round pick become an injury bust? Perry spent all of 2007 on the physically-unable-to-perform list. Added to that are two seasons that he finished on injured reserve, and sundry lesser injuries, and we have a running back who has managed a total of 73 carries in the four years since he was drafted. Rudi Johnson has topped that sum in three consecutive games on more than one occasion. Perry, once a Heisman finalist, is three years younger than Johnson and four years younger than Kenny Watson. There's still a slim chance that Perry can return to form and make a positive contribution.

Adrian Peterson Height: 5-10 Weight: 210 College: Georgia Southern   Draft: 2002/6 (199) Born: 1 July 1979 Age: 29 Risk: Red

Year	Team	G	Runs	Yds	Yd/R	TD	FUM	DVOA	Rk	DYAR	Rk	YAR	Suc%	Rec	Pass	Yds	C%	Yd/C	TD	DVOA	Rk	DYAR	Rk
2005	CHI	16	76	391	5.1	2	1	15.8%	—	77	—	91	53%	7	12	48	58%	6.9	0	-71.3%	—	-40	—
2006	CHI	16	10	41	4.1	2	1	46.6%	—	26	—	30	50%	6	6	88	83%	14.7	0	59.3%	—	30	—
2007	CHI	16	151	510	3.4	3	3	-13.5%	41	-30	40	-53	38%	51	65	420	78%	8.2	0	7.2%	24	70	16
2008	CHI		61	283	4.6	2		21.3%						29	38	250	76%	8.5	1	-12.0%			

As journalists, unusual names like Tarvaris and Laveranues and Adewale drive us crazy, because we have to double-check the spellings all the time, but at least we know off the top of our heads that Tarvaris Jackson plays for Minnesota, Laveranues Coles plays for the Jets, and Adewale Ogunleye plays for Chicago. On the other hand, in the past few years, we have had to deal with two Chris Henrys, two Alex Smiths, two Ricky Williamses, two (An)Tony Gonzalezes, two Steve Smiths, two Mike Williamses, and, yes, two Adrian Petersons. Worse, they play the same position in the same division, and depending on Cedric Benson's legal woes, they each may end up as top rushers for their teams when all is said and done. The Minnesota version is clearly superior, but don't look down at the Chicago rendition. If Matt Forte cuts into this time in the backfield, Peterson will probably be back on special teams, a role he has excelled in for his entire career.

Adrian Peterson Height: 6-2 Weight: 217 College: Oklahoma   Draft: 2007/1 (7) Born: 21 March 1985 Age: 23 Risk: Yellow

Year	Team	G	Runs	Yds	Yd/R	TD	FUM	DVOA	Rk	DYAR	Rk	YAR	Suc%	Rec	Pass	Yds	C%	Yd/C	TD	DVOA	Rk	DYAR	Rk
2007	MIN	14	238	1341	5.6	12	5	16.4%	7	228	4	232	45%	19	29	268	69%	14.1	1	43.5%	3	97	9
2008	MIN		309	1538	5.0	13		20.2%						30	47	321	64%	10.5	1	3.9%			

We all know that Adrian Peterson was the Rookie of the Year and one of the greatest rookies of all time. What you may not know was just how erratic his season was. While there was the NFL record 296-yard game against San Diego and the 224-yard game against Chicago, there was also the 20-carry, 66-yard game against Detroit and the 14-carry, three-yard game against San Francisco. Put it all together, and while Peterson's 96 yards per game led the league, his standard deviation of yards per game was a whopping 78. Based on those numbers, a typical Peterson rushing game ranged anywhere from 17 yards to 174. This, of course, was largely because Peterson and Chester Taylor kept taking turns as the Vikings' starter. In Peterson's nine starts, he averaged 114 yards. If the Vikings commit to Peterson as their top guy and he can stay healthy, it would take a miracle for anyone else to win the rushing title.

Antonio Pittman

Height: 5-11 Weight: 207 College: Ohio State   Draft: 2007/4 (107) Born: 9 Dec. 1985 Age: 22 Risk: Red

Year	Team	G	Runs	Yds	Yd/R	TD	FUM	DVOA	Rk	DYAR	Rk	YAR	Suc%	Rec	Pass	Yds	C%	Yd/C	TD	DVOA	Rk	DYAR	Rk
2007	STL	11	38	139	3.7	0	0	-8.7%	—	0	—	-6	34%	3	9	15	33%	5.0	0	-87.0%	—	-39	—
2008	STL		46	172	3.7	0		-17.5%						13	19	115	68%	8.8	1	9.8%			

Longtime *Pro Football Prospectus* readers will know that most Big Ten running backs (with Minnesota apparently an exception) struggle upon reaching the big leagues. Pittman had a pair of 1,200-yard seasons at Ohio State, was chosen by the Saints in the fourth round, and then got cut before the regular season even started. The Rams picked him after Steven Jackson suffered an early-season injury, and the team managed to find playing time for him even after Jackson returned. St. Louis avoided using him in crucial situations, though; he had 21 carries on first down and only one on third down. He goes into 2008 battling Travis Minor for the third running-back spot in St. Louis behind Jackson and Brian Leonard. Give Pittman the edge in youth and potential: He's more than six years younger than the 29-year-old Minor.

Michael Pittman

Height: 6-0 Weight: 228 College: Fresno State   Draft: 1998/4 (95) Born: 14 Aug. 1975 Age: 33 Risk: Yellow

Year	Team	G	Runs	Yds	Yd/R	TD	FUM	DVOA	Rk	DYAR	Rk	YAR	Suc%	Rec	Pass	Yds	C%	Yd/C	TD	DVOA	Rk	DYAR	Rk
2005	TB	16	70	436	6.2	1	1	7.6%	—	41	—	48	36%	36	46	300	78%	8.3	1	24.7%	9	88	11
2006	TB	16	50	245	4.9	1	1	8.8%	—	32	—	32	39%	47	77	405	58%	8.6	0	-7.7%	40	84	14
2007	TB	10	68	286	4.2	0	1	-4.6%	—	10	—	8	44%	26	39	191	67%	7.3	0	-24.4%	51	-24	51
2008	DEN		99	432	4.4	0	1	-8.7%						32	42	252	76%	7.9	0	-9.9%			

Pittman, Tampa Bay's featured back between Warrick Dunn and Cadillac Williams, was the willing recipient of a Super Bowl ring brought about by a wonderful defense. Since 2005, he's been part of the by-committee approach, and an ankle injury kept him from competing for the spot he used to hold after Williams's season ended early in 2007. Earnest Graham was the latest to usurp him, and searching for a team that would give him more playing time, he signed with Denver as we went to press.

Clinton Portis

Height: 5-11 Weight: 212 College: Miami   Draft: 2002/2 (51) Born: 1 Sept. 1981 Age: 27 Risk: Red

Year	Team	G	Runs	Yds	Yd/R	TD	FUM	DVOA	Rk	DYAR	Rk	YAR	Suc%	Rec	Pass	Yds	C%	Yd/C	TD	DVOA	Rk	DYAR	Rk
2005	WAS	16	352	1516	4.3	11	3	11.0%	10	286	9	212	50%	30	41	216	73%	7.2	0	10.5%	19	57	16
2006	WAS	8	127	523	4.1	7	0	11.6%	8	111	19	86	44%	17	26	170	65%	10.0	0	7.6%	23	41	27
2007	WAS	16	325	1262	3.9	11	6	-3.0%	30	75	26	47	46%	47	58	389	81%	8.3	0	15.4%	18	96	10
2008	WAS		264	1158	4.4	7		-3.7%						40	60	325	67%	8.1	1	-4.3%			

A criminally underrated player, even with his role as the Redskins' unofficial spokesperson and media/blogosphere darling. Portis quietly led the league in carries last year, but his role in the passing game is truly unappreciated. He's a valuable outlet receiver with the smarts to find soft spots in coverage, which puts him in a better position to make plays than most backs. Portis is the best pass-blocking back in the league; his technique isn't flawless by any means, but he makes up for it in brute strength and seemingly boundless energy. An ideal fit for the West Coast offense, he should remain a top-six fantasy pick and Pro Bowl candidate if he stays healthy.

Dominic Rhodes

Height: 5-9   Weight: 203   College: Midwestern State   Draft: 2001/FA   Born: 17 Jan. 1979   Age: 29   Risk: Red

Year	Team	G	Runs	Yds	Yd/R	TD	FUM	DVOA	Rk	DYAR	Rk	YAR	Suc%	Rec	Pass	Yds	C%	Yd/C	TD	DVOA	Rk	DYAR	Rk
2005	IND	13	40	118	3.0	4	0	-18.0%	—	-19	—	-1	50%	13	15	88	80%	6.8	0	-0.3%	—	11	—
2006	IND	16	187	641	3.4	5	2	-9.1%	37	-4	37	3	49%	36	47	251	55%	7.0	0	-8.9%	42	-26	52
2007	OAK	10	75	302	4.0	1	1	-2.0%	—	21	—	38	51%	11	18	70	61%	6.4	0	-36.9%	—	-21	—
2008	IND		95	302	3.2	2		-7.8%						25	32	205	78%	8.2	0	21.6%			

Rhodes is the last in a long line of free agents who learned the hard way that these aren't your father's Raiders. After helping the Colts win Super Bowl XLI with an outstanding, near-MVP performance, Rhodes signed a two-year deal with Oakland, served a four-game substance-abuse suspension, and did little in the Raiders' substandard offense. He's got an effective and defined role in Indianapolis with Joseph Addai, one he's filled well in the past. His 2008 productivity should reflect that.

Ray Rice

Height: 5-8   Weight: 199   College: Rutgers   Draft: 2008/2 (55)   Born: 22 Jan. 1987   Age: 21   Risk: Red

Year	Team	G	Runs	Yds	Yd/R	TD	FUM	DVOA	Rk	DYAR	Rk	YAR	Suc%	Rec	Pass	Yds	C%	Yd/C	TD	DVOA	Rk	DYAR	Rk
2008	BAL		81	317	3.5	4		-14.7%						16	24	153	67%	9.6	0	-6.3%			

Rice reminded several draft analysts of a young Emmitt Smith with his squat, powerful build and his tremendous productivity. Like Smith, Rice doesn't wow you on tape even as he is putting together a big game. The downside to all that productivity is that Rice already has a lot of mileage on his legs and has taken lots of hits to his undersized frame. Rice doesn't have change-of-pace speed and doesn't provide much in the passing game, so he's strictly depth behind Willis McGahee.

Michael Robinson

Height: 6-2   Weight: 217   College: Penn State   Draft: 2006/4 (100)   Born: 6 Feb. 1983   Age: 25   Risk: Red

Year	Team	G	Runs	Yds	Yd/R	TD	FUM	DVOA	Rk	DYAR	Rk	YAR	Suc%	Rec	Pass	Yds	C%	Yd/C	TD	DVOA	Rk	DYAR	Rk
2006	SF	16	38	116	3.1	2	0	-29.5%	—	-41	—	-36	34%	9	12	47	50%	5.2	0	-28.0%	—	-15	—
2007	SF	15	26	121	4.7	0	1	-27.4%	—	-20	—	-13	38%	11	13	73	85%	6.6	0	28.1%	—	26	—
2008	SF		73	284	3.9	1		-2.0%						16	26	118	62%	7.5	0	-22.4%			

Robinson was pigeonholed by former running backs coach Bishop Harris as a special-teams player. It would be tough to find a better core special-teams player in the league, but Robinson could potentially do so much more. With new offensive coordinator Mike Martz, Robinson, a former college quarterback and wide receiver, could have an increased role. Robinson also loves to study and could get himself some increased playing time by learning a complex offense more completely than his fellow backs do.

Marcel Shipp

Height: 5-11   Weight: 228   College: Massachusetts   Draft: 2001/FA   Born: 8 Aug. 1978   Age: 30   Risk: Red

Year	Team	G	Runs	Yds	Yd/R	TD	FUM	DVOA	Rk	DYAR	Rk	YAR	Suc%	Rec	Pass	Yds	C%	Yd/C	TD	DVOA	Rk	DYAR	Rk
2005	ARI	15	157	451	2.9	0	4	-34.6%	45	-169	45	-179	41%	35	44	255	80%	7.3	0	4.1%	26	39	23
2006	ARI	15	17	41	2.4	4	0	10.5%	—	19	—	26	47%	6	11	60	45%	10.0	0	-22.8%	—	-8	—
2007	ARI	16	15	41	2.7	1	0	-19.9%	—	-9	—	-9	40%	4	14	25	29%	6.3	0	-60.6%	—	-33	—
2008	ARI		7	25	3.4	1		10.4%						9	12	62	75%	7.0	0	-38.5%			

Shipp's disappointing season last year ruined Ken Whisenhunt's plan for a two-back system. Shipp has lost most of his speed, and when you average under three yards per carry for three straight years, it takes a lot to stay in the NFL. With his special-teams abilities and a rep as an overachiever, he may be able to stick as a gunner, but J. J. Arrington or Tim Hightower will take on the few carries Shipp earned in recent years.

Steve Slaton

Height: 5-9   Weight: 197   College: West Virginia   Draft: 2008/3 (89)   Born: 4 Jan. 1986   Age: 22   Risk: Red

Year	Team	G	Runs	Yds	Yd/R	TD	FUM	DVOA	Rk	DYAR	Rk	YAR	Suc%	Rec	Pass	Yds	C%	Yd/C	TD	DVOA	Rk	DYAR	Rk
2008	HOU		132	652	4.9	6		-3.1%						29	41	243	71%	8.3	1	15.5%			

Slaton's junior year was a disappointment, and he opted to come out early when Rich Rodriguez departed West

Virginia. Go back to his freshman and sophomore seasons, and you'll find a player who was as explosive as any tail-back in the nation—and not just against poor competition, either. Georgia fans are still smarting from what a then-freshman Slaton did to them in the 2006 Sugar Bowl. He appears to be a perfect fit for a zone-blocking, one-cut of-fense, but may need to bulk up to be more than a third-down guy in the pros.

Kevin Smith
Height: 6-1 Weight: 217 College: Central Florida Draft: 2008/3 (64) Born: 17 Dec. 1986 Age: 21 Risk: Red

Year	Team	G	Runs	Yds	Yd/R	TD	FUM	DVOA	Rk	DYAR	Rk	YAR	Suc%	Rec	Pass	Yds	C%	Yd/C	TD	DVOA	Rk	DYAR	Rk
2008	DET		181	676	3.7	7		0.0%						33	41	276	80%	8.3	1	18.7%			

The Curse of 370? Puh-leeze. For Smith, that's so passé. His 450 carries as a senior had to raise red flags (well, except to Herm Edwards, of course), but the Lions see him as the feature back they haven't had in years. After jettisoning former first-round pick Kevin Jones and returning to a more traditional offense, the Lions will seek to implement Smith as their main man in the backfield as long as he holds up. Smith is a good receiver, so the Lions would be wise to get him out of the backfield once in a while. He also has a Clinton Portis personality: He's offbeat and funny and has an artistic flair. Somehow, that doesn't translate into "Matt Millen type of player."

Kolby Smith
Height: 5-11 Weight: 220 College: Louisville Draft: 2007/5 (148) Born: 15 Dec. 1984 Age: 23 Risk: Red

Year	Team	G	Runs	Yds	Yd/R	TD	FUM	DVOA	Rk	DYAR	Rk	YAR	Suc%	Rec	Pass	Yds	C%	Yd/C	TD	DVOA	Rk	DYAR	Rk
2007	KC	16	112	407	3.6	2	0	-3.4%	31	25	34	53	49%	22	29	148	76%	6.7	0	-8.7%	35	7	37
2008	KC		104	380	3.7	2		-8.4%						29	43	231	67%	8.0	1	-6.5%			

Smith was never a starter during his four-year career at Louisville, but halfway through his rookie season, injuries to Larry Johnson and Priest Holmes thrust him into the starting lineup. He acquitted himself nicely with a nearly league-average performance. Smith has good quickness and should have a nice career as a backup. The drafting of Jamaal Charles returns him to third on the depth chart, but Smith has potential as a third-down back.

Musa Smith
Height: 6-0 Weight: 232 College: Georgia Draft: 2003/3 (77) Born: 31 May 1982 Age: 26 Risk: Red

Year	Team	G	Runs	Yds	Yd/R	TD	FUM	DVOA	Rk	DYAR	Rk	YAR	Suc%	Rec	Pass	Yds	C%	Yd/C	TD	DVOA	Rk	DYAR	Rk
2005	BAL	1	0	0	0.0	0	—	—	—	—	—	—	—	3	3	5	100%	1.7	0	-59.5%	—	-7	—
2006	BAL	12	36	153	4.3	0	1	-13.3%	—	-6	—	-10	39%	22	25	135	76%	6.1	0	-13.1%	45	11	42
2007	BAL	16	75	264	3.5	2	1	-19.2%	—	-31	—	-41	29%	27	34	192	79%	7.1	0	1.8%	29	30	29
2008	NYJ		56	190	3.4	2		-5.5%						20	28	165	71%	8.3	0	-14.8%			

The Ravens showed little interest in retaining Smith after he became an unrestricted free agent. Smith's last visit was with the Jets in May, and he could wind up there as a backup. He has some value as a big third-down back, and he rushed for 83 yards in 22 carries against the Steelers last year. The Jets signed Smith as we went to press.

Jason Snelling
Height: 5-11 Weight: 230 College: Virginia Draft: 2007/7 (244) Born: 29 Dec. 1983 Age: 24 Risk: Red

Year	Team	G	Runs	Yds	Yd/R	TD	FUM	DVOA	Rk	DYAR	Rk	YAR	Suc%	Rec	Pass	Yds	C%	Yd/C	TD	DVOA	Rk	DYAR	Rk
2007	ATL	7	13	43	3.3	1	—	3.0%	—	9	—	10	54%	0	—	0	—	0.0	0	—	—	—	—
2008	ATL		98	386	3.9	3		-10.2%						16	28	129	57%	7.9	1	-11.4%			

One of the most underrated collegiate running backs during his career at Virginia, Snelling is more a "move" full-back than a lead blocker. He was drafted by the Falcons in the seventh round in 2007, put up 172 yards on 39 carries in his first NFL preseason (outgaining Adrian Peterson and Selvin Young), and was subsequently relegated to the practice squad. Placed on the roster in mid-November to avoid a waiver claim by the Cowboys, Snelling excelled in short-yardage situations and on special teams. Atlanta's backfield is very well established, but Snelling could pop off a good game or two if he's given the chance.

Darren Sproles

Height: 5-6   Weight: 181   College: Kansas State   Draft: 2005/4 (130)   Born: 20 June 1983   Age: 25   Risk: Red

Year	Team	G	Runs	Yds	Yd/R	TD	FUM	DVOA	Rk	DYAR	Rk	YAR	Suc%	Rec	Pass	Yds	C%	Yd/C	TD	DVOA	Rk	DYAR	Rk
2005	SD	15	8	50	6.3	0	0	37.3%	—	15	—	14	50%	3	4	10	75%	3.3	0	-79.3%	—	-15	—
2007	SD	15	37	164	4.4	2	0	0.9%	—	13	—	18	41%	10	12	31	83%	3.1	0	-46.2%	—	-21	—
2008	SD		41	203	5.0	2		18.8%						17	27	125	63%	7.2	0	-17.4%			

In two healthy seasons, Sproles caught 13 passes with a career long of 14 yards. In the playoffs against Indianapolis, he took a screen pass 55 yards for a crucial touchdown. Add in a couple of kick return touchdowns in an NBC Sunday night game, also against Indianapolis, and the diminutive running back developed a big-play reputation. Sproles is a good return man, but he is nothing more than depth as a running back. He could be a third-down back on a team with a starting running back who cannot catch the ball, but in San Diego, LaDainian Tomlinson handles the duties on every down.

Aaron Stecker

Height: 5-10   Weight: 213   College: Western Illinois   Draft: 2000/FA   Born: 13 Nov. 1975   Age: 33   Risk: Red

Year	Team	G	Runs	Yds	Yd/R	TD	FUM	DVOA	Rk	DYAR	Rk	YAR	Suc%	Rec	Pass	Yds	C%	Yd/C	TD	DVOA	Rk	DYAR	Rk
2005	NO	15	95	363	3.8	0	2	-11.0%	—	-9	—	10	42%	35	48	281	73%	8.0	0	7.5%	27	52	19
2006	NO	12	4	11	2.8	0	0	10.2%	—	3	—	2	25%	19	28	190	79%	10.0	0	3.5%	28	36	33
2007	NO	16	115	448	3.9	5	1	4.1%	22	64	27	64	50%	36	43	211	86%	5.9	0	5.0%	26	49	23
2008	NO		81	346	4.3	4		15.0%						30	34	236	88%	7.9	0	28.4%			

The Saints have their backfield roles pretty well set. There's Reggie Bush, erstwhile feature back, whose seemingly infinite chasm between potential and reality can only be closed by the presence of Deuce McAllister–like substance in the backfield with him. There's McAllister himself, veteran and erstwhile sort-of-superstar, who now has to share the wealth and who has a bunch of injury concerns. There's erstwhile second-year sleeper Pierre Thomas, the newest member of the Sample Size All-Stars . . . and then there's Stecker, the erstwhile do-it-all guy. He can catch a pass out of the backfield or split wide, he'll impress on special teams, and he filled in quite admirably for Bush when Bush missed the season's last four games with a knee injury. It was Stecker, not any of the other erstwhiles, who posted the only serviceable DYAR among Saints running backs with at least 100 carries. And yet, even the people who talk about Pierre Thomas barely know Stecker's name. The Saints staved off interest from the Buccaneers and signed Stecker to a one-year contract this offseason, so at least they know his erstwhile value.

Jonathan Stewart

Height: 5-11   Weight: 235   College: Oregon   Draft: 2008/1 (13)   Born: 21 March 1987   Age: 21   Risk: Red

Year	Team	G	Runs	Yds	Yd/R	TD	FUM	DVOA	Rk	DYAR	Rk	YAR	Suc%	Rec	Pass	Yds	C%	Yd/C	TD	DVOA	Rk	DYAR	Rk
2008	CAR		202	763	3.8	7		-13.2%						22	25	134	88%	6.0	2	-7.3%			

While many regard Darren McFadden as the rightful heir to Adrian Peterson's "Did you *see* what that guy just *did???*" rookie campaign, many who have seen enough of Stewart's senior year believe that he is the NFL's next great running back. Stewart ran a sub-4.5 40 at the Combine, despite a toe injury that was subsequently fixed. His injury history kept him out of the draft's top ten, but Stewart managed to put up 1,722 rushing yards in his senior season. His versatility will have him on the field for the Panthers right away—Stewart can catch the ball and is an excellent return man for his size. Stewart is generally compared to physical backs like LaDainian Tomlinson, Larry Johnson, and Jamal Lewis, and that bruising style underscores the wisdom of having him split carries with DeAngelo Williams in Carolina.

Chester Taylor

Height: 5-11   Weight: 213   College: Toledo   Draft: 2002/6 (207)   Born: 22 Sept. 1979   Age: 29   Risk: Red

Year	Team	G	Runs	Yds	Yd/R	TD	FUM	DVOA	Rk	DYAR	Rk	YAR	Suc%	Rec	Pass	Yds	C%	Yd/C	TD	DVOA	Rk	DYAR	Rk
2005	BAL	15	117	487	4.2	0	2	-12.2%	39	-17	35	-6	42%	41	52	292	79%	7.1	1	-4.7%	28	23	32
2006	MIN	15	303	1216	4.0	6	4	-7.8%	33	10	33	5	46%	42	51	288	70%	6.9	0	15.8%	15	83	16
2007	MIN	14	157	844	5.4	7	5	8.0%	20	101	20	98	46%	29	43	281	67%	9.7	0	15.7%	17	64	18
2008	MIN		179	802	4.5	6		5.8%						29	39	257	74%	9.0	1	9.6%			

Taylor's 5.4 yards per carry was a shade behind Adrian Peterson's 5.6. Peterson gained 35 percent of his yards at least 10 yards after passing the line of scrimmage, but Taylor was also exceptional in this measure, gaining 31 percent of his yards downfield. Turning to Success Rate, we see Taylor slightly topping Peterson, 46 percent to 45 percent. It would be easy to look at these numbers and assume the two players were very close in quality. There were two main differences between the two. First, there is age. Peterson still has his peak ahead of him. Taylor is now 29, the age at which most running backs begin to fade. Second, there are fumbles. Last season, Peterson put the ball on the ground four times in 238 carries; Taylor fumbled five times in only 157 carries. When the Vikings are trying to kill the clock in the fourth quarter, their fans had better hope that number 28 is in the backfield and number 29 is on the sidelines.

Fred Taylor

Height: 6-1 Weight: 234 College: Florida   Draft: 1998/1 (9) Born: 27 Jan. 1976 Age: 32 Risk: Yellow

Year	Team	G	Runs	Yds	Yd/R	TD	FUM	DVOA	Rk	DYAR	Rk	YAR	Suc%	Rec	Pass	Yds	C%	Yd/C	TD	DVOA	Rk	DYAR	Rk
2005	JAC	11	194	787	4.1	3	0	-11.2%	35	-19	36	40	39%	13	18	83	72%	6.4	0	-8.5%	—	5	—
2006	JAC	15	231	1146	5.0	5	3	11.1%	11	172	12	192	44%	23	28	242	68%	10.5	1	3.4%	29	18	39
2007	JAC	15	223	1202	5.4	5	2	11.1%	16	171	8	165	45%	9	14	58	64%	6.4	0	-17.9%	—	-3	—
2008	JAC		226	1026	4.5	8		5.5%						22	38	226	58%	10.2	1	18.9%			

Memo to Mr. Taylor: Whatever career-rejuvenation secret you've found, there are 30-plus-year-old backs all over the league who would like a sample. The three years' worth of accompanying stats tell the story quite nicely. Taylor has gotten better each of the last two seasons, but at 32, he has to hit the wall sometime, right? Perhaps Taylor is just taking better care of his body these days. Never known as a power back, our game charters noted repeatedly how many tackles he broke last season. Still, you can only fool Father Time for so long. If there are any signs of Taylor slowing down this season—and KUBIAK thinks there will be—the Jaguars will simply slide more of the burden onto Maurice Jones-Drew and Greg Jones.

Anthony Thomas

Height: 6-2 Weight: 225 College: Michigan   Draft: 2001/2 (38) Born: 7 Nov. 1977 Age: 31 Risk: Red

Year	Team	G	Runs	Yds	Yd/R	TD	FUM	DVOA	Rk	DYAR	Rk	YAR	Suc%	Rec	Pass	Yds	C%	Yd/C	TD	DVOA	Rk	DYAR	Rk
2005	DAL	10	43	92	2.1	0	0	-45.4%	—	-9	—	-10	14%	4	4	13	50%	3.3	0	-60.9%	—	-11	—
2006	BUF	16	107	378	3.5	2	1	-25.1%	47	-67	46	-31	37%	22	24	139	83%	6.3	0	-21.3%	—	-17	—
2007	BUF	10	36	89	2.5	0	0	-28.6%	—	-32	—	-23	44%	15	20	95	75%	6.3	1	5.1%	—	18	—

The A-Train looked bad in extended action against the Patriots and Jaguars when Marshawn Lynch got hurt and then tore a calf muscle and ended the season on injured reserve. Thomas is a forever-injured power runner with almost no quickness left. He's probably out of chances, but his excellent pass blocking could keep him around for another year or two.

Pierre Thomas

Height: 5-11 Weight: 210 College: Illinois   Draft: 2007/FA Born: 18 Dec. 1984 Age: 23 Risk: Red

Year	Team	G	Runs	Yds	Yd/R	TD	FUM	DVOA	Rk	DYAR	Rk	YAR	Suc%	Rec	Pass	Yds	C%	Yd/C	TD	DVOA	Rk	DYAR	Rk
2007	NO	12	52	252	4.8	1	0	33.5%	—	87	—	78	60%	17	23	151	83%	8.9	1	25.5%	—	53	—
2008	NO		102	457	4.5	5		4.8%						36	57	243	63%	6.8	0@\B:-16.9%				

As is the case with any undrafted rookie, a few things had to fall into place before Thomas could get a chance in the NFL. There was Deuce McAllister's Week 3 ACL injury, fourth-round pick Antonio Pittman's release, and Reggie Bush's late-season torn knee ligament. When Aaron Stecker and Thomas were the last men standing, they both proved effective; Thomas built on a very solid preseason (190 rushing yards on 33 carries for a 5.8 yards-per-carry average and three touchdowns) with his performance in the season finale. He became the first player in the 41-year history of the Saints franchise to gain over 100 yards rushing and receiving in the same game. The size of his role in 2008 depends in part on Deuce McAllister's health.

LaBrandon Toefield

Height: 5-11 Weight: 232 College: LSU   Draft: 2003/4 (132) Born: 24 Sept. 1980 Age: 28 Risk: Red

Year	Team	G	Runs	Yds	Yd/R	TD	FUM	DVOA	Rk	DYAR	Rk	YAR	Suc%	Rec	Pass	Yds	C%	Yd/C	TD	DVOA	Rk	DYAR	Rk
2005	JAC	9	36	142	3.9	4	0	14.8%	—	34	—	38	47%	3	7	17	43%	5.7	0	-42.5%	—	-11	—
2006	JAC	4	10	22	2.2	0	0	-43.5%	—	-14	—	-13	40%	0	0	0	0%	0.0	0	0.0%	—	0	—
2007	JAC	2	13	27	2.1	1	0	-34.4%	—	-17	—	-16	23%	1	1	4	100%	4.0	0	-1.9%	—	1	—
2008	CAR		64	247	3.9	2		-13.8%						14	17	81	82%	5.9	0	-25.8%			

Fred Taylor's stubborn refusal to age forced Toefield to seek employment elsewhere this offseason, but he can't expect a much bigger role in Carolina, where the Panthers have spent first-round picks on running backs (DeAngelo Williams and Jonathan Stewart) in two of the past three drafts.

LaDainian Tomlinson

Height: 5-10 Weight: 221 College: TCU   Draft: 2001/1 (5)   Born: 23 June 1979   Age: 29   Risk: Green

Year	Team	G	Runs	Yds	Yd/R	TD	FUM	DVOA	Rk	DYAR	Rk	YAR	Suc%	Rec	Pass	Yds	C%	Yd/C	TD	DVOA	Rk	DYAR	Rk
2005	SD	16	339	1462	4.3	18	3	15.8%	6	331	6	280	47%	51	77	370	66%	7.3	2	-19.7%	46	-25	49
2006	SD	16	348	1815	5.2	28	2	23.4%	3	453	1	498	49%	56	80	508	69%	9.1	3	16.0%	14	157	4
2007	SD	16	315	1474	4.7	15	0	13.6%	11	287	2	288	45%	60	86	475	70%	7.9	3	10.7%	22	113	6
2008	SD		331	1439	4.3	20		18.3%						44	69	409	64%	9.2	2	12.1%			

After Tomlinson's MVP performance in 2006, last season was perceived by some as a disappointing year. Perhaps the bar is a bit too high, as Tomlinson ranked second in DYAR, the fifth time in six years he has been in the top six. Even a back as great as Tomlinson is reliant on the blocking of his offensive line. He had four 100-yard games in the six games started by Jeromey Clary at right tackle and only two in the 10 games started by Shane Olivea. You also might notice that big fat zero under "fumbles." At age 29, Tomlinson is now approaching the end of his prime. The good news is that many great backs like Tomlinson first show their decline by poor performance as a receiver, giving us a heads-up that their overall production is about to slip. Last year, Tomlinson remained extremely productive as a receiver, still capable of serving as much more than a dump-off option. He did take a public hit for sitting out after two carries in the AFC Championship game with a bruised knee. Tomlinson has missed *one* game in his entire career and played 2004 with nagging injuries that hurt his performance. Only those who average one sick day every three years should be allowed to criticize his toughness.

Michael Turner

Height: 5-10 Weight: 237 College: Northern Illinois   Draft: 2004/5 (154)   Born: 13 Feb. 1982   Age: 26   Risk: Red

Year	Team	G	Runs	Yds	Yd/R	TD	FUM	DVOA	Rk	DYAR	Rk	YAR	Suc%	Rec	Pass	Yds	C%	Yd/C	TD	DVOA	Rk	DYAR	Rk
2005	SD	16	57	335	5.9	3	0	24.4%	—	74	—	80	51%	0	1	0	0%	0.0	0	-110.5%	—	-4	—
2006	SD	13	80	502	6.3	2	0	34.7%	—	142	—	137	55%	3	3	47	67%	15.7	0	79.7%	—	22	—
2007	SD	16	71	316	4.5	1	1	-27.4%	—	-52	—	-41	28%	4	7	16	57%	4.0	0	-60.5%	—	-19	—
2008	ATL		215	807	3.8	2		-24.2%						35	60	233	58%	6.6	0	-26.2%			

Small sample sizes can be misleading. In 2005 and 2006, Turner was highly productive in limited carries. This past year, he looked awful. Obviously, he is somewhere in between. Turner is tricky to project because what little data we have is skewed by a handful of plays. His career average of 5.5 yards per carry is certainly impressive, but over 18 percent of his career yards came on three runs over 70 yards, adding a full yard to his career yards-per-carry average. His breakaway speed is certainly an asset, but there is a fluke factor in those long runs. LaDainian Tomlinson, not exactly a plodder, only has two 70-plus-yard rushes in 10 times as many carries. Turner's promise landed him a big contract, but he will be likely to split carries with another back who posted impressive yards-per-carry totals in limited action. Turner should reach the projected 215 carries; the poor yards-per-carry projection is a reflection of the serious downgrade in offensive line from San Diego to Atlanta. Turner is probably overrated in fantasy circles; our yards-per-carry projections may seem low, but they reflect an environment with few opportunities for those long runs that would give your fantasy team a good chance to win each week.

Darius Walker

Height: 5-10 Weight: 206 College: Notre Dame   Draft: 2007/FA   Born: 21 Oct. 1985   Age: 23   Risk: Red

Year	Team	G	Runs	Yds	Yd/R	TD	FUM	DVOA	Rk	DYAR	Rk	YAR	Suc%	Rec	Pass	Yds	C%	Yd/C	TD	DVOA	Rk	DYAR	Rk
2007	HOU	4	58	264	4.6	1	0	10.7%	—	46	—	48	48%	13	15	81	87%	6.2	0	25.0%	—	37	—
2008	HOU		60	261	4.3	2		-5.2%						18	25	154	72%	8.7	1	12.0%			

After coming out of Notre Dame as a junior and then going undrafted, Walker will always be a poster child for the stay-in-school campaign. He latched on with the Texans and turned in a better year than expected. Houston thought enough of him to bring him back for a second season, but not so much to keep the Texans from acquiring a free agent (Chris Brown) and drafting Steve Slaton in the third round.

Derrick Ward

Height: 5-11 Weight: 233 College: Ottawa (Kansas) Draft: 2004/7 (235) Born: 30 Aug. 1980 Age: 28 Risk: Red

Year	Team	G	Runs	Yds	Yd/R	TD	FUM	DVOA	Rk	DYAR	Rk	YAR	Suc%	Rec	Pass	Yds	C%	Yd/C	TD	DVOA	Rk	DYAR	Rk
2005	NYG	14	35	123	3.5	0	0	3.4%	—	16	—	7	37%	2	5	13	40%	6.5	0	-37.6%	—	-5	—
2006	NYG	8	0	0	0.0	0	—	—	—	—	—	—	—	0	—	0	—	0.0	0	—	—	—	—
2007	NYG	8	125	602	4.8	3	2	13.0%	13	112	18	108	46%	26	40	179	65%	6.9	1	-20.4%	47	-15	48
2008	NYG		99	446	4.5	4		20.7%						26	37	267	70%	10.1	1	11.1%			

Before Ahmad Bradshaw emerged as the Brandon Jacobs counterpunch, Ward was very effective, both as a complementary back to Jacobs and as a starter when the big man was hurt. Unfortunately, Ward himself struggles with injuries—he went down in Week 7, returned to rush for 154 yards against the Bears in Week 13, and then broke his leg at the end of the game and missed the rest of the Giants' season. Ward comes from the "Keep It Simple, Stupid" family of backs, identifying his hole and hitting it as quickly as possible. He's a distinct number three on the depth chart behind Jacobs and Bradshaw, but with the injury problems likely to afflict at least one of the two, Ward will get on the field at some point in 2008.

Leon Washington

Height: 5-9 Weight: 199 College: Florida State Draft: 2006/4 (117) Born: 29 Aug. 1982 Age: 26 Risk: Red

Year	Team	G	Runs	Yds	Yd/R	TD	FUM	DVOA	Rk	DYAR	Rk	YAR	Suc%	Rec	Pass	Yds	C%	Yd/C	TD	DVOA	Rk	DYAR	Rk
2006	NYJ	16	151	650	4.3	4	1	14.0%	7	133	15	129	49%	25	31	270	55%	10.8	0	17.9%	11	70	20
2007	NYJ	16	71	353	5.0	3	1	2.3%	—	30	—	37	37%	36	51	213	71%	5.9	0	-10.4%	37	10	36
2008	NYJ		68	250	3.7	1		9.5%						28	40	251	70%	8.9	1	-19.5%			

Washington earned team MVP honors because of his kick returns and big-play ability. His first-down DVOA was 30.4%, but his Success Rate on later downs was terrible (30 percent). He was a minus in the receiving game because he produced a nonnourishing diet of three-yard receptions. Washington's offensive stats would look much better if the Jets' offense became more multidimensional, but the team would be wise to limit his carries and get the most from him as a return man.

Kenny Watson

Height: 5-11 Weight: 220 College: Penn State Draft: 2001/FA Born: 13 March 1978 Age: 30 Risk: Red

Year	Team	G	Runs	Yds	Yd/R	TD	FUM	DVOA	Rk	DYAR	Rk	YAR	Suc%	Rec	Pass	Yds	C%	Yd/C	TD	DVOA	Rk	DYAR	Rk
2006	CIN	16	25	138	5.5	1	0	35.4%	—	41	—	42	52%	23	32	213	73%	9.3	0	29.5%	4	88	13
2007	CIN	16	178	763	4.3	7	3	13.0%	12	162	10	178	56%	52	67	374	78%	7.2	0	-4.7%	31	32	28
2008	CIN		131	578	4.4	4		4.4%						37	51	334	73%	8.9	1	18.4%			

Watson took advantage of a string of injuries to Rudi Johnson to establish himself as Cincinnati's primary running back last year, topping the rushing total of the former Pro Bowler by more than 250 yards on a similar number of carries. Assuming both backs are healthy, they will probably be used in tandem this season, though if Watson proves substantially more effective than Johnson again, the Penn State alum will presumably get most of the carries. Watson struggled as a third-down runner last year (-39.8% DVOA on 16 attempts), so Johnson may well keep the short-yardage role.

Brian Westbrook

Height: 5-8 Weight: 203 College: Villanova Draft: 2002/3 (91) Born: 2 Sept. 1979 Age: 29 Risk: Green

Year	Team	G	Runs	Yds	Yd/R	TD	FUM	DVOA	Rk	DYAR	Rk	YAR	Suc%	Rec	Pass	Yds	C%	Yd/C	TD	DVOA	Rk	DYAR	Rk
2005	PHI	12	156	617	4.0	3	0	-5.3%	26	20	27	10	40%	61	96	616	64%	10.1	4	15.9%	16	157	2
2006	PHI	15	240	1217	5.1	7	2	23.9%	2	314	2	299	48%	77	109	699	66%	9.1	4	4.7%	27	142	8
2007	PHI	15	278	1333	4.8	7	1	19.9%	3	334	1	318	53%	90	120	771	75%	8.6	5	12.5%	21	189	1
2008	PHI		280	1376	4.9	12		23.8%						66	89	518	74%	7.8	4	7.9%			

If you polled 100 football fans, how many would say Westbrook was the best running back in football? Five? Ten? Doesn't matter. Last year, he was. Whereas most players will lose some performance as their workload increases, Westbrook set a career high in both carries and receptions while improving his catch rate and his Success Rate. Compare him to, say, Adrian Peterson. Purple Jesus might be a more talented rusher, but Westbrook's ability to catch the ball, block, and produce consistent yardage adds more points to the scoreboard. Westbrook's ability to protect the ball (fumbling once in every 135 touches) also makes him superior to a player like Peterson, who fumbled twice as frequently in 2008. By keeping his workload manageable, the Eagles have ensured that Westbrook can remain at this level of performance for at least another year or two. If the Eagles can come close to matching our projection for them as a team, then Westbrook will be a favorite for league MVP.

LenDale White

Height: 6-2   Weight: 235   College: USC   Draft: 2006/2 (45)   Born: 20 Dec. 1984   Age: 23   Risk: Green

Year	Team	G	Runs	Yds	Yd/R	TD	FUM	DVOA	Rk	DYAR	Rk	YAR	Suc%	Rec	Pass	Yds	C%	Yd/C	TD	DVOA	Rk	DYAR	Rk
2006	TEN	13	61	244	4.0	0	1	-2.3%	—	15	—	21	35%	14	20	60	60%	4.3	0	-12.5%	—	23	—
2007	TEN	16	303	1110	3.7	7	5	-6.5%	34	26	33	61	46%	20	31	114	65%	5.7	0	-17.4%	44	-6	43
2008	TEN		242	1024	4.2	6		-0.2%						23	31	118	74%	5.1	0	-21.0%			

White had minor arthroscopic knee surgery in February, and the Titans hedged their bets by selecting Chris Johnson in the first round of the draft. White may still be the featured runner, but workhorse backs are supposed to provide more consistency, more receiving ability, and more plain-old yardage than White offered for 20-plus carries per game. White also battled weight issues and a minor knee injury for much of the season. The best-case scenario is that the big, lumbering White and the small, speedy Johnson provide the Titans with a great thunder-and-lightning one-two punch. But with Johnson in town, don't expect White to carry the ball 300 times again this year.

Cadillac Williams

Height: 5-11   Weight: 217   College: Auburn   Draft: 2005/1 (5)   Born: 21 April 1982   Age: 26   Risk: Red

Year	Team	G	Runs	Yds	Yd/R	TD	FUM	DVOA	Rk	DYAR	Rk	YAR	Suc%	Rec	Pass	Yds	C%	Yd/C	TD	DVOA	Rk	DYAR	Rk
2005	TB	14	290	1178	4.1	6	3	-7.9%	30	8	30	65	43%	20	25	81	80%	4.1	0	-30.6%	50	-24	47
2006	TB	14	225	798	3.5	1	3	-11.8%	41	-28	42	-69	39%	30	44	196	75%	6.5	0	8.0%	21	83	17
2007	TB	4	54	208	3.9	3	2	10.6%	—	44	—	32	52%	3	5	17	60%	5.7	0	-108.4%	—	-24	—
2008	TB		59	249	4.2	4		-0.2%						34	42	260	81%	7.7	2	44.6%			

None of the top three collegiate backs in 2005 have performed as expected. Cedric Benson's ineffectiveness, not to mention his boating escapades, have the Bears looking anew for ground-game difference-makers. Miami's Ronnie Brown has been effective when healthy, but a pathetic offense around him and his own injury problems have stunted his growth. And then there's Cadillac Williams, Tampa Bay's first-round pick in 2005. His rookie season had people seeing a very bright future, but offensive-line difficulties and injuries derailed his 2006 season. In the fourth game of the 2007 season, Williams took a hard tackle from Carolina safety Chris Harris and left the field with what was later diagnosed as a torn patellar tendon. Williams is saying all the right things about his rehab, but some in the Buccaneers' organization quietly believe that his career may be over. The good news is that the Bucs have enough depth at running back to avoid pushing him back into the rotation too early, assuming there's still a chance for a return.

DeAngelo Williams

Height: 5-10   Weight: 217   College: Memphis   Draft: 2006/1 (27)   Born: 25 April 1983   Age: 25   Risk: Red

Year	Team	G	Runs	Yds	Yd/R	TD	FUM	DVOA	Rk	DYAR	Rk	YAR	Suc%	Rec	Pass	Yds	C%	Yd/C	TD	DVOA	Rk	DYAR	Rk
2006	CAR	13	121	501	4.1	1	1	-1.5%	25	36	29	30	47%	33	36	313	86%	9.5	1	50.6%	1	175	2
2007	CAR	16	144	717	5.0	4	1	11.9%	15	104	19	109	41%	23	38	175	63%	7.6	1	-25.9%	52	-25	52
2008	CAR		222	926	4.2	5		-2.7%						43	61	292	70%	6.8	1	-4.3%			

February 15, 2008: "Okay, DeAngelo . . . here's the good news. We released DeShaun Foster, leaving you as the team's feature back. You certainly earned it by gaining five yards per carry despite an offense that was going door-to-door in the greater Charlotte area looking for quarterbacks. We might draft another back to keep you from breaking down, but we like what you've done. We see you as our clear number one back in 2008."

April 26, 2008: "Okay, DeAngelo . . . slight change of plans. After favoring Foster last season despite the fact that you were far more productive, we've got a situation in which you might be the second man again. With our 13th overall draft pick, we selected Oregon's Jonathan Stewart, the five-foot-eleven, 235-pound monster who ran a sub-4.5 40 at the Combine and can leap tall buildings in a single bound. Now, we know that you're a team play—Hello? DeAngelo?"

Ricky Williams

Height: 5-10   Weight: 228   College: Texas   Draft: 1999/1 (5)   Born: 21 May 1977   Age: 31   Risk: Red

Year	Team	G	Runs	Yds	Yd/R	TD	FUM	DVOA	Rk	DYAR	Rk	YAR	Suc%	Rec	Pass	Yds	C%	Yd/C	TD	DVOA	Rk	DYAR	Rk
2005	MIA	12	168	743	4.4	6	1	8.9%	12	120	12	135	48%	17	20	93	85%	5.5	0	-2.5%	—	13	—
2007	MIA	1	6	15	2.5	0	0	-66.7%	—	-16	—	-16	50%	0	—	0	—	0.0	0	—	—	—	—
2008	MIA		100	411	4.1	2		-6.6%						14	18	104	78%	7.3	0	-4.4%			

There are famous athletes, and then there are athletic curiosities: guys like Dennis Rodman, Manute Bol, Mike Tyson, and José Canseco, who become far more famous for their sideshow than what they bring to the field. This type of player isn't technically washed up—Rodman could still rebound during his transvestite era, and Canseco could simultaneously hit home runs and humiliate himself—but they quickly wear out their welcome, because we like our backup forwards/designated hitters/changeup running backs seen and not heard. Teams also like their reserve running backs to contribute on special teams, so Williams might not be worth a roster spot, regardless of his conduct. Williams is fast descending into sideshow territory; he has already done a stint on *Pros vs. Joes* and seems destined for reality TV.

Garrett Wolfe

Height: 5-8   Weight: 186   College: Northern Illinois   Draft: 2007/3 (93)   Born: 17 Aug. 1984   Age: 24   Risk: Red

Year	Team	G	Runs	Yds	Yd/R	TD	FUM	DVOA	Rk	DYAR	Rk	YAR	Suc%	Rec	Pass	Yds	C%	Yd/C	TD	DVOA	Rk	DYAR	Rk
2007	CHI	13	31	85	2.7	0	1	-40.8%	—	-34	—	-35	23%	9	13	117	69%	13.0	0	4.8%	—	12	—
2008	CHI		12	54	4.5	0		7.8%						10	19	83	53%	8.3	0	-79.2%			

A hometown hero, Wolfe starred at Chicago's Holy Cross High School and then Northern Illinois University, where he led the NCAA in rushing in 2006 with 1,928 yards. When the Bears drafted him in the third round in 2007, general manager Jerry Angelo compared him to Warrick Dunn, who Angelo drafted when he was director of player personnel in Tampa Bay. The comparison is obvious: At five foot seven and 186 pounds, Wolfe is a slightly shorter, stockier version of the five foot nine, 187-pound Dunn. If he can play like Dunn, zipping through small holes on draw plays and swinging out for screen passes, he could be a big help to the Bears, who face a lot of third-and-longs. The drafting of Matt Forte in the second round, however, might have ended those plans; the Bears put Forte above Wolfe on the depth chart before training camp even opened. For every Dunn, there are a dozen quick, tiny backs who are too small to cut it in the NFL. Wolfe is probably one of the dozen and not the Dunn.

Dwayne Wright

Height: 6-0   Weight: 228   College: Fresno State   Draft: 2007/4 (111)   Born: 2 June 1983   Age: 25   Risk: Red

Year	Team	G	Runs	Yds	Yd/R	TD	FUM	DVOA	Rk	DYAR	Rk	YAR	Suc%	Rec	Pass	Yds	C%	Yd/C	TD	DVOA	Rk	DYAR	Rk
2007	BUF	15	29	94	3.2	0	1	-5.0%	—	5	—	11	45%	3	3	17	100%	5.7	0	-67.0%	—	-10	—
2008	BUF		56	248	4.4	0		-4.1%						14	20	124	70%	8.6	1	11.2%			

Wright is a halfback/fullback tweener who got a long look as Marshawn Lynch's changeup as a rookie but was overshadowed by Fred Jackson in the second half of the year. He's an old sophomore at 25 and will have to prove himself as either a special-teams ace or short-yardage runner to stick with the team.

Jason Wright

Height: 5-10   Weight: 210   College: Northwestern   Draft: 2004/FA   Born: 12 July 1982   Age: 26   Risk: Red

Year	Team	G	Runs	Yds	Yd/R	TD	FUM	DVOA	Rk	DYAR	Rk	YAR	Suc%	Rec	Pass	Yds	C%	Yd/C	TD	DVOA	Rk	DYAR	Rk
2005	CLE	3	11	27	2.5	1	0	-11.8%	—	-1	—	-2	36%	3	3	15	100%	5.0	0	-8.0%	—	1	—
2006	CLE	13	62	189	3.0	0	1	-18.0%	—	-23	—	-51	40%	6	11	82	64%	13.7	0	-6.0%	—	5	—
2007	CLE	16	60	277	4.6	1	1	5.6%	—	37	—	50	50%	24	37	233	65%	9.7	0	16.5%	16	63	19
2008	CLE		100	430	4.3	2		4.7%						24	35	218	69%	9.1	1	-3.6%			

Before the start of last year, Wright dipped himself in the magic waters of Lake Erie along with all the other Browns backs, a purifying act that transformed him from a fringe player to an effective running back. No? Okay, the more likely explanation is that he benefited from the same improved line that boosted the DVOA ratings of Jamal Lewis and James Harrison. Barring an injury to Lewis, Wright will again be nothing more than a spot player, though he's worth a roster spot because of his skills as a receiver, pass blocker, and kick gunner.

Deshawn Wynn

Deshawn Wynn Height: 5-10 Weight: 232 College: Florida Draft: 2007/7 (228) Born: 9 Oct. 1983 Age: 25 Risk: Red

Year	Team	G	Runs	Yds	Yd/R	TD	FUM	DVOA	Rk	DYAR	Rk	YAR	Suc%	Rec	Pass	Yds	C%	Yd/C	TD	DVOA	Rk	DYAR	Rk
2007	GB	7	50	203	4.1	4	0	13.4%	—	45	—	29	36%	9	14	73	64%	8.1	0	11.4%	—	18	—
2008	GB		53	287	5.4	3		34.2%						10	14	129	71%	12.7	1	61.6%			

The knock on Wynn when he left the University of Florida was that he didn't run as hard as a 230-pounder should. But Wynn ran hard enough before suffering a Week 8 neck injury. He showed promise in limited action as a goal line runner (8 carries for 29 yards and a 56 percent Success Rate in the red zone) and has some potential as a receiver. He may be a better fit as Ryan Grant's changeup runner than Brandon Jackson is, but Mike McCarthy may find roles for everyone. Remember last year, when the Packers had no good running backs? You'll notice KUBIAK really loves the position of "Green Bay second-stringer" this year—that's related to team variables more than it is related to the individuals involved.

Selvin Young

Selvin Young Height: 6-0 Weight: 212 College: Texas Draft: 2007/FA Born: 1 Oct. 1983 Age: 25 Risk: Red

Year	Team	G	Runs	Yds	Yd/R	TD	FUM	DVOA	Rk	DYAR	Rk	YAR	Suc%	Rec	Pass	Yds	C%	Yd/C	TD	DVOA	Rk	DYAR	Rk
2007	DEN	15	140	729	5.2	1	2	8.4%	19	92	23	82	43%	35	43	231	81%	6.6	0	-7.7%	34	14	33
2008	DEN		230	1075	4.7	7		13.8%						27	38	109	71%	4.0	0	-26.7%			

The undrafted free agent emerged after injuries to Travis Henry, and like seemingly a dozen Denver backs before him, Young became a quality performer. He far outpaced Henry in both conventional and advanced statistics. The Broncos are convinced the diminutive back cannot succeed in an every-down role, so Young seems destined to torture fantasy owners for at least the next few seasons. He'll make a big impact for the Broncos as a 12- to 15-touch committee back.

Going Deep

Chris Barclay, NO: A fringe-level running back, Barclay finished last season with the Saints, a team with one of the deepest running-back depth charts in the league. So he's doomed. He can also return kicks and punts, so there's always a chance some team will sign him as an all-purpose backup.

Jackie Battle, KC: An oversized runner at 235 pounds, Battle could eventually convert to fullback but hopes to hang on as a short-yardage back. He rushed for 935 yards and 15 touchdowns at Houston in 2006, another example of a plowhorse back excelling against dime defenders in a spread offense (see Ironhead Heyward and Mike Rozier). He is a physical specimen, so even if Kansas City cuts him, he may get another shot elsewhere. (2007: 14 rushes for 47 yards and a touchdown, 8.6% DVOA, 10 DYAR.)

Yvenson Bernard, STL: Oregon State's Bernard ran a 4.83 at the Combine, which really isn't going to get it done when you are an undersized running back trying to convince teams you can contribute as a return specialist. With St. Louis's crying need for kickoff men, Bernard is in as good a situation as any, but he's a long shot to make the final roster.

Cory Boyd, TB: Boyd got lost in a ridiculously overcrowded class of running backs, and some off-field issues clouded the beginning of his college career at South Carolina. Still, he's a tough inside runner with pass-catching ability and who could contribute right away. His performances at the Shrine Game and Combine indicate a bright future.

Jamaal Branch, FA: Branch broke his leg in December and was waived by the Saints in May. He was signed off the team's practice squad after Reggie Bush's season-ending knee injury, but he couldn't survive the special-teams grind. (2006: 10 carries for 29 yards, 3.9% DVOA, 5 DYAR; five catches for 14 yards and a touchdown. No stats in 2007.)

Thomas Brown, ATL: Brown would have ranked much higher than a sixth-round prospect had he been able to stay healthy at any level of competition, but he's missed time each year since his senior season of high school with a smorgasbord of injuries, including a broken leg, a hamstring pull, two shoulder sprains (2005 and 2007), a torn ACL, and a broken collarbone. When he can get on the field, this Georgia alum's size (five foot nine, 204 pounds), speed, and versatility make him a good fit as a backup and return man behind Jerious Norwood and Michael Turner.

Brian Calhoun, DET: Calhoun tore his ACL in 2006, returned to camp a little too soon last year, played four games, and then went back on injured reserve because his recovery was incomplete. If he's back to full speed, he can be a valuable complementary back who can run inside and outside and catch the ball. He's obviously not durable enough to be a bell cow. (2007: seven carries for 35 yards, 24.7% DVOA, 10 DYAR, plus five catches for 35 yards.)

Aveion Cason, DET: After seven full seasons in the NFL, Cason finally found steady work as a full-time kickoff returner last season. He performed well, averaging 24.8 yards per return. As an offensive player, he's really a last-resort third-down guy. (2007: 11 carries for 38 yards and a fumble, -28.4% DVOA, -9 DYAR.)

P. J. Daniels, BAL: Daniels spent last season on injured reserve after not seeing any action as a rookie in 2006. He'll lose his roster spot to Ray Rice.

Clifton Dawson, IND: An undrafted rookie in 2007, Dawson had a bit of late-season action when the Colts were making everyone reconsider the whole "lying down when you have your division won" thing. He finished his collegiate career as the Ivy League's all-time leader in rushing yards, rushing touchdowns, career points, career touchdowns, and career all-purpose yards. That would get Dawson a lot more currency in the earliest days of pro football, but in the NFL's modern era, such feats get you on the practice squad of the world champs, hoping that you won't be swept away in a roster move. (2007: 30 carries for 64 yards and a touchdown, -31.0% DVOA, -26 DYAR.)

Adimchinobe Echemandu, OAK: Echemandu was with the Texans last year, and his highlight was a 10-carry, 62-yard performance against San Diego. It wasn't good enough to keep him in Houston, and it's hard to see how Echemandu will stick on a Raiders team with a much deeper set of running backs. (2007: 20 carries for 85 yards and a fumble, -25.5% DVOA, -14 DYAR.)

Jerome Felton, DET: If genetics have anything to do with it, Felton will find it impossible to fail at the NFL level. Failure is not an option in his high-achievement family. Felton's mother, a former Olympic gymnast, is now a college science teacher. His birth father works for the government in Washington, D.C., and his stepfather owns his own veterinary practice. (Stop us if this sounds like the start of Superstar Mode in your favorite video game.) His older brother has served 18-month tours of duty in Iraq and Afghanistan, and his younger brother is taking premed courses at age 15 and plans to enter medical school within two years. On the field at Furman, Felton proved to be one of the NCAA's best scoring threats, and he'll give the Lions a short-yardage and third-down option.

Justin Forsett, SEA: Tulane's Matt Forte put up the best performance of any running back in the Senior Bowl, but Cal's Forsett impressed as well. He's been living under the radar despite 1,546 rushing yards as Marshawn Lynch's successor in 2007. At five foot eight and 194 pounds, he's a little thin in the lower body to apply for true "Pocket Hercules" status, but like Maurice Jones-Drew, he can contribute as a returner and change-of-pace back.

Justise Hairston, IND: It's only the finer offenses in life for Hairston, who was waived by the Patriots after training camp, only to catch on with the Colts. The addition of Dominic Rhodes could cost him a roster spot.

Alex Haynes, CAR: Now entering his fourth season, Haynes is primarily known as UCF's all-time leading rusher before Kevin Smith showed up. He's bounced on and off of Carolina's practice squad, but they re-signed him for 2008.

Verron Haynes, FA: Haynes' major accomplishment in 2007 was being selected as one of Pittsburgh's 25 most beautiful people by *Pittsburgh Magazine*. He re-signed with the team when Willie Parker broke his leg in December, but he was a free agent at press time and is near the end of his run as a changeup back. (2006: 15 carries for 78 yards and a fumble, 7.2% DVOA, 11 DYAR, plus 14 catches for 95 yards. One catch for 12 yards in 2007.)

Noah Herron, GB: Herron lost all of 2007 to a training-camp knee injury. The third-down back will probably be crowded out by the Packers' trio of second-year runners. Herron is a fine special-teamer with good receiving skills, so he'll find work. (2006: 37 carries for 150 yards with a fumble and a touchdown, -6.8% DVOA, 3 DYAR, plus 27 catches for 211 yards and two touchdowns.)

Tim Hightower, ARI: The one guy everyone compares Hightower to is Marion Barber III, but Hightower probably would have come off the board before the fifth round if that were accurate. He gained over 1,900 yards in his senior year with Richmond, and like Barber, he hits the hole with all the velocity he's got. He'll have to beat out J. J. Arrington for a roster spot.

Wali Lundy, FA: Lundy was cut by the Texans in training camp and appears to have gone underground. His chances of following a David Johansen–esque career path depend on his abilities with makeup. (2006: 124 carries for 476 yards and a touchdown, -3.6% DVOA, 25 DYAR, plus 24 catches for 204 yards.)

Reno Mahe, PHI: Mahe rejoined the Eagles in Week 2 last season after Greg Lewis and Ryan Moats played hot-potato as punt returners in the season opener. Eighty-nine players returned at least one punt last season, and 75 of them finished with more value than Mahe, though none of them was Greg Lewis or Ryan Moats. Rookie wide receiver DeSean Jackson has been handed the punt-return duties, which means Mahe is probably finished. For the record, we thought the same thing when the Eagles signed Bethel Johnson, drafted Jeremy Bloom, drafted Moats …

Xavier Omon, BUF: The good news: Omon was one of only three running backs in the history of college football to run for more than 7,000 yards in a four-year career, and the first to rush for at least 1,500 yards in each season. The bad news: He did it for Division II Northwest Missouri State, against such juggernauts as Washburn and Emporia State. How that translates to professional production is open to debate, but Omon will get a shot on special teams and preseason chances to earn reps behind Marshawn Lynch.

Alvin Pearman, SEA: Primarily a kick returner and not a particularly good one. His career punt-return average of 8.6 places him in a massive tie for 171st place all time. Among those he's tied with: Chris Warren, Ed Podolak, and Emlen Tunnell. (2006: 19 carries for 89 yards and a touchdown, -0.2% DVOA, 7 DYAR. One catch in 2007 for one yard.)

Artose Pinner, DET: Last year, Pinner achieved the rare feat of gaining more yards in his longest run than he did in all his runs combined. If that's tripping you out, here's how it breaks down: Pinner rushed for 49 yards on a fake punt against Tennessee. His other four carries gained a total of—ready?—minus-three yards. Pinner's only career 100-yard game came in 2006 for Minnesota against Detroit. Perhaps that's why Detroit reacquired him. That sounds like something Matt Millen would do.

Cory Ross, BAL: Are you ready to play the *$25,000 Pyramid*? Here are your clues: Chris Taylor, Willie Parker, Bruce Perry, Jamaal Branch, Eric McCoo, and now Cory Ross. Do you know the category? It's "Undrafted Free-Agent Running Backs Plucked Off the Practice Squad to Play in Week 17." Unfortunately, only Willie Parker could actually win on the *Pyramid*. (2007: 12 carries for 72 yards and a touchdown, 54.2% DVOA, 27 DYAR.)

Gary Russell, PIT: Russell may manage to claw his way onto Pittsburgh's roster at the expense of Najeh Davenport. Though not as versatile a player as Davenport, Russell will come cheaper and Pittsburgh would be forgiven for economizing on what's probably a fourth-string tailback. Russell is a solid power runner when in shape, but he had weight and motivation issues in college. (2007: seven carries for 21 yards, 10.7% DVOA, 6 DYAR.)

Marcus Thomas, SD: This is the former UTEP back who was drafted in the fifth round, not the Broncos' defensive lineman who has legal issues. It's an open competition behind LaDainian Tomlinson, but the plodding Thomas isn't likely to fill the role.

Tyson Thompson, FA: A local guy from Irving, Thompson came to the Dallas Cowboys as a straight-line runner and return man but never evolved into anything more. There weren't many carries to go around in the Cowboys' backfield, and after breaking his ankle in 2006, Thompson struggled to recover last year. He wasn't tendered a contract following the season. (2007: 14 carries for 54 yards, -27.8% DVOA, -9 DYAR.)

Ryan Torain, DEN: Remember the days when every Denver Broncos running back had a chance of gaining 1,000 yards merely by getting the magic touch from Mike Shanahan? Man, 2006 was awesome. Torain's an interior runner who could follow the Mike Anderson/Reuben Droughns career path by starting at fullback.

Chauncey Washington, JAC: That Washington managed 157 carries in USC's seven-tailback rotation speaks to his talent. The Jaguars could use him as Maurice Jones-Drew Lite if the real deal got hurt, but "MJD Lite" just seems wrong. "MJD Thick?"

Quincy Wilson, CIN: A regular participant at Bengals training camp and a reliable running back in August—reliably cut by the end of September. The highlight of his career remains two carries for two yards against the Patriots in 2006.

FULLBACKS

Fullbacks with at least 10 carries or passes in 2007 or a projection of at least 50 yards in 2008 are listed below.

Name	2007	G	Runs	Yds	TD	DVOA	DYAR	Rec	Pass	Yds	CPct	Yd/C	TD	DVOA	Rank	DYAR	Rank	2008	RuYd	Rec	RcYd	TD	Age
B. J. Askew	TB	13	0	0	0	—	—	18	20	175	90%	9.7	0	64.0%	—	86	—	TB	4	20	131	1	28
Jameel Cook	TB	12	8	24	0	-35.5%	-10	6	8	61	75%	10.2	1	3.7%	—	10	—	HOU	22	10	92	1	29
Mike Cox	—	0	0	0	0	—	—	0	0	0	—	—	0	—	—	—	—	KC	16	19	140	1	23
Carey Davis	PIT	16	17	68	0	-16.8%	-4	12	14	49	86%	4.1	0	-23.8%	—	-7	—	PIT	45	22	170	1	27
Kyle Eckel	NE	12	33	90	2	-19.3%	-16	1	1	6	100%	6.0	0	28.8%	—	3	—	NE	60	1	8	2	27
Heath Evans	NE	16	34	121	3	16.9%	48	4	6	43	67%	10.8	0	19.4%	—	12	—	NE	93	6	41	3	30
Casey FitzSimmons	DET	16	0	0	0	—	—	8	10	85	80%	10.6	1	39.5%	—	34	—	DET	0	10	89	1	28
Justin Griffith	OAK	16	7	27	0	-19.3%	-2	26	36	165	72%	6.3	1	1.8%	28	34	26	OAK	53	29	196	1	27
Ahmard Hall	TEN	11	1	8	0	73.7%	5	9	12	60	75%	6.7	0	-3.7%	—	6	—	TEN	12	11	93	1	29
Korey Hall	GB	14	0	0	0	—	—	8	11	49	73%	6.1	0	-4.0%	—	6	—	GB	1	10	76	1	25
Jacob Hester	—	0	0	0	0	—	—	0	0	0	—	—	0	—	—	—	—	SD	220	14	82	2	23
Brad Hoover	CAR	16	12	39	0	7.3%	9	10	14	58	71%	5.8	0	-7.3%	—	6	—	CAR	50	14	85	1	32
Jeremi Johnson	CIN	16	7	25	0	-13.7%	-2	6	7	32	86%	5.3	1	10.1%	—	14	—	CIN	35	4	25	2	28
Greg Jones	JAC	16	42	119	2	-6.3%	4	11	19	99	58%	9.0	2	11.5%	—	34	—	JAC	210	6	36	3	27
Mike Karney	NO	16	11	17	2	-12.8%	-3	13	19	78	68%	6.0	0	-8.9%	—	6	—	NO	22	20	121	3	27
Vonta Leach	HOU	12	2	2	1	41.5%	6	25	33	61	76%	2.4	1	-30.9%	55	-37	55	HOU	1	9	65	2	27
Le'Ron McClain	BAL	16	8	18	0	-29.3%	-7	9	13	55	69%	6.1	1	-33.1%	—	-15	—	BAL	12	18	111	1	24
Jason McKie	CHI	16	6	17	1	-2.5%	2	9	15	33	60%	3.7	0	-50.6%	—	-37	—	CHI	17	19	106	1	28
Ovie Mughelli	ATL	16	6	7	1	-20.9%	-5	6	10	36	60%	6.0	0	-38.2%	—	-14	—	ATL	21	15	86	1	28
Lorenzo Neal	SD	13	13	32	0	-19.7%	-9	8	11	23	73%	2.9	1	-53.0%	—	-25	—	FA	0	0	0	0	38
Moran Norris	SF	16	7	17	0	3.9%	5	6	11	38	55%	6.3	0	-32.3%	—	-12	—	SF	14	19	127	1	30
Tony Richardson	MIN	14	7	13	0	3.8%	5	11	16	89	69%	8.1	0	-3.2%	—	9	—	NYJ	13	16	113	1	37
Cecil Sapp	DEN	16	18	59	2	8.8%	14	14	20	51	70%	3.6	1	-40.7%	—	-35	—	DEN	66	18	165	2	30
Owen Schmitt	—	0	0	0	0	—	—	0	0	0	—	—	0	—	—	—	—	SEA	93	7	53	3	23
Mike Sellers	WAS	14	26	78	2	-4.1%	7	17	24	117	71%	6.9	1	-16.7%	—	-4	—	WAS	69	21	129	2	33
Thomas Tapeh	PHI	16	5	18	0	-15.2%	-3	8	11	50	73%	6.3	0	-20.6%	—	-4	—	MIN	15	12	76	1	28
Lawrence Vickers	CLE	16	15	43	0	5.5%	15	13	24	91	54%	7.0	2	2.3%	—	25	—	CLE	29	21	149	1	25
Leonard Weaver	SEA	16	33	146	1	16.0%	40	39	52	313	75%	8.0	0	17.3%	14	87	11	SEA	97	16	121	1	26
Kris Wilson	KC	16	0	0	0	—	—	24	50	132	48%	5.5	3	-35.0%	57	-59	58	PHI	1	11	79	1	27

Deon Anderson, DAL: You see some unusual school names in the bios of NFL players, but one of the best is Anderson's high school: Avon Old Farms School, an all-boys academy in Connecticut. Here's guessing that they used a lot of Skin So Soft on the old farm. Anderson moved on to UConn, only to get kicked off the team his junior season. He was allowed back on the team his senior year, but he had to pay his own way. At the end of his senior season, he was voted team MVP. Oliver Hoyte's departure to Kansas City leaves Anderson the top fullback in Dallas.

B. J. Askew, TB: Tampa Bay's starting fullback after the injury that derailed Mike Alstott for good, Askew is an underrated receiver who has been saying for years that he would like to get reps at tailback. We're not sure if that will happen, but we'd like to know: How do you get "B. J." out of "Bobby DeAngelo"?

Darian Barnes, BUF: Barnes found his way into Eric Mangini's doghouse after getting into a yapping match with Joey Porter about whether the Goo Goo Dolls or Soul Asylum represents the absolute nadir of American rock. Mangini brought in a washed-up boxer, who told Barnes the answer was obviously Days of the New. Barnes made his way to Buffalo, where he could play a valuable role clearing space for Marshawn Lynch this year.

Jon Bradley, DET: The Jon Bradley Saga: (1) Bradley stars at running back and linebacker at Barton High School in Arkansas, rushing for over 4,000 yards in his junior and senior years. (2) Bradley bulks up to 305 pounds and tears up the Sun Belt Conference as a defensive tackle. The Buccaneers sign him. (3) After a few seasons on the Bucs practice squad, he follows Rob Marinelli to Detroit. The Lions turn him into a 310-pound fullback. (4) Bradley converts a fourth-and-one against the Redskins in Week 7. Mike Martz decides he's a better short-yardage option than, say, T. J. Duckett. (5) A few failed conversions later, Bradley fumbles on third-and-short against the Broncos. It's his last carry of the season, thanks to Martz's one-and-done policy on fumbles. There's only one place to go from here: *Dancing with the Stars*.

Rock Cartwright, WAS: In hindsight, it's downright funny that Cartwright was with the Redskins for four seasons before anyone thought to give him a serious try at kick returner. He just missed the top 10 in kickoff return value in 2006 and ranked sixth last season, two spots ahead of Devin Hester. He's pretty fast, breaks some tackles, and can hold on to the ball. Of course, Ladell Betts is listed as the kickoff returner going into camp, and the Redskins have Antwaan Randle El ready to pounce if Betts's offensive role gets reduced. Maybe they should try letting Cartwright play some fullback.

Jameel Cook, HOU: Never more than a serviceable fullback, Cook will have to fight off Chris Taylor in camp to keep his job in Houston.

Mike Cox, KC: Cox is an undrafted rookie from Georgia Tech. He's a 260-pound load with a rep as a good lead blocker and adequate receiver. He touched the ball just 18 times in his final college season (six runs, 12 catches), so he doesn't expect to be the focal point of the offense. He will compete with former Cowboys fullback Oliver Hoyte, a converted college linebacker with minimal ball skills.

Zack Crockett, TB: Zack Crockett's 2007 season: September 2: Cut by Tampa Bay. Oct. 10: Re-signed by Tampa Bay. Oct. 21: Gets his only carry of the season against Detroit. The play gains no yards. October 24: Cut by Tampa Bay. December 12: Re-signed by Tampa Bay. December 16: Inactive against Atlanta. December 19: For the third time in less than four months, cut by Tampa Bay. December 20: Signed by Dallas. December 22: Inactive against Carolina. December 24: Cut by Dallas. Before you call the Cowboys cruel for cutting Crockett on Christmas Eve, remember that he was paid more than $48,000 for showing up and doing nothing for four days.

Kenneth Darby, TB: Darby threatened Shaun Alexander's rushing record at Alabama and then was drafted by Tampa Bay in the seventh round in 2007. He'll battle B. J. Askew, Byron Storer, and this year's seventh-rounder, Cory Boyd, for the fullback job. Darby should throw some coins into a wishing well and hope the Bucs hand him a contract and say, "Sign your name."

Carey Davis, PIT: Davis replaced Dan Kreider at fullback due to Davis's added versatility, then was used exactly as

Kreider had been for the past two seasons. Kreider is gone, so the Steelers won't be the only team in the league with a fullback controversy.

Jeff Dugan, MIN: We're not sure who wrote Dugan's Wikipedia page, but we suspect it was Jeff Dugan. "Keep your eyes and ears on this guy Viking fans," writes our anonymous analyst. "Look on the field for number 83, and see what he really can do for the Vikings." In four seasons with Minnesota, Dugan has rushed twice for seven yards. But keep your eyes and ears on him!

Kyle Eckel, NE: A solid special-teamer (12 total tackles) and fine young man, this Navy alum carried the ball 10 times for 40 yards and a touchdown in the Pats' 56-10 romp over the Bills. He's a good enough runner to protect a 46-point lead.

Heath Evans, NE: Solid all-purpose fullback who can run the ball at the goal line or line up as a single setback. He even splits out wide on occasion. Evans gets more carries than most fullbacks because the Patriots love running the fullback dive on third-and-short, and because he gets some garbage-time carries. Another nifty complementary performer for a team that makes role players look special.

Casey FitzSimmons, DET: Jon Kitna threw four first-down passes to Casey FitzSimmons last season. FitzSimmons lined up as a fullback on each play, then ran a short flat or circle route into the softest part of a zone defense. He caught each pass for 10, 10, 22, and 21 yards, which gave him a first down DVOA of 91.6%. If only such production could be bottled. Unfortunately, FitzSimmons was open only because he's the kind of backup tight end/H-back that teams throw to once per month.

Nick Goings, CAR: Goings's 2007 season was marred by concussions that placed him on injured reserve, and his totals have declined in each of the last four years. He may compete for a roster spot, or he may retire and avoid becoming another cautionary tale in the long, sad history of concussion-related issues suffered by current and former players. We're hoping for the latter.

Justin Green, BAL: Green was in line to be the starting fullback before the Ravens drafted Le'Ron McClain, but now he only gets on the field when the team needs a pass-catching fullback. Judging from his two receptions in 2007, that's not very often.

Justin Griffith, OAK: The head-banging fullback has proven to be a willing and fairly able lead blocker. When not colliding with linebackers, Griffith catches passes. He led the Raiders running backs in receptions but may take a backseat to Darren McFadden this year. At least that's the plan.

Boomer Grigsby, MIA: Grigsby is a testament to the importance of special teams and the limitations of being a specialist. The Chiefs kept him for several years on account of his ability to cover kicks, but his inability to develop from a linebacker into an offensive player eventually got him cut. He signed in Miami.

Ahmard Hall, TEN: A block-first fullback who has a fascinating personal story: He joined the Marines out of college, spent four years on active duty, then enrolled at Texas. He was a solid player for the Longhorns, surprised a lot of people by making the Titans' roster in 2006 as a 27-year-old rookie, and is now their best blocking fullback. He rarely touches the ball.

Korey Hall, GB: A star linebacker and team captain at Boise State, Hall switched to fullback and started 10 games for the Packers, blocking well but rarely touching the ball. You know, the Packers really needed more rookies in the backfield last year.

Madison Hedgecock, NYG: An underrated key to the Giants' success last season, Hedgecock offers tight-end size (six foot three, 266 pounds) out of the backfield. His blocking in the stead of the injured Jim Finn covered a lot of deficiencies along the offensive line and opened some holes for Brandon Jacobs and friends, although Hedgecock can get flat-footed in pass protection. Also, let posterity note that it was Hedgecock who dumped Gatorade on Tom Coughlin at the end of Super Bowl XLII.

Jacob Hester, SD: Hester was a tweener at LSU, alternating between fullback and tailback. With longtime fullback Lorenzo Neal released in February, Hester is the obvious choice to take that position for the Chargers. San Diego sent a 2008 fifth-round and a 2009 second-round pick to New England to move up and ensure that it would get Hester in the third round. General Manager A. J. Smith likes Hester as a versatile option, but given San Diego's aversion to the single-back set (only the Bengals lined up with fewer one-back formations), don't be surprised to see him helping to establish rushing lanes for LaDainian Tomlinson.

Lex Hilliard, MIA: Hilliard missed the entire 2006 season with a torn Achilles tendon, but recovered fully for his senior year. He's a blue-collar blocker who scored 50 rushing touchdowns in 49 games at the University of Montana. With his size and determination, he's not a joy to tackle. Hilliard could play some tailback at the next level if need be.

Brad Hoover, CAR: The Panthers re-signed Hoover to a three-year deal in the offseason. He started 12 games at fullback last season and was an adequate lead blocker; the Panthers no longer give him three or four touches per game, which is a good thing. He'll stick to blocking this year, as his power back/outlet receiver role will be reduced with the arrival of Jonathan Stewart.

Jeremi Johnson, CIN: Another guard-in-the-backfield, Johnson doesn't pose much of a receiving threat (six catches for 32 yards in 2007) or a rushing one (seven carries for 25 yards), but he isn't expected to do so. What he does provide is solid run-blocking and an additional player surnamed Johnson to confuse opponents. Or Football Outsiders editors.

Greg Jones, JAC: A year ago, we speculated about Jones's chances of making the Jaguars roster as he returned from the second ACL tear of his career. Well, David Garrard isn't the only man in Jacksonville to enjoy a fairy-tale rise. Meet the new holder of the title "highest-paid fullback in NFL history." Jones earned that designation after paving the way for Fred Taylor and Maurice Jones-Drew. He also has the versatility to spell those two and carry the ball now and then, something he may get a few more chances to do with LaBrandon Toefield gone via free agency.

Mike Karney, NO: Karney is part of a dying breed, one of the last old-school fullbacks whose necks are bigger than their heads, and whose ability to dish out punishment is occasionally spiced up with fits of improbable production. In Karney's case, this last occurred in a Week 5 loss to the Panthers, when he bulled through the pile for a touchdown. Karney is a bit of a misfit in the high-speed two-back set the Saints would like to run, but he's also the short-yardage option you want in a backfield dominated by shifty-nifty Reggie Bush.

Dan Klecko, PHI: Klecko's moved from defensive tackle to full-time fullback, turning a curiosity into a full-time position. You know, like being a blogger. For one out of every 10,000 bloggers or so, it works. The other ones still have to keep their day jobs. Klecko should've held on to his.

Dan Kreider, FA: Fullback platoons are clearly the next great offensive innovation. Or not. Kreider was better at blocking than Carey Davis was, but poses no threat as a receiver, so Kreider came in for short-yardage situations and whenever the Steelers were trying to run down the clock. Kreider was a 31-year-old free agent at press time who touched the ball 11 times in the last two years. He's done.

John Kuhn, GB: A 250-pound thumper and special-teamer who sees some action in the Packers' full-house backfield. He re-signed in the offseason and will have a similar role this year.

Vonta Leach, HOU: The Texans matched an $8 million offer sheet with $1.6 million in guarantees that Leach signed with the Giants before the season, and then they let him carry the ball twice all season for a grand total of two yards and one touchdown. Of course, Leach isn't there to tote the ball but to clear lanes for whoever happens to be playing halfback for Houston.

Reagan Mauia, MIA: The Dolphins' sixth-round pick last season is a 270-pound load best known for crashing through a wall and shouting "I'm the Juggernaut, bitch!" on a YouTube video. Yes, Mauia appeared in a viral video based on a movie quote based on a viral video; somehow that makes him the ultimate Randy Mueller–era Dolphins draft choice. Mauia worked out briefly at tailback in Dolphins camp last year, then broke his hand in August and missed the start of the season. He allegedly has ball skills, but Tony Sparano wants his fullbacks to block, not run, catch passes, or quote X-Men movies.

Le'Ron McClain, BAL: After losing one of the best blocking fullbacks in the league in Ovie Mughelli, Ozzie Newsome found a replacement in the draft. McClain was the consensus top fullback prospect in the 2007 draft and quickly worked his way into the starting lineup. At six foot even and 265 pounds, McClain is built like Lorenzo Neal or Mack Strong, but he has the athleticism to play some H-back in addition to being a lead blocker.

Jason McKie, CHI: An undrafted free agent out of Temple in 2002, McKie passed through the Eagles and Cowboys organizations before finally sticking with the Bears. In 2004, he caught two touchdown passes, which tied for the team lead. That's pathetic. McKie spends his offseasons working with his foundation to help out soldiers and their families, particularly to provide scholarships to children whose parents have been injured or killed. That's not pathetic. The Bears use McKie as a blocker first and foremost; when they used a two-back set, they ran the ball 66 percent of the time, the fifth-highest rate in the league.

Ovie Mughelli, ATL: Regarded as perhaps the NFL's best blocking fullback in Baltimore, Mughelli signed with Atlanta before the 2007 season in a contract that was (at the time) the largest ever given a fullback. He then spent a lot of time on the sidelines as a misfit in Bobby Petrino's allegedly "brilliant" offense. Under new offensive coordinator Mike Mularkey, who prefers the power game, Mughelli will get to do what he does very well—knock linebackers on their butts and clear the way for his teammates in the backfield.

Lorenzo Neal, FA: Fullbacks have a tendency to get full recognition after they reach their prime. Mack Strong finally made Pro Bowls just before hitting the road. Neal garnered appreciation as the best fullback in football just in time to be gradually phased out by San Diego, making the All-Pro team last year when he was only a part-time player. Nonetheless, Neal was arguably the preeminent blocking back of the last two decades.

Moran Norris, SF: Norris's name showed up in a few news stories after he tried to start a fight with rookie free-agent linebacker Lance Brandenburgh. The reason? Brandenburgh was covering Norris on pass routes, and doing a good job of it. The nerve of that guy. Norris's role will shrink in Mike Martz's offense, but he'll hit the field for the occasional short-yardage play.

Patrick Pass, NYG: Pass played in one game for the Giants last season: the 41-17 loss to Minnesota. Does he get a Super Bowl ring for that? He won three with New England, so if he gets one for last year, that means Pass has as many Super Bowl rings as Peyton Manning and Tom Brady combined.

Allen Patrick, BAL: A seventh-round project out of Oklahoma, Patrick started his college career at defensive back before switching over to offense. He has the size to generate three yards and a cloud of dust, which means he'll fit in just fine in Baltimore.

Andrew Pinnock, SD: Injuries hurt in more way than one. The release of Lorenzo Neal meant Pinnock was in line to be the starting fullback. When he suffered a minor hairline fracture in his foot, however, the Chargers drafted Jacob Hester, a tweener who blocks well enough to play fullback in the Chargers' system.

Lousaka Polite, CHI: A four-year starter at fullback at Pittsburgh, Polite was also the school's first three-year captain. His game-worn and autographed 2003 Continental Tire Bowl uniform was going for a little more than $800 in an online auction this spring. Bargain! … Originally signed as an undrafted free agent by the Cowboys in 2004, he'll back up Jason McKie in Chicago this season.

Tony Richardson, NYJ: No team grabbed Richardson out of Auburn in the 1994 draft. He wound up in training camp with the Cowboys, but they had a pretty good fullback themselves at the time (guy named Moose Something-or-other), so they let Richardson go to Kansas City, where he played for 11 seasons. He returned to college for his bachelor's degree in 2000 and earned his MBA from Webster University in 2004. That same season, he was second-team All-Pro. A former NFL Man of the Year candidate who works with the Special Olympics, he signed for "less than $2 million" with the Jets to block for Thomas Jones. To recap: Richardson is stronger than you, tougher than you, smarter than you, works harder than you, is wealthier than you, and does more for children than you do. But who's counting?

Cecil Sapp, DEN: Sapp was a sought-after commodity, but actually took a pay cut to stay in Denver; that tells you all you need to know about the esteem fullbacks are held in nowadays. Sapp can slide to tailback in a pinch, and while he's not a thumping run blocker, he gets through the line quickly and occupies linebackers.

Owen Schmitt, SEA: The best college fullback in the nation in 2007, Schmitt is already being lauded more for his wide Mohawk, dry humor, and coaster-eating persona than his play. At West Virginia, the media fell in love with him, fans named their dogs after him, and the 11 broken facemasks he caused seemed to make him more a character in one of those really dodgy "This guy is all heart" football movies than a real person. Schmitt is certainly real, but some of his college stats—like the fact that he was only tackled behind the line of scrimmage twice in his entire time at WVU—must be adjusted for a spread offense. Still, the Seahawks are switching back to a more powerful running style that hasn't been seen since Mack Strong was in his prime, and Schmitt could be a big part of that.

Derek Schouman, BUF: Robert Royal Junior. A tough gym rat with hands like garden pavers. Could find a role on a Bills team that always makes roster space for special-teams thumpers.

Mike Sellers, WAS: There's more to Walla Walla, Washington, than sweet onions and a prison. Take Sellers, for instance, whose only collegiate experience came at Walla Walla Community College. He left school at 19 to play in the CFL, then joined the Redskins in 1998 at the age of 23. He lasted there for three seasons and then moved to Cleveland and back to the CFL before rejoining the Skins in 2004. At 284 pounds, Sellers hits like a train, but he often whiffs entirely. He's the Rob Deer of fullbacks.

Paul Smith, FA: Smith put together an eight-year career by transferring from a decent fullback with some skill carrying the ball to a solid special-teamer. Those players lose their value as they enter their thirties, but Smith made a rather nice living by doing the dirty work.

Terrelle Smith, ARI: Smith was a college defensive end who converted to fullback and presumably motivates himself by annihilating players he wasn't able to beat out at the position. Unfortunately for him, Tim Castille was getting the first-team reps in minicamp, so Smith could be moving on shortly.

Byron Storer, TB: Only 226 pounds, Storer is one of the smallest fullbacks you'll ever see. He started three games late last year, catching two passes for 3 yards. He is one of four fullbacks going into Tampa Bay's training camp hoping to replace Mike Alstott.

Naufahu Tahi, MIN: *USA Today* named Tahi the top player in the state of Utah during his senior year at Granger High, and in his freshman season at BYU, he led the team in rushing. He then put his football career on hold to undertake a three-year Mormon mission to Jacksonville. When he returned in 2003, he rushed for 872 yards. He began his NFL career with the Bengals in 2006 as a 25-year-old rookie. Last season in Minnesota, he finally made it into a regular-season game. Ten of them, in fact. And you thought the careers of third-string fullbacks were boring!

Thomas Tapeh, MIN: After terrorizing defenders in the NFC East for years (he was witnessed putting Michael Strahan on his back at least once last season), Tapeh leaves Philadelphia and returns to Minnesota, where the native Liberian played high school ball in St. Paul and college ball with the Golden Gophers. Yes, that means the blocking for Adrian Peterson will be better in 2008.

Lawrence Vickers, CLE: Vickers was named a Pro Bowl alternate in just his second season, and his development as a blocker had a lot to do with Jamal Lewis's resurgence. Vickers and Lewis developed their chemistry by watching game film together, and it paid off with a late-season surge, as Lewis racked up 563 yards in December.

Leonard Weaver, SEA: Another success story from our first annual Top 25 Prospects list in *Pro Football Prospectus 2007*, Weaver took over as Seattle's starting fullback after Mack Strong retired. An I-formation with Weaver making room was basically the only way Shaun Alexander earned any yardage last season, and in a few plays, Weaver even played single back and carried the ball. It remains to be seen what the drafting of Owen Schmitt means for his future.

Kris Wilson, PHI: A versatile H-back, Wilson was actually an asset on the inept Kansas City offense, despite his poor DVOA and DYAR totals. He's a fine all-around blocker, and his receiving skills are better than his production was last year. The Chiefs are trying to open their offense a bit, so the Eagles swooped up a talented player who should be creatively employed in their offensive system. The Eagles gave him a fullback's uniform number, and he should take to the position well, because he often lined up in the backfield in Kansas City.

Wide Receivers

If the NFL is truly a copycat league, the years to come will see more teams build their receiving corps the way that New England built their 2007 juggernaut. That doesn't mean "Acquire a receiver with Hall of Fame talent when his value is lowest," although that's a solid plan for both NFL general managers and fantasy players alike. Instead, we'll likely see teams applying more focus on the types of receivers they acquire and fitting them into a coherent offensive scheme together, which led to the Patriots' success in 2007.

The perfect example of that is Wes Welker, who the Patriots acquired from the Dolphins as a restricted free agent. Welker's a very good player who is perfect for his role in the Patriots' scheme, that being to isolate himself against linebackers and safeties and run away from them on outs, ins, and quick hitches. Welker frees up space for Randy Moss, who does the same for Welker in return. They both created room for Donte' Stallworth to go downfield, and for Benjamin Watson to split the seams in the middle of the field. For the Patriots' receivers, the sum was truly more than the individual parts. Cleveland brought in Stallworth this offseason because they're trying to create a similar mix, with Braylon Edwards as the deep threat, Joe Jurevicius as the slot possession guy, and Kellen Winslow as an even better version of Watson.

We'll also likely see teams spreading the ball to more receivers to attempt to mitigate blitz packages and isolate favorable matchups. That's something both the Patriots and the Colts do very well; the latter not only spread the ball well, but do so with unique offensive players like Dallas Clark and Anthony Gonzalez. While the former is listed as a tight end and the latter as a wideout, they both play similar roles in the Colts' offense, lining up in the slot and taking advantage of nickel backs or linebackers. Clark lines up so often as a slot receiver that we consider him to be a wide receiver, not a tight end, despite his official position. As wide receivers get bigger and tight ends faster, the lines between wideouts and tight ends become blurred. "Receiver" truly is becoming the postmodern position of professional football; it's only in most fantasy leagues that the lines will be distinct.

In the following section, we give the last three years worth of statistics as well as a 2008 projection for every wide receiver and tight end who played a significant role in 2007, or is expected to play a significant role in 2008.

HOW TO READ THE WIDE RECEIVER AND TIGHT END STATISTICS TABLES

The first line contains biographical data—each player's name, height, weight, college, draft position, birth date, and age. **Height** and **weight** are the best data we could find; weight, of course, can fluctuate during the off-season. **Age** is very simple, the number of years between the player's birth year and 2008, but birth date is provided if you want to figure out exact age.

Draft position gives draft year and round, with the overall pick number. In the sample table, it says that Hines Ward was chosen in the 1998 draft in the third round with the 92nd overall pick. Undrafted free agents are listed as "FA" with the year they came into the league, even if they were only in training camp or on a practice squad.

Receiver Statistics Sample

Hines Ward   Height: 6-0   Weight: 205   College: Georgia   Draft: 1998/3 (92)   Born: 8-Mar-1976   Age: 32   Risk: Red

Year	Team	G	Rec	Pass	Yds	C%	Yd/Cs	TD	YAC	Rk	DVOA	Rk	DYAR	Rk	YAR	Short	Mid	Deep	Bomb
2005	PIT	15	69	114	975	61%	14.1	11	4.5	26	23.1%	6	325	6	321	24%	55%	17%	4%
2006	PIT	14	74	127	975	59%	13.2	6	4.6	19	12.6%	24	252	11	135	29%	44%	20%	7%
2007	PIT	13	71	113	732	64%	10.3	7	3.1	61	1.8%	43	124	41	144	30%	50%	19%	2%
2008	PIT		56	103	742	54%	13.3	4			-9.6%								

To the far right of the first line is the player's **Risk** for fantasy football in 2008. The players most likely to match their projected stats in 2008 are marked Green, the players who are riskier but still somewhat dependable are marked Yellow, and everyone else is marked Red. The Risk variable is explained further in the introduction to the Quarterbacks section.

Next we give the last three years of player stats. Note that rushing stats are not included for wide receivers, but that any receiver with at least three carries last year has those stats appear in his team's chapter. In the wide receiver and tight end tables, the first column after the year and team for which that receiver played that year is games played (**G**). This is the official NFL total and may include games in which a player appeared on special teams, but did not play at receiver. Receptions (**Rec**) counts passes caught, while Passes (**Pass**) counts passes thrown to this player, complete or incomplete. The next four columns list receiving yards (**Yds**), catch rate (**C%**), yards per catch (**Yd/C**), and receiving touchdowns (**TD**).

Catch rate, or receptions divided by total passes, is an attempt to rectify a major problem in conventional statistics, which lay the blame for incomplete passes entirely on quarterbacks. Historical study shows that receivers definitely have an impact on whether a ball is complete or incomplete. We're still working to break down the degree to which the responsibility for an incomplete is shared by the quarterback and receiver, but it is clearly closer to 50-50 than it is to the 100-0 currently reflected in NFL stats. Wide receivers and tight ends that are used in longer pass patterns will generally catch a lower percentage of passes. Last year, the average wide receiver had a catch rate of 58 percent, while the average tight end had a catch rate of 65 percent. (Note: Incomplete pass does not mean dropped pass; dropped passes are not specified in publicly available play-by-play, and, while we have the data from game charting, it is not yet merged into our other statistics.)

Next comes Yards After Catch (**YAC**), based on information from the game charting project, and rank (**Rk**) in Yards After Catch. That is followed by five columns with our advanced metrics for receiving: **DVOA** (Defense-Adjusted Value Over Average), **DYAR** (Defense-Adjusted Points Above Replacement), and **YAR** (Yards Above Replacement), along with the player's rank in both DVOA and DYAR. These metrics compare every pass intended for a receiver and the results of that pass to a league-average baseline based on the game situations in which passes were thrown to that receiver. DVOA and DYAR are also adjusted based on the opposing defense. The methods used to compute these numbers are described in detail in the "Statistical Toolbox" introduction in the

front of the book. The important distinctions between them are: 1) DVOA is a rate statistic, while DYAR is a cumulative statistic. Thus, a higher DVOA means more value per pass play, while a higher DYAR means more aggregate value over the entire season; 2) Because DYAR is defense-adjusted and YAR is not, a player whose DYAR is higher than his YAR faced a harder-than-average schedule. A player whose DYAR is lower than his YAR faced an easier-than-average schedule.

To qualify for ranking in YAC, receiving DVOA, or receiving DYAR, a wide receiver must have had 50 passes thrown to him in that season, while a tight end must have 25 targets. We ranked 86 wide receivers in 2007, 83 in 2006, and 89 in 2005, while we ranked 44 tight ends in 2007, 43 in 2006, and 45 in 2005.

The final four columns break down pass length based on the Football Outsiders charting project. The categories are **Short** (5 yards or less), **Mid** (6-15 yards), **Deep** (16-25 yards), and **Bomb** (26 or more yards). These numbers are based on distance in the air only and include both complete and incomplete passes.

The italicized row of statistics for the 2008 season is our 2008 KUBIAK projection based on a complicated regression analysis that takes into account numerous variables including projected role, past performance, projected team offense and defense, projected quarterback statistics, historical comparables, height, age, and strength of schedule. This year, for the first time, KUBIAK projects some of our advanced metrics as well, including DVOA as well as passes and catch rate.

It is difficult to accurately project statistics for a 162-game baseball season, but it is exponentially more difficult to accurately project statistics for a 16-game football season because of the small size of the data samples involved. With that in mind, our projections are not predictions of exact numbers, but the mean of a range of possible performances. What's important is not so much the exact number of yards and touchdowns we project, but whether or not we're projecting a given player to improve or decline. Touchdown numbers will vary more than yardage numbers.

A few low-round rookies, guys listed at seventh on the depth chart, and players who are listed as receivers but really only play special teams are briefly discussed at the end of this chapter in a section we call "Going Deep."

Two notes regarding our advanced metrics: We cannot yet fully separate the performance of a receiver from the performance of his quarterback. Be aware that one will affect the other. In addition, these statistics measure only passes thrown to a receiver, not performance on plays when he is not thrown the ball, such as blocking and drawing double teams.

Top 20 WR by DYAR (Total Value), 2007

Rank	Player	Team	DYAR
1	Randy Moss	NE	569
2	Terrell Owens	DAL	449
3	Reggie Wayne	IND	443
4	Wes Welker	NE	384
5	Marques Colston	NO	351
6	Chad Johnson	CIN	305
7	Greg Jennings	GB	302
8	Larry Fitzgerald	ARI	291
9	Andre Johnson	HOU	288
10	Bobby Engram	SEA	270
11	Santonio Holmes	PIT	259
12	Torry Holt	STL	244
13	Jerricho Cotchery	NYJ	240
14	Anthony Gonzalez	IND	239
15	T.J. Houshmandzadeh	CIN	238
16	Joey Galloway	TB	230
17	Anquan Boldin	ARI	229
18	Donald Driver	GB	224
19	Brandon Stokley	DEN	219
20	Dwayne Bowe	KC	207

Top 20 WR by DVOA (Value per Pass), 2007

Rank	Player	Team	DVOA
1	Anthony Gonzalez	IND	43.5%
2	Greg Jennings	GB	31.5%
3	Andre Johnson	HOU	29.9%
4	Randy Moss	NE	29.3%
5	Terrell Owens	DAL	28.2%
6	Santonio Holmes	PIT	26.2%
7	Brandon Stokley	DEN	25.7%
8	Reggie Williams	JAC	25.6%
9	Jabar Gaffney	NE	22.5%
10	Reggie Wayne	IND	22.5%
11	Wes Welker	NE	21.3%
12	Patrick Crayton	DAL	19.6%
13	Antwaan Randle El	WAS	16.9%
14	Marques Colston	NO	16.8%
15	Nate Washington	PIT	16.5%
16	Joey Galloway	TB	16.4%
17	Anquan Boldin	ARI	16.3%
18	Justin Gage	TEN	14.5%
19	Bobby Engram	SEA	12.9%
20	Donte' Stallworth	NE	12.2%

Top 10 TE by DYAR (Total Value), 2007

Rank	Player	Team	DYAR
1	Antonio Gates	SD	278
2	Jason Witten	DAL	256
3	Tony Gonzalez	KC	206
4	Heath Miller	PIT	194
5	Donald Lee	GB	164
6	Tony Scheffler	DEN	149
7	Owen Daniels	HOU	127
8	Chris Cooley	WAS	121
9	Dallas Clark	IND	107*
10	Benjamin Watson	NE	104

Top 10 TE by DVOA (Value per Pass), 2007

Rank	Player	Team	DVOA
1	Heath Miller	PIT	38.9%
2	Ben Utecht	IND	33.6%
3	Donald Lee	GB	30.2%
4	Antonio Gates	SD	30.0%
5	Tony Scheffler	DEN	26.1%
6	Marcus Pollard	SEA	25.8%
7	Benjamin Watson	NE	23.0%
8	Billy Miller	NO	21.8%
9	Jason Witten	DAL	21.1%
10	Daniel Graham	DEN	16.3%

*On our web site and in the 2007 rankings that follow, Clark is considered a wide receiver, not a tight end.

Aundrae Allison

Height: 6-1   Weight: 192   College: East Carolina   Draft: 2007/5 (146)   Born: 25-Jun-1984   Age: 24   Risk: Red

Year	Team	G	Rec	Pass	Yds	C%	Yd/C	TD	YAC	Rk	DVOA	Rk	DYAR	Rk	YAR	Short	Mid	Deep	Bomb
2007	MIN	11	8	18	122	44%	15.3	0	6.0	—	-35.6%	—	-33	—	-35	19%	50%	13%	19%
2008	MIN		19	33	270	58%	14.5	1			-1.4%								

Allison's primary contribution as a rookie was on special teams. The Vikings ranked ninth in the league in kick returns, led by Allison's 20 returns for a 28.7-yard average, including a 104-yard touchdown against Detroit. Allison has a similar skill set to projected starters Bernard Berrian and Sidney Rice, so he's somewhat redundant as a fourth receiver. Perhaps the team intends to use him like the Bears use Devin Hester, tying their offense in knots to get him the ball "in space." Because that always works so well.

David Anderson

Height: 5-11   Weight: 195   College: Colorado State   Draft: 2006/7 (251)   Born: 28-Jul-1983   Age: 25   Risk: Red

Year	Team	G	Rec	Pass	Yds	C%	Yd/C	TD	YAC	Rk	DVOA	Rk	DYAR	Rk	YAR	Short	Mid	Deep	Bomb
2006	HOU	9	1	1	27	100%	27.0	0	22.0	—	99.9%	—	12	—	12	—	—	—	—
2007	HOU	8	12	17	131	71%	10.9	1	1.8	—	18.8%	—	43	—	42	40%	47%	13%	0%
2008	HOU		22	33	282	67%	12.8	2			0.2%								

On a team with only one standout receiver, there are opportunities for just about everyone. Anderson, one of our top 25 prospects from last year's book, made the most of limited playing time in 2007 and showed good hands. He heads to training camp with a chance to earn more playing time at the fourth receiver spot, and could also get a look returning punts.

Devin Aromashodu

Height: 6-2   Weight: 203   College: Auburn   Draft: 2006/7 (233)   Born: 23-May-1984   Age: 24   Risk: Red

Year	Team	G	Rec	Pass	Yds	C%	Yd/C	TD	YAC	Rk	DVOA	Rk	DYAR	Rk	YAR	Short	Mid	Deep	Bomb
2007	IND	6	7	17	96	41%	13.7	0	5.6	—	-24.0%	—	-15	—	-12	53%	27%	7%	13%
2008	IND		17	26	251	65%	14.4	1			23.7%								

The son of a Nigerian immigrant, Aromashadu was the big-play threat on the 2004 Auburn football team that went 13-0. He led the team that season with 21.4 yards per catch, and scored a touchdown in the Tigers' 16-13 win over Virginia Tech in the Sugar Bowl. Still, despite starting every game, he was fourth on the team in catches, and guys who are fourth options in college aren't supposed to make it in the NFL. The Dolphins drafted him in the seventh round in 2006. He signed with Miami but never played, then repeated that feat with Houston. The Colts cut him in training camp, but were forced to bring him back when injuries decimated their receiving corps. He actually started the team's regular season finale against Tennessee. It will likely be the only start of his NFL career, although there's always the possibility he'll start this year's season finale. And next year's. And the year after that.

Miles Austin

Height: 6-3   Weight: 219   College: Monmouth (NJ)   Draft: 2006/FA   Born: 30-Jun-1984   Age: 24   Risk: Red

Year	Team	G	Rec	Pass	Yds	C%	Yd/C	TD	YAC	Rk	DVOA	Rk	DYAR	Rk	YAR	Short	Mid	Deep	Bomb
2007	DAL	16	5	10	76	50%	15.2	0	8.6	—	34.0%	—	44	—	37	25%	33%	17%	25%
2008	DAL		13	22	183	59%	13.7	1			2.4%								

The Cowboys didn't select a wide receiver in the draft, and Austin is part of the reason why. The undrafted free agent out of Monmouth has filled in as a part-time returner and special teams guy over the past two years, and he got to run some pass routes when the Cowboys were shutting things down for the playoffs in Weeks 16 and 17. He's currently sixth on the Cowboys depth chart, but the coaches like him, and good special teamers have a way of sticking.

Jason Avant

Height: 6-1   Weight: 210   College: Michigan   Draft: 2006/4 (109)   Born: 20-Apr-1983   Age: 25   Risk: Red

Year	Team	G	Rec	Pass	Yds	C%	Yd/C	TD	YAC	Rk	DVOA	Rk	DYAR	Rk	YAR	Short	Mid	Deep	Bomb
2006	PHI	8	7	15	68	47%	9.7	1	3.7	—	-14.2%	—	-2	—	-22	50%	17%	17%	17%
2007	PHI	15	23	33	267	70%	11.6	2	2.3	—	20.1%	—	85	—	74	26%	55%	16%	3%
2008	PHI		38	57	468	67%	12.2	3			10.1%								

Your standard-issue backup Eagles wide receiver. Avant can find some holes in some zones, runs solid routes, shows up on special teams, and generally considers the area ten yards past the line of scrimmage to be the Forbidden Zone from *Planet of the Apes*. KUBIAK assumes he'll have an increased role in the offense, which is possible in Philly, where you can't tell one receiver from another without a program. With this skill set, his performance level is already maxed out.

Donnie Avery

Height: 5-11   Weight: 186   College: Houston   Draft: 2008/2 (33)   Born: 12-Jun-1984   Age: 24   Risk: Red

Year	Team	G	Rec	Pass	Yds	C%	Yd/C	TD	YAC	Rk	DVOA	Rk	DYAR	Rk	YAR	Short	Mid	Deep	Bomb
2008	STL		29	51	382	57%	13.3	2			-17.6%								

Avery was projected as a fourth-round pick in the days leading up to the draft. When he was named as the first wideout off the board by the Rams, everyone from mock draft writers to Rams fans got that collective confused-dog face. Avery's out of Conference USA, which has contributed three number-one wideouts to the league (Roddy White, Roydell Williams, and Deion Branch), so the mid-major level of competition shouldn't be an issue. He'll start in the slot, which should alleviate concerns about his ability to break press coverage. Avery's been timed as low as 4.2 in the 40, so he's got elite speed, but his small stature and seeming lack of desire to go over the middle reminds us of another Conference USA product: Todd Pinkston.

Hank Baskett
Height: 6-4　Weight: 215　College: New Mexico　　Draft: 2006/FA　　Born: 4-Sep-1982　Age: 26　Risk: Red

Year	Team	G	Rec	Pass	Yds	C%	Yd/C	TD	YAC	Rk	DVOA	Rk	DYAR	Rk	YAR	Short	Mid	Deep	Bomb
2006	PHI	16	22	43	464	51%	21.1	2	4.9	—	8.3%	—	68	—	85	21%	29%	24%	26%
2007	PHI	16	16	22	142	73%	8.9	1	2.4	—	-2.5%	—	17	—	6	43%	48%	10%	0%
2008	PHI		16	25	142	64%	8.9	1			-2.6%								

Another useful player with a low ceiling: the difference between Baskett and Jason Avant is that Baskett is six foot four. Baskett's also a good blocker on the outside, which makes him a more viable option for increased playing time. Learning how to bust the jam consistently could earn Baskett several million dollars; if he's limited to being just a slot guy, he doesn't have the speed or the explosiveness to make him worth anyone's while.

Arnaz Battle
Height: 6-1　Weight: 217　College: Notre Dame　　Draft: 2003/6 (197)　Born: 22-Feb-1980　Age: 28　Risk: Red

Year	Team	G	Rec	Pass	Yds	C%	Yd/C	TD	YAC	Rk	DVOA	Rk	DYAR	Rk	YAR	Short	Mid	Deep	Bomb
2005	SF	10	32	54	363	59%	11.3	3	3.7	38	-11.9%	72	3	72	23	39%	52%	7%	2%
2006	SF	16	59	86	686	70%	11.6	3	4.1	29	8.8%	27	142	35	122	46%	37%	11%	6%
2007	SF	16	50	104	600	48%	12.0	5	3.1	57	-31.3%	84	-151	87	-122	36%	43%	13%	8%
2008	SF		67	107	760	63%	11.3	3			-3.3%								

What happened to Arnaz Battle? The former quarterback at Notre Dame had a catch rate of 70 percent in 2006 and wasn't credited with a drop that year. Playing with four quarterbacks in 2007 and uninspired offense, Battle dropped seven passes. His quarterback background should help him understand the new Mike Martz offense and Battle remains one of the best blockers at his position.

Drew Bennett
Height: 6-5　Weight: 206　College: UCLA　　Draft: 2000/FA　　Born: 26-Aug-1978　Age: 30　Risk: Yellow

Year	Team	G	Rec	Pass	Yds	C%	Yd/C	TD	YAC	Rk	DVOA	Rk	DYAR	Rk	YAR	Short	Mid	Deep	Bomb
2005	TEN	13	58	109	738	53%	12.7	4	3.1	56	-11.2%	71	13	71	31	32%	46%	9%	12%
2006	TEN	16	46	97	737	47%	16.0	3	2.7	65	-9.4%	63	24	60	14	12%	45%	27%	16%
2007	STL	14	33	73	375	45%	11.4	3	2.8	70	-24.5%	78	-68	79	-70	21%	49%	21%	8%
2008	STL		51	100	604	51%	11.8	4			-9.7%								

Bennett will go into training camp as a starting wide receiver by default; the Rams simply have no other options. Bennett shined in 2003 with Tennessee, leading the league in DVOA but with only 54 passes. He then broke out in 2004, catching 80 passes for 1,247 yards and 11 touchdowns, including eight scores in one stretch of three games. (Those three games are amazing to behold even years later: 28 catches, 517 yards, eight touchdowns. The Titans lost all three games. Let's move on.) He's never been close to that good again, dropping below average in DVOA in 2005 and 2006 and finally dropping below replacement level last year, his first with the Rams. At six foot five, he's at least four inches taller than any other receiver on the roster, so he will offer Marc Bulger and company the biggest target they can find. Bennett's most amazing athletic achievement may have been accomplished before he ever entered the NFL. He played quarterback and wide receiver at UCLA, where one spring evening, he decided to enter the L.A. Marathon. This was no small undertaking, because the marathon was the next day. With no training, Bennett completed the 26-plus-mile course.

Earl Bennett
Height: 6-0　Weight: 209　College: Vanderbilt　　Draft: 2008/3 (70)　Born: 23-Mar-1987　Age: 21　Risk: Red

Year	Team	G	Rec	Pass	Yds	C%	Yd/C	TD	YAC	Rk	DVOA	Rk	DYAR	Rk	YAR	Short	Mid	Deep	Bomb
2008	CHI		33	57	396	58%	11.9	2			-3.9%								

Bennett was another one of the draft day wideout risers, going before conference-mate Early Doucet, who was purported to be a first-round pick. Bennett put up 75+ catches in each of his three years as Vanderbilt, becoming the first SEC receiver to do so. He's not really a possession receiver, but more your typical zone-buster out of the slot—think the Giants' Steve Smith. Bennett should be one of the team's starters by the end of the year or once they've given up on Devin Hester, whichever comes first.

Bernard Berrian   Height: 6-1   Weight: 183   College: Fresno State   Draft: 2004/3 (78)   Born: 27-Dec-1980   Age: 27   Risk: Yellow

Year	Team	G	Rec	Pass	Yds	C%	Yd/C	TD	YAC	Rk	DVOA	Rk	DYAR	Rk	YAR	Short	Mid	Deep	Bomb
2005	CHI	11	13	25	246	52%	18.9	0	3.7	—	9.0%	—	41	—	30	30%	15%	20%	35%
2006	CHI	15	51	102	775	50%	15.2	6	4.1	32	-16.7%	74	-32	76	-5	26%	33%	13%	28%
2007	CHI	16	71	128	951	55%	13.4	5	3.5	46	-6.9%	64	58	60	68	26%	41%	20%	12%
2008	MIN		67	125	977	54%	14.5	9			11.0%								

There's a lot of pressure on Bernard Berrian this season. No less a source than Adrian Peterson is counting on him to change the fortunes in Minnesota. Specifically, Peterson said that the deep threat Berrian provides should stop opposing defenses from stuffing the box. "When they had nine, 10 guys in the box last year, we were still kind of able to get the work done," Peterson told the *St. Paul Pioneer Press*. "It's kind of scary to see what we're capable of doing this year." Here's what else should be scary for Peterson: He and his team are putting their faith in the hands of a receiver who has never gone over 1,000 yards, and has posted below average DVOA ratings three out of four seasons in his career. Granted, the quarterbacks throwing to him were terrible, but that won't change in Minnesota. On the other hand, the only season he posted a positive DVOA was in 2005, when an astonishing 55 percent of his targets were either "deep" or "bomb" range. So sending Berrian deep downfield and blindly lobbing the ball his way (as appears to be the Vikings' plan) may be the best use of his skills.

Anquan Boldin   Height: 6-1   Weight: 218   College: Florida State   Draft: 2003/2 (54)   Born: 3-Oct-1980   Age: 28   Risk: Red

Year	Team	G	Rec	Pass	Yds	C%	Yd/C	TD	YAC	Rk	DVOA	Rk	DYAR	Rk	YAR	Short	Mid	Deep	Bomb
2005	ARI	14	102	171	1402	60%	13.7	7	5.2	13	3.9%	34	221	17	265	37%	35%	20%	7%
2006	ARI	16	83	152	1203	55%	14.5	4	4.5	21	0.8%	49	155	30	113	25%	48%	15%	12%
2007	ARI	12	71	100	853	71%	12.0	9	5.3	10	16.3%	17	229	17	237	46%	35%	14%	5%
2008	ARI		82	141	1018	58%	12.5	6			-4.8%								

The heavily back-loaded contract the Cardinals created for Larry Fitzgerald has caused headaches in Arizona. Fitzgerald finally re-structured the deal so he wasn't making eight figures. Nevertheless, it prompted Boldin to bellyache about a new contract. Don't read too much into Boldin's complaints: he later backed off his statements, and he's too much of a competitor to let his frustrations spill onto the field. Boldin has grown into one of the best blocking receivers in the game, but that's not what makes him special: it's his ability to take over a game (14 receptions against the Ravens in Week 3, 13 against the Falcons in Week 16), his YAC ability, and his talent for working the middle of the field. The Fitzgerald-Boldin combination should be around for a few more seasons, and the competition between them makes them both better.

Marty Booker   Height: 6-0   Weight: 212   College: Louisiana-Monroe   Draft: 1999/3 (78)   Born: 31-Jul-1976   Age: 32   Risk: Red

Year	Team	G	Rec	Pass	Yds	C%	Yd/C	TD	YAC	Rk	DVOA	Rk	DYAR	Rk	YAR	Short	Mid	Deep	Bomb
2005	MIA	15	39	86	686	45%	17.6	3	7.1	5	-5.0%	56	52	55	49	24%	38%	29%	10%
2006	MIA	14	55	90	747	61%	13.6	6	4.9	15	6.4%	34	130	37	166	32%	45%	17%	6%
2007	MIA	15	50	105	556	48%	11.1	1	2.6	75	-27.3%	80	-122	84	-114	34%	35%	26%	5%
2008	CHI		45	93	627	48%	13.9	2			-19.8%								

Booker briefly looked like number-one receiver material for the Bears in 2001 and 2002, when he caught 197 passes in two seasons. His DVOA in his best seasons was negative, a sign that a) the offenses he played for weren't very good and b) Booker's production wasn't all that it seemed. He slipped badly in 2003, but the Dolphins traded Adewale Ogunleye for him, then rewarded him with a $28-million, seven-year contract to play second fiddle to Chris Chambers. Booker was an adequate supporting actor, but when the Dolphins traded Chambers, Booker became the go-to guy. The results were a lot like that last season of *Good Times,* when Willona down the hall filled in for Florida Evans. He had eight catches in the win over the Ravens, only to be upstaged by Greg Camarillo. Released in a cap move on Blue Monday, Booker signed a one-day contract with the Bears so he could retire as . . . wait, he signed a real contract to play for the Bears? Go figure.

Dwayne Bowe

Height: 6-3   Weight: 212   College: LSU   Draft: 2007/1 (23)   Born: 21-Sep-1984   Age: 24   Risk: Yellow

Year	Team	G	Rec	Pass	Yds	C%	Yd/C	TD	YAC	Rk	DVOA	Rk	DYAR	Rk	YAR	Short	Mid	Deep	Bomb
2007	KC	16	70	118	995	59%	14.2	5	5.2	12	10.0%	27	207	20	226	29%	39%	19%	13%
2008	KC		66	125	795	53%	12.1	6			-6.4%								

Rookie receivers are supposed to struggle, but Bowe joined a team with a poor offense and questionable quarterbacks and was immediately productive. His rookie numbers suggest greatness, but beware. There are some similarities between Bowe and Michael Clayton, who burst on the scene a few years ago with a similarly exceptional season. Both were big, physical receivers and talented blockers. For a number of reasons, including injury and focus lapses, Clayton's career stalled, and he has gained roughly as many yards in his past three seasons as he did when he was a rookie. Bowe was always more productive in the open field than Clayton and could just as easily follow the Anquan Boldin path, but it is always useful to learn from the mistakes of the past: stardom is never guaranteed.

Mark Bradley

Height: 6-1   Weight: 201   College: Oklahoma   Draft: 2005/2 (39)   Born: 29-Jan-1982   Age: 26   Risk: Red

Year	Team	G	Rec	Pass	Yds	C%	Yd/C	TD	YAC	Rk	DVOA	Rk	DYAR	Rk	YAR	Short	Mid	Deep	Bomb
2005	CHI	7	18	36	230	50%	12.8	0	4.5	—	-20.1%	—	-21	—	-25	34%	38%	21%	7%
2006	CHI	10	14	23	282	61%	20.1	3	6.2	—	40.1%	—	91	—	85	33%	33%	10%	24%
2007	CHI	15	6	17	71	35%	11.8	1	3.3	—	-44.9%	—	-45	—	-33	33%	28%	17%	22%
2008	CHI		44	99	566	44%	13.0	2			-18.3%								

Bradley's career got off to a promising start—his numbers for 2005 project to 41 catches over 16 games, not bad for a rookie—but came crashing down when he tore his ACL that year. After he caught only 20 passes the next two years, you'd think the Bears would phase Bradley out, but he would beg to differ. "In my eyes, I'm that confident that I'm the number one guy," Bradley told the *Chicago Tribune.* "That's what they drafted me for in the second round, to be the number one guy. I've just had some injuries and some minor setbacks. Now I'm recovered and ready to be that guy." We would never describe a torn ACL as a "minor setback," but then, it's not our knee.

Deion Branch

Height: 5-9   Weight: 193   College: Louisville   Draft: 2002/2 (65)   Born: 18-Jul-1979   Age: 29   Risk: Red

Year	Team	G	Rec	Pass	Yds	C%	Yd/C	TD	YAC	Rk	DVOA	Rk	DYAR	Rk	YAR	Short	Mid	Deep	Bomb
2005	NE	16	78	125	998	62%	12.8	5	3.2	54	14.6%	16	262	11	220	30%	44%	17%	8%
2006	SEA	14	53	101	725	52%	13.7	4	3.5	45	-16.5%	73	-29	74	56	11%	60%	22%	7%
2007	SEA	11	49	85	661	58%	13.5	4	4.2	29	1.8%	44	97	51	106	41%	33%	16%	10%
2008	SEA		19	31	249	61%	13.4	2			2.2%								

When general manager Tim Ruskell announced that he had traded Seattle's 2007 first-round pick to the Patriots to acquire Branch, he justified the high price by citing a draft study he conducted while a personnel guru for the Buccaneers. "This is a known commodity," Ruskell said at the time, referring to Branch. "The first round can be a crap shoot, from top to bottom. Fifty percent were busts." That may be true, but after two injury-riddled years of underwhelming performance, it's clear that Branch is not the "known commodity" that Ruskell imagined him to be. He tore his ACL in January, and this projection assumes he gets back on the field around November.

Steve Breaston

Height: 6-0   Weight: 193   College: Michigan   Draft: 2007/5 (142)   Born: 20-Aug-1983   Age: 25   Risk: Red

Year	Team	G	Rec	Pass	Yds	C%	Yd/C	TD	YAC	Rk	DVOA	Rk	DYAR	Rk	YAR	Short	Mid	Deep	Bomb
2007	ARI	16	8	14	92	57%	11.5	0	4.6	—	-19.4%	—	-8	—	-9	29%	50%	14%	7%
2008	ARI		29	45	294	63%	10.3	1			1.6%								

Breaston was used as the primary return man as a rookie last year, but he'll compete for the third receiver spot now that Bryant Johnson is gone. It's a significant role, even with Anquan Boldin and Larry Fitzgerald on the roster, because Ken Whisenhunt uses three receivers or more 54 percent of the time. Last year, Johnson, who's now with the 49ers, had 88 passes tossed his way. Breaston could see similar opportunities if he can hold off rookie Early Doucet.

Reggie Brown

Height: 6-1 Weight: 197 College: Georgia | Draft: 2005/2 (35) Born: 13-Jan-1981 Age: 27 Risk: Red

Year	Team	G	Rec	Pass	Yds	C%	Yd/C	TD	YAC	Rk	DVOA	Rk	DYAR	Rk	YAR	Short	Mid	Deep	Bomb
2005	PHI	16	43	79	571	54%	13.3	4	4.8	18	-5.4%	57	46	57	28	33%	34%	19%	13%
2006	PHI	16	46	92	816	50%	17.7	8	4.0	37	-3.6%	55	66	56	158	24%	38%	19%	20%
2007	PHI	16	61	111	780	55%	12.8	4	2.8	69	-7.3%	66	47	61	31	29%	44%	20%	7%
2008	PHI		54	105	785	51%	14.6	5			0.4%								

We noted last year that Brown needed to get better on intermediate routes in order to become a complete NFL wideout. Instead, Brown decided it would be easier to just stop going deep. He went long on 20 percent of passes in 2006 but just 7 percent of the time last year. While things seemed so promising this time last year, the chances of Brown becoming an elite wide receiver have decreased dramatically. This is a huge year for Brown, who could take a huge step forward, get a new contract, and emerge as the number-one receiver the Eagles desperately need; alternatively, he could continue down the Alvin Harper career path. KUBIAK predicts the latter, making Brown perhaps the only Philadelphia player it doesn't love unconditionally.

Isaac Bruce

Height: 6-0 Weight: 188 College: Memphis | Draft: 1994/2 (33) Born: 10-Nov-1972 Age: 36 Risk: Red

Year	Team	G	Rec	Pass	Yds	C%	Yd/C	TD	YAC	Rk	DVOA	Rk	DYAR	Rk	YAR	Short	Mid	Deep	Bomb
2005	STL	11	36	71	525	51%	14.6	3	3.7	36	-14.7%	75	-11	74	10	27%	30%	27%	17%
2006	STL	16	74	126	1098	59%	14.8	3	3.6	43	9.7%	26	225	13	211	27%	34%	26%	13%
2007	STL	14	55	101	733	54%	13.3	4	2.5	76	0.9%	49	110	45	97	18%	47%	26%	10%
2008	SF		59	109	810	54%	13.7	3			-1.6%								

The Rams' all-time leader in receptions, yards, and touchdowns, Bruce has moved on to San Francisco, the latest example of a Hall of Fame athlete ending his career in a strange uniform. This is nothing new—Johnny Unitas with the Chargers, Joe Namath with the Rams, Brett Favre with whatever team signs him in October when he's bored—but there will still be gnashing and wailing and moaning, and some will insist that the NFL institute some kind of loophole in the salary cap for players who have spent their entire career with one team. In reality, the salary cap has little to do with the situation. The bottom line is this: The Rams didn't want to pay Bruce what he thought he was worth, but the 49ers did. So Bruce gets his money, the 49ers get their guy, and the Rams don't have to invest in a guy whose non-sentimental value is dwindling by the day. This begs the question of why the 49ers were so eager to sign Bruce to a two-year, $6 million contract. Bruce is far from washed up, but his once-elite speed has left him. He still has the skills to get behind coverage, but he can no longer run down deep balls. Passes that would have been long touchdowns a few years ago turned into overthrows last season. He's going to a team that needs a number-one wideout and has a lousy quarterback situation. This can't end well.

Antonio Bryant

Height: 6-1 Weight: 192 College: Pittsburgh | Draft: 2002/2 (63) Born: 9-Mar-1981 Age: 27 Risk: Red

Year	Team	G	Rec	Pass	Yds	C%	Yd/C	TD	YAC	Rk	DVOA	Rk	DYAR	Rk	YAR	Short	Mid	Deep	Bomb
2005	CLE	16	69	123	1009	56%	14.6	4	3.3	45	3.4%	38	154	25	153	20%	46%	21%	13%
2006	SF	14	40	91	733	44%	18.3	3	4.1	33	0.9%	48	96	46	17	15%	32%	33%	19%
2008	TB		25	55	408	45%	16.1	2			-10.5%								

Bryant was persona non grata last year, with nary a team willing to take on a player facing a two-game suspension who was suing the league at the same time. The lawsuit (Bryant contested that the league could not drug test him if he wasn't on a roster; details of the resolution weren't released) ended in December, but Bryant didn't catch on until March, when he signed a deal with the Buccaneers. The talent is still there, and he's only 27. Irving Fryar and Cris Carter, both of whom had early-career personal problems, started to figure things out around that age, so his career can still have a big second act. At the same time, he's a bad training camp away from washing out of the league.

Nate Burleson
Height: 6-0   Weight: 192   College: Nevada   Draft: 2003/3 (71)   Born: 19-Aug-1981   Age: 27   Risk: Red

Year	Team	G	Rec	Pass	Yds	C%	Yd/C	TD	YAC	Rk	DVOA	Rk	DYAR	Rk	YAR	Short	Mid	Deep	Bomb
2005	MIN	12	30	52	328	58%	10.9	1	2.6	72	-3.4%	48	39	60	24	29%	46%	15%	10%
2006	SEA	16	18	37	192	49%	10.7	2	2.0	—	-35.8%	—	-63	—	-16	27%	39%	21%	12%
2007	SEA	16	50	95	694	53%	13.9	9	3.9	35	1.2%	45	107	48	139	23%	41%	26%	11%
2008	SEA		49	88	774	56%	15.7	4			9.4%								

It's increasingly clear that Burleson will never repeat his 68-catch, 1,006-yard, 35.3% DVOA performance from 2004. At the same time, he didn't fall off the cliff like Michael Clayton (the Tampa receiver, not George Clooney). Burleson played better as the year progressed (20 of his 50 receptions came in December), and his unbelievable catch in the third quarter of the Seahawks-Redskins playoff game literally saved Seattle's season, so perhaps the upward trend will continue in 2008. Hey, somebody has to catch passes in Seattle, right?

Plaxico Burress
Height: 6-5   Weight: 226   College: Michigan State   Draft: 2000/1 (8)   Born: 12-Aug-1977   Age: 31   Risk: Yellow

Year	Team	G	Rec	Pass	Yds	C%	Yd/C	TD	YAC	Rk	DVOA	Rk	DYAR	Rk	YAR	Short	Mid	Deep	Bomb
2005	NYG	16	76	166	1214	46%	16.0	7	3.3	46	-7.2%	63	72	46	65	24%	41%	25%	10%
2006	NYG	15	63	121	988	52%	15.7	10	3.6	42	6.6%	33	182	22	105	25%	36%	23%	16%
2007	NYG	16	70	141	1025	50%	14.6	12	4.0	34	-0.6%	53	139	32	114	24%	37%	21%	18%
2008	NYG		82	156	1208	53%	14.8	12			13.3%								

A member of Hero Squad. The word "gritty" is usually reserved for scrappy little quarterbacks, but it truly applies to Burress, who spent the entire year playing on a mangled ankle, added a separated shoulder as the season went along, and then nearly missed the Super Bowl with another leg injury. Despite all that, Burress made it through all 16 games, remained the team's best downfield threat, and although he was running on fumes in the playoffs, single-handedly ended Al Harris's career as a Pro Bowl cornerback with one of the most dominating displays you'll ever see in a playoff game. Burress always has a low catch rate, but he also runs deeper routes than any number-one wide receiver in football (except perhaps Roddy White), is an excellent downfield blocker, and makes a great security blanket for Eli Manning. He's also getting hyped by Lil' Wayne, which is a step up from Lil' Ronnie.

Andre Caldwell
Height: 6-1   Weight: 200   College: Florida   Draft: 2008/3 (97)   Born: 15-Apr-1985   Age: 23   Risk: Red

Year	Team	G	Rec	Pass	Yds	C%	Yd/C	TD	YAC	Rk	DVOA	Rk	DYAR	Rk	YAR	Short	Mid	Deep	Bomb
2008	CIN		19	31	222	61%	11.7	1			1.1%								

Unlike his older brother Reche, this Caldwell has eyes of normal human size and a reputation for fearlessness; unfortunately, like his older brother Reche, this Caldwell is injury-prone. He's a great downfield blocker and has very good hands, so he'll be the short-range slot-receiver in Cincinnati's offense (with Jerome Simpson as the deep threat) before battling Simpson for a starting role in 2009. If Chad Johnson is traded before the season, this projection changes to 37 receptions for 472 yards and three touchdowns.

Reche Caldwell
Height: 5-11   Weight: 194   College: Florida   Draft: 2002/2 (48)   Born: 28-Mar-1979   Age: 29   Risk: Red

Year	Team	G	Rec	Pass	Yds	C%	Yd/C	TD	YAC	Rk	DVOA	Rk	DYAR	Rk	YAR	Short	Mid	Deep	Bomb
2005	SD	16	28	43	352	65%	12.6	1	2.6	—	0.1%	—	42	—	32	24%	41%	14%	22%
2006	NE	16	61	102	760	60%	12.5	4	3.2	48	-2.0%	54	83	50	101	41%	29%	21%	9%
2007	WAS	8	15	22	141	68%	9.4	0	1.4	—	-0.7%	—	22	—	17	45%	30%	15%	10%
2008	STL		15	25	167	60%	10.9	1			-11.0%								

Caldwell didn't make it out of training camp with the Patriots, only a year after leading them in receiving. He went to Washington and caught 15 passes late in the season, but he might as well have disappeared from the NFL. Caldwell's a talented player who runs good routes and creates separation from defensive backs, but he has the Todd Pinkston stench on him by now. St. Louis brought him in on a one-year deal.

Greg Camarillo

Height: 6-1 Weight: 190 College: Stanford — Draft: 2006/FA — Born: 18-Apr-1982 — Age: 26 — Risk: Red

Year	Team	G	Rec	Pass	Yds	C%	Yd/C	TD	YAC	Rk	DVOA	Rk	DYAR	Rk	YAR	Short	Mid	Deep	Bomb
2007	MIA	15	8	10	160	80%	20.0	2	8.4	—	82.1%	—	72	—	76	20%	50%	30%	0%
2008	MIA		14	24	171	58%	12.0	1			-12.7%								

As unlikely a season hero as you'll ever find: a skinny second-year special teamer who leapfrogged Derek Hagan on the depth chart late in the season. Camarillo followed his game-winning touchdown against the Ravens with solid efforts against the Patriots and Bengals, so he should stick as a gunner and third or fourth wideout. He'll never be a star, but he's earned a permanent place in the trivia question Hall of Fame.

Drew Carter

Height: 6-3 Weight: 200 College: Ohio State — Draft: 2004/5 (163) — Born: 5-Sep-1981 — Age: 27 — Risk: Red

Year	Team	G	Rec	Pass	Yds	C%	Yd/C	TD	YAC	Rk	DVOA	Rk	DYAR	Rk	YAR	Short	Mid	Deep	Bomb
2005	CAR	3	5	15	103	33%	20.6	1	1.6	—	7.6%	—	25	—	17	7%	14%	21%	57%
2006	CAR	14	28	51	357	55%	12.8	3	2.4	75	-6.9%	58	23	62	3	31%	39%	12%	18%
2007	CAR	16	38	75	517	51%	13.6	4	2.9	67	-6.6%	63	38	64	43	32%	27%	15%	26%
2008	OAK		46	82	491	56%	10.8	2			-3.9%								

Selected in the fifth round of the 2004 draft, Carter was supposed to be a super-fast deep threat for the Panthers. He provided some playmaking ability, but he wasn't going to transcend the team's quarterback situation in 2007. His ability to split the field was on display in a loss to the Packers, when he gained 132 yards on only five catches. More common were Loser League specials consisting of two or three catches for less than 30 yards. Oakland is the perfect place for speed merchants with iffy production, and that's where Carter will play in 2008.

Tim Carter

Height: 6-0 Weight: 200 College: Auburn — Draft: 2002/2 (46) — Born: 21-Sep-1979 — Age: 29 — Risk: Red

Year	Team	G	Rec	Pass	Yds	C%	Yd/C	TD	YAC	Rk	DVOA	Rk	DYAR	Rk	YAR	Short	Mid	Deep	Bomb
2005	NYG	15	10	24	186	42%	18.6	0	2.2	—	-16.2%	—	-6	—	-13	14%	36%	23%	27%
2006	NYG	16	22	49	253	45%	11.5	2	1.9	—	-30.3%	—	-65	—	-65	18%	45%	21%	16%
2007	CLE	16	8	22	117	36%	14.6	1	2.4	—	-23.7%	—	-19	—	-17	25%	45%	10%	20%
2008	HOU		15	28	227	54%	14.9	1			-9.1%								

After being traded for Reuben Droughns last offseason, Carter failed to make an impression as the Browns' fourth wideout and departed this offseason for the Texans. The book on Carter is of a talented wide receiver that can't stay healthy, but he had sixteen games to impress last year in a pass-happy attack and barely made a dent. Whether the injuries have sapped his talents or the talents just were never there, he's waiver wire fodder at this point.

Chris Chambers

Height: 5-11 Weight: 210 College: Wisconsin — Draft: 2001/2 (52) — Born: 12-Aug-1978 — Age: 30 — Risk: Red

Year	Team	G	Rec	Pass	Yds	C%	Yd/C	TD	YAC	Rk	DVOA	Rk	DYAR	Rk	YAR	Short	Mid	Deep	Bomb
2005	MIA	16	82	166	1118	49%	13.6	11	4.2	29	-8.0%	65	61	52	59	28%	37%	17%	18%
2006	MIA	16	59	153	677	39%	11.5	4	3.2	51	-41.3%	82	-348	83	-314	31%	31%	24%	14%
2007	MIA	6	31	68	415	47%	13.4	0	2.8	—	-11.5%	—	6	—	-9	16%	46%	31%	7%
2007	SD	10	35	63	555	56%	15.9	4	1.9	78	3.6%	58	80	54	90	19%	41%	27%	13%
2008	SD		56	109	828	51%	14.7	8			11.0%								

One of the biggest differences between statistical analysis of baseball and football is how dramatically a player's value can change by virtue of his situation and role. A hitter with a .300 EQA is going to rake anywhere he goes, but a football player who changes situations can see his value shift dramatically. Chambers skill set is simple: He's a fast guy with incredible leaping ability who can get downfield and make big plays. He also drops the occasional pass, doesn't run great routes, and doesn't help his quarterbacks by adjusting well to poor throws. In Miami, he was absolutely miscast as a number-one receiver—he simply doesn't have the possession receiver traits that an elite receiver has. When he was traded to San Diego, he immediately became the team's "3A" receiver behind Antonio Gates and LaDainian Tomlinson, and alongside Vincent Jackson, and he was allowed to roam downfield in single coverage. That puts Chambers in the best situation possible for him to succeed, which he did. With the return of Eric Parker and the expected improvement of Buster Davis, Chambers's biggest problem is going to be finding passes in such a crowded lineup. Although the meme of Chambers being a number-one guy at any point in his career should be dead and buried, he can be an effective deep threat and fade target by the goal line for at least a couple more seasons.

Antonio Chatman
Height: 5-9   Weight: 177   College: Cincinnati   Draft: 2003/FA   Born: 12-Feb-1979   Age: 29   Risk: Red

Year	Team	G	Rec	Pass	Yds	C%	Yd/C	TD	YAC	Rk	DVOA	Rk	DYAR	Rk	YAR	Short	Mid	Deep	Bomb
2005	GB	16	49	86	549	57%	11.2	4	3.1	57	-3.6%	51	61	54	46	35%	38%	24%	3%
2006	CIN	3	3	5	22	60%	7.3	0	3.7	—	-29.0%	—	-6	—	-4	40%	20%	20%	20%
2007	CIN	13	19	29	149	66%	7.8	1	3.5	—	-11.9%	—	2	—	6	48%	34%	17%	0%
2008	CIN		34	49	379	69%	11.1	2			2.0%								

An outsider in the great 2008 Cincinnati training camp wide receiver spectacle, Chatman will hope that the offseason departures of Chris Henry, Tab Perry, and (perhaps) Chad Johnson will have opened up playing time for the Bengals' lesser lights. Unfortunately for him, Cincinnati drafted Jerome Simpson, Andre Caldwell, and Mario Urrutia. As well as chipping in with a reception or two in most games (most of which seem to have been dumpoffs from Carson Palmer on third-and-long), Chatman can be used as a punt returner, though he was below average in 2007. Odds are that once again he will see the field in three- and four-receiver packages, but we can't make any guarantees as long as Ocho Cinco keeps the Bengals in limbo with his extended sulk-o-rama.

Mark Clayton
Height: 5-10   Weight: 193   College: Oklahoma   Draft: 2005/1 (22)   Born: 2-Jul-1982   Age: 26   Risk: Red

Year	Team	G	Rec	Pass	Yds	C%	Yd/C	TD	YAC	Rk	DVOA	Rk	DYAR	Rk	YAR	Short	Mid	Deep	Bomb
2005	BAL	14	44	86	471	51%	10.7	2	4.5	25	-23.3%	88	-72	88	-65	42%	31%	11%	17%
2006	BAL	16	67	112	939	60%	14.0	5	5.3	6	6.7%	32	167	26	117	37%	44%	9%	10%
2007	BAL	16	48	89	531	54%	11.1	0	2.2	81	-18.4%	76	-41	76	-27	25%	53%	16%	6%
2008	BAL		58	103	698	56%	12.1	4			-3.3%								

It's hard to know how much to blame the receivers for the murky morass that was Brian Billick's offense, but there is no question that Clayton regressed last year. Clayton played in all 16 games, starting 12, but his total completions, yardage, and average per catch numbers all dropped alarmingly. His biggest problems occurred on third down, when he caught just 15 of the 34 passes thrown to him, and in the red zone, where he was six-of-12 with zero touchdowns. Clayton turned it on in the second half of the season, but it's unclear if that will be enough to hang onto his starting job, as new offensive coordinator Cam Cameron prefers bigger receivers who can attack the field vertically and provide quality blocking on the edges.

Michael Clayton
Height: 6-3   Weight: 197   College: LSU   Draft: 2004/1 (15)   Born: 13-Oct-1982   Age: 26   Risk: Red

Year	Team	G	Rec	Pass	Yds	C%	Yd/C	TD	YAC	Rk	DVOA	Rk	DYAR	Rk	YAR	Short	Mid	Deep	Bomb
2005	TB	14	32	55	372	58%	11.6	0	5.2	14	-17.8%	81	-22	77	-14	45%	43%	11%	0%
2006	TB	12	33	65	356	51%	10.8	1	3.2	50	-9.6%	64	16	66	-34	33%	48%	15%	5%
2007	TB	14	22	40	301	55%	13.7	0	5.7	—	-14.3%	—	-5	—	-3	42%	31%	19%	8%
2008	TB		25	44	344	57%	13.6	1			-5.8%								

Since his 80-catch rookie year, Clayton has seen his career derailed by injuries, drops, and an inability to make himself into a complete NFL receiver. The hope is that the 16-catch stretch in the last four games of the regular season is an indicator of better things to come, but time is running out and it feels as if the Bucs are moving on with Clayton as a secondary option at best.

Keary Colbert
Height: 5-10   Weight: 193   College: USC   Draft: 2004/2 (62)   Born: 21-May-1982   Age: 26   Risk: Red

Year	Team	G	Rec	Pass	Yds	C%	Yd/C	TD	YAC	Rk	DVOA	Rk	DYAR	Rk	YAR	Short	Mid	Deep	Bomb
2005	CAR	16	25	55	282	45%	11.3	2	3.5	39	-19.4%	84	-30	81	-29	29%	37%	27%	8%
2006	CAR	12	5	12	56	42%	11.2	0	4.4	—	-21.7%	—	-8	—	-22	20%	50%	20%	10%
2007	CAR	12	32	69	332	46%	10.4	0	3.3	54	-34.6%	86	-122	85	-109	41%	36%	12%	11%
2008	DEN		35	67	426	53%	12.2	3			-7.3%								

When Steve Smith broke his leg and missed most of the 2004 season, Colbert set Carolina rookie records for receptions, yards, and touchdowns. He was installed as the team's secondary target in 2005, but he was never able to live up to that rookie promise. The primary issue has been an ability to hold on to the ball; Colbert hasn't managed a catch rate of over 50 percent since that first season. He underperformed in 2005 and 2007, and basically fell off the face of the earth in 2006. The Broncos signed Colbert to a three-year, $7.2 million contract in March, after which Mike Shanahan compared Colbert to Ed McCaffrey. We beg to differ.

Laveranues Coles

Height: 5-11 Weight: 193 College: Florida State   Draft: 2000/3 (78) Born: 29-Dec-1977 Age: 30 Risk: Yellow

Year	Team	G	Rec	Pass	Yds	C%	Yd/C	TD	YAC	Rk	DVOA	Rk	DYAR	Rk	YAR	Short	Mid	Deep	Bomb
2005	NYJ	16	73	131	845	56%	11.6	5	2.5	79	-4.7%	54	82	42	77	22%	54%	14%	10%
2006	NYJ	16	91	151	1098	60%	12.1	6	3.2	49	-1.9%	53	128	38	93	35%	43%	14%	9%
2007	NYJ	12	55	89	646	62%	11.7	6	2.6	73	5.7%	36	130	39	135	37%	35%	17%	12%
2008	NYJ		67	120	833	56%	12.4	5			-3.0%								

The Jets signed Coles to a contract extension in the offseason, meaning they expect him to recover from the ankle sprain that sidelined him at the end of 2007. A former big-play threat, Coles settled into a role as a possession receiver four years ago. He and Chad Pennington have great timing on hitches and in routes, and Coles gets a clean release and sets up defenders well. He's also 30 years old, small, and coming off an injury. Coles has job security because there's no starting-caliber receiver on the Jets bench to challenge him (Brad Smith is strictly a slot guy), but the Jets should start thinking about a better option in 2009.

Marques Colston

Height: 6-4.5 Weight: 212 College: Hofstra   Draft: 2006/7 (252) Born: 5-Jun-1983 Age: 25 Risk: Green

Year	Team	G	Rec	Pass	Yds	C%	Yd/C	TD	YAC	Rk	DVOA	Rk	DYAR	Rk	YAR	Short	Mid	Deep	Bomb
2006	NO	14	70	115	1038	61%	14.8	8	5.2	8	20.5%	11	306	6	251	33%	44%	17%	6%
2007	NO	16	98	144	1202	68%	12.3	11	4.1	30	16.8%	14	351	5	341	43%	43%	10%	4%
2008	NO		94	154	1208	61%	12.9	11			16.5%								

Colston's got your "fluke" designation right here, pal. His remarkable rookie season, in which he was drafted three picks before Mr. Irrelevant and wound up seventh in the NFL in receiving DYAR, seemed impossible to follow. In his second season, he topped his previous marks in catches, yards, and touchdowns. His 168 receptions in his first two seasons is the highest total in NFL history, and there's no doubt that he's Drew Brees's primary target and one of the league's elite receivers. Colston, guard Jahri Evans, and undrafted running back Pierre Thomas are three examples of the excellence displayed by the Saints' front office when it comes to targeting talent in the nether regions of the collegiate personnel pile.

Terrance Copper

Height: 5-10 Weight: 204 College: East Carolina   Draft: 2004/FA Born: 12-Mar-1982 Age: 26 Risk: Red

Year	Team	G	Rec	Pass	Yds	C%	Yd/C	TD	YAC	Rk	DVOA	Rk	DYAR	Rk	YAR	Short	Mid	Deep	Bomb
2005	DAL	16	1	4	5	25%	5.0	0	5.0	—	-61.4%	—	-15	—	-14	67%	0%	33%	0%
2006	NO	15	23	42	385	55%	16.7	3	4.3	—	9.4%	—	75	—	50	21%	47%	21%	11%
2007	NO	15	15	21	126	71%	8.4	2	3.9	—	4.2%	—	27	—	26	50%	35%	15%	0%
2008	NO		16	24	184	67%	11.8	1			-10.5%								

The Saints wanted to retain all their receivers for the 2008 season, which is why Devery Henderson and David Patten got shiny new contracts. Copper is often overlooked, but he was good enough on special teams to merit a two-year, $2.25 million deal.

Jerricho Cotchery

Height: 6-0 Weight: 199 College: North Carolina State   Draft: 2004/4 (108) Born: 16-Jun-1982 Age: 26 Risk: Red

Year	Team	G	Rec	Pass	Yds	C%	Yd/C	TD	YAC	Rk	DVOA	Rk	DYAR	Rk	YAR	Short	Mid	Deep	Bomb
2005	NYJ	16	19	31	251	61%	13.2	0	3.2	—	10.5%	—	54	—	59	34%	45%	10%	10%
2006	NYJ	16	82	125	961	66%	11.7	6	4.3	25	8.1%	28	210	16	197	40%	42%	17%	1%
2007	NYJ	15	82	127	1130	65%	13.8	2	4.9	16	11.6%	21	240	13	221	38%	39%	15%	8%
2008	NYJ		73	120	931	61%	12.8	3			0.6%								

When we compare current players to legends of the past, we often talk about "context." You can't compare Paul Warfield to Marvin Harrison without understanding context: Warfield played in an era when some teams threw about 15 passes per game and cornerbacks were allowed to bring billy clubs onto the field for bump 'n' run coverage. When analyzing Cotchery, you must also account for context. The Jets had no offensive line and no running game last year. Their quarterbacks were either inexperienced or soggy-armed. Cotchery still caught 82 passes with fine peripherals. Cotchery is one of the best receivers in the league at route running and exploiting zone coverage. He has great hands and a no-nonsense attitude. On a better team, he would have scored 10 touchdowns and averaged 16 yards per catch. He's a true number-one receiver whose numbers are held back by his supporting cast. If the Jets offense improves this year, Cotchery's production will grow as well.

Patrick Crayton

Height: 6-1 Weight: 205 College: Northwest Oklahoma State Draft: 2004/7 (216) Born: 7-Apr-1979 Age: 29 Risk: Red

Year	Team	G	Rec	Pass	Yds	C%	Yd/C	TD	YAC	Rk	DVOA	Rk	DYAR	Rk	YAR	Short	Mid	Deep	Bomb
2005	DAL	11	22	35	341	63%	15.5	2	7.6	—	15.1%	—	71	—	75	29%	57%	11%	4%
2006	DAL	16	36	48	516	75%	14.3	4	5.8	—	37.1%	—	186	—	191	31%	46%	18%	5%
2007	DAL	15	50	81	697	62%	13.9	7	5.7	5	19.6%	12	205	21	186	29%	48%	11%	13%
2008	DAL		48	81	753	59%	15.7	2			6.4%								

Crayton got the chance to start in 2007 after the injury to Terry Glenn. He wasn't as good as Glenn was in 2006, but he was no slouch. Crayton has your standard small white slot guy skill set—deceptively fast, good at finding the hole in zone, better in the slot than on the line of scrimmage—but because he's black and talks a lot of trash, he doesn't get that sort of publicity. As the third option in the passing game behind T. O. and Jason Witten, Crayton's a great value with his new four-year, $14 million deal. Glenn returned from multiple knee injuries for the playoffs, but Crayton has done nothing to deserve losing his job; considering Glenn's injury risk, he likely won't lose it for long if he does.

Josh Cribbs

Height: 6-1 Weight: 192 College: Kent State Draft: 2005/FA Born: 9-Jun-1983 Age: 25 Risk: Red

Year	Team	G	Rec	Pass	Yds	C%	Yd/C	TD	YAC	Rk	DVOA	Rk	DYAR	Rk	YAR	Short	Mid	Deep	Bomb
2005	CLE	14	1	1	7	100%	7.0	0	5.0	—	31.6%	—	4	—	4	—	—	—	—
2006	CLE	16	10	15	91	67%	9.1	0	4.9	—	-23.2%	—	-12	—	-29	36%	57%	7%	0%
2007	CLE	16	3	6	37	67%	12.3	0	9.5	—	-32.6%	—	-10	—	-7	67%	17%	17%	0%
2008	CLE		10	16	117	63%	11.7	2			-14.5%								

Usually coaches are afraid to risk starting players by putting them on special teams, but Cribbs's situation is just the reverse; he's simply more valuable knocking out 30 yards a kickoff than he is as a fourth wide receiver. Cribbs was a quarterback in college and the team could put together a few slash packages for him to run, but don't expect a lot of offensive snaps.

Ronald Curry

Height: 6-2 Weight: 220 College: North Carolina Draft: 2002/FA Born: 28-May-1979 Age: 29 Risk: Red

Year	Team	G	Rec	Pass	Yds	C%	Yd/C	TD	YAC	Rk	DVOA	Rk	DYAR	Rk	YAR	Short	Mid	Deep	Bomb
2005	OAK	2	2	2	12	100%	6.0	0	0.0	—	46.9%	—	8	—	5	50%	50%	0%	0%
2006	OAK	16	62	89	727	70%	11.7	1	3.1	53	7.4%	30	137	36	157	32%	54%	10%	4%
2007	OAK	16	55	97	717	57%	13.0	4	4.0	31	1.0%	48	106	49	102	39%	34%	14%	13%
2008	OAK		43	79	491	54%	11.3	2			-14.4%								

Curry was one of the few incumbents to survive the revamping of the Raiders' receiving corps. He also has the distinction of being the highest-rated Raiders offensive player in DVOA when the team finished 2-14 in 2006. With the offense on the rise last year, the team expected more from Curry, but it's difficult to find continuity when a receiver never knows who's going to be the quarterback. With Jerry Porter now gone, Curry could move into the primary role, but it's more unlikely he gets upstaged by newcomers Javon Walker and Drew Carter.

Kevin Curtis

Height: 5-11 Weight: 186 College: Utah State   Draft: 2003/3 (74) Born: 17-Jul-1978 Age: 30 Risk: Green

Year	Team	G	Rec	Pass	Yds	C%	Yd/C	TD	YAC	Rk	DVOA	Rk	DYAR	Rk	YAR	Short	Mid	Deep	Bomb
2005	STL	16	60	97	801	62%	13.4	6	4.6	22	-0.6%	43	92	38	115	33%	30%	21%	16%
2006	STL	16	40	57	479	70%	12.0	4	2.9	59	19.4%	13	144	33	160	53%	21%	17%	9%
2007	PHI	16	77	135	1110	57%	14.4	6	4.6	22	5.1%	37	195	22	186	28%	36%	22%	13%
2008	PHI		65	107	892	61%	13.7	7			5.1%								

The consolation prize when Philadelphia missed out on Wes Welker, Curtis stepped right in and became the Eagles' best wide receiver. His yards per catch were actually higher than Reggie Brown's, a bet you never would have been able to get us to take last season. His catch rate decreased as he ran deeper routes, but should rebound a bit this year, even if he continues to average 14+ yards per catch. Curtis is a very good number two stretched as a number one, which is a problem, because Reggie Brown was a good number three last year stretched as a number two. This is business as usual in Philadelphia.

Devard Darling

Height: 6-1 Weight: 213 College: Washington State   Draft: 2004/3 (82) Born: 16-Apr-1982 Age: 26 Risk: Red

Year	Team	G	Rec	Pass	Yds	C%	Yd/C	TD	YAC	Rk	DVOA	Rk	DYAR	Rk	YAR	Short	Mid	Deep	Bomb
2007	BAL	16	18	39	326	46%	18.1	3	4.4	—	4.3%	—	53	—	59	19%	32%	32%	16%
2008	KC		53	100	622	53%	11.6	2			-11.3%								

Darling moved off of special teams into a supporting role in Baltimore last year, but left after the season for a chance to start in Kansas City. Darling can get down the field and has decent hands, but he's barely played since college. He'll compete with practice standout Jeff Webb for the starting job across from Dwayne Bowe.

Andre' Davis

Height: 6-1 Weight: 195 College: Virginia Tech   Draft: 2002/2 (47) Born: 12-Jun-1979 Age: 29 Risk: Red

Year	Team	G	Rec	Pass	Yds	C%	Yd/C	TD	YAC	Rk	DVOA	Rk	DYAR	Rk	YAR	Short	Mid	Deep	Bomb
2005	NE	9	9	24	190	38%	21.1	1	6.6	—	-4.6%	—	15	—	23	12%	24%	6%	59%
2006	BUF	16	2	7	13	29%	6.5	0	5.0	—	-90.0%	—	-37	—	-31	40%	20%	20%	20%
2007	HOU	14	33	63	583	52%	17.7	3	3.1	60	2.5%	42	75	58	80	25%	43%	17%	15%
2008	HOU		35	64	564	54%	16.1	3			-0.3%								

Davis has never put it all together as a receiver, but he's more than earned his spot on the roster with his kick-return exploits. He was the league's second-most valuable kick returner last season, trailing Cleveland's Joshua Cribbs (not counting the value Devin Hester creates by forcing squib kicks). He'll compete with Jacoby Jones for the slot position and serve as a deep threat. A decent route-runner, he doesn't always pursue the ball with optimum effort, and tends to get it jarred loose on big collisions.

Chris Davis

Height: 5-10 Weight: 182 College: Florida State   Draft: 2007/4 (128) Born: 23-Jan-1984 Age: 24 Risk: Red

Year	Team	G	Rec	Pass	Yds	C%	Yd/C	TD	YAC	Rk	DVOA	Rk	DYAR	Rk	YAR	Short	Mid	Deep	Bomb
2007	TEN	12	5	9	38	56%	7.6	0	5.0	—	-84.0%	—	-49	—	-45	63%	38%	0%	0%
2008	TEN		26	52	344	50%	13.2	2			-13.0%								

A fourth-round pick out of Florida State in 2007, Davis caught a few passes and handled the Titans' punt-return duties, reminding Titans fans how badly they missed Pac-Man Jones on special teams. He should play a larger role in the regular offense this season.

Craig "Buster" Davis

Height: 6-1 Weight: 203 College: LSU   Draft: 2007/1 (30) Born: 5-Oct-1985 Age: 23 Risk: Red

Year	Team	G	Rec	Pass	Yds	C%	Yd/C	TD	YAC	Rk	DVOA	Rk	DYAR	Rk	YAR	Short	Mid	Deep	Bomb
2007	SD	14	20	34	188	59%	9.4	1	3.7	—	-0.3%	—	35	—	32	44%	41%	13%	3%
2008	SD		18	31	229	58%	12.7	1			-1.0%								

Davis contributed very little as a rookie, but that's common with rookie wideouts. He got the chance to start early but produced little and then suffered through nagging ankle and heel injuries which led to the acquisition of Chris

Chambers. Now, he is battling for playing time with Eric Parker (if he's healthy) and Legedu Naanee. If Davis does not work out, he will be a prime example of one of the great challenges of evaluating college talent. Davis was the third part of the LSU passing game taken in the first round of the 2007 draft. His job was obviously made easier by playing with JaMarcus Russell and across from Dwayne Bowe. Even LSU's number-three receiver, Early Doucet, was drafted in the third round this season. In any case, Davis has the skill-set to develop as a solid possession receiver over the next several seasons and a nice compliment to the more explosive Vincent Jackson.

Rashied Davis Height: 5-9 Weight: 180 College: San Jose State   Draft: 2005/FA   Born: 24-Jul-1979   Age: 29   Risk: Red

Year	Team	G	Rec	Pass	Yds	C%	Yd/C	TD	YAC	Rk	DVOA	Rk	DYAR	Rk	YAR	Short	Mid	Deep	Bomb
2006	CHI	16	22	56	303	39%	13.8	2	2.9	60	-41.8%	83	-122	82	-52	30%	39%	20%	11%
2007	CHI	16	17	31	165	55%	9.7	0	3.3	—	-24.1%	—	-26	—	-31	57%	20%	20%	3%
2008	CHI		21	34	295	62%	14.3	1			-19.5%								

Also known as "the kick returner on the Bears who is not Devin Hester," Davis went undrafted after playing at San Jose State, then spent 4 seasons with the San Jose SaberCats of the Arena Football League. The Bears originally signed him as a cornerback, then switched him to wide receiver, where he has been horrible for 2 seasons. So, faced with a 29-year-old player who had contributed nothing as a wide receiver and whose skills as a kick returner were terribly redundant, what did the Bears do? If you guessed "signed him to a three-year extension worth up to $3.9 million," you win! To be fair, Davis contributes on kick coverage teams as well, and there was word that Kansas City and other teams were bidding for his services. Also, it's doubtful that Davis will see all of that money. The first escalator clause in his contract will kick in if he catches 45 passes, which is six more than he has caught in the first 29 years of his life.

Early Doucet Height: 6-0 Weight: 212 College: LSU   Draft: 2008/3 (81)   Born: 28-Oct-1985   Age: 23   Risk: Red

Year	Team	G	Rec	Pass	Yds	C%	Yd/C	TD	YAC	Rk	DVOA	Rk	DYAR	Rk	YAR	Short	Mid	Deep	Bomb
2008	ARI		33	59	392	56%	12.0	3			-12.1%								

Draft analysts had Doucet going earlier than the third round. He was stuck behind Craig Davis and Dwayne Bowe for most of his career at LSU, then averaged just 9.2 yards per catch on 54 receptions when he finally earned a starting job. Doucet is known as a tough, competitive player who will work the middle and isn't shy about blocking. But he lacks long speed, has short arms, and battled groin injuries in college. He is similar to Anquan Boldin in some ways (good blocker, quicker-than-fast, slipped in the draft). The Cardinals would be happy with a second lightning strike.

Harry Douglas Height: 5-11 Weight: 176 College: Louisville   Draft: 2008/3 (84)   Born: 16-Sep-1984   Age: 24   Risk: Red

Year	Team	G	Rec	Pass	Yds	C%	Yd/C	TD	YAC	Rk	DVOA	Rk	DYAR	Rk	YAR	Short	Mid	Deep	Bomb
2008	ATL		16	29	159	55%	10.1	1			-38.6%								

Douglas is a waterbug receiver from Louisville (yes, he played for Bobby Petrino, but we've run out of jokes) who caught our attention in the media room of the 2008 Scouting Combine when he took an unplugged NFL Network microphone and crashed the press conference of Brian Brohm, his longtime quarterback. When Douglas asked Brohm to talk about his receivers, Brohm replied that he liked them all, but that he "wasn't sure about number 85." . . . Brohm may have been joking, but there are those who weren't sure about Douglas for real after average performances at the Senior Bowl and the Combine. When evaluating a five-foot-eleven, 176-pound pass-catcher, scouts want to see better than the 4.51 40 he ran at the Combine and his Pro Day. Douglas's ability to get behind defenders and break off big gains belies his timed speed, and he's got a great work ethic. He'll get time in the slot as a part of the crowded Falcons receiver corps behind Roddy White.

Donald Driver Height: 6-0 Weight: 188 College: Alcorn State   Draft: 1999/7 (213)   Born: 2-Feb-1975   Age: 33   Risk: Yellow

Year	Team	G	Rec	Pass	Yds	C%	Yd/C	TD	YAC	Rk	DVOA	Rk	DYAR	Rk	YAR	Short	Mid	Deep	Bomb
2005	GB	16	86	146	1221	59%	14.2	5	4.0	33	16.7%	12	351	4	319	27%	41%	23%	10%
2006	GB	16	92	172	1295	53%	14.1	8	5.6	3	-0.2%	51	168	25	109	33%	36%	19%	12%
2007	GB	15	82	122	1048	67%	12.8	2	4.8	17	10.2%	25	224	18	222	40%	44%	8%	8%
2008	GB		73	124	1033	59%	14.3	8			14.9%								

Driver was helped by the emergence of Jennings and James Jones. His raw numbers were off, but the Packers will trade ten receptions and 200 yards for 50 passes that were distributed to other receivers. Driver is 33 and coming off a year full of aches and pains, but his replacements are already on the roster, and he's the kind of player who can slide into a slot role and ring up a few more 50-catch seasons. His low touchdown total last year was a fluke.

Tim Dwight

Height: 5-9 Weight: 180 College: Iowa State Draft: 1998/4 (114) Born: 13-Jul-1975 Age: 33 Risk: Red

Year	Team	G	Rec	Pass	Yds	C%	Yd/C	TD	YAC	Rk	DVOA	Rk	DYAR	Rk	YAR	Short	Mid	Deep	Bomb
2005	NE	16	19	34	332	56%	17.5	3	6.6	—	19.7%	—	85	—	81	31%	31%	14%	24%
2006	NYJ	9	16	19	112	84%	7.0	0	3.6	—	-2.4%	—	16	—	10	61%	39%	0%	0%
2007	OAK	6	6	15	98	40%	16.3	2	1.2	—	-6.1%	—	7	—	10	7%	43%	21%	29%

When the Raiders punt return game was faltering, they hired Dwight, but he didn't provide any flash. Dwight still has sprinter's speed but little else. This might be the end for him.

Braylon Edwards

Height: 6-3 Weight: 211 College: Michigan Draft: 2005/1 (3) Born: 21-Feb-1983 Age: 25 Risk: Red

Year	Team	G	Rec	Pass	Yds	C%	Yd/C	TD	YAC	Rk	DVOA	Rk	DYAR	Rk	YAR	Short	Mid	Deep	Bomb
2005	CLE	10	32	59	512	54%	16.0	3	5.8	10	3.2%	39	71	47	79	16%	53%	15%	16%
2006	CLE	16	61	125	884	49%	14.5	6	5.5	5	-10.5%	65	20	63	13	25%	45%	17%	13%
2007	CLE	16	80	153	1289	52%	16.1	16	4.0	32	3.3%	40	189	23	212	31%	32%	30%	7%
2008	CLE		73	148	1087	49%	15.0	12			6.1%								

For his first two seasons, Edwards was so immature and difficult to handle that the Browns considered trading him before the 2007 draft. Instead they hired Wes Chandler to coach the receivers and found a quarterback who could get Edwards the ball, and the result was a breakout season. Edwards is a matchup nightmare for defensive backs because he has the speed to beat them deep and the size to overwhelm them in the short and medium passing game. Edwards's season looks a bit less dominant through the prism of our advanced metrics than it does when you just look at his raw totals, primarily because he had the lowest catch rate of any receiver in the top 20 in DYAR. Derek Anderson's inconsistency is partly to blame, but Edwards still has room to grow and get better.

Bobby Engram

Height: 5-10 Weight: 188 College: Penn State Draft: 1996/2 (52) Born: 7-Jan-1973 Age: 35 Risk: Yellow

Year	Team	G	Rec	Pass	Yds	C%	Yd/C	TD	YAC	Rk	DVOA	Rk	DYAR	Rk	YAR	Short	Mid	Deep	Bomb
2005	SEA	13	67	97	778	69%	11.6	3	4.0	31	3.9%	35	128	30	157	36%	44%	13%	7%
2006	SEA	7	24	36	290	67%	12.1	1	2.8	—	12.1%	—	65	—	76	29%	46%	21%	4%
2007	SEA	16	94	134	1147	70%	12.2	6	3.9	37	12.9%	19	270	10	293	34%	45%	16%	4%
2008	SEA		85	125	1043	68%	12.3	9			22.9%								

In May, the normally mild-mannered, unassuming Engram skipped Seahawks minicamp due to frustrations over his contract. Engram is due $1.7 million in 2008, roughly half of what fellow underpeforming wide receivers Nate Burleson ($3.25 million) and Deion Branch ($4.2 million including roster bonus) will make this year, so you can see why he might be frustrated. Then again, Joey Galloway is scheduled to make $1.8 million this year and he's still pretty good, plus the Seahawks surely have learned from Shaun Alexander that it you shouldn't pay for past performance. Engram may miss a chunk of training camp, but Hasselbeck has repeatedly said he can throw to him "with his eyes closed" so it shouldn't affect his numbers.

We used to call Engram "The First Down Machine" because of his ability to move the chains. He was targeted a team-high 34 times on third down last year, but his third-down DVOA (0.1%) wasn't up to his usual high standards. Luckily, he posted a 36.4% DVOA on 59 first down attempts. Maybe he's going from a third-down threat to a first-down threat late in his career. At age 53, he'll excel on second downs.

Lee Evans

Height: 5-10 Weight: 197 College: Wisconsin   Draft: 2004/1 (13)   Born: 11-Mar-1981   Age: 27   Risk: Red

Year	Team	G	Rec	Pass	Yds	C%	Yd/C	TD	YAC	Rk	DVOA	Rk	DYAR	Rk	YAR	Short	Mid	Deep	Bomb
2005	BUF	16	48	92	743	53%	15.5	7	5.8	9	-4.1%	52	61	53	90	30%	41%	8%	20%
2006	BUF	16	82	137	1292	60%	15.8	8	4.6	18	16.2%	17	301	7	308	21%	45%	16%	18%
2007	BUF	16	55	113	849	49%	15.4	5	3.5	48	-10.3%	72	21	69	26	25%	41%	17%	17%
2008	BUF		72	130	1054	55%	14.7	8			11.5%								

Deep-threat receivers need big-armed quarterbacks, so it makes sense that Evans would be more productive when J. P. Losman, not Trent Edwards, was under center. Evans did have some of his best games when Losman was starting, including a nine-catch, 165-yard effort against the Bengals. At the same time, he caught just five passes for 29 yards in his first three games, all of them Losman starts, but perked up with six catches for 72 yards when Edwards took over. Evans hauled in 52- and 74-yard passes from Edwards, so he'll still have some opportunities to go long if Edwards starts. He doesn't need a cannon-armed quarterback; he needs a consistent one. Evans and the Bills were taking baby steps toward a contract extension at press time. The Bills may wait until the season starts to see if Evans adjusts to the new offense before opening their nearly-empty coffers.

Robert Ferguson

Height: 6-1 Weight: 209 College: Texas A&M   Draft: 2001/2 (41)   Born: 17-Dec-1979   Age: 28   Risk: Red

Year	Team	G	Rec	Pass	Yds	C%	Yd/C	TD	YAC	Rk	DVOA	Rk	DYAR	Rk	YAR	Short	Mid	Deep	Bomb
2005	GB	11	27	57	366	47%	13.6	3	2.0	86	-6.4%	60	29	64	29	20%	41%	19%	20%
2006	GB	4	5	13	31	38%	6.2	1	-0.2	—	-29.9%	—	-18	—	-40	17%	58%	0%	25%
2007	MIN	15	32	62	391	52%	12.2	1	3.8	38	-17.9%	75	-26	75	-42	25%	44%	12%	19%
2008	MIN		22	36	261	62%	11.6	1			-2.9%								

Ferguson hasn't been above average in DVOA since 2003, but the Vikings re-signed him over the offseason. He seems a lock to make the team; his other competitors for the fifth receiver spot are undrafted rookie Jaymar Johnson and Martin Nance, who has played one game in his two-year career. Ferguson carries virtually no downfield menace at this point in his career; he caught only two of 14 passes thrown at least 20 yards downfield last season. Conversely, he caught 24 of 35 passes (69 percent) within 10 yards of the line of scrimmage, so he can still be a useful player, picking up third-and-shorts here and there like a poor man's Ike Hilliard.

Larry Fitzgerald

Height: 6-2 Weight: 223 College: Pittsburgh   Draft: 2004/1 (3)   Born: 31-Aug-1983   Age: 25   Risk: Green

Year	Team	G	Rec	Pass	Yds	C%	Yd/C	TD	YAC	Rk	DVOA	Rk	DYAR	Rk	YAR	Short	Mid	Deep	Bomb
2005	ARI	16	103	165	1409	62%	13.7	10	3.4	43	10.4%	22	296	9	322	32%	31%	24%	13%
2006	ARI	13	69	111	946	62%	13.7	6	2.6	67	22.0%	10	292	8	270	29%	38%	26%	7%
2007	ARI	15	100	167	1409	60%	14.1	10	2.7	72	9.1%	28	291	8	301	23%	48%	18%	11%
2008	ARI		93	161	1193	58%	12.8	10			5.5%								

Fitzgerald's looming contract negotiations impacted the Cardinals' ability to sign other free agents, but not everybody is as savvy with the specter of uncapped years as Jerry Jones. When Arizona signed Fitzgerald to a four-year, $40-million contract in mid-March, they retained one of the game's top receivers. Physical enough to frustrate cornerbacks who dare to jam him at the line, well-versed enough with routes to find openings in any coverage, and talented enough to contort himself into nearly impossible catch situations, he's a key part of the team's desire to ascend to the NFL's elite. What he'll need to do that is a quarterback situation that isn't so Deadspin-accessible.

Malcom Floyd

Height: 6-5 Weight: 225 College: Wyoming   Draft: 2004/FA   Born: 8-Sep-1981   Age: 27   Risk: Red

Year	Team	G	Rec	Pass	Yds	C%	Yd/C	TD	YAC	Rk	DVOA	Rk	DYAR	Rk	YAR	Short	Mid	Deep	Bomb
2006	SD	12	15	32	210	47%	14.0	3	3.1	—	-6.5%	—	15	—	0	27%	40%	10%	23%
2007	SD	6	7	13	97	54%	13.9	0	1.3	—	-3.8%	—	9	—	10	31%	15%	46%	8%
2008	SD		15	23	162	65%	11.1	2			6.3%								

Tall guys who can run are endlessly attractive to NFL teams, but at a certain point they have to develop fundamentals and show a willingness to block. Floyd kept sliding farther and farther down the depth chart as these deficiencies overcame the raw talent. The Chargers retained their rights to Floyd, so they are still not giving up on him, but this year is likely his last chance with San Diego.

Mike Furrey

Height: 6-0   Weight: 185   College: Northern Iowa   Draft: 2003/FA   Born: 12-May-1977   Age: 31   Risk: Green

Year	Team	G	Rec	Pass	Yds	C%	Yd/C	TD	YAC	Rk	DVOA	Rk	DYAR	Rk	YAR	Short	Mid	Deep	Bomb
2006	DET	16	98	146	1086	67%	11.1	6	3.1	54	4.2%	39	181	23	208	36%	43%	19%	2%
2007	DET	16	61	91	664	67%	10.9	1	3.0	62	6.5%	33	136	33	131	45%	29%	22%	3%
2008	DET		13	20	135	65%	10.7	1			-12.8%								

Furrey's 2006 numbers were an aberration. His 2007 stat line better represents what he's capable of when he's not targeted 140 times in a season. He's now 31, but he should have a long Derrick Mason–type late career as a slot receiver or a starter who runs nothing but shallow option routes. His numbers will drop if the Lions offense is as run-oriented as new coordinator Jim Colletto says it will be, but Furrey will contribute.

Jabar Gaffney

Height: 6-1   Weight: 193   College: Florida   Draft: 2002/2 (33)   Born: 1-Dec-1980   Age: 28   Risk: Red

Year	Team	G	Rec	Pass	Yds	C%	Yd/C	TD	YAC	Rk	DVOA	Rk	DYAR	Rk	YAR	Short	Mid	Deep	Bomb
2005	HOU	16	55	90	492	61%	8.9	2	2.1	85	-16.2%	77	-25	79	-21	50%	37%	9%	4%
2006	NE	10	11	20	142	55%	12.9	1	2.2	—	-25.5%	—	-21	—	24	41%	18%	18%	24%
2007	NE	16	36	50	449	72%	12.5	5	3.3	53	22.5%	9	144	31	135	51%	32%	9%	9%
2008	NE		37	59	483	63%	13.0	3			12.9%								

The operating thought was that Gaffney would be the odd man out following the Patriots' buying in bulk at wide receiver last offseason, but Gaffney beat out Reche Caldwell for a roster spot and excelled as the team's fourth wideout, putting up a DVOA comparable to Wes Welker's while eventually moving past Donte' Stallworth on the depth chart. Gaffney re-upped for one year and $2 million in the offseason; that means you could get half a team of him for what it would take to get one Javon Walker.

Justin Gage

Height: 6-4   Weight: 208   College: Missouri   Draft: 2003/5 (143)   Born: 25-Jan-1981   Age: 27   Risk: Red

Year	Team	G	Rec	Pass	Yds	C%	Yd/C	TD	YAC	Rk	DVOA	Rk	DYAR	Rk	YAR	Short	Mid	Deep	Bomb
2005	CHI	15	31	55	346	56%	11.2	2	2.5	82	-2.7%	46	45	58	48	30%	41%	23%	7%
2006	CHI	8	4	8	68	50%	17.0	0	4.0	—	-42.5%	—	-19	—	-21	25%	38%	13%	25%
2007	TEN	16	55	85	750	65%	13.6	2	4.3	26	14.5%	18	189	24	200	26%	41%	16%	17%
2008	TEN		67	101	778	66%	11.6	5			8.6%								

Gage is an excellent athlete who played college basketball and has the height and leaping ability that scouts like to see. He's not good enough to be a number-one receiver on most teams, but that's what he will likely be this season after re-signing with the receiver-starved Titans for four years and $14 million.

Joey Galloway

Height: 5-11   Weight: 197   College: Ohio State   Draft: 1995/1 (8)   Born: 20-Nov-1971   Age: 37   Risk: Red

Year	Team	G	Rec	Pass	Yds	C%	Yd/C	TD	YAC	Rk	DVOA	Rk	DYAR	Rk	YAR	Short	Mid	Deep	Bomb
2005	TB	16	83	152	1287	55%	15.5	10	4.7	19	7.9%	25	243	14	235	28%	39%	20%	13%
2006	TB	16	62	141	1057	44%	17.0	7	4.7	16	1.7%	46	161	29	31	20%	37%	25%	17%
2007	TB	15	57	98	1014	58%	17.8	6	6.6	3	16.4%	16	230	16	250	27%	39%	18%	16%
2008	TB		70	130	1143	54%	16.3	9			18.6%								

The altitude is rather thin for wide receivers having great seasons past the age of 33. Seventeen receivers have gained over 1,000 yards during a year in which they celebrated their 34th birthday; Jerry Rice was the most productive. The pickins' are even slimmer at age 35—only nine receivers have amassed over 1,000 yards at that milestone. At 36? Fuhgeddaboutit. Three receivers cracked a grand at that age, and no 37-year-old has ever accomplished it. Joey Galloway is the only receiver in NFL history to gain over 1,000 yards at ages 34, 35, and 36. He has done this despite few complementary targets and some very iffy quarterback situations in Tampa Bay, not to mention the up-and-down tenures with the Seahawks and Cowboys earlier in his career and a five-year gap between 1,000-yard seasons from 1999 through 2004. When Rice broke 1,000 at the ages of 39 and 40 with the Raiders, becoming the greatest old receiver of all time as well as the GOAT overall, it was hardly a surprise. That Galloway has accomplished this, and appears to be on track to do it again at age 37 if he stays healthy, makes his career a true anomaly. How many NFL players are more defined by what they accomplish half a decade past average retirement age than in their supposed prime? George Blanda leaps to mind first. Galloway isn't far behind him.

Bryan Gilmore   Height: 6-0   Weight: 200   College: Midwestern State   Draft: 2000/FA   Born: 21-Jul-1978   Age: 30   Risk: Red

Year	Team	G	Rec	Pass	Yds	C%	Yd/C	TD	YAC	Rk	DVOA	Rk	DYAR	Rk	YAR	Short	Mid	Deep	Bomb
2005	MIA	15	5	20	105	25%	21.0	1	5.0	—	-41.1%	—	-44	—	-40	18%	59%	6%	18%
2006	SF	16	8	31	150	26%	18.8	1	4.4	—	-62.0%	—	-121	—	-103	25%	50%	15%	10%
2007	SF	10	7	19	111	37%	15.9	0	3.0	—	-25.3%	—	-18	—	-12	19%	38%	19%	25%
2008	SF		9	18	135	50%	15.0	0			-18.4%								

Gilmore still has some speed, and he's tough enough to play special teams, but he never developed into a consistent receiver. He should be crowded out of a job this year, though his special teams value could allow him to keep a back-of-the-bench spot.

Ted Ginn   Height: 5-11   Weight: 178   College: Ohio State   Draft: 2007/1 (9)   Born: 12-Apr-1985   Age: 23   Risk: Red

Year	Team	G	Rec	Pass	Yds	C%	Yd/C	TD	YAC	Rk	DVOA	Rk	DYAR	Rk	YAR	Short	Mid	Deep	Bomb
2007	MIA	16	34	71	420	48%	12.4	2	5.1	13	-25.9%	79	-71	80	-67	40%	33%	11%	16%
2008	MIA		56	102	762	55%	13.6	6			-6.7%								

The outgoing coaching staff delivered a scathing indictment of Ginn's rookie season in that brief, awkward period when they weren't certain they were an outgoing coaching staff. Receivers coach Terry Robiskie questioned Ginn's ability to grow into a number-one receiver, citing his durability, shiftiness, and field smarts as shortcomings that might not drastically improve. Robiskie didn't say anything that a hundred draft experts didn't say in the weeks leading up to the 2007 draft: Ginn was a return man and a deep-threat receiver, not a go-to guy who can get open for a dozen passes per game. Randy Meuller is one of the few Americans who disagreed. The upside for Ginn is that he might grow into a Lee Evans role as the designated bomb threat on a weak team with an unstable quarterback situation. That's not a great return on a guy drafted before Anthony Gonzalez and James Jones.

Terry Glenn   Height: 5-11   Weight: 195   College: Ohio State   Draft: 1996/1 (7)   Born: 23-Jul-1974   Age: 34   Risk: Red

Year	Team	G	Rec	Pass	Yds	C%	Yd/C	TD	YAC	Rk	DVOA	Rk	DYAR	Rk	YAR	Short	Mid	Deep	Bomb
2005	DAL	16	62	118	1136	53%	18.3	7	3.0	62	13.8%	17	252	12	246	17%	38%	17%	28%
2006	DAL	16	70	111	1047	63%	15.0	6	3.8	40	15.0%	20	244	12	266	24%	41%	20%	15%
2007	DAL	1	0	1	0	0%	0.0	0	0.0	—	-77.4%	—	-5	—	-7	0%	100%	0%	0%
2008	DAL		35	65	572	54%	16.2	2			-0.8%								

Glenn missed the first 15 weeks of the season following two microfracture surgeries on an ailing knee, and had a dire playoff game against the Giants upon his return. Patrick Crayton filled in admirably for Glenn in the latter's absence, and there's no reason to think that the Cowboys would bump aside Crayton for a 34-year-old. Glenn's about to enter the itinerant veteran wideout stage of his career, one he can kick off to a lucrative start by staying healthy and putting up a decent season in the Cowboys offensive scheme. Beware, though; the end for Glenn could come very quickly.

Anthony Gonzalez   Height: 6-0   Weight: 193   College: Ohio State   Draft: 2007/1 (32)   Born: 18-Sep-1984   Age: 24   Risk: Yellow

Year	Team	G	Rec	Pass	Yds	C%	Yd/C	TD	YAC	Rk	DVOA	Rk	DYAR	Rk	YAR	Short	Mid	Deep	Bomb
2007	IND	13	37	51	576	73%	15.6	3	5.4	9	43.5%	1	239	14	237	30%	45%	13%	11%
2008	IND		65	99	1085	66%	16.6	10			28.5%								

The Colts drafted Gonzalez to replace Marvin Harrison, but it wasn't supposed to happen in 2007. Opportunity was thrust upon the rookie, however, and he made the most of it, leading all wide receivers in DVOA (minimum 50 passes). Gonzalez was especially productive in December, posting 16 catches for 264 yards and 3 touchdowns, on only 22 targets. He showed up in the playoff loss to San Diego too, catching 4 passes for 79 yards and a score. The former Ohio State star may mirror the career of teammate Reggie Wayne, who spent several years excelling in the shadow of a legend before supplanting that legend as the Colts' top receiver. Harrison's mysterious medical status and even more mysterious legal woes probably move Gonzalez's breakout forward a couple years—to right now.

D. J. Hackett

Height: 6-2   Weight: 199   College: Colorado   Draft: 2004/5 (157)   Born: 31-Jul-1981   Age: 27   Risk: Red

Year	Team	G	Rec	Pass	Yds	C%	Yd/C	TD	YAC	Rk	DVOA	Rk	DYAR	Rk	YAR	Short	Mid	Deep	Bomb
2005	SEA	13	28	43	400	65%	14.3	2	2.6	—	26.3%	—	140	—	153	43%	26%	11%	20%
2006	SEA	14	45	66	610	68%	13.6	4	4.2	27	17.4%	15	148	31	223	28%	56%	12%	4%
2007	SEA	6	32	47	384	68%	12.0	3	4.3	—	12.8%	—	99	—	100	40%	46%	15%	0%
2008	CAR		59	97	782	61%	13.3	4			7.4%								

We keep waiting for this guy to break out—just look at those catch rates!—but every year seems to end with Hackett sidelined with some fluke injury. If he could have managed to stay healthy last year, Hackett probably would have parlayed his performance into a Nate Clements-like mega deal. As it was, he had to settle for a two-year, $3 million "prove it" deal with the Panthers. If he can stay healthy, Hackett will finally provide the Panthers and Jake Delhomme with the long awaited threat opposite of Steve Smith. That's a mighty big if.

Derek Hagan

Height: 6-2   Weight: 202   College: Arizona State   Draft: 2006/3 (82)   Born: 21-Sep-1984   Age: 24   Risk: Red

Year	Team	G	Rec	Pass	Yds	C%	Yd/C	TD	YAC	Rk	DVOA	Rk	DYAR	Rk	YAR	Short	Mid	Deep	Bomb
2006	MIA	16	21	37	221	57%	10.5	1	2.4	—	-16.3%	—	-11	—	-1	9%	71%	11%	9%
2007	MIA	16	29	59	373	49%	12.9	2	2.3	79	-6.3%	62	29	67	28	19%	47%	22%	12%
2008	MIA		40	66	473	61%	11.9	3			-1.3%								

Outgoing Dolphins coach Terry Robiskie believed that Hagan's receiving skills would improve if he wore a ring. A wedding ring. "The biggest thing is for him to get married. Single guys don't have the focus of married guys. He's focusing on the rims of his car, on 'Am I Cingular or T-Mobile?' and other things that are so irrelevant. He's got too many focuses." Great advice, coach: there's nothing like a couple of kids running around, babbling about Pokemon, to improve a young man's focus. (Note: this very event occurred while writing this player comment.) Hagan caught eight passes against the Bills in Week 14, but for most of the year he was an indifferent third or fourth wideout on a team desperate for anyone, particularly a former third-round pick, to step up. There's a starting job gift-wrapped for Hagan if he can get his head out of his hubcaps this season. The third-year pro is lucky that Robiskie is now in Atlanta: the coach was planning to set him up with Liz Taylor.

Marques Hagans

Height: 5-10   Weight: 205   College: Virginia   Draft: 2006/5 (144)   Born: 29-Dec-1982   Age: 25   Risk: Red

Year	Team	G	Rec	Pass	Yds	C%	Yd/C	TD	YAC	Rk	DVOA	Rk	DYAR	Rk	YAR	Short	Mid	Deep	Bomb
2007	STL	4	8	15	101	53%	12.6	0	2.8	—	-8.2%	—	5	—	7	27%	53%	20%	0%
2008	STL		23	39	287	59%	12.3	1			-7.6%								

Hagans is a long shot to make the Rams after the team drafted Donnie Avery in the second round and Keenan Burton in the fourth. He finished minicamp dueling with Derek Stanley for the fifth receiver role. He does have two things going for him, however. The first is versatility; in 2007, Hagans served as the team's emergency quarterback. Given the nature of the Rams' line last year, it's somewhat remarkable he never spent time under center. Hagans dueled Matt Schaub for the quarterback position at Virginia (rest easy, Texans fans; Schaub won the duel by a wide margin), then took over at quarterback after Schaub graduated. That leads us to Hagans's second advantage: At Virginia, he formed a solid friendship with Chris Long, the defensive end the Rams selected with the second overall pick in the draft. "I know Marques (Hagans) real well," Long said at his introductory news conference. "I was very excited for the fact that we will be reunited here. He's one of the best teammates I've ever had." Now the Rams are not going to let the rookie pass rusher make roster decisions, but it can't hurt to have friends in high places. The projection is higher than you might expect because Hagans isn't going to make the roster if the Rams aren't going to use him.

Dante Hall

Height: 5-8 Weight: 187 College: Texas A&M   Draft: 2000/5 (153) Born: 1-Sep-1978 Age: 30 Risk: Red

Year	Team	G	Rec	Pass	Yds	C%	Yd/C	TD	YAC	Rk	DVOA	Rk	DYAR	Rk	YAR	Short	Mid	Deep	Bomb
2005	KC	16	34	51	436	67%	12.8	3	3.7	37	15.6%	13	112	33	108	45%	27%	11%	16%
2006	KC	15	26	40	204	65%	7.8	2	2.8	—	-5.8%	—	21	—	15	46%	30%	24%	0%
2007	STL	7	5	12	27	42%	5.4	0	3.6	—	-55.1%	—	-37	—	-38	42%	42%	8%	8%
2008	STL		15	22	178	68%	12.2	1			-4.5%								

Hall will be involved in an important race for the record books this year. Hall's next kick return for a touchdown will be his 13th, which will tie him with Brian Mitchell for the most in NFL history. There is a problem for Hall, however, and his name is Devin Hester. Hester has 11 kick return touchdowns in his two-year career (not counting his missed field-goal return in 2006) and seems destined to shatter all remaining records. Can Hall get two scores before Hester gets three and become, momentarily, the league's all time king? He has a better shot at the kickoff return touchdown title, where he has six, which is already tied with five other players for the most ever. Hall only needs one more to stand alone atop the mountain. He should pull that off, but then he'll look down and see a bevy of challengers looking to take his throne; there are seven active players under 30 years old with at least three kickoff returns for scores. Gentlemen, start your engines.

Roy Hall

Height: 6-3 Weight: 240 College: Ohio State   Draft: 2007/5 (169) Born: 8-Dec-1983 Age: 25 Risk: Red

Year	Team	G	Rec	Pass	Yds	C%	Yd/C	TD	YAC	Rk	DVOA	Rk	DYAR	Rk	YAR	Short	Mid	Deep	Bomb
2008	IND		16	23	186	70%	11.6	1			25.4%								

Hall missed a great deal of his 2007 season with a separated shoulder, but the Colts like his potential as a slot receiver. He starts the 2008 season fourth on a depth chart that's more fluid than it used to be.

James Hardy

Height: 6-6 Weight: 220 College: Indiana   Draft: 2008/2 (41) Born: 24-Dec-1985 Age: 22 Risk: Red

Year	Team	G	Rec	Pass	Yds	C%	Yd/C	TD	YAC	Rk	DVOA	Rk	DYAR	Rk	YAR	Short	Mid	Deep	Bomb
2008	BUF		16	34	258	47%	16.0	1			-14.2%								

The Bills ranked 22nd in offensive passing DVOA in 2007, and though rookie Trent Edwards proved to be a capable field general, there have been major concerns about the abilities of Buffalo's receivers to produce consistent results in the red zone. The Bills threw only 12 touchdown passes last year, tied for second-worst in the NFL behind only the Dolphins. Hardy should be able to alleviate that problem to a point—his six-foot-six frame and 36 receiving touchdowns (16 in 2007 alone) for Indiana indicate that he could be that prototypical tall target needed if this team is to take the next step in the AFC East. However, pulling a gun on your own father, as Hardy allegedly did in May, isn't exactly going to spread sunshine on your scouting report. Hardy's status was in the air at press time. The Bills could really use some better luck.

Marvin Harrison

Height: 6-0 Weight: 175 College: Syracuse   Draft: 1996/1 (19) Born: 25-Aug-1972 Age: 36 Risk: Red

Year	Team	G	Rec	Pass	Yds	C%	Yd/C	TD	YAC	Rk	DVOA	Rk	DYAR	Rk	YAR	Short	Mid	Deep	Bomb
2005	IND	15	82	132	1146	62%	14.0	12	3.0	61	11.2%	20	251	13	298	28%	40%	15%	17%
2006	IND	16	95	148	1366	64%	14.4	12	2.8	63	25.2%	7	442	3	468	25%	42%	18%	14%
2007	IND	5	20	32	247	63%	12.4	1	2.0	—	2.3%	—	40	—	36	28%	47%	6%	19%
2008	IND		52	80	741	65%	14.3	5			13.3%								

No one seems certain about the status of Harrison's knee, a bad wheel that cost him the bulk of the 2007 campaign. He played against the Chargers in the playoffs, but was clearly still hurting, catching just two passes for 27 yards. It's doubtful that Harrison will be 100 percent when training camp opens, but the Colts are hopeful he'll be ready to go for the season opener. Nobody is suggesting that Harrison should retire, but not a lot of 36-year-old wide receivers come off knee surgery and make major contributions. The Colts didn't seem to miss him much in 2007, at least after Anthony Gonzalez blossomed. That had to be reassuring to the team and their fans, but it was probably disconcerting for Harrison.

Devery Henderson

Height: 5-11 Weight: 191 College: LSU   Draft: 2004/2 (50)   Born: 26-Mar-1982   Age: 26   Risk: Red

Year	Team	G	Rec	Pass	Yds	C%	Yd/C	TD	YAC	Rk	DVOA	Rk	DYAR	Rk	YAR	Short	Mid	Deep	Bomb
2005	NO	14	22	50	343	44%	15.6	3	4.6	24	-9.0%	69	15	70	25	22%	41%	20%	17%
2006	NO	13	32	54	745	59%	23.3	5	4.9	13	36.4%	1	210	17	248	17%	37%	17%	28%
2007	NO	16	20	43	409	47%	20.5	3	3.8	—	9.7%	—	78	—	66	14%	36%	26%	24%
2008	NO		31	59	551	53%	17.5	2			-3.3%								

The idea was that Henderson had finally discarded his "track-star-disguised-as-receiver" suit and was ready to make a big dent as an integral part of the Saints' newly explosive offense. When he finished first in DVOA in 2006, it looked like a lock. But his follow-up season was marred by dropped passes—10 drops to 20 catches is about as bad a ratio as we can imagine for a player who still cashes checks with a team logo on them. Understandably, Drew Brees threw to him less and less as the season went on. Amazingly, New Orleans gave Henderson a do-over with a one-year, $2 million contract; they're clearly still banking on some of that 2006 magic. Contract aside, if Robert Meachem's healthy and Lance Moore continues to develop, Henderson could be the odd man out.

Chris Henry

Height: 6-4 Weight: 197 College: West Virginia   Draft: 2005/3 (83)   Born: 17-May-1983   Age: 25   Risk: Red

Year	Team	G	Rec	Pass	Yds	C%	Yd/C	TD	YAC	Rk	DVOA	Rk	DYAR	Rk	YAR	Short	Mid	Deep	Bomb
2005	CIN	14	31	50	422	62%	13.6	6	1.8	89	10.1%	23	86	40	72	28%	47%	9%	16%
2006	CIN	13	36	75	605	48%	16.8	9	4.0	34	22.2%	9	200	20	107	11%	54%	15%	20%
2007	CIN	8	21	39	343	55%	16.3	2	3.0	—	5.9%	—	56	—	65	24%	44%	15%	32%

Having finally exhausted Cincinnati's patience with his legal troubles, it's highly unlikely that Henry will catch on with another team—and it's rather probable that Roger Goodell would have words to say about the state of affairs if he did. As a result, this rather checkered career is probably over. It's hard not to wonder what might have been, even as late as this year. With Chad Johnson whining his way out of town, Henry would likely have started for the Bengals, playing deep threat to T. J. Houshmandzadeh's possession receiver. Would he have been a success? It's hard to say, of course, since he's always had two great receivers ahead of him, making it easy for Henry to get open against safeties and nickel defenders. As it is, we'll never know. A pity, though Steelers and Ravens fans irritated by Henry's penchant for big games against his divisional rivals probably won't mind.

Devin Hester

Height: 5-11 Weight: 185 College: Miami   Draft: 2006/2 (57)   Born: 4-Nov-1982   Age: 26   Risk: Red

Year	Team	G	Rec	Pass	Yds	C%	Yd/C	TD	YAC	Rk	DVOA	Rk	DYAR	Rk	YAR	Short	Mid	Deep	Bomb
2007	CHI	16	20	39	299	51%	15.0	2	6.4	—	-21.1%	—	-27	—	-27	36%	39%	6%	19%
2008	CHI		16	33	237	48%	14.5	2			-19.9%								

He's perhaps the greatest kick returner any of us has ever seen, he's an explosive (though erratic) wide receiver, and he's upset about his contract. Hester's rookie deal lasts for two more seasons and is slated to pay him less than $1 million in that time. The Bears approached Hester's agent Eugene Parker at the Combine about inking Hester to an extension, but negotiations are going to be tricky. First of all, Hester is not the only Bear upset with his contract; defensive stars Brian Urlacher and Tommie Harris have also been hunting for new deals. Second, the Bears are not interested in tearing up Hester's current deal. They're hoping that a hefty bonus and long-term stability will make up for the low salary he earns in 2009 and 2010. Finally, there is Hester himself: his skills are so unique, it's difficult to measure his worth in dollars and cents. What should Hester be paid compared to a Leon Washington or a Josh Cribbs, two of the other premier kick returners in the league? How do you put a dollar figure on Hester as a wide receiver, where he has a terribly low floor but a ridiculously high ceiling? One way or another, Hester will be in a Bears uniform this fall—they can't afford to let another receiver go—and three or four times, he will make an entire stadium stand in awe of what they have just witnessed.

Johnnie Lee Higgins

Height: 5-11 Weight: 186 College: UTEP   Draft: 2007/3 (99)   Born: 8-Sep-1983   Age: 25   Risk: Red

Year	Team	G	Rec	Pass	Yds	C%	Yd/C	TD	YAC	Rk	DVOA	Rk	DYAR	Rk	YAR	Short	Mid	Deep	Bomb
2007	OAK	16	6	8	47	75%	7.8	0	0.3	—	-21.3%	—	-4	—	-4	38%	38%	13%	13%
2008	OAK		16	28	184	57%	11.7	1			-10.9%								

Higgins will compete with Drew Carter for the role of deep threat. A raw speedster coming out of UTEP, Higgins didn't see much playing time last year. He could take a big leap his sophomore year, particularly if the Raiders are behind a lot and the big-armed JaMarcus Russell has to play catch-up.

Jason Hill

Height: 6-1 Weight: 204 College: Washington State   Draft: 2007/3 (76)   Born: 20-Feb-1985   Age: 23   Risk: Red

Year	Team	G	Rec	Pass	Yds	C%	Yd/C	TD	YAC	Rk	DVOA	Rk	DYAR	Rk	YAR	Short	Mid	Deep	Bomb
2007	SF	5	1	2	6	50%	6.0	0	0.0	—	-69.6%	—	-9	—	-8	50%	50%	0%	0%
2008	SF		25	50	324	50%	12.9	1			-15.2%								

Every time Jason Hill was ready to get on the field, he got hurt. But coaches and fans have high hopes for the 2006 third-round pick from Washington State. He was voted the hardest receiver to cover in a canvass of Pac-10 defensive backs two years ago. Hill will get every opportunity to challenge for the third-receiver role in training camp.

Ike Hilliard

Height: 5-11 Weight: 210 College: Florida   Draft: 1997/1 (7)   Born: 5-Apr-1976   Age: 32   Risk: Red

Year	Team	G	Rec	Pass	Yds	C%	Yd/C	TD	YAC	Rk	DVOA	Rk	DYAR	Rk	YAR	Short	Mid	Deep	Bomb
2005	TB	16	35	53	282	66%	8.1	1	2.8	68	-8.1%	66	20	68	23	63%	33%	5%	0%
2006	TB	16	34	55	339	62%	10.0	2	4.0	35	2.5%	42	64	57	-2	49%	44%	7%	0%
2007	TB	15	62	86	722	72%	11.6	1	5.0	14	5.8%	35	122	42	134	51%	37%	8%	4%
2008	TB		59	86	680	69%	11.5	3			4.0%								

Hilliard's career has been a long stretch of league-average seasons as the "wily possession receiver." He's never put up elite numbers, though his 2007 season was a bit of a renaissance. He had to fight through back and knee problems last year, and the Tampa Bay depth chart is filling up at the receiver position. Hilliard will get another go, but the Bucs have to start developing younger talent like Paris Warren and Dexter Jackson. This could limit his reps in 2008.

Santonio Holmes

Height: 5-11 Weight: 190 College: Ohio State   Draft: 2006/1 (25)   Born: 3-Mar-1984   Age: 24   Risk: Yellow

Year	Team	G	Rec	Pass	Yds	C%	Yd/C	TD	YAC	Rk	DVOA	Rk	DYAR	Rk	YAR	Short	Mid	Deep	Bomb
2006	PIT	16	49	86	824	57%	16.8	2	5.1	10	27.1%	5	279	9	210	21%	60%	11%	8%
2007	PIT	13	52	85	942	61%	18.1	8	4.9	15	26.2%	6	259	11	274	16%	42%	22%	19%
2008	PIT		73	135	1214	54%	16.7	11			25.9%								

It's unusual to write the phrase "made the best of limited opportunity" about a team's primary receiver. Holmes has replaced the gracefully aging Hines Ward in menace if not yet number of targets. But Pittsburgh throws the ball relatively infrequently and have enough deserving pass-catchers that Holmes doesn't see as many passes as he needs to establish himself as a truly top-tier deep threat. He'll see more of the ball as Hines Ward fades and he and Roethlisberger enter their prime together as perhaps the most promising young quarterback/receiver tandem in the league. (That's assuming, of course, that both can stay healthy, which may be something of a challenge for Roethlisberger, given the state of Pittsburgh's offensive line.) Given the conservative offensive philosophy prevailing in the Steel City, Holmes is unlikely to make as big a splash as the top wideouts in New England or Indianapolis, but he's well on his way to replacing Ward as the AFC's least-hyped Pro Bowl receiver.

Glenn Holt

Height: 6-1 Weight: 195 College: Kentucky   Draft: 2006/FA   Born: 31-Jul-1984   Age: 24   Risk: Red

Year	Team	G	Rec	Pass	Yds	C%	Yd/C	TD	YAC	Rk	DVOA	Rk	DYAR	Rk	YAR	Short	Mid	Deep	Bomb
2006	CIN	11	1	2	3	50%	3.0	0	5.0	—	-38.7%	—	-3	—	-11	50%	50%	0%	0%
2007	CIN	16	16	23	143	70%	8.9	1	3.1	—	9.3%	—	46	—	51	43%	39%	13%	4%
2008	CIN		19	28	223	68%	11.7	2			-12.8%								

An average kick returner and part-time slot receiver (only three of his 16 receptions came after Chris Henry's return in Week 9), Holt will be in training camp competition with Antonio Chatman and draft picks Jerome Simpson, Andre Caldwell, and Mario Urrutia for the second, third, and fourth receiver roles behind T. J. Houshmandzadeh. Holt will likely stick on the roster regardless of where he ends up in the receiver pecking order because of his return skills, but a player who averaged 8.9 yards per catch last season isn't going to convince Marvin Lewis he has the deep-threat credentials to replace Chad Johnson.

Torry Holt

Height: 6-0 Weight: 190 College: North Carolina State Draft: 1999/1 (6) Born: 5-Jun-1976 Age: 32 Risk: Green

Year	Team	G	Rec	Pass	Yds	C%	Yd/C	TD	YAC	Rk	DVOA	Rk	DYAR	Rk	YAR	Short	Mid	Deep	Bomb
2005	STL	14	102	163	1331	63%	13.0	9	2.6	73	5.9%	31	233	16	274	32%	32%	26%	11%
2006	STL	16	93	179	1188	52%	12.8	10	3.0	57	-11.5%	67	16	65	72	25%	38%	22%	15%
2007	STL	16	93	149	1189	62%	12.8	7	2.3	80	7.9%	31	244	12	245	26%	42%	23%	9%
2008	STL		73	142	972	51%	13.3	8			-7.4%								

Isaac Bruce is gone; will Torry Holt be the next legendary Rams wide receiver to play for another team? At a charity golf event Holt hosts with his brother, Carolina Panthers safety Terrence Holt, Torry Holt spoke to Raleigh, N.C., television station WRAL. "I wanted to just send in my resignation to the Rams and join him down here," he said in a televised interview. "What better place to come and play football than in your home state?" Holt is a native of Greensboro, North Carolina, and went to school at N.C. State. Though the tone of the interview was in obvious jest, Holt was more serious when he talked to St. Louis reporters a few days later at Rams minicamp. "The real story is that I have this year and next year, and hopefully I can finish those years out," Holt said. "Then I will see where I am at. I will see where I am at physically and emotionally and financially. Then, if they would like to do something here, I will consider it. If not, then I will have the option to go and explore and give my services somewhere else. If that happens, Carolina will definitely be my first choice." For 2008, Holt will definitely be back with the Rams. His numbers are projected to take a hit; his team won't be any good, and at age 32, he should begin to decline any time now.

Joe Horn

Height: 6-1 Weight: 206 College: Itawamba J.C. Draft: 1996/5 (135) Born: 16-Jan-1972 Age: 36 Risk: Red

Year	Team	G	Rec	Pass	Yds	C%	Yd/C	TD	YAC	Rk	DVOA	Rk	DYAR	Rk	YAR	Short	Mid	Deep	Bomb
2005	NO	13	49	103	654	48%	13.3	1	2.0	87	-20.9%	87	-65	87	-55	13%	54%	25%	9%
2006	NO	10	37	61	679	61%	18.4	4	4.4	23	29.2%	3	207	19	187	16%	48%	25%	11%
2007	ATL	12	27	52	243	52%	9.0	1	1.9	85	-32.1%	85	-79	81	-72	39%	41%	15%	4%
2008	ATL		15	28	221	54%	15.2	1			-7.6%								

Horn's primary contribution in 2007 was a work ethic that rubbed off on a group of young Falcons receivers on a team in complete turmoil. He'll be on the bench if Laurent Robinson lives up to his promise. Hamstring injuries hurt his season, but Horn will get a shot to stay with a team that needs leadership at key positions in a drastic rebuild. What he won't get is much of a chance with the Falcons going forward if he keeps his preseason "I wanna be traded/I'm not gonna work out, 'cause I'm not starting!" act going. That wears thin under the best of circumstances, and overpaid 36-year-old receivers really should be seen and not heard.

T. J. Houshmandzadeh

Height: 6-1 Weight: 197 College: Oregon State Draft: 2001/7 (204) Born: 26-Sep-1977 Age: 31 Risk: Green

Year	Team	G	Rec	Pass	Yds	C%	Yd/C	TD	YAC	Rk	DVOA	Rk	DYAR	Rk	YAR	Short	Mid	Deep	Bomb
2005	CIN	14	78	115	956	68%	12.3	7	4.2	30	21.0%	7	303	8	265	34%	49%	13%	4%
2006	CIN	14	90	132	1081	68%	12.0	9	3.5	47	20.1%	12	341	4	274	39%	39%	17%	5%
2007	CIN	16	112	170	1143	66%	10.2	12	3.1	58	5.1%	38	238	15	223	40%	39%	15%	6%
2008	CIN		87	142	972	61%	11.2	8			10.1%								

For the first time since he was in high school, Houshmandzadeh will (maybe) not be playing alongside Chad Johnson next year. Traditionally when one member of such a highly-rated double act leaves you'd expect the other to receive more touches as a result, but Houshmandzadeh led the league in receptions (tied with Wes Welker) and targets last year, so how many more passes can he really be thrown? Ocho Cinco has been ever-present for Cincinnati during and after Houshmandzadeh's breakout 2004 season, so there's nothing to go on for how Hooch will deal with coverage that is slanted toward him or facing off against the opposition's top cornerback. Still, it's harder to shut down a possession receiver with double coverage than it is a deep threat, and there are many top wideouts in the league who don't have Houshmandzadeh's skills. He'll produce less than last year perhaps, but he's still one of the best in the league.

With Chad Johnson still in town as we go to press, this projection is for Houshmandzadeh as the number-two option. If Johnson is dealt, our projection changes to 92 receptions for 1,031 yards and 11 touchdowns.

Sam Hurd
Height: 6-2 Weight: 187 College: Northern Illinois   Draft: 2006/FA   Born: 24-Apr-1985   Age: 23 Risk: Red

Year	Team	G	Rec	Pass	Yds	C%	Yd/C	TD	YAC	Rk	DVOA	Rk	DYAR	Rk	YAR	Short	Mid	Deep	Bomb
2006	DAL	15	5	11	75	45%	15.0	0	2.6	—	-33.3%	—	-17	—	-6	36%	36%	18%	9%
2007	DAL	16	19	37	314	51%	16.5	1	5.2	—	9.0%	—	64	—	61	21%	62%	9%	9%
2008	DAL		17	26	255	65%	14.7	2			-8.7%								

Hurd is your standard-issue deep threat in the progress of developing into a wide receiver. He's at his best matched up in single coverage against safeties, who have to respect his speed, leaving plenty of space for the curl and out routes that make up Hurd's limited route tree. He's ahead of Isaiah Stanbeck and Miles Austin for the fourth-wide-out position, so if Terrell Owens and Terry Glenn leave after this year, Hurd could see significant playing time come 2009. That's enough for keeper league players to take a late, late flyer on him.

Chad Jackson
Height: 6-1 Weight: 206 College: Florida   Draft: 2006/2 (36)   Born: 6-Mar-1985   Age: 23 Risk: Red

Year	Team	G	Rec	Pass	Yds	C%	Yd/C	TD	YAC	Rk	DVOA	Rk	DYAR	Rk	YAR	Short	Mid	Deep	Bomb
2006	NE	12	13	19	152	68%	11.7	3	3.1	—	20.7%	—	50	—	36	59%	6%	12%	24%
2008	NE		20	34	275	59%	13.9	2			9.7%								

The Patriots' second-round pick in 2006, Jackson was a rookie disappointment before tearing his ACL. The injury wiped out most of the 2007 season, as there was no need to rush Jackson back when the Patriots fielded a Dream Team of wide receivers. Jackson is healthy and will get a chance to slide into Donte' Stallworth's role as a big-play slot guy, but nothing will be handed to him.

Darrell Jackson
Height: 6-0 Weight: 201 College: Florida   Draft: 2000/3 (80)   Born: 6-Dec-1978   Age: 30 Risk: Red

Year	Team	G	Rec	Pass	Yds	C%	Yd/C	TD	YAC	Rk	DVOA	Rk	DYAR	Rk	YAR	Short	Mid	Deep	Bomb
2005	SEA	6	38	55	482	69%	12.7	3	3.3	47	17.3%	11	131	28	147	30%	35%	17%	19%
2006	SEA	13	63	112	956	56%	15.2	10	4.0	38	2.0%	45	125	39	179	24%	46%	17%	13%
2007	SF	15	46	104	497	44%	10.8	3	1.9	84	-27.9%	81	-126	86	-112	28%	39%	20%	13%
2008	DEN		18	33	183	55%	10.3	1			12.8%								

Everyone in San Francisco was excited when Jackson arrived for a mere fourth-round choice. Little did they know how close Jackson was to the end of the line. He dropped passes, didn't get open, and avoided contact. Jackson always dropped too many passes, and if he has lost a bit of quick-twitch athleticism, he's too unreliable to play.

DeSean Jackson
Height: 6-0 Weight: 178 College: California   Draft: 2008/2 (49)   Born: 1-Dec-1986   Age: 22 Risk: Red

Year	Team	G	Rec	Pass	Yds	C%	Yd/C	TD	YAC	Rk	DVOA	Rk	DYAR	Rk	YAR	Short	Mid	Deep	Bomb
2008	PHI		28	49	398	57%	14.1	2			-12.8%								

The Eagles picked up Jackson even after they traded out of the first round. It was an interesting move because Jackson is everything the Eagles don't normally look for in receivers. Jackson's a speed merchant who doesn't block, runs mediocre routes, and could be the best athlete on the team. Of course, for all that ability, he only averaged 11.7 yards per catch at Cal last year. Jackson's not likely to help all that much this year, but he should be an upgrade over Correll Buckhalter as a return man immediately, and should at least provide the Eagles with an option to keep opposing safeties honest against Kevin Curtis and Reggie Brown. On the other hand, it's also worth noting that the best wide receiver to be produced by a Jeff Tedford-led offense is Samie Parker. Maybe that's the real Tedford curse.

Dexter Jackson

Height: 5-10   Weight: 182   College: Appalachian State   Draft: 2008/2 (58)   Born: 5-Aug-1986   Age: 22   Risk: Red

Year	Team	G	Rec	Pass	Yds	C%	Yd/C	TD	YAC	Rk	DVOA	Rk	DYAR	Rk	YAR	Short	Mid	Deep	Bomb
2008	TB		16	24	218	67%	13.9	1			2.7%								

DeSean Jackson was the most highly-touted small receiver of the 2008 draft. But this Jackson could surprise a lot of people, as he did when he caught two touchdowns against Michigan in Appalachian State's upset win last year. He impressed at the Shrine Game, the Senior Bowl, and the Combine, but he'll need a little development as a route-runner in the pros. Short-term, he'll be asked to contribute on special teams and take some of the heat off Joey Galloway. Over time, he could find his way to the top of a younger cadre of receivers.

Vincent Jackson

Height: 6-5   Weight: 241   College: Northern Colorado   Draft: 2005/2 (61)   Born: 14-Jan-1983   Age: 25   Risk: Red

Year	Team	G	Rec	Pass	Yds	C%	Yd/C	TD	YAC	Rk	DVOA	Rk	DYAR	Rk	YAR	Short	Mid	Deep	Bomb
2005	SD	7	3	8	59	38%	19.7	0	1.7	—	-4.7%	—	5	—	3	29%	0%	43%	29%
2006	SD	16	27	56	453	48%	16.8	6	3.0	56	12.7%	23	106	44	71	24%	33%	13%	30%
2007	SD	16	41	81	623	51%	15.2	3	2.7	71	-1.8%	57	68	59	59	22%	36%	22%	21%
2008	SD		45	87	741	52%	16.5	5			1.2%								

Jackson was the Chargers' star in the playoffs. He averaged 100 yards per game and scored two touchdowns in three games. His worst output was 6 catches and 93 yards in the AFC Championship game. As a result, Jackson's stock has never been higher, but should we really ignore his regular season? During those 16 games, Jackson only once topped 90 yards and only had three total touchdowns total. KUBIAK obviously believes the regular season is the true level. Still, Jackson is growing more polished every season. He entered the NFL as a low-percentage deep threat, but now runs better routes and has become more consistent. The postseason may represent a new level of performance for Jackson, who has the physical tools to be an upper echelon receiver.

Dwayne Jarrett

Height: 6-4   Weight: 219   College: USC   Draft: 2007/2 (45)   Born: 11-Sep-1986   Age: 22   Risk: Red

Year	Team	G	Rec	Pass	Yds	C%	Yd/C	TD	YAC	Rk	DVOA	Rk	DYAR	Rk	YAR	Short	Mid	Deep	Bomb
2007	CAR	7	6	13	73	46%	12.2	0	0.2	—	-49.6%	—	-34	—	-29	33%	25%	33%	8%
2008	CAR		22	38	325	58%	14.8	2			-3.1%								

There were screaming red flags about Dwayne Jarrett's character in college. The fact that the Panthers ignored them would raise questions about the team's recent draft acumen, if the questions weren't already there. The team hoped that Jarrett, selected in the second round of the 2007 draft, would give the Panthers a playmaking mismatch, especially on jump balls, not unlike Southern Cal alum Keyshawn Johnson did in 2006. Jarrett's attitude and work ethic reminded many of another USC receiver—Mike Williams, one of the more spectacular busts in recent memory. After his rookie season was over, Jarrett wasn't even the most productive receiver in Carolina's draft. That honor went to fifth-round tight end Dante Rosario. Jarrett's March 11 DWI stop caused teammate Steve Smith to call him out publicly and drove the Panthers to outbid three other teams for D. J. Hackett. This is a career that could be over before it even begins.

Michael Jenkins

Height: 6-4   Weight: 217   College: Ohio State   Draft: 2004/1 (29)   Born: 18-Jun-1982   Age: 26   Risk: Red

Year	Team	G	Rec	Pass	Yds	C%	Yd/C	TD	YAC	Rk	DVOA	Rk	DYAR	Rk	YAR	Short	Mid	Deep	Bomb
2005	ATL	14	36	71	508	51%	14.1	3	2.7	71	-3.6%	50	49	56	58	18%	37%	24%	21%
2006	ATL	16	39	83	436	47%	11.2	7	2.5	69	-11.2%	66	10	67	-34	27%	42%	19%	11%
2007	ATL	15	53	85	532	62%	10.0	4	3.5	47	0.5%	51	85	56	98	51%	43%	3%	4%
2008	ATL		40	74	391	54%	9.8	2			-11.1%								

Jenkins is to Atlanta what Bryant Johnson was to the Arizona Cardinals—an ill-advised first-round pick, later challenged and defeated by better receivers for elite status, who still makes contributions in limited doses. For Jenkins, that meant subjugating any prestige and becoming Atlanta's man in the slot behind Roddy White and Joe Horn. Jenkins put up career highs in receptions and yards, and while he certainly should have done more with his size and speed to this point, he's managed to avoid complete bustitude and may actually surprise in what will hopefully be a more stable offense.

Greg Jennings

Height: 5-11 Weight: 192 College: Western Michigan   Draft: 2006/2 (52)   Born: 21-Sep-1983   Age: 25   Risk: Yellow

Year	Team	G	Rec	Pass	Yds	C%	Yd/C	TD	YAC	Rk	DVOA	Rk	DYAR	Rk	YAR	Short	Mid	Deep	Bomb
2006	GB	14	45	105	632	43%	14.0	3	7.0	1	-17.3%	75	-39	77	-99	33%	37%	13%	17%
2007	GB	13	53	84	920	63%	17.4	12	7.7	1	31.5%	2	302	7	284	39%	35%	8%	18%
2008	GB		70	128	1044	55%	14.8	9			16.7%								

Packers receivers led the NFL in yards after catch, and Jennings led the Packers with a YAC average of 7.7. Like a lot of deep threat receivers, Jennings picks up his share of YAC by waltzing 20 yards to the end zone at the end of a 50-yard pass. But Jennings also produced his share of juking, ankle-breaking highlights, like his 57-yard catch-and-run against the Chargers, the quick hitch he turned into a 20-yard gain against the Lions in their first meeting, and the 43-yard reception against the Cowboys when he made Nate Jones trip over his own feet. Jennings's catch-and-run ability is a big part of the Packers offense, as is his home run capability. He's the ideal number-two receiver and just another reason why Aaron Rodgers is a sweet fantasy football sleeper.

Andre Johnson

Height: 6-2 Weight: 221 College: Miami   Draft: 2003/1 (3)   Born: 11-Jul-1981   Age: 27   Risk: Yellow

Year	Team	G	Rec	Pass	Yds	C%	Yd/C	TD	YAC	Rk	DVOA	Rk	DYAR	Rk	YAR	Short	Mid	Deep	Bomb
2005	HOU	13	63	114	688	55%	10.9	2	3.5	40	-16.0%	76	-31	82	-7	31%	38%	22%	10%
2006	HOU	16	103	164	1147	63%	11.1	5	4.2	26	0.2%	50	166	27	114	44%	31%	14%	12%
2007	HOU	9	60	86	851	70%	14.2	8	4.2	28	29.9%	3	288	9	273	27%	45%	15%	13%
2008	HOU		88	132	1253	67%	14.3	12			26.4%								

Project Johnson's numbers last year over a full season, and they were scary: better than 1,500 yards and 14 touchdowns. Instead, a knee injury robbed him of seven midseason games. He returns healthy and could be a major beneficiary of what is expected to be an upgraded running game in Houston, which will mean more time for Matt Schaub to find his favorite target. Johnson's and Schaub's injuries didn't overlap last year, meaning the pair only played five games together. Another full year in the offseason program should project to a big year for Johnson, although he may not see the ball quite as often if the Texans are more effective running it.

Bryant Johnson

Height: 6-2 Weight: 214 College: Penn State   Draft: 2003/1 (17)   Born: 7-Mar-1981   Age: 27   Risk: Red

Year	Team	G	Rec	Pass	Yds	C%	Yd/C	TD	YAC	Rk	DVOA	Rk	DYAR	Rk	YAR	Short	Mid	Deep	Bomb
2005	ARI	14	40	72	432	56%	10.8	1	3.3	48	-19.8%	85	-41	83	-24	25%	46%	21%	9%
2006	ARI	16	40	74	740	54%	18.5	4	6.0	2	19.0%	14	174	24	158	30%	38%	20%	12%
2007	ARI	16	46	88	528	52%	11.5	2	1.8	87	-10.2%	71	17	71	12	26%	55%	12%	7%
2008	SF		66	120	889	55%	13.4	6			-2.8%								

Johnson is a former first-round pick with the tools to be a solid possession receiver, but he's not going to beat a lot of double coverage. His production in Arizona was steady. He would start a handful of games, either as an injury replacement or in a three-wideout offense. He would catch about 45 passes, usually with very little big-play sizzle. It's not the résumé to be the number one, but he'll get a chance in San Francisco.

Calvin Johnson

Height: 6-5 Weight: 239 College: Georgia Tech   Draft: 2007/1 (2)   Born: 25-Sep-1985   Age: 23   Risk: Red

Year	Team	G	Rec	Pass	Yds	C%	Yd/C	TD	YAC	Rk	DVOA	Rk	DYAR	Rk	YAR	Short	Mid	Deep	Bomb
2007	DET	15	48	93	756	52%	15.8	4	3.4	51	-0.3%	52	90	52	79	21%	31%	36%	11%
2008	DET		64	117	842	55%	13.1	5			-11.5%								

Every Lions comment comes with bonus "he said, she said" material, as if the team were run by the kids from De-Grassi Junior High. Johnson's midseason swoon allegedly occurred because he didn't know the playbook; that, plus a few dropped passes, put him in Mike Martz's spacious doghouse. Not true, said all parties after the season: Johnson's lingering back injury limited his flexibility and led to some drops, but he knew the plays just fine. Johnson looked like a future star when he wasn't playing hot potato, and he should shine as the second receiver behind Roy Williams in a more conventional, balanced offense. These are the Lions, of course, so Johnson may also soon fall prey to some lingering injury or develop some ill-defined character flaw that makes him persona non grata.

Chad Johnson

Height: 6-1 Weight: 192 College: Oregon State Draft: 2001/2 (36) Born: 9-Jan-1978 Age: 30 Risk: Red

Year	Team	G	Rec	Pass	Yds	C%	Yd/C	TD	YAC	Rk	DVOA	Rk	DYAR	Rk	YAR	Short	Mid	Deep	Bomb
2005	CIN	16	97	155	1432	63%	14.8	9	3.3	51	19.7%	8	412	2	409	21%	49%	17%	12%
2006	CIN	16	87	152	1369	57%	15.7	7	3.6	41	25.8%	6	461	1	302	18%	47%	19%	16%
2007	CIN	16	93	161	1440	58%	15.5	8	3.2	56	10.9%	24	305	6	291	19%	44%	26%	11%
2008	CIN		84	150	1146	56%	13.6	10			13.8%								

The Incredible Sulk is, depending on who you believe: a) the victim of a media circus of his own creation; b) a convenient scapegoat for an underachieving team; c) the latest stop for the Drew Rosenhaus Ego Train; or d) a fair-weather friend trying to run out on the Bengals in their time of need. What isn't open to dispute is that a) he's signed with Cincinnati through 2011; b) the Bengals seem determined to hold him to that to the point of self-destruction; and c) he is a Pro Bowl receiver. If fences can be mended or a trade agreed to (though it's hard to imagine the Bengals getting a better offer than the one they've already turned down) then there's little doubt that Ocho Cinco could return to terrorizing defenses once again, and a player of his experience won't be seriously hurt by missing training camp. We tossed him into KUBIAK as the usual number-one Bengals option. Honestly, we have no idea what will happen with his stats this year. Just ... be nice to him, OK? He's sensitive.

Brandon Jones

Height: 6-1 Weight: 208 College: Oklahoma Draft: 2005/3 (96) Born: 6-Oct-1982 Age: 26 Risk: Red

Year	Team	G	Rec	Pass	Yds	C%	Yd/C	TD	YAC	Rk	DVOA	Rk	DYAR	Rk	YAR	Short	Mid	Deep	Bomb
2005	TEN	10	23	47	299	49%	13.0	2	3.4	—	-16.0%	—	-13	—	4	28%	43%	20%	9%
2006	TEN	16	27	54	384	50%	14.2	4	2.5	70	3.5%	41	66	54	64	20%	42%	18%	20%
2007	TEN	9	21	34	248	62%	11.8	2	3.2	—	-4.0%	—	24	—	19	29%	43%	14%	14%
2008	TEN		18	34	185	53%	10.2	1			-30.3%								

Late in 2006, Jones looked like he was coming into his own as a receiver, but 2007 represented a step backward, as his nagging injuries prevented him from ever getting into the flow of the Titans' offense. He had arthroscopic surgery after Week 4, hobbled back for a few productive games (five catches against Jacksonville in Week 10), then hit the shelf for good with a December groin injury. He could be decent as a third receiver, but he doesn't look like a number one, which is what the Titans once hoped he could be. Jones is a good athlete who also played baseball in the Yankees' organization.

Jacoby Jones

Height: 6-3 Weight: 210 College: Lane Draft: 2007/3 (73) Born: 26-Dec-1985 Age: 22 Risk: Red

Year	Team	G	Rec	Pass	Yds	C%	Yd/C	TD	YAC	Rk	DVOA	Rk	DYAR	Rk	YAR	Short	Mid	Deep	Bomb
2007	HOU	14	15	24	149	63%	9.9	0	3.6	—	-19.0%	—	-12	—	-18	55%	36%	9%	0%
2008	HOU		26	45	359	58%	13.7	2			1.6%								

Jones didn't contribute much as a rookie coming out of tiny Lane College, but showed flashes of ability and the Texans have high hopes for his development. On a team where there's a huge drop-off between the top receiver (Andre Johnson) and everyone else, Jones will be given every opportunity to prove he belongs in the NFL.

James Jones

Height: 6-1 Weight: 207 College: San Jose State Draft: 2007/3 (78) Born: 31-Mar-1984 Age: 24 Risk: Red

Year	Team	G	Rec	Pass	Yds	C%	Yd/C	TD	YAC	Rk	DVOA	Rk	DYAR	Rk	YAR	Short	Mid	Deep	Bomb
2007	GB	16	47	80	676	59%	14.4	2	4.7	18	-10.0%	70	17	70	18	38%	39%	15%	8%
2008	GB		50	78	735	64%	14.6	4			18.0%								

Some experts speculate that Jones, who spent most of his life in San Jose, had trouble playing in cold weather last season. He was held without a catch in the NFC Championship game and in a road game at Soldier Field, and he caught just four passes in four December games. It's more likely that Jones wore down in the second half of the year and that expectations were too high after he caught 23 passes in his first five games. Jones played pretty well in the winter wonderland playoff game against the Seahawks (three catches, 42 yards), and he didn't play very well in his December dome game against the Rams (two receptions). Now that he's survived a Green Bay winter, Jones should have little trouble playing in icy conditions. He's a great third wideout who is ready for a starting job as soon as one becomes available.

Matt Jones

Height: 6-6   Weight: 242   College: Arkansas   Draft: 2005/1 (21)   Born: 22-Apr-1983   Age: 25   Risk: Red

Year	Team	G	Rec	Pass	Yds	C%	Yd/C	TD	YAC	Rk	DVOA	Rk	DYAR	Rk	YAR	Short	Mid	Deep	Bomb
2005	JAC	16	36	69	432	52%	12.0	5	2.8	69	-7.1%	62	29	62	38	36%	39%	10%	15%
2006	JAC	14	41	76	643	54%	15.7	4	4.4	22	4.1%	40	102	45	86	22%	41%	22%	14%
2007	JAC	12	24	50	317	48%	13.2	4	3.5	50	-8.6%	67	15	73	18	27%	41%	20%	12%
2008	JAC		19	34	295	56%	15.2	4			6.0%								

Jones has athleticism to die for—no one that big should move that fast—and despite having played quarterback in college he has the hands and coordination to come up with a jaw-dropping catch. So what's missing? Desire would seem to be the obvious answer. When a former first-round pick is routinely left on the inactive list early in his third season, something is clearly amiss. With Reggie Williams showing improvement, and Jerry Porter imported with a sizable free-agent deal, it looks like the Jaguars are close to pulling the plug on Jones. If so, Jones will start to receive Christmas cards from Mike Mamula for knocking the latter out of the Workout Warrior Hall of Fame.

Joe Jurevicius

Height: 6-5   Weight: 230   College: Penn State   Draft: 1998/2 (55)   Born: 23-Dec-1974   Age: 33   Risk: Green

Year	Team	G	Rec	Pass	Yds	C%	Yd/C	TD	YAC	Rk	DVOA	Rk	DYAR	Rk	YAR	Short	Mid	Deep	Bomb
2005	SEA	16	55	84	694	65%	12.6	10	4.3	27	19.5%	9	214	19	243	32%	51%	13%	4%
2006	CLE	13	40	65	495	62%	12.4	3	2.5	72	15.5%	19	142	34	119	22%	61%	11%	6%
2007	CLE	16	50	81	614	62%	12.3	3	4.7	19	4.6%	39	112	44	126	32%	52%	12%	4%
2008	CLE		33	52	367	63%	11.1	3			-4.4%								

It was nice to see Jurevicius have a solid season on a good team after the Ohio native gave the Browns a hometown discount in 2006 when he signed as a free agent. Jurevicius was considered a disappointment with his original team, the Giants, but he turned his career around during stops in Tampa Bay, Seattle, and now Cleveland. Jurevicius has indicated that this will be his final season, but at 34, he still has the size and hands to be a nice complementary receiver, and while the Browns signed Donte' Stallworth to take over starting duties, Jurevicius should still see time in three-receiver sets.

Malcolm Kelly

Height: 6-4   Weight: 218   College: Oklahoma   Draft: 2008/2 (51)   Born: 30-Dec-1986   Age: 21   Risk: Red

Year	Team	G	Rec	Pass	Yds	C%	Yd/C	TD	YAC	Rk	DVOA	Rk	DYAR	Rk	YAR	Short	Mid	Deep	Bomb
2008	WAS		39	74	604	53%	15.6	4			-10.1%								

Kelly dropped like a stone in the draft when he ran two slow 40s on his Pro Day and then blamed the Oklahoma staff for attempting to sabotage his performance to punish him for one reason or another. While we can't speak to that, Kelly's performance on the college level revealed he was a smart receiver who runs good routes and has good hands, traits that make him a perfect fit for the West Coast offense. Some scouts graded him as the best blocking receiver in the draft, which will also help him find the field. Even if he's not the most talented receiver in the draft, he's probably the one most ready to transition to the professional ranks, and the situation he was drafted into should make him the most productive rookie receiver of 2008.

Eddie Kennison

Height: 6-1   Weight: 201   College: LSU   Draft: 1996/1 (18)   Born: 20-Jan-1973   Age: 35   Risk: Red

Year	Team	G	Rec	Pass	Yds	C%	Yd/C	TD	YAC	Rk	DVOA	Rk	DYAR	Rk	YAR	Short	Mid	Deep	Bomb
2005	KC	16	68	108	1102	63%	16.2	5	5.2	12	27.7%	2	344	5	342	28%	41%	21%	10%
2006	KC	16	53	101	860	52%	16.2	5	2.1	80	2.5%	43	118	41	120	20%	35%	33%	12%
2007	KC	8	13	26	101	50%	7.8	0	1.8	—	-36.8%	—	-49	—	-58	31%	31%	23%	15%

Kennison has one of the oddest careers in recent NFL history. He was part of the amazing 1996 draft class, but after an impressive rookie season he nearly busted out of the league. In his first five and a half seasons, he played for four teams and never reached 1,000 yards. After his "retirement" from the Broncos in 2001, he signed with the Chiefs a couple weeks later and was reborn as a deep threat. He produced five seasons between 853 and 1,102 yards with impressive DYARs to match. His injuries and decline last year were among the main reasons the Chiefs offense fell apart. He's probably gone for good; he was far more one-dimensional than most of his class of 1996 colleagues, and that dimension is rapidly disappearing.

Ashley Lelie Height: 6-3 Weight: 200 College: Hawaii   Draft: 2002/1 (19) Born: 16-Feb-1980 Age: 28 Risk: Red

Year	Team	G	Rec	Pass	Yds	C%	Yd/C	TD	YAC	Rk	DVOA	Rk	DYAR	Rk	YAR	Short	Mid	Deep	Bomb
2005	DEN	16	42	88	770	48%	18.3	1	5.1	15	-3.5%	49	62	51	61	18%	35%	16%	31%
2006	ATL	15	28	68	430	41%	15.4	1	2.3	77	-13.4%	70	-4	70	-46	12%	42%	20%	26%
2007	SF	15	10	26	115	38%	11.5	0	1.3	—	-52.7%	—	-82	—	-74	27%	27%	23%	23%
2008	SF		21	44	242	48%	11.4	0			-19.9%								

The Niners' plan when they signed Lelie was to have a deep threat to draw the safety out of the box and keep him from pestering Frank Gore. Even if Lelie never caught a pass, defenses would have to float a safety over the top, because if they didn't, Lelie could get past the cornerback for big plays. The problem was that Lelie didn't work hard enough in practice to warrant much playing time, much less the starting spot. However, receivers coach Jerry Sullivan said Lelie did start putting work in late in the season and could see more plays on the field in 2008.

Greg Lewis Height: 6-0 Weight: 180 College: Illinois   Draft: 2003/FA Born: 12-Feb-1980 Age: 28 Risk: Red

Year	Team	G	Rec	Pass	Yds	C%	Yd/C	TD	YAC	Rk	DVOA	Rk	DYAR	Rk	YAR	Short	Mid	Deep	Bomb
2005	PHI	16	48	105	561	46%	11.7	1	2.5	76	-19.2%	83	-53	85	-72	26%	42%	16%	17%
2006	PHI	16	24	37	348	65%	14.5	2	3.3	—	28.9%	—	113	—	95	15%	59%	7%	19%
2007	PHI	15	13	23	265	57%	20.4	3	4.0	—	31.8%	—	85	—	91	18%	32%	18%	32%
2008	PHI		11	17	96	65%	9.1	1			3.1%								

Sometimes, the young players you sign early to long-term deals pan out, and you've got a bargain. Some other times, even the smart kids end up with a Terrence Long or a Greg Lewis. Lewis's viability as a starting wide receiver is a trendline perfectly expressed by his season-by-season reception numbers: 6, 17, 48, 24, 13. The next step in this progression is high school coach.

Brandon Lloyd Height: 6-0 Weight: 184 College: Illinois   Draft: 2003/4 (124) Born: 5-Jul-1981 Age: 27 Risk: Red

Year	Team	G	Rec	Pass	Yds	C%	Yd/C	TD	YAC	Rk	DVOA	Rk	DYAR	Rk	YAR	Short	Mid	Deep	Bomb
2005	SF	16	48	109	733	44%	15.3	5	3.0	60	-14.2%	74	-13	75	4	13%	55%	15%	18%
2006	WAS	15	23	58	365	41%	15.9	0	2.5	68	-18.3%	76	-25	73	-60	17%	46%	12%	25%
2007	WAS	8	2	11	14	18%	7.0	0	8.0	—	-85.3%	—	-59	—	-54	25%	13%	25%	38%
2008	CHI		19	37	256	51%	13.7	1			-1.9%								

The debate about whether Adam Archuleta or Brandon Lloyd was the worse 2006 acquisition by the Redskins has no winner. It's like comparing a myopia of suck versus a maze of suck. Lloyd was the maze, because it took the Redskins two years to get out. Lloyd's now Chicago property; maybe the Bears got confused and thought they were an AAFL franchise, and had the rights to their local guys.

Dane Looker Height: 6-0 Weight: 194 College: Washington   Draft: 2000/FA Born: 5-Apr-1976 Age: 32 Risk: Red

Year	Team	G	Rec	Pass	Yds	C%	Yd/C	TD	YAC	Rk	DVOA	Rk	DYAR	Rk	YAR	Short	Mid	Deep	Bomb
2005	STL	16	23	27	237	85%	10.3	0	3.4	—	22.1%	—	71	—	75	37%	44%	15%	4%
2007	STL	13	6	14	38	43%	6.3	0	1.8	—	-42.7%	—	-33	—	-39	43%	50%	7%	0%
2008	STL		14	21	154	67%	11.1	1			-4.7%								

Western Washington University, a small liberal arts college squeezed between the mountains and the sea in Bellingham, Washington, has officially produced four NFL players and one *Pro Football Prospectus* author. The player with the longest NFL tenure is Erik Norgard, who stuck to the bottom of the Oilers' roster for eight seasons in the mid-90s. That will likely be surpassed, however, by current Falcons punter Michael Koenen, who is three years into his career and doing fine. On behalf of the other Western Washington alumni, Vince Verhei would like to welcome Dane Looker back into the fold. Looker played two seasons at WWU before transferring to Washington. How did he fare against the football teams of the Great Northwest Athletic Conference? He didn't—he played basketball at the school, not football. Looker will be given a chance to win the third receiver spot with the Rams this season, but he'll have to beat out Dante Hall and second-round draft pick Donnie Avery to do it.

Mario Manningham

Height: 6-0 Weight: 181 College: Michigan   Draft: 2008/3 (95) Born: 25-May-1986 Age: 22 Risk: Red

Year	Team	G	Rec	Pass	Yds	C%	Yd/C	TD	YAC	Rk	DVOA	Rk	DYAR	Rk	YAR	Short	Mid	Deep	Bomb
2008	NYG		12	20	158	60%	12.7	1			-0.9%								

Based on his production in college, Manningham should have been a first-round pick. Based on the pre-draft silly season, he was a sixth-round pick at best. Manningham ran a slow 4.59 40-yard dash at the Combine, mishandled a report that he tested positive for marijuana while in college, and interviewed poorly with teams. He reportedly scored a "6" on the Wonderlic and actually skipped an interview with the Cowboys, two signs that he may not have NFL mental make-up. Manningham caught 72 passes for Michigan in 2007 but also dropped several passes against Ohio State, further clouding his scouting report. The Giants split the difference and used a late third-rounder on what seems like a pick with significant upside. This year, he will battle Super Bowl hero David Tyree for the fourth receiver position.

Brandon Marshall

Height: 6-4 Weight: 230 College: UCF   Draft: 2006/4 (119) Born: 23-Mar-1984 Age: 24 Risk: Red

Year	Team	G	Rec	Pass	Yds	C%	Yd/C	TD	YAC	Rk	DVOA	Rk	DYAR	Rk	YAR	Short	Mid	Deep	Bomb
2006	DEN	15	20	37	309	54%	15.5	2	5.5	—	-6.2%	—	19	—	19	23%	48%	19%	10%
2007	DEN	16	102	170	1325	60%	13.0	7	5.2	11	-1.3%	55	152	28	157	39%	40%	13%	8%
2008	DEN		71	124	909	57%	12.8	8			2.2%								

A breakout second season for Marshall made Denver fans very happy. Marshall's offseason did the opposite. He severely injured his forearm, including nerve damage, in an altercation with a widescreen TV. This non-football injury has little or no precedent, and the impact on Marshall's performance is almost impossible to predict. Needless to say, it cannot be a positive. Marshall's DVOA is low because his exceptional yards after catch ability led to an offense that too frequently isolated him and hoped he worked his magic. He also led the league in drops, a sign that he's prone to attention lapses (injuring yourself on a television is another sign). His catches may go down, but the Broncos would be better served working him down the field and letting him use his physical strength before he catches the ball instead of after.

Ruvell Martin

Height: 6-4 Weight: 217 College: Saginaw Valley State   Draft: 2006/FA Born: 10-Aug-1982 Age: 26 Risk: Red

Year	Team	G	Rec	Pass	Yds	C%	Yd/C	TD	YAC	Rk	DVOA	Rk	DYAR	Rk	YAR	Short	Mid	Deep	Bomb
2006	GB	13	21	43	358	49%	17.0	1	3.2	—	12.0%	—	82	—	47	25%	50%	18%	7%
2007	GB	15	16	28	242	57%	15.1	4	3.8	—	22.2%	—	88	—	95	20%	37%	13%	30%
2008	GB		19	34	253	56%	13.2	1			-8.1%								

Martin doesn't get a lot of playing time, but he has rung a lot of DVOA bells in the last two seasons. He was 4-for-5 on red zone receptions last year, scoring touchdowns on three of them. He was 7-of-10 on third down receptions for a DVOA of 83.3%. Eventually, a six-foot-four deep threat with the ability to produce in high-leverage situations is going to fight his way onto the field. If Donald Driver gets old quickly or James Jones's late-season slump continues into September, Martin could have a breakout season.

Glenn Martinez

Height: 6-2   Weight: 182   College: Saginaw Valley State   Draft: 2004/FA   Born: 30-Nov-1981   Age: 27   Risk: Red

Year	Team	G	Rec	Pass	Yds	C%	Yd/C	TD	YAC	Rk	DVOA	Rk	DYAR	Rk	YAR	Short	Mid	Deep	Bomb
2005	DET	5	1	7	11	14%	11.0	0	6.0	—	-87.7%	—	-35	—	-37	33%	67%	0%	0%
2007	DEN	12	14	24	175	58%	12.5	0	2.9	—	-2.0%	—	19	—	12	32%	55%	9%	5%
2008	DEN		17	30	222	57%	13.3	1			0.4%								

Thanks to injuries, Martinez at one point found himself as the Broncos third receiver. He added some value to his otherwise fringy existence by returning kicks and punts. Unfortunately, he excelled at neither and will have to make the Broncos this year purely as a receiver. With the importation of Samie Parker, Keary Colbert, and Darrell Jackson, that will be easier said than done.

Derrick Mason

Height: 5-10   Weight: 190   College: Michigan State   Draft: 1997/4 (98)   Born: 17-Jan-1974   Age: 34   Risk: Green

Year	Team	G	Rec	Pass	Yds	C%	Yd/C	TD	YAC	Rk	DVOA	Rk	DYAR	Rk	YAR	Short	Mid	Deep	Bomb
2005	BAL	16	86	135	1073	64%	12.5	3	2.5	83	2.9%	40	157	23	141	35%	36%	23%	7%
2006	BAL	16	68	112	750	61%	11.0	2	2.1	79	6.1%	35	163	28	70	30%	53%	10%	7%
2007	BAL	16	103	164	1087	63%	10.6	5	2.9	68	-6.0%	61	88	53	89	43%	40%	14%	3%
2008	BAL		63	113	685	56%	10.9	4			0.3%								

If the Tennessee version of McNair-to-Mason was an unexpected smash hit, the Baltimore version was a weaker but still worthwhile sequel, the *Harold and Kumar Escape from Guantanamo Bay* of quarterback-receiver pairings. Now McNair is gone and the 34-year-old Mason is stuck waiting for a new co-star to emerge while he still has something left in the tank. Last year Mason saw 164 passes, 52 more than in 2006, as the Ravens compensated for the injuries to Todd Heap and the uneven play by the rest of the receivers. He won't see that many passes again, but Mason is the only Ravens receiver guaranteed to start this season, and he should continue to be a solid producer.

Keenan McCardell

Height: 6-1   Weight: 191   College: UNLV   Draft: 1991/12 (326)   Born: 6-Jan-1970   Age: 38   Risk: Red

Year	Team	G	Rec	Pass	Yds	C%	Yd/C	TD	YAC	Rk	DVOA	Rk	DYAR	Rk	YAR	Short	Mid	Deep	Bomb
2005	SD	16	70	108	917	65%	13.1	9	2.5	78	24.0%	5	308	7	274	28%	45%	19%	9%
2006	SD	14	36	51	437	71%	12.1	0	2.1	81	15.7%	18	110	43	85	24%	54%	15%	7%
2007	WAS	10	22	31	256	71%	11.6	1	2.6	—	24.0%	—	88	—	79	23%	55%	19%	3%

Maybe it is coincidence, but in McCardell's long and illustrious career he almost always played for teams with an above average passing attack. McCardell first caught more than 10 passes in 1995 for the Cleveland Browns. From 1995 through 2007, he played for four different teams and with five different primary quarterbacks, and only once, in 2001, did his team have a below average passing DVOA. McCardell has managed to amass the eighth most receptions in history while never being a team's highest profile receiving threat except for the year Keyshawn Johnson quit on the Bucs. He is on his last legs as he pushes towards 40 and will have trouble finding a job.

Justin McCareins

Height: 6-2   Weight: 215   College: Northern Illinois   Draft: 2001/4 (124)   Born: 11-Dec-1978   Age: 29   Risk: Red

Year	Team	G	Rec	Pass	Yds	C%	Yd/C	TD	YAC	Rk	DVOA	Rk	DYAR	Rk	YAR	Short	Mid	Deep	Bomb
2005	NYJ	16	43	102	713	42%	16.6	2	3.1	58	-12.7%	73	0	73	-13	22%	35%	23%	20%
2006	NYJ	16	23	39	347	59%	15.1	1	4.4	—	3.3%	—	51	—	36	24%	29%	18%	29%
2007	NYJ	16	19	46	232	41%	12.2	0	2.0	—	-23.6%	—	-42	—	-67	18%	56%	18%	9%
2008	NYJ		34	57	396	60%	11.6	3			3.1%								

A former 2B or 3A receiver, McCareins's stats have been in steady decline for four years. He started a handful of games last season when Laveranues Coles got hurt but made little impact; when Coles was healthy, Brian Schottenheimer was often more comfortable with Chris Baker as his fourth wideout than McCareins. Now back in Tennessee, McCareins will get another shot at a starting job, but he's more likely to be released than to have another 46-catch season like 2004.

Shaun McDonald

Height: 5-10 Weight: 183 College: Arizona State   Draft: 2003/4 (106) Born: 13-Jun-1981 Age: 27 Risk: Red

Year	Team	G	Rec	Pass	Yds	C%	Yd/C	TD	YAC	Rk	DVOA	Rk	DYAR	Rk	YAR	Short	Mid	Deep	Bomb
2005	STL	16	46	74	523	62%	11.4	0	3.0	63	-7.0%	61	32	61	44	26%	53%	18%	3%
2006	STL	16	13	19	136	68%	10.5	1	1.2	—	-31.8%	—	-28	—	-4	44%	33%	11%	11%
2007	DET	16	79	126	943	63%	11.9	6	3.2	55	-1.6%	56	108	46	102	31%	47%	15%	8%
2008	DET		40	68	409	59%	10.1	2			-7.4%								

Mike Martz loves five-foot-ten, 180-pound slot receivers with good hands and courage in traffic. Players like McDonald, Mike Furrey, and Kevin Curtis can produce big numbers in Martz's system because it's filled with shallow drags, deep crosses, and other opportunities to run unhindered into some nickelback's zone. McDonald led the Lions in targets last season because he was healthier than Roy Williams and Mike Furrey and more reliable than Calvin Johnson. He made the most of his chances, but he won't be nearly as effective in a more run-oriented scheme, and his size and skill set don't make an ideal starter. His best bet is to bide his time for a year, then try to land in San Francisco.

Robert Meachem

Height: 6-2 Weight: 214 College: Tennessee   Draft: 2007/1 (27) Born: 28-Sep-1984 Age: 24 Risk: Red

Year	Team	G	Rec	Pass	Yds	C%	Yd/C	TD	YAC	Rk	DVOA	Rk	DYAR	Rk	YAR	Short	Mid	Deep	Bomb
2008	NO		27	47	410	57%	15.4	3			4.8%								

Yeah, that first-round receiver thing is always such a great idea, isn't it? Meachem added his name to the ever-increasing list of cautionary tales by showing up for his first training camp out of shape and missing his rookie season with a knee injury after appearing singularly unimpressive in the preseason. It should be mentioned that he missed every game in an interesting fashion—as a healthy inactive. All reports indicate that he's coming back solidly for a second chance, and the Saints could certainly use even a fraction of the potential that made Meachem the fourth receiver taken in the 2007 draft.

Lance Moore

Height: 5-9 Weight: 177 College: Toledo   Draft: 2006/FA Born: 31-Aug-1983 Age: 25 Risk: Red

Year	Team	G	Rec	Pass	Yds	C%	Yd/C	TD	YAC	Rk	DVOA	Rk	DYAR	Rk	YAR	Short	Mid	Deep	Bomb
2006	NO	4	1	3	10	33%	10.0	0	7.0	—	-24.8%	—	-3	—	-8	100%	0%	0%	0%
2007	NO	16	32	50	302	64%	9.4	2	1.8	86	6.3%	34	76	57	61	33%	41%	16%	10%
2008	NO		32	47	361	68%	11.1	2			0.2%								

Moore was a decent third option for the Saints when Robert Meachem was lost for the year with a knee injury and Devery Henderson started using Koren Robinson Brand Reverse Stickum. Moore will probably start training camp as the fifth receiver, but there are opportunities to move up the bottom end of this receiver corps. You may hear his name more than expected.

Aaron Moorehead

Height: 6-3 Weight: 200 College: Illinois   Draft: 2003/FA Born: 5-Nov-1980 Age: 28 Risk: Red

Year	Team	G	Rec	Pass	Yds	C%	Yd/C	TD	YAC	Rk	DVOA	Rk	DYAR	Rk	YAR	Short	Mid	Deep	Bomb
2005	IND	2	7	11	75	64%	10.7	0	-0.5	—	-9.7%	—	2	—	5	0%	100%	0%	0%
2006	IND	12	8	16	82	50%	10.3	1	1.5	—	-20.9%	—	-10	—	-4	50%	50%	0%	0%
2007	IND	8	8	22	65	36%	8.1	0	0.8	—	-44.7%	—	-54	—	-66	14%	57%	14%	14%

After 28 games over four seasons in Indianapolis, Moorehead finally had a few starts in 2008. Against the Chargers he caught four passes for 39 yards; against the Chiefs, he was shut out. He was not re-signed after the season, and it's doubtful that any team will take a flier on him—at 28 years old, he's not likely to get any better.

Sean Morey

Height: 5-11 Weight: 200 College: Brown   Draft: 1999/7 (241) Born: 26-Feb-1976 Age: 32 Risk: Red

Year	Team	G	Rec	Pass	Yds	C%	Yd/C	TD	YAC	Rk	DVOA	Rk	DYAR	Rk	YAR	Short	Mid	Deep	Bomb
2006	PIT	15	2	4	29	50%	14.5	0	0.0	—	54.8%	—	17	—	7	0%	50%	50%	0%
2007	ARI	15	8	17	131	47%	16.4	0	8.6	—	-24.4%	—	-15	—	-16	38%	44%	13%	6%
2008	ARI		7	11	80	64%	11.4	1			-10.4%								

Morey was released and then re-signed in March; it's rarely a good sign to learn that your roster spot is tenuous six months before camp starts. A Ken Whisenhunt transplant from Pittsburgh, Morey might have a tough time staying on the team at the crowded receiver spot. Morey had four catches against the Niners in Week 12 last year. Before that, he never had more than two catches in a season.

Randy Moss   Height: 6-4   Weight: 200   College: Marshall   Draft: 1998/1 (21)   Born: 13-Feb-1977   Age: 31   Risk: Yellow

Year	Team	G	Rec	Pass	Yds	C%	Yd/C	TD	YAC	Rk	DVOA	Rk	DYAR	Rk	YAR	Short	Mid	Deep	Bomb
2005	OAK	16	60	124	1005	48%	16.8	8	2.6	74	3.8%	37	157	24	143	13%	38%	28%	22%
2006	OAK	13	42	97	553	43%	13.2	3	2.4	73	-24.2%	80	-84	80	-56	12%	48%	19%	20%
2007	NE	16	98	160	1493	61%	15.2	23	3.3	52	29.3%	4	569	1	562	27%	41%	18%	14%
2008	NE		96	156	1482	62%	15.5	18			34.0%								

The top ten wide receiver seasons in DYAR, from 1995-2007:

Player	Team	Year	DYAR
Michael Irvin	DAL	1995	627
Randy Moss	NE	2007	569
Jerry Rice	SF	1995	549
Marvin Harrison	IND	2001	537
Steve Smith	CAR	2005	497
Chad Johnson	CIN	2006	496
Reggie Wayne	IND	2004	496
Randy Moss	MIN	2003	482
Marvin Harrison	IND	2002	478
Isaac Bruce	STL	1995	472

Psychoanalyzing the species receiverus primadonnus is a futile business. Those who thought that Moss would be clubhouse poison in New England, or that he would be released at the end of training camp, ate their words just hours after the season started. Those who wrote glowing prose about Moss's Patriots redemption began sweating late in the year, when Moss sleepwalked through pass routes and battled domestic violence allegations. Moss, a free agent in the offseason, told all suitors that he really, really wanted to stay in New England, but that didn't stop teams like the Eagles (who played headcase roulette with Terrell Owens three years ago) from placing bids. As Owens showed in Philly, the half life on this breed of player is short. Moss's desire to return to Foxboro was born of self-interest, not loyalty, so we must be ready to hit the fallout shelter once some bee crawls in his bonnet. That could never happen, or it may have already happened when you read this. The only thing that is certain is that two years of grousing and phoning in performances in Oakland didn't cause skill deterioration. Moss proved last year that he's still one of the three or four best athletes in the game, capable of making impossible catches and running past cornerbacks with alleged 4.4 speed. He can bring serious production whenever he wants to. We just can't predict when he will want to.

Santana Moss   Height: 5-10   Weight: 185   College: Miami   Draft: 2001/1 (16)   Born: 1-Jun-1979   Age: 29   Risk: Red

Year	Team	G	Rec	Pass	Yds	C%	Yd/C	TD	YAC	Rk	DVOA	Rk	DYAR	Rk	YAR	Short	Mid	Deep	Bomb
2005	WAS	16	84	134	1483	63%	17.7	9	7.4	4	25.5%	3	402	3	388	41%	35%	11%	13%
2006	WAS	14	55	100	790	54%	14.4	6	4.6	20	2.0%	44	114	42	76	35%	35%	17%	14%
2007	WAS	14	61	115	808	53%	13.2	3	3.1	59	-9.9%	69	25	68	10	40%	30%	16%	15%
2008	WAS		53	106	737	50%	13.8	7			2.2%								

Moss had a terrible season, marred by injuries to his groin, hamstring, and heel, none of which should have affected his hands. Regardless, Moss seemed to drop key pass after key pass in 2007, culminating in the second Todd Collins interception in the wild card game, where Moss gave up on an overthrown ball, watched Marcus Trufant pick the pass off, and then fruitlessly attempted to chase him down while the Seattle corner returned it for six. All of Moss's metrics are declining—look at the trends above—and KUBIAK thinks it will continue.

Sinorice Moss

Height: 5-8 Weight: 185 College: Miami Draft: 2006/2 (44) Born: 28-Dec-1983 Age: 24 Risk: Red

Year	Team	G	Rec	Pass	Yds	C%	Yd/C	TD	YAC	Rk	DVOA	Rk	DYAR	Rk	YAR	Short	Mid	Deep	Bomb
2006	NYG	6	5	11	25	45%	5.0	0	4.6	—	-52.1%	—	-36	—	-47	88%	0%	0%	13%
2007	NYG	13	21	37	225	57%	10.7	0	3.4	—	-26.2%	—	-39	—	-47	36%	48%	9%	6%
2008	NYG		27	40	271	68%	10.2	2			-3.4%								

Santana's younger brother has not developed into the receiver he was expected to be coming out of Miami. While Moss showed the ability to be a viable downfield target in college, he's turned into a possession receiver and "smoke" route target in New York. The selection of Mario Manningham is the biggest indictment of Moss's stagnation, and if he doesn't emerge this year, chances are that he never will.

Eric Moulds

Height: 6-2 Weight: 210 College: Mississippi State Draft: 1996/1 (24) Born: 17-Jul-1973 Age: 35 Risk: Red

Year	Team	G	Rec	Pass	Yds	C%	Yd/C	TD	YAC	Rk	DVOA	Rk	DYAR	Rk	YAR	Short	Mid	Deep	Bomb
2005	BUF	15	81	129	816	63%	10.1	4	3.2	52	-8.6%	68	41	59	43	40%	43%	10%	8%
2006	HOU	16	57	77	557	74%	9.8	1	3.8	39	-1.2%	52	69	53	91	54%	38%	7%	1%
2007	TEN	16	32	52	342	62%	10.7	0	3.7	41	-4.2%	59	35	66	32	38%	38%	17%	8%

You can be forgiven if you had forgotten that Moulds is still in the league, but in the last two years with the Texans and Titans, he has actually managed to have a fairly solid final act to his career as a possession receiver. He looks absolutely nothing like the guy who had 1,368 receiving yards and averaged 20.4 yards a catch for the 1998 Bills—he had 461 DYAR that year, just missing the top ten list in Randy Moss's comment—but if he plays somewhere in 2008 (as of press time he's a free agent) he can contribute.

Muhsin Muhammad

Height: 6-2 Weight: 217 College: Michigan State Draft: 1996/2 (43) Born: 5-May-1973 Age: 35 Risk: Red

Year	Team	G	Rec	Pass	Yds	C%	Yd/C	TD	YAC	Rk	DVOA	Rk	DYAR	Rk	YAR	Short	Mid	Deep	Bomb
2005	CHI	15	64	136	750	47%	11.7	4	2.5	81	-17.7%	80	-57	86	-66	31%	35%	18%	15%
2006	CHI	16	60	117	863	51%	14.4	5	2.8	64	-12.6%	68	1	68	81	20%	41%	29%	9%
2007	CHI	16	40	81	570	49%	14.3	3	4.7	20	-5.9%	60	43	62	46	23%	48%	21%	8%
2008	CAR		31	60	471	52%	15.0	2			-6.6%								

Carolina made two noteworthy acquisitions at wide receiver this offseason. The first was Muhsin Muhammad, a former Panther who set career highs in 2004 with 1,405 yards and 16 touchdowns, then promptly left town for Chicago. He was Chicago's top receiver for two years, including on the 2006 Super Bowl team, but was fourth on the team in receptions in 2007 and released after the season. The second acquisition was FO binky D. J. Hackett, who was outstanding in Seattle when he was healthy enough to get on the field. One was a grizzled veteran making a sentimental return to the city that had seen his greatest success; the other was a potential breakout star who seems ready to take off. Yet come minicamp, there was Muhsin Muhammad, taking snaps with the first-team offense. When the Bears were ahead last year, Muhammad's catch rate was only 39 percent and he averaged just 10.7 yards per catch. Those numbers climbed to 52 percent and 11.5 when the Bears were tied, and soared to 54 percent and 17.4 when the Bears were trailing.

Legedu Naanee

Height: 6-2 Weight: 225 College: Boise State Draft: 2007/5 (172) Born: 16-Sep-1983 Age: 25 Risk: Red

Year	Team	G	Rec	Pass	Yds	C%	Yd/C	TD	YAC	Rk	DVOA	Rk	DYAR	Rk	YAR	Short	Mid	Deep	Bomb
2007	SD	13	8	13	69	62%	8.6	0	6.6	—	-30.1%	—	-17	—	-12	46%	38%	8%	8%
2008	SD		16	28	214	57%	13.7	1			-7.2%								

Naanee is the most recent example of a team-wide trend in San Diego: acquire great athletes and gradually turn them into wide receivers. He happens to be the one with the coolest name. Naanee played wide receiver, tight end, and quarterback at times for Boise State while setting school weightlifting records. The Chargers toyed with using him as sort of a hybrid tight end/fullback/receiver, but he showed enough promise to switch full-time to receiver. He is probably a season or two away from being a regular contributor but will get a chance to compete for the third receiver job this year.

WIDE RECEIVERS 391

Jordy Nelson

Height: 6-3 Weight: 217 College: Kansas State — Draft: 2008/2 (36) Born: 31-May-1985 Age: 23 Risk: Red

Year	Team	G	Rec	Pass	Yds	C%	Yd/C	TD	YAC	Rk	DVOA	Rk	DYAR	Rk	YAR	Short	Mid	Deep	Bomb
2008	GB		10	19	81	53%	7.9	1			-6.4%								

The Packers' modus operandi in the post-Favre era seems simple—we may not have our Hall-of-Fame quarterback any more, but we'll kill your defense with a stacked roster of big receivers who can block and produce after the catch. Green Bay led the NFL in YAC in 2007 and put up a 61.4% DVOA in four-receiver, single-back formations. Nelson, who caught 122 passes as a senior, will fit that skillset perfectly. The obligatory pigment-impaired receiver comparison in this case is Ed McCaffrey.

Dennis Northcutt

Height: 5-11 Weight: 175 College: Arizona — Draft: 2000/2 (32) Born: 22-Dec-1977 Age: 30 Risk: Red

Year	Team	G	Rec	Pass	Yds	C%	Yd/C	TD	YAC	Rk	DVOA	Rk	DYAR	Rk	YAR	Short	Mid	Deep	Bomb
2005	CLE	16	42	77	441	55%	10.5	2	3.1	55	-20.8%	86	-49	84	-63	32%	46%	7%	16%
2006	CLE	13	22	45	228	49%	10.4	0	4.5	—	-21.3%	—	-30	—	-59	46%	32%	5%	16%
2007	JAC	15	44	73	601	60%	13.7	4	2.9	66	11.1%	23	132	38	120	24%	50%	20%	6%
2008	JAC		51	81	753	63%	14.8	4			13.3%								

With their crew of redwood-sized receivers and tight ends, Northcutt's stature alone makes him a nice change-of-pace cog in the Jacksonville passing game. In his first season with the Jaguars, he developed a nice rapport with David Garrard and turned in his highest reception total since 2003. He's also still a passable punt-return man, registering as just above-average in that department last year. KUBIAK seems to think he'll take another step forward with Jerry Porter helping to occupy the safeties.

Ben Obomanu

Height: 6-1 Weight: 198 College: Auburn — Draft: 2006/7 (249) Born: 30-Oct-1983 Age: 25 Risk: Red

Year	Team	G	Rec	Pass	Yds	C%	Yd/C	TD	YAC	Rk	DVOA	Rk	DYAR	Rk	YAR	Short	Mid	Deep	Bomb
2007	SEA	13	12	29	180	41%	15.0	1	4.5	—	-25.5%	—	-30	—	-20	32%	29%	32%	7%
2008	SEA		11	19	118	58%	10.8	0			5.1%								

Is that horrific catch rate an abberation or a harbinger of bad things to come? According to our game charters, Obomanu had only two drops—though that's two too many when you only catch 12 passes on the year—and he seemed to struggle to get open when on the field. Don't be surprised if fellow Auburn alumnus Courtney Taylor eats into his already limited playing time.

Terrell Owens

Height: 6-3 Weight: 226 College: Tennessee-Chattanooga — Draft: 1996/3 (89) Born: 7-Dec-1973 Age: 35 Risk: Yellow

Year	Team	G	Rec	Pass	Yds	C%	Yd/C	TD	YAC	Rk	DVOA	Rk	DYAR	Rk	YAR	Short	Mid	Deep	Bomb
2005	PHI	7	47	92	763	51%	16.2	6	7.7	2	6.0%	28	133	26	102	32%	41%	14%	13%
2006	DAL	16	85	152	1180	56%	13.9	13	4.0	36	5.7%	36	216	14	266	34%	28%	23%	15%
2007	DAL	15	81	141	1355	57%	16.7	15	4.3	25	28.2%	5	449	2	435	25%	43%	19%	13%
2008	DAL		82	147	1304	56%	15.9	14			7.8%								

What separated Owens's performance last year from previous seasons is where he was making his plays—Owens' 16.7 yards per catch average was his best full-season mark since 1998. Because deep threat Terry Glenn was injured, Owens ran deeper patterns, with Patrick Crayton and Jason Witten taking most of the underneath work. Romo and Owens mastered a devastating over-the-shoulder fade route, then used it to set up an almost indefensible hitch-and-go.

Eric Parker

Height: 6-0 Weight: 180 College: Tennessee — Draft: 2002/FA Born: 14-Apr-1979 Age: 29 Risk: Red

Year	Team	G	Rec	Pass	Yds	C%	Yd/C	TD	YAC	Rk	DVOA	Rk	DYAR	Rk	YAR	Short	Mid	Deep	Bomb
2005	SD	16	57	80	725	71%	12.7	3	2.9	65	24.7%	4	236	15	214	25%	49%	17%	9%
2006	SD	15	48	70	659	69%	13.7	0	2.7	66	23.0%	8	188	21	184	22%	44%	21%	13%
2008	SD		29	50	509	58%	17.3	3			-4.1%								

The most underrated possession receiver in football from 2004-2006, Parker's toe injury was a major factor in the Chargers' slow start. Parker should be 100 percent this fall, but his role on the team is far from certain. The Chargers have stockpiled a bevy of young receivers in recent years. At age 29, Parker needs to be healthy early this year, or the Chargers may just cut their losses and move on with the young receivers. If he does return to health, the Chargers will suddenly have one of the very top receiving corps in football. When their offense is among the best in the league, remember to note all of Parker's crucial third-down conversions.

Samie Parker   Height: 5-10 Weight: 178 College: Oregon   Draft: 2004/4 (105) Born: 25-Mar-1981 Age: 27 Risk: Red

Year	Team	G	Rec	Pass	Yds	C%	Yd/C	TD	YAC	Rk	DVOA	Rk	DYAR	Rk	YAR	Short	Mid	Deep	Bomb
2005	KC	12	36	58	533	62%	14.8	3	1.9	88	12.0%	19	114	32	105	13%	54%	28%	6%
2006	KC	16	41	68	561	60%	13.7	1	3.0	58	14.4%	21	145	32	130	29%	43%	21%	7%
2007	KC	15	24	39	298	62%	12.4	2	3.8	—	6.9%	—	62	—	68	37%	39%	16%	8%
2008	DEN		14	23	176	61%	12.5	1			8.7%								

The speedy Parker never developed as a consistent receiver. He was inconsistent in his route running and never able to gain consistent separation. The Chiefs waved goodbye, and Parker heads to the Broncos to compete for playing time. A brittle Brandon Stokley could open up playing time for Parker going forward.

Roscoe Parrish   Height: 5-9 Weight: 168 College: Miami   Draft: 2005/2 (55) Born: 16-Jul-1982 Age: 26 Risk: Red

Year	Team	G	Rec	Pass	Yds	C%	Yd/C	TD	YAC	Rk	DVOA	Rk	DYAR	Rk	YAR	Short	Mid	Deep	Bomb
2005	BUF	10	15	25	148	60%	9.9	1	3.8	—	-10.7%	—	3	—	0	58%	21%	16%	5%
2006	BUF	16	23	40	320	58%	13.9	2	6.5	—	-20.2%	—	-23	—	-22	44%	28%	8%	20%
2007	BUF	16	35	58	352	60%	10.1	1	3.6	44	-13.5%	74	-4	74	-21	45%	35%	5%	15%
2008	BUF		34	55	389	62%	11.6	2			-1.2%								

Parrish is a quick-twitch athlete in the Devin Hester class who is very effective on short hitches and comeback routes. Despite his speed, he doesn't get great separation on deep routes, though he out-leaped Ellis Hobbs for a 47-yard touchdown in Week 11 and toasted Corey Webster on a bomb in Week 16. He's well-suited to the slot receiver/punt returner role, though he could develop into a Derrick Mason–type undersized possession receiver.

David Patten   Height: 5-10 Weight: 190 College: Western Carolina   Draft: 1997/FA Born: 19-Aug-1974 Age: 34 Risk: Red

Year	Team	G	Rec	Pass	Yds	C%	Yd/C	TD	YAC	Rk	DVOA	Rk	DYAR	Rk	YAR	Short	Mid	Deep	Bomb
2005	WAS	9	22	53	217	42%	9.9	0	4.6	21	-32.7%	89	-82	89	-102	35%	47%	12%	7%
2006	WAS	5	1	4	25	25%	25.0	0	0.0	—	-67.4%	—	-16	—	-6	50%	0%	50%	0%
2007	NO	16	54	88	792	61%	14.7	3	4.6	21	6.6%	32	136	35	133	30%	37%	19%	14%
2008	NO		45	80	617	56%	13.6	2			-1.8%								

Drew Brees's second receiver behind Marques Colston, Patten had his best season in years. He led the team in yards after catch, which became invaluable in the last month of the season as Brees was forced more and more to make short throws under pressure. Patten signed a two-year deal in the offseason, and he's helping Robert Meachem—the second-year receiver who may move him to the slot—rehab and overcome the knee injury that ruined his rookie season. Wherever he plays, Patten will provide reliability and value for a team with an increasingly crowded cadre of young receivers.

Jerry Porter   Height: 6-2 Weight: 220 College: West Virginia   Draft: 2000/2 (47) Born: 14-Jul-1978 Age: 30 Risk: Yellow

Year	Team	G	Rec	Pass	Yds	C%	Yd/C	TD	YAC	Rk	DVOA	Rk	DYAR	Rk	YAR	Short	Mid	Deep	Bomb
2005	OAK	16	76	142	942	54%	12.4	5	2.9	64	-4.3%	53	92	37	63	28%	43%	23%	6%
2006	OAK	4	1	4	19	25%	19.0	0	0.0	—	-3.0%	—	2	—	-3	0%	50%	25%	25%
2007	OAK	16	44	102	705	43%	16.0	6	4.3	27	-10.7%	73	16	72	16	20%	38%	22%	20%
2008	JAC		56	101	909	55%	16.2	8			15.3%								

Porter's one-man strike of 2006 came to an end with the hiring of Lane Kiffin. His return to the field, however, was not so successful. The Raiders' hapless passing attack would devolve at times to a desperate attempt to throw deep to Porter, with the usual result an incompletion. He signed one last big contract with Jacksonville, where he will compete for a starting role. As a number-one receiver, Porter may disappoint due to his inability to consistently get open on intermediate routes. If the team looks to him as a secondary big-play option, he can be very productive. If this projection seems high to you, go back to the quarterbacks and read Byron Leftwich's comment.

Antwaan Randle El

Height: 5-10 Weight: 186 College: Indiana   Draft: 2002/2 (62) Born: 17-Aug-1979 Age: 29 Risk: Red

Year	Team	G	Rec	Pass	Yds	C%	Yd/C	TD	YAC	Rk	DVOA	Rk	DYAR	Rk	YAR	Short	Mid	Deep	Bomb
2005	PIT	16	35	70	558	50%	15.9	1	6.0	8	-8.1%	67	25	66	33	25%	39%	23%	13%
2006	WAS	16	32	63	351	51%	11.0	3	2.5	71	-8.1%	60	23	61	-51	40%	23%	23%	15%
2007	WAS	15	51	77	728	66%	14.3	1	3.6	43	16.9%	13	179	27	183	29%	45%	15%	10%
2008	WAS		45	87	686	52%	15.1	2			-8.6%								

Randle El took a step forward to remove himself from the "We Were the Busts of 2006" group that should have a re-union show on VH-1 sometime soon. He emerged as a number-two receiver, increasing his catch rate dramatically. That screams fluke to us, and while Randle El might keep it in the 58-61 percent range, a 15 percent rise in catch rate simply doesn't happen all that frequently. The selections of Malcolm Kelly and Devin Thomas in the second round should push Randle El back into his preferred slot role.

Josh Reed

Height: 5-10 Weight: 208 College: LSU   Draft: 2002/2 (36) Born: 1-May-1980 Age: 28 Risk: Red

Year	Team	G	Rec	Pass	Yds	C%	Yd/C	TD	YAC	Rk	DVOA	Rk	DYAR	Rk	YAR	Short	Mid	Deep	Bomb
2005	BUF	16	32	53	449	60%	14.0	2	6.5	6	4.0%	33	69	48	77	40%	43%	15%	2%
2006	BUF	13	34	48	410	71%	12.1	2	4.3	—	9.9%	—	79	—	83	51%	32%	12%	5%
2007	BUF	15	51	87	578	59%	11.3	0	4.0	33	-7.3%	65	36	65	35	44%	40%	16%	0%
2008	BUF		56	94	619	60%	11.0	3			-6.3%								

Most teams like to pair their deep threat receiver with a big possession type who can work the middle of the field and move the chains. The Bills just loaded up on deep threats in recent years, surrounding Lear jet Lee Evans with players like Reed, a five-foot-ten shake 'n' bake artist who was a failure as a chain mover (-41.1% DVOA, 39 percent catch rate on third downs). Reed is a slot receiver who gets miscast as a starter: throw him a few jet screens and hitches per game and he'll help you, but six targets per week are too many. James Hardy will gobble up some of his playing time.

Sidney Rice

Height: 6-4 Weight: 200 College: South Carolina   Draft: 2007/2 (44) Born: 1-Sep-1986 Age: 22 Risk: Red

Year	Team	G	Rec	Pass	Yds	C%	Yd/C	TD	YAC	Rk	DVOA	Rk	DYAR	Rk	YAR	Short	Mid	Deep	Bomb
2007	MIN	13	31	53	396	58%	12.8	4	3.0	63	11.5%	22	100	50	87	29%	48%	6%	17%
2008	MIN		47	83	571	57%	12.3	4			-4.0%								

It was a promising rookie campaign for Sidney Rice, all things considered. This second-rounder from South Caro-lina started only four games, but still finished second on the team in receiving yards and led the team in touchdown catches. In his sophomore season, the first improvement Vikings are hoping for will be production on the road. Rice averaged 3.3 catches for 37 yards in seven games in the Metrodome, but only 1.6 catches for 27 yards away from home, a number that is pumped up by one 60-yarder in Giants Stadium. Rice will be starting alongside Bernard Berrian this season, and both will have the same assignment: produce enough big plays that teams are afraid to stuff the line of scrimmage to stop Adrian Peterson and Chester Taylor.

Koren Robinson

Height: 6-1 Weight: 205 College: North Carolina State   Draft: 2001/1 (9) Born: 19-Mar-1980 Age: 28 Risk: Red

Year	Team	G	Rec	Pass	Yds	C%	Yd/C	TD	YAC	Rk	DVOA	Rk	DYAR	Rk	YAR	Short	Mid	Deep	Bomb
2005	MIN	14	22	37	347	59%	15.8	1	5.1	—	9.9%	—	70	—	57	41%	25%	13%	22%
2006	GB	4	7	16	89	44%	12.7	0	2.7	—	4.5%	—	20	—	2	19%	38%	31%	13%
2007	GB	9	21	34	241	62%	11.5	1	5.7	—	-15.7%	—	-8	—	4	45%	42%	9%	3%

The Packers released Robinson after the draft. Most of his production last season came in a 34-0 rout over the

Vikings and a rest-the-starters affair in Week 17. Robinson made a positive contribution as a kick returner but couldn't nudge James Jones and Ruvall Martin aside for playing time. Once a 1,000-yard receiver, Robinson's best bet to stay in the NFL is to find a new employer, make an impact on returns, and have a churchmouse-quiet year off the field.

Laurent Robinson   Height: 6-2   Weight: 199   College: Illinois State   Draft: 2007/3 (75)   Born: 20-May-1985   Age: 23   Risk: Yellow

Year	Team	G	Rec	Pass	Yds	C%	Yd/C	TD	YAC	Rk	DVOA	Rk	DYAR	Rk	YAR	Short	Mid	Deep	Bomb
2007	ATL	15	37	74	437	50%	11.8	1	3.5	45	-29.5%	82	-98	82	-84	32%	35%	17%	15%
2008	ATL		55	105	589	52%	10.7	5			-12.4%								

Roddy White is Number One, and Mike Jenkins is Number Three. The Falcons would like to point to Robinson, *Prisoner*-style, and say, "You are the new Number Two," as Joe Horn fades into the distance. Robinson showed some potential at the team's fourth receiver in 2007, especially in a seven-catch Week 16 performance in which he torched Arizona's Antrell Rolle for his first career touchdown. Coming out of Illinois State as a third-round pick last year, Robinson blew people away with a 4.36 40 at the Combine and surprised his new team with fearlessness in traffic that belied his thin frame and speedster status. He's a player to watch.

Ryne Robinson   Height: 5-9   Weight: 179   College: Miami (OH)   Draft: 2007/4 (118)   Born: 4-Nov-1984   Age: 24   Risk: Red

Year	Team	G	Rec	Pass	Yds	C%	Yd/C	TD	YAC	Rk	DVOA	Rk	DYAR	Rk	YAR	Short	Mid	Deep	Bomb
2007	CAR	16	4	8	35	50%	8.8	0	4.3	—	-37.5%	—	-16	—	-14	50%	50%	0%	0%
2008	CAR		19	32	280	59%	14.6	1			-1.1%								

Robinson left Miami of Ohio as the nation's active career leader in punt return yardage and touchdowns. Drafted in the fourth round by the Panthers, he saw a lot of time on special teams and got a cup of coffee late in the season as a receiver. The Panthers are looking at him more as a return man; they're hoping for Roscoe Parrish-style results.

Eddie Royal   Height: 5-10   Weight: 184   College: Virginia Tech   Draft: 2008/2 (42)   Born: 21-May-1986   Age: 22   Risk: Red

Year	Team	G	Rec	Pass	Yds	C%	Yd/C	TD	YAC	Rk	DVOA	Rk	DYAR	Rk	YAR	Short	Mid	Deep	Bomb
2008	DEN		16	29	176	55%	10.8	1			-13.6%								

The Denver Broncos fell to the Chicago Bears in Week 12 in about as good a game as two non-playoff teams can play. In the game, Devin Hester returned two kicks for touchdowns. The Broncos decided to try and get their own dominant return man by drafting Royal in the second round. Nobody has Hester's skills in the open field, but Royal should be a big upgrade, particularly on punts: he returned three for touchdowns in 2006 and 2007 for Virginia Tech. He also showed some toughness as a receiver, though he's undersized and dropped some passes. He'll be a dynamic return man when healthy, but he tweaked a hammy in the Senior Bowl, had some muscular irregularities in his leg in 2005, and doesn't have a great reputation for playing through pain.

Jerome Simpson   Height: 6-2   Weight: 190   College: Coastal Carolina   Draft: 2008/2 (46)   Born: 4-Feb-1986   Age: 22   Risk: Red

Year	Team	G	Rec	Pass	Yds	C%	Yd/C	TD	YAC	Rk	DVOA	Rk	DYAR	Rk	YAR	Short	Mid	Deep	Bomb
2008	CIN		25	47	381	53%	15.0	2			-1.4%								

The Bengals' recent track record for unearthing talented receivers in the draft is unmatched in the NFL, which makes their selection of the small-school Simpson so intriguing. Simpson comes from Coastal Carolina with a rep for great hands and acrobatic catches. The Bengals hope that he can immediately supply the deep threat previously provided by Chris Henry and eventually develop into a complete receiver. If the Bengals are without Chad Johnson, however, Simpson will have to take the accelerated class and make the transition from the Big South to the NFL in his first year. If Johnson is traded before the season, this projection changes to 41 receptions for 600 yards and four touchdowns.

Brad Smith

Height: 6-2   Weight: 210   College: Missouri   Draft: 2006/4 (103)   Born: 12-Dec-1983   Age: 24   Risk: Yellow

Year	Team	G	Rec	Pass	Yds	C%	Yd/C	TD	YAC	Rk	DVOA	Rk	DYAR	Rk	YAR	Short	Mid	Deep	Bomb
2006	NYJ	16	9	14	61	64%	6.8	0	4.1	—	-27.6%	—	-16	—	-18	58%	42%	0%	0%
2007	NYJ	16	32	67	325	48%	10.2	2	3.8	39	-23.7%	77	-57	77	-81	39%	32%	21%	8%
2008	NYJ		25	44	247	57%	9.8	2			1.5%								

For a nifty, shifty, trick play specialist, Smith rarely racks up many yards after the catch. He picked up 19 yards on a shovel pass against the Dolphins and produced a 29-yard catch-and-run against the Titans, but for all the effort the Jets make getting him the ball in space, he doesn't do anything in the open field that your typical slot receiver couldn't do. Factor in the dropped passes (five at least) and the inexperience (he gives up on deep passes and doesn't help his quarterbacks much on shorter routes) and you have an awful third wideout on a team that needs production from the position. Smith has purpose as an all-purpose special teamer, emergency quarterback, and bit player, but four targets and an end-around per game is too much attention.

Marcus Smith

Height: 6-2   Weight: 221   College: New Mexico   Draft: 2008/4 (106)   Born: 11-Jan-1985   Age: 23   Risk: Red

Year	Team	G	Rec	Pass	Yds	C%	Yd/C	TD	YAC	Rk	DVOA	Rk	DYAR	Rk	YAR	Short	Mid	Deep	Bomb
2008	BAL		15	28	174	54%	11.6	1			-13.9%								

Smith is a fourth-round pick out of New Mexico who had a very productive senior season for the Lobos, notching 91 receptions for 1,125 yards and four touchdowns. He was recruited as a running back and still has work to do on his route running, but he can contribute immediately on special teams. His future is probably lining up in the slot in three- and four-receiver sets, and given the lack of receiver depth in Baltimore, he might be playing more than people expect.

Steve Smith

Height: 5-9   Weight: 179   College: Utah   Draft: 2001/3 (74)   Born: 12-May-1979   Age: 29   Risk: Yellow

Year	Team	G	Rec	Pass	Yds	C%	Yd/C	TD	YAC	Rk	DVOA	Rk	DYAR	Rk	YAR	Short	Mid	Deep	Bomb
2005	CAR	16	103	150	1563	69%	15.2	12	7.5	3	28.6%	1	497	1	504	44%	27%	16%	13%
2006	CAR	14	83	139	1166	60%	14.0	8	5.2	7	16.8%	16	323	5	206	34%	30%	21%	15%
2007	CAR	15	87	148	1002	58%	11.5	7	5.5	8	-9.1%	68	42	63	51	43%	34%	11%	12%
2008	CAR		86	142	1154	61%	13.4	11			20.1%								

At some point, Steve Smith's productivity had to fall off. You simply can't expect one player to be a team's only consistently explosive threat for three straight years, surround him with bargain-basement "complementary" players, and whistle a merry tune as he somehow manages to exploit double coverages over and over. The breaking point for Smith last year was the Panthers quarterback situation. He gained 281 of his 1,002 yards in the season's first three games. Common denominator: Jake Delhomme. After Delhomme's Week 3 injury, Smith managed only two 100-yard games the rest of the year. With Delhomme returning to health, the addition of D. J. Hackett, the return of Mushin Muhammad, and a re-fortified power running game, Smith should finally have the talent around him to do some real damage again. Even if he doesn't, he'll still do better than most in his position.

Steve Smith

Height: 6-0   Weight: 197   College: USC   Draft: 2007/2 (51)   Born: 6-May-1985   Age: 23   Risk: Red

Year	Team	G	Rec	Pass	Yds	C%	Yd/C	TD	YAC	Rk	DVOA	Rk	DYAR	Rk	YAR	Short	Mid	Deep	Bomb
2007	NYG	5	8	14	63	57%	7.9	0	2.5	—	-15.8%	—	-4	—	-14	31%	46%	0%	23%
2008	NYG		39	62	496	63%	12.8	1			0.8%								

The other Steve Smith missed most of the campaign with a shoulder injury, and when he came back, he pulled a hammy and missed three more weeks. He wasn't activated until Week 15, and he didn't do much at the end of the regular season, but once the playoffs rolled around, he was suddenly an excellent third wideout operating out of the slot. He caught more passes (14) in the playoffs than he did in the regular season, showing off excellent hands, the intelligence to find openings on plays that were breaking down, and a good rapport with Eli Manning, who found Smith almost exclusively on crossing patterns. Smith should replace Amani Toomer in the starting lineup as early as this season, but he'll need to stay healthy to stay there.

Donte' Stallworth

Height: 6-0   Weight: 197   College: Tennessee   Draft: 2002/1 (13)   Born: 10-Nov-1980   Age: 28   Risk: Red

Year	Team	G	Rec	Pass	Yds	C%	Yd/C	TD	YAC	Rk	DVOA	Rk	DYAR	Rk	YAR	Short	Mid	Deep	Bomb
2005	NO	16	70	129	945	54%	13.5	7	3.3	49	0.5%	42	131	27	129	21%	48%	23%	8%
2006	PHI	12	38	78	725	49%	19.1	5	5.6	4	1.0%	47	84	49	134	19%	37%	29%	15%
2007	NE	16	46	74	697	62%	15.2	3	6.8	2	12.2%	20	150	29	146	42%	34%	8%	15%
2008	CLE		56	109	811	51%	14.5	4			0.9%								

What you see is what you get: a hashmark-to-boundry, screen and bomb, 2b or 3a receiver whose opinion of his own value is slightly higher than his real value. The Browns can afford Stallworth because they have a true number-one receiver (Braylon Edwards), a great tight end (Kellen Winslow), and a solid possession receiver (Joe Jurevicius), allowing them to shop for offensive rims and trim. Stallworth caught 33 passes in the eight games from October 1 through November 25 but just 21 in his other 11 games (including the postseason).

Brandon Stokley

Height: 5-11   Weight: 197   College: Louisiana-Lafayette   Draft: 1999/4 (105)   Born: 23-Jun-1976   Age: 32   Risk: Red

Year	Team	G	Rec	Pass	Yds	C%	Yd/C	TD	YAC	Rk	DVOA	Rk	DYAR	Rk	YAR	Short	Mid	Deep	Bomb
2005	IND	15	41	67	543	61%	13.2	1	5.4	11	3.9%	36	84	41	102	42%	34%	22%	3%
2006	IND	4	8	11	85	73%	10.6	1	3.6	—	48.8%	—	45	—	28	25%	42%	17%	17%
2007	DEN	13	40	71	635	56%	15.9	5	3.0	64	25.7%	7	219	19	207	14%	55%	20%	11%
2008	DEN		38	63	521	60%	13.7	2			1.1%								

Stokley's 2004 season stuck out as a fluke: Peyton Manning's third receivers have years like those. Two unproductive, injury-plagued seasons followed that breakout, so the Broncos took a big risk by signing him. Score one for Mike Shanahan, as Stokley remained reasonably healthy and highly productive as a second option. Stokley worked down the field more in Denver than he did in Indianapolis, but he still has a knack for making the important catch. Also, Stokley is an adept open-field blocker, helping runners to break big plays. Unfortunately, his age and injury history make him risky on a year-to-year basis.

Maurice Stovall

Height: 6-5   Weight: 222   College: Notre Dame   Draft: 2006/3 (90)   Born: 21-Feb-1985   Age: 23   Risk: Red

Year	Team	G	Rec	Pass	Yds	C%	Yd/C	TD	YAC	Rk	DVOA	Rk	DYAR	Rk	YAR	Short	Mid	Deep	Bomb
2006	TB	9	7	13	102	54%	14.6	0	3.5	—	8.0%	—	21	—	6	30%	50%	20%	0%
2007	TB	15	10	13	86	77%	8.6	1	2.3	—	7.6%	—	20	—	21	38%	54%	0%	8%
2008	TB		17	29	178	59%	10.2	1			-6.6%								

If you're going to be a possession receiver, it helps to have a high catch rate. Stovall tied Wes Welker for the third-highest catch rate among receivers with at least 10 passes. Of course, Welker was targeted ten times more often, so there is a sample size alert here. There's speculation that Stovall could wind up anywhere from the starting three to the practice squad, but he'll most likely bump up his catches a bit more and make a bigger contribution among the herd of receivers competing for reps behind Joey Galloway.

Chansi Stuckey

Height: 5-11   Weight: 197   College: Clemson   Draft: 2007/7 (235)   Born: 4-Oct-1983   Age: 25   Risk: Red

Year	Team	G	Rec	Pass	Yds	C%	Yd/C	TD	YAC	Rk	DVOA	Rk	DYAR	Rk	YAR	Short	Mid	Deep	Bomb
2008	NYJ		30	61	376	49%	12.4	2			-19.2%								

Stuckey, a seventh-round draft choice out of Clemson, was well on his way to winning the slot receiver job with the Jets last year when he suffered a season-ending foot injury in training camp. He's healthy now, and early reports are that Stuckey is running as the third receiver in OTAs. Like incumbent Brad Smith, Stuckey is a former quarterback, but his speed and lateral quickness make him a better fit in the slot. Stuckey's primary competition for playing time might not come from the other receivers but from first-round pick Dustin Keller, a receiving tight end who figures to see a lot of time split out wide.

Limas Sweed

Height: 6-4 Weight: 212 College: Texas   Draft: 2008/2 (53) Born: 25-Dec-1984 Age: 23 Risk: Red

Year	Team	G	Rec	Pass	Yds	C%	Yd/C	TD	YAC	Rk	DVOA	Rk	DYAR	Rk	YAR	Short	Mid	Deep	Bomb
2008	PIT		34	62	560	55%	16.4	4			22.0%								

Most mock drafts had Sweed as one of the first couple receivers off the board. Instead, he was the ninth receiver taken. He landed in a good home in Pittsburgh, where he will be the tall receiver that Ben Roethlisberger requested. Sweed was limited in his senior season due to a wrist injury, but he caught 46 passes and had 12 touchdowns in 2006 and could become a top red zone threat. He needs to develop more consistent intermediate routes to become a starter in the NFL. In his favor, spending every day with Hines Ward and Santonio Holmes is a good way to develop into a complete receiver.

Courtney Taylor

Height: 6-2 Weight: 204 College: Auburn   Draft: 2007/6 (197) Born: 7-Apr-1984 Age: 24 Risk: Red

Year	Team	G	Rec	Pass	Yds	C%	Yd/C	TD	YAC	Rk	DVOA	Rk	DYAR	Rk	YAR	Short	Mid	Deep	Bomb
2007	SEA	8	5	6	38	83%	7.6	0	2.8	—	-5.0%	—	4	—	9	67%	17%	0%	17%
2008	SEA		28	46	360	61%	12.7	3			1.9%								

Much like former Seahawks receiver D. J. Hackett, Taylor is tall, runs precise routes, and has good hands. Like Hackett, he seems to hurt himself whenever he steps onto the field. Taylor missed all of Seattle's May minicamps with an undefined injury and seems to be fading from the competition to be the Seahawks' third wide receiver this year.

Devin Thomas

Height: 6-2 Weight: 215 College: Michigan State   Draft: 2008/2 (34) Born: 15-Nov-1986 Age: 22 Risk: Red

Year	Team	G	Rec	Pass	Yds	C%	Yd/C	TD	YAC	Rk	DVOA	Rk	DYAR	Rk	YAR	Short	Mid	Deep	Bomb
2008	WAS		19	36	247	53%	12.9	1			-19.5%								

Thomas is a one-year wonder, going from six catches in 2006 to 79 in 2007. As a result, his selection is all upside and scouting wonder. Although the Redskins chose him ahead of Malcolm Kelly, Kelly's the far-more-ready pro prospect at the moment, so expect Kelly to be a better bet than Thomas in fantasy terms this year.

James Thrash

Height: 6-0 Weight: 200 College: Missouri Southern State   Draft: 1997/FA Born: 28-Apr-1975 Age: 33 Risk: Red

Year	Team	G	Rec	Pass	Yds	C%	Yd/C	TD	YAC	Rk	DVOA	Rk	DYAR	Rk	YAR	Short	Mid	Deep	Bomb
2005	WAS	12	14	30	194	47%	13.9	0	3.5	—	-10.3%	—	5	—	-1	43%	39%	9%	9%
2006	WAS	16	12	20	151	60%	12.6	1	1.7	—	12.9%	—	42	—	27	21%	47%	21%	11%
2007	WAS	12	9	18	107	50%	11.9	2	3.3	—	-3.5%	—	13	—	17	39%	17%	17%	28%
2008	WAS		25	41	255	61%	10.3	1			-2.3%								

When Donovan McNabb's Hall of Fame case is officially made, his presenter should merely state that McNabb made the NFC Championship game three times with Thrash as a starting receiver. In all fairness, Thrash was wildly ill-suited for a role as a go-to receiver, but as a third or fourth receiver who plays special teams, he is a real asset.

Amani Toomer

Height: 6-3 Weight: 208 College: Michigan   Draft: 1996/2 (34) Born: 8-Sep-1974 Age: 34 Risk: Red

Year	Team	G	Rec	Pass	Yds	C%	Yd/C	TD	YAC	Rk	DVOA	Rk	DYAR	Rk	YAR	Short	Mid	Deep	Bomb
2005	NYG	16	60	109	684	55%	11.4	7	2.6	75	6.0%	30	165	22	137	28%	48%	14%	11%
2006	NYG	8	32	50	360	64%	11.3	3	1.4	82	7.7%	29	81	51	88	26%	46%	17%	11%
2007	NYG	16	59	104	760	57%	12.9	3	3.5	49	3.1%	41	133	37	120	32%	42%	22%	4%
2008	NYG		60	103	790	58%	13.2	4			2.8%								

The other Giant who spent last offseason going through a messy, public divorce, Toomer returned from a torn ACL to put up competent second-wideout numbers despite eight drops during the regular season. Of course, in the playoffs, Toomer caught everything thrown in his direction. Toomer has always used his six-foot-three frame well to shade defensive backs from the ball, which comes in handy when you're almost exclusively running slants and ins. Toomer can still be a useful player at this level of performance, but with Sinorice Moss, Steve Smith, and now Mario Manningham all finding their way to the blue side of the swamp in the draft, even the slightest slip could mean the end of Toomer's career as a first-division starter. KUBIAK's expectation of Eli Manning improvement balances out the expectation of Toomer decline.

David Tyree
Height: 6-0 Weight: 205 College: Syracuse Draft: 2003/6 (211) Born: 3-Jan-1980 Age: 28 Risk: Red

Year	Team	G	Rec	Pass	Yds	C%	Yd/C	TD	YAC	Rk	DVOA	Rk	DYAR	Rk	YAR	Short	Mid	Deep	Bomb
2005	NYG	13	5	9	52	56%	10.4	1	4.4	—	-7.5%	—	3	—	2	44%	33%	22%	0%
2006	NYG	16	19	33	197	58%	10.4	2	2.4	—	-0.8%	—	31	—	0	43%	43%	14%	0%
2007	NYG	12	4	5	35	80%	8.8	0	4.5	—	-17.1%	—	-2	—	-3	60%	20%	20%	0%
2008	NYG		16	25	207	64%	13.0	1			-9.2%								

Good at catching balls against his helmet. What, you expected us to mention his special teams play? The man who launched a million nicknames made arguably the greatest play in Super Bowl history—certainly, the greatest since Mike Jones stopped Kevin Dyson on the one-yard line, or when the ol' googly-eye from New England long snapper Lonie Paxton caused John Kasay to shank the final kickoff out of bounds. Either way, Tyree's moment in history is complete. As an actual player rather than a legend, he's a useful special teams guy who might get caught up in the numbers game in New York. What happened in Arizona was special, but shouldn't count for anything extra come training camp.

Jerheme Urban
Height: 6-3 Weight: 212 College: Trinity International Draft: 2003/FA Born: 26-Nov-1980 Age: 28 Risk: Red

Year	Team	G	Rec	Pass	Yds	C%	Yd/C	TD	YAC	Rk	DVOA	Rk	DYAR	Rk	YAR	Short	Mid	Deep	Bomb
2005	SEA	4	7	10	151	70%	21.6	0	5.3	—	62.6%	—	64	—	64	11%	22%	67%	0%
2007	ARI	10	22	38	329	58%	15.0	2	3.7	—	22.4%	—	101	—	92	20%	43%	29%	9%
2008	ARI		23	39	273	59%	11.9	1			-5.4%								

Urban, who spent four years knocking around the Seahawks and Cowboys rosters, was surprisingly productive in his two starts last year: nine catches, 164 yards, one touchdown. But he'll really have to show something to compete with Steve Breaston and Early Doucet for the third-receiver role.

Bobby Wade
Height: 5-10 Weight: 193 College: Arizona Draft: 2003/5 (139) Born: 25-Feb-1981 Age: 27 Risk: Red

Year	Team	G	Rec	Pass	Yds	C%	Yd/C	TD	YAC	Rk	DVOA	Rk	DYAR	Rk	YAR	Short	Mid	Deep	Bomb
2005	CHI	14	14	29	120	48%	8.6	0	2.7	—	-58.6%	—	-98	—	-92	57%	38%	5%	0%
2006	TEN	16	33	58	461	57%	14.0	2	5.0	11	7.2%	31	88	48	76	40%	20%	32%	8%
2007	MIN	16	54	83	647	65%	12.0	3	3.0	65	8.5%	30	133	36	132	43%	43%	9%	6%
2008	MIN		43	76	476	57%	11.1	2			-3.3%								

Wade wins the prize for "Minnesota's most valuable wide receiver in 2007." There is a joke to be made here about the skinniest kid at fat camp, but we don't want to insult overweight children by comparing them to the Vikings receivers. It also says something that the top receiver in Minnesota played for both Chicago and Tennessee in a span of less than two years, and neither team was sad to see him go. Wade is a possession receiver and nothing more; 72 percent of his targets came within 10 yards of the line of scrimmage, and 93 percent came within 20 yards. The acquisition of Bernard Berrian means Wade will be lining up in the slot, making him Minnesota's poverty-level answer to Bobby Engram. With Mewelde Moore departing for Pittsburgh, Wade may also take over as the team's primary punt returner, and that's not good. The two split time roughly evenly in 2007, but Moore was clearly superior (a 10-yard average with a long of 42, compared to Wade's 7-yard average with a long of 17).

Javon Walker
Height: 6-3 Weight: 220 College: Florida State Draft: 2002/1 (20) Born: 14-Oct-1978 Age: 30 Risk: Red

Year	Team	G	Rec	Pass	Yds	C%	Yd/C	TD	YAC	Rk	DVOA	Rk	DYAR	Rk	YAR	Short	Mid	Deep	Bomb
2005	GB	1	4	5	27	80%	6.8	0	0.5	—	10.1%	—	12	—	11	25%	75%	0%	0%
2006	DEN	16	69	126	1084	55%	15.7	8	5.0	12	14.3%	22	267	10	206	29%	40%	14%	18%
2007	DEN	8	26	50	287	52%	11.0	0	4.5	24	-30.2%	83	-66	78	-49	34%	53%	9%	4%
2008	OAK		47	87	525	54%	11.1	4			-11.8%								

Walker appears to only play well in even-numbered years. In 2006, he surpassed all expectations by recovering from an ACL injury and joining Denver as a big-play receiver. Last season, however, his knee flared up and rendered him nearly useless. The Raiders gave him a clean bill of health and signed him to a contract commensurate with his upside. Ignoring the risk is a poor move by Al Davis, but Walker has been a top receiver when healthy. Unless his knee completely falls apart, he should give the Raiders some productive seasons.

Kevin Walter

Height: 6-3   Weight: 221   College: Eastern Michigan   Draft: 2003/7 (255)   Born: 4-Aug-1981   Age: 27   Risk: Red

Year	Team	G	Rec	Pass	Yds	C%	Yd/C	TD	YAC	Rk	DVOA	Rk	DYAR	Rk	YAR	Short	Mid	Deep	Bomb
2005	CIN	16	19	29	211	66%	11.1	1	3.7	—	10.1%	—	55	—	57	38%	42%	15%	4%
2006	HOU	16	17	21	160	81%	9.4	0	2.7	—	18.5%	—	51	—	27	38%	52%	0%	10%
2007	HOU	16	65	106	800	61%	12.3	4	2.6	74	8.9%	29	182	26	182	27%	50%	12%	12%
2008	HOU		60	92	747	65%	12.5	4			9.5%								

Walter was one of Houston's pleasant surprises last year. Nabbing a starting spot after signing as a little-regarded free-agent, he was a steady performer all year. His numbers did get a boost when Andre Johnson missed seven games—he caught 41 passes for 528 yards during that stretch, which included a 12-catch, 160-yard performance against Jacksonville in Week 6. Still, the margin between Walter and those chasing him on the depth chart (Jacoby Jones, David Anderson) is a thin one.

Troy Walters

Height: 5-7   Weight: 172   College: Stanford   Draft: 2000/5 (165)   Born: 15-Dec-1976   Age: 31   Risk: Red

Year	Team	G	Rec	Pass	Yds	C%	Yd/C	TD	YAC	Rk	DVOA	Rk	DYAR	Rk	YAR	Short	Mid	Deep	Bomb
2005	IND	16	14	19	152	74%	10.9	3	3.4	—	20.2%	—	49	—	53	42%	50%	8%	0%
2006	ARI	15	23	35	209	66%	9.1	2	3.5	—	-5.3%	—	20	—	31	59%	25%	9%	6%
2007	DET	13	9	10	101	90%	11.2	1	2.2	—	42.1%	—	44	—	40	50%	30%	20%	0%
2008	DET		8	12	80	67%	10.0	1			-20.4%								

It's been a long time since Walters was the Colts' slot receiver and top return man. He spent last season as the Lions' fifth wideout and sometime return man. He caught nine of the 10 passes thrown his way in early season action but got hurt when the Lions actually needed him, suffering a concussion on a late-season punt return at the same time that Roy Williams went on the IR. He's a replacement level spare part who should stick for another year or two as a safe hands guy on punts.

Hines Ward

Height: 6-0   Weight: 205   College: Georgia   Draft: 1998/3 (92)   Born: 8-Mar-1976   Age: 32   Risk: Red

Year	Team	G	Rec	Pass	Yds	C%	Yd/C	TD	YAC	Rk	DVOA	Rk	DYAR	Rk	YAR	Short	Mid	Deep	Bomb
2005	PIT	15	69	114	975	61%	14.1	11	4.5	26	23.1%	6	325	6	321	24%	55%	17%	4%
2006	PIT	14	74	127	975	59%	13.2	6	4.6	19	12.6%	24	252	11	135	29%	44%	20%	7%
2007	PIT	13	71	113	732	64%	10.3	7	3.1	61	1.8%	43	124	41	144	30%	50%	19%	2%
2008	PIT		56	103	742	54%	13.3	4			-9.6%								

It's second-and-6. Ben Roethlisberger takes the snap and pitches the ball to Willie Parker, who breaks right. Willie Colon and Heath Miller seal the edge while the left guard pulls and leads Parker out to the second level, holding off the strong-side linebacker long enough for Fast Willie to hit the hole and make it into the secondary. By the time the free safety finally hauls him down, the Steelers have first-down yardage and more. Why? Because Pittsburgh's receivers blocked the cornerbacks out of the play. Ward has been one of the best blocking receivers in the NFL for years, and he has helped raise a young corps of pass-catchers in his image who are willing and able to help out with the running game. The Steelers were substantially better running outside than up the middle in 2007, and Ward and his protégés have something to do with that. Ward remains a useful possession receiver, but he had knee surgery in January and has seen his production drop four seasons in a row, so time is running out.

Paris Warren

Height: 6-0   Weight: 213   College: Utah   Draft: 2005/7 (225)   Born: 6-Sep-1982   Age: 26   Risk: Red

Year	Team	G	Rec	Pass	Yds	C%	Yd/C	TD	YAC	Rk	DVOA	Rk	DYAR	Rk	YAR	Short	Mid	Deep	Bomb
2006	TB	8	5	7	63	71%	12.6	0	3.8	—	53.7%	—	33	—	16	40%	40%	20%	0%
2008	TB		23	33	288	70%	12.3	1			20.3%								

Were the four touchdowns Warren caught in the 2007 preseason a fluke, or the start of something big? We never found out because he suffered a dislocated ankle in the exhibition finale, a game in which he caught seven passes for 110 yards and two of those scores. The injury shut Warren down for the regular season just as he was on the verge of gaining a roster spot, which is why he'll get a long look at this year's training camp. Anything close to a repeat performance will have him in the mix.

Nate Washington

Height: 6-1   Weight: 185   College: Tiffin   Draft: 2005/FA   Born: 28-Aug-1983   Age: 25   Risk: Red

Year	Team	G	Rec	Pass	Yds	C%	Yd/C	TD	YAC	Rk	DVOA	Rk	DYAR	Rk	YAR	Short	Mid	Deep	Bomb
2006	PIT	16	35	69	624	51%	17.8	4	3.1	55	29.0%	4	213	15	143	22%	38%	22%	18%
2007	PIT	16	29	56	450	52%	15.5	5	2.5	77	16.5%	15	124	40	133	9%	44%	26%	20%
2008	PIT		14	22	213	64%	15.2	1			-4.9%								

Washington repeated his impressive 2006 season, recording statistics that might suggest he is ready for an expanded role in the offense. On the downside, his catch rate was awful, the lowest in the league for a receiver with a DVOA in excess of 20%. Washington has the speed and agility to beat most of the coverage he faces, but he drops too many passes—five last season in limited work. This unreliability, plus so-so performances when filling in as a starter last year, led the Steelers to draft Limas Sweed as a better long-term replacement for Hines Ward. Washington was listed as the third wideout in May minicamp and has familiarity with the offense, but Sweed will be hard to hold off.

Reggie Wayne

Height: 6-0   Weight: 203   College: Miami   Draft: 2001/1 (30)   Born: 17-Nov-1978   Age: 30   Risk: Green

Year	Team	G	Rec	Pass	Yds	C%	Yd/C	TD	YAC	Rk	DVOA	Rk	DYAR	Rk	YAR	Short	Mid	Deep	Bomb
2005	IND	16	83	122	1055	68%	12.7	5	4.0	32	9.3%	24	218	18	270	32%	50%	12%	6%
2006	IND	16	86	137	1310	63%	15.2	9	2.3	76	29.9%	2	456	2	429	21%	46%	19%	14%
2007	IND	16	104	156	1510	67%	14.5	10	3.8	40	22.5%	10	443	3	440	32%	35%	18%	14%
2008	IND		101	162	1295	62%	12.8	12			14.7%								

When the Jaguars selected two defensive ends in the 2007 draft, they must have had visions of Reggie Wayne streaking through their heads. In his last five games against Jacksonville, Wayne has dominated the action, catching 33 passes for 562 yards, an average of 17.0 yards per catch. Apparently, the Jaguars have given up on ever covering Wayne, deciding instead to try to knock Peyton Manning down before he can ever pass the ball. If Jack Del Rio and company can find a way to stop Wayne, they may be the first to do so. Wayne paced the league with 1,510 yards in 2007; that figure and his 104 catches were both career highs, which mean he is likely to regress at least a little in 2008. Of course, when you're talking about the Indianapolis offense, regression means slipping from "best in the league" to "ordinary Pro Bowl starter." The machine rolls along. ...

Jeff Webb

Height: 6-2   Weight: 200   College: San Diego State   Draft: 2006/6 (190)   Born: 31-Jan-1982   Age: 26   Risk: Green

Year	Team	G	Rec	Pass	Yds	C%	Yd/C	TD	YAC	Rk	DVOA	Rk	DYAR	Rk	YAR	Short	Mid	Deep	Bomb
2006	KC	10	3	4	23	75%	7.7	0	0.0	—	6.6%	—	6	—	5	0%	100%	0%	0%
2007	KC	16	28	57	313	49%	11.2	1	2.0	83	-39.6%	87	-115	83	-106	27%	40%	18%	15%
2008	KC		28	47	317	60%	11.4	2			-0.7%								

Webb picked up a few starts late in the year and showed just enough potential to compete for a starting job opposite Dwayne Bowe this season. Webb is six foot two with long arms, making him a perfect specimen for a possession role. Herm Edwards said as much in January, saying that Webb was best suited to an "X-receiver" role (generally the split end who must beat the jam off the line) and praising Webb's physicality. Webb needs to develop a better short game to be anything more than a replacement-level starter, but he deserves a chance to play for an offense that isn't curled into the fetal position.

Wes Welker

Height: 5-9 Weight: 190 College: Texas Tech | Draft: 2004/FA | Born: 1-May-1981 | Age: 27 | Risk: Red

Year	Team	G	Rec	Pass	Yds	C%	Yd/C	TD	YAC	Rk	DVOA	Rk	DYAR	Rk	YAR	Short	Mid	Deep	Bomb
2005	MIA	16	29	52	434	56%	15.0	0	6.2	7	7.3%	26	79	43	67	26%	52%	15%	7%
2006	MIA	16	67	100	687	67%	10.3	1	4.1	30	-3.9%	57	66	55	85	53%	34%	8%	5%
2007	NE	16	112	145	1175	77%	10.5	8	5.7	6	21.3%	11	384	4	354	65%	29%	6%	0%
2008	NE		90	126	1049	71%	11.7	7			33.5%								

An interesting comparison to Welker is Terrance Mathis. Mathis was a short, shifty receiver and return man who hung around the Jets for several seasons in the early 1990s, catching 20-something passes per year and running a few end-arounds. He then signed with the June Jones's run-'n'-shoot Falcons, where he caught 111 passes in 1994 as the nominal second fiddle to a mercurial ultra-talented number-one receiver (Andre Rison). Mathis's slants-and-options game was perfect for the Falcons' offense, and he was able to use experience to compensate for declining skills once he reached his 30s, so he had three more 1,000-yard seasons and several other 60-catch level campaigns. Welker should be good for that level of production over the next half decade or so, but he has an advantage over Mathis: Tom Brady will deliver more good passes than Bobby Hebert or Chris Chandler did.

Roddy White

Height: 6-1 Weight: 201 College: Alabama-Birmingham | Draft: 2005/1 (27) | Born: 2-Nov-1981 | Age: 27 | Risk: Red

Year	Team	G	Rec	Pass	Yds	C%	Yd/C	TD	YAC	Rk	DVOA	Rk	DYAR	Rk	YAR	Short	Mid	Deep	Bomb
2005	ATL	16	29	68	446	43%	15.4	3	2.5	77	-9.1%	70	20	69	24	11%	53%	11%	25%
2006	ATL	16	30	64	506	47%	16.9	0	2.2	78	-8.6%	62	19	64	-14	15%	45%	13%	27%
2007	ATL	16	83	137	1202	61%	14.5	6	5.5	7	1.2%	46	148	30	167	34%	41%	16%	10%
2008	ATL		71	132	987	54%	13.9	8			7.9%								

It was hard to tell in the debacle that was Atlanta's offense, but White enjoyed a breakout season in 2007 after two disappointing seasons that belied his status as the team's first-round draft pick in 2005. White's catch rate shot up last season after awful totals in 2005 and 2006, and he's developed into a consistent after-catch gainer as well as a deep threat. In the short term, he'll be an underrated receiver due to a prevalent "wait-and-see" attitude. Over time, White and Matt Ryan could do some special things together. Either way, the journey from number-one receiver by default to number-one receiver by choice comes this year.

Ernest Wilford

Height: 6-3 Weight: 220 College: Virginia Tech | Draft: 2004/4 (120) | Born: 14-Jan-1979 | Age: 29 | Risk: Red

Year	Team	G	Rec	Pass	Yds	C%	Yd/C	TD	YAC	Rk	DVOA	Rk	DYAR	Rk	YAR	Short	Mid	Deep	Bomb
2005	JAC	16	41	74	681	55%	16.6	7	3.3	50	19.1%	10	181	21	207	21%	40%	22%	18%
2006	JAC	16	36	74	524	49%	14.6	2	3.5	46	-16.0%	72	-19	72	-6	18%	40%	25%	17%
2007	JAC	16	45	74	518	61%	11.5	3	2.2	82	10.2%	26	136	34	142	16%	60%	15%	8%
2008	MIA		55	95	556	58%	10.1	3			-4.3%								

It turns out that Wilford's promising 2005 campaign was just a tease. When pressed into a bigger role as a starter in 2006, he bombed. He returned to his rightful place as complementary receiver in 2007 and—despite the occasional drop—made important catches to move the chains. In Miami, he is part of a woeful passing attack and will likely see a good number of balls thrown in his direction. As a result, his conventional numbers should rise. Unfortunately, many of those balls will fall incomplete, and his advanced statistics should return to their disappointing 2006 levels.

Demetrius Williams

Height: 6-2 Weight: 191 College: Oregon | Draft: 2006/4 (111) | Born: 28-Mar-1983 | Age: 25 | Risk: Red

Year	Team	G	Rec	Pass	Yds	C%	Yd/C	TD	YAC	Rk	DVOA	Rk	DYAR	Rk	YAR	Short	Mid	Deep	Bomb
2006	BAL	16	22	45	396	49%	18.0	2	5.6	—	11.1%	—	81	—	53	11%	54%	22%	14%
2007	BAL	9	20	47	290	43%	14.5	0	1.5	—	-28.9%	—	-63	—	-47	16%	45%	20%	18%
2008	BAL		33	58	482	57%	14.7	2			0.7%								

Williams was 0-for-9 on red zone passes thrown to him. Part of the problem was Kyle Boller, who can't find tight spots near the red zone, but a better receiver would have caught three or four of those passes ... The Ravens are rumored to be moving to a base three receiver offense. That would mean a lot more playing time for Williams, who would line up on the outside while Derrick Mason or Mark Clayton slid into the slot receiver role. Williams was side-lined for much of the season with a high ankle sprain, but when healthy has the speed to be a vertical threat. He still needs to do a better job of hanging onto the ball.

Mike Williams Height: 6-5 Weight: 229 College: USC Draft: 2005/1 (10) Born: 4-Jan-1984 Age: 24 Risk: Yellow

Year	Team	G	Rec	Pass	Yds	C%	Yd/C	TD	YAC	Rk	DVOA	Rk	DYAR	Rk	YAR	Short	Mid	Deep	Bomb
2005	DET	14	29	57	350	51%	12.1	1	4.6	23	-16.5%	78	-17	76	-20	27%	52%	14%	7%
2006	DET	8	8	18	99	44%	12.4	1	3.2	—	-42.7%	—	-40	—	-23	27%	33%	33%	7%
2007	OAK	8	7	23	90	30%	12.9	0	4.0	—	-62.7%	—	-79	—	-82	36%	50%	9%	5%
2008	TEN		15	27	176	56%	12.0	2			-12.5%								

A change of scenery was apparently not what Williams needed to jumpstart a floundering career, as the Raiders cut him midseason. He simply does not have the speed or elusiveness to get open in the NFL, and his weight remains a major issue. Williams may not be one of the 200 best NFL wide receivers in the world, but because he was a star at USC, he got another shot in Tennessee. His college coordinator, Norm Chow, is no longer with the Titans, so Williams will be on a short leash. He reportedly lost 30 pounds, and this probably is his last chance to prove he is sufficiently dedicated to be an NFL player.

Reggie Williams Height: 6-3 Weight: 223 College: Washington Draft: 2004/1 (9) Born: 17-May-1983 Age: 25 Risk: Red

Year	Team	G	Rec	Pass	Yds	C%	Yd/C	TD	YAC	Rk	DVOA	Rk	DYAR	Rk	YAR	Short	Mid	Deep	Bomb
2005	JAC	16	35	63	445	56%	12.7	0	3.4	41	-18.2%	82	-26	80	-15	31%	33%	25%	11%
2006	JAC	16	52	91	616	57%	11.8	4	4.7	17	-13.2%	69	-4	69	13	47%	36%	11%	5%
2007	JAC	15	38	60	629	63%	16.6	10	5.8	4	25.6%	8	183	25	183	33%	37%	23%	7%
2008	JAC		35	60	475	58%	15.3	3			10.0%								

In the case of Williams, less is more. As a high draft pick, the Jaguars kept trying to push Williams into the starting line-up, only to watch him unable to consistently produce. Last season, Williams was relegated to third and fourth receiver and proved more than capable of beating nickel and dime corners for important first downs. The 10 touch-downs on 38 passes is an impressive but not remotely repeatable feat, so Williams is safely ignored in fantasy circles. Still, it is nice to see a guy who seemed like a certain bust turn into an important contributor.

Roy Williams Height: 6-2 Weight: 212 College: Texas Draft: 2004/1 (7) Born: 20-Dec-1981 Age: 26 Risk: Green

Year	Team	G	Rec	Pass	Yds	C%	Yd/C	TD	YAC	Rk	DVOA	Rk	DYAR	Rk	YAR	Short	Mid	Deep	Bomb
2005	DET	13	45	94	687	48%	15.3	8	3.4	42	-2.2%	44	78	44	63	25%	46%	15%	14%
2006	DET	16	82	151	1310	54%	16.0	7	4.2	28	5.5%	37	209	18	228	16%	39%	30%	15%
2007	DET	12	64	105	838	61%	13.1	5	4.6	23	1.1%	47	115	43	111	28%	42%	18%	12%
2008	DET		82	146	970	56%	11.9	8			5.3%								

The Lions spent most of the offseason deflecting Williams trade rumors. Williams took a step back from 2006 to 2007, but the PCL injury which ended his season is partly to blame, and it's hard to top 83 receptions when three other receivers are getting targeted eight or nine times per game. Rod Marinelli firmly denied all trade rumors, but it's easy to see how they started. The Lions seem perpetually dissatisfied with their best players for not turning into MVP-caliber superstars; instead of building around them, they criticize their shortcomings and move on to the next master plan. Williams is inconsistent and will drop some passes, but he's the guy opponents game-planned to stop last season, not Mike Furrey or Shaun McDonald. Williams and Calvin Johnson could be one of the five best 1-2 punches in the league if the Lions let them play football instead of politics.

Roydell Williams

Height: 6-0   Weight: 192   College: Tulane   Draft: 2005/4 (136)   Born: 14-Mar-1981   Age: 27   Risk: Red

Year	Team	G	Rec	Pass	Yds	C%	Yd/C	TD	YAC	Rk	DVOA	Rk	DYAR	Rk	YAR	Short	Mid	Deep	Bomb
2005	TEN	11	21	39	299	54%	14.2	2	3.8	—	-7.6%	—	15	—	14	18%	50%	8%	24%
2006	TEN	14	8	21	121	38%	15.1	0	4.7	—	-18.9%	—	-10	—	-19	19%	38%	13%	31%
2007	TEN	16	55	93	719	59%	13.1	4	3.9	36	-1.1%	54	85	55	96	36%	44%	8%	12%
2008	TEN		47	82	635	57%	13.5	3			-1.0%								

Williams has the speed to be a deep threat, but that's not the way the Titans have used him. He was the top red zone target in the offense, but he caught just 6 of the 13 passes thrown to him there, and he led the team in third down targets (34) but produced a -19.1% DVOA. The Titans need Justin McCariens or Alge Crumpler to be a better possession target, and their quarterback needs more patience. If Vince Young can get more confident sitting in the pocket and waiting for things to develop in front of him, he might start to find Williams downfield more often, and that would be better both for Williams and for the Titans.

Troy Williamson

Height: 6-1   Weight: 203   College: South Carolina   Draft: 2005/1 (7)   Born: 30-Apr-1983   Age: 25   Risk: Red

Year	Team	G	Rec	Pass	Yds	C%	Yd/C	TD	YAC	Rk	DVOA	Rk	DYAR	Rk	YAR	Short	Mid	Deep	Bomb
2005	MIN	14	24	52	372	46%	15.5	2	8.8	1	-5.5%	58	29	63	13	32%	29%	10%	29%
2006	MIN	14	37	76	455	49%	12.3	0	4.9	14	-19.9%	78	-44	78	-75	29%	41%	9%	21%
2007	MIN	11	18	38	240	47%	13.3	1	2.8	—	-19.5%	—	-21	—	-25	22%	54%	3%	22%
2008	JAC		34	65	558	52%	16.4	3			2.5%								

From the "We Are Not Making This Quote Up" department comes this gem from Jaguars receiving coach Todd Monken, on the acquisition of Troy Williamson from the Vikings: "I'm thrilled to have him. You want to work with guys you think you can improve." Apparently Monken likes Herculean tasks; past coaches have tried everything, including eye surgery, to help Williams achieve his potential. "His troubles in catching the ball have come down the field when it was obvious he was going to go the distance," Monken continued. And who wouldn't want a guy with a reputation for dropping wide-open long touchdown passes? Willamson was taken seventh overall in the 2005 draft, which produced a number of first-round busts at wide receiver: Williamson, Mike Williams, and Matt Jones. The jury is still out on Mark Clayton and Roddy White, but the only first-round wideout taken that year to be an unqualified success has been Braylon Edwards. The good projection here is the power of Jacksonville and David Garrard, not any real improvement from Williamson.

Cedrick Wilson

Height: 5-10   Weight: 183   College: Tennessee   Draft: 2001/6 (169)   Born: 17-Dec-1978   Age: 29   Risk: Red

Year	Team	G	Rec	Pass	Yds	C%	Yd/C	TD	YAC	Rk	DVOA	Rk	DYAR	Rk	YAR	Short	Mid	Deep	Bomb
2005	PIT	16	26	53	451	49%	17.3	0	2.3	84	-6.1%	59	26	65	26	20%	41%	20%	20%
2006	PIT	15	37	69	504	54%	13.6	1	3.5	44	9.9%	25	123	40	47	7%	58%	18%	17%
2007	PIT	16	18	30	207	60%	11.5	1	2.4	—	1.9%	—	33	—	41	20%	63%	17%	0%

The Steelers cut Wilson after he was charged in a domestic violence case, but there's no guarantee he would have made the roster anyway. After losing playing time to Antwaan Randle El, then to Santonio Holmes, and finally to Nate Washington, his cap figure of $2.6 million was excessive for a fourth receiver with little special teams value. His solid production in limited 2007 action suggests that if his legal troubles are resolved and Hanging Judge Goodell approves, Wilson might sign on with a wideout-needy team.

Going Deep

Sam Aiken, NE: An excellent career special teamer; Steve Tasker without the PR. Now in New England, where he's got his best chance of getting the PR.

Adrian Arrington, NO: Their patience with Devery Henderson shows that the Saints don't mind athletic receivers who need time to develop, and Marques Colston's success proves that seventh-rounders needn't be doomed to the practice squad. For Arrington, who was part of the mass exodus that followed Rich Rodriguez's installation of the spread offense at Michigan, the challenge will be to prove that he was wise in coming out early. Between his Combine numbers, various disciplinary issues, and an alarming lack of collegiate experience (not only did he declare for the NFL as a junior, but he missed most of the 2005 season with an ankle injury), it's going to be an uphill battle. Arrington's two-touchdown performance against Florida in the Capital One Bowl shows his potential.

Shaun Bodiford, GB: Bodiford is a high-effort player from Portland State who hung around the Lions practice squad for two years before signing with the Packers. His lone catch last year came in the meaningless Week 17 game. He could stick on special teams, but of course we could say that about almost literally every wide receiver in this section.

John Broussard, JAC: Broussard has blazing speed, but didn't get much of a chance to show it after injuring an ankle. He's got work to do to make the Jacksonville roster after they imported a couple of free-agent receivers in the offseason. If it doesn't happen for him, well, he'll have that 31.5 career yards-per-catch figure to take with him to old age. (2007: four catches for 126 yards and a touchdown, -7.7% DVOA, 5 DYAR.)

Jason Carter, CAR: Carter saw time as a quarterback, tailback, split end, flanker, slot receiver, kickoff returner, and punt returner during his time at Texas A&M. He spent most of 2007 on Carolina's practice squad, and the team re-signed him in February. Carter has some special teams ability, but there probably isn't enough for a real shot as a receiver at the professional level.

Brian Clark, TB: Most of Clark's value comes as a kick returner ... and he is only valuable to his team's opponents. In 23 kick returns for Denver in 2006, he managed to be worth seven points of field position below average, worst in the league. Michael Spurlock and rookie Dexter Jackson are ahead of Clark on the depth chart at both wide receiver and kick returner, so he'll be looking for a new job sooner rather than later. (2007: four catches for 23 yards, -79.9% DVOA, -25 DYAR.)

Thomas Clayton, SF: Last year's seventh-round pick spent the entire season on the practice squad, but he has a chance to jump to the active roster, particularly after a good showing in the team's first minicamp.

David Clowney, NYJ: The Packers cut Clowney in camp last year because he dropped too many passes. The Jets put him on their practice squad, then slipped him onto the IR with a minor excuse of an injury. Clowney was a track star at Virginia Tech and may get a look as a return man, but he's too frail for a regular role.

Chris Davis, NYJ: Davis has spent the last two seasons bouncing back and forth between the Jets practice squad and the Montreal Alouettes of the CFL. He was activated for two games in 2007—he rushed one time for three yards against Washington and caught one pass for three yards against Miami. If you need three yards, Chris Davis is your man.

Eddie Drummond, KC: Once a Pro Bowl kick returner, Drummond was a disaster last year, providing absolutely no big plays on kicks and punts. In a post-Devin Hester world, teams would be wise to remember the short life of a player like Drummond when spending valuable resources on what has long been considered a fungible role.

Biren Ealy, TEN: Ealy is one of the gaggle of young receivers trying to take advantage of the fact that the Titans seem intent on subjecting Vince Young to the pre-T.O. Donovan McNabb experience. Ealy caught two balls in the playoff loss against San Diego, which was twice as many receptions as he made during the regular season.

Jimmy Farris, WAS: "I'm always on the bubble," Farris told the *Washington Post* after he was cut by the Redskins just before the 2005 season started. He came back to play for Washington that season and again in 2007, but at age 30, it's likely that his bubble has burst.

Yamon Figurs, BAL: Figurs's singular offensive highlight occurred in Week 15 against the Dolphins when he hauled in a 36-yard pass. That was it. Figurs was drafted primarily for his return ability, a role that he performed deftly, but he's going to struggle to get on the field as a receiver.

Brian Finneran, ATL: Zombies don't need knee ligaments, right? Back from the dead following two consecutive torn ACL's is Finneran, with the mystery being how much of the speed his game depends upon was left on the operating table. Thirty-two year-old receivers who rely primarily on their speed aren't a great idea even if they're healthy, let alone coming off two lost seasons. With a new coaching staff that has no connection to Finneran's glory days, it'll be a small miracle if Finneran even makes the team, let alone makes any serious contribution. (2005: 50 catches for 611 yards and 2 touchdowns, -2.3% DVOA, 66 DYAR.)

Chris Francies, GB: Francies's bio on the Green Bay Packers' Web site is a fine example of PR work. Apparently Francies is a "sure-handed receiver," a "surprisingly smooth and polished route runner" who is "quick out of the break." If that's true, then why was he undrafted coming out of UTEP in 2006? Why has he been shuttled back and forth between the practice squad and the full roster? Something's fishy here.

Will Franklin, KC: Franklin's an athlete who rose in the draft by virtue of his 4.37 40-yard dash at the Combine. He's a talented player who, by all accounts, entered Missouri with a chip on his shoulder and exited as a team leader. He does, however, have a confirmed learning disability, so it might take him some time to work his way through the Chiefs' playbook and onto the playing field. He's one to watch for in 2009.

Pierre Garcon, IND: The Colts' sixth-round pick was a star at D-III powerhouse Mount Union, where he averaged over 18 yards per catch. Garcon is a blocking dynamo and has good hands, so he should catch on somewhere, if not necessarily Indy.

David Givens, FA: Givens underwent a third knee surgery in February and was released by the Titans at the end of that month. His football career is probably over.

Skyler Green, NO: Playing with the Bengals in 2007, Green got three receptions in the early season, returned punts before losing the job to Antonio Chatman, then was cut to clear a spot when Chris Henry returned from suspension. Green will attend training camp in New Orleans and probably fail to make the roster, he's a pumped-up little guy who lacks the flat-out speed to be a top return man, but he's too small to do much else. It's our loss: the NFL needs more people named "Skyler." (2007: three catches for 33 yards, 15.6% DVOA, 9 DYAR.)

Justin Harper, BAL: Harper is a big receiver who put up good numbers while playing in Frank Beamer's run-heavy offense at Virginia Tech. He averaged 16.1 yards per catch, which will get you drafted when you're six foot three more often than not. It's a muddled situation at the bottom of the Ravens' receiver depth chart, and Harper has a decent chance to stick.

Lavell Hawkins, TEN: Hawkins was a reach in the fourth round. He's a good athlete with the potential to be a good kick returner at this level, but he's not a great athlete like a Chris Johnson or a James Hardy. He barely started in college despite transferring twice, was unimpressive at the scouting combine, and by all accounts, runs awful routes. That's not exactly what Vince Young needs. As far as famous people from Stockton, California go, he's a ways behind Stephen Malkmus and the Diaz brothers when it comes to brilliance in their respective fields. If he was a quarterback, we'd make superfluous references to him being rattled by the rush.

Marcus Henry, NYJ: Between Henry and Dustin Keller, the Jets are trying to fortify their receiver corps with tall red-zone targets. Henry caught ten touchdowns as a senior at Kansas after three prior seasons of little distinction.

Domenik Hixon, NYG: Hixon's season started with a near-tragedy: He was the player that Bills tight end Kevin Everett was trying to tackle when Everett suffered a neck injury that nearly cost him his life. He returned 12 kicks for the Broncos, with a net value around four points worth of field position below average. He was released, and the Giants pounced. He played much better in New York, with a net value nearing six points over average and several important returns late in the year and in the postseason. He'll be the top kickoff returner again for the Giants this season.

Carlyle Holiday, FA: The former Notre Dame quarterback is currently an unemployed wide receiver, and is likely to remain jobless. He played exactly five offensive snaps of the first game in 2007, then was placed on the injured reserve list with a "chronic knee problem." There's a pretty low demand for 26-year-old receivers with nine career catches and bum knees. (2006: nine catches for 126 yards, 11.6% DVOA, 26 DYAR.)

Paul Hubbard, CLE: With Joe Jurevicius entering what is likely his final year with Cleveland, the Browns were on the market for a replacement and Hubbard fit the bill. Hubbard missed five games his senior season due to a right knee sprain, but when healthy he is a big target with impressive athleticism. Hubbard only caught 14 balls in his final season at Wisconsin, but he averaged 21.8 yards per catch.

Taylor Jacobs, DEN: Jacobs may be out of chances after failing in both San Francisco and Denver last year. Do you think the University of Florida alumni who washed out in the NFL could do reenactments of Florida games, Civil War-style? Surely Danny Wuerffel, Jacquez Green, and Reidel Anthony can't have much more to do with their time. (2007: three catches for 40 yards and a touchdown, -8.1% DVOA, 3 DYAR.)

Adam Jennings, ATL: A sixth-round selection in 2006, Jennings has seen time on special teams, in multi-receiver sets, and in certain garbage-time situations. However, with new offensive coordinator Mike Mularkey vowing to use more fullbacks and H-backs and fewer spread receiver sets, Jennings's chances to see the field will diminish. (2007: six catches for 62 yards and a touchdown, 69.3% DVOA, 37 DYAR.)

Steve Johnson, BUF: Johnson led the SEC in receiving yards and touchdowns as a senior, but he'll have to overcome concerns about his route-running and overall skill development if he's to make a dent in an increasingly crowded stable of Bills receivers.

Jordan Kent, SEA: According to Seahawks wide receivers coach Keith Gilbertson, the issue with Kent is "can he consistently catch?" Sort of an important skill for a wide receiver. Kent is in the mix for a third or fourth wideout role. The Seahawks are going to camp with a quarterback who cannot throw (Charlie Frye), so why not a receiver who cannot catch? Or a running back who can't ru … oh, well, Shaun Alexander's gone.

Michael Lewis, SF: We hope this isn't the end of the road for the 36-year-old former beer truck driver. It's always fun to look up a school on a player's bio and find "no college." Lewis was above average as a punt returner last year for the 49ers, thanks mainly to a 51-yard return against Arizona. Never forget, this man led the NFL in punt return and kick return yards in 2002, when the Saints put up the highest special teams DVOA in history, just ahead of last year's Bears.

Chad Lucas, TB: Lucas was an NFL Europe project back when there were such quaint artifacts; now he spends his time working toward keeping his spot as a backup in Tampa Bay. He caught five passes in the season finale against Carolina when Jon Gruden was resting just about everybody, gaining 82 yards with 69.5% DVOA and 34 DYAR.

Jerome Mathis, FA: Once a standout kick returner, Andre Davis took over that role in Houston and made Mathis expendable. The Redskins picked him up temporarily in the offseason, but cut him two months after Mathis was arrested for assaulting his pregnant wife. We commented last year on how similar the measurables of Ted Ginn and Mathis were coming out of college—the biggest difference wasn't that Ginn was selected in the first round, but that he's not crazy.

Brandon Middleton, DET: Middleton was signed from the practice squad after Roy Williams was injured, and he had a little success as an underneath receiver. The promotion came four years after he left University of Houston. Middleton never gave up after stops in Dallas's training camp, on St. Louis's practice squad, and in the now defunct NFL Europa. He was a kick return specialist in Europe, a trait that will increase his chances of making the team, but he's more likely headed back to the practice squad. (2007: eight catches for 70 yards and a touchdown, 27.7% DVOA, 34 DYAR.)

Anthony Mix, WAS: The Giants had him, perhaps because he was the spitting image of Plaxico Burress, but let him go to sign Domenik Hixon. Now, the Redskins will probably cut him to make room for Devin Thomas and Malcolm Kelly. Showing up to minicamp 10 pounds overweight won't do much to help, but for a guy who appeared to be doing a Kate Moss impression, the difference isn't that noticeable.

Marcus Monk, CHI: Monk caught a school-record 27 touchdowns while at Arkansas, but he missed the first seven games of his senior season with a knee injury that required two surgeries to correct. Monk has good speed for a big receiver, and with Chicago in such dire straits at the wide receiver position, he could earn playing time right away.

Kenneth Moore, DET: By our metrics, the Lions had the NFL's worst kick return value in 2007, and the punt returns weren't much better. Moore can help to solve that problem, and he can also help as a receiver—he set an ACC record last year with 98 receptions. The Lions are loaded at wide receiver, so Moore may have to wait his turn on offense.

Josh Morgan, SF: The 49ers sixth-round pick is a likely special teams contributor who could see some action in five-wideout sets on fly routes. He gets low marks as a teammate, which should help him fit in just fine in San Francisco.

Kassim Osgood, SD: Osgood feels he has been pigeonholed as a special teams ace and wants a chance to play receiver. The Chargers control his rights for two more years and disagree. He's one of the league's best special-teamers, but he'll become expendable if he becomes a headache.

Logan Payne, SEA: He's yet to appear in a regular season game, but that may change this year for the undrafted second-year player out of Minnesota. GM Tim Ruskell loves him, and Payne spent a lot of time in the slot during May minicamp. As an aside, Payne played his prep football at Land o' Lakes High School in Florida—their mascot is a Gator, not a squaw sitting in the lotus position.

Willie Reid, PIT: 2006 third-round pick who has spent as many months on injured reserve as he has career receptions (four). Drafted to return punts, of which he fumbled several last preseason, prompting Mike Tomlin to trade for Allen Rossum. (2007: four catches for 54 yards, -4.9% DVOA, 3 DYAR.)

Courtney Roby, CIN: Roby was a third-round pick for the Titans in 2005, but he only lasted two seasons in Tennessee. Roby spent a year in Cincinnati before landing on the Colts practice squad. Roby is the cousin of former Dolphins punter and, somehow, professional wrestling cameraman Reggie Roby.

Bobby Sippio, KC: Well, somebody finally took a chance on this star of the Arena League, who starred for the 2006 Arena Bowl champion Chicago Rush. The Chiefs badly need receivers, so he might see the field. Who knows, maybe he'll even see the field on defense—he was a pretty good cornerback in his early Arena days. His website, sippio.com, may be the most intricate web site in the history of practice squad receivers.

Matt Slater, NE: The Patriots must really like Slater, because they traded up in the fifth round to get him despite the fact that many draft analysts had Slater graded as undrafted free agent material. Slater, the son of Hall of Fame Rams lineman Jackie Slater, was a defensive back at UCLA before switching over to offense. Slater will make his mark at the pro level as a return specialist, but he has the kind of versatility that Bill Belichick craves.

Michael Spurlock, TB: Spurlock's place in NFL lore is already etched in stone. His kickoff return touchdown against Atlanta last year was the first in franchise history. Spurlock benefited from great blocking on the play, catching the ball at the 10 and running straight upfield to the 25. At that point he cut right, zipping through a gaping hole created by Alex Smith, who took out two Falcons with one block. Spurlock then turned on the jets down the sideline, blowing by Lewis Sanders and into the end zone. On the season, Spurlock's kick returns were worth 5.6 points of field position above average, tenth in the league.

Isaiah Stanback, DAL: Stanback is still adjusting to his new position after serving as the quarterback for the University of Washington. Seneca Wallace, Stanbeck's closest comp, took three years to get on the field. The quote on his Myspace page says "I'm focused," so that bodes well, we guess.

Brett Swain, GB: Swain led the San Diego State Aztecs in receptions in each of his last two seasons, and he's got a good reputation as a solid player who can catch in short areas and turn upfield for extra yards. Unfortunately, the Packers have approximately 500 receivers with that same ability, so his best hope is to impress in the preseason and catch on somewhere else.

Travis Taylor, CAR: Released by the Raiders and Rams in 2007, Taylor was taken on a flyer basis late in the season by Carolina. He might get a chance in camp, but the career outlook is not good for this one-time Ravens first-round pick. (2006: 56 catches for 647 yards and four touchdowns, -7.7% DVOA, 34 DYAR.)

Craphonso Thorpe, JAC: Originally drafted by Kansas City in 2005, Thorpe was waived five times (by the Chiefs twice, then the Texans, then the Lions, then the Colts) in less than two years without ever playing a single game. The Colts re-signed him after Marvin Harrison's injury last season, and Thorpe finally made it onto the field, catching 12 passes for 70 yards (-30.3% DVOA, -28 DYAR). In the third quarter of what could be Thorpe's final NFL game, he scored the only touchdown of his career, a three-yard strike from Jim Sorgi that momentarily put the Colts ahead in a meaningless Week 17 contest. If Hollywood ever makes "Craphonso" (starring Eddie Griffin), that catch will be a Hail Mary that wins a playoff game. In reality, the Titans came back to win 16-10. Such is life. Thorpe will go to training camp this year with Jacksonville, but the Jaguars have no room for him.

Mario Urrutia, CIN: The Bengals carpet-bombed the receiver position in the draft as they prepared for life without Chris Henry and possibly Chad Johnson, taking Jerome Simpson, Andre Caldwell and finally Urrutia in the seventh round. Urrutia suffered through an injury-marred senior season at Louisville, but at six foot five and 230 pounds, he has the size and speed to be an intriguing deep threat.

Mike Walker, JAC: Walker is an intriguing player who merits a close eye in training camp. He was the talk of camp last season before the Jaguars decided a knee injury suffered in college wasn't fully healed and stashed him on injured reserve. If healthy, he as all the tools to secure a roster spot and eventually become a contributor.

Kelley Washington, NE: The Patriots re-signed Washington in 2008 primarily as a kick gunner, but he could also be a useful possession receiver if called into duty. (2006: nine catches for 115 yards and a touchdown, 48.8% DVOA, 59 DYAR.)

Paul Williams, TEN: Williams was Tennessee's third-round pick in the 2007 draft, and his scouting reports say that he's a good athlete with the speed to get deep and the ability to go up and make big-time catches. For the moment his scouting reports will have to do, because Williams didn't suit up at all last season.

Matt Willis, BAL: Willis only played two years of football at UCLA, but he was invited to training camp and secured a roster spot with the Ravens. He's a developmental prospect who is likely to spend most of his career on the practice squad.

Travis Wilson, CLE: The track record for Oklahoma receivers hasn't been particularly impressive in recent years, and Wilson is doing nothing to improve it. "T-Money" didn't get into a single game last year, and unless he impresses in training camp, he may find himself looking for work come September.

Wallace Wright, NYJ: Wright started the Jets season finale and caught two passes, including a 36-yarder. He's solid on special teams, so he'll earn a roster spot and could compete for an offensive role. (2007: six catches for 87 yards, -7.7% DVOA, 4 DYAR.)

Tight Ends

For an explanation of how to read the tight end statistics tables, see the Wide Receivers section.

Chris Baker
Height: 6-3   Weight: 258   College: Michigan State   Draft: 2002/3 (88)   Born: 18-Nov-1979   Age:29   Risk: Red

Year	Team	G	Rec	Pass	Yds	C%	Yd/C	TD	YAC	Rk	DVOA	Rk	DYAR	Rk	YAR	Short	Mid	Deep	Bomb
2005	NYJ	8	18	25	269	72%	14.9	1	7.2	2	38.0%	1	71	12	70	50%	29%	21%	0%
2006	NYJ	16	31	45	300	67%	9.7	4	4.2	21	8.7%	11	51	15	51	53%	37%	9%	0%
2007	NYJ	15	41	61	409	67%	10.0	3	3.5	26	9.0%	15	69	16	62	51%	43%	7%	0%
2008	NYJ		32	50	324	64%	10.1	3			5.6%								

Baker caught 17 of 19 passes thrown to him on first down for 209 yards, 51.4% DVOA, and 75 DYAR. It was essentially the same play over and over: Baker lined up as the tight end in a trips formation or as a slot receiver, ran a flat pattern or a short hitch against a linebacker, turned upfield for a few steps, then hit the ground after a healthy 8-to-10 yard gain. Good stuff, but nothing that 25 tight ends can't do just as well or better, which is why the Jets signed Bubba Franks and drafted Dustin Keller. Baker's numbers don't look as swell when you realize how often he lined up as a third or fourth wideout. The Jets are playing Pete Kendall ball with Baker at press time, disavowing all knowledge of a verbal commitment to a contract extension. With Keller and Franks in the fold, Baker could be elsewhere by September.

Anthony Becht
Height: 6-5   Weight: 272   College: West Virginia   Draft: 2000/1 (27)   Born: 8-Aug-1977   Age:31   Risk: Green

Year	Team	G	Rec	Pass	Yds	C%	Yd/C	TD	YAC	Rk	DVOA	Rk	DYAR	Rk	YAR	Short	Mid	Deep	Bomb
2005	TB	16	16	25	112	64%	7.0	0	3.1	38	-31.8%	42	-37	40	-42	57%	43%	0%	0%
2006	TB	16	18	26	115	69%	6.4	1	2.9	39	-38.8%	43	-53	39	-53	75%	21%	4%	0%
2007	TB	16	5	7	20	71%	4.0	2	2.0	—	-4.1%	—	2	—	2	86%	0%	14%	0%
2008	STL		11	17	67	65%	6.1	2			-23.9%								

An unrestricted free agent after the final three years of his Tampa Bay contract were voided, Becht was signed by the Rams as a run-blocker and occasional goal-line scoring threat. His primary functions in St. Louis will be run-blocking and making everyone feel better about cutting Dominique Byrd.

Martellus Bennett
Height: 6-6   Weight: 259   College: Texas A&M   Draft: 2008/2 (61)   Born: 10-Mar-1987   Age:21   Risk: Red

Year	Team	G	Rec	Pass	Yds	C%	Yd/C	TD	YAC	Rk	DVOA	Rk	DYAR	Rk	YAR	Short	Mid	Deep	Bomb
2008	DAL		10	14	62	71%	6.2	1			-8.2%								

Bennett showed that he could block like a monster and catch footballs at Texas A&M, but in the media saturation festival that is the Dallas Cowboys, he'll also be doing something else—stealing quotes from the superstars. It's hard not to like a guy who unleashed the following bon mots at the Combine: "I know a lot of people think I'm goofy—which I am—but I am mature." "I think I will be one of the best talkers in the league if I have a chance." "I couldn't talk that well until I was seven (years old). Ever since then I haven't stopped talking." "I don't do much trash talking on the field. Most of the time I let the other guys do the trash-talking. I just tell them, 'God Bless You,' and they get real mad." "I would say football is my wife, and basketball is my mistress." Ben Riley, Mr. This Week in Quotes, you have been warned.

Kevin Boss

Height: 6-7　Weight: 252　College: Western Oregon　　Draft: 2007/5 (153)　Born: 11-Jan-1984　Age:24　Risk: Red

Year	Team	G	Rec	Pass	Yds	C%	Yd/C	TD	YAC	Rk	DVOA	Rk	DYAR	Rk	YAR	Short	Mid	Deep	Bomb
2007	NYG	13	9	14	118	64%	13.1	2	3.7	—	43.9%	—	48	—	47	31%	46%	23%	0%
2008	NYG		20	30	220	67%	11.0	2			1.1%								

Boss performed admirably in the playoffs after Jeremy Shockey broke his leg. He showed reliable hands and the ability to accelerate after the catch, most famously in the Super Bowl. He's by no means a complete player, or Jeremy Shockey's caliber, but he's a useful second tight end, particularly in passing formations.

Kyle Brady

Height: 6-6　Weight: 278　College: Penn State　　Draft: 1995/1 (9)　Born: 14-Jan-1972　Age:36　Risk: Red

Year	Team	G	Rec	Pass	Yds	C%	Yd/C	TD	YAC	Rk	DVOA	Rk	DYAR	Rk	YAR	Short	Mid	Deep	Bomb
2005	JAC	16	18	26	157	69%	8.7	1	3.4	35	-39.0%	44	-52	42	-52	60%	24%	16%	0%
2006	JAC	15	5	8	37	63%	7.4	0	2.4	—	-29.4%	—	-12	—	-12	57%	43%	0%	0%
2007	NE	14	9	16	70	56%	7.8	2	2.7	—	-8.8%	—	-2	—	-3	67%	13%	13%	7%

Released by the Patriots in late February. Brady still has value as a glorified right tackle, but there are younger, cheaper players who can do the same things and make a bigger impact on special teams.

Dan Campbell

Height: 6-5　Weight: 263　College: Texas A&M　　Draft: 1999/3 (79)　Born: 13-Apr-1976　Age:32　Risk: Red

Year	Team	G	Rec	Pass	Yds	C%	Yd/C	TD	YAC	Rk	DVOA	Rk	DYAR	Rk	YAR	Short	Mid	Deep	Bomb
2005	DAL	16	3	7	24	43%	8.0	1	6.3	—	-12.6%	—	-3	—	-4	86%	14%	0%	0%
2006	DET	16	21	32	308	66%	14.7	4	5.2	6	29.0%	2	79	8	79	44%	33%	19%	4%
2007	DET	2	1	1	1	100%	1.0	0	0.0	—	-96.8%	—	-7	—	-7	100%	0%	0%	0%
2008	DET		12	17	115	71%	9.6	3			-13.2%								

Campbell missed 14 games in 2007 with a back injury; fortunately, the Saints signed Eric Johnson to replace him in the role of soon-to-be-injured tight end. He'll enter training camp behind Eric Johnson and Billy Miller on the depth chart. His survival depends on how much Sean Payton needs blocking from the tight end position.

John Carlson

Height: 6-5　Weight: 251　College: Notre Dame　　Draft: 2008/2 (38)　Born: 12-May-1984　Age:24　Risk: Red

Year	Team	G	Rec	Pass	Yds	C%	Yd/C	TD	YAC	Rk	DVOA	Rk	DYAR	Rk	YAR	Short	Mid	Deep	Bomb
2008	SEA		34	48	412	71%	12.1	3			14.6%								

The tight end position has been a dead spot for the Seahawks ever since Mike Holmgren took over in 1999. This has been unsettling for a coach who relies on tight ends to help his offense go as much as any in the NFL. Christian Fauria gave way to the unfulfilled potential of Jerramy Stevens, and the quietly effective production of Itula Mili didn't last long enough. After losing out to the Broncos on free agent Daniel Graham (actually, the Seahawks got the better of that deal—Patrick Kerney chose Seattle over Denver), the Seahawks picked up the 35-year-old Marcus Pollard as a stopgap, which is exactly how Pollard played. This is Holmgren's last year in Seattle, and the Carlson selection reflects the team's need to get this right—right now. He is not the most athletic at his position in this draft class, but Carlson is the one prospect who is game-ready enough to read coverage and contribute as a pass blocker. Had Holmgren been planning to stick around a while longer, he may have gone with a developmental player, but Carlson will start right away. Given the turmoil at the wide receiver position, he could catch the 50 balls that the team foolishly projected for Pollard last season.

Brent Celek

Height: 6-6　Weight: 260　College: Cincinnati　　Draft: 2007/5 (162)　Born: 25-Jan-1985　Age:23　Risk: Red

Year	Team	G	Rec	Pass	Yds	C%	Yd/C	TD	YAC	Rk	DVOA	Rk	DYAR	Rk	YAR	Short	Mid	Deep	Bomb
2007	PHI	16	16	22	178	73%	11.1	1	4.5	—	23.3%	—	45	—	45	43%	43%	10%	5%
2008	PHI		23	33	209	70%	9.1	3			-13.3%								

The University of Cincinnati product impressed the Eagles in training camp, then stepped up late in the season with eight receptions in the final three games. Celek has a little Kevin Boss in him: he's an an athletically-limited tight end who puts out significant effort in the running game and has sure hands. Offseason surgery on a chronic shoulder condition that's bothered him since college could hinder his chance to win more playing time, and L. J. Smith is back for one more season. But by the end of the year, Celek could replace Smith in the starting lineup.

Dallas Clark

Height: 6-3 Weight: 257 College: Iowa   Draft: 2003/1 (24) Born: 12-Jun-1979 Age:29 Risk: Green

Year	Team	G	Rec	Pass	Yds	C%	Yd/C	TD	YAC	Rk	DVOA	Rk	DYAR	Rk	YAR	Short	Mid	Deep	Bomb
2005	IND	15	37	51	488	73%	13.2	4	4.9	16	30.5%	3	132	4	138	39%	35%	22%	4%
2006	IND	12	30	57	367	53%	12.2	4	4.3	20	-6.8%	29	8	26	5	44%	31%	17%	8%
2007	IND	15	58	101	616	57%	10.6	11	3.7	42	0.6%	50	107	47	102	41%	38%	15%	5%
2008	IND		58	88	746	66%	12.9	7			24.8%								

The Colts made sure that the little kid in Peyton Manning's head will be whispering "Clark" for years to come when they signed the human security blanket to a six-year contract in February. No matter where Clark goes, Manning will find him; he caught 12 passes on the left sideline, 12 on the left side, 10 up the middle, 10 to the right, and 14 along the right sideline. Calling Clark a tight end is something of a misnomer—he spends the majority of his time lined up as a slot receiver—but he still fills the traditional role of a tight end in a passing scheme, catching passes for short gains near the line of scrimmage. Only five of his receptions gained 20 or more yards in 2007; his remaining 52 catches averaged just 8.8 yards per catch. Whenever Manning gets in trouble, he'll look across the field for Clark, just beyond the line of scrimmage, season after season. Note that Clark's ranks are among wide receivers, not tight ends. Your fantasy league will still call him a tight end, but at Football Outsiders, we're living in reality.

Desmond Clark

Height: 6-3 Weight: 255 College: Wake Forest   Draft: 1999/6 (179) Born: 20-Apr-1977 Age:31 Risk: Red

Year	Team	G	Rec	Pass	Yds	C%	Yd/C	TD	YAC	Rk	DVOA	Rk	DYAR	Rk	YAR	Short	Mid	Deep	Bomb
2005	CHI	16	24	49	229	49%	9.5	2	3.0	40	-17.9%	38	-34	38	-38	62%	29%	5%	5%
2006	CHI	16	45	80	626	56%	13.9	6	4.7	13	19.4%	4	142	3	136	37%	49%	10%	3%
2007	CHI	16	44	66	545	67%	12.4	4	5.3	10	16.1%	11	99	11	92	44%	40%	16%	0%
2008	CHI		31	56	382	55%	12.3	3			-3.8								

Clark has been an above-average receiving tight end for several seasons, but he is 31, and the Bears have second-year player Greg Olsen waiting in the wings—which makes it curious that Chicago would re-sign Clark through 2010 to a deal that included a $2 million signing bonus. But Clark plays an important role in the offense, even when Olsen is also on the field. The Bears have learned that Clark does his best work when he's working downfield; his worst year in Chicago was in 2005, when nearly two-thirds of his passes were in the "short" category. Since then, he has run more mid-range routes, and his DVOA has improved. Last season, among tight ends with at least 30 catches, only Kellen Winslow and Antonio Gates averaged more yards per catch than Clark.

Daniel Coats

Height: 6-3 Weight: 257 College: BYU   Draft: 2007/FA Born: 12-Apr-1984 Age:24 Risk: Red

Year	Team	G	Rec	Pass	Yds	C%	Yd/C	TD	YAC	Rk	DVOA	Rk	DYAR	Rk	YAR	Short	Mid	Deep	Bomb
2007	CIN	15	12	16	122	75%	10.2	0	4.2	—	33.8%	—	39	—	37	75%	13%	13%	0%
2008	CIN		13	19	125	68%	9.6	2			-0.7%								

An undrafted free agent out of Brigham Young who latched onto the 2007 roster, Coats's willingness as a special teams gunner (he had six special teams tackles in 2007) and solid blocking are more likely to win him a roster spot than any pass-catching skills he might evince, especially after the addition of restricted free agent Ben Utecht to the Bengals' tight end corps.

Chris Cooley

Height: 6-3 Weight: 265 College: Utah State   Draft: 2004/3 (81) Born: 11-Jul-1982 Age:26 Risk: Green

Year	Team	G	Rec	Pass	Yds	C%	Yd/C	TD	YAC	Rk	DVOA	Rk	DYAR	Rk	YAR	Short	Mid	Deep	Bomb
2005	WAS	16	71	103	774	69%	10.9	7	7.0	3	10.8%	12	127	6	122	64%	23%	10%	2%
2006	WAS	16	57	95	734	57%	12.9	6	7.9	1	-0.2%	24	53	14	51	47%	33%	18%	3%
2007	WAS	16	66	110	786	60%	11.9	8	4.3	16	9.4%	14	121	8	114	40%	39%	17%	5%
2008	WAS		60	98	747	61%	12.5	4			21.8%								

Cooley remains one of the league's most versatile tight ends, a player who can move from fullback to the slot without sacrificing anything. He's been the Redskins only over-the-middle target in recent years, but even if rookie receiver Malcolm Kelly or tight end Fred Davis provides another inside threat, Cooley will get his touches. It's up to Jim Zorn to take full advantage of Cooley's unique skill set; unfortunately, he might not remember what it's like to have a talented tight end after spending so long in Seattle.

Brad Cottam
Height: 6-8   Weight: 270   College: Tennessee   Draft: 2008/3 (76)   Born: 28-Nov-1984   Age:24   Risk: Red

Year	Team	G	Rec	Pass	Yds	C%	Yd/C	TD	YAC	Rk	DVOA	Rk	DYAR	Rk	YAR	Short	Mid	Deep	Bomb
2008	KC		12	19	113	63%	9.4	1			-6.7%								

He's not Tony Gonzalez's heir apparent, but Cottam could be a productive player for the Chiefs if he can just stay on the field. New offensive coordinator Chan Gailey likes two-tight end sets, and the Chiefs lined up in that formation 33 percent of the time in 2007 anyway. Cottam is a six-foot-eight target who has suffered hand, shoulder, and wrist injuries through his time at Tennessee. That's why he started only seven of the 38 games he played in college. The collegiate totals of 21 catches for 341 yards and one touchdown must be taken in context—Cottam's a very big ball of potential that may never be seen.

Alge Crumpler
Height: 6-2   Weight: 262   College: North Carolina   Draft: 2000/2 (35)   Born: 23-Dec-1977   Age:30   Risk: Red

Year	Team	G	Rec	Pass	Yds	C%	Yd/C	TD	YAC	Rk	DVOA	Rk	DYAR	Rk	YAR	Short	Mid	Deep	Bomb
2005	ATL	16	65	118	877	55%	13.5	5	4.3	25	-3.3%	23	31	20	29	30%	45%	22%	3%
2006	ATL	16	56	103	780	51%	13.9	8	4.6	16	0.2%	23	60	13	42	21%	55%	17%	7%
2007	ATL	14	42	70	444	60%	10.6	5	6.2	4	0.4%	24	35	19	37	61%	31%	8%	0%
2008	TEN		48	74	501	65%	10.4	3			7.1%								

Crumpler's farewell tour with the Falcons was certainly interesting. He was the first of many players to publicly bash Bobby Petrino for his in-game decisions, as he felt that the team's new offensive schemes didn't play to his strengths. In his final game in Atlanta, Crumpler showed he can still play when he scored two touchdowns against Seattle and embarrassed Lofa Tatupu on a post pattern. Atlanta's primary aerial threat through seasons of terrible receivers, Crumpler took his great career production and balky knees to Tennessee, where he signed a two-year contract. The Falcons responded by signing former Titans tight end Ben Hartsock, who's more a Band-Aid than a true replacement.

Tony Curtis
Height: 6-5   Weight: 265   College: Portland State   Draft: 2006/FA   Born: 11-Feb-1983   Age:25   Risk: Red

Year	Team	G	Rec	Pass	Yds	C%	Yd/C	TD	YAC	Rk	DVOA	Rk	DYAR	Rk	YAR	Short	Mid	Deep	Bomb
2007	DAL	16	3	3	18	100%	6.0	3	0.0	—	127.4%	—	38	—	37	67%	33%	0%	0%
2008	DAL		19	27	255	70%	13.4	1			2.9%								

The biggest play of Curtis's career came on special teams, when he recovered the onside kick that set up the game-winning field goal in Dallas's crazy come-from-behind win over Buffalo on Monday Night Football last October. With Anthony Fasano now in Miami, Curtis will battle second-round pick Martellus Bennett out of Texas A&M for the second tight end spot.

Owen Daniels
Height: 6-3   Weight: 250   College: Wisconsin   Draft: 2006/4 (98)   Born: 9-Nov-1982   Age:26   Risk: Yellow

Year	Team	G	Rec	Pass	Yds	C%	Yd/C	TD	YAC	Rk	DVOA	Rk	DYAR	Rk	YAR	Short	Mid	Deep	Bomb
2006	HOU	14	34	51	352	67%	10.4	5	5.2	8	14.7%	6	82	7	81	61%	27%	9%	2%
2007	HOU	16	63	94	768	67%	12.2	3	3.3	30	12.7%	13	127	7	118	33%	49%	17%	1%
2008	HOU		52	71	659	73%	12.7	4			22.0%								

Daniels has the pass-catching skills of a wide receiver. He also has the blocking skills of a wide receiver, which is why Mark Bruener is still drawing a paycheck in Houston. He's a smooth route-runner who can do the little things, like deke a defender to get the extra foot for a first down. He did commit six false-start penalties, second-most among all non-offensive linemen.

Fred Davis

Height: 6-4 Weight: 248 College: USC Draft: 2008/2 (48) Born: 15-Jan-1986 Age:22 Risk: Red

Year	Team	G	Rec	Pass	Yds	C%	Yd/C	TD	YAC	Rk	DVOA	Rk	DYAR	Rk	YAR	Short	Mid	Deep	Bomb
2008	WAS		12	20	120	60%	10.0	1			-21.3%								

Davis won the Mackey award as the nation's top tight end, catching 62 passes and eight touchdowns at USC in 2007. His reward for all that work was a seat on the bench behind Chris Cooley. New Redskins coach Jim Zorn is a West Coast Offense guy, so he probably won't run as many two-tight end sets as Joe Gibbs and Al Saunders did. When Davis does take the field, he'll have to prove himself as a blocker, which wasn't his strong point in college. Like Cooley, Davis is fast enough to do damage when in the slot or flexed out. Look for Zorn to try to create mismatches by putting Cooley and Davis on the field, sending them on deep patterns, and teaching Jason Campbell to throw to the one who is covered by a linebacker.

Vernon Davis

Height: 6-3 Weight: 253 College: Maryland Draft: 2006/1 (6) Born: 31-Jan-1984 Age:24 Risk: Red

Year	Team	G	Rec	Pass	Yds	C%	Yd/C	TD	YAC	Rk	DVOA	Rk	DYAR	Rk	YAR	Short	Mid	Deep	Bomb
2006	SF	10	20	42	265	48%	13.3	3	7.5	2	-13.8%	35	-16	35	-39	47%	27%	20%	7%
2007	SF	14	52	85	509	61%	9.8	4	3.4	29	-8.6%	30	-7	31	6	45%	36%	13%	7%
2008	SF		43	67	547	64%	12.7	3			0.9%								

Davis is a subject of endless debate on 49ers blogs. Is he good? Not good? Will he ever fulfill his abundant promise? Does he understand the playbook? Is Mike Martz going to use him more, or less? Those who say he's a superstar-in-waiting cite his 52 catches in a dreadful offense that featured four different quarterbacks. Critics point to his constant mistakes and the fact that his alleged 4.5 40 doesn't translate to the field, plus some inopportune drops. Davis did forget the snap count at times, ran the wrong routes, and was tentative on read routes. If he doesn't spend lots of time learning the Mike Martz offense, the new offensive coordinator will have no qualms benching Davis for those who know the offense and snap count. Davis is a very good blocker, and his athletic potential remains intriguing. If he progresses, he could be the most complete tight end in the game. If he doesn't, Martz will run four-wide sets 80 percent of the time.

Greg Estandia

Height: 6-8 Weight: 255 College: UNLV Draft: 2006/FA Born: 18-Nov-1982 Age:26 Risk: Red

Year	Team	G	Rec	Pass	Yds	C%	Yd/C	TD	YAC	Rk	DVOA	Rk	DYAR	Rk	YAR	Short	Mid	Deep	Bomb
2007	JAC	10	9	16	136	56%	15.1	0	4.1	—	16.5%	—	24	—	18	19%	44%	38%	0%
2008	JAC		15	23	182	65%	12.1	2			9.2%								

Estandia is yet another enormous target who showed flashes in 2007. He could steal playing time from George Wrighster, particularly if he improves his run-blocking. Like all of Jacksonville's tight ends, he has the size and/or athleticism to be a potential matchup nightmare for opposing defenses.

Anthony Fasano

Height: 6-5 Weight: 255 College: Notre Dame Draft: 2006/2 (53) Born: 20-Apr-1984 Age:24 Risk: Red

Year	Team	G	Rec	Pass	Yds	C%	Yd/C	TD	YAC	Rk	DVOA	Rk	DYAR	Rk	YAR	Short	Mid	Deep	Bomb
2006	DAL	16	14	24	126	58%	9.0	0	4.0	—	-18.0%	—	-16	—	-18	44%	44%	6%	6%
2007	DAL	16	14	21	143	67%	10.2	1	3.9	—	-2.5%	—	7	—	3	45%	45%	9%	0%
2008	MIA		28	43	272	65%	9.7	2			-0.7%								

Fasano is a 1970s style tight end. He blocks well in-line, he's an adequate receiver over the middle, and he's a master of the moving pick (call it a "mesh" and it sounds more NFL legal) on crossing routes. He knows Tony Sparano's system and fits it well, so he'll be a perfect fit in Miami. He may be the nominal starter at tight end, but he won't be targeted often.

Jermichael Finley

Height: 6-5 Weight: 243 College: Texas Draft: 2008/3 (91) Born: 26-Mar-1987 Age:21 Risk: Red

Year	Team	G	Rec	Pass	Yds	C%	Yd/C	TD	YAC	Rk	DVOA	Rk	DYAR	Rk	YAR	Short	Mid	Deep	Bomb
2008	GB		10	16	80	63%	8.0	1			9.6%								

Finley is one of the new breed of athletic hybrid tight ends with great athleticism and iffy blocking skills who fit best in pseudo-spread offenses like Green Bay's. The real question is how long it will take Finley to catch up with the speed of the NFL game. Unlike Martellus Bennett or Dustin Keller, Finley is dealing with an experience gap that any rookie would suffer if he declared for the NFL as a third-year sophomore. The Packers love to throw as many big, athletic pass-catchers on the field as possible, so he's in the best possible situation. He probably gave up a full two rounds as a draft pick by coming out so early, but family concerns will override football concerns at times.

Bryan Fletcher

Height: 6-5   Weight: 235   College: UCLA   Draft: 2002/6 (210)   Born: 23-Mar-1979   Age:29   Risk: Red

Year	Team	G	Rec	Pass	Yds	C%	Yd/C	TD	YAC	Rk	DVOA	Rk	DYAR	Rk	YAR	Short	Mid	Deep	Bomb
2005	IND	16	18	27	202	67%	11.2	3	5.5	6	29.9%	4	63	14	63	50%	46%	4%	0%
2006	IND	14	18	25	202	68%	11.2	2	3.9	26	15.2%	5	40	20	39	50%	29%	13%	8%
2007	IND	15	18	27	143	67%	7.9	0	2.3	43	-12.0%	33	-8	32	-5	64%	28%	8%	0%

The good news for Fletcher is that the Colts re-signed him to a one-year deal over the offseason, while allowing fellow tight end Ben Utecht to leave for the Bengals. The bad news is that the Colts spent not one, but two picks on tight ends in the draft, and then cut Fletcher in May. Posting a negative receiving DVOA when Peyton Manning is your quarterback is a remarkable achievement, particularly when you consider that Fletcher would have been the defense's fifth concern on every play.

Bubba Franks

Height: 6-6   Weight: 263   College: Miami   Draft: 2000/1 (14)   Born: 6-Jan-1978   Age:30   Risk: Red

Year	Team	G	Rec	Pass	Yds	C%	Yd/C	TD	YAC	Rk	DVOA	Rk	DYAR	Rk	YAR	Short	Mid	Deep	Bomb
2005	GB	10	25	37	207	65%	8.3	1	2.6	44	-15.9%	36	-23	35	-19	36%	42%	12%	9%
2006	GB	16	25	53	232	47%	9.3	0	4.6	15	-37.5%	42	-98	43	-97	57%	38%	2%	2%
2007	GB	8	18	32	132	56%	7.3	3	2.7	40	-18.2%	35	-24	35	-29	61%	25%	14%	0%
2008	NYJ		16	26	129	62%	8.1	2			-2.5%								

Franks reprised his role as a red zone specialist last year, with four catches in eight attempts and three touchdowns in eight games. Franks's real asset remains his run blocking, which keeps him on the field in all of those third-and-goal situations. Replacement level is rising to meet him, but he's been a fun player for a long time. He left Green Bay for the Jets this past offseason.

Michael Gaines

Height: 6-2   Weight: 275   College: UCF   Draft: 2004/7 (232)   Born: 30-Mar-1980   Age:28   Risk: Red

Year	Team	G	Rec	Pass	Yds	C%	Yd/C	TD	YAC	Rk	DVOA	Rk	DYAR	Rk	YAR	Short	Mid	Deep	Bomb
2005	CAR	11	12	16	155	75%	12.9	2	4.6	—	30.6%	—	44	—	41	50%	17%	25%	8%
2006	CAR	16	15	28	146	57%	9.7	0	3.8	29	-11.4%	34	0	32	-5	45%	45%	5%	5%
2007	BUF	15	25	35	215	71%	8.6	2	6.7	3	5.9%	18	32	21	33	74%	20%	6%	0%
2008	DET		19	30	184	63%	9.7	2			-5.0%								

Gaines was signed by the Bills in early September and became the starter in their two-tight end offense when Kevin Everett got hurt. The 275-pounder enjoyed his best season as a receiver, catching a pass in every game after Week 2 and posting career highs in everything from first downs to yards after catch. Now in Detroit, his production will return to catch-a-game level, but his blocking will be an asset to a team trying to reestablish the run.

Antonio Gates

Height: 6-4   Weight: 260   College: None   Draft: 2003/FA   Born: 18-Jun-1980   Age:28   Risk: Red

Year	Team	G	Rec	Pass	Yds	C%	Yd/C	TD	YAC	Rk	DVOA	Rk	DYAR	Rk	YAR	Short	Mid	Deep	Bomb
2005	SD	15	89	140	1101	64%	12.4	10	4.7	18	22.1%	6	270	1	255	43%	39%	16%	2%
2006	SD	16	71	120	924	59%	13.0	9	4.1	24	7.4%	12	110	4	124	34%	42%	21%	2%
2007	SD	16	75	117	984	64%	13.1	9	3.5	27	30.0%	4	278	1	266	32%	39%	23%	6%
2008	SD		74	112	921	66%	12.4	10			26.7%								

In normal situations, Gates is about the easiest player to project in the whole NFL. The big question mark is whether he will suffer lingering effects from the foot injury that limited him in the playoffs. The current timetable has him recovering in time for the start of the regular season, but he will be extremely limited in the offseason. If he looks healthy as the season approaches, he obviously is the top fantasy tight end. Odds are, however, that he will lose half a step early. Speed is just a small part of Gates's game, but as the Chargers amass more and more talented wide receivers, a slow-starting Gates could see some of his catches migrate to the receivers.

Tony Gonzalez

Height: 6-4 Weight: 248 College: California Draft: 1997/1 (13) Born: 27-Feb-1976 Age:32 Risk: Yellow

Year	Team	G	Rec	Pass	Yds	C%	Yd/C	TD	YAC	Rk	DVOA	Rk	DYAR	Rk	YAR	Short	Mid	Deep	Bomb
2005	KC	16	78	116	905	67%	11.6	2	3.5	34	14.8%	9	169	3	159	38%	43%	16%	3%
2006	KC	15	73	104	900	70%	12.3	5	3.7	31	29.4%	1	266	1	256	31%	52%	16%	0%
2007	KC	16	99	154	1172	64%	11.8	5	2.8	39	14.1%	12	206	3	208	32%	48%	18%	1%
2008	KC		72	105	848	69%	11.8	6			7.6								

So is this the year that Gonzalez starts to decline? We have been predicting a decline for years, but he just put up the second highest catch total of his career. No precedent exists for such amazing performance for a 32-year-old tight end, so we will keep predicting a decline. One year we will be right, but Gonzalez should remain productive as Dwayne Bowe develops and attracts defensive attention. Of note for fantasy players is that Gonzalez is no longer a top red zone threat, averaging only four touchdowns per year over the past three seasons. The Chiefs still throw him the ball inside the 20 (a team high 17 targets last season), but he caught just five of the passes and doesn't post up defenders as easily as he once did. Gonzalez's decline as a fantasy tight end should not obscure the fact that he remains the most complete tight end in the AFC and a much better blocker than Antonio Gates.

Daniel Graham

Height: 6-3 Weight: 257 College: Colorado Draft: 2002/1 (21) Born: 16-Nov-1978 Age:30 Risk: Red

Year	Team	G	Rec	Pass	Yds	C%	Yd/C	TD	YAC	Rk	DVOA	Rk	DYAR	Rk	YAR	Short	Mid	Deep	Bomb
2005	NE	11	16	25	235	64%	14.7	3	11.9	1	16.3%	8	36	18	33	52%	32%	16%	0%
2006	NE	12	21	34	235	62%	11.2	2	4.6	14	9.7%	9	43	17	42	53%	27%	20%	0%
2007	DEN	15	24	33	246	73%	10.3	2	4.3	18	16.3%	10	54	18	50	68%	19%	13%	0%
2008	DEN		21	31	168	68%	8.0	2			-15.0%								

Graham is the latest in a loooooong line of recent New England Patriots players who have flopped after signing free agent contracts with other teams. Signed for his blocking prowess, Graham was merely average in two tight-end sets and did not appear all that athletic. He has always been only a marginal receiver and will not see many balls behind Tony Scheffler.

Ben Hartsock

Height: 6-3 Weight: 264 College: Ohio State Draft: 2004/3 (68) Born: 5-Jul-1980 Age:28 Risk: Red

Year	Team	G	Rec	Pass	Yds	C%	Yd/C	TD	YAC	Rk	DVOA	Rk	DYAR	Rk	YAR	Short	Mid	Deep	Bomb
2005	IND	6	2	2	8	100%	4.0	0	0.0	—	-35.5%	—	-5	—	-4	—	—	—	—
2006	TEN	6	6	15	68	33%	11.3	0	6.3	—	-51.0%	—	-44	—	-45	36%	55%	9%	0%
2007	TEN	16	12	19	138	63%	11.5	0	5.9	—	-7.5%	—	0	—	1	58%	37%	5%	0%
2008	ATL		25	40	249	63%	10.0	2			-20.9%								

Hartsock is a good blocker and special teams player who can occasionally make plays as a receiver, mostly on play-action passes when the defense thinks he's staying in to block. The Falcons are his third team in the last three years and probably the best fit for his skills.

Todd Heap

Height: 6-5 Weight: 252 College: Arizona State Draft: 2001/1 (31) Born: 16-Mar-1980 Age:28 Risk: Red

Year	Team	G	Rec	Pass	Yds	C%	Yd/C	TD	YAC	Rk	DVOA	Rk	DYAR	Rk	YAR	Short	Mid	Deep	Bomb
2005	BAL	16	75	114	855	66%	11.4	7	3.4	36	9.2%	13	120	8	110	44%	36%	19%	1%
2006	BAL	16	73	116	765	63%	10.5	6	3.5	34	4.8%	16	96	6	96	45%	43%	10%	2%
2007	BAL	6	23	34	239	68%	10.4	1	2.9	38	3.2%	20	25	24	33	40%	43%	10%	7%
2008	BAL		59	92	618	64%	10.5	3			-2.2%								

Todd Heap is that rarest of commodities in Baltimore, a Pro Bowl skill position player, but he has so much trouble staying healthy that John Harbaugh might want to keep him wrapped in cellophane during the week. Last year a torn hamstring limited Heap to just six games, but when he was in, he produced at his usual level. The new offense is tight end-friendly, so if Heap can stay on the field, he'll put up solid numbers.

Steve Heiden   Height: 6-5   Weight: 265   College: South Dakota State   Draft: 1999/3 (69)   Born: 21-Sep-1976   Age:32   Risk: Red

Year	Team	G	Rec	Pass	Yds	C%	Yd/C	TD	YAC	Rk	DVOA	Rk	DYAR	Rk	YAR	Short	Mid	Deep	Bomb
2005	CLE	15	43	60	401	72%	9.3	3	4.2	28	3.4%	17	45	16	53	54%	41%	2%	4%
2006	CLE	16	36	46	249	80%	6.9	2	4.4	18	1.4%	20	27	22	28	73%	19%	8%	0%
2007	CLE	16	12	21	104	57%	8.7	0	2.5	—	-34.1%	—	-35	—	-36	62%	29%	10%	0%
2008	CLE		15	22	56	68%	3.7	1			-27.8%								

Heiden is strictly a blocking tight end and special teams player, and he has the numbers to prove it. The ten-year veteran has averaged eight catches per season over the last three years, and with Kellen Winslow and now Martin Rucker on the offense, that number isn't going to change much.

Will Heller   Height: 6-6   Weight: 250   College: Georgia Tech   Draft: 2003/FA   Born: 28-Feb-1981   Age:27   Risk: Red

Year	Team	G	Rec	Pass	Yds	C%	Yd/C	TD	YAC	Rk	DVOA	Rk	DYAR	Rk	YAR	Short	Mid	Deep	Bomb
2005	MIA	7	1	2	1	50%	1.0	1	0.0	—	34.6%	—	7	—	6	50%	50%	0%	0%
2006	SEA	16	4	5	32	80%	8.0	1	2.0	—	28.8%	—	11	—	10	25%	75%	0%	0%
2007	SEA	16	13	26	82	50%	6.3	3	3.7	25	-26.7%	41	-36	36	-34	63%	25%	8%	4%
2008	SEA		15	21	126	71%	8.4	2			12.9%								

At the conclusion of Seattle's May minicamps, head coach Mike Holmgren stated that even though the Seahawks drafted John Carlson, Heller "had a heck of a camp." Whether this is a genuine position battle or good old-fashioned motivational coach-speak is anyone's guess, but Heller is an excellent blocker and a nice red-zone target (seven catches on 10 attempts last year), so keep an eye on training camp. There should be a role for both players in the Seahawks offense.

Eric Johnson   Height: 6-3   Weight: 256   College: Yale   Draft: 2001/7 (224)   Born: 15-Sep-1979   Age:29   Risk: Red

Year	Team	G	Rec	Pass	Yds	C%	Yd/C	TD	YAC	Rk	DVOA	Rk	DYAR	Rk	YAR	Short	Mid	Deep	Bomb
2006	SF	13	34	49	292	69%	8.6	2	4.2	22	-9.8%	33	-5	34	-5	71%	15%	12%	2%
2007	NO	14	48	63	378	76%	7.9	2	3.1	36	-3.2%	27	18	26	7	63%	32%	5%	0%
2008	NO		29	38	248	76%	8.6	2			8.9%								

It's been true throughout his career—when Johnson can actually manage to stay healthy, as he did for his 82-catch season in 2004 with San Francisco, he's one of the better pass-catching threats at his position. But his 2007 season told the more common tale, as Johnson's struggles with a groin injury (not to mention his bottomed-out production) scared potential investors to the point that he was best-served by signing a one-year deal to return to New Orleans. Most likely, he'll continue to alternate injury frustration with the occasional eye-popping "What If?" performance.

Dustin Keller   Height: 6-3   Weight: 242   College: Purdue   Draft: 2008/1 (30)   Born: 25-Sep-1984   Age:24   Risk: Red

Year	Team	G	Rec	Pass	Yds	C%	Yd/C	TD	YAC	Rk	DVOA	Rk	DYAR	Rk	YAR	Short	Mid	Deep	Bomb
2008	NYJ		28	46	332	61%	11.9	4			-10.1%								

No team threw the four-wide, one-back formation on the field more often in 2007 than the Jets, 194 times in 756 total snaps. That they totaled a -25.0% DVOA out of that formation indicates that personnel was an issue. Keller is primed to change this from the word go—of all the receiving tight ends on the 2008 draft class, he's the most "receiver-y." He actually started his Purdue career as a 185-pound receiver and bulked up to his current H-back size. His 4.53 40-yard dash at the Combine and overall versatility have the Jets wondering if Keller can't be their version of Dallas Clark. The Jets are already pushing Chris Baker out the door, so Keller will get a chance to start pretty quickly.

Reggie Kelly

Height: 6-4 Weight: 255 College: Mississippi State Draft: 1999/2 (42) Born: 22-Feb-1977 Age:31 Risk: Red

Year	Team	G	Rec	Pass	Yds	C%	Yd/C	TD	YAC	Rk	DVOA	Rk	DYAR	Rk	YAR	Short	Mid	Deep	Bomb
2005	CIN	15	15	18	90	83%	6.0	1	2.3	—	-13.8%	—	-7	—	-9	78%	17%	6%	0%
2006	CIN	16	21	33	254	64%	12.1	1	4.1	25	12.0%	8	44	16	41	52%	23%	26%	0%
2007	CIN	15	20	27	211	74%	10.6	0	2.5	42	8.5%	17	25	25	22	60%	16%	24%	0%
2008	CIN		19	27	185	70%	9.7	1			-0.3%								

More of a blocker than a receiving tight end, Kelly's role in the Cincinnati offense is likely to shrink with the arrival of Indianapolis's Ben Utecht. Conversely, the role of tight end in the Bengals offense will probably expand, given that two of Cincinnati's top three receivers have left (well, unless Chad Johnson stops whining) and their replacements are likely to get fewer targets. All in all, it's likely to add up to a season much the same as the last for Kelly, except that he'll get a breather when Utecht is on the field.

Jeff King

Height: 6-5 Weight: 253 College: Virginia Tech Draft: 2006/5 (155) Born: 19-Feb-1983 Age:25 Risk: Red

Year	Team	G	Rec	Pass	Yds	C%	Yd/C	TD	YAC	Rk	DVOA	Rk	DYAR	Rk	YAR	Short	Mid	Deep	Bomb
2006	CAR	12	1	4	1	25%	1.0	1	0.0	—	-37.8%	—	-10	—	-10	67%	33%	0%	0%
2007	CAR	16	46	80	406	58%	8.8	2	3.0	37	-20.1%	37	-68	40	-76	55%	38%	5%	1%
2008	CAR		29	42	309	69%	10.7	2			0.4%								

Though King caught 46 passes in 2007 and appeared to have the starting job in hand, he's been debited for fading after Jake Delhomme's early-season injury. A 10-catch performance against the Colts in Week 8 set things straight, but rookie Dante Rosario impressed coaches enough to compete for time, and the 2008 selection of Louisville's Gary Barnidge creates open competition at the position. The Panthers need a power-blocking tight end for their rushing emphasis, and King might not be the best fit.

Jim Kleinsasser

Height: 6-3 Weight: 272 College: North Dakota Draft: 1999/2 (44) Born: 31-Jan-1977 Age:31 Risk: Green

Year	Team	G	Rec	Pass	Yds	C%	Yd/C	TD	YAC	Rk	DVOA	Rk	DYAR	Rk	YAR	Short	Mid	Deep	Bomb
2005	MIN	16	22	28	171	79%	7.8	0	4.1	29	-18.3%	39	-19	34	-22	77%	23%	0%	0%
2006	MIN	16	7	16	47	44%	6.7	0	2.3	—	-47.2%	—	-41	—	-43	64%	18%	9%	9%
2007	MIN	16	4	10	43	40%	10.8	1	4.5	—	-23.5%	—	-11	—	-9	86%	0%	14%	0%
2008	MIN		10	16	104	63%	10.4	1			-4.3%								

A North Dakota native, Kleinsasser usually lines up at the end of the offensive line, sometimes in the backfield, but let's be honest: This is not a tight end, this is not a fullback, this is a slightly undersized tackle who occasionally, perhaps accidentally, finds the ball in his hands. In 117 career games, all with Minnesota, Kleinsasser has averaged less than two catches per game and has only caught six touchdowns. In the past two seasons, he has played in all 32 games, including 22 starts, and caught only 11 passes. No, Kleinsasser and his 272 pounds are out there to block, and as the linebackers of the NFC North will tell you, he is good at his job. In May, his name came up in a news story involving a boat, which had to make the Vikings front office wince, but this time there was no scandal. Along with Steve Hutchinson, Kleinsasser was participating in a charity walleye fishing trip. Is that not the most quintessential upper Midwest story you've ever heard?

Joe Klopfenstein

Height: 6-6 Weight: 245 College: Colorado Draft: 2006/2 (46) Born: 9-Nov-1983 Age:25 Risk: Red

Year	Team	G	Rec	Pass	Yds	C%	Yd/C	TD	YAC	Rk	DVOA	Rk	DYAR	Rk	YAR	Short	Mid	Deep	Bomb
2006	STL	16	20	34	226	62%	11.3	1	4.8	12	6.0%	15	32	21	30	48%	24%	28%	0%
2007	STL	16	2	3	37	67%	18.5	1	11.5	—	36.1%	—	9	—	11	33%	67%	0%	0%
2008	STL		11	17	109	65%	9.9	2			-2.4%								

With just 22 catches in 32 career games, Klopfenstein is obviously a blocking tight end, not a receiver. That would be fine, if he were any kind of competent blocker at all. Game charters, however, were less than thrilled with his blocking, and pined for the days of Brandon Manumaleuna. Klopfenstein was drafted out of Colorado in 2006 in the second round. Second-round tight ends are supposed to bring a lot to the table, but so far that hasn't been the case with Klopfenstein. Maybe football isn't his bag. Maybe he should join his cousin Scott, who sings and plays trumpet, drums and guitar for ska band Reel Big Fish, whose songs include "Beer," "Everything Sucks," and "Somebody Hates Me." Sounds like the perfect soundtrack for a Rams fan, doesn't it? Reel Big Fish also does a snazzy cover of a-ha's "Take On Me." Just wanted to share.

Donald Lee Height: 6-3 Weight: 255 College: Mississippi State Draft: 2003/5 (156) Born: 31-Aug-1980 Age:28 Risk: Red

Year	Team	G	Rec	Pass	Yds	C%	Yd/C	TD	YAC	Rk	DVOA	Rk	DYAR	Rk	YAR	Short	Mid	Deep	Bomb
2005	GB	15	33	55	294	60%	8.9	2	4.9	15	-12.2%	30	-18	33	-30	67%	18%	11%	4%
2006	GB	15	10	21	150	48%	15.0	0	8.0	—	-16.4%	—	-14	—	-13	29%	50%	21%	0%
2007	GB	15	48	63	575	76%	12.0	6	5.6	6	30.2%	3	164	5	168	54%	38%	5%	3%
2008	GB		42	57	506	74%	12.0	3			5.6%								

Lee signed a long-term contract during the 2007 season and should be the Packers starting tight end for at least two more years. He's a pumped up wide receiver, but in five NFL seasons he has developed into a good enough blocker to stay on the field full time. Lee caught exactly four passes in each of the Packers first four games, then three in the next three games, then four passes, then five before catching just one pass on Thanksgiving day. In other words, his role in the offense is pretty defined.

Marcedes Lewis Height: 6-6 Weight: 255 College: UCLA Draft: 2006/1 (28) Born: 19-May-1984 Age:24 Risk: Red

Year	Team	G	Rec	Pass	Yds	C%	Yd/C	TD	YAC	Rk	DVOA	Rk	DYAR	Rk	YAR	Short	Mid	Deep	Bomb
2006	JAC	14	13	21	126	62%	9.7	1	4.4	—	3.4%	—	17	—	17	44%	39%	11%	6%
2007	JAC	16	37	57	391	65%	10.6	2	3.3	31	0.0%	25	28	22	23	35%	44%	20%	0%
2008	JAC		33	48	390	69%	11.8	3			13.5%								

Potential breakout player alert! Lewis appeared to be putting it all together at the end of last season, catching 15 passes over a four-game stretch late in the year. He's blessed with good hands and a tremendous ability to go up and get the ball like a much lighter man. He also impressed with his run-blocking last year, but still needs to improve route-running.

John Madsen Height: 6-5 Weight: 220 College: Utah Draft: 2006/FA Born: 9-May-1983 Age:25 Risk: Red

Year	Team	G	Rec	Pass	Yds	C%	Yd/C	TD	YAC	Rk	DVOA	Rk	DYAR	Rk	YAR	Short	Mid	Deep	Bomb
2006	OAK	15	11	19	146	58%	13.3	1	3.3	—	-13.2%	—	-5	—	-3	25%	50%	6%	19%
2007	OAK	16	8	12	102	67%	12.8	1	4.3	—	20.2%	—	22	—	24	58%	33%	0%	8%
2008	OAK		14	20	149	70%	10.6	1			13.1%								

Madsen has mainly been used as a blocker so far in his career. Lane Kiffin runs a lot of two-tight end sets, but the second tight end is strictly a blocker. Madsen's a big target who runs well, so he could do minor damage if anything happens to Zach Miller.

Brandon Manumaleuna Height: 6-2 Weight: 288 College: Arizona Draft: 2001/4 (129) Born: 4-Jan-1980 Age:28 Risk: Red

Year	Team	G	Rec	Pass	Yds	C%	Yd/C	TD	YAC	Rk	DVOA	Rk	DYAR	Rk	YAR	Short	Mid	Deep	Bomb
2005	STL	14	13	20	129	65%	9.9	1	6.8	—	-34.9%	—	-38	—	-34	56%	31%	6%	6%
2006	SD	16	14	17	91	82%	6.5	3	4.7	—	17.9%	—	27	—	28	88%	13%	0%	0%
2007	SD	16	10	15	86	67%	8.6	1	5.1	—	-9.0%	—	-2	—	0	83%	8%	8%	0%
2008	SD		13	20	114	65%	8.8	3			-3.0%								

An interesting thing happened when All-Pro tight end Antonio Gates was rendered mostly useless in the playoffs: The Chargers passing game still played at a high level. That performance had nothing to do with the enormous Manumaleuna's ability as a receiver. But Manumaleuna's presence on the field led to more max protect calls, which allowed receivers to make plays down the field. Philip Rivers was a much more comfortable quarterback with time to throw. The Chargers are gradually shifting from a two-back offense to a three-receiver offense, but their best look may be two tight ends with Gates flexed out into the slot on most plays.

David Martin

Height: 6-4 Weight: 260 College: Tennessee   Draft: 2001/6 (198) Born: 13-Mar-1979 Age:29 Risk: Red

Year	Team	G	Rec	Pass	Yds	C%	Yd/C	TD	YAC	Rk	DVOA	Rk	DYAR	Rk	YAR	Short	Mid	Deep	Bomb
2005	GB	12	27	39	224	69%	8.3	3	3.0	41	9.0%	14	42	17	35	46%	38%	11%	5%
2006	GB	11	21	36	198	58%	9.4	2	3.5	35	-5.2%	26	4	30	-2	47%	28%	17%	8%
2007	MIA	15	34	50	303	68%	8.9	2	2.3	44	-9.3%	31	-7	30	-8	46%	46%	6%	2%
2008	MIA		26	41	245	64%	9.4	2			-3.0%								

The Packers spent five years trying to turn Martin into a starting tight end. All they got for their trouble was a pumped-up slot receiver who couldn't block and lacked top-end speed. The Dolphins signed him, started him 15 times, and enjoyed a string of three-catch, 18-yard stat lines to go with the lousy blocking. Martin should return to the bench this season.

Sean McHugh

Height: 6-5 Weight: 262 College: Penn State   Draft: 2004/FA Born: 27-May-1982 Age:26 Risk: Red

Year	Team	G	Rec	Pass	Yds	C%	Yd/C	TD	YAC	Rk	DVOA	Rk	DYAR	Rk	YAR	Short	Mid	Deep	Bomb
2005	DET	3	0	1	0	0%	0.0	0	0.0	0	-88.5%	—	-4	—	-4	0%	0%	0%	0%
2006	DET	6	3	5	25	60%	8.3	0	0.0	0	22.1%	—	11	—	10	0%	0%	0%	0%
2007	DET	15	17	29	252	59%	14.8	0	8.6	1	-2.6%	26	10	27	9	67%	19%	15%	0%
2008	DET		18	26	172	69%	9.6	1			-5.6%								

A former Penn State fullback and Packers practice-squader, McHugh saw significant action for the first time last season as a tight end and produced a few big plays, including a 46-yard catch against the Broncos and a 37-yarder against the Cowboys. Michael Gaines is now the Lions tight end, but McHugh deserves a chance to stick as a full-back or H-back.

Randy McMichael

Height: 6-3 Weight: 250 College: Georgia   Draft: 2002/4 (114) Born: 28-Jun-1979 Age:29 Risk: Red

Year	Team	G	Rec	Pass	Yds	C%	Yd/C	TD	YAC	Rk	DVOA	Rk	DYAR	Rk	YAR	Short	Mid	Deep	Bomb
2005	MIA	16	60	104	582	58%	9.7	5	4.9	14	-16.3%	37	-61	43	-55	61%	30%	8%	1%
2006	MIA	16	62	96	640	66%	10.3	3	5.3	4	3.0%	18	72	10	72	55%	35%	8%	1%
2007	STL	16	39	67	429	58%	11.0	3	3.7	23	8.9%	16	72	15	63	55%	31%	13%	2%
2008	STL		48	79	507	61%	10.6	5			0.7%								

Known most of his career as primarily a receiving tight end, Randy McMichael spent more time throwing blocks in 2007, on both passes and runs. Though he was very good in that role (our game charters noted that when the Vikings played Seattle, McMichael lined up at fullback on one play and laid out Pro Bowl linebacker Lofa Tatupu), he'd like to see the ball in his hands more often—which is why he was so happy when St. Louis hired Al Saunders to be their offensive coordinator. "(Saunders) said the funniest thing to me the first time I met him," McMichael said to the *Bellville News-Democrat*. "He said, 'I've had a Pro Bowl tight end eight straight years.'" Saunders was referring to the success he had with Tony Gonzalez in Kansas City and Chris Cooley in Washington. McMichael has put up big numbers before—he caught 73 passes for 791 yards with the Dolphins in 2004—so Saunders's goals for the tight end are optimistic, but not unrealistic.

Billy Miller

Height: 6-3 Weight: 230 College: USC   Draft: 1999/7 (218) Born: 24-Apr-1977 Age:31 Risk: Red

Year	Team	G	Rec	Pass	Yds	C%	Yd/C	TD	YAC	Rk	DVOA	Rk	DYAR	Rk	YAR	Short	Mid	Deep	Bomb
2006	NO	10	14	22	129	55%	9.2	0	2.5	—	-26.4%	—	-36	—	-27	56%	31%	13%	0%
2007	NO	16	27	38	328	71%	12.1	2	7.0	2	21.8%	8	79	13	85	59%	24%	16%	0%
2008	NO		23	32	223	72%	9.7	2			-1.3%								

Miller was one of the Saints' few bright spots late in the season, when it seemed like half the projected starting offense was hurt and the other half was determined to get Drew Brees killed with the minimum amount of protection possible. When Eric Johnson was sidelined with his annual injury festival, Miller stepped up and gained 138 yards in the season's last four games. He could parlay that into a starting role in 2008.

Heath Miller

Height: 6-5 Weight: 256 College: Virginia   Draft: 2005/1 (30) Born: 22-Oct-1982 Age:26 Risk: Yellow

Year	Team	G	Rec	Pass	Yds	C%	Yd/C	TD	YAC	Rk	DVOA	Rk	DYAR	Rk	YAR	Short	Mid	Deep	Bomb
2005	PIT	16	39	52	459	75%	11.8	6	4.7	19	27.2%	5	123	7	124	41%	43%	13%	2%
2006	PIT	16	34	55	393	62%	11.6	5	5.3	5	3.8%	17	43	18	42	43%	39%	18%	0%
2007	PIT	16	47	61	566	77%	12.0	7	4.4	15	38.9%	1	194	4	201	40%	42%	18%	0%
2008	PIT		43	70	575	61%	13.4	5			7.3%								

One of the NFL's more underrated offensive skill position players, Miller is rarely mentioned as an elite tight end despite leading the league in DVOA by almost 15 percentage points. The Steelers would prefer to use Miller more in the passing game, but their horrible offensive line frequently requires him to stay in and help with pass protection—at which he excels, sometimes looking like the best pass blocker on the team. Ben Roethlisberger has been quoted several times as saying he prefers to throw to taller targets, and the six-foot-five Miller certainly qualifies, meaning that if Pittsburgh's line improves Miller will likely get more touches in the passing game. Unfortunately, the line won't be much better this year, so another season of the same beckons.

Zach Miller

Height: 6-4 Weight: 256 College: Arizona State   Draft: 2007/2 (38) Born: 12-Nov-1985 Age:23 Risk: Red

Year	Team	G	Rec	Pass	Yds	C%	Yd/C	TD	YAC	Rk	DVOA	Rk	DYAR	Rk	YAR	Short	Mid	Deep	Bomb
2007	OAK	16	44	69	444	64%	10.1	3	3.3	32	-6.1%	29	5	28	13	44%	41%	13%	3%
2008	OAK		45	66	467	68%	10.4	3			-11.7%								

Last year, with a shifting cadre of quarterbacks, Miller was productive. Offensive coordinator Greg Knapp has always liked throwing to the tight end and Miller could fit in well with new starting quarterback JaMarcus Russell, who will be schooled to look short first. Miller averaged just 7.7 yards per catch in September but improved to 11.8 yards per catch by December. He can help the offense if his season average stays close to the latter figure. How good could he become?

Martrez Milner

Height: 6-4 Weight: 252 College: Georgia   Draft: 2007/4 (133) Born: 8-Aug-1984 Age:24 Risk: Red

Year	Team	G	Rec	Pass	Yds	C%	Yd/C	TD	YAC	Rk	DVOA	Rk	DYAR	Rk	YAR	Short	Mid	Deep	Bomb
2007	ATL	8	9	9	50	100%	5.6	0	2.8	—	-18.6%	—	-6	—	-8	78%	22%	0%	0%
2008	ATL		20	35	215	57%	10.8	2			-13.3%								

If one tight end could rise and emerge from the soup of tight ends on the Falcons' roster in Alge Crumpler's wake, it's Milner. The local hero was taken in the fourth round of the 2007 draft after catching 30 passes in his senior campaign for Georgia. Milner could get a lot of looks as an H-back in Atlanta's revamped offense.

Greg Olsen

Height: 6-6 Weight: 254 College: Miami   Draft: 2007/1 (31) Born: 11-Mar-1985 Age:23 Risk: Red

Year	Team	G	Rec	Pass	Yds	C%	Yd/C	TD	YAC	Rk	DVOA	Rk	DYAR	Rk	YAR	Short	Mid	Deep	Bomb
2007	CHI	14	39	66	391	59%	10.0	2	3.8	22	-9.4%	32	-9	33	-18	48%	29%	22%	2%
2008	CHI		38	65	434	58%	11.4	4			0.8%								

The top tight end of the 2007 draft will spend at least one more season as the understudy in Chicago. Desmond Clark signed a deal that will keep him in Chicago through 2010, but the contract is modest enough to allow Clark to move to the bench once Olsen overtakes him as a receiving threat. Between the grizzled vet Clark, the promising youngster Olsen, and rookie Kellen Davis, the Bears are among the deepest teams in the league at tight end—which is great news, considering the state of their wide receivers. Olsen finished second to Bernard Berrian with 12 red zone targets last season (five catches, 64 yards, 16.7% DVOA). With Berrian gone and no obvious red zone target on the roster, Olsen could get a disproportionate share of red zone throws, making him an appealing fantasy option.

Ben Patrick

Height: 6-3 Weight: 252 College: Delaware   Draft: 2007/7 (215) Born: 23-Aug-1984 Age:24 Risk: Red

Year	Team	G	Rec	Pass	Yds	C%	Yd/C	TD	YAC	Rk	DVOA	Rk	DYAR	Rk	YAR	Short	Mid	Deep	Bomb
2007	ARI	8	7	12	73	58%	10.4	2	4.1	—	8.9%	—	15	—	21	60%	20%	20%	0%
2008	ARI		24	36	290	67%	12.1	3			11.5%								

The Cardinals are high on the former seventh-round pick, who's fearless going over the middle. He's smart, versatile, and hard-nosed, giving him three advantages over the more highly-touted Leonard Pope, and he played well when he started three games after Pope broke his leg last season.

Justin Peelle

Height: 6-4 Weight: 255 College: Oregon   Draft: 2002/4 (103) Born: 15-Mar-1979 Age:29 Risk: Red

Year	Team	G	Rec	Pass	Yds	C%	Yd/C	TD	YAC	Rk	DVOA	Rk	DYAR	Rk	YAR	Short	Mid	Deep	Bomb
2005	SD	16	11	20	38	55%	3.5	1	3.5	—	-57.7%	—	-69	—	-67	65%	29%	6%	0%
2006	MIA	15	16	18	116	94%	7.3	1	3.9	—	10.4%	—	23	—	23	85%	15%	0%	0%
2007	MIA	16	29	47	228	62%	7.9	2	5.4	8	-19.7%	36	-40	37	-40	88%	12%	0%	0%
2008	MIA		18	28	117	64%	6.5	1			-10.4%								

A block-first tight end imported from San Diego a year before Cam Cameron and seemingly tailor-made for the coach's system. Peelle once averaged 3.5 yards per catch for a full season, and he averaged 6.9 yards per catch in 2007 if you take away his career-long 35-yard scamper against the Raiders. Throwing an average of three passes per game to Peelle is a sign of institutional madness. He may fall victim to a football analogy in training camp, as Anthony Fasano : Tony Sparano : Peelle : Cameron.

Marcus Pollard

Height: 6-3 Weight: 247 College: Bradley   Draft: 1995/FA Born: 8-Feb-1972 Age:36 Risk: Yellow

Year	Team	G	Rec	Pass	Yds	C%	Yd/C	TD	YAC	Rk	DVOA	Rk	DYAR	Rk	YAR	Short	Mid	Deep	Bomb
2005	DET	16	46	78	516	59%	11.2	3	4.7	20	-13.5%	32	-32	37	-27	41%	39%	20%	0%
2006	DET	15	12	17	100	71%	8.3	0	4.7	—	-13.5%	—	-8	—	-9	76%	24%	0%	0%
2007	SEA	14	28	35	273	80%	9.8	2	4.6	12	25.8%	6	82	12	76	49%	51%	0%	0%
2008	NE		13	20	124	65%	9.5	1			-0.2%								

During the preseason last year, Mike Holmgren said that he believed Pollard could have 50 catches in 2007. That was ridiculous of course—Shannon Sharpe and Wesley Walls are the only two tight ends in NFL history to put up those kinds of numbers at Pollard's age—but Pollard proved to be a respectable stop-gap after the Seahawks lost out on signing Daniel Graham. Seahawks fans, don't be too bitter about those passes Pollard dropped in the January playoff game against the Packers. You weren't going to win that game anyway, and it wouldn't be a Seahawks playoff game without a few dropped passes by a tight end.

Leonard Pope

Height: 6-8 Weight: 250 College: Georgia   Draft: 2006/3 (72) Born: 9-Sep-1983 Age:25 Risk: Red

Year	Team	G	Rec	Pass	Yds	C%	Yd/C	TD	YAC	Rk	DVOA	Rk	DYAR	Rk	YAR	Short	Mid	Deep	Bomb
2006	ARI	16	16	23	161	70%	10.1	0	4.0	—	-8.3%	—	0	—	2	65%	35%	0%	0%
2007	ARI	13	23	34	238	68%	10.3	5	3.4	28	3.6%	19	26	23	27	50%	32%	9%	9%
2008	ARI		18	27	159	67%	8.8	2			-6.0%								

An ankle injury will likely keep Pope out until the middle of training camp. He's talented and should be a red zone superstar, but constant mistakes are making the Cardinals turn more to Ben Patrick.

Jeb Putzier

Height: 6-4 Weight: 256 College: Boise State   Draft: 2002/6 (191) Born: 20-Jan-1979 Age:29 Risk: Red

Year	Team	G	Rec	Pass	Yds	C%	Yd/C	TD	YAC	Rk	DVOA	Rk	DYAR	Rk	YAR	Short	Mid	Deep	Bomb
2005	DEN	16	37	58	481	64%	13.0	0	5.9	5	13.6%	10	82	10	81	43%	37%	19%	2%
2006	HOU	14	13	22	125	59%	9.6	0	6.1	—	-9.2%	—	-2	—	-3	47%	47%	6%	0%
2007	HOU	8	6	10	39	60%	6.5	1	2.8	—	-10.5%	—	-2	—	-3	78%	22%	0%	0%
2008	SEA		16	24	160	67%	10.0	2			5.7%								

He's only 28, but he can't stay healthy and virtually every metric shows a steady decline in performance over the past three seasons. He even missed time in May minicamp with an unspecified injury, allowing Will Heller to establish himself as the best veteran on the roster. It's not as if the Seahawks are loaded at talent at tight end, but Putzier will have to fight hard for a roster spot. If he manages to stick around in Seattle, perhaps he can team up with Mariners closer J. J. Putz to open a chain of "Putz & Putzier" steakhouses or something.

Dante Rosario

Height: 6-4　Weight: 250　College: Oregon　　Draft: 2007/5 (155)　Born: 25-Oct-1984　Age:24　Risk: Red

Year	Team	G	Rec	Pass	Yds	C%	Yd/C	TD	YAC	Rk	DVOA	Rk	DYAR	Rk	YAR	Short	Mid	Deep	Bomb
2007	CAR	16	6	7	108	86%	18.0	2	6.0	—	88.4%	—	54	—	54	29%	29%	43%	0%
2008	CAR		19	26	184	73%	9.7	2			4.2%								

Thought to be a fullback prospect after his career at Oregon, Rosario flashed potential as a tight end late in the season with a 54-yard catch against the Seahawks and a touchdown catch in the finale against the Buccaneers. He started the team's first 2008 minicamp at the top of the depth chart, and with a good training camp, he could be a sleeper.

Robert Royal

Height: 6-4　Weight: 257　College: LSU　　Draft: 2002/5 (160)　Born: 15-May-1979　Age:29　Risk: Red

Year	Team	G	Rec	Pass	Yds	C%	Yd/C	TD	YAC	Rk	DVOA	Rk	DYAR	Rk	YAR	Short	Mid	Deep	Bomb
2005	WAS	15	18	35	131	51%	7.3	1	6.9	4	-35.9%	43	-68	45	-70	81%	13%	6%	0%
2006	BUF	16	23	39	233	59%	10.1	3	4.5	17	0.3%	22	20	24	19	51%	31%	11%	6%
2007	BUF	16	25	38	248	66%	9.9	3	5.9	5	-14.7%	34	-18	34	-21	66%	23%	6%	6%
2008	BUF		28	44	252	64%	9.0	2			-6.9%								

One of the worst starters in the NFL at any position. Royal has hands like patio blocks, fumbles too many of the passes he does catch, and gets flagged too often to justify his rep as a blocking tight end. Even his three-catch, 42-yard, two-touchdown effort against the Dolphins in Week 14 comes with a grain of salt: he bobbled his 28-yard touchdown for about five seconds before finally hauling it in. His DVOA and DYAR stats never fall off the cliff because no team is crazy enough to throw him more than 40 passes in a season.

Bo Scaife

Height: 6-2　Weight: 249　College: Texas　　Draft: 2005/6 (179)　Born: 6-Jan-1981　Age:27　Risk: Red

Year	Team	G	Rec	Pass	Yds	C%	Yd/C	TD	YAC	Rk	DVOA	Rk	DYAR	Rk	YAR	Short	Mid	Deep	Bomb
2005	TEN	16	37	55	273	67%	7.4	2	4.3	24	-13.9%	34	-26	36	-33	79%	17%	4%	0%
2006	TEN	14	29	56	370	55%	12.8	2	5.0	10	-6.4%	27	7	28	6	49%	31%	16%	4%
2007	TEN	16	46	78	421	59%	9.2	1	3.2	34	-22.8%	38	-80	41	-69	47%	35%	15%	3%
2008	TEN		34	49	325	69%	9.6	2			3.5%								

Scaife has a good rapport with his old Texas teammate, Vince Young, but let's face it: Scaife was terrible last season. If you're only going to catch 59 percent of your passes, you'd better be catching a lot of deep balls, but Scaife wasn't. His longest catch went for just 26 yards. With Alge Crumpler now in Tennessee, Scaife won't get quite as much playing time.

Tony Scheffler

Height: 6-6　Weight: 260　College: Western Michigan　　Draft: 2006/2 (61)　Born: 15-Feb-1983　Age:25　Risk: Yellow

Year	Team	G	Rec	Pass	Yds	C%	Yd/C	TD	YAC	Rk	DVOA	Rk	DYAR	Rk	YAR	Short	Mid	Deep	Bomb
2006	DEN	13	18	37	286	49%	15.9	4	3.9	27	9.4%	10	41	19	37	21%	45%	24%	9%
2007	DEN	16	49	65	549	75%	11.2	5	4.1	19	26.1%	5	149	6	145	45%	33%	15%	6%
2008	DEN		38	54	384	71%	10.1	4			6.1%								

Quietly, Scheffler has emerged as a highly productive receiver. He and Jason Witten are the only tight ends to rank in the top 10 in DVOA both of the last two seasons. Scheffler is not the greatest blocker in the world, so he does not stay on the field all the time. His versatility, however, allows the Broncos to spread him out wide as a receiver and give defenses different looks. Some year, Scheffler will be targeted more than 65 times and might start putting up Wittenesque counting stats as well. It probably won't be this year.

Matt Schobel

Height: 6-5　Weight: 257　College: TCU　　Draft: 2002/3 (67)　Born: 4-Nov-1978　Age:30　Risk: Red

Year	Team	G	Rec	Pass	Yds	C%	Yd/C	TD	YAC	Rk	DVOA	Rk	DYAR	Rk	YAR	Short	Mid	Deep	Bomb
2005	CIN	16	18	25	193	72%	10.7	1	3.5	33	1.4%	20	13	23	12	37%	47%	16%	0%
2006	PHI	16	14	22	214	64%	15.3	2	10.7	—	6.6%	—	24	—	20	60%	20%	13%	7%
2007	PHI	15	11	21	108	52%	9.8	1	2.4	—	-14.5%	—	-11	—	-11	35%	45%	20%	0%
2008	PHI		11	15	101	73%	9.2	2			-1.2%								

Schobel had two catches in Week 3 and nine other weeks with one catch. Schobel is more of a tweener than your standard tight end, running good routes and doing a much better job of blocking linebackers than chipping on defensive ends. The uncalled helmet-to-helmet hit from Ken Hamlin that laid out Schobel in Week 15 was gruesome and left Schobel with a concussion. Brent Celek did well in his absence, so Schobel will be fighting for the second-string spot this year.

Visanthe Shiancoe

Height: 6-4   Weight: 250   College: Morgan State   Draft: 2003/3 (91)   Born: 18-Jun-1980   Age:28   Risk: Red

Year	Team	G	Rec	Pass	Yds	C%	Yd/C	TD	YAC	Rk	DVOA	Rk	DYAR	Rk	YAR	Short	Mid	Deep	Bomb
2005	NYG	16	8	17	91	47%	11.4	0	3.4	—	-25.6%	—	-20	—	-22	57%	29%	14%	0%
2006	NYG	16	12	14	81	85%	6.8	0	3.3	—	-13.0%	—	-4	—	-7	83%	17%	0%	0%
2007	MIN	16	27	43	323	63%	12.0	1	4.6	13	-6.0%	28	3	29	0	37%	39%	16%	8%
2008	MIN		35	56	396	63%	11.3	3			10.0%								

After four seasons as a part-timer with the Giants, Shiancoe joined the Vikings in 2007 and "exploded" with career highs in catches and yards. This is not to say he had a great season, but his DVOA and other stats weren't terrible when you factor in the state of the Vikings passing game. The projection system expects him to set career highs again in 2008, including a whopping three touchdowns. If quarterback Tarvaris Jackson makes any progress as a passer, Shiancoe is likely to benefit. Mobile quarterbacks have a tendency to rely on their tight ends (Randall Cunningham had Keith Jackson in Philadelphia, Steve McNair had Frank Wycheck in Tennessee, Michael Vick had Alge Crumpler in Atlanta). As long as Adrian Peterson is in Minneapolis, though, the tight end's first job will be blocking, not receiving.

Jeremy Shockey

Height: 6-5   Weight: 253   College: Miami   Draft: 2002/1 (14)   Born: 18-Aug-1980   Age:28   Risk: Green

Year	Team	G	Rec	Pass	Yds	C%	Yd/C	TD	YAC	Rk	DVOA	Rk	DYAR	Rk	YAR	Short	Mid	Deep	Bomb
2005	NYG	15	65	122	891	53%	13.7	7	4.9	13	5.9%	16	103	9	121	29%	51%	12%	8%
2006	NYG	15	66	115	623	57%	9.4	7	2.9	38	0.5%	21	61	12	59	36%	49%	14%	1%
2007	NYG	14	57	93	619	61%	10.9	3	4.1	20	3.0%	21	63	17	63	39%	40%	18%	2%
2008	NYG		52	80	595	65%	11.4	5			5.3%								

Shockey-bashing became a popular pastime on New York talk radio this winter. Kevin Boss played very well down the stretch, and the Giants got hot and won the Super Bowl. Therefore, sportstalk logic insists that Boss is better than Shockey, whose season ended when he broke his leg in Week 15. Correlation, as you may have heard, is not causation, and the Giants winning streak has nothing to do with Shockey's absence. Shockey is a far better blocker than Boss, and while Shockey drops a few passes, that's because he runs much tougher and deeper routes than Boss. It's great to root for the underdog, and Shockey's outsized ego probably won him some enemies in New York, but he's a great player, not a guy who should be looking over his shoulder.

Alex Smith

Height: 6-4   Weight: 258   College: Stanford   Draft: 2005/3 (71)   Born: 22-May-1982   Age:26   Risk: Red

Year	Team	G	Rec	Pass	Yds	C%	Yd/C	TD	YAC	Rk	DVOA	Rk	DYAR	Rk	YAR	Short	Mid	Deep	Bomb
2005	TB	16	41	60	367	68%	9.0	2	4.1	30	-4.1%	24	12	25	27	67%	24%	8%	2%
2006	TB	14	35	53	250	66%	7.1	3	3.5	36	-26.1%	39	-64	41	-67	72%	15%	11%	2%
2007	TB	14	32	53	385	60%	12.0	3	4.3	17	2.3%	22	34	20	34	40%	33%	23%	5%
2008	TB		31	46	362	67%	11.7	2			0.6%								

It's a shame that this young man is the "other Alex Smith," when he's the only one of the Alex Smiths drafted in 2005 with any real NFL productivity. The Bucs ran a lot of two-tight-end sets with Smith and Anthony Becht in 2007, and Smith was the main man from a production perspective. He hasn't hit the elite level—any tight end with a 60 percent catch rate is going to raise questions, and he blocks about as well as that other Alex Smith would—but he's a good fulcrum around which a receiving game in transition from veterans to youngsters can build.

L. J. Smith

Height: 6-3 Weight: 258 College: Rutgers Draft: 2003/2 (61) Born: 13-May-1980 Age:28 Risk: Yellow

Year	Team	G	Rec	Pass	Yds	C%	Yd/C	TD	YAC	Rk	DVOA	Rk	DYAR	Rk	YAR	Short	Mid	Deep	Bomb
2005	PHI	16	61	107	682	57%	11.2	3	4.8	17	-7.8%	28	-4	28	-6	53%	35%	12%	0%
2006	PHI	16	50	80	611	63%	12.2	5	5.2	7	7.0%	14	78	9	78	51%	41%	5%	3%
2007	PHI	10	22	44	236	50%	10.7	1	3.2	35	-24.2%	39	-52	38	-53	34%	46%	15%	5%
2008	PHI		35	56	329	63%	9.4	4			-3.0%								

Smith received the franchise tag following the season. If it could, the franchise tag would've hired a lawyer and sued for character defamation. Smith had a middling season, with much of his production coming on dumpoffs and screens. He fumbles so often that his initials should be J. L., for "jarred loose." Smith has become a better blocker, but he's not such a good blocker as to justify such a concerted effort to retain him; 2008 will almost certainly be his last season in Philadelphia.

Matt Spaeth

Height: 6-7 Weight: 270 College: Minnesota Draft: 2007/3 (77) Born: 24-Nov-1983 Age:25 Risk: Red

Year	Team	G	Rec	Pass	Yds	C%	Yd/C	TD	YAC	Rk	DVOA	Rk	DYAR	Rk	YAR	Short	Mid	Deep	Bomb
2007	PIT	14	5	6	34	83%	6.8	3	2.8	—	70.2%	—	35	—	37	83%	17%	0%	0%
2008	PIT		13	20	143	65%	11.0	2			20.0%								

In his first two regular season games in Pittsburgh, Spaeth caught three passes for 15 yards and two touchdowns, and it seemed that Ben Roethlisberger had a new goal-line target. Then he missed the next two games with an injury, and that section of the playbook got misfiled: Spaeth finished the year with just three red zone targets, and he only caught two more passes all year. Spaeth needs to work on his blocking, as he was weak in run support at times last year, but he showed enough signs of developing into a solid second tight end that the Steelers were happy to send Jerame Tuman off to Arizona.

Jerramy Stevens

Height: 6-7 Weight: 260 College: Washington Draft: 2002/1 (28) Born: 13-Nov-1979 Age:29 Risk: Red

Year	Team	G	Rec	Pass	Yds	C%	Yd/C	TD	YAC	Rk	DVOA	Rk	DYAR	Rk	YAR	Short	Mid	Deep	Bomb
2005	SEA	16	45	68	554	66%	12.3	5	2.9	42	19.9%	7	132	5	134	25%	63%	11%	2%
2006	SEA	11	22	48	231	48%	10.5	4	1.7	43	-27.2%	40	-58	40	-58	28%	62%	7%	3%
2007	TB	15	18	21	189	86%	10.5	4	2.7	—	53.5%	—	88	—	87	60%	20%	15%	5%

Stevens finished with the best DYAR among all secondary tight ends, the product of a late-season jag of productivity in which he caught four touchdowns in the last five games. He's always been an attractive red zone target, and his size and athleticism will have some desperate team looking him up before training camp, but there will come a time when Stevens' off-field troubles will catch up with him and leave him with no options. In January and February of 2008, a *Seattle Times* multi-part expose of the University of Washington's football team and what they got away with during Stevens's time there brought some fairly horrifying facts to light regarding Stevens, other players, the program, and Washington's justice system. Stevens's past was prologue; he's been in so many scrapes with the law during his NFL career, even the more astute observers have lost count. As long as he can catch a ball, however, he'll be in play somewhere in 2008. More's the pity.

Quinn Sypniewski

Height: 6-7 Weight: 265 College: Colorado Draft: 2006/5 (166) Born: 14-Apr-1982 Age:26 Risk: Red

Year	Team	G	Rec	Pass	Yds	C%	Yd/C	TD	YAC	Rk	DVOA	Rk	DYAR	Rk	YAR	Short	Mid	Deep	Bomb
2006	BAL	16	2	2	15	100%	7.5	0	5.0	—	42.3%	—	6	—	6	100%	0%	0%	0%
2007	BAL	15	34	52	246	65%	7.2	1	2.7	41	-25.3%	40	-63	39	-51	49%	43%	4%	4%

Sypniewski was going to compete with Daniel Wilcox for the second-string tight end spot behind Todd Heap until he suffered a particularly gruesome knee injury—his ACL was ripped from the bone, and a bone connected to the ligament was shattered. He's out for the season.

David Thomas

Height: 6-3   Weight: 245   College: Texas   Draft: 2006/3 (86)   Born: 5-Jul-1983   Age:25   Risk: Yellow

Year	Team	G	Rec	Pass	Yds	C%	Yd/C	TD	YAC	Rk	DVOA	Rk	DYAR	Rk	YAR	Short	Mid	Deep	Bomb
2006	NE	15	11	16	159	69%	14.5	1	8.3	—	31.3%	—	42	—	42	60%	33%	7%	0%
2007	NE	2	1	1	9	100%	9.0	0	3.0	—	31.4%	—	5	—	4	0%	100%	0%	0%
2008	NE		17	23	192	74%	11.3	2			11.0%								

Thomas was Vince Young's safety valve at Texas, and according to Mack Brown, only dropped one ball in his entire four years. He showed enough promise in 2006 that the Patriots were satisfied letting Dan Graham leave for bigger bucks elsewhere. Then he injured himself during the team's offseason conditioning program and was placed on the PUP list. (So much for conditioning, we suppose.) He returned by Week 3 to catch only one pass before re-injuring himself and landing on injured reserve. When Bill Belichick was asked why the Patriots constantly kept throwing the ball from spread formations late, one of the reasons he fell back on was that not having Thomas limited his personnel for running formations. Sure, Bill, you were limited to Stephen Spach and Marcellus Rivers, but you were also up by four touchdowns. Thomas is expected to be at full strength for 2008, but that didn't prevent the Patriots from signing 97-year-old Marcus Pollard to compete for their second tight end role.

Ben Troupe

Height: 6-4   Weight: 262   College: Florida   Draft: 2004/2 (40)   Born: 1-Sep-1982   Age:26   Risk: Red

Year	Team	G	Rec	Pass	Yds	C%	Yd/C	TD	YAC	Rk	DVOA	Rk	DYAR	Rk	YAR	Short	Mid	Deep	Bomb
2005	TEN	15	55	80	530	69%	9.6	4	5.2	10	-5.0%	26	12	24	25	67%	24%	9%	0%
2006	TEN	10	13	29	150	45%	11.5	2	7.3	3	-24.2%	38	-30	38	-31	52%	44%	4%	0%
2007	TEN	16	5	9	47	56%	9.4	0	7.4	—	-30.6%	—	-16	—	-12	56%	11%	33%	0%
2008	TB		18	27	188	67%	10.4	2			-11.5%								

Troupe caught 55 passes in 2005, but he had trouble learning Norm Chow's system, fractured his ankle in 2006, battled injuries throughout camp last year, and wound up a little-used third stringer. He has good speed and hands, and Jon Gruden loves retread tight ends almost as much as he loves heady 30-something quarterbacks (remember, Gruden once gave Ricky Dudley a job). If Troupe stays healthy and focused, he could enjoy a minor bounce-back.

Ben Utecht

Height: 6-6   Weight: 249   College: Minnesota   Draft: 2004/FA   Born: 30-Jun-1981   Age:27   Risk: Red

Year	Team	G	Rec	Pass	Yds	C%	Yd/C	TD	YAC	Rk	DVOA	Rk	DYAR	Rk	YAR	Short	Mid	Deep	Bomb
2005	IND	12	3	12	59	25%	19.7	2	0.0	—	-19.7%	—	-10	—	-11	0%	71%	14%	14%
2006	IND	14	37	53	377	70%	10.2	0	4.9	11	12.3%	7	69	11	68	44%	48%	8%	0%
2007	IND	14	31	37	364	84%	11.7	1	5.3	9	33.6%	2	100	10	103	53%	39%	8%	0%
2008	CIN		30	42	330	71%	11.0	3			6.6%								

The Bengals haven't seen a tight end catch 30 passes since Rodney Holman pulled in 34 in 1997, so they signed a guy who has topped that figure in each of the past two years. He pulled that off as the blocking tight end in Indianapolis while Dallas Clark lined up in the slot; now it will be Utecht going out for passes while Reggie Kelly opens running lanes. "This is what I've always hoped for," Utecht told the *Dayton Daily News*. "To go to a team that will take advantage of my strength. I had to be the point-of-attack guy with the Colts. I had to learn how to block. Now I'm in a situation where I can do what I do best—stretch the field and put the defense in a tough position." Unless he misses half the season, Utecht should at least notch another 30 catches. One of our projects for 2008 is to spread the use of his name as an exclamation whenever your favorite team fumbles the ball away or throws a game-changing interception. Utecht!

Delanie Walker

Height: 6-2   Weight: 215   College: Central Missouri State   Draft: 2006/6 (175)   Born: 12-Aug-1984   Age:24   Risk: Red

Year	Team	G	Rec	Pass	Yds	C%	Yd/C	TD	YAC	Rk	DVOA	Rk	DYAR	Rk	YAR	Short	Mid	Deep	Bomb
2006	SF	7	2	4	30	50%	15.0	0	15.5	—	-17.8%	—	-3	—	-3	50%	50%	0%	0%
2007	SF	16	21	42	174	50%	8.3	1	5.6	7	-39.4%	42	-90	42	-86	76%	12%	10%	2%
2008	SF		16	25	209	64%	13.1	1			3.0%								

The former college wide receiver started badly last year, but caught up at the end of the year when he learned the offense better and became more confident. Mike Martz does throw some two-tight end sets into his otherwise wide-open offense, so Walker can work his way into a regular role next to Vernon Davis. Walker has a Vulcan mindmeld with Shaun Hill, so if Hill somehow wins the starting job, you can double this projection.

Benjamin Watson

	Height: 6-3		Weight: 253		College: Georgia						Draft: 2004/1 (32)		Born: 18-Dec-1980		Age:27		Risk: Green	

Year	Team	G	Rec	Pass	Yds	C%	Yd/C	TD	YAC	Rk	DVOA	Rk	DYAR	Rk	YAR	Short	Mid	Deep	Bomb
2005	NE	15	29	54	441	54%	15.2	4	4.9	12	13.4%	11	73	11	75	35%	33%	29%	2%
2006	NE	13	49	91	643	54%	13.1	3	4.1	23	-6.5%	28	7	27	9	38%	35%	16%	11%
2007	NE	12	36	49	389	73%	10.8	6	3.2	33	23.0%	7	104	9	101	54%	23%	23%	0%
2008	NE		46	64	525	72%	11.4	4			22.1%								

Watson hurt his ankle when "tackled from behind" (ahem) by Dallas' Roy Williams in a Week 6 win over the Cowboys. He missed a total of four regular-season games and underwent surgery after the season to repair cartilage damage. He still finished high in DYAR for tight ends, and he could easily enjoy a breakout season in New England's explosive offense if he can steer clear of defenders who have rules countermanding illegal maneuvers named after them. Special bonus: Watson is the only player in this book who attended a panel on analytics in football (moderated by Football Outsiders) when MIT Sloan hosted a sports business conference this past February.

Daniel Wilcox

	Height: 6-1		Weight: 245		College: Appalachian State						Draft: 2001/FA		Born: 23-Mar-1977		Age:31		Risk: Yellow	

Year	Team	G	Rec	Pass	Yds	C%	Yd/C	TD	YAC	Rk	DVOA	Rk	DYAR	Rk	YAR	Short	Mid	Deep	Bomb
2005	BAL	13	20	28	154	71%	7.7	1	5.5	8	-5.7%	27	3	27	0	68%	29%	4%	0%
2006	BAL	14	20	27	166	74%	8.3	3	3.6	33	-9.4%	32	-4	33	-5	72%	24%	4%	0%
2007	BAL	5	6	11	18	55%	3.0	1	-0.2	—	-59.8%	—	-43	—	-45	50%	50%	0%	0%
2008	BAL		21	33	144	64%	6.9	2			-7.1%								

Quinn Sypniewski's injury might extend Wilcox's tenure as a reserve blocking tight end and special teams player for one more season. It will give Wilcox more time to indulge his paintball obsession on the company dime.

Kellen Winslow

	Height: 6-4		Weight: 243		College: Miami						Draft: 2004/1 (6)		Born: 21-Jul-1983		Age:25		Risk: Yellow	

Year	Team	G	Rec	Pass	Yds	C%	Yd/C	TD	YAC	Rk	DVOA	Rk	DYAR	Rk	YAR	Short	Mid	Deep	Bomb
2006	CLE	16	89	120	875	76%	9.8	3	3.7	32	7.1%	13	107	5	112	48%	38%	10%	4%
2007	CLE	16	82	148	1106	55%	13.5	5	4.4	14	0.5%	23	75	14	85	29%	50%	19%	2%
2008	CLE		86	125	978	69%	11.4	8			15.2%								

Winslow was reunited last year with his college offensive coordinator and tight ends coach Rob Chudzinski, and he responded with the kind of season the Browns were envisioning when they made him the fifth overall selection in 2004. Winslow did a majority of his damage on the left side, catching 28 passes for 412 yards while coming across the field after Braylon Edwards cleared out the defenders. With his speed and athleticism, Winslow can line up just about anywhere and cause problems, and he's fiercely competitive when the ball is in the air. As long as he can resist the urge to pop wheelies in the Browns parking lot, Winslow will continue putting up elite numbers.

Jason Witten

	Height: 6-5		Weight: 257		College: Tennessee						Draft: 2003/3 (69)		Born: 6-May-1982		Age:26		Risk: Green	

Year	Team	G	Rec	Pass	Yds	C%	Yd/C	TD	YAC	Rk	DVOA	Rk	DYAR	Rk	YAR	Short	Mid	Deep	Bomb
2005	DAL	16	66	89	757	74%	11.5	6	4.2	26	31.2%	2	217	2	213	41%	49%	11%	0%
2006	DAL	16	64	91	754	70%	11.8	1	3.9	28	23.8%	3	175	2	170	32%	49%	12%	6%
2007	DAL	16	96	141	1145	68%	11.9	7	3.9	21	21.1%	9	256	2	230	32%	53%	13%	2%
2008	DAL		83	102	1056	81%	12.7	6			17.8%								

In the four years that Witten's been a full-time starter, his worst year (2006) was far superior to Dallas Clark's best (2007). Somehow, the latter gets far more hype, but Witten is probably the best all-around tight end in football. Any advantage Antonio Gates has in DYAR is more than accounted for by Witten's drastically superior blocking, specifically in the pass game. Witten's numbers will drop some if Terry Glenn returns and/or the Dallas offense takes an overall dip, but something between his 2006 and 2007 levels of performance would be both acceptable and likely. By the way, how come no one ever criticized Witten or Bobby Carpenter for heading to Cabo during wild card week? Tight ends and linebackers have to study game film too, you know.

George Wrighster Height: 6-3 Weight: 260 College: Oregon Draft: 2002/4 (104) Born: 1-Apr-1981 Age:27 Risk: Red

Year	Team	G	Rec	Pass	Yds	C%	Yd/C	TD	YAC	Rk	DVOA	Rk	DYAR	Rk	YAR	Short	Mid	Deep	Bomb
2005	JAC	16	13	23	120	57%	9.2	2	5.1	—	-17.8%	—	-16	—	-18	55%	20%	20%	5%
2006	JAC	16	39	63	353	63%	9.1	3	2.7	40	-7.4%	31	5	29	4	45%	38%	15%	2%
2007	JAC	11	17	24	123	71%	7.2	1	4.3	—	-15.8%	—	-15	—	-20	78%	9%	9%	4%
2008	JAC		18	28	210	64%	11.7	2			6.7%								

Wrighster lends a veteran presence to the Jacksonville tight end group. He was the solid number two behind Marcedes Lewis last season, but that position could be in jeopardy if Greg Estandia and/or Richard Angulo or Isaac Smolko emerge in training camp this fall. He's a decent-enough pass-catcher, but not a great run-blocker. He'll need to perform above replacement level in order to hang on to his spot in the pecking order.

GOING DEEP

Courtney Anderson, BUF: Anderson is a big tight end who had decent numbers or the Raiders in 2004 and 2005, but he fell off precipitously with the Falcons in 2007, appearing in four games and not catching a single pass. He'll try to get it back with the Bills in 2008. (2006: 25 catches for 285 yards and two touchdowns, 2.2% DVOA, 24 DYAR.)

Richard Angulo, JAC: Jacksonville offensive coordinator Dirk Koetter's fondness for multiple-tight end sets is a boost to this ex-Viking's chances of making the roster. He's a huge target who will likely battle Isaac Smolko for a spot on the team. (2007: eight catches for 81 yards and a touchdown, 33.7% DVOA, 28 DYAR.)

Billy Bajema, SF: A special teamer, specifically a long-snapper. Has no catches in two seasons despite eight starts at tight end. Listed ahead of Delanie Walker on the team's depth chart, which has to be some kind of practical joke.

Gary Barnidge, CAR: The fifth-rounder out of Louisville is a receiving tight end who will compete for reps with Jeff King and Dante Rosario. He's putting on weight and working on his blocking, which would help his prospects, as the team was very impressed with the end of Rosario's 2007 season.

Troy Bienemann, ARI: More a blocker than a receiver, this third-year undrafted free agent out of Washington State is the kind of try-hard guy who sticks on a roster—especially in an undefined positional grouping like Arizona's tight ends. (2007: seven catches for 46 yards and a touchdown, -17.2% DVOA, -8 DYAR.)

Dwayne Blakley, TEN: Blakley took the Atlanta-Nashville shuttle along with Alge Crumpler. Just like he did in Atlanta, he'll play special teams and block in two-tight end sets. (2007: seven catches for 48 yards, -18.6% DVOA, -6 DYAR.)

Mark Bruener, HOU: Bruener was a first-round pick for the Steelers back in 1995, but he never eclipsed the 28 receptions he made his rookie year. These days he's moved from "infrequent target" to "complete non-factor" in the passing game. At 35, Bruener is still a capable blocker who should see time in Houtson's heavy packages, but he's not going to take any passes away from Owen Daniels.

Dominique Byrd, STL: In his 14-game career with the Rams, Byrd had more arrests (2) than touchdowns (1). When the Rams released him, they explained on their Web site that Byrd "failed to live up to expectations." Were they expecting the ratio to be inverted? (2007: four catches for 44 yards, 49.4% DVOA, 15 DYAR.)

Kellen Davis, CHI: Davis was a two-way player at Michigan State, spending some time at defensive end in addition to being the primary tight end. He's six foot six with great wingspan, and he may well have been the most athletic tight end in the draft. His stock dropped because of some off-the-field issues, but Davis could prove to be a fifth-round steal if he develops.

Darnell Dinkins, CLE: Unless the Browns plan on carrying four tight ends, Dinkins is locked in a battle with Steve Heiden for the final spot behind Kellen Winslow and rookie Martin Rucker. Last year Dinkins caught one pass for eight yards. It's not an encouraging sign.

Joel Dreessen, HOU: With Jeb Putzier gone and Mark Bruener getting on in years, Dreessen has a chance to see the field as the Texans' blocking tight end. (2007: four catches for 55 yards and two touchdowns, 70.0% DVOA, 33 DYAR.)

Kevin Everett, BUF: Everett can now walk without support and is regaining the use of his hands. He toured the nation to promote his book, works with the Miami Project to Cure Paralysis, and has started a business that creates soap scum resistant-sheeths for showers, a prosaic little job that must seem a million miles from gridiron glory. Everett's fiancé, Wiande Moore, put Everett's injury and recovery in their proper perspective during his book tour. "It makes you complain less and be grateful for things you have on a daily basis, We take those who we love for granted. Sometimes, we forget to say, 'I love you,' every day. But it's the little things that matter. Because your life can go in an instant." Amen, Wiande and Kevin.

Christian Fauria, CAR: The 13-year veteran was signed by the Panthers in September and caught five of six passes for 39 yards and two touchdowns (63.1% DVOA, 33 DYAR). He probably spent more time answering questions about Spygate than he did on the field (he played in New England from 2002 through 2005). Retirement is a distinct possibility.

Derek Fine, BUF: This former Kansas Jayhawk offers a good combination of blocking end receiving skills. He caught 46 passes in 2007, a school record for tight ends, and can be effective in motion. Not a speed player by any means; Fine's contributing will be in extending drives on underneath routes. He should move to the top of the Bills depth chart quickly; Robert Royal and journeyman Courtney Anderson won't be able to hold off a good prospect for long.

John Gilmore, TB: After spending the first six years of his career in Chicago, Gilmore suddenly finds himself the number-two tight end in Tampa Bay behind Alex Smith. The Bucs were eighth in the league last season in two-tight end sets, so Gilmore should have no problem topping his career highs of 10 catches for 130 yards, both set in his rookie season in 2002. (2007: three catches for 14 yards, -54.5% DVOA, -23 DYAR.)

Tory Humphrey, GB: Perpetual project tight end who missed all of 2007 with a broken ankle and most of 2006 with a bad hammy. Could stick in Green Bay with Bubba Franks gone.

Nate Jackson, DEN: Jackson missed most of 2007 with a torn groin, but he returns in 2008 as the third tight end and a special teams performer. (2007: three catches for 34 yards and a touchdown, -47.5% DVOA, 18 DYAR.)

Teyo Johnson, BUF: Johnson 1) started his college career as a redshirt quarterback at Stanford, 2) lettered in basketball for two years, 3) moved to wide receiver, then to tight end, bulking up to 245 pounds, 4) entered the NFL draft early and joined the Raiders as a second round pick in 2003, 5) spent two years proving to the Raiders that he was a square peg, 6) fell out of the NFL after a venti latte with the Cardinals in 2005. He signed a one-year deal with the Bills in February to help them sort out their tight end problem. Will be released by mid-August.

Ryan Krause, HOU: In 2003, Krause was a senior wide receiver for the Nebraska-Omaha Mavericks, trying to prove to dubious scouts that he had the talent to play in the NFL. Five years later, he's still trying. At six foot three, 244 pounds, he's a receiving tight end only. He'll have to beat out Joel Dreessen to make the Texans.

Tim Massaquoi, BUF: The Bills tried out about 50 H-back types last season after Kevin Everett got hurt. Massaquoi, a Michigan alum who spent the 2006 season in Miami, saw action in four games but didn't distinguish himself. He's part of the crowded Coutney Anderson/Robert Royal/Derek Fine field.

Michael Matthews, NYG: Plays the "third tackle" role of bruising blocker. He's powerful, but he's still got to refine his technique and contribute something in the passing game before he'll see snaps outside of obvious running downs. (2007: six catches for 28 yards and two touchdowns, -60.8% DVOA, -47 DYAR.)

Mike Merritt, KC: Mike Merritt is an American bassist best known for playing with The Max Weinberg 7 on the late night television show *Late Night with Conan O'Brien*. Hmmm... we probably should stop cut-and-pasting from Wikipedia. Merritt's a blocking tight end out of Central Florida who can lay down a mean line during show openings.

Garrett Mills, MIN: Mills was part of a waiver claim by the Vikings from the Patriots on Cutdown Day last year, with Bill Belichick threatening to claim a Vikings practice squad player of his choosing if the Vikings dared pluck the Pats' fourth-string tight end. They did, Belichick didn't grab anyone in response, and the next week, Spygate broke. Mills-gate was quickly forgotten ... until now, when we mentioned it. Mills has played all of one game in two seasons.

Richard Owens, STL: When the Rams cut undrafted free agent Brandon McAnderson from Kansas, Owens's roster spot was delivered. A special-teamer and tight end, Owens is listed as the backup fullback on the Rams' depth chart. Since first-string fullback Brian Leonard is also the second-string running back behind Steven Jackson, an injury to either one would push Owens into a starting role.

Marcellus Rivers, NE: The Patriots' third-string tight end is a blocker first, second, third, and fourth. When the Patriots want to run the ball, he could play the same role Kyle Brady did last year.

Martin Rucker, CLE: Rucker erased Kellen Winslow's career reception record at Missouri, and now he finds himself backing up Winslow's son in Cleveland. Rucker has soft hands and is a good route runner, and his bloodlines are good, as his brother Mike played for the Panthers. He's a Junior Winslow injury away from seeing significant playing time in a pass-happy offense.

Sean Ryan, MIA: Ryan is a poor man's Kyle Brady, a big-bodied blocker with limited ability in the passing game. The Jets liked to motion Ryan into the backfield to use as a lead blocker on running plays, and he figures to be used in much the same way down in Miami, freeing up David Martin and Anthony Fasano to run patterns. (2007: three catches for 46 yards, -11.1% DVOA, -1 DYAR.)

Craig Stevens, TEN: This third-round pick out of California was considered one of the best blocking tight ends in college football, and the Titans liked his maturity and overall game, although his lack of speed is a concern.

Tony Stewart, OAK: Stewart's two biggest professional moments where when he nominated his third grade teacher to be the NFL's 2004 Teacher of the Year (she won) and when he met NASCAR driver Tony Stewart and was featured in a pre-race ceremony highlighting the fact that there were two people named "Tony Stewart." When you're an eight-year veteran who has never caught more than 21 passes in a season, it's good to have other things to pad out your resume with. Stewart played 16 games in 2007 without a single catch.

Jerame Tuman, ARI: Mommy, what happens to good Steelers when they lose their role in the team? They go to Canton, dear. But then, what happens to bad Steelers? Oh, they go to Arizona.

Lee Vickers, BAL: Baltimore quarterbacks might have been better off throwing the ball away than sending it in the direction of Vickers, who last year caught two-of-five balls thrown to him for a total of four yards, with both catches occurring on first down. He's here to block, to play special teams, and to hope the Turk doesn't notice him come August. Not related to Cleveland fullback Laurence Vickers.

Todd Yoder, WAS: Yoder didn't have a great year in 2007, dropping too many passes and struggling on too many blocks to remain an effective contributor. The Redskins responded by drafting Fred Davis in the second round, so Yoder's roster spot is in question this year. (2007: seven catches, 97 yards with one touchdown, 20.9% DVOA, 21 DYAR.)

Keith Zinger, ATL: Zinger returned to the field in 2007 after a 2006 stomach illness almost ended his football career. He started 10 games and played in all 13 for LSU in his senior season, catching two passes and blocking for the national champs. Durability is an issue, but Zinger's blocking makes him a good fit for a power game.

Kicker and Defense Projections

KICKERS

Because of the inconsistency of field-goal percentage from year to year, kickers are projected almost entirely based on team forecasts. Individual factors play a role in these projections in only three ways: 1) Kickers generally improved in their second year; 2) Kickers with a better career field-goal percentage tend to get more attempts, although they are not necessarily more accurate; 3) Field-goal percentage on kicks over 40 yards tends to regress to the mean.

Kicker	Team	FG	Pct	XP	Pts	Risk
Stephen Gostkowski	NE	30-34	88%	59	149	Yellow
David Akers	PHI	30-35	86%	45	135	Red
Adam Vinatieri	IND	27-33	82%	50	131	Yellow
Nate Kaeding	SD	26-33	79%	46	124	Green
Mason Crosby	GB	27-31	87%	40	121	Yellow
John Kasay	CAR	27-31	87%	38	119	Red
Matt Prater	DEN	26-33	79%	39	117	Red
Josh Scobee	JAC	24-30	80%	44	116	Green
Ryan Longwell	MIN	26-29	90%	38	116	Red
Jeff Reed	PIT	24-29	83%	43	115	Yellow
Lawrence Tynes	NYG	25-29	86%	40	115	Red
Rob Bironas	TEN	27-32	84%	30	111	Yellow
Nick Folk	DAL	23-28	82%	42	111	Green
Kris Brown	HOU	23-27	85%	40	109	Yellow
Phil Dawson	CLE	24-29	83%	37	109	Yellow
Brandon Coutu	SEA	23-29	79%	39	108	Red
Mike Nugent	NYJ	23-29	79%	37	106	Green
Matt Bryant	TB	23-29	79%	36	105	Red
Neil Rackers	ARI	24-29	83%	32	104	Yellow
Josh Brown	STL	23-28	82%	34	103	Yellow
Taylor Mehlhaff	NO	21-29	72%	41	104	Red
Shayne Graham	CIN	22-29	76%	36	102	Green
Jason Hanson	DET	24-28	86%	31	103	Red
Matt Stover	BAL	24-29	83%	31	103	Green
Sebastian Janikowski	OAK	24-30	80%	30	102	Red
Shaun Suisham	WAS	23-29	79%	32	101	Red
Jay Feely	MIA	23-28	82%	30	99	Red
Rian Lindell	BUF	22-27	81%	32	98	Green
Robbie Gould	CHI	23-29	79%	28	97	Green
Joe Nedney	SF	23-27	85%	27	96	Red
Bill Cundiff	KC	21-26	81%	32	95	Red
Jason Elam	ATL	21-27	78%	25	88	Red

Alternate Possibilities

Kicker	Team	FG	Pct	XP	Pts	Risk
John Carney	KC	20-25	80%	32	92	Red
Dave Rayner	MIA	21-26	81%	31	94	Red
Nick Novak	KC	18-23	78%	32	86	Red

DEFENSES

The method for projecting defensive points is in *PFP 2006*, key conclusions are: 1) Schedule strength is important for projecting fantasy defense; 2) Categories used for scoring in fantasy defense have no consistency from year-to-year , with the exception of sacks and interceptions. The 2008 projections will look very different from the fantasy defense values from the 2007 season. The first column represents leagues with just defense; the second column represents leagues that include both defense and special teams. Our generic fantasy scoring formula is based on 1 point for a sack, 2 points for a fumble recovery, safety, or interception, and 6 points for a touchdown.

Team	Def	Def/ST	Risk
BAL	133	139	Red
PHI	132	138	Red
NE	130	136	Yellow
MIN	130	136	Red
TB	127	133	Yellow
GB	124	130	Red
SEA	123	129	Yellow
NYG	123	129	Green
NO	122	128	Red
DEN	120	126	Yellow
ARI	113	119	Green
CAR	112	118	Red
KC	110	116	Yellow**
SD	110	116	Green
PIT	107	111	Yellow**
DAL	107	113	Green
NYJ	105	114	Yellow
WAS	105	111	Red
JAC	104	110	Green
STL	103	106	Green
HOU	101	107	Red
DET	98	104	Green
CHI	97	121	Green*
BUF	97	106	Green*
TEN	95	101	Green
CLE	93	102	Green*
IND	92	96	Green
ATL	91	97	Green
MIA	91	97	Green
CIN	90	94	Yellow**
OAK	88	94	Green
SF	81	87	Green

*Yellow in leagues with special teams
** Green in leagues with special teams

Fantasy Risers and Fallers

By Bill Barnwell

Most fantasy football magazines project performance from players as if they were almost entirely static. If a guy had 1,400 yards last year, well, there's every reason to think he'll do it again! Of course, that's not reality. Only three of the top 10 running backs in fantasy football in 2006 repeated in 2007: LaDainian Tomlinson, Frank Gore, and Brian Westbrook. Injuries, age, or a change in the performance of the team around them can dramatically affect the fantasy performance of players.

Those changes are integrated into KUBIAK, our fantasy projection system. Its regression analysis takes into account both previous performance as well as body types, personnel turnover, the linkage between different skill-position players on a team, and offensive scheme, among many other variables, to spit out projections on how a player will do based upon his situation in 2008—not in 2007.

Here, we highlight 20 players, 10 of whom should be underrated in your fantasy draft, and 10 who are likely to be overrated. These players should be rising and falling on your board come Draft Day. Players are ranked according to a simple scoring system of one point for 10 yards rushing or receiving, one point for 20 yards passing, four points for a passing touchdown, six for a rushing or receiving touchdown, and minus two points for an interception.

Top Ten Fantasy Risers

Marshawn Lynch   RB   Buffalo Bills

2007: 280 carries	1,115 rushing yards	18 receptions	184 receiving yards	7 TD	Rank: 12
2008: 330 carries	1,438 rushing yards	23 receptions	229 receiving yards	10 TD	Rank: 5

Lynch's huge projection comes with several factors in mind. His ankle should be 100 percent. He'll be playing on a team that should have a better defense in 2008, with a strong offensive line that's had a year to gel and improve. With a questionable passing game, Buffalo will also need to find a way to move the ball reliably. All signs point to Lynch's becoming an elite fantasy back.

Ryan Grant   RB   Green Bay Packers

2007: 188 carries	956 rushing yards	30 receptions	145 receiving yards	8 TD	Rank: 17
2008: 290 carries	1,296 rushing yards	39 receptions	252 receiving yards	10 TD	Rank: 9

In Grant's seven starts last year, he averaged 124.5 rushing yards and a touchdown per game. Those are MVP numbers over a full year. While the lack of Brett Favre should allow teams to focus more effort on stopping the run, Favre's absence also means that the Packers will need to run more. If Grant can withstand the workload, he could be a fantasy dynamo in 2008.

DeAngelo Williams   RB   Carolina Panthers

2007: 144 carries	717 rushing yards	24 receptions	175 receiving yards	5 TD	Rank: 41
2008: 222 carries	926 rushing yards	43 receptions	292 receiving yards	6 TD	Rank: 29

Even though the Panthers drafted Jonathan Stewart in the first round, Williams should move from being the secondary back to the primary one in Carolina this year. He averaged 5.0 yards per attempt last season despite having nary a semblance of a passing game to support him. Although he's not projected to be used as frequently as some other backs might be used, Williams represents an excellent value pick in the third round of your draft.

Earnest Graham   RB   Tampa Bay Buccaneers

2007: 222 carries	898 rushing yards	49 receptions	324 receiving yards	10 TD	Rank: 37
2008: 273 carries	1,230 rushing yards	47 receptions	432 receiving yards	8 TD	Rank: 7

Graham made Cadillac Williams look like a Pinto after the latter went down for the year with a torn-up knee, averaging a full half-yard per carry more than Williams had the previous year. With the former third-overall pick still recovering from his injuries, Graham should have the starting role all to himself at the beginning of the season. Jon Gruden loves to pound the rock inside the five, and once he's identified a goal-line back, he tends to stick with him. Even if Williams returns earlier than expected, Graham will still have the chance to pick up touchdowns in reserve.

Eli Manning   QB   New York Giants

2007: 3,161 yards	23 TD	20 INT	Rank: 13
2008: 3,987 yards	26 TD	15 INT	Rank: 7

Manning improved his accuracy in the playoffs, but a league-high 20 interceptions in 2007 showed that he wasn't always on the same page with his wide receivers. Even though it doesn't know about the playoff magic, KUBIAK expects Manning to have his best year as a pro in 2008, thanks to a number of factors, including experience, offensive-line continuity, and the third-down rebound effect. With anywhere from eight to 10 players in line for serious touches, Manning should be spoiled for choice when it comes to targets. He may never be unstoppable, but we'll take less stoppable.

Peyton Manning   QB   Indianapolis Colts

2007: 4,033 yards	31 TD	14 INT	Rank: 3
2008: 4,359 yards	38 TD	13 INT	Rank: 2

It seems strange to list big brother Peyton as a fantasy riser considering the stratospheric heights he reached earlier in his career, but Manning should easily improve on his 2007 numbers. Marvin Harrison is expected to be back, but more important than not being without Harrison is not being without Harrison, Anthony Gonzalez, and Dallas Clark simultaneously. The offensive line should be healthier and sturdier, decreasing a sack rate that was Manning's highest since 2001, the Colts' last losing season. With the ripening of fellow fantasy riser Gonzalez, Manning could even approach his 2004 numbers in a season-long shootout with Tom Brady. Manning's incredible consistency and ability to avoid injury also make him one of the safer picks in any fantasy draft.

Matt Schaub   QB   Houston Texans

2007: 2,241 yards	9 TD	9 INT	Rank: 23
2008: 3,917 yards	22 TD	15 INT	Rank: 15

What looks like a pedestrian line has a lot to do with the fact that Schaub only got to play four full games with Andre Johnson. In his four games with Johnson available, Schaub averaged 250 yards passing and threw seven touchdowns against three interceptions. In the six non-Johnson games, Schaub averaged 200 yards and threw only two touchdowns and six interceptions. Both Schaub and Johnson should be healthy in 2008, and the pair could reveal themselves to be an elite connection.

Santonio Holmes   WR   Pittsburgh Steelers

2007: 56 receptions	942 yards	8 TD	Rank: 18
2008: 73 receptions	1,214 yards	11 TD	Rank: 7

Holmes should emerge as Ben Roethlisberger's top target this year; his 18.1 yards per catch for a starting receiver attests to his ability to create separation downfield, while back-to-back top-15 showings in yards after catch prove his ability to make people miss in the open field. Holmes won't get the 150 throws that most number one receivers get, because of Pittsburgh's scheme, but he'll make the most of the throws he does see.

Arnaz Battle   WR   San Francisco 49ers

2007: 50 receptions	600 yards	5 TD	Rank: 43
2008: 67 receptions	760 yards	3 TD	Rank: 48

Two years ago, Mike Furrey went from converted safety to NFC receptions leader by virtue of lining up in the slot and catching 100 quick hitches. That role in San Francisco is a perfect fit for Battle, who's not a great receiver by any means, but could be a far better fantasy receiver than real-life one in 2008. If Battle doesn't win the role, it could fall to Jason Hill, who would be expected to do similar things.

Anthony Gonzalez   WR   Indianapolis Colts

2007: 37 receptions	576 yards	3 TD	Rank: 61
2008: 65 receptions	1,085 yards	10 TD	Rank: 12

Once Gonzalez learned the Colts' offense and got playing time after the injury to Marvin Harrison, he emerged as—you guessed it—another terrifying weapon in the Colts' arsenal. He has gravity-gun-esque hands that allowed him to catch 73 percent of the passes thrown to him while still averaging nearly 16 yards per catch. Gonzalez could emerge as a fantasy stud as early as this year, depending on the availability of Harrison. It's sacrilegious to say, but if the future Hall of Famer can't answer the bell in 2008, the Colts' offense shouldn't miss a beat.

Top Ten Fantasy Fallers

Willie Parker   RB   Pittsburgh Steelers

2007: 321 carries	1,316 rushing yards	23 receptions	164 receiving yards	2 TD	Rank: 16
2008: 261 carries	1,057 rushing yards	25 receptions	238 receiving yards	6 TD	Rank: 24

Parker has always been a boom-and-bust back, but a heavy workload in 2007 sapped his speed and big-play ability as the year went along. While the Steelers' selection of Rashard Mendenhall was generally regarded as the team's taking the vaunted Best Available Player, you don't take a player if you don't plan on using him, which the Steelers will do with the superior talent, style, and health of Mendenhall. Parker might not lose his job this year, but his run of 1,200-yard seasons is over, starting now.

Frank Gore   RB   San Francisco 49ers

2007: 260 carries	1,102 rushing yards	53 receptions	436 receiving yards	6 TD	Rank: 9
2008: 233 carries	922 rushing yards	60 receptions	551 receiving yards	7 TD	Rank: 15

Gore was the same player in 2007 that he was in 2006, but the rest of the team collapsed around him. While Mike Martz has insisted that he'll build his offense around the talents of Gore, Martz isn't known for being particularly pliant with his schemes and philosophies; even if Gore is the focal point, the nature of his role will probably change to more of a Roger Craig–style back than a traditional running back. That's less useful in most fantasy leagues, and no matter how Gore is used, his catalog of injuries threatens to bite back at any time.

Justin Fargas   RB   Oakland Raiders

2007: 222 carries	1,009 rushing yards	23 receptions	188 receiving yards	4 TD	Rank: 23
2008: 179 carries	707 rushing yards	25 receptions	190 receiving yards	3 TD	Rank: 45

Fargas is a talented back who got a contract extension to stay in Oakland, only for the Raiders to draft Darren McFadden with the fourth overall pick. He'll be squeezed by McFadden from above and Michael Bush from below, and with a team that's not likely to be running out the clock in too many games, Fargas will struggle to get the playing time he needs to put up fantasy numbers.

Jay Cutler   QB   Denver Broncos

2007: 3,497 yards	20 TD	14 INT	Rank: 11
2008: 3,140 yards	24 TD	20 INT	Rank: 19

The placement of Jay Cutler on this list has nothing to do with the talents of the man himself, who for all the world looks to be a very good NFL quarterback. It has to do with an offensive line that mixes inexperienced youngsters with veterans coming off injury. He also has to deal with the fact that his only receiver of any merit, Brandon Marshall, lost a fight to the Hamburgler this offseason. The quarterback simply can't do it all himself.

Tony Romo   QB   Dallas Cowboys

2007: 4,211 yards	36 TD	19 INT	Rank: 2
2008: 3,926 yards	26 TD	17 INT	Rank: 8

Romo defied his placement on this list last year by putting up similar numbers to his 2006 season, but there are still many reasons to think that he could see his numbers fall off in 2008. Romo's offensive line stayed healthy last year, which kept him upright. Even though the man stayed healthy for the most part, his fearless but reckless style of play easily lends itself to injury. When Romo hurt his thumb against the Eagles in Week 15, he lost all accuracy and was unable to do anything offensively. It's the nagging injuries of that nature that Romo is less likely to avoid in 2008. Combine those factors with the circus of a Terrell Owens contract year, the addition of Asante Samuel to the NFC East, and the return of Carlos Rogers, and you find enough problems running interference to think that Romo could see a decline in 2008.

Jon Kitna   QB   Detroit Lions

2007: 4,068 yards	18 TD	20 INT	Rank: 14
2008: 3,128 yards	20 TD	18 INT	Rank: 26

Kitna stayed on the field despite suffering a concussion and being the most hit quarterback in football last year, one of the virtues of Mike Martz's offensive scheme. Kitna moves into a more traditional scheme this year, but still doesn't have the offensive line or backfield to do anything besides chuck the ball up and hope that one of his receivers gets underneath it. The scheme change would be enough to put him on this list, but the wear and tear of the last two years and his advanced age means that the end is closer for Kitna than his statistics make it appear.

Vincent Jackson   WR   San Diego

2007: 41 receptions	623 yards	3 TD	Rank: 53
2008: 45 receptions	741 yards	5 TD	Rank: 42

Jackson was brilliant in the playoffs, but that also came while LaDainian Tomlinson was injured. It didn't mesh with a regular season in which Jackson failed to solidify his spot as a starting wide receiver. With Chris Chambers, Eric Parker, and Buster Davis all looking for playing time at wide receiver, and all of them waiting in line for touches behind Tomlinson and Antonio Gates, Jackson's playoff performance might not indicate anything more than a flash in the pan. While fantasy faller seems odd for a player projected to slightly improve, a stagnant 2008 for Jackson would bode very poorly for the rest of his career.

Reggie Williams   WR   Jacksonville

2007: 38 receptions	629 yards	10 TD	Rank: 28
2008: 31 receptions	535 yards	3 TD	Rank: 68

The only reason anyone cares about Williams as a fantasy player are those 10 touchdowns last year—so, how likely are they to occur? Since 1983, 11 players have caught between 30 and 40 passes in a year and scored eight or more touchdowns. Chris Henry was one of them in 2006, but we're going to throw him out of the data since his 2007 performance wasn't indicative of anything football related. The year after their touchdown heroics, the other 10 receivers averaged 4.4 touchdowns. To put it another way, Williams averaged a touchdown every 3.8 receptions last year. Over the time mentioned, there were only seven instances of a player having a reception-to-touchdown ratio below 4.0; again, one was Chris Henry. The other six averaged a touchdown every 7.5 receptions the year afterward. Would 38/629/4 seem that exciting? Yes, 2007 was a fluke.

Hines Ward   WR   Pittsburgh

2007: 71 receptions	732 yards	7 TD	Rank: 31
2008: 56 receptions	742 yards	5 TD	Rank: 45

Ward's rank in yards after catch the last three seasons: 26, 19, 61. While Ward's still a consummate blocker, he's never had spectacular hands—it's been his elusiveness that's allowed him to thrive as an NFL receiver. A troublesome knee led to surgery in the offseason—if the surgery solved the problem, then the 32-year-old Ward could approach his previous levels of success. In all likelihood, though, Ward's simply not going to be as agile as he once was, which basically puts him on the Eric Moulds career path to relative irrelevance.

Derrick Mason WR   Baltimore

2007: 103 receptions	1,087 yards	5 TD	Rank: 20
2008: 63 receptions	685 yards	4 TD	Rank: 50

Mason set a career high in receptions last year, but that had less to do with Mason and more with the fact that Todd Heap was hurt and Mark Clayton was hobbled all season. Mason's unimpressive yards per catch points to a receiver who was being forced the ball as if the Ravens were going to make foie turf out of him. Of the passes thrown to him, 43 percent were short throws, up from 30 percent the year before. With Heap back, Clayton healthy, and Mason now 34 years old, his numbers are likely to drop like a rock this year.

Painkillers: The Dirty Secret

Will Carroll

Ronnie Lott cut off his finger to play. We talk about his toughness.

Brett Favre talks about taking "eight or nine" Vicodin before a game. The adult dosage is four to six—per day. We talk about his streak.

Mike Ditka walks, if you can call it that, like a 90-year-old. He's almost 70 and hasn't taken a step without pain for most of his life. We talk about his passion.

Painkillers in all their forms are the dirty little secret of football. While the focus here will be on the usage in the NFL, don't kid yourself that this is just a professional problem. Colleges, high schools, and even Pop Warner have their own abuses. *Friday Night Lights*—the book, not the movie or TV show—first exposed the widespread usage of painkillers in high school. It hasn't gotten better since that late 1980s classic. In today's sports world, where drugs are "bad" and steroids are something just short of the plague in most fans' minds, painkillers are ignored … or worse, justified.

In the NFL, fans, coaches, and even teammates feed this "must play" mentality, which combined with the secrecy ingrained in the culture, ends up pushing players toward the use of painkillers. When Calvin Johnson states that he was taking two Vicodin pills to get through a game due to a lower back injury, he's not just putting himself at risk; he's putting his life at risk. Beyond the risks of addiction, Johnson and the hundreds—yes, hundreds—of other players taking narcotics and injections to play are subject not just to the analgesic effect, but also to the systemic effects of the narcotics. "If people knew how many guys were stoned out on the field," one sports physician told me, "they'd freak out. The NFL will never let that happen, so we'll never hear about it as a problem. They'll spin it into talk about toughness and macho."

That point is true, but to spin, NFL teams would have to address the issue, something they're not likely to do. In fact, no one is willing to address the issue. I spent better than two months researching and writing this story, yet very few people I spoke with—doctors, players, coaches, front office types—would even discuss the issue, let alone go on record. As with steroids, it's a problem that's invisible and that can be waved away. When people like Alan Schwarz of the *New York Times* started shining a light on the concussions problem, the NFL couldn't ignore it, because fans had seen Zach Thomas, Dan Morgan, and others lying on the field unconscious. The reverse is true with painkillers. Instead of seeing someone carted off, the use of painkillers allows many players who would otherwise be sidelined to be on the field, playing.

That invisibility of effect makes it nearly impossible to measure the true cost. Outside of a few cases like Brett Favre, we don't have much of an example of painkiller addiction in the NFL. But this might be the result of the level of pain. "People think that opiates eat pain," I was told by a pain management specialist who consults with two NFL teams and therefore could not speak openly. "That's backwards. Pain eats opiates. If you see people in hospice care, they're not 'stoned' unless you've gone well over the dose necessary, and at that point, they normally just sleep. If pain was convenient and gave us dosages, we'd know exactly how much to give, but even today, we're always hit or miss with the general painkillers, the opiates." Players always want to take "just one more," he said. And for good reason.

It's the "one more" that is the greatest danger. According to one team's athletic trainer, "the game isn't one of yards and seconds anymore. It's inches and milliseconds. A guy who's just a bit overmedicated or undermedicated is going to miss out, be a step slow, zig when he should have zagged." At that point, the risk goes up exponentially. A missed block, a missed assignment, or a highlight-reel hit—all of them could be symptoms of painkiller abuse. So why are players willing to risk it?

"Money" was the clear answer I was given by two NFL players, both of whom refused to speak on the record. Neither man was a star-level player with guaranteed money or someone who had pocketed a big bonus coming into the league. For them, playing wasn't just a paycheck that comes each week. It was a tool to make sure that the paycheck kept coming. "The [salary] cap is a ticking clock. By the time I'm a free agent, some kid younger than me is cheaper than me, too. If I miss a game, it's like back in school. It goes on my permanent record." But aren't they worried about the longer-term consequences? "If I stay in the league three, four more years," one said, "then the future is [the ability to] do whatever I want. Back to school? Kids in college? Buy a business? It's all in making sure that I keep getting that check, and if that means popping some pills or taking the spike, I have to."

It was that attitude—"I have to"—that seems the most sinister. It is often said that steroids and other performance enhancers creep into the game because athletes see one athlete doing it and feel the need to keep up. A small population, if winning, does create that perception, something I've called the Romanowski Effect in football.

Wherever Bill Romanowski went in the NFL, steroids followed, largely because he used them openly and his teammates saw the results. Super Bowl rings. Endorsement deals. A beautiful wife and a beautiful house, all the things David Byrne dreamed of.

If a player refuses to play in pain, he's attacking not just the "warrior's code," but also his team. LaDainian Tomlinson will face that kind of stare coming into the 2008 season after refusing to play on a damaged knee in the AFC Championship game. At the same time, Philip Rivers was playing through a torn ACL, creating a contrast that even the best running back in the NFL may struggle to overcome.

In order to combat the problem, the NFL must first recognize that there is a problem. For the most part, the league has things in order. It has in place an excellent Employee Assistance Program that can help with addiction issues if the situation gets to that point. Admittedly, the program does not often reach this far, and when it does, it's usually only when a player is out of the league, when the pain begins to leave his body and he's left with an addiction. There is a program in place that audits the use of prescription painkillers given out by team physicians. The players I spoke with knew about the program and laughed. "Our doctor squeezes us on meds," one said, indicating that it was tough to get high-level painkillers from team physicians. It just drives him to other sources. "Guys have their own docs. Guys share. Guys know guys," the same player said. The audits are then mere window dressing.

If the NFL is going to get serious about this, it needs to take three steps. First, it needs to make it a league rule that painkillers not prescribed by team physicians are banned. Second, the league needs to add painkillers to the current drug screens. By matching positive test results with team medical records, finding players who have violated the rule should be easy. The procedure would be much the same as with Therapeutic Use Exemptions, but a negative procedure rather than a proactive one. Finally, the league needs to make transparent the use of painkillers by players. A simple addition to the league's weekly injury reports could denote a player on high-level medications, whether he was playing or injured.

It is this last issue that should worry the NFL the most. While safeguarding the health of players should be paramount, we have seen that the league is willing to overlook common medical practices to keep the game profitable. What it cannot afford to lose is its integrity. The injury report is jealously guarded and strictly enforced, largely because a player or team hiding an injury could mean millions to bettors. The transparency of the injury report combats the abuse of the game by gamblers.

Except those same gamblers know about painkillers, often before the teams themselves do. A player told me the story of another NFL player's personal assistant. "His agent helped him find a guy to get stuff done, pick up his clothes, keep the house up, stuff like that. Turns out the dude was counting pills and calling Vegas, too, making a little extra on the side."

Addiction and pain may be the least of the game's worries unless the painkiller problem is addressed now.

The Injury Effect

Bill Barnwell

Injuries provide NFL teams, fans, and media with infinite ways to reinterpret performance and success. More than anything else, though, injuries are used as a scapegoat for a poor season. After all, when was the last time you heard a player say that his team did well because they didn't get hurt all year?

Of course, injuries have a realistic effect on a team that struggles, but what's forgotten is how the opposite is also true: Teams which stay healthy, even if they don't mention it, are benefiting from the absence of injury.

What hasn't been measured up to this point, at least publicly, is exactly how injuries affect teams on a year-to-year basis. Do team injury levels tend to regress to the mean? Are there positions where players who get hurt tend to stay hurt? Is there a position where losing players to injury is less likely to affect team performance? The answers to these questions could be worth millions of dollars, as teams construct their teams under the confines of the salary cap and attempt to place value on depth and the ability of their players to stay healthy. It can also help make our projections of team performance more accurate on a year-to-year basis by allowing us to anticipate likely injury rates and their effects.

First, a quick primer on injury data. Each week, the NFL releases an injury report that details the status of players and their likelihood of playing that week. A player who's **Probable** is said to have a 75 percent chance of playing in the next week's game; a **Questionable** player, 50 percent; **Doubtful**, 25 percent; and players who are **Out** are not expected to see any action in that week's game. A player can also be placed at any point on **Injured Reserve (IR)**, which immediately disqualifies him from playing any more games for his team for the rest of the season; before the season, he can also be placed on the **Physically Unable to Perform (PUP)** list, which prevents the player from playing with the team for at least the first six weeks of the season. The team is then given four weeks to take the player off the list and move him to the active roster or move him to IR, which happens automatically if he doesn't make it off the list after Week 10.

Those percentages have been criticized by league observers, using Tom Brady as an example. For three years running, as some sort of bizarre protest to the league, the Patriots have listed their All-World quarterback as Probable on the league's injury report with a right shoulder injury. Of course, Brady hasn't missed a game in this timeframe and was never expected to.

With that in mind, we began to create a more authentic injury database. First, we combined the IR and PUP lists with the standard NFL injury reports that were released each week. We checked that against the official NFL play-by-play to determine whether a player started, played at all, or sat the game out. That allowed us to calculate the true likelihood that a player who was listed as probable, questionable, or doubtful would play in the next week's game.

In previous versions of this research published on the Patriots Daily website, we used a four-point scale to account for injuries based upon the NFL's description of injuries; after finding the true values, and wanting to adjust the impact to more accurately reflect the effect of losing a player altogether as opposed to simply having him as a sub, we switched to a six-point scale and changed the weighting of the values to an empirical system (Table 1). We're calling that new injury measure Adjusted Value, or AV.

Table 1. Creating Adjusted Value for Injuries

Category	Total 2001-2007	Played	DNP	Original Value (OV)	Adjusted Value (AV)
Probable	9046	89.0%	11.0%	1	0.7
Questionable	9194	52.9%	47.1%	2	2.8
Doubtful	1929	8.4%	91.6%	3	5.5
Out/IR/PUP	12762	0.4%	99.6%	4	6.0

Because not all injuries are of equal importance to a team, we went through each injury report and separated players into different buckets, removing players who never played for a team and spent their entire career on IR or the practice squad. We then separated players into two groups. The Starters group consists of players who started for the team or were supposed to start at the beginning of training camp; for example, LeCharles Bentley would have been a starter in 2006 in Cleveland, but not in 2007 because he wasn't expected to play. Also in that group are situational players who saw significant time, such as third wideouts, nickel backs, or pass-rush specialists, as well as New Starters, which are players who took over as starters when the original starter got hurt (Kurt Warner and Ryan Grant last year, for example). Despite the presence of these other players, we'll call this group Starters to make things simpler. The other group is basically everyone else, who we consider to be Reserves. We computed injury values for the team as a whole (including both Starters and Reserves) and then for only the Starters.

The final metric we'll introduce is the one we're going to quote to provide a simple, easy-to-understand implementation of injury probabilities: Adjusted Games Lost, or AGL. The formula for AGL is, simply, AV/6. You can apply it in a number of ways. Take a team whose injury report has one guy listed as

Probable, three guys as Questionable, two guys as Doubtful, and four as Out. The total adjusted value for those four players is 44.1, so their Games Lost would be 7.35—in other words, the team would expect to have 7.35 players miss the game based on the average likelihood that each player with his given injury definition would miss the game.

We computed AGL for each team from 2001 through 2007, the seven years in which we have reliable injury data, and compared it to wins, total DVOA, and offensive and defensive passing and rushing DVOA for the season in question, as well as the ones before and after each given season (except for 2007, obviously).

EFFECTIVENESS IN PREDICTING PERFORMANCE

After making all these delineations and running the numbers for each team on a year-by-year basis, we discovered that a team's injury status has a dramatic effect on explaining a team's performance as well as in predicting future performance. The most closely correlated effect is that comparing the difference between a team's AGL year-to-year to the same difference in wins or DVOA (Table 2). A correlation of -.44 and -.45 is enormous for professional football.

As a whole, the correlations when using the Starters group specifically as opposed to Starters and Reserves are significantly higher, so in the interest of keeping this essay as readable as possible, we're going to focus most of our attention on them.

The results of Table 2 are borne out in the huge shifts seen when teams who were remarkably injured one year get healthy in the next, or when teams that were healthy get ransacked by injuries. Table 3 shows the five biggest shifts in games lost on either side of the coin; note that both sides feature a number of the same teams. The 2005 Titans, the lone team who got healthier and didn't improve their record by six games, broke up their team after the 2004 season after an injury-riddled year left them unwilling to maneuver the salary cap long enough to retain their core. If they had understood that their injury problems were likely to revert the next year, the Titans may have been more aggressive about retaining their players and may have possibly been able to keep their core together for another season. Indeed, one of the lessons learned from injury research may very well be understanding where teams stand on the success cycle.

Table 3. Biggest Shifts in AGL, Starters Only

Team	Year	Shift	Wins Y1	Wins Y2	Change
Cleveland	2007	-52.5	4	10	+6
New York Jets	2006	-51.2	4	10	+6
Atlanta	2004	-47.0	5	11	+6
Tennessee	2005	-46.9	5	4	-1
Tampa Bay	2005	-42.4	5	11	+6
New York Jets	2005	+57.4	10	4	-6
Tennessee	2004	+51.4	12	5	-7
Chicago	2002	+47.1	13	4	-9
Cleveland	2004	+46.1	5	4	-1
Cleveland	2006	+43.5	6	4	-2

OFFENSE VERSUS DEFENSE

Splitting games lost by offense and defense and then comparing them to relevant metrics reveals interesting effects that can reshape everything from defining replacement level to analyzing roster construction and draft value. We'll explain how as we go along.

First, let's look at how the different splits match up on a year-to-year basis. Offensive injuries have a much more dramatic effect on performance than defensive injuries (Table 4), but defensive injuries turn out to be a stronger predictor of future success.

That fact about defensive performance went into our team projections for the first time last year. The five least-injured defenses in 2006 were (in order) Kansas City, San Francisco, Oakland, St. Louis, and the New York Jets. Only Kansas City remained significantly healthy on defense, but all were among the worst teams in football. The healthiest defenses in 2007 were Tampa Bay, Kansas City, Detroit, Tennessee, and Seattle. It's reasonable to expect that a decline in performance by those teams could be indicated by a defense stretched by injury.

The fact that offensive injuries have a far greater impact on performance than defensive injuries could play a huge role in how teams construct their rosters. It implies that the dropoff in available offensive talent is more significant than that defensively, and that it's easier to plug in a defensive player and succeed than it is an offensive one. That means durable offensive players would be more valuable than is perhaps perceived, and a team should also focus its budget for reserves on offensive players while being more content to use replacement-level defensive players where need be.

Table 2. Correlations Between Injury Metrics and Performance, 2001-2007

Metric	Wins			DVOA		
	Same Year	Change from Prev. Year	Change Next Year	Same Year	Change from Prev. Year	Change Next Year
AGL w/ Reserves	-0.12	-0.18	+0.19	-0.11	-0.19	+0.16
AGL w/Reserves, year-to-year change	-0.17	-0.32	+0.21	-0.13	-0.29	+0.23
AGL w/ Starters Only	-0.22	-0.34	+0.29	-0.22	-0.38	+0.23
AGL w/ Starters Only, year-to-year change	-0.25	-0.46	+0.32	-0.18	-0.45	+0.22

Table 4. Offensive/Defensive Splits by AGL

Metric	Wins			DVOA		
	Same Year	Change from Prev. Year	Change Next Year	Same Year	Change from Prev. Year	Change Next Year
Offensive AGL	-0.28	-0.29	+.20	-0.29	-0.32	+.14
Change in Offensive AGL	-0.22	-0.37	+.20	-0.16	-0.35	+.09
Defensive AGL	-0.06	-0.23	+.24	-0.05	-0.26	+.22
Change in Defensive AGL	-0.17	-0.33	+.30	-0.12	-0.34	+.25

That description matches almost to a tee the management principles and salary cap construction of the Indianapolis Colts. Ironically, they were the league's most injured team in 2007 and barely took a performance hit in the process. The one set of injuries that clearly contributed to a loss and a few close calls was at an offensive position, wide receiver.

Injuries at specific positions naturally affect teams less than their injury rate as a whole. As you might expect, the difference in a team's quarterback AGL from year to year bears the strongest correlation with past wins (-.29) and serves as the strongest indicator of wins the next year (+.22). Interestingly, a team's AGL at linebacker bears the same correlations. Neither of these are foolproof indicators by any means, but they still bear enough of a relationship to wins to merit paying attention to.

Another interesting way to look at this data is to isolate a part of the game, such as running the ball, and analyze how DVOA is affected by injury rates. Last year saw players such as Earnest Graham and Ryan Grant step in and, without a hiccup, produce at the level of a much more expensive player. That sort of interchangeability is now built into our replacement-level models and is borne out in our injury research. When correlating the year-to-year difference in a team's rushing DVOA to AGL or simply correlating a team's AGL at each position to their rushing DVOA for that year, running backs aren't particularly important (Table 5). Quarterback injuries actually affect the running game more than running back injuries, likely owing to the cascading effect of losing a quarterback, which allows defenses to focus more on the run, which then puts more defenders in the box for running backs to beat.

Table 5. Effects of AGL on Rushing DVOA

Position	Correlation, Same Year AGL	Correlation, Change from Previous Year
QB	-0.18	-0.24
RB	-0.05	-0.17
WR/TE	-0.03	-0.07
OL	-0.10	-0.20

No such effect exists on defense, where the performance of players is significantly more muddled and intertwined.

AGE

It's easy to compare football players' bodies to our own and assume that older players are more likely to break down and be injured. For example, repeated injuries to Dan Morgan prevented an otherwise excellent player from continuing his career.

As players grow older, though, and become more expensive, mediocre players are weeded out because of their cost and lack of projectability. They're replaced by younger players, but those players who are valuable enough to stay on the roster, surprisingly, don't get hurt more. Because they're better players, the majority know how to use their bodies to maximum effect by being in better shape or employing superior fundamentals or both. Although that's a form of selection bias built into the system, the fact still stands that there's no significant relationship between the average age of a team's starter(s) at a position and their Adjusted Games Lost for the year at said position (Table 6). In fact, some positions, particularly defensive linemen, see injury rates decline as players get older.

Table 6. Correlation of AGL to Average Age of Starters by Position

Position	Correlation
QB	-0.08
RB	0.03
WR/TE	-0.13
OL	0.01
DL	0.13
LB	-0.03
DB	-0.01

CONCLUSION

This essay just scratches the surface of what we can learn by studying injury trends. Topics we will be analyzing in the future include recovery rates for certain injuries or injury locations, the effects of changing systems or head coaches, the likelihood of injuries to recur, and which positions see a higher rate of injury recurrence.

The research that we've included in this essay, though, already has dramatic implications for understanding how teams should be built and in understanding both past and future performance. Injury data represents only a small portion of the many variables that go into our team projection system on a year-to-year basis, but it is one of the easiest things to understand and discuss. After all, fans have been kvetching about injuries since the beginning of time. We're just letting you know when the proper time to kvetch is.

Rating the 32 Medical Staffs

Bill Barnwell and Will Carroll

If football is a game of inches, a team's medical staff might be worth a foot. Think about how many games—how many seasons—have been turned by a player being available or less than 100 percent. Would Terrell Owens be available for Super Bowl XXXIX? How was Tom Brady's ankle after the AFC Championship? What happens when Edgerrin James injures his knee? We could go on and on, but football teams and their fans still treat injuries as if they're just part of the game, a random occurrence that can't be controlled or at least minimized.

A hard look at the data (we specialize in that sort of thing around here) reveals what we'd expect. Some teams are simply better than others when it comes to keeping their players on the field, getting them back on the field, or overcoming injuries. While our metrics aren't perfect and can't get a hard look at limitations—when a player isn't 100 percent but gets out there anyway—or at the replacement player's effect on the game, losing one of your best 22 for a week is a clear problem for any team.

More than just a simple counting stat, the final version we've come up with is called Adjusted Games Lost (further explained in the previous essay, "The Injury Effect"). Teams are ranked according to AGL over the past three years; right now, it is not weighted towards the most recent season, although that may change in the future. That's just one of the ideas we have to improve this system in the coming years, but although there are still plenty of factors we need to address, this is the first real look we've ever seen at which medical staffs get the best results. Every medical staff is made up of qualified hard-working people that put their lives on the back burner during the season, but results come across the board. We think you'll be surprised, and we hope that the teams use this as a hard look in the mirror.

Dallas

Head ATC: Jim Maurer
Adjusted Games Lost, 2007: 47.5 (18)
Three-Year Rank: 1

Trend: Slightly negative. The Cowboys' incredible health is covered more closely in their chapter, but in short, Dallas barely lost anyone last year for any intermediate period of time. That said, the two guys they did lose were starters (Terry Glenn and Jason Ferguson), and they were gone for the whole regular season. The second place team in three-year rank (Pittsburgh) is closer to tenth than to first. No team can be this lucky this long. The medical staff in Dallas is trying to prove that it's not luck.

Pittsburgh

Head ATC: John Norwig
Adjusted Games Lost, 2007: 20.1 (3)
Three-Year Rank: 2

Trend: Negative. The Steelers have been a relatively healthy team for three years despite having very breakable players. Last year's late-season injury run (Aaron Smith, Willie Parker, and Troy Polamalu) feels more like the tip of the iceberg than an aberration; furthermore, Mike Tomlin's "We're going to ride Willie [Parker] until the wheels fall off" style of management doesn't show the public level of caution you want a head coach to show. For all the injuries that befell Ben Roethlisberger in 2006, he started 15 games; the system doesn't adjust for how poorly he played while hurt.

Tennessee

Head ATC: Brad Brown
Adjusted Games Lost, 2007: 13.3 (1)
Three-Year Rank: 3

Trend: Slightly positive. After some woeful injury years early in the decade, Tennessee's only notable long-term injury of the past two seasons was free agent wideout David Givens. A defense that was remarkably healthy in 2007— even when you consider Albert Haynesworth's midseason hamstring issues—is likely to see more injuries this year.

Houston

Head ATC: Kevin Bastin
Adjusted Games Lost, 2007: 53.8 (23)
Three-Year Rank: 4

Trend: Negative. Very healthy in 2005, healthiest in football in 2006, pretty bad in 2007. Their secondary was extremely healthy in 2005 and 2006 but fell apart last year. If the defensive line continues to improve, the Texans will be able to better deal with having replacement-level guys back there.

Atlanta

Head ATC: Rod Medlin
Adjusted Games Lost, 2007: 48.5 (19)
Three-Year Rank: 5

Trend: Negative. Their offensive line pretty much went to pieces last year, which should bode for a nice little happy bump back towards the mean this year, but too many pieces are going to be finding their place in unfamiliar systems. We don't know whether Michael Turner can take the workload of a starting back. That's a risk.

Kansas City

Head ATC: David Price
Adjusted Games Lost, 2007: 22.8 (4)
Three-Year Rank: 6

Trend: Neutral. There's no correlation between injury and age in our database. It's possible that we could be underestimating the fog, but the older players who survive the onset of age and diminished physical ability seem to have better fundamentals and conserve their bodies, allowing them to remain healthy despite being older and more easily breakable. The Chiefs are going young, but they don't get a boost in our injury ratings for that. Chiefs fans should hope that Larry Johnson's broken foot was a wake-up call to a team that hasn't emphasized keeping its core assets healthy, something that has nothing to do with the work of Head Athletic Trainer David Price.

New York Giants

Head ATC: Ronnie Barnes
Adjusted Games Lost, 2007: 30.5 (10)
Three-Year Rank: 7

Trend: Slightly positive. They require redundancy at running back because all three of their backs are injury-prone. Their front seven was remarkably healthy (except for the season-ending broken leg suffered by Mathias Kiwanuka in Week 11) after being full of problems in 2005 and 2006. Their offensive line was among the healthiest in football, with the only significant injury coming to Shaun O'Hara, causing him to miss a playoff game, which isn't tracked.

Carolina

Head ATC: Ryan Vermillion
Adjusted Games Lost, 2007: 27.0 (7)
Three-Year Rank: 8

Trend: Neutral. Their starters were remarkably healthy except for Jake Delhomme's injury and Dan Morgan's concussion, which our system mostly ignores since no one really expected him to play. Delhomme will be healthier, but the rest of the team will be hurt more. That's neutral.

Green Bay

Head ATC: Pepper Burruss
Adjusted Games Lost, 2007: 19.9 (2)
Three-Year Rank: 9

Trend: Positive. Green Bay had abnormally high injury rates for their wideouts in 2005 and 2006. It's easy to paint some scenario where Brett Favre's gunslinger tendencies get his wideouts laid out, but they were fine in 2003 and 2004, and they returned to health in 2007. The bigger concern is a sec-

ondary with two aging cornerbacks, both of whom have an injury history. Defensive back injuries as a whole are trending up over the 3-year span. When we talk about players getting weeded out as they get older because of their reckless style of play, Atari Bigby is exactly the type of player we're talking about.

Seattle

Head ATC: Sam Ramsden
Adjusted Games Lost, 2007: 29.4 (8)
Three-Year Rank: 10

Trend: Slightly negative. Deion Branch is already out for part of 2008 with a torn ACL, while Marcus Tubbs will definitely miss time after complications from surgery to fix the ACL he tore in the 2007 preseason. Bailing on the injury-prone D. J. Hackett helps, as does losing Shaun Alexander, whose injury woes were caused by the Curse of 370 and not related to the work of Sam Ramsden and his crew. Their injury profile in 2005 and 2007 was eerily similar, with the whole team healthy except for the receivers.

Minnesota

Head ATC: Eric Sugarman
Adjusted Games Lost, 2007: 23.5 (5)
Three-Year Rank: 11

Trend: Positive. The Vikings have had back-to-back top-seven seasons the last two years, keeping the core of their team—their front seven—healthy. Keeping the Williams brothers healthy is an absolutely essential task, even more so than keeping Jesus in purple. Having Jared Allen around should allow the team to rotate the tackles out on passing downs, keeping them fresher and healthier.

San Diego

Head ATC: James Collins, Jr.
Adjusted Games Lost, 2007: 24.7 (6)
Three-Year Rank: 12

Trend: Slightly negative. Antonio Cromartie's relatively perfect health since his selection seems unlikely. They had two years with a goodly amount of linebacker injuries, and then were pretty healthy there last year. Keep in mind that Shawne Merriman and Shaun Phillips are often operating on the line of scrimmage, going up against offensive linemen who outweigh them by 50 pounds. It will be interesting to track outside linebacker injuries across San Diego and Dallas to see whether it's Wade Phillips's system or the players involved or both. Note: Since Adjusted Games Lost does not include the playoffs, postseason injuries to Philip Rivers and LaDainian Tomlinson are not factored into their rating; that's another element to explore adding to our injury ratings in future years.

Detroit

Head ATC: Al Bellamy
Adjusted Games Lost, 2007: 30.5 (10)
Three-Year Rank: 13

Trend: Positive. They get to use Jesus to heal Jon Kitna, but that's not factored into the equation. They've managed to keep their offense healthier for three consecutive years; it's down to a relatively unsustainable level at this point, so they should likely give some of that back this year. Adding Kevin "450 Carries" Smith seems like a logical place to give some weeks back.

Denver

Head ATC: Steve Antonopulos
Adjusted Games Lost, 2007: 57.5 (26)
Three-Year Rank: 14

Trend: Very negative. Management brought in a whole bunch of defensive linemen, only to see their line blow up. That's an issue with bringing new players into a new system; sometimes, they can't get out of their own way and end up getting hurt. Finally giving up on Rod Smith will save them some grief on the injury front, but Brandon Marshall is finding new ways to get hurt and Brandon Stokley has always struggled to be healthy. They had eight starters miss time last year.

Washington

Head ATC: John Burrell
Adjusted Games Lost, 2007: 56.4 (25)
Three-Year Rank: 15

Trend: Neutral. The Redskins' offensive linemen appear to be chronically injured; Jon Jansen, for example, has suffered an injury in Week 1 or the preseason in three out of the last six seasons. The injuries suffered by players such as Orlando Pace over the past few years appear to point to offensive linemen being more susceptible to repeated injuries, although we have not done the research to say that definitively yet. With a new offense, odds of a Redskins receiver getting a concussion on an unfamiliar route package this year are astronomical. (For those wondering, the Adjusted Games Lost rating includes the Sean Taylor injury until his murder.)

St. Louis

Head ATC: Jim Anderson
Adjusted Games Lost, 2007: 58.6 (28)
Three-Year Rank: 16

Trend: Negative. In the St. Louis chapter, we compare the Rams offensive line to Europe during the bubonic plague. What else do you need to know? Quarterback Marc Bulger has been consistently fragile, and although the Rams are rebuilding, they have a very old core that is relied upon to do a lot of the heavy lifting. Because the injuries were so heavily weighted towards the offensive line, they won't get the boost from returning defensive players that teams with this level of injury often get.

Arizona

Head ATC: John Omohundro
Adjusted Games Lost, 2007: 50.7 (21)
Three-Year Rank: 17

Trend: Slightly positive. We don't know what the two-quarterback system will mean if they choose to stick with it for the long-term, but we already know that Kurt Warner is easily breakable. Matt Leinart's collarbone is more likely an isolated incident than it is Charles Rogers 2.0. Their old field was anecdotally one of the worst stadiums in the league with regards to safety, so the move to the University of Phoenix Is Not Actually in Phoenix Stadium has helped push them back towards the light.

Tampa Bay

Head ATC: Todd Toriscelli
Adjusted Games Lost, 2007: 39.8 (15)
Three-Year Rank: 18

Trend: Neutral. Their injury problems were primarily due to Luke Petitgout and Cadillac Williams, and by now, the Buccaneers know not to rely on either. Even with those devastating injuries, the Bucs still finished ahead of their three-year rank on what appears to be a fluke. An incredibly low defensive injury rate isn't likely to recur given their injury problems of the past. Someone will probably blame it on age, but as we've shown, there's no evidence that that is an important factor.

New Orleans

Head ATC: Scottie Patton
Adjusted Games Lost, 2007: 35.9 (14)
Three-Year Rank: 19

Trend: Positive. There are two Deuce McAllister torn ACLs in there, which makes their injury status look a little worse than it actually is. One shocking bit of serendipity: The Saints haven't had an injury to their starting quarterback in three years. Drew Brees is too fragile for that to continue.

Oakland

Head ATC: Rod Martin
Adjusted Games Lost, 2007: 49.6 (20)
Three-Year Rank: 20

Trend: Negative. The Raiders will start an inexperienced quarterback behind a mediocre offensive line and are giving him an undersized running back learning a new system. Oh, and their top wide receiver is coming off two injury-riddled seasons in three years, while their paid-as-stud defensive tackle missed half the season with his own knee injury. It's hard to imagine any sort of progressive thought going on inside the Raiders offices. Sorry, Raiders' medical staff—we know it's not your fault.

Cincinnati

Head ATC: Paul Sparling
Adjusted Games Lost, 2007: 46.2 (17)
Three-Year Rank: 21

Trend: Neutral. In 2005, the linebackers were healthy and the Bengals won 11 games; in 2006 and 2007, the linebackers were all hurt and the Bengals won 15 total. Remember how Peter Boulware broke down after playing under Marvin Lewis? Remember how LaVar Arrington broke down the year after he played under Marvin Lewis? There's not necessarily fire here, but there's lots of smoke.

Buffalo

Head ATC: Bud Carpenter
Adjusted Games Lost, 2007: 70.0 (31)
Three-Year Rank: 22

Trend: Extremely positive. They were simply overloaded with defensive back injuries last year while attempting to patch up Nate Clements' old role. A freak injury to Paul Posluszny cost them a defensive leader and picked up a lot of injury points that aren't likely to recur in 2008. That should be a nice little boost to a team that, honestly, could use it.

Chicago

Head ATC: Tim Bream
Adjusted Games Lost, 2007: 58.4 (27)
Three-Year Rank: 23

Trend: Positive. Mike Brown is the biggest culprit here. The team is likely giving up on Brown as a starter, so he'll come off the starter books and they'll see a boost. Perhaps more than any team this decade, the Bears have been dramatically affected by team health. Nowadays, as goes Tommie Harris, so go the Bears.

San Francisco

Head ATC: Jeff Ferguson
Adjusted Games Lost, 2007: 52.1 (22)
Three-Year Rank: 24

Trend: Slightly positive. This number is slightly deceptive since it includes Jonas Jennings's so-called injury, which was really just a way to get him out of the locker room. After Kurt Warner, Mike Martz has the reputation for killing his quarterbacks for life, but Jon Kitna was actually pretty healthy last season despite leading the NFL in quarterback knockdowns (sacks plus hits) for two straight seasons. The 49ers are a smart front office and will not overuse Frank Gore, but

keeping their star running back on the field is still equal parts proper planning and hope.

Philadelphia

Head ATC: Rick Burkholder
Adjusted Games Lost, 2007: 34.8 (13)
Three-Year Rank: 25

Trend: Neutral. Donovan McNabb stayed healthy! At this point, that occurrence is so rare that it deserves an exclamation point and probably an upside-down one at the beginning of the sentence as well. McNabb's speed was back by the end of the season, but it looks like he's still struggling to trust it—when he doesn't have a choice, such as when he's flushed out of the pocket and has to run for his life, the McNabb of December looked like the McNabb of old. The defensive backfield is approaching Patriots-like levels of consistent injury, and ... Hey, who's that walking in the door. ... Hello, Asante Samuel! The Eagles' defensive backs have been in the top eight for most injured secondaries three out of the last five years; the Eagles will hope that Samuel, the sturdiest of the Patriots' defensive backs, can retain his health in Philadelphia.

New York Jets

Head ATC: John Mellody
Adjusted Games Lost, 2007: 42.0 (16)
Three-Year Rank: 26

Trend: Slightly negative. They brought in a lot of new players, who have to learn a new system. Think of it like a position switch in baseball. If you're thinking about where you're supposed to be going instead of knowing where that is, you're not paying as much attention as you should to the lineman who's coming at your knees. Starting Chad Pennington would up this to flat-out negative.

New England

Head ATC: Jim Whalen
Adjusted Games Lost, 2007: 33.8 (12)
Three-Year Rank: 27

Trend: Negative. They had a better year in 2007, but their injury-prone players get hurt seemingly every year and they simply refuse to add three or four linebackers to replace Vrabel, Seau, and Bruschi. Mayo helps, but even Adalius Thomas is already 31. An injury to Randy Moss, who was in tatters by the end of 2007, could have a dramatic knockdown effect on their offense—maybe even worse than losing Brady.

Miami

Head ATC: Kevin O'Neill
Adjusted Games Lost, 2007: 64.2 (30)
Three-Year Rank: 28

Trend: Positive. As a whole, age doesn't correlate well with injury in the NFL. For the Dolphins, though, age was a ticking time bomb. Mixing in a few old guys is fine; building a whole defense around them, particularly injury-prone players such as Zach Thomas and very large defensive tackles, is not so fine.

Cleveland

Head ATC: Marty Lauzon
Adjusted Games Lost 2007: 29.7 (9)
Three-Year Rank: 29

Trend: Flukish. Cleveland was among the most-injured teams in 2005 and 2006. Their injury numbers for receivers alone from 2005-2007 went 106.2, 65.4, 16.8. If you can find an online sports book that will give you an over-under on the number of games missed by the Jurevicius/Stallworth/Edwards/Winslow/Lewis skill position group, take the over.

Jacksonville

Head ATC: Michael Ryan
Adjusted Games Lost, 2007: 54.1 (24)
Three-Year Rank: 30

Trend: Positive. Although their defensive line got healthier in 2007, it wasn't healthy, and it was supplemented by injuries to the offensive line and secondary. That contributed to the Jaguars selecting Derrick Harvey. The defense should see continued improvement this year.

Baltimore

Head ATC: Bill Tessendorf
Adjusted Games Lost, 2007: 61.4 (29)
Three-Year Rank: 31

Trend: Positive. Steve McNair and Jonathan Ogden (likely) leaving means that two injury-prone players are off the roster. Defensive Adjusted Games Lost over the past three years: 30.3, 10.3, 35.0. Guess which year was the successful one? Our system includes non-football injuries, so Samari Rolle's battle with epilepsy counts in the Ravens' injury calculations from a year ago. Although it wasn't football-related, it still affected the team and forced them to use players in roles they weren't expected—or good enough—to play in.

Indianapolis

Head ATC: Hunter Smith
Adjusted Games Lost, 2007: 71.5 (32)
Three-Year Rank: 32

Trend: Very negative. The Colts had the worst injury record in the league last year by a huge margin and ranked in the bottom five in 2006. They should rebound, but part of the reason they won't totally bounce back is that they draft undersized players who move into starting roles very quickly. These players cost less but get hurt more. As we say over at Baseball Prospectus, fungibility's a bitch when you're the fungi.

2008 College Football Projections

Brian Fremeau

For some pro football fans, the major college football landscape is bizarrely unfamiliar territory, with four times as many teams as in the NFL; an assortment of wishbone, spread-option, and other non-pro-style offenses; completely unbalanced scheduling; and a two-team "playoff" for the national championship determined by a collection of human voters and computer systems. For others, the Saturday games are simply the appetizer on an ultimate football weekend menu. And for many more, college football's history and traditions are unmatched in professional sports. These fans embrace all the college game's idiosyncrasies, including—and perhaps most important—the annual debate over which team is number one.

The Fremeau Efficiency Index (FEI) was created in 2003 and has been further developed each year since with that particular passionate debate in mind. Just as Defensive-Adjusted Value Over Average (DVOA) is refined to determine not only how the top teams stack up but why, FEI is interested in answering the same questions for college football. The data analysis begins with drive data instead of play-by-play data, but FEI shares similar principles with DVOA. A team is rewarded for playing well against good teams, win or lose, and is punished more severely for playing poorly against bad teams than it is rewarded for playing well against bad teams.

To calculate FEI, each of the nearly 20,000 offensive possessions every season in major college football is first filtered to eliminate first-half clock-kills and end-of-game garbage drives and scores. A scoring rate analysis of the remaining possessions then determines the baseline possession-efficiency expectations against which each team is measured. Game Efficiency is the composite possession-by-possession efficiency of a team over the course of a game, a measurement of the success of its offensive, defensive, and special-teams units' essential goals: to maximize the team's own scoring opportunities and to minimize those of its opponent. Finally, each team's FEI rating synthesizes its season-long Game Efficiency data, adjusted for the strength of its opposition; special emphasis is placed on quality performance against good teams, win or lose.

Since the final FEI ratings also fairly represent each team's possession efficiency above or below that of an average team, a comparison of top teams can be made across individual seasons. Table 1 presents the best individual college football teams in the last five seasons, according to FEI.

It would be closed-minded and, for rabid college football fans, quite disappointing to believe that a statistical model can actually settle the "Who is number one?" debate, but FEI and other developing college football analysis at Football

Table 1. Top 10 FEI Final Ratings, 2003-2007

Rank	Team	W-L	FEI	Year Rank
1	2004 USC	13-0	.351	1
2	2005 Texas	13-0	.349	1
3	2006 Florida	12-1	.328	1
4	2005 USC	12-1	.325	2
5	2006 USC	11-2	.315	2
6	2004 Auburn	12-0	.306	2
7	2003 LSU	12-1	.295	1
8	2005 Ohio State	10-2	.287	3
9	2007 LSU	12-2	.285	1
10	2005 Penn State	11-1	.283	4

Team records and all FEI data represent Football Bowl Subdivision (FBS, formerly Division 1-A) games only. Games involving Football Championship Subdivision (FCS, formerly Division 1-AA) teams or other lower divisions are ignored.

Outsiders.com can contribute substantially to the discussion. For this *Pro Football Prospectus* volume, however, the challenge becomes whether FEI can solve an even more perplexing problem: Who is going to be number one?

In many ways, college football is better suited for year-to-year statistical projection than pro football is. The NFL is engineered for parity, providing more opportunities for bad teams to quickly develop into better teams through the draft and free agency, while better teams are forced to jettison important players because of the salary cap. College football's elite teams and conferences, on the other hand, fiercely protect their power by controlling the lion's share of television and bowl revenue; maintaining the best facilities, coaches, and recruits; and determining their own favorable schedules. Certainly, scholarship limitations and increasingly abundant talent give the have-nots much more of a fighting chance than they had 20 or 30 years ago, but by and large, the best college football teams can be reasonably expected to continue to be among the best, year-in and year-out. As illustrated in Table 2, the correlation of same-stat data in college football is significantly stronger than in pro football.

Table 2. Year-to-Year Correlation of Team Stats, 2003-2007

Stat	College	NFL
Winning Percentage	.60	.26
Pythagorean Win Pct	.68	.33
DVOA/FEI	.77	.42

To develop an even stronger projection model than just last year's FEI, I first developed a multiple-year rating model called Program FEI. This rating is calculated in precisely the same way as single-year FEI, inputting five years of possession efficiency data as though that span were a single season. Table 3 lists the top 10 team ratings in Program FEI heading into the 2008 season.

Table 3. Top 10 Program FEI Ratings, 2003-2007

Rank	Team	W-L	Program FEI	Best Year Rank	Worst Year Rank
1	USC	59-6	.311	1	2
2	LSU	54-10	.261	1	20
3	Georgia	48-14	.243	4	14
4	Ohio State	51-11	.237	3	16
5	Virginia Tech	46-16	.226	5	20
6	Florida	43-18	.217	1	22
7	Texas	53-10	.216	1	26
8	Auburn	46-14	.215	2	31
9	Michigan	46-16	.212	8	22
10	Oklahoma	54-13	.209	4	24

The list isn't particularly earth-shattering. USC has dominated college football over the last five seasons, losing only six games by a total of 20 points, and the remaining teams have all won or contended for championships in that span. No fewer than six and as many as eight of these teams have appeared in the top 10 Associated Press preseason and final postseason polls every year since 2003. The consistency of program power is not limited to the teams at the top, however. And since Program FEI more closely approximates each team's year-to-year trend line, it boasts a stronger correlation to next year's FEI than does single-year FEI. As would be expected, an even stronger correlation is yielded from a Program FEI model that gives more weight to recent-year data.

I then refined the projection further through a regression analysis of a handful of potential "transition" factors. Returning starters, quarterback experience, head coach experience, and conference strength and schedule were each tested as independent variables to determine their impact, if any, on team efficiency swings. Of each of these factors, only offensive and defensive returning starters had a measurable impact in improving the projection model. With the inclusion of an adjustment for returning starters, the correlation of Projected FEI to next year's FEI improves to 0.80. Finally, I created a projected record for each team based on its expected win probability for each FBS game scheduled in 2008 as a function of the Projected FEI ratings. The correlation of Projected Win Percentage to actual Win Percentage is 0.64.

Following this methodology, Table 4 presents the Projected FEI ratings of the top 40 teams in college football for 2008. A breakdown of the top 10 and several other teams of interest follows. If you are looking to follow FEI during the season, ratings and commentary are published on Football Outsiders.com each week, beginning with the release of the first official Bowl Championship Series (BCS) ratings in October.

No. 1   Ohio State Buckeyes (10-1)

#8 FEI 2007; #4 Program FEI; 9 ORS; 9 DRS: Ohio State is poised for a run at a third straight BCS game, but having lost the title game in its last two appearances by a combined 41 points, that distinction may induce more dread than elation in Columbus. In a showdown at USC this fall, the Buckeyes will have an almost immediate opportunity to shake the perception that those championship whiffs squandered their right to contend again in 2008. A win in the L.A. Coliseum would almost certainly position Ohio State in the driver's seat for the remainder of the year, but even a competitive loss could still set the stage for a championship season. A slew of starters returns on both sides of the ball, but the defense will anchor the team again in 2008. Last season, Ohio State's defense allowed less than a point per possession and forced opponents into three-and-outs on a whopping 52 percent of their offensive drives.

Key Games: 9/13 at USC, 10/4 at Wisconsin, 10/25 vs. Penn State, 11/22 vs. Michigan

No. 2   USC Trojans (10-2)

#2 FEI 2007; #1 Program FEI; 4 ORS; 7 DRS: The most dominant team in college football will need to bring it week-in and week-out in 2008 or risk falling just short of a title yet again. Every team on USC's schedule this year ranks among the top 60 in Projected FEI, and the lowest-rated of the bunch, Stanford, won in Los Angeles last year. Like Ohio State, USC hung its hat last season on a stifling defensive unit that gave up a grand total of only 40 points all year on 81 opponent possessions begun at or inside the opponent's own 25-yard line. With a Pac-10 and nonconference gauntlet granting virtually no breathers, the Trojans' defense will need to set the tone early while the relatively inexperienced offense learns each other's names.

Key Games: 9/13 vs. Ohio State, 10/4 vs. Oregon, 10/11 vs. Arizona State, 11/8 vs. California

No. 3   Georgia Bulldogs (9-2)

#6 FEI 2007; #3 Program FEI; 7 ORS; 9 DRS: The Bulldogs cruised through the last month of the season in 2007 making a strong argument that they were one of the hottest and best teams in the country. This year, with expectations at an all-time high, they will need to be at their best from the start in order to navigate one of the toughest schedules of any SEC team. The Bulldogs were young last season, and the offense sometimes struggled to get into the end zone even when it moved the ball well. In 19 possessions of 10 plays or more over the course of the season, Georgia scored a touchdown only eight times.

Key Games: 9/20 at Arizona State, 10/11 vs. Tennessee, 10/25 at LSU, 11/1 vs. Florida, 11/15 at Auburn

No. 4   Florida Gators (9-2)

#5 FEI 2007; #6 Program FEI; 7 ORS; 8 DRS: Heisman Trophy winner Tim Tebow is back for at least one more year to lead the Gators' offensive highlight-reel attack. In 2007, Florida scored a touchdown on 49 percent of its offensive possessions and put itself into field-goal range on an addi-

Table 4. 2008 Projected Top 40 Teams by FEI

Rank	Team	Proj 2008 FEI	Proj 2008 W-L	2007 Rank	2007 W-L	PROG FEI Rank	ORS	DRS
1	Ohio State	.292	10-1	8	10-2	4	9	9
2	USC	.269	10-2	2	11-2	1	4	7
3	Georgia	.265	9-2	6	10-2	3	7	9
4	Florida	.264	9-2	5	8-4	6	7	8
5	LSU	.245	9-2	1	12-2	2	6	5
6	Auburn	.231	9-2	13	8-4	8	9	6
7	Oklahoma	.216	9-2	7	11-3	10	8	6
8	West Virginia	.213	9-2	4	11-2	14	8	4
9	Clemson	.202	8-2	11	8-4	17	7	8
10	Wisconsin	.196	9-2	35	8-4	15	8	9
11	Oregon	.184	9-3	3	9-4	21	6	7
12	Boston College	.181	8-3	20	10-3	12	6	7
13	Tennessee	.181	9-3	17	10-4	18	8	6
14	Virginia Tech	.175	9-2	12	10-3	5	6	4
15	Texas Tech	.165	8-2	32	8-4	33	10	8
16	Texas	.161	9-3	26	10-3	7	6	4
17	California	.159	8-4	24	7-6	13	5	7
18	Missouri	.156	9-2	9	11-2	38	6	9
19	BYU	.155	9-2	14	10-2	37	10	3
20	Florida State	.154	6-4	37	7-6	11	8	7
21	Penn State	.151	8-3	38	9-4	22	8	7
22	South Florida	.148	8-3	10	8-4	51	10	6
23	Arizona State	.148	7-4	16	10-3	30	7	7
24	Michigan	.145	8-4	22	9-3	9	3	7
25	Alabama	.142	8-4	27	6-6	34	9	6
26	South Carolina	.129	6-5	30	5-6	44	6	10
27	Kansas	.121	7-4	19	11-1	49	6	9
28	Notre Dame	.119	8-4	74	3-9	25	9	7
29	Wake Forest	.111	8-4	34	9-4	31	5	9
30	Utah	.107	8-3	36	9-4	26	8	6
31	Maryland	.100	6-5	43	5-7	24	9	5
32	Rutgers	.096	7-4	42	7-5	50	7	8
33	Louisville	.095	7-4	46	5-6	20	3	6
34	Arkansas	.091	5-6	21	7-5	32	5	5
35	Oregon State	.091	6-6	18	8-4	29	7	3
36	TCU	.091	8-3	48	8-5	42	8	6
37	UCLA	.090	5-7	23	6-7	36	5	5
38	Michigan State	.083	6-6	33	7-6	40	7	7
39	Pittsburgh	.080	7-5	49	4-7	46	8	7
40	Arizona	.080	6-6	28	4-7	59	10	3

Data on Offensive Returning Starters (ORS) and Defensive Returning Starters (DRS) was collected from team and conference media information available as of May 1.

tional 11 percent of its drives, an absurd level of production in college football. A third of the teams in the nation, including five Florida opponents in 2008, couldn't match that scoring production in a single game in 2007. On the other end of the spectrum, eight returning defensive starters will need to step up and shore up the SEC's least efficient defense from a year ago if Florida wants to contend for a national championship.

Key Games: 9/20 at Tennessee, 10/11 vs. LSU, 11/1 vs. Georgia, 11/29 at Florida State

No. 5   LSU Tigers (9-2)

#1 FEI 2007; #2 Program FEI; 6 ORS; 5 DRS: The defending national champions have plenty of holes to fill on both sides of the ball in 2008, but the Tigers have an easier schedule than most in the SEC, with no marquee out-of-conference games. Head coach Les Miles flirted with departure, but is now firmly entrenched at the strongest program in the strongest conference in the country. If LSU is going to contend for another title, it will require bold, courageous, and sometimes downright crazy leadership to pay off, just as it did last season. No other team in the country seemed to step up in this department as often as the Tigers did in 2007, converting a national best 81 percent of its fourth-down conversions, many with the game on the line and often in dramatic fashion.

Key Games: 9/20 at Auburn, 10/11 at Florida, 10/25 vs. Georgia, 11/8 vs. Alabama

No. 6   Auburn Tigers (9-2)

#13 FEI 2007; #8 Program FEI; 9 ORS; 6 DRS: If it seemed as if every game in the SEC last year came down to the wire, it was positively true for Auburn. The Tigers played 85 percent of their 2007 possessions under nail-biter conditions, with neither team holding a lead of more than a single score. Winning tight games was made possible last season by a defense that dominated its side of the field. In 20 opponent possessions last season begun at the 50-yard line or in Tigers territory, Auburn gave up only six touchdowns. The Tigers' offense needs to step up and produce to be considered among the SEC elite. Auburn's offensive efficiency in 2007 wasn't in the same ballpark as that of LSU, Florida, Georgia, and Tennessee, and the Tigers scored a grand total of 20 second-half points in their four losses.

Key Games: 9/20 vs. LSU, 9/27 vs. Tennessee,10/23 at West Virginia, 11/15 vs. Georgia, 11/29 at Alabama

No. 7   Oklahoma Sooners (9-2)

#7 FEI 2007; #10 Program FEI; 8 ORS; 6 DRS: Ohio State may be getting grief for its last two BCS appearances, but Oklahoma is on a BCS meltdown streak of its own, losing in each of its last four bowl appearances. Not coincidentally, this skid mirrors the dwindling national power of the Big 12 Conference over the same stretch according to FEI. The Sooners have created some separation recently from the rest of their league, but unless they can dominate the conference, their FEI rating isn't likely to propel them ahead of the SEC powerhouses. The offense was very productive in 2007, scoring efficiently from any starting field position, but Oklahoma will need to be more consistent, particularly out of the gate. In three losses, the Sooners averaged only 1.3 points per first-half possession, compared with 3.6 points per first-half possession in their victories.

Key Games: 10/11 vs. Texas, 10/18 vs. Kansas, 11/22 vs. Texas Tech

No. 8   West Virginia Mountaineers (9-2)

#4 FEI 2007; #14 Program FEI; 8 ORS; 4 DRS: The Big East Conference has only played three full seasons with its current roster of teams, and West Virginia positioned itself over that stretch as the league leader under Rich Rodriguez. New head coach Bill Stewart will need to prove that he can sustain that success against several up-and-comers in the Big East, but with a manageable schedule in 2008, he shouldn't struggle too much to get a strong, if not championship-contending, season under his own belt. Stewart got off to a rousing start—and secured the head coaching job in the wake of

the Rodriguez skedaddle—by whipping Oklahoma in the Fiesta Bowl. Pat White leads a juggernaut offense that ran wild last year when he was healthy, and was virtually impossible to pin deep. On possessions begun inside their own 20-yard line, the Mountaineers averaged a remarkable 42 yards per drive in 2007.

Key Games: 10/23 vs. Auburn, 12/6 vs. South Florida

No. 9   Clemson Tigers (8-2)

#11 FEI 2007; #17 Program FEI; 7 ORS; 8 DRS: Clemson fans have anticipated a breakthrough season for years, and it may finally happen in 2008. A solid core of starters returns for a school that was on the cusp last season and should benefit from the projected drop-off of last year's top ACC team, Virginia Tech. Flying almost entirely under the radar, Clemson's defense last season devastated opposing offenses, and eight starters return for another round of punishment. On 26 drives begun inside the opponent's 20-yard line, the Tigers surrendered only 10 points all year and recorded two safeties. With SEC showdowns bookending its conference season, Clemson should have no shortage of opportunities to impress and position itself to be a sleeper contender this year.

Key Games: 8/30 vs. Alabama, 11/1 at Boston College, 11/8 at Florida State, 11/29 vs. South Carolina

No. 10   Wisconsin Badgers (9-2)

#35 FEI 2007; #15 Program FEI; 8 ORS; 9 DRS: Wisconsin is projected to make one of the biggest FEI ranking leaps from last season to this season on the strength of its 17 returning starters and solid Program FEI profile. The Badgers are one of only 10 teams with a winning record in the last five seasons against the Program FEI top 10. The timing is good, too, with a rebuilding year projected for the Big Ten's perennial number two Michigan. Running undefeated through a consecutive-week gauntlet of the Wolverines, Buckeyes, and Nittany Lions is probably too much to ask, but the remainder of the schedule should be easy to manage. The Badgers weren't world beaters on either side of the ball last year, but they were one of the most balanced offenses in the country.

Key Games: 9/27 at Michigan, 10/4 vs. Ohio State, 10/11 vs. Penn State

OTHER 2008 PROJECTED FEI TEAMS OF NOTE

No. 19   BYU Cougars (9-2)

#14 FEI 2007; #37 Program FEI; 10 ORS; 3 DRS: With Boise State in 2006 and Hawaii in 2007 grabbing BCS berths, it would be convenient to assume that the WAC has been the best non-BCS conference in football. FEI, however, suggests the Mountain West has been even stronger, boasting the best non-BCS team in college football four years running. The league leader is currently BYU, heading into 2008 fresh off of back-to-back double-digit win campaigns that actually rated better than both the 2006 Broncos and the 2007 Warriors. The Cougars were led last year by a veteran defense that held offenses to only 1.4 points per possession, but only four starters return. BYU will need to duplicate that effort with a young squad in order to run the table to a BCS game in 2008, but 10 offensive starters return to the second-most efficient Mountain West team from last season.

Key Games: 9/13 vs. UCLA, 10/16 at TCU, 11/22 at Utah

No. 28 Notre Dame Fighting Irish (8-4)

#74 FEI 2007; #25 Program FEI; 9 ORS; 7 DRS: A triple-over-time loss to annual foe Navy for the first time since the days of Roger Staubach was one of several historic black eyes suffered by the 2007 Fighting Irish en route to a nightmarish 3-9 season. The 2007 Irish football season marked the biggest disparity between Program FEI and single-season FEI on record, an outlier of significant proportion from the projection model. Converging on South Bend last fall was a confluence of factors, including (but not limited to) coaching and preparation mistakes, an unusually small group of returning starters, and a schedule not conducive to development of young talent. These last two factors shouldn't affect the 2008 season, giving Charlie Weis a golden opportunity to return his team to the top 25, though probably not BCS contention. The overall efficiency of the defense made baby steps in 2007 and performed quite well in protecting long fields (70 yards or longer). As frequently mismatched as Notre Dame appeared to be throughout the 2007 season, the inept Irish offense scored only nine fewer points in long field possessions than their opponents managed against them.

No. 65 Illinois Fighting Illini (4-7)

#29 FEI 2007; #76 Program FEI; 6 ORS; 6 DRS: On the other end of the spectrum, Illinois vastly outperformed its Program FEI rating in a Rose Bowl season that seemingly came out of nowhere. Illinois had won only five FBS games over the previous four seasons, but 18 returning starters plus the immediate impact of freshman talent launched the Illini past a handful of Big Ten teams in the midst of a swoon. Illinois knocked off conference champion Ohio State by expertly controlling the clock and limiting the Buckeyes to three total second-half possessions. It was a great game plan, but not easily executed consistently over the course of a season. Against USC in the Rose Bowl, the ground game and momentum were fumbled away by Illinois in the blink of an eye. A place at the top of the Big Ten's middle tier isn't a stretch for the team's near future, but that tier is jam-packed in this league. And since Ohio State, Wisconsin, and Penn State (Illini victories in 2007) are expected to each take a step forward this year, Illinois is reciprocally projected to regress back to its Program FEI this fall and find itself fighting to qualify for a bowl.

CONFERENCE PROJECTIONS

For the Conference Standing Projections, the projected conference record for each team is based on its expected win probability for each conference game scheduled in 2008, as a function of the Projected FEI ratings of the two teams in a particular matchup. As such, the projected conference record and overall record are not intended to identify the specific winner of individual games, but more accurately reflect the likely winning percentage of the team over the course of the season.

Projected ACC Standings

Team	Proj. Conf. W-L	Proj. FEI	Proj. Overall Rank	Proj. Overall W-L
Atlantic Division				
Clemson	6-2	.202	9	8-2
Boston College	5-3	.181	12	8-3
Florida State	5-3	.154	20	6-4
Wake Forest	5-3	.111	29	8-4
Maryland	4-4	.100	31	6-5
North Carolina State	2-6	-.013	66	3-8
Coastal Division				
Virginia Tech	6-2	.175	14	9-2
Virginia	4-4	.057	46	5-6
Miami	4-4	.047	48	5-6
Georgia Tech	3-5	.052	47	4-6
North Carolina	3-5	.036	53	5-6
Duke	1-7	-.061	79	3-8

Projected Big 12 Standings

Team	Proj. Conf. W-L	Proj. FEI	Proj. Overall Rank	Proj. Overall W-L
North Division				
Missouri	6-2	.156	18	9-2
Kansas	5-3	.121	27	7-4
Colorado	4-4	.058	45	5-6
Nebraska	3-5	.013	58	6-6
Kansas State	2-6	-.007	64	4-7
Iowa State	2-6	-.049	74	4-7
South Division				
Oklahoma	7-1	.216	7	9-2
Texas Tech	6-2	.165	15	8-2
Texas	5-3	.161	16	9-3
Oklahoma State	4-4	.044	50	6-5
Texas A&M	3-5	-.024	67	5-7
Baylor	1-7	-.119	93	1-10

Projected Big East Standings

Team	Proj. Conf. W-L	Proj. FEI	Proj. Overall Rank	Proj. Overall W-L
West Virginia	6-1	.213	8	9-2
South Florida	5-2	.148	22	8-3
Rutgers	4-3	.096	32	7-4
Louisville	4-3	.095	33	7-4
Pittsburgh	3-4	.080	39	7-5
Cincinnati	3-4	.064	43	7-5
Connecticut	3-4	.059	44	6-5
Syracuse	0-7	-.117	92	1-10

Projected Big Ten Standings

Team	Proj. Conf. W-L	Proj. FEI	Proj. Overall Rank	Proj. Overall W-L
Ohio State	7-1	.292	1	10-1
Wisconsin	6-2	.196	10	9-2
Penn State	5-3	.151	21	8-3
Michigan	5-3	.145	24	8-4
Michigan State	4-4	.083	38	6-6
Iowa	4-4	.069	41	7-4
Purdue	3-5	.032	55	4-7
Minnesota	3-5	.028	56	5-6
Northwestern	3-5	.001	61	5-6
Illinois	2-6	-.012	65	4-7
Indiana	2-6	-.056	78	4-7

Projected Pac-10 Standings

Team	Proj. Conf. W-L	Proj. FEI	Proj. Overall Rank	Proj. Overall W-L
USC	8-1	.269	2	10-2
Oregon	6-3	.184	11	9-3
California	6-3	.159	17	8-4
Arizona State	5-4	.148	23	7-4
Oregon State	4-5	.091	35	6-6
UCLA	4-5	.090	37	5-7
Arizona	4-5	.080	40	6-6
Washington State	3-6	.039	51	5-7
Washington	3-6	.039	52	3-9
Stanford	2-7	.018	57	4-8

Projected SEC Standings

Team	Proj. Conf. W-L	Proj. FEI	Proj. Overall Rank	Proj. Overall W-L
East Division				
Georgia	6-2	.265	3	9-2
Florida	6-2	.264	4	9-2
Tennessee	5-3	.181	13	9-3
South Carolina	4-4	.129	26	6-5
Kentucky	2-6	.035	54	5-6
Vanderbilt	2-6	-.044	72	3-9
West Division				
LSU	6-2	.245	5	9-2
Auburn	6-2	.231	6	9-2
Alabama	4-4	.142	25	8-4
Arkansas	3-5	.091	34	5-6
Mississippi State	2-6	.003	60	4-7
Mississippi	2-6	-.006	63	4-7

The NFL Fan's Guide to College Football 2008

Russell Levine

What follows is our fourth-annual NFL fan's guide to the coming college football season. It is intended to serve not only as an introduction to the players Mel Kiper will be hyperventilating about next April but also as a guided tour of many of the best games this upcoming college season. Clip it out and plan your weekends accordingly.

All statistics are from 2007 unless otherwise noted. The rankings that appear with each team are Fremeau Efficiency Index 2008 projections, which can be found in the previous essay. Note that all players listed in bold are seniors eligible for the 2009 NFL Draft except those denoted by the following:

* * Juniors who are eligible for the 2009 and 2010 drafts
* ** Sophomores who are eligible for the 2010 and 2011 drafts (or 2009 if they have redshirted)

August 30

#25 Alabama at #9 Clemson: Alabama head coach Nick Saban has been making headlines in recruiting, but the Clemson roster will have NFL scouts drooling this fall. The Tigers may have the nation's best backfield duo in **James Davis** (1,064 yards on just 214 carries in 2007) and **C. J. Spiller*** (5.3 yards per carry last year on 145 carries, 7.3 yards per carry the year before on 129 carries). Splitting time has held down the overall totals of these two, but it makes them more attractive to NFL teams who appreciate a talented tailback with lots of tread left on his tires. Clemson **QB Cullen Harper** (2,991 yards, 65.1% completions, 27 TDs, 6 INTs) could have another monster year throwing to **WR Aaron Kelly** (88 catches, 1,081 yards, 11 TDs). For Alabama, players to watch include **OT Andre Smith***, rated by some as the top tackle in the nation, and **FS Rashad Johnson**.

#38 Michigan State at #17 California: He's not as exciting as the departed DeSean Jackson, but Cal **C Alex Mack** may be the best in the nation at his position, while Michigan State is led by explosive **RB Javon Ringer** (1,447 yards while sharing carries last year).

#50 Oklahoma State at #51 Washington State: This game features a couple of talented pass catchers in Washington State **WR Brandon Gibson** (67 catches, 1,180 yards, 9 TDs) and Oklahoma State **TE Brandon Pettigrew** (35 receptions, 15.4 yards per catch).

September 6

#35 Oregon State at #21 Penn State: This should be an interesting intersectional matchup between teams with high aspirations this season. Oregon State's best player can be found on the offensive line in **G Jeremy Perry**. Another name to watch is **WR Sammie Stroughter**, who returns after missing last season. In 2006, he amassed 1,293 yards receiving. Penn State's usually stout defense is led by **DE Maurice Evans*** (12.5 sacks, 21.5 tackles for loss).

#43 Cincinnati at #7 Oklahoma: Cincinnati very quietly won 10 games in 2007 and this rising program has its eye on the Big East's BCS bid. **CB Mike Mickens** is a first-round talent who grabbed six interceptions last season. Oklahoma has serious national-title aspirations thanks to a typically loaded roster. The offense has stars at every level, including **G George "Duke" Robinson**, **OT Phil Loadholt**, and **TE Jermaine Gresham** (11 TDs on 37 receptions) on the line. In the backfield, **QB Sam Bradford**** (3,121 yards, 69.5% completions, 36 TDs, 8 INTs) and **RB DeMarco Murray**** (6.0 YPC, 13 TDs on 127 carries) are expected to put up big numbers this fall.

September 13

#1 Ohio State at #2 USC: It doesn't bother this Michigan grad to admit that Ohio State deserves much credit for its nonconference scheduling in recent years. Wait, yes it does. USC schedules tough every year, and this is perhaps the single biggest game on the regular-season slate entering 2008. As always, both rosters are chock-full of NFL prospects; here we focus on the Ohio State offense and the USC defenders. The Buckeyes are led by the efficient **QB Todd Boeckman** (2,379 yards, 25 TDs), who will throw it plenty to reliable **WR Brian Robiskie** (55 catches, 935 yards, 11 TDs). The brightest star is **RB Chris "Beanie" Wells*** (1,609 yards, 5.9 YPC, 15 TDs), who could put himself atop the Heisman list with a big performance running behind **OT Alex Boone** in this contest. Nothing will come easy against a USC defense with its typical roster of first-round talents, including **LBs Rey Maualuga** and **Brian Cushing**, **DBs Taylor Mays***, **Kevin Ellison**, and **Josh Pinkard**, and **DT Fili Moala**. Of those, Maualuga and Cushing, who both have tremendous athleticism, are the best prospects.

#34 Arkansas at #16 Texas: Gone is the Razorbacks' stud tailback tandem of Darren McFadden and Felix Jones, but this year's team still has some prized prospects, one on each side of the ball. **DE Antwain Robinson** anchors the defensive line, while **C Jonathan Luigs** should be gone by the middle rounds at the latest. The headliner at Texas is **QB Colt McCoy***, who endured a sophomore slump (18 INTs) but still managed to throw for 3,303 yards and 22 touchdowns. **OT Adam Ulatoski*** heads a line that has turned out many high NFL picks.

#11 Oregon at #55 Purdue: Oregon was hit hard by graduation, but the Ducks still have talent enough to challenge in the Pac-10. The Ducks' best NFL prospects are **SS Patrick Chung** (117 tackles, 2 INTs) and **OT Max Unger**. Purdue's offense is led by **QB Curtis Painter**, who has NFL size at six foot four and 230 pounds. He lit up Big Ten defenses to the tune of 3,846 yards and 29 touchdowns, with just 11 interceptions.

#40 Arizona at #68 New Mexico: This isn't exactly a headline game, but it's worth keeping an eye on New Mexico **CB DeAndre Wright** (3 INTs), who should spend plenty of time locked up with Arizona **WR Mike Thomas** (83 receptions, 1,038 yards, 11 TDs).

September 20

#5 LSU at #6 Auburn: The first big test of the SEC conference schedule is also our first opportunity to check out the latest crop of NFL-ready talents at both schools. LSU is as loaded as ever, particularly up front on both sides of the ball. Here we focus on the offense. **OT Ciron Black*** should be among the first tackles off the board in round one whenever he decides to come out. **OL Herman Johnson**, who can play both guard and center, won't last a whole lot longer than Black when draft day arrives. With erstwhile starting QB Ryan Perrilloux booted from the team, LSU's top offensive weapon might be **WR Demetrius Byrd** (35 catches, 621 yards, 7 TDs). Pay attention to the matchup between the LSU offensive line and Auburn **DT Sen'Derrick Marks*** (9 TFL, 2 sacks, 1 INT), yet another candidate for going in the first round of whichever draft he enters.

#4 Florida at #13 Tennessee: NFL teams will spend this fall taking a long, hard look at Florida **QB Tim Tebow***. He's obviously a physical specimen and a freakish athlete, but can he play quarterback in the pros? For now, the mock drafters are suggesting that he'll be snatched up in the first few picks, but he still has a lot to prove in the eyes of pro scouts. **WR/RB Percy Harvin*** (764 yards rushing, 858 receiving, 10 TDs) is slight, but unbelievably fast and elusive. The NFL will find a way to use him somehow. For Tennessee, the talent level has dropped a bit in recent years, which is why the Vols haven't been competing for national championships. If **RB Arian Foster** (1,193 yards, 12 TDs) has his head on straight after several off-field issues, he'll merit the consideration of NFL scouts.

#3 Georgia at #23 Arizona State: On the heels of a dominant performance in the Sugar Bowl, Georgia will begin the season atop many preseason polls. If the Bulldogs are to win their first national championship since Herschel Walker's freshman season of 1980, they'll need huge years out of **QB Matthew Stafford*** (2,523 yards, 19 TDs) and **RB Knowshon Moreno**** (1,334 yards, 14 TDs), who has drawn many comparisons to the aforementioned Walker. This game is also the rarest of tests for the Bulldogs: a nonconference road date in another time zone. Arizona State, coming off a surprising 10-win season in Dennis Erickson's first year at the helm, has some dangerous offensive weapons, including **RB Keegan Herring** (815 yards on just 154 carries, 6 TDs) and **QB Rudy Carpenter** (3,202 yards, 25 TDs, 10 INTs). It will be the job of Georgia **DT Jeff Owens** (22 QB hurries), who is a three-year starter, to get into the ASU backfield and disrupt things.

#41 Iowa at #39 Pittsburgh: Pittsburgh could surprise some teams in the Big East this season, after ending 2007 with an epic upset of West Virginia. Coach Dave Wannstedt has been hitting the recruiting trail hard, turning up gems such as **RB LeSean McCoy**** (1,324 yards, 14 TDs as a freshman). Times have been rough in Iowa City in recent seasons, but the Hawkeyes have an outstanding offensive lineman in **G Dan Doering***.

#90 Ball State at #78 Indiana: This is not normally a game that would warrant mentioning, even among college football diehards. But this is the NFL fan's guide, which is why we would have you keep an eye on Ball State's trio of offensive weapons: **QB Nate Davis*** (MAC-best 3,667 yards, 30 TDs, 6 INTs), **TE Darius Hill** (65 catches, 926 yards, 11 TDs), and **WR Dante Love** (100 catches, 1,398 yards, 10 TDs). All three should earn NFL paychecks one day. Indiana **DE Greg Middleton***, who led the nation with a school-record 16 sacks last year, needs to apply some pressure if the Hoosiers are to slow the Ball State attack.

September 27

#10 Wisconsin at #24 Michigan: The Badgers are expected to be Ohio State's primary competition for the Big Ten title. The typical grind-it-out offense is bolstered by several future pros, including **TE Travis Beckum** (75 catches, 982 yards, 6 TDs), **RB P. J. Hill*** (1,212 yards, 14 TDs), and **G Kraig Urbik**. This could be a difficult year for Michigan as it copes with the transition to Rich Rodriguez's spread option, but the defense still has some talent, including **DT Terrance Taylor** (3.5 sacks, 8.5 TFL).

#14 Virginia Tech at #58 Nebraska: The Cornhuskers should be playing a more familiar brand of football under new head coach Bo Pelini, who has scrapped Bill Callahan's West Coast offense and will run some option. That's good news for **RB Marlon Lucky** (1,019 yards, 9 TDs). Virginia Tech lost plenty of talent in the most recent NFL Draft, but Frank Beamer's cupboard isn't entirely bare. **CB Victor "Macho" Harris** (5 INTs) should be a first-day pick, as could **G Sergio Render***.

October 4

#11 Oregon at #2 USC: Anytime USC takes the field in the Pete Carroll era, it's a good bet plenty of NFL scouts are watching. The offense isn't quite as loaded as it was a year ago, but **QBs Mark Sanchez** (695 yards, 7 TDs as backup in 2007) and **Mitch Mustain*** (a top high-school recruit when he signed at Arkansas in 2006) are both likely draft picks. The Trojans also have a pair of explosive tailbacks in **Stafon

Johnson* (98 carries, 689 yards) and **Joe McKnight**** (94 carries, 610 yards). Oregon hopes to challenge USC in the Pac-10, but the Ducks will need a big year from **RB Jeremiah Johnson***, who is coming off an injury-shortened season in which he carried just 54 times.

October 11

#5 LSU at #4 Florida: This could be the SEC Game of the Year between a pair of teams with serious national-title aspirations—and the talent to match. Future NFL Gators not already covered include **TE Cornelius Ingram**, who averaged nearly 15 yards on 34 receptions and caught seven touchdown passes, and **LB Brandon Spikes***, who led Florida with 131 tackles. LSU's defensive talent is concentrated on the line, where **DT Al Woods*** and **DEs Tyson Jackson** and **Ricky-Jean Francois*** reside. All three played in the considerable shadow of Glenn Dorsey the last few seasons, but none will last long on draft day—particularly Jackson, who lives in opposing backfields.

October 18

#47 Georgia Tech at #9 Clemson: Expect plenty of fireworks from Clemson's offense this season, but the defense should also be strong, thanks to the presence of players such as **DE Ricky Sapp*** (6 sacks, 9.5 TFL), **FS Chris Clemons** (78 tackles, 2 INTs), and **SS Michael Hamlin** (80 tackles, 4 INTs). Sapp could play defensive end or outside linebacker in the pros, making him ideal for a 3-4 or 4-3 team that needs an edge-rusher. Georgia Tech has a new head coach, Paul Johnson, and a new offense, but it has two future high draft picks on the defensive line. **DE Michael Johnson** (21 tackles, 6 TFL) and **DT Vance Walker** (8.5 sacks, 14 TFL) could both be first-rounders.

#73 Western Michigan at #82 Central Michigan: QB Dan LeFevour* of Central Michigan is a legitimate NFL prospect from a conference—the MAC—that has turned out many pros at the position. The incredibly mobile LeFevour ran for 1,122 yards, while throwing for 3,652 yards and 27 touchdowns, completing 65.4 percent of his passes. Even against MAC competition, those are eye-opening numbers for NFL scouts.

October 23

#6 Auburn at #8 West Virginia: Rodriguez may be gone to Michigan, but he left behind plenty of talent at West Virginia, a team that could be in the mix for the BCS Championship. The headline-maker on offense is elusive **QB Pat White** (195 carries, 1,335 yards, 14 TDs), who projects to wide receiver in the NFL. **OT Ryan Stanchek**, a two-year starter at left tackle, is another pro prospect. He lacks ideal height for the NFL (six foot four) but could bulk up and move inside to guard.

October 25

#65 Illinois at #10 Wisconsin: This isn't the biggest game of the day—that would be Georgia at LSU in the SEC, teams that have been covered already—but this Big Ten tilt features some excellent prospects on defense. Although Illinois lost some key players on offense, the defense returns **CB Vontae Davis*** (76 tackles, 4 INTs), who showed off his athleticism in the Rose Bowl by chasing down USC tailback Joe McKnight from behind. Wisconsin's best defensive player is **DE Matt Shaughnessy** (5 sacks, 18 TFL).

November 1

#16 Texas at #15 Texas Tech: The Red Raiders' pass-happy offense always produces ridiculous numbers, but few of Mike Leach's quarterbacks and receivers have had an NFL impact. That is likely to change with **WR Michael Crabtree****, who caught 134 passes. For 1,962 yards. And 22 touchdowns. As a redshirt freshman. The redshirt means Crabtree, who has NFL size at six foot three and 208 pounds, could be eligible for the 2009 draft if he so chooses.

November 8

#7 Oklahoma at #67 Texas A&M: We've covered Oklahoma's offensive prospects; here, we turn to the defense. The line features **DE Auston English*** (9.5 sacks, 13 TFL) and **DT Gerald McCoy**** (19 tackles, 6.5 TFL), who could make life miserable for Texas A&M **RBs Mike Goodson*** (153 carries, 711 yards, 4 TDs) and 268-pound **Jorvorskie Lane** (169 carries, 780 yards, 16 TDs). Should the Aggies' backs get through the line, waiting for them will be the imposing **FS Nic Harris** (74 tackles, 2 INTs), a sure tackler with good cover skills.

November 15

#12 Boston College at #20 Florida State: Boston College will be in rebuilding mode in Year One A.R. (after Ryan), but **TE Ryan Purvis** (54 catches, 553 yards, 4 TDs) is one of the nation's best returning players at his position. Things have gone downhill fast for Florida State, and it doesn't look like the Bobby Bowden era is destined for a happy ending. But despite the Seminoles' offensive limitations, NFL scouts will love the six-foot-six size of **WR Greg Carr** (45 catches, 795 yards, 4 TDs). On defense, the FSU player to watch is **SS Myron Rolle*** (67 tackles), one of the nation's top players coming out of high school two years ago. He could play himself into a first-round pick if he has a big year.

#32 Rutgers at #22 South Florida: These are two programs that have come from nowhere to join the BCS discussion the past two seasons, and you don't accomplish that without stockpiling talent. Even after losing Ray Rice, the Scarlet Knights have offensive weapons in **QB Mike Teel** and **WR Tiquan Underwood** (65 catches, 1,100 yards, 7 TDs). Teel was hampered by a thumb injury as a junior but still threw for 3,147 yards and 20 touchdowns. He has NFL size at six foot four and 220 pounds, while the six-foot-two Underwood could stand to add some weight to his 180-pound frame and must cut down on drops. On defense, **SS Courtney Greene** (101 tackles, 1 INT) should be selected in the middle rounds. South Florida has rapidly built a powerhouse program that briefly held the top spot in the BCS standings last season by mining Florida high schools for speedy players. The best of the bunch is six-foot-four, 242-pound **DE George Selvie***, a Jevon Kearse clone who led the nation with 31.5 TFL last seasons. **FS Nate Allen*** (86 tackles, 4 INTs) is another pro prospect in a secondary that sent both its starting corners to the NFL last season.

November 22

#24 Michigan at #1 Ohio State: Don't look now, but Ohio State could very well be playing for a third consecutive BCS title-game berth when it takes on Michigan in Columbus. Michigan's offense should be much improved by the time this game rolls around, but nothing comes easy against the likes of **LBs James Laurinaitis** and **Marcus Freeman**. Laurinaitis (121 tackles, 5 sacks, 2 INTs) made great strides as a junior, and by opting to return for his senior year could go in the top half of round one. Freeman led the Buckeyes with 66 solo stops and was third with 9.5 TFL. He's not quite as good a prospect as Laurinaitis, but Freeman should still be a first-day pick. The first Buckeye taken could be **CB Malcolm Jenkins** (4 INTs), another player who could have come out early. He is a favorite to be the first corner off the board in April. Michigan also has strength in the secondary, where **CBs Morgan Trent and Donovan Warren*** and **S Brandon Harrison** should make life difficult for opposing receivers while polishing their NFL résumés.

November 28

#63 Ole Miss at #60 Mississippi State: The annual Egg Bowl has a little added luster thanks to some top-notch talent. Ole Miss has potential first-rounders on each side of the ball. **OT Michael Oher**, of *The Blind Side* fame, looks like he will fulfill the promise predicted for him as an itinerant high schooler in Michael Lewis's best-selling book. He's still raw, but he's a potential franchise left tackle in the NFL. **DE Greg Hardy*** (10 sacks, 18.5 TFL) could be joined on day one of the draft by **DTs Jerrell Powe** and **Peria Jerry**—provided Powe is academically eligible. Mississippi State, which finally turned a corner last year under coach Sylvester Croom, is led by **FS Derek Pegues** (5 INTs, 50 tackles), another possible first-day pick.

November 29

#18 Missouri vs. #27 Kansas (at Kansas City): Missouri was one of many surprising teams to play a part in the national-championship discussion last year after going 12-2, and the Tigers have plenty of talent returning to make another run at the Big 12 title and a BCS bid. The offense starts with **QB Chase Daniel** (4,306 yards, 33 TDs, 11 INTs), who should still get a look on draft day despite being undersized. The best player is **WR Jeremy Maclin**** (80 catches, 1,055 yards receiving, 2,776 all-purpose yards), while **TE Chase Coffman** (52 catches, 531 yards, 7 TDs) is Daniel's security blanket. On defense, **FS William Moore** (8 INTs, 115 tackles, 9 TFL) and **LB Sean Weatherspoon** (127 tackles, 9.5 TFL) are both potential first-day picks. Kansas got a BCS bid over Missouri last season, despite the Tigers winning the head-to-head battle, so things could get heated this time around. Kansas is not as loaded with pro-caliber talent, but the defense is led by NFL prospect **LB Joe Mortensen** (106 tackles, 15 TFL).

Building a Better Draft Value Chart

Ben Riley

When he looks back upon his life's accomplishments, Jimmy Johnson should take pride in a lot. Two Super Bowl wins with the Dallas Cowboys. An NCAA Championship with the Miami Hurricanes. His cameo in *The Waterboy*.

And then there's the NFL Draft Value Chart, the spreadsheet that Johnson helped create in the early 1990s to make sure the Cowboys were getting fair value in their draft-day trades. Although not as readily identified with Johnson as, say, his helmet hair, the draft value chart remains his enduring legacy in the NFL. Virtually every team in the league uses some modified version of his original chart.

Unfortunately, the Johnson chart is deeply flawed. In an interview with the *Dallas Morning News* in 2004, former Cowboys executive Mike McCoy explained how he developed the chart for Johnson after studying four years' worth of draft-day trade data. "The more I played with it, the more obvious it became that there was a real, definite trend," McCoy said. "You were able to plot on a graph that showed historically that trades valued draft picks in certain ways. And from that graph, I made up a chart that assigned a numerical value to every single draft pick from the first in the first round to the last in the last round."

Note the circularity of McCoy's methodology: essentially, he established the market value of picks (in 1991) using the market valuation of four years' worth of prior trades. The problem is that this doesn't tell you what the picks *should* be worth unless you assume perfect market efficiency, which is controversial when valuing corporations, much less something as uncertain as a football player. In other words, having established how teams were valuing picks, McCoy created a chart that simply solidified those valuations due to its widespread use. Behavioral economists refer to this as the anchoring phenomena, the tendency to rely too heavily on one piece of information when making a decision, and it certainly seems to have infected the NFL.

Thus, there is a growing recognition that the Johnson chart is in dire need of an overhaul. Enter Football Outsiders and professors Cade Massey and Richard Thaler, authors of "The Winner's Curse: Overconfidence vs. Market Efficiency in the National Football League." Two years ago, Massey and Thaler published this seminal economic study of the NFL draft that analyzed whether the market for young NFL players was inefficient and "plagued by the inability to measure fundamental value." As part of their study, Massey and Thaler tracked the average number of games started for every player taken in the NFL draft between 1991 and 2003 as well as the average number of Pro Bowl starts per round. For example, on average, the first overall pick in the draft plays about 12 games per year over his first five seasons and .10 Pro Bowls, compared to six games for the average second-round pick (.04 Pro Bowls), and so on down the line—although the odds of finding a Pro Bowl player flatten after round three.

At our request, Massey and Thaler generously agreed to share some of their unpublished data with us, which we then used to create our new actual draft value chart (Figure 1). (An earlier version of this chart appeared in an April issue of *ESPN the Magazine*. The ADV chart in *Pro Football Prospectus 2008* is further modified to account for the higher quality of players chosen in earlier rounds.) The major difference between the ADV chart and the Johnson chart is that the ADV chart reduces the absurd overvaluation placed on early picks. Under the old chart, the seventh overall pick in the draft is worth 1500 points, exactly 50 percent of the value of the first overall pick. In contrast, under the new ADV chart, that same pick is worth 2805 points, approximately 94 percent of the value of the first overall pick (Table 1). Indeed, according to the new chart, you have to wait until the 45th pick in the draft (the 13th pick in the second round) before pick values drop below 50 percent of the first overall pick.

The results of this year's draft neatly illustrate this difference in valuation between the new chart and the old. Many experts believe that LSU defensive tackle Glenn Dorsey was the best player available and could end up as the next Warren Sapp, yet for reasons outside his control he fell to the Chiefs with the fifth pick. According to the Johnson chart, this means that Dorsey is presently valued at only 57 percent of Miami's new left tackle, Jake Long. Does that sound right to you? And what about last year's first overall selection, JaMarcus Russell? Does anyone besides Al Davis think

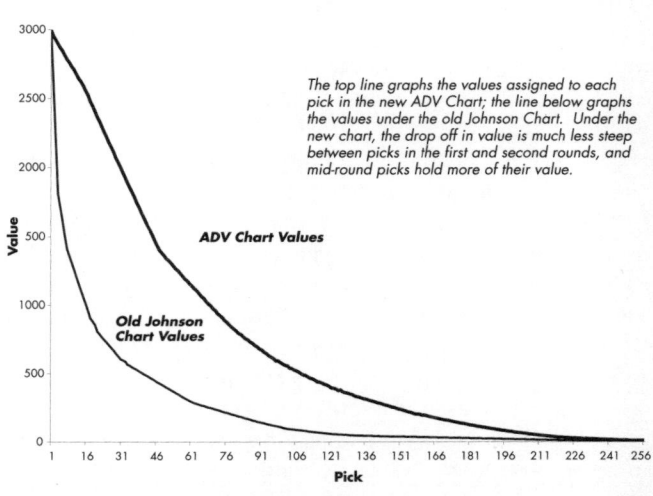

The top line graphs the values assigned to each pick in the new ADV Chart; the line below graphs the values under the old Johnson Chart. Under the new chart, the drop off in value is much less steep between picks in the first and second rounds, and mid-round picks hold more of their value.

Figure 1

Table 1. Johnson Values vs. ADV Values*

Round	Pick	Overall	Johnson	ADV
1	1	1	3000	3000
1	2	2	2600	2950
1	3	3	2200	2920
1	4	4	1800	2890
1	5	5	1700	2860
1	6	6	1600	2835
1	7	7	1500	2805
1	8	8	1400	2775
1	9	9	1350	2750
1	10	10	1300	2720
1	15	15	1050	2580
1	20	20	850	2395
1	25	25	720	2210
2	1	33	580	1915
2	13	45	450	1495
3	1	65	265	1075
4	1	100	100	570
5	1	132	40	325
6	1	171	26	169
7	1	201	12	61

*Assumes an average number of supplemental picks in rounds 3-6.

Table 2. Average Value to Team Trading Down, 2005-2008

Year	Old Chart	ADV Chart
2005	3.92	149
2006	6.87	238
2007	8.94	322
2008	-9.57	273
Average	2.54	246

clusion: The teams that make draft-day trades are definitely still hewing closely to the Johnson chart when determining value. (The entire Football Outsiders ADV chart can be found in the Statistical Appendix.)

As Table 2 also shows, however, 2008 was the first year that the average value of a trade to the teams moving down inched into negative territory. One year does not make a trend, but this suggests that some teams are starting to recognize the benefit of stockpiling picks in later rounds by trading down, even if the Johnson chart doesn't support the deal. More interestingly, when we revalue the trades using the new ADV chart, it reveals that on average, teams that have traded down over the past four years gain approximately 250 points in value per trade, the equivalent of an extra mid fifth-round pick (147th overall). Thus, at least in theory, a team is almost always better off trading down than up.

We then examined the number of trades made by each team to look for discernible patterns over the past four years (Table 3). One team stands out with a flashing neon green-and-yellow sign that says "We Love to Trade Down." Clearly, Ted Thompson of the Green Bay Packers understands the benefits of accumulating mid-round picks. The fact that he was named the NFL's Executive of the Year this past season is not a coincidence. In contrast, if there's one general manager who mistakenly believes he needs to leapfrog up the board on draft day, it's Lions general manager Matt Millen, who—also not coincidentally—was just named the NFL's Laughingstock of the Decade. The 49ers have also traded up four times, as have the Raiders.

Table 3. Five or More Draft-Day Trades, 2005-2008

Team	Down	Up	Net Down	Total
Dallas	7	6	1	13
Green Bay	11	1	10	12
New England	7	3	4	10
Philadelphia	6	4	2	10
Detroit	2	7	-5	9
NY Jets	3	5	-2	8
Jacksonville	5	2	3	7
Chicago	2	3	-1	5
Minnesota	2	3	-1	5
St. Louis	2	3	-1	5
Oakland	1	4	-3	5
Tennessee	3	1	2	4

that Russell is twice as valuable as seventh overall selection Adrian Peterson? Of course not, and the new ADV chart better reflects the incremental—rather than monumental—drop-off between each pick in the first round.

The astute reader may be wondering, "Does this new chart account for the huge contractual obligations that accompany early picks?" Actually no—at least, not yet. In part, this is because it's hard to quantify and combine performance measures such as games started and Pro Bowls with a genuinely objective measure of a pick's financial impact—every team may have the same salary cap, but the Cowboys can still afford to whiff on an early pick far more than the Bills can. In addition, if teams are genuinely concerned about the guaranteed money they pay their early picks, nothing is stopping them from passing on their selection and dropping to a later slot. The fact that no team has ever voluntarily done this may be telling. For now, we'll assume that teams make their draft trades taking into account their feelings about how the signing bonuses for those picks fit within their specific team budgets. The point of our analysis is to make the expectation of player performance from each spot in the draft better match reality, salary aside.

Using both the new ADV chart and the Johnson chart, we then analyzed the past four years of draft trades. Looking only at trades that excluded future picks or players, we expected to find a growing gap in the values of what teams were giving up to move up or down in the draft—that is, we expected that teams in recent years were executing trades using different values than those predicted by the Johnson chart. But of the 59 trades we examined, the average difference in the values of picks exchanged was a miniscule 2.5 points according to the classic Johnson chart (Table 2). Con-

Our new chart suggests trading down is rarely a good idea, but just how bad an idea is it? To answer that question, we took a look at some of the biggest draft-trade "fleeces" according to our new numbers (Table 4). For example, in this year's draft the Jaguars mortgaged their future to grab defensive end Derrick Harvey from Florida, trading four picks to Baltimore to move up 18 slots in the first round. What looks like a huge net loss for the Ravens under the Johnson chart valuation (-273 points) ends up being a huge gain using our new values—a whopping 1420 points, which is the equivalent of an extra mid second round pick. Unfortunately, general manager Ozzie Newsome then went and squandered his good fortune by trading away his newly acquired picks to the Texans in the second-biggest fleecing on our list.

If the Derrick Harvey trade seemed vaguely reminiscent of a similar trade during last year's draft, that's because it was. In 2007, the Broncos traded a third- and fifth-round pick to, ironically, the Jaguars, so they could move up four slots in the first round to take defensive end Jarvis Moss from Florida. Moss promptly broke his leg in Week 5. In contrast, the Jaguars selected Florida safety Reggie Nelson with their first-round pick—he started all 16 games last year and had five interceptions—and then added Iowa tackle Marshall Yanda and Ohio State center Doug Datish to build depth on the offensive line. Net gain to Jacksonville: 648 points, the equivalent of an extra third-round pick.

In another trade that just narrowly missed out being included in the table, in 2006 the Patriots traded with Green Bay to move up 16 slots in the second round. The Patriots selected Florida wide receiver Chad Jackson, who spent most of last season on the inactive list, and the Packers took Western Michigan WR Greg Jennings (920 yards and 12 TDs in 13 games last year) and Louisville offensive lineman Jason Spitz, who played 14 games in 2007 and helped turn Ryan Grant into a fantasy football stud. Net gain to Green Bay: 405 points.

To be fair to the Patriots, this trade was somewhat of an outlier to their usual practice of trading down or trading for early picks in future drafts or both. Although our study focused primarily on draft-day trades involving picks in the same year, we also calculated the value of trades involving future-year picks between 2005 and 2008. Conventional wisdom holds that future draft picks are discounted by a round, that is, to acquire a third-round pick in 2008, a team needs to offer a second-round pick in 2009. The Cowboys, the Eagles, and the Patriots like to bank future picks this way, and they are wise to do so: On average, the team that trades a present-year pick to acquire one in the future gains an impressive 738 points in value, the equivalent of an extra third-round selection.

That's not to say trading down *always* works out for the team that slides back. Three years ago, Carolina agreed to drop nine slots in the second round in exchange for two fourth-round picks from Seattle. Apparently, someone in the Panthers scouting department fell in love with Bobby Petrino's college offense, because they selected Louisville running back Eric Shelton in the second round and quarterback Stefan Lefors in the fourth. Then they dealt the other fourth-round pick to (surprise!) Green Bay so they could move up in the third round. In theory, this trade resulted in a net gain of 540 points to Carolina. In reality, the Seahawks selected USC linebacker Lofa Tatupu and never looked back. Lesson: Scouting departments still matter.

Table 4. Trades That Earned >500 FO Points, 2005–2008

Year	Trade	Winner	Old	New
2008	Baltimore trades their first-round selection (8th overall) to Jacksonville for Jacksonville's first-round selection, two third-round selections, and fourth-round selection (26th, 71st, 89th, and 125th).	Baltimore	-273	1420
2008	Houston trades their first-round selection (18th overall) to Baltimore for the first-round and third-round selections Baltimore acquired from Jacksonville earlier and a sixth-round selection (26th, 89th, and 173rd).	Houston	98	1060
2006	St. Louis trades their first-round selection (11th overall) to Denver for the Broncos' first and third-round picks (15th and 68th overall).	St. Louis	50	905
2007	Carolina trades their first and sixth-round picks (14th and 191st overall) to the Jets for their first, second, and fifth-round picks (25th, 59th and 164th overall).	Carolina	-59.2	870
2006	The Giants trade their first-round pick (25th overall) to Pittsburgh for the Steelers' first, third, and fourth-round picks (32nd, 96th and 129th overall).	Giants	29	695
2007	Jacksonville trades their first-round selection (17th overall) to Denver for the Broncos' first, third, and fifth-round picks (21st, 86th, and 198th overall).	Jacksonville	23.2	648
2007	Detroit trades their second-round pick (34th overall) to Buffalo for the Bills' second and third-round picks (43rd and 74th).	Detroit	130	595
2007	Philadelphia trades their first-round pick (26th overall) to Dallas for the Cowboys' second, third, and fifth-round picks (36th, 87th, and 159th overall).	Philadelphia	23.8	553
2005	Carolina trades their second-round pick (45th overall) to Seattle for the Seahawks' second-round selection and two fourth-round picks (54th, 121st and 126th overall).	Carolina (in theory)	8	540

The College Spread Offense: Bridging the Evaluation Gap

Doug Farrar

I don't want to be a product of my environment. I want my environment to be a product of me.
JACK NICHOLSON

The art and science of finding and developing optimal NFL talent from the collegiate ranks has never been a simple process. So many elements, both tangible and intangible, go into it. The number of first-round busts and late-round steals each year proves that while scouting and evaluation tools become more advanced, there are just as many players who slip through the draft as there are high-investment selections holding their teams back with expensive inefficiency. The primary shortcut to success, if there is one, is the ability to project how players fit your system. The secondary shortcut is the ability to recognize when strategies that work in college don't translate to the NFL, and how players in those systems are affected.

Chief among the difficulties in recent years from the NFL perspective are the schematic presets in the college spread offense and the false positives that offense presents on offense and defense. Many NFL offenses have incorporated elements of the spread over time, but it has proven to be a liability unless it is integrated into a much larger game plan. Yet more and more colleges are going to the spread to keep up with the excitement and high scores it produces at the college level. As this happens, the evaluation gap between the NCAA and the NFL becomes wider and the ability to project how a player will fit into your offense grows more difficult. Although some teams are bemoaning this new trend, others are taking advantage of the change with their own hybrid spread systems.

How did the spread become so prevalent in college football, why doesn't it work in the NFL, and what are the best ways to bridge that gap?

A BRIEF HISTORY

The spread offense and all its variations grew out of a need for college programs to establish schematic advantage, especially against superior opponents. College football has any number of top-heavy games in which major and smaller schools collide, with the smaller schools generally just hoping not to get blown out. The spread offense is an equalizer that allows underdogs to determine both the game's tempo and the opposing defense's strategy.

The current spread offense has its roots in the run-and-shoot, the offense designed in the 1950s and 1960s by Glenn "Tiger" Ellison of Middletown High School in Ohio and then Ohio State and popularized in the 1970s by Mouse Davis at Portland State. Davis became the first coach to take this offense past the collegiate ranks, first as head coach of the USFL's Denver Gold and then as offensive coordinator of the Detroit Lions from 1989 to 1992. The idea behind the run-and-shoot was to throw multiple-receiver sets at opposing defenses, using wide spreads to elongate and predetermine defensive formations. Against these formations, quarterbacks threw to receivers running shorter routes and gaining more yards after the catch. Single-back sets and tight ends sent outside as receivers eliminated backside protection as a concept, but the thought was that the tempo of the offense would always offset that issue. The shotgun later used in different variances of the spread was less prevalent in the run-and-shoot; short routes and backfield options ruled the day.

It was a sharp break from the old-school approach to the passing game. Although the offenses that Bill Walsh created in Cincinnati in the 1970s and ran in San Francisco in the 1980s with great success featured a shorter passing game, the lower-percentage long pass had been an NFL constant from Joe Namath to Terry Bradshaw to John Elway. The run-and-shoot was also different from the Walsh offense because there was generally less time for quarterbacks to read through their progressions. But as the run-and-shoot developed in college football and as a response to blitz-happy defenses such as Buddy Ryan's 46, the league took notice and those formations made their way into the NFL.

The run-and-shoot experienced varying degrees of success in a few cities: Davis's high-powered offense in Detroit, the Houston Oilers of the late 1980s and early 1990s under Jerry Glanville and Jack Pardee, and the Atlanta Falcons under Glanville and June Jones from 1990 through 1995. Glanville, who ran it more than any other head coach at the professional level, went 60-69 in the regular season and 3-4 in the playoffs. Eventually, those who disparaged the offense as gimmicky—Ryan famously called it the "chuck-and-duck"—and thought it vulnerable to the faster, more talented defenders of the NFL had their way as the run-and-shoot fell out of favor. Steve Spurrier tried his own "fun-and-gun" variation with the Washington Redskins in 2002 and 2003, but it didn't take. Spurrier was replaced by Joe Gibbs after posting a 12-20 record, and this breed of offense was basically dead in the NFL.

Why didn't it work? Greg Cosell of NFL Films, producer of ESPN's *NFL Matchup*, puts it succinctly. "Number one, when you spread your offense out like that with no tight ends, you have a short corner on both sides. So if a defense chooses to, they can always pressure the quarterback. So your quarterback will take many more hits in that style of offense than he would in a more traditional offense. Over time, that's a problem. Number two, that's an offense in which there's no real physicality. Teams would have success in yards running the ball at times, but it was all that spread run stuff based on seams and getting the defense spread out. It's not an offense that encourages physicality, and teams that can't line up and be physical in games don't win championships."

In college, that wasn't the case, and the abilities of some personnel executives to isolate players and project their abilities to succeed in the NFL have become hindered by the prevalence of the spread offense. Scout.com's Tom Marino, a former NFL scout who helped build the "Greatest Show on Turf" Rams, believes that the spread offense "affects everything—every position. You've got offensive linemen coming off two-point stances presnap. It gives you a false sense of what the running backs are doing because the splits are so wide and there are five receivers [or four wide receivers with a back that can catch out of the backfield or split wide]. You don't have a standard 4-3 set or an eight-man front [to face] anymore. You basically have a four-man front, and if you can break something, you have a big, long run. So you get a false read there. The receivers catch half their balls behind the line of scrimmage, or on shallow crosses, or slip screens, or hitches, or whatever the case may be, and that's another false read. You have receivers catching 90 or 100 balls, but when you look at it, how many of those balls are longer than three yards beyond the line of scrimmage? The whole route tree's affected."

San Francisco 49ers general manager Scot McCloughan talked about these "false positives" at the 2008 Scouting Combine. "It makes it tougher for some positions to figure out. It's kind of nice when you go watch a college team on tape like USC when you can see an NFL-type offense. It's, 'Oh, it's easy to see what the guy can or can't do.' It's the same for every team."

It's not the same for every position, however. Spread quarterbacks are by far the most affected in the transition to the pros. The answer to the question of "why?" is simple—they are in no way developed to survive in the National Football League. And this is where we begin when discussing how the spread has changed scouting.

QUARTERBACKS

Cosell says that the problem begins presnap, with the formation itself. "First, [the spread quarterback is] not dropping back from center, and there are a lot of footwork and technique talents—all kinds of fundamental issues—that need to be taught. That doesn't happen overnight. Second, he doesn't have any concept of play action, which is a significant part of the NFL offense. When you turn your back to the defense, even if it's only for a second or a second and a half, that's a very long time. You have to learn that and get used to it. These guys who have played in spread offenses have never done that.

"The routes run in spread offenses are not really NFL-type routes. They do a lot of screens and hitches—obviously the NFL does this, too, but these are the basic route concepts of spreads. So there are a whole set of routes these quarterbacks never see that are basic parts of NFL offenses. There isn't a lot of reading progression in the spread that is similar to what they do in the NFL. You're really almost starting from scratch with these guys—they're just not in an offense that projects or transitions to the NFL from the standpoint of the passing game."

Although the 2007 New England Patriots were called a spread offense by some, Cosell says that's a misnomer. "I think the Patriots were a little different (last) year in how much they had Tom Brady in the shotgun—it was over 70 percent of the time, and that was unusual and unconventional," he said. "But having three receivers on the field . . . I wouldn't define that as spread. They still had a tight end." Table 1 shows the teams that most often ran the most popular spread formation—four receivers, one back, and a shotgun formation—and which teams were most effective.

Finally, Marino believes that without extensive experience with the timing involved in longer routes, college quarterbacks are denied the ability to make the throws they will need to make when faced with go-ahead or comeback situations in the NFL. "The 7-route, the 9-route—these are the throws you can only hope they make at the right time."

Table 1. Offenses—Four Receivers, One Back, Shotgun Formation

Rank	Plays		Yards Per Play		DVOA	
1	NYJ	194	SF	8.8	SEA	74.6%
2	DET	175	GB	8.7	DAL	69.0%
3	NE	138	CHI	8.7	SF	68.8%
4	WAS	127	NE	8.2	GB	61.4%
5	ARI	119	TEN	7.9	NE	59.4%
6	PIT	108	CAR	7.7	JAC	57.8%
7	BUF	82	OAK	7.4	PIT	54.2%
8	GB	76	DAL	7.3	CIN	48.2%
9	STL	72	JAC	7.3	NO	36.6%
10	KC	67	SD	7.2	TEN	35.8%

When Scot McCloughan took Alex Smith of Utah first overall in the 2005 NFL draft, he recognized that there would be an adjustment to the pro system. Smith ran Urban Meyer's offense predominantly out of the shotgun, and though Meyer's option system was a bit more power-based than the four- and five-wide spread offenses seen elsewhere, Smith would require an almost complete change in fundamentals. That he has toiled under three different offensive coordinators in his first three seasons with the San Francisco 49ers hasn't helped. Smith now has Mike Martz, who is the closest thing to a true spread advocate successfully working in the NFL today, as his fourth offensive coordinator.

RECEIVERS

The traditional tight end isn't often seen in the spread; think of him more as a larger slot receiver. The two most athletic tight ends with the biggest blocking concerns in the 2008 draft class, Dustin Keller of Purdue and Jermichael Finley of Texas, were taken by the New York Jets and the Green Bay Packers, respectively. The Packers ranked sixth last season in the number of four-wide sets they ran with 19 percent. The Jets ranked second, behind only the Lions, with 25 percent of their plays marked by four-receiver sets. The Lions offense was run by Martz, who was famous for the multireceiver sets he ran with the Rams and his almost total devaluation of the tight end as a receiving option.

The 49ers ran four-wide eight percent of the time last season, and they set up with two tight ends 25 percent of the time. Expect those numbers to be reversed in 2008. McCloughan alluded to the change at the Combine when he told the assembled media to expect tight end Vernon Davis, more of a hybrid receiver at heart, to find himself outside in more formations.

It can be hard to scout wide receivers because of the lack of deep routes, although this is less of a problem because certain NFL teams have adapted to this trend with great success. When Wes Welker went from the Dolphins to the Patriots, he entered a system in which his ability to gain midrange yardage on short routes was of real value to a team running four-wide 22 percent of the time. How was Welker so adept at doing that? He had gained over 1,000 receiving yards for Mike Leach's Texas Tech spread offense in both 2003 and 2004.

The Packers, who led the NFL in yards after catch last year, are cornering the market on big receivers who can either take short passes and shoot upfield or provide excellent downfield blocking. Their selection of Kansas State's Jordy Nelson in the second round made perfect sense. "His versatility (stood out)," head coach Mike McCarthy said after the draft. "Just a big, strong, physical receiver. Loved his toughness, particularly yards after the catch was the thing I admired the most. If you watch our receivers the last two years, the production that we've been able to obtain in our three-step and five-step passing game, he's a perfect fit."

RUNNING BACKS

As NFLDraftScout.com pointed out before the draft, none of the top four running backs in the 2008 draft class played in a traditional pro-style offense. Arkansas's Darren McFadden and Felix Jones were often in the same backfield, and there were times when McFadden would take a direct snap himself or hand off to Jones. Rashard Mendenhall of Illinois and Jonathan Stewart of Oregon both played in option offenses, rarely running behind a fullback. Oklahoma's Adrian Peterson, 2007's best back, ran between the tackles more often, and this is why all the McFadden-Peterson comparisons could turn out to be off target.

"The difference is that NFL offenses, in the running game . . . you're running counter, you're running power, you're running zone. You have to have patience and vision," Cosell said. "You have to have a sense of pace and tempo. It's the old saying, 'It's not speed *to* the hole; it's speed *through* the hole.' [But in the spread], the field is spread, it's out of the shotgun, and the seams are pretty much defined. You're simply taking the ball and running straight through seams, or you're just running wide around a corner. There's no real sense of instinct, of vision, of reading. None of that is in the spread offense for a running back, so you're trying to transition a player to the NFL, and you have to project whether a player can do that.

"It's like Darren McFadden this year. Darren McFadden has hardly ever run NFL runs. He can run very fast in a straight line. Does that mean he'll be a great NFL back? I can't answer that question."

At the Combine, McCloughan pointed out that the spread has deemphasized the power game, especially drive-blocking. His concerns have echoed others' about the lack of play in the spread and how that transfers negatively to the NFL. Of the top 10 teams in number of four-wide, one-back plays, Pittsburgh was the only team to take one of the draft's top four running backs when Mendenhall fell to them at 23. Of course, the Steelers are known for a more physical style of offense.

Backs that have run in the spread will have to adjust to defensive formations they've rarely seen, in unfamiliar offensive formations. "You have to watch a little more tape with these guys," Colts general manager Bill Polian told the *Chicago Tribune* before the draft. "You might see them run from an I-formation with a fullback five times a game instead of 25 times, so you have fewer opportunities to see how well he does what you're looking for." Fullbacks are a dying breed in this offense, but Owen Schmitt benefited from West Virginia's wide splits as a pass-catcher under Rich Rodriguez and was drafted by Seattle in the fifth round.

OFFENSIVE LINE

In the spread, offensive linemen often operate out of a preset, two-point stance. This limits the ability to come out of a base stance and explode into a defender. "You don't see a lot of drive blocking from the O-linemen. You see a lot of finesse because of the position," McCloughan said. In addition, the splits between linemen are wider in the spread, which works against college defenses set on their heels with the threat of misdirection. Against NFL teams with elite speed rushers, not so much.

Perhaps the primary indicator of this trend and how it's affected the draft-readiness of linemen is the advantage that blockers have in pro-style offenses. And when McCloughan mentioned that it's a relief to see a team such as USC, this was a big part of what he was talking about. When asked how much the spread has debited elite linemen, Cosell's non-answer was an answer in itself: There aren't many elite linemen in a spread.

"You know, in watching college tape, I don't think it affected line play that dramatically," he said. "I watched all the tackles in the 2008 class, all the guards, and three centers. I didn't get the sense that the linemen I was watching were any different than the linemen I'd watched in previous years in terms of style of play.

"(Michigan's) Jake Long played in a pro-style offense. (Boston College's Gosder) Cherilus: pro-style. (Vanderbilt's) Chris Williams played in a hybrid—there are some concerns there. With tackles, they still look more for pass blocking, which then becomes more a function of your movement skills and your feet. Still, you have to have a certain level of toughness. [Current Jets and former Virginia tackle] D'Brickashaw Ferguson has played two years in the NFL, and he's not very good, and he was the fourth overall pick in the [2006] draft. One reason he's not very good is that he lacks a certain physicality and toughness. No matter how quick you are in the NFL, you still have to drive-block and play with some power."

DEFENSE

How are defenses affected by playing against the spread, and what are the differences in personnel? Speed is at a premium at every position. Smaller, faster linebackers who can react to the splits and the quickness of the game will succeed in college. When they get to the NFL, and they have to shift through traffic in more complicated defenses, things get problematic. A player like Colorado's Jordon Dizon, he of the 463 career tackles and six foot, 230-pound frame, could make a dent in a defense such as the Cover-2 espoused by the Detroit Lions, who took him in the second round.

Secondaries who play three- and four-deep against the spread are, according to Cosell, emblematic of a larger issue. "You rarely see corners play press coverage in college because press is all about technique. A lot of the corners drafted this year—and everybody talked about what a great class it was—are poor in their fundamentals. That can be taught, but most college corners are 'off corners.' They play six, seven yards off the receiver. That's less a function of the spread offense than it is the fact that corners aren't taught anything in college. You get 20 hours a week, and they don't teach corners technique. So in college, you're watching corners playing as athletes."

LOST IN TRANSLATION

Given the problems presented by the spread offense and the transition to the NFL, should thought be given to decreasing the number of spread teams and getting things more in line with NFL-style offenses? According to Cosell and Marino, that's not going to happen because there are two types of college players: the pro-style players who go to the pro-style offenses and the ones for whom the NCAA is the end of the road.

"No, because there are always going to be Pat Whites," Cosell said, when asked if teams would benefit from a change in philosophy. "There are always going to be six-foot, 190-pound guys who are phenomenal athletes and want to play quarterback in college. A lot of the kids who play other positions in the NFL played quarterback in college. But if you're a six foot four, 220-pound kid who can throw the ball, you're not going to go to Michigan [formerly one of the bastions of the pro-style offense] and play for Rich Rodriguez. And he's not going to be recruiting that kid. He's going to be recruiting Pat White!

"So, I don't think it will go away, but I do think that players who believe they have NFL futures at quarterback are going to go to pro-style offenses. When Rodriguez went to Michigan, Ryan Mallett, who was at Michigan last year and was a big recruit, transferred to Arkansas and Bobby Petrino because he wants to be a pro quarterback. Whether he is or not, time will tell."

Marino says that if the NFL is looking at the NCAA as an ad hoc minor league and complaining about an evaluation gap, they're barking up the wrong tree. "It's a small price to pay for what the NFL is getting for free," he said. "They have a 600-team minor league, and they don't pay a penny for it. That's a small consequence. Major League Baseball teams have five and six minor league teams, and instructional leagues, and winter ball . . . teams spend millions and millions of dollars on player development, and they have 40-50 scouts per team. They have 100 players, and they know that only 10 of them are prospects. The rest are just there to play games, so the NFL's got it pretty good."

In the end, the question is less about whether the evaluation gap can be reduced than it is about how best to bridge it. In taking certain aspects of the spread offense and adding them to their traditional and successful offenses, teams such as the Packers and Patriots are ahead of the curve and can more easily transition players from a system that doesn't seem to fit. Making the right fits happen is what player evaluation is all about. Seeing things that others don't see is what *great* player evaluation is all about.

Five Seconds Can Be a Lifetime

Bill Barnwell

The Combine is the NFL's version of the SAT, a test designed to take similarly experienced people from across the country and measure their abilities on a level playing field. Much like the SAT, an applicant's Combine numbers can be a valuable tool in determining his viability at the next level, but at the same time, using a SAT score as the ultimate measure of a student's intelligence is obviously foolhardy. Zach Morris's 1530 on the SAT comes to mind.

It's the job of scouts, player personnel mavens, and draftniks to analyze those Combine numbers in concert with college performance to determine a player's value. This analysis process involves projecting the tools on display at the Combine into skills that the players themselves may not have, often by comparing the athlete in question to an NFL player who had the same strengths or weaknesses when entering the NFL. This allows the "40 times don't matter" camp to set up a base in the corner of Jerry Rice, ignoring that Rice was the exception to a rule; in reality, if 40 times didn't matter at all, NFL scouts would be drafting wideouts who ran 4.8 40s in the first round. Rice proved that it's possible to succeed without a great 40, just like you can start a billion-dollar company as a college dropout. That doesn't mean every dude working at Safeway after he graduates high school will turn into Bill Gates.

David Lewin's Lewin Career Forecast, which made its debut in *Pro Football Prospectus 2006*, was the first real attempt to analyze the tools and statistics available to NFL general managers coming out of the draft. Its findings were remarkably accurate and yet incredibly simple: The only two factors that really matter for a quarterback taken in the first two rounds of the NFL Draft when predicting future performance are completion percentage and games started. That's it.

With quarterback success so remarkably predictable with only two metrics, it follows that we might be able to do the same with running backs using a similar analysis. The benefit to projecting skill-position players is that we have metrics such as yards, DVOA, and DYAR to determine what success is; with other positions, we're left to metrics that have too much noise in their data to delineate positional value, or we're forced to use measurements such as games started that aren't able to truly account for performance.

For running backs, we took every runner who entered the NFL Draft from 1999 through 2007 and gathered as much predraft data as we could. For most players, that consists of their Combine data, although Pro Day data was gathered for as many players as we could find. We did not mix and match this data because of the inherent differences between a Combine performance and a Pro Day performance, as evidenced by the laments of Malcolm Kelly this offseason. Just like we wouldn't compare the performance of two students who took two different SAT prep tests, the fact that the context is different eliminates our ability to reliably compare the two.

Not everyone performs in every event at the Combine. Although players projected to be late-round picks often perform every drill to give teams a reason to notice and draft them, players with huge reputations skip out on Combine events that they might be weak in to avoid giving teams a reason to push them down their board. The percentage of players available who performed in each of the drills available to them at the Combine is listed in Table 1.

Table 1. Combine Participation, 1999-2007

Drill	Participation
40-Yard Dash	87.6%
20-Yard Dash	62.1%
10-Yard Dash	62.1%
Bench Press (225 lb.)	57.4%
Vertical Jump	62.9%
Broad Jump	54.4%
Shuttle	45.6%
Three-Cone Drill	46.8%
Wonderlic Test	55.6%

Because our college stats database currently goes back to 1999 through 2007, we have only partial data for players drafted through 2001. As a result, any attempts to project the professional performance of running backs using collegiate statistics is strictly preliminary right now. Even with that in mind, there's little significance to be found with college statistics up to this point.

We compared the Combine data to three metrics of NFL performance, measured three ways. Those metrics are carries, rushing yards, and DYAR, each measured as a standard average for each season that the player participated on the NFL level, a sum for his career performance, and the method we're going to use primarily in this essay, which is a modified average that measures the total carries, yards, or DYAR accrued by the player divided by the number of years since he was drafted. The result is an average that penalizes players who have missed years due to injury or are otherwise out of the league, while rewarding players who have stuck around. It also provides us a fair basis for comparing players from 1999 with players from 2006, which is necessary considering the relatively small player pool we're working with.

Consider the careers of Edgerrin James and Ricky Williams. Before the 2007 season, James had averaged 1,298 yards per season; Williams, 1,213. The issue is that James

Table 2. Combine Correlations

Drill	Modified Avg		
	DYAR	Yards	Carries
40-Yard Dash	-.34	-.35	-.35
20-Yard Dash	-.23	-.28	-.26
10-Yard Dash	-.33	-.29	-.28
Bench Press	-.02	.04	.02
Vertical Jump	.24	.29	.30
Broad Jump	.14	.23	.19
Shuttle	.30	.19	.13
Three-Cone Drill	.00	.01	.01
Wonderlic Test	.06	.01	.00
Height	.13	.17	.19
Weight	.10	.20	.20
BMI	.01	.11	.09
40-Yard Speed Score	.37	.46	.46

lost a half-season to injury, which artificially lowers his score some, while Williams's missed seasons are ignored. Because James participated in every one of the seasons, his modified average remained 1,298 yards, but Williams's average dropped down all the way to 911 yards. The latter is much more indicative of the value they've provided to their teams since their selection, which is what we're trying to measure here.

Comparing the Combine numbers for all relevant players to their pro success as defined by their modified averages in each of the three statistics mentioned reveals that some Combine drills are significantly more important than others, at least for running backs (Table 2). Immediately, we can throw out a running back's bench press, broad jump, three-cone drill, and Wonderlic test as signs of his NFL viability. In addition, during this time period, neither height nor weight nor BMI seems to bear a relationship to NFL success by itself. The 20-yard dash, 10-yard dash, and shuttle drills bear at least a somewhat anecdotal relationship with NFL success but aren't enough by themselves to say much.

Although the vertical jump offers a decent correlation to NFL success, the simplest raw metric that bears a strong connection to performance is the 40-yard dash. Some selection bias is inherently built in because players who run fast 40-yard dashes are more likely to be noticed (such as Chris Johnson), but across all draft grades and rounds, the 40-yard dash reigns supreme among raw metrics.

The reason that's *raw metrics* and not all metrics is because of a new metric we put together while conducting our research, one that bears more resemblance to NFL success than any other. This metric is a complicated equation that remains simply elegant and sits on an easy-to-understand scale. Please welcome our new friend, the Speed Score.

Table 3 compares the measurable data for two running backs taken in back-to-back years during the first round of the NFL Draft. Player A played in a big college conference on a prominent team, and Player B played at a midmajor Division I school. Player A had a middle-of-the-first-round grade, and Player B was considered an upper first-round

pick. Their measurables are eerily similar, with Player A having the slightest of edges except for one facet: his weight. That's factored into the calculation of the two players' Speed Scores.

Table 3. First-Round Mystery Backs

	Height (in)	40 Time	20 Time	10 Time	BP	Wonderlic	Weight	Speed
Player A	70.5	4.44	2.59	1.53	18	21	193	99.3
Player B	70.2	4.46	2.59	1.54	18	13	221	111.7

Player A is Trung Canidate, a player who wasn't fast enough to run away from linebackers in the pros or big enough to break tackles and stay healthy. Player B is LaDainian Tomlinson, who does all that and sits on the bench in the playoffs, too.

What Speed Score does is more accurately reflect how a player's 40 time comes into play in reality. It increases the importance of each hundredth of a second while adjusting the value to account for the frame that is being pushed through those steps. The result is a formula that, in less than five seconds, can give a reasonable assumption about a running back's value on the NFL level. The formula is

$$\frac{(WEIGHT * 200)}{(40\ TIME)^4}$$

Although dividing weight by 40 time is intuitive, the weights and exponents used may seem strange. First, the 40 time is raised to the fourth power to more accurately reflect the huge difference between a 4.30 dash and a 4.50. Without any weighting of the numbers, the difference between the two is only 4 percent. Raising it to the fourth power increases the difference to a much more accurate (in NFL terms) 16 percent. The player's weight, meanwhile, is multiplied by 200 to make the number more palatable as a simple figure. The average Speed Score for all running backs who ran at the Combine is 98.5, while the average Speed Score for all drafted running backs is 102.5. As a quick-and-dirty rule, an average Speed Score of 100 is safe.

Despite the fact that Speed Score enjoys a stronger correlation with NFL success than a player's 40-yard dash or any other statistic or measurable, taking it as a foolproof indicator of NFL success is incorrect for a variety of reasons. First, there is a built-in selection bias: Teams draft fast, big players more than they do slow, small ones. This is mitigated by the fact that late-round picks with very good Speed Scores tend to have longer NFL careers and enjoy more success than those with mediocre ones.

That also explains one of the ways a back's Speed Score is different from the Lewin Career Forecast. Although the quarterback projections in our system are only accurate for players taken in the first two rounds, the Speed Score can be considered for players on all levels. On the other hand, the Speed Score is nowhere near as authoritative a figure as the projections of the Lewin Career Forecast. Players with high Speed Scores should not necessarily be marked above players with lower Speed Scores. Instead, the scores should be

Table 4. Speed Score Hits and Misses

Year	Speed Score Approved	Speed Score Disapproved
1999	Edgerrin James (117.4)	Kevin Faulk (94.0)
	Ricky Williams (112.9)	Joe Montgomery (98.8)
		Mike Cloud (92.5)
		J. J. Johnson (92.3)
		Olandis Gary (87.8)
		Amos Zereoue (96.4)
2000		Trung Canidate (99.3)
		Reuben Droughns (95.2)
2001	LaDainian Tomlinson (111.7)	Travis Henry (98.8)
	Deuce McAllister (117.4)	James Jackson (98.0)
	Michael Bennett (112.5)	
	LaMont Jordan (107.4)	
	Kevan Barlow (108.7)	
	Rudi Johnson (104.1)	
	Correll Buckhalter (107.3)	
	Derrick Blaylock (107.4)	
2002	Rock Cartwright (118.7)	DeShaun Foster (101.8)
	Josh Scobey (114.2)	William Green (98.7)
		Maurice Morris (98.8)
		Lamar Gordon (99.9)
		Brian Westbrook (91.7)
		Chester Taylor (96.8)
2003	Willis McGahee (113.7)	Domanick Williams (96.8)
	Chris Brown (111.2)	Quentin Griffin (96.8)
	Musa Smith (118.3)	Artose Pinner (95.5)
	Justin Fargas (122.2)	
	Earnest Graham (109.7)	
2004	Steven Jackson (117.8)	Chris Perry (102.7)
	Kevin Jones (123.4)	Mewelde Moore (89.4)
	Greg Jones (116.2)	Cedric Cobbs (87.6)
	Michael Turner (116.6)	
	Tatum Bell (116.3)	
2005	Ronnie Brown (121.0)	Darren Sproles (93.7)
	J. J. Arrington (114.2)	Maurice Clarett (89.7)
	Brandon Jacobs (123.5)	Alvin Pearman (90.5)
	Eric Shelton (116.8)	
	Ryan Grant (111.7)	
2006	Joseph Addai (114.2)	Brian Calhoun (92.2)
	Maurice Jones-Drew (111.5)	P. J. Daniels (92.3)
	Jerious Norwood (112.0)	
	Leon Washington (105.3)	
2007	Adrian Peterson (115.8)	Lorenzo Booker (96.5)
	Chris Henry (122.7)	Brandon Jackson (98.9)
	DeShawn Wynn (116.2)	Ahmad Bradshaw (92.9)
	Kolby Smith (107.3)	

but the versatility of his skillset made him attractive to the Eagles in the third round. Westbrook's 40 wasn't indicative of his actual speed, and although he is not a blazer in the open field, he is an elite receiver out of the backfield, an agile, intelligent runner, and an excellent blocker, which mitigate any concerns about his velocity. Just like Jerry Rice, though, the fact that one Brian Westbrook exists doesn't mean that any running back who runs a slow 40 is unfairly slagged off.

If we go year by year and look at the prominent running backs selected and what Speed Score thought of them, more often than not the Speed Score gets them right. Remember that a Speed Score of 105 in the fourth round is slightly more impressive than the same score in the first round, so players with similar scores might show up on either side of the equation.

The perception that the 2008 draft presented an elite crop of running backs is borne out in the Speed Scores of the players involved. The draft contained four of the top 24 Speed Scores of the past ten years, all of which belong to players selected in the first round (Table 5).

Table 5. Speed Scores for Class of 2008 Running Backs

Player	College	Speed Score	NFL Team	Round
Darren McFadden	Arkansas	120.0	OAK	1
Jonathan Stewart	Oregon	116.7	CAR	1
Felix Jones	Arkansas	103.7	DAL	1
Rashard Mendenhall	Illinois	114.8	PIT	1
Chris Johnson	East Carolina	121.9	TEN	1
Matt Forte	Tulane	109.7	CHI	2
Ray Rice	Rutgers	99.7	BAL	2
Kevin Smith	Central Florida	98.6	DET	3
Jamaal Charles	Texas	108.7	KC	3
Steve Slaton	West Virginia	96.9	HOU	3
Tashard Choice	Georgia Tech	104.9	DAL	4
Jalen Parmele	Toledo	112.2	MIA	6
Xavier Omon	NW Missouri St.	101.0	BUF	6
Mike Hart	Michigan	85.2	IND	6

The best Speed Score of the draft, and seventh-highest of the last 10 years, belongs to Titans first-round pick **Chris Johnson** (121.9), who could find himself moving to wide receiver in the long term when you consider how poor the Titans' wideouts are. Right behind him was **Darren McFadden** (120.0), who will be a better back than Johnson, but will need his line to improve to put up the numbers that people might be expecting from him out of the gate. **Jonathan Stewart** (116.7) could very well end up being the draft's best back; not only did he have an excellent Speed Score, but he had the best vertical of any running back in the draft and did so on a turf toe injury that forced him to have surgery two weeks after the Combine. He also played in the Pac-10, which tends to produce underrated backs. **Rashard Mendenhall** (114.8) will have to split time with Willie Parker, and he played in a college conference (the Big Ten) that tends to produce overrated backs by virtue of the number of attempts they get, but Mendenhall should be an above-average back for the next several seasons.

taken in context and used as truer markers of speed and NFL viability than other raw measurables. With a five-second timespan on a given day, it's also possible that a player could be hurt, slip, or otherwise simply run a slow 40.

A good example is Brian Westbrook, whose 91.71 is the lowest Speed Score a successful running back has produced since 1999. Westbrook ran a 4.58 40 at the Combine in 2001,

One player who didn't produce a high Speed Score was **Felix Jones** (103.7), whose 4.47 40 was too slow for a runner of his size. He also didn't run at his Pro Day and is coming out of a trick offense in college. Both **Ray Rice** (99.7) and **Kevin Smith** (98.6) have slow 40s compounded by overuse in college, and no back has ever succeeded with a Speed Score as slow as **Mike Hart**'s (85.2). If you are looking for a Speed Score-approved sleeper, sixth-rounder **Jalen Parmele** (112.2) is playing behind two veterans, one coming off an ACL tear and the other prone to taking unexpected "vacations."

Although Speed Score isn't a quick-and-dirty measure of the viability of NFL running backs, it provides an insight into that viability that surpasses any other metric or measurable on draft day. With the availability of predicative data for quarterbacks and running backs, it stands to reason that similar information exists for all positions. As access to data grows and ventures such as the Football Outsiders game charting project continue to gather new information about the game, the horizon looms with the possibility of someday improving draft accuracy by combining scouting and character study with quantitative analysis of every single young player.

Wide Receivers: Size Matters

by Rob Pitzer

Wide receivers are like the dogs of the football world—they come in all shapes and sizes. While most positions have fairly small ranges between the minimum and maximum heights required to be successful, wide receivers span a much larger gamut. Put simply, you can be short, tall or anywhere in between and still catch a football. The modern NFL passing game developed to take advantage of this fact by developing specialized roles for receivers with radically different body types. Need a slot receiver who can attack the seam and force the safety to stay in the middle of the field? You're probably talking about a small, quick player around 5-foot-8, 5-foot-9. Looking for a red zone specialist to run fades and fade stops in the corner of the end zone? You'll want a guy who is 6-foot-3 or taller to go up and get the ball at its highest point. Are you running a West Coast Offense that relies on the receiver to generate yards after the catch? Sign a few receivers with the bulk to stand up to contact over the middle and the athleticism to turn short passes into long gains.

And yet despite all the specialization, teams haven't gotten any better at gauging which college receivers are most likely to succeed at the next level. No other position has such a low rate of return in the first round. Busts like Charles Rogers, David Terrell, Peter Warrick, and Mike Williams litter the top end of the draft, and there aren't nearly enough hits like Torry Holt or Andre Johnson to even out the ledger. With so many different kinds of receivers to choose from, is there some way that teams can separate the future stars from the future busts? As it turns out, yes there is.

For the purposes of this study, I looked only at the NFL Draft Combine data for the years 1998-2007. Based on cursory analysis, there is no reason to believe the results do not extend backwards beyond 1998. Additionally, the measure of a receiver's success in the NFL here is based on career yards per game, not the advanced Football Outsiders stats like DYAR or DVOA. However, the results are so clear-cut that it's unlikely any valid measure of receiver performance would change the central finding much.

The original data set for the research included only basic information such as draft position, collegiate division, height, and weight. The initial analysis produced minimal results. Draft position, while imperfect, was somewhat predictive of a player's career performance. Wide receivers under 180 pounds (the "Pinkston Line") virtually never panned out. These were all very general findings, and not especially useful in categorizing the vast majority of receivers chosen each year.

However, despite differences in height and weight, Randy Moss, Chad Johnson, and Marvin Harrison have something in common physically. Likewise, Larry Fitzgerald, Anquan Boldin, and Hines Ward share some physical characteristic. That characteristic is body mass index, or BMI.

BMI measures a person's density, incorporating both height and weight into a single number. Even though Moss is a few inches taller than Johnson or Harrison, all three players are slightly built relative to other receivers, with BMIs of approximately 25 or 26. On the other hand, Fitzgerald, Boldin, and Ward are all a bit thicker than their peers, with BMIs between 28 and 29.

These thickly-built players clearly outperform their peers once we account for draft position. Ward, Darrell Jackson, Chris Chambers, and Anquan Boldin were not second- and third-round flukes; they were thickly built wide receivers who had a statistically meaningful advantage.

What about the average wide receiver, who has a BMI between 26 and 28? Something else is needed in order to separate first-round busts such as Troy Williamson, David Terrell, and Travis Taylor from stars such as Steve Smith, Plaxico Burress, and Torry Holt. That second ingredient is height. The successful receivers with BMI closer to average are nearly all either shorter than six feet, or taller than 6-foot-2. Williamson, Terrell, and Taylor fall in between those bounds. Clearly, certain body types work better than others for NFL receivers.

Table 1 lists the top 25 wide receivers drafted from 1998 through 2007, according to receiving yards per game played. No adjustments have been made to account for years in the league, quarterback quality, or other factors.

When we look at a visual grid made up of the height and BMI ranges of these 25 players—with height measured to tenths of an inch and BMI measured to tenths of a unit—we get clear and unequivocal results (Figure 1).

Starting with the left-hand box and moving clockwise, the four boxes are labeled Slight (average height, low BMI), Short (short, average BMI), Thick (average height, high BMI) and Tall (tall, average BMI). The box outlines are the smallest possible perimeter that incorporates all the receivers within each category. The outlines should be considered slightly "fuzzy"—after all, we are separating receivers by very small units, and there's always the possibility that a wide receiver will fall on one side of a line or the other based on how much breakfast he ate that morning, or what company manufactured the scale. In addition, while these boxes are very good approximations of the four body types that are a prerequisite for elite success in NFL wide receivers, they are not definitive. The Slight box in particular is still subject to revision.

Only 63 of the approximately 165 receivers drafted in the first four rounds of this ten-year period have a height/BMI

Table 1. Top 25 Wide Receivers Drafted 1998-2007 in Yards per Game

Player	Yd/G	Height	Weight	BMI	WR Group
Torry Holt	83.5	72.2	190	25.6	Slight
Anquan Boldin	80.3	72.5	217	29.0	Thick
Randy Moss	79.2	75.3	210	26.0	Slight
Chad Johnson	77.5	73.0	192	25.3	Slight
Larry Fitzgerald	75.7	74.7	226	28.5	Thick
Marques Colston	74.7	76.5	231	27.8	Tall
Andre Johnson	68.6	74.0	222	28.5	Thick
Roy Williams	66.4	74.4	211	26.8	Tall
Steve Smith	64.4	69.0	185	27.3	Short
Reggie Wayne	64.1	72.0	198	26.9	Short
Braylon Edwards	63.9	74.7	215	27.1	Tall
Plaxico Burress	63.2	77.3	232	27.3	Tall
David Boston	62.7	73.2	240*	31.5	Thick/Other
Darrell Jackson	62.5	71.6	206	28.3	Thick
Dwayne Bowe	62.2	74.2	221	28.2	Thick
Santonio Holmes	60.9	70.5	189	26.7	Short
Laveranues Coles	60.4	71.2	193	26.8	Short
Lee Evans	58.2	70.7	197	27.7	Short
Santana Moss	57.9	69.5	200**	29.1	Short/Other
Greg Jennings	57.5	71.1	197	27.4	Short
Chris Chambers	56.8	71.5	210	28.9	Thick
Hines Ward	56.7	71.5	205	28.2	Thick
Donald Driver	54.5	72.2	190	25.6	Slight
T.J. Houshmandzadeh	54.2	73.2	199	26.1	Slight
Javon Walker	53.0	74.6	215	27.2	Tall

* Final playing weight; drafted at 215 pounds.
** Current playing weight; drafted at 181 pounds.

combination that places them in one of these categories. However, 23 of the 25 top receivers in this group (as measured by yardage per game) fit into one of these categories, with Santana Moss and David Boston being the exceptions (for the moment). The odds that 23 of the top 25 receivers would come from these areas by random chance are roughly 36 million to one. Using other metrics than receiving yards per game may change the results slightly, but the central finding remains unchanged: Elite wide receivers come from relatively small intersections of height and BMI.

Fourteen of the 46 first-round receivers chosen between 1998 and 2007 (30 percent) are among the 25 receivers with the most yards per game. By comparison, there have been 63 wide receivers drafted in the first four rounds who played at a height/BMI combination that put them inside one of the "good" boxes and 20 of those 63 receivers (32 percent) appear on our top 25 list. Three of the other five players on our list fit in the boxes, but were drafted in the seventh round: Marques Colston, Donald Driver, and T. J. Houshmandzadeh. The final two players, Moss and Boston, spent their best seasons at an ideal size, but no longer qualify due to weight variation. In short, a receiver's build is more predictive of NFL success than first-round draft status.

Obviously, not every single good wide receiver is going to fall within these four specific categories. Two other sections on the graph in particular seem to produce a fair number of

useful, but not elite, receivers: the area to the left of the Slight category (players with BMI below 25, including Bernard Berrian) and the top right section of the chart (above the Thick category, where shorter route technicians like Deion Branch and Troy Brown reside).

Why does a certain body build provide some receivers with an objective advantage? One possibility has to do with the incredibly narrow margins that NFL passing games are built on—and the frequently-discussed concepts of "separation" and a receiver "using his body" to create space for the quarterback. Perhaps our height/BMI combinations are a quantitative measure of which players have the ability to get separation from cornerbacks (for Slight and Short players), or provide a larger target for his quarterback and shield a defender from the ball (for Thick and Tall receivers). One obvious area for further research would be to look at the height and weight of NFL defensive backs; it is possible they do not share any of the four "ideal" receiver builds, and that those receivers with elite body types have a natural physical advantage as a result.

The most important secondary finding is that drafted receivers must be at their natural playing weight when evaluated, and teams must put a premium on finding ideally built wide receivers who are disciplined enough to maintain their body weight once they enter the NFL. Since height doesn't change, the only thing that can move a player away from an ideal build is weight change. Some notable first-round busts, such as Mike Williams and Charles Rogers, entered the league with ideal builds, but lost them almost immediately.

On the other side of the coin, some receivers, such as Braylon Edwards and Germane Crowell, entered the league without ideal builds, but grew into them by adding a few pounds. This is where Santana Moss becomes an interesting study. The 5-foot-9 Moss entered the league at 181 pounds, which is less than the ideal weight for his height. However, during his first seven years in the league he added 19 pounds, and his current playing weight is listed as 200 pounds.

Access to year-by-year weights for NFL players is not readily available, but it would be an interesting exercise to link Moss's career path and weight as he moved into and then back out of his ideal weight range in the Short box. Based on the analysis above, there's a good argument to be made that Moss's most successful seasons were a result of acquiring an ideal body type, which he has since lost. Could the Redskins have saved a second-round pick in this year's draft by having Moss lose 15 pounds instead?

The possibility of weight change will always make drafting receivers something of a crapshoot. Even with perfect knowledge at the time of the draft, it will be difficult to predict which players will end up at a playing weight that leaves them with a less than ideal build. David Boston, the other player in the top 25 who hasn't spent his entire career inside one of the four boxes, is a good example; Boston came into the league with a BMI of 28.2, on the left edge of the "Thick"

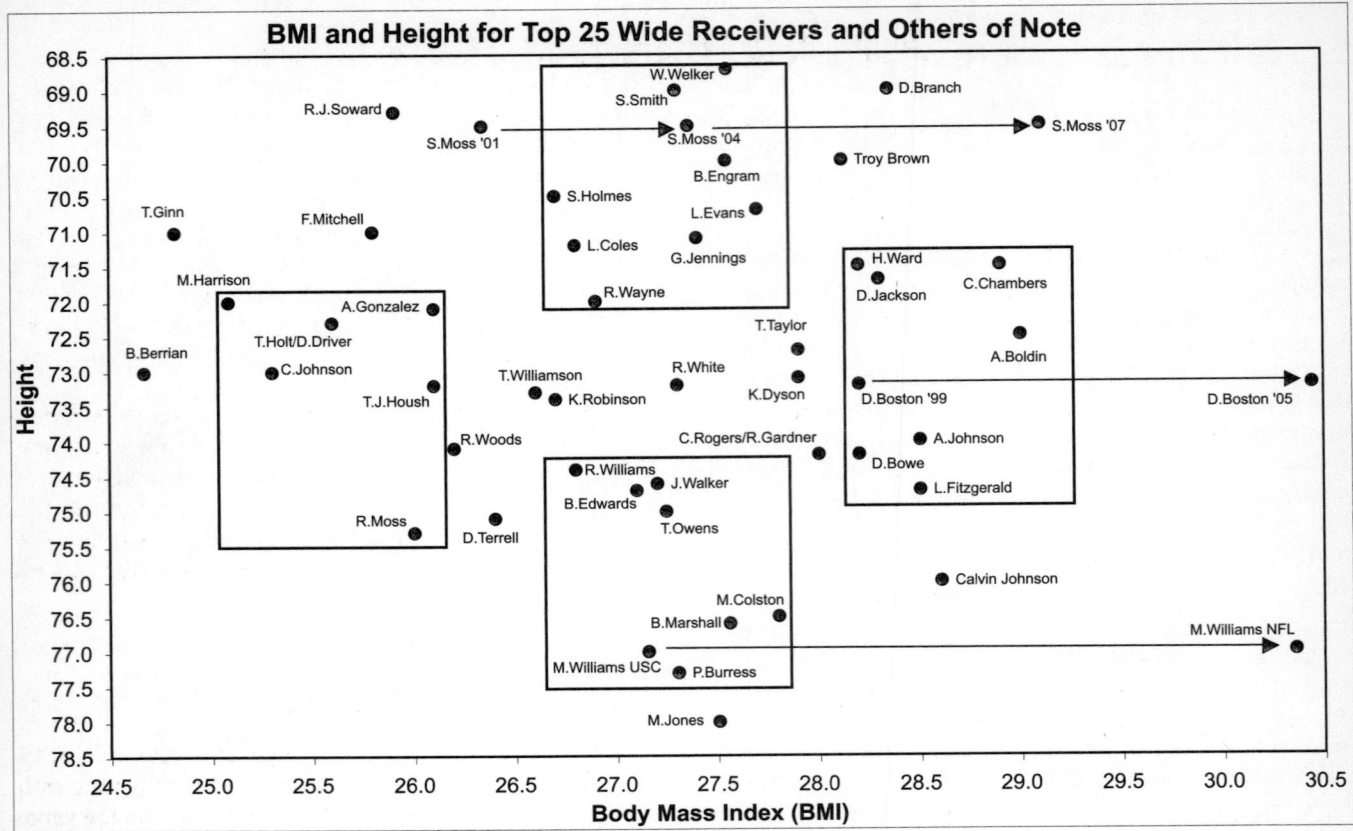

BMI and Height for Top 25 Wide Receivers and Others of Note

body type. Gradually, through what we might call "questionable nutritional choices," Boston bulked up to 240 pounds, growing his way out of the right side of the "Thick" box and out of the NFL as well.

Of the 44 players who had an ideal build at the time of the Combine, 12 subsequently lost it by changing weight. And of the 63 players who ended up with an ideal playing build, roughly half arrived there after the Combine. This would be another excellent area for further research—finding the predictors for players who can maintain their weight or who can change weights enough to achieve an ideal playing build.

Not every receiver can change weight and maintain his basic skill at running and catching, but almost all players who do not fit into these boxes would be better served to change weight and move to an ideal build if possible. It

seems fairly clear that *on average* receivers who change weight and move into an ideal build have dramatically longer and more productive careers as a result, doing so.

Finally, it is important to realize that having the right build is a necessary, but *not sufficient* requirement to become an elite receiver in the NFL. Roughly one-half of all wide receivers who have an ideal height/BMI combination and are drafted in the first four rounds still do not pan out. Some of these players are no doubt subjectively misevaluated in terms of their ability to run and catch. Some play behind more talented receivers. Some get injured, or play for teams with horrible passing games. But no elite receiver in the last ten years has fallen outside of the Four Boxes—Slight, Short, Thick, and Tall—and teams that ignore a receiver's body build do so at their peril.

Top 25 Prospects

Aaron Schatz

Since the early days of *Pro Football Prospectus*, one of the most common questions from readers has been, "Why doesn't *Pro Football Prospectus* write about up-and-coming prospects, the way *Baseball Prospectus* does?"

The answer is obvious, when you think about it. The men who will be NFL stars in 2010 are not hidden away in the Florida State League, playing every night to 2,000 fans. You can see them every Saturday on regional or national television, playing big-time college football. Hundreds of websites are devoted to these players: sites with mock NFL drafts for three years hence, sites for fans of each individual college, even sites that follow the high school recruiting process. You don't need *Pro Football Prospectus* to tell you that James Laurinaitis has good instincts.

On the other hand, what happens to these college stars after draft day? If they don't start immediately, players who started every game in the ACC or Big Ten disappear as role players on NFL rosters. Hardcore fans know every player on their favorite team but not necessarily every player around the league. Meanwhile, the obsessive subculture of NFL draftniks has moved on to the next crop of 21-year-olds.

That's the gap we wanted to fill with our first-ever top prospects list in *Pro Football Prospectus* 2007. We tried to identify 25 young, up-and-coming players who were already in the NFL but had not yet reached stardom or even the starting lineup. Some of the players were already well-known and continued their growth in 2007, primarily the backup running backs: Marion Barber, Brandon Jacobs, and Michael Turner. However, we also spotted Bengals tackle Stacy Andrews, who had only three career starts before 2007 but is now important enough to Cincinnati that they put the franchise tag on him this offseason; Cortland Finnegan, a little-known seventh-round pick who became a starting cornerback for the league-leading defense in Tennessee; and Leonard Weaver, who became the starting fullback in Seattle when Mack Strong retired.

That's not to say that all our picks were perfect. Anybody know what Junior Glymph is doing these days?

To be considered for our top prospects list, players have to meet the following criteria:

- Drafted or signed between 2005 and 2007
- Drafted in rounds three through seven, or undrafted
- Less than five career games started
- Still on a free agent contract or their original contract

The last rule is new for this year's list, and you can think of it as the "Marion Barber rule." Even though Barber made the Pro Bowl, he has only three career regular-season starts.

The fact that the Cowboys were weirdly addicted to starting Julius Jones doesn't make Barber a prospect. Both Barber and Justin Tuck have already fulfilled a large part of their potential and have been handsomely rewarded for it. Thus, they are no longer prospects.

However, our top prospect for 2008 has yet to be handsomely rewarded for his amazing performance in his first two seasons. In fact, his team went out and spent a bunch of money on a similar, older player, which keeps him second on the depth chart. For the second straight year, the *Pro Football Prospectus* top 25 prospects list urges the Atlanta Falcons to free Jerious Norwood!

1. Jerious Norwood, RB, Falcons

A third-round draft pick in 2006, Norwood put up a 6.0 yards per carry average in 2007 behind the NFL's worst run-blocking line. He has now led all running backs with at least 99 carries in DVOA for two straight seasons. Splitting time with new back Michael Turner could have Norwood on the verge of a breakout season, but how much splitting will there be? We don't think they gave Turner that money to run the ball just 160 times. Norwood is small (six feet, 205 pounds), so perhaps he couldn't handle a 300-carry load on his own. However, as we point out in the Atlanta chapter, Turner didn't do anything in San Diego that Norwood didn't do himself—and better—in Atlanta over the last two years. If the Falcons don't give Norwood an equal share of the carries, they are making a huge mistake.

2. Jason Hatcher, DE, Dallas

A valuable backup in Dallas's defensive end rotation, this 2006 third-rounder out of Grambling is an intelligent player who simply overpowers offensive linemen with an explosive first step. At 295 pounds, Hatcher could also move inside with a little more bulk, which is exactly what was rumored around draft time. In a part-time role, Hatcher had seven quarterback hurries and four quarterback hits. Starters Chris Canty and Marcus Spears had six hurries and three hits *combined*. Once he's mastered more in the way of technique, Hatcher will take Spears's place in the starting lineup. If it doesn't happen this season, the Cowboys will let Spears go elsewhere when his contract ends and hand Hatcher the job in 2009.

3. Brandon McDonald, CB, Browns

For three years now, we've been doling out Leigh Bodden man-love in our Cleveland chapters, but it was the presence of young talent like Brandon McDonald that gave general manager Phil Savage the confidence to trade Bodden away to Detroit. McDonald's 67 percent Success Rate and 5.8 adjusted yards allowed per pass both led the Browns last year. In fact, among players with at least 20 charted passes, only eight allowed fewer yards per pass and only two, Brian McFadden of Pittsburgh and Joselio Hanson of Philadelphia, had a higher Success Rate. The highlight of McDonald's season may have been his Week 12 performance, when he had three passes defensed and picked off a pass to Andre Johnson to help preserve a fourth-quarter lead.

4. Tarell Brown, CB, 49ers

Last year's fifth-round pick spent a year learning the system and should have the edge over rookie Reggie Smith and veteran Shawntae Spencer for the nickel spot. At some point, Walt Harris will wake up and realize he is 34 years old, and Brown may be the heir apparent. Brown is athletic, with speed and good ball skills. He has the strength to jam receivers at the line and to make an open field tackle in run support. Brown fell in the draft because of a broken foot that hobbled him during his senior year at Texas and because of character concerns—he was suspended for the Ohio State game because of a handgun incident at the beginning of the season. The 49ers definitely think they got a steal.

5. Aaron Rouse, SS, Packers

Good news, NFL officials. You may not have to draw out those flags against the Green Bay Packers quite so often this year—at least, not if 2007 third-rounder Aaron Rouse can beat out Atari Bigby as the Packers starting strong safety. Rouse has the size to hit guys up in the box—he started as an outside linebacker at Virginia Tech—and he has reasonably good coverage ability despite the kind of height (six foot four) that usually creates problems with defensive backs moving their hips and changing directions. Last year's *ESPN Draft Magazine* compared Rouse to Arizona's Adrian Wilson. Oh, Packers fans, you can only dream.

6. Jerome Harrison, RB, Browns

Quick, who led the Pac-10 in rushing yardage in 2005? Well, if it was Reggie Bush, we wouldn't be writing this under the name "Jerome Harrison," would we? Harrison led all of Division I with 1,900 rushing yards in 2005 but fell to the fifth round because of size concerns (he's five foot nine, 210 pounds). Harrison gained just 60 yards in 20 carries as a rookie, but last year he made the most of the few touches he got when Cleveland gave the resurgent Jamal Lewis a breather. He had 145 yards on 23 carries for 45 DYAR and a 74 percent Success Rate, plus a few catches. As long as Lewis remains effective, Harrison is stuck in a reserve role, but he adds an extra dimension to Cleveland's ground game and the coaching staff would be wise to give him more opportunities and keep the not-so-old man (Lewis is only 29, seemingly going on 67) fresh.

7. Marques Harris, LB, Chargers

Harris is a pass-rush specialist who has turned out a lot better than the scouts expected back when Harris was at that infamous football factory, Southern Utah. The Chargers brought him in as an undrafted free agent and ended up with Shaun Phillips Lite to stick on the bench behind Shaun Phillips Classic. Last year, Harris had an 82 percent Stop Rate, plus 1.5 sacks and two hurries in limited action. The year before, he had a 74 percent Stop Rate and three sacks and became a bit of a folk hero in San Diego when he did a back flip on the field after a sack that forced a Damon Huard fumble. With more and more teams considering a 3-4 defensive scheme, don't be surprised if Harris is targeted in restricted free agency next offseason. Dolphins have been known to do the occasional back flip, right?

8. Ahmad Bradshaw, RB, Giants

Bradshaw became the back that every fan wished his team had as the playoffs went along, a scatback with enough power to break tackles but also the ability to cut back without going down like so much Shaun Alexander. Bradshaw isn't incredibly fast, but he is lightning-quick in and out of his cuts, is assertive in his gap recognition, and is a patient, instinctive runner. He still needs to work on pass protection and catching the ball out of the backfield, and he may be easily breakable if given a larger workload. For 100 carries, though, Bradshaw could be a top-10 DVOA guy.

9. Josh Beekman, G, Bears

From Tom Nalen and Pete Kendall to Dan Koppen and Chris Snee, Boston College has been one of the NFL's top sources for offensive linemen in recent years. Beekman, Chicago's new left guard, is the latest lineman to make his way off Chestnut Hill and into an NFL starting lineup. Beekman is an A-1 road grader who could become Cedric Benson's savior (or Matt Forte's best friend). However, scouts felt he had to work on pass blocking coming out of college, and there was some worry that at a little under six foot two he is a bit short for an NFL lineman.

10. Tank Tyler, DT, Chiefs

Once upon a time Tank Tyler was that guy in the film next to Mario Williams, but soon Tyler will be the guy who gets all the sacks and quarterback hurries because the offense has to double-team Glenn Dorsey. Tyler is a physical beast who shows good upfield rush for a big guy, though he can sometimes be pushed around on runs. He might still be a year away, because Alfonso Boone had a good year last year and will be hard to unseat.

11. Andy Alleman, G, Saints

Ah, now here's a prospect in the baseball sense of the word—a guy who simply isn't ready yet because he's learning something new, like when Rick Ankiel went back down to the minors to become a slugging outfielder. Drafted in the third round of the 2007 draft, Alleman started out as a defensive end at Pitt, and then transferred to Akron and was converted to guard. He's played the position for only three years and still needs time to learn proper technique, but he's a tremendous athlete. When Alleman puts it all together, his on-field mean streak and impressive work ethic will have him competing for starting time.

12. Dusty Dvoracek, DT, Bears

Dvoracek, a third-round pick in 2006, missed his entire rookie year with a foot injury but played well enough to win the starting job coming out of training camp a season later. He injured his knee in the first game of the season and was lost for the year again. He should be healthy heading into the 2008 season, and his speed will help improve the pass rush from the Chicago front four—an important factor for a defensive scheme that rarely includes the blitz. Dvoracek would be ranked higher based on talent, but as our man Will Carroll always says, "Health is a skill."

13. Brent Celek, TE, Eagles

Draft experts can put together all the big boards and top-200 lists they want, but once you get into the middle rounds of the NFL Draft, the talent differentiation becomes small enough from pick to pick that a player's ability to fit your system becomes more important. And thus did Brent Celek, a tight end born to play in the West Coast Offense, find his way from the University of Cincinnati to Andy Reid and the Philadelphia Eagles. Celek is a smart route runner with outstanding hands who opened eyes at the 2007 East-West Shrine Game. When blocking, he makes up for his lack of natural talent with competitiveness. The Eagles put the franchise tag on L. J. Smith because this year's free agent class was low on tight ends, but he's not wowing everyone with that -24.2% DVOA and 50 percent catch rate. Celek will get more time in 2008 and is in line to start in 2009.

14. Pierre Thomas, RB, Saints

Compared to the big, bold, billboard-size lettering that was teammate Rashard Mendenhall, Thomas was a footnote in eight-point font. You won't find a video on YouTube called "Pierre Thomas Ultimate Highlights." The Saints brought him in as an undrafted free agent, and he started the year fifth on the depth chart. But with the release of Antonio Pittman, Deuce McAllister's knee injury, and Reggie Bush's relative ineffectiveness as a feature back, Thomas got more and more reps as the season went on, particularly after Bush was lost for the last month with an injury. He became the first Saints player to gain 100 yards rushing and receiving in the same game in the season finale against Chicago, and his 87 DYAR ranked second in the NFL among running backs with less than 100 carries. Depending on McAllister's future, Thomas could be a big part of the Saints offense in 2008.

15. Ben Patrick, TE, Cardinals

The Arizona Cardinals have not had a lot of luck when it comes to finding tight ends this decade. They spent three years starting Freddie Jones, Jedi Master of the three-catch, eight-yard stat line. They spent 2005 with a couple of undrafted free agents who were unimpressive, Adam Bergen and Eric Edwards. In 2006 they spent a third-round pick on Leonard Pope—he's been reasonable according to DVOA, but from the lack of growth in his role in the offense, you can tell he's not impressing the Cardinals. That may open things up for last year's seventh-round pick out of Delaware to steal the starting job. Some people considered Patrick the most well-rounded tight end in the class of 2007. He is smart, runs good routes, and can block, and apparently he's over the conditioning problems that caused him to drop all the way to the end of the draft.

16. H. B. Blades, LB, Redskins

A long line of intelligent, intuitive, short linebackers far outperformed their draft position and became not just starters but Pro Bowl-caliber players: Zach Thomas, Tedy Bruschi, London Fletcher. Five-foot-ten H. B. Blades, a sixth-round pick in 2007, wants to be the latest in that line. The only problem is that Thomas, Bruschi, and Fletcher made up for their short height not only with smarts but also with athleticism. The scouts aren't sure Blades has enough of that either. What he does have is the classic throwback linebacker approach to playing defense, outstanding ball skills, and the kind of instinctive football knowledge that comes from being the son and nephew of two outstanding NFL stars of the eighties (Dad Bennie was a Lions defensive back, and uncle Brian was a Seahawks wideout).

17. Kevin Boss, TE, Giants

Boss played so well following Jeremy Shockey's broken leg that a good portion of Giants fans wanted Shockey shipped away afterwards. It is important not to overrate Boss by confusing correlation with causation. He wasn't one of the main reasons the Giants won the Super Bowl, and Shockey's the better player, particularly because of his blocking. Nonetheless, Boss has sure hands and is a sound blocker. He's not going to get much better than this, but he's going to be able to maintain this level of play for several years, and on a rookie salary, that's a bargain.

18. Troy Smith, QB, Ravens

The former Heisman Trophy winner saw action in four games at the end of the year, including starts against Seattle and Pittsburgh, and while he didn't set the world on fire, he was the only Baltimore quarterback to post a positive DVOA on the season. He has natural leadership skills and was apparently commanding attention in the Baltimore locker room before he even entered the starting lineup. With first-round pick Joe Flacco waiting in the wings, the odds are stacked against Smith in Baltimore, but if he can beat out Kyle Boller in camp and put together a few quality starts, he might hang onto the starting job all year, which could set him up for a chance with another team or at least a long NFL career as a Charlie Batch-level backup.

19. Kevin Payne, SS, Bears

This 2007 fifth-rounder made his first NFL start against the Lions and promptly broke his arm, thus ending his rookie season. Payne is big and physical, known for a strong work ethic as well as versatility—he was a tailback and wide receiver in his first couple years at Louisiana-Monroe before switching to the defensive side of the ball. Payne will battle Brandon McGowan, who struggled as Adam Archuleta's replacement last season, for Chicago's starting job at strong safety.

20. Jared Gaither, OT, Ravens

Gaither could be a stud if he could just get his act together. The guy is absolutely huge, 350 pounds and the tallest player in the NFL at six foot nine. Scout.com rated him the nation's seventh-best offensive lineman coming out of high school, and he started eight games as a true freshman at Maryland in 2005. According to Maryland coaches, he didn't allow a single sack. However, he was inconsistent as a sophomore and then had academic issues. If he had stuck around and had a strong junior year, he would have been a first- or second-round pick. Instead, with Terrapins coach Ralph Friedgen threatening to suspend him for 2007, Gaither declared for the NFL supplemental draft, and Baltimore traded in a fifth-round pick to grab him. If Adam Terry can't fill the shoes of Jonathan Ogden, Gaither might get his chance. Maybe taking over for one of the greatest left tackles to ever play the game would finally motivate Gaither to fulfill his potential.

21. James Marten, OT, Cowboys

Here's another player from Boston College, where apparently they just pump NFL-ready blockers out of an offensive line cloning machine. In the Dallas chapter, we discuss the Cowboys' absurdly good injury record, particularly along the offensive line. At some point, one of those guys is going to get hurt, and Marten is probably the man who will need to step up and fill in. A 2007 third-round pick, Marten has experience playing both guard and tackle. He's a hard worker with long arms who understands stunts and other defensive line tricks, but he struggled with speed rushers in college.

22. Courtney Taylor, WR, Seahawks

A sixth-round pick out of Auburn, Taylor runs smooth routes and has had one year to digest the Mike Holmgren West Coast playbook. He's not fast or explosive, but he's big and can use his body to shield guys away from the ball like a slow version of Randy Moss. He peaked early in college and was inconsistent as a junior and senior, which is how he fell in the draft. Still, the Seahawks desperately need one of their young wide receivers to emerge this year—Ben Obomanu looked unimpressive in limited action last year—so Taylor may see a lot of time on the field as the third option behind Bobby Engram and Nate Burleson. One warning sign: Taylor needs to bulk up to get out of the wide receiver middle area described in the essay "Size Matters."

23. David Thomas, TE, Patriots

Thomas missed the final 13 games of the season with a foot injury, but anyone who saw his sprawling, diving touchdown catch against the Jaguars in 2006 will not soon forget the soft hands and physical abilities of Vince Young's old target. Thomas will need to compete for playing time and targets in the crowded New England passing game, but as long as he doesn't walk away from the team in midseason, he should stay in the coaching staff's good graces.

24. Aundrae Allison, WR, Vikings

As Minnesota's fifth-round fifth receiver, this rookie wasn't just rawer than sushi—he was rawer than a live fish flopping around on a bed of seaweed on shore. He caught only eight passes for 122 yards last season, but he also averaged 28.7 yards per kick return, including a 104-yard touchdown. Allison has the speed to be a major deep threat, and like most of the writers of this book, he has better hands than Troy Williamson. He still needs to better learn how to run routes and read coverages, but he'll battle Robert Ferguson for the fourth receiver job behind Bernard Berrian, Bobby Wade, and Sidney Rice.

25. Mansfield Wrotto, G, Seahawks

Seahawks general manager Tim Ruskell loves to draft players whose stock falls on draft day because they are undersized. Mansfield Wrotto is not one of those players. Wrotto is six foot three and 310 pounds and was chosen with the fourth-round pick that the Seahawks acquired in the Darrell Jackson trade. He played defensive tackle for three seasons at Georgia Tech before converting to offensive lineman in his senior season, so he's sort of Andy Alleman Lite. (Actually, neither of these gentlemen could qualify as "light" anything.) Wrotto spent all of last year on the practice squad, but Mike Solari, the Seahawks new offensive line coach, excels at teaching technique.

Honorable Mention

Michael Bush, RB, Raiders
Dashon Goldson, FS, 49ers
Martrez Milner, TE, Falcons
Dante Rosario, TE, Panthers
Lyle Sendlein, C, Cardinals
Chansi Stuckey, WR, Jets
Tyler Thigpen, QB, Chiefs
Guy Whimper, OT, Giants

Statistical Appendix A: Fantasy Projections

Here are the top 215 players according to the KUBIAK projection system, ranked by projected fantasy value (**FANT**) in 2008. We've used the following generic scoring system:

- 1 point for each 10 yards rushing, 10 yards receiving, or 20 yards passing.
- 6 points for each rushing or receiving TD, 4 points for each passing TD.
- -2 points for each interception.
- 1 point for each extra point, 3 points for each field goal.
- Team defense: 2 points for a fumble recovery, interception, or safety, 1 point for a sack, and 6 points for a touchdown.

Note that fantasy totals may not exactly equal these calculations, because each touchdown projection is not necessarily a round number. (For example, a quarterback listed with 2 rushing touchdowns may actually be projected with 2.4 rushing touchdowns, which will add 14 fantasy points to the player's total rather than 12.) Fantasy value does not include adjustments for week-to-week consistency, but we have listed each player's **Risk** for 2008, based on the likelihood that the player will fail to meet his projection because of injury or decline. The risk colors are:

- Red: Standard risk
- Yellow: Less than usual risk
- Green: Least amount of risk

Players are ranked in order based on marginal value of each player, the idea that you draft based on how many more points a player will score compared to the worst starting player at that position, not how many points a player scores overall. The ranks in this table are based on a 12-team league that starts 1 QB, 2 RB, 2 WR, 1 FLEX (RB/WR), 1 TE, 1 K, and 1 DEF. The rankings also include half value for the first running back on the bench, and reduce the value of kickers and defenses to reflect the general drafting habits of fantasy football players. *Pro Football Prospectus* urges you to draft using common sense, not a strict reading of these rankings.

The final two columns list each player's value in a league that adds one point per reception (**PPR**) as well as draft value rank (**Rk**) for a 12-team PPR league.

A customizable spreadsheet featuring these projections will be available at FootballOutsiders.com for a nominal fee. This spreadsheet will include updates based on injuries and changing forecasts of playing time during the preseason, as well as a version which includes individual defensive players.

Rk	Player	Team	Bye	Pos	PaYd	PaTD	INT	Ru	RuYd	RuTD	Rec	RcYd	RcTD	XP	FG	Fant	Risk	PPR	Rk
1	LaDainian Tomlinson	SD	9	RB	0	0	0	331	1439	20	44	409	2	0	0	316	Green	360	1
2	Brian Westbrook	PHI	7	RB	0	0	0	280	1376	12	66	518	4	0	0	285	Green	351	3
3	Adrian Peterson	MIN	8	RB	0	0	0	309	1538	13	30	321	1	0	0	273	Yellow	303	6
4	Randy Moss	NE	4	WR	0	0	0	0	0	0	96	1482	18	0	0	255	Yellow	351	2
5	Steven Jackson	STL	5	RB	0	0	0	289	1246	8	65	539	2	0	0	240	Yellow	305	4
6	Marshawn Lynch	BUF	6	RB	0	0	0	330	1438	9	23	229	1	0	0	224	Yellow	248	25
7	Joseph Addai	IND	4	RB	0	0	0	287	1248	8	48	391	1	0	0	221	Green	269	13
8	Maurice Jones-Drew	JAC	7	RB	0	0	0	230	1032	11	41	426	2	0	0	222	Red	263	17
9	Earnest Graham	TB	10	RB	0	0	0	273	1230	6	47	432	2	0	0	219	Yellow	266	16
10	Tom Brady	NE	4	QB	4415	37	10	26	57	1	0	0	0	0	0	362	Red	362	14
11	Ryan Grant	GB	8	RB	0	0	0	290	1296	9	39	252	1	0	0	216	Yellow	255	24
12	Terrell Owens	DAL	10	WR	0	0	0	0	0	0	82	1304	14	0	0	212	Yellow	294	7
13	Laurence Maroney	NE	4	RB	0	0	0	234	1092	11	25	299	1	0	0	211	Red	236	34
14	Peyton Manning	IND	4	QB	4359	38	13	14	19	1	0	0	0	0	0	354	Green	354	21
15	Reggie Wayne	IND	4	WR	0	0	0	0	0	0	101	1295	12	0	0	203	Green	304	5
16	Andre Johnson	HOU	8	WR	0	0	0	0	0	0	88	1253	12	0	0	198	Yellow	285	8
17	Larry Johnson	KC	6	RB	0	0	0	310	1170	9	43	288	0	0	0	200	Red	243	28
18	Clinton Portis	WAS	10	RB	0	0	0	264	1158	7	40	325	1	0	0	197	Red	237	30
19	Brandon Jacobs	NYG	4	RB	0	0	0	253	1095	9	21	214	2	0	0	197	Yellow	218	50
20	Plaxico Burress	NYG	4	WR	0	0	0	0	0	0	82	1208	12	0	0	196	Yellow	277	10
21	Darren McFadden	OAK	5	RB	0	0	0	264	1219	8	34	227	0	0	0	196	Red	230	38
22	Frank Gore	SF	9	RB	0	0	0	233	922	5	60	551	2	0	0	190	Red	251	26
23	Marion Barber	DAL	10	RB	0	0	0	250	1109	7	33	231	2	0	0	190	Red	223	44
24	Marques Colston	NO	9	WR	0	0	0	0	0	0	94	1208	11	0	0	188	Green	281	9
25	Ronnie Brown	MIA	4	RB	0	0	0	256	1150	6	47	358	0	0	0	190	Red	237	32
26	Santonio Holmes	PIT	6	WR	0	0	0	0	0	0	73	1214	11	0	0	187	Yellow	260	18
27	Jamal Lewis	CLE	5	RB	0	0	0	287	1215	9	23	90	0	0	0	185	Yellow	208	55
28	Steve Smith	CAR	9	WR	0	0	0	0	0	0	86	1154	11	0	0	183	Yellow	269	12
29	Braylon Edwards	CLE	5	WR	0	0	0	0	0	0	73	1087	12	0	0	183	Red	255	23
30	Rashard Mendenhall	PIT	6	RB	0	0	0	221	1057	7	34	279	1	0	0	182	Red	216	51
31	Antonio Gates	SD	9	TE	0	0	0	0	0	0	74	921	10	0	0	151	Red	225	20
32	Chris Johnson	TEN	6	RB	0	0	0	179	945	5	53	460	2	0	0	181	Red	234	36
33	Willis McGahee	BAL	10	RB	0	0	0	310	1142	7	41	229	0	0	0	179	Green	220	46
34	Fred Taylor	JAC	7	RB	0	0	0	226	1026	8	22	226	1	0	0	177	Yellow	199	59
35	Larry Fitzgerald	ARI	7	WR	0	0	0	0	0	0	93	1193	10	0	0	177	Green	270	11
36	Kellen Winslow	CLE	5	TE	0	0	0	0	0	0	86	978	8	0	0	148	Yellow	233	15
37	Chad Johnson	CIN	8	WR	0	0	0	0	0	0	84	1146	10	0	0	173	Red	258	22
38	Jason Witten	DAL	10	TE	0	0	0	0	0	0	83	1056	6	0	0	143	Green	226	19
39	Anthony Gonzalez	IND	4	WR	0	0	0	0	0	0	65	1085	10	0	0	168	Yellow	233	35
40	Cedric Benson	CHI	8	RB	0	0	0	267	1015	6	35	299	1	0	0	170	Yellow	205	58
41	Joey Galloway	TB	10	WR	0	0	0	0	0	0	70	1143	9	0	0	166	Red	236	31
42	Willie Parker	PIT	6	RB	0	0	0	261	1057	6	25	238	1	0	0	166	Red	191	68
43	Edgerrin James	ARI	7	RB	0	0	0	285	1061	6	30	204	0	0	0	163	Green	193	65
44	Thomas Jones	NYJ	5	RB	0	0	0	292	1149	6	16	80	0	0	0	162	Green	177	81
45	Bobby Engram	SEA	4	WR	0	0	0	0	0	0	85	1043	9	0	0	159	Yellow	244	27
46	Greg Jennings	GB	8	WR	0	0	0	0	0	0	70	1044	9	0	0	159	Yellow	229	39
47	Reggie Bush	NO	9	RB	0	0	0	146	677	5	74	521	2	0	0	159	Red	233	37
48	Selvin Young	DEN	8	RB	0	0	0	230	1075	7	27	109	0	0	0	160	Red	187	73
49	Ben Roethlisberger	PIT	6	QB	3824	28	15	38	108	3	0	0	0	0	0	301	Red	301	54
50	Lee Evans	BUF	6	WR	0	0	0	0	0	0	72	1054	8	0	0	156	Red	227	40
51	Donovan McNabb	PHI	7	QB	3851	29	12	35	134	0	0	0	0	0	0	300	Yellow	300	56
52	DeAngelo Williams	CAR	9	RB	0	0	0	222	926	5	43	292	1	0	0	154	Red	197	61
53	Drew Brees	NO	9	QB	4225	30	19	16	24	0	0	0	0	0	0	297	Green	297	57
54	Donald Driver	GB	8	WR	0	0	0	0	0	0	73	1033	8	0	0	152	Yellow	224	42
55	LenDale White	TEN	6	RB	0	0	0	242	1024	6	23	118	0	0	0	153	Green	176	82

Rk	Player	Team	Bye	Pos	PaYd	PaTD	INT	Ru	RuYd	RuTD	Rec	RcYd	RcTD	XP	FG	Fant	Risk	PPR	Rk
56	Bernard Berrian	MIN	8	WR	0	0	0	0	0	0	67	977	9	0	0	152	Yellow	219	47
57	Tony Gonzalez	KC	6	TE	0	0	0	0	0	0	72	848	6	0	0	122	Yellow	193	41
58	Wes Welker	NE	4	WR	0	0	0	0	0	0	90	1049	7	0	0	149	Red	239	29
59	Roddy White	ATL	7	WR	0	0	0	0	0	0	71	987	8	0	0	148	Red	219	48
60	T.J. Houshmandzadeh	CIN	8	WR	0	0	0	0	0	0	87	972	8	0	0	148	Green	235	33
61	Dallas Clark	IND	4	TE	0	0	0	0	0	0	58	746	7	0	0	118	Green	177	53
62	David Garrard	JAC	7	QB	3898	23	13	40	169	2	0	0	0	0	0	291	Yellow	291	62
63	Eli Manning	NYG	4	QB	3987	26	15	36	115	0			0	0	0	289	Green	289	64
64	Stephen Gostkowski	NE	4	K	0	0	0	0	0	0	0	0	0	59	30	149	Yellow	149	63
65	Torry Holt	STL	5	WR	0	0	0	0	0	0	73	972	8	0	0	144	Green	217	49
66	Chester Taylor	MIN	8	RB	0	0	0	179	802	6	29	257	1	0	0	145	Red	174	88
67	Roy Williams	DET	4	WR	0	0	0	0	0	0	82	970	8	0	0	143	Green	224	43
68	Matt Forte	CHI	8	RB	0	0	0	220	761	4	31	323	1	0	0	143	Red	174	89
69	Sammy Morris	NE	4	RB	0	0	0	166	708	7	26	230	1	0	0	143	Yellow	169	100
70	Brandon Marshall	DEN	8	WR	0	0	0	0	0	0	71	909	8	0	0	141	Red	212	52
71	Anquan Boldin	ARI	7	WR	0	0	0	0	0	0	82	1018	6	0	0	140	Red	222	45
72	Kevin Smith	DET	4	RB	0	0	0	181	676	7	33	276	1	0	0	140	Red	173	90
73	Jonathan Stewart	CAR	9	RB	0	0	0	202	763	7	22	134	2	0	0	140	Red	162	117
74	Julius Jones	SEA	4	RB	0	0	0	203	859	7	11	47	1	0	0	140	Green	150	139
75	Jerry Porter	JAC	7	WR	0	0	0	0	0	0	56	909	8	0	0	137	Yellow	193	66
76	Tony Romo	DAL	10	QB	3926	26	17	23	75	1	0	0	0	0	0	279	Yellow	279	72
77	Chris Brown	HOU	8	RB	0	0	0	183	819	5	29	167	1	0	0	134	Red	164	114
78	Kevin Curtis	PHI	7	WR	0	0	0	0	0	0	65	892	7	0	0	134	Green	199	60
79	Chris Chambers	SD	9	WR	0	0	0	0	0	0	56	828	8	0	0	132	Red	189	70
80	Aaron Rodgers	GB	8	QB	3729	25	13	34	79	1	0	0	0	0	0	275	Red	275	76
81	David Akers	PHI	7	K	0	0	0	0	0	0	0	0	0	45	30	135	Red	135	75
82	Felix Jones	DAL	10	RB	0	0	0	164	760	6	16	156	1	0	0	131	Red	147	144
83	Chris Cooley	WAS	10	TE	0	0	0	0	0	0	60	747	4	0	0	100	Green	160	67
84	Carson Palmer	CIN	8	QB	3780	26	13	25	37	0	0	0	0	0	0	272	Yellow	272	79
85	Adam Vinatieri	IND	4	K	0	0	0	0	0	0	0	0	0	50	27	131	Yellow	131	80
86	Ravens D	BAL	10	D	0	0	0	0	0	0	0	0	0	0	0	133	Red	133	84
87	Eagles D	PHI	7	D	0	0	0	0	0	0	0	0	0	0	0	132	Red	132	85
88	Philip Rivers	SD	9	QB	3667	26	16	32	65	1	0	0	0	0	0	268	Red	268	87
89	Bryant Johnson	SF	9	WR	0	0	0	0	0	0	66	889	6	0	0	123	Red	189	69
90	Tarvaris Jackson	MIN	8	QB	3376	21	18	73	343	2	0	0	0	0	0	266	Red	266	93
91	Patriots D	NE	4	D	0	0	0	0	0	0	0	0	0	0	0	130	Yellow	130	94
92	Vikings D	MIN	8	D	0	0	0	0	0	0	0	0	0	0	0	130	Red	130	95
93	Rudi Johnson	CIN	8	RB	0	0	0	201	774	6	16	65	0	0	0	120	Red	137	161
94	Nate Kaeding	SD	9	K	0	0	0	0	0	0	0	0	0	46	26	124	Green	124	96
95	Jeremy Shockey	NYG	4	TE	0	0	0	0	0	0	52	595	5	0	0	90	Green	142	83
96	Matt Hasselbeck	SEA	4	QB	3793	24	14	27	49	0	0	0	0	0	0	264	Green	264	98
97	Jeff Garcia	TB	10	QB	3582	23	11	38	94	1	0	0	0	0	0	262	Yellow	262	99
98	Owen Daniels	HOU	8	TE	0	0	0	0	0	0	52	659	4	0	0	89	Yellow	141	86
99	Buccaneers D	TB	10	D	0	0	0	0	0	0	0	0	0	0	0	127	Yellow	127	101
100	Michael Turner	ATL	7	RB	0	0	0	215	807	2	35	233	0	0	0	118	Red	154	137
101	Steve Slaton	HOU	8	RB	0	0	0	132	652	4	29	243	1	0	0	118	Red	147	149
102	Heath Miller	PIT	6	TE	0	0	0	0	0	0	43	575	5	0	0	88	Yellow	131	112
103	Matt Schaub	HOU	8	QB	3917	22	15	27	45	0	0	0	0	0	0	261	Yellow	261	105
104	Packers D	GB	8	D	0	0	0	0	0	0	0	0	0	0	0	124	Red	124	103
105	Mason Crosby	GB	8	K	0	0	0	0	0	0	0	0	0	40	27	121	Yellow	121	104
106	Laveranues Coles	NYJ	5	WR	0	0	0	0	0	0	67	833	5	0	0	116	Yellow	183	74
107	Calvin Johnson	DET	4	WR	0	0	0	0	0	0	64	842	5	0	0	116	Red	180	77
108	Kenny Watson	CIN	8	RB	0	0	0	131	578	4	37	334	1	0	0	117	Red	154	135
109	Jerious Norwood	ATL	7	RB	0	0	0	133	668	2	47	385	0	0	0	117	Red	163	116
110	Seahawks D	SEA	4	D	0	0	0	0	0	0	0	0	0	0	0	123	Yellow	123	106

Rk	Player	Team	Bye	Pos	PaYd	PaTD	INT	Ru	RuYd	RuTD	Rec	RcYd	RcTD	XP	FG	Fant	Risk	PPR	Rk
111	Santana Moss	WAS	10	WR	0	0	0	0	0	0	53	737	7	0	0	116	Red	169	97
112	Giants D	NYG	4	D	0	0	0	0	0	0	0	0	0	0	0	123	Green	123	109
113	Saints D	NO	9	D	0	0	0	0	0	0	0	0	0	0	0	122	Red	122	110
114	John Kasay	CAR	9	K	0	0	0	0	0	0	0	0	0	38	27	119	Red	119	111
115	Dwayne Bowe	KC	6	WR	0	0	0	0	0	0	66	795	6	0	0	114	Yellow	180	78
116	Jerricho Cotchery	NYJ	5	WR	0	0	0	0	0	0	73	931	3	0	0	113	Red	186	71
117	Matt Prater	DEN	8	K	0	0	0	0	0	0	0	0	0	39	26	117	Red	117	120
118	Josh Scobee	JAC	7	K	0	0	0	0	0	0	0	0	0	44	24	116	Green	116	121
119	Randy McMichael	STL	5	TE	0	0	0	0	0	0	48	507	5	0	0	82	Red	130	113
120	Broncos D*	DEN	8	D	0	0	0	0	0	0	0	0	0	0	0	120	Yellow	120	122
121	Ryan Longwell	MIN	8	K	0	0	0	0	0	0	0	0	0	38	26	116	Red	116	123
122	Jeff Reed	PIT	6	K	0	0	0	0	0	0	0	0	0	43	24	115	Yellow	115	124
123	Jake Delhomme	CAR	9	QB	3640	22	14	40	86	0	0	0	0	0	0	254	Yellow	254	126
124	Ted Ginn	MIA	4	WR	0	0	0	0	0	0	56	762	6	0	0	110	Red	166	102
125	Todd Heap	BAL	10	TE	0	0	0	0	0	0	59	618	3	0	0	80	Red	140	91
126	Lawrence Tynes	NYG	4	K	0	0	0	0	0	0	0	0	0	40	25	115	Red	115	128
127	Donte' Stallworth	CLE	5	WR	0	0	0	0	0	0	56	811	4	0	0	108	Red	164	108
128	Reggie Brown	PHI	7	WR	0	0	0	0	0	0	54	785	5	0	0	108	Red	161	118
129	Shaun Alexander	FA	--	RB	0	0	0	166	661	7	4	10	1	0	0	109	Red	113	204
130	Justin Fargas	OAK	5	RB	0	0	0	179	707	3	25	190	0	0	0	109	Red	133	171
131	Derek Anderson	CLE	5	QB	3365	26	19	26	51	2	0	0	0	0	0	249	Green	249	132
132	Cardinals D	ARI	7	D	0	0	0	0	0	0	0	0	0	0	0	113	Green	113	131
133	Justin Gage	TEN	6	WR	0	0	0	0	0	0	67	778	5	0	0	106	Red	172	92
134	Marvin Harrison	IND	4	WR	0	0	0	0	0	0	52	741	5	0	0	104	Red	156	130
135	Ahman Green	HOU	8	RB	0	0	0	144	597	5	24	132	0	0	0	106	Red	130	178
136	Benjamin Watson	NE	4	TE	0	0	0	0	0	0	46	525	4	0	0	76	Green	123	134
137	Nate Burleson	SEA	4	WR	0	0	0	0	0	0	49	774	4	0	0	104	Red	153	136
138	Amani Toomer	NYG	4	WR	0	0	0	0	0	0	60	790	4	0	0	104	Red	164	115
139	Vincent Jackson	SD	9	WR	0	0	0	0	0	0	45	741	5	0	0	102	Red	147	145
140	Isaac Bruce	SF	9	WR	0	0	0	0	0	0	59	810	3	0	0	102	Red	161	119
141	Derrick Ward	NYG	4	RB	0	0	0	99	446	4	26	267	1	0	0	103	Red	129	179
142	D.J. Hackett	CAR	9	WR	0	0	0	0	0	0	59	782	4	0	0	101	Red	160	125
143	Ladell Betts	WAS	10	RB	0	0	0	118	482	3	37	284	1	0	0	102	Red	139	157
144	Pierre Thomas	NO	9	RB	0	0	0	102	457	5	36	243	0	0	0	101	Red	137	160
145	Vernon Davis	SF	9	TE	0	0	0	0	0	0	43	547	3	0	0	72	Red	115	141
146	Hines Ward	PIT	6	WR	0	0	0	0	0	0	56	742	4	0	0	100	Red	155	133
147	Ahmad Bradshaw	NYG	4	RB	0	0	0	129	560	5	13	135	1	0	0	101	Red	114	202
148	Donald Lee	GB	8	TE	0	0	0	0	0	0	42	506	3	0	0	71	Red	112	151
149	Kevin Walter	HOU	8	WR	0	0	0	0	0	0	60	747	4	0	0	99	Red	159	127
150	Dennis Northcutt	JAC	7	WR	0	0	0	0	0	0	51	753	4	0	0	98	Red	149	138
151	Marc Bulger	STL	5	QB	3345	26	21	22	77	1	0	0	0	0	0	242	Green	242	143
152	Jay Cutler	DEN	8	QB	3140	24	20	40	154	3	0	0	0	0	0	242	Yellow	242	142
153	Matt Leinart	ARI	7	QB	3526	21	19	47	128	1	0	0	0	0	0	241	Red	241	148
154	Arnaz Battle	SF	9	WR	0	0	0	0	0	0	67	760	3	0	0	97	Red	164	107
155	James Jones	GB	8	WR	0	0	0	0	0	0	50	735	4	0	0	97	Red	147	146
156	Travis Henry	DEN	8	RB	0	0	0	155	620	4	8	41	1	0	0	95	Red	103	209
157	Zach Miller	OAK	5	TE	0	0	0	0	0	0	45	467	3	0	0	67	Red	112	152
158	Alge Crumpler	TEN	6	TE	0	0	0	0	0	0	48	501	3	0	0	66	Red	114	147
159	Derrick Mason	BAL	10	WR	0	0	0	0	0	0	63	685	4	0	0	94	Green	157	129
160	John Carlson	SEA	4	TE	0	0	0	0	0	0	34	412	4	0	0	65	Red	99	173
161	Greg Olsen	CHI	8	TE	0	0	0	0	0	0	38	434	4	0	0	65	Red	103	164
162	Tony Scheffler	DEN	8	TE	0	0	0	0	0	0	38	384	4	0	0	62	Yellow	100	169
163	Mark Clayton	BAL	10	WR	0	0	0	0	0	0	58	698	4	0	0	91	Red	149	140
164	Patrick Crayton	DAL	10	WR	0	0	0	0	0	0	48	753	2	0	0	90	Red	137	158
165	T.J. Duckett	SEA	4	RB	0	0	0	115	494	5	12	100	0	0	0	89	Red	101	212

Rk	Player	Team	Bye	Pos	PaYd	PaTD	INT	Ru	RuYd	RuTD	Rec	RcYd	RcTD	XP	FG	Fant	Risk	PPR	Rk
166	Visanthe Shiancoe	MIN	8	TE	0	0	0	0	0	0	35	396	3	0	0	60	Red	95	181
167	Alex Smith	SF	9	QB	3699	17	17	39	125	0	0	0	0	0	0	231	Red	231	159
168	Panthers D	CAR	9	D	0	0	0	0	0	0	0	0	0	0	0	112	Red	112	154
169	Rob Bironas	TEN	6	K	0	0	0	0	0	0	0	0	0	30	27	111	Yellow	111	155
170	Nick Folk	DAL	10	K	0	0	0	0	0	0	0	0	0	42	23	111	Green	111	156
171	Brandon Jackson	GB	8	RB	0	0	0	93	509	2	21	217	1	0	0	88	Red	109	207
172	Laurent Robinson	ATL	7	WR	0	0	0	0	0	0	55	589	5	0	0	87	Yellow	142	153
173	Ike Hilliard	TB	10	WR	0	0	0	0	0	0	59	680	3	0	0	86	Red	145	150
174	Marcedes Lewis	JAC	7	TE	0	0	0	0	0	0	33	390	3	0	0	57	Red	90	186
175	Desmond Clark	CHI	8	TE	0	0	0	0	0	0	31	382	3	0	0	57	Red	87	192
176	Brodie Croyle	KC	6	QB	2990	22	18	53	106	3	0	0	0	0	0	230	Red	230	165
177	Chiefs D	KC	6	D	0	0	0	0	0	0	0	0	0	0	0	110	Yellow	110	162
178	Drew Bennett	STL	5	WR	0	0	0	0	0	0	51	604	4	0	0	84	Yellow	135	163
179	Sidney Rice	MIN	8	WR	0	0	0	0	0	0	47	571	4	0	0	84	Red	130	176
180	LaMont Jordan	OAK	5	RB	0	0	0	116	467	3	26	191	0	0	0	85	Red	111	206
181	L.J. Smith	PHI	7	TE	0	0	0	0	0	0	35	329	4	0	0	55	Yellow	90	188
182	Dustin Keller	NYJ	5	TE	0	0	0	0	0	0	28	332	4	0	0	54	Red	82	198
183	Kellen Clemens	NYJ	5	QB	3099	20	17	45	178	2	0	0	0	0	0	229	Red	229	170
184	Phil Dawson	CLE	5	K	0	0	0	0	0	0	0	0	0	37	24	109	Yellow	109	167
185	Kris Brown	HOU	8	K	0	0	0	0	0	0	0	0	0	40	23	109	Yellow	109	168
186	Malcolm Kelly	WAS	10	WR	0	0	0	0	0	0	39	604	4	0	0	83	Red	121	191
187	Limas Sweed	PIT	6	WR	0	0	0	0	0	0	34	560	4	0	0	82	Red	116	197
188	Aaron Stecker	NO	9	RB	0	0	0	81	346	4	30	236	0	0	0	84	Red	114	203
189	Antwaan Randle El	WAS	10	WR	0	0	0	0	0	0	45	686	2	0	0	82	Red	128	183
190	Cadillac Williams	TB	10	RB	0	0	0	59	249	4	34	260	2	0	0	83	Red	117	199
191	Brandon Coutu	SEA	4	K	0	0	0	0	0	0	0	0	0	39	23	108	Red	108	172
192	Roydell Williams	TEN	6	WR	0	0	0	0	0	0	47	635	3	0	0	81	Red	128	182
193	Alex Smith	TB	10	TE	0	0	0	0	0	0	31	362	2	0	0	51	Red	82	200
194	Ben Utecht	CIN	8	TE	0	0	0	0	0	0	30	330	3	0	0	51	Red	80	205
195	Mike Nugent	NYJ	5	K	0	0	0	0	0	0	0	0	0	37	23	106	Green	106	177
196	Kolby Smith	KC	6	RB	0	0	0	104	380	2	29	231	1	0	0	79	Red	108	208
197	Jason Wright	CLE	5	RB	0	0	0	100	430	2	24	218	1	0	0	81	Red	105	210
198	Chris Baker	NYJ	5	TE	0	0	0	0	0	0	32	324	3	0	0	49	Red	81	201
199	Josh Reed	BUF	6	WR	0	0	0	0	0	0	56	619	3	0	0	78	Red	135	166
200	Jason Campbell	WAS	10	QB	3496	19	20	28	102	0	0	0	0	0	0	221	Red	221	184
201	Chargers D	SD	9	D	0	0	0	0	0	0	0	0	0	0	0	110	Green	110	180
202	Devard Darling	KC	6	WR	0	0	0	0	0	0	53	622	2	0	0	77	Red	130	175
203	Marty Booker	CHI	8	WR	0	0	0	0	0	0	45	627	2	0	0	77	Red	122	189
204	Greg Jones	JAC	7	RB	0	0	0	102	463	3	13	91	0	0	0	78	Red	91	215
205	Javon Walker	OAK	5	WR	0	0	0	0	0	0	47	525	4	0	0	76	Red	123	187
206	David Patten	NO	9	WR	0	0	0	0	0	0	45	617	2	0	0	77	Red	122	190
207	Matt Bryant	TB	10	K	0	0	0	0	0	0	0	0	0	36	23	105	Red	105	185
208	Ernest Wilford	MIA	4	WR	0	0	0	0	0	0	55	556	3	0	0	75	Red	131	174
209	Ben Patrick	ARI	7	TE	0	0	0	0	0	0	24	290	3	0	0	45	Red	69	211
210	Jason Snelling	ATL	7	RB	0	0	0	98	386	3	16	129	1	0	0	75	Red	92	214
211	Vince Young	TEN	6	QB	2783	13	15	71	440	1	0	0	0	0	0	213	Red	213	193
212	Adrian Peterson	CHI	8	RB	0	0	0	61	283	2	29	250	1	0	0	70	Red	99	213
213	Jon Kitna	DET	4	QB	3128	20	18	24	75	1	0	0	0	0	0	212	Green	212	196
214	Steelers D	PIT	6	D	0	0	0	0	0	0	0	0	0	0	0	107	Yellow	107	194
215	Cowboys D	DAL	10	D	0	0	0	0	0	0	0	0	0	0	0	107	Green	107	195

*Note: In leagues where defensive team scoring includes special teams, the Chicago Bears D/ST should be ranked next to Denver.

Statistical Appendix B: Actual Draft Value Chart

The table below gives the value of each pick in the NFL draft according to the Actual Draft Value Chat introduced in the article "Building a Better Draft Value Chart."

Beginning in the third round, we've added an average number of supplemental picks in each round.

Round 1		Round 2		Round 3		Round 4		Round 5		Round 6		Round 7	
Pick	Value	Pick	Value	Pick	Value	Pick	Value	Pick	Value	Pick	Value	Pick	Value
1	3000	33	1915	65	1075	100	570	132	325	166	169	201	60.6
2	2950	34	1880	66	1055	101	560	133	320	167	165	202	58.3
3	2920	35	1845	67	1040	102	550	134	315	168	161	203	56.0
4	2890	36	1810	68	1020	103	545	135	310	169	158	204	53.8
5	2860	37	1775	69	1000	104	530	136	305	170	154	205	51.6
6	2835	38	1735	70	985	105	525	137	300	171	150	206	49.5
7	2805	39	1700	71	965	106	515	138	295	172	147	207	47.4
8	2775	40	1665	72	950	107	510	139	290	173	143	208	45.4
9	2750	41	1630	73	930	108	500	140	285	174	140	209	43.3
10	2720	42	1595	74	915	109	490	141	280	175	136	210	41.3
11	2695	43	1560	75	900	110	480	142	275	176	133	211	39.4
12	2665	44	1530	76	880	111	475	143	270	177	129	212	37.5
13	2635	45	1495	77	865	112	465	144	265	178	126	213	35.6
14	2610	46	1460	78	845	113	455	145	260	179	123	214	33.7
15	2580	47	1425	79	830	114	450	146	255	180	119	215	31.9
16	2545	48	1390	80	815	115	440	147	250	181	116	216	30.1
17	2510	49	1370	81	800	116	430	148	245	182	113	217	28.4
18	2470	50	1350	82	785	117	425	149	240	183	110	218	26.7
19	2435	51	1330	83	775	118	420	150	235	184	107	219	25.0
20	2395	52	1315	84	760	119	410	151	230	185	103	220	23.3
21	2355	53	1295	85	745	120	405	152	225	186	100	221	21.7
22	2320	54	1275	86	735	121	395	153	220	187	97	222	20.1
23	2285	55	1255	87	720	122	385	154	215	188	95	223	18.5
24	2245	56	1240	88	710	123	380	155	210	189	92	224	17.9
25	2210	57	1220	89	695	124	375	156	205	190	89	225	17.3
26	2170	58	1200	90	685	125	365	157	200	191	86	226	16.6
27	2135	59	1180	91	670	126	365	158	195	192	83	227	15.9
28	2100	60	1165	92	660	127	355	159	193	193	81	228	15.2
29	2060	61	1145	93	645	128	350	160	190	194	78	229	14.5
30	2025	62	1130	94	635	126	365	161	185	195	75	230	13.8
31	1990	63	1110	95	620	127	355	162	185	196	73	231	13.1
32	1950	64	1095	96	610	128	350	163	180	197	70	232	12.4
				97	600	129	345	164	176	198	68	233	11.7
				98	585	130	340	165	173	199	65	234	11.0
				99	580	131	335			200	63	235	10.4
												236	9.7
												237	9.0
												238	8.3
												239	7.6
												240	6.9

Statistical Appendix C

This section contains a number of lists based on stats from either game charting or play-by-play analysis.

Many of these statistics are defined in the "Statistical Toolbox" near the front of the book. All stats are for 2007 only.

Top 20 Players in Offensive Penalties

Rk	Player	Team	Penalties
1	R.Gallery	OAK	17
2	A.Barron	STL	16
3	F.Adams	DAL	14
3	B.Sims	OAK	14
5	K.Winslow	CLE	13
6	J.Brown	NO	11
6	W.Colon	PIT	11
8	M.Colombo	DAL	10
9	G.Foster	DET	10
10	M.Gandy	ARI	10
11	T.Gonzalez	KC	10
12	F.Miller	CHI	10
13	A.Sears	TB	10
14	J.Trueblood	TB	10
15	V.Davis	SF	9
15	C.Green	OAK	9
15	D.Joseph	TB	9
15	D.Lutui	ARI	9
15	R.Moss	NE	9
15	T.Owens	DAL	9
15	C.Terry	KC	9
15	R.White	ATL	9

Includes declined and offsetting, but not special teams.

Top 20 Players in Defensive Penalties

Rk	Player	Team	Penalties
1	C.Woodson	GB	12
2	A.Harris	GB	11
2	J.Taylor	MIA	11
4	A.Haynesworth	TEN	9
5	A.Bigby	GB	8
5	T.Brown	TEN	8
5	E.Dumervil	DEN	8
5	K.Jenkins	CAR	8
5	S.Rogers	DET	8
5	D.Ware	DAL	8
11	N.Clements	SF	7
11	T.Harris	CHI	7
11	C.Ivy	BAL	7
11	Q.Jammer	SD	7
11	A.Odom	TEN	7
11	D.Revis	NYJ	7
11	B.Scott	BAL	7
11	T.Suggs	BAL	7
19	15 tied with 6		

Includes declined and offsetting, but not special teams.

Top 10 Intended Receivers on Interceptions

Rk	Player	Team	Total
1	D.Bennett	STL	10
2	T.J.Houshmandzadeh	CIN	9
2	L.Fitzgerald	ARI	9
2	T.Owens	DAL	9
2	J.Porter	OAK	9
6	C.Johnson	CIN	8
6	T.Holt	STL	8
6	P.Burress	NYG	8
6	B.Berrian	CHI	8
6	S.McDonald	DET	8

Top 10 Rate of Intended Receiver on Interceptions
(minimum 50 passes)

Rk	Player	Team	Total	Pct	
1	D.Bennett	STL	10	14%	74
2	B.Smith	NYJ	6	9%	67
3	J.Porter	OAK	9	9%	103
4	M.Jenkins	ATL	6	7%	85
5	D.Jackson	SF	7	7%	105
6	K.Walter	HOU	7	7%	107
7	J.Shockey	NYG	6	6%	94
8	T.Owens	DAL	9	6%	141
9	R.Ferguson	MIN	4	6%	63
10	S.McDonald	DET	8	6%	127

Top 20 Players in Blown Blocks

Rk	Player	Team	Total
1	J.Backus	DET	11.0
1	D.Diehl	NYG	11.0
3	B.Sims	OAK	8.5
4	C.Terry	KC	8.0
5	G.Foster	DET	7.5
5	E.Salaam	HOU	7.5
7	N.Kaczur	NE	7.0
7	F.Miller	CHI	7.0
7	K.Simmons	PIT	7.0
10	M.Brown	STL	6.5
10	T.Pashos	JAC	6.5
10	A.Snyder	SF	6.5
10	J.Trueblood	TB	6.5
14	L.Brown	ARI	6.0
14	A.Clement	NYJ	6.0
14	D.Ferguson	NYJ	6.0
14	C.Liwienski	MIA	6.0
14	B.McKinnie	MIN	6.0
14	E.Pears	DEN	6.0
14	J.Staley	SF	6.0

Top 20 Players in Defeats

Rk	Player	Team	Total
1	D.Johnson	KC	35
2	D.Ware	DAL	34
3	J.Allen	KC	32
3	L.Briggs	CHI	32
3	T.Cole	PHI	32
3	K.Morrison	OAK	32
7	W.Witherspoon	STL	31
8	M.Boley	ATL	30
8	E.Henderson	MIN	30
8	T.Howard	OAK	30
8	S.Merriman	SD	30
8	L.Tatupu	SEA	30
8	B.Urlacher	CHI	30
8	P.Willis	SF	30
15	J.Harrison	PIT	29
15	J.Tuck	NYG	29
17	A.Schobel	BUF	28
18	K.Dansby	ARI	27
18	R.Marshall	CAR	27
18	A.Ogunleye	CHI	27

Top 20 Defenders in Quarterback Hits

Rk	Player	Team	Total
1	K.Vanden Bosch	TEN	22
2	A.Kampman	GB	20
3	A.Carter	WAS	14
3	D.Dockett	ARI	14
3	A.Odom	TEN	14
3	D.Ware	DAL	14
3	K.Wimbley	CLE	14
8	J.Abraham	ATL	12
8	L.Glover	STL	12
8	S.Rogers	DET	12
8	W.Smith	NO	12
8	T.Suggs	BAL	12
8	T.Warren	NE	12
14	J.DeVries	DET	11
14	R.Geathers	CIN	11
14	A.Ogunleye	CHI	11
14	J.Tuck	NYG	11
14	K.Udeze	MIN	11
14	O.Umenyiora	NYG	11
20	Five tied with 10		

Adjusted based on official scorer tendencies.

Top 20 Defenders in QB Knockdowns (Sacks + Hits)

Rk	Player	Team	Total
1	A.Kampman	GB	32
1	K.Vanden Bosch	TEN	32
3	D.Ware	DAL	27
4	J.Allen	KC	24
4	A.Carter	WAS	24
4	P.Kerney	SEA	24
7	D.Dockett	ARI	23
7	O.Umenyiora	NYG	23
9	E.Dumervil	DEN	22
9	A.Odom	TEN	22
9	J.Tuck	NYG	22
12	T.Cole	PHI	21
12	S.Merriman	SD	21
12	A.Ogunleye	CHI	21
15	J.Harrison	PIT	20
15	J.Abraham	ATL	20
15	S.Rogers	DET	20
18	M.Strahan	NYG	19
18	J.Taylor	MIA	19
20	K.Wimbley	CLE	18

Adjusted based on official scorer tendencies.

Top 20 Defenders in QB Hurries

Rk	Player	Team	Total
1	A.Kampman	GB	21
2	D.Burgess	OAK	20
3	J.Abraham	ATL	19
3	R.Geathers	CIN	19
3	A.Odom	TEN	19
3	D.Ware	DAL	19
7	J.Smith	CIN	18
7	K.Vanden Bosch	TEN	18
9	J.Allen	KC	17
9	J.Farrior	PIT	17
9	J.Green	NE	17
9	P.Kerney	SEA	17
9	A.Ogunleye	CHI	17
9	K.Wimbley	CLE	17
15	T.Suggs	BAL	16
15	J.Taylor	MIA	16
15	K.Udeze	MIN	16
18	T.Hali	KC	15
18	C.Pace	ARI	15
18	M.Strahan	NYG	15
18	M.Vrabel	NE	15

Adjusted based on game charter tendencies.

Top 20 Quarterbacks in QB Knockdowns (Sacks + Hits)

Rk	Player	Team	Total
1	J.Kitna	DET	88
2	D.McNabb	PHI	73
2	K.Warner	ARI	73
4	T.Brady	NE	70
5	B.Roethlisberger	PIT	68
6	J.Garcia	TB	65
7	D.Huard	KC	62
7	M.Hasselbeck	SEA	62
9	P.Rivers	SD	60
10	J.Harrington	DET	57
11	M.Bulger	STL	56
12	K.Boller	BAL	55
12	E.Manning	NYG	55
12	T.Jackson	MIN	55
12	C.Palmer	CIN	55
16	J.Campbell	WAS	54
16	P.Manning	IND	54
16	C.Pennington	NYJ	54
19	D.Garrard	JAC	53
20	J.Cutler	DEN	52

Adjusted based on official scorer tendencies.

Top 10 Quarterbacks in Knockdowns per Pass (minimum 200 passes)

Rk	Player	Team	Total	Pct
1	C.Pennington	NYJ	54	18.3%
2	J.Garcia	TB	65	18.0%
3	K.Boller	BAL	55	17.9%
4	T.Jackson	MIN	55	17.4%
5	R.Grossman	CHI	44	17.3%
6	D.Huard	KC	62	16.3%
7	T.Dilfer	SF	41	16.0%
8	J.McCown	OAK	35	15.7%
9	K.Clemens	NYJ	43	15.0%
10	K.Warner	ARI	73	14.9%

Adjusted based on official scorer tendencies.

Bottom 10 Quarterbacks in Knockdowns per Pass (minimum 200 passes)

Rk	Player	Team	Total	Pct
29	M.Hasselbeck	SEA	62	10.1%
30	P.Manning	IND	54	9.8%
31	M.Schaub	HOU	31	9.7%
32	S.Rosenfels	HOU	24	9.7%
33	E.Manning	NYG	55	9.4%
34	C.Palmer	CIN	55	8.9%
35	T.Romo	DAL	44	7.8%
36	B.Favre	GB	45	7.7%
37	D.Anderson	CLE	38	6.8%
38	D.Brees	NO	45	6.5%

Adjusted based on official scorer tendencies.

Top 10 Quarterbacks in Rate of Passes Dropped (minimum 200 passes)

Rk	Player	Team	Total	Pct
1	E.Manning	NYG	49	9.3%
2	J.Garcia	TB	28	8.7%
3	T.Dilfer	SF	17	7.9%
4	R.Grossman	CHI	17	7.7%
5	B.Croyle	KC	17	7.6%
6	J.Campbell	WAS	31	7.5%
7	B.Griese	CHI	19	7.4%
8	D.Brees	NO	47	7.2%
9	T.Jackson	MIN	20	6.9%
10	D.Anderson	CLE	35	6.7%

Bottom 10 Quarterbacks in Rate of Passes Dropped (minimum 200 passes)

Rk	Player	Team	Total	Pct
29	B.Roethlisberger	PIT	20	5.0%
30	J.Cutler	DEN	23	5.0%
31	M.Bulger	STL	18	4.8%
32	K.Warner	ARI	21	4.7%
33	P.Rivers	SD	21	4.6%
34	T.Edwards	BUF	12	4.5%
35	K.Boller	BAL	12	4.4%
36	S.McNair	BAL	8	3.9%
37	M.Schaub	HOU	9	3.2%
38	C.Pennington	NYJ	8	3.1%

Top 10 Quarterbacks in Rate of Passes Overthrown
(minimum 200 passes)

Rk	Player	Team	Total	Pct
1	A.Smith	SF	30	16.6%
2	M.Bulger	STL	51	14.1%
3	T.Edwards	BUF	34	13.4%
4	T.Dilfer	SF	27	13.4%
5	B.Croyle	KC	28	13.2%
6	C.Palmer	CIN	73	13.1%
7	K.Clemens	NYJ	31	12.9%
8	R.Grossman	CHI	27	12.8%
9	D.Anderson	CLE	63	12.5%
10	S.McNair	BAL	23	12.0%

Includes plays marked "Overthrown" and "Thrown Ahead."

Bottom 10 Quarterbacks in Rate of Passes Overthrown
(minimum 200 passes)

Rk	Player	Team	Total	Pct
29	P.Manning	IND	40	8.2%
30	V.Young	TEN	33	7.9%
31	J.Garcia	TB	23	7.3%
32	B.Favre	GB	37	7.1%
33	M.Schaub	HOU	19	7.0%
34	D.Brees	NO	42	6.7%
35	D.Culpepper	OAK	12	6.5%
36	S.Rosenfels	HOU	14	6.1%
37	J.Cutler	DEN	28	6.0%
38	C.Pennington	NYJ	14	5.7%

Includes plays marked "Overthrown" and "Thrown Ahead."

Top 10 Quarterbacks in Rate of Passes Underthrown
(minimum 200 passes)

Rk	Player	Team	Total	Pct
1	D.Culpepper	OAK	21	11.4%
2	C.Lemon	MIA	25	8.4%
3	B.Roethlisberger	PIT	30	7.3%
4	J.Cutler	DEN	34	7.3%
5	D.Anderson	CLE	35	6.9%
6	T.Edwards	BUF	16	6.3%
7	K.Clemens	NYJ	15	6.2%
8	E.Manning	NYG	31	6.1%
9	D.McNabb	PHI	27	5.8%
10	J.Kitna	DET	31	5.8%

Includes plays marked "Underthrown" and "Thrown Behind."

Bottom 10 Quarterbacks in Rate of Passes Underthrown
(minimum 200 passes)

Rk	Player	Team	Total	Pct
29	J.McCown	OAK	8	4.3%
30	B.Croyle	KC	9	4.2%
31	T.Jackson	MIN	12	4.2%
32	J.Garcia	TB	13	4.2%
33	C.Palmer	CIN	23	4.1%
34	K.Boller	BAL	10	3.8%
35	M.Bulger	STL	13	3.6%
36	S.McNair	BAL	6	3.1%
37	J.Campbell	WAS	11	2.7%
38	S.Rosenfels	HOU	6	2.6%

Includes plays marked "Underthrown" and "Thrown Behind."

Top 10 Quarterbacks in Rate of Passes Defensed
(minimum 200 passes)

Rk	Player	Team	Total	Pct
1	S.Rosenfels	HOU	31	13.0%
2	M.Bulger	STL	48	12.8%
3	K.Clemens	NYJ	30	12.2%
4	T.Dilfer	SF	26	12.1%
5	J.Cutler	DEN	56	12.1%
6	C.Lemon	MIA	35	11.4%
7	V.Young	TEN	43	11.3%
8	C.Pennington	NYJ	29	11.2%
9	D.Anderson	CLE	57	11.0%
10	K.Warner	ARI	49	10.9%

Bottom 10 Quarterbacks in Rate of Passes Defensed
(minimum 200 passes)

Rk	Player	Team	Total	Pct
29	D.Garrard	JAC	26	8.0%
30	S.McNair	BAL	16	7.8%
31	D.Brees	NO	51	7.8%
32	B.Roethlisberger	PIT	31	7.7%
33	D.McNabb	PHI	34	7.2%
34	J.Kitna	DET	40	7.1%
35	C.Palmer	CIN	40	7.0%
36	T.Jackson	MIN	19	6.6%
37	T.Brady	NE	37	6.4%
38	J.Garcia	TB	12	3.7%

Top 20 Players in Dropped Passes

Rk	Player	Team	Drops
1	B.Marshall	DEN	15
2	B.Edwards	CLE	12
3	R.Moss	NE	11
3	D.Bowe	KC	11
3	D.Henderson	NO	11
6	C.Johnson	CIN	10
6	T.Owens	DAL	10
6	R.Bush	NO	10
6	B.Jacobs	NYG	10
10	K.Curtis	PHI	9
10	B.Westbrook	PHI	9
10	S.Moss	WAS	9
10	D.Jackson	SF	9
10	D.Clark	IND	9
10	J.Jurevicius	CLE	9
10	E.Graham	TB	9
17	D.Mason	BAL	8
17	S.Smith	CAR	8
17	P.Burress	NYG	8
17	R.White	ATL	8
17	A.Toomer	NYG	8
17	M.Booker	MIA	8

Top 20 Players in Percentage of Passes Dropped (minimum 5 drops)

Rk	Player	Team	Drops	Pass	Pct
1	B.Jacobs	NYG	10	38	26.3%
2	D.Henderson	NO	11	43	25.6%
3	C.Benson	CHI	6	27	22.2%
4	K.Keith	IND	5	23	21.7%
5	S.Alexander	SEA	5	25	20.0%
6	D.Ward	NYG	7	40	17.5%
7	J.Fargas	OAK	5	32	15.6%
8	L.Betts	WAS	5	32	15.6%
9	D.Hester	CHI	6	39	15.4%
10	M.Gaines	CAR	5	35	14.3%
11	E.Graham	TB	9	69	13.0%
12	T.Williamson	MIN	5	39	12.8%
13	M.Clayton	TB	5	40	12.5%
14	W.Dunn	ATL	7	59	11.9%
15	J.Jurevicius	CLE	9	82	11.0%
16	R.Bush	NO	10	98	10.2%
17	M.Jones	JAC	5	50	10.0%
18	K.Wilson	KC	5	50	10.0%
19	L.Weaver	SEA	5	52	9.6%
20	E.Johnson	NO	6	63	9.5%

Top 20 First Downs/Touchdowns Allowed in Coverage

Rk	Player	Team	Total
1	J.Joseph	CIN	45
2	C.Griffin	MIN	43
2	J.Reeves	DAL	43
4	T.McGee	BUF	42
5	N.Clements	SF	41
5	J.David	NO	41
7	I.Taylor	PIT	39
8	M.Trufant	SEA	38
8	L.Bodden	CLE	38
8	D.Revis	NYJ	38
11	S.Madison	NYG	37
12	E.Hobbs	NE	36
12	F.Brown	STL	36
14	R.Hood	ARI	35
14	C.Finnegan	TEN	35
14	N.Harper	TEN	35
14	M.McCauley	MIN	35
14	C.Houston	ATL	35
14	D.Florence	SD	35
20	E.Wright	CLE	34
20	A.Harris	GB	34

Top 20 Passing Yards Allowed in Coverage

Rk	Player	Team	Total
1	J.David	NO	1051
2	C.Griffin	MIN	925
3	N.Clements	SF	909
4	I.Taylor	PIT	853
5	J.Reeves	DAL	818
6	E.Hobbs	NE	748
7	S.Madison	NYG	746
8	M.Trufant	SEA	744
9	C.Ivy	BAL	740
10	D.Florence	SD	733
11	K.Jennings	SEA	732
12	D.Bly	DEN	720
13	J.Joseph	CIN	717
14	L.Bodden	CLE	708
15	F.Brown	STL	702
16	C.Houston	ATL	699
17	D.Revis	NYJ	697
18	R.Hood	ARI	696
19	C.Finnegan	TEN	695
20	M.McCauley	MIN	692

Top 20 Yards After Catch Allowed in Coverage

Rk	Player	Team	Total
1	J.David	NO	321
2	A.Rolle	ARI	310
3	N.Clements	SF	295
4	C.Greenway	MIN	266
5	D.Bly	DEN	262
6	C.Griffin	MIN	244
7	J.Reeves	DAL	224
8	D.Florence	SD	223
9	T.Howard	OAK	222
10	S.Brown	PHI	221
11	P.Surtain	KC	220
12	S.Madison	NYG	205
13	V.Hutchins	HOU	197
14	C.Ivy	BAL	194
15	K.Lucas	CAR	191
16	J.Craft	NO	190
17	D.Hall	ATL	187
18	Q.Jammer	SD	185
19	D.Johnson	KC	181
20	J.Joseph	CIN	180
20	D.Revis	NYJ	180

Top 10 Kickers, Gross Kickoff Value over Average

Rk	Kicker	Team	Kick Pts+	Net Pts+	Kicks
1	N.Rackers	ARI	10.3	6.6	73
2	S.Gostkowski	NE	6.2	7.3	108
3	R.Bironas	TEN	6.0	5.9	75
4	J.Brown	SEA	5.4	-0.4	82
5	O.Mare	NO	4.8	-0.3	48
6	S.Janikowski	OAK	4.6	1.2	64
7	K.Brown	HOU	3.5	7.9	74
8	M.Koenen	ATL	3.1	0.8	60
9	M.Nugent	NYJ	3.0	-6.7	59
10	A.Vinatieri	IND	2.8	-15.5	86

Min. 20 kickoffs; squibs and onside kicks not included.

Bottom 10 Kickers, Gross Kickoff Value over Average

Rk	Kicker	Team	Kick Pts+	Net Pts+	Kicks
24	J.Wilkins	STL	-0.6	-18.4	61
25	D.Akers	PHI	-0.7	-2.4	74
26	L.Tynes	NYG	-1.0	-6.1	74
27	N.Kaeding	SD	-2.3	9.7	68
28	J.Carney	JAC/KC	-2.5	7.9	54
29	J.Kasay	CAR	-2.6	-7.8	50
30	M.Bryant	TB	-2.7	-0.8	71
31	R.Gould	CHI	-3.2	6.0	73
32	N.Folk	DAL	-3.6	-3.6	90
33	S.Suisham	WAS	-6.1	-6.4	71

Min. 20 kickoffs; squibs and onside kicks not included.

Top 10 Punters, Gross Punt Value over Average

Rk	Punter	Team	Punt Pts+	Net Pts+	Punts
1	A.Lee	SF	22.0	18.1	105
2	M.Scifres	SD	11.0	6.8	82
3	S.Lechler	OAK	9.9	-5.8	74
4	C.Kluwe	MIN	9.8	0.9	81
5	M.McBriar	DAL	7.4	-0.6	63
6	D.Jones	STL	6.6	6.1	78
7	N.Harris	DET	6.0	4.3	68
8	M.Koenen	ATL	5.5	11.2	88
9	D.Sepulveda	PIT	4.8	2.8	68
10	D.Colquitt	KC	4.4	5.9	96

Bottom 10 Punters, Gross Punt Value over Average

Rk	Punter	Team	Punt Pts+	Net Pts+	Punts
26	C.Hanson	NE	-2.8	0.8	45
27	D.Frost	WAS	-3.0	6.1	75
28	P.Ernster	DEN	-3.2	-2.5	12
29	S.Rocca	PHI	-3.4	-10.3	73
30	T.Sauerbrun	DEN	-5.2	-10.7	49
31	A.Podlesh	JAC	-5.4	-2.1	55
32	C.Hentrich	TEN	-5.9	-4.6	71
33	R.Plackemeier	SEA	-6.3	-2.9	86
34	M.Barr	ARI	-7.4	-21.5	60
35	J.Ryan	GB	-8.9	-3.7	63

Top 10 Kick Returns, Value over Average (minimum eight returns)

Rk	Player	Team	Pts+	Returns
1	J.Cribbs	CLE	29.9	56
2	A.Davis	HOU	19.1	31
3	L.Washington	NYJ	16.8	45
4	D.Sproles	SD	7.4	37
5	J.Wilson	SEA	7.0	13
6	R.Cartwright	WAS	6.9	52
7	D.Hester	CHI	6.3	41
8	M.Spurlock	TB	5.6	16
9	R.Davis	CHI	5.4	10
10	A.Allison	MIN	5.3	20

Bottom 10 Kick Returns, Value over Average (minimum eight returns)

Rk	Player	Team	Pts+	Returns
54	C.Carr	OAK	-3.1	59
55	C.Ross	BAL	-3.2	9
56	L.Moore	NO	-3.8	17
57	D.Williams	CAR	-3.9	13
58	D.Rhodes	OAK	-4.1	15
59	S.Breaston	ARI	-4.6	61
60	C.Buckhalter	PHI	-5.4	36
61	B.Sapp	KC	-5.7	15
62	E.Drummond	KC	-6.3	37
63	N.Goings	CAR	-6.6	9

Top 10 Punt Returns, Value over Average (minimum eight returns)

Rk	Player	Team	Pts+	Returns
1	D.Hester	CHI	19.8	42
2	R.Parrish	BUF	12.4	27
3	J.Cribbs	CLE	9.2	30
4	N.Burleson	SEA	8.6	58
5	T.Rushing	IND	8.3	19
6	D.Hall	STL	6.3	19
7	W.Blackmon	GB	5.4	8
8	S.Breaston	ARI	4.7	42
9	D.Sproles	SD	4.2	24
10	N.Clements	SF	3.1	8

Bottom 10 Punt Returns, Value over Average (minimum eight returns)

Rk	Player	Team	Pts+	Returns
34	A.Jennings	ATL	-3.4	30
35	R.W.McQuarters	NYG	-4.1	42
36	C.Davis	TEN	-4.2	31
37	P.Buchanon	TB	-4.7	16
38	B.Wade	MIN	-4.7	16
39	T.Dwight	OAK	-4.8	9
40	A.Randle El	WAS	-5.6	34
41	E.Drummond	KC	-6.1	32
42	J.Higgins	OAK	-8.8	20
43	A.Rossum	PIT	-9.1	36

Top 10 Offenses, Points per Drive

Rk	Team	Pts/Dr
1	NE	3.37
2	IND	2.70
3	JAC	2.42
4	DAL	2.42
5	GB	2.18
6	PIT	2.15
7	CIN	2.05
8	CLE	2.01
9	SD	1.96
10	HOU	1.95

Bottom 10 Offenses, Points per Drive

Rk	Team	Pts/Dr
23	NYJ	1.40
24	OAK	1.39
25	CHI	1.37
26	CAR	1.37
27	BAL	1.35
28	ATL	1.34
29	STL	1.29
30	BUF	1.23
31	KC	1.15
32	SF	1.08

Top 10 Defenses, Points per Drive

Rk	Team	Pts/Dr
1	SEA	1.39
2	SD	1.40
3	NE	1.42
4	TB	1.43
5	IND	1.44
6	PIT	1.48
7	MIN	1.52
8	GB	1.55
9	PHI	1.55
10	WAS	1.56

Bottom 10 Defenses, Points per Drive

Rk	Team	Pts/Dr
23	BAL	1.94
24	OAK	1.96
25	ATL	1.96
26	CIN	2.03
27	NO	2.03
28	DEN	2.08
29	STL	2.15
30	HOU	2.15
31	DET	2.21
32	MIA	2.40

Top 10 Offenses, Yards per Drive

Rk	Team	Yds/Dr
1	NE	41.63
2	IND	37.03
3	JAC	35.28
4	CIN	32.93
5	DAL	32.92
6	GB	32.75
7	NO	32.10
8	PHI	32.01
9	DEN	31.69
10	HOU	31.01

Bottom 10 Offenses, Yards per Drive

Rk	Team	Yds/Dr
23	BAL	26.30
24	MIA	25.82
25	STL	25.40
26	BUF	25.19
27	ATL	24.92
28	CAR	24.82
29	OAK	23.17
30	KC	22.66
31	CHI	22.57
32	SF	18.41

Top 10 Defenses, Yards per Drive

Rk	Team	Yds/Dr
1	SEA	24.24
2	TB	24.37
3	PIT	24.75
4	NYG	25.38
5	TEN	25.95
6	WAS	26.13
7	BAL	26.16
8	NE	26.43
9	KC	26.72
10	CHI	26.79

Bottom 10 Defenses, Yards per Drive

Rk	Team	Yds/Dr
23	NO	30.49
24	CLE	30.51
25	DEN	31.10
26	ATL	31.16
27	NYJ	31.38
28	CIN	31.39
29	HOU	32.03
30	DET	32.18
31	MIA	32.28
32	BUF	33.92

Top 10 Offenses, Average Line of Scrimmage to Start Drive

Rk	Team	LOS
1	CHI	34.4
2	TB	33.3
3	CLE	33.3
4	SF	32.4
5	TEN	32.4
6	PIT	32.3
7	NE	32.0
8	ARI	31.9
9	DAL	31.8
10	WAS	31.8

Bottom 10 Offenses, Average Line of Scrimmage to Start Drive

Rk	Team	LOS
23	BAL	29.5
24	HOU	29.5
25	PHI	29.1
26	NO	28.6
27	STL	28.4
28	CAR	28.3
29	DEN	28.1
30	MIN	27.8
31	MIA	27.7
32	KC	27.6

Top 10 Defenses, Average Line of Scrimmage to Start Drive

Rk	Team	LOS
1	TB	26.9
2	NE	27.0
3	TEN	28.6
4	ATL	28.6
5	GB	28.7
6	IND	28.8
7	NYJ	29.1
8	SD	29.3
9	CHI	29.3
10	SF	29.3

Bottom 10 Defenses, Average Line of Scrimmage to Start Drive

Rk	Team	LOS
23	ARI	31.9
24	HOU	31.9
25	DET	32.0
26	PHI	32.0
27	CIN	32.0
28	CLE	32.1
29	STL	33.0
30	CAR	33.2
31	MIA	34.6
32	BAL	35.1

Top 10 Offenses, Better DVOA on Play Action

Rk	Team	PA	No PA	Dif
1	NYJ	67.4%	-17.3%	84.7%
2	TB	76.3%	-2.6%	78.9%
3	DAL	89.2%	15.1%	74.0%
4	CLE	54.3%	0.6%	53.6%
5	OAK	13.4%	-33.8%	47.2%
6	CHI	20.7%	-24.9%	45.6%
7	BUF	35.1%	-10.4%	45.5%
8	SF	-0.6%	-45.9%	45.3%
9	CAR	18.3%	-25.8%	44.0%
10	CIN	48.2%	19.1%	29.0%

Bottom 10 Offenses, Better DVOA on Play Action

Rk	Team	PA	No PA	Dif
23	ARI	9.8%	8.6%	1.2%
24	IND	40.6%	43.5%	-2.9%
25	DEN	16.3%	20.4%	-4.2%
26	MIA	-16.8%	-10.7%	-6.1%
27	GB	20.8%	27.9%	-7.2%
28	JAC	34.3%	41.6%	-7.3%
29	PIT	11.5%	28.1%	-16.6%
30	BAL	-25.5%	-7.3%	-18.2%
31	SD	-12.9%	11.3%	-24.2%
32	WAS	-8.0%	22.0%	-30.1%

Top 10 Defenses, Better DVOA on Play Action

Rk	Team	PA	No PA	Dif
1	SF	9.9%	24.3%	-14.4%
2	TB	-20.1%	-7.6%	-12.4%
3	TEN	-21.5%	-17.4%	-4.1%
4	HOU	20.2%	22.1%	-1.9%
5	WAS	-3.9%	-2.6%	-1.3%
6	OAK	-1.6%	-1.3%	-0.3%
7	SEA	0.9%	0.9%	-0.1%
8	DAL	-4.4%	-4.8%	0.4%
9	MIN	16.0%	13.0%	3.0%
10	STL	22.0%	17.9%	4.1%

Bottom 10 Defenses, Better DVOA on Play Action

Rk	Team	PA	No PA	Dif
23	CLE	42.1%	13.4%	28.6%
24	CAR	35.0%	5.2%	29.8%
25	JAC	20.7%	-11.3%	32.0%
26	NYG	29.4%	-3.0%	32.4%
27	CIN	50.6%	16.4%	34.2%
28	NE	24.2%	-12.7%	36.9%
29	GB	33.5%	-5.2%	38.6%
30	DEN	55.0%	0.0%	55.0%
31	NO	82.8%	15.5%	67.3%
32	KC	58.9%	-22.5%	81.4%

Top 10 Offenses, Better DVOA with Shotgun

Rk	Team	Shot	Not	Dif
1	PIT	41.0%	-3.4%	44.4%
2	JAC	58.7%	14.6%	44.1%
3	SEA	45.8%	2.7%	43.1%
4	GB	37.8%	4.0%	33.8%
5	SD	30.0%	-1.6%	31.6%
6	IND	48.4%	20.1%	28.3%
7	NE	56.9%	30.2%	26.7%
8	WAS	18.7%	-2.9%	21.7%
9	ARI	13.9%	-4.0%	17.9%
10	NO	22.0%	7.0%	15.0%

Bottom 10 Offenses, Better DVOA with Shotgun

Rk	Team	Shot	Not	Dif
23	CLE	1.1%	7.8%	-6.7%
24	STL	-24.5%	-16.8%	-7.7%
25	CHI	-27.4%	-18.9%	-8.5%
26	MIN	-4.4%	5.3%	-9.7%
27	TB	-0.6%	10.0%	-10.6%
28	PHI	1.1%	14.0%	-12.9%
29	SF	-39.9%	-26.6%	-13.4%
30	MIA	-19.3%	-5.2%	-14.0%
31	HOU	-11.4%	7.1%	-18.4%
32	CAR	-35.5%	-11.7%	-23.8%

Top 10 Defenses, Better DVOA vs. Shotgun

Rk	Team	Shot	Not	Dif
1	NYJ	-18.4%	18.6%	-37.0%
2	DEN	-14.9%	11.4%	-26.3%
3	KC	-21.5%	3.9%	-25.4%
4	CIN	-2.0%	13.8%	-15.8%
5	PHI	-11.8%	-0.3%	-11.6%
6	CAR	-6.4%	2.6%	-9.0%
7	JAC	-7.8%	-1.4%	-6.4%
8	NYG	-4.5%	-2.3%	-2.2%
9	DAL	-6.4%	-5.5%	-0.9%
10	IND	-11.3%	-10.6%	-0.7%

Bottom 10 Defenses, Better DVOA vs. Shotgun

Rk	Team	Shot	Not	Dif
23	DET	23.9%	10.5%	13.4%
24	BAL	4.4%	-9.2%	13.6%
25	HOU	27.3%	9.3%	18.0%
26	MIN	12.8%	-6.2%	19.0%
27	NO	29.0%	6.3%	22.7%
28	TEN	4.4%	-18.4%	22.8%
29	NE	10.6%	-13.2%	23.8%
30	BUF	18.3%	-8.6%	26.9%
31	MIA	39.7%	9.7%	30.0%
32	ARI	30.6%	-0.3%	30.9%

Author Biographies

LEAD WRITER AND STATISTICIAN

Aaron Schatz is the creator of FootballOutsiders.com and the proprietary statistics within *Pro Football Prospectus*. This past season, he wrote simultaneously for ESPN.com, FOXSports.com, AOL Sports, and *ESPN the Magazine*, thus establishing himself as the greatest crossover artist since Ray Charles topped the *Billboard* Country and Western charts. He has also written for *The New York Times, The Boston Globe, The New York Sun*, The New Republic Online, and Slate.com, and has done custom research for a number of NFL teams. Before creating FootballOutsiders.com, he was a radio disc jockey and spent three years tracking search trends online as the writer and producer of the Internet column "The Lycos 50." He has a BA in Economics from Brown University and lives in Framingham, Massachusetts with his wife Kathryn and daughter Mirinae.

CONTRIBUTORS

Dr. Benjamin Alamar is the founding editor of the *Journal of Quantitative Analysis in Sports* and has consulted for various NFL and NBA franchises. He holds a doctorate in Economics from the University of California at Santa Barbara.

Bill Barnwell runs the FO West Coast Office out of the Mission District in San Francisco, where he serves as the Sports Editor for IGN.com. Yes, that means his job is writing about sports and playing video games. To steal a line from The Wrens, he's the best 16-year-old ever. After writing Scramble for the Ball weekly for the last two years on FootballOutsiders.com, he'll be writing a new column in 2008, analyzing the 49ers offense on a weekly basis as they learn to love Mike Martz. He has also written for *ESPN the* Magazine and on the web at ESPN.com, Rotoworld.com, and PatriotsDaily.com.

Will Carroll is a fantasy owner's best friend and a thorn in the side of the NFL's control over injury information. A three-time Fantasy Sports Writers Association award winner, Will came over to Football Outsiders and brought the same edge to the funny-shaped pigskin ball that he did to the spherical horsehide one.

He lives in Indianapolis and is awaiting the 2009 Baseball Winter Meetings and 2012 Super Bowl while trying to figure out who to give his author's copy of *PFP 2008* to this year (since handing last year's edition to Peter King worked out pretty well for the company).

Born in Milan, Italy and reared in Denver, **Doug Farrar** fell in love with pro football as a wee lad, when Broncomania filled the mile-high air, Lyle Alzado was more than a cautionary tale, and Woody Paige wrote books. Though he once dreamed of returning punts like Rick Upchurch, it was the allure of the guitar and pen that took Doug through his adolescent years. A Seattleite since 1985, Doug now holds true allegiance to the Emerald City and all she possesses. In 2002, he traded in his home studio for a Frank Deford-wannabe license and started writing for Seahawks.NET, where he's been Editor-in-Chief for four years. He was Football Outsiders' first West Coast draft pick in 2006, and through FO has written for FOXSports.com, *The New York Sun*, and ESPN.com.

Briton **Stuart Fraser** joined the Football Outsiders writing staff in July 2007, and removed the "U" key from his keyboard shortly thereafter. Fraser still lives near his alma mater Cambridge University, but maintains a long-distance relationship with the Pittsburgh Steelers. When he isn't writing for Football Outsiders, he can be found battling the transatlantic time zone difference with doctoral research in nanotechnology.

Brian Fremeau contributes the Fremeau Efficiency Index (FEI) and other college football stats and analysis to FootballOutsiders.com. Unofficially created in 2002 in an attempt to quantify momentum, FEI's roots actually extend to an early-1990s NCAA hoops tournament forecasting project Brian still hopelessly maintains today. Living in South Bend, Indiana with his wife and daughter, he spends every home Saturday cheering his beloved alma mater from the south end zone, with the outstretched arms of Touchdown Jesus signaling into the blue, gray sky.

Football is not just a Sunday passion for Web producer and Michigan graduate **Russell Levine**, who covers the college game for *The New York Sun* and in the weekly Football Outsiders column "Confessions of a Football Junkie." He also hosts a weekly college picks podcast on FootballOutsiders.com called "Seventh Day Adventure." Russell lives in West Orange, New Jersey, with his wife, Susan, and their kids, Trevor and Lindsay, where together they spend Saturdays pretending the Appalachian State game never happened.

Kevin Lynch first found football interesting when he was told to sit quietly on the couch after mistakenly breaking the first of many windows in his youth. His eight-year-old eyes opened wide watching a full-faced Roman Gabriel behind a single-bar facemask. Since then he has covered the league and the San Francisco 49ers since 1988 for many publications including the *San Francisco Chronicle*. He writes the 49ers Insider blog for sfgate.com and will also write a blog on environmental issues for sfgate.com beginning this summer.

Ned Macey is a recent University of Michigan law school graduate who hopes to delay inevitably earning the actual title of lawyer in a desperate attempt to stay young. He writes the weekly column "Any Given Sunday," analyzing the week's biggest upset Football Outsiders' style. His work has appeared in various places supporting the Outsiders, most frequently on FOX Sports.com and AOL Sports. He lives with his wife Melanie and one-year-old daughter Katie and this fall returns to his native Indianapolis, where he last lived when Jim Harbaugh was quarterback, one year before the Manning era.

Sean McCormick is a graduate of the University of Pennsylvania and holds an MFA in Creative Writing from Arizona State University. In addition to being a regular contributor at FootballOutsiders.com, his draft coverage has appeared at FOXSports.com. As of June, he will be indulging his inner masochist as a contributing writer for TheJetsBlog.com. He is the proud owner of the lone Richard Todd jersey still in existence.

Boston native **Bill Moore** graduated from Babson College and is currently a hedge fund portfolio manager in New York City when he is not coordinating the activities of over two dozen volunteers each week for the Football Outsiders Game Charting Project. Although his probation period of ten years has expired, his wife has still not completely forgiven him for kicking a hole in their couch during Super Bowl XXXI.

Rob Pitzer resides in Arlington, Virginia and works for the Smithsonian Institution. He is a graduate of West Virginia University and The Darden School of Business at the University of Virginia.

Ben Riley is a Deputy Attorney General for the State of California and a diehard Seattle Seahawks fan — yes, there are two on staff. Prior to joining Football Outsiders, Ben enjoyed filing lawsuits against various NFC West teams, including the San Francisco 49ers for conducting (allegedly) unconstitutional pat-down searches before home games. During the season, he masterminds The Week in Quotes on FootballOutsiders.com. His work has also appeared in *ESPN the Magazine* and various volumes of California Appellate Reporter.

Michael David Smith's weekly feature, "Every Play Counts," was described by the *Wall Street Journal*'s Daily Fix as "packing more game analysis into a single column than many beat writers display over a full season." He is a contributor to both AOL FanHouse and ProFootballTalk.com, and the main writer at College-FootballTalk.com. He has also written for multiple publications and websites including the *New York Times*, *New York Sun*, *Orange County Register*, FOXSports.com, Deadspin.com, The New Republic Online, and *ESPN the Magazine*. Contrary to popular belief, he never appears on *Around the Horn*; that's a different Michael Smith. Our Michael lives in Chicago with his wife Sarah, a lawyer.

Mike Tanier has been part of the Football Outsiders team since 2005. He writes the weekly Rundown column for FOXSports.com and has also written for *ESPN the Magazine*, *Maxim*, Rotoworld, Deadspin, and other outlets. He lives in South Jersey with his wife Karen, sons C.J. and Michael, and dog Rosie. He teaches at Audubon High School, and is proud to have known Joe Flacco when he was only 6-foot-3.

Vince Verhei is a jack of all trades for Football Outsiders. As copy editor, he reads, proofs and lays out nearly every story that appears on the Web site. As a writer, he has filled in numerous different columns online and contributed to a number of chapters in this book where his name may not appear. As an avid game watcher, he has been involved with the game charting project since 2005. A graduate of Western Washington University, Verhei has worked on the editorial staff of an outdoors magazine in the Seattle area for more than eight years despite the fact that his last fishing trip came in elementary school. His other night job is as a writer and podcast host for pro wrestling/MMA web site Figurefouronline.com.

Ryan Wilson currently holds down full-time two jobs: freelance sportswriter and stay-at-home dad. When not changing diapers, he contributes to AOL FanHouse and the Steelers Scout.com site ("Steel City Insider"), and his work has also appeared on ESPN.com and in the *New York Sun*. Ryan attended the College of William and Mary when Mike Tomlin was known as just a wide receiver, and he currently lives in upstate New York with his wife, Audrey, and son Kai.

ACKNOWLEDGEMENTS

We are grateful for the support of Prospectus Entertainment Ventures, Inc., particularly Nate Silver, Christina Karl, Steven Goldman, and Joe Sheehan. They have made it possible for us to write three books—and not just by giving us the title. We also thank Matt Silverman for editing help, plus Cherise Fisher and Mary Pomponio at Plume and Christine Marra at Marrathon Production Services.

We cannot express enough gratitude to all the volunteers who have participated in the Football Outsiders game charting project over the last three years. There are too many contributors to name everyone, but we do want to mention those charters who have done the most to build the data. They include Andrew Apold, Sergio Becerril Lopez, Dave DuPlantis, James Gibson, Tom Gower, Dan Haverkamp, Trevor Hoskins, Jason Hutt, Peter Koski, Shawn Krest, Andrew Lee, Louis Mazza, Chris (don't call me Luke or Josh) McCown, Brian McIntyre, Scott Metcalf, Dave Nicoloro, Jason Paradise, Kyle Peters, Gwyn Price, Matt Raymond, Nate Richards, Vince Rocchi, Michael Rutter, Nevin Sharma, Rob Stewart, and Nick Walters, as well as a number of writers in this book. Thanks to Michael Mulvihill of FOX Sports for providing game telecasts that we needed for the charting project, and to Bill Benetti and Chris Boylan for helping maintain archives of broadcasts online. Thanks to a number of NFL teams for providing 1995 play-by-play data, and to Alex Rubin for his trip to the Hall of Fame to mimeograph anything we were missing.

As an ex-radio jock who can't stop talking, Aaron Schatz sends extra thanks to Dale Arnold, Michael Holley, and James Stewart at WEEI for getting him back in a radio studio, and also to Bill Simmons and the producers of the B.S. Podcast for helping spread his babble nationwide. Thanks as well to Max Kellerman, Papa Joe Chevalier, and everyone else who has invited Football Outsiders onto the airwaves.

We want to acknowledge the support and friendship of many other folks, including Daniel Adler, Bruce Allen, John Banks, Carl Bialik, Ed Bunnell, Matt Burke, Scott Burton at *ESPN the Magazine*, Greg Cosell and the entire *NFL Matchup* production team, Chris Davidson at Sloan Business School, Kevin Demoff (don't tell the main man we mention you in the book), Doug Drinen, Gregg Easterbrook, Eddie Epstein, Stefan Fatsis, Mike Florio (for giving MDS the shot at ProFootballTalk. com), Mike Frazier, Bob Ganley, Bob Goetz at the *New York Times*, Jascha Hoffman, John Hollinger, Chris Holtege at the NFL, Sam Hudson and Steve Deutsch at Foley-Hoag, Richard Hurtado, Ron Jaworski, K. C. Joyner, Jason Klabacha, King Kaufman, Bill Kent and everybody at Sports Management Worldwide (visit SMWW.com), Peter King, Sydelle Kramer, William Krasker, Aaron Kuriloff, Russ Lande, Will Leitch, David Leonhardt, Josh Levin at Slate.com, Trip MacCracken, Paraag Marathe, Daryl Morey, Matt Mosley, Jamie Mottram, Rob Neyer, Dean Oliver, Kevin Pelton, Bill Polian, Mike Reiss, Gregg Rosenthal, Bob Ryan, Mike Sando, David Schoenfeld, Jim Schwartz, Tom Seeley, Michael "not David" Smith, Sheldon Spencer, Patrick Steigman, Samir Suleiman, Neil Zender, all the people from Scout.com, the brothers of Zeta Delta Xi at Brown University, and anybody who has written about us anywhere at any time.

Special acknowledgement goes to Roland Beech of TwoMinuteWarning.com and 82games.com for the original ideas that spawned our individual defense statistics, to Russ Lande of *Sporting News* and GM Jr. for advice on our Top 25 Prospects list, and to Cade Massey and Richard Thaler for sharing some of their research on draft value.

Thanks to all the readers of Football Outsiders, particularly everyone who participates in the online discussions. Thanks to everyone who did a guest spot on the Seventh Day Adventure podcast last season. Thanks to the interns who helped compile data for this book: Matthew Accornero, Wes Bunting, Peter DeBaz, James Doyle, Dan Haverkamp, Derek Marr, Roger Shaw, Devon Teeple, Parker Woodard, and Mark Zajack. Thanks to the folks from Football Outsiders whose work you won't see in this book, particularly cartoonist Jason Beattie, programmers Pat Laverty and Sean McCall, quarterback projection maven David Lewin, drive stats guru Jim Armstrong, and departed writers Al Bogdan, Ian Dembsky, and Vivek Ramgopal. Thanks to Eliot Horowitz and Dennis Doughty, who wrote the data parser, John Argentiero, who writes all the stat compilers, and Chris Povirk, who has done a little bit of everything. Thanks to designer Benjy Rose and programmer Elias Holman, currently working on a redesign of FootballOutsiders.com from back end to front page. Thanks to Mike McGibbon for help covering the league this offseason while we were busy writing the book. Thanks to anyone we mistakenly forgot.

Finally, infinite gratitude goes to our wives and children, for putting up with this silliness.